盘江煤矸石发电厂
Panjiang coal gangue power plant

建成的贵定海螺盘江水泥建设项目
Built Guiding Conch Panjiang Cement construction projects

Guizhou Panjiang Investment Holdings (Group) Co., Ltd. Is one of the National 520 key state-owned enterprises, 50 enterprises of China's coal enterprises in coal production, one of the top ten enterprises in Guizhou Province, formerly known as the former Ministry of Coal belongs to Panjiang Bureau of Mines. Corporate Reform in 1997, renamed Panjiang Coal (Group) Co., Ltd.. In 2010, and renamed Guizhou Panjiang Investment Holdings (Group) Co., Ltd., approved business transformation by Guizhou Province SASAC, headquartered in Guizhou Panxian moved to Guiyang City, Guizhou Province. Panjiang Group, which owns 35 wholly owned subsidiary, subsidiaries, holding companies and joint stock companies. Until to May 2012, with a staff of 50,000 people.

In recent years, the company adhere to the "coal-based, multi-industry simultaneously, scientific development" strategy, the Group's business realized by the production and management to capital management, industrial development, the successful transformation of strategic control, the initial establishment of a specialized division of labor, group collaboration, intensive management, large-scale development pattern. Currently, the planning and the formation of "coal, coal chemical, coal bed methane, electricity, ferro alloys, building materials, equipment manufacturing, specialty real estate" 15 industry sections, of which the coal industry ranks first in the south of the Yangtze River in China, coal bed methane industry in low-density gas in power generation and installed capacity ranks first in the country, cement and other industries have become the leading enterprises in the region.

In 2011, the company has the strong support of the Ninth National Games, wine Fair and other major events, throughout the year to donate to sponsor 20 million yuan; 32 pairs of helping Guizhou local small coal mines; "electricity security and people's livelihood" work of Guizhou Province supply coal electricity 8.1 million tons in the province, profits of 1.2 billion yuan...... won the Guizhou Province the most socially responsible enterprises and so on.

In 2011, sales revenue for the first time surpassed the ten billion mark, reaching 14.1 billion yuan, total assets increased from 14.3 billion in 2010 to more than 26 billion yuan, profits and taxes reached 2.1 billion yuan and 1.9 billion yuan, respectively, an increase of 47.6% and 41.6%, per capita income of 54,000 yuan, an increase of 15%, major economic indicators record the best score, to achieve the "12th Five-Year" a good start.

盘江矿区选煤厂
Panjiang Coal Preparation Plant

新建的盘江松河煤矿
The new Panjiang Songhe coal mine

中煤盘江重工建设项目
The China Coal Panjiang Heavy construction projects

瓦斯发电站
Gas power stations

“洼地崛起”谋跨越

"Depression rise" to seek leapfrog

信息服务当“尖兵”

Information services as "Vanguard"

中国移动通信集团贵州有限公司紧紧围绕“正德厚生·臻于至善”的核心价值观，致力于促进企业与社会共同发展，为全省经济社会实现“洼地崛起”贡献应有的力量。公司拥有省内规模最大、技术最优、覆盖最广的移动通信精品网络，全省各类服务网点超过5万个，网上营业厅、短信营业厅等电子化服务渠道24小时提供优质服务。客户规模发展至2300万户，增长了79倍。上缴税收累计超过53亿元。2011年业务收入突破100亿元。

作为全省通信运营行业的领跑者和主力军，中国移动贵州公司积极打造覆盖广、质量优的精品移动通信网络，通信基础设施建设投资年均超过40亿元，以消除城乡数字鸿沟为核心的“村通”工程投资累计约55亿元，具有我国自主知识产权的第三代移动通信技术TD-SCDMA网络已在全省所有市、州及县城城区实现连续覆盖。此外，中国移动贵州公司已在全省配备了80个具有超强抗灾能力的基站、17辆包括卫星应急通信车在内的应急通信车，以高科技、全方位的通信应急保障系统打造“天地一体”的应急通信保障网络，确保在危难险急时刻做好通信服务保障，为抢险救灾、抢救人民生命和财产安全提供有力支持。

基于自身网络、技术优势，中国移动贵州公司正以“移动改变生活”为目标，着力实施“信息化便民、信息化兴业、信息化助政”，全面推进社会信息化建设。

为第九届全国民族运动会提供通信保障

Provide communications support for the Ninth National Ethnic Games

贵州移动无线城市业务受到市民青睐

Guizhou Mobile wireless city business favored by the public

贵州移动优质的服务遍布村村寨寨

Guizhou Mobile quality of service throughout the village and stockaded

Guizhou Co., Ltd., China Mobile Communications Group, closely around the dedicated core values of "benefiting the people and strive for continuous improvement", to promoting the common development of enterprises and society, to achieve the province's economic and social "depression rise", to contribue the force. The company has the province's largest scale, best technical, most extensive coverage of the mobile communication network quality, the province's various types of more than 50,000 service outlets, online business, SMS Business Hall of electronic service channels 24 hours to provide quality services. Customers scale developed to 23 million, an increase of 79 times. Paid taxes total more than 5.3 billion yuan. In 2011, revenue exceeded 10 billion yuan.

贵州移动与绥阳县委共同搭建的党务服务中心，实实在在为老百姓办实事

Guizhou Mobile and Suiyang county built party service centers, really do practical things for the people

As the province's leader and the main force of the industry communications operators, China Mobile Guizhou Company actively to build a wide coverage, quality and excellent quality mobile communication networks, communications infrastructure investment is an annual average of over 4 billion yuan, in order to eliminate the digital divide in urban and rural areas as the core "connect to village" project total investment of about 5.5 billion yuan, China's independent intellectual property rights of third generation mobile communication technology TD-SCDMA network is in the province of all city, state and county city to achieve continuous coverage. In addition, China Mobile, Guizhou province has equipped with 80 super resilient base stations, 17 emergency communications vehicles, including satellite emergency communications vehicles, including high-tech, all-round communication emergency support system to create "Heaven and Earth one" emergency communications support network to ensure that the anxious moments of distress risk, and providing communications services, to provide effective support for protecting, rescuing and disaster relief, rescuing people's lives and property security.

贵州移动在各种灾害和重大事件中，应急通信保障做到了第一时间响应、第一时间到位、第一时间工作，确保了关键时刻通信"生命线"的畅通

Guizhou Mobile in a variety of disasters and major events, emergency communications support to do the first time response, the first time in place, the first time to ensure the smooth, flow of the "lifeline" of the critical moment communication

Based on its own network, technical superiority, China Mobile Guizhou Company takes "mobile life-changing" as goals, focus on the implementation of "information technology convenience, information prspers the business, the information technology to help government", and comprehensively promote the construction of social information.

贵州移动现代化的移动通信机房

Modernization of Guizhou Mobile's Mobile Communications Equipment

工程技术人员上铁塔进行检修

Engineering and technical personnel on the Tower overhaul

水 钢

Shui Steel

省委书记栗战书视察水钢

Provincial Party Committee Secretary Li Zhanshu to inspect the Shui Steel

2011年，水钢按照贵州省“加速发展、加快转型、推动跨越”主基调和实施“工业强省、城镇化带动”战略的要求，在力保重大技改项目按期竣工投产的同时，坚持一切以效益为中心，实施市场倒逼机制，着力对标挖潜、降本增效，努力抓好购销两头市场、控制中间生产环节，有效推进节能降耗、产品研发等工作。成功研发冷镦钢、30硅预应力钢棒等系列产品；承担的国家科技支撑计划《高性能SWRS82B盘条研发与产业化》项目通过国家科技部委托省科技厅组织的验收，成功用人工时效代替自然时效，将盘条原15天的时效检验缩短到1天，减少产品在库时间及资金占用，该项产品质量检验技术尚属国际首例。企业主要产品产量、营业收入大幅提高，生产经营继续保持安全、稳定、高效、经济运行，实现了钢铁主业产能规模从300万吨到500万吨的跨越。

水钢双高产品——82B钢筋

Double high Shui Steel products - 82B reinforced steel

新投运棒材生产线

Newly put into operation rod production line

In 2011, Shui steel is according to the Guizhou Province "accelerate the development, speed up transformation, push span" the main tone and implementation of the stragegic requirements "the industrial strong the province, urbanization led", preserve major technology projects on schedule to be completed and commissioned at the same time, adhere to all focus on efficiency, the implementation of the forced mechanism of market, to focus on the standard maximization, cost reduction and efficiency, efforts to grasp the purchase and sale of two markets, to control the middle of production processes, to effectively promote energy saving, product research and development work. Successful development of cold heading steel, 30 silicon prestressed steel bars and other products; undertaken by the National Science and Technology Support Program, "high-performance SWRS82B coil R & D and Industrialization" project commissioned by the National Science and Technology, acceptance of Provincial Science and Technology Organization, the successful use of artificial aging instead of natural aging, the rod of the original 15-day aging test reduced to one day, reduce the products in the library time and funds used, the product quality inspection technology is still the first in the international. A substantial increase of the output of main products, and operating income, production and management continue to maintain a safe, stable, efficient and economic operation, to achieve a leap forward of the main iron and steel industry production capacity from 3 million tons to 500 tons.

新投运的4号高炉

New No. 4 blast furnace operation

GUIZHOU STATISTICAL YEARBOOK

贵州统计年鉴

2012

贵州省统计局　国家统计局贵州调查总队　编

Compiled by Guizhou Provincial Bureau of Statistics　NBS Survey Office in Guizhou

GUIZHOU STATISTICAL YEARBOOK

（京）新登字 041 号

图书在版编目（CIP）数据

贵州统计年鉴．2012 ／ 贵州省统计局，国家统计局贵州调查总队编．-- 北京 ：中国统计出版社，2012.9

ISBN 978-7-5037-6680-0/C.2743

Ⅰ．①贵… Ⅱ．①贵… ②国… Ⅲ．①统计资料－贵州省－2012－年鉴 Ⅳ．① C832.73-54

中国版本图书馆 CIP 数据核字 (2012) 第 208718 号

贵州统计年鉴 -2012

作　　者／ 贵州省统计局　国家统计局贵州调查总队
责任编辑／ 佘竞雄
封面设计／华健在线
出版发行／ 中国统计出版社
通信地址／ 北京市西城区月坛南街 57 号　邮编 100826
办公地址／ 北京市丰台区西三环南路甲 6 号
电　　话／ (010)63376907
网　　址／ http://csp.stats.gov.cn
印　　刷／ 北京卡梅尔彩印厂
经　　销／ 新华书店
开　　本／ 890 × 1240 毫米　1/16
字　　数／1563.6 千字
印　　张／53.75 印张
印　　数／ 1-1600 册
版　　别／ 2012 年 9 月第 1 版
版　　次／ 2012 年 9 月第 1 次印刷
书　　号／ ISBN 978-7-5037-6680-0/C · 2743
定　　价／330.00 元

本书附同版本 CD-ROM 一张，光盘内容以书面文字为准。

中国统计版图书，如有印装错误，本社发行部负责调换。

编 者 说 明

一、《贵州统计年鉴 -2012》收录了2011年贵州省国民经济和社会发展等各方面的统计数据，改革开放以来特别是2006年以来的主要统计数据，以及2011年全国、各省（区、市）主要统计数据，是反映贵州省情的重要工具书。

二、本年鉴包括29个部分：综合；国民经济核算；人口；就业人员和职工工资；固定资产投资；对外经济贸易；能源；财政税收；价格指数；人民生活；城市概况；资源和环境；农业；工业；建筑业；运输和邮电；批发和零售业；住宿、餐饮业和旅游业；金融业；教育和科技；文化、体育和卫生；社会服务及其他；非公有制经济；民族自治地方；经济强县；扶贫与开发；地县资料；全国各省（区、市）资料；历年资料。为便于使用统计数据，在每部分之后附有主要统计指标解释。

三、本年鉴中，凡由有关部门（单位）提供的数据都在表式的注释中说明了数据来源；部分统计指标的范围以及口径变化在表下均有注释。

四、本年鉴中部分数据合计数或相对数由于计算单位或取舍不同而产生的计算误差，均未作机械调整。

五、本年鉴表中的符号使用说明："…"表示数据不足最小计量单位；"空格"表示该统计指标数据不详或无数据；"#"表示该指标的其中项。

本年鉴在编辑、出版、发行过程中，得到了有关部门（单位）的大力支持和帮助，在此谨致衷心感谢!

Editor's Notes

I. Guizhou Statistical Yearbook 2012 is an annual statistical publication, which reflects comprehensively the economic and social development of Guizhou Province. It covers data for 2011, key statistical data for the years since Reform and Opening-up especially the year 2006, and Main Statistics of Province (autonomous regions, municipalities) as well as the whole country. It is a useful reference book to thoroughly know Guizhou.

II. The Yearbook contains 29 chapters: General Survey; National Accounts; Population; Employment and Wages; Investment in Fixed Assets; Foreign Trade and Economic Cooperation; Energy; Finance and Taxation; Price Index; People's Living Conditions; General Survey of Cities; Resources and Environment; Agriculture; Industry; Construction; Transport, Postal and Telecommunication Services; Wholesale and Retail Trades; Hotel, Catering Services and Tourism; Financial Intermediation; Education, Science and Technology; Culture, Sports and Public Health; Social Services and Others; Non-public Sectors of the Economy; Minority Nationality Autonomous Areas; Economically Strong Counties; Anti-poverty and Development; Main Statistics of Prefectures and Counties; Main Statistics of Provinces(autonomous regions, municipalities)in the Whole Country; Historical Statistics. Explanatory Notes on Main Statistical Indicators is attached to the end of each chapter to use the statistical data conveniently in this book.

III. Notes are taken under the data tables in which the data are provided by relative departments other than statistical divisions, or the statistical coverage has been changed. Please pay attention when you use it.

IV. Statistical discrepancies due to rounding are not adjusted in the yearbook.

V. Notations used in the yearbook: "…"indicates that the figure is not large enough to be measured with the smallest unit in the table; "blank space" indicates that data are unknown or are not available; "#"indicates a major breakdown of the total.

Thanks for enthusiastic of many relational departments and individuals to the editing, publication and distribution of the Yearbook!

《贵州统计年鉴－2012》编辑委员会

Editorial Board

《贵州统计年鉴－2012》编辑人员

主　　　编：陶谋立　朱新武　钟赛梅

副　主　编：冯育毅　刘带春　张贵平　张北平　王宪筑　潘　康　杨大昆
何友才　王正潮　唐晓川　杨天禄　廖金昌　袁金发　王　渝

编辑部主任：彭　龙　魏龙斌

编辑部副主任：王　瑛　聂坤琪

分 科 主 编：（按姓氏笔画为序）
毛　敏　王朝晖　白文英　张小芳　张学进　李诗刚　沈先发　肖　瑶
邵　蔚　陈应芳　周　蓉　胡　刚　倪　明　龚　勇　董安娜　廖建伟

编 辑 人 员：（按姓氏笔画为序）
万朝晖　王练练　王贵森　邓伟庆　冯　璐　刘光淋　刘继海　刘　强
张仕英　李平惠　汪明峰　肖高萍　周　莲　周惠云　胡国阳　赵世玲
赵媛媛　董建巍　谢小清

英 文 翻 译：侯佳佳

电 脑 排 版：李立丹

编 务 人 员：韦　博　黄　河

Editorial Staff of Guizhou Statistical Yearbook 2012

Editor-in-chief: Tao Mouli Zhu Xinwu Zhong Saimei

Deputy Editor-in-chief:

Feng Yuyi Liu Daichun Zhang Guiping Zhang Beiping Wang Xianzhu Pan Kang
Yang Dakun He Youcai Wang Zhengchao Tang Xiaochuan Yang Tianlu Liao Jinchang
Yuan Jinfa Wang Yu

Directors of Editorial Department:

Peng Long Wei Longbin

Vice Directors of Editorial Department:

Wang Ying Nie Kunqi

Editor-in- chief by Section(in order of strokes of chinese surname):

Mao Min Wang Zhaohui Bai Wenying Zhang Xiaofang Zhang Xuejin Li Shigang
Shen Xianfa Xiao Yao Shao Wei Chen Yingfang Zhou Rong Hu Gang
Ni Ming Gong Yong Dong Anna Liao Jianwei

Editorial Staff(in order of strokes of chinese surname):

Wan Zhaohui Wang Lianlian Wang Guisen Deng Weiqing Feng Lu Liu Guanglin
Liu Jihai Liu Qiang Zhang Shiying Li Pinghui Wang Mingfeng Xiao Gaoping
Zhou Lian Zhou Huiyun Hu Guoyang Zhao Shiling Zhao Yuanyuan Dong Jianwei
Xie Xiaoqing

English Translators: Hou Jiajia

Computer Typesetting: Li Lidan

Staff for Editorial Affairs: Wei Bo Huang He

目 录

CONTENTS

一 综 合
General Survey

二 国民经济核算
National Accounts

三 人 口
Population

四 就业人员和职工工资
Employment and Wages

五 固定资产投资
Investment in Fixed Assets

六 对外经济贸易
Foreign Trade and Economic Cooperation

九 价格指数
Price Index

十 人民生活
People's Living Conditions

十一 城市概况
General Survey of Cities

十二 资源和环境
Resources and Environment

十三 农 业
Agriculture

十四 工 业
Industry

十五 建筑业
Construction

十六 运输和邮电
Transport, Postal and Telecommunication Services

十七 批发和零售业
Wholesale and Retail Trades

十八 住宿、餐饮业和旅游业
Hotel, Catering Services and Tourism

十九 金融业
Financial Intermediation

二十 教育和科技
Education, Science and Technology

二十一 文化、体育和卫生
Culture, Sports, and Public Health

二十二 社会服务及其他
Social Services and Others

二十八 全国各省（区、市）资料
Main Statistics of Provinces (autonomous regions, municipalities) in the Whole Country

二十九 历年资料
Historical Statistics

机构风采

Institutions Highlights

贵州省民委

Guizhou Provincial Ethnic Affairs Commission

2011年10月8日，赵克志省长、谌贻琴部长、谢庆生副省长在吴军主任的陪同下视察民族文化宫

October 8, 2011, Zhao Kezhi governor, Minister Chen Yiqin, Xie Qingsheng vice governor accompanied by Wu Jun Director inspected Cultural Palace of Nationalities

2011年10月11日，吴军主任、黄平副主任在镇远县尚寨民族乡调研帮扶工作

October 11, 2011, Wu Jun director, Huang Ping deputy director had research of helping work in Zhenyuan county Shangzhai Minority clan Township

2011年是“十二五”规划的开局之年。一年来，贵州省民委认真贯彻落实中央和省委、省政府关于民族工作的决策部署，各项民族工作取得了新的进展。

一是依靠党委政府，全面部署了“十二五”全省民族工作。省政府召开了第四次民族工作联席会。报请省政府批准实施了《贵州省少数民族事业发展“十二五”规划》，出台了《关于繁荣我省优秀少数民族文化的意见》，转发了《关于实施“十二五”少数民族事业发展十大推进计划》，下发了《关于做好少数民族和民族地区数据监测统计工作的通知》。

二是加大协调力度，努力营造民族工作良好氛围。按照民族工作社会化的要求，积极整合各个方面的力量推动民族工作的发展。省民委先后与省直20多个部门沟通协商，达成了共同推进民族地区各项事业发展的共识。

三是狠抓措施落实，确保各项重点工作扎实推进。积极承担争取国务院出台扶持贵州加快发展政策的前期工作，先后起草了《加快内陆民族地区转变经济发展方式试验区的请示》等文稿上报给国家民委和省委、省政府。2012年1月12日，国务院以国发[2012]2号文正式下发了《意见》，为加快贵州经济社会发展争取到了更加优惠的政策措施。

四是成功承办了第九届全国民族运动会。在省委、省政府和组委会的领导下，办出了特色、办出了水平、办出了影响，在运动会规模、运动会的组织、竞赛和表演项目的数量、贵州代表团的获奖情况和民族运动会的社会影响等方面产生了良好的反响。

开幕式领导

The Leadership of the opening ceremony

闭幕式领导

The leadership of the closing ceremony

开幕式

Opening ceremony

开幕式点火仪式
Opening ceremony of the Lighting Ceremony

开幕式
Opening ceremony

开幕式——吉祥物圆圆
Opening ceremony - the mascot Yuanyuan

2011 is the first year of the "12th Five-Year Plan". Over the past year, Guizhou Provincial Ethnic Affairs Commission to seriously implement the central and provincial party committee, provincial government deployed on the work of national decision-making, the nation's work has made new progress.

The first is to rely on the party committee and government, the full deployment of the "12th Five-Year" the province's ethnic work. The provincial government held the Fourth National Joint Council. Submitted to the provincial government approved the implementation of "Guizhou Province minority career development '12th Five-Year Plan'", the introduction of the "opinion on the prosperity of the province of outstanding minority cultures", and transmitted "on the implementation of '12th Five-Year Plan' minority business development Top 10 Promotion Plan", issued on the "data monitoring and statistical work to increase minority and ethnic minority areas".

The second is to increase coordination, and strive to create a good atmosphere of the national work. In accordance with the requirements of the socialization of ethnic work, and actively integrate all aspects of the forces to promote the development of the national work. Provincial Ethnic Affairs Commission has communication and consultation with more than 20 departments, and the provincial reached a consensus to jointly promote the development of various undertakings in ethnic areas.

The third is to pay close attention to the implementation of the measures to ensure that the priority tasks to push forward. Positive commitment to the fight for the State Council to support the introduction of Guizhou to speed up the development policies of the preliminary work, has drafted a "speed up the landlocked nation of the transformation of economic development pilot area to consult" presentation reported to the State Ethnic Affairs Commission and the provincial committee, government. January 12, 2012, the State Council to the State [2012] 2 text formally issued the "Opinions" in order to secure a more favorable policies and measures to speed up the Guizhou economic and social development.

The fourth is to successfully host the Ninth National Ethnic Games. Under the leadership of the provincial committee, government and the organizing committee, to do a feature, do the level, do that affect the number of the organization of the Games scale, Games, contests and performances, the winners of the Guizhou delegation of a good response and the social impact of the national Games.

闭幕式
Closing ceremony

闭幕式——火炬熄灭
Closing ceremony - torch extinguished

构建体育精神高地　打造体育文化品牌
为加快贵州经济社会发展提供精神动力

To build the spirit of sport Heights　To build sports culture brand

Provide the motive power to accelerate the Guizhou's economic and social development

56朵民族体育之花齐聚贵阳为九届民族运动增光添彩
The flower of the 56 national sports gathered in Guiyang to add luster to the Ninth National Ethinic Sports

2011年是贵州体育发展史上具有里程碑意义的一年。全年成功举办了第九届民族运动会等国内外大型赛事活动达17项之多，并在赛事组织、运动成绩、场地建设、体育宣传等方面取得了丰硕成果，全省体育事业取得了重大成效。

一、成功举办第九届全国民族运动会

2011年 9 月10日至18日，第九届全国少数民族传统体育运动会在贵阳隆重举行。全国31个省（区、市）和解放军、新疆建设兵团及台湾等34个代表团6790运动员参加16个大项、188个表演项目的比赛，竞赛项目、表演项目和参赛运动员均创历届新高。本届运动会改革奖励办法，取消金银铜牌设置，改设一、二、三等奖。

贵州代表团1千余名运动员参加了15个竞赛项目、39个表演项目比赛，夺得竞赛项目一等奖28个、二等奖31个、三等奖31个，表演项目一等奖7个、二等奖23个、三等奖9个，取得了竞赛项目获奖总数和一等奖个数、表演项目获奖总数“三个全国第一”的好成绩，实现了重大历史性突破。贵州代表团和龙舟、独竹漂等12个队33人获得体育道德风尚奖，实现了竞赛成绩和体育道德风尚双丰收的目标。

本届民族运动会贵州省体育局还圆满完成了竞赛组织工作，火炬传递任务；新建和改扩建体育场馆7个，总投资达2.1亿元；通过市场运作获得省内外企业总价值2.5亿资金、物资、服务的赞助支持，创历届民族运动会集资新高。

WSB世界拳王争霸赛
WSB World Boxing Champion Competition

2011 is Guizhou sports development milestone in the history of the year. Successfully held throughout the year of the Ninth National Ethnic Games and other major domestic and foreign competitions as much as 17, and in the organization of events, sports scores, venue construction, sports publicity achieved fruitful results, the province's sports has made significant results.

First, successful holding of the Ninth National Ethnic Games

September 10 to 18, 2011, the Ninth National Minorities Traditional Sports was held in Guiyang. 34 Delegation 6,790 athletes in the country's 31 provinces (autonomous regions, municipalities) and the People's Liberation Army, the Xinjiang Production and Construction Corps, and Taiwan to participate in a game of 16, 188 performances, the competition events, performances and athletes were all made the previous record high. The current games to reform the incentives and the abolition of the gold and silver bronze settings, re-established as the first, second, third prize.

农民体育健身工程
Fitness Project for Peasants

Guizhou delegation of a thousand athletes participated in 15 competitions, 39 performances contest, to contest the first prize of 28, second prize of 31, and 31 third prizes, performances of the first prize 7, 23 second prize, third prize 9, Contest winning total and the first prize number, award-winning performances to the total number of "three national good" results, made a major historic breakthrough. Guizhou delegation and dragon boat, alone bamboo drift such as 12 teams of 33 persons won Sportsmanship Award, to achieve the goal of the competition results and sportsmanship double-win.

This session of the ethnic movement Guizhou Province Sports Bureau successfully completed the organization of the competitions; torch passing tasks; new construction and renovation and expansion stadiums 7, a total investment of 210 million yuan; through the operation of the market total value of inside and outside the province 250 million yuan of funds, materials, services, sponsorship support, create a new high of the previous national games set owned.

2011中国梵净山环梵公路自行车挑战赛
2011 China the Fanjingshan Huanfan road bike challenge

二、继续加强体育民生工程建设

2011年全民健身工程列入省50项重点工作和十大民生工程。完成了200条全民健身路径工程，440个农体工程，4个 “雪炭工程”建设。全年组团参加了第八届全国残疾人运动会，第二届全国智力运动会。举办了贵州省第六届老年人运动会，开展了“健身大拜年”、“全民健身日”、多彩贵州龙舟系列活动和省直机关职工体育活动等。

三、竞技体育力争奥运参赛资格

名将邹市明夺得全国和世界锦标赛冠军，获2012年伦敦奥运会参赛资格。小将常勇夺得2011年亚洲拳击锦标赛52公斤级冠军，体现积极向上的发展势头。皮划艇静水女运动员李章丽，在全国皮划艇冠军赛上取得两个第二名、一个第三名的好成绩，目前个人排位全国第二位；女子四人皮艇500米项目在皮划艇世界杯第三站获得第六名，为取得奥运会参赛资格奠定基础。贵州省有运动员、教练员、科研人员共29人次在国家队训练，积极备战2012年伦敦奥运会。

竞技体育取得国际国内比赛冠军19个，亚军30个，季军41个，四至八名108个。举办了WSB世界拳王争霸赛、中国拳击公开赛、第九届全国越野跑锦标赛、全国艺术体操集体锦标赛和个人冠军赛和全国皮划艇激流回旋冠军赛第二、三站比赛。

四、体育产业品牌赛事引领，助推体育旅游发展

今年举办了中国贵州“紫云格凸”国际攀岩交流大会，晴隆24道拐公路汽车爬坡，黄果树国际半程马拉松赛，黔东南超100公里跑国际挑战赛，“环梵”公路自行车挑战赛等一系列特色鲜明的国内外品牌赛事，加强贵州山地户外运动资源宣传推介，以格凸河攀岩运动为代表的山地户外休闲体育旅游呈现良好发展势头。启动《中国贵州山地户外运动大省专项建设规划》编制工作。体育彩票继续保持稳定发展，全省销售体育彩票11.77亿元。

2011中国贵州格凸河国际攀岩交流大会举办具有民族特色的开幕式
2011 China's Guizhou the Getu river international climbing Exchange Conference held the opening ceremony of the national characteristics

2011“紫云格凸”国际攀岩交流大会运动员晚上观看露天电影

2011 the "Ziyun Getu" the international rock climbing Exchange Conference athletes at night to watch the outdoor movie

2011中国贵州格凸河国际攀岩交流大会

2011 China Guizhou the Getu river international rock climbing Exchange Conference

Second, continue to strengthen the sports livelihood projects

In 2011, National Fitness Project is included in the 50 key work and 10 livelihood projects. 200 of the National Fitness Route, 440 agricultural and engineering, 4 snow carbon project" construction. Annual delegation to participate in the Eighth National Games for the Disabled, the Second National Mind Sports Games. Held in the sixth Games of older people in Guizhou Province, launched a "fitness New Year," "National Fitness Day" Colorful Guizhou Dragon Boat series of activities and provincial organs of employee sports activities.

Third, competitive sports strive Olympic eligibility

Champion Zou Shiming won national and world champion, won the 2012 London Olympic qualification. Teenager Chang Yong won the 52 kg class title of the 2011 Asian Boxing Championship, reflecting the positive momentum of development. Li Zhangli, canoeing hydrostatic female athletes in the national canoeing championship two second ranks, one third rank good results, individual qualifying National No.2; women's four-person kayak 500 meters project plan in the skin boats World Cup, finished sixth in the third leg of the foundation to achieve Olympic qualification. Guizhou Province, athletes, coaches, researchers, a total of 29 people in the national team training, and actively preparing for the 2012 London Olympics.

Competitive sports made 19 international and domestic champion, the second place 30, the third place 41, fourth to eighth place 108. Organized WSB World Boxing Champion Competition, Chinese Boxing Open, the ninth national cross-country running championships, the National Rhythmic Gymnastics Championships and the individual championship and the National Canoe Slalom Championships, the second and third races.

Fourth, the sports industry in brand events lead, boost sports tourism development

Held in this year in Guizhou, China the "Ziyun Getu" international rock climbing Exchange Conference, Qinglong 24 Daoguai cars climbing, Huangguoshu International Half Marathon, the Qiandongnan over 100 kilometers to run the International Challenge, "Huanfan" road bike challenge competitions, a series of distinctive characteristics of domestic and foreign brand events, strengthen Guizhou mountain outdoor sports resource publicity and promotion the Getu river rock climbing, mountain outdoor leisure and sports tourism have shown good momentum of development. Start "the largest province of China Guizhou mountain outdoor sports special construction plan" preparation work. Sports lottery to maintain the stable development, the province's sale of sports lottery of 1.177 billion yuan.

贵州省公安厅

Guizhou Province Public Security Department

领导关怀
Leading Care

研究部署全省公安工作
Study the deployment of the province's public security work

2011年，是全省公安工作任务极其繁重的一年，是风险和挑战最大的一年，压力、挑战和考验前所未有，取得的成绩也前所未有。

一年来，全省公安机关始终坚持围绕中心，服务大局，强化公安机关职能作用，为经济社会又好又快更好更快发展创造了和谐稳定的社会环境。圆满完成了抗凝救灾、抗旱救灾、抗洪抢险等一系列抢险救灾任务，圆满完成了建党90周年大庆、民族九运会安保、酒博会暨投洽会安保、旅游发展大会安保等重大活动安保和重大警卫任务，成功圆满处置了安顺“7·26”、黔西“8·11”群体性事件和福泉“11·1”爆炸事故等突发事件，狠抓对敌斗争，坚持严打黑恶势力犯罪、拐卖妇女儿童犯罪等违法犯罪活动，有力地维护了全省社会大局的持续稳定。

一年来，全省公安机关始终坚持人民公安为人民，以作风建设为突破口，深入开展“三个建设年”、“四帮四促”、“大走访”开门评警、主题教育实践、干部下基层、队伍集中教育整顿等活动，全面推进队伍建设，涌现出以潘琴、张斌等为代表的一大批英雄模范人物，公安队伍整体素质有了新的提高，全省人民群众安全感和对公安机关的满意度持续五年上升。

一年来，全省公安机关始终坚持解放思想，与时俱进，勇于创新，涌现了许多“亮点”，创造了社区戒毒社区康复“阳光工程”、瓮安由大乱到大治等一批可圈可点的经验做法，公安业务建设和队伍建设上取得了新突破。

九运安保表彰
Recognition of 9th National Games security protection

打击毒品犯罪

To combat drug-related crimes

销毁非法伪劣产品

Destruction of illicit and counterfeit products

In 2011, the province's public security tasks were extremely heavy, the risks and challenges were biggest of the year, unprecedented pressures, challenges and tests, and the achievements of the year are most than ever.

Over the past year, the province's public security organs always adhere around the center, serving the overall situation, strengthen the functional role of the public security organs, to create a harmonious and stable social environment for sound and rapid, better and faster economic development. The successful completion of the anticoagulant relief, drought relief, flood fighting and a series of rescue and relief missions, the successful completion of the major events of the 90th anniversary of National Games security, wine expo-cum-Fair security, Tourism Development Conference Security, etc. security and critical security missions, the successful consummation disposal Anshun "7·26", Qianxi "8·11" mass incidents and Fuquan "11·1" explosion accident emergencies, pay close attention to the struggle against the enemy, adhere to strike hard black evil crime, trafficking in women and children, crime and other criminal activities, effectively safeguarding the continuity of the province's overall social stability.

Over the past year, the province's public security organs always adhere to the People's Public Security serve for the people, take the style of construction as a breakthrough, to carry out the "three construction year", "four to four help and promote", "visits" to open the door assessment police, the theme of educational practice, cadres grass-roots level, the team focus on activities such as education and rectification, and comprehensively promote team building, the emergence of the Pan Qin, Zhang Bin and other representative of a large number of heroes and models, the overall quality of the police contingent has been enhanced, the people of the province their sense of safety and the satisfaction of the public security organs continue to rise for five years.

Over the past year, the province's public security organs always adhere to set free minds, catch up with the time, be creative and innovative, emerged many "bright spots", to create a community drug treatment community-based rehabilitation "Sunshine Project", Weng'an from chaos to peace and order and a number of ring point of the experiences and practices, the public security of business-building and team building to achieve a breakthrough.

抗洪抢险救灾

Flood rescue and relief

深入田间地头开展便民服务

Go to the fields in a convenience service

贵州省公安厅交警总队

Guizhou Province Public Security Bureau Traffic Police Corps

2011年1月，省委副书记、省长赵克志，省委常委、政法委书记、公安厅长崔亚东视察贵阳市交通管理工作
January 2011, the Provincial Committee, vice governor Zhao Kezhi, Provincial Standing Committee, secretary of the Political and Law Commission, Public Security Bureau director Cui Yadong visited Guiyang City the traffic management

2011年凝冻期间，黄康生副省长、王泽洪常务副厅长深入贵新路实地检查调研
2011 Freezing period, Huang Kangsheng deputy governor of the province, executive vice director Wang Zehong had depth inspection research of the Guixin road site

3月22日，省政府召开全省道路交通安全工作电视电话会议，省委常委、副省长黄康生在会上作了重要讲话
March 22, the provincial government held the province's road traffic safety, television and telephone conference, the Provincial Party Standing Committee, Vice Governor Huang Kangsheng made an important speech at the meeting

2011年，全省公安交警部门以科学发展观为统领，认真贯彻落实省委、省政府“三个建设年”相关部署，按照最大限度增加和谐因素，最大限度减少不和谐因素的总要求，以回应人民群众的新期待，满足人民群众的新要求为着力点，以解放思想、改革创新为动力，不断破解交通管理发展难题、提升服务保障水平，全力服务贵州加速发展、加快转型、推动跨越的主基调，开展了一系列工作，圆满完成了各项工作任务，有效保障了全省道路交通的安全和畅通。

全省共发生道路交通事故1566起，造成1020人死亡，2270人受伤，同比事故次数减少254起，下降13.96%；死亡人数减少157人；下降13.34%；受伤人数减少463人，下降19.87%，连续8年实现省委、省政府提出的“双降目标”，道路交通安全整体形势保持了持续平稳态势。同时，全省交警部门还致力于强化社会管理创新，不断提升便民利民工作水平。在车驾管工作上，力推亲民爱民惠民三项举措；在资源整合方面，实现了异地缴纳交通罚款；在拓展交通业务办理渠道方面，开通了988个“警邮交通管理服务站”，平均每日收缴罚款966笔，处理非现场交通违法330起，极大方便了群众办理各项交通管理业务。

2011年4月，交警总队召开全省道路交通管理工作社会管理创新座谈会，崔亚东同志出席会议并讲话

April 2011, the traffic police corps held a provincial road traffic management and society management innovation forum Cui Yadong attended the meeting and delivered a speech

In 2011, the province's public security traffic police department took the scientific development concept as a guide and conscientiously implement the provincial government "three construction year" deployment, in accordance with the maximum increase harmonious factors and minimize the total requirements of the factors of disharmony, to respond to the people's new expectations, to meet the new demands of the masses of the people as the focal points, took emancipate the mind, reform and innovation as the driving force, continue to crack the problem of the development of traffic management, improve service level of protection, full service for Guizhou to accelerate the development, accelerate the transition, and promote leap the main tone, carried out a series of work, the successful completion of various tasks, and effectively protect the province's road traffic safety and smoothness.

The province road traffic accidents in 1,566, 1,020 people were killed, 2,270 injured, the number of accidents decreased by 254 cases, a decrease of 13.96%; number of deaths decreased by 157 people; a decrease of 3.34%; reduce the number of injured 463 people, decreased by 9.87%, for eight consecutive years to achieve the provincial party committee and provincial government put forward the goal of "double down", the road traffic safety situation has maintained a sustained and stable trend. Meanwhile, the traffic police department in the province is also committed to strengthen social management innovation, and improve the convenience and benefit level. In the Car driving management work, pushing close to the love people benefit people three initiatives; in the integration of resources, to achieve the off-site to pay traffic fines; expand the traffic channels of business process, the opening of the 988 "Post, police traffic control service station", the average daily collection of a fine of 966, pen to deal with off-site traffic offense to 330, a great convenience to the masses to handle the various traffic management business.

2011年6月，总队领导带队深入黔西南州检查指导抗洪救灾交通安保工作

June 2011, the Corps leadership led in-depth the Qianxinan check the guidance of security, transport of the flood relief work

2011年6月，总队召开全省通报点评集中整治道路交通安全专项行动工作视频会议

June 2011, the Corps held the entire province reviews focus on the regulation of road traffic safety special action video conferencing

8月29日，总队就在全省推行的“三项便民利民措施”召开新闻通气会

August 29, the Corps implemented in the province, "three of the convenience and benefit measures" held a news briefing

贵州省民营经济发展局（贵州省中小企业局）

Guizhou Province Private Economic Development Bureau
(Guizhou Provincial SME Bureau)

龙超亚局长调研都匀市中小企业发展
Director Long Chaoya has research of Duyun SME development

“十佳民营企业家”获奖现场
"Top Ten private entrepreneurs", award-winning site

3月28日，全省加快民营经济发展暨表彰大会现场
March 28, to accelerate the development of private economy and the commendation of the General Assembly site

为认真贯彻落实《中共贵州省委贵州省人民政府关于进一步加快全省民营经济发展的意见》（黔党发〔2011〕10号），在原省中小企业局（省非公有制经济办公室）并入省经信委后的中小企业办公室（非公有制经济办公室）的基础上，成立了省民营经济发展局（省中小企业局），履行全省民营经济、中小企业发展工作管理、协调和服务职责。

2011年是贵州民营经济发展历史上最不平凡的一年，是环境改善最多的一年。全省民营经济增加值占全省经济总量的比重达到36.9%，比2005年提高12.5个百分点。全省私营企业、个体工商户分别达到9.46、75.5万户，分别比2005年增长72.6%、48.7%。在全国民营企业推动贵州发展大会上，全省共签订了5833.6亿元民营企业合作项目，其中园区建设和工业项目签约金额3988.6亿元，占全部签约金额的68.4%。民营经济拥有中国驰名商标件数18件，占全省的66.7%，民营经济主体新增“贵州名牌产品”86件，占全省的55%。全年民营经济专利申请量2327件，同比增加113.6%；专利授权1120件，同比增加34.3%。我省民营高新企业占全省138家高新技术企业的48.6%。

2011年，改善民营经济、中小企业发展，推动民营经济、中小企业加速发展、加快转型初显成效：

全国民营企业助推贵州发展大会现场
Private enterprises to boost Guizhou Development Conference site

省民营经济发展局（省中小企业局）挂牌仪式举行
Provincial and private economy Development Bureau (SME Bureau) held the listing ceremony

省推动非公有制经济中小企业发展工作联席会议现场
Province to promote the non-public economic development of SME in the work of the joint meeting site

省中小企业局与农业银行省分行签署战略合作协议
Provincial SME Bureau and the provincial branch of Agricultural Bank of China signed a strategic cooperation agreement

In order to conscientiously implement the "CPC Guizhou Provincial Committee Guizhou Provincial People's Government to further accelerate the development of the province's private economy"(Guizhou Party Issued [2011] No. 10), on the basis of the former province SME bureau(provincenon-public economy office) combined into the province SME Office of the Information Commission (the non-public economy office), the establishment of a private economic development bureau (Provincial SME Bureau), to fulfill functions of the province's private economy, the management of SME development, coordination and service.

In 2011, the Guizhou private economic development in the history of the most extraordinary year, is the largest year of environmental improvement. The province of private economic added value accounted for 36.9% of the province total economy, increased by 12.5 percentage points more than in 2005. The province's private enterprises, individual businesses to reach 94,600, 755,000 , respectively, compared with in 2005, has an increase 72.6%, 48.7%. In the Private enterprises to promote Guizhou development General Assembly, the province signed a total of 583.36 billion yuan of private enterprise cooperation projects, including park construction and industrial projects contracted amount of 398.86 billion yuan, accounting for 68.4% of the total contracted amount. The private economy has a well-known trademarks in China 18, accounting for 66.7% of the whole province's , and private economic agents to new added "Guizhou Famous Brand" 86, accounting for 55% of the province. The annual private economy of patent applications in 2,327, an increase of 113.6%; patents of 1,120, an increase of 34.3%. The province of private high-tech enterprises accounted for 48.6% of the province's 138 high-tech enterprises.

In 2011, to improve the private economy, the development of SMEs, to promote the private economy, accelerated development of small and medium enterprises, to accelerate the transition is paying off:

2011“多彩贵州”旅游商品两赛一会颁奖典礼
2011 "Colorful Guizhou" Tourist Commodities two race one meeting prize presentation ceremony

两赛一会千人大赛获中国基尼斯记录
The two race one meeting won the thousands of people contest Guinness record in China

组团参加2011香港中小企业国际博览会开幕式
Delegation to participate in the opening ceremony of the 2011 Hong Kong SMEs International Fair

2011年“多彩贵州”旅游商品两赛一会比赛现场
2011 "Colorful Guizhou" tourism commodities two race one meeting race scene

召开了全省加快民营经济发展暨表彰大会。大会出台了促进民营经济、中小企业发展的《中共贵州省委贵州省人民政府关于加快全省民营经济发展的意见》。大会还对“十佳民营企业家”、“贵州省十佳民营企业纳税大户”、“贵州省十佳民营经济发展县市区”、“贵州省十佳民营经济服务机构”、“贵州省十佳服务民营经济金融机构”和“贵州省百佳创业小老板”、“贵州省百佳个体工商户”等250个先进集体和个人给予了表彰。

实施“民营经济三年倍增计划”。“民营经济三年倍增计划”提出到2013年底，贵州民营经济增加值达到3200亿元以上，民间投资达到4000亿元，民营经济注册资本达到4000亿元，新增就业30万人以上。2011年三年倍增指标除市场主体中“私营企业”和“个体工商户”数量指标未达到预计目标，其余指标均实现超额完成。

加大支持力度。省中小企业发展专项资金2011年安排项目190个，资金13000万元，拉动投资86483万元。其中民营经济项目158个，资金11100万元，拉动投资79799万元，分别占总数的83.15%、85.4%、92.3%。省中小企业局争取到国家扶持中小企业发展的各类资金2.35亿元，项目251个，注重利用专项资金推进万户小老板工程，支持了2202户创业的小老板，新增就业岗位2万多个。

改善融资服务环境。构建融资合作平台，省民营经济发展局分别于国家开发银行省分行、中国农业银行省分行签订了战略合作协议。进一步放宽小额贷款公司试点条件，并率先在全国实行对小额贷款公司进行业务补助和风险补偿。截止年底，全省融资性担保机构214户，注册资金161亿元；全省小额贷款公司167户，注册资本44.5亿元。

加快中小企业社会化服务体系建设。省民营经济发展局充分发挥全省推动非公经济中小企业工作联席会议办公室的作用，统筹协调全省民营经济发展工作，积极向上争取，向下放权，汇总情况，协调问题，加快中小企业社会化服务体系建设，集聚更多要素向民营经济倾斜。

永红食品清洁生产车间
The Yonghong food cleaning production workshop

航天成功汽车装配生产线
The successful aerospace automotive assembly line

Held the province to speed up the development of private economy and the commendation of the General Assembly. The Assembly introduced to promote private economy, the development of SMEs "CPC Guizhou Provincial Committee Guizhou Provincial People's Government views on accelerating the development of private economy in the province." The Assembly also on the "Top Ten private entrepreneurs," "the top ten private enterprises in Guizhou Province taxpayer", "Guizhou Province the top ten private economic development of counties and cities", "Guizhou Province the top ten private economic services agency", "Guizhou Province ten good service private economic and financial institutions" and the "Guizhou Province Pokka entrepreneurial small business owners", "Guizhou Province Pokka individual industrial and commercial households" and 250 advanced collectives and individuals who were commended.

Implementation of the "private economy a three-year plan to double." "The private economy for three years doubling plan" put forward by the end of 2013, Guizhou private economic value added more than 320 billion yuan, private investment reached 400 billion yuan, the private economy in the registered capital of 400 billion yuan, new jobs to more than 300,000 people. 2011 to three years doubled indicators in addition to the quantitative indicators of the main players in the market in the "private sector" and "individual businesses" does not meet the projected targets, the remaining targets were exceeded.

Strengthen their support. Provincial SME development funds in 2011 arrangements 190 projects, 130 million yuan of funds, stimulating investment of 864.83 million yuan. 158 private economic projects, 111 million yuan of capital, stimulating investment of 797.99 million yuan, respectively accounting for 83.15%, 85.4%, 92.3% of the total amount. Provincial SME Bureau to secure state support for the development of small and medium-sized enterprises of all types of funds of 235 million yuan, 251 projects, advancing the engineering of ten thousand small business owners focus on the use of special funds to support the 2,202 entrepreneurial small business owners, more than 20,000 new jobs.

Improve the financing environment. Build a financing platform for cooperation, provincial and private Economic Development Bureau of the State Development Bank provincial branches, the provincial branch of Agricultural Bank of China signed a strategic cooperation agreement. Further relaxation of the experimental conditions of the small loan companies, and the first in the country of small loan companies, business subsidies and risk compensation. Up to the end of the year, the province's financing guarantee institutions 214, registered capital of 16.1 billion yuan; 167 small loan companies in the province, the registered capital of 4.45 billion yuan.

Accelerate the development of the social service system. Provincial and private Economic Development Bureau to give full play to the role of the province to promote the non-public economy SME Office of the Joint Conference, co-ordination of the province of private economic development, strive for positive downward decentralization summary of the situation, coordination problems, and accelerate the development of social service system, gathering more elements to tilt to the private economy.

贵州省民政厅

Guizhou Province Civil Affairs Department

贵州省第七届双拥模范城（县）命名表彰大会
Guizhou Province Seventh double support model city (county) named in recognition of the General Assembly

丁治学厅长慰问因雪凝灾滞留在贵新高速公路的乘客
Ding Zhixue director condolences passengers stranded in Guixin highway due to Snow Storm Disaster

按照“黔北民居”风格修建的遵义市汇川区板桥镇五保供养中心
Zunyi City Huichuan district Banqiao Town five guarantees supportting center is built accord with "Qianbei residential" style

2011年是经济社会发展“十二五”规划的开局之年。全省各级民政部门紧紧围绕“两加一推”的主基调，围绕保障和改善民生、加强和创新社会管理、服务经济发展、促进社会和谐的工作主线，经过上下共同努力，圆满完成了全年的各项工作目标任务。

2011年，全省民政事业费总支出116447.6万元，增长51.9%。城镇居民最低生活保障费支出143028.5万元，增长40.7%；农村居民最低生活保障费支出549880万元，增长73.2%。其他农村社会救济支出29994.8万元，增长104.4%。其他城镇社会救济支出4455.1万元，增长98.8%。社会福利支出60325.3万元，增长316.6%。

2011年末，全省共有城市低保对象54.3万人，增长0.6%。低保资金支出14.3亿元，增长40.7%。2011年末，全省有农村低保对象530.9万人，全年支出农村低保资金54.99亿元，增长73.3%。2011年末，全省共有五保供养对象13.9万人，农村传统救济1.7万人。农村医疗救助人数536.9万人，城市医疗救助52.2万人。2011年，全省直接募集社会捐赠款13769.1万元，捐赠衣被5.6万件，其他捐赠物资折款77.7万元。2011年，全省共有社区服务设施6593个，社区服务从业人员为14089人。2011年，全省共有收养性福利单位1185个，床位44025张，年末收养人员27203人。2011年，全省国家抚恤、补助对象223071人，比上年增加31083人。2011年，全省共有救助管理站59个，全年救助6.9万人次。2011年末，全省设6个地级市、3个民族自治州、56个县、11个民族自治县、7个县级市、13个市辖区、2个特区。2011年，全省共有社团4851个。2011年，全省办理内地居民结婚登记373423对。2011年，全省共有殡仪服务单位119个。

清镇市暗流乡穿洞村村委会换届选举“海选”现场
Qingzhen City Anliu Township Chuandong village general election "sea election" on-site

村民积极参加村委会换届选举投票
Villagers participate actively in the village committee general elections

民政干部给灾区群众送水
Civil affairs cadres send water to people in disaster areas

紫云抗旱救灾粮
Food of the Ziyun drought relief

向雪灾被困群众送食品
Send food to stranded people in the snowstorm

2011 is the first year of the economic and social development "Twelfth Five-Year" plan. The main tone of the provincial civil affairs departments at all levels closely around the "two plus one push", around protect and improve people's livelihood, strengthen and innovate the public administration, serve economic development, promote social harmony main line of work, through concerted efforts, the successful completion of the objectives and tasks of the year.

In 2011, the total expenditure of the provincial Civil Affairs 1.164476 billion yuan, an increase of 51.9%. The minimum living guarantee for urban residents expenses 1.430285 billion yuan, up 40.7%; rural areas the minimum living expenses of 5.4988 billion yuan, an increase of 73.2%. Other rural social assistance expenditure of 299.948 million yuan, an increase of 104.4%. Other urban social relief expenditure of 44.551 million yuan, an increase of 98.8%. Social welfare spending of 603.253 million yuan, an increase of 316.6%.

By the end of 2011, the province's total urban minimum target of 543,000, an increase of 0.6%. Subsistence allowances and capital expenditures of 1.43 billion yuan, an increase of 40.7%. By the end of 2011, the province's rural minimum target of 5,309,000 annual, expenditure of rural subsistence allowances capital of 5.499 billion yuan, an increase of 73.3%. By the end of 2011, the total beneficiaries of the province to support object 139,000 people, 17,000 of the traditional rural relief. The number of rural medical assistance 5,369,000 people, 522,000 people in urban medical assistance. In 2011, the province directly raise social donations 137.691 million yuan, donated clothing 56,000, donations of goods converted into money 777,000 yuan. In 2011, the province totally has community service facilities 6,593, and community services employing 14,089 people. In 2011, the province adoption welfare units 1,185, beds 44,025, at the end of the yeae, adoptions to 27,203 people. In 2011, the province's National Subsidy objects 223,071, an increase of 31,083 people over the previous year. In 2011, the province relief management station 59, the annual salvage of 69,000 people. By the end of 2011, six prefecture-level cities and 3 ethnic autonomous prefectures and 56 counties, 11 autonomous counties, 7 county-level cities, 13 municipal districts, 2 of the SAR. In 2011, the province has a total of Societies 4,851. In 2011, the province to handle matters of Mainland residents for marriage registration of 373,423 pairs. In 2011, the province funeral service unit 119.

贵州省农业委员会

Guizhou Province Agricultural Committee

领导深入田间地头调研
Leadership go to the fields to have depth research

放心农资下乡
Assured agricultural funds to rural areas

2011年，全省各级农业部门在省委、省政府的坚强领导下，紧紧围绕“两加一推”和“三化同步”重大部署，积极应对严重干旱和市场波动等不利影响，大力推进农业结构调整和产业化经营，切实保障主要农产品供给，为全省经济社会又好又快发展做出了重要贡献。

主要农产品取得较好收成。通过科技救灾和恢复生产，最大限度地减轻了灾害影响。全年粮食总产876.9万吨。油菜籽产量71.8万吨，比上年增长39.1%。肉类总产量179.97万吨，蛋类13.65万吨，奶类4.85万吨，水产品10.88万吨，分别增长0.5%、9.1%、5.7%和23.8%。

规范化种植高产玉米
Standardized planting high-yield corn

农民人均纯收入大幅提升。通过不断夯实农业基础、发展山地现代农业、广辟农民就业增收渠道，加上农产品价格上涨等因素，实现减灾增收。全年农牧渔业总产值同比增长1.4%。农民人均纯收入4145.4元，实际增长14%。

特色优势产业加快发展。畜牧业稳定发展，草食牲畜比重提升。特色优势农产品较快发展，蔬菜、马铃薯面积分别达到1062.8万亩、1002万亩，茶园、果园面积分别达到294.6万亩、253.5万亩，中药材、花生、食用菌等特色作物持续发展。大鲵存池29.1万尾。休闲农业与乡村旅游接待2837万人次，实现营业收入18.5亿元。

贵州省现代农业展示区一角
Guizhou Province modern agricultural demonstration corner

In 2011, the province's agricultural sector at all levels under the strong leadership of the provincial committee, government to focus on "two plus one push" and "three synchronization" significant deployment, actively respond to the adverse effects of severe drought and market volatility, and vigorously promote agricultural restructuring and industrial management, and effectively protect the main supply of agricultural products, made an important contribution to the province's economic and social good and fast development.

The main agricultural products to obtain a good harvest. Relief and restore production through science and technology, to minimize the impact of disasters. Annual total grain production of 8.769 million tons. Rapeseed production is 718,000 tons, an increase of 39.1% over the previous year. Total meat output of 1.7997 million tons, eggs 136,500 tons, 48,500 tons of milk, aquatic products 108,800 tons, respectively, an increase of 0.5%, 9.1%, 5.7% and 23.8%.

The per capita net income of farmers has increased significantly. Constantly reinforce the foundation of agriculture, the development of mountain modern agriculture, is necessary to find the income sources of farmers' employment, coupled with the prices of agricultural products and other factors, income for disaster reduction. The total output value of animal husbandry and fishery throughout the year an increase of 1.4%. The rural per capita net income was 4,145.4 yuan, an increase of 14% in real terms.

Accelerate the development of industries with local advantages. Animal husbandry got stable development, to enhance the proportion of herbivorous livestock. The characteristics and advantages of agricultural products is relatively fast development, vegetables, potato area of 1,062.8 mu, 1,002 mu, tea garden, the orchard area of 294.6 mu and 253.5 mu, herbs, peanuts, edible fungi and other characteristics of crops had sustainable development. Giant salamander deposit pool 291,000. Leisure agriculture and rural tourism received 28.37 million passengers, operating income of 1.85 billion yuan.

贵州辣椒销往外地
The Guizhou pepper sold to other place

牛场乡黑木耳标准化生产
Standardized black fungus production in Niuchang township

贵州省农委扶持农户发展的养鸡场
Guizhou Provincial Agricultual Committee support the development of farmers chicken farms

惠水优质苹果基地
Huishui quality apple base

农业结构调整成效突出。经济作物（含茶果）面积占农作物总面积的比重达到43.3%，比上年提高1.7%，畜牧业和经济作物增加值占农业增加值的比重分别提高1.5%和2.3%。目前，绿茶、辣椒及部分药材生产规模居全国第一，马铃薯、火龙果居全国第二，蔬菜即将进入全国前五，牛、猪存栏分别排名第六和第十一位。产业布局进一步优化，农产品品质结构加快改善。

农业产业化经营深入推进。全省规模以上农产品加工业年总产值完成483亿元，同比增长28.8%。251家省级以上重点龙头企业资产年末总额200亿元，实现销售收入225亿元，建设带动原料基地800万亩，带动农户360万户。累计注册农民专业合作社8000家，增长32%。农村土地流转面积达到300万亩。

农产品质量水平稳步提高。畜禽产品、蔬菜、水产品平均监测合格率分别达99.8%、95%和92.5%，农产品质量总体安全可靠，保障九运会工作圆满完成。累计通过无公害农产品认证1112个，新增认证绿色食品15个，获农业部地理标志登记保护农产品5个，19种农产品被评为省名牌产品。

农业农村基础设施继续改善。通过农机补贴项目新增购置各类机具12.89万台（套）、温室大棚68万平方米，农机总动力达到1851万千瓦。建成农村户用沼气13.1万户、大中型沼气工程231处、农村清洁工程80处，基层农技推广、农产品质量安全等服务体系等建设进展顺利。新农村建设17个“整乡推进”试点有序实施，农垦农场4700户危房改造全部开工，农村经济和社会事业全面协调发展。

高山牧场
Gaoshan pastures

贵州省农业展示区培育的福禄寿瓜
Gods melon cultivated by agricultural display area in Guizhou Province

The effectiveness of the adjustment of agricultural structure is prominent. The area of economic crops (including tea and fruit) accounted for the proportion of the total agricultural area of 3.3%, over the previous year increased by 1.7%, livestock and cash crops to increase the proportion of the value of total agricultural added value increased by 1.5% and 2.3% respectively. At present, the scale of production of green tea, pepper and some herbs in the nation ranks first, potato, dragon ranks second, vegetables is about to enter the country five, cattle, pig herds were ranked sixth and eleventh. Industrial layout to further optimize, the structure to accelerate the improvement of quality of agricultural products.

Further promote the industrialized operation of agriculture. Over the province scale, agricultural product processing industry annual output value of 48.3 billion yuan, an increase of 28.8%. More than 251 provincial key leading enterprise of assets at the end of the year the total income of 20 billion yuan, sales income of 22.5 billion yuan, construction driven by raw material base of 8 million mu, driven 3.6 million farmers. Registered professional farmers cooperatives of 8,000, an increase of 32%. Rural land circulation area of 3 million mu.

The level of quality of agricultural products has increased steadily. Livestock and poultry products, vegetables, aquatic products mean monitoring the passing rate of 99.8%, 95% and 92.5%, the overall quality of agricultural products safe and reliable, protection of the Ninth National Games work satisfactorily completed. Accumulated through the pollution-free agricultural products certification for 1,112, 15 new certified green food, the Ministry of Agriculture registration of geographical indications protection of agricultural products 5, 19 kinds of agricultural products as a provincial famous brand.

Agricultural and rural infrastructure continues to improve. New agricultural subsidy programs to purchase various types of equipment 128,900 units (sets), 680,000 square meters of greenhouses, agricultural machine power reached 18.51 million kilowatts. Built rural household biogas 131,000, 231 large and medium-sized biogas project, 80 rural cleaning projects, the primary agricultural extension, agricultural products quality and safety of service system construction progressing smoothly. 17 new rural construction "the whole township to promote" the pilot ordered, the implementation of the 4,700 renovation of dilapidated buildings of the land reclamation farm all work has started, the rural economy and social undertakings got comprehensive and coordinated development.

贵州省扶贫办

Guizhou Poverty Alleviation Office

省扶贫办主任叶韬在赫章县查看核桃种植
Poverty Alleviation Office director Ye Tao to view the walnut planting in Hezhang County

黎平就地转移——手工刺绣培训
The Liping place transfer - hand embroidery training

2011年，贵州省深入实施“扶贫脱贫攻坚第一民生工程”，扶贫开发不断取得新成效。全年减少农村贫困人口60万人，50个国家扶贫开发工作重点县农民人均纯收入增长17%。在全国扶贫开发工作绩效考评中，贵州省从2008年全国挂末的位置上升到2011年全国第十名，位次前移21位。2011年，贵州省共获中央财政扶贫资金23.0251亿元，占全国8.5%，增幅36%，排全国第一。

产业化致富。近年来，贵州省确定了“东油西果、南药北茶中蔬、面上牛羊和核桃”的产业布局，在革命老区、贫困地区大力实施乡村旅游扶贫。通过创新机制、整合资源，在产业化扶贫开发上进行了多种模式的有益探索，产业化扶贫涵盖了第一、二、三产业，取得了良好成效。

同心协力，共谋致富。十年来，中央省直单位和大连、青岛、深圳、宁波及社会各界人士共投入近80亿元资金给予贵州无私帮助，彰显博爱情怀。

石漠化治理。贵州石漠化面积占全省国土面积的21.34%。2008年国家启动的100个石漠化综合治理试点县中，贵州就有55个。新阶段扶贫开发以来，贵州省在石漠化先后探索出了晴隆县种草养畜的“晴隆模式”、贞丰县种植花椒的“顶坛模式”、长顺县“一品为主、多品共荣”的“长顺做法”等，实现了石漠化治理生态效益和农民增收共赢的目标。

石阡县乡村旅游扶贫点——楼上古寨

Shiqian rural tourism for poverty alleviation - Loushang ancient village

乡村旅游扶贫点——苗王城风雨桥

Rural tourism for poverty alleviation - Miao Wang City Fengyu bridge

In 2011, Guizhou Province got in-depth implementation of "poverty alleviation and tackling poverty as the first livelihood project", poverty alleviation and development continue to achieve new results. Throughout the year to reduce rural poverty population of 600,000 people, 50 national poverty alleviation and development priorities ounties farmers' per capita net income growth of 17%. Performance evaluation of the national poverty alleviation work, Guizhou Province rose from the position at the end of 2008 the country hang to 2011 the tenth, ranking forward 21. In 2011, Guizhou Province won a total central financial funds 2.30251 billion yuan, accounting for 8.5% of the nation, an increase of 36%, ranked first in the country.

Industrialization to get rich. In recent years, Guizhou Province has identified "East oil west fruit and South medicine north tea middle vegetables, the surface of cattle and sheep and walnuts" the industrial layout, vigorously implemented the rural tourism to poverty alleviation in old revolutionary base areas, and poor areas. Through innovative mechanisms, integration of resources, and useful exploration of the multiple modes of industrialization poverty alleviation development, industrialization poverty alleviation covering the first, second and tertiary industries, which have achieved good results.

Work together to seek common wealth. Over the past decade, the central government provincial units and Dalian, Qingdao, Shenzhen, Ningbo and the community who invested a total of nearly 8 billion yuan of funds given to Guizhou selfless help to highlight the fraternity feelings.

Rocky desertification control. Guizhou rocky desertification area accounts for 21.34% of the total land area. In 2008 Countries started 100 pilot counties of rocky desertification, of which 55 in Guizhou. Sice the new stage of poverty alleviation and development, in Guizhou Province in the rock desertification has explored a forage for raising livestock in Qinglong County "the Qinglong mode", Zhenfeng County planting pepper "Dingtan mode" Changshun County "a product-based, multi- goods and common prosperity" and " Changshun practices" and so on, to achieve ecological benefits and win-win goal of increasing farmers' income for rocky desertification control.

茶产业扶贫基地之一——黎平县茶产业基地

One of the poverty alleviation bases of the tea industry - tea industry base of Liping County

种养结合

Planting and breeding combination

贵州省商务厅

Guizhou Province Department of Commerce

商务部陈健副部长来黔调研
Vice Minister of the Ministry of Commerce Chen Jian has research in Guizhou

原省委常委、常务副省长王晓东、副省长蒙启良率商务厅相关同志到商务部汇报对接酒博会相关事宜
Former Provincial Standing Committee, Executive Vice Governor Wang Xiaodong, the vice governor Meng Qiliang led the Department of Commerce comrades to the Commerce Department report on the related issues of docking wine expo

2011年，全省实现社会消费品零售总额1750亿元，同比增长18%。其中，城镇1434亿元，同比增长19.7%，乡村316亿元，同比增长18.8%；批发业168.2亿元，同比增长38.9%，零售业1404.7亿元，同比增长17.9%，住宿业13.9亿元，同比增长20.9%，餐饮业163.1亿元，同比增长16.7%。

2011年，全省进出口实现历史新高，完成货物进出口48.8亿美元，同比增长55.2%，列居全国第四，在西部十二省区中列居第三。其中，出口29.8亿美元，同比增长55.5%；进口19亿美元，同比增长54.8%。

2011年，全省共批准外商直接投资项目70个，同比增长89.19%，合同外资金额合计170785万美元，同比增长279.32%，实际利用外资金额合计67322万美元，同比增长127.85%。

按照《贵州省开发区扩区和调整区位的原则和审批程序》《贵州省省级开发区的基本原则和审批程序》，积极推进原有开发区扩区调位有序开展，鼓励和支持有条件工业园区申报省级开发区。2011年，完成12个省级开发区扩区调位审核报批工作，经省政府正式批准新建17个省级开发区，超额完成全年目标任务。开发区完成固定资产投资1118亿元，完成工业总产值1889亿元。同时加大政策资金支持力度，省级财政安排专项资金1亿元，重点支持开发区基础设施和标准厂房建设。

2011年，全省共完成对外承包工程、劳务合作、设计咨询2.9亿美元，同比增长32%。项目涉及斯里兰卡、哈萨克斯坦、加纳、利比亚、印尼等28个国家和地区。落实中英基础项目五期2010万元，省农委草场开发、牲畜管理和畜种改良培训项目66万元。

省商务厅申晓庆厅长陪同中科院海外院士、徐传毅博士在金阳高新区相关企业调研
Minister of Department of Commerce Shen Xiaoqing, accompanied by overseas academicians of Chinese Academy of Sciences, Dr. Xu Chuanyi to have research in Jinyang high-tech related businesses

蒙启良副省长、省商务厅申晓庆厅长会见沃尔玛中国副总裁廖红晖一行
Meng Qiliang Vice Governor, Minister of Provincial Department of Commerce Shen Xiaoqing met with Wal-Mart vice president Liao Honghui and his team

2011年全省商务工作会议暨产业园区建设现场会现场
2011 the province's commercial business conference and industrial park construction meetings site

2011年8月18日，中国（贵州）国际酒类博览会暨2011中国•贵阳投资贸易洽谈会在贵阳隆重开幕

August 18, 2011, China (Guizhou) International Wine Expo 2011 China • Guiyang Investment and Trade Fair grand opening in Guiyang

贵州上海经贸合作项目签约仪式现场

Guizhou and Shanghai economic and trade cooperation project signing ceremony site

In 2011, the province to achieve 175 billion yuan of total retail sales of social consumer goods, an increase of 18%. Among which, the towns of 143.4 billion yuan, an increase of 19.7%, the rurals of 31.6 billion yuan, an increase of 18.8%; wholesale trade of 16.82 billion yuan, an increase of 38.9%, retail trade of 140.47 billion yuan, an increase of 17.9%, the lodging industry of 1.39 billion yuan, an increase of 20.9%, food and beverage industry of 16.31 billion yuan, an increase of 16.7%.

In 2011, the province's import and export to achieve a record high, cargo import and export of $ 4.88 billion, an increase of 55.2%, ranking the fourth in the nation, ranking third in western twelve provinces. Among which, exports of $ 2.98 billion, an increase of 55.5%; imported $ 1.9 billion, an increase of 54.8%.

In 2011, the province had approved 70 foreign direct investment projects, an increase of 89.19% total contracted foreign investment of $ 1,707,850,000, an increase of 279.32%, the actual utilization of foreign investment total of $ 67,322 million, an increase of 127.85%

省政府召开外贸进出口联席会议

The provincial government held the import and export joint

第三届泛珠三角区域口岸合作联席会议暨口岸大通关签约仪式

Third Fanzhu Triangle Area Port Cooperation Joint Conference and the port customs clearance signing ceremony

黔川经贸合作项目签约仪式现场

Guizhou and Sichuan economic and trade cooperation project signing ceremony site

In accordance with "the expanding area and adjust the location of Guizhou Province Development Zone principles and approval procedures" "the basic principles and the approval process of provincial development zone in Guizhou Province", actively promote original development zone extended regional survey conducted in an orderly, encourage and support conditions of industrial parks to declare a provincial development zone. In 2011, complete the 12 provincial development zone extended regional survey audit approval, the provincial government formally approved a new 17 provincial development zones, exceeding the annual objectives and tasks. Development Zone in fixed assets investment of 111.8 billion yuan, 188.9 billion yuan of industrial output value. Increase policy financial support, the provincial financial arrangements of 100 million yuan of special funds, and focus on supporting the development zone infrastructure and standard factory building.

In 2011, the province completed a total of foreign contracted projects, labor cooperation, design and consulting of $ 290 million, an increase of 32%. The project involves 28 countries and regions in Sri Lanka, Kazakhstan, Ghana, Libya, Indonesia and so on. 20.1 million yuan o fthe implementation of the Sino-British NO.V infrastructure projects, Provincial Angriculture Committee pasture development, livestock management and livestock improvement training program of 660,000 yuan.

贵州省工商局

Guizhou Provincial Industrial and Commercial Bureau

2月21日，省政府新闻办公室、新工商局等单位召开新闻发布会，就第九届全国民族运动会特殊标志保护内容、注册备案情况、许可使用和管理以及净化广告市场等方面的情况进行了发布

February 21, the unit of the Provincial Government Information Office, Industrial and Commercial Bureau held a news conference on the special logo to protect the content, registration and record the circumstances, permit the use and management, and purification advertising market release of the ninth National Games

2011年3月，全国工商系统打击侵犯知识产权和制售假冒伪劣商品专项行动现场会在仁怀召开

March 2011, the national industrial and commercial systems to combat IPR infringement and selling counterfeit and shoddy goods special action on-site meetings to be held in Renhuai

6月21日，省工商局党组被省直机关工委表彰为“先进党组”

June 21, Provincial Industrial and Commercial Bureau party was recognized as "advanced party group" by the working committee of the provincial authorities

2011年，贵州省工商系统坚持“两加一推”主基调，认真实施工业强省战略和城镇化带动战略，把服务科学发展作为第一要务，把市场监管作为第一职责，把消费维权作为重要使命，将党的建设和队伍建设作为政治保证，全面完成了各项工作任务。省工商局领导班子被省直机关工委评为2009-2011年度“学习型领导班子”，省局被中宣部、司法部、全国普法办联合表彰为“五五”普法先进单位，被国家工商总局评为“打击侵犯知识产权和制售假冒伪劣商品专项行动先进集体”，被省保密委、省国家保密局评为2010-2011年度贵州省保密法制宣传教育先进单位，被中央文明委授予第三批“全国文明单位”，省局党组被省直机关工委评为党建工作先进党组，省局12315申诉举报处被贵州省“巾帼建功”活动协调小组授予“巾帼文明岗”称号。

法治建设。圆满完成省委、省政府交办的行政审批前置许可事项清理工作；全面清理行政审批事项；梳理行政职权、编制行政职权目录、细化行政处罚自由裁量权；继续做好行政复议委员会试点工作和行政诉讼工作。

反垄断与反不正当竞争执法。紧紧围绕以转变执法理念，创新监管方式，坚持以改革创新市场监管体系，促进经济社会又好又快、更好更快的发展为主线，以维护公平竞争市场秩序为目标，以营造公平、公正竞争市场环境为主题，以治理商业贿赂专项整治、医药纠风、反公用企业和打击侵犯知识产权违法行为为工作重点，严厉查处经济领域各类违法行为。

直销监督管理。全省打击传销工作取得明显成效，初步建立了“党委领导、政府负责、社会协同、公众参与”的打击传销工作机制，基本形成了部门联动、各司其职、相互配合、权责一致的工作格局。

消费者权益保护。一是切实加强12315“四个平台”建设，进一步完善消费维权长效机制；二是开展“家电下乡”、太阳能热水器、纸巾纸产品、汽车轮胎、电动自行车、电线电缆和机动车制动液等专项整治；三是继续推进12315“五进”工作，全面建设“一会两站”；四是及时有效处理消费者投诉，努力提升消费维权社会服务水平。

6月24日，贵州省工商系统庆祝建党90周年专题党课在贵阳国际会议中心举行
June 24, the topic of industrial and commercial system in Guizhou Province celebrate its 90th anniversary gave lectures held at the Guiyang International Conference Center

2011年，省工商局处以上领导干部与紫云县水塘镇62户困难户结成了帮扶对子
In 2011, leading cadres above the provincial Industrial and Commercial Bureau with Ziyun County Shuitang Town 62 needy households formed helping pairs

2011年，全省工商系统广泛开展“访企业、解难题”活动
In 2011, the province's industrial and commercial systems extensively to "visit enterprises, and solve problems" activities

In 2011, Guizhou Province industrial and commercial systems to adhere to the "two plus one push" the main tone, and earnestly implement the strategy of industrial province strategy and urbanization led, the service of scientific development as the top priority, market supervision as the first duty, the consumer rights as important mission, party building and team building as a political guarantee, complete all tasks. Provincial Industrial and Commercial Bureau of the leading bodies of provincial organs as 2009 - 2011 "learning leadership", the Provincial Joint recognition of the Central Propaganda Department, the Justice Department, the National Propaganda Law Department "55" propaganda law advanced units, the State SAIC "to combat IPR infringement special action of making and selling fake and shoddy goods advanced collective", be the province confidentiality of the Commission, the State Secrets Bureau as the 2010 - 2011 Guizhou Province confidentiality law publicity and education advanced unit, the Central Committee of civilization awarded the third installment of "National Civilized Unit", the provincial bureau party group of provincial organs as the advanced party group of the work of party building, the provincial bureau 12315 complaints and reports, the Department of Guizhou Province "women achievement" Activities Coordination Group awarded the title of "women civilization station".

Rule of law. Successful completion of the provincial party committee and gorvenment the administrative examination and approval of pre-licensing matters assigned by the provincial government to clean-up work; comprehensive clean-up of administrative examination and approval; combing the administrative authority, the preparation of administrative authority directory, refine the discretion of the administrative penalty; continue to do the pilot work of administrative reconsideration committee and administrative proceedings.

The anti-monopoly and anti-unfair competition law enforcement. Closely around the main line to change the philosophy of the law enforcement, innovative forms of regulation, persist in reform and innovation to the market supervision system, and promote sound and rapid, better and faster economic and social development, in order to maintain a fair competitive market order as the goal, to create a fair, fair competitive market environment, to combat bribery in business regulation, the rectification of medicine, anti-public enterprises and the fight against infringement of intellectual property violations as the key work, severely crack down on the various types of violations of the economic sphere.

Direct supervision and management. Province-wide crack down on pyramid schemes made remarkable initial achievements, establishment of the "Party committee leadership, government responsibility, social coordination, public participation" in the fight against pyramid selling mechanism, the basic form of departmental interaction, carry out their duties, cooperate with each other, the same powers and responsibilities pattern.

2011年，全省共建立食品流通行业协会81个，行业协会分会357个，会员51620户
In 2011, the province had set up 81 food distribution industry associations, industry associations Branch 357, Member 51,620

2011年，全省工商系统共查处公平交易执法案件6071件，“傍名牌”案件329件，商业贿赂案件50件，公用企业限制竞争案件11件，有效维护了贵州省公平竞争的市场秩序
In 2011, provincial industrial and commercial systems were investigated and handled fair trade enforcement cases 6,071, cases of "illegal use of the famous brand" 329, 50 cases of commercial bribery, public enterprises to limit competition in cases of 11, effectively safeguarding the market order of fair competition in Guizhou Province

市场规范管理。认真做好商品交易市场分类监管工作；扎实开展“农资打假”行动，有力维护农村市场经济秩序和农民合法权益；认真开展文明集市创建活动。

食品流通监督管理。一是加强市场主体准入管理，切实规范证照核发工作；二是扎实开展了对食品非法添加和滥用食品添加剂、“瘦肉精”等专项整治；三是充分发挥检测体系作用；四是深入推进流通环节食品行业自律体系建设。

市场主体注册登记。全系统坚持“畅通、变通和沟通”的服务方式，落实“非禁即允”的要求，最大限度降低门槛、最大限度放宽条件、最大努力缩短办事时限，全力服务市场主体膨胀。

市场主体信用监督管理。积极开展市场主体信用体系建设和信用分类监管，推进社会诚信建设。

广告监督管理。一是加大力度打击以药品、保健食品、医疗、涉性广告为重点的虚假违法广告；二是加强行政指导；三是在“酒博会”、“九运会”期间对媒体发布广告进行事前咨询和开展行政提醒；四是积极开展户外广告、固定形式印刷品广告和部分商品滥用“特供”、“专供”标识整治行动；五是认真处理消费者的申诉和举报；六是认真组织全国助理广告师、广告师职业水平首次考试；七是加大广告监测力度。

商标管理。一是全省商标申请快速增长；二是驰名、著名商标稳步发展；三是农产品商标、地理标志步入快车道；四是加大商标法律法规宣传；五是贯彻落实商标富农与社会主义新农村建设；六是加大市场主体实施商标战略行政指导力度；七是加大《贵州省著名商标认定和保护办法》立法调研工作的步伐；八是召开了第九届民族运动会特殊标志保护及净化广告市场新闻发布；九是开展打击侵犯知识产权和制售假冒伪劣商品专项行动。

2011年年初凝冻期间，全省工商执法人员加大市场监管力度，有效维护市场秩序
Freezing during the beginning of the year, in 2011, the province's law enforcement officers to increase market supervision, effectively maintaining the market order

2011年，全省工商机关共指导签订农业订单合同10.4568万份，合同涉及金额13.17亿元
In 2011, the province's industrial and commercial authorities guided and signed an agricultural contract orders 104,568 copies, contracts involving an amount of 1.317 billion yuan

Consumer Protection. First, strengthen the construction of 12315 "four platforms", and further improve the long-term mechanism of consumer rights; second, is to carry out the "home appliances to village", solar water heaters, paper products, automobile tires, electric bicycles, wire and cable, and motor vehicle brake fluid and other special regulation; third, 12315 "5 into" work continue to promote the comprehensive construction of "one meet two stations"; fourth, timely and effective handling of consumer complaints, and strive to enhance consumer rights level of social services.

Market Regulation. Earnestly do well the commodity trading market supervision; carry out the "agricultural counterfeiting" action, effectively maintaining the order of market economy in rural areas and farmers' legitimate rights and interests; seriously to create civilized bazaar activities.

The food circulation supervision and management. The first is to strengthen the management of access to market players, effectively regulate the licenses issued by the work; the second is to carry out illegally added to food and abuse of food additives, "lean meat" special rectification; the third is to give full play to the role of inspection system; the fourth is to further promote the food industry self-regulation of the circulation system.

Registration of the main players in the market. System-wide adhere to the "smooth, flexibility and communication" services, the implementation of "non-forbidden or allowed" requirements, to minimize the threshold, the maximum relaxation of the conditions, the maximum effort to shorten the work time limits, full service of the market main body expansion.

Market players credit supervision and management. Active in the market the main credit system and credit classification regulation, promote social integrity.

Advertising supervision and control. First, greater efforts to crack down on false and illegal advertisements of medicines, health food, health care, involving sexual advertisement; second, the strengthening of administrative guidance; third, "Wine Expo", "Ninth National Games" period released to the media advertising prior consultation and carry out administrative alert; fourth, is active in outdoor advertising, fixed form printed advertisement and some of the goods to the abuse of "special use", "designed for using" identifies the remediation action; fifth, is to seriously deal with consumer complaints and reporting; sixth, seriously organize assistant advertising division, advertising division professional level exam for the first time; seventh, intensify advertising monitoring.

The administration of trademarks. First, the rapid growth of the province's trademark applications; second, is well-known, famous trademark got steady development; third, agricultural product trademarks, geographical indications into the fast lane; fourth, is to increase the publicity of the trademark law and regulations propaganda; fifth, is to implement the trademark rich farmers with the socialist new rural construction; sixth, increase the market main body administrative guidance and implementation of trademark strategy; seventh, is to increase the pace of legislative research work in "Guizhou Province famous trademark identification and protection measures"; eighth, is the convening of the Ninth National Games the distinctive emblems of protection and purification of the advertising market press release; ninth, special actions to combat IPR infringement and selling counterfeit and shoddy goods.

2011年以来，省工商局加大食品安全检测力度，确保了"酒博会"、"九运会"、"省旅发大会"等大型活动的食品安全，确保了全省流通环节无重、特大食品安全事故

Since 2011, the Provincial Industrial and Commercial Bureau to increase food safety testing efforts, to ensure the "Wine Expo", "Ninth National Games", "Provincial Tourism Conference" and other large-scale ctivities food safety, to ensure that no re-circulation in the province, serious food safety incidents

2011年贵州遭受特大干旱以来，全省工商系统600多个红盾应急分队奋战在为群众送水的一线

Since Guizhou suffered from severe drought in 2011, the provincial industrial and commercial systems over 600 Hongdun emergency unit fought in the first line of bottled water for the masses

贵州省水利厅

Department of Water Resources of Guizhou Province

息峰鱼简河水库
Xifeng Yujianhe reservoir

紫云格八水库
The Ziyungeba reservoirs

水利投入创历史新高。全年共完成水利投资151.78亿元，比2010增长48.8%，是“十一五”年平均投入的3.25倍，创下历史新高。

重点工程建设取得突破性进展。加快推进民生水利新发展。全面加快直接关系到群众切身利益的水利基础设施建设。全年新增解决农村饮水安全330万人，兑现了政府“十大民生”工程中关于农村饮水安全问题的庄严承诺。

水利规划和项目前期工作扎实推进。防汛抗旱减灾成效显著。

荔波大七孔电站（摄影/杨争红）
Libo seven holes power station (Photography / Yang Zhenghong)

油菜河水库
Rapeseed River Reservoir

水利改革发展取得了新成效。一是稳定增长的水利投融资机制初步建立，积极搭建各级水利投融资平台。二是进一步扩大了水务一体化管理体制改革范围。三是基层水利服务体系建设进一步加强。

最严格的水资源管理制度启动实施。依法治水管水能力进一步提升。水文和水利科技支撑不断加强。

Water input made a new high history record. Water conservancy investment throughout the year completed a total of 15.178 billion yuan, up 48.8% compared with 2010, "the 11th Five-Year Plan" average of 3.25 times, made a new high history record.

Construction of key projects is a breakthrough. Accelerate the development of people's livelihood water conservancy. Full speed the water conservancy infrastructure construction which is directly related to the vital interests of the mass. Throughout the year to add rural drinking water safety around 3.3 million people, and to honor the solemn commitment of the government "Ten people's livelihood" projects on the problem of rural drinking water safety.

Water Resources Planning and project preparatory work pushed forward steadily. Flood Control and Drought Relief made remarkable results.

Water reform and development has made new achievements. First, the steady growth of the investment and finance mechanisms initially established, positive structures at all levels of the investment and finance platform. Second, the further expansion of water affairs management system. Third, the primary water services system was strengthened.

The most stringent water management system to start implementation. Law pipes of water was further enhanced. Hydrology and water resources science and technology support has been constantly strengthened.

贵州省文化厅

Guizhou Provincial Department of Culture

贵州省庆祝中国共产党成立90周年大型文艺晚会《迎七一•促跨越》
Guizhou Province to celebrate the Communist Party of China 90th anniversary large-scale variety show "welcome 7•1, promote across"

《多彩贵州风》赴美国新泽西州演出现场
"Colorful Guizhou" live performances to the United States, New Jersey

中国•贵州“印度尼西亚之夜”文艺演出
Guizhou• China, "Indonesia Night" theatrical performance

第五届亚州青年动漫大赛开幕式
5th Asian Youth Animation Competition opening ceremony

一年来，贵州省文化厅围绕省委、省政府“加速发展、加快转型、推动跨越”这一主线，立足特色、创新思路、真抓实干，努力推进全省文化建设又好又快、更好更快发展。

公共文化服务体系建设深入推进。全省公共图书馆、文化馆（站）基本实现免费开放。全省“十大民生工程”目标任务全面完成。成功举办“第九届贵州省少儿艺术节”。开展艺术之乡评定。完成全省文化馆评估定级。组织大规模基层文化骨干培训。

艺术生产和重大文化活动取得新成绩。文化市场不断繁荣规范。文化遗产保护取得实效。对外文化交流工作取得新成绩。文化体制改革深入推进。积极加强横向联系与协作。

Over the past year, the Guizhou Provincial Department of Culture around the provincial committee, government "to accelerate the development, accelerate the transition, to promote across" the main line, based on the features, innovative ideas, solid work, make efforts to promote sound and rapid cultural construction in the province, and better and faster development.

In-depth progress of the construction of public cultural service system. The province's public libraries, cultural centers (stations) is basically free to the public. The objectives and tasks of the province's "10 livelihood projects" completed. The successful holding of the "Ninth Guizhou Province Children Arts Festival. To carry out the hometown of the arts assessment. Complete the province's cultural centers, assessment grading. Organization of large-scale grass-roots cultural backbone of the training.

Artistic production and major cultural activities to achieve new results. Cultural market is increasing prosperity and specifications. Protection of cultural tangible heritage to achieve results. Cultural exchanges with foreign made new achievements. Further promote the reform of cultural system. Actively to strengthen the horizontal linkages and collaboration.

贵州省林业厅

Forestry Department of Guizhou Province

牛角山生态茶园
The Niujiaoshan ecological tea garden

2011年，全省森林面积731万公顷，森林覆盖率达41.53%，活立木蓄积量3.89亿立方米。

2011年，全省完成营造林面积27.6万公顷，完成封山育林面积14.48万公顷，完成退耕还林荒山造林1.87万公顷，完成天保工程封山育林面积0.6万公顷。

2011年，全省发生森林火灾430起，森林火灾受害率为0.127‰。森林病虫鼠害面积27.18万公顷，森林病虫鼠害无公害防治率98.29%。

2011年，全省林业系统自然保护105个，其中国家级7个，省级3个，市州级13个，县级82个；自然保护区面积81.42万公顷，约占全省国土面积的5.6%。

2011年，全省森林公园72个，其中国家级22个，省级31个；森林公园面积26.07万公顷，约占全省国土面积的1.79%。

郁郁葱葱的册亨桉树林
The lush Ceheng eucalypt forests

In 2011, the province's forest area was 7.31 million hectares, the forest coverage rate reached 41.53%, 389 million cubic meters of stumpage.

In 2011, the province completed the afforestation area of 276,000 hectares, closing off an area of 144,800 hectares, completion of returning farmland to forest afforestation of 18,700 hectares, the completion of the Natural Forest Protection Project closing off an area of 6,000 hectares.

In 2011, the province's 430 cases of forest fires, forest fire victims rate of 0.127 ‰. Forest pest and rodent area of 271,800 hectares, forest pest and rodent pollution prevention and control rate of 98.29%.

In 2011, 105 Nature Conservation of the province's forestry system, including seven national and three provincial, 13 of city and state level, 82 at the county level; Nature Reserve with an area of 814,200 hectares, accounting for about 5.6% of the total land area.

In 2011, the 72 province's forest parks, 22 national and 31 provincial level; Forest Park area of 260,700 hectares, accounting for 1.79% of the total land area.

贵州省地方税务局

Guizhou Local Taxation Bureau

税收志愿者小分队深入基层
Tax volunteer teams to the grassroots

2011年，全省地税系统严格坚持依法治税、科学治税、服务优税、人才兴税、创新强税，认真履行工作职责，充分发挥税收职能作用。全年共组织各项收入547.16亿元，比上年同期增长36.75%。其中，税收收入和教育费附加两项收入520亿元，比上年同期增长33.89%，超序时进度16.38个百分点，实现我省地税机构成立以来税收收入总量的历史性突破；代征文化事业建设费、地方教育附加、煤炭价格调节基金、残疾人就业保障金等非税收入27.16亿元，比上年同期增长1.29倍。

坚持依法组织收入，全省地税收入突破500亿元。组织收入实现“两大历史性突破”；六个税种”位次前移；呈现四大增收“亮点”。积极发挥税收职能作用，全力支持地方经济发展。强化科技支撑，税收征管质效稳步提升。

福泉市局税收志愿者进超市
The Fuquan Board tax volunteer to enter the supermarket

In 2011, the province's land tax system strictly adhere to the tax according to law, science taxation, excellent tax service, and talent prospering tax, innovation strong tax. conscientiously perform their duties, and give full play to the tax functions. Were organized throughout the year the income of 54.716 billion yuan, an increase of 36.75% over the same period of last year. Which, income tax and education surtax two revenue of 52 billion yuan, an increase of 33.89% over the same period of last year, 16.38 percent points of the super-sequence progress, to achieve a historic breakthrough of the Local Tax Bureau in our province since the founding of the total tax revenue; levied by the culture construction costs, local education additional coal price adjustment fund, the employment of persons with disabilities security payments and other non-tax revenue of 2.716 billion yuan, 1.29 times more than the same period of last year.Adhere to the law to organize the income, the province's land tax revenue exceeded 50 billion yuan. "Two historic breakthrough" in organizational revenue; ranking forward "six taxes"; showing the four income "bright spot". Actively play the tax functional role, to support local economic development. Strengthen the scientific and technological support, steady improvement of tax collection and quality efficiency.

贵阳海关

Guiyang Customs

2011年，贵阳海关坚持“以人为本、文化兴关、建设特色海关”的工作思路，贯彻“依法行政、为国把关、服务经济、促进发展”的工作方针，落实海关总署党组提出的“把好国门、搞好服务、防好风险、带好队伍”的要求，超额完成全年各项工作任务，努力推动地方开放型经济跨越式发展。2011年，贵阳海关共监管进出口转关运输货物231万吨，总值11.01亿美元；征收关税和进口环节税8.8亿元人民币；审批减免税6762万美元；加工贸易合同备案156个，合同金额2.44亿美元；监管进出境旅客5.17万人（次），监管行李物品10.4万件。

2011年，贵阳海关继续优化人力资源配置，改善干部梯次结构；应收尽收，强化税收征管；优化服务，促进外贸发展；提高打私效能，维护经济秩序；转变作风，加强队伍建设。

2011年11月26日，海关总署署长于广洲与贵州省省长赵克志在贵阳签署《海关总署·贵州省合作备忘录》
November 26, 2011, the Director of General Administration of Customs Yu Guangzhou andGuizhou Province Governor Zhao Kezhi signed the "Customs General Administration of Guizhou Province Memorandum of Cooperation " in Guiyang

2011年12月7日，贵阳海关党组书记、关长宋立强赴开磷集团息烽小寨坝生产基地进行考察调研
December 7, 2011, party secretary of Guiyang Customs and Excise Song Liqiang went Kailin Group the Xifeng Xiaozhai dam production base to carry out investigation and study

In 2011, the Guiyang Customs insist on "people-oriented culture proper the customs, building characteristics of Customs" work ideas, and implement the "administration according to law, proposed for the country to ensure the service economy and promote development" the working principle, the implementation of the General Administration of Customs party of the requirements "the excess of good country, good service, anti-good risk with a good team", to complete the various tasks for the whole year, efforts to promote the development of local open economy by leaps and bounds. In 2011, Guiyang Customs supervision of import and export transit transport of goods of 2.31 million tons, worth $ 1,101,000,000; tariffs and import taxes of 880 million yuan; approval of tax reduction and exemption of $ 67,620,000; processing trade contracts for the record 156, the contract amount $ 244 million; regulatory inward and outward passengers to 51,700 persons (times), the regulatory baggage 104,000.

In 2011, Guiyang Customs will continue to optimize the allocation of human resources, improve the echelon structure of cadres; due taxes, strengthening tax collection and management; optimization services, promote the development of foreign trade; increase smuggling and performance, maintain the economic order; change their work style, to strengthen the team building.

贵州省公路局

Guizhou Province Highway Bureau

省公路局“四帮四促”工作组走村串户走访、看望和慰问特困户
Provincial highway "four help and four promote" Working Group vis t villages, went to visit the destitute familiesc

贵州省公路局系贵州省交通运输厅领导下的副厅级事业单位，负责管养国省干线公路，对县乡公路的管理、改造和养护进行行业管理和业务指导，并承担部分高速公路建设任务，实行“条块结合、以条为主”的管理体制。

2011年，贵州省公路局全力推进高速公路、农村公路建设，认真抓好国省干线公路改造，统筹协调重点加强工业园区周边线路国省干线大中修，固定资产投资完成创历史新高，全年完成固定资产投资196.8亿元。加强公路养护管理，国省干线公路路况良好，行车安全通畅，标志标线醒目，安保设施齐全，环境和谐舒适，被交通运输部评为“‘十一五’全国干线公路养护管理工作进步单位”。国省干线公路优良率64.4%，县公路好路率提高到80.8%，乡村公路好路率60.5%。公路服务能力和水平有较大提升，农村公路通达深度进一步提高，路网结构进一步完善。路政管理日趋规范，信息化建设逐步推进，安全生产态势基本平稳。

普安高速公路风姿（普定至安顺及安顺西绕城高速公路开通收费）
The Expressway Puan grace (Puding to Anshun Anshun West Ring Expressway opened fees)

公路预防性养护新工艺演示
Highway preventive maintenance technology demonstration

积极开展应急救援演练
Actively carry out emergency rescue drill

Guizhou Province Highway Bureau is under the leadership of the deputy departmental level institutions of Guizhou Province Department of Transportation, responsible for the custody of the national and provincial trunk highways, industry management and operational guidance on the management, transformation and maintenance of the county road, and bear part of the highway construction task, the implementation of "compartmentalized integration of the article" management system.

In 2011, the Guizhou Province Highway Bureau make efforts to promote highway, rural road construction, a good grasp of the national and provincial trunk highway upgrade, the integrated and coordinated focus on strengthening the industrial park surrounding the line of national and provincial trunk large and medium-sized repair, investment in fixed assets hit a record high, the annual fixed asset investment of 19.68 billion yuan. To strengthen the management of road maintenance, national and provincial trunk highway traffic, smooth road safety, eye-catching signs and markings, security facilities, harmonious and comfortable environment, the Ministry of Transport awarded it as the "'Eleventh Five-Year' national trunk highway maintenance and management progress unit". National and provincial trunk highway rate of 64.4%, good way of county highway rate to 80.8%, rural roads good road rate of 60.5%. A larger increase highway capacity and level, to further improve the rural road accessible depth, to further improve the road network structure. Road administration has become increasingly standardized, the information construction pushed step by step, the production safety situation is basically stable.

稳价安民　服务发展　构建和谐
贵州省物价局

Stabilize Price and People's livelihood　Serve Development　Build harmony

Guizhou Provincial Price Bureau

2011年，全省居民消费价格指数CPI累计同比上涨5.1%，低于全国0.3个百分点，优化和营造了有利的价格服务环境，切实促进了经济加快发展与社会和谐稳定。一是努力保持价格总水平基本稳定。扶持农业生产，切实稳定农产品价格，完善流通体系，强化重要商品储备、调运，加强监测预警分析和调控引导，稳定社会预期，督促各项稳控物价措施的落实。二是充分发挥基金作用。全省全年共征收价调基金约7.5亿元，切实用于扶持生产、保障供应、稳定价格、安定民生和促进经济可持续发展等。三是积极疏导价格矛盾。两次调整疏导电价，缓解煤电价格矛盾，保障电力供应。四是加强价格监督检查。全省共查处价格违法案件735件，切实维护了市场价格秩序。五是加强民生价格监管。加强医疗服务、教育、住房、旅游等价费管理，建立并启动最低生活保障和失业保险金标准与物价上涨挂钩联动机制。六是加大清费治乱力度。全省共清理取消、停止征收收费项目130项，降低收费标准11项。

2012年2月28日，赵克志省长到省物价局调研指导工作
February 28, 2012, Zhao Kezhi Governor to the Provincial Price Bureau research to guide the work

2011年5月5日，省物价局陈仁贵局长（右二）在榕江县农贸市场调研市场物价
May 5, 2011, Provincial Price Bureau director Chen Rengui (second from right) had research of the market prices in Rongjiang County farmers' market

2011年3月9日，省物价局陈仁贵局长在铜仁地区调研市场物价召开座谈会
March 9, 2011, Provincial Price Bureau director Chen Rengui held a forum to research the market price in Tongren Prefecture

2012年4月26日，省物价局在都匀市召开全省稳控物价暨推进平价商店建设工作现场会，图为参会领导和代表实地考察都匀市平价商店建设情况
April 26, 2012, the Provincial Price Bureau held the province's stability control prices cum promote fair-price shops meetings in Duyun City, the picture shows leaders and representatives participants ispect the field trips Duyun fair-price shops construction

In 2011, the province's consumer price index (CPI) cumulative increase rose 5.1%, 0.3 percentage points lower than the national, optimize and create a favorable price environment, and effectively promote and accelerate economic development and social harmony and stability. First, efforts to maintain the basic stability of the overall price level. To support agricultural production, and effectively stabilize the prices of agricultural products, improve the circulation system, and strengthen the reserves of important commodities, transporting, and strengthen monitoring and early warning analysis and regulatory guidance, stabilize social expectations, and urge the implementation of the stability control price measures. Second, is to give full play of the fund role. The province throughout the year levied a total of about 750 million yuan price adjustment fund, and effectively used to support production and ensure supply, stable prices, stability of people's livelihood and promote sustainable economic development. Third, is positive to ease the price of contradictions. Two adjustments to ease electricity, coal and electricity price mitigation conflicts, protect the power supply. Fourth, is to strengthen the price supervision and inspection. The province investigated 735 cases of illegal price, to effectively maintain the market price of the order. Fifth, strengthen the people's livelihood and price control. Strengthen medical services, education, housing, tourism equivalent fee management, the establishment and start of the minimum living allowance and the unemployment insurance payment and price increases linked to the linkage mechanism. Sixth, is to intensify efforts to combat confusion and clear fee. Province were cleared, canceled, to cease the levying of fees 130, 11 lower fees.

贵州盐业集团

Congjiang County

2011年全省盐业工作会议在贵阳召开
2011 the province's salt industry work conference held in Guiyang

贵州盐业集团于2000年11月8日经贵州省政府同意挂牌成立，是省管国有大型企业之一。主要职责是认真落实食盐专营政策措施，保证全省合格碘盐供应，致力于消除碘缺乏危害；努力推进集团改革发展、做大做强，实现国有资产的保值增值。集团现有成员单位85个，职工3789人。集团公司与省盐务局一套人马、职责分开、合署办公。贵州省国资委是集团的上级主管部门，贵州省经信委是盐政管理的行业主管部门。

2011年，集团总资产21.04亿元、净资产9.13亿元、营业收入12.81亿元、税利1. 3亿元。集团调整转型初显成效，盐和非盐收入比例调整为7:3。市场网络、房地产业、酒店旅游和资本运作“四大业务”基本形成。11年来，集团累计供应碘盐200多万吨，有效保证了全省食盐正常供应，推动我省防治碘缺乏病工作取得了显著成效。

贵州盐业集团与贵州省农信社签定《战略合作框架协议》，省国资委党委副书记、常务副主任谢谦（后排左六）出席会议并作重要讲话

Guizhou Salt Group and Guizhou Province Rural Credit Cooperative signed a "strategic cooperation framework agreement", provincial SASAC deputy party secretary, deputy director Xieqian (sixth from left in back row) attended the meeting and make an important speech

贵州盐业集团与重庆盐业集团签订战略合作框架协议和出资协议书（前排右二为贵盐集团董事长刘仰瑞，前排左二为重盐集团董事长陈逸根）

The Guizhou Salt Group and Chongqing Salt Industry Group signed a strategic cooperation framework agreement and the contribution agreement (second from right in the front row is Guizhou Salt Group chairman Liu Yangrui, second from left is in the front row is Diazonium Group chairman Chen Yigen)

Guizhou Salt Group is agreed to formally established by Guizhou provincial government on November 8, 2000, is one of the management of the provincial state-owned large enterprises. The main responsibility is to conscientiously implement the salt monopoly policies and measures, to ensure the supply of qualified iodized salt in the province, and work towards the elimination of iodine deficiency hazards; to make efforts to promote reform and development of the Group, the bigger and stronger, increasing the value of state assets. The Group currently has 85 member units, staff of 3,789 people.Corporation and the Salt Bureau is a suit of troops, segregation of duties, under one roof. Guizhou Province SASAC is the higher authorities of the Commission by letter of Guizhou Province, is the industry department in charge of the Salt Administration management.

In 2011, total assets of 2.104 billion yuan, net assets of 913 million yuan, sales income of 1.281 billion yuan, profits and taxes 130 million yuan. Adjustment and transformation of the Group is paying off, adjust the salt and salt-income ratio is 7:3. Market network, real estate, hotels and tourism, and capital operation of "four main business" is basically formed. In 11 years, the Group's cumulative supply over 20 million tons of iodized salt, and effectively to ensure the normal supply of the province's salt, made remarkable achievements to promote the province to combat iodine deficiency disorders.

贵州储备物资管理局

Guizhou Material Reserve Authority

贵州国储物流有限公司揭牌仪式上，全国政协常委、贵州省原政协副主席吴嘉甫（左二），贵州储备物资管理局党组书记、局长张映芳（左一），贵州省发改委铁建办主任陈熵（右一），中石化贵州分公司总经理何建新（右二）为公司揭牌

Guizhou State Reserve Logistics Co., Ltd. opening ceremony, the CPPCC Standing Committee, the CPPCC Vice Chairman of Guizhou Province Wu Jiafu (second from left), the party secretary of Guizhou Material Reserve Authority, the Director Zhang Yingfang (first from left), Guizhou Province Development and Reform Commission of Railwany Building Office Director Chen Shang (first from right), general manager of Sinopec Guizhou branch He Jianxin (second from right) for the company inaugurated

贵州国储物流有限公司揭牌仪式上，贵州国储物流有限公司董事长、总经理汪元发（左）与中石油贵州分公司总经理张宏（右）签订合作协议

The opening ceremony of the Guizhou State Reserve Logistics Co., Ltd., chairman of the State Reserve in Guizhou Logistics Co., Ltd., general manager Wang Yuanfa (left) and Guizhou Branch of CNPC general manager Zhang Hong(right) signed a cooperation agreement

国家发展改革委国家物资储备局分类推进事业单位改革领导小组办公室副主任刘毅军（中）到贵州储备物资管理局调研改革工作

National Development and Reform Commission and the National Material Reserve Classification promoting institutions Reform Leading Group Office of the Deputy Director Liu Yijun (middle) to Guizhou Material Reserve Authority has research and reform of work

2011年，贵州储备物资管理局认真履行“服务国防建设、应对突发事件、参与宏观调控，维护国家安全”的职责，在履行职责中主动服务地方经济建设，在服务地方经济建设中壮大贵州储备事业的发展，取得了积极成效。

在管好国储物资的同时，及时出库数万吨成品油，缓解贵州出现的“油荒”；完成“十二五”事业发展规划；完成五三一处安改扩建工程，启动一五八处油库扩容建设，启动六三一处铁路专用线建设。

按照国家发展改革委国家物资储备局推进事业单位改革的总体部署，贵州储备物资管理局以事企分开为切入点，以规范经营性活动为主要内容，通过对事业单位所属全部企业进行资产清查，合并新设贵州国储物流有限公司，于2011年5月26日通过贵州省工商行政管理局注册，7月28日揭牌正式成立。公司成立后，贵州储备物资管理局所属各基层事业单位彻底剥离经营业务，所有业务向公司移交。公司同时控股贵州华储石化公司，自主经营成品油批发业务。通过事企职能分开、机构分开、财务分开、人员分开，清晰划分了事企界面，分类推进事业单位改革迈出坚实一步。

贵州国储物流有限公司目前主营通用物资仓储业务、石化产品仓储经营业务和铁路专用线货物代理业务。公司在贵州省共设立7个管理部，1家控股子公司，自有各类仓库总面积超过12万平米，货场总面积8万余平米，铁路专用线6条，油罐总罐容数十万立方米，下属控股子公司贵州华储石化有限公司，注册资本3010万元，拥有成品油批发经营资质。2011年，公司实现经营收入2800万余元。

贵州储备物资管理局党组书记、局长张映芳（左三）陪同国家发展改革委国家物资储备局副局长芮执多（右三）调研六三一处在安顺市的专用线建设工作

Party secretary of Guizhou Material Reserve Authority, the Secretary Zhang Yingfang (third from left), accompanied by the National Development and Reform Commission and State Reserves Bureau deputy director of Rui Zhiduo (third from right) have survey of the special line construction work in 631 in Anshun City

贵州储备物资管理局党组书记、局长张映芳（前排左）陪同国家发展改革委国家物资储备局副局长芮执多（前排中）检查五三一处高坪铺仓库物流工作

Party secretary of Guizhou Material Reserve Authority, the Secretary Zhang Yingfang (left in the front row), accompanied by the National Development and Reform Commission and State Reserves Bureau deputy director of Rui Zhiduo (middle in the front row) check 531 Gaopingpu warehouse logistics

贵州储备物资管理局党组书记、局长张映芳（前）在一五八处油库扩容建设仪式上讲话

Party secretary of Guizhou Material Reserve Authority, the Secretary Zhang Yingfang (former) had speech in the ceremony of 158 depot expansion construction

In 2011, Guizhou's Material Reserve Authority conscientiously fulfill "the service of national defense construction, to respond to emergencies, to participate in the macro-control, and safeguarding national security" duties, in discharging their duties in active service in local economic construction, and growth in services in local economic construction in Guizhou the development of reserves, and achieved positive results.

In the management of the State Reserve materials, in a timely manner to the library a few million tons of refined oil, to ease the southwestern province of Guizhou "oil shortage"; completion of the "12th Five-Year" development planning; completed 531 security renovation and expansion project, to start 158 oil tanks expansion construction, to start 631 special railway line construction.

贵州储备物资管理局党组书记、局长张映芳陪同国家发展改革委国家物资储备局副局长刘小江检查油库工作

Party secretary of Guizhou Material Reserve Authority, the Secretary Zhang Yingfang, accompanied by the National Development and Reform Commission and State Reserves Bureau, deputy director Liu Xiaojiang check the oil depot work

Overall arrangements to promote the reform of the institutions in accordance with the National Development and Reform Commission and State Material Reserves Bureau, Guizhou Materials Reserve Authority to separate enterprises and institutions as starting point, to regulate business activities, asset inventory of all enterprises and institutions merge the new Logistics Co., Ltd. of Guizhou State Reserve, Guizhou Province Administration for Industry and registered on May 26, 2011, inauguration was formally established in July 28. After its establishment, the Guizhou Materials Reserve Authority belongs to the grass-roots institutions completely stripped the business, all business transferred to the company. The company also holding the Guizhou Huachu petrochemical companies, operating independently of the wholesale business of refined oil products. By separation of the functions of enterprises and institutions, institutions separate financial affairs, the separation of a clear division of the trouble enterprises interface classification to promote the reform of the institutions has taken a solid step forward.

Guizhou State Reserve Logistics Co., Ltd. is the main general-purpose materials storage operations, warehousing operations of petrochemical products and special railway lines, freight forwarding business. In Guizhou Province has set up 7 Department of Management, a holding subsidiaries, own all kinds of warehouse total area of over 120,000 square meters, the freight yard of the total area of 80,000square meters, special railway lines 6, total tank capacity of 100,000 cubic meters, controlled subsidiary Guizhou TACT Petrochemical Co., Ltd., registered capital of 30.1 million yuan, with the qualification of refined oil wholesale business. In 2011, the company achieved operating income of 28 million yuan.

贵州储备物资管理局成品油经营油罐

The Guizhou Material Reserve Authority refined oil business tank

贵州省烟草专卖局（公司）

Guizhou Province Tobacco Monopoly Bureau (company)

国家烟草专卖局副局长何泽华在贵州省黔南布依族苗族自治州福泉市藜山乡罗坳村实地调研烟叶受灾情况

National Tobacco Monopoly Bureau, deputy director He Zehua has field research in Qiannan Buyi-Miao Autonomous Prefecture of Guizhou Province the Fuquan City Lishan Luoao Village tobacco affected the situation

贵州省烟草产业发展大会在贵阳召开

Guizhou Province Tobacco Industry Development Summit held in Guiyang

省局（公司）举办“相聚党旗下、永远跟党走”党史党建知识竞赛

Organized by the provincial bureau (company) to "meet under the party's flag, and follow the party forever" Party Building Knowledge Contest

贵州省烟草专卖局组建于1983年9月，中国烟草总公司贵州省公司组建于1981年11月，下辖贵阳、遵义、安顺、六盘水市，黔南、黔东南、黔西南自治州、毕节、铜仁地区9个地市级烟草专卖局（公司）及中国烟草贵州进出口有限责任公司、贵州烟草科学研究所及贵州烟草投资管理有限公司，控股管理贵州烟叶复烤有限责任公司。9个地市级烟草专卖局（公司）下设85个县级烟草专卖局（分公司）。截至2011年年底，公司拥有资产总额190亿元，其中，固定资产35.7亿元，流动资产140亿元，所有者权益149亿元。实现“两烟”主营业务收入314亿元，同比增长11.34%；实现税利78.8亿元，增长10.9%。全省烟草商业系统从业人员23297人，在岗员工18915人。

全年查处假冒商标卷烟案件923起，查获假烟2731.2万支、真品卷烟2429.3万支、烟叶烟丝1080.8吨。破获较大规模制售假烟团伙网络案件17起。公安、司法机关依法刑事拘留犯罪嫌疑人134人、逮捕60人、判刑109人。县级局查处5万元以上大要案件164起。

全省种植烟叶292万亩，户均种植规模19.21亩，同比增加1.52亩，签订种植收购合同15.2万份。收购烟叶27.44万吨（548.8万担）。销售烟叶30.164万吨（603.28万担）。实现烟叶税利30.7亿元，下降1.2%。

全省销售卷烟662.8亿支（132.56万箱），同比增长3.91%。销售一类烟57.35亿支（11.47万箱），增长8.65%；销售二类烟20.75亿支（4.15万箱），增长3.13%；销售三类烟183.35亿支（36.67万箱），增长24.6%；销售四类烟291.6亿支（58.32万箱），增长3.9%；销售五类烟109.7亿支（21.94万箱），下降30.1 %。卷烟税利48.3亿元，增长26.7%。2011年，省公司被贵州省企业联合会、贵州省企业家协会评为“2011贵州100强企业”第二名。

贵州烟叶复烤有限责任公司为“胡平伦希望小学“捐资
Guizhou tobacco redrying limited liability company donate to "Hu Pinglun Hope Primary School"

贵阳烟草烟技员和烟农一起运水抗旱
Guiyang tobacco smoke technical staff and farmers had water transport and fight for the drought together

假冒伪劣卷烟销毁现场
Counterfeit cigarettes destroyed the site

卷烟零售终端形象店
The image of cigarette retail store

增温补光系统助力优质壮苗培育
Increase temprature add light system power quality strong seedling cultivation

Guizhou Province Tobacco Monopoly Bureau was established in September 1983, Guizhou Province, China National Tobacco Corporation was established in November 1981, under the jurisdiction of Guiyang, Zunyi, Anshun, Liupanshui City, Qiannan, Qiandongnan Autonomous State, Bijie, Tongren Prefecture, nine municipal Tobacco Monopoly Bureau (company) and the China National Tobacco Guizhou Import and Export Co., Ltd., Guizhou Tobacco Science Research Institute and Guizhou Tobacco Investment Management Limited, the holding management Guizhou tobacco redrying limited liability company. 9 municipal Tobacco Monopoly Bureau (Company) consists of 85 county-level Tobacco Monopoly Bureau (Branch). At the end of 2011, the company has total assets of 19 billion yuan, of which 3.57 billion yuan fixed assets, current assets of 14 billion yuan, 14.9 billion yuan of owner's equity. The "two smoke" main business income of 31.4 billion yuan, an increase of 11.34%; profits and taxes 7.88 billion yuan, an increase of 10.9%. The province's tobacco business systems industry employees 23,297 people, in the post 18,915 people.

Throughout the year investigated 923 cases of counterfeit trademark cigarette cases, and seized 27.312 million counterfeit cigarettes, genuine cigarettes 24,293,000, 1,080.8 tons of tobacco leaf tobacco. Uncovered large-scale manufacturing and selling counterfeit cigarettes from 17 cases of gang network. The public security, judicial organs for 134 criminal detention of criminal suspects, arrested 60 people, sentenced to 109 people. County-level Bureau investigated 164 major cases of more than 50,000 yuan.

2.92 million mu of tobacco cultivation in the province, the average household scale cultivation of 19.21 acres, an increase of 1.52 acres, the signing of the growing purchasing contract 152,000. Acquisition of tobacco 274,400 tons (5.488 million dan). Sale of tobacco 301,640 tons (6,032,800 dan). Tobacco taxes and profits of 3.07 billion yuan, down 1.2%.

The province's sales of 66.28 billion cigarettes (1,325,600 boxes), an increase of 3.91%. Sales of 5.735 billion first class of tobacco (114,700 boxes), an increase of 8.65%; sales of second class of tobacco 2.075 billion, an increase of 3.13% (41,500 boxes); 18.335 billion sale of third class of tobacco (366,700 boxes), an increase of 24.6%; 29.16 billion sale of fourth class of tobacco, an increase of 3.9% (583,200 boxes); 10.97 billion sale of fifth class tobacco (219,400 boxes), a decrease of 30.1%. Cigarette taxes and profits of 4.83 billion yuan, an increase of 26.7%. In 2011, the company was approved by Enterprise Association of Guizhou Province, Guizhou Province Entrepreneur Association as "2011 Guizhou 100 companies" the second.

乐山烟叶工场全景图
The Leshan tobacco factory panorama

中国电信贵州公司

China Telecom Guizhou Branch

中国电信贵州公司促进3G应用推广普及
China Telecom Guizhou Branch promote and popularized 3G applications

2011年，全省各级企业面对激烈的市场竞争环境，紧紧围绕集团、省公司战略部署和工作安排，努力拓展生存空间、全力以赴开拓全业务市场、持续深入推进转型，全面完成集团公司下达的各项经营目标。

统筹兼顾，全业务经营协同发展。全年以移动、宽带、ICT三大重点业务为主要拉动力，统筹固网业务与移动业务、基础业务与转型业务、增量拓展与存量保有。全业务收入市场份额保持相对稳定。

聚焦客户感知，全业务服务支撑能力进一步强化。推进客户服务全过程管控。组织新版全业务客户服务标准贯标及推出“五个一”服务举措，全业务客户服务标准达标率达98.89%，被集团公司评为“全业务客户标准落实标杆单位”。 强化服务质量监督。创新渠道管理模式，提高营销服务能力。持续优化运维体系，“三项精品网络”打造初见成效，全面完成集团各项运行维护考核指标。IT支撑能力持续提高。

第九届全国少数民族传统体育运动会期间，中国电信贵州公司提供优质的通信服务保障
During the Ninth National Traditional Ethnic Minority Sports, the China Telecom Guizhou Branch to provide quality communication services insurance

深化精确管理，管理效率和效益逐步提升。加强营销管理，本着“套餐标准化、促销本地化”的原则，逐步将用户集中到主流套餐。进一步推进财务集中管理。深化人力资源管理创新。加强对市场前端的支撑，从后端和管控部门选拔专业人员输送到市场前端部门工作。适应全业务发展调整组织架构。完成省、地两级前端组织架构优化调整。加强网间结算收支管理，降低异常结算损失。协调网间通信质量，重点解决天翼产品互联互通。加强信息安全管理。

全面保障，形成企业发展活力。深入开展“创先争优”活动。“四好班子”建设全部达标。初步形成党风廉政建设惩防考核评价体系。扎实开展特色文化建设，加强员工关怀。公司连续七年获得中华全国总工会、国家安监局授予全国“安康杯”优胜企业称号。

中国电信贵州公司入驻中小企业总部基地
China Telecom Guizhou Branch assigned to the headquarters base for SMEs

中国电信贵州公司应急抢险队赴望谟开展抗洪保通信工作
China Telecom Guizhou Branch emergency rescue team went to Wangmo to carry out anti-flood communication work insurance

In 2011, the province at all levels enterprises face the fierce market competition, closely around the Group, the provincial strategic plan and organization of work, efforts to expand the living space, go all out to develop full-service market, continued to further promote the transition, to fully complete the Group the company issued the business objectives.

天翼3G网络率先实现全省乡镇全覆盖
Tianyi 3G network is the first to achieve full coverage of the province's township

Integrated and coordinated all business development. Year to the mobile, broadband, ICT business as the three major main pull, driving force to co-ordinate fixed-line business and mobile services, basic services and transformation services, incremental expansion and stock ownership. Full-service revenue market share remained relatively stable.

中国电信贵州公司组织开展"天翼飞扬之五心服务我最优"客户服务技能竞赛
China Telecom Guizhou Branch company organized "Tianyi flying the optimal five cardiac services" customer service skills competition

Focus on customer perception, full service support capabilities further strengthened. Promote the customer service process control. New full-service organization implementing standards and customer service standards introduced "five-one" service initiatives, full-service customer service standards compliance rate of 98.89%, was named by the group "full implementation of the standard benchmark for business clients unit." Enhance service quality supervision. Innovative channel management model to improve the marketing services capabilities. Continue to optimize operation and maintenance system, "three quality network" to create initial success, the Group completed a comprehensive operation and maintenance assessment indicators. IT support capabilities continue to improve.

Deepen the precise management, management efficiency and effectiveness increased gradually. Strengthen the marketing management, the spirit of "standardized packages, promotions localization" principle, and gradually the user focus to the mainstream packages. Further promote the centralized financial management. Deepen the human resource management innovation. Strengthen the support of the front end of the market, and control department from the back-end selection of professional front-end delivery to the market sector. Adjusted to adapt to the whole business development organization. Complete the provincial and prefectural levels optimization to adjust the front organization. Strengthen the interconnection revenue and expenditure management, reduce abnormal settlement loss. Coordination the quality cmong the network, focused on solving surfing products interoperability. Strengthen information security management.

Comprehensive protection, the formation of business development activity. Carry out the "to be first and fight for excellence" activities. "Four good team" build all the standards. The initial formation of honest government, punishment and prevention assessment system. To solidly carry out characteristics culture, to enhance staff care. The company received seven consecutive years, the ACFTU, the State Administration of Work Safety Bureau awarded the national "Ankang Cup" winning business title.

中国联通贵州省分公司

China Unicom Guizhou Province Branch

省长赵克志到中国联通贵州省分公司指导检查工作
Provincial Governor Zhao Kezhi had guide and inspection work in China Unicom Guizhou Province Branch

中国联通贵州省分公司党委书记、总经理张哲
China Unicom Guizhou branch party secretary, general manager Zhang Zhe

提升服务、创造价值——10010客户服务中心
Improve service, create value - 10010 Customer Service Center

遍布城乡的联通营业网点为广大用户提供优质、高效和便捷的服务
Outlets throughout the urban and rural areas of China Unicom to provide customers with high quality, efficient and convenient services

中国联合网络通信有限公司贵州省分公司（简称“中国联通贵州省分公司”）主要经营移动通信、固定通信、数据通信、宽带互联网接入和各类增值电信业务，下辖9个市州分公司和96个区县分公司，总资产逾45亿元，年收入规模达17亿元，全省从业人员4000余人，各类通信用户总数超过350万户，拥有覆盖全省、结构合理、技术先进、功能强大的现代通信网络，在推进全省国民经济和社会信息化建设进程中发挥了重要的支撑保障作用。致力于成为“信息生活的创新服务领导者”，中国联通贵州省分公司始终将“引领创新”作为推动企业持续快速发展、构筑差异化竞争优势的战略基点，不断推动企业加快提升综合实力和运营效率，以全面满足社会各界和广大用户的信息通信服务需求，并在全省加速发展、加快转型、推进跨越的宏伟进程中努力发挥排头兵和主力军作用。

“选3G ，就选沃”——联通“沃3G”品牌得到社会各界的高度认可
"Choose 3G, we chose the WO" - China Unicom "Wo 3G" brand was highly recognized by all sectors of society

China United Network Communications Co., Ltd. Guizhou Province Branch (referred to as "China Unicom Guizhou Province branch") mainly engaged in mobile communications, fixed communications, data communications, broadband internet access and various value-added telecom services, under the jurisdiction of the 9 city state companies and 96 districts branches, total assets of over 4.5 billion yuan, the annual income of 1.7 billion yuan, the province's 4,000 employees, the total number of various types of communications users over 3.5 million, which covers the whole province, reasonable structure, technology advanced and powerful modern communications network, has played an important supporting role in safeguarding in the process of promoting the province's national economy and social informatization construction. Committed to being the "information life leader of innovative services", China Unicom Guizhou Province Branch will always be "Leading Innovation" as a sustained and rapid development to promote the enterprise to build competitive differentiation and advantage of the strategic basis, and constantly promote the enterprises to accelerate and enhance the comprehensive strength and operational efficiency, in order to fully meet the needs of the community and the majority of users of information and communication services, and make efforts to play a vanguard and main force in the grand process to accelerate the development, accelerate the transformation, advancing leap-fog in the province.

1

One

综　合

General Survey

1-1 行政区划(2011)

Divisions of Administrative Areas

单位:个 (unit)

市(州)名称	City (State,Prefecture)	地级单位 Units at Prefectural Level	#市 Cities	县级单位 Units at County Level	县 Counties	自治县 Autonomous Counties	县级市 Cities at County Level	市辖区 Districts under the Jurisdiction of City
全省合计	**Total**	**9**	**6**	**88**	**56**	**11**	**7**	**13**
贵阳市	Guiyang	1	1	10	3		1	6
六盘水市	Liupanshui	1	1	4	2			1
遵义市	Zunyi	1	1	14	8	2	2	2
安顺市	Anshun	1	1	6	2	3		1
毕节市	Bijie	1	1	8	6	1		1
铜仁市	Tongren	1	1	10	4	4		2
黔西南布依族苗族自治州	Qianxinan	1		8	7		1	
黔东南苗族侗族自治州	Qiandongnan	1		16	15		1	
黔南布依族苗族自治州	Qiannan	1		12	9	1	2	

注:资料来源于省民政厅(下表同)。
Note:Date in the table are obtained from the department of civil affairs(the same applies to the next table).

1-1 续表 continued

市(州、地)名称	City (State,Prefecture)	特区 Special District	镇 Town	街道办事处 Urban Subdistrict Office	乡 Township	#民族乡 Ethnic Community Township	城市社区居民委员会 Neighbourhood Committees	村民委员会 Village Committees
全省合计	**Total**	**1**	**694**	**113**	**751**	**250**	**1705**	**17583**
贵阳市	Guiyang		29	44	48	18	471	1156
六盘水市	Liupanshui	1	30	4	64	50	150	1019
遵义市	Zunyi		164	17	62	8	304	1689
安顺市	Anshun		38	7	42	11	100	1837
毕节市	Bijie		101	10	142	77	148	3602
铜仁市	Tongren		71	5	93	54	120	2201
黔西南布依族苗族自治州	Qianxinan		75	12	49	3	117	1097
黔东南苗族侗族自治州	Qiandongnan		89	7	115	17	168	3307
黔南布依族苗族自治州	Qiannan		97	7	136	12	127	1675

1–2 各市（州）、县（市、区、特区）名称(2011)

Name of Each City(State,Prefecture) and County(City,District,Special Region)

市(州)名称 City(State,Prefecture)	县(市、区、特区)名称 County(City,District,Special Region)
贵阳市 Guiyang	南明区 Nanming　云岩区 Yunyan　小河区 Xiaohe　花溪区 Huaxi　乌当区 Wudang　白云区 Baiyun　清镇市 Qingzhen　开阳县 Kaiyang　息烽县 Xifeng　修文县 Xiuwen
六盘水市 Liupanshui	钟山区 Zhongshan　六枝特区 Liuzhi　盘县 Panxian　水城县 Shuicheng
遵义市 Zunyi	红花岗区 Honghuagang　汇川区 Huichuan　赤水市 Chishui　仁怀市 Renhuai　遵义县 Zunyi　桐梓县 Tongzi　绥阳县 Suiyang　正安县 Zhengan　凤冈县 Fenggang　湄潭县 Meitan　余庆县 Yuqing　习水县 Xishui　道真仡佬族苗族自治县 Daozhen　务川仡佬族苗族自治县 Wuchuan
安顺市 Anshun	西秀区 Xixiu　平坝县 Pingba　普定县 Puding　关岭布依族苗族自治县 Guanling　镇宁布依族苗族自治县 Zhenning　紫云布依族苗族自治县 Ziyun
毕节市 Bijie	七星关区 Qixingguan　大方县 Dafang　黔西县 Qianxi　金沙县 Jinsha　织金县 Zhijin　纳雍县 Nayong　赫章县 Hezhang　威宁彝族回族苗族自治县 Weining
铜仁市 Tongren	碧江区 Bijiang　万山区 Wanshan　江口县 Jiangkou　石阡县 Shiqian　思南县 Sinan　德江县 Dejiang　沿河土家族自治县 Yanhe　松桃苗族自治县 Songtao　玉屏侗族自治县 Yuping　印江土家族苗族自治县 Yinjiang
黔西南布依族苗族自治州 Qianxinan	兴义市 Xingyi　兴仁县 Xingren　普安县 Puan　晴隆县 Qinglong　安龙县 Anlong　望谟县 Wangmo　贞丰县 Zhenfeng　册亨县 Ceheng
黔东南苗族侗族自治州 Qiandongnan	凯里市 Kaili　黄平县 Huangping　施秉县 Shibing　三穗县 Sansui　镇远县 Zhenyuan　岑巩县 Cengong　天柱县 Tianzhu　锦屏县 Jinping　剑河县 Jianhe　台江县 Taijiang　黎平县 Liping　榕江县 Rongjiang　从江县 Congjiang　雷山县 Leishan　麻江县 Majiang　丹寨县 Danzhai
黔南布依族苗族自治州 Qiannan	都匀市 Duyun　福泉市 Fuquan　荔波县 Libo　贵定县 Guiding　瓮安县 Wengan　平塘县 Pingtang　罗甸县 Luodian　长顺县 Changshun　龙里县 Longli　惠水县 Huishui　独山县 Dushan　三都水族自治县 Sandu

1-3 社会经济主要指标

指　　标	Item	总量指标 1978	2000	2005
人口与就业	**Population and Employment**			
人口	**Population**			
年末常住人口(万人)	Total Population at the Year-end (10000 persons)	2686.40	3755.72	3730
#城镇人口	Urban Population	323.97	896.49	1002.25
乡村人口	Rural Population	2362.43	2859.23	2727.75
#男性人口	Male	1364.82	1968.00	1920.55
女性人口	Female	1321.58	1787.72	1809.45
年平均人口(万人)	Annual Average Population(10000 persons)	2663.27	3732.89	3717.61
就业	**Employment**			
就业人员(万人)	Year-end Employees (10000 persons)	1053.67	1866.28	1944.29
#非私营单位职工人数	Staff and Workers	171.19	193.96	202.02
城镇登记失业人数（万人）	Urban Registeration Unemployment (10000 persons)		10.23	12.13
宏观经济	**Macro Economy**			
国民经济核算	**National Accounting**			
生产总值(亿元)	Gross Domestic Product (100 million yuan)	46.62	1029.92	2005.42
第一产业	Primary Industry	19.42	271.20	368.94
第二产业	Secondary Industry	18.73	391.20	821.16
工　业	Industry	15.24	328.73	707.35
建筑业	Construction	3.49	62.47	113.81
第三产业	Tertiary Industry	8.47	367.52	815.32
固定资产投资	**Investment in Fixed Assets**			
全社会固定资产投资(亿元)	Total Investment in Fixed Assets in the Whole Province (100 million yuan)	10.93	402.50	1018.25
消费	**Consumption**			
社会消费品零售总额(亿元)	Total Retail Sales of Consumer Goods(100 million yuan)	21.23	355.58	615.75
对外贸易	**Foreign Trade**			
进出口总额（亿美元）	Total Value of Imports and Exports(USD 100 million)	0.16	6.60	14.04
#出口额	Total Exports	0.03	4.21	8.59
利用外资	**Utilization of Foreign Capital**			
签订合同项目(个)	Projects of Agreements and Contracts(unit)		59	61
实际利用外资金额(万美元)	Foreign Capital Actually Absorbed(USD 10000)	※148	19545	19568
财政	**Government Finance**			
财政总收入(亿元)	Total Financial Revenue(100 million yuan)	14.20	153.04	366.16
#财政一般预算收入(亿元)	Local Financial Revenue (100 million yuan)	6.26	85.23	182.50
财政一般预算支出(亿元)	Financial Expenditure (100 million yuan)	12.30	201.57	520.73
价格指数(上年=100)	**Price Indices(preceding year=100)**			
居民消费价格总指数	Consumer Price Index	100.3	99.5	101.0
商品零售价格总指数	Retail Price Index	100.3	97.3	101.3
农业生产资料价格总指数	General Price Index of Means of Agricultural Production	△102.1	100.6	110.2
工业生产者出厂价格指数	Ex-Factory Price Index of Industrial Producer		100.4	107.2
工业生产者购进价格指数	Purchasing Price Index of Industrial Producer		102.9	107.4

Major Social and Economic Indicators

Aggregate Indicators						速度指标 (%) Indices and Growth Rates (%)					
2006	2007	2008	2009	2010	2011	指数（2011为以下各年）Index (2011 as Percentage of the Following Years)				平均增长速度 Average Annual Growth Rate	
						1978	2000	2006	2010	1979–2011	2001–2011
3690	3632	3596	3537	3479	3469	129.1	92.4	94.0	99.7	0.8	-0.7
1013.27	1025.68	1046.79	1057.21	1176.25	1212.76	374.3	135.3	119.7	103.1	4.1	2.8
2676.73	2606.32	2549.21	2479.79	2302.75	2256.24	95.5	78.9	84.3	98.0	-0.1	-2.1
1908.85	1879.70	1868.73	1827.56	1797.43	1801.21	132.0	91.5	94.4	100.2	0.8	-0.8
1781.15	1752.30	1727.27	1709.44	1681.57	1667.79	126.2	93.3	93.6	99.2	0.7	-0.6
3710	3661	3614	3566.50	3508	3474	130.4	93.1	93.6	99.0	0.8	-0.7
1953.24	1872.64	1867.20	1841.92	1770.90	1792.80	170.1	96.1	91.8	101.2	1.6	-0.4
201.87	207.53	199.76	206.44	210.67	225.90	132.0	116.5	111.9	107.2	0.8	1.4
12.12	12.13	12.56	12.34	12.18	12.51		122.3	103.2	102.7		1.8
2338.98	2884.11	3561.56	3912.68	4602.16	5701.84	2266.1	341.4	184.6	115.0	9.9	11.8
382.06	446.38	539.19	550.27	625.03	726.22	443.3	152.8	121.9	101.2	4.6	3.9
967.54	1124.79	1370.03	1476.62	1800.06	2194.33	3660.6	384.0	188.6	117.9	11.5	13.0
839.13	978.86	1195.30	1252.67	1516.87	1829.20	4000.5	380.5	185.9	117.8	11.8	12.9
128.41	145.93	174.73	223.95	283.19	365.13	2139.3	407.4	204.8	118.3	9.7	13.6
989.38	1312.94	1652.34	1885.79	2177.07	2781.29	4835.7	432.8	207.1	116.5	12.5	14.2
1197.68	1488.80	1864.45	2450.99	3186.28	5101.55	46674.7	1267.5	426.0	160.1	19.0	23.2
710.00	858.15	1075.24	1247.25	1482.68	1751.62	8250.7	492.6	246.7	118.1	14.3	15.6
16.17	22.73	33.70	23.07	31.47	48.84	29692.4	740.0	302.0	155.2	18.8	20.0
10.39	14.65	19.01	13.59	19.20	29.85	104747.7	709.8	287.4	155.5	23.5	19.5
59	51	50	39	42	70		118.6	118.6	166.7		1.6
18413	15333	17379	18027	34026	71674		366.7	389.3	210.6		12.5
448.88	556.98	674.58	779.59	969.57	1329.99	9366.1	869.0	296.3	137.2	14.7	21.7
226.82	285.14	349.55	416.48	533.73	773.08	12349.5	907.0	340.8	144.8	15.7	22.2
610.64	795.40	1055.39	1372.27	1631.48	2249.40	18287.8	1115.9	368.4	137.9	17.1	24.5
101.7	106.4	107.6	98.7	102.9	105.1						
100.9	104.2	107.2	97.6	103.0	105.5						
105.4	105.1	113.4	96.2	101.1	111.1						
104.3	105.0	112.4	95.1	104.7	105.4						
107.3	107.5	112.5	93.5	109.8	115.0						

1-3 续表1

指　　标	Item	总量指标		
		1978	2000	2005
能源生产与消费	**Total Production and Consumption of Energy**			
一次能源生产总量（万吨标准煤）	Total Production of Primary Energy(10000 tons of SCE)	1204.51	3288.83	7957.07
能源消费总量(万吨标准煤)	Total Energy Consumption(10000 tons of SCE)	674.50	4278.60	5641.25
产　业	**Industry**			
农业	**Agriculture**			
年末常用耕地面积(千公顷)	Cultivated Land at the Year-end(1000 hectares)	1905.33	1843.33	1753.50
农业从业人员(万人)	Agriculture Employment(10000 persons)	851.79	1372.12	1268.09
主要农产品产量(万吨)	Output of Major Farm Products(10000 tons)			
粮　　食	Grain	643.36	1161.30	1152.06
油　　料	Oil-bearing Crops	9.89	74.34	84.89
#油菜籽	Rapeseed	7.34	66.20	76.51
烤　　烟	Flue-cured Tobacco	8.11	31.09	34.45
肉类总产量	Meat	12.80	124.06	187.01
水产品	Aquatic Products	0.37	6.24	9.46
工业	**Industry**			
规模以上工业企业	Industrial Enterprises above Designated Size			
增加值（亿元）	Added Value(100 million yuan)		216.99	585.85
#轻工业	Light Industry		82.16	177.19
重工业	Heavy Industry		134.83	408.66
主营业务收入(亿元)	Revenue from Principal Business(100 million yuan)		593.80	1577.16
利税总额(亿元)	Total Profits(100 million yuan)		87.44	232.49
主要工业产品产量	Output of Major Industrial Products			
原煤(万吨)	Coal(10000 tons)	1669	3677	10615
发电量(亿千瓦小时)	Electricity(100 million kwh)	41.43	404.70	786.78
铝(万吨)	Aluminum(10000 tons)	2.32	27.19	41.99
成品钢材(万吨)	Rolled Steel(10000 tons)	4.95	150.93	214.85
水泥(万吨)	Cement(10000 tons)	130.93	783.88	1557.97
磷矿石(万吨)	Phosphorite(10000 tons)	169.02	588.70	878.79
茅台酒(吨)	Mao-Tai Chiew(ton)	1067	5397	8885
卷烟(万箱)	Cigarettes(10000 cases)	31.60	187.40	208.21
建筑业	**Construction**			
建筑业总产值(亿元)	Gross Output Value of Construction(100 million yuan)	4.40	109.06	271.23
房屋建筑施工面积(万平方米)	Floor Space of Buildings under Construction(10000 sq.m)	313	1792	3153
房屋建筑竣工面积(万平方米)	Floor Space of Buildings Completed(10000 sq.m)	164	824	1150
交通运输业	**Transportation**			
运输线路长度(公里)	Length of Transportation Routes(km)			
铁路营业里程	Length of Railways	1365	1641	1986
公路线路里程	Length of Highways in Operation	25954	34643	46893
客运量(万人)	Passenger Traffic(10000 persons)	3294	53032	64450
旅客周转量(亿人公里)	Passenger-Kilometers(100 million passenger-km)	25.50	238.36	312.40
货运量(万吨)	Freight Traffic(10000 tons)	3467	15615	21771
货物周转量(亿吨公里)	Freight Ton-Kilometers(100 million ton-km)	79.60	404.07	646.55

continued

Aggregate Indicators						速度指标 (%) Indices and Growth Rates (%)					
						指数（2011为以下各年）Index (2011 as Percentage of the Following Years)				平均增长速度 Average Annual Growth Rate	
2006	2007	2008	2009	2010	2011	1978	2000	2006	2010	1979–2011	2001–2011
8089.39	8480.62	9262.34	11070.09	13100.00	12739.97	1057.7	387.4	157.5	97.3	7.4	13.1
6172.45	6799.72	7083.99	7566.33	8175.43	9067.85	1344.4	211.9	146.9	110.9	8.2	7.1
1753.36	1751.86	1754.05	1757.82	1761.56	1754.90	92.1	95.2	100.1	99.6	-0.2	-0.4
1247.08	1203.62	1202.06	1207.08	1188.27	1165.32	136.8	84.9	93.4	98.1	1.0	-1.5
1038.00	1100.86	1158.00	1168.27	1112.30	876.90	136.3	75.5	84.5	78.8	0.9	-2.5
68.24	69.66	68.39	78.68	60.34	78.85	797.3	106.1	115.5	130.7	6.5	0.5
63.18	64.59	60.38	70.40	51.62	71.81	978.3	108.5	113.7	139.1	7.2	0.7
30.71	31.22	37.71	36.92	37.02	32.50	400.7	104.5	105.8	87.8	4.3	0.4
163.70	150.60	161.46	169.60	179.09	179.97	1406.0	145.1	109.9	100.5	8.3	3.4
6.71	7.68	7.80	8.03	8.79	10.88	2940.5	174.4	162.1	123.8	10.8	5.2
747.38	890.48	1051.26	1170.29	1227.17	1723.58		448.1	202.8	122.6		14.6
218.52	267.87	302.25	352.38	413.99	563.48		424.5	187.5	123.7		14.0
528.86	622.61	749.01	817.91	813.18	1160.10		451.4	210.6	122.1		14.7
1948.57	2430.62	2922.35	3234.59	3926.01	5290.90		891.0	271.5	134.8		22.0
299.09	403.49	453.53	470.60	671.39	924.04		1056.8	309.0	137.6		23.9
11817	10864	11798	10001	12656	14015	839.7	381.1	118.6	110.7	6.7	12.9
974.66	1166.32	1192.08	1363.09	1358.69	1359.01	3280.3	335.8	139.4	100.0	11.2	11.6
56.28	75.07	58.15	80.27	88.79	90.36	3894.8	332.3	160.6	101.8	11.7	11.5
256.57	328.14	337.52	337.62	391.04	462.77	9348.9	306.6	180.4	118.3	14.7	10.7
1799.40	1943.10	2048.94	2664.78	3694.84	5250.89	4010.5	669.9	291.8	142.1	11.8	18.9
1034.60	1198.83	1317.18	1360.66	1579.21	2084.18	1233.1	354.0	201.4	132.0	7.9	12.2
9719	10789	11308	12161	12911	15523	1454.8	287.6	159.7	120.2	8.5	10.1
211.73	220.71	226.74	232.24	239.24	245.23	776.0	130.9	115.8	102.5	6.4	2.5
312.34	348.79	393.88	523.91	622.96	824.72	18743.6	756.2	264.0	132.4	17.2	20.2
3369	3813	4230	4953	5756	6779	2168.5	378.2	201.2	117.8	9.8	12.9
1108	1204	1216	1244	1350	1530	933.3	185.7	138.1	113.3	7.0	5.8
2014	2012	1962	1983	2002	2070	151.6	126.1	102.8	103.4	1.3	2.1
113278	123247	125365	142561	151644	157820	608.1	455.6	139.3	104.1	5.6	14.8
69270	74440	80056	84981	97793	120554	3659.8	227.3	174.0	123.3	11.5	7.8
349.82	369.20	407.59	430.56	514.41	631.74	2477.4	265.0	180.6	122.8	10.2	9.3
24709	26788	33576	34844	40310	44890	1294.8	287.5	181.7	111.4	8.1	10.1
680.96	721.26	809.93	897.38	1012.20	1060.69	1332.5	262.5	155.8	104.8	8.2	9.2

1–3 续表2

指　标	Item	总量指标		
		1978	2000	2005
邮电通信业	**Post and Telecommunication**			
邮路总长度(公里)	Number of Postal Routes(km)		63538	64926
函件(万件)	Number of Letters(10000 pcs)	3880	6943	5728
交换机容量(万门)	Capacity of Telephone Exchanges(10000 lines)	8.95	260.46	1369.55
年末固定电话用户(万户)	Number of Telephones Subscribers at the Year-end(10000 subscribers)	3.80	153.70	466.49
移动电话用户(万户)	Number of Mobile Telephones Subscribers(10000 subscribers)		79.70	509.42
互联网宽带接入端口(万个)	Number of Subscribers of Internet Service(10000 subscribers)			51.21
旅游业	**Tourism**			
旅游总人数(万人次)	**Total Number of Visitors(10000 persons)**		1998.39	3127.08
#入境旅游人数	Number of International Tourists Inbound		18.39	27.62
旅游总收入(亿元)	**Total Tourism Income(100 million yuan)**		62.94	251.14
#国际旅游外汇收入(万美元)	International Earnings from Tourism (USD 10000)		6092	10141
金融业	**Financial Intermediatio**			
全部金融机构人民币存款余额(亿元)	Total Savings Deposit Balancen(100 million yuan)	18.05	1106.64	2777.54
#储蓄存款	Savings Deposit	1.84	539.49	1350.90
全部金融机构人民币贷款余额(亿元)	Total Loan Balance n(100 million yuan)	21.62	1064.82	2303.93
教育、文化	**Education and Culture**			
教育	**Education**			
专任教师数	**Full-time Teachers**			
普通高等学校(万人)	Regular Institutions of Higher Education (10000 persons)	0.28	0.72	1.44
普通中学(万人)	Regular Secondary Schools (10000 persons)	5.42	8.12	12.27
小　学(万人)	Primary Schools(10000 persons)	15.59	17.48	18.37
在校学生数	**Students Enrollmen**			
普通高等学校(万人)	Regular Institutions of Higher Education (10000 persons)	1.33	7.55	20.68
普通中学(万人)	Regular Secondary Schools(10000 persons)	137.17	157.20	254.96
小学(万人)	Primary Schools(10000 persons)	423.60	500.21	473.76
学龄儿童入学率(%)	Enrollment Rate of School-age Children (%)	89.5	98.5	98.3
文化	**Culture**			
图书总印数(万册)	Number of Books Printed Copies (10000 copies)	5842	10289	9993
杂志总印数(万册)	Number of Magazines Printed Copies(10000 copies)	69	994	1349
报纸总印数(万份)	Number of Newspapers Printed Copies(10000 copies)	11930	28799	35172
家庭生活	**Family and People's Living Conditions**			
家庭	**Household**			
城镇居民平均每户常住家庭人口(人)	Average Persons Per Urban Household(person)	5.41	3.11	3.06
农村居民平均每户常住人口(人)	Average Persons Per Rural Household(person)	5.80	4.52	4.40
婚姻	**Marital**			
准予登记结婚(万对)	Marriage Registration Permitted(10000 households)	△7.02	28.02	21.13
离婚人数(万人)	Divorce(10000 persons)	△0.38	1.54	8.21
居住	**Residence**			
城镇人均住宅建筑面积(平方米)	Per Capita Building Space in Urban Areas(sq.m)	5.45	17.60	26.40
农村居民人均住房面积(平方米)	Per Capita Living Space in Rural Areas(sq.m)		19.75	23.50
生活	**Per Capita Standard of Living**			
城镇居民人均可支配收入(元)	Per Capita Annual Disposable Income of Urban Households(yuan)	261	5121	8147
农村居民人均纯收入(元)	Per Capita　Annual Net Income of Rural Residents(yuan)	109	1374	1877

continued

Aggregate Indicators						速度指标 (%) Indices and Growth Rates (%)					
						指数（2011为以下各年）Index (2011 as Percentage of the Following Years)				平均增长速度 Average Annual Growth Rate	
2006	2007	2008	2009	2010	2011	1978	2000	2006	2010	1979–2011	2001–2011
62936	60747	65236	61854	96174	99155		156.1	157.5	103.1		4.1
6859	5735	6566	6768	5939	5041	129.9	72.6	73.5	84.9	0.8	-2.9
1639.41	2334.67	2858.70	3182.88	3673.01	5423.48	60597.5	2082.3	330.8	147.7	21.4	31.8
493.91	521.19	499.61	451.13	432.61	403.96	10630.5	262.8	81.8	93.4	15.2	9.2
646.20	834.05	1185.84	1583.28	1964.40	2175.22		2729.3	336.6	110.7		35.1
67.44	96.65	119.89	163.63	231.69	437.87			649.3	189.0		
4747.89	6262.89	8190.23	10439.95	12913.02	17019.36		851.7	358.5	131.8		21.5
32.14	43.00	39.54	39.95	50.01	58.51		318.2	182.0	117.0		11.1
387.05	512.28	653.13	805.23	1061.23	1429.48		2271.2	369.3	134.7		32.8
11516	12918	11697	11044	12958	13507		221.7	117.3	104.2		7.5
3300.08	3826.37	4736.93	5898.26	7363.92	8742.79	48436.5	790.0	264.9	118.7	20.6	20.7
1596.86	1790.14	2237.05	2676.09	3244.99	3934.48	213830.4	729.3	246.4	121.2	26.2	19.8
2696.11	3128.63	3569.27	4656.50	5747.53	6841.92	31646.3	642.5	253.8	119.0	19.1	18.4
1.54	1.70	1.80	1.96	2.04	2.19	793.9	301.9	141.9	107.4	6.5	10.6
12.83	13.11	13.54	13.93	14.25	14.74	271.8	181.6	114.9	103.4	3.1	5.6
18.88	19.20	20.00	19.92	19.79	19.71	126.4	112.7	104.4	99.6	0.7	1.1
22.15	24.17	26.75	29.91	32.33	34.41	2587.2	455.8	155.3	106.4	10.4	14.8
256.31	256.00	261.78	269.45	275.68	282.71	206.1	179.8	110.3	102.6	2.2	5.5
474.38	466.31	469.79	456.87	433.50	408.74	96.5	81.7	86.2	94.3	-0.1	-1.8
98.6	98.6	97.2	98.4	97.9	98.6	110.2	100.2	100.0	100.7	0.3	0.0
9402	8626	10457	9263	8069	8492	145.4	82.5	90.3	105.2	1.1	-1.7
1380	1376	1420	1358	1300	1413	2047.8	142.2	102.4	108.7	9.6	3.2
32026	34676	35110	36286	37004	44931	376.6	156.0	140.3	121.4	4.1	4.1
3.02	3.02	3.07	3.04	3.03	2.98	55.1	95.8	98.7	98.3	-1.8	-0.4
4.43	4.43	4.40	4.38	4.34	4.32	74.5	95.6	97.5	99.5	-0.9	-0.4
21.31	23.49	26.32	30.79	37.51	37.34		133.3	175.2	99.6		2.6
8.43	9.17	10.24	11.59	12.79	14.44		936.3	171.4	112.9		22.5
26.42	27.52	26.95	27.57	27.42	27.83	510.6	158.1	105.3	101.5	5.1	4.3
23.84	24.54	25.27	26.43	27.26	29.63		150.0	124.3	108.7		3.8
9117	10678	11759	12863	14143	16495	978.3	245.2	149.6	110.8	7.2	8.5
1985	2374	2797	3005	3472	4145	626.0	224.7	170.4	114.0	5.7	7.6

1–3 续表3

指　　标	Item	总量指标		
		1978	2000	2005
社会保险	**Social Insurance**			
社会保险基金收入(亿元)	Revenue of Social Insurance Fund (100 million yuan)		22.87	57.34
社会保险基金支出(亿元)	Expenses of Social Insurance Fund (100 million yuan)		23.41	53.78
卫生	**Health Care**			
医院、卫生院(个)	Number of Hospitals and Health Centers(unit)	4510	1878	1843
执业(助理)医师(万人)	Number of Licensed (Assistant) Doctors (10000 persons)	2.12	4.57	3.55
医院、卫生院床位数(万张)	Number of Beds(10000 beds)	3.75	5.51	5.84
城市市政建设	**City Construction**			
供水总量(万立方米)	Volume of Tap Water Supply(10000 cu.m)	5389	45693	63705
城市排水管道长度(公里)	Length of Sewer Pipelines(km)	214	1665	4313
人工煤气供应量(万立方米)	Volume of Coal Gas Supply(10000 cu.m)			19209
出租汽车(辆)	Taxi(unit)	☆33	7352	12386
年末公共交通运营数(辆)	Number of Public Vehicles under Operation at Year-end (Buses and Trolley Buses, etc.)(unit)	●326	●4144	5814
年末实有道路长度(公里)	Length of Paved Roads at Year-end(km)	184	1679	3518
城市园林绿地面积(公顷)	Area of Parks and Green Land (hectare)	1037	9939	31161
环境	**Environment**			
环保资金投入(亿元)	Environment Protection Investment(100 million yuan)	☆0.17	10.98	33.26
环境污染事故(起)	Accident of Environment Pollution(unit)			28
污染事故直接经济损失(万元)	Direct Economy Losing for Pollute Accident(10000 yuan)			57.90
火灾、交通事故	**Basic Statistics on Fires and Traffic Accidents**			
火灾发生数(起)	Number of Fires(case)	2501	1608	2299
直接财产损失(万元)	Losses Converted into Cash(10000 yuan)	1734.21	2814.70	1078.50
交通事故发生数(起)	Number of Traffic Accidents(case)	3104	2593	3315
损失折款(万元)	Losses Converted into Cash(10000 yuan)	236.07	1899.62	2507.06

注：1.年末总人口及分项指标1978、2000年为常住一年口径，2005年为常住半年口径，2006年–2009年数据已根据第六次人口普查数据进行修订。2.本表速度指标中，生产总值、工业增加值和城乡居民收入及分项指标均按可比价格计算，全社会固定资产投资及分项指标平均增长速度按累计法计算。3.原煤产量1978–2007年为全社会口径。4.工业生产者出厂价格指数2010年及以前为全部工业品出厂价格指数，工业生产者购进价格指数2010年及以前为全部原材料、燃料、动力价格指数，统计口径不变。5.储蓄存款2010年及以前为城乡居民储蓄存款(以下相关表同)。6、"△"为1979年数据；"☆"为1981年数据；"※"为1985年数据；"●"为"标台"。

continued

Aggregate Indicators						速度指标 (%) Indices and Growth Rates (%)					
						指数（2011为以下各年）Index (2011 as Percentage of the Following Years)				平均增长速度 Average Annual Growth Rate	
2006	2007	2008	2009	2010	2011	1978	2000	2006	2010	1979–2011	2001–2011
73.72	90.86	140.50	17[illegible].40	201.56	256.94		1123.6	348.5	127.5		24.6
67.77	80.57	98.24	122.73	151.41	181.74		776.2	268.2	120.0		20.5
1855	1939	1934	1982	2005	2071	45.9	110.3	111.6	103.3	-2.3	0.9
4.11	4.21	3.88	4.02	4.22	4.40	207.4	96.4	107.0	104.5	2.2	-0.3
6.26	7.14	7.81	9.12	9.75	10.80	287.8	195.9	172.6	110.8	3.3	6.3
71568	68297	64871	61971	63572	67766	1257.5	148.3	94.7	106.6	8.0	3.6
4485	4724	4796	5047	5507	5977	2792.9	359.0	133.3	108.5	10.6	12.3
21650	23491	26613	26886	26963	30515			140.9	113.2		
13540	13411	13768	14700	15087	17196		233.9	127.0	114.0		8.0
3687	5083	5140	4864	4984	5364						
3474	3772	3836	3933	4081	4487	2438.7	267.3	129.2	110.0		9.3
40682	41410	41841	43781	45500	48024	4631.1	483.2	118.0	105.5		15.4
32.79	48.88	50.74	69.78	89.52	106.70		971.8	325.4	119.2		23.0
23	18	10	4	4	7			30.4	175.0		
13.40	673.20	14.70	10.00	107.30	450.00			3358.2	419.4		
1919	833	800	869	1630	1170	46.8	72.8	61.0	71.8	-2.3	-2.8
1194.20	3075.20	3436.52	3435.55	4416.80	6625.40	382.0	235.4	554.8	150.0	4.1	8.1
2734	2292	2219	1816	1764	1566	50.5	60.4	57.3	88.8	-2.1	-4.5
1869.39	1848.85	1480.23	1214.50	1208.00	1611.39	682.6	84.8	86.2	133.4	6.0	-1.5

Note:1.As to total population at the year-end and subitems in this table,the year 1978 and 2000 refer to permanent population in one year scope,the year 2005 refer to permanent population in half a year scope, additionly the year 2006 to 2009 had been amendmented on the base of the result of the Sixth National Population Census.2.As to growth rates,GDP, value-added of industry, per capita annual disposable income of urban households and per capita annual net income of rural residents and their sub items were calculated at constant price.The average annual growth rate of total investment in fixed assets in the whole province and its sub items were calculated by accumulation method .3.Output of raw coal in the year 1978 to 2007 refer to the scope of the whole province.4.The year 2010 and before , Ex-Factory price index of industrial product refere to the ex-factory price index of the whole industrial products and purchasing price index of industrial producer refer to the price index of the whole raw materials,fuels and power.The statistics caliber isn't changed.5.The year 2010 and before,savings deposit refer to resident savings deposit of urban and rural(The relative tables in this chapter are the same).6.Data with "△" refer to the year 1979,with "☆" refer to the year 1981,with "※" refer to the year 1985,and with "●" refer to standard unit.

1–4 社会经济主要指标结构

Composition Indicators on National Economic and Social Development

单位：% (%)

指 标	Item	2006	2007	2008	2009	2010	2011
人口与就业	**Population and Employment**						
人口	**Population**						
城镇、乡村结构	Grouped by Urban and Rural Area						
城 镇	Urban Population	27.5	28.2	29.1	29.9	33.8	35.0
乡 村	Rural Population	72.5	71.8	70.9	70.1	66.2	65.0
性别结构	Grouped by Sex						
男	Male	51.7	51.8	52.0	51.7	51.7	51.9
女	Female	48.3	48.2	48.0	48.3	48.3	48.1
就业	**Employment**						
就业人员结构	Grouped by Three Industries						
第一产业	Primary Industry	76.2	74.1	72.3	70.5	68.3	66.6
第二产业	Secondary Industry	8.9	9.2	9.7	10.7	11.5	12.0
第三产业	Tertiary Industry	14.9	16.7	18.0	18.7	20.2	21.3
宏观经济	**Macro Economy**						
国民经济核算	**National Accounting**						
生产总值结构	In GDP						
#第一产业	Primary Industry	16.3	15.5	15.1	14.1	13.6	12.7
第二产业	Secondary Industry	41.4	39.0	38.5	37.7	39.1	38.5
第三产业	Tertiary Industry	42.3	45.5	46.4	48.2	47.3	48.8
#公有经济	Public-Owned Economic Unit	69.1	68.7	67.6	66.9	65.0	63.1
非公有经济	Non-public-owned Economic Unit	30.9	31.3	32.4	33.1	35.0	36.9
投资	**Investment in Fixed Assets**						
全社会固定资产投资结构	Structure of Total Investment in Fixed Assets in the Whole Province						
#中央	Central	19.0	16.1	16.5	14.2	10.2	8.2
地方	Local	81.0	83.9	83.5	85.8	89.8	91.8
#国有经济	State-owned Economic Unit	50.3	46.9	48.8	51.0	50.4	47.3
非国有经济	Non-State-owned Economic Unit	49.7	53.1	51.2	49.0	49.6	52.7
资金来源结构	Grouped by Source of Funds						
国家预算内资金	State Budgetary Appropriation	4.3	5.0	6.4	8.9	8.7	11.0
国内贷款	Domestic Loans	24.4	22.7	22.2	22.3	20.8	15.6
利用外资	Foreign Investment	1.0	0.9	0.7	0.3	0.3	0.3
自筹资金	Self-raising Funds	49.3	50.7	50.7	44.6	45.5	51.5
其他投资	Others	21.0	20.7	20.1	23.9	24.8	21.6
对外贸易	**Foreign Trade**						
出 口	Total Exports	64.2	64.5	56.4	58.9	61.0	61.1
进 口	Total Imports	35.8	35.5	43.6	41.1	39.0	38.9
财政	**Government Finance and Tax**						
地方财政收入结构	Structure of Local Financial Revenue						
省 级	Provincial Level	24.0	24.7	25.6	22.6	20.3	21.4
地 级	Prefectural Level	21.1	21.0	20.2	21.3	23.3	21.9
县 级	County level	35.0	39.7	39.8	43.3	44.0	45.7
乡 级	Township Level	19.9	14.5	14.4	12.8	12.4	11.0

1-4 续表1 continued

单位：% (%)

指 标	Item	2006	2007	2008	2009	2010	2011
能源	**Energy**						
一次能源生产总量结构	Structure of Total Energy Production						
原煤	Coal	95.5	91.5	86.7	88.3	89.9	91.4
水电	Hydro-power	4.5	8.5	13.3	11.7	10.1	8.6
能源终端消费总量结构	Structure of Total Energy Consumption						
#原煤	Coal	47.7	45.6	45.4	47.6	48.0	48.8
天然气	Natural Gas	1.2	1.1	1.0	0.8	0.8	0.6
电力	Electricity	32.7	33.1	32.0	32.4	33.3	33.2
产 业	**Industry**						
农业	**Agriculture**						
农林牧渔业增加值结构	Structure of Value-added of FFAFS						
农 业	Farming	58.4	58.3	57.1	60.1	61.7	59.3
林 业	Forestry	4.4	4.1	4.3	4.6	4.5	4.4
畜牧业	Animal Husbandry	30.7	32.6	33.9	30.5	28.7	30.7
渔 业	Fishery	1.3	1.3	1.3	1.3	1.4	1.8
农林牧渔服务业	FFAF Services	5.2	3.6	3.4	3.6	3.7	3.8
工业	**Industry**						
规模以上工业增加值	In the Industrial Enterprises above Designated Size						
#轻工业	Light Industry	29.2	30.1	28.8	30.1	33.7	32.7
重工业	Heavy Industry	70.8	69.9	71.2	69.9	66.3	67.3
#大型企业	Large Industry	49.3	46.0	40.9	37.0	38.0	37.2
中型企业	Medium-sized Industry	25.3	28.2	26.5	28.4	24.6	23.9
小型企业	Small Industry	25.4	25.8	32.7	34.6	37.4	36.6
建筑业	**Construction**						
建筑业总产值结构	Structure of Gross Output Value of Construction						
国有经济	State-owned	79.4	77.9	77.0	77.9	79.6	79.9
非国有经济	Non-state-owned	20.6	22.1	23.0	22.1	20.4	20.1
交通运输业	**Transportation**						
货运量结构	Structure of Freight Traffic						
铁 路	Railways	27.6	27.2	19.9	20.1	19.8	16.1
公 路	Highways	70.0	70.3	77.9	77.6	77.9	81.7
水 运	Waterways	2.4	2.5	2.2	2.3	2.3	2.2
客运量结构	Structure of Passenger Traffic						
铁 路	Railways	3.7	4.0	4.0	3.8	3.5	3.3
公 路	Highways	95.0	94.5	94.1	94.2	94.5	94.9
水 运	Waterways	1.4	1.5	1.9	2.0	2.0	1.8
旅游业	**Tourism**						
来黔涉外旅游人数结构	Structure of Tourists Visiting Guizhou						
外国人	Foreigners	33.3	36.0	46.1	40.8	37.2	40.4
港澳同胞	Compatriots from Hong Kong and Macao	29.0	30.3	27.3	27.1	27.3	28.9
台湾同胞	Compatriots from Taiwan	37.7	33.7	26.6	32.1	35.5	30.7
金融业	**Financial Intermediation**						
金融机构存款结构	Structure of Total Savings Deposit Balance						
#财政存款	Treasury Deposit	2.8	3.8	4.7	5.1	4.9	5.1
储蓄存款	Savings Deposit	48.4	46.8	47.2	45.4	44.1	45.0

1-4 续表2 continued

单位：% (%)

指 标	Item	2006	2007	2008	2009	2010	2011
金融机构贷款结构	Structure of Total Loan Balance						
#短期贷款	Short-Term Loan	31.3	27.5	25.0	23.4	17.7	18.9
中长期贷款	Middle-Term • Long-Term Loan	66.0	69.6	72.5	73.7	79.7	79.5
教育	**Education**						
教育(学历教育口径)	**Education**						
在校学生结构	Structure of Students Enrollment						
#高等教育阶段	Higher Education	2.9	3.2	3.5	4.0	4.4	4.7
高中阶段	Senior Secondary Schools	7.1	7.3	7.4	7.7	8.4	9.5
初中阶段	Junior Secondary Schools	27.0	27.0	27.1	27.9	28.8	29.5
小学阶段	Primary Schools	63.0	62.5	62.0	60.4	58.5	56.3
专任教师结构	Structure of Full-time Teachers						
#高等教育阶段	Higher Education	4.6	5.0	5.1	5.5	5.6	6.0
高中阶段	Senior Secondary Schools	8.5	8.6	8.6	8.8	9.2	9.9
初中阶段	Junior Secondary Schools	30.1	30.0	29.7	30.1	30.3	30.3
小学阶段	Primary Schools	56.8	56.5	56.6	55.6	54.9	53.8
生活、环境保护	**People's Living Conditions and Environment**						
人民生活	**People's Living Conditions**						
城市居民消费结构	Consumption Structure of Urban Residents						
#食品类	Food	38.7	40.2	43.1	41.5	39.9	40.2
衣着类	Clothing	12.2	11.7	10.2	11.2	11.0	10.7
居 住	Residence	9.2	9.3	10.0	8.3	8.9	9.7
家庭设备用品及服务	Household Facilities,Articles and Services	6.5	6.0	6.3	6.5	6.7	7.6
医疗保健	Medicines and Medical Services	4.8	4.6	5.6	5.9	5.4	5.1
交通和通信	Transport and Communications	11.3	11.5	10.4	10.9	12.6	12.3
教育文化娱乐服务	Education, Cultural and Recreation Services	13.7	13.4	11.2	12.7	12.5	11.7
农村居民消费结构	Consumption Structure of Rural Residents						
#食品类	Food	51.5	52.2	51.7	45.2	46.3	47.6
衣着类	Clothing	5.4	5.2	5.2	5.2	4.8	5.4
居 住	Residence	16.3	17.2	19.7	24.3	21.8	18.5
家庭设备、用品及服务	Household Facilities,Articles and Services	4.0	3.7	4.4	4.8	4.8	5.6
医疗保健	Medicines and Medical Services	4.7	4.1	4.5	5.5	6.2	7.1
交通和通信	Transport and Communications	7.5	8.1	7.4	7.2	8.1	8.8
文教、娱乐、用品及服务	Recreation,Education and Cultural Articles and Services	8.5	7.7	5.6	6.3	6.5	5.3
卫生	**Health Care**						
卫生机构结构	Structure of Various Health Care Institutions						
#医院、卫生院	Hospitals and Health Centers	30.2	32.8	33.1	34.6	35.6	36.4
卫生机构床位结构	Structure of Beds of Health Care Institutions						
#医院、卫生院	Hospitals and Health Centers	94.2	94.2	94.0	93.5	92.6	91.9
卫生技术人员结构	Structure of Medical Technical Personnels						
#执业(助理)医师	Licensed(Assistant) Doctors	50.0	49.4	43.5	42.2	41.1	39.2
环境	**Environment**						
环境保护投入资金结构	Structure of Environment Protection Investment						
#老工业污染源治理资金	Old Industry Pollute Fountain Treatment	30.7	16.2	20.1	12.8	7.6	13.2
城市环境基础设施建设	Urban Environment Infrastructure Investment	31.2	27.5	30.4	38.2	32.3	35.6

1-5 社会经济主要指标比例、效益

Major Indicators on Proportions and Efficiency in Economic Social Development

指 标	Item	2006	2007	2008	2009	2010	2011
人口与就业	**Population and Employment**						
人口出生率(‰)	Birth Rate(‰)	13.97	13.28	13.49	13.65	13.96	13.31
人口死亡率(‰)	Death Rate(‰)	6.71	6.60	6.77	6.69	6.55	6.93
人口自然增长率(‰)	Natural Growth Rate(‰)	7.26	6.68	6.72	6.96	7.41	6.38
城镇登记失业率(%)	Registered Unemployment Rate in Urban Areas(%)	4.11	3.97	3.98	3.81	3.63	3.63
国民经济核算	**National Accounting**						
人均生产总值(元)	Per Capita Gross Domestic Product(yuan)	6305	7878	9855	10971	13119	16413
固定资产投资	**Investment in Fixed Assets**						
全社会固定资产投资相当于生产总值比例(%)	Proportion of Investmetn in Fixed Assets to GDP(%)	51.2	51.6	52.3	62.6	69.2	89.5
全社会房屋建筑面积竣工率(%)	Rate of Total Floor Space of Buildings Completed in the Whole Province (%)	39.7	40.2	34.2	38.9	36.8	33.4
消费	**Consumption**						
社会消费品零售总额相当于生产总值比例(%)	Proportion of Retail Sales of Consumer Goods to GDP(%)	30.4	29.8	30.2	31.9	32.2	30.7
人均社会消费品零售额(元)	Per Capita Ratail Sales of Consumer Goods(yuan)	1914	2344	2975	3497	4227	5042
对外贸易	**Foreign Trade**						
进出口总额相当于生产总值比例(%)	Proportion of Total Value of Imports and Exports as Percentage to GDP(%)	5.3	5.4	6.6	4.0	4.6	5.5
财政	**Government Finance**						
财政总收入相当于生产总值比例(%)	Proportion of Total Financial Revenues to GDP(%)	19.2	19.3	18.9	19.9	21.1	23.3
一般预算支出相当于生产总值比例(%)	Proportion of General Budget Expenditure to GDP (%)	26.1	27.6	29.6	35.1	35.5	39.5
能源	**Energy**						
能源生产弹性系数	Elasticity Ratio of Energy Production	0.13	0.32	0.82	1.71	1.43	
电力生产弹性系数	Elasticity Ratio of Electricity Production	2.18	1.35	1.27	1.39	0.03	
能源消费弹性系数	Elasticity Ratio of Energy Consumption	0.74	0.69	0.37	0.60	0.63	0.73
电力消费弹性系数	Elasticity Ratio of Electricity Consumption	1.52	1.01	0.13	0.92	0.89	0.87
每万元生产总值能耗(吨标准煤/万元)(可比价)	Energy Consumption Per Unit of GDP (ton of SCE/10000 yuan) (equivalent value)	2.7283	2.6173	2.4495	2.3480	2.2480	1.7140
农业	**Agriculture**						
每亩播种面积农产品产量	Output of Farm Crops Per Mu of Sowning Area						
粮 食(公斤)	Grain(kg)	244	260	264	261	244	191
油 料(公斤)	Oil-bearing Crops(kg)	106	107	100	102	76	98

1–5 续表1 continued

指　　标	Item	2006	2007	2008	2009	2010	2011
工业(规模以上)	**Industry(above Designated Size)**						
总资产贡献率(%)	Ratio of Total Assets to Industrial Output Value(%)	11.93	12.89	12.96	10.69	12.84	14.13
资本保值增值率(%)	Capital Maintenance and Appreciation Rate (%)	114.61	114.86	124.99	106.87	125.32	127.96
流动资产周转次数(次/年)	Number of Times of Turnover of Circulating Fund (times/year)	1.81	2.04	1.92	1.88	1.75	1.92
成本费用利润率(%)	Ratio of Profits to Industrial Cost(%)	6.95	8.10	6.42	6.56	9.04	9.63
全员劳动生产率(元/人, 按增加值计算)	All-personnel Labour Productivity (yuan/person) (account by value-added)	111168	133663	141433	160077	152823	183433
建筑业	**Construction**						
建筑业劳动生产率(元/人)(按增加值计算)	Overall Labour Productivity in Construction(yuan/person) (account by value-added)	22864	25096	28116	70294	89177	98494
技术装备率(元/人)	Value of Machinery Per Laborer (yuan/person)	7553	7531	8248	7398	8232	34182
产值利税率(%)	Ratio of Per-tax Profits to Gross Output Value(%)	4.4	4.7	5.8	5.1	5.9	5.9
交通运输业	**Transportation**						
铁路网密度(公里/万平方公里)	Railway Density(km/10000 sq.km)	114.33	114.21	111.37	112.57	113.64	117.50
公路网密度(公里/万平方公里)	Highway Density(km/10000 sq.km)	6430.26	6996.15	7116.38	8092.52	8608.12	8958.70
邮电通信业	**Postal and Telecommunication Services**						
电话普及率(包括移动电话)(部/百人)	Popularization Rate of Telephone (set/100 persons)	30.90	37.31	46.87	57.52	68.90	74.35
移动电话普及率(部/百人)	Popularization Rate of Mobile Telephone (set/100 persons)	17.51	22.96	32.97	44.76	56.46	62.71
旅游业	**Tourism**						
每一来黔境外旅游者消费支出(美元/人天)	Daily Expenditure of Per Tourists Visiting Guizhou(USD)	163.68	171.54	169.30	169.12	171.76	168.68
金融	**Finance**						
金融机构存款相当于生产总值比例(%)	Deposit of Financial Institutions as Percentage of GDP(%)	141.1	132.7	133.0	150.7	160.0	153.3
金融机构贷款相当于生产总值比例(%)	Loans of Financial Institutions as Percentage of GDP(%)	115.3	108.5	100.2	119.0	124.9	120.0

1-5 续表2 continued

指 标	Item	2006	2007	2008	2009	2010	2011
教 育	**Education**						
学龄儿童入学率(%)	Enrollment Rate of School-age Children(%)	98.6	98.6	97.2	98.4	97.9	98.6
初中阶段毛入学率(%)	Enrollment Rate of Primary School Graduates Entering into Junior Secondary Schools(%)	100.5	97.5	95.9	98.2	97.6	94.2
高中阶段毛入学率(%)	Enrollment Rate of Junior secondary School Graduates Entering into Senior secondary Schools(%)	37.7	42.2	47.9	53.4	55.0	58.9
高等教育毛入学率(%)	Enrollment Rate of Senior secondary School Graduates Entering into Institution of Higher Learning(%)	11.0	11.5	11.8	18.4	20.0	23.2
教师负担学生系数(学生/教师)	Student-Teacher Ratio (student/teacher)						
普通高校	Regular Institution of Higher Education	14.39	14.25	14.83	15.23	15.89	15.74
普通高中	Regular Senior Secondary Schools	18.88	18.68	18.56	18.51	18.75	19.02
普通初中	Regular Junior Secondary Schools	20.29	19.77	19.56	19.58	19.52	19.23
小 学	Primary Schools	25.13	24.29	23.49	22.94	21.90	20.74
城乡收入比例	**Urban-rural income ratio**						
城市与农村居民收入比例(以农民人均纯收入＝1)	Ratio of Annual Income of Urban Residents to Rural(rural resident=1)	4.59	4.50	4.20	4.28	4.07	3.98
卫 生	**Health Care**						
每万人拥有执业(助理)医师数(人)	Number of Licensed(Assistant) Doctors Per 10000 Persons(person)	11.1	11.5	10.7	11.3	12.0	10.4
每万人拥有医院、卫生院床位数(张)	Number of Beds in Hospitals and Health Centers Per 10000 Persons(bed)	16.9	19.5	21.6	25.6	27.8	25.5
城市建设	**City Construction**						
人均公园绿地面积(平方米)	Per Capita Area of Parks and Green Land (sq.m)	4.25	4.23	4.44	4.65	5.33	5.50
用水普及率(%)	Percentage of Population with Access to Tap Water(%)	81.0	79.7	83.2	85.4	86.5	86.9
燃气普及率(%)	Percentage of Households with Access to Tap Gas(%)	50.3	51.1	54.1	54.2	54.5	55.0
环境、灾害	**Environment and Disaster**						
环保投入相当于生产总值比例(%)	Environment Protection Investment as Percentage to GDP(%)	1.4	1.7	1.4	1.8	1.9	1.9
平均每起环境污染事故直接经济损失(万元)	Average Loss Converted into Cash Per Pollution Accident(10000 yuan)	0.6	37.4	1.5	2.5	26.8	64.3
亿元生产总值生产安全事故死亡人数(人/亿元)	Deaths of Industrial Accidents per Unit of GDP(person/100 million yuan)	1.22	0.96	0.73	0.56	0.42	0.29
平均每起火灾损失(万元)	Average Loss of Per Fire(10000 yuan)	0.62	3.69	4.30	3.95	2.71	5.66
平均每起交通事故损失(万元)	Average Loss of Per Traffic Accident (10000 yuan)	0.68	0.81	0.67	0.67	0.68	1.03

1-6 贵州社会经济主要指标占全国比重
Proportion of Guizhou's Main Economic and Social Indicators to the Whole Country

指标	Item	全国 China		贵州 Guizhou		贵州占全国比重(%) Proportion of Guizhou to China(%)	
		2006	2011	2006	2011	2006	2011
土地面积(万平方公里)	**Area of Territory(10000 sq.km)**	**960**	**960**	**17.62**	**17.62**	**1.8**	**1.8**
人口	**Population**						
年末总人口(万人)	Total Population at the Year-end (10000 persons)	131448	134735	3690	3469	2.8	2.6
就业	**Employment**						
就业人员(万人)	Employees(10000 persons)	74978	76420	1953.24	1792.80	2.6	2.3
非私营单位职工平均工资(元)	Average Wage of Staff and Workers(yuan)	20856	41799	16815	37331	80.6	89.3
国民经济核算	**National Accounting**						
生产总值(亿元)	Gross Domestic Product(100 million yuan)	216314	471564	2338.98	5701.84	1.1	1.2
第一产业	Primary Industry	24040	47712	382.06	726.22	1.6	1.5
第二产业	Secondary Industry	103720	220592	967.54	2194.33	0.9	1.0
第三产业	Tertiary Industry	88555	203260	989.38	2781.29	1.1	1.4
人均生产总值(元)	Per Capita Gross Domestic Product(yuan)	16500	35083	6305	16413	38.2	46.8
固定资产投资	**Investment in Fixed Assets**						
全社会固定资产投资(亿元)	Total Investment in Fixed Assets (100 million yuan)	109998	311022	1197.68	5101.55	1.1	1.6
消费	**Consumption**						
社会消费品零售总额(亿元)	Total Retail Sales of Consumer Goods (100 million yuan)	79145	183919	710.00	1751.62	0.9	1.0
对外贸易	**Foreign Trade**						
进出口总额(亿美元)	Total Value of Imports and Exports (USD 100 million)	17604	36421	16.17	48.84	0.1	0.1
#出口	Total Exports	9690	18986	10.39	29.85	0.1	0.2
财政	**Government Finance**						
财政一般预算收入(亿元)	Local Financial Revenue(100 million yuan)	18304	52434	226.82	773.08	1.2	1.5
财政一般预算支出(亿元)	Financial Expenditure (100 million yuan)	30431	92415	610.64	2249.40	1.2	2.4
能源	**Energy**						
一次能源生产总量(万吨标准煤)	Total Production of Primary Energy(10000 tons of SCE)	232167	317800	8089.39	12739.97	3.5	4.0
能源终端消费总量(万吨标准煤)	Consumption of Energy(10000 tons of SCE)	258676	347800	5574.99	8359.80	2.2	2.4
农业	**Agriculture**						
粮食产量(万吨)	Output of Grain(10000 tons)	49804	57121	1038	877	2.1	1.5
油料产量(万吨)	Output of Oil-bearing Crops (10000 tons)	2640	3307	68.24	78.85	2.6	2.4
工业	**Industry**						
原煤产量(亿吨)	Output of Coal(100 million tons)	25.3	35.2	1.18	1.30	4.7	4.0
发电量(亿千瓦小时)	Output of Electricity (100 million kwh)	28657	46037	975	1344	3.4	2.9
卷　烟(亿支)	Output of Cigarettes(100 million pieces)	20218	24474	1058.65	1226.20	5.2	5.0

注：表中2011年工业产品产量为全部年主营业务收入2000万元及以上工业企业数据。
Note:Output of industrial products refer to the industrial enterprises above designaled size that revenue from principal business is zo million yuan.

1-6 续表 continued

指 标	Item	全 国 China		贵 州 Guizhou		贵州占全国比重(%) Proportion of Guizhou to China(%)	
		2006	2011	2006	2011	2006	2011
交通运输业	**Transportation**						
铁路营业里程(万公里)	Length of Railways(10000 km)	7.7	9.3	0.20	0.21	2.6	2.2
公路里程(万公里)	Length of Highways(10000 km)	346	411	11.33	15.78	3.3	3.8
旅客周转量(亿人公里)	Passenger-Kilometers(100 million passenger-km)	19197	30984	349.82	631.74	1.8	2.0
货物周转量(亿吨公里)	Freight Ton-Kilometers(100 million ton-km)	88840	159324	680.96	1060.69	0.8	0.7
邮电通信业	**Post and Telecommunication**						
电信业务总量(亿元)	Business Revenue of Telecommunications (100 million yuan)	14595	11772	215.85	204.35	1.5	1.7
邮政业务总量(亿元)	Business Volume of Post (100 million yuan)	731	1608	8.02	14.97	1.1	0.9
旅游业	**Tourism**						
入境旅游人数(万人次)	Number of Visitor Arrivals(10000 person-times)	12494	13542	32.14	58.51	0.3	0.4
国内旅游人数(亿人次)	Domestic Tourists(100 million person-times)	13.9	26.4	0.47	1.70	3.4	6.4
国际旅游外汇收入(亿美元)	International Earnings from Tourism (USD 100 million)	340	485	1.15	1.35	0.3	0.3
国内旅游收入(亿元)	Domestic Earnings from Tourism (100 million yuan)	6230	19305	377.79	1420.70	6.1	7.4
金融业	**Finance**						
金融机构人民币存款余额(亿元)	Total Savings Deposit Balance(100 million yuan)	335460	809368	3300.08	8742.79	1.0	1.1
金融机构人民币贷款余额(亿元)	Total Loan Balance(100 million yuan)	225347	547947	2696.11	6841.92	1.2	1.2
教育	**Education**						
普通高等学校(所)	Regular Institutions of Higher Education(unit)	1867	2409	36	48	1.9	2.0
普通高等学校专任教师(万人)	Full-time Teachers of Regular Institutions of Higher Education(10000 persons)	107.6	139.3	1.54	2.19	1.4	1.6
普通高校在校大学生(万人)	Students Enrollment of Regular Institutions of Higher Education(10000 persons)	1738.8	2308.5	22.15	34.41	1.3	1.5
文化	**Culture**						
广播人口覆盖率(%)	Radio Coverage Rate of the Population(%)	95.0	97.1	83.7	88.0	-11.3 (百分点)	-9.1 (百分点)
电视人口覆盖率(%)	TV Coverage Rate of the Population(%)	96.2	97.8	90.7	92.8	-5.5 (百分点)	-5.0 (百分点)
卫生	**Health Care**						
医院、卫生院(个)	Number of Hospitals and Health Centers(unit)	19000	22000	1855	2071	9.8	9.4
执业(助理)医师(万人)	Number of Licensed(Assistant) Doctors (10000 persons)	209.9	246.6	4.11	4.40	2.0	1.8
医院、卫生院床位(万张)	Number of Beds in Hospitals and Health Centers(10000 beds)	256.0	370.5	6.26	10.80	2.4	2.9
人民生活	**People's Livelihood**						
城镇居民人均可支配收入(元)	Per Capita Annual Disposable Income of Urban Households(yuan)	11760	21810	9117	16495	77.5	75.6
农村居民人均纯收入(元)	Annual Per Capita Net Income of Rural Residents(yuan)	3587	6977	1985	4145	55.3	59.4

主要统计指标解释

行政区划 指国家对行政区域的划分。根据有关法规规定，我国的行政区域划分如下：(1)全国分为省、自治区、直辖市；(2)省、自治区分为自治州、县、自治县、市；(3)自治州分为县、自治县、市；(4)县、自治县分为乡、民族乡、镇；(5)直辖市和较大的市分为区、县；(6)国家在必要时设立的特别行政区。

国民经济行业分类 自2003年定期报表开始使用新的《国民经济行业分类》（GB/T4754-2002）。该分类是由国家统计局组织修订，经国家质量监督检验检疫总局批准，于2002年5月10日发布实施。这次修订是在1994年分类标准的基础上，参照联合国《全部经济活动的国际标准产业分类》（ISIC/Rev.3）进行的。修订后的《国民经济行业分类》（GB/T4754-2002）共有门类20个，大类95个，中类396个，小类913个。新增门类4个，大类增加3个，中类增加28个，小类增加67个。

企业（单位）登记注册类型 是以在工商行政管理机关登记注册的各类企业为划分对象，以工商行政管理部门对企业登记注册的类型为依据，将企业登记注册类型分为内资企业、港澳台商投资企业和外商投资企业三大类。内资企业包括国有企业、集体企业、股份合作企业、联营企业、有限责任公司、股份有限公司、私营公司和其他企业；港澳台商投资企业和外商投资企业分别包括合资经营企业、合作经营企业、独资经营企业和股份有限公司。对不在工商行政管理部门进行登记注册的行政机关、事业单位和社会团体，主要按其经费来源和管理方式进行划分。

国有企业 指企业全部资产归国家所有，并按《中华人民共和国企业法人登记管理条例》规定登记注册的非公司制的经济组织。不包括有限责任公司中的国有独资公司。

集体企业 指企业资产归集体所有，并按《中华人民共和国企业法人登记管理条例》规定登记注册的经济组织。

股份合作企业 指以合作制为基础，由企业职工共同出资入股，吸收一定比例的社会资产投资组建，实行自主经营，自负盈亏，共同劳动，民主管理，按劳分配与按股分红相结合的一种集体经济组织。

联营企业 指两个及两个以上相同或不同所有制性质的企业法人或事业单位法人，按自愿、平等、互利的原则，共同投资组成的经济组织。联营企业包括国有联营企业、集体联营企业、国有与集体联营企业和其他联营企业。

有限责任公司 指根据《中华人民共和国公司登记管理条例》规定登记注册，由两个以上、五十个以下的股东共同出资，每个股东以其所认缴的出资额对公司承担有限责任，公司以其全部资产对其债务承担责任的经济组织。有限责任公司包括国有独资公司以及其他有限责任公司。

股份有限公司 指根据《中华人民共和国公司登记管理条例》规定登记注册，其全部注册资本由等额股份构成并通过发行股票筹集资本，股东以其认购的股份对公司承担有限责任，公司以其全部资产对其债务承担责任的经济组织。

私营企业 指由自然人投资设立或由自然人控股，以雇佣劳动为基础的营利性经济组织。包括按照《公司法》、《合伙企业法》、《私营企业暂行条例》规定登记注册的私营有限责任公司、私营股份有限公司、私营合伙企业和私营独资企业。

其他内资企业 指上述企业之外的其他内资经济组织。

与港澳台商合资经营企业 指港澳台地区投资者与内地企业依照《中华人民共和国中外合资经营企业法》及有关法律的规定，按合同规定的比例投资设立、分享利润和分担风险的企业。

与港澳台商合作经营企业 指港澳台地区投资者与内地企业依照《中华人民共和国中外合作经营企业法》及有关法律的规定，依照合作合同的约定进行投资或提供条件设立、分配利润和分担风险的企业。

港澳台商独资经营企业 指依照《中华人民共和国外资企业法》及有关法律的规定，在内地由港澳台地区投资者全额投资设立的企业。

港澳台商投资股份有限公司 指根据国家有关规定，经外经贸部依法批准设立，其中港、澳、台商的股本占公司注册资本的比例达25%以上的股份有限公司。凡其中港、澳、台商的股本占公司注册资本的比例小于25%的，属于内资企业中的股份有限公司。

中外合资经营企业 指外国企业或外国人与中国内地企业依照《中华人民共和国中外合资经营企业法》及有关法律的规定，按合同规定的比例投资设立、分享利润和分担风险的企业。

中外合作经营企业 指外国企业或外国人与中国内地企业依照《中华人民共和国中外合作经营企业法》及有关法律的规定，依照合作合同的约定进行投资或提供条件设立、分配利润和分担风险的企业。

外资企业 指依照《中华人民共和国外资企业法》及有关法律的规定，在中国内地由外国投资者全额投资设立的企业。

外商投资股份有限公司 指根据国家有关规定，经外经贸部依法批准设立，其中外资的股本占公司注册资本的比例达25%以上的股份有限公司。凡其中外资股本占公司注册资本的比例小于25%的，属于内资企业中的股份有限公司。

行政机关、事业单位和社会团体 参照企业登记注册类型，主要按其经费来源和管理方式划分。具体规定如下:

(1) 行政机关: 包括国家机关和政党机关，原则上均列为“国有”。但有特殊规定的，如供销社等，则列为“集体”

(2) 事业单位: 包括经国家机构编制部门和有关业务主管部门批准成立的各类事业单位，不包括实行企业化管理的事业单位。事业单位的划分办法如下:

①由国家财政预算拨款或列入财政预算外资金管理以及经费主要来源于国有主管部门或国有上级单位的事业单位，列为“国有”。

②经费主要来源于集体单位的事业单位，列为“集体”。

③公民个人（或个人合伙）开办的事业单位，列为“私营”。

④上述以外的其他事业单位，如果其经费来源不明确，按管理方式进行归类。

(3) 社会团体: 包括经民政部门批准成立以及未纳入社会团体管理条例范围的工会、妇联等各类社会团体。社会团体的划分办法如下:

①未纳入民政部社会团体管理条例范围的工会、妇联、共青团、青联、工商联、科协、侨联等社会团体，国家拨款设立的基金会或基金管理组织以及经费主要来源于国有业务主管部门或国有上级单位的社会团体，列为“国有”。

②经费主要来源于集体单位的社会团体，列为“集体”。

③公民个人（或个人合伙）开办的社会团体，划为“私营”。

④上述以外的其他社会团体，如果其经费来源不明确，改按管理方式进行归类。

Explanatory Notes on Main Statistical Indicators

Divisions of Administrative Areas refers to the division of administrative areas by the state. The relative laws stipulate that: 1) The whole country is divided into provinces, autonomous regions and municipalities directly under the central government; 2) Provinces and autonomous regions are divided into autonomous prefectures, counties, autonomous counties and cities; 3) Autonomous prefectures are divided into counties, autonomous counties and cities; 4) Counties and autonomous counties are divided into townships, nationality townships and towns; 5) Municipalities and large cities are divided into districts and counties, 6) The state shall, when necessary, establish special administrative regions.

Industrial Classification of the National Economy The new Industrial Classification of the National Economy (GB/T 4754-2002) is introduced starting from the compilation of 2003 annual statistics. The revision, based on the 1994 classification, was organized by the National Bureau of Statistics taking into consideration of the International Standards of the Industrial Classification of All Economic Activities (ISIC/Rev.3) of the United Nations. The new Classification was promulgated by the National Administration of Quality Supervision, Inspection and Quarantine on May 10, 2002. The revised version of the Industrial Classification of the National Economy (GB/T 4754-2002) is composed of 20 major divisions, 95 divisions, 396 major groups and 913 groups, of which 4 major divisions, 3 divisions, 28 major groups and 67 groups are new respectively

Registration Status of Enterprises Enterprises are classified into 3 categories, namely domestic-funded enterprises, enterprises with investment from Hong Kong, Macau and Taiwan, and enterprises with foreign investment, in the light of the registration status of an enterprise in industrial and commercial administration agencies. Domestic-funded enterprises include state-owned enterprises, collective-owned enterprises, cooperative enterprises, joint ownership enterprises, limited liability corporations, share-holding corporations Ltd., private enterprises and other enterprises. Included in the enterprises with investment from Hong Kong, Macau and Taiwan and enterprises with foreign investment are joint-venture enterprises, cooperative enterprises, sole investment enterprises and share-holding corporations Ltd. For government agencies, institutions and social organizations which are not requested to be registered in industrial and commercial administration agencies, they are classified mainly by their sources of funds and way of management.

State-owned Enterprises refer to non-corporation economic units where the entire assets are owned by the state and which have registered in accordance with the Regulation of the Peoples Republic of China on the Management of Registration of Corporate Enterprises. Excluded from this category are sole state-funded corporations in the limited liability corporations.

Collective-owned Enterprises refer to economic units where the assets are owned collectively and which have registered in accordance with the Regulation of the Peoples Republic of China on the Management of Registration of Corporate Enterprises.

Cooperatve Enterprises refer to a form of collective economic units (enterprises) where capitals come mainly from employees as their shares, with certain proportion of capital from the outside, where production is organized on the basis of independent operation, independent accounting for profits and losses, joint work, democratic management, and a distribution system that integrates remuneration according to work with dividend according to capital share.

Joint Ownership Enterprises refer to economic units established by two or more corporate enterprises or corporate institutions of the same or different ownership, through joint investment on the basis of equality, voluntary participation and mutual benefits. They include state joint ownership enterprises, collective joint ownership enterprises, joint state-collective enterprises, other joint ownership enterprises.

Limited Liability Corporations refer to economic units established with investment from 2-50 investors and registered in accordance with the Regulation of the Peoples Republic of China on the Management of Registration of Corporations, each investor bearing limited liability to the corporation depending on its share of investment, and the corporation bearing liability to its debt to the maximum of its total assets. Limited liability corporations include exclusive state-funded limited liability corporations and other limited liability corporations.

Share-holding Corporations Ltd. refer to economic units registered in accordance with the Regulation of the Peoples Republic of China on the Management of Registration of Corporations, with total registered capitals divided into equal shares and raised through issuing stocks. Each investor bears limited liability to the corporation depending on the holding of shares, and the corporation bears liability to its debt to the maximum of its total assets.

Private Enterprises refer to profit-making economic units invested and established by natural persons, or controlled by natural persons using employed labour. Included in this category are private limited liability corporations, private share-holding corporations Ltd., private partnership enterprises and private-funded enterprises registered in accordance with the Corporation Law, Partnership Enterprises Law and Interim Regulations on Private Enterprises .

Other Domestic-funded Enterprises refer to domestic-funded economic units other than those mentioned above.

Joint-venture Enterprises with Funds from Hong Kong, Macau and Taiwan refer to enterprises jointly established by investors from Hong Kong, Macau and Taiwan with enterprises in the mainland of China in accordance with the Law of the Peoples Republic of China on Sino-foreign Joint Venture Enterprises and other relevant laws, where the share of investment, profits and risks is stipulated in the contract.

Cooperative Enterprises with Funds from Hong Kong Macau and Taiwan established by investors from Hong Kong, Macau and Taiwan with enterprises in the mainland of China in accordance with the Law of the Peoples Republic of China on Sino-foreign Cooperative Enterprises and other relevant laws, where the investment or provision of facilities, and the share of profits and risks is stipulated in the cooperative contract.

Enterprises with Sole (exclusive) Investment from Hong Kong, Macau and Taiwan refer to enterprises established in the mainland of China with exclusive investment from investors from Hong Kong, Macau and Taiwan in accordance with the Law of the Peoples Republic of China on Foreign-Funded Enterprises and other relevant laws.

Share-holding Corporations Ltd. with Investment from Hong Kong, Macau and Taiwan refer to share-holding corporations Ltd. established with the approval from the Ministry of Foreign Trade and Economic Relations in line with relevant state regulations, where the share of investment from Hong Kong, Macau or Taiwan businessmen exceeds 25% of the total registered capital of the corporation. In case the share of investment from Hong Kong, Macau or Taiwan is less than 25% of the total registered capital, the enterprise is to be classified as domestic-funded share-holding corporation Ltd.

Joint-venture Enterprises with Foreign Investment refer to enterprises jointly established by foreign enterprises or foreigners with enterprises in the mainland of China in accordance with the Law of the Peoples Republic of China on Sino-foreign Joint Venture Enterprises and other relevant laws, where the share of investment, profits and risks is stipulated in the contract.

Cooperation Enterprises with Foreign Investment refer to enterprises jointly established by foreign enterprises or foreigners with enterprises in the mainland of China in accordance with the Law of the Peoples Republic of China on Sino-foreign Cooperative Enterprises and other relevant laws, where the investment or provision of facilities, and the share of profits and risks is stipulated in the cooperative contract.

Enterprises with Sole (exclusive) Foreign Investment refer to enterprises established in the mainland of China with exclusive investment from foreign investors in accordance with the Law of the Peoples Republic of China on Foreign-Funded Enterprises and other relevant laws.

Share-holding Corporations Ltd. with Foreign Investment refer to share-holding corporations Ltd. established with the approval from the Ministry of Foreign Trade and Economic Relations in line with relevant state regulations, where the share of investment from foreign investors exceeds 25% of the total registered capital of the corporation. In case the share of foreign investment is less than 25% of the total registered capital, the enterprise is to be classified as domestic-funded share-holding corporation Ltd.

Government Agencies, Institutions and Social Organizations are classified into following categories by source of funds and way of management taking reference of the registration status of enterprises:

(1) Government agencies: include state and party agencies, classified in principle as “state-owned”. There are exceptions, such as supply and marketing cooperatives which are classified as “collective”.

(2) Institutions: include institutions of various types established with the approval by organization and staffing departments of the government, but exclude institutions where enterprise management system is introduced. Institutions are further classified as follows:

(a) Institutions whose main budget is listed in the government budget appropriations or extra-budget funds, or allocated from the budget of their competent government agencies. Such institutions are classified as “state-owned”.

(b) Institutions whose budget mainly comes from collective units. Such institutions are classified as “collective".

(c) Social organizations established by individual or a group of citizens, which are classified as “private”.

(d) Institutions other than those mentioned above whose source of budget is not clear. Such institutions are classified by way of management.

(3) Social organizations: include social organizations established with the approval from the Ministry of Civil Affairs, and organizations that are not covered by social organization management regulations such as trade unions, women's federations etc. Social organizations are further classified as follows:

(a) Social organizations that are not covered by social organization management regulations of the Ministry of Civil Affairs such as trade unions, women's federations, communist youth leagues, youth associations, industrial and commerce associations, scientists associations, overseas Chinese associations, etc., foundations and fund management organizations established with funds from the state, and social organizations whose funds mainly come from the budget of their competent government agencies. Such institutions are classified as “state-owned".

(b) Social organizations whose budget mainly comes from collective units. Such institutions are classified as “collective".

(c) Social organizations established by individual or a group of citizens, which are classified as “private".

(d) Social organizations other than those mentioned above whose source of budget is not clear. Such organizations are classified by way of management.

2

Two

国民经济核算

National Accounts

2-1 全省生产总值

Gross Domestic Product

单位：亿元 (100 million yuan)

指　标	Item	2006	2007	2008	2009	2010	2011	2011年比2010年增长(%) Increase Rate in 2011 over 2010(%)
地区生产总值	**Gross Domestic Product**	**2338.98**	**2884.11**	**3561.56**	**3912.68**	**4602.16**	**5701.84**	**15.0**
第一产业	Primary Industry	382.06	446.38	539.19	550.27	625.03	726.22	1.2
第二产业	Secondary Industry	967.54	1124.79	1370.03	1476.62	1800.06	2194.33	17.9
工业	Industry	839.13	978.86	1195.30	1252.67	1516.87	1829.20	17.8
建筑业	Construction	128.41	145.93	174.73	223.95	283.19	365.13	18.3
第三产业	Tertiary Industry	989.38	1312.94	1652.34	1885.79	2177.07	2781.29	16.5
交通运输、仓储和邮政业	Transport, Storage and Post	192.95	282.04	370.65	399.77	480.32	590.91	15.3
批发和零售业	Wholesale and Retail Trade	161.70	198.79	248.83	293.53	367.52	448.77	14.4
住宿和餐饮业	Hotel and Catering Services	57.07	90.09	130.41	153.41	180.73	224.40	10.7
金融业	Financial Intermediation	89.43	122.25	151.55	194.44	231.51	297.27	17.0
房地产业	Real Estate	80.24	93.19	104.81	136.15	139.64	160.30	6.0
其他服务业	Other Services	407.99	526.58	646.09	708.49	777.35	1059.64	21.3
营利性服务业	For-profit Services	126.94	168.46	213.55	250.39	283.45	398.09	23.1
非营利性服务业	Non-profit Services	281.05	358.12	432.54	458.10	493.90	661.55	20.3
人均生产总值(元)	**Per Capita Gross Domestic Product(yuan)**	**6305**	**7878**	**9855**	**10971**	**13119**	**16413**	**16.1**

注：人均生产总值及增速按人口普查修订后常住半年人口计算(以下相关表同)。

Note: per capital GDP and its growth rate were caculated based on permanent population in half a year scope which had been adjusted on the basis of the National Population Census(the related tables in the chapter are the same).

2-2 全省生产总值构成

Composition of Gross Domestic Product

单位：% (%)

指　标	Item	2006	2007	2008	2009	2010	2011
地区生产总值	**Gross Domestic Product**	**100.0**	**100.0**	**100.0**	**100.0**	**100.0**	**100.0**
第一产业	Primary Industry	16.3	15.5	15.1	14.1	13.6	12.7
第二产业	Secondary Industry	41.4	39.0	38.5	37.7	39.1	38.5
工业	Industry	35.9	33.9	33.6	32.0	33.0	32.1
建筑业	Construction	5.5	5.1	4.9	5.7	6.1	6.4
第三产业	Tertiary Industry	42.3	45.5	46.4	48.2	47.3	48.8
交通运输、仓储和邮政业	Transport Storage and Post	8.2	9.8	10.4	10.2	10.4	10.4
批发和零售业	Wholesale and Retail Trade	6.9	6.9	7.0	7.5	8.0	7.9
住宿和餐饮业	Hotel and Catering Services	2.4	3.1	3.7	3.9	3.9	3.9
金融业	Financial Intermediation	3.8	4.2	4.3	5.0	5.0	5.2
房地产业	Real Estate	3.4	3.2	2.9	3.5	3.0	2.8
其他服务业	Other services	17.6	18.3	18.1	18.1	17.0	18.6
营利性服务业	For-profit Services	5.4	5.8	6.0	6.4	6.2	7.0
非营利性服务业	Non-profit Services	12.2	12.5	12.1	11.7	10.8	11.6

2-3 全省生产总值(按支出法计算)
Gross Domestic Product(Accounted by Expenditure Approach)

指 标	Item	2006	2007	2008	2009	2010	2011	2011年比2010年增长(%) Increase Rate in 2011 over 2010(%)
绝对数(亿元)	**Absolute Value(100 million yuan)**							
地区生产总值	**Gross Domestic Product**	**2338.98**	**2884.11**	**3561.56**	**3912.68**	**4602.16**	**5701.84**	**15.0**
最终消费	Final Consumption Expenditure	1854.35	2087.54	2354.11	2603.31	2931.13	3438.71	9.7
居民消费	Household Consumption	1408.54	1560.80	1763.74	1945.99	2181.37	2566.78	8.8
农村居民	Rural Households	478.54	553.35	623.42	689.41	770.06	908.51	6.3
城镇居民	Urban Households	930.00	1007.45	1140.32	1256.58	1411.31	1658.27	10.2
政府消费	Government Consumption	445.81	526.74	590.37	657.32	749.76	871.93	12.0
资本形成总额	Gross Capital Formation	1180.30	1442.35	1782.31	2100.53	2575.27	3229.30	17.1
固定资本形成总额	Gross Fixed Capital Formation	1153.87	1363.42	1691.89	2046.84	2510.39	3147.46	17.2
库存增加	Changes in Inventories	26.43	78.93	90.42	53.69	64.88	81.84	14.3
货物和服务净出口	Net Outflow of Goods and Services	-695.67	-645.78	-574.86	-791.16	-904.24	-966.17	
构成(%)	**Composition(%)**							
以最终消费为100	Final Consumption Expenditure=100							
居民消费	Household Consumption	76.0	74.8	74.9	74.8	74.4	74.6	
政府消费	Government Consumption	24.0	25.2	25.1	25.2	25.6	25.4	
以居民消费为100	Household Consumption=100							
农村居民	Rural Households	34.0	35.5	35.3	35.4	35.3	35.4	
城镇居民	Urban Households	66.0	64.5	64.7	64.6	64.7	64.6	
最终消费率(%)	**Final Consumption Rate(%)**	**79.3**	**72.4**	**66.1**	**66.5**	**63.7**	**60.3**	
资本形成率(%)	**Capital Formation Rate(%)**	**50.5**	**50.0**	**50.0**	**53.7**	**56.0**	**56.6**	
城乡居民人均消费水平对比(农村居民=1)	**Urban/Rural Consumption Ratio (rural households=1)**	**5.21**	**4.72**	**4.55**	**4.36**	**3.92**	**3.49**	

注：表中居民消费按常住半年人口计算,城乡居民人均消费水平对比根据第六次人口普查数据进行修订，2007–2010年居民消费数据根据新农合数据进行修订。

Note:The Data of Household Consumption in the table are calculated based on permanent population in half a year scope.Urban/Rural Consumption ratio is adjusted according to the result of the sixth National population census.The year 2007 to 2010,the data of household consumption were adjusted according to the data of New cooperatrie Medical.

2-4 三次产业对全省生产总值增长的拉动

Contribution of the Three Strata of Industry to GDP Growth

单位：百分点 (percentage points)

指 标	Item	2006	2007	2008	2009	2010	2011
地区生产总值	**Gross Domestic Product**	**12.8**	**14.8**	**11.3**	**11.4**	**12.8**	**15.0**
第一产业	Primary Industry	0.8	0.6	1.0	0.6	0.6	0.2
第二产业	Secondary Industry	5.5	5.4	3.3	4.8	6.6	7.0
#工 业	Industry	4.9	5.0	3.1	3.5	5.3	5.9
第三产业	Tertiary Industry	6.5	8.8	7.0	6.0	5.6	7.8

2-5 三次产业贡献率

Share of the Contributions of the Three Strata of Industry to the Increase of the GDP

单位：% (%)

指 标	Item	2006	2007	2008	2009	2010	2011
地区生产总值	**Gross Domestic Product**	**100.0**	**100.0**	**100.0**	**100.0**	**100.0**	**100.0**
第一产业	Primary Industry	6.6	3.8	9.2	5.5	5.0	1.1
第二产业	Secondary Industry	42.8	36.6	29.2	41.8	51.1	46.8
#工 业	Industry	37.9	33.7	27.0	30.8	41.6	39.2
第三产业	Tertiary Industry	50.6	59.6	61.6	52.7	43.9	52.1

主要统计指标解释

国内生产总值（GDP） 指按市场价格计算的一个国家（或地区）所有常住单位在一定时期内生产活动的最终成果。国内生产总值有三种表现形态，即价值形态、收入形态和产品形态。从价值形态看，它是所有常住单位在一定时期内生产的全部货物和服务价值超过同期投入的全部非固定资产货物和服务价值的差额，即所有常住单位的增加值之和；从收入形态看，它是所有常住单位在一定时期内创造并分配给常住单位和非常住单位的初次收入之和；从产品形态看，它是所有常住单位在一定时期内最终使用的货物和服务价值与货物和服务净出口价值之和。在实际核算中，国内生产总值有三种计算方法，即生产法、收入法和支出法。三种方法分别从不同的方面反映国内生产总值及其构成。

对于一个地区来说，称为地区生产总值或地区 GDP。

三次产业 三次产业的划分是世界上较为常用的产业结构分类，但各国的划分不尽一致。我国的三次产业划分是：

第一产业是指农业、林业、畜牧业、渔业和农林牧渔服务业。

第二产业是指采矿业，制造业，电力、煤气及水的生产和供应业，建筑业。

第三产业是指除第一、二产业以外的其他行业。

劳动者报酬 指劳动者因从事生产活动所获得的全部报酬。包括劳动者获得的各种形式的工资、奖金和津贴，既包括货币形式的，也包括实物形式的，还包括劳动者所享受的公费医疗和医药卫生费、上下班交通补贴、单位支付的社会保险费、住房公积金等。

生产税净额 指生产税减生产补贴后的余额。生产税指政府对生产单位从事生产、销售和经营活动以及因从事生产活动使用某些生产要素（如固定资产、土地、劳动力）所征收的各种税、附加费和规费。生产补贴与生产税相反，指政府对生产单位的单方面转移支出，因此视为负生产税，包括政策亏损补贴、价格补贴等。

固定资产折旧 指一定时期内为弥补固定资产损耗按照规定的固定资产折旧率提取的固定资产折旧，或按国民经济核算统一规定的折旧率虚拟计算的固定资产折旧。它反映了固定资产在当期生产中的转移价值。各类企业和企业化管理的事业单位的固定资产折旧是指实际计提的折旧费；不计提折旧的政府机关、非企业化管理的事业单位和居民住房的固定资产折旧是按照统一规定的折旧率和固定资产原值计算的虚拟折旧。原则上，固定资产折旧应按固定资产当期的重置价值计算，但是目前我国尚不具备对全社会固定资产进行重估价的基础，所以暂时只能采用上述办法。

营业盈余 指常住单位创造的增加值扣除劳动者报酬、生产税净额和固定资产折旧后的余额。它相当于企业的营业利润加上生产补贴，但要扣除从利润中开支的工资和福利等。

支出法国内生产总值 是从最终使用的角度反映一个国家（或地区）一定时期内生产活动最终成果的一种方法，包括最终消费支出、资本形成总额及货物和服务净出口三部分。计算公式为：

支出法国内生产总值 = 最终消费支出 + 资本形成总额 + 货物和服务净出口

最终消费支出 指常住单位为满足物质、文化和精神生活的需要，从本国经济领土和国外购买的货物和服务的支出。它不包括非常住单位在本国经济领土内的消费支出。最终消费支出分为居民消费支出和政府消费支出。

居民消费支出 指常住住户在一定时期内对于货物和服务的全部最终消费支出。居民消费支出除了直接以货币形式购买的货物和服务的消费支出外，还包括以其他方式获得的货物和服务的消费支出，即所谓的虚拟消费支出。居民虚拟消费支出包括如下几种类型：单位以实物报酬及实物转移的形式提供给劳动者的货物和服务；住户生产并由本住户消费了的货物和服务，其中的服务仅指住户的自有住房服务和付酬的家庭雇员提供的家庭和个人服务；金融机构提供的金融媒介服务。

政府消费支出 指政府部门为全社会提供的公共服务的消费支出和免费或以较低的价格向居民住户提供的货物和服务的净支出，前者等于政府服务的产出价值减去政府单位所获得的经营收入的价值，后者等于政府部门免费或以较低价格向居民住户提供的货物和服务的市场价值减去向住户收取的价值。

资本形成总额 指常住单位在一定时期内获得减去处置的固定资产和存货的净额，包括固定资本形成总额和存货增加两部分。

固定资本形成总额 指常住单位在一定时期内获得的固定资产减处置的固定资产的价值总额。固定资产是通过生产活动生产出来的，且其使用年限在一年以上、单位价值在规定标准以上的资产，不包括自然资产。可分为有形固定资本形成总额和无形固定资本形成总额。有形固定资本形成总额包括一定时期内完成的建筑工程、安装工程和设备工器具购置（减处置）价值，以及土地改良、新增役、种、奶、毛、娱乐用牲畜和新增经济林木价值。无形固定资本形成总额包括矿藏的勘探、计算机软件等获得减处置。

存货增加　指常住单位在一定时期内存货实物量变动的市场价值，即期末价值减期初价值的差额，再扣除当期由于价格变动而产生的持有收益。存货增加可以是正值，也可以是负值，正值表示存货上升，负值表示存货下降。存货包括生产单位购进的原材料、燃料和储备物资等存货，以及生产单位生产的产成品、在制品和半成品等存货。

货物和服务净出口　指货物和服务出口减货物和服务进口的差额。出口包括常住单位向非常住单位出售或无偿转让的各种货物和服务的价值；进口包括常住单位从非常住单位购买或无偿得到的各种货物和服务的价值。由于服务活动的提供与使用同时发生，一般把常住单位从非常住单位得到的服务作为进口，非常住单位从常住单位得到的服务作为出口。货物的出口和进口都按离岸价格计算。

Explanatory Notes on Main Statistical Indicators

Gross Domestic Product(GDP) refers to the final products at market prices produced by all resident units in a country (or a region) during a certain period of time. Gross domestic product is expressed in three different perspectives, namely value, income, and products respectively. GDP in its value perspective refers to the total value of all goods and services produced by all resident units during a certain period of time, minus the total value of input of goods and services of the nature of non-fixed assets; in other words, it is the sum of the value-added of all resident units. GDP from the perspective of income includes the primary income created by all resident units and distributed to resident and non-resident units. GDP from the perspective of products refers to the value of all goods and services for final demand by all resident units plus the net exports of goods and services during a given period of time. In the practice of national accounting, gross domestic product is calculated from three approaches, namely production approach, income approach and expenditure approach, which reflect gross domestic product and its composition from different angles.

For a region, it is called as Gross Regional Product(GRP) or regional GDP.

Three Strata of Industry Classification of economic activities into three strata of industry is a common practice in the world, although the grouping varies to some extent from country to country. In China economic activities are categorized into the following three strata of industry:

Primary industry refers to agriculture, forestry, animal husbandry and fishery and services in support of these industries.

Secondary industry refers to mining and quarrying, manufacturing, production and supply of electricity, water and gas, and construction.

Tertiary industry refers to all other economic activities not included in the primary or secondary industries.

Compensation of Employees refers to the total payment of various forms to employees for the productive activities they are engaged in. It includes wages, bonuses and allowances, which the employees earn in cash or in kind. It also includes the free medical services provided to the employees and the medicine expenses, transport subsidies and social insurance, and housing fund paid by the employers.

Net Taxes on Production refers to taxes on production less subsidies on production. The taxes on production refers to the various taxes, extra charges and fees levied on the production units on their production, sale and business activities as well as on the use of some factors of production, such as fixed assets, land and labour in the production activities they are engaged in. In contrast to taxes on production, subsidies on production refer to the unilateral government transfer to the production units and are therefore regarded as negative taxes on production. They include subsidies on the loss due to implementation of government policies, price subsidies, etc.

Depreciation of Fixed Assets refers to the depreciation of fixed assets in a given period, drawn in accordance with the stipulated depreciation rate for the purpose of compensating the wear-and-tear loss of the fixed assets or the depreciation of fixed assets imputed in accordance with the stipulated unified depreciation rate in the national economic accounting system. It reflects the value of transfer of the fixed assets in the production of the current period. The depreciation of fixed assets in various enterprises and institutions managed as enterprises refers to the depreciation expenses actually drawn. In government agencies and institutions not managed as enterprises which do not draw the depreciation expenses, as well as for the houses of residents, the depreciation of fixed assets is the imputed depreciation, which is calculated in accordance with the stipulated unified depreciation rate. In principle, the depreciation of fixed assets should be calculated on the basis of the re-purchased value of the fixed assets. However, currently the conditions in China do not facilitate the revaluation of all the fixed assets. Therefore, only the above-mentioned methods can be adopted at present.

Operating Surplus refers to the balance of the value added created by the resident units after deducting the labourers remuneration, net taxes on production and the depreciation of fixed assets. It is equivalent to the business profit of the enterprises plus subsidies to production, but the wages and welfare expenses paid from the profits should be deducted.

GDP by Expenditure Approach refers to the method of measuring the final results of production activities of a country (region) during a given period from the perspective of final uses. It includes final consumption expenditure, gross capital formation and net export of goods and services. The formula for computation is.:

GDP by expenditure approach = final consumption expenditure + gross capital formation + net export of goods and services

Final Consumption Expenditure refers to the total expenditure of resident units for purchases of goods and services from both the domestic economic territory and abroad to meet the needs of material, cultural and spiritual life. It does not include the expenditure of non-resident units on consumption in the economic territory of the country. The final consumption expenditure is broken down into household consumption expenditure and government consumption expenditure.

Household Consumption Expenditure refers to the total expenditure of resident households on the final consumption of goods and services. In addition to the consumption of goods and services bought by the households directly with money, the household consumption expenditure also includes expenditure on goods and services obtained by the households in other ways, i.e. the so-called imputed consumption expenditure, which includes the following: (a) the goods and services provided to households by employers in the form of payment in kind and transfer in kind; (b) goods and services produced and consumed by the households themselves, in which the services refer to the owner-occupied housing and services offered by payed family employees; (c) financial intermediate services provided by financial institution.

Government Consumption Expenditure refers to the consumption expenditure spent for the provision of public services provided by the government to the whole country and the net expenditure on the goods and services provided by the government to households free of charge or at reduced prices. The former equals to the output value of the government services minus the value of operating income obtained by the government departments. The latter equals to the market value of the goods and services provided by the government free of charge or at reduced prices to the households minus the value received by the government from the households.

Gross Capital Formation refers to the fixed assets acquired less disposals and the net value of inventory, thus including gross fixed capital formation and changes in inventories.

Gross Fixed Capital Formation refers to the value of acquisitions less those disposals of fixed assets during a given period. Fixed assets are the assets produced through production activities with unit value above a specified amount and which could be used for over one year. Natural assets are not included.Gross fixed capital formation can be categorized into total tangible fixed capital formation and total intangible fixed capital formation. Total tangible fixed capital formation includes the value of the construction projects and installation projects completed and the equipment, apparatus and instruments purchased (less those disposed) as well as the value of land improved, the value of draught animals, breeding stock and animals for milk, for wool and for recreational purposes and the newly increased forest with economic value. Total intangible fixed capital formation includes the prospecting of minerals and the acquisition of computer software minus the disposal of them.

Changes in Inventories refers to the market value of the change in the physical volume of inventory of resident units during a given period, i.e. the difference between the values at the beginning and at the end of the period minus the gains due to the change in prices. The changes in inventories can have a positive or a negative value. A positive value indicates an increase in inventory while a negative value indicates a decrease in inventory. The inventory includes raw materials, fuels and reserve materials purchased by the production units as well as the inventory of finished products, semi-finished products and work-in-progress.

Net Export of Goods and Services refers to the exports of goods and services subtracting the imports of goods and services. Exports include the value of various goods and services sold or gratuitously transferred by resident units to non-resident units. Imports include the value of various goods and services purchased or gratuitously acquired resident units from non-resident units. Because the provision of services and the use of them happen simultaneously, the acquisition of services by resident units from abroad is usually treated as import while the acquisition of services by non-resident units in this country is usually treated as export. The exports and imports of goods are calculated at FOB.

3

Three

人口

Population

3–1 历次人口普查主要指标
Main Indicators on National Population Census in 1953,1964,1982,1990,2000 and 2010

单位：万人 (10000 persons)

指标名称	Item	第一次 1953年 The First	第二次 1964年 The Second	第三次 1982年 The Third	第四次 1990年 The Forth	第五次 2000年 The Fifth	第六次 2010年 The Sixth
总人口	**Total Population**	**1503.73**	**1714.05**	**2855.29**	**3239.11**	**3524.77**	**3474.65**
按城镇、乡村分	**Grouped by Residence**						
城镇人口	Urban population	109.91	203.55	540.22	623.17	844.51	1174.78
乡村人口	Rural population	1393.82	1510.51	2315.07	2615.94	2680.25	2299.87
城镇人口比重（%）	The proportion of urban population(%)	7.31	11.88	18.92	19.24	23.96	33.81
按男女分	**Grouped by Male and Female**						
男	Male	759.8	868.48	1464.08	1676.88	1846.45	1795.15
女	Female	743.93	845.57	1391.21	1562.22	1678.32	1679.5
性别比(以女性为100)	Sex Ratio(female=100)	102.13	102.71	105.24	107.34	110.02	106.89
人口年平均增长率（%）	The growth rate of Annual Average Population(%)		1.32	2.89	1.59	0.82	-0.14
家庭总户数（万户）	Total Number of Household (10000 households)	340.15	390.96	565.93	721.04	923.94	1038.96
户均规模（人/户）	Average Family Size(person/household)	4.42	4.38	4.93	4.41	3.74	3.24
人口自然变动（‰）	**Natural Change of Population(‰)**						
出生率	Birth Rate	38.43	52.62	24.81	23.09	20.59	13.96
死亡率	Death Rate	17.61	20.66	7.6	7.9	7.53	6.55
自然增长率	Natural Growth Rate	20.82	31.96	17.21	15.19	13.06	7.41
年龄结构（%）	**Age Composition (%)**						
0–14	Aged 0-14	37.88	38.82	40.88	32.68	30.17	25.22
15–64	Aged 15-64	58.52	58.42	54.45	62.71	63.87	66.21
65岁及以上	Aged 65 and Over	3.59	2.76	4.66	4.61	5.97	8.57
民族	**Population by Ethnicity**						
汉族	Han	1109.84	1312.89	2112.95	2114.88	2191.17	2219.85
占总人口比重（%）	% to Total Population(%)	73.81	76.61	74	65.29	62.16	63.89
年均增长率（%）	Annual average growth rate(%)		0.37	-0.35	-1.24	-0.49	0.27
少数民族	Minority	393.89	401.16	742.35	1124.23	1333.6	1254.8
占总人口比重（%）	% to Total Population(%)	26.19	23.39	26	34.71	37.84	36.11
年均增长率（%）	Annual average growth rate(%)		-1.12	1.06	2.93	0.87	-0.46
受教育程度	**Education Attainments**						
小学	Primary School		352.71	822.65	1210.75	1535.3	1368.07
初中	Junior Secondary School		53.8	325.86	475.78	727.48	1035.07
高中	Senior Secondary School		13.38	84.72	127.5	199.67	253.02
大专以上	Junior College and Above		3.96	11.09	25.06	67.49	183.88
文盲人口	Illiterate Population			1202.24	969.11	598.58	303.85
文盲率（%）	Illiterate Rate(%)			42.11	29.92	16.98	8.74
每十万人口拥有的各种受教育程度人口（人）	**Population with Various Education Attainments Per 10 0000 Persons (person)**						
大专及以上	Junior College and Above				774	1915	5292
高中/中专	Senior Secondary School and Technical Secondary School				3973	5665	7282
初中	Junior Secondary School				14688	20639	29789
小学	Primary School				37379	43557	39373

注：表中数据来源于历次人口普查公报。
Note:Data in this table come from the communique of the six national population censuses.

3-2 第六次人口普查各民族人口数

Population of all ethnic groups on the Sixth National Population Census

单位：万人 (10000 persons)

指标名称	Item	2010年
总人口	Total Population	3474.86
男	Male	1790.55
女	Female	1684.31
汉族	Han	2234.42
男	Male	1151.79
女	Female	1082.63
蒙古族	Mongolian	4.16
男	Male	2.32
女	Female	1.84
回族	Hui	18.48
男	Male	9.50
女	Female	8.98
苗族	Miao	396.84
男	Male	204.09
女	Female	192.75
彝族	Yi	83.45
男	Male	42.96
女	Female	40.49
壮族	Zhuang	5.26
男	Male	2.65
女	Female	2.61
布依族	Bouyei	251.06
男	Male	127.11
女	Female	123.95
满族	Manchu	2.31
男	Male	1.19
女	Female	1.12
侗族	Dong	143.19
男	Male	75.02
女	Female	68.17
瑶族	Yao	4.09
男	Male	2.14
女	Female	1.95
白族	Bai	17.95
男	Male	9.59
女	Female	8.36
土家族	Tujia	143.70
男	Male	73.65
女	Female	70.05
畲族	She	3.66
男	Male	1.91
女	Female	1.75
水族	Shui	34.87
男	Male	18.03
女	Female	16.84
仫佬族	Mulam	2.50
男	Male	1.33
女	Female	1.17
羌族	Qiang	0.16
男	Male	0.09
女	Female	0.07
毛南族	Maonan	2.73
男	Male	1.42
女	Female	1.31
仡佬族	Gelao	49.52
男	Male	25.89
女	Female	23.62
未定族称人们共同体	Undetermined called People Community	61.28
男	Male	32.01
女	Female	29.27

注：表中数据来源于第六次人口普查机器汇总数。

Note:Data in this table are obtained from the Sixth Population Census.

3-3 常住人口(半年口径)

Permanent Resident Population (at least half a year)

单位：万人 (10000 persons)

指 标	Item	2006	2007	2008	2009	2010	2011
年末总人口	**Total Population at the Year-end**	**3690**	**3632**	**3596**	**3537**	**3479**	**3469**
按城镇、乡村分	Grouped by Residence						
城 镇	Urban	1013.27	1025.68	1046.79	1057.21	1176.25	1212.76
乡 村	Rural	2676.73	2606.32	2549.21	2479.79	2302.75	2256.24
按性别分	Grouped by Sex						
男	Male	1908.85	1879.70	1868.73	1827.56	1797.43	1801.21
女	Female	1781.15	1752.30	1727.27	1709.44	1681.57	1667.79
性别比(以女性为100)	Sex Ratio(female=100)	107.17	107.27	108.19	106.91	106.89	108.00
年平均人口	Annual Average Population	3710.00	3661.00	3614.00	3566.50	3508.00	3474.00
家庭年末总户数(万户)	Total Number of Household (10000 households)	1043.60	1056.84	1053.61	1046.28	1038.96	1066.13
家庭户规模(人/户)	Average Family Size(person/household)	3.44	3.34	3.31	3.28	3.24	3.16
人口自然变动	**Natural Change of Population**						
出生人数	Number of Birth	51.83	48.62	48.75	48.68	48.52	46.24
出生率(‰)	Birth Rate(‰)	13.97	13.28	13.49	13.65	13.96	13.31
死亡人数	Number of Death	24.89	24.16	24.47	23.86	22.76	24.07
死亡率(‰)	Death Rate(‰)	6.71	6.60	6.77	6.69	6.55	6.93
自然增长人数	Natural Increase of Population	26.94	24.46	24.28	24.82	25.76	22.17
自然增长率(‰)	Natural Growth Rate(‰)	7.26	6.68	6.72	6.96	7.41	6.38

注：2006年—2009年数据根据第六次人口普查数据进行修订。
Note:Data from 2006 to 2009 had been adjusted according to the result of the Sixth National Population Census.

3-4 户籍人口
Household Registered Population

单位：万人 (10000 persons)

指　　标	Item	2006	2007	2008	2009	2010	2011
年末总人口	**Total Population at the Year-end**	**3921.91**	**3985.04**	**4036.75**	**4090.78**	**4189.00**	**4238.44**
农　业	Agriculture	3295.08	3346.09	3385.66	3429.36	3512.92	3551.18
非农业	Non-agriculture	626.83	638.95	651.09	661.43	676.07	687.26
构成(以年末总人口=100)(%)	**Composition (total population at the year-end=100)(%)**						
农　业	Agriculture	84.0	84.0	83.9	83.8	83.9	83.8
非农业	Non-agriculture	16.0	16.0	16.1	16.2	16.1	16.2

注：资料来源于省公安厅。
Note:Data in the table above are obtained from the Public Security Department of Guizhou Province.

3-5 计划生育
Family Planning

单位：万人 (10000 persons)

指　　标	Item	2006	2007	2008	2009	2010	2011
符合政策出生人数	Number of Birth in Legality	51.79	49.78	47.00	47.95	46.22	40.70
生育政策符合率(%)	Family Planning Rates(%)	94.6	94.5	94.1	92.5	92.8	93.9
采取节育措施人数	Number of Contraception Users	633.07	649.53	596.74	621.67	563.07	572.94
避孕率(含复合使用药具)(%)	Contraception Rates(Including Using contraceptives)(%)	90.8	90.1	90.3	89.6	88.2	88.1

注：资料来源于省人口计生委。
Note:Data in the table are provided from the Committee of Population and Family Planning of Guizhou Provincial.

主要统计指标解释

人口数 指一定时点、一定地区范围内的有生命的个人的总和。年度统计的年末人口数指每年 12 月 31 日 24 时的人口数。

城镇人口和乡村人口 城镇人口是指居住在城镇范围内的全部常住人口；乡村人口是除上述人口以外的全部人口。

出生率（又称粗出生率） 指在一定时期内（通常为一年）一定地区的出生人数与同期内平均人数（或期中人数）之比，用千分率表示。本资料中的出生率指年出生率，其计算公式为：

$$出生率=\frac{年出生人数}{年平均人数}\times 1000‰$$

式中：出生人数指活产婴儿，即胎儿脱离母体时（不管怀孕月数），有过呼吸或其他生命现象。年平均人数指年初、年底人口数的平均数，也可用年中人口数代替。

死亡率（又称粗死亡率） 指在一定时期内（通常为一年）一定地区的死亡人数与同期内平均人数（或期中人数）之比，用千分率表示。本资料中的死亡率指年死亡率，其计算公式为：

$$死亡率=\frac{年死亡人数}{年平均人数}\times 1000‰$$

人口自然增长率 指在一定时期内（通常为一年）人口自然增加数（出生人数减死亡人数）与该时期内平均人数（或期中人数）之比，用千分率表示。计算公式为：

$$人口自然增长率=\frac{本年出生人数-本年死亡人数}{年平均人数}\times 1000‰$$

$$=人口出生率-人口死亡率$$

Explanatory Notes on Main Statistical Indicators

Total Population refers to the total number of people alive at a certain point of time within a given area. The annual statistics on total population is taken at midnight, the 31st of December.

Urban Population and Rural Population Urban population refers to all people residing in cities and towns, while rural population refers to population other than urban population.

Birth Rate (or Crude Birth Rate) refers to the ratio of the number of births to the average population (or mid-period population) during a certain period of time (usually a year), expressed in ‰. Birth rate in the chapter refers to annual birth rate. The following formula is used:

$$\text{Birth Rate}=\frac{\text{Number of Births}}{\text{Annual Average Population}}\times 1000‰$$

Number of births in the formula refers to live births, i.e. when a baby has breathed or showed any vital phenomena regardless of the length of pregnancy.

Annual average population is the average of the number of population at the beginning of the year and that at the end of the year. Sometimes it is substituted by the mid-year population.

Death Rate(or Crude Death Rate) refers to the ratio of the number of deaths to the average population (or mid-period population) during a certain period of time (usually a year), expressed in ‰. Death rate in the chapter refers to annual death rate. The following formula is used:

$$\text{Death Rate}=\frac{\text{Number of Death}}{\text{Annual Average Population}}\times 1000‰$$

Natural Growth Rate of Population refers to the ratio of natural increase in population (number of births minus number of deaths) in a certain period of time (usually a year) to the average population (or mid-period population) of the same period, expressed in ‰. The following formula is applied:

$$\text{Natural Growth Rate of Population}=\frac{\text{Number of Births-Number of Deaths}}{\text{Annual Average Population}}\times 1000‰$$

Natural Growth Rate of Population = Birth Rate-Death Rate

就业人员和职工工资

4

Four

Employment and Wages

4-1 就业人员及劳动报酬
Number of Employed Personnels and Wages

指 标	Item	2006	2007	2008	2009	2010	2011	2011年比2010年增长(%) Increase Rate in 2011 over 2010(%)
就业人员(万人)	**Number of Employed Persons (10000 persons)**	**1953.24**	**1872.64**	**1867.20**	**1841.92**	**1770.90**	**1792.80**	**1.2**
按产业分	**Grouped by Three Strata of Industry**							
第一产业	Primary Industry	1487.40	1388.02	1350.32	1299.29	1209.55	1194.39	-1.3
第二产业	Secondary Industry	174.17	172.31	180.73	197.60	203.52	215.86	6.1
第三产业	Tertiary Industry	291.67	312.31	336.15	345.03	357.82	382.55	6.9
按城乡分	**Grouped by Urban and Rural**							
城镇	Urban Area	478.85	489.96	501.33	512.95	525.76	554.14	5.4
乡村	Rural Area	1474.39	1382.67	1365.87	1328.96	1245.14	1238.66	-0.5
非私营单位职工人数总计(万人)	**Total Number of Staff and Workers (10000 persons)**	**201.87**	**207.53**	**199.76**	**206.44**	**210.67**	**225.91**	**7.2**
国有单位	State-owned Unit	137.86	141.48	140.97	141.79	146.81	158.26	7.8
集体单位	Collective-owned Unit	8.86	8.10	7.42	6.69	6.41	7.17	11.9
其他单位	Others	55.15	57.95	51.37	57.96	57.45	60.47	5.3
非私营单位职工工资总额(亿元)	**Total Wages of Staff and Wokers (100 million yuan)**	**350.16**	**439.24**	**509.54**	**572.67**	**649.55**	**830.11**	**27.8**
国有单位	State-owned Unit	251.39	320.64	377.51	416.87	470.49	606.80	29.0
集体单位	Collective-owned Unit	11.35	13.47	15.21	14.65	15.72	22.12	40.7
其他单位	Others	87.42	105.13	116.82	141.15	163.34	201.19	23.2
非私营单位在岗职工平均工资(元)	**Average Wage of Staff and Workers(yuan)**	**16815**	**20668**	**24602**	**28245**	**31458**	**37331**	**18.7**
国有单位	State-owned Unit	17638	22106	25874	29956	32718	38914	18.9
集体单位	Collective-owned Unit	12873	16893	20914	22167	24703	31601	27.9
其他单位	Others	15365	17668	21659	24772	29006	33851	16.7

注：2006—2009年就业人员总数及分产业、分城乡就业数据根据第六次人口普查结果修订。

Note:From 2006 to 2009，total number of employed persons and data of employment by three strata of industry and urban and rural have been adjusted according to the result of the Six National population census.

4-2 非私营单位就业人员年末人数(2011)

Number of Employed Persons in Non-private Units at Year-end

单位：人 (person)

指 标	Item	就业人员 Number of Employed	国有单位 State-owned Unit	集体单位 Collective-owned Unit	其他单位 Unit of Other Type of Ownership
总 计	**Total**	**2410482**	**1705366**	**76640**	**628476**
按企事业、机关分组	**By Enterprises,Institutions and Agencies**				
企 业	Enterprises	1337964	643659	70718	623587
事 业	Institutions	731652	721325	5816	4511
机 关	Agencies	340866	340382	106	378
按产业分	**By Three Strata of Industry**				
第一产业	Primary Industry	18663	16385	254	2024
第二产业	Secondary Industry	900041	460125	42837	397079
第三产业	Tertiary Industry	1491778	1228856	33549	229373
按国民经济行业分组	**By Sector**				
农、林、牧、渔业	Farming,Forestry,Animal Husbandry and Fishing	18663	16385	254	2024
采矿业	Mining and Quarrying	135445	53242	5727	76476
制造业	Manufacturing	398782	136656	11134	250992
电力、燃气及水的生产和供应业	Production and Supply of Electricity, Gas and Water	83107	64043	955	18109
建筑业	Construction	282707	206184	25021	51502
交通运输、仓储和邮政业	Transportation,Storage and Post	96691	80685	2121	13885
信息传输、计算机服务和软件业	Information Transmit,Computer Services and Software Trade	26787	11944		14843
批发和零售业	Wholesale and Retail Trade	106332	35826	5507	64999
批发业	Wholesale	63772	30529	2621	30622
零售业	Retail	42560	5297	2886	34377
住宿和餐饮业	Hotels and Catering Services	29414	7504	935	20975
金融业	Financial Intermediation	71546	22311	10183	39052
房地产业	Real Estate	42834	7674	1699	33461
租赁和商务服务业	Leasing and Commerce Services	31271	10618	4665	15988
租赁业	Leasing Services	1523	930	15	578
商务服务业	Commerce Services	29748	9688	4650	15410
科学研究、技术服务和地质勘查业	Scientific Research,Technic Serviced and Geological Prospecting	46388	40768	263	5357
水利、环境和公共设施管理业	Water Conservancy,Environment and Public Facilities Services	38289	35158	1993	1138
居民服务和其他服务业	Services to Households and Other Services	12799	5700	771	6328
教 育	Education	425384	413066	4474	7844
卫生、社会保障和社会福利业	Health Care,Social Securities and Social Welfare	130764	126803	818	3143
#卫 生	Health Care	125878	122174	737	2967
社会保障业	Social Securities	3431	3424		7
文化、体育和娱乐业	Culture,Sports and Entertainment	19489	17359	47	2083
#新闻出版社	News Publishing Company	3007	2800		207
广播、电视、电影和音像业	Broadcasting,Television,Film and Video Trade	6030	5534	13	483
体 育	Sports	3775	3771		4
公共管理和社会组织	Public Administration and Social Organization	413790	413440	73	277

4-3 非私营单位女性就业人员年末人数(2011)

Number of Employed Female in Non-private Units at the Year-end

单位：人 (person)

行业	Sector	女性就业人员数 Number of Female Employed	国有单位 State-owned Unit	集体单位 Collective-owned Unit	其他单位 Unit of Other Type of Ownership
总计	**Total**	**785066**	**560600**	**20865**	**203601**
农、林、牧、渔业	Farming,Forestry,Animal Husbandry and Fishing	5114	4265	62	787
采矿业	Mining and Quarrying	18579	8256	1025	9298
制造业	Manufacturing	131635	46297	4085	81253
电力、燃气及水的生产和供应业	Production and Supply of Electricity, Gas and Water	22111	17598	288	4225
建筑业	Construction	31457	19808	3303	8346
交通运输、仓储和邮政业	Transportation,Storage and Post	27669	22493	687	4489
信息传输、计算机服务和软件业	Information Transmit,Computer Services and Software Trade	11981	6478		5503
批发和零售业	Wholesale and Retail Trade	43295	12355	2441	28499
批发业	Wholesale	21778	10054	1104	10620
零售业	Retail Trade	21517	2301	1337	17879
住宿和餐饮业	Hotels and Catering Services	17592	4668	444	12480
金融业	Financial Intermediation	33412	10133	4358	18921
房地产业	Real Estate	15316	3158	578	11580
租赁和商务服务业	Leasing and Commerce Services	9681	3737	601	5343
租赁业	Leasing Services	602	424	5	173
商务服务业	Commerce Services	9079	3313	596	5170
科学研究、技术服务和地质勘查业	Scientific Research,Technic Services and Geological Prospecting	12375	10769	69	1537
水利、环境和公共设施管理业	Water Conservancy,Environment and Public Facilities Services	18648	17138	1032	478
居民服务和其他服务业	Services to Households and Other Services	5471	2093	296	3082
教育	Education	174703	169100	1017	4586
卫生、社会保障和社会福利业	Health Care,Social Securities and Social Welfare	78557	76044	516	1997
#卫生	Health Care	76066	73691	472	1903
社会保障业	Social Securities	1693	1688		5
文化、体育和娱乐业	Culture,Sports and Entertainment	7995	6915	19	1061
#新闻出版社	News Publishing Company	1489	1425		64
广播、电视、电影和音像业	Broadcasting,Television,Film and Video Trade	2349	2122	4	223
体育	Sports	996	995		1
公共管理和社会组织	Public Administration and Social Organization	119475	119295	44	136

4–4 非私营单位各行业在岗职工年末人数(2011)

Working Staff and Workers in Non-private units at the Year-end by Sector

单位：人 (person)

行业	Sector	职工人数 Number of Staff and Workers	国有单位 State-owned Unit	集体单位 Collective-owned Unit	其他单位 Unit of Other Type of Ownership
总　计	**Total**	**2259081**	**1582623**	**71716**	**604742**
按企事业、机关分组	**By Enterprises,Institutions and Agencies**				
企　业	Enterprises	1251425	585502	65818	600105
事　业	Institutions	693622	683571	5792	4259
机　关	Agencies	314034	313550	106	378
按产业分	**By Three Strata of Industry**				
第一产业	Primary Industry	16929	14805	254	1870
第二产业	Secondary Industry	834155	412241	39008	382906
第三产业	Tertiary Industry	1407997	1155577	32454	219966
按国民经济行业分组	**By Sector**				
农、林、牧、渔业	Farming,Forestry,Animal Husbandry and Fishing	16929	14805	254	1870
采矿业	Mining and Quarrying	134334	53160	5602	75572
制造业	Manufacturing	387452	132500	10888	244064
电力、燃气及水的生产和供应业	Production and Supply of Electricity,Gas and Water	81217	62569	949	17699
建筑业	Construction	231152	164012	21569	45571
交通运输、仓储和邮政业	Transportation,Storage and Post	89128	74118	1990	13020
信息传输、计算机服务和软件业	Information Transmit,Computer Services and Software Trade	25989	11499		14490
批发和零售业	Wholesale and Retail Trade	104093	34970	5230	63893
批发业	Wholesale	62030	29808	2446	29776
零售业	Retail Trade	42063	5162	2784	34117
住宿和餐饮业	Hotels and Catering Services	28561	7221	923	20417
金融业	Financial Intermediation	67441	21669	9970	35802
房地产业	Real Estate	40460	7318	1630	31512
租赁和商务服务业	Leasing and Commerce Services	30271	10232	4357	15682
租赁业	Leasing Services	1484	896	15	573
商务服务业	Commerce Services	28787	9336	4342	15109
科学研究、技术服务和地质勘查业	Scientific Research,Technic Services and Geological Prospecting	44040	38784	233	5023
水利、环境和公共设施管理业	Water Conservancy,Environment and Public Facilities Services	31786	28695	1978	1113
居民服务和其他服务业	Services to Households and Other Services	11977	5100	761	6116
教　育	Education	410555	398571	4474	7510
卫生、社会保障和社会福利业	Health Care,Social Securities and Social Welfare	121941	118113	790	3038
#卫　生	Health Care	117208	113637	709	2862
社会保障业	Social Securities	3398	3391		7
文化、体育和娱乐业	Culture,Sports and Entertainment	19121	17001	47	2073
#新闻出版社	News Publishing Company	2976	2769		207
广播、电视、电影和音像业	Broadcasting,Television,Film and Video Trade	5925	5429	13	483
体　育	Sports	3681	3677		4
公共管理和社会组织	Public Administration and Social Organization	382634	382286	71	277

4–5 非私营单位在岗职工工资总额(2011)
Total Wages Bill of Working Staff and Workers in Non-private units

单位：亿元 (100 million yuan)

指标	Item	工资总额 Total Wage Bill	国有单位 State-owned Unit	集体单位 Collective-owned Unit	其他单位 Unit of Other Type of Ownership
总　计	**Total**	**830.11**	**606.80**	**22.12**	**201.19**
按企事业、机关分	**By Enterprises,Institutions and Agencies**				
企　业	Enterprises	479.83	259.45	20.57	199.81
事　业	Institutions	236.24	233.41	1.53	1.30
机　关	Agencies	114.05	113.94	0.02	0.08
按产业分	**By Three Strata of Industry**				
第一产业	Primary Industry	4.32	3.95	0.04	0.32
第二产业	Secondary Industry	310.54	179.25	8.33	122.95
第三产业	Tertiary Industry	515.26	423.60	13.75	77.91
按国民经济行业分	**By Sector**				
农、林、牧、渔业	Farming,Forestry,Animal Husbandry and Fishing	4.32	3.95	0.04	0.32
采矿业	Mining and Quarrying	53.71	20.46	1.44	31.82
制造业	Manufacturing	137.23	62.64	2.16	72.44
电力、燃气及水的生产和供应业	Production and Supply of Electricity,Gas and Water	43.71	35.62	0.26	7.83
建筑业	Construction	75.88	60.54	4.47	10.87
交通运输、仓储和邮政业	Transportation,Storage and Post	34.88	30.07	0.48	4.34
信息传输、计算机服务和软件业	Information Transmit,Computer Services and Software Trade	11.88	5.35		6.53
批发和零售业	Wholesale and Retail Trade	36.08	18.68	0.98	16.42
批发业	Wholesale	26.25	17.21	0.56	8.48
零售业	Retail Trade	9.83	1.47	0.43	7.94
住宿和餐饮业	Hotels and Catering Services	6.54	1.88	0.29	4.37
金融业	Financial Intermediation	51.69	15.22	9.25	27.22
房地产业	Real Estate	11.42	2.04	0.34	9.04
租赁和商务服务业	Leasing and Commerce Services	8.10	3.60	0.74	3.75
租赁业	Leasing Services	0.38	0.25	0.00	0.13
商务服务业	Commerce Services	7.72	3.35	0.74	3.62
科学研究、技术服务和地质勘查业	Scientific Research,Technic Services and Geological Prospecting	15.15	13.48	0.04	1.63
水利、环境和公共设施管理业	Water Conservancy,Environment and Public Facilities Services	8.95	8.45	0.28	0.22
居民服务和其他服务业	Services to Households and Other Services	3.27	1.87	0.15	1.26
教　育	Education	144.62	141.88	0.99	1.76
卫生、社会保障和社会福利业	Health Care,Social Securities and Social Welfare	41.79	40.78	0.17	0.85
#卫　生	Health Care	40.73	39.76	0.15	0.81
社会保障业	Social Securities	0.68	0.68		0.00
文化、体育和娱乐业	Culture,Sports and Entertainment	5.76	5.25	0.02	0.48
#新闻出版社	News Publishing Company	0.85	0.80		0.05
广播、电视、电影和音像业	Broadcasting,Television,Film and Video Trade	1.83	1.68	0.01	0.13
体　育	Sports	1.25	1.25		0.00
公共管理和社会组织	Public Administration and Social Organization	135.13	135.07	0.01	0.05

4–6 非私营单位各行业在岗职工平均工资(2011)

Average Wages of Working Staff and Workers in Non-private units by Sector

单位：元 (yuan)

指　标	Item	平均工资 Average Wage	国有单位 State-owned Unit	集体单位 Collective-owned Unit	其他单位 Unit of Other Type of Ownership
总　计	**Total**	**37331**	**38914**	**31601**	**33851**
按企事业、机关分	**By Enterprises,Institutions and Agencies**				
企　业	Enterprises	39452	46214	31543	33977
事　业	Institutions	34486	34582	26039	30197
机　关	Agencies	36959	36979	19714	22416
按产业分	**By Three Industries**				
第一产业	Primary Industry	25637	26867	17567	17135
第二产业	Secondary Industry	37930	44312	21746	32711
第三产业	Tertiary Industry	37119	37154	43725	35976
按国民经济行业分	**By Sector**				
农、林、牧、渔业	Farming,Forestry,Animal Husbandry and Fishing	25637	26867	17567	17135
采矿业	Mining and Quarrying	41113	39633	26095	43279
制造业	Manufacturing	35753	47489	20325	30018
电力、燃气及水的生产和供应业	Production and Supply of Electricity,Gas and Water	53927	56992	27640	44464
建筑业	Construction	34002	38193	21062	25027
交通运输、仓储和邮政业	Transportation,Storage and Post	39555	40936	24433	33919
信息传输、计算机服务和软件业	Information Transmit,Computer Services and Software Trade	46661	47227		46208
批发和零售业	Wholesale and Retail Trade	35354	54860	19200	26106
批发业	Wholesale	42025	59262	23188	28706
零售业	Retail Trade	24140	29329	15675	23804
住宿和餐饮业	Hotels and Catering Services	23364	25656	31401	22133
金融业	Financial Intermediation	78071	70907	96174	77493
房地产业	Real Estate	28430	28123	21639	28843
租赁和商务服务业	Leasing and Commerce Services	27239	35552	18578	24069
租赁业	Leasing Services	25115	26395	16923	23211
商务服务业	Commerce Services	27315	36478	18583	24102
科学研究、技术服务和地质勘查业	Scientific Research,Technic Services and Geological Prospecting	36124	36620	19662	33148
水利、环境和公共设施管理业	Water Conservancy,Environment and Public Facilities Services	28789	30155	14768	18848
居民服务和其他服务业	Services to Households and Other Services	27482	37046	19419	20591
教　育	Education	35459	35827	22147	23758
卫生、社会保障和社会福利业	Health Care,Social Securities and Social Welfare	35167	35438	21617	28308
#卫　生	Health Care	35389	35846	21412	28928
社会保障业	Social Securities	22036	22170		15143
文化、体育和娱乐业	Culture,Sports and Entertainment	30293	31165	40293	22973
#新闻出版社	News Publishing Company	28724	29148		23134
广播、电视、电影和音像业	Broadcasting,Television,Film and Video Trade	30727	31034	24500	27812
体　育	Sports	34158	34214		14500
公共管理和社会组织	Public Administration and Social Organization	35776	35792	14099	18465

注：在岗职工平均工资包含劳务派遣人员。
Note:The average wages of working staff and workers include labor dispatching personnel.

4-7 城乡私营企业户数和就业人员(2011)

Number of Private Enterprises and Employed Persons in Urban and Rural Areas by Sector

指　标	Item	户数(户) Number of Enterprises (unit)	城镇 Urban Areas	乡村 Rural Areas	就业人员(人) Number of Employees (Person)	城镇 Urban Areas	乡村 Rural Areas
总　计	**Total**	**94625**	**56620**	**38005**	**740579**	**410722**	**329857**
农、林、牧、渔业	Farming,Forestry,Animal Husbandry and Fishing	4407	1634	2773	33611	14112	19499
采掘业	Mining and Quarrying	5350	1250	4100	52139	12246	39893
制造业	Manufacturing	10870	5578	5292	165689	88367	77322
电力、燃气及水的生产和供应业	Production and Supply of Electricity,Gas and Water	998	471	527	9608	4458	5150
建筑业	Construction	3865	2635	1230	39264	26149	13115
交通运输、仓储和邮政业	Transportation,Storage and Post	2151	1185	966	16841	9362	7479
信息传输、计算机服务和软件业	Information Transmit,Computer Services and Software Trade	3665	2319	1346	16617	8209	8408
批发和零售业	Wholesale and Retail Trade	39128	25630	13498	208220	120547	87673
住宿和餐饮业	Hotels and Catering Services	1363	921	442	17694	9339	8355
房地产业	Real Estate	5138	3371	1767	53181	31895	21286
租赁和商务服务业	Leasing and Commerce Services	7941	5710	2231	41599	29017	12582
居民服务和其他服务业	Services to Households and Other Services	4437	2741	1696	25808	14806	11002
卫生、社会保障和社会福利业	Health Care,Social Securities and Social Welfare	360	247	113	4643	3247	1396
文化、体育和娱乐业	Culture,Sports and Entertainment	590	417	173	5820	3524	2296
其他行业	Others	4362	2511	1851	49845	35444	14401

注：资料来源于省工商局(下表同)。
Note:Data in the table are obtained from Guizhou Provincial Industrial and Commercial Bureau(the same applies to the next table).

4–8 城乡个体工商户数和就业人员(2011)
Number of Household and Self-Employed Individuals in Urban and Rural Areas

指　标	Item	户数(户) Number of Enterprises (unit)	城镇 Urban Areas	乡村 Rural Areas	就业人员（人） Number of Employed (Person)	城镇 Urban Areas	乡村 Rural Areas
总　计	**Total**	**755135**	**397842**	**357293**	**1201351**	**632807**	**568544**
农、林、牧、渔业	Farming,Forestry,Animal Husbandry and Fishing	9062	2903	6159	14872	4607	10265
采掘业	Mining and Quarrying	3969	1121	2848	13169	3128	10041
制造业	Manufacturing	43904	23102	20802	85609	40503	45106
电力、燃气及水的生产和供应业	Production and Supply of Electricity,Gas and Water	443	190	253	1035	413	622
建筑业	Construction	4164	2912	1252	13793	7539	6254
交通运输、仓储和邮政业	Transportation,Storage and Post	25052	10514	14538	35581	13842	21739
信息传输、计算机服务和软件业	Information Transmit,Computer Services and Software Trade	4040	1790	2250	6298	2780	3518
批发和零售业	Wholesale and Retail Trade	492568	258412	234156	718728	372639	346089
住宿和餐饮业	Hotels and Catering Services	79236	48632	30604	157036	97139	59897
房地产业	Real Estate	89	70	19	306	266	40
租赁和商务服务业	Leasing and Commerce Services	6270	3813	2457	12631	7421	5210
居民服务和其他服务业	Services to Households and Other Services	64300	32924	31376	106458	63046	43412
卫生、社会保障和社会福利业	Health Care,Social Securities and Social Welfare	3055	1978	1077	6992	4101	2891
文化、体育和娱乐业	Culture,Sports and Entertainment	3869	2647	1222	9351	6617	2734
其他行业	Others	15114	6834	8280	19492	8766	10726

4−9 城镇新就业人数和失业人数

Number of Newly Employed Persons and Unemployed Persons in Urban Areas

单位：万人 (10000 persons)

指 标	Item	2006	2007	2008	2009	2010	2011	2011年比2010年增长(%) Increase Rate in 2011 over 2010(%)
新就业人数总计	Total Incremental Employed Personnels	20.1	22.4	21.12	21.10	27.71	35.94	29.7
城镇登记失业人数	Number of Registered Unemployed Persons in Urban Areas	12.12	12.13	12.56	12.34	12.18	12.51	2.7
城镇登记失业率(%)	Registered Unemployment Rate in Urban Areas(%)	4.11	3.97	3.98	3.81	3.63	3.63	持平

注：资料来源于省人力资源社会保障厅(以下相关表同)。

Note: Data in the table are obtained from Guizhou Department of Human Resources and Social Security(the related tables in the chapter are the same).

4−10 下岗失业人员享受再就业优惠政策情况

Statistics of Re-employment Preferential Policies for Laid-off Workers

单位：人 (person)

指 标	Item	2010	2011	2011年比2010年增长(%) Increase Rate in 2011 over 2010(%)
下岗失业人员	Laid-off Workers	96146	108060	12.4
#就业困难对象	Residents Experiencing Employment Difficulty	55968	49438	-11.7
消除零就业家庭(户)	Number of Househoulds rased Zero-employment Families(househould)	1530	683	-55.4
促进零就业家庭成员就业	Promoting Zero-employment Families Employed	1697	713	-58.0
从事公益性岗位人数	Number of Persons Engaged in Public-service Jobs	41123	103460	151.6
享受职业培训补贴人数	Number of Persons Receiving Professional Training Subsidies	104640	154626	47.8
享受职业介绍补贴人数	Number of Persons Receiving Job Services Subsidies	35034	16952	-51.6
享受技能鉴定补贴人数	Number of Persons Receiving Skill Identification Subsidies	26382	42925	62.7
享受社会保险补贴人数	Number of Persons Receiving Social Insurance Subsidies	132998	119711	-10.0
使用就业再就业资金(万元)	Using Employment and Re-employment Fund(10000 yuan)	131891	175915	33.4
#社会保险补贴	Social Insurance Subsidies	38441	49470	28.7
岗位补贴	Post Subsidies	60635	87877	44.9
职业培训补贴	Professional Training	12089	25919	114.4
职业介绍补贴	Job Services	1554	917	-41.0
扶持公共就业服务	Supporting Public Employment Service	3494	2300	-34.2

4−11 职业技能鉴定

Occupation Skill Appraisal

单位:人 (person)

指标名称	Item	2006	2007	2008	2009	2010	2011
参加职业技能鉴定	Number of Persons Joining in Occupation Skill Appraisal	84421	96145	87352	77735	82135	114691
获取证书人数	Number of Persons With Qualification Certificates	75523	86067	79352	69781	73717	105141
#高级技工	Advanced Mechanic	5509	5148	6274	6205	5989	11322
#技 师	Technician	2222	1315	1272	487	372	615
#高级技师	Advanced Technician	307	190	230	161	163	138

4-12 劳动力市场需求人员、求职人员及构成

Components of Persons Required by Labor Market and Applying for a Job

单位：人 (person)

行业分组	by Sector	2010 绝对数 Level	2010 构成(%) Composition	2011 绝对数 Level	2011 构成(%) Composition	2011年比2010年增长(%) Increase Rate in 2011 over 2010(%)
劳动力市场需求人员合计	**Number of Persons Required by Labor Market**	**274614**	**100.0**	**278542**	**100.0**	**1.4**
农林牧渔业	Farming,Forestry,Animal Husbandry and Fishing	4995	1.8	4264	1.5	-14.6
采矿业	Mining and Quarrying	2324	0.8	4391	1.6	88.9
制造业	Manufacturing	74144	27.0	55877	20.1	-24.6
电力煤气和水的生产和供应业	Production and Supply of Electricity, Gas and Water	2927	1.1	4937	1.8	68.7
建筑业	Construction	6456	2.4	7405	2.7	14.7
交通运输、仓储和邮政业	Transportation,Storage and Post	7301	2.7	12409	4.5	70.0
信息传输、计算机服务和软件业	Information Transmit,Computer Services and Software Trade	5791	2.1	10051	3.6	73.6
批发和零售业	Wholesale and Retail Trade	57142	20.8	63141	22.7	10.5
住宿和餐饮业	Hotels and Catering Services	48349	17.6	45767	16.4	-5.3
金融业	Financial Intermediation	1897	0.7	1490	0.5	-21.5
房地产业	Real Estate	4541	1.7	5215	1.9	14.8
租赁和商务服务业	Leasing and Commerce Services	4402	1.6	5190	1.9	17.9
科学研究、技术服务和地质勘查业	Scientific Research,Technic Services and Geological Prospecting	440	0.2	247	0.1	-43.9
水利、环境和公共设施管理业	Water Conservancy,Environment and Public Facilities Services	501	0.2	294	0.1	-41.3
居民服务和其他服务业	Services to Households and Other Services	30848	11.2	37989	13.6	23.1
教育	Education	4040	1.5	1951	0.7	-51.7
卫生、社会保障和社会福利业	Health Care,Social Securities and Social Welfare	5637	2.1	1303	0.5	-76.9
文化、体育和娱乐业	Culture,Sports and Entertainment	11940	4.3	15583	5.6	30.5
公共管理与社会组织	Public Administration and Social Organization	939	0.3	1038	0.4	10.5
劳动力市场求职人员合计	**Number of Person Applying for A Job**	**241422**	**100.0**	**223260**	**100.0**	**-7.5**
新成长的失业青年	New grown Unemployed Youngth	44550	18.5	41798	18.7	-6.2
#应届高校毕业生	Graduating Students from higer School	21014	8.7	22773	10.2	8.4
就业转失业人员	Working Staff Transmiting into Unemployed	76846	31.8	65848	29.5	-14.3
其他失业人员	Other Unempolyed	18644	7.7	29088	13.0	56.0
在业人员	Working Staff	5987	2.5	5751	2.6	-3.9
下岗职工	Laid-off Workers	17303	7.2	12297	5.5	-28.9
退休人员	Retired	415	0.2	529	0.2	27.5
在学人员	Enrollment	4115	1.7	5552	2.5	34.9
本市农村人员	Persons of Domesitc Country	46359	19.2	38382	17.2	-17.2
外埠人员	Outside	27203	11.3	24015	10.8	-11.7

主要统计指标解释

就业人员　指在16周岁及以上，从事一定社会劳动并取得劳动报酬或经营收入的人员。这一指标反映了一定时期内全部劳动力资源的实际利用情况，是研究我国基本国情国力的重要指标。

单位就业人员　指在各级国家机关、政党机关、社会团体及企业、事业单位中工作，取得工资或其他形式的劳动报酬的全部人员。包括在岗职工、再就业的离退休人员、民办教师以及在各单位中工作的外方人员和港澳台方人员、兼职人员、借用的外单位人员和第二职业者。不包括离开本单位仍保留劳动关系的职工。各单位的就业人员反映了各单位实际参加生产或工作的全部劳动力。

城镇私营和个体就业人员　城镇私营就业人员指在工商管理部门注册登记，其经营地址设在县城关镇（含县城关镇）以上的私营企业就业人员，包括私营企业投资者和雇工。城镇个体就业人员指在工商管理部门注册登记，并持有城镇户口或在城镇长期居住，经批准从事个体工商经营的就业人员，包括个体经营者和在个体工商户劳动的家庭帮工和雇工。

国有单位　指资产归国家所有的经济组织。包括按《中华人民共和国企业法人登记管理条例》规定登记注册的非公司制的经济组织，以及中央、地方各级国家机关、事业单位和社会团体。

集体单位　指生产资料归集体所有，并按《中华人民共和国企业法人登记管理条例》规定登记注册的经济组织。

其他单位　包括股份合作单位、联营单位、有限责任公司、股份有限公司、港澳台商投资单位以及外商投资单位等其他登记注册类型单位。

在岗职工　指在本单位工作并由单位支付工资的人员，以及有工作岗位，但由于学习、病伤产假等原因暂未工作，仍由单位支付工资的人员。

工资总额　指各单位在一定时期内直接支付给本单位全部就业人员的劳动报酬总额。工资总额的计算原则应以直接支付给就业人员的全部劳动报酬为根据。各单位支付给就业人员的劳动报酬以及其他根据有关规定支付的工资，不论是计入成本的还是不计入成本的，不论是按国家规定列入计征奖金税项目的，还是未列入计征奖金税项目的，不论是以货币形式支付的还是以实物形式支付的，均包括在工资总额内。

平均工资　指企业、事业、机关单位的就业人员在一定时期内平均每人所得的货币工资额。它表明一定时期职工工资收入的高低程度，是反映就业人员工资水平的主要指标。计算公式为：

$$平均工资=\frac{报告期实际支付的全部就业人员工资总额}{报告期全部就业人员平均人数}$$

平均工资指数　指报告期就业人员平均工资与基期就业人员平均工资的比率，是反映不同时期就业人员货币工资水平变动情况的相对数。计算公式为：

$$平均工资指数=\frac{报告期就业人员平均工资}{基期就业人员平均工资}\times 100\%$$

城镇登记失业人员　指有非农业户口，在一定的劳动年龄内（16周岁至退休年龄），有劳动能力，无业而要求就业，并在当地就业服务机构进行求职登记的人员。

城镇登记失业率　城镇登记失业人员与城镇单位就业人员（扣除使用的农村劳动力、聘用的离退休人员、港澳台及外方人员）、城镇单位中的不在岗职工、城镇私营业主、个体户主、城镇私营企业和个体就业人员、城镇登记失业人员之和的比。计算公式为:

$$城镇登记失业率=\frac{城镇登记失业人数}{\begin{array}{l}(城镇单位就业人员-使用的农村劳动力-聘用的离退休人员-聘用的港澳\\台及外方人员)+不在岗职工+城镇私营业主+城镇个体户主+城镇私营企\\业及个体就业人员+城镇登记失业人数\end{array}}\times 100\%$$

Explanatory Notes on Main Statistical Indicators

Employed Persons refer to persons aged 16 and over who are engaged in gainful employment and thus receive remuneration payment or earn business income. This indicator reflects the actual utilization of total labour force during a certain period of time.

Persons Employed in Various Units refer to all the persons working in government agencies of various levels, political and party organizations, social organizations, enterprises and institutions, and receiving wages or other forms of payment. They include fully-employed staff and workers, re-employed retirees, teachers in the schools run by the local people, foreigners and Chinese compatriots from Hong Kong, Macao, and Taiwan working in various units, part-time employees, employees of other units working temporarily at current posts, and employees holding the second job, but do not include persons who have left their working units while keeping their labour contract (employment relation) unchanged. This indicator reflects the total number of laborers actually engaged in production or other operations in various units.

Persons Employed in Private Enterprises and Self-Employed Individuals in Urban Areas Persons employed in private enterprises refer to the persons employed in the private enterprises which have been registered at the departments of industrial and commercial administration for which the business operation are situated at a county town (i.e. a town where the county government is located), or at urban areas with administrative hierarchy higher than a county town. The self-employed individuals in urban areas refer to persons who hold the certificates of residence in urban areas or have resided in the urban areas for a long time and have been registered at the departments of industrial and commercial administration and approved to be engaged in individual industrial or commercial business, including self-employed persons as well as helpers and hired labourers who work in individual households.

State-owned Units refer to economic units whose assets are owned by the state, including non-corporation units registered according to Regulation of the People's Republic of China on the Registration of Enterprises and Corporations, state organs, institutions and social organizations at the central-level and local levels.

Collective-owned Units refer to economic units registered according to Regulation of the People's Republic of China on the Registration of Enterprises and Corporations where the means of production are collectively owned.

Units of Other Types of Ownership refer to units registered with other types of ownership, including cooperative units, joint ownership units, limited liability corporations, share holding corporations, units funded by entrepreneurs from Hong Kong, Macao, and Taiwan, and foreign- funded units.

Employed Staff and Workers refer to persons who work in, and receive wages from their working units, including persons who have their work posts but are temporarily absent from work for reasons of study or on sick, injury or maternal leave and still receive wages from their working units.

Total Wage Bill refers to the total remuneration payment to employed persons in various units during a certain period of time. The calculation of total wage bill is based on the total remuneration payment to employed persons . Therefore, all the wages and salaries and other payments to employed persons are included in the total wage bill regardless of sources, reckoning the cost of production or not, category, listing as items of premium taxation or not, and forms, paying in cash or in kind.

Average Wage refers to the average wage in money terms per person during a certain period of time for employed persons in enterprises, institutions, and government agencies, which reflects the general level of wage income during a certain period of time and is calculated as follows:

$$\text{Average Wage}=\frac{\text{Total Wage Bill of Employed Persons at Reference Time}}{\text{Average Number of Persons Employed at Reference Time}}$$

Average Wage Indices refers to the ratio of average wage of employed persons the reference period to that at the base period, which reflects the change of wage of employed persons at the different period. It is calculated as follows:

$$\text{Average Wage Indices}=\frac{\text{Average Wage of Employed Persons at Reference Time}}{\text{Average Wage of Persons Employed at Base Period}}\times 100\%$$

Registered Unemployed Persons in Urban Areas refer to the persons with non-agricultural household registration at certain working ages (16 years old to retirement age), who are capable of working, unemployed and willing to work, and have been registered at the local employment service agencies to apply for a job.

Registered Unemployment Rate in Urban Areas refers to the ratio of the number of the registered unemployed persons to the sum of the number of persons employed in various units (minus the employed rural labour force, re-employed retirees, and Hong Kong, Macao, Taiwan or foreign employees), laid-off staff and workers in urban units, owners of private enterprises in urban areas, owners of self-employed individuals in urban areas, employees of private enterprises in urban areas, employee of self-employed individuals in urban areas, and the registered unemployed persons in urban areas. The formula is as follows:

$$\text{Registered unemployment rate in urban areas}=\frac{\text{unmber of registered urban unemployed persons}}{\begin{array}{c}\text{number of persons employed in urban units-employed}\\ \text{rural labour forcere-empioyed retirees-Hong Kong,Macao}\\ \text{Taiwan or foreign employees +laid-off staff and workers}\\ \text{of urban private enterprises+owners of urban self-employed}\\ \text{individuals +employees of urban self-employed individuals}\\ \text{+registered unemployed persons in urban areas}\end{array}}\times 100\%$$

5 Five

固定资产投资

Investment in Fixed Assets

5-1 全社会固定资产投资
Total Investment in Fixed Assets in the whole Province

单位：亿元 (100 million yuan)

指　标	Item	2006	2007	2008	2009	2010	2011	2011年比2010年增长(%) Increase Rate in 2011 over 2010(%)
全社会固定资产投资	**Total Investment in Fixed Assets in theWhole Province**	**1197.68**	**1488.80**	**1864.45**	**2450.99**	**3186.28**	**5101.55**	**60.1**
#房地产开发	Real Estate Development	187.05	249.67	311.26	371.25	556.69	873.48	56.9
按隶属关系分	Grouped by Jurisdiction of Management							
中央	Central	227.34	239.96	308.09	348.79	324.62	418.64	29.0
地方	Local	970.34	1248.84	1556.36	2102.20	2861.66	4682.91	63.6
按经济类型分	Grouped by Registration Status							
国有经济	State-owned Units	602.50	697.68	910.69	1250.42	1605.82	2412.97	50.3
集体经济	Collective-owned Units	12.93	17.27	25.23	29.70	29.01	57.23	97.3
个体经济	Self-employed Units	82.56	93.86	108.74	144.07	172.91	254.97	47.5
联营经济	Joint Ownership Units	2.21	1.84	3.68	0.42	2.16	4.68	116.4
股份制经济	Share Holding Units	303.61	382.27	466.73	523.58	774.14	1404.00	181.4
外商投资经济	Foreign Funded Units	21.47	18.57	31.31	54.21	35.85	38.21	6.6
港澳台商投资经济	Units with Funds from Hong Kong,Macao and Taiwan	8.51	14.85	18.78	19.70	34.18	86.78	153.9
其他经济	Others	163.89	262.46	299.29	428.89	532.21	842.72	58.3
按构成分	Grouped by Structure							
建筑安装工程	Construction and Installation	697.35	874.47	1118.74	1607.26	2010.16	3599.46	79.1
设备工具器具购置	Purchase of Equipment and Instruments	277.31	329.11	381.20	431.77	494.07	689.24	39.5
其他费用	Others	223.02	285.22	364.51	411.96	682.04	812.85	19.2
按三次产业分	Grouped by Three Industries							
第一产业	Primary Industry	27.07	29.32	50.87	73.42	80.71	163.20	102.2
第二产业	Secondary Industry	516.23	647.85	794.79	911.72	1087.87	1852.10	70.3
工业	Industry	513.27	644.88	787.60	905.01	1074.55	1821.24	69.5
建筑业	Construction	2.96	2.97	7.19	6.70	13.32	30.86	131.6
第三产业	Tertiary Industry	654.38	811.63	1018.79	1465.85	2017.70	3086.25	53.0
资金来源合计	**Total Sources of Funds**	**1376.73**	**1725.63**	**2157.38**	**3192.06**	**4108.87**	**6111.46**	**48.7**
国家预算内资金	State Budget	58.93	86.36	138.06	283.38	355.96	669.68	88.1
国内贷款	Domestic Loans	335.47	391.62	479.25	710.79	852.62	952.72	11.7
利用外资	Foreign Investment	14.41	15.56	14.33	10.89	10.71	18.05	68.6
自筹资金	Self-raising Funds	679.38	874.97	1092.78	1424.18	1869.01	3150.30	68.6
其他资金	Others	288.54	357.12	432.96	762.82	1020.58	1320.70	29.4
房屋建筑面积(万平方米)	**Floor Space of Buildings(10000 sq.m)**							
施工面积	Floor Space under Construction	6938	8112	9383	12176	14456	18160	25.6
#住宅	Residential Buildings	4811	5814	6791	8535	10123	11939	17.9
竣工面积	Floor Space Completed	2752	3259	3207	4734	5325	6065	13.9
#住宅	Residential Buildings	2189	2527	2500	3782	4054	4274	5.4

5-2 全社会工业投资
Industry Investment in the Whole Province

单位：亿元 (100 million yuan)

指　标	Item	2008	2009	2010	2011	2011年比2010年增长(%) Increase Rate in 2011over 2010(%)
工业投资	**Industry Investment**	**787.60**	**905.01**	**1074.55**	**1821.24**	**69.5**
按隶属关系分	**Grouped by Jurisdiction of Management**					
中央	Central Investment	228.51	205.47	152.19	204.56	34.4
地方	Local Investment	559.09	699.54	922.36	1616.68	75.3
按国民经济行业分	**By Sector**					
采矿业	#Mining	184.23	272.87	374.61	522.83	39.6
#煤炭开采和洗选业	#Mining and Washing of Coal	162.90	252.26	337.39	448.88	33.0
黑色金属矿采选	Mining and Processing of Ferrous Metal Ores	1.20	1.04	1.68	5.42	222.0
有色金属矿采选	Mining and Processing of Non-Ferrous Metal Ores	9.05	7.12	9.92	22.89	130.7
制造业	Manufacturing	321.80	354.98	428.33	952.08	122.3
#化学原料及化学制品制造	#Manufacture of Raw Chemical Materials and Chemical Products	77.64	72.07	65.09	89.40	37.3
黑色金属冶炼及压延加工	Smelting and Pressing of Ferrous Metals	19.28	20.32	32.89	85.53	160.0
有色金属冶炼及压延加工	Smelting and Pressing of Non-ferrous Metals	62.40	38.02	49.90	89.92	80.2
电力、燃气及水的生产和供应业	Production and Supply of Electricity, Gas and Water	281.57	277.15	271.61	346.34	27.5
#电力、热力的生产和供应业	#Production and Supply of Electric Power and Heat Power	263.94	252.19	254.12	312.04	22.8
项目个数(个)	**Number of Projects(unit)**					
#施工项目个数	#Number of Projects under Construction	3102	3574	3754	4850	29.2
#新开工项目个数	#Number of Projects Newly Started	2175	2520	2436	3618	48.5
#投产项目个数	#Number of Projects Put into Use	1798	1821	2029	3079	51.7
自年初累计资金来源合计	**Total Funds this Year**	**832.89**	**1149.27**	**1215.89**	**2196.36**	**80.6**
上年末结余资金	Fund Left Last Year	28.27	133.33	73.36	110.25	50.3
本年资金来源小计	Total Funds of This Year	804.62	1015.94	1142.54	2086.11	82.6
国家预算内资金	State Budget	11.74	32.15	43.20	59.51	37.8
国内贷款	Domestic Loans	208.42	270.32	237.55	264.80	11.5
利用外资	Foreign Investment	6.56	8.72	6.69	4.17	-37.7
自筹资金	Self-raising Funds	531.22	660.11	808.97	1721.87	112.8
各项应付款合计	**Total Account Payables**	**49.96**	**74.12**	**98.20**	**202.68**	**106.4**

5-3 固定资产投资新增主要生产能力(2011)

Newly Increased Production Capacity through Capital Construction and Innovation

生产能力名称	Production Capacity	数 量 Amount
原煤开采(万吨/年)	Coal Mining(10000 tons/year)	7196.70
洗煤(万吨/年)	Coal Washing(10000 tons/year)	4126.60
焦炭(万吨/年)	Coke(10000 tons/year)	92.00
生铁(万吨/年)	Pig Iron(10000 tons/year)	40.20
铁合金(折标万吨/年)	Iron Alloy(10000 tons/year)	46.10
水力发电(万千瓦)	Hydropower(10000 kw)	30.50
火力发电(万千瓦)	Thermal Power(10000 kw)	120.00
输电线路长度(11万伏及以上)(公里)	Transmit Electricity Line (110000 Volt-amper Level and above)(km)	2441.26
水泥(万吨/年)	Cement(10000 tons/year)	800.00
电石(万吨/年)	Calcium Carbide(10000 tons/year)	
氮肥(万吨/年)	Nitrogen Fertilizers(10000 tons/year)	10.18
磷肥(万吨/年)	Phosphate Fertilizers(10000 tons/year)	24.01
白酒(万吨/年)	Liquor(10000 tons/year)	2.48
新建公路(公里)	Length of New Highways(km)	4509.30
#高速公路(公里)	#Freeway(km)	489.00
改建公路(公里)	Length of Reconstructed Highways(km)	5696.30
新建独立公路桥梁(延长米)	New Independent Highway Bridge(extending.m)	2194.00
(座)	New Independent Highway Bridge(bridge)	7
新(扩)建公路客、货运站(个)	Newly-built or Expanded Passenger Transport and Freight Station(unit)	127.00
新(扩)建公路客、货运站面积(平方米)	Newly-built or Expanded Passenger Transport and Freight Station(sq.m)	88151.00
城市自来水供水能力(万吨/日)	Volume of Tap Water Supply in Cities(10000 ton/day)	2.10
城市公共交通车辆购置(辆)	Vehicle Purchase of Public Transportation in Cities(unit)	420.00
城市污水处理能力(万吨/日)	Disposal Capacity of Sewage in Cities(10000 tons/year)	9.00

注:本表统计口径为计划总投资50万元及以上的城镇固定资产投资和农村非农户投资。

Note:Data in the table refer to those projects planned to invest 500,000 yuan at least in urban areas and projects funded by rural non-farm households.

5-4 按行业、隶属关系和注册类型分固定资产投资(2011)

单位：亿元

指标	Item	固定资产投资 Investment in Fixed Assets
固定资产投资	**Investment in Fixed Assets**	**4892.10**
农、林、牧、渔业	Agriculture, Forestry, Animal Husbandry and Fishery	129.18
#农业	#Farming	57.89
畜牧业	Animal Husbandry	22.88
农、林、牧、渔服务业	Services in Support of Agriculture	32.11
采矿业	Mining	522.83
#煤炭开采和洗选业	#Mining and Washing of Coal	448.88
制造业	Manufacturing	951.83
#饮料制造业	#Manufacture of Beverages	75.47
烟草制品业	Manufacture of Tobacco	8.76
造纸及纸制品业	Manufacture of Paper and Paper Products	6.26
石油加工、炼焦及核燃料加工业	Processing of Petroleum, Coking, Processing of Nuclear Fuel	36.99
化学原料及化学制品制造业	Manufacture of Raw Chemical Materials and Chemical Products	89.40
医药制造业	Manufacture of Medicines	16.92
非金属矿物制品业	Manufacture of Non-metallic Mineral Products	156.84
黑色金属冶炼及压延加工业	Smelting and Pressing of Ferrous Metals	85.53
有色金属冶炼及压延加工业	Smelting and Pressing of Non-ferrous Metals	89.92
交通运输设备制造业	Manufacture of Transport Equipment	103.77
电力、燃气及水的生产和供应业	Production and Supply of Electricity, Gas and Water	346.34
#电力、热力的生产和供应业	#Production and Supply of Electric Power and Heat Power	312.04
建筑业	Construction	30.86
#房屋和土木工程建筑业	#Construction of Buildings and Civil Engineering	24.00
交通运输、仓储和邮政业	Transport, Storage and Post	781.87
#铁路运输业	#Railway Transport	168.86
道路运输业	Road Transport	555.89
仓储业	Storage	26.56
信息传输、计算机服务和软件业	Information Transmission, Computer Services and Software	46.19
#电信和其他信息传输服务业	#Telecommunications and Other Information Transmission Services	45.69
批发和零售业	Wholesale and Retail Trades	49.77
住宿和餐饮业	Hotels and Catering Services	52.66
金融业	Financial Intermediation	4.62
#银行业	#Bank	3.92
房地产业	Real Estate	1045.42
租赁和商务服务业	Leasing and Business Services	13.38
租赁业	Leasing	0.80
商务服务业	Business Services	12.59
科学研究、技术服务和地质勘查业	Scientific Research, Technical Service and Geologic Prospecting	10.61
#研究与试验发展	#Research and Experimental Development	1.87
水利、环境和公共设施管理业	Management of Water Conservancy, Environment and Public Facilities	680.77
#水利管理业	Management of Water Conservancy	78.21
居民服务和其他服务业	Services to Households and Other Services	10.55
教育	Education	85.85
卫生、社会保障和社会福利业	Health, Social Security and Social Welfare	39.17
#卫生	#Health	31.35
文化、体育和娱乐业	Culture, Sports and Entertainment	31.94
#文化艺术业	#Cultural and Art Activities	9.21
公共管理和社会组织	Public Management and Social Organization	58.27

注：本表统计口径为计划总投资50万元及以上的城镇投资、农村非农户投资和房地产开发投资。

Investment in Fixed Assets by Sector, Jurisdiction of Management and Registration Status

(100 million yuan)

按隶属关系分 Grouped by Jurisdiction of Management		按注册类型分 Grouped by Registration Status			
中央 Central Investment	地方 Local Investment	内资企业 Domestic Funds	港、澳、台商投资企业 Hong Kong, Macao and Taiwan	外商投资企业 Foreign Funded	个体经营 Self-employed Individual
418.64	**4473.46**	**4721.59**	**86.78**	**38.21**	**45.51**
0.97	128.20	124.69	0.63	0.43	3.43
0.83	57.05	55.95	0.02	0.32	1.59
	22.88	21.51	0.61		0.76
0.09	32.02	31.62		0.03	0.46
1.13	521.69	490.38	13.42	4.08	14.94
1.03	447.86	422.25	13.31	0.65	12.68
52.27	899.55	899.18	30.91	12.68	9.06
	75.47	69.18	4.23	0.95	1.12
2.44	6.31	8.73			0.03
	6.26	6.22			0.04
	36.99	28.29	8.70		
0.45	88.95	81.10	0.78	6.13	1.39
	16.92	15.81	0.75	0.29	0.06
2.15	154.69	137.86	13.64	1.76	3.57
0.27	85.26	84.78	0.44	0.31	
4.12	85.80	89.69	0.03	0.13	0.07
33.44	70.33	103.49		0.03	0.25
151.16	195.18	345.97		0.26	0.12
149.63	162.41	311.88		0.05	0.10
0.40	30.46	30.43	0.04	0.15	0.24
0.39	23.60	23.64		0.15	0.21
177.17	604.69	778.53	2.86	0.22	0.25
163.66	5.20	168.86			
0.57	555.32	555.89			
2.14	24.43	23.26	2.86	0.22	0.23
22.45	23.75	37.73	0.36	7.94	0.16
22.45	23.24	37.39	0.36	7.94	
2.43	47.34	46.05	0.27	1.45	2.00
0.03	52.63	48.25	0.18	0.22	4.01
0.32	4.30	4.62			
0.25	3.67	3.92			
3.63	1041.79	992.03	36.18	8.98	8.23
	13.38	13.33			0.05
	0.80	0.74			0.05
	12.59	12.59			
0.63	9.98	10.00		0.62	
0.63	1.25	1.26		0.62	
1.18	679.60	675.94	1.94	1.01	1.88
0.28	77.92	78.06		0.15	
0.14	10.41	10.24			0.31
0.10	85.76	85.56		0.01	0.28
4.03	35.14	39.07			0.10
3.88	27.47	31.25			0.10
	31.94	31.37		0.15	0.42
	9.21	9.15			0.05
0.61	57.66	58.24		0.01	0.02

Note:Data in the table refer to those projects planned to invest 500,000 yuan at least in urban areas,projects funded by rural non-farm households and real estate development.

5-5 按行业分50万元以上固定资产投资施工项目(2011)

Number of Construction Projects over 500 Thousand Yuan under Construction by Sector

行业	Sector	本年施工项目(个) Number of Projects under Construction This Year (unit)	#本年新开工 Number of Projects Started This Year	本年投产项目(个) Number of Projects Put into Use (unit)	项目建成投产率(%) Percentage of Projects Completed and Putinto Use
总计	**Total**	**15781**	**12953**	**10841**	**68.7**
农、林、牧、渔业	Agriculture, Forestry, Animal Husbandry and Fishery	1397	1248	1165	83.4
#农、林、牧、渔服务业	Service in Support of Agriculture	340	293	290	85.4
采矿业	Mining	1611	936	992	61.6
#煤炭开采和洗选业	Mining and Washing of Coal	1221	575	692	56.6
制造业	Manufacturing	2440	2063	1589	65.1
#饮料制造业	Manufacture of Beverages	249	207	157	63.1
烟草制品业	Manufacture of Tobacco	36	32	24	66.9
造纸及纸制品业	Manufacture of Paper and Paper Products	36	34	26	73.1
石油加工、炼焦及核燃料加工业	Processing of Petroleum, Coking and Processing of Nuclear Fuel	24	9	9	38.4
化学原料及化学制品制造业	Manufacture of Raw Chemical Materials and Chemical Products	211	173	151	71.3
医药制造业	Manufacture of Medicines	72	53	48	66.3
非金属矿物制品业	Manufacture of Non-metallic Mineral Products	503	446	378	75.1
黑色金属冶炼及压延加工业	Smelting and Pressing of Ferrous Metals	105	86	62	58.8
有色金属冶炼及压延加工业	Smelting and Pressing of Non-ferrous Metals	70	49	33	48.1
交通运输设备制造业	Manufacture of Transport Equipment	112	76	57	50.6
电力、燃气及水的生产和供应业	Production and Supply of Electricity,Gas and Water	799	619	498	62.4
#电力、热力的生产和供应业	Production and Supply of Electric Power and Heat Power	581	445	346	59.5
建筑业	Construction	124	112	92	74.3
#房屋和土木工程建筑业	Construction of Buildings and Civil Engineering	79	69	52	65.5
交通运输、仓储和邮政业	Transport, Storage and Post	1966	1702	1334	67.9
#铁路运输业	Railway Transport	11	1		
道路运输业	Road Transport	1795	1574	1241	69.1
仓储业	Storage	96	76	57	59.2

5-5 续表 continued

行 业	Sector	本年施工项目(个) Number of Projects under Construction This Year (unit)	#本年新开工 Number of Projects Started This Year	本年投产项目(个) Number of Projects Put into Use (unit)	项目建成投产率(%) Percentage of Projects Completed and Put into Use
信息传输、计算机服务和软件业	Information Transmission, Computer Services and Software	413	380	369	89.4
#电信和其他信息传输服务业	Telecommunications and Other Information Transmission Services	403	371	360	89.4
批发和零售业	Wholesale and Retail Trades	300	259	211	70.4
住宿和餐饮业	Hotels and Catering Services	241	218	162	67.2
金融业	Financial Intermediation	52	42	31	59.2
#银行业	Bank	44	33	24	54.2
房地产业	Real Estate	1257	1065	905	72.0
租赁和商务服务业	Leasing and Business Services	58	48	39	67.9
租赁业	Leasing	3	2	2	75.0
商务服务业	Business Services	55	46	37	67.6
科学研究、技术服务和地质勘查业	Scientific Research, Technical Service and Geologic Prospecting	63	53	44	69.4
#研究与试验发展	Research and Experimental Development	13	11	8	64.7
水利、环境和公共设施管理业	Management of Water Conservancy, Environment and Public Facilities	2541	2111	1772	69.7
#水利管理业	Management of Water Conservancy	659	556	518	78.7
居民服务和其他服务业	Services to Households and Other Services	85	73	59	69.6
教育	Education	1164	995	705	60.6
卫生、社会保障和社会福利业	Health, Social Security and Social Welfare	407	309	276	67.9
#卫生	Health	259	179	179	69.0
文化、体育和娱乐业	Culture, Sports and Entertainment	230	185	158	68.8
#文化艺术业	Cultural and Art Activities	109	83	67	61.5
公共管理和社会组织	Public Management and Social Organization	633	534	439	69.2

5–6 房地产开发企业基本情况(2011)

单位：亿元

指　标	item	总 计 Toatal	内资企业 Domestic Funded
企业个数(个)	**Number of Enterprises(unit)**	**1946**	**1902**
年末从业人员总计(人)	**Number of Employed Persons at the Year-end (person)**	**41104**	**40038**
本年完成投资	**Investment Completed This Year**	**873.48**	**828.05**
按工程用途分	By Use of Project		
#商品住宅	Residential Buildings	576.44	541.10
办公楼	Office Building	19.11	16.69
商业营业用房	House for Business Used	123.43	118.52
其他	Others	154.50	151.74
按构成分	By Type of Construction		
建筑工程	Construction	677.59	635.77
安装工程	Installation	30.28	30.07
设备工器具购置	Purchase of Equitment and Instruments	11.72	11.48
其他费用	Others	153.89	150.73
本年资金来源合计	**Total Source of Funds This Year**	**1533.83**	**1478.75**
#国内贷款	Domestic Loans	172.78	162.18
利用外资	Foreign Investment	4.47	0.06
自筹资金	Fundraising	526.09	500.88
其他资金来源	Others	542.13	532.67
#个人按揭贷款	Personal Housing Mortgage Loans	190.90	186.52
土地购置费	Land Acquisition Costs	65.61	65.04
待开发土地面积(万平方米)	Land Space to Be Developed (10000 sq.m)	1171.18	974.51
本年购置土地面积(万平方米)	Land Space Purchased This Year(10000 sq.m)	882.78	874.70
主营业务收入	Revenue From Principal Business	4948.02	4841.27
税金总额	Total Tax	539.53	531.00
资产总计	Total Assets	30235.99	29159.67
负债合计	Total Liabilities	24252.74	23436.48
所有者权益合计	Total Owners Equities	5983.25	5723.20
资产负债率(%)	Assets-Liability Ratio(%)	80.2	80.4
施工房屋面积(万平方米)	Floor Space Under Construction(10000 sq.m)	10260.58	9921.36
竣工房屋面积(万平方米)	Floor Space of Completed(10000 sq.m)	1455.24	1376.67
房屋建筑面积竣工率(%)	Rate of Floor Space Completed(%)	14.18	13.88
本年新开工房屋面积(万平方米)	**Floor Space Started This Year(10000 sq.m)**	**2885.07**	**2751.55**
#住宅	Residential Buildings	2170.66	2058.52
办公楼	Office Building	13.61	13.04
商业营业用房	House for Business Used	407.20	400.62
其他	Others	293.60	279.37

Real Estate Development Enterprises

(100 million yuan)

#国 有 企 业 State-owned Enterprises	#私营有限 责任公司 Private Limited Liability Company	#私营股份 有限公司 Private Share-holding Corporations Limited	港澳台商 投资企业 Enterprises with Funds from HongKong, Macao and TaiWan	外商投 资企业 Foreign Funded Enterprises
77	**702**	**89**	**33**	**11**
1704	**13314**	**1651**	**836**	**230**
62.33	**206.21**	**24.64**	**36.95**	**8.48**
39.06	137.55	13.60	30.32	5.02
0.16	2.99	0.98	1.54	0.89
3.07	26.07	3.81	2.88	2.03
20.04	39.60	6.25	2.22	0.54
40.05	164.44	18.45	33.52	8.29
2.42	5.41	1.41	0.17	0.04
0.35	2.61	0.47	0.23	0.00
19.51	33.74	4.31	3.02	0.14
118.79	**338.61**	**52.28**	**44.09**	**10.99**
10.69	49.80	4.95	7.46	3.15
	0.03		4.41	
63.01	108.45	25.04	20.49	4.72
23.85	128.35	13.87	7.07	2.38
3.50	50.88	5.93	3.26	1.12
14.78	15.05	2.64	0.57	
78.52	136.92	81.53	196.07	0.60
82.34	189.90	97.88	8.08	
550.21	883.32	248.81	73.85	32.91
39.49	98.94	17.75	4.70	3.83
3034.28	7201.61	1001.79	759.89	316.43
1972.27	5861.66	858.98	506.27	309.99
1062.01	1339.95	142.81	253.61	6.44
65.0	81.4	85.7	66.6	98.0
547.53	2806.15	461.04	233.34	105.88
52.31	457.05	102.28	63.04	15.53
9.55	16.29	22.18	27.02	14.67
154.74	**865.09**	**118.28**	**57.00**	**76.52**
125.62	653.38	76.80	38.88	73.25
0.08	5.24	0.55	0.58	
11.98	124.94	24.06	6.30	0.28
17.05	81.54	16.86	11.24	2.99

5-7 房地产开发投资主要指标

Main Indicator on Real Estate Development

指　标	Item	2006	2007	2008	2009	2010	2011	2011年比2010年增长(%) Increase Rate in 2011 over 2010(%)
本年土地购置面积(万平方米)	**Land Space Purchased This Year (10000 sq.m)**	**787**	**661**	**590**	**373**	**1027**	**883**	**-14.0**
本年完成投资额(亿元)	**Investment Completed This Year (100 million yuan)**	**187.05**	**249.67**	**311.26**	**371.25**	**556.69**	**873.48**	**56.9**
#住　宅	Residential Buildings	104.77	156.07	195.49	249.46	328.63	576.44	75.4
资金来源合计(亿元)	**Source of Funds(100 million yuan)**	**319.74**	**444.77**	**520.31**	**773.47**	**1135.61**	**1533.83**	**35.1**
#国内贷款	Domestic Loans	70.75	95.81	79.98	133.11	160.10	172.78	7.9
利用外资	Foreign Investment	3.98	2.24	1.20	0.26	0.72	4.47	520.8
自筹资金	Self-raising Funds	81.25	109.36	160.40	168.24	268.68	526.09	95.8
房屋建筑面积(万平方米)	**Floor Space of Buildings(10000 sq.m)**							
施工面积	Floor Space under Construction	3309	4277	5229	6101	7906	10261	29.8
#本年新开工面积	Floor Space Started This Year	1289	1575	1594	1755	2871	2885	0.5
#住　宅	Residential Buildings	2506	3369	4210	4715	5971	7689	28.8
竣工面积	Floor Space Completed	642	695	721	1224	1048	1455	38.8
#住　宅	Residential Buildings	522	559	589	1041	826	1102	33.4

5-8 商品房屋销售面积(2011)

Floor Space of Commercialized Buildings

单位：万平方米 (10000 sq.m)

指标	Item	商品房屋销售面积 Floor Space of Commercialized Buildings Sold	#住宅 Residential Buildings
总计	**Total**	**1882.10**	**1698.52**
#现房	#Existing House	281.21	240.79
期房	Forward House	1600.89	1457.73
#内资企业	#Domestic Funded Enterprises	1862.26	1681.71
#国有企业	State-owned Enterprises	108.67	100.09
集体企业	Collective-owned Enterprises	0.28	0.28
其他有限责任公司	Other Limited Liability Corporations	1014.89	912.29
股份有限公司	Share-holding Corporations Ltd.	106.47	100.96
私营独资企业	Private-funded Enterprises	23.82	22.09
私营有限责任公司	Private Limited Liability Corporations	508.63	456.40
私营股份有限公司	Private Share-holding Corporations Ltd.	78.80	69.67
港澳台商投资企业	Enterprises with Funds from Hong Kong,Macao and Taiwan	12.24	9.89
#与港澳台商合资经营企业	#Joint-venture Enterprises	4.06	2.88
港澳台商独资经营企业	Enterprises with Sole Fund	8.18	7.01
外商投资企业	Foreign Funded Enterprises	7.61	6.91
#中外合资经营企业	#Joint-venture Enterprises	2.34	2.32
外资企业	Enterprises with Sole Fund		

5-9 商品房屋销售额(2011)

Total Sale of Commercialized Buildings

单位：万元 (10000 yuan)

指标	Item	商品房屋销售额 Total Sale of Commercialized Buildings Sold	#住宅 Residential Buildings
总计	**Total**	**7319072**	**5927327**
#现房	#Existing House	951614	723561
期房	Forward House	6367458	5203766
#内资企业	#Domestic Funded Enterprises	7199384	5838837
#国有企业	#State-owned Enterprises	438748	374759
集体企业	Collective-owned Enterprises	531	531
其他有限责任公司	Other Limited Liability Corporations	4294820	3458370
股份有限公司	Share-holding Corporations Ltd.	379480	333539
私营独资企业	Private-funded Enterprises	68349	62176
私营有限责任公司	Private Limited Liability Corporations	1677195	1318571
私营股份有限公司	Private Share-holding Corporations Ltd.	292266	246542
港澳台商投资企业	Enterprises with Funds from Hong Kong,Macao and Taiwan	82576	58631
#与港澳台商合资经营企业	#Joint-venture Enterprises	30749	20003
港澳台商独资经营企业	Enterprises with Sole Fund	51827	38628
外商投资企业	Foreign Funded Enterprises	37112	29859
#中外合资经营企业	#Joint-venture Enterprises	8084	7933
外资企业	Enterprises with Sole Fund		

主要统计指标解释

全社会固定资产投资 是以货币形式表现的在一定时期内全社会建造和购置固定资产的工作量以及与此有关的费用的总称。该指标是反映固定资产投资规模、结构和发展速度的综合性指标，又是观察工程进度和考核投资效果的重要依据。全社会固定资产投资按登记注册类型可分为国有、集体、个体、联营、股份制、外商、港澳台商、其他等。

城镇固定资产投资 指城镇各种登记注册类型的企业、事业、行政单位及个体户进行的计划总投资 50 万元及以上的建设项目投资和房地产开发投资。县城及以上区域内发生的投资，县及县以上各级政府及主管部门直接领导、管理的建设项目和企业事业单位的投资均为城镇固定资产投资。

房地产开发投资 指各种登记注册类型的房地产开发公司、商品房建设公司及其他房地产开发法人单位和附属于其他法人单位实际从事房地产开发或经营活动的单位统一开发的包括统代建、拆迁还建的住宅、厂房、仓库、饭店、宾馆、度假村、写字楼、办公楼等房屋建筑物和配套的服务设施，土地开发工程（如道路、给水、排水、供电、供热、通讯、平整场地等基础设施工程）的投资；不包括单纯的土地交易活动。

农村投资 包括在农村区域范围内进行固定资产投资活动的企业、事业、行政单位及农户投资。

固定资产投资的资金来源 根据固定资产投资的资金来源不同，分为国家预算内资金、国内贷款、利用外资、自筹资金和其他资金。

(1) 国家预算内资金：分为财政拨款和财政安排的贷款两部分。包括中央财政的基本建设基金（分经营性基金和非经营性基金两部分）、专项支出（如煤代油专项等）、收回再贷、贴息资金，财政安排的挖潜改造和新产品试制支出、城建支出、商业部门简易建筑支出、不发达地区发展基金等资金中用于固定资产投资的资金；地方财政中由国家统筹安排的资金等。

(2) 国内贷款：指报告期固定资产投资单位向银行及非银行金融机构借入的用于固定资产投资的各种国内借款，包括银行利用自有资金及吸收的存款发放的贷款、上级主管部门拨入的国内贷款、国家专项贷款、地方财政专项资金安排的贷款、国内储备贷款、周转贷款等。

(3) 利用外资：指报告期收到的用于固定资产建造和购置的国外资金（包括设备、材料、技术在内）。包括对外借款（外国政府、国际金融组织贷款、出口信贷、外国银行商业贷款、对外发行债券和股票）、外商直接投资及外商其他投资。不包括我国自有外汇资金（国家外汇、地方外汇、留成外汇、调剂外汇和中国银行自有资金发行的外汇贷款等）。计算利用外资时，需要折算成人民币，折算中所使用的外汇汇率按现汇计算，即按使用外汇时的汇率计算。

(4) 自筹资金：指固定资产投资单位报告期收到的，由各地区、各部门及企、事业单位筹集用于固定资产投资的预算外资金，包括中央各部门、各级地方和企、事业单位的自筹资金。

(5) 其他资金：指在报告期收到的除以上各种资金之外其他用于固定资产投资的资金，包括企业或金融机构通过发行各种债券筹集到的资金、群众集资、个人资金、无偿捐赠的资金及其他单位拨入的资金等。

固定资产投资按国民经济行业分 根据建设项目建成投产后的主要产品或主要用途及社会经济活动性质来确定国民经济行业。一般情况下，一个建设项目或一个企业、事业单位只能属于一种国民经济行业。

固定资产投资按隶属关系分 是按建设单位或企业、事业、行政单位的主管上级机关确定的。

（1）中央：是指中共中央、人大常委会和国务院各部、委、局、总公司以及直属机构直接领导的建设项目和企业、事业、行政单位。这些单位的固定资产投资计划由国务院各部门直接编制和下达，建设中所需物资、主要设备以及建设中的问题都由中央有关部门安排和解决。

（2）地方：是由省（自治区、直辖市）、地区（州、盟、省辖市）、县（旗、县级市）三级政府及业务主管部门直接领导和管理的建设项目、企业、事业、行政单位。地方项目还包括不隶属以上各级政府及主管部门的建设项目和企业、事业单位，如外商投资企业和无主管部门的企业等。

固定资产投资按建设性质分 根据整个建设项目情况来确定。建设项目的性质一般分为新建、扩建、改建和技术改造、迁建、恢复。房地产开发单位、农村投资、城镇工矿区私人建房投资不划分建设性质。

(1) 新建：一般指从无到有开始建设的企业、事业和行政单位或建设项目。有的单位原有基础很小，经过建设后新增的固定资产价值超过该企业、事业、行政单位原有固定资产价值（原值）三倍以上的也应作为新建。

(2) 扩建：指在厂内或其他地点，为扩大原有产品的生产能力（或效益）或增加新的产品生产能力，而增建主要的生产车间（或主要工程）、分厂、独立的生产线。行政、事业单位在原单位增建业务用房（如学校增建教学用房、医院增建门诊部、病房等）也作为扩建。

现有企业、事业单位为扩大原有主要产品生产能力或增加新的产品生产能力，增建一个或几个主要生产车间（或主要工程）、分厂，同时进行一些更新改造工程的，也应作为扩建。

(3) 改建和技术改造：指现有企业、事业单位，对原有设施进行技术改造或更新（包括相应配套的辅助性生产、生活福利设施）的建设项目。现有企业、事业单位为适应市场变化的需要，而改变企业的主要产品种类（如军工企业转产民用品等）的建设项目，应作为改建。原有产品生产作业线由于各工序（车间）之间能力不平衡，为填平补齐充分发挥原有生产能力而增建不增加本企业主要产品设计能力的车间，也应作为改建。技术改造是指企业、事业单位在现有基础上，用先进的技术代替落后的技术，用先进的工艺和装备代替落后的工艺和装备，以改变企业落后的技术经济面貌，实现以内涵为主的扩大再生产，达到提高产品质量、促进产品更新换代、节约能源、降低消耗、扩大生产规模、全面提高社会经济效益的目的。技术改造具体包括以下内容：机器设备和工具的更新改造；生产工艺改革、节约能源和原材料的改造；厂房建筑和公共设施的改造；劳动条件和生产环境的改造等。

固定资产投资按构成分　固定资产投资活动按其工作内容和实现方式分为建筑安装工程，设备、工具、器具购置，其他费用三个部分。

(1) 建筑安装工程（建筑安装工作量）：指各种房屋、建筑物的建造工程和各种设备、装置的安装工程。包括各种房屋建造工程；各种用途设备基础和各种工业窑炉的砌筑工程及金属结构工程；为施工而进行的各种准备工作和临时工程以及完工后的清理工作等；铁路、道路的铺设，矿井的开凿及石油管道的架设等；水利工程；防空地下建筑等特殊工程；列入房屋工程预算内的暖气、卫生、通风、照明、煤气等设备的价值及装设油饰工程；列入建筑工程预算内的各种管道（蒸汽、压缩空气、石油、给排水等管道）、电力、电讯电缆导线等的敷设工程；以及各种机械设备的安装工程；为测定安装工程质量，对设备进行的试运工作；房地产开发单位进行的商品房屋开发建设工程、土地开发工程。

在安装工程中，不包括被安装设备本身的价值。

(2) 设备、工具、器具购置：指建设单位或企、事业单位购置或自制的，达到固定资产标准的设备、工具、器具的价值。新建单位及扩建单位的新建车间，按照设计或计划要求购置或自制的全部设备、工具、器具，不论是否达到固定资产标准均计入"设备、工具、器具购置"中。

(3) 其他费用：指在固定资产建造和购置过程中发生的，除上述几项内容以外的各种应分摊计入固定资产的费用。

施工项目　指报告期内进行过建筑或安装施工活动的项目。凡是报告期内施过工的建设项目，不论施工时间长短，均作为施工项目统计。施工项目个数可以反映一定时期固定资产投资的实际规模，与同期全部建成投产项目个数相比，可以从建设速度的角度反映固定资产投资的效果。根据建设项目施工活动的不同性质，施工项目又分为：本年正式施工项目、本年收尾项目和以前年度全部停缓建项目。

全部建成投产项目　工业项目指设计文件规定形成生产能力的主体工程及其相应配套的辅助设施全部建成，经负荷试运转，证明具备生产设计规定合格产品的条件，并经过验收鉴定合格或达到竣工验收标准，与生产性工程配套的生活福利设施可以满足近期正常生产的需要，正式移交生产的建设项目。非工业项目指设计文件规定的主体工程和相应的配套工程全部建成，能够发挥设计规定的全部效益，经验收鉴定合格或达到竣工验收标准，正式移交使用的建设项目。

新增生产能力（或工程效益）　指通过固定资产投资活动而增加的设计能力（或工程效益），该指标是以实物形态表现的反映固定资产投资成果的指标，也是考核投资经济效果的重要依据之一。

新增生产能力（或工程效益）一般有以下几种表现形式：

(1) 用产品数量表示，以工程在单位时间内（一般是一年）所能生产的产品数量（即年产量）表示。如原煤开采用万吨/年表示，化学农药用吨/年表示，拖拉机制造用台/年表示等。某些化工产品由于含量差别较大，按其设计含量计算折合量表示，如硫酸、纯碱、烧碱等。

(2) 用单位时间内所能处理的原料数量表示，以工程每天（或小时）所能处理原料的数量表示。如机制糖工程日处理原料吨，食用植物油日处理原料吨，城市污水处理能力用万吨/日表示等。

(3) 用新增加的主要设备的数量或容量表示，如新增棉布织机、丝织机等台数，毛纺锭等锭数，发电厂新增发电机组容量用千瓦表示等。

(4) 用建筑物容积、容量、面积、长度表示，是非工业项目或工程新增效益的一种表现形式。如铁路投产里程、新建公路、水库容量、粮食仓库、学校学生席位、医院病床、有效灌溉面积等。

根据工程的特点，有时需要用两种或两种以上的复合计量单位表示新增生产能力（或工程效益），如新增内燃机生产能力同时用年产台数、千瓦数表示等。

为了规范新增生产能力（或工程效益）的名称和计算单位，国家统计局制订了《新增生产能力（或工程效益）目录及代码》。各固定资产投资单位在统计新增生产能力（或工程效益）时，必须按目录中规定的名称、计量单位和代码填报。

房屋建筑面积　指房屋建筑物勒脚以上外墙外围的水平截面面积，包括房屋建筑物的有效面积和结构面积。该指标是从实物形态上反映建设规模和建设成果的重要指标之一，也是检查工程形象进度、计算工程造价、分析投资效果、研究施工任务和建筑材料之间平衡情况的重要依据。

住宅建筑面积　指施工和竣工房屋建筑面积中供居住用的房屋建筑面积。

施工面积　指报告期内施工的全部房屋建筑面积。包括本期新开工的面积和上期开工跨入本期继续施工的房屋面积，以及上期已停建在本期恢复施工的房屋面积。本期竣工和本期施工后又停缓建的房屋，其建筑面积仍计入本期房屋施工面积中。

竣工面积　指在报告期内房屋建筑按照设计要求已经全部完工，达到住人和使用条件，经验收鉴定合格（或达到竣工验收标准），正式移交使用单位的各栋房屋建筑面积的总和。

房屋建筑面积竣工率　指一定时期内房屋竣工面积占同期房屋施工面积的比率。

新增固定资产　指报告期内已经完成建造和购置过程，并已交付生产或使用单位的固定资产价值。该指标是表示固定资产投资成果的价值指标，也是反映建设进度，计算固定资产投资效果的重要指标。

项目建成投产率　指一定时期内全部建成投产项目个数与同期施工项目个数的比率。该指标是从建设单位建设速度的角度反映投资效果的指标。

固定资产交付使用率　指一定时期新增固定资产与同期完成投资额的比率。该指标是反映固定资产动用速度，衡量建设过程中宏观投资效果的综合指标。由于新增固定资产是较长时期内形成的结果，而投资额则是当年完成的，因此，该指标一般适宜于反映较长时期内固定资产的动用情况。

商品房销售面积　指报告期内出售商品房屋的合同总面积（即双方签署的正式买卖合同中所确定的建筑面积）。由现房销售建筑面积和期房销售建筑面积两部分组成。

商品房销售额　指报告期内出售商品房屋的合同总价款（即双方签署的正式买卖合同中所确定的合同总价）。该指标与商品房销售面积同口径，由现房销售额和期房销售额两部分组成。

经济适用房　指根据经济适用房计划安排建设的政策性住宅。经济是指房屋建筑造价和销售价格低于一般商品住宅；适用是指适合中低收入家庭购买使用。经济适用房主要是由国家统一下达投资计划，房地产公司开发，对外销售；用地一般采用行政划拨或招标投标方式，免收土地出让金；对各种经批准的收费减半征收，开发利润不超过 3%；销售价格实行政府指导价。该指标可以分析房地产投资结构，反映中低收入家庭商品住宅的供求平衡情况。

Explanatory Notes on Main Statistical Indicators

Total Investment in Fixed Assets in the Whole Province refers to the volume of activities in construction and purchases of fixed assets of the whole province and related fees, expressed in monetary terms during the reference period. It is a comprehensive indicator which shows the size, structure and growth of the investment in fixed assets, providing a basis for observing the progress of construction projects and evaluating results of investment. Total investment in fixed assets in the whole province includes, by type of ownership, the investment by State-owned units, collective-owned units, individuals, joint ownership units, share-holding units, as well as investments by entrepreneurs from foreign countries and from Hong Kong, Macao and Taiwan, and by other units.

Urban Investment in Fixed Assets refers to construction projects involving a total planned investment of 500,000 yuan and over by enterprises of various types of ownership, institutions, administrative units and individuals in urban areas, investment in real estate development. In other words, all investments that take place in county towns and urban areas, investment in construction projects under the direct leadership and management of government agencies at and above county levels and investments by enterprises and institutions at and above county levels are covered in urban investment in fixed assets.

Investment in Real Estate Development refers to investment by real estate development companies, commercialized buildings construction companies and other real estate development units of various types of ownership in the construction of buildings, such as residential buildings, factory buildings, warehouses, hotels, guesthouses, holiday villages, office buildings, and the complementary service facilities and land development projects, such as roads, water supply, water drainage, power supply, heating supply, telecommunications, land leveling and other infrastructural projects. It does not include activities in pure land transactions.

Investment in Rural Areas refers to investment in fixed assets by enterprises, institutions, administrative units and households in rural areas.

Sources of Funds for Investment in Fixed Assets are categorized as funds from the State budget, domestic loans, foreign investment, self-raised funds, and others, depending on the sources of investment.

(1) Fund from the State budget consists of budgetary appropriation and loans from the State budget. More specifically, it includes, from the budget of the central government, capital construction fund (operation fund and non-operational fund), special expenses (e.g. expenses on substituting petroleum with coal), loans from repayment, discount fund, expenses on innovation and trial production of new products, expenses on urban construction, expenses on temporary construction from business departments, development fund for less developed areas, as well as local budgetary fund transferred from the central budget.

(2) Domestic loans refer to loans of various forms borrowed by investing units from banks and non-bank financial institutions during the reference period for the purpose of investment in fixed assets, including loans issued by banks from their self-owned funds and deposit, loans appropriated by higher authorities, special loans by government, loans arranged by local government from special funds, domestic reserve loan, and working loan.

(3) Foreign investment refers to foreign funds received during the reference period for the construction and purchase of investment in fixed assets (covering equipment, materials and technology), including foreign borrowings (loans from foreign governments and international financial institutions, export credit, commercial loans from foreign banks, issue of bonds and stocks overseas), foreign direct investment and other foreign investments. Excluded from this category is capital in foreign exchanges owned by China (foreign exchanges owned by the central and local governments, foreign exchanges retained by enterprises, foreign exchanges by enterprises through the regulating mechanism, loans in foreign exchanges issued by the Bank of China with its own fund, etc.).In calculating the utilization of foreign capital, foreign

currencies are converted into Chinese Renminbi applying the current exchange rate when the foreign capitals are actually used.

(4) Self-raised funds refer to extra-budgetary funds for investment in fixed assets received during the reference period by investing units from central government ministries, local governments, enterprises and institutions, including their self-raised funds.

(5) Others refer to funds for investment in fixed assets received from sources other than those listed above, including capital raised through issuing bonds by enterprises or financial institutions, funds raised from individuals and through donations, and funds transferred from other units.

Investment in Fixed Assets by Sector The classification of construction projects by sector is determined by the major products or the purpose of the projects when they are put into production or use, and by the nature of their social economic activities. In general, one project or one enterprise or institution can only be classified into one sector.

Investment in Fixed Assets by Jurisdiction of Management refers to the classification of investment by the competent authorities under which investment is made by construction units, enterprises, institutions or administrative units.

(1) Central investment refers to the investment in projects or by enterprises, institutions or administrative units which are under the direct leadership and management of the State Council and of the national commissions, ministries, agencies and State-owned large corporations. Various ministries and departments of the State Council prepare and implement plans for investment in fixed assets by those departments, and arrange and ensure the supply of materials and key equipment required for the projects.

(2) Local investment refers to the investment in projects or by enterprises, institutions or administrative units which are under the direct leadership and management of departments under the provincial, prefecture and county governments. Also included are projects by foreign-invested enterprises and enterprises without competent managing authorities.

Investment in Fixed Assets by Type of Construction Construction projects in general can be classified, by the type of construction, into new construction, expansion, reconstruction and technical transformation, moving and restoration. However, investment by type of construction is not applied to investment by real-estate development units, investment in rural areas and private investment in housing construction in urban areas and in industrial and mining areas.

(1) New construction in general refers to construction projects, which start from scratch, of enterprises, institutions, administrative agencies. In case the size of the existing unit is quite small, and the value of newly added fixed assets is more than three times of the the original value, the expansion will be considered as new construction.

(2) Expansion refers to construction of new major production workshop, branch factory or independent production line within a factory or in other locations, for the purpose of increasing the production capacity (or improving efficiency) or adding new production capacity. Newly constructed accommodation for the operation of institutions and administrative organizations (such as newly constructed buildings for teaching in schools, buildings for clinics or wards in hospitals, etc.) are also classified as expansion.

Also included in expansion are investments by existing enterprises or institutions in building major production line(s) or branch factory(ies) along with some work on innovation, for the purpose of expanding the production capacity of original products or producing new products.

(3) Reconstruction and technical transformation refers to construction projects by existing enterprises or institutions in innovation or technical transformation of the old facilities (including auxiliary production equipment and welfare facilities). Also considered as reconstruction is the construction of new workshops by the existing enterprises or institutions to change the variety of products to meet the market demand (such as the production of civil products by defence industries), or to bring the designed production capacity into full play through a more balanced production process on production lines. Technical transformation refers to replacement of old technology or equipment by new technology or equipment, in order to expand the reproduction through improvement of technology contents in production, to improve product quality, to promote new products, to save energy, to reduce consumption, to expand

the production scale and to improve overall social-economic efficiency. Contents of technical transformation include: updating of machinery, equipment and tools; reforming production process by using energy or materials saving technology; construction of factory workshops and transformation of public facilities; improvement of working conditions and environment, etc.

Investment in Fixed Assets by Structure By their contents and the mode of implementation, investment activities are classified into 3 categories, i.e. construction and installation, purchase of equipment and instrument, and other expenses.

(1) Construction and installation (work volume of construction and installation) refers to the construction of houses and buildings and the installation of various kinds of equipment and instruments. They include construction of houses; equipment foundations, industrial kilns and stoves, and metal structure work; preparation works and temporary works for project construction, and clearing up works post project construction; pavement of railways and roads, drilling of mines and putting up of oil pipes; construction of water conservancy; construction of underground air-raid shelters and construction of other special projects; value of equipment for heating, sanitation, ventilation, lighting, gas, painting, etc. that are covered by the budget of housing projects; laying out of various pipelines (for steam, compressed air, petroleum, tap water and sewage) and wiring and cabling for electric power and for communications; installation of various machinery and equipment; testing operation for pre-testing the quality of installation projects, and land and other development work conducted by real estate developers for commercialized housing. The value of equipment installed is itself not included in the value of installation projects.

(2) Purchase of equipment and instruments refers to the total value of equipment, tools, and instruments purchased or self-produced which come up to the cut-off point for fixed assets by the construction units or investing enterprises or institutions. Equipment, tools and instruments purchased or self-produced for new workshops by newly established or expanded units are categorized as "purchase of equipment and instruments" no matter whether they come up to the cut-off point for fixed assets.

(3) Other expenses refer to expenses arising during the construction or purchase of fixed assets other than those mentioned above.

Projects under Construction refer to projects with construction and installation activities undertaken in the reference period. All projects that have construction activities undertaken during the reference period are reported as projects under construction irrespective of the length of construction work. The number of projects under construction can reflect the actual size of investment in fixed assets during a given period, and when compared with the number of projects completed and put into use during the same period, it demonstrates the results of investment in fixed assets from the angle of the speed of the construction. Depending on the nature of construction activities, projects under construction can also be classified into projects beginning construction in current year, winding-up projects in current year and stopped or suspended projects in previous years (with resumption of work in current year).

Projects Completed and Put into Use Industrial projects refer to the major projects and anxilliary facilities having been completed in accordance with the design documents, resulting in forming production capacity and having checked and accepted after relevant tests, while the living and welfare facilities having been completed and being capable of ensuring normal production. Non-industrial projects refer to the major projects and anxilliary facilities which have been completed in accordance with the design documents ; have been checked, accepted after relevant examination; and have been formally delivered for use.

Newly Increased Production Capacity (or Project Efficiency) refers to the increase in design capacity (or project efficiency) through investment in fixed assets, which reflects the accomplishment of investment in fixed assets in physical form and serves as an important basis for evaluating the economic efficiency of investment.

The newly increased production capacity (project efficiency) are usually expressed in one of the following forms:

(1) volume of output of products, i.e. the volume of output that the project can produce during a given period (usually a year). For instance, the capacity in coal mining is expressed in 10,000 tons/year, the capacity in producing chemical pesticides expressed in ton/year, the capacity in producing tractors in tractor/year, etc. For some chemical products

where the effective contents differ significantly, the production capacity is expressed as the designed effective content equivalent, such as in the case of sulphuric acid, soda ash, caustic soda, etc;

(2) volume of raw materials processed per unit of time, i.e. the volume of raw materials that could be processed by the project per day (or per hour), such as tons of materials processed per day by a sugar refining project or edible vegetable oil project, or tons of urban sewage processed per day;

(3) number or capacity of major equipment increased, such as number of cotton or silk looms increased, wool spindles increased, or capacity (in kilowatts) of power generators increased; and

(4) physical measures (volume, capacity, area, and length) of construction, which is typical for non-industrial projects, for instance, the length of railways put into operation, the length of highways, the capacity of reservoirs, the capacity of warehouses, the floor space of housing projects, capacity for new students in schools or beds in hospitals, areas under new irrigation project, etc.

The special features of projects may sometimes call for the combined use of two or more measurements to reflect the increase in production capacity (or project efficiency); for instance, the new capacity for the production of internal combustion engines is expressed in sets per year and kilowatts per year simultaneously.

To standardize the nomenclature and unit of measurement for newly increased production capacity (or project efficiency), the National Bureau of Statistics has developed the Nomenclature and Codes for New Production Capacity (Project Efficiency). All reporting units with investment activities are required to follow these two nomenclatures in reporting statistics on new production capacity (project efficiency).

Floor Space of Buildings under Construction refers to the total floor space of the horizontal section of outer walls above the plinth of the building, including the effective area and the area occupied by the structure. This indicator is one of the important indicators in physical terms to reflect the scale and accomplishment of the construction industry and also an important basis for monitoring the progress, calculating the cost, analyzing the efficiency and studying the supply of building materials in relation to the construction projects.

Floor Space of Residential Buildings refers to the floor space of the residential buildings among the total space of buildings under construction or completed.

Floor Space under Construction refers to total floor space of all buildings under construction during the reference period, including floor space of newly started buildings during the reference period, floor space of construction extended from the previous period to the current period, and floor space of construction suspended during the previous period and resumed in the current period. Floor space of construction completed in the current period, and floor space of construction started and then suspended in the current period are also included in the floor space under construction of the current year.

Floor Space Completed refers to the floor space of all buildings completed in the reference period, which have been appraised and accepted (or come up to the designed standards) and have been transferred to owner units.

Completion Rate of Floor Space of Buildings refers to the ratio of the floor space of buildings completed in a certain period of time to the floor space of buildings under construction in the same period.

Newly Increased Fixed Assets refer to the newly increased value of fixed assets, constructed or purchased, that have been transferred to the investors. This is an indicator that demonstrates the results of investment in fixed assets in monetary terms, and an important indicator to reflect the speed of construction and to calculate the efficiency of investment.

Rate of Construction Projects Completed and Put into Use refers to the ratio of the number of construction projects completed and put into use in a certain period of time to the number of projects under construction in the same period. This reflects the investment efficiency from the perspective of the speed of projects construction.

Rate of Projects of Fixed Assets Completed and Put into Operation refers to the ratio of the newly increased fixed assets to the total investment made in the same period. This is a comprehensive indicator reflecting the speed of the employment of fixed assets and the investment efficiency at the macro-level. As the newly increase fixed assets is the result of a long period while the investment is completed in the current year, this indicator is expected to be used to reflect the employment of fixed assets over a long period of time.

Area of Commercialized Housing Sold refers to total contracted area of commercialized housing (i.e. area of floor space as designated in the formal contracts signed by both sides) during the reference time. It constitutes floor space of completed housing and floor space of future housing.

Value of Commercialized Housing Sold refers to the total contracted value (i.e. value of sales/purchase for selling/purchase of commercialized housing as designated in the contract signed by both sides) during the reference time. This indicator has the same coverage as the area of commercialized housing sold, which constitutes floor space of completed housing and floor space of housing yet to be completed.

Economically Affordable Housing refers to housing constructed according to the State Plan for economically affordable housing. The features of houses of this category are low cost of construction and low prices, and therefore are affordable to mid-income and low income households. Economically affordable housing projects are developed by real estate companies under the State Investment Plan, with the land provided through government allocation or tendering procedures. Developers are exempted from land utilization fees and enjoy another 50% exemption of all other legitimate fees, while their profits are limited to less than 3%, and the completed houses are sold under government-guided prices. This indicator helps to analyze the investment structure of the real estate industry and the demand and supply of housing for mid-income and low income households.

6 Six

对外经济贸易

Foreign Trade and Economic Cooperation

6-1 进出口总额

Total Value of Imports and Exports

指标	Item	2006	2007	2008	2009	2010	2011	2011年比2010年增长(%) Increase Rate in 2011 over 2010(%)
进出口总额(万元)	**Total Value of Imports and Exports(RMB 10000 yuan)**	**1240471**	**1558266**	**2350249**	**1576427**	**2132280**	**3163005**	**48.3**
出口总额	Total Exports	796641	1004493	1324260	928258	1299881	1933198	48.7
进口总额	Total Imports	443830	553773	1025989	648169	832399	1229807	47.7
进出口差额	Balance	352811	450720	298271	280089	467482	703391	50.5
进出口总额(万美元)	**Total Value of Imports and Exports(USD 10000)**	**161745**	**227285**	**337037**	**230732**	**314680**	**488440**	**55.2**
出口总额	Total Exports	103874	146513	190084	135856	192018	298531	55.5
进口总额	Total Imports	57871	80772	146953	94876	122662	189909	54.8
进出口差额	Balance	46003	65741	43131	40980	69356	108622	56.6

注：资料来源于贵阳海关(以下相关表同)。
Note:Data in the table are obtained from Guiyang Customhouse(the same applies to the relative tables below) .

6-2 按地区分的出口商品总额

Foreign Export Trade with Related Countries(Territories)

单位：万美元 (USD 10000)

地区名	Country (Territory)	2006	2007	2008	2009	2010	2011
总　计	**Total**	**103874**	**146513**	**190084**	**135856**	**192018**	**298531**
亚　洲	Asia	68524	84784	111949	88831	120024	186319
非　洲	Africa	2528	4306	5594	5514	5307	8302
欧　洲	Europe	13554	20061	23111	13711	18937	23746
拉丁美洲	Latin America	2424	12672	10551	3859	8998	29283
北美洲	North America	14854	18716	23009	13331	22826	35285
大洋洲	Oceania	1990	5974	15870	10610	15926	15596

6-3 按地区分的进口商品总额

Foreign Import Trade with Related Countries(Territories)

单位：万美元 (USD 10000)

地区名	Country (Territory)	2006	2007	2008	2009	2010	2011
总　计	**Total**	**57871**	**80772**	**146953**	**94876**	**122662**	**189909**
亚　洲	Asia	28293	44453	69268	32219	64064	78758
非　洲	Africa	1582	3053	8083	9538	8595	22185
欧　洲	Europe	7923	11844	13333	14004	7770	9946
拉丁美洲	Latin America	3654	3247	3203	12271	14950	22722
北美洲	North America	8901	11364	41685	9304	11670	18644
大洋洲	Oceania	7518	6811	11381	17540	15613	37654

6–4 海关出口商品分类

单位：万美元

指　标	Item	2006
总　计	**Total**	**103874**
活动物；动物产品	Live Animals;Animal Products	45
植物产品	Vegetable Products	457
动、植物油、脂及其分解产品；精制的食用油脂；动、植物蜡	Animal or Vegetable Oils,Fats and Their Cleavage Products; Refined Edible Oils and Fats;Animal or Vegetable Wax	127
食品；饮料、酒及醋；烟草及烟草代用品的制品	Food;Beverages, Liquor and Vinegar;Tobacco and Manufactured Tobacco Substitutes	5743
矿产品	Mineral Products	8525
化学工业及其相关工业的产品	Products of Chemical Industries and Related Industies	38915
塑料及其产品；橡胶及其产品	Plastics and Related Products;Rubber and Related Products	8804
生皮、皮革、毛皮及其制品；鞍具及挽具；旅行用品、手提包及类似物品；动物肠线(蚕胶丝除外)制品	Raw Hides, Leather, Furs and Related Products; Saddle;Travel Articles, Handbags and Similar Containers;Containers;Articles of Animal Gut(Other Than Silk-Worm Gut)	128
木及木制品；木炭；软木及软木制品；稻草、秸秆、针茅或其他编结材料制品；篮筐及柳条编织品	Wood and Wooden Products;Charcoal;Corkand Related Products; Straws,Straws,Plaited Products;Baskets and Wickerwork	12
木浆及其他纤维状纤维素浆；回收(废碎)纸或纸板；纸、纸板及其制品	Paper Pulp and Cellulose Pulp;Paper and Waste Paper; Paperboard and Related Products	10
纺织原料及纺织制品	Textile Materials and Products	1098
鞋、帽、伞、杖、鞭及其零件；已加工的羽毛及其制品；人造花；人发制品	Footwear, Headgear,Umbrellas,Canes,Whips and Parts Thereof; Processed Feather, and Articles Made Therewith;Artificial Flowers;Wigs	3
石料、石膏、水泥、石棉、云母及类似材料的制品；陶瓷产品；玻璃及其制品	Gypsum, Cement, Asbestos,Mica or Similar Materials;Ceramic Products;Glass and Glassware	832
珠宝、贵金属及制品	Jewelry, Precious Metal and Rolled Precious Metal	2
贱金属及其制品	Base Metals and Related Products	23644
机器、机械器具、电气设备机器零件、录音机及放声机、电视图象、声音的录制和重放设备及其零件、附件	Machinery,Electric Equipment and Accessories,Recorders, Videorecorderand Accessories	12999
车辆、航空器、船舶及有关运输设备	Vehicles, Aircraft,Ship and Related Transportation Equipment	2056
光学、照相、电影、计量、检验、医疗或外科用仪器及设备、精密仪器及设备，钟表，乐器及其零附件	Optical,Photographic,Film,Measuring, Checking, PrecisionMedical or Surgical Instruments and Equipment; Clocks, Musical and Related Parts and Accessories	271
杂项制品	Miscellaneous Products	203
艺术品、收藏品及古物	Art,Collection and Antique	

Value of Export Commodities by Category

(USD 10000)

2007	2008	2009	2010	2011	2011年比2010年增长(%) Increase Rate in 2011 over 2010(%)
146513	**190084**	**135856**	**192018**	**298531**	**55.5**
83	47	101	97	116	19.5
489	384	448	457	721	58.0
158	342	215	413	335	-18.9
6516	9797	13560	17476	20772	18.9
10433	31326	8133	12790	11192	-12.5
68668	74712	53762	100049	171897	71.8
11466	12457	12324	19117	28879	51.1
92	92	46	44	419	845.7
54	165	96	52	3	-95.0
14	14	15	107	144	33.8
3973	1401	739	994	1635	64.4
15	24	39	128	164	27.7
514	890	1211	2201	5919	169.0
1	2	3	4	5	33.2
24806	28242	6678	6415	10857	69.2
15752	25643	34252	28060	37544	33.8
2696	3460	2664	2137	2451	14.7
305	370	801	333	577	73.0
478	716	769	1144	4796	319.1
				105	

6–5 海关进口商品分类

Value of Import Commodities by Category

单位：万美元 (USD 10000)

指　标	Item	2006	2007	2008	2009	2010	2011	2011年比2010年增长(%) Increase Rate in 2011 over 2010(%)
总　计	**Total**	**57871**	**80772**	**146953**	**94876**	**122662**	**189909**	**54.8**
植物产品	Vegetable Products	3	5	4	27	30	21	**-30.6**
食品；饮料、酒及醋；烟草及烟草代用品的制品	Food,;Beverages, Liquor and Vinegar; Tobacco and Tobacco Substitutes	20	18	31	25	13	18	36.8
矿产品	Mineral Products	32653	53697	108189	53620	73337	135047	84.2
化学工业及其相关工业的产品	Products of Chemical Industries and Related Industies	1513	1616	2736	1763	1712	1471	-14.1
塑料及其产品；橡胶及其产品	Plastics and Related Products;Rubber and Related Products	9002	11348	16005	11900	25366	28578	12.7
生皮、皮革、毛皮及其制品;旅行用品、手提包及类似品;动物肠线制品	Raw Hides, Leather, Furs and Related Products; Saddle;Travel Articles, Handbags and Similar Containers; Containers;Articles of Animal Gut (Other Than Silk-Worm Gut)						4	
木及木制品;木炭;软木及软木制品；稻草、秸秆、针茅或其他编结材料制品;篮筐及柳条编结品	Wood and Wooden Products; Charcoal;Corkand Related Products;Straws,Straws,Plaited Products;Baskets and Wickerwork						15	
木浆及其他纤维状纤维素浆；回收(废碎）纸或纸板；纸、纸板及其制品	Paper Pulp and Cellulose Pulp;Paper and Waste Paper;Paperboard and Related Products	174	333	376	387	382	849	122.2
纺织原料及纺织制品	Textile Materials and Products	19	33	68	10	19	65	245.1
鞋、帽、伞、杖、鞭及其零件;已加的羽毛及其制品;人造花;人发制品	Footwear, Headgear,Umbrellas, Canes,Whips and Parts Thereof; Processed Feather, and Articles Made Therewith;Artificial Flowers; Wigs						8	

6-5 续表 continued

单位：万美元 (USD 10000)

指　标	Item	2006	2007	2008	2009	2010	2011	2011年比2010年增长(%) Increase Rate in 2011 over 2010(%)
石料、石膏、水泥、石棉、云母及类似材料的制品；陶瓷产品；玻璃及其制品	Gypsum, Cement, Asbestos,Mica or Similar Materials;Ceramic Products; Glass and Glassware	8	9	27	63	210	62	-70.4
天然或养殖珍珠、宝石或半宝石、贵金属、包贵金属及其制品,仿首饰,硬币	Natural or Cultured Pearls,Precious or Semi-Precious Stones,Precious Metals,Metals Clad With Precious Metal and Stones, Precious Metals,Metals Clad With Precious Metal and Articles Thereof;Imitation Jewellery;Coin						2	
贱金属及其制品	Base Metals and Related Products	2032	1471	2706	7649	6079	7308	20.2
机电、音像设备及其零件机及放声机、电视图象、声音的录制和重放设备及其零件、附件	Machinery, Electric Equipment and Accessories,Recorders,Videorecorder and Accessories	10683	9918	9552	15654	10629	10552	-0.7
车辆、航空器、船舶及有关运输设备	Vehicles, Aircraft,Ship and Related Transportation Equipment	333	491	5691	603	2311	1766	-23.6
光学、照相、电影、计量、检验、医疗或外科用仪器及设备、精密仪品及设备， 钟表，乐器及其零附件	Optical,Photographic,Film,Measuring, Checking, PrecisionMedical or Surgical Instruments and Equipment; Clocks, Musical and Related Parts and Accessories	1406	1830	1503	3162	2550	3904	53.1
杂项制品	Miscellaneous Products	25	2	65	13	24	239	908.3
艺术品、收藏品及古物	Art,Collection and Antique		1					

6-6 利用外资
Foreign Capital Absorbed

指　标	Item	2006	2007	2008	2009	2010	2011
项目数(个)	**Number of Signed Contracts(unit)**	**59**	**51**	**50**	**39**	**42**	**70**
#直接利用外资	Direct Foreign Investment	55	50	40	37	37	66
#合资企业	Joint Venture	23	18	13	19	4	26
合作经营企业	Cooperative Venture	7	7	11	2	7	6
独资企业	Sole-foreign Enterprise	25	25	16	16	26	34
签订合同金额(万美元)	**Contracted Foreign Capital(USD 10000)**	**25845**	**53610**	**59402**	**37397**	**45024**	**170785**
#直接利用外资	Direct Foreign Investment	23275	43610	59402	16397	45024	170785
#合资企业	Joint Venture	4055	10643	4355	9738	8591	73566
合作经营企业	Cooperative Venture	3711	8901	6269	2380	5486	9922
独资企业	Sole-foreign Enterprise	15509	24066	48778	4279	30947	87297
实际利用外资额(万美元)	**Foreign Capital Actually Absorbed(USD 10000)**	**18413**	**15333**	**17379**	**18027**	**34026**	**71674**
#直接利用外资	Direct Foreign Investment	9384	12651	14904	13364	29546	51541
#合资企业	Joint Venture	2438	4288	4401	5230	8885	23856
合作经营企业	Cooperative Venture	608	52	3783	228	73	657
独资企业	Sole-Foreign Enterprise	6338	8311	6720	7906	20588	27028
外商投资企业基本情况	**Registered Foreign-funded Enterprise**						
年末实有外商投资企业(个)	Number of Foreign-funded Enterprises at the year-end(unit)	601	603	601	622	603	644
#本年登记户数(户)	Number of Registered Enterprises at the year-end(unit)	34	50	30	32	31	46
投资总额(万美元)	Total Investment(USD 10000)	263407	279741	321526	356542	413189	568345
注册资本(万美元)	Registered Capital(USD 10000)	163024	169718	193101	213730	250964	321179
#外　方	Capital from Foreign Partners	115071	119505	141801	158456	186005	255181

注：1.资料来源于省发改委、省商务厅。2.2011年起签订(合同)项目、实际利用外资统计口径变化。

Note:1.Data in the table are obtained from the provincial development and reform commission,the provincial department of commerce.2.From 2011, the standard of the signed (the contract) project and the foreign capital actually utilized are changed.

6–7 外商直接投资按行业分项目个数

Number of Projects for Contracted Foreign Direct Investment by Sector

单位：个 (unit)

行业	Sector	2006	2007	2008	2009	2010	2011
总计	**Total**	**55**	**50**	**40**	**37**	**37**	**66**
农、林、牧、渔业	Farming,Forestry,Animal Husbandry and Fishery	4	3	3	5	6	6
采矿业	Mining and Quarrying	1	10	3		2	2
制造业	Manufacturing	29	17	19	11	8	16
电力、燃气及水的生产和供应业	Electric Power,Gas and Water Production and Supply	1		3	2	1	7
建筑业	Construction		2	1		1	2
交通运输、仓储和邮政业	Transport, Storage and Post	1			1	3	
信息传输、计算机服务和软件业	Information Transmission,Computer Services and Software		1			1	1
批发和零售业	Wholesale and Retail Trade		3	2	8	7	7
住宿和餐饮业	Hotel and Catering Services	7	4		1	2	
金融业	Financial Intermediation					1	2
房地产业	Real Estate	6	6	2	1		5
租赁和商务服务业	Leasing and Business Services	4	2	5	7	3	10
科学研究、技术服务和地质勘查业	Scientific Research,Technic Services and Geological Prospecting	1	1			1	3
水利、环境和公共设施管理业	Water Conservancy,Environment and Public Facilities Services		1	1		1	3
居民服务和其他服务业	Services to Households and Other Services				1		1
文化、体育和娱乐业	Culture, Sports and Entertainment	1		1			1

6–8 按行业分外商直接投资协议金额

Agreement Value of Foreign Direct Investment by Sector

单位：万美元 (USD 10000)

行业	Sector	2006	2007	2008	2009	2010	2011
总计	**Total**	**23275**	**43610**	**59402**	**16397**	**45024**	**170785**
农、林、牧、渔业	Farming,Forestry,Animal Husbandry and Fishery	1832	514	2973	3042	12736	8666
采矿业	Mining and Quarrying	70	1657	1233	491	1235	1875
制造业	Manufacturing	10594	16911	27419	5948	16014	55293
电力、燃气及水的生产和供应业	Electric Power,Gas and Water Production and Supply	300		6120	2210	500	15492
建筑业	Construction		1838	3220		20	12083
交通运输、仓储及邮电通讯业	Transport, Storage and Post	483			368	3857	
信息传输、计算机服务和软件业	Information Transmission,Computer Services and Software	-2	14		-50	100	500
批发和零售业	Wholesale and Retail Trade	80	1754	1389	-616	1808	6512
住宿和餐饮业	Hotel and Catering Services	191	8036	-96	15	1720	-8
金融业	Financial Intermediation					1000	5142
房地产业	Real Estate	8852	7514	12019	587	697	24520
租赁和商务服务业	Leasing and Business Services	353	905	3212	3593	2103	27913
科学研究、技术服务和地质勘查业	Scientific Research,Technic Services and Geological Prospecting	472	1113		799	1951	7118
水利、环境和公共设施管理业	Water Conservancy,Environment and Public Facilities Services		3354	410		500	3993
居民服务和其他服务业	Services to Households and Other Services				10		304
文化、体育和娱乐业	Culture, Sports and Entertainment	50		1503		783	1382

6–9 按行业分外商实际直接投资额
Actually Used Amount of Foreign Direct Investment by Sector

单位：万美元 (USD 10000)

指　标	Item	2006	2007	2008	2009	2010	2011
总　计	**Total**	**9384**	**12651**	**14904**	**13364**	**29546**	**51541**
农、林、牧、渔业	Farming, Forestry,Animal Husbandry and Fishery	119	70			4300	8200
采矿业	Mining and Quarrying	145	434	469	372	905	737
制造业	Manufacturing	4193	6111	7641	11370	14318	20078
电力、燃气及水的生产和供应业	Electric Power,Gas and Water Production and Supply			750			7330
建筑业	Construction	8					21
交通运输、仓储和邮政业	Transport, Storage and Post	490					3006
信息传输、计算机服务和软件业	Information Transmission,Computer Services and Software	128					
批发和零售业	Wholesale & Retail Trade and Catering Services	86	400	1275	472	368	1172
住宿和餐饮业	Quarter and Catering Services	237				15	
金融业	Financial Intermediation					1000	
房地产业	Real Estate	3363	4870	1339	617	3125	2272
租赁和商务服务业	Leasing and Business Services	62	104	76	10	3385	6327
科学研究、技术服务和地质勘查业	Scientific Research,Technic Services and Geological Prospecting	497	662		523	2120	1985
水利、环境和公共设施管理业	Water Conservancy,Environment and Public Facilities Services			3354			
居民服务和其他服务业	Services to Households and Other Services	6				10	313
文化、体育和娱乐业	Culture,Sports and Entertainment	50					100

6–10 对外经济合作
Economic Cooperation with Foreign Countries or Territories

指　标	Item	2006	2007	2008	2009	2010	2011
境外经济合作	**Economic Cooperation with Foreigh Countries or Territories**						
签订合同项目(个)	Number of Contracts(unit)	2	4	3	10	24	25
#对外承包工程	Contracted Projects	2	4	3	10	24	25
签订合同金额(万美元)	Value of Contracts(USD 10000)	2419	6774	20000	16461	32431	29649
#对外承包工程	Contracted Projects	2419	6774	20000	16461	32431	29649
实际营业额(万美元)	Actual Turnover(USD 10000)	6608	6065	12425	13700	22003	30015
#对外承包工程	Contracted Projects	6593	6065	12425	13700	22003	30015
年末在外人员(人)	Persons in Abroad(year-end)(person)	775	620	897	1649	1789	1938
#对外承包工程	Contracted Projects	690	620	897	1649	1789	1926
省外经济合作	**Economic Cooperation with Other Provinces**						
引进省外项目(个)	Number of Contracted Projects(unit)	2086	2056	2157		2640	4637
引进省外资金(亿元)	Contracted Value(100 million yuan)	286	401	510		992	2580

注:表中数据不含铝镁设计院及国内国际标项目。

Note: Data in the table don't contain bidding projects of the Magnesium and Design Institute and the domestic and international.

主要统计指标解释

进出口总额 指实际进出我国国境的货物总金额。包括对外贸易实际进出口货物，来料加工装配进出口货物，国家间、联合国及国际组织无偿援助物资和赠送品，华侨、港澳台同胞和外籍华人捐赠品，租赁期满归承租人所有的租赁货物，进料加工进出口货物，边境地方贸易及边境地区小额贸易进出口货物（边民互市贸易除外），中外合资企业、中外合作经营企业、外商独资经营企业进出口货物和公用物品，到、离岸价格在规定限额以上的进出口货样和广告品（无商业价值、无使用价值和免费提供出口的除外），从保税仓库提取在中国境内销售的进口货物，以及其他进出口货物。我国规定出口货物按离岸价格统计，进口货物按到岸价格统计。

利用外资 指我国各级政府、部门、企业和其他经济组织通过对外借款、吸收外商直接投资以及用其他方式筹措的境外现汇、设备、技术等。

对外借款 指通过对外正式签订借款协议，从境外筹措的资金，包括外国政府贷款、国际金融组织贷款、外国银行商业贷款、出口信贷以及对外发行债券等。1996 年及以前还包括对外发行股票。

外商直接投资 指外国企业和经济组织或个人(包括华侨、港澳台胞以及我国在境外注册的企业)按我国有关政策、法规，用现汇、实物、技术等在我国境内开办外商独资企业、与我国境内的企业或经济组织共同举办中外合资经营企业、合作经营企业或合作开发资源的投资（包括外商投资收益的再投资），以及经政府有关部门批准的项目投资总额内企业从境外借入的资金。

外商其他投资 指除对外借款和外商直接投资以外的各种利用外资的形式。包括企业在境内外股票市场公开发行的以外币计价的股票（目前主要是在香港证券市场发行的 H 股和在境内证券市场发行的 B 股）发行价总额，国际租赁进口设备的应付款，补偿贸易中外商提供的进口设备、技术、物料的价款，加工装配贸易中外商提供的进口设备、物料的价款。

对外承包工程 指各对外承包公司以招标议标承包方式承揽的下列业务：(1) 承包国外工程建设项目，(2) 承包我国对外经援项目，(3) 承包我国驻外机构的工程建设项目，(4) 承包我国境内利用外资进行建设的工程项目，(5) 与外国承包公司合营或联合承包工程项目时我国公司分包部分，(6) 对外承包兼营的房屋开发业务。对外承包工程的营业额是以货币表现的本期内完成的对外承包工程的工作量，包括以前年度签订的合同和本年度新签订的合同在报告期内完成的工作量。

对外劳务合作 指以收取工资的形式向业主或承包商提供技术和劳动服务的活动。我国对外承包公司在境外开办的合营企业，中国公司同时又提供劳务的，其劳务部分也纳入劳务合作统计。劳务合作营业额按报告期内向雇主提交的结算数（包括工资、加班费和奖金等）统计。

Explanatory Notes on Main Statistical Indicators

Total Imports and Exports at Customs refer to the value of commodities imported into and exported from the boundary of China. They include the actual imports and exports through foreign trade, imported and exported goods under the processing and assembling trades and materials, supplies and gifts as aid given gratis between gov-ernments and by the United Nations and other international organizations, and contributions donated by overseas Chinese, compatriots in Hong Kong and Macao and Chinese with foreign citizenship, leasing commodities owned by tenant at the expiration of leasing period, the imported and exported commodities processed with imported materi-als. commodities trading in border areas (excluding mutual exchange goods), the imported and exported commodities and articles for public use of the Sino-foreign joint ventures, cooperative enterprises and ventures exclusively with foreign own investment .Also included are import or export of samples and advertising goods for whose CIF or FOB value are beyond the permitted ceUing (excluding goods of no trading or use value and free commodities for export),imported goods sold in China from bonded warehouses and other imported or exported goods.ln accordance with the stipulation of the Chinese government,imports are calculated at CIF. while exports are calcu-lated at FOB.

Utilization of Foreign Capital refers to remittance, equipment and technology financed from abroad, by loans, foreign direct investment and other forms undertaken by the Chinese governments at all levels, by various departments, enterprises and other economic units.

Foreign Borrowings it refers to funds borrowed from abroad through formal signing of borrowing agreements with foreign institutions. including loans of foreign governments. loans of international financial institutions.commercial loans of foreign banks, export credit, and funds raised by Chinese bonds (and shares before 1996) issued abroad.

Foreign Direct Investment refers to the investments inside China by foreign enterprises and economic organizations or individuals (including overseas Chinese,compatriots from Hong Kong and Macao,and Chinese enterprises registered abroad), following the relevant policies and laws of China, for the establishment of ventures exclusively with foreign own investment. Sino-foreign joint ventures and cooperative enterprises or for co-operative exploration of resources with enterprises or economic organizations in China. It includes the re investment of the foreign entrepreneurs with the profits gained from the investment and the funds that enterprises borrow from abroad in the total investment of projects which are approved by the relevant department of the government.

Other Foreign Direct Investment refers to all forms of utilization of foreign capitals other than foreign borrowings and foreign direct investment. It includes the total value of stock shares in foreign currencies issued by enterprises at domestic or foreign stock exchanges (now mainly consisting of H shares issued at Hong Kong Security Market and B shares issued at domestic security markets), rent payable for the imported equipment through international leasing arrangement, cost of imported equipment, technology and materials provided by foreign counterparts in compensation trade and processing and assembly trade.

Overseas Contracted Project refer to projects undertaken by Chinese contractors (project contracting companies) through bidding process.They include: (l)overseas civil engineering construction projects financed by foreign investors; (2)overseas projects financed by the Chinese government through its foreign aid programs; (3)construction projects of Chinese diplomatic missions,trade offices and other institutions stationed abroad; (4)construction projects in China financed by foreign investment; (5)sub-contracted projects to be taken by Chinese contractors through a joint umbrella project with foreign contractor(s); (6)housing development projects.The business income from international contracted projects is the work volume of contracted projects completed during the reference period, expressed in monetary terms, including completed work on projects signed in previous years.

Overseas Labour Services refers to the activities of providing technology and labour services to employers or contractors in the forms of receiving salaries and wages. Labour services providing by contractual joint ventures of Chihe statistics of service cooperation with foreign countries.The business mcome of labour service cooperation is the income in the form of wages and salaries, overtime pay, bonuses and other remuneration received from the employers during the reference period.

中电投贵州金元集团公司

China Power Investment Guizhou Jinyuan Group

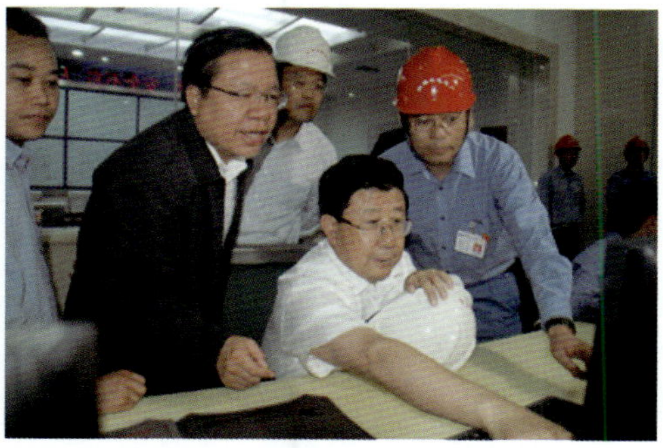

2011年6月12日，贵州省委副书记、省长赵克志（中）视察纳雍电厂
June 12, 2011, the deputy secretary of the Guizhou Province, vice governor Zhao Kezhi (center) visited the Nayong Power Plant

中电投贵州金元集团在中电投集团公司和中共贵州省委、省政府的正确领导下，紧紧围绕“抓发展、调结构、保增长、强管理、防风险、维稳定”的工作方针和“三步走”发展战略，通过体制创新、机制创新，积极发挥区位、产业集群优势，千方百计克服了生产经营困难。在管理、文化、理念方面实现了与中电投集团的全面融合，圆满完成了各项生产经营和发展目标。

金元集团全资及控股电厂全年完成发电量391.13亿千瓦时；完成煤炭产量40万吨，销售完成84万吨；生产铁合金12万吨，销售9.83万吨；销售商品房1786套，销售面积225407平方米；全年实现销售收入125.26亿元，上缴税金15.2亿元。全年完成基建项目投资12.6亿元。

2011年5月3日，集团公司党组书记、总经理陆启洲（左一）到贵州调研，并与省委副书记王福玉（右一）进行了会晤
May 3, 2011, the party secretary of the Corporation, general manager Lu Qizhou (first from left) to Guizhou have research, and met with the Provincial Party Secretary Wang Fuyu (first from right)

2011年2月5日，贵州省副省长孙国强（前排左一）深入系统电厂看望慰问一线干部员工
February 5, 2011, vice governor of Guizhou Province, Sun Guoqiang (first from left in the front row), visited and saluted the front-line cadres and staff in-depth power plants system

公司全资发电厂——纳雍发电总厂，位于毕节地区纳雍县阳长镇
Wholly owned power plants - Nayong Power Plant, located in Bijie region Nayong County Yangchang town

China Power Investment Guizhou Jinyuan Group, under the correct leadership of China Power Investment Corporation and the CPC Guizhou Provincial Committee,the provincial government, closely around the "grasping development, structural adjustment, to maintain growth, strong management, anti-risk peacekeeping and stability" policy and "three steps" development strategy, through institutional innovation, mechanism innovation, and actively play to regional advantages of industrial clusters, do everything possible to overcome difficulties in production and operation. Management, culture, philosophy, to achieve full integration with China Power Investment Corporation and the successful completion of the production and management and development objectives.

Jinyuan Group wholly owned and controlled power plant year to 39.113 billion kwh of electricity generation; completion of the 400,000 tons of coal production, the completion of the sale of 840,000 tons; 120,000 tons of ferroalloy production, sales of 98,300 tons; 1,786 sets of sales of commercial housing, sales area 225,407 square meters; annual sales income of 12.526 billion yuan, taxes of 1.52 billion yuan. Last year's infrastructure projects to invest 1.26 billion yuan.

贵州电网公司

Guizhou Power Grid Corporation

6月1日，公司启动“安全生产月”各项活动
June 1, the company launched "Safety Production Month" activities

11月8日，贵州电网公司庆祝记者节
November 8, Guizhou Power Grid Corporation to celebrate the Reporter

贵州电网公司是中国南方电网有限责任公司的全资子公司，负责贵州电网的统一规划、建设、管理和调度，承担着省内电力供应和西电东送双重任务。供电面积17万平方公里，供电服务人口3798万，供电户数950余万户。2009年实现全省电网覆盖范围内“户户通电”。 2011年，实现售电量1090亿千瓦时，资产总额5 80.7亿元，员工54529人。近年来，贵州电网公司先后荣获全国五一劳动奖状、中央企业先进基层党组织、贵州省和谐企业先进单位、“四好”领导班子先进集体等荣誉。连续蝉联贵州省百强企业榜首。

截至2011年底，贵州电网统调装机2893万千瓦，其中，火电装机1749万千瓦，水电装机1139万千瓦，风电5万千瓦。 贵州电网已拥有110千伏及以上变电站407座，变电容量5616万千伏安，线路长度24683千米，形成以中部500千伏日字型环网为中心，向北、向东延伸的500千伏主干网架，并通过500千伏兴安直流、高肇直流、500千伏天金线、青河双回、黎桂双回“五交两直”通道与南方主网并联运行。黔电送粤能力达到800万千瓦以上，加上外送周边省区，外送能力已超过9 00万千瓦。

“十二五”时期，贵州电网公司迎来了加快发展的大好机遇。贵州电网公司将坚持贯彻科学发展观，认真落实南方电网公司和贵州省委、省政府的工作部署，以“服务好、管理好、形象好”为努力方向，努力创建国内先进电网企业，为贵州经济社会更好更快发展做出更大贡献。

1月9日，电建一公司抗冰保电工作紧张有序地进行
January 9, Power I Company to build an anti-ice protection electrical work in an orderly manner

8月26日，南方电网公司“为民服务创先争优”社会活动日贵阳供电局活动现场
August 26, China Southern Power Grid Company "to excel serving the public" social activities day, Guiyang Power Supply Bureau the active site

1月21日，遵供道真供电局抢修队员正在磨盘山区为台变除冰

January 21,Zungong Daozhen team of the Power Supply Bureau is de-icing for Mopanshan District

9月，贵州电网首次利用载人直升机为主网“体检”

September, Guizhou Power Grid for the first time to use manned helicopter-based to have "medical" of the network

Guizhou Power Grid Corporation is a wholly owned subsidiary of China Southern Power Grid Co., Ltd., is responsible for the Guizhou Power Grid of unified planning, construction, management and scheduling, to bear the supply of electricity in the province and west to east the dual task. Supply electricity area of 170,000 square km, power supply serving a population of 37,980,000, the number of households supply more than 9,500,000. In 2009, the province's power grid coverage of the "Every Households Power". In 2011, electricity sales of 109 billion kwh, the total assets of 8.07 billion yuan, employs 54,529 people. In recent years, Guizhou Power Grid Corporation has won the National Labor Award, the central advanced grassroots party organizations, Guizhou Province advanced unit of harmonious enterprise, "four goods" leading groups advanced group and other honors. Consecutive reelection of the top 100 enterprises of Guizhou Province.

By the end of 2011, Guizhou Power Grid transfer system installed capacity of 28.93 million kilowatts, of which thermal power installed capacity of 17.49 million kilowatts, hydropower installed capacity of 11.39 million kilowatts and 50,000 kilowatts of wind power. Guizhou Power Grid has 407 substations of 110 kV and above, transformer capacity of 56,160,000 kilovolt, line length of 24,683 km, the formation of the Central 500 kV Day-shaped ring as the center, north, east extension of 500 kV backbone frame, and 500 kV Xing'an DC, Gaozhao DC ,500 kV Tianjin line, back to Qinghe Double DC, Li Gui for Double "five cross two straight" channel and the South of the main network operating in parallel. The Qian power to send Guangdong ability to reach more than 8 million kilowatts, plus neighboring provinces delivery, delivery capacity has exceeded 9 million kilowatts.

During the "12th Five-Year Plan" period, the Guizhou Power Grid Corporation ushered in a golden opportunity to accelerate the development. Guizhou Power Grid Corporation will adhere to implement the scientific development concept, to seriously implement the work plans of the Southern Power Grid Company and Guizhou Provincial Party Committee and Provincial Government, take the "good service, good management, good image" for the direction, make efforts to create advanced power grid enterprises in domestic, and make greater contributions for Guizhou economic and social better and faster development.

7月，安顺供电局220千伏两所屯变电站值班人员对站内重要变电设备进行特巡检查和测温

In July, the duty officer of the Anshun Power Supply Bureau, 220 kV and two Tuen substation to have special patrol inspection and temperature of substation equipment in the station

8月9日，都供丹寨供电局抗旱突击队员在当地长青乡排中村帮助村民铺接抽水设备

August 9, Dugong Daizhai Power Supply Bureau drought commandos to help villagers in the local Changqingxiang Township Zhong village to access pumping equipment

贵州送变电工程公司

Guizhou Power Transmission and Distribution Engineering Company

贯彻落实南网中长期战略

Implement the long-term strategy of the South Network

电力天路建成投运

Electricity sky road was put into operation

贵州送变电工程公司是中国南方电网贵州电网公司全资子公司，始建于1958年，经国家住房和城乡建设部核准，具有贵州省唯一的国家电力施工总承包壹级资质和土石方工程专业承包叁级，及消防设施工程专业承包壹级、承装（修、试）类壹级和房屋建筑工程施工总承包叁级资质；具有承包境外送变电工程及境内国际招标工程；以及境外送变电工程所需的设备、材料出口；对外派遣实施境外送变电工程所需的劳务人员；工程设计电力行业（送电工程、变电工程）专业丙级；消防设施工程设计专项乙级；调试资质送变电工程类甲级企业。

公司成立50多年来，共建成110kV及以上输电线路11516km，变电站总容量36625MVA。近年来，公司遵照“完善、规范、巩固、提高”的总体要求，取得了辉煌的业绩。2003-2010年，公司获得国家优质工程银质奖13个。1987-2006年连续20年荣获市级“守合同、重信用”单位称号。2008年荣获得中电联授予的首批“电力行业AAA级信用企业”荣誉。2008年还获得中国南方电网公司抗突抢修复电先进单位，获贵州省抗凝冻保民生工作集体记一等功。2009年公司再次荣获2008年度全国“五一”劳动奖状和贵州省“五一”劳动奖状。公司承建的贵广II回±500kV直流输电工程和500kV金州变电站工程分别荣获2009年和2010年国家优质工程银质奖。1995-2010年连续16年荣获贵州省“守合同、重信用”单位。

柬埔寨金边——马德望电网运维

Phnom Penh, Cambodia - Battambang power grid operation and maintenance

柬埔寨菩萨变施工

Cambodia Buddha substation construction

鏖战两个昼夜打通望谟北部电力动脉

The fight lasting two days and nights to get through the artery of northern Wangmo power

望谟抗洪救灾

Wangmo flood relief

Guizhou Power Transmission and Distribution Engineering Company is a wholly owned subsidiary of Guizhou Power Grid Corporation China Southern Power Grid, was founded in 1958, approved by the Ministry of National Housing and Urban-Rural Development, is the only general contractor with firs-level qualification of the national electric power construction and earthwork engineering contracting third-level in Guizhou Province, and fire facilities engineering contractor first-level, installing the (repair test) class first-level, and housing construction facilities work contract third-level qualification; contracted overseas transmission and distribution engineering and domestic international tendering project; and outside transmission and distribution engineering the necessary equipment and materials for export; to send foreign labor for the outside transmission and distribution engineering; engineering design of the power industry (power transmission engineering, substation engineering) professional grade C; fire-fighting facilities engineering design special grade B; debug qualification of sending substation engineering grade A enterprise.

Since the company's establishment for 50 years, built a total of 110kV and above transmission lines 11,516 km, the substation total capacity 36,625MVA. In recent years, the company pursuant to "improve, standardize, consolidate and enhance"the general requirement to obtain a brilliant achievement. During 2003 - 2010, the company received the National Quality Engineering Silver Medal 13. During 1987 - 2006 for 20 consecutive years won the title of the municipal "observe contract, re-credit" units. In 2008, won the CEC granted to the first "power industry AAA grade credit enterprise" honorary. In 2008, China Southern Power Grid Company won advanced units of anti-emergence and rob repairment, won the collective Merit Citation Class I in the Guizhou Province Anti-Freezing and ensure people's livelihood work. In 2009, the company has once again won the 2008 "May 1" labor certificates and Guizhou Province "May 1" labor certificates. The construction of the Guizhou-Guangdong II back to ± 500kV DC transmission project and 500kV Jinzhou substation project won the silver medal of the National Quality Engineering in 2009 and 2010. During 1995 - 2010 for 16 consecutive years won the Guizhou Province "observe contract, re-credit" units.

普安高速迁改工程

The Puan high-speed moved Engineering

抗击凝冻

The fight against freezing

贵州电力建设第二工程公司

Guizhou Electric Power Construction NO.2 Engineering Company

安顺电厂二期（2×300MW）工程
Anshun Power Plant Phase II (2 x 300MW) project

盘南电厂4台60千瓦机组工程
60 kilowatts Pannan Power Plant 4 Units Project

贵州电力建设第二工程公司始建于1958年，资质等级为国家一级火电建筑安装大型综合性施工企业，并取得中华人民共和国对外承包工程经营资格证书，可承建各类火力发电厂的整体建筑、安装工程；核电站常规岛建筑安装工程；各类工业及民用建筑、安装工程，各种压力等级的锅炉及管道安装工程等。

公司现有职工1600余人，具有各类技术、经济管理职称专业人员702人，现有各类国家级注册执业资格证人员60人。施工力量雄厚、机械装备完善。目前，公司拥有各类先进机械1840台，机械装备总功率达26735千瓦，机具设备等固定资产原值已达2亿1千多万元，具备了大型现代化建筑安装施工的能力。

公司获得了ISO9001：2008质量管理体系、ISO14001：2004环境管理体系、GB/T28001：2001职业健康安全管理体系和ISO10012：2003测量管理体系认证证书；获得中国建筑工程最高奖——鲁班奖；全国优秀施工企业称号、全国五一劳动奖状、中国500家最大建筑企业、全国电力行业用户满意工程先进单位、全国“安康杯”竞赛优胜企业、中国电力行业安全生产先进集体；荣获“中国企业新纪录”、“中国企业诚信经营示范单位”、“中国工程建设社会信用AAA级企业”、“改革开放三十周年贵州省经济发展贡献奖”、“全国电力行业企业信用评价AAA级信用企业”等称号。

公司连续20年获得贵州省“守合同重信用单位”称号，荣列中国500家最佳经济效益建筑企业第166位，堤坝、电站、码头建筑业100家最大经营规模企业第34位，堤坝、电站、码头建筑业100家最佳经济效益第20位，已跨入了中国一流施工企业的先进行列。

发耳电厂4X600MW机组工程

Faer Power Plant 4X600MW Unit Project

Guizhou Electric Power Construction NO.2 Engineering Company was founded in 1958, the level of qualification for the country first class fire electrical construction and installation of large-scale comprehensive construction enterprises, and made the business credentials of foreign contracted projects of the People's Republic of China, can contract the construction of the overall construction of various types of thermal power plant installation works; nuclear power plant, conventional island of construction and installation; kinds of industrial and civil construction, installation works, a variety of pressure levels of the boiler and piping installation works.

Company employees are 1,600 people, with a variety of technical, economic management professionals in 702 titles, 60 of the existing types of national practicing certificate personnel. The construction is strong, equipped machinery. Currently, the company has all kinds of advanced machinery 1,840, the total power of machinery and equipment up to 26,735 kilowatts, machinery and equipment, and other value of fixed assets has reached more than 210 million yuan, with the ability of large-scale installation and construction of modern buildings.

The company obtained ISO9001: 2008 Quality Management System, ISO14001: 2004 environmental management system and GB/T28001: 2001 occupational health and safety management system and ISO 10012: 2003 Measurement management system certification; won the China State Construction Engineering highest Award - Luban Award; National Excellent Construction Enterprise advanced engineering unit, the title of the National Labor Award, the 500 largest construction companies in China, the national power industry customer satisfaction advanced unit, National "Health Cup" contest winners enterprises, the Chinese electricity industry safety in production advanced collectives; won a "new record in Chinese enterprises", "good faith business demonstration unit for Chinese enterprises", "China Construction Social Credit AAA Grade Enterprise", "reform opened 30 years Guizhou Province Economic Development Contribution Award ", the title of the country's electricity industry companies credit rating AAA grade credit enterprise", and so on.

The compant won the "Guizhou Province Credible Unit" for 20 consecutive years, the wing out of the 500 best value for economy efficence construction enterprises 166th, 34th of the 100 largest scale enterprises of the dam, power station, wharf construction, 20th of the 100 the best value for economy efficence of the dams, power station, wharf construction, has entered the advanced ranks of the leading construction companies in China.

施工中的幺铺变全景

Panoramic view of the construction of Yaopu Substation

地球彩带、世界花园、养生福地、避暑天堂——百里杜鹃

Earth Ribbons, the World's Garden, Health and Blessed Land, Summer Paradise -Baili Rhododendron

第七届贵州省旅游产业发展大会在百里杜鹃举行，省委书记栗战书（右一）出席并向民革中央授感谢牌

7th Guizhou Province Tourism Industry Development Conference held in Baili Rhododendron, provincial party secretary Li Zhanshu (first from right) present and grant thank license for the Kuomintang Revolutionary Central Committee

贵州省省长赵克志（前排右二）、省委常委、毕节市委书记秦如培（前排右一）在毕节市人大常委会副主任、百里杜鹃党工委书记黄家耀（前排右三）、管委会主任熊灿平（左一）的陪同下视察工作

Governor of Guizhou Province Zhao Kezhi (second from right in front row), the Provincial Standing Committee, the Bijie municipal secretary Qin Rupei (first from right in front row), accompanied by Bijie City People's Congress Standing Committee, deputy director, Baili Rhododendron Party Work Committee Huang Jiayao (third from right in front row), director of the CMC Xiong Canping (first from left), to have inspections

国家旅游局局长邵琪伟出席在百里杜鹃举行的第七届贵州省旅游产业发展大会

China National Tourism Administration Shao Qiwei, attended the Seventh Conference on Guizhou Province Tourism Development in Baili Rhododendron

毕节市市长张吉勇（前排中）在百里杜鹃检查重大项目和重大工程建设

Bijie City Mayor Zhang Jiyong (middle of front row) Checked for major projects and major construction projects in Baili Rhododendron

各国驻华大使联合授予百里杜鹃为"最值得驻华大使馆向国际推荐的世界最大天然杜鹃花园"

States Ambassador to jointly awarded the Baili Rhododendron as "the most worthy of the world's largest natural rhododendron garden that Embassy recommended to the internationally"

2007年6月，经贵州省委省政府批准同意，贵州省机构编制委员会办公室行文批准设立贵州百里杜鹃风景名胜区（国家级森林公园、自然保护区）党的工作委员会和管理委员会，为中共毕节市委（原中共毕节地委）、毕节市人民政府（原毕节地区行署）的正县级派出机构，行使一级县级政府职能，对贵州百里杜鹃国家森林公园实行统一领导和管理，辖普底乡、大水乡、金坡乡、仁和乡、鹏程办事处等4个少数民族乡，1个办事处，共56个村（居）和九龙山国有林场，行政管理区总面积500平方公里，总人口11万。境内拥有总面积125.8平方公里、世界迄今为止已查明的面积最大的原生杜鹃林带，原生杜鹃林带绵延50余公里，宽1-5公里，故被誉为"百里杜鹃"，百里杜鹃是世界罕见的具有特殊保护价值的森林生态系统和杜鹃种质基因库，具有极高的科研价值和旅游价值，是宝贵的世界自然遗产。百里杜鹃因独特的资源优势、区位优势和景区人民的不懈努力，先后被评为国家森林公园、国家4A级旅游景区、全国低碳旅游实验区、最负国际盛名景区、自然保护区、亚洲•大中华区十大自然原生态旅游景区、贵州省十大影响力景区、贵州省十大魅力景区、最值得驻华大

百里杜鹃国家森林公园
Baili Rhododendron national forest park

米底河瀑布
Midi River Falls

贵州省第七届旅游产业发展大会在百里杜鹃举行
The Seventh Conference on Tourism Development in Guizhou Province are held in the Baili Rhododendron

红军黄家坝阻击战纪念碑
Red Army huangjiaba blocking action Monument

In June 2007, the Guizhou provincial committee, government approved and agreed, the Office of the Committee of Guizhou Province wording approved the establishment of Guizhou Baili Rhododendron scenic spots (national forest parks, nature reserves) the party's Working Committee and Management Committee, is county-level institution dispatched of the CPC Bijie Municipal (former Chinese Communist the Bijie Prefectural Party Committee), Bijie Municipal People's Government (formerly Bijie Prefecture Administrative), by the exercise of a county government functions, unified leadership and management on Guizhou Baili Rhododendron National Forest Park, jurisdiction over Pudi Township, Dashui Township, Jinpo Township, Renhe Township, Pengcheng Office and other 4 minority townships 1 offices a total of 56 villages (neighborhood) and Jiulongshan state-owned forest, the administration of a total area of 500 kilometers, with a total a population of 110,000. The territory has a total area of 125.8 square kilometers, the world have been identified so far the largest area of native rhododendron forest, native rhododendron forest stretches for more than 50 km, 1-5 km wide, it is known as "Baili Rhododendron", Baili Rhododendron is rare in the world with special conservation value forest ecosystems and the rhododendron gene pool of germplasm, with high scientific value and tourist value, is a valuable World Natural Heritage. Baili Rhododendron for its unique advantages in resources, locational advantages and scenic people's unremitting efforts, has been named a national forest park, national 4A level scenic spots, national low-carbon tourism experimental area, the most internationally renowned scenic spots, nature reserves, Asia • Greater China ten natural eco-tourism attractions, the top ten influential scenic spots in Guizhou Province, the top ten charm of scenic spots in Guizhou Province, most notably the excellent eco-tourism places recommended by the Embassy to the world, the title of 2011 the province's tourism industry 10 best tourist attractions, the advanced group of the national

花海中的百里杜鹃会展中心
The flower sea of Baili Rhododendron Convention and Exhibition Center

依山傍水、绿树遮映的附源村
Near the mountain and water, the trees cover mapping Fuyuan village

百里杜鹃度假村
Baili Rhododendron Resort

滚山珠
Rolling mountain bead

祭花神
A memorial ceremony for flower God

使馆向世界推荐的中国优秀生态旅游地、2011年全省旅游行业十佳旅游景区、全国旅游系统先进集体等称号，在刚刚结束的第七届贵州旅游产业发展大会上又被评选为“最值得驻华大使向世界推荐的天然杜鹃大花园”称号。

百里杜鹃党工委、管委会建立五年来，严格按照省委、省政府，市委、市政府将百里杜鹃建设成为“独具特色的杜鹃森林生态休闲旅游度假区”的总体要求和创建国家“5A”级景区的总体目标，遵循“科学规划、依法保护、合理利用、加快发展”的总体思路，按照“地球彩带、世界花园、养生福地、避暑天堂”的发展定位，大力实施“生态立区、旅游强区、工业富区、城镇带区、科教兴区”发展战略，不断创新工作思路，探索工作方法，用“小队伍”撬动“大服务”，全面实现了管景区与管社会的和谐发展。

2011年，完成生产总值11.5亿元，是成立之初的5.71倍；完成全社会固定资产投资21亿元，是成立之初的31.34倍；完成财政总收入5.88亿元，是成立之初的19.6倍，其中地方财政收入3.41亿元，是成立之初的21.86倍；城镇居民人均可支配收入1.5万元，是成立之初的2.19倍；农民人均纯收入4084元，是成立之初的2.45倍，核心景区农民人均纯收入达7000多元。接待游客135万人次，实现旅游综合收入6.2亿元，分别是成立之初的4.1倍和29倍；旅游直接间接就业人数从成立之初的500人增长到6800人；农民旅游纯收入从成立之初的140元增长到1800元。

十二五时期主要预期目标：实现地区生产总值年均增长19%以上，2015年达到21亿元以上；财政收入年均增长20%以上，到2015年达到10亿元以上；全社会固定资产投资年均增长50%以上，到2015年达到90亿元以上；城镇居民可支配收入年均增长17%以上，到2015年达到27879元；农民人均纯收入年均增长15%以上，到2015年达到6500元以上；城镇化率达到30%以上；森林覆盖率提高到70%以上；到2015年，当年接待国内外游客达到160万人次以上，实现旅游总收入达到10亿元以上。

火把节之夜
Torch Festival of the Night

彝族青年男女在杜鹃花王下对歌
Yi minority young men and women antiphonal singing in the rhododendron flower king

百里杜鹃湖
Baili Rhododendron Lake

千年古桑
Millennium ancient mulberry

醉九牛花廊
Flower-drunk nine cattle

五月映山红
May azalea t

tourism system and so on, has been selected as the "the most worthy of the world's largest natural rhododendron garden that Embassy recommended to the world" title in the just concluded 7th Guizhou Conference on Tourism Development.

Since the establishment of Baili Rhododendron Party Working Committee, the CMC, in the past five years, in strict accordance with the provincial committee, government, municipal committee, municipal government build Baili Rhododendron into the overall requirements of "the unique rhododendron forest ecological leisure and tourism resort" and the creation of the State's overall goal of the "5A" level scenic spots, follow the "scientific planning, legal protection, rational use, accelerate the development" the general idea, vigorously implemented in accordance with the "Earth Ribbons, the World's Garden, Health and Blessed Land, Summer Paradise" positioning, vigorously implemented "ecological build the area, tourism strengthen the area, industrial rich the area, the town push the band, science and education propers the area" development strategy, innovative ideas, and explore methods of work, "small team" leveraging the "big service", the full realization of the harmonious development of management of scenic area and management of society.

In 2011, GDP of 1.15 billion yuan, 5.71 times of the establishment of the beginning; completed investment in fixed assets of 2.1 billion yuan, 31.34 times of the establishment of the beginning; completion of the total fiscal revenue of 588 million yuan, is 19.6 times of the establishment of the beginning, which the local revenue of 341 million yuan, is 21.86 times of the establishment of the beginning; urban residents per capita disposable income of 15,000 yuan, 2.19 times of the establishment of the beginning; rural per capita net income of 4,084 yuan, 2.45 times of the establishment of the beginning, the core scenic rural per capita net income of more than 7,000 yuan. 1.35 million people of tourists and tourism revenue of 620 million yuan, respectively, 4.1 times and 29 times at the beginning of the establishment; travel direct and indirect employment growth from the inception of the 500 to 6,800; net income of the farmers from travel increase from the inception of 140 yuan to 1,800 yuan.

The main targets of the Twelfth Five-Year period: average annual GDP growth of more than 19%, reached more than 2.1 billion yuan in 2015; annual fiscal revenue growth of more than 20%, reached more than 1 billion yuan in 2015; fixed assets average annual investment growth of 50%, reached more than 9 billion yuan in 2015 ; the average annual disposable income of urban residents increased by more than 17%, to 27,879 yuan in 2015; the average annual per capita net income of farmers increased by more than 15%, reached more than 6,500 yuan in 2015 ; urbanization rate has reached more than 30%; the forest coverage rate to 70%; in 2015, the domestic and foreign tourists reached more than 1.6 million people, total tourism income reached 1 billion yuan.

百里杜鹃大草原
Baili Rhododendron Prairie

遵义供电局

Zunyi Power Supply Bureau

继电保护技术能手，南网十大杰出青年罗智燃正在带班技术人员
Protection of technical experts, South Network Ten Outstanding Young Lo Zhiran is training the technical personnel

全国劳模申友强在现场抢修
National model workers, Shen Youjiang is repairing on site

2011年1月，习水县仙源的高海拔地带，工作人员正在抢修除冰
In January 2011, Xishui County Xianyuan the high altitudes area, the staff are repair de-icing

由南网捐建的“南网渠”帮遵义习水黄木坪村圆了饮水梦
Donated by the South Network "South Network channels" to help of Zunyi Huangmuping Village to fullfill the drinking Dream

遵义供电局系隶属于中国南方电网公司贵州电网公司的大一型企业，担负着贵州北部14个县、市、区的供电任务，供电面积达3.35万多平方公里，区域内人口约774万（不含遵义市余庆县，含铜仁地区德江县），资产总额达59.55亿元。下辖城区供电分局、桐梓分局等2个直属分局，直管县级供电企业12家。

遵义供电局致力于建设“智能、高效、可靠、绿色”的现代化电网，服务于“西电东送”和黔北经济发展大局。2011年，全年电力供应有序有效，完成售电量128.56亿千瓦时，同比增长13.75%。安全生产总体形势平稳，城市供电可靠率99.855%。电网完成投资24.54亿元。2011年，遵义供电局连续第三届荣获全国文明单位荣誉称号；获得省部级个人荣誉2个；地市级集体荣誉4个、个人荣誉8个。

Zunyi Power Supply Bureau is the larger first-class enterprise belonging to the Guizhou Power Grid Corporation of China Southern Power Grid Company, responsible for 14 counties, city, district supply mission in Guizhou northern part, the power supply area of over 33.5 thousand square kilometers, the region's population of about 7.74 million (excluding Yuqing County Zunyi City, including Tongren Prefecture Dejiang County), with total assets of 5.955 billion yuan. Directly under the branch jurisdiction of the urban power supply branch, Tongzi Branch, directly manage 12 county-level power supply companies.

Zunyi Power Supply Bureau is committed to building a "smart, efficient, reliable and gree"n modern power grid, service in the "West electricity to East" and Qianbei overall economic development. In 2011, the annual electricity supply is orderly and effective, to complete the electricity sales of 12.856 billion kwh, an increase of 13.75%. Production safety and the overall situation is stable, the city power supply reliability rate of 99.855%. Grid to complete the investment of 2.454 billion yuan. In 2011, Zunyi Power Supply Bureau, the third consecutive won the honorary title of National Civilized Unit; and by the provincial and ministerial level 2 personal honor; 4 municipal collective honor, 8 personal honor.

2011年1月12日，“戴孝除冰”的共产党员刘世超奋战在抗冰现场
January 12, 2011, "wearing the mourning to de-icing" Communists Liu Shichao fight in the anti-ice scene

提高供电可靠率，遵义供电局加大带电作业力度，最大限度的减少客户停电时间
Improve power supply reliability rate, Zunyi Power Supply Bureau to increase the live working efforts, to minimize customer outage time

遵义供电局线路人员在习水县除冰保电网
Zunyi Power Supply Bureau line workers are having de-icing for protection of the grid in Xishui

7

Seven

能　源

Energy

7−1 能源生产、消费总量及构成
Total Production and Consumption of Energy and Its Composition

单位：万吨标准煤 (10000 tons of SCE)

指 标	Item	2006	2007	2008	2009	2010	2011
一、绝对数	**Absolute Figure**						
一次能源生产总量	Total Production of Primary Energy	8089.39	8480.62	9262.34	11070.09	13100.00	12739.97
原煤	Coal	7726.30	7760.28	8028.53	9779.48	11778.54	11642.93
水电	Hydro-power	363.09	720.34	1233.81	1290.61	1321.46	1097.04
能源终端消费总量	Final Consumption of Energy	5574.99	6278.96	6486.30	6918.98	7373.10	8359.80
#原煤	Coal	2661.70	2861.98	2947.29	3295.82	3538.23	4079.55
天然气	Natural Gas	66.23	68.36	63.04	55.59	55.71	53.05
电力	Electricity	1821.36	2075.79	2076.32	2241.06	2457.22	2777.89
二、构成(%)	**Composition(%)**						
一次能源生产总量	Total Production of Primary Energy	100.0	100.0	100.0	100.0	100.0	100.0
原煤	Coal	95.5	91.5	86.7	88.3	89.9	91.4
水电	Hydro-power	4.5	8.5	13.3	11.7	10.1	8.6
能源终端消费总量	Final Consumption of Energy	100.0	100.0	100.0	100.0	100.0	100.0
#原煤	Coal	47.7	45.6	45.4	47.6	48.0	48.8
天然气	Natural Gas	1.2	1.1	1.0	0.8	0.8	0.6
电力	Electricity	32.7	33.1	32.0	32.4	33.3	33.2

注:电力、热力按等价热值折算(以下各表同)。

Note:Electric power and heat are converted on the basic of equal caloric value(The same as in the following tables).

7-2 综合能源平衡表
Overall Energy Balance

单位：万吨标准煤 (10000 tons of SCE)

指 标	Item	2006	2007	2008	2009	2010	2011
可供消费的能源总量	**Total Energy Available for Consumption**	**6070.27**	**6632.05**	**6903.39**	**7529.73**	**8237.33**	**9551.40**
一次能源生产量	Primary Energy Output	8089.39	8480.62	9262.34	11070.09	13100.00	12739.97
省外调入	Inflow from Other Provinces	487.75	599.49	695.73	789.95	769.65	1040.78
调出省外(一)	Outflow from Guizhou Province(-)	2434.65	2837.71	3292.89	4323.14	5827.75	4028.72
年初年末库存差额	Stock Changes in the Year	-95.68	239.74	87.52	-94.89	48.17	-200.62
能源消费总量	**Total Energy Consumption**	**6172.45**	**6799.72**	**7083.99**	**7566.33**	**8175.43**	**9067.85**
在总量中：	Consumption by Sector						
农、林、牧、渔、水利业	Farming,Forestry,Animal Husbandry, Fishery and Water Conservancy	138.91	141.28	146.50	152.95	141.96	129.52
工业	Industry	4045.78	4472.19	4613.69	4945.37	5289.48	5895.87
建筑业	Construction	60.90	62.55	63.54	75.65	82.51	76.13
交通运输和邮电通讯业	Transportation,Post and Telecommunications Services	309.40	390.57	453.32	467.62	538.48	597.73
商业、饮食、物资供销和仓储业	Commerce,Catering Services, Materials Supply and Storage	275.71	356.50	415.31	488.22	513.29	554.60
其他	Others	436.13	472.84	534.85	566.35	614.04	675.13
生活消费	Residential Consumption	905.62	903.78	856.78	870.17	995.67	1138.87
在总量中：	Consumption by Usage						
终端消费	Final Consumption	5574.99	6278.96	6486.30	6918.98	7373.10	8359.80
#工业	Industry	3448.31	3951.43	4016.00	4298.02	4487.15	5187.82
加工转换损失量	Losses in Processing and Transformation	435.82	347.55	422.10	452.28	577.64	484.95
#炼焦	Coking	104.50	100.81	91.83	85.60	80.12	67.93
损失量	Other Losses	161.65	173.21	175.59	195.07	224.69	223.10
平衡差额	Balance	-102.19	-167.66	-180.59	-36.60	61.90	483.55

注：2008年发电损失量分摊到电力工业消费量中。

Note:The data of Power Generation Losses have been distributed to electricity industry consumption in 2008.

7-3 煤炭平衡表
Coal Balance Sheet

单位：万吨 (10000 tons)

指 标	Item	2006	2007	2008	2009	2010	2011
可供量	**Total Energy Available for Consumption**	**8869.78**	**9363.87**	**9513.90**	**10867.59**	**11230.30**	**12738.14**
生产量	Output	10816.60	10864.18	11239.72	13691.00	15954.02	15601.02
调出省外(—)	Outflow from Guizhou Province(-)	1784.39	1812.99	1844.95	2747.44	4993.21	2812.84
年初年末库存差额	Stock Changes in the Year	-128.66	318.60	125.13	-188.79	269.49	-217.46
消费量	**Total Energy Consumption**	**8994.57**	**9572.63**	**9732.18**	**10912.47**	**11177.47**	**12084.97**
在消费量中：	Consumption by Sector						
农、林、牧、渔、水利业	Farming,Forestry,Animal Husbandry, Fishery and Water Conservancy	153.22	153.51	159.12	168.62	132.66	115.69
工业	Industry	7356.83	7774.81	7976.40	9054.38	9415.02	10145.51
建筑业	Construction	25.09	24.04	20.08	25.49	24.67	20.26
交通运输和邮电通讯业	Transportation,Post and Telecomm unications Services	5.55	7.85	7.23	12.62	14.06	15.16
商业、饮食、物资供销和仓储业	Commerce,Catering Services, Materials Supply and Storage	262.58	368.86	425.81	507.10	463.13	510.90
其他	Others	362.72	453.10	491.22	529.95	503.30	563.10
生活消费	Residential Consumption	828.58	790.46	652.32	614.31	624.63	714.36
在消费量中：	Consumption by Usage						
终端消费	Final Consumption	3398.47	3688.47	3707.66	4182.50	3976.62	4779.70
#工业	Industry	1760.73	1890.65	1951.88	2324.41	2214.17	2840.74
中间消费(用于加工转换)	Intermediate Consumption (Consumed in Transformation)	5554.60	5856.16	5999.52	6704.97	7165.85	7265.27
#发电	Power Generation	4030.79	4179.22	4130.83	4936.90	4913.10	5557.29
炼焦	Coking	884.13	1149.07	1129.76	1078.70	1005.61	948.43
损失量	Losses in Coal Washing and Dressing	41.50	28.00	25.00	25.00	35.00	40.00
平衡差额	**Balance**	**-124.79**	**-208.76**	**-218.28**	**-44.88**	**52.83**	**653.17**

7–4 电力平衡表
Electricity Balance Sheet

单位：亿千瓦小时 (100 million kwh)

指 标	Item	2006	2007	2008	2009	2010	2011
可供量	**Total Energy Available for Consumption**	**581.98**	**669.09**	**679.18**	**750.30**	**835.52**	**944.13**
生产量	Output	868.91	1042.27	1191.69	1380.03	1385.64	1372.87
水电	Hydropower	108.52	216.57	375.60	400.88	416.58	348.88
火电	Thermal Power	760.39	825.70	816.09	979.15	969.06	1023.99
调出省外(一)	Outflow from Guizhou Province(-)	286.93	373.28	515.84	630.63	550.40	428.74
消费量	**Total Energy Consumption**	**581.98**	**669.09**	**679.18**	**750.30**	**835.52**	**944.13**
在消费量中：	Consumption by Sector						
农、林、牧、渔、水利业	Farming,Forestry,Animal Husbandry, Fishery and Water Conservancy	3.85	5.33	4.22	4.48	4.22	3.89
工业	Industry	466.22	538.21	531.64	578.46	639.64	715.53
建筑业	Construction	6.05	6.87	8.04	10.03	11.10	10.33
交通运输和邮电通讯业	Transportation,Post and Telecommunications Services	16.50	19.96	18.02	20.50	22.71	25.94
商业、饮食、物资供销和仓储业	Commerce,Catering Services, Materials Supply and Storage	7.17	8.16	9.67	10.43	12.42	14.80
其他	Others	19.49	15.86	18.80	20.25	23.26	25.58
生活消费	Residential Consumption	62.70	74.70	88.79	106.15	122.17	145.06
在消费量中：	Consumption by Usage						
终端消费	Final Consumption	544.37	624.09	632.08	696.10	774.62	883.42
#工业	Industry	428.61	493.21	484.54	524.26	578.74	654.82
输配损失量	Losses in Transmission	37.61	45.00	47.10	54.20	60.90	60.71

7-5 分行业能源消费总量

Basic Statistics on Energy Consumption by Sector

单位：万吨标准煤 (10000 tons of SCE)

行 业	Sector	2006	2007	2008	2009	2010	2011
工业	Industry	4045.78	4472.20	4613.69	4945.38	5289.48	5895.87
采掘业	Mining and Quarring	578.64	480.69	483.17	645.89	751.50	685.36
#煤炭采选业	Coal Mining and Dressing	507.56	444.62	430.61	546.11	682.81	606.00
黑色金属矿采选业	Ferrous Metals Mining and Dressing	4.78	2.38	6.22	10.32	9.58	9.85
有色金属矿采选业	Nonferrous Metals Mining and Dressing	7.02	13.23	15.40	14.90	14.08	16.91
非金属矿采选业	Nonmetal Minerals Mining and Dressing	51.05	11.78	21.70	22.50	22.03	27.37
制造业	Manufacturing	3056.54	3606.00	3584.32	3844.63	4028.50	4733.39
食品加工业	Food Processing	12.77	13.70	11.84	14.31	12.76	14.23
食品制造业	Food Production	8.98	9.06	7.35	8.95	9.41	13.13
饮料制造业	Beverage Production	29.42	34.62	46.70	54.51	50.43	73.72
烟草加工业	Tobacco Processing	25.54	30.38	29.85	30.87	22.07	20.51
纺织业	Textile Industry	4.70	5.62	4.18	3.06	2.60	2.73
服装及其他纤维制品制造业	Garments and Other Fiber Products	1.16	1.17	1.50	0.98	1.12	1.43
皮革、毛皮、羽绒及其制品业	Leather,Furs,Down and Related Products	0.04	0.01		0.13	0.16	0.21
木材加工及竹、藤、棕、草制品业	Timber Processing,Bamboo,Cane,Palm Fiber and Straw Products	5.88	7.39	6.50	6.49	6.43	7.50
家具制造业	Furniture Manufacturing	0.70	0.73	0.36	0.03	0.33	0.42
造纸及纸制品业	Papermaking and Paper Products	12.13	12.41	8.28	7.74	10.69	25.27
印刷业,记录媒介的复制	Printing and Record Medium Reproduction	2.33	2.10	2.07	2.00	1.75	1.66
文教体育用品制造业	Cultural,Educational and Sports Articles	0.17	0.20	0.13	0.10	0.31	0.49
石油加工及炼焦业	Petroleum Processing and Coking	140.79	128.25	122.42	91.07	127.21	207.44
化学原料及化学制品制造业	Raw Chemical Materials and Chemical Products	998.11	978.23	1055.77	1034.99	1000.00	1189.63
医药制造业	Medical and Pharmaceutical Products	14.57	14.13	16.45	16.24	13.94	18.56

7-5 续表 continued

行 业	Sector	2006	2007	2008	2009	2010	2011
化学纤维制造业	Chemical Fibers	1.20	0.50	0.66	21.60	22.27	14.06
橡胶制品业	Rubber Products	39.98	44.92	49.41	50.02	51.82	54.92
塑料制品业	Plastic Products	2.92	1.30	4.15	6.77	9.87	9.17
非金属矿物制品业	Nonmetal Mineral Products	521.70	601.75	652.21	829.55	870.29	945.45
黑色金属冶炼及压延加工业	Smelting and Pressing of Ferrous Metals	707.22	897.34	835.45	851.89	955.29	1066.28
有色金属冶炼及压延加工业	Smelting and Pressing of Nonferrous Metals	408.20	739.99	612.57	678.60	759.11	943.84
金属制品业	Metal Products	15.83	18.91	53.57	61.08	28.22	36.74
普通机械制造业	Ordinary Machinery Manufacturing	12.11	13.91	18.93	12.72	17.00	17.34
专用设备制造业	Special Purposes Equipment Manufacturing	8.07	6.59	3.93	8.10	7.72	7.71
交通运输设备制造业	Transportation Equipment Manufacturing	26.97	22.79	20.37	19.70	16.74	17.54
电气机械及器材制造业	Electric Equipment and Machinery	10.51	3.61	3.35	2.64	2.35	3.75
电子及通信设备制造业	Electronic and Telecommunications Equipment	3.07	1.90	2.57	1.77	1.69	2.64
仪器仪表及文化、办公用机械制造业	Instruments,Meters,Cultural and Office Machinery	0.78	0.55	0.52	0.42	0.27	0.27
其他制造业	Others	40.70	13.94	13.22	28.31	26.65	36.74
电力、煤气及水的生产和供应业	Electric Power, Gas and Tap Water Production and Distribution	410.60	385.51	546.20	454.86	509.49	477.12
电力、蒸汽、热水的生产和供应业	Electric Power• Steam and Hot Water Production and Distribution	364.58	363.22	513.34	424.46	471.33	437.02
煤气生产和供应业	Gas Production and Distribution	37.58	10.87	21.76	19.32	26.14	26.59
自来水的生产和供应业	Tap Water Production and Distribution	8.44	11.42	11.09	11.08	12.02	13.51
建筑业	Construction	60.90	62.55	63.54	75.65	82.51	76.13
交通运输、仓储及邮电通信业	Transportation,Storage,Postal & Telecommunications Services	309.40	390.57	453.32	467.62	538.48	597.73
批发和零售贸易餐饮业	Wholesale,Retail Trade and Catering Services	275.71	356.50	415.31	488.22	513.29	554.60
其他行业	Others	436.13	472.84	534.85	566.35	614.04	675.13
生活消费	Residential Consumption	905.62	903.78	856.78	870.17	995.67	1138.87

7-6 能源生产消费弹性系数

Elasticity Ratio of Energy Production and Consumption

指 标	Item	2006	2007	2008	2009	2010	2011
生产总值比上年增长(%)	Growth Rate of Gross Domestic Product (GDP) over Preceding Year	12.8	14.8	11.3	11.4	12.8	15.0
能源生产比上年增长(%)	Growth Rate of Energy Production over Preceding Year	1.7	4.8	9.2	19.5	18.3	-2.8
能源消费总量比上年增长(%)	Growth Rate of Energy Consumption over Preceding Year	9.4	10.2	4.2	6.8	8.1	10.9
电力生产比上年增长(%)	Growth Rate of Electricity Production over Preceding Year	27.9	20.0	14.3	15.8	0.4	-0.9
电力消费比上年增长(%)	Growth Rate of Electricity Consumption over Preceding Year	19.5	15.0	1.5	10.5	11.4	13.0
能源生产弹性系数	Elasticity Ratio of Energy Production	0.13	0.32	0.82	1.71	1.43	
能源消费弹性系数	Elasticity Ratio of Energy Consumption	0.74	0.69	0.37	0.60	0.63	0.73
电力生产弹性系数	Elasticity Ratio of Electricity Production	2.18	1.35	1.27	1.39	0.03	
电力消费弹性系数	Elasticity Ratio of Electricity Consumption	1.52	1.01	0.13	0.92	0.89	0.87

注:生产总值增长速度按可比价格计算。
Note:The growth rates of GDP are calculated at comparable prices.

7-7 生活能源消费量

Energy Consumption for Non-Production Purpose

能源品种	Item	2006	2007	2008	2009	2010	2011
生活能源消费量(万吨标准煤)	**Energy Consumption for Non-Production Purpose (10000 tons of SCE)**	**905.62**	**903.78**	**856.78**	**870.17**	**995.67**	**1138.87**
煤炭(万吨)	Coal (10000 tons)	828.58	790.46	652.32	614.31	624.63	714.36
煤油(万吨)	Kerosene (10000 tons)	0.03	0.48	0.05	0.05	0.04	0.04
液化石油气(万吨)	Liquefied Petroleum Gas (10000 tons)	5.01	7.60	10.12	8.33	8.82	9.55
天然气(亿立方米)	Natural Gas(100 million cu.m)	0.10	0.10	0.10	0.11	0.12	0.13
煤气(亿立方米)	Gas (100 million cu.m)	0.93	0.94	0.94	1.09	1.14	1.28
电力(亿千瓦小时)	Electricity (100 million kwh)	62.70	74.70	88.79	106.15	122.17	145.06

7–8 人均生活能源消费量

Annual Average Per Capita Energy Consumption for Non-Production Purpose

指　标	Item	2006	2007	2008	2009	2010	2011
平均每人生活消费能源（千克标准煤/人）	**Annual Average Non-Productive Consumption Per Capita(kg of SCE/person)**	**241.91**	**240.38**	**226.80**	**229.27**	**287.26**	**327.83**
煤炭(千克)	Coal(kg)	221.33	210.24	172.68	161.85	180.21	205.63
电力(千瓦小时)	Electricity(kwh)	167.49	198.68	235.04	279.67	352.48	417.56
液化石油气(千克)	Liquefied Petroleum Gas(kg)	1.34	2.02	2.68	2.19	2.54	2.75
煤气(立方米)	Gas(cu.m)	2.48	2.50	2.49	2.87	3.29	3.68

7–9 能源利用效率

Using Efficiency of Energy

指标	Item	2006	2007	2008	2009	2010	2011
每万元生产总值能源消费量（吨标准煤/万元）（可比价）	**Energy Consumption Per Unit of GDP (ton of SCE/10000 yuan) (at comparable prices)**	**2.7283**	**2.6173**	**2.4495**	**2.3480**	**2.2480**	**1.7140**
每万元生产总值电力消费量（千瓦小时/万元）	**Electricity Consumption Per Unit of GDP(kwh/10000 yuan)**	**2572.42**	**2575.41**	**2348.47**	**2328.02**	**2297.45**	**1784.56**
每万元生产总值煤炭消费量（吨/万元）	**Coal Consumption Per Unit of GDP (ton/10000 yuan)**	**3.98**	**3.68**	**3.37**	**3.39**	**3.07**	**2.28**
能源消费总量(万吨标准煤)	Total Energy Consumption (10000 tons of SCE)	6172.45	6799.72	7083.99	7566.33	8175.43	9067.85
每吨能源生产的生产总值(万元/吨)	GDP Produced by Per Unit of Energy (10000 yuan/ton)	0.37	0.38	0.41	0.43	0.44	0.58
规模以上工业能源消费量(万吨标准煤)	Energy Consumption of Industry above Designated Size(10000 tons of SCE)	3586.40	3931.63	3827.03	4231.41	4373.38	4803.14
规模以上工业万元增加值能源消费量(吨标准煤/万元)	Energy Consumption Per Unit of Value-added of Industry above Designated Size (ton of SCE/10000 yuan)	5.210	4.890	4.323	4.322	3.857	3.18

注:2011年生产总值和工业增加值按2010年可比价格计算，其余年份按2005年可比价格计算。

Note:In 2011,industry value-added and GDP are calculated at 2010 comparable prices and they in other years were calculated at 2005 comparable prices .

主要统计指标解释

能源生产总量 指一定时期内全省一次能源生产量的总和。一次能源生产量包括原煤，原油，天然气，水电、核能及其他动力能（如风能、地热能等）发电量，不包括低热值燃料生产量、生物质能、太阳能等的利用和由一次能源加工转换而成的二次能源产量。

能源消费总量 指一定时期内全省物质生产部门、非物质生产部门和生活消费的各种能源的总和。能源消费总量包括原煤和原油及其制品、天然气、电力，不包括低热值燃料、生物质能和太阳能等的利用。能源消费总量分为终端能源消费量、能源加工转换损失量和损失量三部分。

(1) 终端能源消费量：指一定时期内全省生产和生活消费的各种能源在扣除了用于加工转换二次能源消费量和损失量以后的数量。

(2) 能源加工转换损失量：指一定时期内全省投入加工转换的各种能源数量之和与产出各种能源产品之和的差额，是观察能源在加工转换过程中损失量变化的指标。

(3) 能源损失量：指一定时期内能源在输送、分配、储存过程中发生的损失和由客观原因造成的各种损失量，不包括各种气体能源放空、放散量。

能源生产弹性系数 是研究能源生产增长速度与地区生产总值增长速度之间关系的指标。计算公式为:

$$能源生产弹性系数 = \frac{能源生产总量年平均增长速度}{地区生产总值年平均增长速度}$$

电力生产弹性系数 是研究电力生产增长速度与地区生产总值增长速度之间关系的指标。一般来说，电力的发展应当快于经济的发展，也就是说电力应超前发展。计算公式为:

$$电力生产弹性系数 = \frac{电力生产量年平均增长速度}{地区生产总值年平均增长速度}$$

能源消费弹性系数 是反映能源消费增长速度与地区生产总值增长速度之间比例关系的指标。计算公式为:

$$能源消费弹性系数 = \frac{能源消费量年平均增长速度}{地区生产总值年平均增长速度}$$

电力消费弹性系数 反映电力消费增长速度与地区生产总值增长速度之间比例关系的指标。计算公式为:

$$电力消费弹性系数 = \frac{电力消费量年平均增长速度}{地区生产总值年平均增长速度}$$

能源加工转换效率 指一定时期内能源经过加工、转换后，产出的各种能源产品的数量与同期内投入加工转换的各种能源数量的比率。它是观察能源加工转换装置和生产工艺先进与落后、管理水平高低等的重要指标。计算公式为:

$$能源加工转换效率 = \frac{能源加工、转换产出量}{能源加工、转换投入量} \times 100\%$$

单位生产总值能耗 指一定时期内，每生产一个单位的生产总值所消耗的能源。计算公式为:

$$单位生产总值能耗 = \frac{能源消费总量}{地区生产总值}$$

单位生产总值电耗 指一定时期内，每生产一个单位的生产总值所消耗的电力。计算公式为:

$$单位生产总值电耗 = \frac{全社会用电量}{地区生产总值}$$

单位工业增加值能耗 指一定时期内，每生产一个单位的工业增加值所消耗的能源。计算公式为:

$$单位工业增加值能耗 = \frac{工业能源消费量}{工业增加值}$$

Explanatory Notes on Main Statistical Indicators

Total Energy Production refers to the total production of primary energy by all energy producing enterprises in the country in a given period of time. The production of primary energy includes that of coal, crude oil, natural gas, hydro-power and electricity generated by nuclear energy and other means such as wind power and geothermal power. However, it excludes the production of fuels of low calorific value, bio-energy, solar energy and the secondary energy converted from the primary energy.

Total Energy Consumption refers to the total consumption of energy of various kinds by material production sectors, non material production sectors and households in the province in a given period of time. It is a comprehensive indicator to show the scale, composition and development of energy consumption. The total energy consumption includes that of coal, crude oil and their products, natural gas and electricity, however, it excludes the consumption of fuel of low calorific value, bio-energy and solar energy. Total domestic energy consumption can be divided into three parts:

(1)End-use Energy Consumption: It refers to the total energy consumption by material production sectors, non material production sectors and households in the country(region)in a given period of time, but excludes the consumption in conversion of the primary energy into the secondary energy and the loss in the process of energy conversion.

(2)Loss During the Process of Energy Conversion: It refers to the total input of various kinds of energy for conversion, minus the total output of various kinds of energy in the country in a given period of time. It is an indicator to show the loss that occurs during the process of energy conversion.

(3)Loss: It refers to the total of the loss of energy during the course of energy transport, distribution and storage and the loss caused by any objective reason in a given period of time. The loss of various kinds of gas due to gas discharges and stocktaking is excluded.

Elasticity Ratio of Energy Production is an indicator to show the relationship between the growth rate of energy production and the growth rate of the national (regional) economy. The formula is:

$$\text{Elasticity Ratio of Energy Production}=\frac{\text{Average Annual Growth Rate of Energy Production}}{\text{Average Annual Growth Rate of National(regional) Economy}}$$

The average annual growth rate of the national(regional) economy can be shown by the gross national(regional) product, gross domestic product and other indicators, depending upon the purposes or needs. The gross (regional) product is used in calculation of the ratio in this chapter.

Elasticity Ratio of Electricity Production is an indicator to show the relationship between the growth rate of electricity production and the growth rate of the national(regional) economy. Generally speaking, the growth rate of electricity production should be higher than that of the national(regional) economy. Its formula is:

$$\text{Elasticity Ratio of Electricity Production}=\frac{\text{Average Annual Growth Rate of Electricity Production}}{\text{Average Annual Growth Rate of National(regional) Economy}}$$

Elasticity Ratio of Energy Consumption is an indicator to show the relationship between the growth rate of energy consumption and the growth rate of the national(regional) economy. The formula is:

$$\text{Elasticity Ratio of Energy Consumption}=\frac{\text{Average Annual Growth Rate of Energy Consumption}}{\text{Average Annual Growth Rate of National(regional) Economy}}$$

Elasticity Ratio of Electricity Consumption is an indicator to show the relationship between the growth rate of electricity consumption and the growth rate of the national(regional) economy. The formula is:

$$\text{Elasticity Ratio of Electricity Consumption}=\frac{\text{Average Annual Growth Rate of Electricity}}{\text{Average Annual Growth Rate of National(regional) Economy}}$$

Efficiency of Energy Processing and Conversion refers to the ratio of the total output of energy products of various kinds after processing and conversion and the total input of energy of various kinds for processing and conversion in the same reference period. It is an important indicator to show the current conditions of energy processing and conversion equipment, production technique and management. The formula is:

$$\text{Efficiency of Energy Processing \& Conversion}=\frac{\text{Output of Energy After Processing \& Conversion}}{\text{Input of Energy for Processing \& Conversion}}\times 100\%$$

Energy Consumption per Unit of GDP refers to the energy consumption per unit of Gross Domestic Product in a country or the Gross Regional Product in a region in the same reference period. The formula is:

$$\text{Energy Consumption per Unit of GDP}=\frac{\text{Total Energy Consumption}}{\text{Gross Domestic(regional) Product}}$$

Electricity Consumption per Unit of GDP refers to the electricity consumption per unit of Gross Domestic Product in a country or the Gross Regional Product in a region in the same reference period. The formula is:

$$\text{Electricity Consumption per Unit of GDP}=\frac{\text{Total Electricity Consumption}}{\text{Gross Domestic (regional)Product}}$$

Energy Consumption per Unit of Industrial Value-added refers to the energy consumption per unit of industrial value-added in a country or region in the same reference period. The formula is:

$$\text{Energy Consumption per Unit of Industrial Value-added}=\frac{\text{Total Energy Consumption}}{\text{Industrial Value-added}}$$

8

Eight

财政税收

Government Finance and Taxation

8-1 财政收入
Financial Revenue

单位：亿元 (100 million yuan)

指　标	Item	2006	2007	2008	2009	2010	2011	2011年比2010年增长(%) Increase Rate in 2011 over 2010(%)
财政总收入	**Total Government Revenue**	**448.88**	**556.98**	**674.58**	**779.59**	**969.57**	**1329.99**	**37.2**
#一般预算收入	Local Financial Revenue	226.82	285.14	349.55	416.48	533.73	773.08	44.8
#增值税	Value-added Tax	38.19	45.94	55.14	57.47	66.00	76.41	15.8
营业税	Business Tax	55.73	68.27	80.33	104.31	136.73	181.73	32.9
企业所得税	Company Income Tax	21.41	29.88	35.70	42.34	51.14	70.69	38.2
个人所得税	Personal Income Tax	11.04	14.72	18.41	21.32	27.42	33.24	21.2
资源税	Resource Tax	3.07	4.32	5.33	8.49	11.01	11.95	8.6
城市维护建设税	Urban Maintenance and Development Tax	15.42	18.89	22.07	24.45	29.18	37.82	29.6
房产税	Tax on Real Estates	5.12	5.78	6.29	7.43	8.41	9.73	15.7
契税	Contract Tax	4.71	6.34	7.85	8.69	13.98	23.91	71.0
土地增值税	Value-added Tax on Land	1.43	3.01	3.73	5.81	11.98	13.76	14.8
国有资本经营收入	State-owned Assets Profit	6.90	6.42	4.34	6.04	4.88	6.38	30.9
罚没收入	Penalty and Confiscatory Income	12.15	12.90	12.67	14.23	16.66	23.50	41.1
行政事业性收费收入	Income from Administrative Fees	16.77	18.48	19.76	19.08	30.06	45.98	53.0
专项收入	Special Project Income	13.92	24.85	40.65	46.56	59.07	85.91	45.4

注:资料来源于省财政厅(以下相关表同)。
Note:Data in the table are provided by the Provincial Department of Finance(The relative tables in this chapter are the same).

8-2 财政支出
Financial Expenditure

单位：亿元 (100 million yuan)

指　标	Item	2007	2008	2009	2010	2011	2011年比2010年增长(%) Increase Rate in 2011 over 2010(%)
总　计	**Total**	**795.40**	**1055.39**	**1372.27**	**1631.48**	**2249.40**	**37.9**
一般公共服务	Common Public Service	148.95	184.21	196.78	212.69	307.21	44.4
国防	National Defence	1.75	1.58	2.81	3.66	4.15	13.2
公共安全	Public Security	57.22	68.07	82.95	101.46	117.31	15.6
教育	Education	166.27	229.77	256.72	292.06	376.86	29.0
科学技术	Science and Technology	9.98	12.99	14.27	16.66	21.68	30.1
文化体育与传媒	Culture,Sports and Media	15.71	17.84	23.62	23.98	35.31	47.3
社会保障和就业	Social Security and Jobs	70.80	107.46	150.04	140.76	194.78	38.4
医疗卫生	Health Care	48.79	67.44	102.84	127.68	173.26	35.7
环境保护	Environmental Protection	26.67	40.44	55.31	54.32	55.45	2.1
城乡社区事务	Urban and Country Community Affairs	27.42	46.51	43.74	53.00	65.52	23.6
农林水事务	Affairs of Agriculture,Forest and Water	87.53	121.71	204.13	246.76	278.47	12.9
交通运输	Transport	48.84	49.39	120.80	109.61	305.16	178.4

8-3 分级一般预算收入(2011)

Local Government Financial Revenue by Level

单位：亿元 (100 million yuan)

指 标	Item	总 计 Provincial Total	省 级 Province	地 级 Prefecture	县 级 County	乡镇级 Villages and Towns
一般预算收入	**Local Financial Revenue**	**773.08**	**165.31**	**169.53**	**353.29**	**84.94**
#增值税	Value-added Tax	76.41	30.56	10.29	25.83	9.72
营业税	Business Tax	181.73	37.89	40.66	73.36	29.82
企业所得税	Company Income Tax	70.69	24.50	14.68	23.04	8.47
个人所得税	Personal Income Tax	33.24	0.06	7.21	18.52	7.45
资源税	Resource Tax	11.95	3.59	1.54	3.98	2.85
城市维护建设税	Urban Maintenance and Development Tax	37.82	…	16.02	17.62	4.17
房产税	Tax on Real Estates	9.73		3.71	5.17	0.85
契税	Contract Tax	23.91		8.11	13.48	2.31
土地增值税	Value-added Tax on Land	13.76		4.05	7.63	2.08
国有资本经营收入	State-owned Assets Profit	6.38	0.08	1.00	5.15	0.15
罚没收入	Penalty and Confiscatory Income	23.50	4.57	4.92	13.65	0.36
行政性收费收入	Income from Administrative Fees	45.98	11.13	8.09	25.23	1.54
专项收入	Special Project Income	85.91	24.86	21.78	37.27	2.00

8-4 分级一般预算支出(2011)

Local Financial Expenditure by Level

单位：亿元 (100 million yuan)

指 标	Item	总计 Total	省 级 Province	地 级 Prefecture	县 级 County	乡镇级 Villages and Towns
一般预算支出	**Local Financial Expenditure**	**2249.40**	**561.30**	**310.07**	**1233.69**	**144.34**
#一般公共服务	Common Public Service	307.21	44.63	43.55	152.77	66.25
国防	National Defence	4.15	1.28	1.57	1.28	0.02
公共安全	Public Security	117.31	32.25	23.37	60.98	0.72
教育	Education	376.86	39.57	35.54	288.53	13.21
科学技术	Science and Technology	21.68	8.72	4.39	8.47	0.10
文化体育与传媒	Culture,Sports and Media	35.31	14.80	8.85	10.24	1.42
社会保障和就业	Social Security and Jobs	194.78	37.32	29.09	120.66	7.70
医疗卫生	Health Care	173.26	14.12	24.90	131.75	2.48
环境保护	Environmental Protection	55.45	5.91	7.36	40.46	1.71
城乡社区事务	Urban and Country Community Affairs	65.52	0.58	17.98	42.17	4.79
农林水事务	Affairs of Agriculture,Forest and Water	278.47	52.64	19.11	175.68	31.04
交通运输	Transport	305.16	261.83	14.87	27.95	0.51

8-5 税收收入(按产业分)
Tax Revenue(by Industry)

单位：亿元 (100million yuan)

项　　目	Item	2006	2007	2008	2009	2010	2011
税收收入合计	**Total**	**375.15**	**464.73**	**577.62**	**660.15**	**807.26**	**1021.39**
第一产业	Primary Industry	…	0.02	0.18	0.57	1.26	1.20
第二产业	Secondary Industry	239.68	287.17	349.16	383.55	448.88	574.26
采矿业	Mining and Quarrying	31.95	42.40	67.05	87.91	118.05	142.59
制造业	Manufacturing	141.82	166.32	194.37	197.47	226.09	293.84
电力、燃气及水的生产和供应业	Production and Distribution of Electric Power,Gas and Water	43.72	55.36	61.80	66.34	60.65	59.42
建筑业	Construction	22.20	23.09	25.94	31.82	44.09	78.41
第三产业	Tertiary Industry	135.47	177.54	228.28	276.04	357.13	445.93
交通运输、仓储及邮政业	Transport,Storage and Post	9.93	13.95	15.04	13.96	16.10	19.04
信息传输、计算机服务和软件业	Information Transmission,Computer Services and Software	6.42	7.15	8.23	11.83	12.14	14.19
批发和零售业	Wholesale and Retail Trade	57.02	78.50	95.46	107.79	131.90	170.04
住宿和餐饮业	Hotel and Catering Services	4.01	4.76	5.65	6.20	7.21	9.05
金融业	Financial Intermediation	10.37	14.77	22.51	28.40	39.12	55.61
房地产业	Real Estates	17.16	26.10	29.24	42.23	69.94	86.88
租赁和商务服务业	Leasing and Business Services	15.19	15.67	17.59	13.99	17.59	24.01
居民服务和其他服务业	Services to Households and Other Services		3.63	8.76	8.12	10.49	20.08
教育	Education	0.49	0.44	0.74	0.89	1.14	1.45
卫生、社会保险和社会福利业	Health,Social Security and Social Welfare		0.43	0.54	0.85	1.61	1.71
文化、体育和娱乐业	Culture,Sports and Entertainment	1.14	1.12	1.55	2.12	2.36	2.80
公共管理和社会组织	Public Management and Social Organization			3.64	5.39	6.39	9.41
其他行业	Others	13.74	11.02	19.33	34.30	41.13	31.65

注：资料来源于省国税局、省地税局(以下相关表同)。

Note:Data in the table are provided by Guizhou Provincial National Taxation Beaura and Local Taxation Beaura of Guizhou Province(the relative tables in this chapter are the same).

8-6 税收收入(按企业类型分)

Taxation Revenue (by Business Entities)

单位：亿元 (100 million yuan)

项 目	Item	2006	2007	2008	2009	2010	2011
总 计	**Total**	**375.15**	**464.73**	**577.62**	**660.15**	**807.26**	**1021.39**
内资企业	Domestic Enterprises	330.72	414.65	511.51	585.25	720.82	914.58
国有企业	State-owned Enterprises	136.31	157.93	192.95	108.23	117.19	126.59
集体企业	Collective-owned Enterprises	8.13	8.01	8.59	10.19	12.57	15.17
股份合作企业	Cooperative Enterprises	1.97	2.95	4.41	4.95	7.67	11.52
联营企业	Joint Ownership Enterprises	0.46	0.58	0.72	0.95	0.78	0.87
#国有控股	State-owned and State-controlled Enterprises	0.09	0.07	0.03	0.03	0.10	0.48
股份公司	Share-holding Corporations Limited	149.13	197.14	238.68	381.45	474.28	636.01
#国有控股	State-owned and State-controlled Enterprises	54.65	69.59	63.69	143.76	177.53	274.39
私营企业	Private Enterprises	26.44	38.52	55.02	65.50	87.90	100.32
其它企业	Other Enterprises	8.28	9.52	11.14	13.98	20.44	24.09
港澳台投资企业	Enterprises with Funds from Hong Kong, Macao and Taiwan	2.72	3.12	3.91	4.44	5.01	5.30
#国有控股	State-owned and State-controlled Enterprises	0.19	0.14	0.24	0.18	0.12	0.46
外商投资企业	Foreign Funded Enterprises	8.95	10.75	12.07	18.24	21.03	24.70
#国有控股	State-owned and State-controlled Enterprises	0.36	0.28	0.24	0.30	0.27	2.71
个体经营	Individual Operators	32.76	36.21	50.12	52.22	60.41	76.79
附：乡(镇)企业	Township and Village Enterprises	18.87	20.04	22.14	26.07	35.23	48.93

8-7 国税税收收入(按产业分)
National Tax Revenue (by Industry)

单位：亿元 (100 million yuan)

项目	Item	2006	2007	2008	2009	2010	2011
税收收入合计	**Total**	**237.37**	**285.04**	**353.45**	**385.38**	**458.13**	**568.60**
第一产业	Primary Industry		0.01	0.15	0.51	1.16	1.03
第二产业	Secondary Industry	186.97	220.02	261.91	275.14	312.66	382.23
采矿业	Mining and Quarrying	23.56	28.23	42.64	51.31	70.37	82.10
制造业	Manufacturing	124.84	144.31	165.91	167.98	189.93	250.64
电力、燃气及水的生产和供应业	Production and Distribution of Electric Power,Gas and Water	38.32	47.03	52.41	54.63	50.66	47.18
建筑业	Construction	0.26	0.45	0.95	1.22	1.69	2.31
第三产业	Tertiary Industry	50.40	65.02	91.39	109.73	144.31	185.33
交通运输、仓储及邮政业	Transport,Storage and Post	0.05	0.24	0.70	1.45	2.48	3.05
信息传输、计算机服务和软件业	Information Transmission,Computer Services and Software	3.36	3.51	3.43	6.57	6.15	7.09
批发和零售业	Wholesale and Retail Trade	37.93	49.21	60.70	68.56	89.03	111.23
住宿和餐饮业	Hotel and Catering Services	0.02	0.03	0.07	0.08	0.12	0.17
金融业	Financial Intermediation	1.93	2.90	5.31	6.50	11.38	19.84
房地产业	Real Estates	1.18	2.03	3.09	7.26	10.73	13.99
租赁和商务服务业	Leasing and Business Services	0.13	0.20	0.43	1.16	1.87	2.25
居民服务和其他服务业	Services to Households and Other Services		0.12	0.55	0.72	0.78	0.89
教育	Education		0.01	0.03	0.06	0.09	0.13
卫生、社会保险和社会福利业	Health,Social Security and Social Welfare		…	0.02	0.05	0.10	0.15
文化、体育和娱乐业	Culture,Sports and Entertainment	…	0.01	0.03	0.18	0.18	0.24
公共管理和社会组织	Public Management and Social Organization			1.65	1.58	2.14	3.91
其他行业	Others	5.79	6.77	15.39	15.55	19.24	22.38

8-8 地方系统税收收入(按产业分)
Local Tax Revenue(by Industry)

单位：亿元 (100 million yuan)

项　　目	Item	2006	2007	2008	2009	2010	2011
税收收入合计	**Total**	**137.78**	**179.69**	**224.17**	**274.78**	**349.13**	**452.79**
第一产业	Primary Industry	…	0.01	0.03	0.05	0.10	0.17
第二产业	Secondary Industry	52.71	67.16	87.25	108.41	136.22	192.03
采矿业	Mining and Quarrying	8.39	14.17	24.41	36.61	47.68	60.49
制造业	Manufacturing	16.98	22.01	28.45	29.49	36.16	43.20
电力、燃气及水的生产和供应业	Production and Distribution of Electric Power,Gas and Water	5.40	8.33	9.39	11.71	9.99	12.24
建筑业	Construction	21.94	22.65	25.00	30.60	42.39	76.10
第三产业	Tertiary Industry	85.08	112.52	136.89	166.32	212.82	260.59
交通运输、仓储及邮政业	Transport,Storage and Post	9.88	13.71	14.34	12.50	13.62	15.99
信息传输、计算机服务和软件业	Information Transmission,Computer Services and Software	3.05	3.64	4.81	5.26	5.99	7.10
批发和零售业	Wholesale and Retail Trade	19.10	29.29	34.76	39.23	42.87	58.81
住宿和餐饮业	Hotel and Catering Services	3.99	4.72	5.58	6.11	7.09	8.88
金融业	Financial Intermediation	8.44	11.87	17.20	21.91	27.73	35.77
房地产业	Real Estates	15.98	24.08	26.15	34.97	59.21	72.89
租赁和商务服务业	Leasing and Business Services	15.06	15.47	17.16	12.82	15.72	21.76
居民服务和其他服务业	Services to Households and Other Services		3.52	8.21	7.40	9.71	19.19
教育	Education	0.49	0.44	0.71	0.83	1.05	1.32
卫生、社会保险和社会福利业	Health,Social Security and Social Welfare		0.43	0.53	0.80	1.51	1.56
文化、体育和娱乐业	Culture,Sports and Entertainment	1.13	1.12	1.52	1.94	2.18	2.56
公共管理和社会组织	Public Management and Social Organization			1.99	3.80	4.25	5.50
其他行业	Others	7.95	4.25	3.94	18.75	21.89	9.27

8–9 国税税收收入(按企业类型分)

National Taxation Revenue(by Business Entities)

单位：亿元 (100 million yuan)

项 目	Item	2006	2007	2008	2009	2010	2011
总 计	**Total**	**237.37**	**285.04**	**353.45**	**385.38**	**458.13**	**568.60**
内资企业	Domestic Enterprises	219.09	263.81	321.67	348.82	412.92	514.21
国有企业	State-owned Enterprises	102.55	117.98	141.34	51.97	59.33	62.20
集体企业	Collective-owned Enterprises	2.29	2.12	2.45	3.56	5.26	7.65
股份合作企业	Cooperative Enterprises	0.63	1.18	1.64	2.71	4.80	7.95
联营企业	Joint Ownership Enterprises	0.37	0.44	0.54	0.73	0.50	0.62
#国有控股	State-owned and State-controlled Enterprises	0.08	0.06	0.03	0.03	0.08	0.47
股份公司	Share-holding Corporations Limited	92.30	116.01	138.23	248.46	289.50	376.54
#国有控股	State-owned and State-controlled Enterprises	40.55	47.15	40.67	116.02	146.25	220.87
私营企业	Private Enterprises	19.28	25.14	36.02	39.68	50.92	55.19
其它企业	Other Enterprises	1.67	0.94	1.46	1.72	2.62	4.06
港澳台投资企业	Enterprises with Funds from Hong Kong, Macao and Taiwan	1.83	2.13	2.97	3.12	3.44	3.30
#国有控股	State-owned and State-controlled Enterprises	0.17	0.13	0.22	0.16	0.10	0.08
外商投资企业	Foreign Funded Enterprises	6.99	8.18	8.33	13.74	15.67	17.83
#国有控股	State-owned and State-controlled Enterprises	0.28	0.20	0.18	0.25	0.23	0.36
个体经营	Individual Operators	9.46	10.93	20.48	19.70	26.10	33.25
附：乡(镇)企业	Township and Village Enterprises	12.06	12.93	14.62	17.38	23.39	32.41

8-10 地方系统税收收入(按企业类型分)

Local Taxation Revenue (by Business Entities)

单位：亿元 (100 million yuan)

项　目	Item	2006	2007	2008	2009	2010	2011
总　计	**Total**	**137.78**	**179.69**	**224.17**	**274.78**	**349.13**	**452.79**
内资企业	Domestic Enterprises	111.63	150.84	189.84	236.43	307.90	400.37
国有企业	State-owned Enterprises	33.76	39.95	51.60	56.26	57.86	64.39
集体企业	Collective-owned Enterprises	5.84	5.89	6.15	6.64	7.31	7.52
股份合作企业	Cooperative Enterprises	1.34	1.77	2.77	2.24	2.87	3.57
联营企业	Joint Ownership Enterprises	0.10	0.14	0.18	0.22	0.27	0.25
#国有控股	State-owned and State-controlled Enterprises	0.01	0.01	0.00	0.01	0.02	0.01
股份公司	Share-holding Corporations Limited	56.83	81.13	100.46	132.99	184.78	259.47
#国有控股	State-owned and State-controlled Enterprises	14.10	22.44	23.02	27.74	31.29	53.52
私营企业	Private Enterprises	7.17	13.38	19.00	25.83	36.98	45.13
其它企业	Other Enterprises	6.61	8.58	9.69	12.26	17.82	20.03
港澳台投资企业	Enterprises with Funds from Hong Kong, Macao and Taiwan	0.89	1.00	0.94	1.32	1.57	2
#国有控股	State-owned and State-controlled Enterprises	0.02	0.01	0.02	0.02	0.02	0.38
外商投资企业	Foreign Funded Enterprises	1.96	2.56	3.74	4.49	5.36	6.87
#国有控股	State-owned and State-controlled Enterprises	0.08	0.08	0.06	0.05	0.03	2.35
个体经营	Individual Operators	23.30	25.29	29.65	32.52	34.31	43.54
附：乡(镇)企业	Township and Village Enterprises	6.81	7.11	7.52	8.69	11.84	16.52

注：表中数据不含契税、耕地占用税(以下相关表同)。
Nota:Data in the table don't include contract tax and farm land occupation tax(The relative tables in this chapter are the same).

8-11 国家税收收入(分行业、分税种)(2011)

单位：万元

项目	Item	合计 Total
合计	**Total**	**5685977**
第一产业	Primary Industry	10336
第二产业	Secondary Industry	3822313
采矿业	Mining and Quarrying	821040
煤炭开采和洗选业	Mining and Washing of Coal	709192
黑色金属矿采选业	Mining and Processing of Ferrous Metals	14490
有色金属矿采选业	Mining and Processing of Non-ferrous Metals	38439
非金属矿采选业	Mining and Processing of Nonmetal Minerals	56760
其他采矿业	Other Minings and Quarryings	2061
制造业	Manufacturing	2506378
农副食品加工业	Processing of Food from Agricultural Products	6157
食品制造业	Manufacture of Foods	24811
饮料制造业	Manufacture of Beverages	333075
#酒制造	Manufacture of Liquors	327229
烟草制品业	Manufacture of Tobacco	1490415
#卷烟制造	Tobacco Leaf Baking	1478285
纺织业	Manufacture of Textile	2078
纺织服装、鞋帽制造业	Manufacture of Textile Wearing Apparel, Footware and Caps	3364
皮革、毛皮、羽毛(绒)制品业	Manufacture of Leather,Furs,Feather and Related Products	364
木材加工及木竹藤棕草制品业	Timber Processing,Manufacture of Wood,Bamboo, Rattan, Manufacture of Furniture	8160
家具制造业	Manufacture of Furniture	1918
造纸及纸制品业	Manufacture of Paper and Paper Products	4949
印刷业和记录媒体的复制	Printing,Reproduction of Recording Media	12824
文教体育用品制造业	Manufacture of Articles For Culture,Education and Sport Activity	14
石油加工、炼焦及核燃料业	Processing of Petroleum,Coking,Processing of Nuclear Fuel	31925
化学原料及化学制品业	Manufacture of Raw Chemical Materials and Chemical Products	76182
医药制造业	Manufacture of Medicines	94833
化学纤维制造业	Manufacture of Chemical Fibers	47

Taxation Revenue of the Central Government (By Industrial Sector and Taxation Category)

(10000 yuan)

国内增值税 Domestic Value-added Tax	#一般纳税人增值税 Value-added Tax from General Taxpayer	国内消费税 Domestic Consumption Tax	企业所得税 Corporate Income Tax	外商投资企业和外国企业所得税 Foreign-invested Enterprises and Foreign Enterprises Income Tax	个人所得税 Personal Income Tax	车辆购置税 Vehicle Purchase Tax
3064426	**2874448**	**1472518**	**744425**	**128751**	**1454**	**274403**
494	283		539	5		9298
2181311	2113266	1363680	208569	56914		11839
777431	763620		12661	27588		3360
697804	687703		9325	6		2057
13895	13784		452			143
10202	9985		529	27571		137
54469	51404		1776	11		504
1058	744		579			424
980103	964069	1363680	136824	21572		4199
3281	2776		2688	70		118
21890	21604		2580	51		290
91199	90390	237888	158	3367		463
87101	86679	237875	60	2069		124
316895	316894	1116706	56687	19		108
308308	308308	1116706	53250	19		2
1975	1954		65			38
1960	1857		1324	21		59
343	325		11			10
7370	5417		674	1		115
1477	1164		374			67
4446	4403		361	100		42
9776	9320		414	2609		25
9	4		1			4
28104	28082	1	3794			26
58344	58229	117	15541	1953		227
91316	91304		972	2408		137
39	38		1			7

8-11 续表1

单位：万元

项　目	Item	合　计 Total
橡胶制品业	Manufacture of Rubber	26648
塑料制品业	Manufacture of Plastics	10221
非金属矿物制品业	Manufacture of Non-metallic Mineral Products	106490
黑色金属冶炼及压延加工业	Smelting and Pressing of Ferrous Metals	82238
有色金属冶炼及压延加工业	Smelting and Pressing of Non-ferrous Metals	49425
金属制品业	Manufacture of Metal Products	22904
通用设备制造业	Manufacture of General Purpose Machinery	30228
专用设备制造业	Manufacture of Special Purpose Machinery	14677
交通运输设备制造业	Manufacture of Transport Equipment	27354
#汽车制造	Automobiles	17080
摩托车制造	Motorcycles	2
电气机械及器材制造业	Manufacture of Electrical Equipment and Machinery	21430
通信设备、计算机及其他电子设备制造业	Manufacture of Communication Equipment, Computers and Other Electronic Equipment	10411
仪表仪器及文化、办公用机械制造业	Manufacture of Measuring Instruments and Machinery for Cultural Activity and Office Work	3832
其他制造业	Other Manufacturing	9404
电力、燃气及水的生产和供应业	Production and Distribution of Electric Power, Gas and Water	471824
电力、热力的生产和供应业	Production and Distribution of Electric Power and Heat Power	460747
#电力生产和供应	Production of Electric Power	458431
燃气生产和供应业	Production and Distribution of Gas	3384
水的生产和供应业	Production and Distribution of Water	7693
建筑业	Construction	23071
房屋和土木工程建筑业	Building and Civil Engineering Construction	9519
建筑安装业	Construction and Installation	9907
建筑装饰业	Construction and Decoration	527
其他建筑业	Other Construction	3118
第三产业	Tertiary Industry	1853328
交通运输、仓储及邮政业	Transport,Storage and Post	30509
交通运输业	Transport	29297
仓储业	Storage	473
邮政业	Post	739

continued

(10000 yuan)

国内 增值税 Domestic Value-added Tax	#一般纳税人 增值税 Value-added Tax from General Taxpayer	国内 消费税 Domestic Consumption Tax	企业 所得税 Enterprises Income Tax	外商投资企业和 外国企业所得税 Foreign Enterprises Income Tax	个人 所得税 Personal Income Tax	车辆 购置税 Vehicle Purchase Tax
18689	18666	7387	564			8
8165	8034		711	1286		59
86654	80935		12780	5909		1147
76161	76104		6008	6		63
47992	47874		1362	23		48
19482	18779		3094	56		272
18271	17864		10089	1605		263
9329	9270		4666	523		159
19368	18056	1562	5072	1208		144
12636	11482	1503	2007	816		118
2	2					
18095	18017		3182	100		53
7265	7256		2894	229		23
3516	3496		282	27		7
8692	5957	19	475	1		217
422328	384370		42152	4996		2348
412480	374664		41860	4631		1776
411580	373770		41679	4631		541
2490	2472		166	320		408
7358	7234		126	45		164
1449	1207		16932	2758		1932
541	529		5673	2745		560
543	472		9081			283
130	65		285			112
235	141		1893	13		977
882621	760899	108838	535317	71832	1454	253266
581	519		3579	726		25623
405	351		3435	181		25276
167	167		43			263
9	1		101	545		84

8-11 续表2

单位：万元

项　　目	Item	合　计 Total
信息传输、计算机服务和软件业	Information Transmission,Computer Services and Software	70900
电信和其他信息传输服务业	Telecommunication and Information Transmission Services	66521
#电信	Telecommunication Services	66169
计算机服务业	Computer Services	2320
批发和零售业	Wholesale and Retail Trade	1112347
批发业	Wholesale	890229
#烟草制品批发	Tabacco	340215
煤炭及制品批发	Coal	69941
石油及其制品批发	Petroleum	36071
汽车及零配件批发	Spare and Component Parts for Automobiles	14141
零售业	Retail	222118
住宿和餐饮业	Hotel and Catering Services	1672
住宿业	Hotel	799
餐饮业	Catering	873
金融业	Financial Intermediation	198445
银行业	Banking Institutions	183150
证券业	Security Institutions	4056
保险业	Insurance Institutions	5454
其他金融	Other Financial Institutions	5785
房地产业	Real Estates	139947
租赁和商务服务业	Leasing and Business Services	22529
租赁业	Leasing	722
商务服务业	Business Services	21807
居民服务和其他服务业	Services to Households and Other Services	8854
教育	Education	1278
卫生、社会保险和社会福利业	Health,Social Security and Social Welfare	1530
文化、体育和娱乐业	Culture,Sports and Entertainment	2431
公共管理和社会组织	Public Management and Social Organization	39067
其他行业	Others	223819

continued

(10000 yuan)

国内 增值税 Domestic Value-added Tax	#一般纳税人 增值税 Value-added Tax from General Taxpayer	国内 消费税 Domestic Consumption Tax	企业 所得税 Enterprises Income Tax	外商投资企业和 外国企业所得税 Foreign Enterprises Income Tax	个人 所得税 Personal Income Tax	车辆 购置税 Vehicle Purchase Tax
3271	2951		6367	60886		376
147	132		5209	60875		290
139	127		5155	60875		
1656	1392		587	11		66
833015	746713	108838	152067	5899		12528
642781	633212	106058	137300	2233		1857
152482	152193	106014	81689			30
62959	62946		6944			38
22757	22744		13295	14		5
10307	10135		3778			56
190234	113501	2780	14767	3666		10671
254	236		965	366		87
234	229		516	3		46
20	7		449	363		41
470	439		195844	701		1430
466	439		181137	556		991
			3898	145		13
			5345			109
4			5464			317
71	66		134656	3012		2208
3481	2806		16130	179		2739
76	70		161			485
3405	2736		15969	179		2254
4160	1226		2777	28		1889
1			434	12		831
33	33		153			1344
1613	1532		465			353
29377			2739			6951
6294	4378		19141	23	1454	196907

8-12 地方系统税收收入(分行业、分税种)(2011)

单位：万元

项　　目	Item	合计 Total	营业税 Business Tax	企业所得税 Enterprises Income Tax
合 计	**Total**	**4527882**	**1817289**	**835114**
第一产业	Primary Industry	1701	654	138
第二产业	Secondary Industry	1920316	637198	359163
采矿业	Mining and Quarrying	604899	58594	142198
制造业	Manufacturing	432028	14770	92260
电力、燃气及水的生产和供应业	Production and Distribution of Electric Power, Gas and Water	122376	10611	28759
建筑业	Construction	761013	553223	95946
第三产业	Tertiary Industry	2605865	1179437	475813
交通运输、仓储及邮政业	Transport,Storage and Post	159886	93710	10382
信息传输、计算机服务和软件业	Information Transmission,Computer Services and Software	71032	53571	2179
批发和零售业	Wholesale and Retail Trade	588071	22634	341934
住宿和餐饮业	Hotel and Catering Services	88774	58153	2207
金融业	Financial Intermediation	357739	233341	2242
房地产业	Real Estates	728862	429160	58887
租赁和商务服务业	Leasing and Business Services	217564	113952	23830
居民服务和其他服务业	Services to Households and Other Services	191878	98873	10857
教育	Education	13234	4210	747
卫生、社会保险和社会福利业	Health,Social Security and Social Welfare	15572	1315	319
文化、体育和娱乐业	Culture,Sports and Entertainment	25589	14342	1767
公共管理和社会组织	Public Management and Social Organization	54960	14467	8751
其他行业	Others	92704	41709	11711

Taxation Revenue of the Local Government
(By Industrial Sector and Taxation Category)

(10000 yuan)

个人所得税 Personal Income Tax	城市维护建设税 Tax on City Maintenance and Construction	房产税 Tax on Real Estates	印花税 Stamp Tax	城镇土地使用税 Tax on the Use of Urban Land	土地增值税 Value-added Tax on Land	其他各税 Other Taxes
829554	**378180**	**97306**	**57200**	**126146**	**137578**	**249515**
314	219	126	110	127	4	9
431362	250746	32658	26422	62303	6148	114316
257767	42339	2312	4120	8934	1443	87192
74016	160121	20236	10731	40975	1200	17719
40181	22020	7294	5129	7934	395	53
59398	26266	2816	6442	4460	3110	9352
397878	127215	64522	30668	63716	131426	135190
38595	6771	3092	3063	3167	327	779
6785	3467	3478	311	1206	33	2
53518	45086	11632	8525	8770	1394	94578
19977	3792	3004	55	1385	201	
61274	15570	7336	3039	1682	403	32852
29231	28253	15113	6944	39304	121634	336
49144	8680	9521	5647	4342	2036	412
59685	7830	6377	1785	2045	2951	1475
6887	270	846	89	185		
13498	72	278	34	56		
7183	964	978	32	196	127	
23762	2485	930	224	177	1564	2600
28339	3975	1937	920	1201	756	2156

主要统计指标解释

财政收入 包括地方财政收入和上划中央增值税、消费税两部分。地方财政收入包括营业税、地方企业所得税、个人所得税、城镇土地使用税、固定资产投资方向调节税、城镇维护建设税、房产税、车船使用税、印花税、屠宰税、农牧业税、农业特产税、耕地占用税、契税、增值税25%部分、证券交易税（印花税）的50%部分和除海洋石油资源税以外的其他资源税。

财政支出 国家财政将筹集起来的资金进行分配使用，以满足经济建设和各项事业的需要，主要包括:

(1) 一般公共服务：指政府提供基本公共管理与服务的支出，包括人大事务、政协事务、政府办公厅（室）及相关机构事务、发展与改革事务、统计信息事务、财政事务、税收事务、审计事务、海关事务、人力资源事务、纪检监察事务、人口与计划生育事务、商贸事务、知识产权事务、工商行政管理事务、国土资源事务、海洋管理事务、测绘事务、地震事务、气象事务、民族事务、宗教事务、港澳台侨事务、档案事务、共产党事务、民主党派事务及工商联事务、群众团体事务、彩票事务等。

(2) 外交：指政府外交事务支出，包括外交行政管理、驻外机构、对外援助、国际组织、对外合作与交流、边界勘界联检等方面的支出。

(3) 国防：指政府用于国防方面的支出，包括用于现役部队、预备役部队、民兵、国防科研事业、专项工程、国防动员等方面的支出。

(4) 公共安全：指政府维护社会公共安全方面的支出，包括武装警察、公安、国家安全、检察、法院、司法行政、监狱、劳教、国家保密、缉私警察等。

(5) 教育：指政府教育事务支出，包括教育行政管理、学前教育、小学教育、初中教育、普通高中教育、普通高等教育、初等职业教育、中专教育、技校教育、职业高中教育、高等职业教育、广播电视教育、留学生教育、特殊教育、干部继续教育、教育机关服务等。

(6) 科学技术：指用于科学技术方面的支出，包括科学技术管理事务、基础研究、应用研究、技术研究与开发、科技条件与服务、社会科学、科学技术普及、科技交流与合作等。

(7) 文化教育与传媒：指政府在文化、文物、体育、广播影视、新闻出版等方面的支出。

(8) 社会保障和就业：指政府在社会保障与就业方面的支出，包括社会保障和就业管理事务、民政管理事务、财政对社会保险基金的补助、补充全国社会保障基金、行政事业单位离退休、企业改革补助、就业补助、抚恤、退役安置、社会福利、残疾人事业、城市居民最低生活保障、其他城镇社会救济、农村社会救济、自然灾害生活救助、红十字事务等。

(9) 医疗卫生：指政府医疗卫生方面的支出，包括医疗卫生管理事务支出、医疗服务支出、医疗保障支出、疾病预防控制支出、卫生监督支出、妇幼保健支出、农村卫生支出等。

(10) 环境保护：指政府环境保护支出，包括环境保护管理事务支出、环境监测与监察支出、污染治理支出、自然生态保护支出、天然林保护工程支出、退耕还林支出、风沙荒漠治理支出、退牧还草支出、已垦草原退耕还草、能源节约利用、污染减排、可再生能源和资源综合利用等支出。

(11) 城乡社区事务：指政府城乡社区事务支出，包括城乡社区管理事务支出、城乡社区规划与管理支出、城乡社区公共设施支出、城乡社区住宅支出、城乡社区环境卫生支出、建设市场管理与监督支出等。

(12) 农林水事务：指政府农林水事务支出，包括农业支出、林业支出、水利支出、扶贫支出、农业综合开发支出等。

(13) 交通运输：指政府交通运输和邮政业方面的支出，包括公路运输支出、水路运输支出、铁路运输支出、民用航空运输支出、邮政业支出等。

(14) 工业商业金融等事务：指政府对工业、商业及金融等方面的支出，包括采掘业支出、制造业支出、建筑业支出、工业和信息产业监管支出、国有资产监管支出、商业流通事务支出、金融业监管支出、旅游业管理与服务支出等。

Explanatory Notes on Main Statistical Indicators

Government Revenue includes the local government revenue and the consumption tax and value added tax transfered to central government.The revenue of the local government includes business tax,income tax of the enterprises subordinated to the local government,personal income tax,tax on the use of urban land,tax on the adjustment of the investment in fixed assets,tax on town maintenance and construction,tax on real estates,tax on the use of vehicles and ships,stamp tax,slaughter tax,tax on agriculture and animal husbandry,tax on special agricultural products,tax on the occupancy of cultivated lan d,contract tax,25% of the value added tax,50% of the tax on stock dealing (stamp tax) and tax on resources other than the ocean petroleum resources.

Government Expenditure refers to the distribution and use of the funds the government finance has raised, so as to meet the needs of economic construction and various causes. It includes the following main items:

(1) Expenditure for general public services: It refers to the spending on the basic public management and services which provided by governments, including the expense on affairs of People's Congress, affairs of People's Political Consultative Conference, affairs of government general office and relative institutions, affairs of development and reform, affairs of statistics, affairs of finance, affairs of taxation, affairs of audit, affairs of customs, affairs of human resources and social security, affairs of discipline inspection and supervision, affairs of population and family planning, affairs of commerce and trade, affairs of intellectual property, affairs of administration for industry and commerce, affairs of land and resources, affairs of oceanic administration, affairs of surveying and mapping, affairs of earthquake, ethnic affairs, religious affairs, affairs of Hong Kong, Macao, Taiwan, and Overseas Chinese, affairs of archives administration, affairs of Chinese Communist Party, affairs of democratic parties and federation of industry and commerce, affairs of mass organization, and affairs of lottery, etc.

(2) Expenditure for foreign affairs: It refers to the spending of government on foreign affairs, including the expense on administration of foreign affairs, missions overseas, external assistance, international organizations, foreign cooperation and communication, surveying and joint inspection on borderline, etc.

(3) Expenditure for national defence: It refers to the spending of government on national defence, including the expense on active force, reserve force, militia, scientific research on national defence, special projects, mobilization of national defence, etc.

(4) Expenditure for public security: It refers to the spending of government on maintaining social and public security, including the expense on armed police force, public security, state security, prosecution, courts, justice, prison, labour education and rehabilitation, protection of state secrecy, anti-smuggling police, etc.

(5) Expenditure for education: It refers to the spending of government on education, including the expense on the administration of education, pre-primary education, primary education, secondary education, high school education, regular higher education, primary vocational education, secondary vocational education, technical school education, vocational high school education and higher vocational education, radio and television education, student abroad education, special education, on the job training of cadres, education authorities services, etc.

(6) Expenditure for science and technology: It refers to the spending of government on science and technology (S&T), including the expense on the administration of S&T, basic research, applied research, research and development, conditions and services of S&T, popularization of social science, science and technology, exchanges and cooperation of S&T, etc.

(7) Expenditure for culture, sport and media: It refers to the spending of government on culture, cultural heritage, sports, radio, film, television, press and publication, etc.

(8) Expenditure for social safety net and employment effort: It refers to the spending of government on social

safety net and employment, including the expense on administration of social safety net and employment, civil affairs, budgetary subsidy on the social insurance funds, subsidy on National Social Security Fund, retirees of administrative units and institutions, subsidy on enterprise reform, subsidy on employment effort, pension, placement of ex-serviceman, social welfare, the handicapped undertakings, the system of cost of living allowances for urban residents, other urban social relief, rural social relief, living relief of natural disasters, affairs of Red Cross Society, etc.

(9) Expenditure for medical and health care: It refers to the spending of government on medical and health care, including the expense on administration of medical and health care, medical services, health care, disease prevention and control, health inspection and supervision, women and children's health, rural health care, etc.

(10) Expenditure for environment protection: It refers to the spending of government on environment protection, including the expense on administration of environment protection, environment monitoring and supervision, pollution control, natural ecology protection, project of virgin forests protection, reforesting farmland, controlling the sources of dust storms, returning pastureland to grassland, returning pastureland to grassland, returning cultivated land to grassland, energy conservation, emissions reduction, comprehensive utilization of renewable energy and resources, etc.

(11) Expenditure for urban and rural community affairs: It refers to the spending of government on urban and rural community affairs, including the expense on administration of urban and rural community, planning and management of urban and rural community, public facilities of urban and rural community, housing of urban and rural community, sanitation of urban and rural community, management and supervision on the construction market, etc.

(12) Expenditure for agriculture, forestry and water conservancy: It refers to the spending of government on agriculture, forestry and water conservancy, including the expense on agriculture, forestry, water conservancy, poverty alleviation, comprehensive agricultural development, etc.

(13) Expenditure for transportation: It refers to the spending of government on transportation and postal services, including the expense on road transportation, waterway transportation, railway transportation, civil aviation transportation, and postal services.

(14) Expenditure for industry, commerce and banking: It refers to the spending of government on industry, commerce and banking, including the expense on mining, manufacturing, construction, industry and information technology supervision and administration, State-owned assets supervision and administration, commerce and circulation affairs, financial intermediation supervision and administration, tourism administration and service, etc.

9

Nine

价格指数

Price Indices

9-1 居民消费价格分类指数
Consumer Price Indices by Category

(上年=100) (preceding year=100)

指　标	Item	2006	2007	2008	2009	2010	2011
居民消费价格总指数	**General Consumer Price Index**	**101.7**	**106.4**	**107.6**	**98.7**	**102.9**	**105.1**
#非食品价格指数	Non-Food Price Index	100.8	101.4	102.5	98.9	100.5	101.2
#服务项目价格指数	Services Price Index	102.1	102.5	102.6	99.9	101.4	101.3
消费品价格指数	Consumer Goods Price Index	101.6	107.6	109.0	98.4	103.4	106.6
食品	**Food**	**103.4**	**116.7**	**117.3**	**98.5**	**107.7**	**113.5**
粮食	Grain	102.9	106.9	107.6	103.0	120.5	116.8
淀粉及薯类	Starches and Tubers	105.8	104.2	104.9	120.1	110.7	108.9
干豆类及豆制品	Beans and Its Products	100.4	107.2	137.4	102.1	109.7	107.9
油脂	Oil or Fat	96.6	147.5	128.3	78.4	100.4	116.5
肉禽及其制品	Meat, Poultry and Their Products	99.9	134.8	124.7	91.0	104.9	124.5
食用畜肉及副产品	Livestock for Slaughtering and Sideline Products	98.5	144.3	129.8	84.9	102.5	129.9
禽	Poultry	101.1	124.4	108.0	97.8	114.7	113.4
肉禽加工制品	Products of Processed Meat and Poultry	104.0	116.1	120.3	100.3	101.9	109.5
蛋	Eggs	94.7	114.2	100.1	98.0	107.3	114.7
水产品	Aquatic Products	103.3	110.5	112.2	95.3	109.7	111.1
鱼	Fish	96.2	110.4	113.0	94.8	111.4	110.7
其他水产品	Other Aquatic Products	120.6	110.2	110.1	95.7	104.5	112.0
菜	Vegetables	112.9	107.8	108.1	114.7	116.6	108.7
鲜菜	Fresh Vegetables	111.9	105.4	107.7	119.0	114.3	108.3
调味品	Flavoring	106.3	109.9	108.9	103.7	105.3	107.3
糖	Sugar	107.8	102.3	105.6	101.0	109.7	111.7
茶及饮料	Tea and Beverages	101.1	101.0	101.8	100.8	100.9	102.6
干鲜瓜果	Dried and Fresh Melons and Fruits	125.3	94.3	108.5	112.7	120.3	112.0
糕点饼干面包	Cake, Biscuit and Bread	102.0	106.6	112.8	101.2	102.3	110.5
奶及奶制品	Milk and Its Products	99.5	100.5	120.0	103.4	101.0	100.5

9-1 续表1 continued

(上年=100) (preceding year=100)

指 标	Item	2006	2007	2008	2009	2010	2011
在外用膳食品	Outward Dinner Food	102.3	114.3	120.7	101.5	101.3	109.5
其他食品及食品加工服务	Other Foods and Manufacturing Services	102.3	101.3	106.7	95.4	100.8	103.5
烟酒及用品	**Tobacco, Liquor and Articles**	**99.0**	**102.2**	**104.0**	**100.9**	**102.0**	**102.4**
烟草	Tobacco	98.7	100.0	99.8	100.1	100.8	99.7
酒	Liquor	99.5	109.5	113.2	102.3	103.8	107.2
白酒	Distilled Spirit	101.0	114.5	117.5	103.5	106.5	110.0
啤酒	Beer	94.6	99.3	107.6	99.4	95.9	103.3
衣着	**Clothing**	**97.5**	**97.8**	**97.8**	**95.6**	**97.4**	**100.3**
服装	Garments	97.3	97.8	98.3	96.7	99.3	100.9
衣着材料	Clothing Materials	101.2	99.6	100.3	101.9	103.1	113.2
鞋袜帽	Footgear and Hats	97.8	97.4	96.4	92.5	92.5	97.1
家庭设备用品及维修服务	**Household Facilities Articles and Repair Services**	**101.0**	**101.8**	**103.5**	**99.6**	**99.3**	**100.2**
耐用消费品	Durable Consumer Goods	100.2	101.3	102.8	98.4	98.6	98.7
家具	Furniture	100.2	100.1	102.8	100.2	100.8	101.7
家庭设备	Household Facilities	100.1	102.2	102.3	98.0	97.6	97.3
室内装饰品	Interior Decorations	106.7	97.4	96.1	97.6	101.0	97.6
床上用品	Bed Articles	100.5	97.3	100.6	97.7	93.2	103.4
家庭日用杂品	Daily Use Household Articles	101.5	102.1	102.7	100.9	99.8	100.7
家庭服务及加工维修服务	Household Services and Manufacturing Upkeep	101.8	109.8	127.1	103.0	109.7	103.2
医疗保健和个人用品	**Health Care and Personal Articles**	**100.1**	**100.6**	**100.7**	**100.9**	**101.3**	**102.6**
医疗保健	Health Care	99.1	99.2	99.2	100.1	100.9	103.5
医疗器具及用品	Medical Instrument and Articles	99.9	99.6	100.3	100.5	101.0	100.8
中药材及中成药	Traditional Chinese Medicine	99.5	99.6	104.4	102.4	103.8	115.1
西药	Western Medicine	98.8	98.2	98.3	100.1	101.1	101.9
保健器具及用品	Health Care Appliances and Articles	101.9	101.0	100.2	99.8	99.5	99.6
医疗保健服务	Health Care Services	98.6	99.6	98.9	99.6	100.3	100.0

9–1 续表2 continued

(上年=100) (preceding year=100)

指　标	Item	2006	2007	2008	2009	2010	2011
个人用品及服务	Personal Articles and Services	101.3	102.4	102.4	102.0	101.8	101.3
化妆美容用品	Cosmetics	100.8	99.8	98.6	100.5	101.7	100.4
卫生用品	Sanitation Articles	99.3	101.7	98.4	100.7	101.9	101.3
个人饰品	Personal Ornaments	103.9	102.1	103.8	98.2	100.1	103.7
个人服务	Personal Services	101.8	104.7	107.1	108.1	103.5	99.9
交通和通讯	**Transportation and Communication**	**100.5**	**100.3**	**100.7**	**98.2**	**100.8**	**100.1**
交　通	Transportation	103.3	102.5	103.4	99.8	102.6	102.9
交通工具	Transportation Facility	98.7	99.7	99.9	99.6	99.8	100.7
车用燃料及零配件	Fuels and Parts	110.1	103.7	110.9	91.0	111.3	109.7
车辆使用及维修	Using and Upkeep Fare	99.8	99.8	102.6	103.3	102.5	108.2
市区公共交通	Incity Traffic Fare	104.0	100.8	102.9	100.4	101.5	99.3
城市间交通	Intercity Traffic Fare	103.9	105.3	106.4	103.0	102.7	104.9
通　信	Communication	98.3	98.6	98.3	96.7	99.1	97.2
通信工具	Communication Facility	87.4	84.3	89.2	91.3	92.6	84.0
通信服务	Communication Service	100.2	101.3	100.4	97.8	100.4	100.6
娱乐教育文化用品及服务	**Recreation,Education and Culture Articles and Services**	**101.6**	**101.3**	**101.6**	**100.2**	**100.4**	**99.9**
文娱用耐用消费品及服务	Durable Consumer Goods and Services for Culture and Recreation	96.2	94.1	94.6	94.0	96.9	96.0
教　育	Education	101.0	101.8	102.3	100.5	101.0	101.4
文化娱乐用品	Cultural and Recreational Articles	102.4	107.6	108.2	102.8	100.3	99.7
文化娱乐	Recreation and Culture	100.7	100.8	99.5	98.2	99.1	99.7
书报杂志	Books,Newspapers and Magazines	102.6	101.2	101.7	102.2	101.1	100.3
文娱费	Recreation Fee	103.8	114.4	115.0	106.0	100.2	99.5
旅游	Touring	111.8	99.8	96.8	105.6	106.2	100.1
居住	**Residence**	**103.9**	**104.9**	**107.5**	**98.4**	**102.4**	**102.8**
建房及装修材料	Building and Building Decoration Materials	101.6	103.9	104.4	100.9	100.4	102.5
租　房	Rent	100.2	111.9	107.4	104.6	102.5	99.5
自有住房	Private Housing	103.0	101.4	99.6	85.6	100.6	102.3
水、电、燃料	Water, Electricity and Fuels	106.0	106.4	112.4	99.8	105.0	103.9

9-2 商品零售价格分类指数

Retail Price Indices by Category

(上年=100) (preceding year=100)

指 标	Item	2006	2007	2008	2009	2010	2011
商品零售价格总指数	**Retail Price Index**	**100.9**	**104.2**	**107.2**	**97.6**	**103.0**	**105.5**
食品类	Food	103.2	117.4	117.8	98.3	108.2	113.9
粮食	Grain	103.2	107.0	108.8	103.7	120.4	117.1
油脂	Oil or Fat	95.0	144.6	123.7	77.0	98.9	116.5
肉禽及其制品	Meat,Poultry and Their products	100.0	134.5	125.9	89.9	104.9	123.6
蛋	Eggs	95.5	114.5	101.7	98.2	107.2	115.7
水产品	Aquatic Products	102.8	110.5	115.5	96.2	108.2	112.3
鲜菜	Frash Vegetables	111.8	105.9	108.1	118.1	114.4	109.5
干菜及菜制品	Dried Vegetables and Its Products	109.4	119.0	107.7	96.0	125.8	110.8
鲜果	Fresh Fruits	127.4	96.2	108.2	117.0	122.1	112.3
干(坚)果及瓜果制品	Dried Fruits and Its Products	107.9	119.8	118.0	101.4	120.8	113.4
在外用膳食品	Outward Dinner Food	102.4	113.9	119.0	101.5	101.3	109.3
饮料、烟酒	Beverages,Tobacco and Liquor	98.7	101.0	102.3	100.6	101.1	101.6
服装、鞋帽类	Garments,Shoes and Hats	98.6	98.7	98.6	96.1	98.3	100.4
纺织品类	Textiles	98.1	97.4	101.0	98.4	99.5	103.8
家用电器及音像器材	Household Appliances, Music and Video Equipment	98.5	98.0	98.1	95.7	97.9	96.3
文化办公用品	Cultural and Office Appliances	100.0	97.1	98.5	99.3	100.1	98.1
日用品	Articles for Daily Use	98.9	102.2	103.8	100.8	100.8	100.8
体育娱乐用品	Sports and Recreation Articles	98.2	100.5	99.8	97.3	99.2	100.3
交通、通信用品	Traffic and Commanication Appliances	96.1	96.3	97.4	98.2	97.6	96.2
家具	Furniture	100.5	100.3	102.7	100.9	99.8	101.9
化妆品类	Cosmetics	96.9	100.2	98.3	98.6	99.7	100.6
金银珠宝类	Gold,Silver and Jewelry	120.6	108.3	113.3	89.7	108.9	111.7
中西药品及医疗保健用品类	Traditional Chinese and Western Medicines & Health Care Articles	100.5	101.4	102.4	101.0	102.6	106.2
书报杂志及电子出版物类	Books, Newspapers, Magazines and Electronic Publications	100.6	99.8	100.3	102.2	100.5	100.2
燃料类	Fuels	113.5	108.1	124.5	93.7	111.2	113.7
建筑材料及五金电料类	Building Materials and Hardware	100.4	105.2	112.7	96.6	102.5	102.7

9-3 工业生产者出厂价格分类指数
Ex-Factory Price Indices of Industrial Products by Gategory

(上年=100) (preceding year=100)

指标	Item	2006	2007	2008	2009	2010	2011
工业生产者出厂价格指数	**Total Ex-Factory Price Index of Industrial Products**	**104.3**	**105.0**	**112.4**	**95.1**	**104.7**	**105.4**
按轻、重工业分	**Grouped by Light or Heavy Industries**						
轻工业	Light Industry	102.6	103.8	107.5	99.7	100.5	102.9
重工业	Heavy Industry	105.4	105.4	114.4	93.3	106.2	106.0
按用途分	**Grouped by Use**						
生产资料	Means of Production	105.1	105.4	114.2	93.8	105.5	106.2
采掘工业	Mining & Quarrying Industry	129.2	106.0	118.1	96.9	116.1	107.2
原材料工业	Raw Materials Industry	106.4	101.6	107.1	97.1	105.4	106.4
加工工业	Manufacturing Industry	98.4	109.3	120.8	89.3	102.1	105.6
生活资料	Consumer Goods	102.2	103.3	105.4	100.6	100.9	102.8
食品类	Food	102.5	104.2	106.1	101.5	101.7	102.8
衣着类	Clothing	108.8	104.0	105.2	106.1	102.4	114.2
一般日用品	Non-Durable Consumer Goods	101.4	100.6	102.8	99.0	100.3	101.6
耐用消费品	Durable Consumer Goods	97.3	97.6	100.2	91.7	92.2	101.5
按工业大类行业分	**Grouped by Sector**						
煤炭开采和洗选业	Mining and Washing of Coal	120.9	109.1	120.9	100.0	117.0	111.9
有色金属矿采选业	Mining and Processing of Non-Ferrous Metal Ores	77.0	106.6	106.4	86.8	105.6	104.5
非金属矿采选业	Mining and Processing of Nonmetal Ores	146.1	94.9	110.4	90.4	106.2	123.6
农副食品加工业	Processing of Food from Agricultural Products	100.2	117.8	126.0	95.0	102.5	111.9
食品制造业	Manufacture of Foods	100.1	104.0	110.5	101.2	98.9	104.4
饮料制造业	Manufacture of Beverages	102.2	100.8	112.1	103.5	102.3	103.0
烟草制品业	Manufacture of Tobacco	102.2	100.5	100.4	101.0	100.6	99.7
纺织业	Manufacture of Textile	100.8	104.1	100.7	87.9	113.0	120.9
纺织服装、鞋、帽制造业	Manufacture of Textile Wearing Apparel, Footware,and Caps	108.1	100.1	101.9	100.6	103.8	104.6
皮革、毛皮、羽毛（绒)及其制品业	Manufacture of Leather, Fur, Feather and Related Products	98.8	100.2	100.0	100.0	100.0	119.0

9-3 续表 Continued

(上年=100) (preceding year=100)

指 标	Item	2006	2007	2008	2009	2010	2011
木材加工及木、竹、藤、棕、草制品业	Processing of Timber,Manufacture of Wood, Bamboo,Rattan,Palm and Straw Products	104.8	101.2	102.7	98.1	100.9	103.2
家具制造业	Manufacture of Furniture	100.1	103.1	104.4	98.6	103.1	119.8
造纸及纸制品业	Manufacture of Paper and Paper Products	100.7	105.1	107.3	101.2	104.4	103.0
印刷业和记录媒介的复制	Printing,Reproduction of Recording Media	100.5	101.8	102.7	98.9	99.3	100.0
文教体育用品制造业	Manufacture of Articles For Culture,Education and Sport Activities	99.9	104.4	100.2	100.0	100.0	109.3
石油加工、炼焦及核燃料加工业	Processing of Petroleum, Coking, Processing of Nuclear Fuel	98.8	107.8	142.1	92.3	110.6	112.4
化学原料及化学制品制造业	Manufacture of Raw Chemical Materials and Chemical Products	95.7	107.1	138.8	83.3	105.8	114.1
医药制造业	Manufacture of Medicines	104.4	108.5	101.6	104.0	103.7	101.9
橡胶制品业	Manufacture of Rubber	108.3	108.0	106.0	100.2	102.0	114.0
塑料制品业	Manufacture of Plastics	99.6	106.1	106.7	96.3	102.3	106.8
非金属矿物制品业	Manufacture of Non-metallic Mineral Products	109.7	105.1	123.8	99.1	93.1	102.2
黑色金属冶炼及压延加工业	Smelting and Pressing of Ferrous Metals	90.8	118.8	124.9	81.2	104.2	105.5
有色金属冶炼及压延加工业	Smelting and Pressing of Non-ferrous Metals	116.2	92.6	95.8	81.3	111.9	108.4
金属制品业	Manufacture of Metal Products	98.9	101.7	114.9	91.8	102.6	101.4
通用设备制造业	Manufacture of General Purpose Machinery	102.2	100.7	104.3	99.4	100.9	100.0
专用设备制造业	Manufacture of Special Purpose Machinery	100.0	102.4	104.9	102.4	99.9	105.0
交通运输设备制造业	Manufacture of Transport Equipment	98.9	99.3	102.4	99.8	97.8	100.0
电气机械及器材制造业	Manufacture of Electrical Machinery and Equipment	107.4	105.3	103.1	94.3	99.2	99.6
通信设备、计算机及其他电子设备制造业	Manufacture of Communication Equipment, Computers and Other Electronic Equipment	88.3	92.6	92.1	85.4	99.0	99.3
仪器仪表及文化、办公用机械制造业	Manufacture of Measuring Instruments and Machinery for Cultural Activity and Office Work	97.5	99.5	97.0	96.9	98.8	101.5
电力、热力的生产和供应业	Production and Distribution of Electric Power and Heat Power	105.8	103.0	104.3	104.5	102.1	101.6
燃气生产和供应业	Production and Distribution of Gas	107.3	116.3	100.0	116.0	120.3	102.4
水的生产和供应业	Production and Distribution of Water	118.5	108.3	104.6	103.3	107.1	104.3

注：工业生产者出厂价格指数2010年及以前为全部工业品出厂价格指数，统计口径不变。

Note:For the year 2010 and before,Ex-Factory Price Index of Industrial Producer referred to Total Ex-Factory Price Index of Industrial Products; statistical standards are unchanged.

9-4 工业生产者购进价格指数

Purchasing Price Index of Industrial Producer

(上年=100)

(preceding year =100)

指　标	Item	2006	2007	2008	2009	2010	2011
工业生产者购进价格指数	**Purchasing Price Index of Industrial Producer**	**107.3**	**107.5**	**112.5**	**93.5**	**109.8**	**115.0**
燃料、动力类	Fuels and Power	110.8	105.0	115.6	101.2	110.1	121.6
黑色金属材料类	Ferrous Metals	98.5	106.5	123.9	86.9	104.0	109.9
#钢　材	Rolled-steel	97.1	106.0	120.7	88.2	103.3	108.0
有色金属材料和电线类	Nonferrous Metals and Wire	131.6	109.4	95.4	85.6	122.5	112.4
化工原料类	Raw Chemical Materials	99.6	106.3	109.8	86.0	110.2	116.4
木材及纸浆类	Timber and Paper Pulps	101.9	103.5	112.9	98.5	105.2	107.8
建筑材料及非金属矿类	Building Materials and Nonmetal Minerals Processing	104.1	105.2	131.2	94.2	96.7	117.8
其他工业原材料及半成品类	Other Industrial Raw Materials and Semi-products	108.9	107.4	108.4	93.3	108.8	106.4
农副产品类	Agricultural Products	106.6	115.2	115.0	90.7	115.1	109.2
纺织原料类	Textile Raw Materials	106.7	104.1	103.4	99.1	105.0	118.1

注：工业生产者购进价格指数2010年及以前为全部原材料、燃料、动力价格指数，统计口径不变。

Note:For the year 2010 and before,Purchasing Price Index of Industrial Producer referred to Total Indices of Purchasing Prices of Raw Materials,Fuels and Power;statistical standards are unchanged.

9-5 农业生产资料价格分类指数

Price Indices of Means of Agricultural Production by Category

(上年=100)

(preceding year =100)

指　标	Item	2006	2007	2008	2009	2010	2011
农业生产资料价格总指数	**General Price Index of Means of Agricultural Production**	**105.4**	**105.1**	**113.4**	**96.2**	**101.1**	**111.1**
小农具	Small Farm Tools	107.1	101.4	107.3	107.9	107.5	105.5
饲　料	Forage	102.3	107.5	108.5	100.6	109.4	104.1
产品畜	Production Livestocks	105.9	129.8	114.9	105.0	97.1	153.9
半机械化农具	Semi-mechanized Farm Tools	113.0	101.2	116.1	106.1	99.3	115.7
机械化农具	Mechanized Farm Machinery	100.1	98.3	110.6	98.8	98.9	106.0
化学肥料	Chemical Fertilizer	102.1	103.5	121.3	91.5	92.7	101.4
农药及农药器械	Pesticide & Its Appliances	97.6	101.8	100.3	100.8	99.1	100.6
化学农药	Chemical Pesticide	99.7	102.5	101.0	103.3	97.6	101.5
农药器械	Appliances for Pesticide	94.2	100.7	99.1	96.7	101.6	96.1
农机用油	Oil for Farm Machinery	109.0	103.4	106.5	95.4	107.5	103.8
其他农业生产资料	Others Means of Agricultural Production	129.3	105.0	103.7	100.6	99.9	107.8

9–6 固定资产投资和房地产销售价格指数

Price Indices of Investment in Fixed Assets and Real Estate

(上年=100) (preceding year =100)

指　标	Item	2006	2007	2008	2009	2010	2011
固定资产投资价格指数	**Price Indices of Investment in Fixed Assets**	**101.1**	**103.5**	**108.9**	**100.5**	**102.7**	**105.4**
建筑安装工程	Price Indices of Construction and Installation	101.5	105.4	114.3	102.1	103.6	107.5
人工费	Manpower	106.6	108.0	115.6	115.1	114.0	111.0
材料费	Materials	100.0	105.6	116.3	98.4	101.2	109.3
钢　材	Steel Products	95.1	106.0	122.8	88.6	102.2	114.6
木　材	Timber	103.4	104.8	108.8	103.6	108.0	110.0
水　泥	Cement	103.8	105.4	117.3	106.8	97.5	102.1
电　料	Electrical Materials	103.2	101.7	109.5	98.7	103.2	106.4
化工材料	Chemical Raw Materials	108.0	105.8	112.5	109.8	106.8	108.6
地方建筑材料	Local Materials	105.2	111.2	110.9	106.2	100.8	106.7
其他材料	Others	103.3	104.1	105.0	105.6	103.4	102.7
机械使用费	Costs for Using Machine	102.2	101.9	104.2	103.0	102.7	101.8
设备、工器具购置	Purchase of Equipment,Tools and Instruments	100.3	100.2	100.6	97.5	100.1	101.0
其他费用	Others	100.6	100.9	101.1	99.3	102.5	102.6
新建住宅价格指数(贵阳市)	**Price Indices of New Residential Housings(Guiyang)**	**104.4**	**106.9**	**106.6**	**103.6**	**108.2**	**104.4**
新建商品住宅价格指数（贵阳市）	Price Indices of New Commodity Residential Housings(Guiyang)	105.4	107.7	106.7	103.6	108.3	104.5

注：新建住宅价格指数2010年及以前为房屋销售价格指数,新建商品住宅价格指数2010年及以前为住宅销售价格指数，统计口径不一致。

Note:For the year 2010 and before,Price Indices of New Residential Housings referred to the Sales Price Indices of Real Estate;Price Indices of New Commodity Residential Housings referred to the Sales Price Indices of Residence Housings;statistical standards are unchanged.

主要统计指标解释

商品零售价格指数 是反映城乡商品零售价格变动趋势和程度的相对数。零售物价的变动直接反映城乡居民的生活支出和国家的财政收入，影响居民购买力和市场供需平衡，影响消费与积累的比例关系。

居民消费价格指数 是反映一定时期内城乡居民所购买的生活消费品价格和服务项目价格变动趋势和程度的相对数。

农产品收购价格指数 是反映国有商业、集体商业、个体商业、外贸部门、国家机关、社会团体等各种经济类型的商业企业和有关部门收购农产品价格的变动趋势和程度的相对数。

工业品出厂价格指数 是反映全部工业产品出厂价格总水平的变动趋势和程度的相对数，包括工业企业售给本企业以外所有单位的各种产品和直接售给居民用于生活消费的产品。

固定资产投资价格指数 是反映固定资产投资额价格变动趋势和程度的相对数。固定资产投资额是由建筑安装工程投资完成额、设备、工器具购置投资完成额和其他费用投资完成额三部分组成的。编制固定资产投资价格指数应首先分别编制上述三部分投资的价格指数，然后采用加权算术平均法求出固定资产投资价格总指数。

农业生产资料价格指数 是反映一定时期内农业生产资料价格变动趋势和程度的相对数。农业生产资料价格指数分为小农具、饲料、产品畜、役畜、半机械化农具、机械化农具、化学肥料、农药及农具械、农机用油、其他农业生产资料十大类。

原材料、燃料和动力价格指数 是反映工业企业作为生产投入，而从物质交易市场和能源、原材料生产企业购买原材料、燃料和动力产品时，所支付的价格水平变动趋势和程度的统计指标，是扣除工业企业物质消耗成本中的价格变动影响的重要依据。

Explanatory Notes on Main Statistical Indicators

Retail Price Index reflects the general change in retail prices of commodities. The change and adjustment in retail prices directly affect the living expenditure of urban and rural residents, government revenue,purchasing power of residents and the equilibrium of market supply and demand,and the ratio of consumption to accumulation.

Consumer Price Index reflects the trend and degree of changes in prices of consumer goods and services purchased by urban and rural residents,and is a composite index derived from the urban consumer price index and the rural consumer price index.

Index of Purchasing Prices of Farm Products reflects the trend and degree of changes in purchasing prices of farm products purchased by state-owned, collective-owned,and individual commercial enterprises,foreign trade sectors,government agencies,social organizations and other units of various types of ownership. It is used to observe the impact of change in purchasing prices of farm products on the cash income of peasants, and serves as basis for the formulation and supervision of pricing policies for farm products.

Ex-factory Price Index of Industrial Products reflects the trend and degree of changes in general ex-factory prices of all industrial products,including sales of industrial products by an industrial enterprise to all units outside the enterprise, as well as sales of consumer goods to residents.

Price Index of Investment in Fixed Assets reflects the trend and degree of changes in prices of investment in fixed assets. The investment in fixed assets consists of three components, namely the investment in construction and installation,the investment in purchases of equipment and instrument,and the investment in other items. Price index of investment in fixed assets is calculated as the weighted arithmetic mean of the price indices of the three components of investment in fixed assets.

Price Indices of Means of Agricultural Production reflect the trend and degree of changes in prices of means of agricultural production during a given period. Price indices of means of agricultural production are composed of 10 categories including small farm tools, feeds, domestic animals for meat, draught domestic animals, semi-mechanized farm machinery, mechanized farm machinery, chemical fertilizers, pesticides and spraying machinery, fuels for farm machinery and other means of agricultural production.

Indices of Purchasing Prices of Raw Materials, Fuels and Power reflect changes in the level and degree of prices paid by industrial enterprises when they purchase production input such as raw materials, fuels and power from the market or from other energy or raw materials producing enterprises. These indices provide important basis for measuring the material consumption of industrial enterprises after removing influence of price changes.

10 Ten

人民生活

People's Living Conditions

10-1 城乡人民生活水平
People's Livelihood in Urban and Rural Areas

指　标	Item	2006	2007	2008	2009	2010	2011
就业	**Employment**						
城镇居民家庭每户就业人口(人)	Average Number of Employed Persons per Urban Household(person)	1.49	1.52	1.37	1.43	1.43	1.43
城镇居民家庭每个就业者赡养人口(人)	Number of Dependents per Employee of Urban Household(person)	2.03	1.99	2.22	2.13	2.11	2.08
城镇平均每户就业面(%)	Proportion of Employment per Urban Household(%)	0.49	0.50	0.45	0.47	0.47	0.48
城镇登记失业人数(万人)	Registered Urban Unemployment Persons (10000 persons)	12.12	12.13	12.56	12.34	12.18	12.51
城镇登记失业率(%)	Registered Urban Unemployment Rate(%)	4.11	3.97	3.98	3.81	3.63	3.63
农村平均每户整、半劳动力(人)	Average Number of Full/Semi Laborer Force per Rural Household(person)	2.86	2.90	2.93	2.95	2.95	2.83
农村居民家庭每一劳动力赡养人口(人)	Number of Dependents per Laborer of Rural Household(person)	1.55	1.52	1.51	1.48	1.47	1.52
收入与支出	**Income and Expenditure**						
城镇居民人均可支配收入(元)	Annual Per Capita Disposable Income of Urban Households(yuan)	9117	10678	11759	12863	14143	16495
城镇居民人均消费性支出(元)	Annual Per Capita Consumption Expenditure of Urban Householdss(yuan)	6848	7759	8349	9048	10058	11353
在岗职工平均工资(元)	Average Wage of Staff and Workers in their Posts(yuan)	16815	20668	24602	28245	31458	37331
农村居民人均纯收入(元)	Annual Per Capita Net Income of Rural Households (yuan)	1985	2374	2797	3005	3472	4145
农村居民人均生活消费支出(元)	Annual Per Capita Living Expenditure of Rural Households (yuan)	1627	1914	2166	2422	2852	3456
生活质量	**Life Quality**						
居民家庭恩格尔系数(%)	**Household's Engle Coefficient(%)**						
城　镇	Urban	38.7	40.2	43.1	41.5	39.9	40.2
农　村	Rural	51.5	52.2	51.7	45.2	46.3	47.7
居住条件	**Residence Condition**						
城镇人均住宅建筑面积(平方米)	Per Capita Building Space in Urban Areas(sq.m)	26.42	27.52	26.95	27.57	27.42	27.83
农村居民人均住房面积(平方米)	Per Capita Living Space in Rural Areas(sq.m)	23.84	24.54	25.27	26.43	27.26	29.63
交通条件	**Traffic Condition**						
城市人均拥有道路面积(平方米)	Per Capita Area of Paved Roads in City(sq.m)	5.57	6.06	5.99	6.03	6.23	6.66
每百户城镇居民拥有家用汽车(辆)	Number of Family Vehicles Per 100 Urban Households(unit)	2.07	2.01	3.29	4.85	5.96	10.48
每百户农村居民拥有家用摩托车(辆)	Number of Motorcycles Per 100 Rural Households(unit)	15.80	17.20	19.60	26.80	30.76	35.98
通信条件	**Communication Condition**						
每百户拥有移动电话(部)	Mobile Telephone Per 100 Households(set)						
城　镇	Urban	140.43	160.87	163.27	177.27	183.54	204.75
农　村	Rural	26.70	34.20	53.80	82.50	102.10	156.96
城市公用设施普及占有率	City Public Utility Rate						
用水普及率(%)	Rate of Access to Tap Water(%)	81.0	79.7	83.2	85.4	86.5	86.9
燃气普及率(%)	Rate of Access to Gas(%)	50.3	51.1	54.1	54.2	54.5	55.0
人均公园绿地面积(平方米)	Per Capita Green Area(sq.m)	4.25	4.23	4.44	4.65	5.33	5.50

10-1 续表 continued

指　标	Item	2006	2007	2008	2009	2010	2011
文化、教育和卫生	**Culture, Education and Health Care**						
文化	**Culture**						
广播综合人口覆盖率(%)	Radio Coverage Rate of the Population (%)	83.7	84.1	86.1	86.6	87.5	88.0
电视综合人口覆盖率(%)	TV Coverage Rate of the Population(%)	90.7	91.1	91.3	91.3	92.5	92.8
每百户彩色电视机拥有量(部/百户)	Number of Color TV per 100 Households(set)						
城镇	Urban	125.23	122.02	118.85	122.03	121.93	115.78
农村	Rural	64.90	72.90	74.60	88.10	91.07	93.93
每百户家用电脑拥有量(部/百户)	Number of Computers per 100 Households(set)						
城镇	Urban	29.81	40.37	43.37	52.47	56.79	63.89
农村	Rural	0.67	1.07	1.07	0.98	1.65	4.11
居民家庭文教娱乐支出比重(%)	Percentage of Household Expenditure on Education,Culture and Entertainment(%)						
城镇	Urban	13.7	13.4	11.2	12.7	12.5	11.7
农村	Rural	8.5	7.7	5.6	6.3	6.5	5.3
教育	**Education**						
学龄儿童入学率(%)	Enrollment Rate of School-age Children(%)	98.6	98.6	97.2	98.4	97.9	98.6
初中阶段毛入学率(%)	Enrollment Rate of Primary School Graduates Entering into Junior Secondary Schools(%)	100.5	97.5	95.9	98.2	97.6	94.2
高中阶段毛入学率(%)	Enrollment Rate of Juniorsecondary School Graduates Entering into Senior secondary Schools(%)	37.7	42.2	47.9	53.4	55.0	58.9
高等教育毛入学率(%)	Enrollment Rate of Senior secondary School Graduates Entering into Institution of Higher Education(%)	11.0	11.5	11.8	18.4	20.0	23.2
卫生	**Health Care**						
居民家庭医疗保健支出比重(%)	Percentage of Resident Expenditure on Health Care(%)						
城镇	Urban	4.8	4.6	5.6	5.9	5.4	5.1
农村	Rural	4.7	4.1	4.5	5.5	6.2	7.1
社会保障	**Social Security**						
基本养老保险参保人数(万人)	Number of People Joining in Basic Pension Insurance(10 000 persons)	193.25	205.93	215.89	235.61	257.31	282.06
#参保职工	Number of Employees	139.14	149.39	156.57	172.14	190.29	210.71
离退休人数	Number of Retirees						
城镇基本医疗保险参保人数(万人)	Number of Persons Joining in Urban Basic Medical Care System (10 000 persons)	199.22	228.22	257.35	279.53	293.52	314.06
失业保险参保人数(万人)	Number of Employees Joining in Unemployment Insurance (10 000 persons)	131.07	134.55	141.36	144.60	152.48	160.52
工伤保险参保人数(万人)	Number of Employees Joining in Injury Insurance (10 000 persons)	90.47	110.50	129.02	143.35	162.18	193.96
生育保险参保人数(万人)	Number of Persons Joining in Maternity Insurance(10 000 persons)	72.11	88.70	135.95	152.49	164.30	198.09
社会保险基金收入(亿元)	Revenue of Social Insurance Fund(100 million yuan)	73.72	90.86	140.50	171.40	201.56	256.94

10–2 城镇居民家庭生活基本情况
Basic Conditions of Urban Households Life

指 标	Item	2006	2007	2008	2009	2010	2011
调查户数(户)	Number of Households Surveyed(household)	1340	1340	1490	1670	1670	1720
平均每户常住家庭人口(人)	Average Household Size(person)	3.02	3.02	3.07	3.04	3.03	2.98
平均每户就业人员(人)	Number of Employed Persons Per Household(person)	1.49	1.52	1.37	1.43	1.43	1.43
平均每户就业面(%)	Proportion of Employment per Household(%)	0.49	0.50	0.45	0.47	0.47	0.48
平均每户国有经济单位职工人数(人)	Number of Staff and Workers in State-owned Units (person)	0.92	0.92	0.80	0.79	0.81	0.74
平均每户城镇集体经济单位职工人数(人)	Number of Staff and Workers in Urban Collective-ownedUnits (person)	0.06	0.05	0.04	0.04	0.03	0.04
平均每户其他各种经济类型单位职工(人)	Number of Staff and Workers in Other Types ofOwnership Units (person)	0.08	0.10	0.09	0.09	0.09	0.10
平均每个就业者赡养人口(人)	Number of Dependents per Employee(person)	2.03	1.99	2.22	2.13	2.11	2.08
平均每人年可支配收入(元)	**Per Capita Annual Disposable Income (yuan)**	**9116.61**	**10678.40**	**11758.76**	**12862.53**	**14142.74**	**16495.01**
平均每人年总收入(元)	**Per Capita Annual Income(yuan)**	**9439.31**	**11066.43**	**12185.62**	**13793.38**	**15138.80**	**17598.87**
工资性收入	Income of Wages and Salaries	6507.12	7750.15	7811.16	9005.57	9627.99	10754.45
工资及补贴收入	Income of Laborage and Allowance	6293.14	7544.09	7503.85	8569.27	9190.47	10359.48
其他劳动收入	Income of other Labor	213.98	206.06	307.32	436.30	437.52	394.97
经营者净收入	Net Business Income	886.32	764.63	770.86	1135.05	1174.02	1614.67
财产性收入	Income from Property	120.92	161.30	110.90	134.34	213.83	356.41
转移性收入	Income from Transfer	1924.96	2390.34	3492.70	3518.42	4122.96	4873.34
#养老金或离退休金	Annuities or Pension	1668.27	1969.84	3002.09	3026.06	3493.33	4229.54
出售财物收入(元)	Income of Selling Property and Goods(yuan)	13.88	1.46	13.87	17.66	181.55	46.61
借贷收入(元)	Income on Loan(yuan)	1508.41	1705.94	1802.29	2277.39	3651.74	4390.30
平均每人消费性支出 (元)	**Per Capita Annual Consumption Expenditure (yuan)**	**6848.39**	**7758.69**	**8349.21**	**9048.29**	**10058.29**	**11352.88**
食 品	Food	2649.02	3122.46	3597.94	3755.61	4013.67	4565.85
衣 着	Clothing	832.74	910.30	851.50	1012.14	1102.41	1209.88
居 住	Residence	627.23	718.65	836.54	747.57	890.75	1102.99
家庭设备用品及服务	Household Facilities, Articles and Services	446.53	463.56	525.70	589.35	673.33	857.55
医疗保健	Health Care and Medical Services	329.77	354.52	471.39	535.43	546.84	578.33
交通和通信	Transport and Communication	775.07	895.04	871.15	983.13	1270.49	1395.28
教育文化娱乐服务	Education, Culture and Recreation Services	938.37	1035.96	934.73	1146.35	1254.56	1331.43
其他商品与服务	Miscellaneous Goods and Services	249.66	258.21	260.27	278.71	306.24	311.57
平均每人消费性支出构成(%)(人均消费性支出=100)	**Composition of Per Capita Annual Consumption Expenditure (%)**						
食 品	Food	38.7	40.2	43.1	41.5	39.9	40.2
衣 着	Clothing	12.2	11.7	10.2	11.2	11.0	10.7
居 住	Residence	9.2	9.3	10.0	8.3	8.9	9.7
家庭设备用品及服务	Household Facilities, Articles and Services	6.5	6.0	6.3	6.5	6.7	7.6
医疗保健	Health Care and Medical Services	4.8	4.6	5.6	5.9	5.4	5.1
交通和通信	Transport and Communication	11.3	11.5	10.4	10.9	12.6	12.3
教育文化娱乐服务	Education, Culture and Recreation Services	13.7	13.4	11.2	12.7	12.5	11.7
其他商品与服务	Miscellaneous Goods and Services	3.6	3.3	3.1	3.1	3.0	2.7

10-3 城镇居民家庭人均现金收支

Per Capita Annual Cash Income and Expenditure of Urban Households

单位：元 (yuan)

指 标	Item	2006	2007	2008	2009	2010	2011
家庭总收入	**Total Households Income**	**9439.31**	**11066.43**	**12185.62**	**13793.38**	**15138.80**	**17598.87**
#可支配收入	Disposable Income	9116.61	10678.40	11758.76	12862.53	14142.74	16495.01
#工资性收入	Income of Wages and Salaries	6507.12	7750.15	7811.16	9005.57	9627.99	10754.45
工资及补贴收入	Income of Laborage and Allowance	6293.14	7544.09	7503.85	8569.27	9190.47	10359.48
其他劳动收入	Income of other Labor	213.98	206.06	307.32	436.30	437.52	394.97
经营净收入	Net Business Income	886.32	764.63	770.86	1135.05	1174.02	1614.67
财产性收入	Income from Property	120.92	161.30	110.90	134.34	213.83	356.41
#利息收入	Interest Income	4.91	2.06	1.71	6.81	10.22	19.03
股息与红利收入	Dividends and Bonus Income	2.91	38.76	6.91	4.70	4.29	12.63
转移性收入	Income from Transfer	1924.96	2390.34	3492.70	3518.42	4122.96	4873.34
#养老金或离退休金	Annuities or Pension	1668.27	1969.84	3002.09	3026.06	3493.33	4229.54
出售财物收入	**Income of Selling Property and Goods**	**13.88**	**1.46**	**13.87**	**17.66**	**181.55**	**46.61**
借贷收入	**Income on Loan**	**1508.41**	**1705.94**	**1802.29**	**2277.39**	**3651.74**	**4390.30**
#提取储蓄存款	Drawing Money from Banks	1396.85	1521.12	1689.76	1922.08	3082.85	3955.57
其他借贷收入	Others	7.53	3.11	2.91	86.91	172.05	37.54
家庭总支出	**Total Households Expenditure**	**8654.79**	**9735.19**	**10236.67**	**12085.93**	**13479.37**	**15558.27**
消费支出	Consumption Expenditure	6848.39	7758.69	8349.21	9048.29	10058.29	11352.88
#服务性消费支出	Services	1840.65	2019.82	2115.23	2350.91	2830.23	3014.21
财产性支出	Property Expenditure	6.00	3.09	4.45	55.23	52.40	88.39
转移性支出	Transfer Expenditure	1196.85	1414.12	1442.97	1857.66	1923.23	2364.36
#交纳的个人收入税	Individual Income Tax	4.96	12.82	9.98	14.96	20.67	15.95
各种非储蓄性保险支出	Various Nonsaving Insurance Expenditure	8.55	10.16	18.80	30.22	32.84	39.87
其他转移性支出	Others	42.43	46.00	45.57	51.66	56.49	73.40
社会保障支出	Social Seurity Expenditure	298.01	347.73	357.08	820.86	859.17	996.60
购房与建房支出	Expenditure of Purchasing or Building House	305.55	211.56	82.96	303.88	586.28	756.04
借贷支出	Expenditure on Loan	1851.27	2265.82	2851.94	3284.53	4725.38	5277.74
#存入储蓄款	Saving Deposits	1588.90	1865.85	2526.66	2903.20	4316.79	4842.53
购置有价证券	Purchasing Seurities	0.04	36.47	2.64	4.28	2.31	17.74
其他借贷支出	Others	10.08	9.66	23.67	39.32	5.51	39.58

10-4 城镇居民家庭人均消费性支出

Per Capita Annual Consumption Expenditure of Urban Household

单位：元 (yuan)

指　标	Item	2006	2007	2008	2009	2010	2011
消费性支出	**Consumption Expenditure**	**6848.39**	**7758.69**	**8349.21**	**9048.29**	**10058.29**	**11352.88**
食品	**Food**	**2649.02**	**3122.46**	**3597.94**	**3755.61**	**4013.67**	**4565.85**
#粮食	Grain	214.72	248.81	303.11	295.28	320.00	374.20
糖、烟、酒、饮料类	Sugar, Cigarette,Liquor and Beverage	404.31	388.28	432.85	470.42	494.98	508.79
在外饮食	Dining Out	511.29	593.27	642.09	741.81	818.58	918.02
衣着	**Clothing**	**832.74**	**910.30**	**851.50**	**1012.14**	**1102.41**	**1209.88**
居住	**Residence**	**627.23**	**718.65**	**836.54**	**747.57**	**890.75**	**1102.99**
#房租	Rent	12.45	14.05	28.11	19.16	24.19	50.08
水费	Water	59.62	71.55	83.12	91.99	98.60	94.38
电费	Electricity	272.33	293.11	332.22	354.97	385.54	412.22
燃料费	Fuels	149.51	150.87	205.27	139.27	147.89	158.01
家庭设备用品及服务	**Household Facilities,Articles and Services**	**446.53**	**463.56**	**525.70**	**589.35**	**673.33**	**857.55**
#耐用消费品	Durable Consumer Goods	159.55	162.60	186.10	212.21	199.59	366.57
医疗保健	**Health Care and Medical Services**	**329.77**	**354.52**	**471.39**	**535.43**	**546.84**	**578.33**
交通和通信	**Transport and Communications**	**775.07**	**895.04**	**871.15**	**983.13**	**1270.49**	**1395.28**
交通	Transport	279.39	386.34	400.19	436.24	606.34	698.37
通信	Communications	495.68	508.70	470.96	546.89	664.15	696.91
教育文化娱乐服务	**Education,Culture and Recreation Services**	**938.37**	**1035.96**	**934.73**	**1146.35**	**1254.56**	**1331.43**
#文化娱乐用品	Recreation Articles	226.57	235.94	221.73	309.29	269.35	323.35
书报杂志	Books,Newspaper and Magazines	33.65	35.34	28.26	30.68	31.26	29.84
文化娱乐服务	Recreation Services	287.84	310.01	276.76	401.43	491.18	520.72
学杂费	Tuition Fee	198.07	248.29	226.11	184.92	209.62	191.07
托幼费	Child-care Fee	37.54	30.80	28.56	35.12	50.76	44.43
其他商品和服务	**Miscellaneous Goods and Services**	**249.66**	**258.21**	**260.27**	**278.71**	**306.24**	**311.57**
恩格尔系数(%)	**Engel Coefficient(%)**	**38.7**	**40.2**	**43.1**	**41.5**	**39.9**	**40.2**

10–5 城镇居民家庭人均购买主要商品数量

Per Capita Annual Purchases of Major Commodities of Urban Houseoulds

单位：公斤 (kg)

指 标	Item	2006	2007	2008	2009	2010	2011
粮 食	Grain	71.98	52.02	59.33	51.92	70.69	78.88
食用植物油	Edible Vegetable Oil	8.63	9.84	9.96	9.16	8.70	9.91
猪 肉	Pork	25.51	24.80	24.80	26.41	25.66	27.89
牛、羊肉	Beef and Mutton	1.63	1.95	1.72	1.71	1.88	2.15
禽 类	Poultry	7.80	7.33	7.24	7.66	8.64	9.41
蛋 类	Eggs	5.16	5.14	5.21	5.09	5.70	6.68
水产品类(元)	Aquatic Products(yuan)	53.51	59.21	66.49	74.64	81.01	86.94
鲜 菜	Fresh Vegetables	87.99	94.62	102.58	98.69	93.57	106.12
糖类(元)	Sugar(yuan)	38.97	39.74	39.74	42.55	43.48	53.33
烟草类(元)	Cigarettes(yuan)	229.70	226.78	258.42	266.26	278.65	277.38
酒 类	Liquor	5.79	4.79	4.85	4.45	4.03	3.59
糕点类	Cake	3.14	2.96	2.65	3.20	3.08	3.34
干鲜瓜果类	Dried and Fresh Melons and Fruits	48.26	46.36	39.45	43.89	41.94	44.08
奶类及制品(元)	Milk and Its Products(yuan)	107.11	118.30	118.35	133.15	154.78	157.23

10–6 每百户城镇居民家庭耐用消费品拥有量

Number of Major Durable Consumer Goods Owned Per 100 Urban Households

单位：台 (set)

指 标	Item	2006	2007	2008	2009	2010	2011
摩托车(辆)	Motorcycle(unit)	7.46	4.92	5.13	6.15	5.79	5.46
家用汽车(辆)	Automobile(unit)	2.07	2.01	3.29	4.85	5.96	10.48
洗衣机	Washing Machine	98.51	98.32	96.73	99.03	99.23	99.15
电冰箱	Refrigerator	88.00	94.22	92.54	94.42	94.56	97.21
彩色电视机	Color TV Set	125.23	122.02	118.85	122.03	121.93	115.78
家用电脑	Household Computer	29.81	40.37	43.37	52.47	56.79	63.89
组合音响(套)	Hi-Fi Stereo Component System(unit)	39.12	38.94	35.41	36.84	37.06	31.22
照相机(架)	Camera(unit)	33.83	32.95	25.25	28.78	28.03	29.01
钢琴	Piano	1.91	1.06	1.84	1.88	1.79	2.07
微波炉	Microwave Oven	39.30	43.70	43.77	45.28	45.71	45.76
空调器	Air Conditioner	9.73	14.69	16.25	17.49	17.00	20.46
淋浴热水器	Water Heater for Shower	58.27	68.61	69.36	72.24	72.42	75.11
健身器材(套)	Healthy Equipment(unit)	2.53	2.04	2.86	4.47	4.20	3.30
固定电话(部)	Telephone(unit)	86.88	80.40	70.87	71.38	71.51	64.94
移动电话(部)	Mobile Phone(unit)	140.43	160.87	163.27	177.27	183.54	204.75

10-7 按收入等级分城镇居民家庭收入、消费情况(2011)

指　标	Item	总平均 Average	最低收入户 (10%) Lowest Income Households (first decile group)
平均每人年总收入(元)	**Per Capita Annual Total Income(yuan)**	**17598.87**	**5153.04**
平均每人年可支配收入(元)	**Per Capita Annual Disposable Income(yuan)**	**16495.01**	**4824.55**
人均购买主要商品数量	**Per Capita Purchases of Major Commodities**		
粮食(千克)	Grain(kg)	78.88	78.99
食用植物油(千克)	Edible Vegetable Oil(kg)	9.91	8.76
猪肉(千克)	Pork(kg)	27.89	19.41
牛肉(千克)	Beef(kg)	2.01	0.74
鸡(千克)	Chicken(kg)	6.51	2.97
鸭(千克)	Duck(kg)	1.36	0.92
鲜蛋(千克)	Eggs(kg)	5.95	3.70
鱼(千克)	Fish(kg)	3.34	1.94
鲜菜(千克)	Fresh Vegetables(kg)	106.12	88.60
糖类(元)	Sugar(yuan)	53.33	19.34
烟草类(元)	Cigarettes(yuan)	277.38	92.93
白酒(千克)	Liquor(kg)	2.09	0.94
鲜果(千克)	Fresh Fruit(kg)	37.44	14.35
糕点(千克)	Cakes(kg)	3.34	0.87
鲜乳品(千克)	Fresh Milk Products(kg)	12.43	2.62
服装(件)	Clothing(unit)	5.77	2.04
每百户耐用消费品拥有量	**Ownership of Major Durable Consumer Goods Per 100 Urban Househoulds**		
摩托车(辆)	Motorcycle(unit)	5.46	5.63
家用汽车(辆)	Automobile(unit)	10.48	0.17
洗衣机(台)	Washing Machine(set)	99.15	86.63
电冰箱(台)	Refrigerator(set)	97.21	81.00
彩色电视机(台)	Color TV Set(set)	115.78	101.07
家用电脑(台)	Household Computer(set)	63.89	19.54
组合音响(套)	Hi-Fi Stereo Component System(unit)	31.22	9.80
照相机(架)	Camera(unit)	29.01	1.83
钢琴(架)	Piano(set)	2.07	
微波炉(台)	Microwave Oven(set)	45.76	14.77
空调器(台)	Air Conditioner(set)	20.46	5.22
淋浴热水器(台)	Water Heater for Shower(set)	75.11	42.65
健身器材(套)	Healthy Equipment(unit)	3.30	0.32
固定电话(部)	Telephone(unit)	64.94	46.03
移动电话(部)	Mobile Phone(unit)	204.75	141.34

Statistics of Income and Consumption of Urban Househoulds by Level of Income

低收入户 (10%) Low Income Households (second decile group)	较低收入户 (20%) Lower Middle Income Households (second quintile group)	中间收入户 (20%) Middle Income Households (third quintile group)	较高收入户 (20%) Upper Middle Income Households (fourth quintile group)	高收入户 (10%) High Income Households (ninth decile group)	最高收入户 (10%) Highest Income Households (tenth decile group)
8537.26	**11881.36**	**16677.64**	**22106.61**	**29915.26**	**43891.44**
7870.06	**11098.07**	**15575.06**	**20742.44**	**28042.65**	**41524.46**
77.66	81.45	78.57	80.43	78.96	70.02
10.04	9.97	10.64	10.41	9.95	8.36
24.84	27.80	30.84	29.91	31.14	30.30
1.22	1.99	2.46	2.59	2.38	2.28
5.09	6.29	7.27	7.89	7.78	8.25
1.19	1.35	1.45	1.54	1.69	1.31
4.45	5.81	6.79	7.05	6.12	7.26
2.36	3.20	3.73	3.98	3.74	4.53
100.67	101.76	112.35	117.01	111.43	107.05
36.21	51.34	53.42	65.77	74.89	82.48
137.98	222.03	256.16	390.35	368.38	604.25
1.58	2.75	2.36	2.15	2.26	1.82
23.41	33.77	42.95	47.78	50.34	51.83
1.94	3.19	3.88	3.74	4.92	5.65
7.77	9.62	14.94	16.68	15.89	22.58
3.79	5.43	6.08	7.05	6.99	10.34
4.77	7.28	7.66	4.13	3.81	2.46
4.60	4.57	9.56	13.45	20.39	24.77
94.30	99.66	101.74	100.58	104.10	102.91
92.38	97.38	100.05	100.83	101.51	101.29
107.58	110.65	115.35	119.44	127.54	131.12
42.72	53.96	62.92	81.20	88.56	92.88
21.11	27.44	28.50	39.14	45.66	45.48
6.88	17.05	29.32	39.83	53.22	56.61
0.93	1.31	2.00	2.78	0.95	6.83
31.44	37.83	45.17	57.83	59.17	71.47
8.85	5.95	15.41	30.49	37.00	50.15
73.44	71.62	75.20	82.45	86.41	90.76
1.17	1.21	2.25	4.03	8.80	7.62
54.32	58.54	65.57	73.86	78.10	75.48
216.29	207.06	202.87	220.17	220.73	209.42

10-8 农村居民家庭生活基本情况
Basic Conditions of Rural Households Life

指　标	Item	2006	2007	2008	2009	2010	2011
调查户数(户)	**Households Surveyed(household)**	**2240**	**2240**	**2240**	**2240**	**2240**	**2240**
平均每户常住人口(人)	Average Number of Persons Per Household (person)	4.43	4.43	4.40	4.38	4.34	4.32
平均每户整、半劳动力(人)	Average Number of Laborers Per Household (person)	2.86	2.90	2.93	2.95	2.95	2.83
平均每一劳动力赡养人口(人)	Average Number Persons Supported by a Laborer (person)	1.55	1.52	1.51	1.48	1.47	1.52
平均每百个劳动力中(人)	In Per 100 Laborers (person)						
文盲或半文盲	Illiterate or Semi-Illiterate	14.50	14.09	13.06	12.93	12.32	10.29
小学程度	Elementary School	37.43	36.23	35.78	35.86	35.70	38.63
初中程度	Junior High School	41.67	42.45	43.29	42.59	42.56	43.23
高中程度	Senior High School	4.21	5.24	5.32	5.98	6.59	3.78
中专程度	Technical Secondary School	1.69	1.74	1.83	1.82	1.91	1.69
大专以上	Junior College	0.50	0.66	0.72	0.83	0.92	1.31
劳动力平均受教育年限(年)	Average Fixed Number of Year of Receiving Education of the Laborers(year)	6.79	6.86	7.02	7.05	7.14	7.07
平均每人年收入(元)	**Per Capita Annual Income (yuan)**						
总收入	Total Income	2799.36	3217.96	3889.69	4050.40	4560.52	5659.58
工资性收入	Income from Wages and Salaries	715.49	846.85	1002.68	1074.32	1303.85	1713.52
家庭经营收入	Income from Household Operations	1881.06	2116.54	2541.26	2502.62	2674.22	3367.61
财产性收入	Income from Properties	36.93	46.69	63.92	81.90	117.19	59.50
转移性收入	Income from Transfers	165.87	207.87	281.83	391.57	465.26	518.96
现金收入	Cash Income	2097.06	2347.33	3013.00	3188.31	3448.33	4439.54
工资性收入	Income from Wages and Salaries	715.49	846.72	1002.52	1072.54	1303.65	1712.31
家庭经营收入	Income from Household Operations	1181.89	1250.95	1670.77	1652.25	1571.86	2169.90
财产性收入	Income from Properties	35.62	45.51	62.60	79.31	114.47	48.31
转移性收入	Income from Transfers	164.06	204.15	277.11	384.22	458.35	509.02
平均每人年纯收入(元)	**Annual Average Net Income Per Capita(yuan)**	**1984.62**	**2373.99**	**2796.93**	**3005.41**	**3471.93**	**4145.35**
工资性收入	Payment for Labour	715.49	846.85	1002.68	1074.32	1303.85	1713.52
家庭经营纯收入	Income from Household Operations	1112.81	1320.06	1512.47	1537.57	1706.33	1980.21
转移性收入	Income from Transfers	119.38	160.39	217.86	311.63	344.56	392.13
财产性收入	Income from Properties	36.93	46.69	63.92	81.90	117.19	59.50
平均每人年总支出(元)	**Annual Average Expenditure Per Capita(yuan)**	**2629.49**	**2960.37**	**3590.51**	**3862.77**	**4350.25**	**5722.46**
#人均生活消费支出	Living Expenditure	1627.07	1913.50	2165.70	2421.95	2852.48	3455.76
人均年末使用房屋面积(平方米)	Average Per Capita Living Space at the Year-end(sq.m)	23.84	24.54	25.27	26.43	27.26	29.63

10–9 农村居民家庭人均年纯收入
Per Capita Annual Net Income of Rural Households

单位：元 (yuan)

指 标	Item	2006	2007	2008	2009	2010	2011
全年纯收入	**Annual Net Income**	**1984.62**	**2373.99**	**2796.93**	**3005.41**	**3471.93**	**4145.35**
工资性收入	Income from Wage	715.49	846.85	1002.68	1074.32	1303.85	1713.52
家庭经营收入	Income from Household Operation	1112.81	1320.06	1512.47	1537.57	1706.33	1980.21
第一产业	Primary Industry	906.06	1116.45	1246.85	1233.79	1396.65	1500.94
农业收入	Farming	690.93	789.52	864.19	899.31	1081.82	1065.10
林业收入	Forestry	24.49	24.94	29.00	34.70	42.99	63.41
牧业收入	Animal Husbandry	188.13	301.20	349.84	296.58	268.61	368.01
渔业收入	Fishery	2.52	0.79	3.82	3.21	3.23	4.41
第二产业	Secondary Industry	39.57	44.94	51.33	60.20	49.97	58.49
工业收入	Industry	17.64	15.36	16.14	21.54	9.30	12.91
建筑业收入	Construction	21.93	29.58	35.19	38.65	40.66	45.57
第三产业	Tertiary Industry	167.18	158.67	214.27	243.58	259.72	420.78
交通运输邮电业收入	Transport, Post and Telecommunication Services	39.22	47.16	65.95	73.49	74.27	146.97
批发贸易餐饮业收入	Wholesale and Retail Trade & Catering Services	78.33	63.71	84.83	93.20	99.41	175.44
社会服务业收入	Social Services	17.67	16.71	24.28	32.52	29.92	39.27
其他家庭经营收入	Others	31.96	31.09	39.20	44.37	56.12	59.10
转移性收入	Income from Transfer	119.38	160.39	217.86	311.63	344.56	392.13
财产性收入	Income from Property	36.93	46.69	63.92	81.90	117.19	59.50

10-10 农村居民家庭人均年总支出
Per Capita Annual Gross Expenditures of Rural Households

单位：元 (yuan)

指 标	Item	2006	2007	2008	2009	2010	2011
全年总支出	**Gross Expenditure**	**2629.49**	**2960.37**	**3590.51**	**3862.77**	**4350.25**	**5722.46**
#生活消费支出	Living Expenditure for Consumption	1627.07	1913.50	2165.70	2421.95	2852.48	3455.76
食 品	Food	838.42	998.39	1119.64	1093.94	1319.43	1646.51
衣 着	Clothing	88.56	99.44	112.46	125.35	137.49	186.22
居 住	Residence	265.54	329.44	427.40	588.42	621.80	639.32
家庭设备、用品及服务	Household Facilities,Articles and Services	64.91	70.93	94.36	115.39	135.64	192.78
医疗保健	Medicines and Medical Services	76.76	79.31	96.38	133.15	178.07	246.28
交通和通信	Transport and Telecommunications	122.47	154.52	159.61	175.08	229.66	304.51
文教娱乐用品及服务	Culture,Education and Recreation Articles and Services	138.13	147.31	122.10	151.59	186.19	183.03
其他商品和服务	**Miscellaneous Goods and Services**	32.28	34.16	33.75	39.03	44.21	57.10
家庭经营费用支出	Expenditure for Household Operation	699.90	722.95	944.61	872.54	871.62	1218.87
#种植业生产支出	Farming Production Costs	223.57	240.83	288.09	298.33	312.74	374.98
牧业生产支出	Animal Husbandry Costs	338.60	429.48	580.29	497.29	484.31	628.23
购置生产用固定资产支出	Expenditure for Purchasing Productive Fixed Assets	96.28	76.66	167.99	166.61	102.89	209.95
税费支出	Taxes	1.40	2.18	1.43	1.64	2.06	2.14
转移性支出	Transfer Expenditures	195.53	235.59	308.48	393.75	508.59	809.31
#寄给和带给在外人口	Posting or Taking to Outside City	27.04	23.75	30.26	30.24	30.67	74.84
财产性支出	Property Expenditures	8.84	5.02	1.51	5.63	8.52	24.55
恩格尔系数(%)	**Engel Coefficient(%)**	**51.5**	**52.2**	**51.7**	**45.2**	**46.3**	**47.7**

10-11 农村居民家庭人均年现金收入

Per Capita Annual Cash Income of Rural Households

单位：元 (yuan)

指　　标	Item	2006	2007	2008	2009	2010	2011
现金收入合计	**Total Annual Cash Income**	**2097.06**	**2347.33**	**3013.00**	**3188.31**	**3448.33**	**4439.54**
工资性收入	Income from Wage	715.49	846.72	1002.52	1072.54	1303.65	1712.31
家庭经营现金收入	Income from Household Business Operation	1181.89	1250.95	1670.77	1652.25	1571.86	2169.90
#出售产品收入	Income from Selling Product	824.00	985.49	1327.84	1263.26	1162.33	1440.86
工业服务性收入	Industry Processing Fee	16.25	11.00	10.62	13.33	8.80	7.72
建筑业收入	Construction	32.88	38.82	39.97	49.43	52.15	65.33
交通运输邮电业收入	Transport, Post and Telecommunication Services	64.80	73.04	105.95	116.47	118.38	271.86
批发和零售贸易餐饮业收入	Wholesale and Retail Trade & Catering Services	172.42	74.61	103.84	113.72	120.40	251.27
社会服务业收入	Social Service	19.96	18.57	25.80	34.60	31.66	45.10
文教卫生业收入	Culture, Education and Health Care	15.51	15.35	15.76	17.60	16.77	34.53
其他家庭经营现金收入	Others	22.04	21.03	29.84	34.23	45.35	35.11
转移性现金收入	Transfer Cash Income	164.06	204.15	277.11	384.22	458.35	509.02
#在外人口寄回和带回	Income from Outside City	20.27	12.87	16.87	31.02	24.65	5.35
亲友赠送	Income from Friends' and Relatives' Presents	48.89	59.47	70.03	84.26	125.70	141.13
抚恤金	Pension	0.76	1.98	1.60	2.03	3.63	3.11
财产性现金收入	Property Cash Income	35.62	45.51	62.60	79.31	114.47	48.31
#租金收入	Rental Income	24.14	22.18	36.42	34.47	26.45	18.26
非收入所得合计	**Reward From Other Way**	**387.08**	**436.75**	**579.71**	**944.54**	**1046.65**	**1690.01**
#银行、信用社贷款	Loans of Bank and Credit Union	58.28	49.11	82.50	121.20	130.30	271.12
借入款	Borrowed Money	109.17	104.74	164.87	244.11	260.04	440.70
收回借出款	Drawing Back Loan	30.03	30.46	26.82	36.19	51.78	54.72
从银行、信用社取回存款	Drawing Money from Banks and Credit Union	46.95	50.16	60.91	114.19	165.05	200.05
收回投资款	Disinvestment	0.21	0.01		0.05		0.10

10-12 农村居民家庭人均年现金支出

Per Capita Annual Cash Expenditures of Rural Households

单位：元 (yuan)

指 标	Item	2006	2007	2008	2009	2010	2011
现金支出合计	**Total Cash Expenditure**	**1948.92**	**2112.32**	**2701.82**	**3039.16**	**3339.45**	**4659.81**
#生产费用支出	Expenditure for Operating Costs	578.04	532.50	806.49	756.46	666.48	1153.38
缴纳税金	Taxes	1.40	2.18	1.43	1.64	2.06	2.14
生活消费支出	Living Expenditure for Consumption	1167.92	1338.85	1585.40	1888.12	2159.14	2670.71
转移性支出	Transfer Expenditures	192.73	233.77	307.00	387.31	503.26	809.03
#寄给在外人口	Posting to Outside City	26.81	23.46	30.26	30.12	30.65	74.84
赠送亲友	Present to Relatives and Friends	156.35	195.54	249.94	331.71	431.91	654.27
非消费性现金支出	Nonconsumptive Expenditure	308.95	333.18	345.89	462.73	599.03	668.28
#归还银行、信用社存款	Deposits of Bank and Credit Union Recession	39.39	51.43	35.07	45.87	64.56	90.04
借出款	Loan	11.09	12.91	12.90	12.06	18.14	25.86
归还借款	Loan Recession	57.79	63.36	78.16	108.81	99.02	150.47
存入银行、信用社	Deposit	166.53	157.26	152.16	186.84	286.23	187.3

注：现金支出合计不包括非消费性现金支出数据在内。
Note:Data of total expenditure in cash don't include the data of non-consumptive expenditure paid in cash.

10-13 农村居民家庭经营情况

Statistics of Household Operations in Rural Households

指 标	Item	2006	2007	2008	2009	2010	2011
经营耕地面积(亩/人)	Management Cultivated Area(mu/person)	1.03	1.07	1.09	1.11	1.10	1.10
年内出售肥猪头数(头/户)	Number of Selling Fattened Hogs in the Year (head/household)	1.61	1.26	1.01	1.11	1.19	0.98
年内自宰肥猪头数(头/户)	Number of Fattened Hogs Slaughtered by Peasants Themselves(head/household)	0.74	0.87	0.79	0.81	0.71	0.77
出售、自宰肥猪肉产量(公斤/户)	Output of Pork Slaughtered by Peasants Themselves and Sold(kg/household)	211.86	189.60	160.94	180.12	178.98	151.17
每头猪肉产量(公斤/头)	Output of Per Slaughtered Hog(kg/head)	90.28	89.16	89.63	93.53	93.85	86.05
年内出售菜羊只数(只/户)	Number of Sold Mutton Sheep and Goat in the Year (head/household)	0.08	0.04	0.05	0.05	0.09	0.13
出售、自宰羊的肉产量(公斤/户)	Output of Mutton Slaught ered by Peasants Themselves and Sold(kg/household)	1.53	0.85	1.02	1.51	2.06	2.68
年内出售肉牛数(头/百户)	Number of Sold Fattened Cattle in the Year (head/100 households)	3.57	3.04	2.86	2.88	2.95	4.15

10–14 农村居民家庭每人主要消费品消费量
Per Capita Annual Consumption of Major Consumer Goods in Rural Households

单位：公斤 (kg)

指　标	Item	2006	2007	2008	2009	2010	2011
粮　食	Grain	186.72	183.69	186.38	173.17	164.63	162.62
#大　米	Rice	139.07	136.05	143.02	136.32	130.26	135.55
食　油	Edible Oil	3.69	3.23	3.36	3.21	3.01	4.34
肉禽及其制品	Meat,Poultry and Related Product	31.26	28.37	27.63	28.46	27.77	25.73
#猪　肉	Pork	28.94	25.98	25.01	25.93	25.21	23.04
家　禽	Poultry	1.80	1.96	2.25	2.04	1.98	2.10
蛋类及蛋制品	Eggs and Their Products	1.41	1.25	1.72	1.66	1.81	1.93
水产品	Aquatic Products	0.49	0.48	0.36	0.41	0.38	0.43
#鱼　类	Fish	0.44	0.42	0.31	0.36	0.33	0.39
蔬　菜	Vegetables	134.44	130.60	133.36	126.10	116.74	110.42
瓜　果	Melon and Fruits	7.86	10.78	8.63	9.11	8.93	10.33
食　糖	Sugar	0.78	0.83	0.89	0.93	0.78	0.68
卷　烟(盒)	Cigarette(pack)	23.24	22.40	22.91	23.69	22.44	25.34
酒	Liquor	6.47	6.30	6.69	6.71	6.83	7.52

10–15 每百户农村居民家庭年末耐用消费品拥有量
Number of Durable Consumer Goods Owned By Per 100 Rural Households at the Year-end

单位：台 (set)

指　标	Item	2006	2007	2008	2009	2010	2011
黑白电视机	Black/White TV Set	10.5	7.0	4.0	2.3	2.1	0.4
彩色电视机	Color TV Set	64.9	72.9	74.6	88.1	91.1	93.9
电冰箱	Refrigerator	8.6	9.8	12.9	19.3	27.2	39.9
洗衣机	Washing Machine	29.8	33.6	36.4	48.7	55.2	62.5
影碟机	Video Disc Player	43.0	44.3	46.7	49.1	51.0	48.6
热水器	Water Heater for Shower	3.1	3.0	3.4	4.3	6.2	9.7
摩托车(辆)	Motorcycle(unit)	15.8	17.2	19.6	26.8	30.8	36.0
自行车(辆)	Bicycle(unit)	8.5	8.5	7.7	6.3	7.1	5.3
电话机(部)	Telephone(unit)	31.3	37.8	38.5	38.1	37.5	17.9
移动电话(部)	Mobile Telephone(unit)	26.7	34.2	53.8	82.5	102.1	157.0

10-16 按收入五等份分农村居民家庭收入、消费情况（2011）
Income and Consumption of Rural Househoulds by Income Quintile

项 目	Item	低收入户 Low Income Households	中低收入户 Lower Middle Income Households	中等收入户 Middle Income Households	中高收入户 Upper Middle Income Households	高收入户 High Income Households
平均每人总收入(元)	**Per Capita Annual Income(yuan)**	**2969.03**	**3998.48**	**5180.51**	**6861.43**	**11119.75**
#现金收入	Cash Income	2008.77	2894.72	3927.51	5495.10	9568.23
平均每人总支出(元)	**Per Capita Annual Expenditures(yuan)**	**4390.78**	**4406.55**	**5211.18**	**6353.24**	**9409.38**
#现金支出	Cash Expenditures	3437.10	3414.15	4142.41	5170.28	8236.93
平均每人纯收入(元)	**Per Capita Annual Net Income(yuan)**	**1617.56**	**2825.38**	**3809.07**	**5159.06**	**8934.21**
平均每人主要消费品消费量(公斤)	**Per Capita Consumption of Majar Consumor Goods(kg)**					
粮 食	Grain	150.93	155.91	164.76	168.99	178.96
#大 米	Rice	124.51	130.36	134.80	142.30	152.04
食 油	Edible Oil	2.99	3.69	4.44	4.69	6.72
肉禽及其制品	Meat,Poultry and Related Product	20.28	22.78	24.60	29.47	34.94
#猪 肉	Pork	18.24	20.27	22.15	26.52	31.00
家 禽	Poultry	1.62	1.97	1.90	2.36	2.95
蛋类及蛋制品	Eggs and Their Products	1.56	1.87	1.88	2.16	2.33
水产品	Aquatic Products	0.28	0.43	0.34	0.51	0.69
#鱼 类	Fish	0.26	0.39	0.31	0.45	0.61
蔬 菜	Vegetables	96.11	98.25	110.41	119.02	138.29
瓜 果	Melon and Fruits	7.38	8.63	8.84	11.90	17.04
食 糖	Sugar	0.56	0.68	0.58	0.82	0.86
卷 烟(盒)	Cigarette(pack)	16.81	20.43	24.62	29.72	40.48
酒	Liquor	5.62	7.18	7.56	7.84	10.37
每百户耐用消费品拥有量	**Number of Durable Consumer Goods Owned By Per 100 Rural Households**					
黑白电视机(台)	Black/White TV Set(set)	0.67	0.22	0.89		
彩色电视机(台)	Color TV Set(set)	88.62	88.84	90.40	99.55	102.23
电冰箱(台)	Refrigerator(set)	26.12	35.71	37.95	44.42	55.36
洗衣机(台)	Washing Machine(set)	48.88	55.36	60.71	70.54	77.00
影碟机(台)	Video Disc Player(set)	45.09	44.87	47.77	46.88	58.48
热水器(台)	Water Heater(set)	5.36	5.36	7.14	13.39	17.41
摩托车(辆)	Motorcycles(set)	27.68	31.25	37.50	39.06	44.42
自行车(辆)	Bicycle(unit)	4.69	4.69	4.02	6.25	6.70
电话机(部)	Telephone(unit)	19.64	18.75	14.96	16.96	19.20
移动电话(部)	Mobile Telephone(unit)	135.04	141.96	148.21	169.87	189.73

10−17 农村居民家庭人均经营费用和生产性固定资产购置
Per Capita Expenditure for Household Operations and Expenditure for Purchasing Productive Fixed Assets of Rural Households

单位：元 (yuan)

指　标	Item	2006	2007	2008	2009	2010	2011
家庭经营费用支出	**Expenditure for Household Operations**	**699.90**	**722.95**	**944.61**	**872.54**	**871.62**	**1218.87**
农业生产支出	Farming	223.57	240.83	288.09	298.33	312.74	374.98
林业生产支出	Forestry	1.45	1.80	2.69	2.13	2.65	8.64
牧业生产支出	Animal Husbandry	338.60	429.48	580.29	497.29	484.31	628.23
渔业生产支出	Fishery	0.76	1.88	2.29	3.34	2.51	1.03
工业生产支出	Industry	7.06	5.13	12.47	6.18	4.50	26.90
建筑业支出	Construction	10.29	7.51	3.78	10.08	10.51	17.15
交通运输邮电业支出	Transport, Post and Telecommunication	17.69	18.47	27.11	26.48	26.82	86.41
批发和零售贸易、餐饮业支出	Wholesale and Retail Trade & Catering Services	92.44	9.16	17.67	18.70	18.40	63.42
社会服务业支出	Social Services	1.82	1.47	1.13	1.42	1.07	4.78
文教卫生支出	Culture, Education and Health Care	4.81	5.10	5.39	4.83	3.62	4.06
其他经营支出	Others	1.39	2.13	3.69	3.78	4.49	3.27
购置生产用固定资产支出	**Expenditure for Purchasing Productive Fixed Assets**	**96.28**	**76.66**	**167.99**	**166.61**	**102.89**	**209.95**
#农林牧渔业机械	Machinery of Farming, Forestry, Animal Husbandry and Fishery	13.76	13.78	15.60	21.61	22.89	52.80
工业机械	Industrial Machinery	3.39	2.06	6.87	3.46	5.74	5.91
运输机械	Transportation Machinery	40.81	19.96	70.27	92.13	36.32	86.99
役畜、产品畜	Draught Animals and Commodity Animals	28.61	30.89	48.53	26.02	16.46	38.80

10-18 农村居民家庭主要产品商品率

Commodity Rate of Major Agricultural Products in Rural Households

单位：% (%)

指　标	Item	2006	2007	2008	2009	2010	2011
大农业	Agriculture	54.2	53.3	60.2	59.6	51.5	54.3
小农业	Farming	41.5	38.9	43.8	46.6	39.9	39.5
#粮　食	Grain	18.9	17.9	17.2	19.1	15.2	26.9
油　料	Oil-bearing Crops	49.7	53.9	32.2	36.0	46.3	36.5
糖　料	Sugar Crops	44.6	88.6	79.4	80.8	83.5	93.5
烟　叶	Tobacco	84.9	92.0	93.7	88.0	91.4	84.7
蔬　菜	Vagetable	29.7	27.7	29.0	27.7	31.6	33.0
果用瓜	Melon	89.6	72.3	94.8	96.3	98.0	92.2
水　果	Fruits	62.6	48.8	71.9	71.5	79.5	75.3
茶　叶	Tea	32.1	26.9	40.0	41.9	26.1	27.3
油桐籽	Tung-oil Seeds	69.2	69.6	89.9	100.0	100.0	100.0
油茶籽	Tea-oil Seeds		36.6	100.0	100.0		100.0
核　桃	Walnuts	35.1	60.3	81.3	82.9	85.4	72.9
出售自宰猪肉	Pork Slaughtered by Peasants Themselves & Sold	62.0	60.7	58.6	61.3	59.7	60.0
出售自宰羊肉	Mutton Slaughtered by Peasants Themselves & Sold	85.7	94.0	95.7	82.9	93.2	95.2
出售自宰家禽	Poultry Slaughtered by Peasants Themselves & Sold	57.5	53.4	57.1	57.3	50.8	70.2
禽　蛋	Poultry and Eggs	31.6	29.0	27.7	33.1	23.1	38.6

10-19 农村居民人均粮食收支存

Per Capita Grain Income,Expense and Stock of Rural Households

单位：公斤 (kg)

指　标	Item	2006	2007	2008	2009	2010	2011
年内粮食收入合计	**Grain Income within Current Year**	**424.84**	**451.54**	**485.84**	**478.34**	**448.93**	**392.63**
家庭经营生产	Household Operations	359.14	391.14	419.08	405.73	376.48	312.08
购　入	Bought Grain	60.85	56.16	63.45	69.95	70.40	80.00
借　入	Borrowed Grain	0.84	1.55	0.10	0.19	0.10	
收回借出粮	Recall of Loaned Grain	2.41	1.61	2.01	1.27	0.93	0.24
其它粮食收入	Other Grain Income	1.60	1.08	1.20	1.20	1.02	0.32
年内粮食支出合计	**Grain Expense within Current Year**	**419.51**	**423.05**	**446.88**	**434.86**	**381.53**	**400.77**
#主食用粮	Staple Food Grain	186.72	183.69	186.38	173.17	164.63	162.62
出　售	Sold Grain	68.02	70.00	72.12	77.67	57.35	83.90
种　籽	Seed	13.15	12.96	5.51	4.56	3.93	8.30
饲　料	Forage	147.49	153.30	181.01	170.46	153.39	145.78
借　出	Loaned Grain	1.48	1.48	0.33	4.58	0.51	
其它粮食支出	Other Grain Expenses	2.37	1.44	1.04	3.85	1.67	0.04
年末结存	**Stock of Grain at the Year-end**	**354.07**	**392.60**	**409.11**	**389.24**	**386.35**	**302.41**

主要统计指标解释

一、城镇住户

城镇家庭人口 指居住在一起，经济上合在一起共同生活的家庭成员。凡计算为家庭人口的成员其全部收支都包括在本家庭中。

城镇就业面 指就业人口占家庭人口的百分比。

城镇就业者负担人数 指家庭人口与就业人口之比。

城镇家庭总收入 指家庭成员得到的工薪收入、经营净收入、财产性收入、转移性收入之和，不包括出售财物收入和借贷收入。

城镇家庭可支配收入 指家庭成员得到可用于最终消费支出和其它非义务性支出以及储蓄的总和，即居民家庭可以用来自由支配的收入。它是家庭总收入扣除交纳的所得税、个人交纳的社会保障支出以及记账补贴后的收入。计算公式为:

可支配收入 = 家庭总收入 - 交纳所得税 - 个人交纳的社会保障支出 - 记帐补贴

城镇家庭总支出 指除借贷支出以外的全部家庭支出。包括消费性支出、购房建房支出、转移性支出、财产性支出、社会保障支出。

城镇家庭消费性支出 指家庭用于日常生活的支出，包括食品、衣着、家庭设备用品及服务、医疗保健、交通和通信、娱乐教育文化服务、居住、杂项商品和服务等八大类支出。

城镇家庭服务性消费支出 指家庭用于支付社会提供的各种非商品性服务费用。

城镇家庭收入分组方法 将所有调查户依户人均可支配收入由低到高排队，按 10%，10%，20%，20%，20%，10%，10% 的比例依次分成: 最低收入户、低收入户、中等偏下收入户、中等收入户、中等偏上收入户、高收入户、最高收入户等七组。总体中最低 5% 的户为困难户。

恩格尔系数 指食物支出金额在生活消费总支出金额中所占的比例。计算公式为:

$$\text{恩格尔系数} = \frac{\text{食品支出金额}}{\text{生活消费总支出金额}} \times 100\%$$

二、农村住户

农村住户 指农村常住户。农村常住户指长期（一年以上）居住在乡镇（不包括城关镇）行政管理区域内的住户，以及长期居住在城关镇所辖行政村范围内的农村住户。户口不在本地而在本地居住一年及以上的住户也包括在本地农村常住户范围内；有本地户口，但举家外出谋生一年以上的住户，无论是否保留承包耕地都不包括在本地农村住户范围内。

常住人口 指全年经常在家或在家居住 6 个月以上，而且经济和生活与本户连成一体的人口。外出从业人员在外居住时间虽然在 6 个月以上，但收入主要带回家中，经济与本户连为一体，仍视为家庭常住人口；在家居住，生活和本户连成一体的国家职工、退休人员也为家庭常住人口。但是现役军人、中专及以上（走读生除外）的在校学生、以及常年在外（不包括探亲、看病等）且已有稳定的职业与居住场所的外出从业人员，不算家庭常住人口。家庭常住人口主要作为计算农村住户平均每人收入、消费和积累水平及分析家庭人口状况的依据。

整、半劳动力 整劳动力指男子 18 周岁到 50 周岁，女子 18 周岁到 45 周岁；半劳动力指男子 16 周岁到 17 周岁，51 周岁到 60 周岁；女子 16 周岁到 17 周岁，46 周岁到 55 周岁，同时具有劳动能力的人。虽然在劳动年龄之内，但已丧失劳动能力的人，不应算为劳动力；超过劳动年龄，但能经常参加劳动，计入半劳动力数内。常住人口中的职工，若这些职工为劳动力，就包括在本户的整半劳动力中。

总收入 指调查期内农村住户和住户成员从各种来源渠道得到的收入总和。按收入的性质划分为工资性收入、家庭经营收入、财产性收入和转移性收入。

工资性收入 指农村住户成员受雇于单位或个人，靠出卖劳动而获得的收入。

家庭经营收入 指农村住户以家庭为生产经营单位进行生产筹划和管理而获得的收入。农村住户家庭经营活动按行业划分为农业、林业、牧业、渔业、工业、建筑业、交通运输业邮电业、批发和零售贸易餐饮业、社会服务业、文教卫生业和其他家庭经营。

财产性收入 指金融资产或有形非生产性资产的所有者向其他机构单位提供资金或将有形非生产性资产供其支配，作为回报而从中获得的收入。

转移性收入 指农村住户和住户成员无须付出任何对应物而获得的货物、服务、资金或资产所有权等，不包括无偿提供的用于固定资本形成的资金。一般情况下，是指农村住户在二次分配中的所有收入。

现金收入 指农村住户和住户成员在调查期内得到以现金形态表现的收入。按来源分成工资性收入、家庭经营现金收入、财产性收入、转移性收入。

纯收入 指农村住户当年从各个来源得到的总收入相应地扣除所发生的费用后的收入总和。计算方法:

纯收入 = 总收入 − 家庭经营费用支出 − 税费支出 − 生产性固定资产折旧 − 赠送农村外部亲友支出

纯收入主要用于再生产投入和当年生活消费支出，也可用于储蓄和各种非义务性支出。“农民人均纯收入”按人口平均的纯收入水平，反映的是一个地区或一个农户农村居民的平均收入水平。

总支出 指农村住户用于生产、生活和再分配的全部支出。家庭经营费用支出、购置生产性固定资产支出、生产性固定资产折旧、税费支出、生活消费支出、财产性支出和转移性支出。

Explanatory Notes on Main Statistical Indicators

I. Urban Households

Population of Urban Households refer to members of the household living and sharing economically together. All income and expenditure of the population of the household are included in the income and expenditure of the household.

Proportion of Urban Employment refer to the proportion of employed population to the population of urban households.

Number of Dependents Per Urban Employee refers to the ratio between number of persons in urban households and the number of dependents.

Total Income of Urban Households refers to the sum of wage and salary, net business income, income from properties, and income from transfers of members of the households, excluding income from selling of properties and income from borrowings.

Disposable Income of Urban Households refers to the actual income at the disposal of members of the households which can be used for final consumption, other non-compulsory expenditure and savings. This equals to total income minus income tax, personal contribution to social security and sample household subsidy for keeping diaries. Following formula is used:

Disposable income = total household income - income tax - personal contribution to social security - sample household subsidy for keeping diaries

Total expenditure of Urban Households refer to all expenditure of the households except expenditure on leading. It includes expenditure on consumption, on purchasing or building houses, on transfers, on properties and on social security.

Consumption Expenditure of Urban Households refers to total expenditure of the sample households for consumption in daily life, including expenditure on eight categories such as food, clothing, household appliances and services, health care and medical services, transport and communications, recreation, education and cultural services, housing, miscellaneous goods and services.

Expenditure of Urban Households on Consumption of Services refers to expenditure of households on services of various kinds provided by the society.

Urban Households by Income Group All households in the sample are grouped, by per capita disposable income of the household, into groups of lowest income, low income, lower middle income, middle income, upper middle income, high income and highest income, each group consisting of 10%, 10%, 20%, 20%, 20%, 10% and 10% of all households respectively. The lowest 5% of households are also referred to as poor households.

Engel Coefficient refers to the percentage of expenditure on food in the total consumption expenditure, using the following formula:

$$\text{Engel Coefficient}=\frac{\text{expenditure on food}}{\text{total consumption expenditure}}\times 100\%$$

II. Rural Households

Rural Households refer to resident households in rural areas. Resident households in rural areas are the households residing for more than one year in the areas under the jurisdiction of administration of township governments(excluding county towns), and in the areas under the jurisdiction of administration of villages in county towns. Migrated households residing in the current addresses for over one year with their household registration in other places are included in the resident households of their current addresses. For households with their household registration in one place but all members of the households moving away for living in another place for over one year, they will not be included in the rural households of the area where they are registered, irrespective of whether they still keep their contracted land.

Resident Population refers to population staying at home permanently or for over 6 months during a year and sharing life economically with the household. Members of the household staying away from the household for over 6 months but keeping a close economic relation with the household by sending the majority of income to the household are regarded as resident population of the household. Government staff and workers or retirees living as close members of the household are also considered as resident population. However, servicemen, students of secondary technical schools or schools of higher education and persons with stable jobs and residence outside the household (excluding those visiting relatives or seeking medical service) are not included as resident population of the household. Resident population is used in calculating income, consumption, accumulation on per capita basis of rural households and in analyzing composition of rural households.

Full/Semi Labour Force Full labour force refers to persons capable of work, aged 18-50 for males and 18-45 for females. Semi labour force refers to persons capable of work, aged 16-17 and 51-60 for males and 16-17 and 46-55 for females. Persons at their working ages but not capable of work are not to be included as labour force. Persons not at working ages but participating regularly in work are included in semi labour force. For staff and workers as resident population of the household, they are included as full or semi labour force of the household if they are in the labour force.

Total Income refers to the sum of income earned from various sources by the rural households and their members during the reference period, and is classified as income from wages and salaries, income from household operations, income from properties and income from transfers.

Income from Wages and Salaries refers to income from labour earned by the members of rural households employed by other units or individuals.

Income from Household Operations refers to income by the rural households as units of production and operations. Operations by rural households are classified by economic activities as agriculture, forestry, animal husbandry, fishery, manufacturing, construction, transportation, post and telecommunications, wholesale, retail and catering, social service, culture, education, health, and other household operations.

Income from Properties refers to the income received as returns by owners of financial assets or tangible non-productive assets by providing capitals or tangible non-productive assets to other institutional units.

Income from Transfers refers to the receipt by rural households and their members of goods, services, capitals or rights of assets without giving or repaying accordingly, excluding capitals provided to them for the formation of fixed assets. In general, it refers to all income received by rural households through redistribution.

Cash Income refers to income received by rural households and their members in the form of cash during the reference period. It is classified, by source of income, into income from wages and salaries, cash income from household operations, income from properties and income from transfers.

Net Income refers to the total income of rural households from all sources minus all corresponding expenses. The formula for calculation is as follows:

Net income = total income - household operation expenses - taxes and fees - depreciation of fixed assets for production - gifts to non-rural relatives

Net income is mainly used as input for reproduction and as consumption expenditure of the year, and also used for savings and non-compulsory expenses of various forms. ?°Per capita net income of farmers?±is the level of net income averaged by population which reflects the average income level of rural households in a given area.

Total Expenditure refers to total expenses of rural households on production, consumption and redistribution, including expenditure on household operations, on purchase of productive fixed assets, depreciation of productive fixed assets, taxes and fees, expenses on household consumption, expenses on properties and expenses on transfer

11

Eleven

城市概况

General Survey of Cities

11-1 城市公用事业
Basic Statistics on City Public Utilities

项　　目	Item	2006	2007	2008	2009	2010	2011
城市建设	**City Areas and Floor Space of Buildings**						
城区面积(平方公里)	Urban Area(sq.km)		4044.45	4042.57	4057.98	4103.09	4108.16
建成区面积(平方公里)	Area of Built Districts(sq.km)	792.40	812.30	821.60	883.56	972.99	986.50
城市建设用地面积(平方公里)	Area of Land Used for Urban Construction (sq.km)	908.16	932.05	952.04	999.81	1002.15	1005.73
征用土地面积(人/平方公里)	Area of Land Put in Requisition for State Construction Projects(persons/sq.km)	19.07	17.45	13.97	16.97	26.03	36.20
城市人口密度(人/平方公里)	Population Density of City Districts (persons/sq.km)	1832	2331	2379	2440	2481	2579
城市供水、燃气	**Supply Water and Gas**						
年末供水综合生产能力(万立方米/日)	Production Capacity of Tap Water Supply at Year-end (10000 cu.m)	371.40	367.70	357.05	348.56	352.11	364.56
全年供水管道长度(公里)	Annual Length of Water Pipelines(km)	6802.00	7401.30	7719.80	8706.10	9376.00	11107.57
建城区城市供水管道密度(公里/平方公里)	Water Pipelines Pensity of Built Districts of city(km/sq.km)	8.6	9.1	9.4	9.85	9.64	11.26
供水总量(万立方米)	Volume of Tap Water Supply (10000 cu.m)	71568	68297	64871	61971	63572	67766
#生活用水	Water Consumption for Residential Use	33586	32278	31560	32584	33064	36091
生产用水	Water Consumption for Productive Use	18575	16555	13850	10517	12109	11335
用水人口(万人)	Number of Residents with Access to Tap Water (10000 persons)	749.46	751.80	800.32	845.78	880.83	920.40
人均日生活用水(升)	Per Capita Daily Consumption of Tap Water for Residential Use (liter)	149.40	141.57	127.72	124.32	116.88	127.82
用水普及率 (%)	Coverage Rate of Urban Population with Access to Tap Water (%)	81.0	79.7	83.2	85.4	86.5	86.9
人工煤气生产能力(万立方米)	Production Capacity of Gaswork Gas (10 000 cu.m)	129.80	190.80	191.80	191.80	191.80	187.00
管道长度(公里)	Length of Gas Pipelines (km)	2653.00	2850.10	2925.10	3051.20	3207.50	3264.27
人工煤气	Coal Gas	2465.00	2639.30	2693.90	2784.40	2829.70	2741.53
液化石油气	Liquefied Petroleum Gas	135.00	136.00	146.16	154.82	182.72	182.72
天然气	Natural Gas	53.00	74.77	85.05	111.93	195.07	340.02
全年供气总量	Annual Volume of Gas Supply						
人工煤气(万立方米)	Coal Gas (10 000 cu.m)	21650	23491	26613	26886	26963	30515
#家庭用量	Consumption of Gaswork Gas for Residential Use	9013	9439	10493	10921	11436	13118
天然气(万立方米)	Natural Gas Supply(10 000 cu.m)	705	1449	1378	2336	3546	5496
#家庭用量	Consumption of Natural Gas for Residential Use	297	1005	1017	1070	1160	674
液化石油气 (吨)	Liquefied Petroleum Gas(ton)	78800	81565	86863	89770	94481	99396
#家庭用量	Consumption of Liquefied Gas for Residential Use	58624	74171	79149	82645	86703	91742
用气人口(万人)	Population with Access to Gas (10 000 persons)	465.48	481.67	520.28	536.53	554.35	582.54
人工煤气	Coal Gas	133.8	145.11	156.15	161.33	166.76	207.69
液化石油气	Liquefied Petroleum Gas	327.55	327.91	355.35	364.88	375.94	350.98
天然气	Natural Gas	4.13	8.65	8.78	10.32	11.65	23.87
燃气普及率(%)	Coverage Rate of Urban Population with Access to Gas (%)	50.3	51.1	54.1	54.2	54.5	55.0
城市市政设施	**Municipal Infrastructure**						
年末实有道路长度(公里)	Length of Paved Roads at Year-end(km)	3474	3772	3836	3933	4081	4487

11-1 续表 continued

项 目	Item	2006	2007	2008	2009	2010	2011
年末实有道路面积(万平方米)	Area of Paved Roads at Year-end(10 000sq.m)	5156	5711	5759	5972	6342	7054
人均拥有道路面积(平方米)	Per Capita Area of Paved Roads(sq.m)	5.57	6.06	5.99	6.03	6.23	6.66
城市排水管道长度(公里)	Length of City Sewage Pipes(km)	4485	4724	4796	5047	5507	5977
城市污水日处理能力(万立方米)	Daily Disposal Capacity of City Sewage (10 000 cu.m)	35.0	57.0	66.0	93.5	170.5	170.5
建城区城市排水管道密度(公里/平方公里)	Density of City Sewage Pipes(km/sq.km)	5.66	5.82	5.84	5.71.	5.66	6.06
城市桥梁(座)	Number of City Bridges (unit)	668	714	715	727	735	776
城市道路照明灯(千盏)	Number of Street Lights (1 000 units)	231	232	260	299	302	391
城市公共交通	**Public Traffic**						
年末公共交通运营数(辆)	Number of Public Vehicles under Operation at Year-end (Buses and Trolley Buses, etc.) (unit)	3687	5083	5140	4864	4984	5364
运营线路网长度(公里)	Network Length (km)	1221	1456	1527	3523	6056	6212
公共交通客运总量(万人次)	Passengers Transported by Public Vehicles (10 000person-times)	88384	98999	103383	109586	120220	130976
出租汽车(辆)	Number of Taxi(unit)	13540	13411	13768	14700	15087	17196
城市绿化和园林	**City Greening**						
城市园林绿地面积(公顷)	Area of Parks and Green Land (hectare)	40682	41410	41841	43781	45500	48024
公园绿地面积	Park Green Areas	3933	3984	4271	4602	5422	5830
人均公园绿地面积(平方米)	Per Capita Area of Parks and Green Land(sq.m)	4.25	4.23	4.44	4.65	5.33	5.50
公园个数(个)	Number of Parks and Zoos(unit)	105	117	121	128	130	146
公园面积(万公顷)	Area of Parks (10 000 hectares)	3675	3914	3773	3965	4622	4941
建成区绿化覆盖率(%)	Green Covered Area as % of Completed Area (%)	21.70	21.48	21.55	22.12	21.83	24.57
城市环境卫生	**Environmental Sanitation**						
清扫保洁面积(万平方米)	Area under Cleaning Program (10 000 sq.m)	4221	4900	4916	5374	5948	6982
生活垃圾清运量(万吨)	Volume of Garbage Disposal (10 000 tons)	393.50	402.90	413.80	426.60	428.51	431.46
市容环卫专用车辆设备总数(台)	Number of Special Vehicles for Environmental Sanitation (unit)	1082	1160	1216	1315	1588	2320
公共厕所(座)	Number of Public Lavatories (unit)	2015	1924	2055	2116	2147	2121
#三类以上	Third Grade and Above	1330	1207	1284	1358	1463	1445

注：资料来源于省住房城乡建设厅、省交通厅(以下相关表同)。

Note:Data are provided by provincial department of transport and department of housing and urban and rural development(The relative tables in the chapter are the same).

11-2 城市气象(2011)
Climate of Major Cities

城市名称	City	年平均气温(℃) Annual Average Temperature(℃)	年降水量(毫米) Annual Precipitation(mm)	年日照时数(小时) Annual Sunshine Hours(hour)	年平均相对湿度(%) Annual Average Relative Humidity(%)
贵 阳 市	Guiyang	14.0	735.2	804.0	78
六盘水市	Liupanshui	12.2	777.9	1384.5	82
遵 义 市	Zunyi	15.9	836.7	1223.1	72
安 顺 市	Anshun	13.6	851.1	1276.4	78
铜 仁 市	Tongren	17.4	941.9	968.0	68
兴 义 市	Xingyi	15.7	612.6	1491.8	77
毕 节 市	Bijie	13.1	665.4	1259.6	82
凯 里 市	Kaili	16.0	1004.6	1404.8	72
都 匀 市	Duyun	14.9	1094.1	1074.7	83
清 镇 市	Qingzhen	14.2	780.5	1235.4	83
赤 水 市	Chishui	18.2	880.7	1342.3	74
仁 怀 市	Renhuai	15.8	864.1	1244.9	74
福 泉 市	Fuquan	14.8	868.4	1113.1	71

注：资料来源于省气象局(下表同)。
Note:Data in the table are provided by the provincial bureau of meteorology(The same applies to the next table).

11-3 主要城市平均气温（2011）
Monthly Average Temperature of Major Cities

单位：℃ ℃

城市名称	City	1月 Jan.	2月 Feb.	3月 Mar.	4月 Apr.	5月 May	6月 June	7月 July	8月 Aug.	9月 Sept.	10月 Oct.	11月 Nov.	12月 Dec.
贵 阳 市	Guiyang	-1.5	7.7	6.8	14.5	19.0	21.3	23.3	23.7	20.2	15.1	14.3	3.6
六盘水市	Liupanshui	-1.9	6.3	5.6	12.8	17.6	19.6	20.9	20.6	17.4	13.3	11.9	2.6
遵 义 市	Zunyi	0.9	8.5	8.6	15.9	21.0	23.0	26.1	26.5	22.6	16.6	15.5	5.4
安 顺 市	Anshun	-1.1	7.3	6.7	14.3	18.5	20.8	22.4	22.3	19.3	14.7	13.7	3.7
铜 仁 市	Tongren	2.5	8.5	10.4	17.7	22.1	25.0	28.9	28.4	24.0	17.9	16.0	7.4
兴 义 市	Xingyi	1.8	9.8	9.5	16.9	20.6	22.8	23.7	23.4	21.3	16.7	15.0	7.0
毕 节 市	Bijie	-1.4	6.3	6.4	13.7	18.6	20.6	22.4	22.6	18.9	14.2	12.3	2.8
凯 里 市	Kaili	0.5	9.0	8.6	16.0	20.6	23.3	26.8	26.5	22.6	16.6	15.5	5.5
都 匀 市	Duyun	-0.8	8.5	7.5	15.3	19.4	22.3	24.5	24.7	21.1	15.7	15.3	4.7
清 镇 市	Qingzhen	-0.8	7.9	7.1	14.6	19.0	21.5	23.1	23.5	20.4	15.3	14.3	4.2
赤 水 市	Chishui	4.5	10.1	11.5	19.1	23.1	25.6	27.5	29.8	23.8	18.4	16.1	8.5
仁 怀 市	Renhuai	0.8	8.4	8.5	16.0	21.1	23.0	25.9	26.7	22.1	16.5	15.2	5.2
福 泉 市	Fuquan	-0.3	8.2	7.8	14.9	19.4	22.2	24.7	24.7	21.1	15.5	14.6	4.3

11–4 城市建设(2011)

Basic Statistics on City Construction

城市名称	City	城区面积 (平方公里) Urban Area (sq.km)	建成区面积 (平方公里) Area of Built Districts (sq.km)	城市建设用地面积 (平方公里) Area of Land Used for Urban Construction (sq.km)
贵 阳 市	Guiyang	414.77	162.00	170.85
六盘水市	Liupanshui	129.00	38.50	58.98
遵 义 市	Zunyi	220.00	62.00	61.81
安 顺 市	Anshun	109.48	36.00	31.15
铜 仁 市	Tongren	38.89	31.90	36.44
兴 义 市	Xingyi	73.40	33.22	37.00
毕 节 市	Bijie	43.87	30.00	36.15
凯 里 市	Kaili	92.04	54.20	38.18
都 匀 市	Duyun	301.50	14.69	14.41
清 镇 市	Qingzhen	51.60	15.17	11.22
赤 水 市	Chishui	91.00	9.00	8.84
仁 怀 市	Renhuai	89.00	12.00	9.92
福 泉 市	Fuquan	19.20	9.60	9.27

11–5 城市设施水平(2011)

Basic Statistics on Level of Public Facilities in Cities

城市名称	City	城市用水普及率 (%) Coverage Rate of Urban Population with Access to Tap Water (%)	城市燃气普及率 (%) Coverage Rate of Urban Population with Access to Gas (%)	每万人拥有公共交通车辆 (标台) Number of Public Transportation Vehicles Per 10 000 Population (unit)	人均城市道路面积 (平方米) Per Capita Area of Paved Roads (sq.m)	人均公园绿地面积 (平方米) Per Capita Park Green Areas (sq.m)
贵 阳 市	Guiyang	89.4	95.5	10.0	5.37	9.39
六盘水市	Liupanshui	96.5	85.6	8.0	9.96	2.40
遵 义 市	Zunyi	100.0	63.9	5.7	5.23	4.89
安 顺 市	Anshun	91.1	37.4	5.3	5.68	1.36
铜 仁 市	Tongren	89.7	34.7	4.4	7.02	3.21
兴 义 市	Xingyi	92.3	29.4	2.4	16.08	7.86
毕 节 市	Bijie	95.2	15.6	2.9	9.14	9.09
凯 里 市	Kaili	83.4	84.1	7.8	8.81	14.84
都 匀 市	Duyun	98.0	73.9	9.7	7.27	8.22
清 镇 市	Qingzhen	84.9	49.7	2.0	3.16	5.82
赤 水 市	Chishui	79.2	52.8	5.0	5.02	5.63
仁 怀 市	Renhuai	92.3	44.1	2.2	5.31	1.62
福 泉 市	Fuquan	98.4	60.9	2.6	7.39	10.12

11-6 城市供水（2011）

Basic Statistics on Tap Water Supply in Cities

城市名称	City	年末供水综合生产能力（万立方米/日）Production Capacity of Tap Water Supply (year-end) (10 000 cu.m/day)	年末供水管道长度（公里）Length of Water Supply Pipelines (year-end) (km)	全年供水总量（万立方米）Total Annual Volume of Water Supply (10 000 cu.m)	#生活用水 For Residential Use	#生产用水 For Productive Use	用水人口（万人）Number of Residents with Access to Tap Water (10 000 persons)	人均日生活用水量（升）Per Capita Daily Consumption of Tap Water for Residential Use(liter)
贵阳市	Guiyang	126.90	3413.16	25238.82	10642.75	4694.07	224.26	169
六盘水市	Liupanshui	10.00	925.08	3217.00	1301.00	1073.00	31.00	167
遵义市	Zunyi	23.40	305.00	4831.00	3326.00	510.00	73.55	137
安顺市	Anshun	8.60	142.80	2083.10	1185.80	446.80	46.80	81
铜仁市	Tongren	14.26	159.50	1600.60	1025.00	219.00	24.05	132
兴义市	Xingyi	13.76	380.00	1635.00	1010.00	345.00	28.42	109
毕节市	Bijie	18.15	445.70	2054.40	993.00	150.70	22.30	136
凯里市	Kaili	8.38	688.77	2055.50	979.40	278.00	23.60	119
都匀市	Duyun	11.80	240.48	1687.82	744.00	339.00	22.53	135
清镇市	Qingzhen	2.50	145.00	416.00	304.00	101.00	11.97	72
赤水市	Chishui	2.00	64.80	366.50	249.00	31.00	9.00	85
仁怀市	Renhuai	3.00	78.00	707.00	510.00	115.00	12.00	127
福泉市	Fuquan	2.19	136.00	801.54	465.67	252.10	7.19	181

11-7 城市燃气(2011)

Basic Statistics on Supply of Gas in Cities

城市名称	City	人工煤气生产能力（万立方米/日）Production Capacity of Gaswork Gas (10 000 cu.m/day)	管道长度（公里）Length of GasPipelines(km)			全年供气总量 Volume of Gas Supply			用气人口（万人）Population with Accessto Gas (10 000 persons)		
			人工煤气 Coal Gas	液化石油气 Liquefied Petroleum Gas	天然气 Natural Gas	人工煤气（万立方米）Coal Gas (10 000 cu.m)	液化石油气（吨）Liquefied Petroleum Gas (ton)	天然气（万立方米）Natural Gas (10 000 cu.m)	人工煤气 Coal Gas	液化石油气 Liquefied Petroleum Gas	天然气 Natural Gas
贵阳市	Guiyang	180	1971		55	25237	36000	2949	174.69	63.00	2.08
六盘水市	Liupanshui	6	637			4723	497		26.00	1.50	
遵义市	Zunyi			10	20		10280	1320		42.00	5.00
安顺市	Anshun				77		4088	9		12.20	7.00
铜仁市	Tongren			91			2005			9.30	
兴义市	Xingyi				21		2454	4		9.00	0.05
毕节市	Bijie				62		480	76		3.20	0.46
凯里市	Kaili				65		6639	148		19.80	4.00
都匀市	Duyun			28			1683			17.00	
清镇市	Qingzhen	1	133			555			7.00		
赤水市	Chishui			4	24		303	831		1.50	4.50
仁怀市	Renhuai				7		456	147		5.13	0.60
福泉市	Fuquan						491			4.45	

11–8 城市市政设施（2011）

Statistics on Municipal Infrastructure in Cities

城市名称	City	年末实有道路长度（公里）Length of Paved Roads (year-end) (km)	年末实有道路面积（万平方米）Area of Paved Roads (year-end) (10 000 sq.m)	城市桥梁（座）Number of City Bridges (unit)	城市排水管道长度（公里）Length of City Sewage Pipes (km)	城市污水日处理能力（万立方米）Daily Disposal Capacity of City Sewage (10 000 cu.m)	城市道路照明灯（千盏）Number of Street Lights (1 000 units)
贵 阳 市	Guiyang	872.0	1347.6	188	2051	58.0	129
六盘水市	Liupanshui	160.0	320.0	25	70	6.5	21
遵 义 市	Zunyi	276.0	385.0	28	222	11.0	21
安 顺 市	Anshun	181.5	292.2	19	297	5.0	12
铜 仁 市	Tongren	184.1	188.3	17	145	5.3	8
兴 义 市	Xingyi	226.1	495.2	25	246	5.5	13
毕 节 市	Bijie	108.0	214.1	35	92	8.0	5
凯 里 市	Kaili	147.8	249.3	24	219	8.0	25
都 匀 市	Duyun	92.0	167.3	30	158	6.0	6
清 镇 市	Qingzhen	38.0	44.6	4	45	5.0	3
赤 水 市	Chishui	42.0	57.0	2	72	2.0	4
仁 怀 市	Renhuai	26.0	69.0	5	40	1.0	4
福 泉 市	Fuquan	65.0	54.0	6	38	1.5	2

11–9 城市绿地和园林(2011)

Basic Statistics on Parks and Green Areas in Cities

城市名称	City	城市园林绿地面积（公顷）Area of Parks and Green Land(hectare)	#公园绿地 Park Green Areas	公园（个）Number of Parks (unit)	公园面积（公顷）Area of Parks (hectare)	建成区绿化覆盖率（%）Green Covered Area as % of Completed Area (%)
贵 阳 市	Guiyang	20551	2357	13	2359	42.1
六盘水市	Liupanshui	216	77	3	72	25.0
遵 义 市	Zunyi	2072	360	4	337	34.6
安 顺 市	Anshun	2228	70	2	70	16.9
铜 仁 市	Tongren	773	86	6	73	25.8
兴 义 市	Xingyi	746	242	7	58	22.5
毕 节 市	Bijie	931	213	4	213	39.4
凯 里 市	Kaili	1203	420	7	680	23.9
都 匀 市	Duyun	577	189	6	129	39.5
清 镇 市	Qingzhen	464	82	1	6	32.8
赤 水 市	Chishui	362	64	2	15	30.2
仁 怀 市	Renhuai	134	21	1	1	15.7
福 泉 市	Fuquan	264	74	3	74	30.8

11-10 城市市容环境卫生(2011)
Basic Statistics on Urban Sanitation in Cities

城市名称	City	清扫保洁面积(万平方米) Area under Cleaning Program (10 000 sq.m)	生活垃圾清运量(万吨) Volume of Garbage Disposal (10 000 tons)	市容环卫专用车辆设备总数(台) Number of Special Vehicles for Environmental Sanitation (unit)	公共厕所(座) Number of Public Lavatories (unit)	#三类以上 Third Grade and Above
贵阳市	Guiyang	1864	77.85	805	531	531
六盘水市	Liupanshui	265	15.30	82	35	8
遵义市	Zunyi	493	33.46	184	310	310
安顺市	Anshun	314	15.28	74	21	21
铜仁市	Tongren	446	10.49	37	117	28
兴义市	Xingyi	138	9.13	27	16	
毕节市	Bijie	87	12.90	156	36	
凯里市	Kaili	328	13.90	34	30	30
都匀市	Duyun	109	10.33	17	36	36
清镇市	Qingzhen	56	5.10	29	18	18
赤水市	Chishui	40	3.43	14	12	12
仁怀市	Renhuai	58	5.10	30	21	16
福泉市	Fuquan	43	6.00	7	20	

主要统计指标解释

供水综合生产能力　指按供水设施取水、净化、送水、出厂输水干管等环节设计能力计算的综合生产能力。包括在原设计能力的基础上，经挖、革、改增加的生产能力。计算时，以四个环节中最薄弱的环节为主确定能力。

年末供水管道长度　指从送水泵至用户水表之间所有管道的长度。不包括新安装尚未使用的管道。

全年供水总量　指报告期供水企业（单位）供出的全部水量。包括有效供水量和漏损水量。

生活用水量　包括公共服务用水和居民家庭用水。公共服务用水指为城市社会公共生活服务的用水。包括行政事业单位、部队营区和公共设施服务、社会服务业、批发零售贸易业、旅馆饮食业以及其他公共服务业等单位的用水。居民家庭用水指城市范围内所有居民家庭的日常生活用水。包括城市居民、农民家庭、公共供水站用水。

用水普及率　指城市用水人口数与城市人口总数的比率。计算公式:

$$\text{用水普及率}=\frac{\text{城市用水人口数}}{\text{城市人口总数}}\times 100\%$$

人工煤气生产能力　指报告期末人工煤气生产厂制气、净化、输送等环节的综合生产能力，不包括备用设备能力。一般按设计能力计算，如果实际生产能力大于设计能力时，应按实际测定的生产能力计算。测定时应以制气、净化、输送三个环节中最薄弱的环节为主。

供气管道长度　指报告期末从气源厂压缩机的出口或门站出口至各类用户引入管之间的全部已经通气投入使用的管道长度。不包括煤气生产厂、输配站、液化气储存站、灌瓶站、储配站、气化站、混气站、供应站等厂（站）内的管道。

全年供气总量　指全年燃气企业（单位）向用户供应的燃气数量。包括销售量和损失量。

用气普及率　指报告期末使用燃气的城市人口数与城市人口总数的比率。计算公式为:

$$\text{用气普及率}=\frac{\text{城市用气人口数}}{\text{城市人口总数}}\times 100\%$$

城市供热能力　指供热企业（单位）向城市热用户输送热能的设计能力。

城市供热总量　指在报告期供热企业（单位）向城市热用户输送全部蒸汽和热水的总热量。

城市供热管道长度　指从各类热源到热用户建筑物接入口之间的全部蒸汽和热水的管道长度。不包括各类热源厂内部的管道长度。

年末道路长度　指年末道路长度和与道路相通的广场、桥梁、隧道的长度，按车行道中心线计算。在统计时只统计路面宽度在 3.5 米（含 3.5 米）以上的各种铺装道路，包括开放型工业区和住宅区道路在内。

城市桥梁　指为跨越天然或人工障碍物而修建的构筑物。包括跨河桥、立交桥、人行天桥以及人行地下通道等。包括永久性桥和半永久性桥。

城市排水管道长度　指所有排水总管、干管、支管、检查井及连接井进出口等长度之和。

城市污水日处理能力　指污水处理厂（或处理装置）每昼夜处理污水量的设计能力。

年末运营车数　指年末公交企业（单位）用于运营业务的全部车辆数。以企业（单位）固定资产台帐中已投入运营的车辆数为准。

城市园林绿地面积　指报告期末用作园林和绿化的各种绿地面积。包括公共绿地、居住区绿地、单位附属绿地、防护绿地、生产绿地、道路绿地和风景林地面积。

不包括:

1. 屋顶绿化、垂直绿化、阳台绿化和室内绿化。
2. 以物质生产为主的林地、耕地、牧草地、果园和竹园等。
3. 城市总体规划中不列入绿地的水域。

公共绿地　指向公众开放的市级、区级、居住区级各类公园、街旁游园，包括其范围内的水域。其中居住区级公园应不小于 1 万平方米，街旁游园的宽度不小于 8 米，面积不小于 400 平方米。

Explanatory Notes on Main Statistical Indicators

Production Capacity of Water Supply refers to the designed overall production capacity of water facilities, covering the four segments of water collection, purification, conveyance, and outflow through trunk pipelines. Increased capacity through transformation and innovation projects is included as well. The capacity is determined mainly on the weakest of the above-mentioned four segments.

Length of Water Supply Pipelines at Year-end refers to the total length of all the pipelines between the water pumps and the user water meters, excluding pipelines newly installed but not used yet, pipeline in the water factory,and pipeline in the user's buildings.

Annual Volume of Water Supply refers to the total volume of water supplied by water-works (units) during the reference period, including both the effective water supply and loss during the water supply.

Consumption of Water for Residential Use refers to water consumption of households for daily life and water consumption of public service facilities. The latter refers to water consumption for urban public services, including the consumption of government agencies and public institutions, military barracks, public facilities, wholesale and retail outlets, restaurants, hotels, and other units providing public services. Household water consumption refers to consumption of water for daily life of all households within the boundary of cities, including households of urban residents and farmers, and public water supply stations.

Coverage Rate of Urban Population with Access to Tap Water refers to the ratio of the urban population with access to tap water to the total urban population. The formula is:

$$\text{Coverage Rate of Urban Population with Access to Tap Water} = \frac{\text{Urban population with access to tap water}}{\text{Urban population}} \times 100\%$$

Production Capacity of Gaswork Gas refers to the overall production capacity of the urban gasworks in gas generation, purification and delivery at the end of the reference period, excluding capacity of the reserved facilities. In general, it is determined by the designed capacity, and when actual production capacity is larger than the designed capacity, the capacity is determined by the actual measurement on the weakest segment in the production, purification and delivery.

Length of Gas Pipelines refers to the total length of pipelines in use between the outlet of the compressor of gas-work or outlet of gas stations and the leading pipe of users, excluding pipelines within gasworks, delivery stations, LPG storage stations, refilling stations, gas-mixing stations and supply stations.

Volume of Gas Supply refers to the total volume of gas provided to users by gas-producing enterprises (units) in a year, including the volume sold and the volume lost.

Coverage Rate of Urban Population with Access to Gas refers to the ratio of the urban population with access to gas to the total urban population at the end of the reference period. The formula is:

$$\text{Coverage Rate of Urban Population with Access to Gas} = \frac{\text{Urban population with access to gas}}{\text{Urban population}} \times 100\%$$

Heating Capacity in Urban Areas refers to the designed capacity of heating enterprises (units) in supplying heating energy to urban users during the reference period.

Quantity of Heat Supplied in Urban Areas refers to the total quantity of heat from steam and hot water supplied to urban users by heating enterprises (units) during the reference period.

Length of Urban Heating Pipelines refers to the total length of steam or hot water pipelines for sources of heat to the leading pipelines of the buildings of the users, excluding internal pipelines in heat generating enterprises.

Length of Paved Roads at Year-end refers to the length of roads with paved surface including bridges and tunnels connected with roads by the end of the year. Length of the roads is measured by the central lines for vehicles for paved roads with a width of 3.5 meters and over, including roads in open-ended factory compounds and residential quarters.

Urban Bridges refer to bridges built to cross over natural or man-made barriers, including bridges over rivers, overpasses for traffic and for pedestrians, underpasses for pedestrians, etc. Both permanent and semi-permanent bridges are included.

Length of Urban Sewage Pipes refers to the total length of general drainage, trunks, branch and inspection wells, connection wells, inlets and outlets, etc.

Daily Disposal Capacity of Urban Sewage refers to the designed 24-hour capacity of sewage disposal by the sewage treatment works or facilities.

Number of Vehicles under Operation at Year-end refers to the total number of vehicles under operation by public transport enterprises (units) at the end of the year, based on the records of operational vehicles by the enterprises (units).

Area of Urban Gardens and Green Areas refers to the total area occupied for green projects at the end of the reference period, including public green land, green land in residential quarters, green land attached to institutions, protection green land, production green land, roadside green land and forest in scenic spots. It does not include the following terms:

(1) Greenery and plants on roofs, balconies, indoors and vertical greening areas;

(2) Forest, cultivated land, grassland, orchards and bamboo grooves that are for the purpose of material production ;

(3) Water areas that are not included in urban master plan as green land.

Public Green Area refers to green areas open to the public such as municipal, community and neighborhood parks and roadside parks, including waters within parks. Neighborhood parks should occupy an area larger than 10,000 square meters, and the width of roadside parks should occupy an area larger than 400 square meters, with a width of more that 8 meters.

12

Twelve

资源和环境

Resources and Environment

12-1 主要河流(省内部分)主要特征值(2011)

Major Feature of Some Part of The Main River

水系	Water System	流域面积(平方公里) Drainage Area(sq.km)	河长(千米) Length of River (1000 m)	平均坡降(‰) Average Slope Falling(‰)
长江流域	**Changjiang River Drainage**	**115747**		
#赤水河	Chishuihe	11412	299	3.81
乌　江	Wujiang	66807	889	3.30
清水江	Qingshuijiang	17145	459	2.82
洪州河	Hongzhouhe	975	81	1.20
㵲阳河	Wuyanghe	6474	258	4.15
锦　江	Jinjiang	4017	168	9.92
松桃河	Songtaohe	1526	88	2.30
宋坎河	Songkanhe	2321	56	6.55
牛栏河	Liunanhe	2014	79	4.30
横江(洛泽河)	Hengjiang(Luozehe)	2874	120	9.65
珠江流域	**Zhujiang River Drainage**	**60420**		
#南盘江	Nanpanjiang	7651	263	1.61
北盘江	Beipanjiang	20982	318	4.36
红水河	Hongshuihe	15978	106	0.57
都柳江	Duliujiang	11586	330	2.97
打狗河	Dagouhe	4184	139	4.78

注：资料来源于省水利厅。

Note:Data in the table are provided by the Provincial Hydrographic Regulatory Burea.

12−2 主要矿产资源(2011)
Major Mineral Resources

名　称	Item	资源储量 Reserves	居全国位次 Order in Whole Country
矿产资源	**Mineral Resources(Ensured Reserves)**		
煤炭(亿吨)	Coal(100 million tons)	488.64	5
锰矿(万吨)	Manganese(10000 tons)	11221.58	3
钒矿(万吨)	Vanadium(10000 tons)	159.43	7
铅矿(万吨)	Plumbum(10000 tons)	67.89	18
锌矿(万吨)	Zincum(10000 tons)	222.41	15
铝土矿(亿吨)	Bauxite Ore(100 million tons)	5.98	4
镁(炼镁白云岩)(万吨)	Magnesium(10000 tons)	5365.41	8
汞矿(万吨)	Hydrargyrum(10000 tons)	3.09	1
锑矿(万吨)	Antimony(10000 tons)	24.63	4
金矿(岩金)(吨)	Gold mine(ton)	260.02	11
冶金用砂岩(万吨)	Gritstone for Metallurgy(10000 tons)	8512.80	2
硫铁矿(亿吨)	Pyrites Ore(100 million tons)	7.68	3
重晶石(万吨)	Barite Ore(10000 tons)	9216.48	1
磷矿(亿吨)	Phosphorus Ore(100 million tons)	30.45	3
稀土矿(万吨)	Rare Earth Mine(10000 tons)	92.09	2
水泥用灰岩(亿吨)	Limestone for Cement(100 million tons)	18.33	21

注：资料来源于省国土资源厅。
Note:Data in this table are obtained from the Provisional Department of Land and Resoures.

12–3 森林资源

Forest Resources

指　　标	Item	2006	2007	2008	2009	2010	2011	2011年比2010年增长(%) Increase Rate in 2011 over 2010(%)
森林面积(含灌丛)(万公顷)	**Areas of Forest(10000 Ha.)**	**703.39**	**703.39**	**703.39**	**703.39**	**713.80**	**732.00**	**2.6**
森林覆盖率(%)	Rate of Forest Covered (%)	39.93	39.93	39.93	39.93	40.52	41.53	1.0(百分点)
活立木总蓄积量(亿立方米)	Total Standing Fovest Stock (100 million stere)	3.10	3.10	3.10	3.10	3.33	3.89	16.8
完成造林面积(万公顷)	Area of Fulfilled Foyestation(10000 Ha.)	7.81	8.20	6.60	9.05	7.27	13.13	80.6
封山育林面积(万公顷)	Area of Seal Mountain Pass for Forestation(10000 Ha.)	13.52	9.19	13.07	17.36	13.39	14.48	8.1
实施退耕还林工程中:	**In Implement Cancel Infield for Forest Project**							
宜林荒山造林(万公顷)	Forestation for Feasible deserted Mountain(10000 Ha.)	4.33	5.30	2.00	1.33	1.33	1.20	-9.8
天然林保护工程中:	**In Savageness Forest Protect Project**							
封山育林(万公顷)	Seal Mountain Pass for Forestation (10000 Ha.)	7.33	3.40	3.50	7.28	4.66	0.60	-87.1
森林保护	**Forest Protection**							
森林火灾(起)	Forest Fire (unit)	1236	1254	2612	1626	2537	430	-83.1
森林火灾受害率(‰)	Rate of Fall Victim for Forest Fire (‰)	0.30	0.27	0.63	0.53	1.29	0.13	–1.2(千分点)
森林病虫鼠害面积(万公顷)	Area of Fall Victim for Insect Pest(10000 ha.)	26.96	26.90	22.94	28.97	26.85	27.18	1.2
森林病虫鼠害防治面积(万公顷)	Prevention Area of Forest Insect Pest(10000 ha.)	23.40	22.60	16.04	25.65	19.63	18.91	-3.7
森林病虫鼠害防治率(%)	Prevention Rate of Forest Insect Pest (%)	86.8	84.0	70.0	88.5	73.1	69.6	–3.5(百分点)

注：资料来源于省林业厅(以下相关表同)。

Note:The data in this table are obtained from Forest Department of Guizhou Province(The relative tables in the chapter are the same).

12-4 自然保护区
Natural Reserves

指 标	Item	2006	2007	2008	2009	2010	2011
自然保护区个数(个)	**Number of Nature Reserves (unit)**	**130**	**130**	**130**	**130**	**130**	**130**
#国家级自然保护区	Nature Reserves of National-level	7	9	9	9	9	9
省级自然保护区	Nature Reserves of Guizhou Province	4	4	4	4	4	4
地市级自然保护区	Nature Reserves of Region	22	21	21	21	21	21
县级自然保护区	Nature Reserves of County	97	96	96	96	96	96
自然保护区面积(万公顷)	Area of Nature Reserves (10000 hectares)	96.10	96.02	96.02	96.02	96.02	96.02
自然保护区面积占全省国土面积(%)	Percentage of Nature Reserves in Guizhou Province Land(%)	5.5	5.5	5.5	5.5	5.5	5.5
自然保护区中：	**In Nature Reserves**						
森林生态系统、野生动、植物类型(个)	Forest Biogeocenose,Wildness Animal and Plant(unit)	120	120	120	120	120	120
内陆湿地类型(个)	Wetlands inside Land(unit)	8	8	8	8	8	8
古生物遗迹类型(个)	Ancient Biology Relic(unit)	1	1	1	1	1	1
地质地貌类型(个)	Geological features(unit)	1	1	1	1	1	1

12-5 森林公园
Forest Parks

指 标	Item	2006	2007	2008	2009	2010	2011	2011年比2010年增长(%) Increase Rate in 2011 over 2010(%)
森林公园(个)	Number of Forest Park (unit)	60	61	65	66	70	72	2.9
#国家级森林公园	Forest Park of National-level	21	21	21	21	21	21	持平
省级森林公园	Forest Park of Guizhou Province-level	26	25	26	26	31	32	3.2
森林公园面积(万公顷)	Area of Forest Park (10000 hectares)	24.0	24.0	24.7	24.7	25.4	26.1	2.6
森林公园面积约占全省国土面积(%)	Percentage of Forest Park Area to the Guizhou Total Land Areas(%)	1.4	1.4	1.4	1.4	1.5	1.5	持平

12—6 水资源和水质监测

Basic Statistics on Water Resource and Monitoring of Water Quality

指 标	Item	2006	2007	2008	2009	2010	2011	2011年比2010年增长(%) Increase Rate in 2011 over 2010(%)
水资源总量(亿立方米)	**Total Water Resources (100 million cu.m)**	**814.63**	**1054.62**	**1140.67**	**910.46**	**956.54**	**626.02**	**-34.6**
#地表水	Surface Water Resources	814.63	1054.62	1140.67	910.46	956.54	626.02	-34.6
人均水资源量(立方米)	Per Capita Water Resources (cu.m)	2060	2649	2824	2226	2284	1805	-21.0
供水总量(亿立方米)	Water Supply(100 million cu.m)	99.95	98.03	101.89	100.38	101.45	99.19	-2.2
#地表水	Surface Water Supply	92.13	91.33	93.51	93.18	93.75	98.89	5.5
用水总量(亿立方米)	Water Use(100 million cu.m)	99.95	98.03	101.89	100.38	101.45	99.19	-2.2
河流水质	**Water Quality of River**							
监测河流(条)	Monitored River (unit)	33	33	33	33	44	44	持平
监测河段断面(个)	Monitored Section of River (unit)	74	74	74	74	85	85	持平
满足规定水质类别的断面占总监测断面百分比(%)	the Sections Meeting the Standard of Water Quality I-III Genus As Percentage of total Monitored Sections(%)	58.1	64.9	67.6	66.2	71.8	72.9	1.1(百分点)
水质良好的出境断面(个)	Number of Favorable Water Quality Section(unit)	11	11	10	10	11	12	9.1
湖泊水质	**Water Quality of Lake**							
监测湖库(个)	Monitored Lake (unit)	8	8	8	8	8	8	持平
监测点(个)	Monitored Point (unit)	25	25	25	25	25	25	持平
满足规定水质类别的监测点(个)	Ratio of the Points Meeting Water Quality I-III Genus(unit)	4	4	8	5	14	11	-21.4
占总监测点百分比(%)	As Percentage of total Monitored Points (%)	16.0	16.0	32.0	20.0	56.0	44.0	-12.0(百分点)

注：资料来源于省水利厅、省环保厅。
Note:Data in the table are provided by the Provincial Department of Water Resources and Provincial Department of Environmental Protection.

12–7 环保系统机构、人员数
Enviornmental Protection Agencies and Persons Engaged

指　标	Item	2006	2007	2008	2009	2010	2011
机构总数(个)	**Number of Agencies(unit)**	**287**	**295**	**311**	**359**	**404**	**400**
#省	Province	11	12	13	13	13	14
地	Prefecture	37	38	45	47	48	53
县	County	239	241	249	258	306	296
年末人员总数(人)	**Number of Staff and Workers at the Year-end(person)**	**2314**	**2454**	**2644**	**2650**	**3220**	**3168**
#省	Province	318	336	372	368	360	380
地	Prefecture	565	579	594	609	649	730
县	County	1431	1526	1665	1661	2137	1984
#科研人员	Scientific and Technical Personnel	102	108	111	109	101	93
监测人员	Monitoring Personal	600	618	693	665	720	838
监察人员	Supervising and Administrative Personnel	703	727	752	727	786	900

注：资料来源于省环保厅(以下相关表同)。
Note: The data in the table are provided by the provinvial Department of Environmental Protection(The relative tables in the chapter are the same).

12–8　环境保护资金投入
Investment in Environmental Protection

单位：亿元　　(100 million yuan)

指　标	Item	2006	2007	2008	2009	2010	2011	2011年比2010年增长(%) Increase Rate in 2011 over 2010(%)
环保资金投入	**Investment in Environmental Protection**	**32.79**	**48.88**	**50.74**	**69.78**	**89.52**	**106.70**	**19.2**
环保资金投入占生产总值比重(%)	Investment in Environmental Protection as Percent of GDP(%)	1.4	1.7	1.4	1.8	1.9	1.9	持平
环保资金投入中：	**In Investment of Environmental Protection**							
#老工业污染源治理	Old Industry Pollution Source Treatment	10.08	7.91	10.20	8.95	6.81	14.05	106.3
建设项目"三同时"污染防治	"Three Simultaneities" Environmental Investment for New Project	1.28	9.73	5.07	7.11	16.47	13.74	-16.6
城市环境基础设施建设	Investment in Urban Environmental Infrastructure	10.24	13.42	15.42	26.63	28.91	37.95	31.3
环境管理能力建设	Construction of Environment Management Capacity	0.61	0.77	1.52	1.92	1.81	1.21	-33.1
工业污染治理设施运行费用	Operating Expense of Industry Pollution Treatment Facilities	10.59	17.05	18.53	25.17	35.52	39.75	11.9
征收排污费总额	**Pollutant Discharge Fees**	**4.15**	**4.43**	**4.48**	**4.51**	**4.47**	**4.58**	**2.5**

注：表中"城市环境基础设施建设"数据2006–2010年由省环保厅提供，2011年由省住房城乡建设厅提供。
Note:The data of investment in urban environmental infrastructure were provided by Provincial Department of Environmental Protection from 2006 to 2010,But they were provided by provincial Department of urban and Rural development in 2011.

12—9 废水治理
Waste Water Treatment

指　标	Item	2006	2007	2008	2009	2010	2011	2011年比2010年增长(%) Increase Rate in 2011 over 2010(%)
废水排放总量(亿吨)	**Total Volume of Waste Water Discharged(100 million tons)**	**5.54**	**5.51**	**5.59**	**5.92**	**8.45**	**7.80**	**-7.7**
工业废水	Volume of Industrial Waste Water Discharged	1.39	1.21	1.17	1.35	2.55	2.07	-18.8
生活废水	Volume of Residential Waste Water Discharged	4.15	4.30	4.42	4.57	5.89	5.73	-2.7
废水中化学需氧排放量(万吨)	**COD Discharged from Industrial Waste Water(10000 tons)**	**22.90**	**22.70**	**22.18**	**21.60**	**34.83**	**34.22**	**-1.8**
工业废水	Industrial Sector	1.83	1.84	1.37	1.30	6.07	6.55	7.9
生活污水	Residential Sector	21.07	20.86	20.81	20.30	22.05	21.49	-2.5
当年完成工业废水治理项目(个)	Item of Industry Waste Water Treatment Completed in This Year(unit)	522	76	76	63	45	82	82.2
新增废水治理能力(万吨/日)	Newly Desinged Treatment and Utilization Capacity of Waste Water(10000 tons/day)	12.03	43.70	47.96	97.00	1.61	29.91	17.6倍
城市污水处理率(%)	Treatment Rate of City Waste Water (%)	21.2	29.0	31.2	42.0	74.8	82.0	7.2(百分点)

注：2010年数据采用污染源普查动态更新数据(以下相关表同)。
Note:The data of 2010 were updated by the methods of survey of pollution sources dynamic(The relative tables in the chapter are the same).

12−10 空气质量及污染治理
Air Quality and Treatment of Industrial Waste Gas

指　标	Item	2006	2007	2008	2009	2010	2011	2011年比2010年增长(%) Increase Rate in 2011 over 2010(%)
城市空气质量	**Atmosphere Quality of City**							
达到国家环境空气质量二级标准城市(个)	Number of Cities Reaching the National Grade Ⅱ Standard of Atmosphere Quality of City (unit)	8	8	7	7	7	11	57.1
占统计城市数(%)	Percentage in Total (%)	66.7	66.7	58.3	58.3	58.3	91.7	33.4
城市空气污染物	**Contamination in City Atmosphere**							
二氧化硫年均浓度值(毫克/立方米)	Annud Average SO_2 Concentration in Downtown(mg/cu.m)	0.06	0.056	0.052	0.05	0.05	0.04	-10.4
达到国家空气质量二级标准城市(个)	Number of Cities Reaching the National Grade Ⅱ Standard of Atmosphere Quality of City (unit)	8	9	7	8	9	12	33.3
二氧化氮年均浓度值(毫克/立方米)	Annual Average NO_2 Concentration in Downtown(mg/cu.m)	0.02	0.019	0.017	0.017	0.018	0.019	5.6
达到国家空气质量一级标准城市(个)	Number of Cities Reaching the National Grade I Standard of Atmosphere Quality of City (unit)	12	12	12	12	12	12	持平
城市可吸入颗粒物年均浓度值(毫克/立方米)	Average Chroma of City Suspend Grain (mg/cu.m)	0.13	0.078	0.073	0.073	0.077	0.078	1.3
达到国家空气质量二级标准城市(个)	Number of Cities Reaching the National Grade Ⅱ Standard of Atmosphere Quality of City (unit)	12	11	12	11	10	11	10.0
废气中污染物排放	**Contamination Discharged of Exhaust Gas**							
二氧化硫排放总量(万吨)	Volume of SO_2 Emission(10000 tons)	146.50	137.51	123.59	117.55	116.17	110.42	-4.9
#工业	Industry	103.97	92.06	74.13	62.37	96.05	90.3	-6.0
生活及其它废气中二氧化硫排放量	Volume of SO_2 from Living and Other Exhaust Gas Emission	42.53	45.45	49.46	55.18	20.13	20.12	-0.1
烟(粉)尘排放总量(万吨)	Total Volume of soot(Dust) Emission (10000 tons)	26.31	29.52	32.62	43.98	29.08	28.97	-0.4
#工业	Industry	18.45	19.11	14.57	11.78	24.88	24.34	-2.2
生活及其它废气中烟(粉)尘排放量	Discharged Volume of soot(Dusts) from Living and Other Exhaust Gas Emission	7.86	10.41	18.05	32.20	3.32	3.69	11.1
空气污染治理	**Air Pollution Treatment**							
工业废气中:	In Industrial Exhaust Gas							
二氧化硫去除率(%)	Rate of SO_2 Removed (%)	22.8	41.2	52.0	67.9	59.9	66.3	6.4
烟(粉)尘去除率(%)	Rate of Soot(Dust) Removed (%)	97.2	97.5	98.6	99.2	98.2	98.9	0.7
当年完成废气治理项目(个)	Item of Exhaust Gas Treatment Fulfilled in This Year (unit)	130	81	154	90	34	29	-14.7
新增废气治理能力(万标立方米/小时)	New Exhaust Gas Treatment Capacity inThis Year (10000 stere/hour)	560.00	3484.70	466.39	562.09	268.31	725.51	170.4
城市燃气普及率(%)	Popularization Rate of City Coal Gas (%)	55.2	57.3	54.1	54.2	54.5	55.0	0.5 (百分点)

注：“烟(粉)尘排放总量”为原“烟尘排放总量”，“烟(粉)尘去除率”为原“烟尘去除率”。

Note:"Total volume of soot(dust)emission"refers to the original"total volume of dust emission"."Rate of soot(dust) removed"refers to the original"Rate of soot removed".

12-11 固体废物生产及处理
Production and Treatment of Industrial Solid Wastes

指　标	Item	2006	2007	2008	2009	2010	2011	2011年比2010年增长(%) Increase Rate in 2011 over 2010(%)
工业固体废物产生量(万吨)	**Volume of Industrial Solid Wastes Produced (10000 tons)**	**5827.27**	**5988.58**	**5843.56**	**7317.37**	**8187.68**	**7660.70**	**-6.4**
工业固体废物倾倒丢弃量	Dumping Volume of Industrial Solid Waste Discarded	137.66	81.88	55.59	94.49	59.76	28.88	-51.7
工业固体废物治理	**Industrial Solid Wastes Treatment**							
当年完成工业固体废物治理项目(个)	Item of Industrial Solid Wastes Fulfilled in This Year (unit)	23	14	6	11	8	4	-50.0
工业固体废物综合利用量(万吨)	Volume of Industrial Solid Wastes Utilized(10000 tons)	2107.56	2251.83	2339.22	3350.67	4174.13	4089.09	-2.0
工业固体废物处置量(万吨)	Volume of Industrial Solid Wastes Treated (10000 tons)	2510.29	2559.34	2126.11	2109.39	2497.55	2102.95	-15.8
工业固体废物综合利用率(%)	Ratio of Industrial Solid Wastes Utilized(%)	36.0	37.5	39.9	45.6	50.9	52.7	1.8 (百分点)
生活垃圾处理	**Consumption Wastes Treatment**							
生活垃圾清运总量(万吨)	Consumption Wastes Collected and Transported (10000 tons)	393.50	402.85	413.83	426.61	428.51	431.46	0.7
生活垃圾处理总量(万吨)	Consumption Wastes Treated (10000 tons)	222.00	214.74	242.55	284.02	294.92	296.47	0.5
#无害化处理量	Volume of Wastes Disposed	123.20	130.85	147.23	169.59	194.62	205.11	5.4
城市生活垃圾无害化处理率(%)	Treatment Rate of Consumption Wastes in Cities(%)	31.3	32.5	35.6	39.8	45.4	47.5	2.1 (百分点)

注：“工业固体废物倾倒丢弃量”为原“工业固体废物排放量”。
Note:"Dumping volume of industrial solid waste discarded" refers to original "volume of industrial solid wastes discharged".

12-12 环境污染事故
Accident of Environment Pollution

指　标	Item	2006	2007	2008	2009	2010	2011	2011年比2010年增　长(%) Increase Rate in 2011 over 2010(%)
环境污染事故(起)	**Number of Environmental Pollution Accidents(unit)**	**23**	**18**	**10**	**4**	**4**	**7**	**75.0**
#重大事故	Fatal Accident	1	5				1	
较大事故	Major Accident						1	
一般事故	Commonly Accident	22	13	10	4	4	5	25.0
#水污染事故	Water Pollution Accident	16	15	4	4	2	5	150.0
空气污染事故	Air Pollution Accident	6	3	1		2	2	持平
污染事故直接经济损失(万元)	**Direct Economy Loss on Pollution Accident(10000 yuan)**	**13.40**	**673.20**	**14.70**	**10.00**	**107.30**	**450.00**	**319.4**

12-13 自然灾害
Natural Disasters

指　标	Item	2006	2007	2008	2009	2010	2011	2011年比2010年增长(%) Increase Rate in 2011 over 2010(%)
遭受自然灾害县个数(个)	Number of Counties Suffering from Natural Disasters(unit)	88	84	88	84	86	88	2.3
受灾人口(万人次)	The Population Affected by Natural Disasters (10000 person-times)	2321.86	1345.39	2935.00	1687.12	2633.40	2883.44	9.5
农作物受灾面积(万公顷)	Area of Crop Affected by Natural Disasters (10000 ha)	138.26	52.47	211.90	89.16	195.64	253.75	29.7
#绝收面积	The Gainless Area of Crop for Natural Disasters	34.61	7.19	52.20	12.85	55.72	51.51	-7.6
因自然灾害造成直接经济损失(亿元)	The Direct Economy Loss for Natural Disasters (100 million yuan)	59.10	38.27	487.22	35.60	179.77	250.67	39.4

注：资料来源于省民政厅。
Note: The data in the table are provided by the provinvial Department of Civil Affairs.

主要统计指标解释

国土 指中华人民共和国国家管辖下的领土、领海和领空。

气候 指地球与大气之间长期能量交换与质量交换所形成的一种自然环境状态，它是多种因素综合作用的结果。气候既是人类生活和生产的环境要素之一，又是供给人类生活和生产的重要资源。气温、降水、湿度等气象要素的多年平均值是用来描述一个地区气候状况的主要参数，而各种气象要素某年、某月的平均值（或总量）则可以反映出该时期天气气候状况的重要特征。

自然资源 指人类可以直接从自然界获得，并用于生产和生活的物质资源。自然资源一般可以分成可再生资源和非再生资源两大类。可再生资源指在较短时间内可以再生、可以循环利用的资源，包括土地资源、水资源、气候资源、生物资源和海洋资源等。非再生资源指在使用后不能再生的资源，包括矿产资源和地热能源。

土地资源 土地指陆地的表层部分，它主要由岩石、岩石的风化物和土壤构成。土地资源按利用类型可以分为农用地、建筑用地和未利用地。农用地包括耕地、园地、林地、牧草地和水面。建筑用地包括居民点及工矿用地、交通用地和水利设施用地。未利用地指农用地和建筑用地以外的土地，包括滩涂、荒漠、戈壁、冰川和石山等。

耕地面积 指经过开垦用以种植农作物并经常进行耕耘的土地面积。包括种有作物的土地面积、休闲地、新开荒地和抛荒未满三年的土地面积。

森林资源 指森林、林木、林地以及依托森林、林木、林地生存的野生动物、植物和微生物。林木指树木和竹子。森林指以乔木为主体的植物群落，是集生的乔木及与共同作用的植物、动物、微生物和土壤、气候等的总体。

活立木总蓄积量 指一定范围内土地上全部树木蓄积的总量，包括森林蓄积、疏林蓄积、散生木蓄积和四旁树蓄积。

森林面积 指由乔木树种构成，郁闭度0.2以上（含0.2）的林地或冠幅宽度10米以上的林带的面积，即有林地面积。森林面积包括天然起源和人工起源的针叶林面积、阔叶林面积、针阔混交林面积和竹林面积，不包括灌木林地面积和疏林地面积。

森林蓄积量 指一定森林面积上存在着的林木树干部分的总材积。它是反映一个国家或地区森林资源总规模和水平的基本指标之一，也是反映森林资源的丰富程度、衡量森林生态环境优劣的重要依据。

森林覆盖率 指一个国家或地区森林面积占土地总面积的百分比。森林覆盖率是反映森林资源的丰富程度和生态平衡状况的重要指标。在计算森林覆盖率时，森林面积包括郁闭度0.2以上的乔木林地面积和竹林地面积，国家特别规定的灌木林地面积、农田林网以及四旁（村旁、路旁、水旁、宅旁）林木的覆盖面积。计算公式为：

$$\text{森林覆盖率}(\%)=\frac{\text{森林面积}}{\text{土地总面积}}\times 100\%$$

水资源 水在自然界中以固体、液体和气态三种聚集状态存在，分布于海洋、陆地（包括土壤）以及大气之中，通过水循环形成水资源。水资源包括经人类控制并直接可供灌溉、发电、给水、航运、养殖等用途的地表水和地下水，以及江河、湖泊、井、泉、潮汐、港湾和养殖水域等。水资源是发展国民经济不可缺少的重要自然资源。

地表水和地下水 陆地上的水因空间分布不同，分为地表水和地下水。地表水指分别存在于河流、湖泊、沼泽、冰川和冰盖等水体中水分的总称，又称陆地水。地下水指储存在地面以下饱和岩土孔隙、裂隙及溶洞中的水。

矿产资源 矿产指由地质作用形成，富集于地壳中或出露于地表达到工农业利用要求的有用矿物。矿产是一种重要的自然资源，是社会发展的重要物质基础。

流域 每条河流都有自己的干流和支流，干支流共同组成这条河流的水系。每条河流都有自己的集水区域，这个集水区域就称为该河流的流域。

气温 指空气的温度，我国一般以摄氏度（℃）为单位表示。气象观测的温度表是放在离地面约1.5米处通风良好的百叶箱里测量的，因此，通常说的气温指的是离地面1.5米处百叶箱中的温度。其统计计算方法为：

月平均气温是将全月各日的平均气温相加，除以该月的天数而得。

年平均气温是将12个月的月平均气温累加后除以12而得。

相对湿度 指空气中实际所含水蒸气密度和同温度下饱和水蒸气密度的百分比值。其统计方法与气温相同。

降水量 指从天空降落到地面的液态或固态（经融化后）水，未经蒸发、渗透、流失而在地面上积聚的深度。其统计计算方法为：

月降水量是将全月各日的降水量累加而得。

年降水量是将 12 个月的月降水量累加而得。

日照时数 指太阳实际照射地面的时间。其统计方法与降水量相同

水资源总量 一定区域内的水资源总量指当地降水形成的地表和地下产水量，即地表径流量与降水入渗补给量之和，不包括过境水量。

用水总量 指分配给用户的包括输水损失在内的毛用水量。按用户特性分为农业、工业、生活和生态用水四大类。

农业用水 包括农田灌溉和林牧渔业用水。林牧渔业用水指林果地灌溉、草地灌溉和鱼塘补水。

工业用水 按新水取用量计，不包括企业内部的重复利用水量。

生活用水 包括城镇生活用水和农村生活用水。城镇生活用水由居民用水和公共用水（含服务业、商饮业、货运邮电业及建筑业等用水）组成；农村生活用水除居民生活用水外，还包括畜用水在内。

工业废水排放量 指经过企业厂区所有排放口排到企业外部的工业废水量。包括生产废水、外排的直接冷却水、超标排放的矿井地下水和与工业废水混排的厂区生活污水，不包括外排的间接冷却水（清污不分流的间接冷却水应计算在内）。

工业废水排放达标量 指报告期内废水中各项污染物指标都达到国家或地方排放标准的外排工业废水量，包括未经处理外排达标的，经废水处理设施处理后达标排放的，以及经污水处理厂处理后达标排放的。

工业废水排放达标率 指工业废水排放达标量占工业废水排放量的百分率，计算公式为:

$$\text{工业废水排放达标率} = \frac{\text{工业废水排放达标量}}{\text{工业废水排放量}} \times 100\%$$

城镇生活污水排放量 指城镇居民每年排放的生活污水中的 COD 的量。用人均系数法测算。测算公式为:

城镇生活污水排放量 = 城镇生活污水排放系数 × 市镇非农业人口 × 365

生活污水中化学需氧量（COD）排放量 指城镇居民每年排放的生活污水中的 COD 的量。用人均系数法测算。测算公式为:

城镇生活污水中 COD 排放量 = 城镇生活污水中 COD 产生系数 × 市镇非农业人口 × 365

工业废气排放量 指报告期内企业厂区内燃料燃烧和生产工艺过程中产生的各种排入大气的含有污染物的气体的总量，以标准状态（273K，101325Pa）计算。测算公式为:

工业废气排放量 = 燃料燃烧过程中废气排放量 + 生产工艺过程中废气排放量

生活及其他 SO_2 排放量 以生活及其他煤炭消费量和其含硫量为基础，根据以下公式计算:

生活及其他 SO_2 排放量 = 生活及其他煤炭消费量 × 含硫量 × 0.8 × 2

工业 SO2 排放量 指报告期内企业在燃料燃烧和生产工艺过程中排入大气的 SO_2 总量，计算公式为:

工业 SO_2 排放量 = 燃料燃烧过程中 SO_2 排放量 + 生产工艺过程中 SO_2 排放量

工业烟尘排放量 指企业厂区内燃料燃烧过程中产生的烟气中夹带的颗粒物排放量。

生活及其他烟尘排放量 指除工业生产活动以外的所有社会、经济活动及公共设施的经营活动中燃烧所排放的烟尘纯重量。以生活及其他煤炭消费量为基础进行测算。

工业粉尘排放量 指企业在生产工艺过程中排放的能在空气中悬浮一定时间的固体颗粒物排放量。如钢铁企业的耐火材料粉尘、焦化企业的筛焦系统粉尘、烧结机的粉尘、石灰窑的粉尘、建材企业的水泥粉尘等。不包括电厂排入大气的烟尘。

工业固体废物产生量 指报告期内企业在生产过程中产生的固体状、半固体状和高浓度液体状废弃物的总量，包括危险废物、冶炼废渣、粉煤灰、炉渣、煤矸石、尾矿、放射性废物和其他废物等；不包括矿山开采的剥离废石和掘进废石（煤矸石和呈酸性或碱性的废石除外）。酸性或碱性废石指采掘的废石其流经水、雨淋水的 pH 值小于 4 或 pH 值大于 10.5 者。

危险废物 指列入国家危险废物名录或根据国家规定的危险废物鉴别标准和鉴别方法认定的，具有爆炸性、易燃性、易氧化性、毒性、腐蚀性、易传染疾病等危险特性之一的废物。

工业固体废物综合利用量 指报告期内企业通过回收、加工、循环、交换等方式，从固体废物中提取或者使其转化为可以利用的资源、能源和其他原材料的固体废物量（包括当年利用往年的工业固体废物贮存量），如用作农业肥料、生产建筑材料、筑路等。综合利用量由原产生固体废物的单位统计。

工业固体废物综合利用率 指工业固体废物综合利用量占工业固体废物产生量（包括综合利用往年贮存量）的百分率。计算公式为:

$$\text{工业固体废物综合利用率} = \frac{\text{工业固体废物综合利用量}}{\text{工业固体废物产生量} + \text{综合利用往年贮存量}} \times 100\%$$

工业固体废物贮存量 指报告期内企业以综合利用或处置为目的，将固体废物暂时贮存或堆存在专设的贮存设施或专设的集中堆存场所内的数量。专设的固体废物贮存场所或贮存设施必须有防扩散、防流失、防渗漏、防止污染大气、水体

的措施。

工业固体废物处置量 指报告期内企业将固体废物焚烧或者最终置于符合环境保护规定要求的场所，并不再回取的工业固体废物量（包括当年处置往年的工业固体废物贮存量）。处置方式有填埋（其中危险废物应安全填埋）、焚烧、专业贮存场（库）封场处理、深层灌注、回填矿井及海洋处置（经海洋管理部门同意投海处置）等。

工业固体废物排放量 指报告期内企业将所产生的固体废物排到固体废物污染防治设施、场所以外的数量，不包括矿山开采的剥离废石和掘进废石（煤矸石和呈酸性或碱性的废石除外）。

“三废”综合利用产品产值 指报告期内利用“三废”作为主要原料生产的产品价值（现行价）；已经销售或准备销售的应计算产品价值，留作生产自用的不应计算产品价值。

生活垃圾清运量 指报告期内收集和运送到垃圾处理厂（场）的生活垃圾数量。生活垃圾指城市日常生活或为城市日常生活提供服务的活动中产生的固体废物以及法律行政规定的视为城市生活垃圾的固体废物。包括：居民生活垃圾、商业垃圾、集市贸易市场垃圾、街道清扫垃圾、公共场所垃圾和机关、学校、厂矿等单位的生活垃圾。

生活垃圾无害化处理率 指报告期生活垃圾无害化处理量与生活垃圾产生量比率。在统计上，由于生活垃圾产生量不易取得，可用清运量代替。计算公式为：

$$\text{生活垃圾无害化处理率}=\frac{\text{生活垃圾无害化处理量}}{\text{生活垃圾产生量}}\times 100\%$$

造林总面积 指报告期内在荒山、荒地、沙丘、退耕地等一切可以造林的土地上，采用人工播种、飞机播种、植苗造林、分植造林等方法新植成片乔木林和灌木林，经过检查验收符合《造林技术规程》要求的单位面积株数，并按《中华人民共和国森林法实施条例》规定，成活率达85%以上（含85%，年降雨量在400毫米以下且无浇灌条件的地区造林成活率达70%以上）的总面积。四旁植树如一侧在四行以上，连片面积0.066公顷（一亩）以上，应统计在造林面积内。造林面积，通常按所有制（国有、国有集体合作、集体和个人）、造林方式（人工、飞机播种）、主要林种用途（用材林、经济林、防护林、薪炭林、特种用途林）分组进行统计。

退耕还林还草工程 是我国林业建设上涉及面最广、政策性最强、工序最复杂、群众参与度最高的生态建设工程。主要解决重点地区的水土流失问题。

自然保护区 指对有代表性的自然生态系统、珍稀濒危野生动植物物种的天然分布区、水源涵养区、有特殊意义的自然历史遗迹等保护对象所在的陆地、陆地水体或海域，依法划出一定面积进行特殊保护和管理的区域。以县及县以上各级人民政府正式批准建立的自然保护区为准（包括“六五”以前由部门或“革委会”批准且现仍存在的自然保护区）。风景名胜区、文物保护区不计在内。

生态示范区 指省级以上环境保护行政主管部门批准，以省、地、县政府为主按批准的生态示范区建设规划实施的行政区域。包括已经过国家或省级环境保护行政主管部门验收的和正在开展试点工作的。

环境污染与破坏事故 指由于违反环境保护法规的经济、社会活动与行为，以及意外因素的影响或不可抗拒的自然灾害等原因，致使环境受到污染，国家重点保护的野生动植物、自然保护区受到破坏，人体健康受到危害，社会经济和人民财产受到损失，造成不良社会影响的突发性事件。

环境污染治理投资 指在工业污染源治理和城市环境基础设施建设的资金投入中，用于形成固定资产的资金。包括工业新老污染源治理工程投资、建设项目“三同时”环保投资，以及城市环境基础设施建设所投入的资金。

Explanatory Notes on Main Statistical Indicators

Territory refers to territorial land, sea and air space under the administration of the People's Republic of China.

Climate refers to the natural environmental status formed by the long-term exchange of energy and mass between the earth and the air, and is the results of interaction of many factors. Climate is both one of the environment factors and the important resources for the living and production activities of the human being. The average values across several years of meteorological factors such as temperature, rainfall and humidity are used as important parameters to describe the climate of a region, while the average values (or total values) of a given year or month of meteorological factors reflect the key characteristics of climate for that period of time.

Natural Resources refer to material resources that could be obtained from the nature by human being and used for production and living. Natural resources in general can be classified as renewable resources and non-renewable resources. Renewable resources refer to resources that could be renewed and recycled during a relatively short period of time, including land resource, water resource, climate resource, biology resource and marine resource. Non-renewable resources include resources that could not be renewed, such as minerals and geothermal resource.

Land Resource Land refers to the surface of the earth, consisting of mainly rocks and its weathering and earth. Land resource can be classified, by its utilization, as land for agriculture, land for construction and unused land. Land for agriculture includes cultivated land, plantation land, forestland, grassland and waters. Land for construction includes land for residential purpose, for manufacturing and mining, for transportation and for water-conservancy projects. Unused land refers to land other than land for agriculture and construction, including beaches, deserts, Gobi, glaciers and rock mountains.

Area of Cultivated Land refers to area of land reclaimed for the regular cultivation of various farm crops, including crop-cover land, fallow, newly reclaimed land and land laid idle for less than 3 years.

Forest Resource refers to forests, trees, forestland and wild animals, plants and microorganism that live on forest and trees. Trees include trees and bamboo. Forest refers to the population of clusters of trees and other plants, animals and microorganism as well as the earth and climate that have interactions with the trees.

Forest Area refers to the area of forest where trees and bamboo grow with canopy density above 0.2, including land of natural woods and planted woods, but excluding bush land and thin forest land. It reflects the total areas of afforestation.

Stock Volume of Forest refers to total stock volume of wood growing in forest area, which shows the total size and level of forest resources of a country or a region. It is also an important indicator illustrating the richness of forest resource and the status of forest ecological environment.

Forest Coverage Rate refers to the ratio of area of afforested land to total land area. It is a very important indicator that reflects the status of abundance of forest resource and ecosystem balance. Forest area includes the area of trees and bamboo grow with canopy density above 0.2, the area of shrubby tree according to regulations of the government, the area of forest land inside farm land and the area of trees planted by the side of villages, farm houses and along roads and rivers. The formula for calculating forest coverage rate is as follows:

$$\text{Forestry coverage rate (\%)} = \frac{\text{Area of Afforested Land}}{\text{Area of Total Land}} \times 100\%$$

Water Resource Water exists in the nature in solid, liquid and gaseous states, is distributed in the ocean, land (including earth) and air, and constitutes the water resource through the circulation of water. Water resource includes the surface water and underground water that is controlled by the human being for irrigation, power-generation, water supply, navigation and cultivation. It also includes rivers, lakes, wells, springs, tides, gulf and water area for cultivation.

Water resource as an important natural resource is indispensable for the development of the national economy.

Surface Water and Underground Water Water on earth can be divided into surface water and underground water according to its distribution. Surface water refers to moisture exists in rivers, lakes, swamps, glaciers, icecaps and so on. It is also called land water. The underground water refers to water deposited underground in the cranny and the hole of saturated rock soil and in the water-eroded cave.

Mineral Resources refer to useful minerals that can be used for industrial or agricultural purposes enriched in lithosphere or on earth due to the geological process. Minerals are important natural resources, and important material base for social development.

Drainage Area Each river has its own main stream and branches to form the water system of the river. Each river has its own catchment's area, which is also called as the drainage area of the river.

Temperature refers to the air temperature. China uses centigrade as the unit. The thermometry used for weather observation is put in a breezy shutter, which is 1.5 meters high from the ground. Therefore, the commonly used temperature refers to the temperature in the breezy shutter 1.5 meters away from the ground. The calculation method is as follows:

Monthly average temperature is the summation of average daily temperature of one month divided by the actual days of that particular month.

Annual average temperature is the summation of monthly average of a year divided by 12 months.

Relative Humidity refers to the ratio of actual water vapor pressure to the saturation water vapor density under the current temperature. The statistical method is the same as that of temperature.

Volume of Precipitation refers to the deepness of liquid state or solid state (thawed) water falling from the sky to the ground that has not been evaporated, infiltrated or run off. The calculation method is as follows:

Monthly precipitation is the summation of daily precipitation of a month.

Annual precipitation is the summation of 12 months precipitation of a year.

Sunshine Hours refer to the actual hours of sun irradiating the earth. The calculation method is the same as that of the precipitation.

Total Water Resources refers to total volume of water resources measured as run-off for surface water from rainfall and recharge for groundwater in a given area, excluding transit water.

Water Use refers to gross water use distributed to users, including loss during transportation, broken down with use by agriculture, industry, living consumption and biological protection.

Water Use by Agriculture includes uses of water by irrigation of farming fields and by forestry, animal husbandry and fishing. Water use by forestry, animal husbandry and fishing includes irrigation of forestry and orchards, irrigation of grassland and replenishment of fishing pools.

Water Use by Industry refers to new withdrawals of water, excluding reuse of water within enterprises.

Water Use by Living Consumption includes use of water for living consumption in both urban and rural areas. Urban water use by living consumption is composed of household use and public use (including services, commerce, restaurants, cargo transportation, posts, telecommunication and construction). Rural water use by living consumption includes both households and animals.

Waste Water Discharged by Industry refers to the volume of waste water discharged by industrial enterprises through all their outlets, including waste water from production process, directly cooled water, groundwater from mining wells which does not meet discharge standards and sewage from households mixed with waste water produced by industrial activities, but excluding indirectly cooled water discharged (It should be included if the discharge is not separated with waste water).

Industrial Waste Water Meeting Discharge Standards refers to volume of industrial waste water discharge which, with or without treatment, reaches national or local standards with regard to all pollutants.

Ratio of Industrial Waste Water Meeting Discharge Standards refers to percentage of industrial waste water meeting discharge standards over total industrial waste water discharge. It is calculated as:

Ratio of industrial waste water meeting discharge standards = industrial waste water meeting discharge standards / total industrial waste water discharge

Urban Non-industrial Waste Water Discharge refers to annual discharge of the amount of COD in non-industrial waste water by urban households. It is estimated by per capita coefficient using the formula:

Urban non-industrial waste water discharge = urban non-industrial waste water discharge coefficient urban non-agricultural population × 365

Volume of Chemical Oxygen Demand(COD) Generated by Urban Non-industrial Waster Water refers to chemical oxygen demand generated through the annual discharge of non-industrial waste water by urban households. It is estimated as:

Volume of chemical oxygen demand(cod) generated by urban non-industrial waster water = Coefficient of COD generated through urban non-industrial waste water urban non-agricultural population × 365

Industrial Waste Air Emission refers to discharge into atmosphere of waste air containing pollutants generated from fuel burning and production process in enterprises within a given period of time. It is calculated at standard status (273K, 101325Pa) as:

Industrial waste air emission = emission through fuel burning + emission through production process

SO_2 Emission through Non-industrial and Other Activities is calculated on the basis of consumption of coal by households and other activities and the sulphur content of coal with the following formula:

SO_2 emission through non-industrial and other activities = consumption of coal by households and other activities × sulphur content × 0.8 × 2

SO_2 Emission through Industrial Activities refers to volume of sulphur dioxide emission from fuel burning and production process by enterprises during a given period of time. It is calculated as:

SO_2 emission through industrial activities = SO_2 emission from fuel burning + SO_2 emission from production process

Industrial Soot Emission refers to volume of soot in smoke emitted in process of fuel burning in premises of enterprises.

Soot Emission by Consumption and Others refers to net volume of soot emitted by fuel burning from all social and economic activities and operation of public facilities other than industrial activities. It is calculated on the basis of coal consumption by households and others.

Industrial Dust Emission refers to volume of dust emitted by production process of enterprises and suspended in the air for a given period of time, including dust from refractory material of iron and steel works, dust from coke-screening systems and sintering machines of coke plants, dust from lime kilns and dust from cement production in building material enterprises, but excluding soot and dust emitted from power plants.

Industrial Solid Wastes Produced refers to total volume of solid, semi-solid and high concentration liquid residues produced by industrial enterprises from production process in a given period of time, including hazardous wastes, slag, coal ash, gangue, tailings, radioactive residues and other wastes, but excluding stones stripped or dug out in mining (gangue and acid or alkaline stones not included). A stone is acid or alkaline depending on the pH value of the water below 4 or above 10.5 when the stone is in, or soaked by, the water.

Hazardous Wastes refers to those included in the national hazardous wastes catalogue or specified as any one of the following properties in the national hazardous wastes identification standards: explosive, ignitable, oxidizable, toxic, corrosive or liable to cause infectious diseases or lead to other dangers.

Industrial Solid Wastes Utilized refers to volume of solid wastes from which useful materials can be extracted or which can be converted into usable resources, energy or other materials by means of reclamation, processing, recycling and exchange (including utilizing in the year the stocks of industrial solid wastes of the previous year). Examples of such utilizations include fertilizers, building materials and road materials. The information shall be collected by the producing units of the wastes.

Ratio of Industrial Solid Wastes Utilized refers to the percentage of industrial solid wastes utilized over industrial solid wastes produced (including stocks of the previous years). It is calculated as:

$$\text{Ratio of industrial solid wastes utilized} = \frac{\text{volume of industrial solid wastes utilized}}{\text{industrial solid wastes produced} + \text{stock of previous years}} \times 100\%$$

Stocks of Industrial Solid Wastes refers to volume of solid wastes placed in special facilities or special sites for purposes of utilization or disposal. The sites or facilities should take measures against dispersion, loss, seepage, and air and water contamination.

Industrial Solid Wastes Disposed refers to quantity of industrial solid wastes which are burnt or placed ultimately in the sites meeting the requirements for environmental protection and not salvaged or recycled (including disposition in the year of those wastes of previous years). The disposition includes landfill (Safe landfills should be conducted for hazardous wastes), incineration, containment spaces, deep underground disposal, backfill in mining pits and disposal at sea.

Industrial Solid Wastes Discharged refers to volume of industrial solid wastes discharged by producing enterprises to disposal facilities or to other sites. The wastes exclude stones stripped or dug from mining (gangue and acid or alkaline waste stones not included).

Output Value of Products Made from Waste Gas, Waste Water and Solid Wastes refers current value of products with waste gas, waste water and solid wastes as main materials of production. Products sold and ready to sell shall be included while those produced for own use shall not be included.

Consumption Wastes Transported refers to volume of consumption wastes collected and transported to disposal factories or sites. Consumption wastes are solid wastes produced from urban households or from service activities for urban households, and solid wastes regarded by laws and regulations as urban consumption wastes, including those from households, commercial activities, markets, cleaning of streets, public sites, offices, schools, factories, mining units and other sources.

Ratio of Consumption Wastes Treated refers to consumption wastes treated over that produced. In practical statistics, as it is difficult to estimate, the volume of consumption wastes produced is replaced with that transported. It is calculated as:

$$\text{Ratio of consumption wastes treated} = \frac{\text{consumption wastes treated}}{\text{consumption wastes produced}} \times 100\%$$

Total Area of Afforestation refers to the total area of land suitable for afforestation, including barren hills, idle land, sand dunes, rain for green land, on which acres of arbores or bushes are planted through manual planting, airplane planting, plant seedlings, etc. in accordance with the required density standards of the Technical Procedures of Afforestation, and with a survival rate of over 85% in line with the Implementing Rules of the Forest Law of the People's Republic of China (or a survival rate of 75% in areas with less that 400 mm of annual rainfall and without irrigation facilities). Included in the this category are trees planted alone the roadsides, riversides, or next to houses that occupy an area over 0.066 hectares, or where more than 4 lines of trees are planted. Total area of afforestation is further classified by ownership (state-owned, state-collective, collective or private), by approach of planting (manual, airplane), and by type of forests (timber, by-products, protection, fuel, special use, etc.).

Projects on Converting Cultivated Land to Forests and Grassland(Grain for Green Projects) aiming at preventing soil erosion in key regions, these projects are ecological construction projects in the development of forest industry that have the widest coverage and most sophisticated procedures, with strong policy implications and most active participation of the people.

Nature Reserves refer to certain areas of land, waters or sea that are representative in natural ecological systems, or are natural habitats for rare or endangered wild animals or plants, or water conservation zones, or the location of important natural or historic relics, which are demarked by law and put under special protection and management.

Nature reserves are designated by the formal approval of governments at and above county level (including those approved by relevant departments or "revolutionary committees" before 1980). Scenic spots and cultural preservationzones are not included.

Ecological Demonstration Zones refer to administrative areas approved by the environment protection agencies of central and provincial governments and established by provincial, prefecture or county governments in line with the approved programme for ecological demonstration zones. They include those evaluated and accepted by the environment protection agencies of central and provincial governments and those under pilot development stage.

Environment Pollution and Destruction Accidents refer to sudden accidents, due to economic or social activities that are in contrast to environment protection laws or due to unforeseen factors or natural disasters, that lead to the environment pollution, the destruction of protected wild animals, plants or nature reserves, the damage to human health, the economic and property losses, and the negative impact on the society.

Investment in Environment Pollution Harnessing Projects refers to the proportion of investment in fixed assets in the total investment in harnessing industrial pollution and in the construction of urban environment infrastructure facilities. It includes investment in harnessing sources of industrial pollution, investment in environment protection facilities designed concurrently with construction projects, and investment in urban environment infrastructure facilities.

13 Thirteen

农　业

Agriculture

13-1 农村基本情况及农业生产条件

Basic Conditions of Rural Areas and Agricultural Production

指 标	Item	2006	2007	2008	2009	2010	2011
农村基层组织	**Rural Grassroots Units**						
乡镇个数(个)	Nunmber of Township and Town Governments(unit)	1449	1449	1449	1446	1446	1445
村委会个数(个)	Nunmber of Villagers' Committees(unit)	19669	18091	17332	17568	17672	17583
农村社会基础设施	**Basic Facilities in Rural Areas**						
自来水受益村数(个)	Number of Villages with Access to Tap Water(unit)	14253	13269	13113	13639	13636	13922
通汽车的村数(个)	Villages with Automobile(unit)	17068	15980	15930	17334	17388	17336
通电话的村数(个)	Villages with Telephone Communication(unit)	15542	15354	15612	16725	16772	16823
通有线广播的村数(个)	Villages with Wire Broadcast(unit)	6415	5655	5913	5912	6332	6690
乡村人口与从业人员	**Rural Population and Laborers**						
乡村户数(万户)	Number of Rural Households(10000 units)	802.44	814.20	826.17	840.08	858.82	879.86
乡村人口数(万人)	Rural Population(10000 persons)	3294.35	3324.98	3358.32	3370.89	3443.72	3484.48
乡村从业人员(万人)	Number of Rural Laborers(10000 persons)	1953.89	1982.08	2006.39	2031.16	2078.64	2115.46
#农业从业人员	Agriculture Laborers	1247.08	1203.62	1202.06	1207.08	1188.27	1165.32
耕 地	**Area of Cultivated Land**						
年末常用耕地面积(千公顷)	Regularly Cultivated Land(year-end)(1000 hectares)	1753.36	1751.86	1754.05	1757.82	1761.56	1754.9
#水 田	Paddy Fields	756.94	754.07	754.01	753.48	756.94	752.25
农业机械化	**Agricultural Mechanization**						
农用机械总动力(万千瓦)	Total Power of Agricultural Machinery(10000 kw)	1207.19	1411.74	1537.50	1606.42	1730.31	1851.40
柴油机	Diesel Engine	851.30	980.69	1055.54	1122.17	1192.24	1308.11
汽油机	Gas Engine	29.15	30.69	45.56	49.39	53.42	60.50
电动机	Electromotor	317.60	393.68	423.94	421.34	472.21	473.46
其他机械	Others	9.14	6.68	12.46	13.52	12.44	9.33
农村主要物资消耗	**Main Materials Consumption for Agricultural Use**						
农用化肥施用量(折纯法)(万吨)	Consumption of Chemical Fertilizer(pure)(10000 tons)	80.23	82.05	83.09	86.54	86.53	94.06
平均每亩耕地化肥施用量(公斤)	Average Per Mu Consumption of Chemical Fertilizer(kg)	30.51	31.22	31.58	32.82	32.75	35.73
农药使用量(吨)	Consumption of Chemical Pesticides(ton)	10637	10722	12920	12464	12938	14469
农用塑料薄膜使用量(吨)	Consumption of Farm Plastic Membrane(ton)	30681	33710	47765	46470	36174	40857
农田水利建设	**Farmland and Water Conservancy**						
有效灌溉面积(千公顷)	Effective Irrigated Area(1000 hectares)	797.70	894.28	987.41	1087.41	1195.33	1266.8
旱涝保收面积(千公顷)	Area that Ensure Stable Yields Despite Droughtor Excessive Rain(1000 hectares)	541.87	570.21	586.55	633.73	646.02	659.31
机电排灌面积(千公顷)	Area with Motorized Drainage and Irrigation Facilities (1000 hectares)	68.49	72.04	74.11	75.14	77.86	80.14

注:表中“农田水利建设”资料来源于省水利厅，“农业机械化”资料来源于省农委(以下相关表同)。

Note:The data of Farmland and Water Conservancy are provided by the provincial department of water resources,and the data of agricultural mechanization are provided by the provincial agricultural commission(The relative tables in the chapter are the same).

13−2 年末主要农业机械拥有量

Major Agricultural Machinery at the Year-end

指 标	Item	2006	2007	2008	2009	2010	2011	2011年比2010年增长(%) Increase Rate in 2011 over 2010(%)
大中型拖拉机(万台)	Large and Medium Agricultural Tractors(10000 sets)	2.17	1.92	2.36	2.50	2.53	3.12	23.2
大中型拖拉机配套农具(万套)	Suited Farm Tools by Large and Medium Agricultural Tractors(10000 sets)	0.52	0.61	1.20	1.29	1.36	1.38	1.1
小型拖拉机(万台)	Mini Agricultural Tractors(10000 sets)	4.76	5.12	4.82	5.34	5.66	6.64	17.4
小型拖拉机配套农具(万套)	Suited Farm Tools by Mini Agricultural Tractors(10000 sets)	1.41	1.55	1.64	2.14	2.47	2.61	5.9
农用排灌电动机(万台)	Number of Drainage and Irrigation Electromotor Engines(10000 units)	16.31	17.56	17.11	18.13	19.03	19.06	0.1
农用排灌柴油机(万台)	Number of Drainage and Irrigation Diesel Engines(10000 units)	12.72	15.42	17.42	18.28	18.72	18.45	-1.4
联合收割机(台)	Combine Harvesters(unit)	280	440	507	602	642	695	8.3

13−3 灌溉、除涝治水

Irrigation, Flood Prevention, Water and Soil Conservation

项 目	Item	2006	2007	2008	2009	2010	2011
水利投入(亿元)	Input of Water Conservancy(100 million yuan)	17.72	24.25	40.40	49.18	102.01	151.78
灌溉面积(千公顷)	Irrigation Area(1000 hectares)	797.70	894.28	987.41	1087.41	1195.33	1266.80
节水灌溉面积(千公顷)	Water-saving Irrigated Area (1000 hectares)			380.00	386.31	391.74	396.00
除涝面积(千公顷)	Areas with Flood Prevention Measures(1000 hectares)			50.47	52.38	54.00	54.81
水土流失治理面积(千公顷)	Area of Soil Erosion under Control(1000 hectares)	2406.50	2490.80	2567.60	2701.50	2811.50	2956.00
堤防长度(公里)	Total Length of Dikes(km)			1534.83	1557.60	1598.40	1634.60
堤防保护面积(千公顷)	Area of Land Protected by Dikes (1000 hectares)			164.45	165.21	167.68	169.12

13-4 农林牧渔业总产值、增加值

Gross Output Value and Value-Added of Farming,Forestry, Animal Husbandry, Fishery and Their Services

单位：亿元 (100 million yuan)

指 标	Item	2006	2007	2008	2009	2010	2011	2011年比2010年增长(%) Increase Rate in 2011over 2010(%)
农林牧渔业总产值	**Gross Output Value of Farming,Forestry, Animal Husbandry and Fishery**	**601.54**	**697.01**	**843.80**	**875.20**	**997.82**	**1165.46**	**1.4**
农 业	Farming	347.97	392.20	464.80	501.52	587.31	655.30	-0.2
林 业	Forestry	25.85	27.77	35.63	36.92	41.01	46.66	7.4
畜牧业	Animal Husbandry	189.79	231.60	291.65	281.53	304.16	381.95	1.2
渔 业	Fishery	7.44	9.04	10.49	11.06	13.82	19.90	25.1
农、林、牧、渔服务业	FFAF Services	30.49	36.40	41.23	44.17	51.52	61.65	10.3
农林牧渔业增加值	**Added Value of FFAFS**	**387.33**	**446.38**	**540.27**	**550.27**	**625.04**	**726.21**	**1.2**
农 业	Farming	226.28	260.30	308.48	330.50	385.61	430.84	-0.3
林 业	Forestry	17.01	18.27	23.44	25.11	28.07	31.99	7.4
畜牧业	Animal Husbandry	118.96	145.68	183.16	167.79	179.51	223.22	1.0
渔 业	Fishery	4.90	5.89	6.84	7.21	8.98	12.78	23.7
农、林、牧、渔服务业	FFAF Services	20.18	16.24	18.35	19.66	22.86	27.38	10.4

注：2006年数据为第二次农业普查修订数(以下相关表同)。
Note:Data were adjusted according to the Second National Agricultural Census in 2006(The same applies to the relative tables below).

13–5 农林牧渔业总产值

Gross Output Value of Farming,Forestry,Animal Husbandry, Fishery and Their Services

单位：亿元 (100 million yuan)

指　标	Item	2006	2007	2008	2009	2010	2011	2011年比2010年增长(%) Increase Rate in 2011over 2010(%)
农林牧渔业总产值	**Gross Output Value of Farming,Forestry, AnimalHusbandry and Fishery**	**601.54**	**697.01**	**843.80**	**875.20**	**997.82**	**1165.46**	**1.4**
农业产值	**Farming**	**347.97**	**392.20**	**464.80**	**501.52**	**587.31**	**655.30**	**-0.2**
谷物及其他作物的种植	Planting of Cereal and other Crops	222.64	240.51	289.75	307.19	340.56	340.36	-9.6
蔬菜、园艺作物的种植	Planting of Vegetable and Gardening Crops	99.51	120.40	140.60	155.83	194.69	249.10	12.0
水果、坚果、饮料和香料作物的种植	Planting of Fruits, nuts, Beverages and Spice Crops	15.46	18.94	20.73	23.61	35.64	46.12	15.3
中药材的种植	Planting of Chinese Traditional Medicine	10.36	12.35	13.71	14.89	16.42	19.72	17.4
林业产值	**Forestry**	**25.85**	**27.77**	**35.63**	**36.92**	**41.01**	**46.66**	**7.4**
林木的培育和种植	Cultivating and planting of forest	4.07	4.15	4.91	5.17	5.49	5.90	3.4
木材和竹材的采运	Logging and Transporting of Timber & bamboo	5.11	5.43	8.88	9.46	11.47	12.51	6.8
林产品的采集	Collecting of Forest Products	16.67	18.19	21.84	22.29	24.04	28.25	8.5
畜牧业产值	**Animal Husbandry**	**189.79**	**231.60**	**291.65**	**281.53**	**304.16**	**381.95**	**1.2**
牲畜的饲养	Animal Raising	26.62	30.60	37.16	39.82	56.13	70.05	持平
猪的饲养	Hogs Raising	133.93	165.62	212.99	195.52	196.23	253.35	0.2
家禽的饲养	Poultry Raising	27.95	33.96	39.84	44.43	50.00	56.69	6.5
狩猎和捕捉动物	Hunting and Catching Animales	0.08	0.09	0.09	0.10	0.09	0.09	持平
其他畜牧业	Others	1.21	1.33	1.57	1.66	1.71	1.76	-0.5
渔业产值	**Fishery**	**7.44**	**9.04**	**10.49**	**11.06**	**13.82**	**19.90**	**25.1**
农林牧渔服务业产值	**Gross Output Value of FFAF Services**	**30.49**	**36.40**	**41.23**	**44.17**	**51.52**	**61.65**	**10.3**

13-6 主要农作物播种面积
Sown Areas of Major Farm Crops

单位：千公顷 (1000 hectares)

指 标	Item	2006	2007	2008	2009	2010	2011	2011年比2010年增长(%) Increase Rate in 2011 over 2010(%)
农作物总播种面积	**Total Sown Areas of Farm Crops**	**4449.43**	**4464.53**	**4619.43**	**4780.69**	**4889.30**	**5021.22**	**2.7**
#粮食作物	Grain Crops	2836.02	2821.84	2919.57	2984.73	3039.50	3055.56	0.5
#稻 谷	Rice	679.62	676.22	691.15	698.24	695.81	681.53	-2.1
小 麦	Wheat	243.93	242.71	262.44	262.93	260.77	257.62	-1.2
玉 米	Corn	734.87	731.20	734.64	751.49	781.14	787.80	0.9
大 豆	Soybeans	121.87	121.26	125.74	126.63	128.95	132.78	3.0
薯 类	Tubers	792.10	788.14	842.53	876.23	894.83	912.94	2.0
#马铃薯	Irish Potato	592.83	604.90	605.76	634.96	645.84	668.01	3.4
油 料	Oil-bearing Crops	430.78	433.13	455.15	513.13	529.14	536.14	1.3
#油菜籽	Rapeseeds	399.91	400.12	412.77	466.88	479.19	488.98	2.0
花 生	Peanuts	24.33	25.40	33.50	38.76	40.81	38.90	-4.7
糖 料	Sugar Crops	18.01	17.15	17.67	16.47	13.74	12.02	-12.5
#甘 蔗	Sugarcane	17.94	17.07	17.63	16.43	13.70	11.98	-12.6
烟 叶	Tobacco	193.40	192.79	207.74	197.82	195.37	212.24	8.6
#烤 烟	Flue-cured Tobacco	177.99	177.39	194.77	184.94	182.74	200.01	9.4
药材类	Crude Drugs	23.76	24.72	24.86	25.60	28.12	44.35	57.7
蔬 菜	Vegetable	494.50	527.85	558.29	599.58	647.92	708.52	9.4

13–7 主要农作物产品产量
Yields of Major Farm Crops

单位：万吨 (10000 tons)

指　标	Item	2006	2007	2008	2009	2010	2011	2011年比2010年增长(%) Increase Rate in 2011 over 2010(%)
粮食作物	**Grain Crops**	**1038.00**	**1100.86**	**1158.00**	**1168.27**	**1112.30**	**876.90**	**-21.2**
#稻　谷	Rice	424.15	449.84	461.10	453.17	445.65	303.93	-31.8
小　麦	Wheat	45.13	47.86	42.81	44.52	24.83	50.38	102.9
玉　米	Corn	336.71	357.10	391.19	405.20	415.43	243.71	-41.3
大　豆	Soybeans	14.08	14.93	16.57	15.87	15.99	7.11	-55.5
薯　类	Tubers	187.64	199.00	214.81	208.84	174.13	239.31	37.4
#马铃薯	Irish Potato	140.43	152.73	150.30	153.50	141.43	189.38	33.9
油料作物	**Oil-bearing Crops**	**68.24**	**69.66**	**68.39**	**78.68**	**60.34**	**78.85**	**30.7**
#油菜籽	Rapeseeds	63.18	64.59	60.38	70.40	51.62	71.81	39.1
花　生	Peanuts	4.12	4.93	6.44	7.31	7.68	6.07	-21.0
甘　蔗	**Sugarcane**	**63.88**	**66.97**	**71.76**	**64.27**	**52.24**	**43.60**	**-16.5**
烤　烟	**Flue-cured Tobacco**	**30.71**	**31.22**	**37.71**	**36.92**	**37.02**	**32.50**	**-12.2**
蔬　菜	**Vegetable**	**788.00**	**877.34**	**991.15**	**1077.81**	**1202.04**	**1250.05**	**4.0**

13–8 主要农作物单产
Yields of Major Farm Crops Per Mu

单位：公斤/亩 (kg/mu)

指　标	Item	2006	2007	2008	2009	2010	2011	2011年比2010年增长(%) Increase Rate in 2011 over 2010(%)
粮食作物	**Grain Crops**	**244**	**260**	**264**	**261**	**244**	**191**	**-21.6**
#稻　谷	Rice	416	443	445	433	427	297	-30.4
小　麦	Wheat	123	131	109	113	63	130	105.4
玉　米	Corn	305	326	355	359	355	206	-41.8
大　豆	Soybeans	77	82	88	84	83	36	-56.5
薯　类	Tubers	158	168	170	159	130	175	34.8
#马铃薯	Irish Potato	158	168	165	161	146	189	29.7
油料作物	**Oil-bearing Crops**	**106**	**107**	**100**	**102**	**76**	**98**	**29.0**
#油菜籽	Rapeseed	105	108	98	101	72	98	36.3
花　生	Peanuts	113	129	128	126	125	104	-17.1
甘　蔗	**Sugarcane**	**2374**	**2615**	**2714**	**2608**	**2542**	**2427**	**-4.5**
烤　烟	**Flue-cured Tobacco**	**115**	**117**	**129**	**133**	**135**	**108**	**-19.9**

13−9 茶叶、水果面积及产量

Total Sown Areas and Yields of Tea,Fruit

指　标	Item	2006	2007	2008	2009	2010	2011	2011年比2010年增长(%) Increase Rate in 2011 over 2010(%)
面　积(千公顷)	**Area(1000 hectares)**							
茶园面积	Tea Field Area	63.60	71.81	105.17	132.19	167.19	196.37	17.5
桑园面积	Mulberry Field Area	6.31	5.35	5.50	5.01	4.63	4.47	-3.3
柞坡面积	Breed Tussah Field Area	4.72	4.11	3.14	3.10	2.79	5.46	95.8
果园面积	Orchards Filed Area	119.14	124.55	133.28	140.83	151.83	169.02	11.3
产　量(万吨)	**Yield(10000 tons)**							
茶　叶	Tea	2.49	2.84	3.49	4.19	5.23	5.84	11.7
水　果	Fruit	109.19	112.86	114.28	119.74	123.47	128.03	3.7
#园林水果	Garden Fruit	54.97	60.32	61.68	64.22	69.61	79.52	14.2
#苹　果	Apples	1.06	1.10	1.22	1.62	1.55	2.17	40.0
梨	Pears	13.94	14.80	16.29	16.77	18.21	19.54	7.3
柑　桔	Citrus	17.70	19.07	19.11	19.42	20.37	20.81	2.2
香　蕉	Bananas	0.87	0.88	0.80	0.79	0.61	0.59	-2.8
杨　梅	Red Bayberry	2.23	2.94	2.33	3.05	2.90	3.19	9.9
猕猴桃	Chinese Gooseberrys	1.11	1.15	1.24	1.18	1.30	1.70	30.7
柿　子	Persimmons	1.40	1.45	1.27	1.28	1.36	1.25	-8.2

13−10 造林及林产品产量

Areas of Forestation and Output of Forest Products

单位：吨 (ton)

指　标	Item	2006	2007	2008	2009	2010	2011	2011年比2010年增长(%) Increase Rate in 2011 over 2010(%)
当年造林面积(千公顷)	**Areas of Forestation in this year(1000 hectares)**	**78.05**	**81.80**	**65.96**	**90.49**	**72.70**	**131.30**	**80.6**
林产品产量	**Output of Forest Products**							
生　漆	Lacquer	1327	1426	1641	1526	1614	2001	24.0
油桐籽	Tung-oil Seed	77630	78147	73395	61796	63815	75769	18.7
油茶籽	Tea-oil Seed	11725	12177	16233	19057	20368	23166	13.7
乌桕籽	Tallow-seed	2917	2839	2874	2396	2468	2487	0.8
五倍籽	Nutgall	1887	1698	1739	1581	2216	1624	-26.7
棕　片	Palm-flake	4864	4615	4510	4396	4365	4530	3.8
松　脂	Pine Resin	7109	11799	9382	7734	8215	12001	46.1
竹笋片	Bamboo Shoot	7674	10934	11719	13780	20382	19897	-2.4
核　桃	Walnuts	8136	12187	12316	13125	15356	17364	13.1
板　栗	Chestnut	13671	17336	16707	17278	19316	22653	17.3

注：表中"造林面积"资料来源于省林业厅。
Note:The areas of forestation in this table are obtained from the Provincial Department of Forest.

13-11 畜牧业生产及水产品
Basic Statistics on Livestock and Aquatic Products

指 标	Item	2006	2007	2008	2009	2010	2011	2011年比2010年增长(%) Increase Rate in 2011 over 2010(%)
当年出栏数	**Number of Slaughtered Fattened Hogs, Ox,Goats and Sheep**							
猪(万头)	Slaughtered Fattened Hogs(10000 heads)	1574.00	1445.40	1561.10	1596.10	1688.67	1689.66	0.1
牛(万头)	Ox by Sold and Killed(10000 heads)	72.20	75.20	84.20	92.14	96.56	97.21	0.7
羊(万头)	Goats by Sold and Killed(10000 heads)	160.30	162.20	178.50	190.10	198.70	197.31	-0.7
肉类总产量(万吨)	**Total Yield of Meat(10000 tons)**	**163.70**	**150.60**	**161.46**	**169.60**	**179.09**	**179.97**	**0.5**
#猪 肉	Pork	138.80	125.60	134.60	140.10	148.09	148.29	0.1
牛 肉	Beef	9.10	9.50	10.20	11.40	11.99	12.00	0.1
羊 肉	Mutton	2.70	2.80	3.00	3.23	3.40	3.37	-0.9
禽 肉	Poultry	12.20	11.70	12.60	13.50	14.12	14.35	1.6
其他畜产品产量	**Others**							
牛 奶(万吨)	Cow Milk(10000 tons)	4.09	4.06	4.30	4.49	4.59	4.85	5.7
禽 蛋(万吨)	Poultry Eggs(10000 tons)	10.00	10.30	10.80	12.20	12.51	13.65	9.1
蜂 蜜(吨)	Honey(ton)	2255.00	1988.00	3093.00	2017.00	1893.50	2029.20	7.2
大牲畜年末存栏数(万头)	**Large Livestock(year-end)(10000 heads)**	**578.78**	**612.10**	**611.51**	**626.21**	**627.64**	**550.82**	**-12.2**
#牛	Cattle and Buffaloes	498.10	513.10	523.40	539.10	541.80	467.11	-13.8
猪年末存栏数(万头)	**Hogs(year-end)(10000 heads)**	**1562.10**	**1548.70**	**1587.50**	**1617.96**	**1616.34**	**1521.60**	**-5.9**
羊年末存栏数(万只)	**Sheep and Goats(year-end)(10000 heads)**	**218.40**	**222.30**	**231.20**	**252.98**	**261.10**	**256.49**	**-1.8**
水产品(万吨)	**Aquatic Products(10000 tons)**	**6.71**	**7.68**	**7.80**	**8.03**	**8.79**	**10.88**	**23.8**

注：表中“水产品”资料来源于省农委。

Note:Data of aquatic products in this table are obtained from the Provincial Agricultural Commission.

主要统计指标解释

农林牧渔业总产值 指以货币表现的农、林、牧、渔业全部产品和对农林牧渔业生产活动进行的各种支持性服务活动的价值总量，它反映一定时期内农业生产总规模和总成果。农业总产值的计算方法通常是按农林牧渔业产品及其副产品的产量分别乘以各自单位产品价格求得；然后将四业产品产值及农林牧渔服务业产值相加即为农业总产值。

粮食产量 指全社会的产量。包括国有经济经营的、集体统一经营的和农民家庭经营的粮食产量，还包括工矿企业办的农场和其他生产单位的产量。粮食除包括稻谷、小麦、玉米、高粱、谷子及其他杂粮外，还包括薯类和豆类。其产量计算方法，豆类按去豆荚后的干豆计算；薯类（包括甘薯和马铃薯，不包括芋头和木薯）1963 年以前按每 4 公斤鲜薯折 1 公斤粮食计算，从 1964 年开始改为按 5 公斤鲜薯折 1 公斤粮食计算。城市郊区作为蔬菜的薯类（如马铃薯等）按鲜品计算，并且不作粮食统计。其他粮食一律按脱粒后的原粮计算。

油料产量 指全部油料作物的生产量。包括花生、油菜籽、芝麻、向日葵籽、胡麻籽（亚麻籽）和其他油料。不包括大豆、木本油料和野生油料。花生以带壳干花生计算。

水产品产量 指人工养殖的水产品和天然生长的水产品的捕捞量。包括海水的鱼类、虾蟹类、贝类和藻类以及内陆水域的鱼类、虾蟹类和贝类，不包括淡水生植物。

猪、牛、羊肉产量 指当年出栏并已屠宰、除去头蹄下水后带骨肉（即胴体重）的重量。

期初（末）畜禽存栏头（只）数 指报告期初（末）农村各种合作经济组织和国营农场、农民个人、机关、团体、学校、工矿企业、部队等单位以及城镇居民饲养的大牲畜、猪、羊、家禽等畜禽的存栏数。

耕地面积 指可以用来种植农作物、经常进行耕锄的田地，包括熟地、当年新开荒地、连续撂荒未满三年的耕地和当年的休闲地（轮歇地），还包括以种植农作物为主并附带种植桑树、茶树、果树和其他林木的土地，以及沿海、沿湖地区已围垦利用的“海涂”、“湖田”等面积。不包括属于专业性的桑园、茶园、果园、果木苗圃、林地、芦苇地、天然或人工草地面积。

农作物播种面积 指实际播种或移植有农作物的面积。凡是实际种植有农作物的面积，不论种植在耕地上还是种植在非耕地上，均包括在农作物播种面积中。在播种季节基本结束后，因遭灾而重新改种和补种的农作物面积，也包括在内。

有效灌溉面积 指具有一定的水源，地块比较平整，灌溉工程或设备已经配套，在一般年景下当年能够进行正常灌溉的耕地面积。

农用化肥施用量 指本年内实际用于农业生产的化肥数量，包括氮肥、磷肥、钾肥和复合肥。化肥施用量要求按折纯量计算数量。折纯量是指把氮肥、磷肥、钾肥分别按含氮、含五氧化二磷、含氧化钾的百分之一百成份进行折算后的数量。复合肥按其所含主要成分折算。

农业机械总动力 指主要用于农、林、牧、渔业的各种动力机械的动力总和。包括耕作机械、排灌机械、收获机械、农用运输机械、植物保护机械、牧业机械、林业机械、渔业机械和其他农业机械〔内燃机按引擎马力折成瓦（特）计算、电动机按功率折成瓦（特）计算〕。不包括专门用于乡、镇、村、组办工业、基本建设、非农业运输、科学试验和教学等非农业生产方面用的动力机械与作业机械。

农林牧渔业劳动力 指全社会直接参加农林牧渔业生产活动的劳动力。

Explanatory Notes on Main Statistical Indicators

Gross Output Value of Agriculture, Forestry, Animal Husbandry and Fishery refers to the total value of products of agriculture, forestry, animal husbandry and fishery, and total value of services in support of agriculture, forestry, animal husbandry and fishery activities. It reflects the total scale and results of agricultural production during a given period.

Gross output value of agriculture is obtained by multiplying the output of each product or by-product by its price, resulting in the output value of each single item. The sum of output values of all products of agriculture, forestry, animal husbandry and fishery and services in support to those industries is then equal to the gross output value of agriculture.

Grain Output refers to the total output in the whole country including grains produced by State farms, collective units, rural households, as well as by farms affiliated to industrial and mining enterprises and other production units. Grain includes rice, wheat, corn, sorghum, millet and other miscellaneous grains as well as tubers and beans. Output of beans refers to dry beans without pods. The output of tubers (sweet potatoes and potatoes, not including taros and cassava) are converted into that of grain at the ratio 4:1, i.e. 4 kilograms of fresh tubers were equivalent to 1 kilogram of grain up to 1963. Since 1964 the ratio for conversion has been 5:1. Tubers supplied as vegetables (such as potatoes) in cities and suburbs are calculated as fresh vegetables and their output is not included in the output of grain. Output of all other grains refers to husked grain.

Output of Oil-bearing Crops refers to the total production of oil-bearing crops of various kinds, including peanuts (dry, in shell), rapeseeds, sesame, sunflower seeds, flax seeds, and other oil-bearing crops. Soybeans, oil-bearing woody plants, and wild oil-bearing crops are not included.

Output of Aquatic Products refers to catches of both artificially cultured and naturally grown aquatic products, including fish, shrimps, crabs and shellfish in sea and inland water as well as seaweed. Freshwater plants are not included.

Output of Pork, Beef, and Mutton refers to the meat of slaughtered hogs, cattle, sheep and goats with head, feet, and offal taken away.

Number of Livestock or Poultry in Stock at Beginning (or End) of Period refers to the total number of large animals, pigs, sheep, fowls, etc. raised by rural cooperative organizations, State farms, rural individuals, government agencies, schools, industrial and mining enterprises, army, and urban residents at the beginning (or end) of the reference period.

Sown Area of Crops refers to area of land sown or transplanted with crops regardless of being in cultivated area or non-cultivated area. Area of land re-sown due to natural disasters is also included.

Irrigated Area refers to area of land that are effectively irrigated, i.e. relatively level land, where there are water sources or complete sets of irrigation facilities to lift and move adequate water for irrigation purpose under normal conditions. Under normal situations, irrigated area is the sum of watered fields and irrigated fields where irrigation systems or equipment have been installed for regular irrigation purpose.

Consumption of Chemical Fertilizers in Agriculture refers to the quantity of chemical fertilizers applied in agriculture in the year, including nitrogenous fertilizer, phosphate fertilizer, potash fertilizer, and compound fertilizer. The consumption of chemical fertilizers is calculated in terms of volume of effective components by means of converting the gross weight of the respective fertilizers into weight containing effective component. Compound fertilizer is converted in regard to its major components.

Total Power of Agricultural Machinery refers to total mechanical power of machinery used in agriculture, forestry, animal husbandry and fishery, including machinery for ploughing, irrigation and drainage, harvesting, transport, plant protection, animal husbandry, forestry and fishery and other agricultural machineries. (For the power of internal combustion engines, it is converted from its horsepower into watts while for electric motors the output power is converted into watts.) Machinery employed for non-agricultural purposes, such as the machines used in township-run and village-run industry, construction, non-agricultural transport, scientific experiments and teaching, are not included. Data are mainly from agricultural machinery agencies.

Labour Force Engaged in Agricultural,Forestry,Animal Husbandry and Fishery refers to the total laborers who are directly engaged in production of agricultural, forestry, animal husbandry and fishery.

14 Fourteen

工　业

Industry

14-1 规模以上工业企业单位数

Number of Industrial Enterprises above Designated Size

单位：个 (unit)

指标	Item	2006	2007	2008	2009	2010	2011
总计	**Total**	**2594**	**2296**	**2676**	**2791**	**2963**	**3687**
#国有控股企业	State-holding Industry Enterprises	760	541	530	523	516	576
按轻重工业分	**Grouped by Type of Light and Heavy Industry**						
轻工业	Light Industry	679	536	578	600	634	842
重工业	Heavy Industry	1915	1760	2098	2191	2329	2845
按企业规模分	**Grouped by Scale of Enterprise**						
大型企业	Large Enterprises	26	25	31	31	30	70
中型企业	Medium-sized Enterprises	257	286	325	340	415	509
小型企业	Small Enterprises	2311	1985	2320	2420	2518	2646
微型企业	Micro-enterprises						462
按登记注册类型分	**By Status of Registration**						
内资企业	Domestic Funded	2483	2200	2570	2686	2861	3590
国有企业	State-owned Enterprises	558	362	331	315	309	349
集体企业	Collective-owned Enterprises	124	92	70	64	59	68
股份合作企业	Cooperative Enterprises	62	59	53	49	41	50
联营企业	Joint Ownership Enterprises	23	17	15	13	12	28
有限责任公司	Limited Liability Corporations	612	598	725	820	844	1100
股份有限公司	Share-holding Corporations Limited	107	101	100	100	113	140
私营企业	Private Enterprises	988	965	1267	1308	1469	1793
其他企业	Other Enterprises	9	6	9	17	14	62
港、澳、台商投资企业	Enterprises with Funds from Hong Kong,Macao and Taiwan	50	46	49	48	51	47
外商投资企业	Foreign Funded Enterprises	61	50	57	57	51	50

注：1、规模以上标准，2011年国家统计局规定为年主营业务收入2000万元及以上工业企业，我省为保持资料的可比性，仍执行500万元及以上标准。(以下相关表除特殊标注外，均同)。2、企业规模从2011年开始，按国家统计局新制定的《统计上大中小微企业划分办法》执行。

Note:1.The scale of the above criteria has been changed the revenue from principal business of more than 20 million of enterprise by National Bureau of statistics since 2011.But to keep the data comparable, our province continue to enforce the standards more than five million (In addition to special label,the same applies to the tables following) 2.From 2011,the designated size of industry is executed according to "Statistics issued by the division of the large, medium, small and micro-enterprises" which is the newly established by National Bureau of Statistics.

14-2 按行业分规模以上工业企业单位数
Number of Industrial Enterprises above Designated Size by Sector

单位：个 (unit)

指 标	Item	2006	2007	2008	2009	2010	2011
总 计	**Total**	**2594**	**2296**	**2676**	**2791**	**2963**	**3687**
采矿业	Mining and Quarring	467	476	745	760	929	1165
#煤炭开采和洗选业	Mining and Washing of Coal	377	372	617	652	827	999
黑色金属矿采选业	Mining and Dressing of Ferrous Metals	19	19	38	29	28	45
有色金属矿采选业	Mining and Dressing of Nonferrous Metals	38	50	47	30	30	44
非金属矿采选业	Mining and Dressing of Nonmetal Minerals	33	34	43	49	44	77
制造业	Manufacturing	1847	1615	1706	1798	1814	2267
#农副食品加工业	Processing of Food from Agricultural Products	144	127	138	150	153	208
食品制造业	Manufacture of Foods	54	40	50	49	56	78
饮料制造业	Manufacture of Beverages	83	77	92	101	133	182
烟草制品业	Manufacture of Tobacco	7	7	8	8	3	6
纺织业	Manufacture of Textile	16	10	11	11	12	16
纺织服装、鞋、帽制造业	Manufacture of Textile Wearing Apparel, Footware and Caps	8	6	5	6	7	13
皮革、毛皮、羽毛(绒)及其制造业	Manufacture of Leather,Furs,Feather and Related Products	1	1	1	1	2	3
木材加工及木、竹、藤、棕、草制品业	Timber Processing,Manufacture of Wood, Bamboo, Rattan,Palm and Straw Products	35	52	64	69	69	85
家具制造业	Manufacture of Furniture	3	2	2	2	5	8
造纸及纸制品业	Manufacture of Paper and Paper Products	36	34	41	44	41	54
印刷业和记录媒介的复制	Printing,Reproduction of Recording Media	49	30	28	26	21	28
文教体育用品制造业	Manufacture of Articles For Culture,Education and Sport Activity	4	3	3	3	3	3

14-2 续表 continued

单位：个 (unit)

指　标	Item	2006	2007	2008	2009	2010	2011
石油加工、炼焦及核燃料加工业	Processing of Petroleum,Coking,Processing of Nuclear Fuel	72	44	49	45	27	35
化学原料及化学制品制造业	Manufacture of Raw Chemical Materials and Chemical Products	213	186	173	188	182	220
医药制造业	Manufacture of Medicines	110	101	98	97	96	107
橡胶制品业	Manufacture of Rubber	12	9	9	9	12	16
塑料制品业	Manufacture of Plastics	52	42	49	55	54	67
非金属矿物制品业	Manufacture of Non-metallic Mineral Products	290	276	299	327	345	457
黑色金属冶炼及压延加工业	Smelting and Pressing of Ferrous Metals	255	212	210	205	185	182
有色金属冶炼及压延加工业	Smelting and Pressing of Non-ferrous Metals	123	117	103	101	97	103
金属制品业	Manufacture of Metal Products	34	25	29	36	38	51
通用设备制造业	Manufacture of General Purpose Machinery	53	47	54	59	63	96
专用设备制造业	Manufacture of Special Purpose Machinery	37	34	33	43	39	49
交通运输设备制造业	Manufacture of Transport Equipment	71	63	67	70	67	82
电气机械及器材制造业	Manufacture of Electrical Equipment and Machinery	39	33	45	47	58	65
通信设备、计算机及其他电子设备制造业	Manufacture of Communication Equipment, Computers and Other Electronic Equipment	19	19	23	25	21	23
仪器仪表及文化、办公用机械制造业	Manufacture of Measuring Instruments and Machinery for Cultural Activity and Office Work	14	8	11	11	12	14
工艺品及其他制造业	Manufacture of Artwork and Other Manufacturing	9	9	9	9	11	12
废弃资源和废旧材料回收加工业	Recycling and Disposal of Waste	1		1	1	2	4
电力、燃气及水的生产和供应业	Production and Distribution of Electric Power, Gas and Water	280	205	225	233	220	255
电力、热力的生产和供应业	Production and Distribution of Electric Power and Heat Power	182	160	180	188	177	190
燃气生产和供应业	Production and Distribution of Gas	5	5	6	6	8	8
水的生产和供应业	Production and Distribution of Water	93	40	39	39	35	57

14-3 规模以上工业增加值

Value added of Industry above Designated Size

单位：亿元 (100 million yuan)

指标	Item	2006	2007	2008	2009	2010	2011	2011年比2010年增长(%) Increase Rate in 2011 over 2010(%)
总计	**Total**	**747.38**	**890.48**	**1051.26**	**1170.29**	**1227.17**	**1723.58**	**22.6**
#国有控股企业	State-holding Industry	518.27	602.51	685.93	732.65	749.55	924.79	13.7
#私营企业	Private Enterprises	96.91	128.40	177.82	196.08	277.96	465.32	36.1
按轻重工业分	**Grouped by Type of Light and Heavy Industry**							
轻工业	Light Industry	218.52	267.87	302.25	352.38	413.99	563.48	23.7
重工业	Heavy Industry	528.86	622.61	749.01	817.91	813.18	1160.10	22.1
按企业规模分	**Grouped by Scale of Enterprise**							
大型企业	Large Enterprises	368.57	409.99	429.49	433.21	465.95	640.70	17.5
中型企业	Medium-sized Enterprises	188.89	250.94	278.14	332.02	302.19	412.05	16.1
小型企业	Small Enterprises	189.92	229.55	343.64	405.06	459.03	631.37	25.3
微型企业	Micro-enterprises						39.46	26.9
按登记注册类型分	**By Status of Registration**							
国有企业	State-owned Enterprises	318.82	375.11	459.98	503.69	356.22	485.22	15.3
集体企业	Collective-owned Enterprises	6.73	6.53	7.75	6.00	6.81	3.09	-14.7
股份合作企业	Cooperative Enterprises	6.08	7.56	12.29	5.75	8.35	4.73	14.0
股份制企业	Share-holding Enterprises	309.82	369.48	449.40	516.72	612.56	854.72	24.7
外商及港澳台商投资企业	Enterprises with Funds from Foreign,Hong Kong, Macao and Taiwan	15.56	20.69	26.26	25.47	40.44	41.39	15.6
其他企业	Other Enterprises	90.37	111.11	95.58	112.65	202.80	334.43	31.8

注：2010年以后工业增加值按收入法计算，增长速度按可比价计算(以下相关表同)。

Note:Value-added of industry above designated size is calculated by income approach and the increase rate is calculated at the comparable scope in 2010(the same as the follows).

14-4 按行业分规模以上工业增加值

Value added of Industry above Designated Size by Sector

单位：亿元 (100 million yuan)

指　　标	Item	2006	2007	2008	2009	2010	2011	2011年比2010年增长(%) Increase Rate in 2011 over 2010(%)
总　计	**Total**	**747.38**	**890.48**	**1051.26**	**1170.29**	**1227.17**	**1723.58**	**22.6**
采矿业	Mining and Quarring	73.45	103.46	153.61	181.10	297.43	486.34	31.5
#煤炭开采和洗选业	Mining and Washing of Coal	59.45	90.85	129.66	158.48	276.68	441.75	29.5
石油和天然气开采业	Extraction of Petroleum and Natural Gas							
黑色金属矿采选业	Mining and Dressing of Ferrous Metals	0.98	2.46	3.57	5.28	5.58	7.71	56.1
有色金属矿采选业	Mining and Dressing of Nonferrous Metals	2.11	4.00	7.18	2.07	3.28	5.83	99.8
非金属矿采选业	Mining and Dressing of Nonmetal Minerals	10.91	6.07	13.08	15.05	11.89	31.04	51.7
制造业	Manufacturing	479.22	576.93	665.32	712.64	721.35	995.21	25.1
#农副食品加工业	Processing of Food from Agricultural Products	8.93	9.47	11.47	14.22	11.50	23.08	31.4
食品制造业	Manufacture of Foods	8.93	8.07	10.24	9.42	15.41	14.99	34.9
饮料制造业	Manufacture of Beverages	49.77	75.21	94.86	112.29	162.79	243.65	28.6
烟草制品业	Manufacture of Tobacco	85.84	101.59	106.27	116.99	152.62	176.21	15.2
纺织业	Manufacture of Textile	1.00	1.10	1.07	0.97	1.12	3.11	42.6
纺织服装、鞋、帽制造业	Manufacture of Textile Wearing Apparel, Footware,and Caps	0.76	0.81	1.06	0.87	0.65	1.99	53.1
皮革、毛皮、羽毛(绒)及其制造业	Manufacture of Leather,Furs,Feather and Related Products	0.12	0.24	0.18	0.43	0.05	0.02	-58.8
木材加工及木、竹、藤、棕、草制品业	Timber Processing,Manufacture of Wood, Bamboo, Rattan,Palm, and Straw Products	1.83	2.45	4.55	6.73	5.55	13.49	120.0
家具制造业	Manufacture of Furniture	0.02	0.01	0.01	0.02	1.30	1.45	9.7
造纸及纸制品业	Manufacture of Paper and Paper Products	1.52	1.66	2.10	4.30	3.81	5.14	34.6
印刷业和记录媒介的复制	Printing,Reproduction of Recording Media	3.44	3.45	3.20	4.11	6.60	6.62	11.0
文教体育用品制造业	Manufacture of Articles For Culture, Education and Sport Activity	0.19	0.23	0.21	0.29	0.32	0.40	9.9
石油加工、炼焦及核燃料加工业	Processing of Petroleum,Coking, Processing of Nuclear Fuel	8.35	10.97	25.68	24.32	13.46	12.34	17.6
化学原料及化学制品制造业	Manufacture of Raw Chemical Materials and Chemical Products	51.96	68.43	79.07	71.49	58.47	100.62	24.0

14-4 续表 continued

单位：亿元 (100 million yuan)

指 标	Item	2006	2007	2008	2009	2010	2011	2011年比2010年增长(%) Increase Rate in 2011 over 2010(%)
医药制造业	Manufacture of Medicines	41.80	46.04	48.31	59.98	40.50	54.31	20.0
橡胶制品业	Manufacture of Rubber	11.23	9.67	12.58	14.18	19.12	15.98	14.6
塑料制品业	Manufacture of Plastics	2.59	3.39	5.20	5.94	4.51	7.39	31.9
非金属矿物制品业	Manufacture of Non-metallic Mineral Products	19.02	21.08	29.41	37.64	47.86	70.29	49.3
黑色金属冶炼及压延加工业	Smelting and Pressing of Ferrous Metals	51.07	72.52	87.86	75.94	54.42	67.42	19.3
有色金属冶炼及压延加工业	Smelting and Pressing of Non-ferrous Metals	71.33	61.70	55.95	58.05	32.92	58.64	18.6
金属制品业	Manufacture of Metal Products	4.48	8.23	9.72	6.49	7.56	10.41	26.6
通用设备制造业	Manufacture of General Purpose Machinery	5.42	5.97	11.98	12.75	14.92	23.54	38.0
专用设备制造业	Manufacture of Special Purpose Machinery	5.81	7.65	7.02	10.66	5.77	7.88	18.1
交通运输设备制造业	Manufacture of Transport Equipment	24.19	29.87	26.30	29.16	31.50	33.58	16.0
电气机械及器材制造业	Manufacture of Electrical Equipment and Machinery	7.30	11.29	12.90	14.48	8.66	8.60	20.4
通信设备、计算机及其他电子设备制造业	Manufacture of Communication Equipment, Computers and Other Electronic Equipment	7.09	8.24	10.46	12.00	8.94	10.87	15.7
仪器仪表及文化、办公用机械制造业	Manufacture of Measuring Instruments and Machinery for Cultural Activity and Office Work	1.60	3.53	3.22	2.66	1.91	3.05	16.2
工艺品及其他制造业	Manufacture of Artwork and Other Manufacturing	3.53	4.04	4.43	6.24	9.05	19.46	71.3
废弃资源和废旧材料回收加工业	Recycling and Disposal of Waste	0.01		…	…	0.07	0.68	40.2
电力、燃气及水的生产和供应业	Production and Distribution of Electric Power,Gas and Water	194.71	210.08	232.33	276.55	208.40	242.03	3.2
#电力、热力的生产和供应业	Production and Distribution of Electric Power and Heat Power	190.26	205.06	228.40	272.24	203.60	236.91	3.0
燃气生产和供应业	Production and Distribution of Gas	1.60	2.16	0.79	0.81	0.67	1.24	24.2
水的生产和供应业	Production and Distribution of Water	2.85	2.86	3.14	3.49	4.13	3.88	12.3

14–5 规模以上工业总产值

Gross Output Value of Industry above Designated Size

单位：亿元 (100 million yuan)

指 标	Item	2006	2007	2008	2009	2010	2011
总 计	**Total**	**2066.77**	**2520.36**	**3111.13**	**3426.69**	**4206.37**	**5794.83**
#国有控股企业	State-holding Enterprises	1360.00	1607.15	1878.69	2094.77	2429.41	2987.30
按轻重工业分	**Grouped by Type of Light and Heavy Industry**						
轻工业	Light Industry	449.67	527.16	641.78	758.14	914.19	1253.14
重工业	Heavy Industry	1617.10	1993.20	2469.34	2668.55	3292.18	4541.70
按企业规模分	**Grouped by Scale of Enterprise**						
大型企业	Large Enterprises	923.32	1065.56	1236.25	1318.12	1523.30	2213.39
中型企业	Medium-sized Enterprises	567.93	764.93	982.98	1122.55	1349.06	1585.19
小型企业	Small Enterprises	575.52	689.87	891.90	986.02	1334.01	1894.07
微型企业	Micro-enterprises						102.18
按登记注册类型分	**By Status of Registration**						
内资企业	Domestic Funded	1997.24	2440.98	2995.35	3300.03	4048.82	5591.28
国有企业	State-owned Enterprises	789.17	1055.98	1068.74	1026.67	1212.22	1504.98
集体企业	Collective-owned Enterprises	20.94	18.21	17.43	14.62	23.28	30.39
股份合作企业	Cooperative Enterprises	10.57	22.68	28.00	22.56	17.22	45.45
联营企业	Joint Ownership Enterprises	6.79	8.69	6.99	6.95	6.18	19.35
有限责任公司	Limited Liability Corporations	553.76	685.00	1003.27	1287.94	1501.31	2012.22
股份有限公司	Share-holding Corporations Limited	321.42	260.52	331.62	378.35	440.28	620.75
私营企业	Private Enterprises	293.57	388.90	536.98	555.24	839.58	1334.71
其他企业	Other Enterprises	1.02	1.00	2.34	7.69	8.74	23.42
港、澳、台商投资企业	Enterprises with Funds from Hong Kong, Macco and Taiwan	21.17	28.07	39.38	44.42	57.93	74.70
外商投资企业	Foreign Funded Enterprises	48.37	51.32	76.39	82.25	99.62	128.86

14–6 按行业分规模以上工业总产值
Gross Output Value of Industry above Designated Size by Sector

单位：亿元 (100 million yuan)

指 标	Item	2006	2007	2008	2009	2010	2011
总 计	**Total**	**2066.77**	**2520.36**	**3111.13**	**3426.69**	**4206.37**	**5794.83**
采矿业	Mining and Quarring	167.02	212.54	399.32	436.46	704.13	1169.11
#煤炭开采和洗选业	Mining and Washing of Coal	129.55	183.82	353.76	403.15	655.72	1062.53
石油和天然气开采业	Extraction of Petroleum and Natural Gas						
黑色金属矿采选业	Mining and Dressing of Ferrous Metals	2.33	4.09	6.66	6.09	7.52	15.69
有色金属矿采选业	Mining and Dressing of Nonferrous Metals	5.99	11.62	22.10	5.82	12.00	23.06
非金属矿采选业	Mining and Dressing of Nonmetal Minerals	29.14	12.74	16.82	21.39	28.89	67.83
制造业	Manufacturing	1346.35	1666.04	1998.82	2135.40	2554.94	3597.34
#农副食品加工业	Processing of Food from Agricultural Products	35.35	46.10	54.54	69.20	83.13	146.66
食品制造业	Manufacture of Foods	24.05	26.95	41.59	40.19	56.53	81.91
饮料制造业	Manufacture of Beverages	80.67	103.64	150.79	179.04	227.04	333.38
烟草制品业	Manufacture of Tobacco	124.00	139.99	164.23	183.12	208.65	253.47
纺织业	Manufacture of Textile	4.17	4.72	4.38	3.69	5.08	8.86
纺织服装、鞋、帽制造业	Manufacture of Textile Wearing Apparel, Footware and Caps	2.65	2.83	3.44	3.48	3.63	5.29
皮革、毛皮、羽毛(绒)及其制造业	Manufacture of Leather,Furs,Feather and Related Products	0.55	0.69	0.94	1.35	1.17	1.95
木材加工及木、竹、藤、棕、草制品业	Timber Processing,Manufacture of Wood, Bamboo, Rattan,Palm and Straw Products	6.10	8.81	16.56	23.80	26.51	53.06
家具制造业	Manufacture of Furniture	0.11	0.08	0.13	0.19	1.63	8.44
造纸及纸制品业	Manufacture of Paper and Paper Products	5.77	6.10	11.05	17.16	24.36	42.61
印刷业和记录媒介的复制	Printing,Reproduction of Recording Media	8.92	10.70	10.09	12.60	13.13	14.96
文教体育用品制造业	Manufacture of Articles For Culture, Education and Sport Activity	0.51	0.64	0.71	0.88	1.09	1.31
石油加工、炼焦及核燃料加工业	Processing of Petroleum,Coking, Processing of Nuclear Fuel	22.39	31.90	62.11	63.83	67.18	78.48

14–6 续表 continued

单位：亿元 (100 million yuan)

指　标	Item	2006	2007	2008	2009	2010	2011
化学原料及化学制品制造业	Manufacture of Raw Chemical Materials and Chemical Products	182.06	244.15	313.02	283.34	336.03	495.93
医药制造业	Manufacture of Medicines	96.12	109.60	119.46	150.87	180.61	238.29
橡胶制品业	Manufacture of Rubber	41.84	48.96	58.76	67.03	85.09	113.97
塑料制品业	Manufacture of Plastics	11.17	13.42	18.18	22.73	23.43	40.15
非金属矿物制品业	Manufacture of Non-metallic Mineral Products	62.79	76.37	104.71	134.71	182.22	314.43
黑色金属冶炼及压延加工业	Smelting and Pressing of Ferrous Metals	218.45	288.80	364.09	330.16	408.41	542.78
有色金属冶炼及压延加工业	Smelting and Pressing of Non-ferrous Metals	197.88	218.44	177.54	171.13	219.70	303.56
金属制品业	Manufacture of Metal Products	18.79	35.10	59.37	47.86	42.33	51.20
通用设备制造业	Manufacture of General Purpose Machinery	16.05	22.42	25.22	25.86	32.62	63.39
专用设备制造业	Manufacture of Special Purpose Machinery	22.60	28.31	23.91	31.99	36.00	40.98
交通运输设备制造业	Manufacture of Transport Equipment	76.88	95.12	109.00	143.13	144.21	183.32
电气机械及器材制造业	Manufacture of Electrical Equipment and Machinery	39.27	50.82	57.70	65.54	75.45	97.52
通信设备、计算机及其他电子设备制造业	Manufacture of Communication Equipment, Computers and Other Electronic Equipment	24.72	25.98	30.18	38.44	43.00	48.72
仪器仪表及文化、办公用机械制造业	Manufacture of Measuring Instruments and Machinery for Cultural Activity and Office Work	4.70	6.68	6.12	8.49	9.24	11.17
工艺品及其他制造业	Manufacture of Artwork and Other Manufacturing	17.22	18.43	10.86	15.51	17.35	17.41
废弃资源和废旧材料回收加工业	Recycling and Disposal of Waste	0.04		0.09	0.09	0.12	4.11
电力、燃气及水的生产和供应业	Production and Distribution of Electric Power, Gas and Water	553.40	641.78	712.99	854.84	947.31	1028.39
#电力、热力的生产和供应业	Production and Distribution of Electric Power and Heat Power	536.45	623.35	687.92	832.87	913.38	987.63
燃气生产和供应业	Production and Distribution of Gas	10.28	11.98	17.41	13.69	24.19	27.79
水的生产和供应业	Production and Distribution of Water	6.68	6.46	7.65	8.27	9.74	12.97

14-7 规模以上工业企业主要经济指标
Major Economic Indicators of Industrial Enterprises above Designated Size

指 标	Item	2006	2007	2008	2009	2010	2011
固定资产净值年平均余额(亿元)	Average Balance of Net Value of Fixed Assets (100 million yuan)	1247.06	1476.49	1645.22	2535.38	2653.16	2721.62
流动资产年平均余额(亿元)	Average Balance of Circulating Funds (100 million yuan)	1045.08	1188.62	1485.62	1716.85	2015.98	2480.37
主营业务收入(亿元)	Revenue from Principal Business (100 million yuan)	1948.57	2430.62	2922.35	3234.59	3926.01	5290.90
利税总额(亿元)	Total Profits and Taxes (100 million yuan)	299.09	403.49	453.53	470.60	671.39	924.04
#利润	Total Profits	110.91	174.41	181.83	191.73	317.63	464.89
产值利税率(%)	Ratio of Pre-Tax Profit to Output Value(%)	14.47	16.01	14.58	13.73	15.96	16.78
资金利税率(%)	Ratio of Pre-Tax Profit to Assets(%)	13.05	15.14	14.49	10.31	12.62	17.76
销售利税率(%)	Ratio of Pre-Tax Profit to Sales(%)	14.92	16.60	15.52	14.55	17.10	16.99
资本保值增值率(%)	Increment Ratio of Capital(%)	114.61	114.86	124.99	106.87	125.32	127.96
总资产贡献率(%)	Ratio of Total Assets to Industrial Output Value(%)	11.93	12.89	12.96	10.69	12.84	14.13
资产负债率(%)	Asset-Liability Ratio(%)	65.78	64.46	66.28	67.00	64.85	64.45
流动资产周转次数(次/年)	Number of Times of Turnover of Circulating Fund(times/year)	1.81	2.04	1.92	1.88	1.75	1.92
成本费用利润率(%)	Ratio of After-tax Profits to Cost and Expenses(%)	6.95	8.10	6.42	6.56	9.04	9.63
全员劳动生产率(元/人、年)	Overall Labor Productivity (yuan/person,year)	111168	133663	141433	160077	152823	183433
产销率(%)	Proportion of Industrial Products Sold(%)	96.57	96.68	95.36	94.8	95.44	95.01

14–8 大中型工业企业主要经济指标

Major Economic Indicators of Large and Medium-sized Industrial Enterprises

指　标	Item	2006	2007	2008	2009	2010	2011
固定资产净值年平均余额(亿元)	Average Balance of Net Value of Fixed Assets (100 million yuan)	1022.22	1179.16	1310.40	1643.79	2009.61	2084.76
流动资产年平均余额(亿元)	Average Balance of Circulating Funds (100 million yuan)	805.11	939.37	1148.78	1317.62	1526.28	1636.84
主营业务收入(亿元)	Revenue from Principal Business (100 million yuan)	1446.61	1779.30	2123.08	2366.97	2752.96	3583.56
利税总额(亿元)	Total Profits and Taxes(100 million yuan)	261.91	343.17	361.47	390.73	516.99	746.51
#利润	Total Profits	106.28	154.16	146.13	166.30	240.89	376.07
资本保值增值率(%)	Increment Ratio of Capital(%)	114.20	115.99	120.58	104.78	122.88	129.90
总资产贡献率(%)	Ratio of Total Assets to Industrial Output Value(%)	11.51	13.36	17.21	11.00	12.72	14.84
资产负债率(%)	Asset-Liability Ratio(%)	65.38	63.99	65.81	67.80	65.46	64.91
流动资产周转次数(次/年)	Number of Times of Turnover of Circulating Fund(times/year)	1.80	1.89	1.85	1.80	1.63	1.76
成本费用利润率(%)	Ratio of After-tax Profits to Cost and Expenses(%)	8.36	9.90	7.76	7.92	9.88	11.56
全员劳动生产率(元/人)	Overall Labor Productivity(yuan/person)	135164	156051	182870	166738	151836	168622
产销率(%)	Proportion of Products Sold(%)	97.80	97.20	95.67	95.65	96.01	95.22

14-9 主要工业产品产量

Output of Major Industrial Products

单位：万吐 (10000 tons)

产品名称	Item	2006	2007	2008	2009	2010	2011
原煤	Coal	11816.60	10864.18	11798.46	10001.00	12656.00	14014.80
粗钢	Steel	332.51	349.36	345.64	343.10	360.48	434.01
成品钢材	Steel Products	256.57	328.14	337.52	337.62	391.04	462.77
铁合金	Iron Alloy	153.57	178.87	156.62	220.87	208.18	263.90
铝	Aluminium	56.28	75.07	58.15	80.27	88.79	90.36
氧化铝	Aluminum Oxide	110.52	128.27	144.28	136.91	134.84	211.03
铝材	Aluminium Material	0.88	1.19	1.33	1.42	1.49	13.16
磷矿石	Phosphorite Mineral	1034.60	1198.83	1317.18	1360.66	1579.21	2084.18
生铁	Pig Iron	343.50	342.61	331.01	374.82	366.65	482.35
农用化肥	Chemical Fertilizer	338.76	321.84	262.21	347.28	384.92	364.66
轮胎外胎(万条)	Tires(10000 units)	387.41	443.90	457.29	517.21	558.59	536.77
水泥	Cement	1799.40	1943.10	2048.94	2664.78	3694.84	5250.89
发电量(亿千瓦小时)	Electricity(100 million kwh)	974.66	1166.32	1192.08	1363.09	1358.69	1359.01
#水电	Hydropower	214.27	340.62	380.86	400.88	389.65	334.66
煤气生产量(亿立方米)	Gas Production (100 million cu.m)	55.34	59.64	64.19	65.18	67.81	84.15
卷烟(万箱)	Cigarettes(10000 cases)	211.73	220.71	226.74	232.24	239.24	245.23
饮料酒(万千升)	Alcohol Beverages(10000 kiloliters)	34.49	35.87	41.65	41.35	48.72	61.80
#白酒	White Spirit	14.21	14.57	18.35	13.79	16.04	25.49
食用植物油	Edible Vegetable Oil	13.15	8.79	5.50	11.20	10.22	12.23
中成药	Traditional Chinese Medicine	4.57	4.65	4.72	4.58	5.00	4.92
家用电冰箱(万台)	Household Refrigerators (10000 units)	102.20	132.24	143.81	168.16	196.35	169.54
彩色电视机(万部)	Color TV Sets(10000 units)	74.51	76.21	79.25	72.56	66.93	77.87

注：2008年及以前原煤产量为全社会口径。

Note:Before 2008,output of Coal refered to the statistical coverage of the whole province.

14-10 规模以上工业企业主要经济指标(2011)

单位：亿元

指　　标	Item	企业单位数(个) Number of Enterprises (unit)	从业人员年平均人数(万人) Annual Average of All Employees (10000 persons)
总　　计	**Total**	**3687**	**93.96**
#国有控股企业	State-holding Enterprises	576	49.37
#农村工业	Rural Industry	169	2.41
按登记注册类型分	**Gorouped by Status of Registration**		
内资企业	Domestic-funded Enterprises	3590	91.03
国有企业	State-owned Industry	349	25.88
中央企业	Central Industry	52	9.12
地方企业	Local Industry	297	16.76
集体企业	Collective-owned Industry	68	0.86
股份合作企业	Cooperative Enterprises	50	1.23
联营企业	Joint Ownership Enterprises	28	0.29
有限责任公司	Limited Liability Corporations	1100	26.29
股份有限公司	Share-holding Enterprises	140	11.56
私营企业	Private Enterprises	1793	24.45
其他企业	Others Enterprises	62	0.47
港、澳、台商投资企业	Enterprises with Funds from Hong kong, Macao and Taiwan	47	0.95
外商投资企业	Foreign Funded Enterprises	50	1.99
按轻重工业分	**Grouped by Light and Heavy Industry**		
轻工业	Light Industry	842	14.36
重工业	Heavy Industry	2845	79.60
按企业规模分	**Grouped by Scale of Enterprise**		
大型企业	Large Enterprises	70	35.01
中型企业	Medium-sized Enterprises	509	27.45
小型企业	Small Enterprises	2646	28.90
微型企业	Micro-enterprises	462	2.60

Main Economic Indicators of Industrial Enterprises above Designated Size

(100 million yuan)

工业总产值 Total Output Value of Industry	工业增加值 Value-Added of Industry	资产合计 Total Assets	主营业务收入 Revenue from Principal Business	利税总额 Total Profits and Taxes	#利润总额 Total Profits
5794.83	**1723.58**	**7384.82**	**5290.90**	**924.04**	**464.89**
2987.30	924.79	5133.05	2908.98	557.77	237.97
95.28	26.68	106.21	91.75	28.75	16.78
5591.28	1682.19	7100.16	5114.44	900.27	448.17
1504.98	485.22	2574.79	1458.22	276.51	164.45
672.52	136.36	1037.68	627.89	36.99	16.69
832.45	348.86	1537.11	830.33	239.52	147.76
30.39	3.09	16.64	26.92	1.56	0.75
45.45	4.73	34.71	34.59	5.35	2.52
19.35	5.02	33.31	18.14	3.06	1.82
2012.22	549.38	2360.28	1818.46	312.99	102.10
620.75	162.17	1066.52	581.10	93.55	56.53
1334.71	465.32	995.90	1152.67	204.73	118.37
23.42	7.26	18.00	24.35	2.51	1.64
74.70	20.07	127.40	68.15	0.61	-1.51
128.86	21.32	157.26	108.31	23.16	18.23
1253.14	563.48	1271.92	1132.83	465.59	221.28
4541.70	1160.10	6112.90	4158.07	458.45	243.61
2213.39	640.70	3515.27	2216.26	539.38	255.14
1585.19	412.05	2139.93	1367.31	207.13	120.93
1894.07	631.37	1559.55	1649.80	171.99	86.89
102.18	39.46	170.07	57.53	5.54	1.93

14-11 规模以上工业企业分行业主要经济指标(2011)

单位：亿元

指　标	Item	企业单位数(个) Number of Enterprises (unit)	从业人员年平均人数(万人) Annual Average of All Employees (10000 persons)
总　　计	**Total**	**3687**	**93.96**
采矿业	Mining and Quarrying	1165	30.35
#煤炭开采和洗选业	Mining and Washing of Coal	999	28.80
黑色金属矿采选业	Mining and Dressing of Ferrous Metals	45	0.43
有色金属矿采选业	Mining and Dressing of Nonferrous Metals	44	0.40
非金属矿采选业	Mining and Dressing of Nonmetal Minerals	77	0.72
其他采矿业	Mining of other Ores		
制造业	Manufacturing	2267	51.69
#农副食品加工业	Processing of Food from Agricultural Products	208	1.42
食品制造业	Manufacture of Foods	78	1.12
饮料制造业	Manufacture of Beverages	182	3.78
#白酒制造	Manufacture of Liquors	87	2.91
烟草制品业	Manufacture of Tobacco	6	1.38
纺织业	Manufacture of Textile	16	0.45
纺织服装、鞋、帽制造业	Manufacture of Textile Wearing Apparel, Footware and Caps	13	0.37
皮革、毛皮、羽毛(绒)及其制造业	Manufacture of Leather,Furs,Feather and Related Products	3	0.05
木材加工及木、竹、藤、棕、草制品业	Timber Processing, Manufacture of Wood, Bamboo, Rattan,Palm and Straw Products	85	1.25
家具制造业	Manufacture of Furniture	8	0.11
造纸及纸制品业	Manufacture of Paper and Paper Products	54	0.49
印刷业和记录媒介的复制	Printing,Reproduction of Recording Media	28	0.29
文教体育用品制造业	Manufacture of Articles For Culture,Education and Sport Activity	3	0.08
石油加工、炼焦及核燃料加工业	Processing of Petroleum, Coking,Processing of Nuclear Fuel	35	0.95

Main Economic Indicators of Industrial Enterprises above Designated Size by Sector

(100 million yuan)

工业总产值 Total Output Value of Industry	工业增加值 Value-Added of Industry	资产合计 Total Assets	主营业务收入 Revenue from Principal Business	利税总额 Total Profits and Taxes	#利润总额 Total Profits
5794.83	**1723.58**	**7384.82**	**5290.90**	**924.04**	**464.89**
1169.11	486.34	1339.43	959.74	245.97	135.47
1062.53	441.75	1275.19	864.36	221.30	118.64
15.69	7.71	13.83	14.83	3.06	1.79
23.06	5.83	16.29	20.37	3.46	1.82
67.83	31.05	34.12	60.19	18.15	13.23
3597.34	995.21	3853.93	3368.77	629.28	320.99
146.66	23.08	62.06	130.43	8.19	5.73
81.91	14.99	44.38	77.28	19.90	15.77
333.38	243.65	569.30	306.95	211.29	142.59
293.14	230.18	534.68	270.17	206.09	139.19
253.47	176.21	204.19	262.01	175.13	23.37
8.86	3.11	5.96	7.07	0.18	
5.29	1.99	6.05	6.28	0.52	0.40
1.95	0.02	1.51	1.91	0.26	0.24
53.06	13.49	27.19	46.60	5.39	3.32
8.44	1.45	3.89	7.30	2.07	1.79
42.61	5.14	48.10	38.51	1.58	0.52
14.96	6.62	18.52	13.41	4.01	3.04
1.31	0.40	0.57	1.08	0.06	0.02
78.48	12.34	49.05	70.53	5.39	2.92

14-11 续表

单位：亿元

指 标	Item	企业单位数(个) Number of Enterprises (unit)	从业人员年平均人数(万人) Annual Average of All Employees (10000 persons)
化学原料及化学制品制造业	Manufacture of Raw Chemical Materials and Chemical Products	220	6.24
医药制造业	Manufacture of Medicines	107	2.65
化学纤维制造业	Manufacture of Chemical Fibers		
橡胶制品业	Manufacture of Rubber	16	1.40
塑料制品业	Manufacture of Plastics	67	0.74
非金属矿物制品业	Manufacture of Non-metallic Mineral Products	457	6.89
黑色金属冶炼及压延加工业	Smelting and Pressing of Ferrous Metals	182	6.10
有色金属冶炼及压延加工业	Smelting and Pressing of Non-ferrous Metals	103	3.74
金属制品业	Manufacture of Metal Products	51	1.46
通用设备制造业	Manufacture of General Purpose Machinery	96	1.49
专用设备制造业	Manufacture of Special Purpose Machinery	49	0.97
交通运输设备制造业	Manufacture of Transport Equipment	82	5.60
电气机械及器材制造业	Manufacture of Electrical Equipment and Machinery	65	1.16
通信设备、计算机及其他电子设备制造业	Manufacture of Communication Equipment, Computers and Other Electronic Equipment	23	0.80
仪器仪表及文化、办公用机械制造业	Manufacture of Measuring Instruments and Machinery for Cultural Activity and Office Work	14	0.26
工艺品及其他制造业	Manufacture of Artwork and Other Manufacturing	12	0.42
废弃资源和废旧材料回收加工业	Recycling and Disposal of Waste	4	0.04
电力、燃气及水的生产和供应业	Production and Distribution of Electric Power, Gas and Water	255	11.92
#电力、热力的生产和供应业	Production and Distribution of Electric Power and Heat Power	190	10.84
电力生产	Production of Electric Power	108	2.87
电力供应	Distribution of Electric Power	82	7.98
燃气生产和供应业	Production and Distribution of Gas	8	0.35
水的生产和供应业	Production and Distribution of Water	57	0.73

continued

(100 million yuan)

工业总产值 Total Output Value of Industry	工业增加值 Value-Added of Industry	资产合计 Total Assets	主营业务收入 Revenue from Principal Business	利税总额 Total Profits and Taxes	#利润总额 Total Profits
495.93	100.62	767.02	570.66	60.58	45.76
238.29	54.31	186.25	182.91	36.81	24.66
113.97	15.98	82.44	104.07	4.74	1.87
40.15	7.39	25.20	34.67	2.36	1.33
314.43	70.29	363.70	261.29	20.07	8.70
542.78	67.42	366.39	496.04	15.12	4.18
303.56	58.64	381.31	276.77	22.45	12.57
51.20	10.41	55.36	52.29	3.72	2.15
63.39	23.54	61.55	55.07	6.50	4.38
40.98	7.88	63.62	35.09	3.34	2.63
183.32	33.58	311.59	179.20	8.11	4.90
97.52	8.60	66.35	76.53	5.23	3.65
48.72	10.87	36.65	45.14	2.93	2.01
11.17	3.05	10.86	9.32	1.53	0.93
17.41	19.46	33.47	16.54	1.69	1.49
4.11	0.68	1.40	3.81	0.13	0.09
1028.39	242.03	2191.45	962.39	48.79	8.42
987.63	236.91	2099.35	923.40	46.68	7.49
379.93	149.98	1513.27	329.76	14.19	-8.82
607.69	86.44	586.08	593.64	32.50	16.31
27.79	1.24	34.97	28.31	1.32	0.84
12.97	3.88	57.13	10.68	0.78	0.09

14-12 规模以上国有控股工业企业主要经济指标(2011)

单位：亿元

指　标	Item	企业单位数(个) Number of Enterprises (unit)	从业人员年平均人数(万人) Annual Average of All Employees (10000 persons)
总　　计	**Total**	**576**	**49.37**
按轻重工业分	**Grouped by Type of Light and Heavy Industry**		
轻工业	Light Industry	120	5.51
重工业	Heavy Industry	456	43.87
按企业规模分	**Grouped by Scale of Enterprise**		
大型企业	Large Enterprises	52	31.49
中型企业	Medium-sized Enterprises	189	12.30
小型企业	Small Enterprises	289	4.16
微型企业	Micro-enterprises	46	1.42
按工业行业分	**Grouped by Industrial Sector**		
采矿业	Mining and Quarrying	79	11.33
#煤炭开采和洗选业	Mining and Washing of Coal	67	11.06
有色金属矿采选业	Mining and Processing of Nonferrous Metal Ores	3	0.08
非金属矿采选业	Mining and Processing of Nonmetal Ores	8	0.20
制造业	Manufacturing	303	26.41
#农副食品加工业	Processing of Food from Agricultural Products	16	0.06
食品制造业	Manufacture of Foods	6	0.14
饮料制造业	Manufacture of Beverages	8	1.79
烟草制品业	Manufacture of Tobacco	5	1.37
纺织业	Manufacture of Textile	4	0.18
纺织服装、鞋、帽制造业	Manufacture of Textile Wearing Apparel, Footware and Caps	3	0.24
木材加工及木、竹、藤、棕、草制品业	Timber Processing , Bamboo , Cane , Palm Fiber and Straw Products	15	0.20

Major Economic Indicators of State-controlled Industrial Enterprises above Designated Size

(100 million yuan)

工业增加值 Value-Added of Industry	资产合计 Total Assets	主营业务收入 Revenue from Principal Business	利税总额 Total Profits and Taxes	#利润总额 Total Profits
2987.30	**5133.05**	**2908.98**	**557.77**	**237.97**
575.03	815.35	572.83	364.44	151.73
2412.27	4317.70	2336.15	193.33	86.25
1972.15	3275.76	2019.29	484.83	211.48
733.46	1402.65	658.16	56.15	21.18
244.09	385.61	227.43	14.42	5.00
37.60	69.02	4.10	2.37	0.32
326.28	586.40	262.22	74.40	38.37
294.38	570.31	233.77	66.14	32.40
3.88	3.52	3.74	0.72	0.33
27.91	12.34	24.64	7.56	5.67
1653.24	2482.33	1703.48	429.98	185.62
6.02	3.68	5.12	0.00	-0.01
3.87	3.19	3.50	0.08	0.02
206.93	461.25	213.24	185.25	127.05
252.62	203.69	261.06	175.13	23.37
1.61	1.31	1.07	0.02	-0.07
3.56	3.32	4.49	0.33	0.29
8.84	3.86	8.36	0.41	0.17

14-12 续表

单位：亿元

指　标	Item	企业单位数(个) Number of Enterprises (unit)	从业人员年平均人数(万人) Annual Average of All Employees (10000 persons)
造纸及纸制品业	Manufacture of Paper and Paper Products	2	0.09
印刷业、记录媒介的复制	Printing,Reproduction of Recording Media	5	0.09
文教体育用品制造业	Manufacture of Articles For Culture, Education and Sport Activity		
石油加工、炼焦及核燃料加工业	Processing of Petroleum,Coking,Processing of Nuclear Fuel	1	0.09
化学原料及化学制品制造业	Manufacture of Raw Chemical Materials and Chemical Products	45	3.96
医药制造业	Manufacture of Medicines	5	0.04
橡胶制品业	Manufacture of Rubber	3	1.10
塑料制品业	Manufacture of Plastics	7	0.12
非金属矿物制品业	Manufacture of Non-metallic Mineral Products	33	2.03
黑色金属冶炼及压延加工业	Smelting and Pressing of Ferrous Metals	10	3.20
有色金属冶炼及压延加工业	Smelting and Pressing of Non-ferrous Metals	14	2.27
金属制品业	Manufacture of Metal Products	9	1.19
通用设备制造业	Manufacture of General Purpose Machinery	21	0.78
专用设备制造业	Manufacture of Special Purpose Machinery	18	0.61
交通运输设备制造业	Manufacture of Transport Equipment	38	5.11
电气机械及器材制造业	Manufacture of Electrical Equipment and Machinery	7	0.47
通信设备、计算机及其他电子设备制造业	Manufacture of Communication Equipment, Computers and Other Electronic Equipment	14	0.67
仪器仪表及文化、办公用机械制造业	Manufacture of Measuring Instruments and Machinery for Cultural Activity and Office.Work	6	0.17
工艺品及其他制造业	Manufacture of Artwork and Other Manufacturing	6	0.38
电力、燃气及水的生产和供应业	Production and Distribution of Electric Power,Gas and Water	194	11.63
#电力、热力的生产和供应业	Production and Distribution of Electric Power and Heat Power	137	10.61
燃气生产和供应业	Production and Distribution of Gas	5	0.32
水的生产和供应业	Production and Distribution of Water	52	0.70

continued

(100 million yuan)

工业增加值 Value-Added of Industry	资产合计 Total Assets	主营业务收入 Revenue from Principal Business	利税总额 Total Profits and Taxes	#利润总额 Total Profits
7.47	29.36	6.54	-1.56	-1.83
1.17	1.48	1.36	0.07	-0.01
18.88	14.79	20.06	1.57	0.73
277.81	613.74	361.88	30.65	20.20
6.59	2.91	4.17	0.53	0.26
103.36	77.19	95.31	4.56	1.83
2.15	5.24	2.26	-0.26	-0.32
52.38	85.31	35.47	3.00	1.47
226.54	222.93	223.11	0.15	-3.44
141.13	242.54	139.94	6.74	0.18
35.68	45.89	39.14	2.80	1.52
25.00	39.44	23.31	3.39	2.49
19.19	41.38	16.71	1.92	1.39
143.39	272.05	142.04	6.60	3.90
38.98	30.23	30.92	2.56	2.03
45.74	34.56	43.17	2.74	1.89
6.79	8.99	5.20	1.40	0.88
15.26	32.90	14.35	1.61	1.47
1007.79	2064.32	943.28	53.40	13.98
968.84	1976.57	906.62	51.39	13.08
26.72	33.58	27.07	1.31	0.84
12.23	54.17	9.59	0.69	0.06

14-13 规模以上集体工业企业主要经济指标(2011)

单位：万元

指 标	Item	企业单位数(个) Number of Enterprises (unit)	从业人员年平均人数(人) Annual Average of All Employees (person)
总 计	**Total**	**68**	**8573**
#亏损企业	Loss Making Enterprise	19	1453
#农村工业	Rural Industry	4	153
按轻重工业分	**Grouped by Type of Light and Heavy Industry**		
轻工业	Light Industry	9	424
重工业	Heavy Industry	59	8149
按企业规模分	**Grouped by Size of Enterprise**		
中型企业	Medium-sized Enterprises	8	4170
小型企业	Small Enterprises	48	4297
微型企业	Micro-enterprises	12	106
按工业行业分	**Grouped by Industrial Sector**		
采矿业	Mining and Quarrying	12	1743
#煤炭开采和洗选业	Mining and Washing of Coal	7	1095
黑色金属矿采选业	Mining and Processing of Ferrous Metal Ores	3	548
有色金属矿采选业	Mining and Processing of Nonferrous Metal Ores		
制造业	Manufacturing	54	6742
#食品制造业	Manufacture of Foods	2	119
饮料制造业	Manufacture of Beverages	3	135

Main Economic Indicators of All Collective-owned Industrial Enterprises above Designated Size

(10000 yuan)

工业增加值 Value-Added of Industry	资产合计 Total Assets	主营业务收入 Revenue from Principal Business	利税总额 Total Profits and Taxes	#利润总额 Total Profits
303926	**166447**	**269166**	**15589**	**7515**
42215	40008	39002	-2076	-3214
37466	7070	31405	144	-322
28798	14549	26835	1742	867
275127	151898	242331	13847	6648
116489	39206	104233	4857	2830
177269	122172	155940	10418	4732
10168	5070	8993	314	-47
48393	31108	44709	3932	1506
25032	22052	21871	1426	-92
17761	6911	17238	1656	748
253616	126110	222841	12102	6492
3154	1964	3154	450	300
7049	9648	5790	919	576

14-13 续表

单位：万元

指　标	Item	企业单位数(个) Number of Enterprises (unit)	从业人员年平均人 数(人) Annual Average of All Employees (person)
造纸及纸制品业	Manufacture of Paper and Paper Products	1	64
印刷业、记录媒介的复制	Printing,Reproduction of Recording Media		
化学原料及化学制品制造业	Manufacture of Raw Chemical Materials and Chemical Products	4	81
塑料制品业	Manufacture of Plastics	2	163
非金属矿物制品业	Manufacture of Non-metallic Mineral Products	14	1610
黑色金属冶炼及压延加工业	Smelting and Pressing of Ferrous Metals	4	1713
有色金属冶炼及压延加工业	Smelting and Pressing of Non-ferrous Metals	3	183
金属制品业	Manufacture of Metal Products	4	429
通用设备制造业	Manufacture of General Purpose Machinery	6	394
交通运输设备制造业	Manufacture of Transport Equipment	4	301
电气机械及器材制造业	Manufacture of Electrical Equipment and Machinery	2	169
电力、燃气及水的生产和供应业	Production and Distribution of Electric Power,Gas and Water	2	88
#电力、热力的生产和供应业	Production and Distribution of Electric Power and Heat Power	2	88

continued

(10000 yuan)

工业总产值 Total Output Value of Industry	资产合计 Total Assets	主营业务收入 Revenue from Principal Business	利税总额 Total Profits and Taxes	#利润总额 Total Profits
2934	1710	2522	-94	-101
6429	2952	7082	227	16
1737	1854	2212	180	-48
42882	42334	39089	4259	2897
51018	19068	50008	2860	1995
25162	6377	17205	558	294
5966	7215	5589	212	-89
15949	10068	12562	512	23
11928	9033	7705	784	221
9827	2844	10287	440	101
1917	9229	1615	-445	-483
1917	9229	1615	-445	-483

14-14 规模以上外商投资和港澳台投资工业企业主要经济指标(2011)

单位：万元

指 标	Item	企业单位数(个) Number of Enterprises (unit)	从业人员年平均人数(人) Annual Average of All Employees (person)
总 计	**Total**	**97**	**29367**
#亏损企业	Loss Making Enterprises	32	4413
#港、澳、台商投资企业	Enterprises with Funds from Hong kong, Macao and Taiwan	47	9463
合资经营企业(港或澳、台资)	Joint Venture Enterprises(with Funds from Hong Kong, Macao and Taiwan)	23	5305
港澳台商独资企业	Enterprises with Sole Funds from Hong Kong,Macao and Taiwan	23	4103
港澳台商投资股份有限公司	Share Holding Enterprises with Funds from Hong kong, Macao and Taiwan	1	55
外商投资企业	Foreign Funded Enterprises	50	19904
中外合资经营企业	Joint-venture Enterprises	24	5059
中外合作经营企业	Cooperation Enterprises	2	991
外资企业	Enterprises Funds with Sole Foreigner	19	6161
外商投资股份有限公司	Share Holding Enterprises with Funds from Foreigner	5	7693
按轻重工业分	**Grouped by Type of Light and Heavy Industry**		
轻工业	Light Industry	30	8691
重工业	Heavy Industry	67	20676
按企业规模分	**Grouped by Size of Enterprise**		
大型企业	Large Enterprises	4	11917
中型企业	Medium-sized Enterprises	17	8136
小型企业	Small Enterprises	69	9103
微型企业	Micro-enterprises	7	211
按工业行业分	**Grouped by Industrial Sector**		
采矿业	Mining and Quarrying	4	7559
#煤炭开采和洗选业	Mining and Washing of Coal	1	7089

Major Economic Indicators of all above Designated Size Industrial Enterprises Funded by Foreigners and Hong kong,Macao and Taiwan

(10000 yuan)

工业总产值 Total Output Value of Industry	资产合计 Total Assets	主营业务收入 Revenue from Principal Business	利税总额 Total Profits and Taxes	#利润总额 Total Profits
2035547	**2846574**	**1764582**	**237742**	**167171**
313561	862433	297201	-57765	-64945
746982	1273998	681463	6097	-15097
443175	997674	394239	-6496	-20983
302914	270555	283670	13655	6957
893	5768	3554	-1063	-1071
1288565	1572577	1083119	231646	182269
393747	363743	371927	58781	46059
199030	246438	198542	93559	93410
447584	515533	408931	60043	30295
248203	446862	103719	19263	12506
635714	684242	521718	104827	71286
1399833	2162333	1242864	132915	95885
449172	675169	301702	49579	34177
712771	1326573	665783	114094	87714
862188	806399	786062	74718	46083
11415	38433	11034	-648	-803
221156	394488	87561	27859	15408
182381	380421	60681	17084	12317

14-14 续表

单位：万元

指　标	Item	企业单位数(个) Number of Enterprises (unit)	从业人员年平均人数(人) Annual Average of All Employees (person)
制造业	Manufacturing	91	20334
#农副食品加工业	Processing of Food from Agricultural Products	4	381
食品制造业	Manufacture of Foods	2	513
饮料制造业	Manufacture of Beverages	5	1434
纺织业	Manufacture of Textile		
纺织服装、鞋、帽制造业	Manufacture of Textile Wearing Apparel, Footware and Caps	1	125
造纸及纸制品业	Manufacture of Paper and Paper Products	2	143
印刷业、记录媒介的复制	Printing,Reproduction of Recording Media	3	467
文教体育用品制造业	Manufacture of Articles For Culture, Education and Sport Activity	1	405
石油加工、炼焦及核燃料加工业	Processing of Petroleum,Coking,Processing of Nuclear Fuel	1	215
化学原料及化学制品制造业	Manufacture of Raw Chemical Materials and Chemical Products	6	489
医药制造业	Manufacture of Medicines	9	3468
橡胶制品业	Manufacture of Rubber	1	64
塑料制品业	Manufacture of Plastics	2	1146
非金属矿物制品业	Manufacture of Non-metallic Mineral Products	24	4005
黑色金属冶炼及压延加工业	Smelting and Pressing of Ferrous Metals	4	1045
有色金属冶炼及压延加工业	Smelting and Pressing of Non-ferrous Metals	7	1812
金属制品业	Manufacture of Metal Products	4	874
通用设备制造业	Manufacture of General Purpose Machinery	2	139
专用设备制造业	Manufacture of Special Purpose Machinery	1	1494
交通运输设备制造业	Manufacture of Transport Equipment	6	871
电气机械及器材制造业	Manufacture of Electrical Equipment and Machinery	2	591
通信设备、计算机及其他电子设备制造业	Manufacture of Communication Equipment,Computers and Other Electronic Equipment	1	61
仪器仪表及文化、办公用机械制造业	Manufacture of Measuring Instruments and Machinery for Cultural Activity and Office Work	2	391
电力、燃气及水的生产和供应业	Production and Distribution of Electric Power,Gas and Water	2	1474
#电力、热力的生产和供应业	Production and Distribution of Electric Power and Heat Power	1	315
水的生产和供应业	Production and Distribution of Water	1	1159

continued

(10000 yuan)

工业总产值 Total Output Value of Industry	资产合计 Total Assets	主营业务收入 Revenue from Principal Business	利税总额 Total Profits and Taxes	#利润总额 Total Profits
1703303	1760011	1582442	257151	201656
54745	10683	42286	977	762
95058	41654	94502	31657	27236
88578	104139	90052	14458	7140
1817	2721	1290	12	5
7379	5423	7368	336	98
65619	64327	43955	18650	14628
5973	3275	3787	13	12
30429	15961	32450	-103	-1008
60324	103321	64622	12784	9650
256563	208045	197923	35043	19620
1704	3002	984	-308	-314
81436	49245	83325	10567	7717
268332	499788	256139	16677	7966
136160	56072	141720	3902	2323
227978	304242	227262	97037	94444
33010	9433	32376	1018	279
2944	1777	2939	149	-3
103106	135363	99640	7897	7819
48544	49148	41488	4330	2792
60067	47399	42658	743	289
59731	10842	59836	1125	878
4956	6397	4427	-513	-821
111088	692076	94579	-47268	-49893
73171	462529	68411	-50350	-51217
37917	229547	26168	3082	1324

14-15 规模以上工业企业主要经济效益指标(2011)

Main Indicators on Economic Efficiency of all Industrial Enterprises above Designated Size

单位：% (%)

指 标	Item	产值利税率 Ratio of Pre-Tax Profit to Output Value	资金利税率 Ratio of Pre-Tax Profit to Asset	销售利税率 Ratio of Pre-Tax Profit to Sales
总 计	**Total**	**15.95**	**13.85**	**17.46**
内资企业	Domestic Enterprises	16.10	14.06	17.60
国有企业	State-owned	18.37	12.28	18.96
中央企业	Central	5.50	3.91	5.89
地方企业	Local	28.77	18.36	28.85
集体企业	Collective-owned	5.13	9.14	5.79
股份合作企业	Cooperation Enterprises	11.76	17.18	15.45
联营企业	Joint-owned Enterprises	15.83	10.08	16.89
有限责任公司	Limited Liability Corporations	15.55	13.98	17.21
股份有限公司	Share Holding Enterprises	15.07	9.62	16.10
私营企业	Private Enterprises	15.34	24.06	17.76
其他企业	Others	10.71	19.93	10.30
港、澳、台商投资企业	Enterprises with Funds from Hong kong,Macao and Taiwan	0.82	0.53	0.89
外商投资企业	Foreign Funded Enterprises	17.98	15.20	21.39
在总计中：	of the Total:			
#国有控股企业	State-controlled Enterprises	18.67	11.86	19.17
在总计中：	of the Total:			
#农村工业	Rural Industry	30.17	35.45	31.33
按轻重工业分	**Grouped by Type of Light and Heavy Industry**			
轻工业	Light Industry	36.95	40.86	41.10
重工业	Heavy Industry	10.08	8.29	11.03
按企业规模分	**Grouped by Size of Enterprise**			
大型企业	Large Enterprises	24.37	16.34	24.34
中型企业	Medium-sized Enterprises	13.07	10.68	15.15
小型企业	Small Enterprises	9.08	11.03	10.42
微型企业	Micro-enterprises	5.42	3.26	9.63
按工业行业分	**Grouped by Industrial Sector**			
采矿业	Mining and Quarrying	21.04	21.45	25.63
#煤炭开采和洗选业	Mining and Washing of Coal	20.83	20.23	25.60
黑色金属矿采选业	Mining and Processing of Ferrous Metal Ores	19.53	27.65	20.66
有色金属矿采选业	Mining and Processing of Nonferrous Metal Ores	14.99	26.18	16.97
非金属矿采选业	Mining and Processing of Nonmetal Ores	26.76	63.50	30.16
制造业	Manufacturing	17.49	18.23	18.68
#农副食品加工业	Processing of Food from Agricultural Products	5.59	16.72	6.28
食品制造业	Manufacture of Foods	24.30	44.68	25.75
饮料制造业	Manufacture of Beverages	63.38	42.73	68.84
烟草制品业	Manufacture of Tobacco	69.09	94.34	66.84
纺织业	Manufacture of Textile	2.07	3.91	2.60
纺织服装、鞋、帽制造业	Manufacture of Textile Wearing Apparel,Footware and Caps	9.73	9.33	8.21
皮革、毛皮、羽毛(绒)及其制造业	Manufacture of Leather,Furs,Feather and Related Products	13.37	19.55	13.65

14-15 续表 continued

单位：% (%)

指 标	Item	产值利税率 Ratio of Pre-Tax Profit to Output Value	资金利税率 Ratio of Pre-Tax Profit to Assets	销售利税率 Ratio of Pre-Tax Profit to Sales
木材加工及木、竹、藤、棕、草制品业	Processing of Timber,Manufacture of Wood, Bamboo,Rattan,Palm and Straw Products	10.17	25.30	11.58
家具制造业	Manufacture of Furniture	24.59	78.73	28.43
造纸及纸制品业	Manufacture of Paper and Paper Products	3.72	3.72	4.12
印刷业、记录媒介的复制	Printing,Reproduction of Recording Media	26.79	23.30	29.88
文教体育用品制造业	Manufacture of Articles For Culture,Education and Sport Activity	4.41	10.45	5.35
石油加工、炼焦及核燃料加工业	Processing of Petroleum,Coking, Processing of Nuclear Fuel	6.87	8.87	7.64
化学原料及化学制品制造业	Manufacture of Raw Chemical Materials and Chemical Products	12.22	8.97	10.62
医药制造业	Maufacture of Medicines	15.45	21.18	20.12
橡胶制品业	Manufacture of Rubber	4.16	6.41	4.55
塑料制品业	Manufacture of Plastics	5.87	10.84	6.80
非金属矿物制品业	Manufacture of Non-metallic Mineral Products	6.38	6.35	7.68
黑色金属冶炼及压延加工业	Smelting and Pressing of Ferrous Metals	2.79	4.64	3.05
有色金属冶炼及压延加工业	Smelting and Pressing of Non-ferrous Metals	7.39	6.65	8.11
金属制品业	Manufacture of Metal Products	7.27	7.33	7.12
通用设备制造业	Manufacture of General Purpose Machinery	10.25	11.99	11.80
专用设备制造业	Manufacture of Special Purpose Machinery	8.15	5.51	9.51
交通运输设备制造业	Manufacture of Transport Equipment	4.42	2.87	4.53
电气机械及器材制造业	Manufacture of Electrical Equipment and Machinery	5.36	9.11	6.83
通信设备、计算机及其他电子设备制造业	Manufacture of Communication Equipment Computers and Other Electronic Equipment	6.02	6.59	6.50
仪器仪表及文化、办公用机械制造业	Manufacture of Measuring Instruments and Machinery for Cultural Activity and Office Work	13.70	15.83	16.44
工艺品及其他制造业	Manufacture of Artwork and Other Manufacturing	9.68	4.77	10.19
废弃资源和废旧材料回收加工业	Recycling and Disposal of Waste	3.19	16.18	3.45
电力、燃气及水的生产和供应业	Production and Distribution of Electric Power, Gas and Water	4.74	2.35	5.05
#电力、热力的生产和供应业	Production and Distribution of Electric Power and Heat Power	4.73	2.35	5.06
燃气生产和供应业	Production and Distribution of Gas	4.76	4.07	4.67
水的生产和供应业	Production and Distribution of Water	6.01	1.42	7.30

14-16 规模以上国有控股工业企业主要经济效益指标(2011)
Major Indicators on Economic Efficiency of State-controlled Industrial Enterprises above Designated Size

单位：% (%)

指 标	Item	产值利税率 Ratio of Pre-Tax Profit to Output Value	资金利税率 Ratio of Pre-Tax Profit to Assets	销售利税率 Ratio of Pre-Tax Profit to Sales
总 计	**Total**	**18.67**	**11.86**	**19.17**
#亏损企业	Loss Making Enterprises	-3.70	-2.23	-4.02
按轻重工业分	**Grouped by Type of Light and Heavy Industry**			
轻工业	Light Industry	62.73	49.11	61.97
重工业	Heavy Industry	8.02	4.87	8.32
按企业规模分	**Grouped by Size of Enterprise**			
大型企业	Large Enterprises	24.58	15.80	24.01
中型企业	Medium-sized Enterprises	7.66	4.95	8.53
小型企业	Small Enterprises	5.91	4.74	6.34
微型企业	Micro-enterprises	6.31	4.44	5.79
按工业行业分	**Grouped by Industrial Sector**			
采矿业	Mining and Quarrying	22.80	14.03	28.37
#煤炭开采和洗选业	Mining and Washing of Coal	22.47	12.77	28.29
黑色金属矿采选业	Mining and Dressing of Ferrous Metals	-18.70	-3.11	-34.16
有色金属矿采选业	Mining and Processing of Nonferrous Metal Ores	18.62	24.94	19.30
非金属矿采选业	Mining and Processing of Nonmetal Ores	27.08	84.32	30.66
制造业	Manufacturing	26.01	19.41	25.24
#农副食品加工业	Processing of Food from Agricultural Products	-0.07	-0.14	-0.09
食品制造业	Manufacture of Foods	2.11	1.62	2.34
饮料制造业	Manufacture of Beverages	89.52	45.57	86.87
烟草制品业	Manufacture of Tobacco	69.32	94.52	67.08
纺织业	Manufacture of Textile	1.01	1.33	1.52
纺织服装、鞋、帽制造业	Manufacture of Textile Wearing Apparel, Footware and Cap	9.38	10.70	7.42
木材加工及木、竹、藤、棕、草制品业	Processing of Timber,Manufacture of Wood, Bamboo,Rattan,Palm and Straw Products	4.60	16.31	4.87
家具制造业	Manufacture of Furniture	12.73	29.45	16.93
造纸及纸制品业	Manufacture of Paper and Paper Products	-20.92	-5.31	-23.90

14-16 续表 continued

单位：% (%)

指 标	Item	产值利税率 Ratio of Pre-Tax Profit to OutputValue	资金利税率 Ratio of Pre-Tax Profit to Assets	销售利税率 Ratio of Pre-Tax Profit to Sales
印刷业、记录媒介的复制	Printing,Reproduction of Recording Media	6.07	4.20	5.20
石油加工、炼焦及核燃料加工业	Processing of Petroleum,Coking, Processing of Nuclear Fuel	8.30	11.90	7.81
化学原料及化学制品制造业	Manufacture of Raw Chemical Materials and Chemical Products	11.03	5.85	8.47
医药制造业	Manufacture of Medicines	8.07	26.06	12.75
橡胶制品业	Manufacture of Rubber	4.42	6.56	4.79
塑料制品业	Manufacture of Plastics	-11.94	-7.30	-11.36
非金属矿物制品业	Manufacture of Rubber	5.72	4.19	8.45
黑色金属冶炼及压延加工业	Smelting and Pressing of Ferrous Metals	0.07	0.08	0.07
有色金属冶炼及压延加工业	Smelting and Pressing of Non-ferrous Metals	4.78	3.18	4.82
金属制品业	Manufacture of Metal Products	7.85	6.47	7.16
通用设备制造业	Manufacture of General Purpose Machinery	13.57	9.43	14.55
专用设备制造业	Manufacture of Special Purpose Machinery	10.01	5.29	11.50
交通运输设备制造业	Manufacture of Transport Equipment	4.60	2.57	4.65
电气机械及器材制造业	Manufacture of Electrical Equipment and Machinery	6.57	12.32	8.28
通信设备、计算机及其他电子设备制造业	Manufacture of Communication Equipment, Computers and Other Electronic Equipment	5.99	6.41	6.34
仪器仪表及文化、办公用机械制造业	Manufacture of Measuring Instruments and Machinery for Cultural Activity and Office Work	20.62	18.23	26.96
工艺品及其他制造业	Manufacture of Artwork and Other Manufacturing	10.57	4.65	11.24
废弃资源和废旧材料回收加工业	Recycling and Disposal of Waste			
电力、燃气及水的生产和供应业	Production and Distribution of Electric Power, Gas and Water	5.30	2.72	5.66
#电力、热力的生产和供应业	Production and Distribution of Electric Power and Heat Power	5.30	2.74	5.67
燃气生产和供应业	Production and Distribution of Gas	4.90	4.19	4.84
水的生产和供应业	Production and Distribution of Water	5.66	1.31	7.21

14-17 规模以上集体工业企业主要经济效益指标(2011)
Main Indicators on Economic Benefit of Collective-owned Industrial Enterprises above Designated Size

单位：% (%)

指 标	Item	产值利税率 Ratio of Pre-Tax Profit to Output Value	资金利税率 Ratio of Pre-Tax Profit to Assets	销售利税率 Ratio of Pre-Tax Profit to Sales
总 计	**Total**	**5.13**	**9.14**	**5.79**
#亏损企业	Loss Making Enterprises	-4.92	-6.32	-5.15
#农村工业	Rural Industry	0.39	1.80	0.46
按轻重工业分	**Grouped by Type of Light and Heavy Industry**			
轻工业	Light Industry	6.05	5.55	6.49
重工业	Heavy Industry	5.03	9.95	5.71
按企业规模分	**Grouped by Size of Enterprise**			
中型企业	Medium-sized Enterprises	4.17	12.39	4.66
小型企业	Small Enterprises	5.88	8.53	6.68
微型企业	Micro-enterprises	3.08	6.18	3.49
按工业行业分	**Grouped by Industrial Sector**			
采矿业	Mining and Quarrying	8.13	11.64	8.80
#煤炭开采和洗选业	Mining and Quarrying	5.70	5.39	6.52
黑色金属矿采选业	Mining and Processing of Ferrous Metal Ores	9.32	26.45	9.61
非金属矿采选业	Mining and Dressing of Nonmetal Minerals	15.18	79.25	15.18
制造业	Manufacturing	4.77	9.83	5.43
#农副食品加工业	Processing of Food from Agricultural Products	2.81	24.62	2.87
食品制造业	Manufacture of Foods	14.26	1.87	14.26
饮料制造业	Manufacture of Beverages	13.04	19.06	15.88
造纸及纸制品业	Manufacture of Paper and Paper Products	-3.19	-6.03	-3.71
石油加工、炼焦及核燃料加工业	Processing of Petroleum,Coking, Processing of Nuclear Fuel			
化学原料及化学制品制造业	Manufacture of Raw Chemical Materials and Chemical Products	3.53	9.32	3.20
橡胶制品业	Manufacture of Rubber	0.45	4.74	0.54
塑料制品业	Manufacture of Plastics	10.35	10.08	8.12
非金属矿物制品业	Manufacture of Non-metallic Mineral Products	9.93	15.15	10.89
黑色金属冶炼及压延加工业	Smelting and Pressing of Ferrous Metals	5.61	14.58	5.72
有色金属冶炼及压延加工业	Smelting and Pressing of Non-ferrous Metals	2.22	8.19	3.24
金属制品业	Manufacture of Metal Products	3.54	2.70	3.78
通用设备制造业	Manufacture of General Purpose Machinery	3.21	6.33	4.08
专用设备制造业	Manufacture of Special Purpose Machinery	7.85	15.77	7.85
交通运输设备制造业	Manufacture of Transport Equipment	6.57	9.27	10.18
电气机械及器材制造业	Manufacture of Electrical Equipment and Machinery	4.48	18.50	4.28
电力、燃气及水的生产和供应业	Production and Distribution of Electric Power, Gas and Wate	-23.21	-3.24	-27.55
#电力、热力的生产和供应业	Production and Distribution of Electric Power and Heat Power	-23.21	-3.24	-27.55

14－18 大中型工业企业主要经济指标占全省规模以上工业比重(2011)

Percentages of Main Indicators of Large and Medium Industrial Enterprises as the whole Industrial Enterprises above Designated Size

单位：亿元 (100 million yuan)

指 标	Item	规模以上工业 Industrial Enterprises above Designated Size	#大中型工业企业 Large and Medium industrial Enterprises		#国有大中型 State-owned Large and Medium Industrial Enterprises	
			绝对数 Absolute Figure	占规模以上工业比重(%) Percentage Taken to Industrial Enterprises above Designated Size(%)	绝对数 Absolute Figure	占规模以上工业比重(%) Percentage Taken to Industrial Enterprises above Designated Size(%)
企业单位数(个)	Number of Industrial Enterprises(unit)	3687	579	15.7	241	6.5
#亏损企业个数(个)	Number of Loss Making Industrial Enterprises(unit)	1028	101	9.8	51	5.0
工业总产值	Gross Output Value of Industry	5794.83	3798.58	65.6	2705.61	46.7
工业增加值	Value-added of Industry	1723.58	1052.75	61.1	818.18	47.5
资产总计	Total Assets	7384.82	5655.20	76.6	4678.41	63.4
#流动资产年平均余额	Average Balance of Circulating Funds	2480.37	1636.84	66.0	557.92	22.5
固定资产净值年平均余额	Annual Average Balance Net Value of Fixed Assets	2721.62	2084.76	76.6	829.59	30.5
负债总计	Total Liabilities	4759.80	3681.37	77.3	3111.82	65.4
主营业务收入	Revenue from Principal Business	5290.90	3583.56	67.7	2677.46	50.6
#产品销售成本	Cost of Sales	4083.11	2661.81	65.2	2027.05	49.6
产品销售税金及附加	Sales Tax and Extra Charges	207.74	183.00	88.1	169.09	81.4
亏损企业亏损额	Total Deficit of Loss Making Industrial Enterprises	74.64	44.61	59.8	32.63	43.7
利税总额	Total Profits and Taxes	924.04	746.51	80.8	540.98	58.5
从业人员年平均人数(万人)	Annual Average Number of All Employees (10000 persons)	93.96	62.46	66.5	43.79	46.6
资金利税率(%)	Ratio of Pre-Tax Profit and Assets(%)	17.76	18.21	102.5	16.94	95.4
全员劳动生产率(元/人)	Overall Labor Productivity (yuan/person)	183433	168622	91.9	186842	107.5

14–19 规模以上大中型工业企业分行业主要经济指标(2011)

单位：亿元

指 标	Item	企业单位数(个) Number of Enterprises (unit)	从业人员年平均人数(万人) Annual Average of All Employees (10000 persons)
总 计	**Total**	**579**	**62.46**
采矿业	Mining and Quarrying	212	19.20
#煤炭开采和洗选业	Mining and Washing of Coal	202	18.81
有色金属矿采选业	Mining and Processing of Nonferrous Metal Ores	1	0.03
非金属矿采选业	Mining and Processing of Nonmetal Ores	6	0.24
制造业	Manufacturing	298	33.27
#农副食品加工业	Processing of Food from Agricultural Products	6	0.30
食品制造业	Manufacture of Foods	9	0.61
饮料制造业	Manufacture of Beverages	17	2.44
烟草制品业	Manufacture of Tobacco	3	1.31
纺织业	Manufacture of Textile	5	0.32
纺织服装、鞋、帽制造业	Manufacture of Textile Wearing Apparel, Footware and Caps	2	0.20
木材加工及木、竹、藤、棕、草制品业	Timber Processing, Manufacture of Wood, Bamboo, Rattan,Palm and Straw Products	7	0.44
造纸及纸制品业	Manufacture of Paper and Paper Products	3	0.14
印刷业、记录媒介的复制	Printing, Reproduction of Recording Media	2	0.11
石油加工、炼焦及核燃料加工业	Processing of Petroleum, Coking, Processing of Nuclear Fuel	6	0.60
化学原料及化学制品制造业	Manufacture of Raw Chemical Materials and Chemical Products	39	4.79
医药制造业	Manufacture of Medicines	21	1.84
橡胶制品业	Manufacture of Rubber	4	1.25
塑料制品业	Manufacture of Plastics	3	0.23
非金属矿物制品业	Manufacture of Non-metallic Mineral Products	37	1.82
黑色金属冶炼及压延加工业	Smelting and Pressing of Ferrous Metals	24	4.30
有色金属冶炼及压延加工业	Smelting and Pressing of Non-ferrous Metals	19	3.01
金属制品业	Manufacture of Metal Products	4	0.98
通用设备制造业	Manufacture of General Purpose Machinery	14	0.86
专用设备制造业	Manufacture of Special Purpose Machinery	8	0.63
交通运输设备制造业	Manufacture of Transport Equipment	33	5.07
电气机械及器材制造业	Manufacture of Electrical Equipment and Machinery	11	0.69
通信设备、计算机及其他电子设备制造业	Manufacture of Communication Equipment, Computers and Other Electronic Equipment	9	0.60
仪器仪表及文化、办公用机械制造业	Manufacture of Measuring Instruments and Machinery for Cultural Activity and Office Work	3	0.15
工艺品及其他制造业	Manufacture of Artwork and Other Manufacturing	3	0.36
电力、燃气及水的生产和供应业	Production and Distribution of Electric Power,Gas and Water	69	10.00
#电力、热力的生产和供应业	Production and Distribution of Electric Power and Heat Power	64	9.50
燃气生产和供应业	Production and Distribution of Gas	2	0.28
水的生产和供应业	Production and Distribution of Water	3	0.21

Main Indicators on Economic of Large and Medium Industrial Enterprises by Sector

(100 million yuan)

工业总产值 Total Output Value of Industry	资产合计 Total Assets	主营业务收入 Revenue from Principal Business	利税总额 Total Profits and Taxes	#利润总额 Total Profits
3798.58	**5655.20**	**3583.56**	**746.51**	**376.07**
603.68	850.85	474.29	168.02	97.34
574.71	836.89	452.66	161.17	93.10
1.88	0.45	1.29	0.09	0.01
23.69	11.32	17.15	6.54	4.09
2319.79	2987.00	2260.62	536.27	269.58
20.13	6.64	17.79	1.38	0.68
47.76	26.06	45.56	15.07	12.81
240.83	497.68	233.81	195.25	134.03
249.72	203.69	258.16	175.13	23.37
3.87	3.87	2.61	0.02	-0.12
3.48	2.44	4.42	0.29	0.26
17.00	8.54	13.23	2.52	2.11
15.35	30.84	14.05	-0.36	-0.76
4.87	7.03	4.82	1.65	1.27
46.89	29.30	43.56	4.49	3.01
374.01	690.62	453.20	51.75	40.63
132.48	112.81	98.82	21.94	13.72
109.81	77.37	100.21	4.56	1.82
10.05	6.88	9.89	1.03	0.64
111.70	155.27	86.78	7.71	4.48
328.83	268.24	312.23	7.30	0.57
233.56	348.10	213.54	19.68	11.98
30.44	32.65	34.09	1.70	0.70
33.33	40.32	29.15	4.59	3.24
26.09	43.77	23.58	2.52	2.10
159.95	290.72	157.04	7.35	4.68
47.59	39.32	38.26	3.88	2.93
36.74	29.90	34.41	2.28	1.56
7.13	5.17	5.60	0.63	0.39
15.08	25.27	13.61	1.47	1.35
875.10	1817.35	848.66	42.22	9.14
844.17	1756.74	819.03	40.27	7.87
25.76	29.79	25.73	1.56	1.14
5.18	30.82	3.90	0.40	0.13

14-20 规模以上工业销售产值(2011)
Industrial Sales Output Value

单位：亿元 (100 million yuan)

类　别	Item	销售产值 Sales Value	#出口交货值 Delivery Value of Industry
总　计	**Total**	**5505.47**	**100.67**
#国有控股企业	State-controlled Enterprises	2869.74	84.64
按登记注册类型分	**Grouped by Registration**		
内资企业	Domestic Enterprises	5316.16	86.97
国有企业	State-owned Enterprises	1453.27	18.78
中央企业	Central	662.06	6.28
地方企业	Local	791.21	12.50
集体企业	Collective-owned Enterprises	28.04	
股份合作企业	Cooperation Enterprises	43.16	
联营企业	Joint-owned Enterprises	20.57	
有限责任公司	Limited Liability Corporations	1911.98	40.04
股份有限公司	Share Holding Enterprises	565.56	22.14
私营企业	Private Enterprises	1271.78	6.00
其他企业	Others	21.80	
港、澳、台商投资企业	Enterprises with Funds from Hong kong,Macao and Taiwan	68.60	7.72
外商投资企业	Foreign Funded Enterprises	120.71	5.98
按轻重工业分	**Grouped by Type of Light and Heavy Industry**		
轻工业	Light Industry	1163.58	13.75
重工业	Heavy Industry	4341.89	86.92
按企业规模分	**Grouped by Scale of Enterprise**		
大型企业	Large Enterprises	2131.55	73.53
中型企业	Medium-sized Enterprises	1490.53	7.44
小型企业	Small Enterprises	1787.22	19.70
微型企业	Micro-enterprises	96.17	

14-21 规模以上工业主要产品产量、销售量和产销率(2011)

Sales Volume of Major Industrial Products and Proportion of Products Sold

产品名称	Item	产 量 Output	销售量 Sales Volume	产销率(%) Ratio of Products Sold(%)	2011年比2010年增长(%) Increase Rate in 2011 over 2010(%) 产 量 Output	销售量 Sales Volume
原煤(万吨)	Raw Coal(10000 tons)	14014.80	10958.46	78.2	8.8	4.5
洗煤(万吨)	Washed Coall(10000 tons)	3938.04	3560.60	90.4	30.3	34.5
煤气生产量(亿立方米)	Volume of Coal Gas Production(100 million cu.m)	84.15			24.1	
发电量(亿千瓦小时)	Electricity(100 million kwh)	1359.01			-0.2	
#水电	Hydropower	334.66			-15.3	
磷矿石(生产量含$P_2O_5$30%)(万吨)	Phosphorite Mineral(10000 tons)	2084.18	1254.41	60.2	33.2	48.0
配混合饲料(万吨)	Forage(10000 tons)	89.82	82.40	91.7	72.9	74.2
成品糖(万吨)	Sugar(10000 tons)	0.43	0.11	24.9	29.8	
乳制品(吨)	Dairy Products(ton)	55133.63	5.51	0.0	25.2	25.3
罐头(吨)	Canned Food(ton)	15924.34	1.57	0.0	50.6	49.7
饮料酒(万千升)	Alcohol Beverages(10000 kiloliter)	61.80	54.11	87.6	23.9	15.8
#白酒	White Spirit	25.49	19.05	74.7	48.4	28.8
啤酒	Beer	36.27	35.06	96.7	11.1	9.7
软饮料(万吨)	Soft Drink(10000 tons)	118.65	108.78	91.7	73.2	61.7
卷烟(万箱)	Cigarettes(10000 cases)	245.23	247.18	100.8	2.5	3.7
纱(万吨)	Yarn(10000 tons)	1.40	1.26	90.0	3.8	-0.8
布(万米)	Cloth(10000 m)	789.37	800.39	101.4	-5.6	-9.3
丝(吨)	Silk(ton)	356.50	176.00	49.4	166.4	51.7
服装(万件)	Garment(10000 pieces)	569.15	478.54	84.1	38.7	59.9
人造板(万立方米)	Artificial Board(10000cu.m)	165.81	129.77	78.3	170.6	170.5
机制纸(万吨)	Machine-made Paper(10000 tons)	27.18	24.33	89.5	60.3	77.0
焦炭(万吨)	Coke(10000 tons)	652.76	515.63	79.0	5.0	11.2
硫酸(折100%)(万吨)	Sulfuric Acid(10000 tons)	733.82	290.37	39.6	19.6	33.1
氢氧化钠(烧碱折100%)(万吨)	Caustic Soda(10000 tons)	13.76	12.92	93.9	59.4	51.5
碳化钙(电石折300升/千克)(万吨)	Calcium Carbide(10000 tons)	46.94	46.81	99.7	26.9	35.5
合成氨(万吨)	Synthetic Ammonia(10000 tons)	170.12	55.01	32.3	-1.0	22.3
农用化学肥料总计(折纯)(万吨)	Chemical Fertilizer(10000 tons)	364.66	341.42	93.6	23.9	14.2
#氮肥(折含N100%)	Nitrogen Fertilizer	165.42	159.14	96.2	9.8	3.5
尿素	Carbamide	85.72	84.38	98.4	9.6	6.0
磷肥(折合$P_2O_5$100%)	Phosphate Fertilizer	197.37	180.69	91.5	39.2	25.2

14–21 续表 continued

产品名称	Item	产 量 Output	销售量 Sales Volume	产销率(%) Proportion of Products Sold(%)	2011年比2010年增长(%) Increase Rate in 2011 over 2010(%) 产 量 Output	销售量 Sales Volume
纯苯(吨)	Pure Benzene(ton)	12359	12306	99.6	-14.3	-14.7
合成洗涤剂(万吨)	Synthetic Detergents(10000 tons)	4.92	2.98	60.5	59.2	-6.1
轮胎外胎(万条)	Tires(10000 tires)	536.77	532.62	99.2	-3.9	-5.4
塑料制品(万吨)	Plastic Products(10000 tons)	30.72	26.81	87.3	39.2	46.1
#农用薄膜(吨)	Rural Use Membrane(ton)	5377.08	3174.00	59.0	68.5	76.5
水泥(万吨)	Cement(10000 tons)	5250.89	4866.33	92.7	51.3	47.5
生铁(万吨)	Pig Iron(10000 tons)	482.35	108.88	22.6	31.6	46.1
粗钢(万吨)	Steel(10000 tons)	434.01	4.47	1.0	20.5	7.9
成品钢材(万吨)	Steel Products(10000 tons)	462.77	457.45	98.9	18.5	16.8
#盘条(线材)	Wire Rod	112.82	111.70	99.0	13.4	12.1
无缝钢管	Seamless Steel Pipe	17.17	16.44	95.7	29.2	28.9
铁合金(万吨)	Iron Alloy(10000 tons)	263.90	259.79	98.4	28.6	30.0
十种有色金属(万吨)	Ten kinds of Nonferrous Metals(10000 tons)	98.33	94.33	95.9	3.1	-0.6
#铅(吨)	Lead(ton)	7923.00	7923.00	100.0	38.3	37.7
锌	Zinc	3.37	1.87	55.3	10.2	-14.9
铝	Aluminium	90.36	87.54	96.9	2.0	-1.2
氧化铝(万吨)	Alumina(10000 tons)	211.03	126.37	59.9	56.5	146.5
铝材(万吨)	Aluminium Material(10000 tons)	13.16	13.00	98.8	774.1	810.4
金属切削机床(台)	Metal-cutting Machine Tools(set)	1150	1408	122.4	15.2	10.9
小型拖拉机(辆)	Mini-tractors(set)	1710	1754	102.6	58.6	53.1
交流电动机(万千瓦)	Alternating Current Motor(10000 kw)	52.75	34.38	65.2	60.7	10.1
家用电冰箱(万台)	Household Refrigerators(10000 sets)	169.54	167.19	98.6	-13.7	-14.8
集成电路(万块)	Semiconductor Integrated Circui(10000 pcs)	1189.82	1009.88	84.9	-42.9	-47.5
彩色电视机(万部)	Color TV Sets(10000 sets)	77.86	76.67	98.5	12.9	12.6

14–22 高技术产业基本情况
Basic Statistics on High-tech Industry

行 业	Item	2006	2007	2008	2009	2010	2011
规模以上工业企业数(个)	Number of Enterprises (unit)	173	155	154	149	155	157
从业人员年平均人数(万人)	Annual Average Number of Employees (10 000 persons)	7.02	6.69	6.66	6.78	6.77	6.82
工业总产值(亿元)	Gross Output Value(100 million yuan)	178.05	204.83	231.56	273.92	320.96	392.87
主营业务收入(亿元)	Revenue from Principal Business (100 million yuan)	137.74	168.03	190.57	225.65	260.26	316.59
利税总额(亿元)	Pre-Tax Profits(100 million yuan)	15.69	21.73	25.67	29.32	33.21	35.18
利润总额(亿元)	Profits (100 million yuan)	9.27	14.07	16.16	18.89	21.38	22.38

主要统计指标解释

工业 指从事自然资源的开采，对采掘品和农产品进行加工和再加工的物质生产部门。具体包括：(1) 对自然资源的开采，如采矿、晒盐等（但不包括禽兽捕猎和水产捕捞）；(2) 对农副产品的加工、再加工，如粮油加工、食品加工、缫丝、纺织、制革等；(3) 对采掘品的加工、再加工，如炼铁、炼钢、化工生产、石油加工、机器制造、木材加工等，以及电力、自来水、煤气的生产和供应等；(4) 对工业品的修理、翻新，如机器设备的修理、交通运输工具（包括小卧车）的修理等。

1984 年以前农村的村及村以下办工业归属农业，1984 年以后划归工业。

工业统计调查单位为独立核算法人工业企业。

独立核算法人工业企业指从事工业生产经营活动的单位。独立核算法人工业企业应同时具备以下条件：①依法成立，有自己的名称、组织机构和场所，能够承担民事责任；②独立拥有和使用资产，承担负债，有权与其他单位签订合同；③独立核算盈亏，并能够编制资产负债表。

本年鉴中涉及的企业登记注册类型：

国有及国有控股企业 指国有企业加上国有控股企业。国有企业（即原全民所有制工业或国营工业）指企业全部资产归国家所有，并按《中华人民共和国企业法人登记管理条例》规定登记注册的非公司制的经济组织。包括国有企业、国有独资公司和国有联营企业。1957 年以前的公私合营和私营工业，后均改造为国营工业，1992 年改为国有工业，这部分工业的资料不单独分列时，均包括在国有企业内。国有控股企业是对混合所有制经济的企业进行的“国有控股”分类。它是指这些企业的全部资产中国有资产（股份）相对其他所有者中的任何一个所有者占资（股）最多的企业。该分组反映了国有经济控股情况。

集体企业 指企业资产归集体所有，并按《中华人民共和国企业法人登记管理条例》规定登记注册的经济组织。是社会主义公有制经济的组成部分。包括城乡所有使用集体投资举办的企业，以及部分个人通过集资自愿放弃所有权并依法经工商行政管理机关认定为集体所有制的企业。

股份合作企业 指以合作制为基础，由企业职工共同出资入股，吸收一定比例的社会资产投资组建，实行自主经营，自负盈亏，共同劳动，民主管理，按劳分配与按股分红相结合的一种集体经济组织。

联营企业 指两个及两个以上相同或不同所有制性质的企业法人或事业单位法人，按自愿、平等、互利的原则，共同投资组成的经济组织。联营企业包括：

国有联营企业指国有企业与国有企业间的联营；

集体联营企业指集体企业与集体企业间的联营；

国有与集体联营企业指国有企业与集体企业间的联营。

有限责任公司 指根据《中华人民共和国公司登记管理条例》规定登记注册，由两个以上，五十个以下的股东共同出资，每个股东以其所认缴的出资额对公司承担有限责任，公司以其全部资产对其债务承担责任的经济组织。

有限责任公司包括国有独资公司以及其他有限责任公司。

股份有限公司 指根据《中华人民共和国企业法人登记管理条例》规定登记注册，其全部注册资本由等额股份构成并通过发行股票筹集资本，股东以其认购的股份对公司承担有限责任，公司以其全部资产对其债务承担责任的经济组织。

私营企业 指由自然人投资设立或由自然人控股，以雇佣劳动为基础的营利性经济组织。包括按照《公司法》、《合伙企业法》、《私营企业暂行条例》规定登记注册的私营有限责任公司、私营股份有限公司、私营合伙企业和私营独资企业。

港、澳、台商投资企业 指企业注册登记类型中的港、澳、台资合资、合作、独资经营企业和股份有限公司之和。

外商投资企业 指企业注册登记类型中的中外合资、合作经营企业、外资企业和外商投资股份有限公司之和。

轻工业 指主要提供生活消费品和制作手工工具的工业。按其所使用的原料不同，可分为两大类：(1) 以农产品为原料的轻工业，是指直接或间接以农产品为基本原料的轻工业。主要包括食品制造、饮料制造、烟草加工、纺织、缝纫、皮革和毛皮制作、造纸以及印刷等工业；(2) 以非农产品为原料的轻工业，是指以工业品为原料的轻工业。主要包括文教体育用品、化学药品制造、合成纤维制造、日用化学制品、日用玻璃制品、日用金属制品、手工工具制造、医疗器械制造、文化和办公用机械制造等工业。

重工业 指为国民经济各部门提供物质技术基础的主要生产资料的工业。按其生产性质和产品用途，可以分为下列三类：(1) 采掘（伐）工业，是指对自然资源的开采，包括石油开采、煤炭开采、金属矿开采、非金属矿开采等工业；(2) 原材料工业，指向国民经济各部门提供基本材料、动力和燃料的工业。包括金属冶炼及加工、炼焦及焦炭、化学、化工原料、水泥、人造板以及电力、石油和煤炭加工等工业；(3) 加工工业，是指对工业原材料进行再加工制造的工业。包括装备国民经济各部门的机械设备制造工业、金属结构、水泥制品等工业，以及为农业提供的生产资料如化肥、农药等工业。

根据上述划分原则，修理业中以重工业产品为修理作业对象的划为重工业，反之划为轻工业。

工业总产值

(1) 定义：工业总产值是以货币形式表现的，工业企业在一定时期内生产的工业最终产品或提供工业性劳务活动的总价值量。它反映一定时间内工业生产的总规模和总水平。

(2) 计算原则：

工业生产的原则，即凡是企业在报告期生产的经检验合格的产品，不管是否在报告期销售，均包括在内。

最终产品的原则，即凡是计入工业总产值的产品，必须是本企业生产的经检验合格的，不需要再进行任何加工的最终产品。如果企业有中间产品（半成品）对外销售，则对外销售的中间产品应视为企业的最终产品。

工厂法原则，即工业总产值是以工业企业作为基本计算（核算）单位，即按企业的最终产品计算工业总产值。按这种方法计算的工业总产值，不允许同一产品价值在企业内部重复计算，不能把企业内部各个车间（分厂）生产的成果相加，但允许企业间的重复计算。

(3) 内容及计算方法：1995 年全国工业普查对工业总产值（原规定）的内容及计算原则和方法做了某些修订，修订后的工业总产值（新规定）包括三项内容：即本期生产成品价值、对外加工费收入、在制品半成品期末期初差额价值三部分。

本期生产成品价值：指企业本期生产，并在报告期内不再进行加工，经检验、包装入库的全部工业成品（半产品）价值合计，包括企业生产的自制设备及提供给本企业在建工程、其他非工业部门和福利部门等单位使用的成品价值。本期生产成品价值为按自备原材料生产的产品的数量乘以本期不含增值税（销项税额）的产品实际销售平均单价计算；会计核算中按成本价格转帐的自制设备和自产自用的成品，按成本价格计算生产成品价值。生产成品价值中不包括用定货者来料加工的成品（半产品）价值。

对外加工费收入：指企业在报告期内完成的对外承接的工业品加工（包括用定货者来料加工产品）的加工费收入和对外工业修理作业所取得的加工费收入。对外加工费收入按不含增值税（销项税额）的价格计算，可根据会计“产品销售收入”科目的有关资料取得。

对于本企业对内非工业部门提供的加工修理、设备安装的劳务收入，如果企业会计核算基础较好，能取得这部分资料，而且这部分价值所占比重较大，应包括在对外加工费收入中。

自制半成品在制品期末期初差额价值：指企业报告期在制品期末减期初的差额价值，本指标一般可以从会计核算资料中取得。如果会计产品成本核算中不计算半成品、在制品的成本，则总产值中也不包括这部分价值，反之则包括。

(4) 工业总产值统计范围变化和计算方法修订情况：

1984 年以前工业总产值不包括村办工业，村办工业总产值划归农业。1984 年以后工业总产值包括村办工业。

1995 年工业普查对工业总产值计算方法做了修订，即从 1995 年始按新修订（新规定）方法计算工业总产值。新规定与原规定的区别如下：

全价与加工费的计算原则不同：新规定为凡自备原材料，不论其生产繁简程度如何，一律按全价计算工业总产值；凡来料加工，允许按加工费计算工业总产值。原规定则视生产加工的繁简程度不同，规定哪些行业按全价，哪些行业按加工费计算工业总产值。

自制半成品、在产品期末期初差额价值的计算原则不同：新规定要求，凡会计产品成本核算时计算了成本的差额价值，总产值中就应包括，否则可不包括；原规定则按生产周期六个月的界限区分，凡生产周期六个月以上的企业，总产值计算中应包括这部分差额价值，否则可不包括。

计算价格不同：新规定按不含增值税（销项税额）的价格计算；原规定则按含增值税（销项税额）的价格计算。

工业增加值 指工业企业在报告期内以货币表现的工业生产活动的最终成果。

工业增加值有两种计算方法：一是生产法，即工业总产出减去工业中间投入加上应交增值税；二是收入法，即从收入的角度出发，根据生产要素在生产过程中应得到的收入份额计算，具体构成项目有固定资产折旧、劳动者报酬、生产税净额、营业盈余，这种方法也称要素分配法。本年鉴中的工业增加值是以生产法计算的。

生产法工业增加值的计算方法为：

工业增加值 = 工业总产出 − 工业中间投入 + 应交增值税

(1) 工业总产出：指工业企业在一定时期内工业生产活动的总成果。工业总产出包括：成品生产价值，对外加工费收入，自制半成品、在产品期末期初差额价值。1995 年后用新规定计算的工业总产值代替。

(2) 工业中间投入：指工业企业在工业生产活动中消耗的外购物质产品和对外支付的服务费用。服务费用包括支付给物质生产部门（工业、农业、批发零售贸易业、建筑业、运输邮电业）的服务费用和支付给非物质生产部门（如保险、金融、文化教育、科学研究、医疗卫生、行政管理等）的服务费用。工业中间投入的确定须遵循以下原则：必须从外部购入的，并已计入工业总产出的产品和服务价值；必须是本期投入生产，并一次性消耗掉（包括本期摊销的低值易耗品等）的产品和服务价值。

工业中间投入包括直接材料费用、制造费用中的工业中间投入、管理费用中的工业中间投入、销售费用中的工业中间投入和利息支出五部分。

资产总计　指企业拥有或控制的能以货币计量的经济资源，包括各种财产、债权和其他权利。资产按流动性分为流动资产、长期投资、固定资产、无形资产、递延资产和其他资产。该指标根据企业会计“资产负债表”中“资产总计”项目的期末数增列。

流动资产平均余额　指企业在报告期内全部流动资产的平均余额。

固定资产净值年平均余额　指固定资产净值在报告期内余额的平均数。计算公式为:

$$\text{固定资产净值年平均余额}=\frac{\text{1至12月各月月初+月末固定资产净值}}{24}$$

该指标根据“资产负债表”中“固定资产原价”、“累计折旧”指标的期初、期末数计算填列。

固定资产净值指固定资产原价减去历年已提折旧额后的净额。计算公式为:

固定资产净值 = 固定资产原价 − 累计折旧

产品销售收入　指企业在报告期内生产的成品、自制半成品和工业性劳务取得的收入。

产品销售成本　指企业在报告期内销售本企业生产的成品、自制半成品和工业性劳务等的实际成本。

产品销售税金及附加　指企业在报告期内销售产品、提供的劳务等主要经营业务应负担的城市维护建设税、消费税、资源税和教育费附加等。

利润总额　指企业生产经营活动的最终成果，是企业在一定时期内实现的盈亏相抵后的利润总额（亏损以“−”号表示），它等于营业利润加上补贴收入加上投资收益加上营业外净收入再加上以前年度损益调整。

本年应交增值税　指企业在报告期内应交纳的增值税额。它等于本年销项税额加上出口退税加上进项税额转出数减去本年进项税额。小规模纳税企业直接按全年计税销售额乘以征收率计算取得。

年末从业人员平均人数　从业人员是指在企业工作并取得劳动报酬的全部人员数。包括在岗职工、再就业的离退休人员、民办教师及在企业工作的外方人员和港澳台方人员、兼职人员、借用的外单位人员和第二职业者。不包括离开本单位但仍保留劳动关系的职工。

从业人员平均人数　是指报告期内每天拥有的从业人员人数。其计算公式为:

$$\text{月平均人数}=\frac{\text{报告月内每天实有人数之和}}{\text{报告月日历日数}}$$

$$\text{季平均人数}=\frac{\text{季内各月平均人数之和}}{3}$$

$$\text{年平均人数}=\frac{\text{年内各月平均人数之和}}{12}$$

总资产贡献率　反映企业全部资产的获利能力，是企业经营业绩和管理水平的集中体现，是评价和考核企业盈利能力的核心指标。计算公式为:

$$\text{总资产贡献率（\%）}=\frac{\text{利润总额+税金总额+利息支出}}{\text{平均资金总额}}\times 100\%$$

公式中：税金总额为产品销售税金及附加与应交增值税之和；平均资产总额为期初期末资产之和的算术平均值。

资产负债率　该指标既反映企业经营风险的大小，也反映企业利用债权人提供的资金从事经营活动的能力。计算公式为

$$\text{资产负债率（\%）}=\frac{\text{负债总额}}{\text{资产总额}}\times 100\%$$

资产与负债均为报告期期末数。

流动资产周转次数　指一定时期内流动资产完成的周转次数，反映投入工业企业流动资金的周转速度。计算公式为:

$$\text{流动资产周转次数}=\frac{\text{产品销售收入}}{\text{全部流动资产平均余额}}$$

公式中：全部流动资产平均余额为期初和期末的流动资产之和的算术平均值。

成本费用利润率 反映企业投入的生产成本及费用的经济效益，同时也反映企业降低成本所取得的经济效益。计算公式为：

$$成本费用利润（\%）=\frac{利润总额}{成本费用总额}\times 100\%$$

公式中：成本费用总额为产品销售成本、销售费用、管理费用、财务费用之和。

Explanatory Notes on Main Statistical Indicators

Industry refers to the material production sector which is engaged in extraction of natural resources and processing and reprocessing of minerals and agricultural products, including (1) extraction of natural resources, such as mining, salt production (but not including hunting and fishing); (2) processing and reprocessing of farm and sideline produces, such as rice husking, flour milling, wine making, oil pressing, silk reeling, spinning and weaving, and leather making; (3) manufacture of industrial products, such as steel making, iron smelting, chemicals manufacturing, petroleum processing, machine building, timber processing; water and gas production and electricity generation and supply; (4) repairing of industrial products such as the repairing of machinery and means of transport (including cars).

Prior to 1984, the rural industry run by villages and cooperative organizations under village was classified into agriculture. Since 1984, it has been grouped into industry.

Units of industrial statistics survey are corporate industrial enterprises with independent accounting system.

Corporate industrial enterprises with independent accounting system refer to enterprises engaging in industrial production activities, which meet the following requirements: ① They are established legally, having their own names, organizations, location,and able to take civil liability; ② They possess and use their assets independently, assume liabilities, and are entitled to sign contracts with other units; ③ They are financially independent and compile their own balance sheets.

Enterprises covered in the industrial statistics in the Yearbook include following categories by their registration:

State-owned and State-Controlled Enterprises refer to state-owned enterprises plus state-holding enterprises. State-owned enterprises(originally known as state-run enterprises with ownership by the whole society) are non-corporate economic entities registered in accordance with the Regulation of the People's Republic of China on the Management of Registration of Legal Enterprises, where all assets are owned by the state. Included in this category are state-owned enterprises, state-funded corporations and state-owned joint-operation enterprises. Joint state-private industries and private industries, which existed before 1957, were transformed into state-run industries since 1957, and into state-owned industries after 1992. Statistics on those enterprises are included in the state-owned industries instead of grouping them separately. State-controlled enterprises is a sub-classification of enterprises with mixed ownership, referring to enterprises where the percentage of state assets (or shares by the state) is larger than any other single share holder of the same enterprise. This sub-classification illustrates the control of the state over a particular industry.

Collective-owned Enterprises refer to economic entities registered in accordance with the Regulation of the People's Republic of China on the Management of Registration of Legal Enterprises, where assets are owned collectively. Collective enterprises constitute an integral part of the socialist economy with public ownership. They include urban and rural enterprises invested by collectives, and some enterprises registered in industrial and commercial administration agency as collective units where funds are pulled together by individuals who voluntarily give up their right of ownership.

Share-holding Cooperative Enterprises refer to economic units set up on cooperative basis, with funding partly from members of the enterprise and partly from outside investment, where the operation and management is decided by the members who also participate in the production, and the distribution of income is based both on work (labour input) and on shares (capital input).

Joint-operation enterprises refer to economic units that are established by joint investment by two or more corporate enterprises or institutions of the same or different types of ownership on voluntary, equal and mutual-beneficial basis. They include:

a) state-owned joint-operation enterprises (joint operation between state-owned enterprises);

b) collective joint-operation enterprises (joint operation between collective enterprises; and

c) state-collective joint-operation enterprises (joint operation between state and collective enterprises).

Limited Liability Corporations refer to economic units registered in accordance with the Regulation of the People's Republic of China on the Management of Registration of Corporations, with capitals from 2 to 49 investors, each investor bears limited liability to the corporation depending on his/her holding of shares, and the corporation bears liability to its debt to the maximum of its total assets.

Share-holding Corporations Ltd. refer to economic units registered in accordance with the Regulation of the People's Republic of China on the Management of Registration of Corporate Enterprises, with total registered capitals divided into equal shares and raised through issuing stocks. Each investor bears limited liability to the corporation depending on the holding of shares, and the corporation bears liability to its debt to the maximum of its total assets.

Private Enterprises refer to economic units invested or controlled(by holding the majority of the shares) by natural persons who hire labours for profit-making activities. Included in this category are private limited liability corporations, private share-holding corporations Ltd., private partnership enterprises and private sole investment enterprises registered in accordance with the Corporation Law, Partnership Enterprise Law and Tentative Regulation on Private Enterprises.

Enterprises with Funds form Hong Kong, Macao and Taiwan refers to all industrial enterprises registered as the joint-venture, cooperative, sole (exclusive) investment industrial enterprises and limited liability corporations with funds from Hong Kong, Macao and Taiwan.

Foreign Funded Enterprises refers to all industrial enterprises registered as the joint-venture, cooperative, sole (exclusive) investment industrial enterprises and limited liability corporations with foreign funds.

Light Industry refers to the industry that produces consumer goods and hand tools. It consists of two categories, depending on the materials used:

(1) Industries using farm products as raw materials. These are branches of light industry which directly or indirectly use farm products as basic raw materials, including the manufacture of food and beverages, tobacco processing, textile, clothing, fur and leather manufacturing, paper making, printing, etc.

(2) Industries using non farm products as raw materials. These are branches of light industry which use manufactured goods as raw materials, including the manufacture of cultural, educational articles and sports goods, chemicals, synthetic fiber, chemical products for daily use, glass products for daily use, metal products for daily use, hand tools, medical apparatus and instruments, and the manufacture of cultural and clerical machinery.

Heavy Industry refers to the industry which produces capital goods, and provides various sectors of the national economy with necessary material and technical basis. It consists of the following three branches according to the purpose of production or the use of products:

(1) Mining, quarrying and logging industry refers to the industry that extracts natural resources, including extraction of petroleum, coal, metal and non-metal ores.

(2) Raw materials industry refers to the industry that provides various sectors of the national economy with raw materials, fuels and power. It includes smelting and processing of metals, coking and coke chemistry, chemical materials and building materials such as cement, plywood, and power, petroleum refining and coal dressing.

(3) Manufacturing industry refers to the industry that processes raw materials. It includes machine-building industry which equips sectors of the national economy, industries of metal structure and cement products, industries producing means of agricultural production, such as chemical fertilizers and pesticides.

According to the above principle of classification, the repairing trades, which are engaged primarily in repairing products of heavy industry are classified into heavy industry while these engaged in repairing products of light industry are classified into light industry.

Gross Industrial Output Value

(1) Definition: Gross industrial output value is the total volume of final industrial products produced and industrial

services provided during a given period. It reflects the total achievements and overall scale of industrial production during a given period.

(2) Principles for calculation:

Statistics on industrial production follow the principle that all products produced by the enterprises and accepted during the reference period are to be included no matter whether they are sold or not during the reference period.

Determination of final products follow the principle that all products that are included in the calculation of grow industrial output value are the final products of the enterprise which have been accepted through quality check and require no further processing. If an enterprise has intermediate (semi-finished) products to sell, these intermediate products are considered as the final products of the enterprise.

Gross industrial output value is calculated following the principle of factory approach, i.e. industrial enterprise is used as the basic accounting unit in calculating the gross industrial output value. By this approach, value of the same product is not to be double counted, and the output value of different workshops (branch factories) should not be added. However, this approach does not exclude the possibility of double counting between enterprises.

(3) Content and calculation method: The old definition of gross industrial output value was modified during the national industrial census in 1995. The revised (new) definition of gross industrial output value consists of 3 components: value of the finished products during the reference period, income from external processing, and value of change in semi-finished products at the end and at the beginning of the reference period.

Value of the finished products during the reference period: refers to the value of all finished (semi-finished) industrial products that are produced during the reference period without the need for further processing, checked for acceptance, packed and put into the warehouse of the enterprise, including the value of own-produced equipment and the value of products provided to the projects under construction of the enterprise, and to other non-industrial or welfare units. Value of finished products during the reference period is calculated by the quantity of products produced using own materials multiplied by the average unit prices at which products are sold (excluding value-added tax). Own-produced equipment and products produced for own use are value at cost prices as in the case of enterprise accounting. Value of finished products does not include the value of finished products (semi-finished products) that are produced using the materials from the clients who make the orders.

Income from external processing: refers to income from contracted external processing of industrial products (including processing of industrial products using materials from the clients), and the income from industrial repairing work provided to other units. Income from external processing is calculated using information from the item "products sales income" in the enterprise accounting at the prices excluding value-added tax.

For income from services such as processing, repairing and installation of equipment provided to non-industrial units within the enterprise, if the accounting work of the enterprise is good enough to separate it from other records, and the share of such services is significant, it should also be included in the income from external processing.

Value of change in semi-finished products at the end and at the beginning of the reference period: refers to the value of change in semi-finished products at the end and at the beginning of the reference period, which generally can be obtained from accounting records of enterprises. If the enterprise accounting excludes the cost of semi-finished products, then it should not be included in the gross industrial output value, and vice versa.

(4) Changes in the coverage and method of calculation of gross industrial output value

Prior to 1984, the value of rural industry run by villages was classified into agriculture instead of industry. Since 1984, it has been included in the gross industrial output value. Method of calculation for the gross industrial output value was modified in the industrial census in 1995. The difference in the new method as compared with the old one is outlined below:

Principle in using full value vs. processing fee: The new method stipulates that all products produced using own materials are to be calculated with full value in reporting the gross industrial output value irrespective of sophistication of production, and for external processing, it allows calculation using processing fee. In the old method, however, the use of full value or processing fee was determined by the degree of sophistication of production in different branches of industries.

Principle in determining the value of change in semi-finished products: The new method requires that value of the change in semi-finished products should be included in the gross industrial output value if it is included in the accounting record of the enterprise, otherwise it should not be included. By the old method, it is determined by the type of enterprises in terms of production cycle. If the production cycle is over 6 months, the value of change in semi-finished products is included in the gross industrial output value, otherwise it is excluded.

Difference in prices: The new method uses prices excluding value-added tax in the calculation of gross industrial output value, while the old method used prices including value-added tax.

Value-added of Industry refers to the final results of industrial production of industrial enterprises in money terms during the reference period.

Industrial value-added can be calculated by two approaches: the production approach, i.e. gross industrial output value minus intermediate input plus value-added tax, and the income approach, i.e. income for various factors used in the course of production, including depreciation of fixed assets, remuneration of labourers, net of production tax, and operating surplus. Value-added of industry in the Yearbook is calculated by production approach as following:

Value-added of industry = gross industrial output-industrial intermediate input + value-added tax

(1) Gross industrial output: refers to the total achievements of industrial production during a given period. Gross industrial output includes value of finished products, income from external processing, and value of change in semi-finished products at the end and at the beginning of the reference period. Since 1995, it was substituted by the gross industrial output value by new method.

(2) Industrial intermediate input: refers to purchased goods and paid services consumed during the industrial production of enterprises. Fees paid for services include fees paid for the services provided by material production sectors (industry, agriculture, wholesale and retail trade, construction, transport, post and telecommunications) and by non-material production sectors (insurance, banking, culture, education, scientific research, health and medical care, public administration, etc.). The determination of industrial intermediate input follows the principle that the goods and services must be purchased from outside and included in the gross industrial output, and that the goods and services are inputted into production and consumed (include low-value consumables) during the reference period.

Industrial intermediate input includes 5 components, namely direct consumption of materials, industrial intermediate input in manufacturing cost, industrial intermediate input in management cost, industrial intermediate input in marketing cost and expenditure on interest.

Total Assets refer to all economic resources, in monetary terms, that are owned or controlled by enterprises, including properties, creditors equity and other economic rights of all forms. Classified by the degree of equitability, total assets include circulating assets, long-term investment, fixed assets, intangible assets and deferred assets, and other assets. Data on this indicator can be obtained by the year-end figures of total assets in the Assets and Liability Table of accounting records of enterprises.

Annual Average of Net Value of Fixed Assets refers to average of the net value of fixed assets during the reference period, calculated with the following formula:

$$\text{Annual Average of Net Value of Fixed Assets} = \frac{\text{sum of net value of fixed assets at the beginning and at the end of each month from January to December}}{24} \times 100\%$$

Information on this indicator can be obtained from the beginning and ending figures of the original value of fixed assets and cumulative depreciation from the Assets and Liability Table of enterprises.

Net value of fixed assets refers to the original value of fixed assets minus depreciation over the years, i.e.:

Net value of fixed assets = original value of fixed assets-cumulative depreciation

Sales Revenue of Industrial Products refers to the revenue from the sales of finished and semi-finished products and from rendering of industrial services by industrial enterprises during the reference period.

Cost of Industrial Products Sold refers to the actual cost of finished and semi-finished products sold and industrial services rendered by industrial enterprises during the reference period.

Tax and Extra Charges on Sales of Products refers to the tax on city maintenance and construction, consumption tax, resources tax and extra charges for education, which should be borne by the enterprises in selling products and providing industrial services during the reference period.

Total Profits refers to the final achievements of production and operation of the enterprises, represented by the total profits after deducting losses (loss is expressed by the negative figure). It is the sum of profits from operation, income from subsidies, investment earnings, net income from activities other than operation, and adjustment of profits and losses of previous years.

Value-added Tax Payable refers to the amount of the value-added tax which should be paid by the enterprises during the reference period. It is the sum of tax on sales, export rebate, and transferred tax on purchases of the current year, minus the tax on purchases of the current year. Value-added tax payable of small-size enterprises is determined by the taxable sales of the year multiplied by the tax rate.

Average Annual Number of Employed Persons Employed persons refer to all those who are employed in enterprises and receive remunerations therefrom, including currently working employees, retirees who are re-employed, teachers of local-run schools, as well as foreigners, staff from Hong Kong, Macao and Taiwan, part-time employees and persons with second job who are employed by the enterprise, and employees of other units temporarily working in the enterprises, but excluding former employees who left the enterprise with their employment records still kept by the enterprises.

Average number of employed persons refers to the number of employees everyday during the reference period, calculated with the following formula:

$$\text{Monthly average number}=\frac{\text{sum of actual employees everyday in reference month}}{\text{number of calendar dates in reference month}}$$

$$\text{Quarterly average number}=\frac{\text{sum of monthly average number in reference quarter}}{3}$$

$$\text{Annual average number}=\frac{\text{sum of monthly average number in reference year}}{12}$$

Ratio of Profits, Taxes and Interests to Average Assets reflects the profit-making capability of all assets of the enterprise and is a key indicator manifesting the performance and management and evaluating the profit-making potential of the enterprise. It is calculated as follows:

$$\text{Ratio of Profits, Taxes and Interests to Average Asset(\%)} = \frac{\text{total profits} + \text{total taxes} + \text{interest payment}}{\text{average assets}}\times 100\%$$

In the above formula, total taxes is the sum of tax and extra charges on the sales of products and value-added tax payable; and average assets is the arithmetic mean of the sum of beginning assets and ending assets.

Ratio of Debts to Assets reflect both the operation risk and the capability of the enterprise in making use of the capital from the creditors. It is calculated as follows:

$$\text{Ratio of Debts to Assets (\%)} = \frac{\text{total debts}}{\text{total assets}}\times 100\%$$

Both assets and debts are figures at the end of the reference period.

Turnover of Working Capital refers to the number of times of turnover of working capital in a given period of time, which reflects the speed of the turnover of working capital of industrial enterprises, and is calculated as follows:

$$\text{Turnover of Working Capital}=\frac{\text{sales revenue of products}}{\text{average balance of total working capital}}$$

In the above formula, average balance of total working capital refers to the arithmetic mean of the sum of working capital at the beginning and at the end of the reference period.

Ratio of Profits to Total Industrial Costs refers to the ratio of profits realized in a given period to the total costs in the same period, which reflects the economic efficiency of input cost and is calculated as follows:

$$\text{Ratio of Profits to Total Industrial Cost(\%)} = \frac{\text{total profits}}{\text{total costs}} \times 100\%$$

Total costs in the above formula is the sum of cost of products sold, marketing cost, management cost and financial cost.

15 Fifteen

建筑业

Construction

15-1 建筑业主要指标

Main Economic Indicators on Construction Enterprises

指　标	Item	2006	2007	2008	2009	2010	2011
建筑业企业个数(个)	**Number of Enterprises (unit)**	**618**	**614**	**609**	**611**	**605**	**581**
年末从业人员(万人)	Number of Emplyed Persons at the Year-end(10000 persons)	30.25	29.12	30.16	33.05	33.83	33.14
自有固定资产原价(亿元)	Fixed Assets Owned(original value)(100 million yuan)	76.30	77.08	77.77	86.38	87.43	92.00
自有固定资产净价(亿元)	Fixed Assets Owned(net value)(100 million yuan)	52.15	51.72	50.78	59.12	57.16	57.33
自有机械设备台数(万台)	Number of Machinery and Equipment Owned(10000 sets)	7.08	6.84	6.22	6.21	7.97	7.26
自有机械设备净值(亿元)	Net Value of Machinery and Equipment Owned (100 million yuan)	22.84	21.93	23.54	24.45	27.85	115.62
自有机械设备总功率(万千瓦)	Total Power of Machinery and Equipment Owned (10000 kw)	121.16	116.79	128.90	113.22	142.88	153.03
建筑业总产值(亿元)	**Gross Output Value of Construction (100 million yuan)**	**312.34**	**348.79**	**393.88**	**523.91**	**622.96**	**824.72**
建筑业增加值(亿元)	**Value Added of Construction(100 million yuan)**	**62.82**	**69.18**	**80.29**	**223.95**	**283.19**	**365.13**
#本年固定资产折旧	Depreciation of Fixed Assets	3.89	3.85	3.38	4.44	5.44	5.56
应付工资	Wages Payable	39.21	43.87	49.94	55.51	75.25	90.07
应付福利费	Welfare Expenses Payable	4.02	3.17	2.90	3.36	4.24	4.85
工程结算税金及附加	Taxes and Extra Charges on Project Settle Accounts	10.14	11.60	13.69	18.00	22.67	29.86
管理费用中的税金	Taxes in Management Expenses	0.41	0.54	0.90	0.60	0.8	0.83
营业利润	Operating Profits	2.46	3.58	6.05	6.84	9.78	14.31
房屋建筑施工面积(万平方米)	**Floor Space of Buildings under Construction (10000 sq.m)**	**3369**	**3813**	**4230**	**4953**	**5756**	**6779**
房屋建筑竣工面积(万平方米)	**Floor Space of Buildings Completed(10000 sq.m)**	**1108**	**1204**	**1216**	**1244**	**1350**	**1530**
利润总额(亿元)	Total Profits(100 million yuan)	3.20	4.08	6.46	6.63	10.48	14.4
税金总额(亿元)	Total Taxes(100 million yuan)	10.54	12.14	16.23	20.24	26.24	34.08
劳动生产率(元/人)	Overall Labor Productivity(yuan/person)						
按总产值计算	In Terms of Gross Output Value	113685	126528	138070	159654	196170	222471
按增加值计算	In Terms of Value-added	22864	25096	28116	70294	89177	98494
技术装备率(元/人)	Value of Machines Per Laborer(yuan/person)	7553	7531	8248	7398	8232	34182
动力装备率(千瓦/人)	Power of Machines Per Laborer(kw/person)	4.01	4.01	4.52	3.43	4.22	4.52
房屋建筑面积竣工率(%)	Ratio of Floor Space of Buildings Completed(•)	32.9	31.6	28.7	25.1	23.5	22.6
产值利润率(%)	Ratio of Profit to Gross Output Value(%)	1.0	1.2	1.6	1.3	1.7	1.7
产值利税率(%)	Ratio of Pre-tax Profit to Gross Output Value(%)	4.4	4.7	5.8	5.1	5.9	5.9

15-2 建筑业企业主要生产指标(2011)

指 标	Item	企业个数(个) Number of Constru-stion Enterp-rises (unit)	年末从业人员(万人) Number of Persons Engaged (10000 persons)	签订合同额(亿元) Value of Signed Contract (100 million yuan)	#本年新签合同额 New Value of Signed Contract in this year
总 计	**Total**	**581**	**33.14**	**1781.06**	**852.58**
#国有及国有控股	State-owned and state-controlled Construction Enterprises	122	21.72	1464.89	648.66
#施工总承包企业	General Contractors	452	32.00	1723.90	829.39
专业承包企业	Special Contractors	129	1.14	57.15	23.19
按登记注册类型分组	**By Registration Status**				
#内资企业	Domestic Funded	580	33.14	1781.06	852.58
#国有企业	State-owned	90	14.02	899.52	453.31
集体企业	Collective-owned	98	2.55	50.53	34.13
股份有限公司	Company Limited with Share Holding	25	0.70	18.14	11.39
私营企业	Private Enterprises	158	3.12	105.07	70.87
按国民经济行业分组	**By Sector**				
房屋和土木工程建筑业	Building and Civil Engineering Construction	423	30.20	1567.41	723.15
房屋工程建筑	Building Engineering Construction	353	20.02	929.51	491.88
土木工程建筑	Civil Engineering Construction	70	10.18	637.90	231.27
建筑安装业	Construction Installation	85	2.43	171.83	113.78
建筑装饰业	Construction Decoration	55	0.34	13.25	7.38
其他建筑业	Others	18	0.16	28.57	8.27

Main Production Indicators on Construction Enterprises

建筑业总产值(亿元) Total Output Value of Construction (100 million yuan)	#在省外完成的产值 Value of Construction Which Fulfilled outside of Guizhou Province	#建筑工程 Output Value of Constr-uction	#安装工程 Output Value of Instal-lation	房屋建筑施工面积(万平方米) Floor Space of Buildings under Constru-ction (10000 sq.m)	#本年新开工面积 Started This Year	#实行投标承包面积 Verified Eligible Area of the First Time	自有机械设备年末净值(万元) Net Value of Machinery and Equipment Owned (10000 yuan)	自有机械设备年末总台数(台) Number of Machinery and Equipment Owned (year-end) (unit)	自有机械设备年末总功率(万千瓦) Total Power of Machinery and Equipment Owned (year-end) (10000 kw)
824.72	**165.91**	**718.01**	**52.65**	**6779**	**2383**	**5525**	**1156248**	**72647**	**153.03**
659.29	160.84	583.10	37.20	5054	1448	4490	1036402	37805	91.60
788.60	165.67	692.36	44.90	6779	2382.479	5525	1140026	70927	146.98
36.12	0.24	25.65	7.75	0	0.48	0	16222	1720	6.05
824.72	165.91	718.01	52.65	6779	2383	5525	1156248	72647	153.03
395.64	107.41	345.04	34.42	4648	1367	4421	139556	30585	49.37
35.12		25.81	1.88	406	224	263	21297	6603	16.11
10.55	0.13	7.48	2.61	124	56	107	10040	1471	2.90
51.26	4.29	43.39	3.26	673	356	376	38567	15647	22.04
711.36	141.53	632.18	31.92	6264	2217	5107	1111022	63762	132.53
482.78	129.50	424.74	13.21	6232	2199	5077	972063	45191	78.55
228.59	12.03	207.43	18.71	32	18	30	138959	18571	53.98
85.35	24.38	61.95	20.04	515	166	419	37073	8169	16.98
10.55		9.69	0.67				260	346	0.32
17.45		14.20	0.02				7893	370	3.21

15-3 建筑业企业主要财务指标(2011)

单位：万元

指 标	Item	年末资产负债 Assets 资产合计 Total Assets	#流动资产小计 Liquid Assets	#固定资产小计 Fixed Assets
总 计	**Total**	**7399665**	**5680027**	**757007**
#国有及国有空股	Construction Enterprises of State-owned and state-controlled	5557633	4236951	484444
#施工总承包企业	General Contractors	6789201	5316483	699235
专业承包企业	Special Contractors	610464	363544	57773
按登记注册类型分组	**By Registration Status**			
#内资企业	Domestic Funded	7397958	5678342	756984
#国有企业	State-owned	3458955	2736957	299811
集体企业	Collective-owned	288565	208459	60373
股份有限公司	Company Limited with Share Holding	150864	106312	20100
私营企业	Private Enterprises	532460	424487	85170
按国民经济行业分组	**By Sector**			
房屋和土木工程建筑业	Building and Civil Engineering Construction	6197387	4732679	663019
房屋工程建筑	Building Engineering Construction	3728653	3167984	361005
土木工程建筑	Civil Engineering Construction	2468734	1564695	302014
建筑安装业	Construction Installation	887369	716458	78621
建筑装饰业	Construction Decoration	122129	112891	4761
其他建筑业	Others	192780	117999	10606

Main Financial Indicators of Construction Enterprises

(10000 yuan)

and Liabilities(year-end)		所有者权益合计	损益及分配 Loss-profit and Allocation			
负债合计 Total Liabilities	#流动负债小计 Liquid Liabilities	Creditors' Equity	工程结算收入 Revenue of Project Settlement Accounts	其他业务收入 Revenue From Other Business	营业利润 Operating Profits	利润总额 Total Profits
5634922	**5264112**	**1764743**	**8185461**	**52831**	**143140**	**144001**
4446439	4131507	1111194	6609887	28378	103908	108577
5223072	4993026	1566130	7860296	43041	121864	122347
411851	271086	198613	325165	9790	21276	21654
5634432	5263622	1763526	8185461	52831	143141	144002
2743592	2567359	715363	4040226	21725	33174	35016
200175	194215	88390	305013	6555	6916	3050
86101	80430	64764	106479	2563	4667	4610
329564	321307	202896	520378	1002	14230	14244
4808456	4540023	1388931	7024146	41611	95049	95656
2925912	2839877	802741	4766148	20114	81446	79053
1882544	1700146	586190	2257998	21497	13603	16603
597820	562966	289549	928380	3910	30810	31106
89956	73999	32173	98461	76	553	621
138689	87124	54091	134474	7233	16729	16619

15-4 建筑业企业房屋建筑(2011)

指　标	Item	竣工面积(平方米) Floor Space of Buildings Completed (sq.m)	#厂房、仓库 Workshop Storehouse	#住 宅 Residential Buildings	#教育用房 Educational Buildings
总　计	**Total**	**15303800**	**415718**	**10227296**	**1219010**
#国有及国有控股	Construction Enterprises of State-owned and state-controlled	8621647	250419	6055448	496153
#施工总承包企业	General Contractors	15299950	412718	10227296	1219010
专业承包企业	Special Contractors	3850	3000		
按登记注册类型分组	**By Registration Status**				
#内资企业	Domestic Funded	15303800	415718	10227296	1219010
#国有企业	State-owned	8097583	204490	5910953	380957
集体企业	Collective-owned	1809085	58200	1079240	223405
股份有限公司	Company Limited with Share Holding	459550	14750	335519	35969
私营企业	Private Enterprises	2316845	69575	1179511	253485
按国民经济行业分组	**By Sector**				
房屋和土木工程建筑业	Building and Civil Engineering Construction	13969904	366296	9370017	1061084
房屋工程建筑	Building Engineering Construction	13905062	331166	9356017	1061084
土木工程建筑	Civil Engineering Construction	64842	35130	14000	
建筑安装业	Construction and Installation	1333896	49422	857279	157926

Basic Statistics on House Buildings by Construction Enterprises

		总造价					
#卫生医疗用房 Medical Buildings	#科研用房 Scientific Research Buildings	(元/平方米) Total cost of Buildings Completed (yuan/sq.m)	#厂房、仓库 Workshop Storehouse	#住宅 Residential Buildings	#教育用房 Educational Buildings	#卫生医疗用房 Medical Buildings	#科研用房 Scientific Research Buildings
538634	**11554**	**1095**	**1459**	**973**	**1162**	**1426**	**1621**
370682	6000	1181	1385	972	1527	1583	1000
538634	11554	1095	1464	973	1162	1426	1621
		765	667				
538634	11554	1095	1459	973	1162	1426	1621
201146	6000	1160	1418	974	1390	1359	1000
34737		920	1750	864	812	1237	
2324		1001	1799	966	1268	816	
85063	3117	1011	1471	1017	950	1132	3174
523084	11554	1093	1397	965	1068	1428	1621
523084	11554	1092	1345	965	1068	1428	1621
		1448	1836				
15550		1117	1664	927	1739	1112	

主要统计指标解释

建筑业统计单位　指从事房屋、构筑物建造和设备安装活动的法人企业。建筑业法人企业应同时具备的条件是：①依法成立，有自己的名称、组织机构和场所，能够承担民事责任；②独立拥有和使用资产，承担负债，有权与其他单位签订合同；③独立核算盈亏，能够编制资产负债表。

建筑业总产值（即自行完成施工产值）　是以货币形式表现的建筑业企业在一定时期内生产的建筑业产品和提供的服务的总和。建筑业总产值包括：

(1) 建筑工程产值：指列入建筑工程预算内的各种工程价值。

(2) 安装工程产值：指设备安装工程价值，不包括被安装设备本身价值。

(3) 其他产值：建筑业总产值中除建筑工程、安装工程以外的产值。包括房屋构筑物修理产值、非标准设备制造产值、总包企业向分包企业收取的管理费以及不能明确划分的施工活动所完成的产值。

a. 房屋构筑物修理产值：指房屋和构筑物修理所完成的产值，但不包括被修理房屋、构筑物本身价值和生产设备的修理价值。

b. 非标准设备制造产值：指加工制造没有定型的非标准生产设备的加工费和原材料价值（如化工厂、炼油厂用的各种罐、槽，矿井生产统一使用的各种漏斗、三角槽、阀门等）以及附属加工厂为本企业承建工程制作的非标准设备的价值。

建筑业增加值　指建筑业企业在报告期内以货币表现的建筑业生产经营活动的最终成果。建筑业现价增加值按生产法和分配法（收入法）两种方法计算，以收入法的计算结果为准，即从收入的角度出发，根据生产要素在生产过程中应得的收入份额计算。

房屋建筑施工面积　指在报告期内施过工的全部房屋建筑面积，包括本期新开工的房屋面积、上期施工跨入本期继续施工的房屋面积、上期停缓建在本期恢复施工的房屋面积、本期竣工的房屋面积及本期施工后又停缓建的房屋面积。

房屋建筑竣工面积　指在报告期内房屋建筑按照设计要求全部完工，达到了住人和使用条件，经验收鉴定合格，正式移交使用单位的房屋建筑面积。

企业总收入　指与企业生产经营直接有关的各项收入，包括工程结算收入和其他业务收入。计算公式为：

企业总收入＝工程结算收入＋其他业务收入

工程结算收入　指企业承包工程实现的工程价款结算收入，以及向发包单位收取的除工程价款以外的按规定列作营业收入的各种款项，如临时设施费、劳动保险费、施工机械调迁费等以及向发包单位收取的各种索赔款。

工程结算利润　指已结算工程实现的利润，如亏损以“－”号表示。计算公式为：

工程结算利润＝工程结算收入－工程结算成本－工程结算税金及附加

Explanatory Notes on Main Statistical Indicators

Statistical Unit in Construction refers to corporate enterprise engaged in the construction of buildings and structures and in the installation of equipment.A corporate construction enterprise should meet the following 3 requirements: ① being set up in line with relevant legal basis,having its full name,organization and location,and capable of taking civil liabilities; ② independently possessing and using its assets and assuming its liabilities,and entitled to sign contracts with other institutions; ③ and making independent accounts of its profits and losses,and capable of compiling its own balance sheet.

Gross Output Value of Construction refers to total of construction products and services, expressed in money terms, produced or rendered by construction and installation enterprises during a given period of time. It includes:

(1) Output value of construction projects: the value of projects covered by the project budgets;

(2) Output value of installation projects: the value of the installation of equipment, (excluding the value of the equipment to be installed);

(3) Other output values: the output value of construction industry apart from that of construction projects and installation projects. It includes: output value of repair of buildings and structures; output value of non-standard equipment manufacturing; overhead expenses received by contracted enterprises from the sub-contracted enterprises and the completed output value of construction activities for which there is no clear definition.

a. Output value of repair of buildings and structures: the value created through the repairs of buildings or structures. It does not include the value of buildings or structures being repaired and the value of the repair of production equipment;

b. Output value of manufactured non-standard equipment: the value of non-standard production equipment, including raw materials and manufacturing cost, made for the construction project (i.e., chemical plant; kettles or tanks used by refineries; various fillers, triangle tanks, valves used by mines). It also includes the output value of equipment manufactured by subsidiary workshops.

Value-added of Construction refers to the final result of the activities of production and operation of enterprises of the construction industry in monetary terms during the reference period. Value-added of construction is calculated by both production approach and income approach, with the figures from the income approach as the final figures., Under the income approach,, calculation starts from the perspective of income and is based on the share of income derived from the production process by the relevant factors of production.

Floor Space of Buildings Under Construction refers to floor space of buildings under construction during the reference period,including newly started buildings,buildings started earlier and continued during the reference period,and buildings suspended earlier but restarted during the reference period, buildings completed during the reference period, and buildings under construction and then suspended during the reference period.

Floor Space of Buildings Completed refers to the floor space of buildings that are completed in the reference period in accordance with the requirements of the design, up to the standard for putting them into use, and have been checked and accepted by concerned departments as qualified ones.

Total Revenue of Enterprises refers to the sum of income from production and operation of enterprises, including income from settlement of projects and other operational income, namely:

Total Revenue of Enterprises=Income from Settlement of Projects+Other Operational Income.

Income from Settlement of Projects refers to the income received by the construction enterprise from the contracted project through settlement procedures, and other charges to the contractoree as operational costs in addition to the value of the project,such as temporary facility fee,labour insurance premium,moving cost of construction equipment,as well as various types of claims to the contractee.

Profit from Settlement of Projects refers to profit realized through settled projects. It is calculated with the following formula:

Profit frcm Settlement of Projects=Income from Settlement of Projects-Settled Cost-Settled Taxes and Other Cost

16

Sixteen

运输和邮电

Transport, Postal and Telecommunication Services

16-1 境内运输线路长度
Length of Transport Routes

单位：公里 (km)

指 标	Item	2006	2007	2008	2009	2010	2011	2011年比2010年增长(%) Increase Rate in 2011 over 2010(%)
铁路营业里程	**Length of Railways in Operation**	**2014**	**2012**	**1962**	**1983**	**2002**	**2070**	**3.4**
#复线里程	Double-tracking Length	559	560	560	604	643	643	持平
公路线路里程	**Total Length of Highways**	**113278**	**123247**	**125365**	**142561**	**151644**	**157820**	**4.1**
按行政等级分	**Classified by Administrative Level**							
国道	State Road	3541	3658	3658	3717	3924	4132	5.3
#国家高速公路	State Highway	831	986	868	1050	1259	1467	16.6
省道	Provincial Road	7204	7217	7210	7346	7463	7769	4.1
县道	County Road	15638	15534	17324	17272	17311	17350	0.2
乡道	Township Road	21149	21079	18432	18459	18465	18447	-0.1
村道	Village Road	65066	75013	78051	95072	103785	109384	5.4
专用公路	Accommodation Highway	680	746	690	697	697	737	5.8
按技术等级分	**Classified by Technical Grade**							
等级公路	Standard Highway	49305	55517	64044	68046	72557	79643	9.8
高速公路	Expressway	678	924	924	1189	1507	2022	34.1
#四车道	Four-lane	674	920	920	1189	1507	1979	31.3
一级	First Class	96	120	139	151	153	164	6.9
二级	Second Class	2750	2658	2706	3171	3578	3831	7.1
三级	Third Class	8139	8650	8412	8309	8222	8367	1.8
四级	Fourth Class	37642	43165	51864	55226	59096	65258	10.4
等外公路	Substandard Highway	63972	67730	61321	74516	79087	78177	-1.2
按路面类型分	**Classified by Pavement**							
有铺装路面(高级)	Paved Road (advanced)	6595	6841	8045	9245	10474	14859	41.9
沥青混凝土	Asphalt Concrete	1838	2002	1919	2867	3663	4512	23.2
水泥混凝土	Cement Concrete	4757	4839	6126	6378	6810	10347	51.9
简易铺装路面	Simple Paved Road	17924	19272	20995	23748	26589	29167	9.7
未铺装路面	Not-paved Road	88759	97135	96325	109569	114581	113794	-0.7
晴雨通车里程	Can be open to traffic in rainy or sunny days	83265	100121	93845	112237	151644	157820	4.1
可绿化里程	Can be green	67855	89026	114213	132813	141768	147643	4.1
养护里程	Maintained Road	86557	109562	125032	142483	151644	157820	4.1
内河航道里程	**Length of Navigable Inland Waterways**	**3322**	**3322**	**3563**	**3563**	**3563**	**3563**	**持平**

注：1、资料来源于省交通运输厅、成都铁路分局(以下相关表同)。2、2006年及以后公路线路里程包括村道里程。

Note:1.Data in the table are obtained from the Provincial Department of Transports and Chengdu Railway Branch(The relative tables in the chapter are the same). 2.Since the year 2006 the total length of highways has included the length of village road.

16–2 民用航空运输

Civil Aviation

指　标	Item	2006	2007	2008	2009	2010	2011	2011年比2010年增长(%) Increase Rate in 2011 over 2010(%)
机场个数(个)	**Numbei of Civil Airports(unit)**	**5**	**5**	**6**	**6**	**6**	**6**	**持平**
通航城市(个)	Cities Reachable (unit)	47	53	51	59	59	61	3.4
#国际及地区城市	International and Regional Cities	4	4	4	5	6	6	持平
起降航班(架次)	Flight Movements (unit)	43232	47829	48990	60680	64835	72009	11.1
进出港旅客(万人次)	**Passengers Get in and Get out of the Airports(10000 person-times)**	**382.86**	**437.27**	**442.93**	**578.24**	**637.59**	**747.02**	**17.2**
#进港旅客	Passengers Get in the Airports	183.11	203.53	213.97	278.86	302.82	353.01	16.6
货物吞吐量(万吨)	**Volume of Freight Handled in Civil Aviation(10000 tons)**	**4.00**	**4.00**	**4.20**	**5.16**	**6.17**	**6.93**	**12.3**

注：资料来源于贵州省机场集团有限公司。

Note:Data in the table are provided by Airports Group Corporation Ltd. of Guizhou Province.

16–3 民用汽车拥有量

Possession of Civil Vehicles

单位：万辆 (10000 units)

指　标	Item	2006	2007	2008	2009	2010	2011	2011年比2010年增长(%) Increase Rate in 2011 over 2010(%)
民用汽车合计	**Total**	**53.74**	**65.05**	**77.15**	**96.83**	**121.30**	**140.12**	**15.5**
#载客汽车	Passenger Vehicles	32.20	40.36	48.95	63.40	82.19	101.14	23.1
载货汽车	Trucks	16.68	19.10	22.26	27.29	32.73	34.23	4.6
#私人汽车	Private Vehicles	35.88	44.74	54.27	71.28	92.77	109.54	18.1

注：资料来源于省交警总队车辆管理所。

Note:Data in the table are obtained from the vehicle management office of the provincial traffic police corps.

16-4 旅客运量及周转量
Passenger Traffic and Passenger-Kilometers

指 标	Item	2006	2007	2008	2009	2010	2011	2011年比2010年增长(%) Increase Rate in 2011 over 2010(%)
旅客运量(万人)	**Total Passenger Traffic(10000 persons)**	**69270**	**74440**	**80056**	**84981**	**97793**	**120554**	**23.3**
铁 路	Railways	2536	2979	3199	3204	3437	3939	14.6
公 路	Highways	65786	70377	75350	80044	92426	114429	23.8
水 运	Waterways	948	1084	1507	1733	1930	2186	13.3
旅客周转量(亿人公里)	**Passenger-Kilometers(100 million passenger-km)**	**349.82**	**369.20**	**407.59**	**430.56**	**514.41**	**631.74**	**22.8**
铁 路	Railways	160.98	160.51	163.00	162.41	189.38	204.58	8.0
公 路	Highways	186.91	206.40	241.15	264.06	320.46	422.01	31.7
水 运	Waterways	1.93	2.29	3.44	4.09	4.57	5.15	12.7

注：2008年以后公路水路运输量采用全国公路水路运输量专项调查数据(下表同)。

Note:Since 2008 the data of highways and waterways freight traffic adopt the data of the special investigation on highways and waterways freight traffic(the same applies to the next table).

16-5 货物运输量及周转量
Freight Traffic and Ton-Kilometers

指 标	Item	2006	2007	2008	2009	2010	2011	2011年比2010年增长(%) Increase Rate in 2011over 2010(%)
货物运输量(万吨)	**Total Freight Traffic (10000 tons)**	**24709**	**26788**	**33576**	**34844**	**40310**	**44890**	**11.4**
铁 路	Railways	6826	7289	6683	6997	7991	7219	-9.7
公 路	Highways	17284	18834	26156	27031	31409	36684	16.8
水 运	Waterways	599	665	737	816	910	987	8.5
货物周转量(亿吨公里)	**Total Freight Ton-Kilometers (100 million ton-km)**	**680.96**	**721.26**	**809.93**	**897.38**	**1012.20**	**1060.69**	**4.8**
铁 路	Railways	557.70	583.85	564.31	644.41	706.45	696.36	-1.4
公 路	Highways	114.48	127.99	234.96	241.60	293.00	350.10	19.5
水 运	Waterways	8.78	9.42	10.66	11.37	12.75	14.23	11.6

16–6 电信主要指标

Major Indicators of Telecommunications

指标	Item	2006	2007	2008	2009	2010	2011	2011年比2010年增长 (%) Increase Rate in 2011 over 2010(%)
电信业务收入(亿元)	Business Revenue of Telecommunications (100 million yuan)	85.26	104.02	123.90	138.11	147.38	164.56	11.7
电信业务总量(亿元)	Business Revenue of Telecommunications (100 million yuan)	215.85	283.31	361.37	453.33	566.40	204.35	22.3
交换机总容量(万门)	Capacity of Telephone Exchanges (10000 line)	1639.41	2334.67	2858.70	3182.88	3673.01	5423.48	47.7
移动电话交换机容量(万户)	Capacity ofMobileTelephoneExchanges (10000 subscribers)	858.80	1442.50	1960.04	2332.20	2724.50	4433.00	62.7
长途光缆线路长度(万公里)	Length of LongDistance OpticalCable Lines(km)	2.33	3.01	2.98	2.86	3.02	3.45	14.2
年末固定电话用户数(万户)	Number of Telephone Subscribers at Year-end (10000 subscribers)	493.91	521.19	499.61	451.13	432.61	403.96	-6.6
#农话用户数	Number of Rural Telephone Subscribers	176.77	209.99	217.60	196.64	184.37	149.07	-19.1
城市电话用户	Number of Local(urban)Telephone Subscribers	317.14	311.20	282.01	254.49	248.24	254.90	2.7
#公　用	Number of Public Telephone Subscribers	42.66	40.97	35.97	34.76	39.29	34.63	-11.9
移动电话用户(万户)	Number of Mobile Telephone Subscribers (10000 subscribers)	646.20	834.05	1185.84	1583.28	1964.40	2175.22	10.7
移动短信业务量(亿条)	Mobile SMS Business Volume (100 million messages)	30.66	45.46	66.63	111.85	120.84	129.26	7.0
互联网宽带接入端口(万个)	Number of Subscribers of Internet Service (10000 subscribers)	67.44	96.65	119.89	163.63	231.69	437.87	89.0
电话普及率(包括移动电话)(部/百人)	Popularization Rate of Telephone (set/100 persons)	30.90	37.31	46.87	57.52	68.90	74.35	7.9
#移动电话普及率	Popularization Rate of Mobile Telephone	17.51	22.96	32.97	44.76	56.46	62.71	11.1
已通电话的行政村比重(%)	Percentage of Administrative Village with Phone Sets(%)		100	100	100	100	100	持平
国内长途电话(万分钟)	Number of Long Distance Telephone Calls Inside Country(10000 minutes)	74939	103754	114322	91235	138922	111354	-19.8
国际及港澳长途电话(万分钟)	Number of Long Distance Telephone Calls outside Country or to Macao、Hong Kong(10000 minutes)	205.57	252.32	313.66	65.00	121.83	111.00	-8.9

注：1、资料来源于省通信管理局。2、国内长途电话、国际及港澳长途电话2008年及以前单位为万次。3、电信业务总量增长速度按可比价计算。

Note:1.Data in the table are obtained from the provincial communications authority bureau. 2.Before 2008,Unit of measuring long- distance-telephone -calls inside and outside the country is 10000 person-time.3.The increase rate of business volume of telecommunication services is calculated at comparable prices.

16-7 邮政主要指标

Major Indicators of Post

指　　标	Item	2006	2007	2008	2009	2010	2011	2011年比2010年增长(%) Increase Rate in 2011 over 2010(%)
邮电局所总数(处)	**Number of Post and Telecommunication Offices(unit)**	**13740**	**8143**	**10995**	**29262**	**19372**	**21496**	**11.0**
邮政	Post	2081	2082	2194	2259	1795	1425	-20.6
电信	Telecommunication	11659	6061	8801	27003	17577	20071	14.2
邮路总长度(公里)	Number of Postal Routes(km)	62936	60747	65236	61854	96174	99155	3.1
#汽车邮路	Number of Highway Postal Routes	23377	25222	24733	28799	55901	58062	3.9
铁路邮路	Number of Railways Postal Routes	6379	6379	6876	6413	6413	6413	持平
邮政业务总量(亿元)	Business Volume of Post (100 million yuan)	8.02	9.08	10.42	11.69	15.50	14.97	34.1
函件(万件)	Number of Letters(10000 pcs)	6859	5735	6566	6768	5939	5041	-15.1
报刊、杂志累计订销数(万份)	Issue of Newspapers and Magazines(10000 copies)	27564	28291	31899	32007	32084	35056	9.3
国内特快专递(万件)	Pieces of Express Mail Services inside Nation (10000 pcs)	425	459	524	926	1115	1529	37.1
国际特快专递(万件)	Pieces of Express Mail Services outside Nation (10000 pcs)	0.75	0.79	0.79	4.20	5.60	4.90	-12.5
邮政储蓄期末余额(亿元)	Post Deposits at the Year-end(100 million yuan)	177.20	195.30	229.20	270.13	336.90	431.56	28.1
集邮业务(万枚)	Stamps for Collection(10000 pcs)	849	901	945	749	1226	1907	55.5
长话业务电路(2M)	Long Distance Cable Lines(2M)	66405	68658	97773	114805	127660	118618	-7.1

注：1、资料来源于省邮政公司。2、2009年起邮电局所总数含电信部门特约代理点。3、2009年起国内、国际特快专递含快递企业数据。4、邮政业务总量增长速度按可比价计算。

Notes:1.Data in the table are obtained from the provincial post company.2.Since 2009，the number of post and telecommunication offices include the special agent point,but not for the year 2008 and before. 3.Since 2009,pieces of express mail services inside and outside the country cover the courier companies. 4.The growth rates of the business volume of postal are calculated at comparable prices.

主要统计指标解释

铁路营业里程　又称营业长度（包括正式营业和临时营业里程），指办理客货运输业务的铁路正线总长度。凡是全线或部分建成双线及以上的线路，以第一线的实际长度计算；复线、站线、段管线、岔线和特殊用途线以及不计算运费的联络线都不计算营业里程。铁路营业里程是反映铁路运输业基础设施发展水平的重要指标，也是计算客货周转量、运输密度和机车车辆运用效率等指标的基础资料。

公路里程　指在一定时期内实际达到《公路工程[WTBZ]技术标准 JTJ01-88》规定的等级公路，并经公路主管部门正式验收交付使用的公路里程数。包括大中城市的郊区公路以及通过小城镇街道部分的公路里程和桥梁、渡口的长度，不包括大中城市的街道、厂矿、林区生产用道和农业生产用道的里程。两条或多条公路共同经由同一路段，只计算一次，不得重复计算里程长度。

内河航道里程　也称内河通航里程，指在一定时期内，能通航运输船舶及排筏的天然河流、湖泊水库、运河及通航渠道的长度。包括全年季节性通航累计三个月以上的航道，不包括仅供零散流放竹、木排的河道。

民用航空航线里程　指民航运输定期班机飞行的航线长度的总和。航线长度按机场之间的距离计算，通常有两种计算方法：一是将每条航线长度相加称为重复计算航线里程；一是将两线或两条以上航线经过同一区段里程，只计算一次航线长度称为不重复计算航线里程，一般常用的是后者。

货（客）运量　指在一定时期内，各种运输工具实际运送的货物（旅客）数量。货运按吨计算，客运按人计算。货物不论运输距离长短、货物类别，均按实际重量统计。旅客不论行程远近或票价多少，均按一人一次客运量统计；半价票、小孩票也按一人统计。

货物（旅客）周转量　指在一定时期内，由各种运输工具运送的货物（旅客）数量与其相应运输距离的乘积之总和。计算货物周转量通常按发出站与到达站之间的最短距离，也就是计费距离计算。计算公式为：

货物（旅客）周转量 = Σ货物（旅客）运输量 × 运输距离

邮电业务总量　指以货币形式表示的邮电企业为社会提供各类邮电服务的总数量，是用于观察邮电业务发展变化总趋势的综合性总量指标。分别按邮政业务总量和电信业务总量统计。邮电业务总量是以各类业务的实物量分别乘以相应的不变单价，得出各类业务的货币量再加总求得。

移动电话用户　指在电信运营企业营业网点办理开户登记手续，通过移动电话交换机进入移动电话网，占用移动电话号码的各类电话用户。包括 GSM 数字移动电话用户、CDMA 数字移动电话用户和电信运营企业发行的报告期末已激活充值的能异地漫游的各种智能卡用户。

固定电话用户　指在电信运营企业营业网点办理开户登记手续并已接入固定电话网上的全部电话用户。包括普通电话用户、公用电话用户、窄带综合业务数字网（N-ISDN）用户、智能网专用接入终端用户等。按行政区划分为城市电话用户和农村电话用户。

城市电话用户　指直辖市、省辖市、地级市、县级市的市区、市郊区及县城（包括县人民政府所在地的县城关区或行政建制相当于县人民政府所在地的镇）范围内接入局用交换机的电话用户数，包括分布在农村地区的独立工矿区、林区、驻军等电话用户数。

乡村电话用户　指县城关区以下的集镇和农村接入局用交换机的电话用户。

住宅电话用户数　指安装在居民住宅或农民家里并按照住宅电话用户登记和收费的电话用户。包括私人付费、单位付费和按规定免费安装的住宅电话用户。

Explanatory Notes on Main Statistical Indicators

Length of Railways in Operation refers to the total length of the trunk line under passenger and freight transportation(including both full operation and temporary operation).The calculation is based on the actual length of the first line even if this line has a full or partial double track or more tracks,excluding double tracks,station sidings, tracks under the charge of stations, branch lines, special-purpose lines and the non-payable connecting lines. The length of railways in operation is an important indicator to show the development of the infrastructure for the railway transport,and also the essential data to calculate volume of passenger freight transport,traffic density and utilization efficiency of the locomotives and carriages.

Length of Highways refers to the length of highways which are built in conformity with the grades specified by the highway engineering standard formulated by the Ministry of Communications, and have been formally checked and accepted by the departments of highways and put into use. The length of highways includes that of the suburb highways at large and medium-sized cities,highways passing through streets at small cities and towns,and also the length of bridges and ferries.It does not include the length of streets in big and medium-sized cities and highways built for the production purpose at factories,mines,forest areas and agricultural areas.If two or more highways go the same section of the way,the length of the section is only calculated for once and no duplication is allowed.

Length of Navigable Inland Waterways an indicator reflecting the size and development of inland water network, it refers to the length of the natural rivers,lakes,reservoirs,canals,and ditches open to navigation during a given period, which enables the transport by ships and rafts. It includes the channels open to navigation for over an accumulative 3 months in a year,yet this does not include the river courses which are only used to float odd logs and bamboo rafts.

Length of Civil Aviation Routes refers to the length of all routes for regular civil aviation flights.There are usually two ways to calculate the distance between airports connected by the route length: One is to put the length of all air routes together, called duplicated calculation of the length of the routes;the other is not to allow the duplication in calculation when two or more routes passing the same section of aviation routes. The latter is usually used,as it can precisely show the size of the civil aviation network and indicate the extent of civil aviation serving the national economy and the people.

Freight(Passenger)Traffic refers to the volume of freight(passenger)transported with various means. Freight transport is calculated in tons and passenger traffic is calculated in the number of persons. Despite the type of freight and travelling distance,the freight transport is calculated in the actual weight of the goods:and despite the travelling distance and ticket price,the passenger traffic is calculated by the principle that one person can be counted only once in one travel. The passenger who travel with a half price ticket or a child ticket is also calculated as one person.

Freight Ton-kilometers(Passenger-kilometers) refer to the sum of the products of the volume of transported cargo (passengers) multiplying by the transport distance,usually using ton-kilometer and passenger-kilometer as units for measurement.Normally, the shortest distance between the departure station and the destination station (i.e., the payable distance) is the basis to calculate the freight ton-kilometers. The formula is as follows:

Freight Ton-kilometers (Passenger-kilometers) =∑{Freight (Passenger) Traffic × Distance of Transportation}

Measuring unit: ton-kilometer (person-kilometer)

Business Volume of Post and Telecommunications refers to the total amount of postal and telecommunication services, expressed in value terms, provided by the post and telecommunications departments for society. This indicator reflects the overall results of development of postal and telecommunication services. It can be classificated as postal services and and telecommunication services. Business volume of post and telecommunications is the sum of all services in kind multiplying with the unit price (constant price) to get the total business value.

Mobile Telephone Subscribers refer to persons who have gone through registration procedures in the operation points of enterprises engaged in telecommunications and are hence connected with the mobile telephone communication network through the mobile telephone switchboards and occupy mobile phone numbers. Included are GSM digital mobile phone subscribers, CDMA digital mobile phone subscribers and subscribers to intelligent phone cards with roaming facility issued by telecommunications enterprises and which have been subscribed to and activated at the end of the reference period.

Local Telephone Subscribers refers to all subscribers who have gone through registration procedures in the operation points of enterprises engaged in telecommunications and are hence connected to the local telecommunications service provider through fixed line network. Included are general subscribers, public telephones subscribers, N-ISDN subscribers and intelligent network terminal subscribers. They are also classified in terms of administrative districts as urban telephone subscribers and rural telephone subscribers according to location.

Urban Telephone Subscribers refers to number of telephone subscribers, located at municipalities, cities under the jurisdiction of province, cities at prefecture level, downtown and suburb of city at county level town and county towns (including country towns where county government located, and towns of county level according to the administrative organizational system), that are connected to the public line telephone network, including rural mineral area, forest area, military area.

Rural Telephone Subscribers refers to telephone subscribers, located at the towns below the level of county town and villages, that are connected to the public line telephone network.

Household Telephone Subscribers refer to telephone sets installed in the dwelling units of urban or rural residents, and registered as residence subscribers for payment, including 3 types of payment for the service: private payment, public payment and free service.

17

Seventeen

批发和零售业

Wholesale and Retail Trades

17-1 社会消费品零售总额
Total Retail Sales of Consumer Goods

单位：亿元 (100 million yuan)

指 标	Item	2006	2007	2008	2009	2010	2011
社会消费品零售总额	**Total Retail Sales of Consumer Goods**	**710.00**	**858.15**	**1075.24**	**1247.25**	**1482.68**	**1751.62**
按地域分	**By Area**						
城镇	Urban	558.10	667.83	838.81	971.37	1213.66	1439.22
乡村	Rural	151.90	190.32	236.43	275.88	269.02	312.40
按行业分	**By Sector**						
批发和零售业	Wholesale and Retail Trade	619.35	720.80	952.04	1114.40	1329.51	1576.66
住宿和餐饮业	Hotel and Catering Services	78.29	121.43	106.90	132.85	153.17	174.96

注：表中2009年及以前的“城镇”数据为市、县消费品零售总额合计数，“乡村”数据为县以下消费品零售额。
Note:The urban data in the table were the total number of cities and counties in total retail sales of consumer goods before 2009.The rural data were under County level in total retail sales of consumer goods.

17-2 限额以上批发业和零售业情况
Basic Conditions of Enterprises above Designated Size in Wholesale and Retail Trade Services

指 标	Item	2006	2007	2008	2009	2010	2011
批发业	**Wholesale Trade**						
法人企业(个)	Number of Corporations(unit)	145	143	248	283	306	332
年末从业人数(人)	Employees at Year-end(person)	24217	38040	66821	38332	41066	45691
商品购进额(亿元)	Total Purchases(100 million yuan)	293.24	316.06	579.92	575.07	776.73	1124.58
商品销售额(亿元)	Total Sales(100 million yuan)	453.41	534.56	815.21	825.77	1095.34	1309.90
期末商品库存额(亿元)	Inventory at year-end(100 million yuan)	44.63	47.02	83.85	80.45	93.47	127.38
零售业	**Retail Trade**						
法人企业(个)	Number of Corporations(unit)	96	108	303	371	494	555
年末从业人数(人)	Employees at Year-end(person)	18485	18085	24998	30806	38154	44045
商品购进额(亿元)	Total Purchases(100 million yuan)	94.74	107.72	200.02	278.82	423.39	588.27
商品销售额(亿元)	Total Sales(100 million yuan)	103.18	127.22	260.20	358.02	487.38	690.58
期末商品库存额(亿元)	Inventory at Year-end(100 million yuan)	9.42	10.75	32.77	28.67	42.11	59.71
年末零售营业面积(万平方米)	Retail Operating Area at year-end(10000 sq.m)	82.20	116.00	142.28	195.96	212.03	230.85

17-3 限额以上批发业企业情况(2011)

单位：万元

指　标	Item	法人企业(个) Number of Corporation (Unit)	从业人数(人) Employees (person)
合　计	**Total**	**332**	**45691**
按登记注册类型分组	**by Types of Registration Status**		
内资企业	**Domestic Funded Enterprises**	**331**	**45371**
国有企业	State-owned Enterprises	63	27126
集体企业	Collective-owned Enterprises	8	360
股份合作企业	Cooperation Enterprises	4	315
联营企业	Joint Ownership Enterprises		
有限责任公司	Limited Liability Corporations	188	13783
股份有限公司	Share-holding Corporations Ltd.	12	1782
私营企业	Private Enterprises	54	1860
其他	Other Enterprises	2	145
港、澳、台商投资企业	**Enterprises with Funds From HongKong, Macao and Taiwan**		
合资经营企业(港或澳、台资)	Joint-venture Enterprises		
合作经营企业(港或澳、台资)	Cooperative Enterprises		
港、澳、台商独资经营企业	Enterpises with Sole Investment		
港、澳、台商投资股份有限公司	Share-holding Corporations Ltd.		
外商投资企业	**Foreign Funded Enterprises**	**1**	**320**
中外合资经营企业	Joint-venture Enterprises	1	320
中外合作经营企业	Cooperation Enterprises		
外资企业	Enterprises with Sole Fund		
外商投资股份有限公司	Share-holding Corporations Ltd.		
按国民经济行业分组	**by Sector**		
农畜产品批发	**Wholesale of Farm Produce and Livestock Products**	**2**	**91**
谷物、豆及薯类批发	Wholesale of Grain, Beans and Potatoes		
种子、饲料批发	Wholesale of Seeds and Feed	2	91
棉、麻批发	Wholesale of Cotton and hemp		
牲畜批发	Wholesale of Livestock		
其他农畜产品批发	Others		
食品、饮料及烟草制品批发	**Wholesale of Food,Beverages and Tobaccos**	**54**	**26919**
米、面制品及食用油批发	Wholesale of Rice,Flour and Edible oil	8	920
糕点、糖果及糖批发	Wholesale of Pastries, Candy and Sugar	2	40
果品、蔬菜批发	Wholesale of Fruit and Vegetables		
肉、禽、蛋及水产品批发	Wholesale of Meat, Poultry, Eggs and Aquatic Products		
盐及调味品批发	Wholesale of Salt and Condiment	12	823
饮料及茶叶批发	Wholesale of Beverages and Tea	17	4248
烟草制品批发	Wholesale of Tobaccos and Related Products	10	20613
其他食品批发	Wholesale of Other Food	5	275
纺织、服装及日用品批发	**Wholesale of Textiles,Garments and Daily Consumer Goods**	**6**	**351**
纺织品、针织品及原料批发	Wholesale of Textiles ,Knitwear and Raw Materials	1	5

Basic Conditions of Enterprises above Designated Size in Wholesale Trade

(10000 yuan)

购进总额 Total Purchases	销售总额 Total Sales	批发 Wholesale Trade	零售 Retail Trade	年末库存额 Inventory (year-end)
11245778	**13098988**	**12079187**	**1019802**	**1273848**
11244292	**13084376**	**12065305**	**1019071**	**1273247**
6133716	7568976	6861240	707736	835371
106164	127409	123837	3572	12366
56459	60315	60315		1054
3502053	3708282	3646489	61793	207514
1056131	1200343	964917	235426	177975
373516	400087	390244	9843	37530
16253	18964	18264	700	1438
1486	**14612**	**13881**	**731**	**602**
1486	14612	13881	731	602
10473	**10774**	**10774**		**123**
10473	10774	10774		123
4890136	**5856261**	**5550163**	**306098**	**793563**
101728	99073	92859	6214	48982
5035	5795	5795		512
49122	75950	75017	933	4958
2361630	2320910	2031072	289838	208693
2342446	3317302	3315025	2277	525363
30176	37232	30395	6837	5055
56497	**58153**	**57727**	**427**	**7860**
7301	7653	7653		1335

17-3 续表

单位：万元

指　　标	Item	法人企业（个）Number of Corporation (Unit)
服装批发	Wholesale of Garments	4
鞋帽批发	Wholesale of Shoes and Hats	
厨房、卫生间用具及日用杂货批发	Wholesale of Kitchen and Lavatory Appliance and Daily Consumer Groceries	
化妆品及卫生用品批发	Wholesale of Cosmetics and Hygiene Products	
其他日用品批发	Wholesale of Other Daily Consumer Goods	1
文化、体育用品及器材批发	**Wholesale of Culture,Sports Goods and Equipments**	**10**
文具用品批发	Wholesale of Stationery	3
体育用品批发	Wholesale of Sports Goods	
图书批发	Wholesale of Books	5
报刊批发	Wholesale of Newspapers and Periodicals	
音像制品及电子出版物批发	Wholesale of Audio and Visual Products and Electronic Publications	
首饰、工艺品及收藏品批发	Wholesale of Jewelry,Arts and Crafts and Collections	
其他文化用品批发	Wholesale of Other Cultural Articles	2
医药及医疗器材批发	**Wholesale of Medicines and Medical Appliances**	**47**
西药批发	Wholesale of Western Medicines	40
中药材及中成药批发	Wholesale of Traditional Chinese Medicines	7
医疗用品及器材批发	Wholesale of Medical Articles and Appliances	
矿产品、建材及化工产品批发	**Wholesale of Mininery Products,Building Materials and Chemical Materials**	**148**
煤炭及制品批发	Wholesale of Coal and Related Products	52
石油及制品批发	Wholesale of Petroleum and Related Products	11
非金属矿及制品批发	Wholesale of Non-metallic Minerals and Related Products	1
金属及金属矿批发	Wholesale of Metal Materials	29
建材批发	Wholesale of Building Materials	7
化肥批发	Wholesale of Chemical Fertilizers	19
农药批发	Wholesale of Pesticide	
农用薄膜批发	Wholesale of Agricultural Film	
其他化工产品批发	Wholesale of Other Chemical Materials	29
机械设备、五金交电及电子产品批发	**Wholesale of Machinery,Hardware,Transport, Electric and Electronic Products**	**54**
农业机械批发	Wholesale of Agricultural Machinery	1
汽车、摩托车及零配件批发	Wholesale of Motor Vehicles, Motorcycles and Parts	20
五金、交电批发	Wholesale of Hardware,Transport and Electric Products	5
家用电器批发	Wholesale of Household Electrical Appliances	8
计算机、软件及辅助设备批发	Wholesale of Computer,Software and Assistance Appliances	4
通讯及广播电视设备批发	Wholesale of Communication , Radio and Television Equipments	3
其他机械设备及电子产品批发	Wholesale of Other Machinery Equipments and Electric Products	13
贸易经纪与代理	**Trade Broker and Agent**	
其他批发	**Others**	**11**
再生物资回收与批发	Wholesale and Reclaim of Regeneration Materials	5
其他未列明的批发	Other Wholesale Unlisted	6

continued

(10000 yuan)

从业人数（人）Employees (person)	购进总额 Total Purchases	销售总额 Total Sales			年末库存额 Inventory (year-end)
			批发 Wholesale Trade	零售 Retail Trade	
246	33232	34376	33949	427	5971
100	15965	16125	16125		554
461	**167358**	**160656**	**159025**	**1631**	**41898**
81	19910	20952	20374	578	7236
328	138748	130585	130375	210	33285
52	8699	9118	8276	842	1377
4364	**653960**	**690183**	**682357**	**7826**	**53315**
3888	589807	616988	610739	6249	47898
476	64153	73196	71619	1577	5417
9131	**3827329**	**4647633**	**3968399**	**679234**	**278798**
3336	1246468	1331780	1331780		25634
3315	686027	1421409	753518	667891	57035
15	8011	7733	7733		1053
606	428337	442054	437270	4784	13203
130	134699	155779	154715	1064	3080
564	163271	197680	192185	5494	20788
1165	1160516	1091198	1091198		158007
4040	**1584920**	**1621276**	**1600280**	**20995**	**92660**
41	14976	14918	13473	1445	2914
848	701203	705989	693881	12108	17350
172	143225	152459	152281	178	4138
1035	221365	226665	226321	344	19425
175	39582	40241	33341	6900	2328
85	22315	23188	23188		2151
1684	442253	457816	457796	21	44355
334	**55107**	**54053**	**50462**	**3591**	**5632**
146	22798	21242	21242		2951
188	32308	32811	29220	3591	2681

17-4 限额以上批发业企业主要财务指标(2011)

Main Financial Indicators of Enterprises above Designated Size in Wholesale Trade

单位：万元 (10000 yuan)

指标	Item	主营业务收入 Revenue from Principal Business	主营业务成本 Cost of Principal Business	主营业务税金及附加 Tax and Extra Charges on Principal Business	销售费用 Selling Expenses	营业利润 Operating Profits
总计	**Total**	**11991042**	**9275403**	**255094**	**536889**	**1566281**
#国有控投	State-Controlled	9092196	6600997	249875	403835	1538728
按登记注册类型分组	**Grouped by Registration Status**					
内资企业	**Domestic-funded Enterprise**	**11978553**	**9266006**	**255061**	**533269**	**1566861**
国有企业	State-owned Enterprise	6850021	4638276	165012	291235	1484641
集体企业	Collective-owned Enterprise	128008	124359	83	2227	-1345
股份合作企业	Copperative Enterprise	20683	17315	48	959	-1262
联营企业	Joint Ownership Enterprises					
有限责任公司	Limited Liability Corporations	3432751	3092073	26274	175783	59236
股份有限公司	Share Holding Co.Ltd	1135969	1018976	62730	41765	21491
私营企业	Private Enterprise	394401	359608	860	20460	3997
其他	Other Enterprises	16721	15399	54	840	104
港、澳、台商投资企业	**Enterprises with Funds From HongKong, Macao and Taiwan**					
合资经营企业(港或澳、台资)	Joint-venture Enterprises					
合作经营企业(港或澳、台资)	Cooperative Enterprises					
港、澳、台商独资经营企业	Enterpises with Sole Investment					
港、澳、台商投资股份有限公司	Share-holding Corporations Ltd.					
外商投资企业	**Foreign Funded Enterprises**	**12489**	**9398**	**33**	**3620**	**-580**
中外合资经营企业	Joint-venture Enterprises	12489	9398	33	3620	-580
中外合作经营企业	Cooperation Enterprises					
外资企业	Enterprises with Sole Fund					
外商投资股份有限公司	Share-holding Corporations Ltd.					
按国民经济行业分组	**by Sector**					
农畜产品批发	**Wholesale of Farm Produce and Livestock Products**	**10398**	**9716**	**3**	**3**	**32**
谷物、豆及薯类批发	Wholesale of Grain, Beans and Potatoes					
种子、饲料批发	Wholesale of Seeds and Feed	10398	9716	3	3	32
棉、麻批发	Wholesale of Cotton and hemp					
牲畜批发	Wholesale of Livestock					
其他农畜产品批发	Others					
食品、饮料及烟草制品批发	**Wholesale of Food,Beverages and Tobaccos**	**5332865**	**3109105**	**182506**	**313071**	**1456356**
米、面制品及食用油批发	Wholesale of Rice,Flour and Edible oil	95718	84519	50	4533	-792
糕点、糖果及糖批发	Wholesale of Pastries, Candy and Sugar	3496	3206	5	250	-10
果品、蔬菜批发	Wholesale of Fruit and Vegetables					
肉、禽、蛋及水产品批发	Wholesale of Meat, Poultry, Eggs and Aquatic Products					
盐及调味品批发	Wholesale of Salt and Condiment	60634	41610	343	5054	3695
饮料及茶叶批发	Wholesale of Beverages and Tea	2016455	575430	47039	130422	1252879
烟草制品批发	Wholesale of Tobaccos and Related Products	3123231	2385896	134813	166029	194775
其他食品批发	Wholesale of Other Food	33331	18444	257	6783	5809
纺织、服装及日用品批发	**Wholesale of Textiles,Garments and Daily Consumer Goods**	**54150**	**51344**	**66**	**1104**	**278**
纺织品、针织品及原料批发	Wholesale of Textiles ,Knitwear and Raw Materials	6543	6394	9	40	-36

17-4 续表 continued

单位：万元 (10000 yuan)

指 标	Item	主营业务收入 Revenue from Principal Business	主营业务成本 Cost of Principal Business	主营业务税金及附加 Tax and Extra Charges on Principal Business	营业费用 Operating Expenses	营业利润 Operating Profits
服装批发	Wholesale of Garments	31482	29048	31	1064	243
鞋帽批发	Wholesale of Shoes and Hats					
厨房、卫生间用具及日用杂货批发	Wholesale of Kitchen and Lavatory Appliance and Daily Consumer Groceries					
化妆品及卫生用品批发	Wholesale of Cosmetics and Hygiene Products					
其他日用品批发	Wholesale of Other Daily Consumer Goods	16125	15903	26		72
文化、体育用品及器材批发	**Wholesale of Culture,Sports Goods and Equipments**	**123858**	**109409**	**192**	**4635**	**5530**
文具用品批发	Wholesale of Stationery	18973	17521	23	397	466
体育用品批发	Wholesale of Sporting Goods					
图书批发	Wholesale of Books	97059	84389	146	3893	5080
报刊批发	Wholesale of Newspapers and Periodicals					
音像制品及电子出版物批发	Wholesale of Audio and Visual Products and Electronic Publications					
首饰、工艺品及收藏品批发	Wholesale of Jewelry,Arts and Crafts and Collectibles					
其他文化用品批发	Wholesale of Other Cultural Articles	7826	7499	24	345	-16
医药及医疗器材批发	**Wholesale of Medicines and Medical Appliances**	**603988**	**558260**	**1338**	**21588**	**2981**
西药批发	Wholesale of Western Medicine	540242	503989	1110	14623	3319
中药材及中成药批发	Wholesale of Chinese Traditional Medicines	63746	54271	227	6965	-338
医疗用品及器材批发	Wholesale of Medical Articles and Appliances					
矿产品、建材及化工产品批发	**Wholesale of Mininery Products,Building Materials and Chemical Materials**	**4361890**	**4017467**	**68769**	**142363**	**89015**
煤炭及制品批发	Wholesale of Coal and Related Products	1304017	1183729	3800	65985	18933
石油及制品批发	Wholesale of Petroleum and products	1238919	1153179	1468	27437	48458
非金属矿及制品批发	Wholesale of Non-metallic Minerals and Products	7310	6963	3	153	55
金属及金属矿批发	Wholesale of Metal Materials	410878	399231	544	6058	3613
建材批发	Wholesale of Building Materials	138814	129629	34	1939	6427
化肥批发	Wholesale of Chemical Fertilizer	195828	189563	123	3677	-2071
农药批发	Wholesale of Pesticide					
农用薄膜批发	Wholesale of Agricultural Film					
其他化工产品批发	Wholesale of Other Chemical Materials	1066124	955173	62797	37115	13601
机械设备、五金交电及电子产品批发	**Wholesale of Machinery,Hardware,Transport, Electric and Electronic Products**	**1451785**	**1371822**	**1825**	**52414**	**12484**
农业机械批发	Wholesale of Agricultural Machinery	13164	11619	10	894	-62
汽车、摩托车及零配件批发	Wholesale of Motor Vehicles, Motorcycles and Parts	631513	606074	671	18385	2787
五金、交电批发	Wholesale of Hardware,Transport and Electric Products	148811	144747	202	757	1636
家用电器批发	Wholesale of Household Electrical Appliances	196713	176814	399	15351	1585
计算机、软件及辅助设备批发	Wholesale of Computer,Software and Assistance Appliances	34635	33522	32	443	133
通讯及广播电视设备批发	Wholesale of Communications and Broadcasting Equipment	24780	23890	24	411	93
其他机械设备及电子产品批发	others	402170	375157	487	16173	6311
贸易经纪与代理	**Trade Broker and Agent**					
其他批发	**Others**	**52109**	**48281**	**395**	**1713**	**-394**
再生物资回收与批发	Wholesale and Reclaim of Regeneration Materials	19876	19676	211	224	-178
其他未列明的批发	Other Wholesale Unlisted	32233	28605	184	1490	-217

17-5 限额以上零售业企业情况(2011)

单位：万元

指　标	Item	法人企业(个) Number of Corporations (Unit)
合　计	**Total**	**555**
按登记注册类型分组	**by Types of Registration Status**	
内资企业	**Domestic Funded Enterprises**	**538**
国有企业	State-owned Enterprises	67
集体企业	Collective-owned Enterprises	7
股份合作企业	Cooperation Enterprises	2
联营企业	Joint Ownership Enterprises	2
有限责任公司	Limited Liability Corporations	247
股份有限公司	Share-holding Corporations Ltd.	13
私营企业	Private Enterprises	192
其他	Other Enterprises	8
港、澳、台商投资企业	**Enterprises with Funds From Hongkong, Macao and Taiwan**	**8**
#合资经营企业(港或澳、台资)	Joint-venture Enterprises	5
合作经营企业(港或澳、台资)	Cooperative Enterprises	
港、澳、台商独资经营企业	Enterprises with Sole Investment	2
港、澳、台商投资股份有限公司	Share-holding Corporations Ltd.	1
外商投资企业	**Foreign Funded Enterprises**	**9**
中外合资经营企业	Joint-venture Enterprises	5
中外合作经营企业	Cooperation Enterprises	
外资企业	Enterprises with Sole Fund	2
外商投资股份有限公司	Share-holding Corporations Ltd.	1
按国民经济行业分组	**by Sector**	
综合零售	**Integrated Retail**	**88**
#百货零售	Retail of General Merchandise	29
超级市场零售	Retail of Supermarkets	50
其他综合零售	Other Integrated Retail	9
食品、饮料及烟草制品专门零售	**Retail of Food,Beverages and Tobaccos**	**21**
粮油零售	Retail of Grain and Oil	3
糕点、面包零售	Retail of Pastries and Bread	
果品、蔬菜零售	Retail of Fruits and Vegetables	
肉、禽、蛋及水产品零售	Retail of Meat, Poultry, Eggs and Aquatic Products	1
饮料及茶叶零售	Retail of Beverages and Tea	14
烟草制品零售	Retail of Tobaccos and Related Products	
其他食品零售	Other Food Retail	3
纺织品、服装及日用品专门零售	**Retail of Textiles,Garments and Daily Consumer Goods**	**20**
纺织品及针织品零售	Retail of Textiles and Knitwear	
服装零售	Retail of Garments	17
鞋帽零售	Retail of Shoes and Hats	

Basic Conditions of Enterprises above Designated Size in Retail Sales

(10000 yuan)

从业人数(人) Employees (person)	购进总额 Total Purchases	销售总额 Total Sales	批发 Wholesale Trade	零售 Retail Trade	年末库存额 Inventory at year-end
44045	**5882662**	**6905778**	**621718**	**6284060**	**597096**
40007	**5405115**	**6430185**	**610165**	**5820021**	**553366**
4014	535918	1081722	146116	935606	38544
187	49070	46746	10647	36099	3235
40	5329	5945		5945	290
47	3124	3396		3396	783
20143	2352838	2475429	79586	2395843	335609
4338	1560307	1821602	324282	1497320	69301
10682	869188	965106	49451	915655	101611
556	29340	30240	83	30158	3995
1320	**249811**	**247765**	**11553**	**236212**	**21994**
910	211127	211188	9520	201668	14910
321	9304	9977	2033	7944	4304
89	29380	26600		26600	2780
2718	**227736**	**227827**		**227827**	**21735**
910	211127	211188	9520	201668	14910
321	9304	9977	2033	7944	4304
89	29380	26600		26600	2780
13979	**875737**	**900477**	**5344**	**895133**	**86911**
4718	595189	598038	1099	596939	20924
8174	246790	265807	1288	264519	53286
1087	33757	36633	2957	33676	12701
498	**71972**	**128136**	**52759**	**75377**	**6458**
115	4997	4160		4160	2187
116		42767	42767		…
226	64551	78035	9992	68043	3898
41	2424	3175		3175	373
2005	**105847**	**117347**	**11969**	**105378**	**21838**
1921	103755	114304	11166	103138	20833

17-5 续表

单位：万元

指　　标	Item	法人企业(个) Number of Corporations (Unit)	从业人数(人) Employees (person)
钟表、眼镜零售	Retail of Horologe and Spectacles	2	58
化妆品及卫生用品零售	Retail of Cosmetics and Hygiene Products		
其他日用品零售	Retail of Other Daily Consumer Use	1	26
文化、体育用品及器材专门零售	**Retail of Culture,Sports Apliances and Equipments**	**47**	**1574**
文具用品零售	Retail of Stationery		
体育用品零售	Retail of Sports Goods	2	148
图书零售	Retail of Books	41	1301
报刊零售	Retail of Newspapers and Periodicals		
音像制品及电子出版物零售	Retail of Audio and Visual Products and Electronic Publications		
珠宝首饰零售	Retail of Jewelry	2	64
工艺美术品及收藏品零售	Retail of Arts and Crafts and Collections	1	38
照相器材零售	Retail of Photographic Equipment	1	23
其他文化用品零售	Retail of Other Cultural Articles		
医药及医疗器材专门零售	**Retail of Medicines and Medical Appliances**	**28**	**4225**
#药品零售	Retail of Medicines	27	4198
医疗用品及器材零售	Retail of Medical Articles and Appliances	1	27
汽车、摩托车、燃料及零配件专门零售	**Retail of Motor Vehicles, Motorcycles, Fuel and Parts**	**244**	**16400**
#汽车零售	Retail of Motor Vehicles	199	9570
汽车零配件零售	Retail of Auto Parts and Accessories	3	102
摩托车及零配件零售	Retail of Motorcycles,Parts and Accessories	12	235
机动车燃料零售	Retail of Fuel of Motor Vehicles	30	6493
家用电器及电子产品专门零售	**Retail of Household Electric Appliances and Electronic Products**	**85**	**4487**
#家用电器零售	Retail of Household Appliances	51	3028
计算机、软件及辅助设备零售	Retail of Computer,Software and Assistant Appliances	25	536
通讯设备零售	Retail of Communication Equipments	8	715
其他电子产品零售	Retail of Other Electronic Products	1	208
五金、家具及室内装修材料专门零售	**Retail of Hardware, Furniture and Interior Decoration Materials**	**7**	**158**
五金零售	Retail of Hardware	2	16
家具零售	Retail of Furniture	1	18
涂料零售	Retail of Paint		
其他室内装修材料零售	Retail of Other Interior Decoration Materials	4	124
无店铺及其他零售	**Non-shop and Other Retails**	**15**	**719**
流动货摊零售	Retail of Flow Stalls		
邮购及电子销售	Distribution of Post and E-commerce		
生活用燃料零售	Retail of life Fuel	5	366
花卉零售	Retail of Flowers		
旧货零售	Retail of Second-hand Goods		
其他未列明的零售	Other Retails Unlisted	10	353

continued

(10000 yuan)

购进总额 Total Purchases	销售总额 Total Sales	批发 Wholesale Trade	零售 Retail Trade	年末库存额 Inventory at Year-end
1570	2251	803	1448	759
522	792		792	247
99137	**101217**	**7431**	**93786**	**10248**
4451	4420		4420	697
87968	89897	7431	82466	7058
3387	3530		3530	2035
1060	1107		1107	107
2271	2263		2263	351
101515	**105442**	**491**	**104951**	**27816**
98042	102468	491	101978	26209
3473	2973		2973	1607
4150996	**5048231**	**483778**	**4564453**	**386936**
2153204	2277889	8811	2269078	288995
21195	20971	10590	10381	1646
10083	10319	375	9945	2582
1966513	2739052	464003	2275049	93714
386762	**424847**	**36927**	**387920**	**38434**
284458	310460	3224	307236	24027
40915	49956	2276	47680	6321
57142	58236	29545	28691	7874
4247	6195	1882	4313	212
36511	**26361**	**10954**	**15408**	**15471**
2555	2579		2579	68
860	680		680	180
33096	23102	10954	12148	15223
54186	**53720**	**12067**	**41653**	**2983**
25424	25395	9520	15875	991
28762	28326	2547	25779	1993

17–6 限额以上零售业企业主要财务指标(2011)

Main Financial Indicators of Enterprises above Designated Size in Retail Trade

单位：万元 (10000 yuan)

指 标	Item	主营业务收入 Revenue from Principal Business	主营业务成本 Cost of Principal Business	主营业务税金及附加 Tax and Extra Charges on Principal Business	销售费用 Selling Expenses	营业利润 Operating Profits
总 计	**Total**	**6088738**	**5477346**	**16684**	**276665**	**222293**
#国有控股	State-Controlled	2318004	2111472	3375	76448	105394
按登记注册类型分组	**by Types of Registration**					
内资企业	**Domestic Funded Enterprises**	**5676764**	**5134235**	**14193**	**240428**	**194044**
国有企业	State-owned Enterprises	948786	844879	1690	34655	54254
集体企业	Collective-owned Enterprises	42736	31727	195	895	9038
股份合作企业	Cooperation Enterprises	5289	4376	17	105	604
联营企业	Joint Ownership Enterprises	2857	2552	18	171	67
有限责任公司	Limited Liability Corporations	2145683	1932787	8028	122227	29045
股份有限公司	Share-holding Corporations Ltd.	1624347	1479401	1906	46559	88099
私营企业	Private Enterprises	878199	812482	2241	34046	13258
其他	Other Enterprises	28867	26032	99	1771	-321
港、澳、台商投资企业	**Enterprises with Funds From HongKong, Macao and Taiwan**	**218970**	**187818**	**1043**	**16471**	**12675**
#合资经营企业(港或澳、台资)	Joint-venture Enterprises	192572	165428	869	13858	13113
合作经营企业(港或澳、台资)	Cooperative Enterprises					
港、澳、台商独资经营企业	Enterpises with Sole Investment	9225	7406	26	1242	-587
港、澳、台商投资股份有限公司	Share-holding Corporations Ltd.	17172	14985	149	1371	149
外商投资企业	**Foreign Funded Enterprises**	**193004**	**155293**	**1448**	**19766**	**15574**
中外合资经营企业	Joint-venture Enterprises	192572	165428	869	13858	13113
中外合作经营企业	Cooperation Enterprises					
外资企业	Enterprises with Sole Fund	9225	7406	26	1242	-587
外商投资股份有限公司	Share-holding Corporations Ltd.	17172	14985	149	1371	149
按国民经济行业分组	**by Sector**					
综合零售	**Integrated Retail**	**776463**	**645731**	**6985**	**80037**	**35190**
#百货零售	Retail of General Merchandise	502598	415397	5192	48025	27371
超级市场零售	Retail of Supermarkets	241157	202478	1642	28913	7571
其他综合零售	Other Integrated Retail	32708	27857	152	3099	247
食品、饮料及烟草制品专门零售	**Retail of Food,Beverages and Tobaccos**	**114376**	**88931**	**516**	**2165**	**20465**
粮油零售	Retail of Grain and Oil	4095	3500		253	-221
糕点、面包零售	Retail of Pastries and Bread					
果品、蔬菜零售	Retail of Fruits and Vegetables					
肉、禽、蛋及水产品零售	Retail of Meat, Poultry, Eggs and Aquatic Products	42767	42617	35	376	-308
饮料及茶叶零售	Retail of Beverages and Tea	64637	40886	464	1483	20327
烟草制品零售	Retail of Tobaccos and Related Products					
其他食品零售	Other Food Retail	2876	1929	17	53	667
纺织品、服装及日用品专门零售	**Retail of Textiles,Garments and Daily Consumer Goods**	**100400**	**81271**	**657**	**14991**	**2053**
纺织品及针织品零售	Retail of Textiles and Knitwear					
服装零售	Retail of Garments	97732	79091	648	14686	1981
鞋帽零售	Retail of Shoes and Hats					

17-6 续表 continued

单位：万元 (10000 yuan)

指 标	Item	主营业务收入 Revenue from Principal Business	主营业务成本 Cost of Principal Business	主营业务税金及附加 Tax and Extra Charges on Principal Business	营业费用 Operating Expenses	营业利润 Operating Profits
钟表、眼镜零售	Retail of Horologe and Spectacles	2012	1732	5	189	49
化妆品及卫生用品零售	Retail of Cosmetics and Hygiene Products					
其他日用品零售	Retail of Other Daily Consumer Use	656	448	5	116	23
文化、体育用品及器材专门零售	**Retail of Culture,Sports Apliances and Equipments**	**84755**	**67630**	**517**	**6710**	**2605**
文具用品零售	Retail of Stationery					
体育用品零售	Retail of Sports Goods	3701	3345	6	296	-228
图书零售	Retail of Books	74758	59144	319	5729	2902
报刊零售	Retail of Newspapers and Periodicals					
音像制品及电子出版物零售	Retail of Audio and Visual Products and Electronic Publications					
珠宝首饰零售	Retail of Jewelry	3127	2662	185	302	-135
工艺美术品及收藏品零售	Retail of Arts and Crafts and Collections	1235	692	6	242	64
照相器材零售	Retail of Photographic Equipment	1934	1788	2	140	2
其他文化用品零售	Retail of Other Cultural Articles					
医药及医疗器材专门零售	**Retail of Medicines and Medical Appliances**	**94848**	**72636**	**374**	**14095**	**1121**
#药品零售	Retail of Medicines	92307	70736	368	14095	1089
医疗用品及器材零售	Retail of Medical Articles and Appliances	2541	1901	6		31
汽车、摩托车、燃料及零配件专门零售	**Retail of Motor Vehicles, Motorcycles, Fuel and Parts**	**4460647**	**4111513**	**6124**	**132393**	**150446**
#汽车零售	Retail of Motor Vehicles	2011330	1871823	3287	58088	30402
汽车零配件零售	Retail of Auto Parts and Accessories	16294	15579	33	292	139
摩托车及零配件零售	Retail of Motorcycles,Parts and Accessories	10138	9078	30	500	-2
机动车燃料零售	Retail of Fuel of Motor Vehicles	2422885	2215032	2774	73512	119906
家用电器及电子产品专门零售	**Retail of Household Electric Appliances and Electronic Products**	**378867**	**341563**	**1216**	**23306**	**7525**
#家用电器零售	Retail of Household Appliances	267537	238976	808	19015	5865
计算机、软件及辅助设备零售	Retail of Computer,Software and Assistant Appliances	41519	39205	72	1106	117
通讯设备零售	Retail of Communication Equipments	64517	59640	242	3161	715
其他电子产品零售	Retail of Other Electronic Products	5295	3741	94	24	828
五金、家具及室内装修材料专门零售	**Retail of Hardware, Furniture and Interior Decoration Materials**	**25874**	**24377**	**61**	**487**	**187**
五金零售	Retail of Hardware	1777	1588	4	78	-5
家具零售	Retail of Furniture	680	600	20	5	65
涂料零售	Retail of Paint					
其他室内装修材料零售	Retail of Other Interior Decoration Materials	23417	22190	37	404	128
无店铺及其他零售	**Non-shop and Other Retails**	**52509**	**43695**	**233**	**2481**	**2701**
流动货摊零售	Retail of Flow Stalls					
邮购及电子销售	Distribution of Post and E-commerce					
生活用燃料零售	Retail of life Fuel	23338	19817	78	1281	1040
花卉零售	Retail of Flowers					
旧货零售	Retail of Second-hand Goods					
其他未列明的零售	Other Retails Unlisted	29170	23878	155	1201	1661

17-7 商品交易市场

Commodity Exchange Markets

单位：个 (unit)

指 标	Item	2006	2007	2008	2009	2010	2011
合 计	**Total**	**1859**	**1940**	**2135**	**2215**	**2216**	**2211**
消费品市场数	**Number of Consumable Markets**	**1742**	**1818**	**2057**	**2173**	**2175**	**2170**
消费品综合市场	Consumable Goods Integrative Market	1150	1178	1252	1195	1190	1176
农副产品市场	Agricultural Subproduct Market	504	543	724	881	890	894
农副产品综合市场	Agricultural Subproduct Integrative Market	462	507	675	836	844	846
农副产品专业市场	Agricultural Subproduct Special Market	42	36	49	45	46	48
工业消费品市场	Industrial Consumable Goods Market	40	43	54	61	59	58
工业消费品综合市场	Industrial Consumable Goods Integrative Market	28	32	45	53	51	50
工业消费品专业市场	Industrial Consumer Goods Special Market	12	11	9	8	8	8
其他消费品市场	Other Consumable Goods Market	48	54	27	36	36	42
生产资料市场数	**Number of Production Market**	**107**	**112**	**78**	**42**	**41**	**41**
生产资料综合市场	Production Integrative Market	30	30	29	5	4	4
工业生产资料市场	Industrial Production Market	30	33	28	27	27	27
机动车交易市场	Motor vehicle market	10	14	11	9	9	11
钢材交易市场	Steel market	10	9	6	6	6	5
煤炭交易市场	Coal market	3	3	1	2	2	2
木材交易市场	Timber market	5	6	6	6	6	5
其他工业生产资料市场	Other Means of Industrial Production Market	2	1	4	4	4	4
农业生产资料市场	Agricultural Production Market	46	46	19	5	5	5
农业生产资料综合市场	Agricultural Production Integrative Market	24	25	15	3	3	3
农业生产资料专业市场	Agricultural Production Special Market	22	21	4	2	2	2
其他生产资料市场	Others	1	3	2	5	5	5

注：资料来源于省工商局。

Note:Data in the table are provided by the provincial administration for industry and commerce.

主要统计指标解释

社会消费品零售总额 指国民经济各行业直接售给城乡居民和社会集团的消费品总额。它是反映各行业通过多种商品流通渠道向居民和社会集团供应的生活消费品总量，是研究国内零售市场变动情况、反映经济景气程度的重要指标。

社会消费品零售总额包括：⑴售给城乡居民作为生活用的商品和修建房屋用的建筑材料；⑵售给社会集团的各种办公用品和公用消费品；⑶售给机关、团体、学校、部队、企业、事业单位的职工食堂和旅店（招待所）附设专门供本店旅客食用，不对外营业的食堂的各种食品、燃料；企业、单位和国营农场直接售给本单位职工和职工食堂的自己生产的产品；⑷售给部队干部、战士生活用的粮食、副食品、衣着品、日用品、燃料；⑸售给来华的外国人、华侨、港澳台同胞的消费品；⑹居民自费购买的中、西药品、中药材及医疗用品；⑺报社、出版社直接售给居民和社会集团的报纸、图书、杂志，集邮公司出售的新、旧纪念邮票、特种邮票、首日封、集邮册、集邮工具等；⑻旧货寄售商店自购、自销部分的商品；⑼煤气公司、液化石油气站售给居民和社会集团的煤气灶具和罐装液化石油气；⑽农民售给非农业居民和社会集团的商品。不包括售给国民经济各部门企业、事业单位（包括国有经济的农场）生产经营用的各种原材料、燃料、设备、工具等和售给批发和零售贸易业、住宿和餐饮业作为转卖用的商品，旧货寄售商店受托寄售卖出的商品，服务业的营业收入，邮局出售邮票的收入，自来水、电力、煤气生产（供应）单位的产品供应收入，也不包括农民之间的商品销售。

批发和零售业商品购进、销售、库存额 指各种登记注册类型的批发和零售业企业（单位）以本企业（单位）为总体的，从国内、国外市场购进的商品总量，销售和出口的商品总量、库存的商品总量等情况。该指标可以反映商品流转过程中商品的购进、销售、库存之间的比例关系和存在的问题。

商品购进总额 指从本企业以外的单位和个人购进（包括从国外直接进口）作为转卖或加工后转卖的商品金额（含增值税）。商品包括：（1）从工农业生产者、批发和零售业企业、住宿和餐饮业企业、出版社或报社的出版发行部门和其他服务业企业购进的商品；（2）从机关团体、事业单位购进的商品；（3）从海关、市场管理部门购进的缉私和没收的商品；（4）从居民收购的废旧商品等，不包括：（1）企业为本单位自身经营用，不是作为转卖而购进的商品，如材料物资、包装物、低值易耗品、办公用品等；（2）未通过买卖行为而收入的商品，如接受其他部门移交的商品、借入的商品、收入代其他单位保管的商品、其他单位赠送的样品、加工回收的成品等；（3）经本单位介绍，由买卖双方直接结算，本单位只收取手续费的业务；（4）销售退回和买方拒付货款的商品；（5）商品溢余。

商品销售总额 指对本单位以外的单位和个人出售的商品金额(包括售给本单位消费用的商品，含增值税)。商品包括(1)售给城乡居民和社会集团消费用的商品；（2）售给农业、工业、建筑业、运输邮电业、服务业、公用事业等国民经济各行业用于生产、经营用的商品，包括售予批发和零售业作为转卖或加工后转卖的商品；（3）对国（境）外直接出口的商品，不包括：（1）未通过买卖行为付出的商品，如随机构变动移交给其他企业单位的商品、借出的商品、归还受其他单位委托代保管的商品、付出的加工原料和赠送给其他单位的样品等；（2）经本单位介绍，由买卖双方直接结算，本单位只收取手续费的业务；（3）购货退回的商品；（4）商品损耗和损失；（5）出售本单位自用的废旧物资。

商品库存额 指报告期末各种登记注册类型的批发和零售业企业（单位）已取得所有权的商品。它反映批发和零售业企业（单位）的商品库存情况和对市场商品供应的保证程度。商品库存包括：(1) 存放在批发和零售业经营单位（如门市部、批发站、经营处）仓库、货场、货柜和货架中的商品；(2) 挑选、整理、包装中的商品；(3) 已记入购进而尚未运到本单位的商品，即发货单或银行承兑凭证已到而货未到的商品；(4) 寄放他处的商品，如因购货方拒绝承付而暂时存放在购货方的商品和已办完加工成品收回手续而未提回的商品；(5) 委托其他单位代销（未作销售或调出）尚未售出的商品；(6) 代其他单位购进尚未交付的商品。不包括所有权不属于本单位的商品、委托外单位加工生产尚未收回成品的商品、外贸企业代理其他单位从国外进口尚未付给订货单位的商品、代国家物资储备部门保管的商品等。

消费品市场成交额 指从事消费品交易的商品市场的全部商品成交金额。消费品市场包括农副产品市场和工业消费品市场。

Explanatory Notes on Main Statistical Indicators

Total Retail Sales of Consumer Goods refer to the sum of retail sales of consumer goods sold by all sectors of the national economy to urban and rural residents and social groups. This indicator is used to show the supply of consumers goods through various channels to households and institutions, and is very important for the study on changes at the domestic retail market, and on economic cycles.

The retail sales of consumer goods include: (1) commodities sold to urban and rural residents for their daily use and building materials sold to them for the construction or repair of houses; (2) office appliances and supplies sold to institutions; (3) food and fuels sold to canteens of institutions, enterprises ,schools ,military units and to canteens of hotels and hostels that only serve their guests ,and commodities produced by enterprises ,institutions or state farms and sold directly to their employees or their canteens; (4) grain and non-staple food, clothing ,daily articles and fuels sold to military personnel; (5)consumer goods sold to foreigners, overseas Chinese, and Chinese compatriots from Taiwan, Hong Kong and Macao during their stay in the mainland of China; (6) Chinese and western medicines, herbs and medical facilities purchased by residents; (7) newspapers, books and magazines directly sold to residents and social groups by publishers, new and old commemorative stamps, special stamps, first-day covers, stamp albums and other stamp-collection articles sold by stamp companies; (8) consumer goods purchased and then sold by second-hand shops; (9) stoves and other heating facilities and liquefied gas sold by gas companies to households and institutions; and (10) commodities sold by farmers to non-agricultural residents and social groups. Excluded under this heading are:raw materials, fuels, equipment, tools sold to enterprises, institutions and state farms for production purpose; commodities sold to trade establishments for re-selling; commissioned sales at second-hand shops; operational income of urban public utilities; stamps sold at post offices; income of water, power, gas production and supply establishments from the supply of their products; and sales of commodities among farmers.

Purchase, Sales and Stock of Commodities by Wholesale and Retail Trades refer to the total volume of commodities purchased, total volume of sales and exports, and the stock of commodities by wholesale and retail enterprises (establishments) of different status of registration from domestic and overseas markets. This indicator reflects the relationship among purchase, sales and stock of commodities in the circulation of goods and reveals the existing problems.

Total Purchases of Commodities refer to the total value of purchases of commodities by enterprises (establishments) from other establishments or individuals (including direct import from abroad) for the purpose of re-selling, either with or without further processing of the commodities purchased. The commodities include: (1) commodities purchased from agricultural and industrial producer, wholesaler, retailer, publishing hourse and other service business; (2) commodities purchased from institutions and government departments; (3) confiscated goods purchased from the custums authorities or market management agencies; (4) second-hand goods and wastes purchased from residents; The commodities exclude 1 commodities purchased by enterprises (establishments) for use in their own business operation, commodities obtained without buying or selling procedures such as materials, consumable goods of low value, office appliances,etc. 2 received goods without trading, such as goods handed over from others, borrowed goods, preserved goods for others, donated goods from others, processed and retrieved goods, etc. 3. goods of direct settlement between buyer and seller with handling fees introduced by others, 4. goods returned or refused to pay by the buyer, 5. excessive goods.

Total Sales of Commodities refer to value of commodities sold by the establishments to other establishments and individuals (including goods sold for self consumption, including the value-added tax). The commodities include: (1) commodities sold to urban and rural residents and social groups for their consumption; (2) commodities sold to establishments in all industries for their production and operation, including agriculture, industry, construction, transportation, post and telecommunications, catering services, and public utility including commodities sold to wholesale and retail establishments for re-selling, with or without further processing; and (3) commodities for direct export to abroad. Excluded are (1) extended commodities without trading, such as goods handed over to other enterprises and institutions becase of the change of organizations, lent goods, returned goods preserved for others, extended processing materials and samples donated to others, (2) goods of direct settlement between buyer and seller with handling fees introduced by others, 3. goods returned after purchase, (4) damaged and spoiled goods, (5) waste and used goods of self use.

Total Stock of Commodities refers to total commodities possessed by wholesaler and retailer of various types of registration status at the end of the reference period, reflecting the commodity stock level of various wholesaler and retailer and the potential for market supply. It includes: (1) commodities located in storage, garages, counters, and shelves of operating places (such as sale stores, wholesale centres, and operating offices); (2) commodities in the process of being selected, sorted, and packed; (3) commodities not arrived but recorded as purchase in the account, i.e. commodities not arrived but payment receipts for the commodities from the sellers or the banks arrived; (4) commodities deposited in other places rather than places mentioned above, for instance: commodities in the hold of purchasers temporarily due to the refusal of payment and commodities not taken back after going through the formalities; (5) commodities entrusted to other units to sell but not sold yet; (6) commodities purchased for other units but not delivered yet. Commodities not included as stock are those not owned by the enterprises (units), commodities on commission for processing but not yet delivered, imported commodities of agency of foreign trade enterprise but not yet delivered to ordering units and finally those put in stock on behalf of the state material reserves units.

Volume of Transaction at Free Markets for Consumer Goods refers to the value of transaction of all goods at the free trade markets for consumer goods, where markets include both free markets for farm and sideline products and for manufactured consumer goods.

18

Eighteen

住宿、餐饮业和旅游业

Hotel, Catering Services and Tourism

18−1 限额以上住宿业和餐饮业情况

Basic Conditions of Enterprises above Designated Size in Hotels and Catering Services

指 标	Item	2006	2007	2008	2009	2010	2011
住宿业	**Hotels**						
法人企业(个)	Number of Corporations(unit)	152	164	180	181	234	260
年末从业人数(人)	Employed Persons(person)	16398	17179	20367	20064	23289	26236
营业额(亿元)	Business Revenue (100 million yuan)	10.56	11.78	15.69	16.91	20.53	27.07
#客房收入	Reveneu From Hotel Rooms	6.26	6.92	9.32	9.65	11.71	15.58
餐费收入	Reveneu from Meals	3.41	3.77	5.16	5.96	7.35	9.30
客房数(万间)	Number of Hotel Rooms(10000 rooms)			2.04	2.11	2.79	3.05
床位数(万位)	Number of Beds(10000 beds)	2.60	2.90	3.59	3.73	5.07	5.20
年末餐饮营业面积(万平方米)	Catering Services Operating Area at year-end(10000 sq.m)	25.00	18.60	19.02	18.65	23.03	49.19
餐饮业	**Catering Services**						
法人企业(个)	Number of corporation Unit (unit)	66	73	111	110	134	153
年末从业人数(人)	Employed Persons(person)	8061	7880	10338	10108	12088	15234
营业额(亿元)	Business Revenue (100 million yuan)	6.73	6.46	9.01	9.45	11.65	15.88
#餐费收入	Reveneu from Meals	6.30	6.00	8.42	8.60	10.45	13.63
年末餐饮营业面积(万平方米)	Catering Services Operational Area at Year-end(10000 sq.m)	15.70	14.90	28.83	20.59	23.51	36.24

18-2 限额以上住宿业企业情况(2011)

单位：万元

项　目	Item	法人企业(个) Number of Corporations (unit)	年末从业人数(人) Employed Persons (person)	营业额 Business Revenue	#客房收入 Revenue from Hotel Rooms	#餐费收入 Reveneu from Meals
合计	**Total**	**260**	**26236**	**270679**	**155843**	**92962**
按登记注册类型分	**by Types of Registration**					
内资企业	**Domestic Funded Enterprises**	**255**	**25223**	**257513**	**149853**	**86373**
国有企业	State-owned Enterprises	52	5294	61425	33732	23475
集体企业	Collective-owned Enterprises	5	259	2586	1716	687
股份合作企业	Cooperation Enterprises					
联营企业	Joint Ownership Enterprises					
有限责任公司	Limited Liability Corporations	91	11517	122911	69051	41853
股份有限公司	Share-holding Corporations Ltd.	2	204	1287	903	360
私营企业	Private Enterprises	97	7410	65139	41913	18696
其他企业	Other Enterprises	8	539	4165	2538	1303
港、澳、台商投资企业	**Enterprises with Funds From Honkong, Macao and Taiwan**	**4**	**805**	**9678**	**4474**	**4855**
合资经营企业	Joint-venture Enterprises	2	600	7784	3681	3909
合作经营企业	Cooperative Enterprises					
独资经营企业	Enterpises with Sole Funds	2	205	1894	793	946
投资股份有限公司	Share-holding Corporations Ltd.					
外商投资企业	**Foreign Funded Enterprises**	**1**	**208**	**3489**	**1516**	**1734**
中外合资经营企业	Joint-venture Enterprises	1	208	3489	1516	1734
中外合作经营企业	Cooperation Enterprises					
外资企业	Enterprises with Sole Fund					
外商投资股份有限公司	Share-holding Corporations Ltd.					
按国民经济行业分	**by Sector**					
旅游饭店	Tourist Hotels	177	19985	206739	113180	75513
一般旅馆	General Hotels	74	5727	59399	39063	16868
其他住宿服务	Other Hotel Services	9	524	4542	3600	582

Basic Conditions of Enterprises above Designated Size in Hotel Services

(10000yuan)

主营业务收入 Revenue from Principal Business	主营业务成本 Cost of Principal Business	主营业务税金及附加 Tax and Extra Charges on Principal Business	主营业务利润 Profits from Principal Business	资产总计 Total Assets	#流动资产合计 Total Current Assets	#固定资产合计 Total Fixed Assets	负债合计 Total Liabilities	所有者权益合计 Total Owners' Equity
269795	**94427**	**15316**	**160052**	**601581**	**193192**	**300664**	**368888**	**232693**
256628	**91891**	**14563**	**150175**	**580366**	**188007**	**294013**	**353075**	**227291**
61247	21703	3518	36026	96226	25502	59665	35786	60440
2569	1780	133	655	1752	418	1142	490	1262
123017	41881	6788	74348	301612	97931	149963	216785	84828
1422	278	79	1064	12190	542	3580	8318	3872
64205	25065	3770	35370	149995	53850	73684	82476	67519
4169	1184	275	2711	18591	9764	5980	9220	9370
9678	**1904**	**550**	**7224**	**12200**	**4755**	**5701**	**8811**	**3390**
7784	1396	443	5945	9673	2982	5067	7207	2466
1894	508	108	1278	2528	1773	634	1604	924
3489	**632**	**203**	**2654**	**9015**	**430**	**950**	**7003**	**2012**
3489	632	203	2654	9015	430	950	7003	2012
206922	73472	11592	121858	491880	147442	247990	312029	179852
58556	19630	3411	35515	98625	40643	48380	51303	47323
4317	1324	313	2680	11076	5106	4294	5557	5519

18–3 限额以上餐饮业企业情况(2011)

单位：万元

项目	Item	法人企业(个) Number of corporation (unit)	年末从业人数(人) Employees (person)	营业额 Business Revenue	#餐费收入 From Meals
合计	**Total**	**153**	**15234**	**158843**	**136334**
按登记注册类型分	**by Types of Registration**				
内资企业	**Domestic funded Enterprises**	**152**	**15174**	**156291**	**133782**
国有企业	State-owned Enterprises	11	1009	11779	6841
集体企业	Collective-owned Enterprises				
股份合作企业	Copperative Enterprises	1	30	226	185
联营企业	Joint Ownership Enterprises				
有限责任公司	Limited Liability Corporations	51	7351	78743	70517
股份有限公司	Share Holding Corporations Ltd.	1	43	725	725
私营企业	Private Enterprises	75	5667	54440	45685
其他企业	Other Enterprises	13	1074	10378	9829
港、澳、台商投资企业	**Enterprises with Funds from Hong Kong,Macao and Taiwan**				
合资经营企业	Joint-venture Enterprises				
合作经营企业	Cooperative Enterprises				
独资经营企业	Corporations with Sole Fund				
投资股份有限公司	Share-holding Corporations Ltd.				
外商投资企业	**Foreign Funded Enterprises**	**1**	**60**	**2552**	**2552**
中外合资经营企业	Joint-venture Enterprises				
中外合作经营企业	Cooperation Enterprises				
外资企业	Enterprises with Sole Fund	1	60	2552	2552
外商投资股份有限公司	Share-holding Corporations Ltd.				
按国民经济行业分	**by Sector**				
正餐服务业	Restaurant Services	149	14800	151155	129413
快餐服务业	Snack Counter Services	3	260	4165	4165
饮料及冷饮服务业	Beverages and Cold Drinks				
其他餐饮服务业	Others	1	174	3523	2757

Basic Conditions of Enterprises above Designated Size in Catering Services

(10000yuan)

主营业务收入 Revenue from Principal Business	主营业务成本 Cost of Principal Business	主营业务税金及附加 Tax and Extra Charges on Principal Business	主营业务利润 Profits from Principal Business	资产总计 Total Assets	#流动资产合计 Current Assets	#固定资产合计 Total Fixed Assets	负债合计 Total Liabilities	所有者权益合计 Total Owners' Equities
156881	**81756**	**8998**	**66127**	**190418**	**93185**	**60545**	**121800**	**68618**
154329	**80944**	**8853**	**64532**	**190138**	**93185**	**60545**	**121800**	**68338**
11230	6179	482	4569	11477	5770	4144	6719	4758
226	119	13	95	297	195	102	123	174
78150	40392	4467	33292	102192	56738	26721	73814	28378
725	220	30	476	666	9	66	9	658
53627	28164	3298	22165	63439	26287	25019	35790	27650
10370	5871	563	3936	12068	4188	4492	5347	6721
2552	**812**	**146**	**1595**	**280**				**280**
2552	812	146	1595	280				280
149459	77474	8716	63268	187465	91096	60023	119903	67562
4165	1479	234	2452	514	71	102	69	445
3257	2802	48	407	2439	2019	420	1828	611

18-4 旅游业主要指标

Basic Statistics on Development of Tourism

指　标	Item	2006	2007	2008	2009	2010	2011
旅行社总数(个)	**Total Number of Travel Agencies(unit)**	**181**	**177**	**218**	**201**	**260**	**270**
国际旅行社	International Travel Agencies	16	17	18	18	11	11
国内旅行社	Domestic Travel Agencies	165	160	200	183	249	259
旅行社职工人数(人)	**Number of Staff and Workers of Travel Agencies(person)**	**2085**	**2215**	**5215**	**4824**	**5384**	**7071**
国际旅行社	International Travel Agencies	850	910	1050	1050	950	1085
国内旅行社	Domestic Travel Agencies	1235	1305	4165	3774	4434	5986
旅游总人数(万人次)	**Total Number of Tourists(10000 person-times)**	**4747.89**	**6262.89**	**8190.23**	**10439.95**	**12913.02**	**17019.36**
入境旅游人数	Total Number of International Tourists Inbound	32.14	43.00	39.54	39.95	50.01	58.51
外国人	Foreigners	10.70	15.48	18.22	16.28	18.61	23.62
港澳同胞	Compatriots from Hong Kong and Macao	9.33	13.05	10.79	10.84	13.64	16.91
台湾同胞	Compatriots from Taiwan	12.11	14.47	10.52	12.83	17.76	17.98
国内旅游人数	Total Number of Domestic Tourists	4715.75	6219.89	8150.69	10400.00	12863.01	16960.85
旅游总收入(亿元)	**Tourism Earnings(100 million yuan)**	**387.05**	**512.28**	**653.13**	**805.23**	**1061.23**	**1429.48**
国际旅游外汇收入(万美元)	Earnings from International Tourism (USD 10000)	11515.66	12917.55	11697.37	11044.40	12957.88	13507.18
国内旅游收入(亿元)	Earnings from Domestic Tourism (100 million yuan)	377.79	504.04	643.82	797.69	1052.64	1420.70
三大旅行社接待入境旅游人数(万人次)	**Number of International Tourists Received by Three Major Travel Service (10000 person-times)**	**3.71**	**3.30**	**3.87**	**5.25**	**1.76**	**1.51**
中国国际旅行社	China International Travel Service	0.98	0.41	1.67	1.31	0.23	0.39
贵州海外旅游总公司	Guizhou Overseas Tourism Corporation	2.55	2.48	2.06	3.83	1.47	0.69
中国青年旅行社	China Youth Travel Service	0.18	0.41	0.14	0.11	0.06	0.43

注：资料来源于省旅游局(以下相关表同)。

Note:Data in the table are obtained from the provincial tourism administration(The relative tables are the same).

18-5 来黔境外旅游人数及人均消费支出

Number of Overseas Tourists Visiting Guizhou and Average Per Capita Spending

类别	Item	2006	2007	2008	2009	2010	2011	2011年比2010年增长(%) Increase Rate in 2011 over 2010(%)
来黔境外旅游人数(万人次)	**Number of Foreign Tourists Visiting Guizhou(10000 person-times)**	**32.14**	**43.00**	**39.54**	**39.95**	**50.01**	**58.51**	**17.0**
外国人	Foreigner	10.70	15.48	18.22	16.28	18.61	23.62	26.9
港澳同胞	Compatriots from Hong Kong and Macao	9.33	13.05	10.79	10.84	13.64	16.91	24.0
台湾同胞	Compatriots from Taiwan	12.11	14.47	10.52	12.83	17.76	17.98	1.2
平均每人逗留天数(天/人)	Average Days Tourists Stay in Guizhou Per Capita (day/person)	2.24	1.86	1.75	1.63	1.43	1.39	-2.8
平均每人每天消费支出(美元/人、天)	Average Per Capita Daily Spending (USD/person-day)	163.68	171.54	169.30	169.12	171.76	168.68	-1.8

18-6 接待外国旅游人数(按地区分)

Number of Overseas Tourists Visiting Guizhou(by Country/Territory)

单位：人次　　(person-time)

地区名	Country (Territory)	2006	2007	2008	2009	2010	2011	2011年比2010年增长(%) Increase Rate in 2011 over 2010(%)
总　计	**Total**	**107006**	**154762**	**182231**	**162792**	**186054**	**236244**	**27.0**
亚　洲	Asia	50403	69077	81560	75042	85383	104624	22.5
非　洲	Africa	569	752	1120	980	1110	1536	38.4
欧　洲	Europe	23547	36234	43325	39094	44799	57619	28.6
拉丁美洲	Latin America	21302	30355	35076	30493	35239	45379	28.8
大洋洲	Oceania	10229	15456	17564	14814	16861	23518	39.5
其　他	Others	956	2888	3586	2369	2662	3568	34.0

18-7 旅游外汇收入
Foreign Exchange Earnings

单位：万美元 (USD 10000)

类别	Item	2006	2007	2008	2009	2010	2011	2011年比2010年增长(%) Increase Rate in 2011 over 2010(%)
总　计	**Total**	**11515.66**	**12917.56**	**11697.37**	**11044.40**	**12957.88**	**13507.18**	**4.2**
长途交通	Long Distance Transportation	3569.85	3100.22	3661.28	3224.96	5001.74	5200.26	4.0
游　览	Visiting	817.61	490.86	432.80	441.78	596.06	540.29	-9.4
住　宿	Accommodation	2360.71	1459.68	1368.59	1336.37	1399.45	1701.9	21.6
餐　饮	Food and Beverage	1450.97	1072.16	959.18	949.82	997.76	729.39	-26.9
商品销售	Shopping	2153.43	3733.18	3193.38	3379.59	2410.17	3241.72	34.5
娱　乐	Entertainment	713.97	477.95	514.68	452.82	583.10	634.84	8.9
邮电通讯	Postal and Communication Services	57.58	426.28	514.68	353.42	362.83	324.17	-10.7
市内交通	Local Transportation	115.16	232.51	362.64	77.31	220.28	108.06	-50.9
其他服务	Other Services	276.38	1924.72	690.14	828.33	1386.49	1026.55	-26.0

18-8 旅馆业接待经营
Operation of Hotels

类　别	Item	2006	2007	2008	2009	2010	2011	2011年比2010年增长(%) Increase Rate in 2011 over 2010(%)
接待能力	**Capacity**							
年末客房数(间)	Guest Rooms (Year-end) (unit)	15805	18625	21278	23578	25191	26120	3.7
年末客房床位数(张)	Guest Beds (Year-end) (bed)	30396	34974	39142	42885	45683	46204	1.1
客房开房率(%)	Room Occupancy Rate(%)	65.0	65.5	63.0	63.5	63.6	64.2	0.6(百分点)
#星级宾馆	Star-rated Hotels	70.1	66.0	64.0	64.5	65.1	64.6	-0.5(百分点)
实际住宿人次数(万人次)	Actual Number of Guests (10000 person-times)	395.53	435.65	510.89	540.32	625.63	740.49	18.4
#海外来黔	Overseas Visitors	32.14	43.00	39.53	39.95	50.01	58.51	17.0
实际住宿人天数(万人天)	Actual Number of Guests and Days of Stay (10000 person-days)	605.11	689.21	748.61	801.35	866.84	997.23	15.0
#海外来黔	Overseas Visitors	72.04	80.01	69.09	65.30	71.39	81.22	13.8
经营和财务	**Management and Financial**							
营业收入(万元)	Operational Revenue(10000 yuan)	155630	171256	180254	187002	195639	228252	16.7

18-9 星级饭店
Star-rated Hotels

单位：个 (unit)

指　标	Item	2006	2007	2008	2009	2010	2011
总　计	**Total**	**214**	**243**	**279**	**323**	**344**	**340**
按经济类型分	**Grouped by Ownership**						
国有经济	State-owned	134	111	97	111	103	90
集体经济	Collective-owned	75	130	175	210	241	250
外商投资经济	Foreign Funded	5	2	7	2		
按规模分	**Grouped by Capacity**						
客房总数300间以上	With Above than 300 Rooms	2	2	2	4	3	3
客房总数200-299间	With 200-299 Rooms	7	8	10	13	14	16
客房总数100-199间	With 100-199 Rooms	38	45	45	65	54	63
客房总数99间以下	With Less than 100 Rooms	167	188	222	241	273	258

18–10　风景名胜区

Scenic Spots

名　称	Name	级 别	地　址
红枫湖风景名胜区	Hongfeng Lake Scenic Spot	国家级	贵州省贵阳市清镇市
黄果树风景名胜区	Huangguoshu Waterfalls Scenic Spot	国家级	贵州省安顺市镇宁县
龙宫风景名胜区	The Dragon Palace Scenic Spot	国家级	贵州省安顺市
织金洞风景名胜区	Zhijin Cave Scenic Spot	国家级	贵州省毕节市织金县
九洞天风景名胜区	Jiudongtian Scenic Spot	国家级	贵州省毕节市
马岭河峡谷风景名胜区	Malinghe Canyon Scenic Spot	国家级	贵州省黔西南州兴义市
㵲阳河风景名胜区	Wuyang River Scenic Spot	国家级	贵州省黔东南州镇远县
黎平侗乡风景名胜区	Liping Dong-Village Scenic Spot	国家级	贵州省黔东南州黎平县
荔波樟江风景名胜区	Libo Zhangjiang Scenic Spot	国家级	贵州省黔南州荔波县
都匀斗篷山——剑江风景名胜区	Duyun Doupeng Mountain----Jianjiang Scenic Spot	国家级	贵州省黔南州
赤水风景名胜区	Chishui Scenic Spot	国家级	贵州省遵义市赤水市
九龙洞风景名胜区	Jiulong Cave Scenic Spot	国家级	贵州省铜仁市
紫云格凸河风景名胜区	Ziyun Getu River Scenic Spot	国家级	贵州省安顺市紫云县
平塘风景名胜区	Pingtang Scenic Spot	国家级	贵州省黔南州平塘县
瓮安江界河风景名胜区	Wengan Jiangjie River Scenic Spot	国家级	贵州省黔南州瓮安县
榕江古榕风景名胜区	Rongjiang Gurong Scenic Spot	国家级	贵州省黔东南州榕江县
石阡温泉群风景名胜区	Shiqian Hot Well Flock Scenic Spot	国家级	贵州省铜仁市石阡县
沿河乌江山峡风景名胜区	Yanhe Wujiang River Sanxia Scenic Spot	国家级	贵州省铜仁市沿河县
百花湖风景名胜区	Baihua Lake Scenic Spot	省级	贵州省贵阳市
花溪风景名胜区	Huaxi Scenic Spot	省级	贵州省贵阳市花溪区
息烽风景名胜区	Xifeng Scenic Spot	省级	贵州省贵阳市息烽县
修文阳明风景名胜区	Xiuwen Yangming Scenic Spot	省级	贵州省贵阳市修文县
香纸沟风景名胜区	Xiangzhigou Scenic Spot	省级	贵州省贵阳市
开阳风景名胜区	Kaiyang Scenic Spot	省级	贵州省贵阳市开阳县
相思河风景名胜区	Xiangsi River Scenic Spot	省级	贵州省贵阳市
清镇暗流河风景名胜区	Qingzhen Undercurrent River Scenic Spot	省级	贵州省贵阳市清镇市
普定梭筛风景名胜区	Puding Suoshai Scenic Spot	省级	贵州省安顺市普定县
关岭花江大峡谷风景名胜区	Guanling Huajiang Canyon Scenic Spot	省级	贵州省安顺市关岭县花江镇
平坝天台山——斯拉河风景名胜区	Pingba Tiantai Mountain ----Sila River Scenic Spot	省级	贵州省安顺市平坝县
百里杜鹃风景名胜区	One-Hundred-Li Azalea Belt Scenic Spot	省级	毕节市大方、黔西县
贵州屋脊赫章韭菜坪风景名胜区	Guizhou Fastigium Hezhang Jiucaiping Scenic Spot	省级	贵州省毕节市赫章县
鲁布革风景名胜区	Lubuge Scenic Spot	省级	贵州省黔西南州兴义市
泥凼石林风景名胜区	Nidang shilin Scenic Spot	省级	贵州省黔西南州兴义市泥凼镇
安龙招堤风景名胜区	Anlong Zhaodi Scenic Spot	省级	贵州省黔西南州安龙县
贞丰三岔河风景名胜区	Zhenfeng Sancha River Scenic Spot	省级	贵州省黔西南州贞丰县

18-10 续表 continued

名　称	Name	级别	地　址
晴隆三望坪风景名胜区	Qinglong Sanwangping Scenic Spot	省级	贵州省黔西南州晴隆县
兴仁放马坪风景名胜区	Xingren Fangmaping Scenic Spot	省级	贵州省黔西南州兴仁县
岑巩龙鳌河风景名胜区	Cengong Longao River Scenic Spot	省级	贵州省黔东南州岑巩县
剑河风景名胜区	Jianhe Scenic Spot	省级	贵州省黔东南州剑河县
麻江下司风景名胜区	Majiang Xiasi Scenic Spot	省级	贵州省黔东南州麻江县
镇远高过河风景名胜区	Zhenyuan Gaoguo River Scenic Spot	省级	贵州省黔东南州镇远县
雷山风景名胜区	Leishan Scenic Spot	省级	贵州省黔东南州雷山县
锦屏三板溪——隆里古城风景名胜区	Jinping Sanbanxi----Longli Scenic Spot	省级	贵州省黔东南州锦屏县
丹寨龙泉山——岔河风景名胜区	Danzhai Longquanshan----Chahe Scenic Spot	省级	贵州省黔东南州丹寨县
从江风景名胜区	Congjiang Scenic Spot	省级	贵州省黔东南州从江县
龙里猴子沟风景名胜区	Longli Monkey Fossa Scenic Spot	省级	贵州省黔南州龙里县
福泉洒金谷风景名胜区	Fuquan Sajingu Scenic Spot	省级	贵州省黔南州福泉市
惠水涟江——燕子洞风景名胜区	Huishui Lianjiang--Yanzi Cave Scenic Spot	省级	贵州省黔南州惠水县
长顺杜鹃湖——白云山风景名胜区	Changshun Dujuan Lake--Baiyun Mountain Scenic Spot	省级	贵州省黔南州长顺县
三都都柳江风景名胜区	Sandu Duliu River Scenic Spot	省级	贵州省黔南州三都县
贵定洛北河风景名胜区	Guiding Luobei River Scenic Spot	省级	贵州省黔南州贵定县
独山深河桥风景名胜区	Dushan Shenhe Bridge Scenic Spot	省级	贵州省黔南州独山县
遵义娄山风景名胜区	Zunyi Loushan Mountain Scenic Spot	省级	贵州省遵义市遵义县板桥镇
绥阳宽阔水风景名胜区	Suiyang Kuankuoshui Scenic Spot	省级	贵州省遵义市绥阳县
仁怀茅台风景名胜区	Renhuai Moutai Scenic Spot	省级	贵州省遵义仁怀市茅台镇
习水风景名胜区	Xishui Scenic Spot	省级	贵州省遵义市习水县东皇镇
余庆大乌江风景名胜区	Yuqing Wujiang River Scenic Spot	省级	贵州省遵义市余庆县白泥镇
湄潭湄江风景名胜区	Meitan Scenic Spot	省级	贵州省遵义市湄潭县
梵净山——太平河风景名胜区	Fanjing Mountain----Taiping River Scenic Spot	省级	贵州省铜仁市江口县
印江木黄风景名胜区	Yinjiang Muhuang Scenic Spot	省级	贵州省铜仁市印江县
思南乌江白鹭洲风景名胜区	Sinan Wujiang River Bailuzhou Scenic Spo	省级	贵州省铜仁市思南县
松桃豹子岭——寨英风景名胜区	Songtao Baozi Mountain----Zhaiying Scenic Spot	省级	贵州省铜仁市松桃县
万山夜郎谷风景名胜区	Wanshan Yelang Canyon Scenic Spot	省级	贵州省铜仁市万山区
玉屏北洞萧笛之乡风景名胜区	Yuping Beidong Xiaodi-Village Scenic Spot	省级	贵州省铜仁市玉屏县
六枝牂牁江风景名胜区	Liuzhi Zangke River Scenic Spot	省级	贵州省六盘水市六枝特区
盘县古银杏风景名胜区	Panxian Ancientry Gingko Scenic Spot	省级	贵州省六盘水市盘县石桥镇
盘县大洞竹海风景名胜区	PanXian Dadong Banboo Sea Scenic Spot	省级	贵州省六盘水市盘县珠东乡、老厂镇
盘县坡上草原风景名胜区	PanXian Grassland on Mountain Scenic Spot	省级	贵州省六盘水市盘县四格乡、坪地乡
南开风景名胜区	Nankai Scenic Spot	省级	贵州省六盘水市水城县
务川洪渡河风景名胜区	Wuchuan hongduhe Scenic Spot	省级	贵州省遵义市务川县
罗甸大小井风景名胜区	Luodian daxiaojin Scenic Spot	省级	贵州省黔南州罗甸县
德江乌江傩文化风景名胜区	Dejiang Wjiang Riverside Scenic Spot	省级	贵州省铜仁市德江县

18-11 全国重点文物保护单位

Historical and Cultrual Relics under Key Protection

文物单位名称	Name	市	县
平坝天台山伍龙寺	Pingba Tiantai Wulong Temple	安顺市	平坝县
云山屯古建筑群(含本寨)	The Ancientry Construction Yunshantun	安顺市	西秀区
安顺文庙	Anshun State Joss House	安顺市	西秀区
穿洞遗址	Chuandong,the Stone Cave	安顺市	普定县
宁谷遗址	The Site of Ninggu	安顺市	西秀区
黔西观音洞遗址	The Site of Kwan-yin Cave Qianxi	毕节市	黔西县
赫章可乐遗址	The Site of Kele Hezhang	毕节市	赫章县
织金古建筑群	The Ancientry Construction Zhijin	毕节市	织金县
川滇黔省革命委员会旧址	Finish the committee old address of Chuan Dian Qian province revolution	毕节市	大方县
奢香墓	The Mausoleum of Lady She Xiang	毕节市	大方县
大屯土司庄园	Datun Headman's Castle	毕节市	毕节市
马头寨古建筑群	The Ancientry Construction Matouzhai	贵阳市	开阳县
阳明洞和阳明祠	Yangming Cave and Yangming Ancestral Temple	贵阳市	修文县、云岩区
文昌阁和甲秀楼	Wenchang Pavilion and Jiaxiu Floor	贵阳市	贵阳市
息烽集中营旧址(含玄天洞)	The Site Concentration Camp Xifeng(including Tien-dong)	贵阳市	息烽县
大洞遗址	The Site of Dadong Cave	六盘水市	盘县
郎德上寨古建筑群	The Ancientry Construction Langdeshangzhai	黔东南州	雷山县
地坪风雨桥	Diping Pavilion Bridge	黔东南州	黎平县
飞云崖古建筑群	The Ancientry Construction Feishanya	黔东南州	黄平县
旧州古建筑群	The Ancientry Construction Jiuzhou	黔东南州	黄平县
黎平会议会址	The Site of Liping Conference	黔东南州	黎平县
和平村旧址	Peace village sit	黔东南州	镇远县
青龙洞	Qinglong Cave	黔东南州	镇远县
增冲鼓楼	Zengchong Drum-tower	黔东南州	从江县
福泉城墙	Fuquan Ming Dynasty Wall	黔南州	福泉市
葛镜桥	Gejing BrBridge	黔南州	福泉市
交乐墓群	The Cemetery Jiaole	黔西南州	兴仁县
“二十四道拐”抗战公路	"twenty-four Shui" road war	黔西南州	晴隆县
石阡万寿宫	Shiqian Wanshou Palace	铜仁市	石阡县
万山汞矿遗址	The Site of Wanshan Hydrargyrum	铜仁市	万山区
东山古建筑群	The Ancientry Construction Dongshan	铜仁市	铜仁市
寨英古建筑群	The Ancientry Construction Zhaiying	铜仁市	松桃县
思唐古建筑群	The Ancientry Construction Sitang	铜仁市	思南县
黔东特区革命委员会旧址	The site of Qiandong SAR revolution committee	铜仁市	沿河县、德江县、印江县
遵义会议会址	The Site of Zunyi Conference	遵义市	红花岗区
遵义海龙屯	Zunyi Hailongtun	遵义市	汇川区
杨粲墓	Yangcan Tomb	遵义市	汇川区
红军四渡赤水战役旧址	The ferry station monument of Red Army "four Dus red water"s soil city	遵义市	习水县、仁怀市、汇川区
湄潭浙江大学旧址	Meitan former Zhejiang University	遵义市	湄潭县

注：资料来源于省文化厅。
Note:Data in this table come from the Provinvial Department of Culture.

18-12 星级饭店

Star-rated Hotels

名　称	Name	星级 Level	评定日期 Date of Assess	客房数 Rooms	床位数 Beds	地　址 Address	电　话 Telephone
贵州天怡豪生大酒店	Guizhou Tianyi Haosheng Hotel	5	2005.03	310	439	贵阳市枣山路29号	0851-6518888
贵阳喜来登贵航酒店	Xilaideng Hotel	5	2010.08	346	629	贵阳市中华南路49号	0851-5888888
黔西南金州翠湖宾馆	Qianxinan Jinzhou Cuihu Hotel	5	2010.12	203	294	兴义市瑞金南路60号	0859-3619999
贵州饭店	Guizhou Hotel	4	1998.07	382	660	贵阳市北京路66号	0851-6823888
贵阳华美达神奇酒店	Guiyang Shenqi Hotel	4	1999.12	230	339	贵阳市贵开路1号	0851-6771888
贵阳神奇金筑酒店	Guiyang Shenqijinzhu Hotel	4	2000.07	180	230	贵阳市延安东路2号	0851-6825888
贵州鲜花酒店	Guizhou Xuanhua Hotel	4	2001.12	260	403	贵阳市中华南路1号	0851-5867888
贵州柏顿酒店	Guizhou Bodun Hotel	4	2001.05	254	343	贵阳市延安东路18号	0851-5827888
贵州丽豪大饭店	Guizhou Lihao Hotel	4	2005.07	220	355	贵阳市瑞金北路115号	0851-6521888
贵龙饭店	GuiLong Bodun Hotel	4	2001.06	168	316	贵阳市神奇路52号	0851-5593888
能辉酒店	Nenghui Hotel	4	2003.12	125	205	贵阳市瑞金南路38号	0851-5898888
贵州武岳酒店	Guizhou Wuyue Hotel	4	2007.09	192	306	贵阳市南厂路1号	0851-8651777
贵州雅迪尔国际大酒店	Guizhou Yadier International Hotel	4	2010.04	218	342	贵阳市中华南路7号	0851-5578888
凯里嘉瑞禾腾龙酒店	Kaili Jiaruihe Tenglong Hotel	4	2004.05	166	311	凯里市宁波东路	0855-8066666
凯里金冠酒店	Kaili Jinguan Hotel	4	2006.11	168	316	凯里市支庄路18号	0855-8068888
贵州省兴义民航酒店	Guizhou Xingyi Civil Aviaton Hotel	4	2003.07	180	230	兴义市瑞金南路	0859-3126666
兴义黔山度假酒店	Xingyi Qianshan Hotel	4	2006.12	199	355	兴义市瑞金北路20号	0859-3116669
安顺天瀑大酒店	Anshun Tianpu Hotel	4	2006.08	230	339	安顺市贵黄东路电力城	0853-3516888
安顺凯旋大酒店	Anshun Kaixuan Hotel	4	2006.12	246	403	安顺市开发区南马广场	0853-3461999
毕节腾龙凯悦酒店	Bijie Tenglong Kaiyue Hotel	4	2006.12	254	343	毕节市桂花路2号	0857-8291111
铜仁宝鑫大酒店	Tongren Baoxin Hotel	4	2006.07	151	280	铜仁市东太大道88号	0856-5937888
荔波县三力酒店	Libo Sanli Hotel	4	2007.09	152	293	荔波县玉屏镇思铭大道	0854-3615888
贵侯苑商务大酒店	Guihouyuan Business Hotel	4	2009.03	85	138	都匀市开发区龙山大道	0854-7121111
金鹏国际酒店	Jinpeng International Hotel	4	2009.08	88	126	都匀市剑江中路67号	0854-7127777
伯爵花园酒店	Bojue Huayuan Hotel	4	2009.01	149	204	都匀市开发区	0854-8759999
毕节大酒店	Bijie Hotel	4	2008.09	151	269	毕节市砂石路	0857-8689999
金凯帝豪酒店	Jinkaidihao Hotel	4	2008.09	109	187	凯里市北京西路	0855-8276688
遵义大世界酒店	Zunyi Dasijie Hotel	4	2008.12	167	238	遵义市汇川区珠海路一号	0852-8666666
遵义东方酒店	Zunyi Dongfang Hotel	4	2008.12	204	327	遵义市中华南路2号	0852-8867777
赤水中悦大酒店	Chishui zhongyue Hotel	4	2008.12	140	250	赤水市南正街22号	0852-2823888
六盘水时代假日酒店	Liupanshui Shidai Holiday Hotel	4	2009.08	265	381	六盘水钟山区钟山中路66号	0858-8108888
六盘水凤凰祥林大酒店	Liupanshui Phoenix Xianglin Hotel	4	2010.12	130	224	六盘水市凤凰新区青峰路18号	0858-8296789
贵州峰润喀斯特酒店	Guizhou Runfeng Kasite Hotel	4	2011.01	197	309	南明区神奇路1号	0851-8196888
金芦笙小镇精品特色酒店	Jinlongsheng town Characteristic and Boutique Hotal	4	2011.04	138	245	宝山南路88号	0851-5623999
毕节红都假日酒店	Bijie Hongdu Holiday Hotel	4	2011.05	115	198	毕节市拥军路军分区内	0857-8237772
贵州民族大酒店	Guizhou National Hotel	4	2011.08	121	209	南明区箭道街23号	0851-5571888
贵阳蓝天宾馆	Guiyang Lantian Hotel	4	2011.08	112	191	南明区解放路158号	0851-5795988
西苑锦润酒店	Xiyuanjinrun Hotel	4	2011.08	134	214	小河区锦江路5号	0851-5975555
西湖花园大酒店	West Lake Garden Hotel	4	2011.08	252	451	宝山北路133号	0851-5292802
宏洲国际大酒店	Hongzhou International Hotel	4	2011.10	203	298	织金县城关镇金北路151号	0857-7758888
都市怡景酒店	Dushiyijing Hotel	4	2011.10	117	202	贵阳市都司路122号	0851-5848888
贵州铝厂宾馆	Guizhou Aluminum Plant Hotel	4	2011.11	78	134	贵阳市白云区刚玉街57号	0851-4896111
贵阳夏日康桥酒店	Guiyang Summer Cambridge Hotel	4	2011.11	89	141	贵阳市白云区白云南路299号	0851-4439655
六盘水红果大酒店	Liupangshui Hongguo Hotel	4	2011.12	189	353	盘县红果经济开发区凤鸣路	0858-3631888
遵义森林大酒店	Zunyi Forest Hotel	4	2011.12	121	212	遵义市汇川区深圳路新客运大楼	0852-8988888
三都福丰假日酒店	Sandu Fufeng Holiday Hotel	4	2011.12	165	236	三都县三合镇龙嘴角移民新村	0854-3029999
贵州华联酒店	Guizhou Hualian Hotel	3	1999.09	141	261	贵阳市中华中路137号	0851-5810999
贵阳山林大酒店	Guizhou Shanlin Hotel	3	1999.09	158	300	贵阳市山林路118号	0851-6523000
黔灵大酒店	Qianling Hotel	3	2000.04	152	273	贵阳市北京路225号	0851-8271521

18-12 续表1 continued

名 称	Name	星级 Level	评定日期 Date of Assess	客房数 Rooms	床位数 Beds	地 址 Address	电 话 Telephone
贵阳神奇星岛酒店	Guiyang Shenqi Xingdao Hotel	3	2002.09	101	180	贵阳市贵开路1号	0851-6751888
贵州立云酒店	Guizhou Liyun Hotel	3	2002.12	254	468	贵阳市浣沙路5号	0851-8126666
紫林宾馆	Zilin Hotel	3	2004.02	195	365	贵阳市延安中路110号	0851-5283000
久远饭店	Jiuyuan Hotel	3	2004.08	169	300	贵阳市瑞金南路36号	0851-5849999
贵州腾飞电信酒店	Guizhou Tengfeidianxin Hotel	3	2004.12	83	153	贵阳市市南路69号	0851-5529888
修文珍珠岛度假中心	Xiuwen zhenzhudao Hotel	3	2004.11	89	220	贵阳修文酒长镇	0851-2436002
贵阳市金品大酒店	Guiyang Jinpin Hotel	3	2004.12	112	196	贵阳朝阳洞路建材巷1号	0851-8216666
贵阳南翔酒店	Guiyang Nanxiang Hotel	3	2004.12	63	108	贵阳市延安西路185号	0851-6522888
贵州宏业宾馆	Guizhou Hongye Hotel	3	2005.02	75	143	贵阳市解放路87号	0851-5566755
贵阳久泰大酒店	Guiyang Jiutai Hotel	3	2005.01	120	191	贵阳市瑞金北路116号	0851-6685998
花溪溪山酒店	Huaxi Xishan Hotel	3	2006.01	49	96	贵阳市花溪区迎宾路	0851-3630166
贵阳山水大酒店	Guiyang Shanshui Hotel	3	2006.11	38	41	贵阳市沙冲路198号	0851-3831838
新联大厦	Xinlian Hotel	3	1997.12	120	200	贵阳市外环东路227号	0851-6765555
红阳宾馆	Hongyang Hotel	3	2005.01	73	140	贵阳花溪区150号信箱	0851-3853306
金泉酒店	Jinquan Hotel	3	2007.01	91	172	贵阳花溪区花谷路6号	0851-3851484
贵阳方源酒店	Guiyang Fangyuan Hotel	3	2007.08	95	152	贵阳市小河区香江路6号	0851-8316655
贵阳机场宾馆	Guiyang JiChang Hotel	3	2007.11	168	315	贵阳市	0851-5498585
黔景宾馆	Qianjing Hotel	3	2007.12	117	246	贵阳市	0851-3990188
京瑞宾馆	Jingrui Hotel	3	2005.06	134	300	贵阳市北京路194号	0851-6891602
贵阳瑞金酒店	Guiyang Ruijin Hotel	3	2008.06	168	312	贵阳市瑞金南路62号	0851-5209999
贵州铁路通达饭店	Guizhou Tielu Tongda Hotel	3	2008.11	234	468	贵阳市遵义路86号	0851-8213888
贵阳皇嘉大酒店	Guiyang Huangjia Hotel	3	2009.09	50	77	贵阳市小河区黄河路608号	0851-3808131
贵阳益宏酒店有限公司	Guiyang Yihong Hotel Co., Ltd.	3	2009.12	99	157	贵阳市油榨街2号	0851-3818888
云岩浣溪假日大酒店	Yunyan Huanxi Holiday Hotel	3	2010.05	138	230	贵阳市浣沙路104号	0851-8598888
燕安大酒店	Yanan Hotel	3	1997.12	81	167	安顺市贵黄路5公里处	0853-3228988
安顺西秀山宾馆	Anshun Xixiushan Hotel	3	2002.04	92	153	安顺市南华路48号	0853-3223900
神奇福运大酒店	Shenqi Fuyun Hotel	3	2002.09	90	160	安顺市外环西南路3号	0853-3290000
黔中大厦	Qianzhong Hotel	3	2005.07	66	113	安顺市南华路68好	0853-3292019
白马湖山庄	Baimahu Hotel	3	2005.07	33	59	安顺市镇宁县白马哨	0853-6791111
安顺若飞宾馆	Anshun Ruofei Hotel	3	2001.04	41	73	安顺市南华路48号	0853-3225325
龙宫酒店	Longgong Hotel	3	2006.01	41	79	安顺市龙宫风景名胜区	0853-3661388
关岭黔岭宾馆	Guanling Qianling Hotel	3	2006.11	50	92	关岭县外环路128号	0853-7228888
安顺纽曼宾馆	Anshun Niuman Hotel	3	2008.03	36	70	安顺市	0853-3467777
龙宫水电宾馆	Anshun Longgong Shuidian Hotel	3	2009.11	31	60	安顺市龙宫风景名胜区	0853-3661166
廊桥华油酒店	Langqiao Huayou Hotel	3	2010.07	82	152	安顺市塔山西路15号	13308530111
平坝白云大酒店	Pingba Baiyun Hotel	3	2010.07	47	52	平坝县城关镇高新区	
遵义港澳大酒店	Zunyi Gangao Hotel	3	2005.11	81	148	遵义市澳门路8号	0852-8716655
遵义宾馆	Zunyi Hotel	3	2000.01	181	329	遵义市石龙路3号	0852-8224902
金城大酒店	Jincheng Hotel	3	2000.01	150	256	遵义市香港路中段	0852-8621666
遵义京腾丽湾酒店	Zunyi Jintengliwan Hotel	3	2006.11	140	252	遵义市北京路	0852-8649898
茅园宾馆	Maoyuan Hotel	3	2004.01	56	110	遵义仁怀市茅台镇	0852-2386290
习水绿洲酒店	Xishui Lvzhou Hotel	3	2006.11	83	150	遵义习水县经济开发区	0852-2732100
遵义县顺天酒店	Zunyi Shuntian Hotel	3	2007.09	44	80	遵义县南白镇万寿广场	0852-7232188
遵义市维多利亚大酒店	Zunyi Weiduoliya Hotel	3	2007.09	191	335	遵义市外环路	0852-8717818
广电酒店	Guangdian Hotel	3	2007.09	109	192	遵义市中华北路广电大厦	0852-8700888
仁怀市名酒宾馆	Renhuai Mingjiu Hotel	3	2007.09	60	100	仁怀市国酒大道	0852-3226999
嘉联宾馆	Jialian Hotel	3	2008.12	64	110	赤水市人民南路运管大厦	0852-2820222
鹏程大酒店	Pengcheng Hotel	3	2010.01	51	92	余庆县城内	0852-4625868
赤天化宾馆	Chitianhua Hotel	3	2010.01	95	170	赤水市	0852-2887081

18-12 续表2 continued

名 称	Name	星级 Level	评定日期 Date of Assess	客房数 Rooms	床位数 Beds	地 址 Address	电 话 Telephone
都匀港龙大酒店	Duyun Ganglong Hotel	3	2002.08	126	210	都匀市河滨路134号	0854-8222895
五月花景山酒店	Wuyuehua Jingshan Hotel	3	2005.01	89	121	都匀市剑江中路112号	0854-8756999
都匀神奇星岛酒店	Duyun Shenqi Xingdao Hotel	3	2006.11	89	144	都匀市建江北路152号	0854-8752888
西苑假日酒店	XiYuan Holiday Hotel	3	2007.09	54	96	都匀市开发区	0854-8758888
锦绣园	Jingxiu Hotel	3	2005.09	48	101	龙里县城郊	0854-5669508
顺庆大酒店	Shunqing Hotel	3	2005.03	98	218	荔波樟江北街	0854-3610388
荔波吉妮丽吉大酒店	Libo Jiniliji Hotel	3	2006.11	86	170	荔波县教师新村	0854-3619666
神泉大酒店	Shenquan Hotel	3	2005.03	46	96	罗甸县政府路	0854-7620758
都匀市桥城宾馆	Duyun Qiaocheng Hotel	3	2007.09	92	166	都匀市文明路50号	0854-8222189
独山县南方大酒店	Dushan Nanfang Hotel	3	2007.09	61	91	独山县四通路十八号	0854-3238525
荔波县金谷宾馆	Libo Jingu Hotel	3	2007.09	53	120	荔波县樟江北路	0854-3613888
纪龙大酒店	JiLong Hotel	3	2005.09	44	80	龙里县	0854-5620333
贵定县环岛大酒店	Guiding Huandao Hotel	3	2009.01	38	78	贵定县城关镇八一村	0854-5221000
瓮安县金福大酒店	Wen'an Jinfu Hotel	3	2009.03	49	83	瓮安县文峰中路	0854-2635100
荔波县大鹏商务酒店	Libo Dapeng Bussiness Hotel	3	2008.03	95	178	荔波县漳江中路12号	0854-3615499
平塘县西苑俊华酒店	Pingtang Xiyuan Junhua Hotel	3	2008.03	37	55	平塘县西苑俊华酒店	0854-7222588
独山县翠泉宾馆	Dushan Cuiquan Hotel	3	2009.04	62	116	独山县	0854-3239018
凯里凯莱酒店	Kaili Kevin Hotel	3	2006.12	96	182	凯里市韶山南路21号	0855-8277888
国泰大酒店	Guotai Hotel	3	2004.07	73	135	凯里市北京东路6号	0855-8269888
凯里鸿祺宾馆	Kaili Hongqi Hotel	3	2006.08	84	140	凯里市韶山南路3号	0855-8275555
黎平大酒店	Liping Hotel	3	2006.11	80	148	黎平德风镇富民北路	0855-6210666
贵州清酒醉翁宾馆	Guizhou Qingjiu Zuiweng Hotel	3	2004.05	46	92	镇远县	0855-5823238
施秉县三丰迎宾馆	Shibing Sanfeng Hotel	3	2004.05	89	190	施秉县平宁桥	0855-4227188
凯铁大酒店	kaitie Hotel	3	2008.09	63	121	凯里市清江路	0855-3811999
凯里大酒店	Kaili Hotel	3	2008.09	156	275	凯里市韶山北路	0855-8277778
忠德园假日酒店	Zhongdeyuan Holiday Hotel	3	2008.09	70	160	凯里市环城东路	0855-8538888
港赛大酒店	Gangsai Hotel	3	2008.09	63	114	黎平县城内	0855-6230888
久格里吉温泉度假酒店	Jiugeliji Wenquan Hotel	3	2008.09	60	115	剑河县温泉风景区内	0855-5158288
清源酒店	Qingyuan Hotel	3	2008.12	30	56	下司镇皮划艇激流回旋训练基地	0855-2685666
营盘坡民族宾馆	Yingpanpo Minzu Hotel	3	2009.07	92	163	凯里市	0855-3837779
凯里市天华宾馆	Kaili Tianhua Hotel	3	2009.07	82	153	凯里市	0855-8276411
镇远县铁溪度假酒店	Zhenyuan Tiexi Holiday Hotel	3	2009.07	33	57	镇远县	0855-5721888
剑河县馨泉山庄	Jianhe Xinquan Hotel	3	2009.11	38	74	剑河县	0855-5158168
凯里宾馆	Kaili Hotel	3	2010.04	57	130	凯里市	0855-8066100
从江县奥悦酒店	Congjiang Aoyue Hotel	3	2009.11	33	66	从江县	0855-6411808
金正酒店	Jinzheng Hotel	3	2010.06	67	107	凯里市经济开发区	0855-8558988
麻江县怡景湾酒店	Majiang Yijing Hotel	3	2010.08	34	48	麻江县下司镇	0855-2684777
城城大厦	Chengcheng Hotel	3	2005.07	68	128	兴义市神奇路159号	0859-3112222
龙宇大酒店	Longyu Hotel	3	2007.11	56	112	兴义市神奇西路26号	0859-3126888
盘江宾馆	Panjiang Hotel	3	2005.07	123	231	兴义市盘江西路4号	0859-3223456
兴义神禧大酒店	Shenxi Hotel	3	2008.05	80	158	兴义市坪东路	0859-3818188
贞丰县贞丰宾馆	Zhenfeng Hotel	3	2009.09	120	214	贞丰县金丰大道29号	0859-6777777
贞丰县怡景酒店	Zhenfeng Yijing Hotel	3	2009.09	36	60	贞丰县	0859-6613777
兴义市三生酒店	Xingyi Sansheng Hotel	3	2009.09	111	200	兴义市瑞金北路中段	0859-3244888
六盘水金三角大酒店	LiuPanshui Jinsanjiao Hotel	3	2006.12	44	79	六盘水市明湖路3号	0858-8233888
雨田酒店	Yutian Hotel	3	2005.07	75	126	六盘水钟山西路48号	0858-8261888
夜郎酒肆大酒店	Yelang Jiusi Hotel	3	2009.03	66	117	六盘水市钟山区其林路	0858-8204096
铜仁天源大酒店	Tongren Tianyuan Hotel	3	2005.03	48	91	铜仁市东太大道	0856-5930555
源丰商务酒店	Yuanfeng Commerce Hotel	3	2005.07	62	99	铜仁市锦江南路1号	0856-5222222

18-12 续表3 continued

名 称	Name	星级 Level	评定日期 Date of Assess	客房数 Rooms	床位数 Beds	地 址 Address	电 话 Telephone
思南远航大酒店	Sinan Yuanhang Hotel	3	2009.06	62	110	思南县城北街29号	0856-7220777
江口县索菲特大酒店	Jiangkou Suofeite Hotel	3	2009.12	57	112	江口县三星西路17号	0856-6622288
德江县金平大酒店	Dejiang Jinpin Hotel	3	2009.12	44	83	德江县清龙镇	0856-8527555
铜仁市金顶酒店	Tongren Jinding Hotel	3	2009.12	41	73	铜仁市清水大道80号	0856-5211168
毕节天工大酒店	Bijie Tiangong Hotel	3	1999.06	66	150	毕节市洪山路60号	0857-2136188
威宁县黑颈鹤大酒店	Weining Heijinghe Hotel	3	2008.07	78	162	威宁建设东路79号	0857-6224426
金沙县黄金大酒店	Jinsha Huangjin Hotel	3	2008.07	95	179	金沙县长安街138号	0857-7258888
洪南大酒店	Hongnan Hotel	3	2008.09	81	117	毕节市迎宾大道	0857-8292888
赫章夜郎大酒店	Hezhang Yelang Hotel	3	2008.12	145	255	赫章县城南路	0857-3238998
煌都帝豪酒店	Huangdu Dihao Hotel	3	2008.09	78	120	黔西县城内	0857-4888888
铜仁市梵天索菲特酒店	Tongren Fantian Suofeite Hotel	3	2010.12	57	97	铜仁锦江大道8号	0856-5218888
沿河沙洲大酒店	Yanhe Shazhou Hotel	3	2010.11	55	87	铜仁市沿河县沙坨电站	0856-6998666
玉屏宾馆	Yuping Hotel	3	2010.12	66	114	玉屏县平溪镇人民路333号	0856-3227888
三江宏晟度假酒店	Sanjianghongsheng Holiday Hote	3	2010.08	30	40	福泉市金山办事处双桥村金鸡山	0854-2210999
怡景苑宾馆	Yijingyuan Hotel	3	2010.08	54	108	荔波县漳江北街42号	0854-3618300
华通大酒店	Huatong Hotel	3	2010.11	45	70	独山县五星花园二期	0854-3222399
夜郎大酒店	Yelang Hotel	3	2010.12	70	126	惠水县和平镇建设路	0854-6234567
沿河金红大酒店	Yanhe Jinhong Hotel	3	2010.12	57	130	铜仁市沿河县城南路	0856-8228055
华侨大酒店	Huaqiao Hotel	3	2010.11	70	110	三穗城关	0855-3855555
柏悦酒店	Boyue Hotel	3	2010.11	56	101	凯里市	0855-8270000
万豪酒店	Wanhao Hotel	3	2010.11	72	128	凯里市	0855-8603999
湄潭大酒店	Meitan Hotel	3	2010.12	82	136	湄潭县兴湄北路35号	0852-4366595
花溪玉龙宾馆	Huaxiyulong Hotel	3	2011.03	35	70	花溪区大吉路1号	0851-3863865
聚鑫酒店	Juxin Hotel	3	2011.04	114	189	贵阳市环城北路228号	0851-6851999
黔西化屋度假酒店	Qianxi Huawu Holiday Hotel	3	2011.08	36	66	黔西县新仁乡化屋村	0857-4634166
纳雍华熙酒店	Nayong Huaxi Hotel	3	2010.01	114	173	纳雍县城南大道	0857-3685777
龙都大酒店	Longdu Hotel	3	2011.06	139	216	铜仁市清水大道128号	0856-4133333
贵武花园大酒店	Guiwu Garden Hotel	3	2011.09	91	151	贵阳市金阳新区云潭南路	0851-5625678
大正酒店	Dazheng Hotel	3	2011.09	60	126	贵阳市南明区翠微巷60号	0851-5515666
桂花园度假酒店	Guihuayuan Holiday Hotel	3	2011.09	80	150	贵州省都匀市大河村村卫生院对面	0854-8190559
南江度假酒店	Nanjiang Holiday Hotel	3	2011.07	146	257	开阳南江大峡谷景区内	0851-7524089
金海大酒店	Jinhai Hotel	3	2011.09	67	120	毕节市洪南路	0857-8615555
草海大酒店	Caohai Hotel	3	2011.09	108	188	威宁威双大道	0857-7115388
红楼酒店	Honglou Hotel	3	2004.06	48	90	大方县奢香大道南段	0857-5233712
和泰大酒店	Hetai Hotel	3	2010.06	101	175	大方县城利民路中段	0857-5250998
红枫湖旅游度假村	Hongfeng lake Tourist Resort	3	2011.07	126	207	清镇市望城坡	0851-8575042
清镇皇朝大酒店	Qingzhen Dynasty Hotel	3	2011.07	90	144	清镇市云岭东路	0851-2581888
金竹大酒店	Jinzhu Hotel	3	2011.12	100	189	赤水市文化办财神涂	0852-2853555
枫叶山庄	Fengye Hill	2	2000.01	66	129	贵阳市红枫发电总厂内	0851-2554168
贵州铝厂宾馆	Guizhou Aluminum Plant Hotel	2	2004.06	92	152	贵阳市白云区刚玉街	0851-4896111
天洋楼大酒店	Tianyanglou Hotel	2	2004.09	42	100	贵阳市民权路5号	0851-5832088
贵州民族宾馆	Guizhou Minzu Hotel	2	2004.12	86	170	贵阳市市北路68号	0851-8633666
开阳金都宾馆	Kaiyang Jindu Hotel	2	2004.01	41	87	贵阳市开阳县环城北路	0851-5832088
金黔宾馆	Jinqian Hotel	2	2005.09	62	120	贵阳市新华路106号	0851-5500315
仁达饭店	Renda Hotel	2	2004.09	112	300	贵阳市中华北路319号	0851-6825301
开阳尚怡宾馆	Kaiyang Shangyi Hotel	2	2009.04	22	41	开阳	
开阳江南宾馆	Kaiyang Jiangnan Hotel	2	2010.05	35	65	开阳县城关镇环城北路	
安顺凤凰山大酒店	Anshun Fenghuangshan Hotel	2	1999.12	41	73	安顺市塔山东路58号	0853-3343413
腾达酒店	Tengda Hotel	2	2005.06	27	54	安顺市	0853-7228886

18-12 续表4 continued

名 称	Name	星级 Level	评定日期 Date of Assess	客房数 Rooms	床位数 Beds	地 址 Address	电 话 Telephone
安顺情源宾馆	Anshun Qingyuan Hotel	2	1994.11	86	151	安顺普定县城内	0853-8221999
长城宾馆	Great Wall Hotel	2	2009.07	29	48	安顺平坝县武装部	0853-4227333
钟山宾馆	Zhongshan Hotel	2	1994.11	138	330	六盘水钟山中路52号	0858-8223285
六枝工矿迎宾馆	Liuzhi Gongkuang Hotel	2	2002.05	57	114	六枝特区团结路13号	0858-5713548
凯豪大酒店	Kaihao Hotel	2	2007.01	40	72	六枝特区交通西路	0858-5319999
六枝宾馆	Liuzhi Hotel	2	2005.01	65	160	六枝平寨镇友谊路	0858-5322660
行署会议中心	Xingshu Huiyi Hotel	2	2005.06	40	76	铜仁市花果山路100号	0856-4127888
东山酒店	Dongshan Hotel	2	2006.01	35	63	铜仁市铜江大道12号	0856-5236888
印江腾龙大酒店	Yinjiang Tenglong Hotel	2	2003.08	55	100	印江县城西环开发区	0856-6228888
石阡宾馆	Shiqian Hotel	2	2005.06	61	115	石阡县汤山镇	0856-7652777
石阡临江宾馆	Shiqian Linjiang Hotel	2	2005.09	41	82	石阡县汤山镇河西街	0856-8957399
沿河天龙大酒店	Yanhe Tianlong Hotel	2	2005.09	96	350	沿河县城南路23号	0856-8228054
思南县明星宾馆	Sinan Mingxing Hotel	2	2009.12	26	54	思南县民政局内	0856-7225085
玉屏贵阳大酒店	Yuping Guiyang Hotel	2	2010.08	30	60	玉屏火车站附近	0856-3228886
洪山宾馆	Hongshan Hotel	2	2004.08	208	388	毕节市洪山路1号	0857-8251829
黔西雍和酒店	Qianxi Yonghe Hotel	2	2008.01	38	71	黔西县城内	0857-4220888
金辉酒店	Jinhui Hotel	2	2006.07	60	102	金沙县城内	0857-7251999
毕节迎宾馆	Bijie Yingbin Hotel	2	2009.07	49	90	毕节市环东路1号	0857-8312222
大方东风宾馆	Dafang Dongfeng Hotel	2	2009.07	55	107	大方县西大街	0857-5252222
织金平远酒店	ZhiJin Pingyuan Hotel	2	2009.07	43	83	织金县沿河路	0857-7636999
威宁明珠酒店	Weining Mingzhu Hotel	2	2009.07	27	51	威宁县开发区	0857-6233088
威宁穗苑宾馆	Weining Suiyuan Hotel	2	2009.07	30	66	威宁县星光路	0857-6282222
赫章维尔乐宾馆	Hezhang Wei'erle Hotel	2	2009.07	20	33	赫章县南环路	0857-3239898
瑞海酒店	Ruihai Hotel	2	2001.12	74	108	遵义市外环路沙坝	0852-8866333
名族酒店	Mingzu Hotel	2	2004.06	46	86	遵义市红花岗武装部	0852-8433888
蓝天宾馆	Lantian Hotel	2	2005.12	138	248	遵义市北京路99号	0852-8622916
通达酒店	Tongda Hotel	2	2001.06	148	276	遵义市北京路134号	0852-8822925
正华大酒店	Zhenghua Hotel	2	2002.05	46	105	桐梓县娄山关镇	0852-6657869
娄山宾馆	Loushan Hotel	2	2004.09	30	85	桐梓县城河滨南路	0852-6652868
利永宾馆	Liyong Hotel	2	2004.05	83	136	仁怀市国酒中路	0852-2250882
聚贤楼宾馆	Juxianlou Hotel	2	2005.12	33	50	绥阳县博雅苑陈列馆内	0852-6233848
娄山关生态乐园酒店	Loushanguan Shengtaileyuan Hotel	2	2009.01	27	49	桐梓县娄山关镇娄山村	0852-6825333
彩阳酒店	Caiyang Hotel	2	2008.12	35	49	桐梓县城	0852-3208788
金马大酒店	Jinma Hotel	2	2008.12	45	90	桐梓县河滨大道南大门	0852-6661118
博雅宾馆	Boya Hotel	2	2008.12	40	76	绥阳县北大街	0852-6223855
香山宾馆	Xiangshan Hotel	2	2008.12	67	129	遵义市红花岗区大兴路狮子桥头	0852-8234444
赤水大酒店	Chishui Hotel	2	2008.12	36	74	赤水市西内环路106号	0852-2821334
云门囤宾馆	Yunmentun Hotel	2	2009.01	38	71	遵义县三渡镇花桥村	0852-6581555
枫香温泉	Fengxiang Spa Hotel	2	2009.01	38	82	遵义县枫香镇	0852-7572608
凤岗宾馆	Fenggang Hotel	2	2009.01	57	105	凤岗县县府路	0852-5224567
恒源酒店	Hengyuan Hotel	2	2009.01	37	66	凤岗县政通路	0852-5222768
明星宾馆	Mingxing Hotel	2	2009.01	24	43	凤岗县商贸街	0852-5220088
安龙县麗月鸿钰酒店	Anlong Liyuehongyu Hotel	2	2010.01	36	63	安龙县	0859-5216111
凯里市西湖大酒店	Kaili West lake Hotel	2	2002.12	44	83	凯里市北京西路74号	0855-3826888
国穗大酒店	Guosui Hotel	2	2003.01	28	52	凯里市国税务局大院内	0855-8276888
雷山县苗都酒店	Leishan Hotel	2	2007.09	28	50	雷山县雷公山大道	0855-3336588
岑巩县凯华大酒店	Cengong Kaihua Hotel	2	2007.01	65	128	岑巩县	0855-3895988
从江宾馆	Congjiang Hotel	2	2008.12	34	67	从江县	0855-6418669
仁和大酒店	Renhe Hotel	2	2008.12	29	43	从江县	0855-6412900

18-12 续表5 continued

名 称	Name	星级 Level	评定日期 Date of Assess	客房数 Rooms	床位数 Beds	地 址 Address	电 话 Telephone
雷山县圣城嘉源酒店	Leishan Shengchengjiayuan Hotel	2	2008.12	27	51	雷山县	0855-3336718
麻江县下司第一楼	Majiang Xiasi NO.1 Building	2	2008.12	32	65	麻江县	0855-2684000
金鼎龙大酒店	Jindinglong Hotel	2	2009.04	22	41	雷山县城关镇	0855-5158168
剑河温泉剑泉山庄	Jianhewenquan Jianquan Hotel	2	2008.05	33	61	剑河县	0855-5158088
马家岩大酒店	Majiayan Hotel	2	2010.05	36	70	黄平县	0855-2431199
凯里香山大酒店	Kaili Xiangshan Hotel	2	2010.07	40	68	凯里市北京西路39号	0855-8601099
西苑酒店	Xiyuan Hotel	2	2006.04	50	104	都匀市剑江中路	0854-8682132
都匀丽都酒店	Dunyun Lidu Hotel	2	2005.09	63	97	都匀州地税局培训中心	0854-8318869
樟江大厦	Zhangjiang Hotel	2	2003.04	34	66	荔波县城内	0854-3618888
荔波宾馆	Libo Hotel	2	2003.04	46	93	荔波县政府大院内	0854-3612169
鲁黔宾馆	Luqian Hotel	2	2003.04	20	52	荔波县樟江中路	0854-3617098
政协宾馆	Zhengxie Hotel	2	2003.04	24	48	荔波县城内	0854-3615573
锦源宾馆	Jinyuan Hotel	2	2004.01	21	47	荔波县广场东路	0854-3618818
水上人间	Shuishang Renjian Hotel	2	2003.12	15	27	荔波县内	0854-8939979
松源宾馆	Songyuan Hotel	2	2003.12	31	56	荔波县内	0854-8967651
东方宾馆	Dongfang Hotel	2	2003.04	20	40	荔波县内	0854-3618968
青旅大酒店	Qinglv Hotel	2	2006.05	35	70	荔波县广场东路	0854-3613158
再富酒店	Zaifu Hotel	2	2006.05	38	76	荔波县城樟江北街	0854-3618118
晟圆酒店	Shengyuan Hotel	2	2006.05	20	40	荔波县广场东路	0854-8971162
蓝天宾馆	Lantian Hotel	2	2003.04	32	63	荔波县城	0854-3619831
荔伊宾馆	Liyi Hotel	2	2006.05	27	52	荔波县城樟江北街	0854-8808668
荔波南江宾馆	Libo Nanjiang Hotel	2	2006.09	21	48	荔波	13985787238
荔波前锦宾馆	Libo Qianjing Hotel	2	2006.09	45	57	荔波	13595418295
世纪鑫酒店	Shijixin Hotel	2	2003.04	22	56	独山县环城东路	0854-3238688
怡心宾馆	Yixin Hotel	2	2005.09	15	24	三都三启镇县府路	0854-3927818
黄金大酒店	Huangjin Hotel	2	2006.01	30	50	三都县三合镇振兴路	0854-3927778
望月宾馆	Wangyue Hotel	2	2006.04	48	87	罗甸县委	0854-7611554
沙梨园宾馆	Shaliyuan Hotel	2	2007.05	18	48	荔波县城	0854-3618258
腾龙宾馆	Tenglong Hotel	2	2006.09	27	46	平塘县	0854-7222888
银河大酒店	Yinhe Hotel	2	2008.12	23	41	平塘县	0854-7230988
金胜宾馆	Jinsheng Hotel	2	2008.12	25	44	平塘县	0854-7223688
富源宾馆	Fuyuan Hotel	2	2008.12	20	44	荔波县	0854-3619298
金容宾馆	Jinrong Hotel	2	2008.12	30	60	荔波县	0854-3613818
祥和宾馆	Xianghe Hotel	2	2008.12	30	62	荔波县	0854-3616177
金林宾馆	Jinlin Hotel	2	2008.12	30	57	荔波县	0854-3619780
玉屏镇信合宾馆	Yupinzhen Xinhe Hotel	2	2008.12	36	69	荔波县	0854-3615828
东篱宾馆	Dongli Hotel	2	2008.12	30	60	荔波县	0854-3619758
名豪大酒店	Minghao Hotel	2	2008.12	41	69	瓮安县	0854-2625555
东利酒店	Dongli Hotel	2	2008.12	30	50	瓮安县	0854-2621889
水电宾馆	Shuidian Hotel	2	2008.12	26	47	瓮安县	0854-2624584
杜鹃苑宾馆	Dujuanyuan Hotel	2	2008.12	48	87	长顺县	0854-6936222
凤凰宾馆	Fenghuang Hotel	2	2008.12	40	90	三都县	0854-3927898
都柳江宾馆	Duliujiang Hotel	2	2008.12	38	72	三都县	0854-3928888
三林时尚酒店	Sanlinshishang Hotel	2	2008.12	52	88	都匀市	0854-8239828
惠水县百联商务酒店	Huishui Bailian Bussiness Hotel	2	2009.12	32	58	惠水县涟江中路中段	0854-6283989
荔波县溪桥宾馆	Libo Xiqiao Hotel	2	2009.12	55	103	荔波县樟江东路17号	0854-3618666
荔波县齐鲁宾馆	Libo Qilu Hotel	2	2009.12	26	51	荔波县玉屏镇文明路24号	0854-3617118
贵储酒店	Guichu Hotel	2	2010.06	35	50	贵定县	0854-5236666
贵定飞龙大酒店	Guiding Feilong Hotel	2	2010.06	28	54	贵定县	0854-5233298

18-12 续表6 continued

名 称	Name	星级 Level	评定日期 Date of Assess	客房数 Rooms	床位数 Beds	地 址 Address	电 话 Telephone
三都地中海宾馆	Sandu Dizhonghai Hotel	2	2010.07	22	35	三都县城中心	0854-3028777
三都润丰宾馆	Sandu Runfeng Hotel	2	2010.07	23	27	三都县三合镇团结路	0854-3929123
南昆宾馆	Nankun Hotel	2	2004.11	44	69	兴义市顶效开发区	0859-2282188
兴义市心意酒店	Xingyi xinyi Hotel	2	2007.05	61	118	兴义市	0859-3811658
盘江紫薇园宾馆	Panjiang Hotel	2	2006.09	42	87	安龙县	0859-5211888
安龙招提宾馆	Anlong Zhaoti Hotel	2	2007.02	20	40	安龙县	0859-5210721
黔西南州隆泰酒店	Qianxinan Longtai Hotel	2	2007.07	27	53	兴义市	0859-3290555
贞丰县金舟宾馆	Zhenfeng Jinzhou Hotel	2	2009.09	30	56	贞丰县	0859-6818777
沿河壹加壹假日酒店	Yanhe Yijiayi Holiday Hotel	2	2010.12	39	59	沿河县开发区团结大道东段	0856-8230000
祥华酒店	Xianghua Hotel	2	2010.08	26	55	龙里县龙山镇青龙路	0854-5636088
馨豪酒店	Xinhao Hotel	2	2010.08	40	78	龙里县龙山镇兴龙路	0854-5635789
育才宾馆	Yucai Hotel	2	2010.11	32	64	荔波县建设西路41号	0854-3619852
虹泰宾馆	Hongtai Hotel	2	2010.09	15	27	平塘县平湖镇环城路	0854-7225888
聚丰园宾馆	Jufengyuan Hotel	2	2010.09	20	30	平塘县新区大道	0854-7230568
银都宾馆	Yindu Hotel	2	2010.11	38	63	贵定县红旗大道1号	0854-5231878
纳雍良源大酒店	Nayong Liangyuan Hotel	2	2009.12	40	100	纳雍县农贸街1号(法院旁)	0857-3536116
金沙宾馆	Jinsha Hotel	2	2005.01	32	60	长安路237号	0857-7252222
金沙富豪大酒店	Jinsha Fuhao Hotel	2	2010.08	17	27	新武装部旁	0857-7235555
万乐商务酒店	Wanle Hotel	2	2011.11	65	87	贵阳市白云区同心路1号	0851-6617999
一家快捷酒店	Yijia Inn	2	2011.11	43	48	贵阳市白云区白云南路402号	0851-4485308
息烽县人民政府招待所	Xifeng Government Hotel	2	2011.11	28	54	息烽县永靖镇县府路50号	0851-7721123
君安宾馆	Junan Hotel	2	2011.10	92	148	贵阳黔灵西路62号	0851-6816999
七天连锁酒店花溪行政中心店	7 days Inn Huaxi administrative center shop	2	2011.12	93	99	贵阳市花溪区清溪路493号	0851-8516677
新怡龙湾酒店	Xinyilongwan Hotel	2	2011.11	21	42	清镇市云岭西路	0851-2600678
平达快捷酒店	Pingda Hotel	2	2011.11	38	47	开阳县城关镇环城北路68号	0851-7228369
温馨宾馆	Wenxin Hotel	2	2011.11	20	35	开阳县城关镇三中小区	0851-7250839
南江农庄	Nanjiang Hotel	2	2011.12	21	30	开阳县南江乡杉木冲	13595005415
开阳舜熙酒店	Kaiyang Shunxi Hotel	2	2011.12	21	32	开阳县城关镇吉祥路	0851-7315399
鸿雁宾馆	Hongyan Hotel	1	2004.06	39	97	黔西县东路	0857-4225666
鑫源大酒店	Xinyuan Hotel	1	2005.09	14	26	三都县环城北路	0854-3921729
亲情宾馆	Qinqing Hotel	1	2006.09	19	34	平塘县	13985085075
玖玖宾馆	Jiujiu Hotel	1	2006.09	15	34	平塘县	13385185973
紫金大酒店	Zijin Hotel	1	2006.09	29	51	平塘县	13885455082
思南县电力宾馆	Sinan Dianli Hotel	1	2003.07	25	53	思南县中山街55号	0856-7229948
从江文广宾馆	Congjiang Wenguang Hotel	1	2007.03	28	47	从江县	0855-6418316
从江观音阁山庄	Congjiang Guanyinge Hotel	1	2007.03	30	52	从江县	0855-6418488
黄平谦和大酒店	Huangping Qianhe Hotel	1	2006.12	27	54	黄平	0855-2436366
黄平丰丰宾馆	Huangping Fengfeng Hotel	1	2006.12	43	86	黄平	0855-2438298
岑巩兴岑大酒店	Cengong Xingcen Hotel	1	2007.09	15	25	岑巩县	0855-3575333
岑巩万向宾馆	Cengong Wanxiang Hotel	1	2007.09	17	30	岑巩县	0855-3573086
瑞权宾馆	Ruiquan Hotel	1	2010.06	70	110	黔西南州	0859-3815588
青松宾馆	Qingsong Hotel	1	2010.12	78	143	罗甸县	0854-7620518
天竹名人酒店	Tianzhumingren Hotel	1	2011.10	32	108	贵阳市乌当区航天大道1号	0851-6402020
港湾快捷酒店	Gangwan Hotel	1	2011.08	42	65	贵阳市白云区建设路4号	0851-4611112
赛菲尔商务宾馆	Saifeier Hotel	1	2011.11	38	45	贵阳市白云区金塘北街四合院	0851-4480899
博纳快捷酒店	Bona Hotel	1	2011.11	43	62	贵阳市白云区大山洞尖山路	0851-5619999

主要统计指标解释

住宿业 指有偿为顾客提供临时住宿的服务活动。不包括：提供长期住宿场所的活动（如出租房屋、公寓等），列入7210（房地产开发经营）。

餐饮业 指在一定场所，对食物进行现场烹饪、调制，并出售给顾客主要供现场消费的服务活动。

营业额 指住宿和餐饮业法人企业（单位）在经营活动中因提供服务或销售商品等取得的收入。包括：客房收入、餐费收入、商品销售额和其他收入。其中，客房收入指住宿和餐饮业法人企业（单位）在经营活动中因提供住宿服务取得的收入。餐费收入指住宿和餐饮业法人企业（单位）因为顾客提供就餐服务取得的收入，包括经烹饪、调制加工后出售的各种食品，如主食、炒菜、凉拌菜等的收入。

旅游者人数

(1) 入境旅游人数：指报告期内来我国观光、度假、探亲访友、就医疗养、购物、参加会议或从事经济、文化、体育、宗教活动的外国人、港澳台同胞等入境游客。统计时，外国人、港澳台同胞每入境一次统计1人次。

(2) 国内旅游人数：指在报告期内在中国（大陆）观光游览、度假、探亲访友、就医疗养、购物、参加会议或从事经济、文化、体育、宗教活动的中国（大陆）居民人数，其出游的目的不是通过所从事的活动谋取报酬。统计时，国内游客按每出游一次统计1人次。

国际旅游（外汇）收入 指入境游客在中国（大陆）境内旅行、游览过程中用于交通、参观游览、住宿、餐饮、购物、娱乐等全部花费。

国际旅行社 指经营对外招徕并接待外国人、华侨、港澳同胞和台湾同胞来中国、归国或回内地旅游业务的旅行社。

国内旅行社 指负责经营招徕、组团、接待国内旅客的旅游业务，以及不对外招徕，负责经营接待国际旅行社或其它涉外部门组织的外国人、华侨、港澳同胞和台湾同胞来中国、归国或回内地的旅游业务的旅行社。

国内旅游收入 又称旅游总花费指国内游客在国内旅行、游览过程中用于交通、参观游览、住宿、餐饮、购物、娱乐等全部花费。

星级饭店 指设备、设施、服务符合《旅游饭店星级的划分与评定》（GB/T14308-2003），通过相关旅游管理部门评定，并取得星级饭店称号的饭店（含预备星级饭店）。

Explanatory Notes on Main Statistical Indicators

Hotel Services refer to the activities of enterprises providing paid services of lodging to the customer, excluding the activities of providing long period of services of lodging (such as leased house and apartments), which are shown in 7210 (Development and operation of real estate).

Catering Services refer to the activities of enterprises prvideing on-the-spot services of selling food cooked and prepared to the customer in certain sites

Business Revenue refers to revenue received from providing services or selling commodities by enterprises and establishments engaged in hotels and catering services, including income from hotels, from catering services, from selling of commodities and from other services. Income from hotels refers to income of enterprises and establishments engaged in hotels and catering services by providing lodging services. Income from catering services refers to income of enterprises and establishments engaged in hotels and catering services by providing catering services, including selling of cooked or prepared foods, such as staple food, cooked dishes, or cold dishes.

Number of Tourists:

(1) Visitor arrivals refer to the number of foreigners, Chinese compatriots from Hong Kong, Macao and Taiwan Chinese (mainland) who come to China (mainland) for sight-seeing, vacation, visiting relatives, medical treatment, shopping, attending conference, or to engage in economic, cultural, sports and religious activities. In compiling statistics, each time of entering China is counted as one person-time.

(2) Number of domestic tourists refers to the number of Chinese (mainland) residents who travel within China (mainland) for sight-seeing, vacation, visiting relatives, medical treatment, shopping, attending conference, or to engage in economic, cultural, sports and religious activities. In compiling statistics, each time of travelling is counted as one person-time.

Foreign Exchange Earnings from International Tourism refer to the total expenditure of foreigners, overseas Chinese, Chinese compatriots from Hong Kong, Macao and Taiwan during their stay in the mainland of China on transportation,sighting, accommodation, food, shopping and entertainment.

International Travel Agencies refer to travel agencies engaged in the promotion, solicitation, organization and reception of tours to the mainland of China by foreigners, overseas Chinese, Chinese compatriots from Hong Kong, Macao and Taiwan.

Domestic Travel Agencies refer to travel agencies engaged in the promotion, solicitation, organization and reception of domestic tourists, and in the reception of foreigners, overseas Chinese, Chinese compatriots from Hong Kong, Macao and Taiwan organized by international travel agencies or other departments concerned, without their own promotion and solicitation programmes.

Income from Domestic Tourism refers to expenditure of domestic tourists on transportation, sighting, accommodation, food, shopping and entertainment while they travel.

Star-rated Hotels refer to hotels rated with stars as assessed by the relevant tourism authorities according to GB/T14308-2003 standard with reference to their infrastructure, facilities and service levels.

中国人民银行贵阳中心支行

The People Bank of China Guiyang Centre Branch

9月28日，人民银行贵阳中心支行与贵阳市政府联合举办“贵阳市科技金融推进会暨科技企业信用体系建设”签约仪式

September 28, the People Bank of China Guiyang Centre Branch and the Guiyang Municipal Government jointly organized the signing ceremony "the Guiyang City, Technology and Finance advanced will and Technology enterprise credit system construction"

2011年2月12日，人民银行贵阳中心支行召开全行职工大会

February 12, 2011, the People Bank of China Guiyang Centre Branch held a full line TUC

2011年，中国人民银行贵阳中心支行紧密结合贵州省经济金融运行实际和省委、省政府“两加一推”发展主基调，认真履行中央银行分支机构职责，各项工作取得明显成效。

一是认真贯彻落实金融宏观调控政策，加强货币政策工具管理和运用，进一步优化信贷结构，加大对重大项目和战略性新兴产业的信贷支持，完善金融支持社会薄弱环节和“三农”发展工作机制，为地方经济平稳较快发展提供了有力支持。

二是进一步加强农村信用社专项票据兑付后续监测考核，促进了农村信用社持续健康发展。

三是着力加强外汇管理与服务创新，强化跨境资金流动监测与监管，促进贸易投资便利化，维护外汇市场秩序和涉外经济金融安全，支持我省涉外经济稳健发展。

四是进一步提升金融服务和管理水平。

In 2011, the People Bank of China Guiyang Centre Branch is in the close connection with the Guizhou Province Economic and Financial practical and the provincial party committee and provincial government "two-plus one push" the development of the main tone, earnestly fulfill the responsibilities of the central bank branches, all work achieved remarkable results.

First, earnestly implement the financial macro-control policies, strengthen the management and use of monetary policy tools, to further optimize the credit structure, increase credit support for major projects and strategic emerging industries, and improve financial support for social weaknesses and "three rurals" development mechanisms, provide a strong support for the stable and rapid development of the local economy.

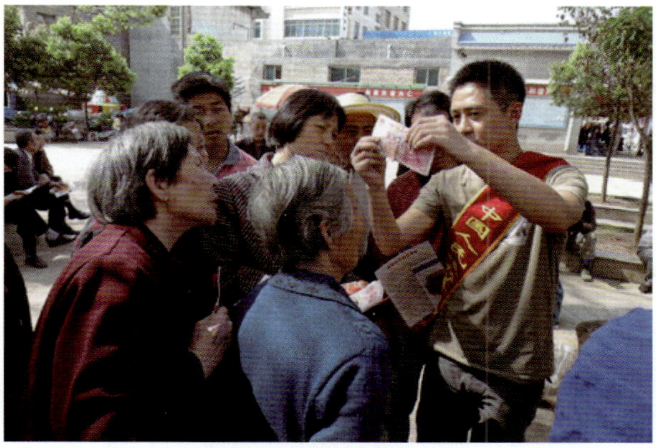

4月26日，人民银行贵阳中心支行深入黔西南州兴仁县开展“金融知识进社区”活动

April 26, People Bank of Guiyang Centre Branch in-depth Qianxinan Xingren to carry out the activities of "financial knowledge into the community"

Second, is to further strengthen the rural credit cooperatives, special bill payment follow-up monitoring assessment, and promote sustained and healthy development of rural credit cooperatives.

Third, is to focus on strengthening foreign exchange management and service innovation, and strengthen monitoring and supervision of cross-border capital flows, and promote trade and investment facilitation, maintaining the order of the foreign exchange market and foreign-related economic and financial security, and support the stability of the foreign-related economic development in our province.

Fourth, is to further improve financial services and management level.

中国银行贵州省分行多措并举
合力推进业务持续发展

The Bank of China Guizhou Province Branch take many measures

Work together to promote sustainable business development

中共贵阳市委常委、贵阳市人民政府副市长周道许一行访问贵州省分行，就我省金融业发展与该行领导进行座谈

CPC Guiyang Municipal Committee, Guiyang Municipal People's Government Vice Mayor Zhou Daoxu and his entourage visit Guizhou Province Branch, held a discussion with the bank leadership on the financial industry in our province

中国银行贵州省分行热烈庆祝中国银行成立100周年文艺汇演，蔡虎行长致词

The Bank of China Guizhou Province Branch to celebrate the Bank of China, the 100th anniversary of the variety show, Cai Hu President had speech

2011年，中国银行贵州省分行认真落实“调结构、扩规模、防风险、上水平”和“创新发展、转型发展、跨境发展”的工作方针，解放思想、正视困难，将“保证有充足的存款来源”作为发展的首要问题，将“扩规模调结构、控制风险”作为发展的重要课题，认真部署扎实推进各项工作，取得了良好的经营业绩。截至12月末，各货币汇总折人民币总资产427亿元；各货币汇总折人民币负债合计420亿元；本外币一般性存款余额为403亿元，人民币各项贷款余额323亿元，实现中间业务净收入23138万元。

业务发展模式实现“五创新”，合力推进业务持续发展。一是产品创新，有力促进中间业务良性发展。二是融资渠道创新，综合营销，业务稳步攀升。三是信贷结构优化创新，贷款规模有效控制、资本管理能力加强。四是联动营销创新，夯实发展基础。五是业务架构整合创新，拓展市场发展空间。

2011年，中国银行贵州省分行在自身业务发展的基础上，多措并举，以多元化融资渠道帮助企业解决融资难问题、利用海外资源创新业务发展，融通资金、保值增值，成立信贷工厂，服务中小企业，积极介入民生领域等积极支持地方经济发展，提供优质高效的金融服务。

2012年2月，中行贵州省分行举办"百年中行百年辉煌"全辖员工文艺汇演活动
February 2012, the Bank of China Guizhou Province Branch held "a hundred years the Bank of China a hundred years brilliant" full jurisdiction over employees Arts Festival activities

中国银行贵州省分行与贵州省经济和信息化委员会签署《银政战略合作协议》
Bank of China Guizhou Province Branch and Guizhou Province Economic and Information Technology Commission signed the "Silver political and strategic cooperation agreement"

In 2011, the Bank of China Guizhou Province Branch, earnestly implement the "structural adjustment, expand the scale, anti-risk, up new level" and "innovation development, restructuring development, cross-border development" approach, emancipate the mind, face difficulties, and take "ensure adequate sources of deposits" as the most important issue for development, expand "the scale of readjusting the structure, control risk" as an important issue for development, serious plans to push forward the work and achieved good operating results. At the end of December, the monetary aggregate discount RMB total assets of 42.7 billion yuan; each monetary aggregate discount of RMB 42 billion yuan total liabilities; general of the foreign currency deposits amounted to 40.3 billion yuan and loan balance of RMB 32.3 billion yuan, intermediate business net income of 231,380,000 yuan.

中国银行贵州省分行宽敞明亮的营业大厅
Bright and spacious business hall of the Bank of China Guizhou Province Branch

The business model realize "five innovation", work together to promote sustainable business development. First, product innovation, and effectively promote the sound development of intermediary business. Second, financing channels for innovation, marketing mix, and business is steadily rising. Third, the credit structure optimization and innovation, and effective control of the size of loans and capital management capabilities to enhance. Fourth, the linkage of marketing innovation, consolidate the foundation for the development. Fifth, integration innovation of the business structure, expand the market space for development.

In 2011, the Bank of China Guizhou Province Branch on the basis of their own business development, take many measures, help to diversify financing channels for enterprises to solve the problem of financing, use of overseas resources development of innovative business, financial intermediation, increasing the value to set up a credit factory services to small and medium-sized enterprises, and actively involved in the areas of people's livelihood, to actively support local economic development, provide quality and efficient financial services.

工行贵州省分行

Guizhou Province Branch of ICBC

2011年，针对省内能源、交通、煤磷化工等重大项目资金需求，工行贵州分行在加大传统信贷市场投放力度的同时，还采用票据承销、发行理财产品以及私募等多种融资方法

2011, funding requirements for the major projects of the provincial energy, transportation, coal and phosphorus chemical etc, the Guizhou branch of the ICBC put in efforts to increase the traditional credit markets, while also notes underwriting, distribution of financial products and private equity and other financing methods

2011年，工行贵州省分行将总行发展导向与省委、省政府“两加一推”发展战略有机结合，紧盯市场不放松，以发展促转型，在转型中求发展，一方面实施了积极的业务发展结构调整，一方面在调整中不断加大对地方经济发展支持的力度。

工行贵州分行一直重视不断以金融创新提升服务水平回馈社会

The Guizhou branch of the ICBC has always attached importance to continue to financial innovation, improve service levels to contribute to the community

该行深入开展“贵州在加速，我们怎么办”大讨论活动和“金点子”征集活动，集中全行智慧谋发展。召开发展战略研讨会，制定规划，统一全行发展战略。在业务发展中，对企业客户、机构客户、个人客户金融服务再上台阶，经营效益良好，社会效益显著。该行是“全国金融职工代表大会制度建设示范单位”，也是全省金融系统唯一一家荣获贵州省表彰的“2011年度职工素质建设工程先进单位”。该行非常重视公益事业，彰显了负责任大行形象。

工行贵州分行先后在省内开展多种活动，凝聚了人心，团结了群众

Guizhou branch of ICBC has a wide range of activities in the province, the combination of people, unity of the masses

工行贵州分行积极支持省内小微企业发展，小微企业贷款近年来节节攀升

The Guizhou branch of the ICBC to actively support the development of the province of small micro-enterprises, small micro-enterprise loans has been rising in recent years

工行贵州分行秉承一贯的社会责任意识，积极参与各类社会公益活动

The Guizhou branch of the ICBC to uphold the sense of social responsibility and actively participate in various social welfare activities

In 2011, Guizhou Province Branch of ICBC head office development-oriented provincial committee, government development strategy of "two plus one push" organic integration, focused their attention on the market does not relax, to develop and promote the transformation and development in the transition, on the one hand, the implementation of a positive business development, structural adjustment, on the other hand, the adjustment continued to increase efforts to support local economic development.

The bank has depth development "Guizhou is accelerating, how do we do" a big discussion activities and the "golden idea" solicitation to focus on the wisdom of pursuing development of the whole bank. Development Strategy Seminar convened to develop the plan, a unified development strategy of the bank. In business development, corporate clients, institutional clients and individual customers of financial services to a higher level, operational efficiency, significant social benefits. The bank is "a national financial workers' congress system construction demonstration unit", is also the only one of the financial system in the province won the Guizhou Province in recognition of "2011 the quality of employees construction projects advanced units". The bank attaches great importance to the public welfare, highlight responsible bank image.

建设银行贵州省分行

China Construction Bank Guizhou Branch

建设银行贵州省分行与贵州省卫生厅签署医疗健民合作协议
China Construction Bank Guizhou Branch and Guizhou Province Health Department to sign the medical and health cooperation agreement

建设银行贵州省分行与贵州省农业委员会举行“三农”战略合作协议暨涉农中小微企业借款合同签字仪式
China Construction Bank Guizhou Branch and Guizhou Province Agriculture Committee held a "three rural" strategic cooperation agreement, agriculture-related small and medium-sized micro-enterprise loan contract signing ceremony

由建设银行贷款支持的贵州玉凯高速公路项目
Guizhou, Yu-Kai expressway projects supported by the Construction Bank loans

2011年，中国建设银行股份有限公司贵州省分行以创先争优统领全局，积极抢抓历史机遇，主动适应监管变化，加快转变发展方式，业务规模再创新高，经营效益稳步提升，资产质量不断夯实，收入结构不断优化。截至12月末，各项存款余额1350.2亿元，较年初新增196.17亿元，增幅17.00%。各项贷款余额867.20亿元，比年初新增124.96亿元，增幅16.84%。全年实现拨备前利润26.50亿元，增长率32.15%。不良贷款率为0.84%，较年初下降0.02个百分点。实现中间业务收入9.83亿元，同比增速37.89%。

全年累计向公路、铁路、机场、电力、煤炭、燃气等涉及国计民生领域重点基础设施项目发放贷款179.07亿元。小企业业务加速发展，全力打造“社区金融”营销服务平台。加快个人信贷投放，个人贷款余额成功实现三年翻番。

In 2011, the China Construction Bank Corporation. Guizhou Province Branch excel commanding the overall situation, actively seize the historical opportunity to take the initiative to adapt to regulatory changes, to speed up the transformation of development mode, the scale of business made a new high record, steady improvement in operating efficiency, asset quality constantly consolidate, and improve the income structure. By the end of December, the deposits of 135.02 billion yuan,the new added 19.617 billion yuan over the beginning of the year, an increase of 17.00%. The loan balance of 86.72 billion yuan, the new added 12.496 billion yuan over the beginning of the year, an increase of 16.84%.Full-year pre-provision profit of 2.65 billion yuan, an increase of 32.15%.Performing loan ratio was 0.84%, down 0.02 percentage points than that in the beginning of the year. The intermediate business income of 983 million yuan, increasing 37.89% over the same period of the last year.

The annual total 17.907 billion yuan loans to the roads, railways, airports, electricity, coal, gas and other issues involving the national economy and the field of basic infrastructure projects. Business to accelerate the development of small enterprises, to create a "community financial" marketing services platform. Speed up the personal credit, personal loans successfully achieved three years to double.

国家开发银行贵州省分行

China Development Bank Guizhou Province Branch

2011年，国开行贵州省分行在省委省政府的高度关心和指导下，紧密围绕贵州“十二五”发展的主基调和主战略，充分发挥开发性金融的独特优势，抢抓贵州跨越发展的战略机遇，在“十二五”规划开局之年全力推进开发性金融在贵州的实践工作，为全省经济社会发展目标做出了突出贡献。

开行与贵州省举行高层联席会
CDB and Guizhou Province to hold high-level Joint

开发银行支持扶贫开发，与省扶贫办签署百亿合作协议
CDB Bank supports poverty alleviation and development, and with Poverty Alleviation signed ten billion cooperation agreement

截止年底，分行管理资产余额达1181.89亿元，较年初增加282.2亿元，其中：表内贷款余额达870亿元，余额新增达160亿元，较去年增长23%，增幅居全省第一；全年发放表内人民币贷款239.44亿元，表外发放126.02亿元，表外较去年增长31.88%；表外受托业务余额312.01亿元，较年初增加112.78亿元；外汇贷款余额2.04亿美元，较年初增加1.49亿美元，居全省首位。其中，国际合作业务贷款余额1.14亿美元，较年初增加0.7亿美元；新增人民币中长期评审承诺409.89亿元，外币评审承诺1.49亿美元。国开行贵州省分行全年为贵州筹集各类建设资金384亿元，其中分行直接发放贷款245亿元，引入信托50亿元、社保15亿元、夹层投资4亿元，承兑汇票13亿元，保理代付9亿元，落实银团贷款48亿元。年末，分行贷款余额在全省占比12.53%，比上年提升1个位次，位居第3。非个人中长期贷款余额达808.88亿元，比年初增加151.48亿元，全省占比20.66%，较年初提升1个百分点，全省排名提升至第一。

开行独家支持建设的九运会主场馆
CDB exclusive support the construction of the main stadium of the 9th National Games

开发银行支持的塘寨电厂
Development Bank to support Tong Village power plant

开行支持的贵州最大水电站——构皮滩水电站
CDB to support the largest hydropower station in Guizhou - Goupitan Hydropower Station

In 2011, China Development Bank Guizhou Province Branch under the high degree of care and guidance of provincial committee and government, closely around the main tone and the main strategy of Guizhou, "the 12th Five Year Plan" development, give full play to the unique advantages of the development of the financial, seize Guizhou leapfrog development of strategic opportunities, in the first year of "the 12th Five Year Plan", make efforts to promote the practice of development finance in Guizhou, made an outstanding contribution to the province's economic and social development goals.

开行融资支持的厦蓉高速——格都段乌细沟特大桥
CDB financing support of the Xiamen-Chengdu Expressway - Gedu section Wuxigou Bridge

By the end of the year, branches balance of assets under management amounted to 118.189 billion yuan, an increase of 28.22 billion yuan over the beginning of the year, including: Table loan balance of 87 billion yuan, the balance add up to 16 billion yuan, an increase of 23% compared with last year, an increase of the province's first one; annual payment of 23.944 billion yuan of RMB loans in the table, table outside paid 12.602 billion yuan, off-balance table growth of 31.88% over last year; table outside the fiduciary activities of the balance 31.201 billion yuan, an increase of 11.278 billion yuan over the beginning of the year; balance of $ 204 million of foreign exchange loans, an increase of $ 149 million of the beginning of the year,, ranking the province first. Among which international cooperation business loan balance of $ 114,000,000, an increase of $ 70 million compared to the beginning of the year; assessment of new RMB medium-and long-term commitment to 40.989 billion yuan, while foreign currency review pledged $ 149 million. CDB Guizhou Province Branch 38.4 billion yuan to raise all kinds of construction funds throughout the year in Guizhou, which branch direct loans of 24.5 billion yuan, the introduction of the Trust 5 billion yuan, 1.5 billion yuan of social security, mezzanine investments of 400 million yuan, acceptance money order of 1.3 billion yuan, factoring paid on behalf of 900 million yuan, the implementation of the syndicated loan of 4.8 billion yuan. At the end of the year, branch loan balance in the province, accounting for 12.53% over the previous year to enhance one ranking, ranking No. 3. Non-personal medium-and long-term loans reached 80.888 billion yuan, an increase of 15.148 billion yuan over the beginning of the year, the province accounted for 20.66% and increases by 1 percentage point compared with the beginning of the year, be the first in the province.

家庭困难学生正在申请开发银行助学贷款
Students from poor families are applying for student loans from development banks

贵阳农村商业银行

Guiyang Rural Commercial Bank

董事长索美英
Chairman Suo Meiying

行长安德治
Governor An Dezhi

宽敞明亮的营业部大厅
Bright and spacious hall of the business department

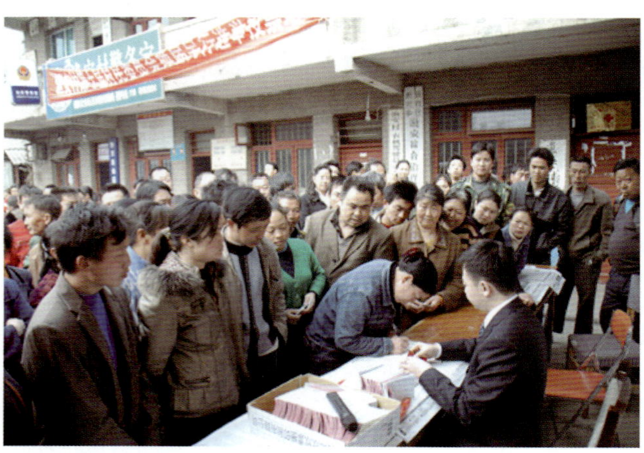

送金融服务下乡
Send financial services to rural areas

贵阳农村商业银行股份有限公司（简称贵阳农村商业银行）是经省政府同意，银监会批准，以贵阳市南明区农村信用合作联社、小河区农村信用合作联社、白云区农村信用合作联社、云岩农村合作银行为基础，通过增资扩股，按照市场化原则合并新设成立的贵州省首家农村商业银行。78个营业网点遍布贵阳市，可为广大客户提供各类定活期存款、项目融资、理财咨询、结算业务、代收代付、代理业务、企业贷款、个人信贷等多种金融服务项目。

截至2011年末，总资产280余亿元，各项存款余额156亿元，各项贷款余额100亿元，实现经营利润4.6亿元，不良贷款率为3.85%，资本充足率为19.83%，核心资本充足率为16.99%。拨备覆盖率为150.11%。

坚持服务三农，做“支农”主力军。坚持服务中小微企业，做中小微企业的好伙伴。打造特色银行，助力地方经济发展。强化内控与风险管理，实现协调发展。积极履行社会责任，品牌影响力快速提升。

Guiyang Rural Commercial Bank Co., Ltd. (hereinafter referred to Guiyang Rural Commercial Bank) is the consent of the provincial government, the CBRC approved, which is based on Nanming District of Guiyang City Rural Credit Cooperative Union, Xiaohe District Rural Credit Cooperative Union, Baiyun District Rural Credit Cooperative Union, Yunyan Rural Cooperative Bank, the new establishment of the province's first rural commercial banks to increase their investment, the merger in accordance with market principles. 78 outlets in Guiyang City, can provide clients with various types of fixed demand deposits, project finance, financial consulting, settlement services, collecting payment, the agency business, business loans, personal credit and other financial services.

At the end of 2011, total assets of over 28 billion yuan, the balance of deposits of 15.6 billion yuan, the loan balance of 10 billion yuan, an operating profit of 460 million yuan, non-performing loan rate of 3.85% capital adequacy ratio was 19.83%, core capital adequacy ratio was 16.99%. The provision coverage ratio was 150.11%.

Insist on Three Rural Problems services, to be the main force of "agriculture support". Adhere to serve the small and medium-sized micro-businesses, be the partners of small and medium-sized and micro enterprises. To creat characteristics banks, boost local economic development.Strengthen internal control and risk management, and achieve coordinated development. Actively fulfill their social responsibilities, and rapid promotion of brand influence.

省市领导、省银监局、省联社领导出席贵阳农商行开业仪式

Provincial and municipal leaders, the provincial banking regulatory bureaus, the leadership of the provincial association leaders to attend the opening ceremony of Guiyang Rural Commercial Bank

整洁有序的支行营业厅

Neat and orderly Office of the Branch

贵阳农商行总行营业部

Guiyang Rural Commercial Bank Head Office

中国人寿贵州省分公司

China Life Insurance Company Guizhou Branch

龙永图代表中国人寿向贵州省春晖行动发展基金会捐赠100万元人民币
Long Yongtu on behalf of China Life Insurance, donated one million yuan to Guizhou Province Spring Sunlight Foundation

贵州国寿党委书记、总经理江龙海在“贵州保险业3.15国际消费者权益保护日暨行业服务标准发布会”上宣读寿险服务标准
Party secretary of China Life Insurance Guizhou Province Branch, General Manager Jiang Longhai took the life standards of service in the insurance industry in "Guizhou 3.15 International Consumer Rights Protection Day-cum-industry service standards conference"

捐助10万元，贵州国寿全力投入望谟“6.06”抗洪抢险工作，贵阳市周副市长和贵州国寿纪委书记郑万里在捐赠仪式上
The donation of 100,000 yuan, China Life Insurance Guizhou Province Branch devote Wangmo, "6.06" flood fighting and rescue work, Guiyang City Deputy Mayor Zhou, China Life Insurance Guizhou Province Branch Commission for Discipline Inspection secretary, Zheng Wanli are at the donation ceremony

2011年，中国人寿贵州省分公司全年实现总保费收入25.86亿元，市场份额为39.35%，继续保持省内领先地位。截至年末，公司共有员工1414人。全省系统机构总数为314个，其中省级分公司1个、市级分公司9个、县支公司91个、县级以下营业部16个、营销服务部197个。全省系统个险渠道新增人力2854人，总持证人力达到8132人；银保渠道客户经理新增人力212人，总人数达到519人；团险渠道优化队伍结构，调整充实120人。

建立健全教育培训组织架构。9个市级分公司均成立了教育培训部；省、市公司均建立了专门的培训职场；围绕销售及管理全年共举办了各类培训班139期，受训人数达7680余人次；以推广个险新人育成体系和初级主管育成体系为重点，实施新人扬帆启航、初级主管训练营项目；组织全省系统员工进行E学堂学习，员工专业技能和经营管理能力得到明显提升。

品牌形象有效提升。在“3.15”国际消费者权益日召开质量监督员座谈会，认真听取客户及各行业的质量监督员的意见或建议；组织开展以“牵手国寿、绿动中国”为主题的2011年国寿客户节活动，向全社会倡导节能环保意识和低碳生活方式；积极参与贵州保监局主办、行协组织的庆祝建党九十周年文艺汇演暨第五届“保险之星”、第三届“诚信建设先进单位”表彰活动。稳步推进农村小额信贷保险，切实履行金融服务“三农”社会职责。勇于承担社会责任，有效展示了中国人寿良好的品牌形象和社会影响力。

中国人寿形象代言人姚明
Yao Ming, spokesperson of the China Life Insurance image

In 2011, China Life Insurance Company Guizhou Branch to achieve a total premium income of 2.586 billion yuan, 39.35% of market share, continue to maintain a leading position in the province. As the end of the year, the company employs were 1,414 people. System agencies in the province has a total of 314, including a provincial branch, 9 municipal branches, County branch of the 91, 16 below the county level sales department, marketing services 197. The province's system of insurance channels new human 2,854, the total permittee manpower up to 8,132 people; Bancassurance Channel Account Manager 212 new human, the total number of 519; group insurance channel to optimize the team structure, adjust to enrich 120 people.

Establish and improve the education and training organizational structure. 9 municipal sub-companies have set up a Ministry of Education and Training; provinces, municipalities and companies to establish a special training for the workplace; around the sales and management throughout the year organized a total of 139 training classes, the number of trainees reached 7,680 people; to promote the breeding system and a junior executive of a risk the new incubation system, focusing on the implementation of the new man to have sail, junior executive training camp project; organization of the province's system staff E school learning, staff professional skills and management capacity improved significantly.

为庆祝建党90周年，中国人寿贵州省分公司组织“心手相牵、血脉相连”义务献血活动
To celebrate the 90th anniversary of founding of the party, China Life Insurance Guizhou Province Branch have organization "Hands in hands, blood and blood" donation activities

Effectively enhance the brand image."3.15" World Consumer Rights Day held a quality supervisor seminars, listened carefully to the opinions or suggestions of the customers and the industry's quality supervisor; organizations to "hand China Life, the green China" movement as the theme of 2011 China Life Festival of customers, the whole of society to promote awareness of energy saving and environmental protection and low-carbon lifestyle; actively participate in Guizhou Insurance Regulatory Commission for hosting the line co-celebrate the founding of the organization's 90th Anniversary Arts Festival and the fifth "Insurance Star", the third "advanced unit building of the integrity" recognition activities. Steady progress in the rural micro-credit insurance, and earnestly implement the "three rural" social responsibility of financial services. Bravely to have the social responsibility, effective display of China Life Insurance a good brand image and social influence.

中国人寿捐资50万元援建的黔西南兴义市敬南镇“国寿春晖白古小学”建成投用
China Life Insurance donated 500,000 yuan aided in southwest Guizhou Xingyi City, Jingnan town "China Life the Chunhui Baigu elementary school" put into use

平安养老保险股份有限公司贵州分公司
Ping An Annuity Insurance Company Guizhou Branch

2011年分公司年终会上王胜总经理做工作报告
2011 Branch on the end of the year will, general manager Wang Sheng made a work report

2011年，平安养老保险股份有限公司贵州分公司在总公司的领导和社会各界的大力支持下，认真贯彻落实2011年全省保险工作会议精神，紧紧围绕监管“转方式、调结构、防风险、促发展”的工作要求，和总公司“大刀阔斧、精细经营、巩固领先、健康发展”的经营方针，加快业务结构调整，通过重点抓管理、抓队伍、抓积累，力促保进度、保达成、保合规等一系列举措，业务呈现持续快速发展的良好势头。截至2011年12月13日，平安养老险贵州分公司各项业绩如下表：

单位：万元	短险	非健险	长险	企业年金	集合计划
2009	4313	1465	1806	5356	2193
2010	4322	2424	2677	14678	1326
2011	4799	2954	5309	8525	1704
上年增长率	11%	21. 8%	98%	-72%	28. 5%

2011年分公司年终会上表彰优秀员工
2011 Branch on the end of the year will, the recognition of outstanding employees

In 2011, Ping An Annuity Insurance Co., Ltd. Guizhou branch, under the strong support of the Corporation's leadership and the community, earnestly implement the spirit of the 2011 provincial insurance work conference, closely around the regulation "transfer mode, adjust the structure, anti-risk, and promote development" work requirements, with the head office "drastic, fine business, strengthening its leadership, and healthy development" operating principles, and accelerate business restructuring, to focus on management, focus on grasping the team, caught accumulation, urged the security progress, ensure the achievement, ensure compliance and a series of initiatives, the business showed a good momentum of sustained and rapid development. By the end of December 13, 2011, Ping An Annuity Guizhou branch of the performance the following table:

Unit: million	Short-term insurance	Non-health insurance	Long-term insurance	Enterprise annuity	Integrated Plan
2009	4313	1465	1806	5356	2193
2010	4322	2424	2677	14678	1326
2011	4799	2954	5309	8525	1704
On the annual growth rate	11%	21. 8%	98%	-72%	28. 5%

分公司全体内外勤员工参加业务培训
Branch of all inside and outside the ground staff to participate in business training

19

Nineteen

金 融 业

Financial Intermediation

19−1 金融机构人民币存贷款余额(含外资)

Total Deposits and Total Loans of Financial Institutions (Including Foreign Investment)

单位：亿元 (100 million yuan)

指 标	Item	2006	2007	2008	2009	2010	2011	2011年比2010年增长(%) Increase Rate in 2011 over 2010(%)
资金来源合计	**Funds Sources**	**3476.46**	**3524.42**	**4290.47**	**5280.86**	**7029.92**	**8300.17**	**18.1**
各项存款	Total Deposits	3300.08	3826.37	4736.93	5898.26	7363.92	8742.79	18.7
财政存款	Fiscal Deposits	93.83	146.05	223.69	301.77	361.52	447.67	23.8
储蓄存款	Savings Deposit	1596.86	1790.14	2237.05	2676.09	3244.99	3934.48	21.2
资金运用合计	**Funds Uses**	**3476.47**	**3524.42**	**4290.47**	**5280.86**	**7029.92**	**8300.17**	**18.1**
各项贷款	Total Loans	2696.11	3128.63	3569.27	4656.50	5747.53	6841.92	19.0
#短期贷款	Short-term Loans	844.64	860.81	890.77	1090.72	1015.30	1293.00	27.4
中长期贷款	Medium-term & Long-term Loans	1779.24	2177.66	2586.49	3433.03	4582.34	5439.64	18.7

注：1、资料来源于中国人民银行贵阳中心支行。2、储蓄存款2010年及以前为城乡居民储蓄存款。

Note:1.Data in the table are obtained from Guiyang Central Branch of PBC.2.The year 2010 and brfore, savings deposit refer to resident savings deposit of urban and rural.

19-2 保险系统机构数

Number of Institutions in Insurance System

单位：个 (unit)

项 目	Item	2006	2007	2008	2009	2010	2011	2011年比2010年增长(%) Increase Rate in 2011 over 2010(%)
总计	**Total**	**548**	**652**	**774**	**854**	**883**	**930**	**5.3**
按行政区划分	By Administrative Areas							
省级分公司	Provincial Branches	12	15	18	19	20	22	10.0
地市级分公司	Branches at Prefecture Level	57	70	91	102	110	117	6.4
县级支公司	Branches at County Level	183	207	220	268	328	384	17.1
办事处或营业部	Business Offices and Departments	42	42	40	39	38	38	持平
营销服务部	Marketing Deparements	254	318	405	426	387	369	-4.7
按经济区划分	By Economic Level							
一级分公司	First Level Filiales	12	15	18	19	20	22	10.0
二级分公司	Second Level Filiales	57	70	91	102	110	117	6.4
支公司	Branches	183	207	220	268	328	384	17.1
办事处或营业部	Offices or Business Departments	42	42	40	39	38	38	持平
营销服务部	Marketing Departments	254	318	405	426	387	369	-4.7

注：资料来源于中国保险监督管理委员会贵州监管局(以下相关表同)。
Note:Data in the table are obtained from the provincial insurance regulatory bureau(the same applies to relative tables below).

19-3 保险系统职工人数

Number of Employed Persons in Insurance System

单位：人 (person)

项 目	Item	2006	2007	2008	2009	2010	2011	2011年比2010年增长(%) Increase Rate in 2011over 2010(%)
总计	**Total**	**4543**	**6615**	**7331**	**9421**	**10472**	**11283**	**7.7**
按行政区划分	By Administrative Areas							
省级分公司	Provincial Branches	1166	1803	1926	2296	2552	2666	4.5
地市级分公司	Branches at Prefecture Level	2102	2635	3068	3914	4650	5444	17.1
县级支公司	Branches at County Level	982	1638	1729	2421	2546	2597	2.0
办事处或营业部	Business Offices and Departments	43	47	23	39	60	33	-45.0
营销服务部	Marketing Departments	250	492	585	751	664	543	-18.2
按经济区划分	By Economic Level							
一级分公司	First Level Filiales	1166	1803	1926	2296	2552	2666	4.5
二级分公司	Second Level Filiales	2102	2635	3068	3914	4650	5444	17.1
支公司	Branches	982	1638	1729	2421	2546	2597	2.0
办事处或营业部	Offices or Business Departments	43	47	23	39	60	33	-45.0
营销服务部	Marketing Departments	250	492	585	751	664	543	-18.2

19-4 财产保险公司业务

Major Business Indicators of Property Insurance Companies

单位：万元 (10000 yuan)

指　标	Item	2006	2007	2008	2009	2010	2011	2011年比2010年增长(%) Increase Rate in 2011 over 2010(%)
保费收入	**Premium**	**178778**	**239669**	**300413**	**377293**	**489187**	**617886**	**26.3**
企业财产保险	Enterprise Property Insurance	14849	16012	21091	22231	28222	38138	35.1
机动车辆保险	Motor Vehicle Insurance	140979	186426	226527	301561	392399	480928	22.6
货物运输保险	Freight Transport Insurance	4722	5521	6696	5824	7289	7290	…
责任保险	Liability Insurance	6574	9926	13428	16396	20552	29781	44.9
信用保证保险	Credit Guarantee Insurance	292	286	544	494	1346	7624	466.4
农业保险	Agriculture Insurance	95	7058	7150	5516	920	2119	130.3
其他保险	Other Insurance	11267	14440	24978	25271	38459	52006	35.2
储金	**Deposits**	**5673**	**7386**	**6996**	**6446**	**4362**	**5822**	**33.5**
赔案件数(万件)	**Cases of Claims(10000 cases)**	**20**	**38**	**57**	**53**	**42**	**50**	**17.4**
赔款支出	**Claim and Payment**	**88348**	**107672**	**188553**	**253010**	**192351**	**262491**	**36.5**
企业财产保险	Enterprise Property Insuance	7602	7370	32791	80899	6159	10467	69.9
机动车辆保险	Motor Vehicle Insurance	73560	91040	133453	145450	163175	225500	38.2
货物运输保险	Freight Transport Insurance	755	593	679	805	408	517	26.7
责任保险	Liability Insurance	1898	3179	5503	7064	8013	10904	36.1
信用保证保险	Credit Guarantee Insurance	15	79	95	73	68	193	182.3
农业保险	Agriculture Insurance	16	162	7836	8531	1686	1311	-22.3
其他保险	Other Insurance	4502	5249	8196	10187	12842	13598	5.9
未决赔款	**Unsettled Claim**	**34826**	**43893**	**147554**	**85005**	**117217**	**189131**	**61.4**

注：本表包括人保、太保产险、平安产险、天安保险、安邦保险、阳光产险、大地产险、国寿产险、都邦产险、太平保险、华安产险、鼎和产险12家财产保险分公司数据(下表同)。

Note:.Data in this table include figures of the Guizhou Branches of PICC,Pacific Property Insurance Company, Ping'an Property Insurance Company, Tianan Insurance Company,Anbang Insurance Company,Yangguang Property Insurance Company, Dadi Property Insurance Company, China Life Property & Casualty Insurance Company, Du-Bang Insurance,and Ding-he Insurance Company (the same applies to the next table) .

19-5 财产保险主要指标(2011)

Major Indicators on Property Insurance

指　　标	Item	合　计 Total	企业财产保险 Enterprise Property Insurance	家庭财产保险 Family Property Insurance	机动车辆保险 Transportation Equipment Insurance	工程保险 Engineering Insurance	责任保险 Responsibility Insurance	保证保险 Pledge Insurance
承保件数(万件)	Amount Insured (10000 cases)	374	2	3	271	…	8	…
保险金额或责任限额(亿元)	Insurance Value or Liability Limit (100 million yuan)	24079.16	3133.82	108.87	6053.21	684.63	9839.04	12.99
签单保费(万元)	Premium of Sign Bill (10000 yuan)	615559	38205	2313	480839	21114	27825	7357
赔付件数(万件)	Amount Claim and Payment (10000 cases)	50	…	…	46	…	…	…
已决赔款(万元)	Indemnity Expenditure (10000 yuan)	251341	10708	1281	215312	2028	10319	201
未决赔款(万元)	Indefinite Expenditure (10000 yuan)	189131	24896	256	135526	5393	14325	161

19-5 续表　continued

指　　标	Item	船舶保险 Boats and Ships Insurance	货物运输保险 Freight Transport Insurance	特殊风险保险 Special Risk Insurance	农业保险 Agricultural Insurance	健康险 Health Insurance	意外伤害保险 Unforeseen Injury Insurance	其他险 Others
承保件数(万件)	Amount Insured(10000 cases)	…	11		…	4	74	…
保险金额或责任限额 (亿元)	Insurance Value or Liability Limit (100 million yuan)	1.04	710.43	6.11	7.43	1026.21	2489.90	5.49
签单保费(万元)	Premium of Sign Bill(10000 yuan)	206	7284	277	2120	8344	19150	523
赔付件数(万件)	Amount Claim and Payment (10000 cases)		…		…	2	…	…
已决赔款(万元)	Indemnity Expenditure(10000 yuan)	59	586	12	1277	4547	4767	245
未决赔款(万元)	Indefinite Expenditure(10000 yuan)	122	313	400	448	2025	5200	67

19-6 人寿保险公司业务

Major Business Indicators of Life Insurance Companies

单位：万元 (10000 yuan)

指 标	Item	2006	2007	2008	2009	2010	2011	2011年比2010年增长(%) Increase Rate in 2011 over 2010(%)
保费收入	**Premium**	**312233**	**349758**	**498647**	**574137**	**735914**	**700228**	**-4.8**
#新单保费	Premium of New Guarantee Slip	149081	178006	309841	341664	423733	368371	-13.1
#个人业务	Personal Business	278894	319447	475109	543109	702187	670327	-4.5
人寿保险	Life Insurance	252922	293387	445525	513918	662714	624908	-5.7
意外伤害险	Accident Injury Insurance	10238	9663	10965	9846	11983	13608	13.6
健康险	Health Insurance	15735	16397	18619	19345	27490	31811	15.7
团体业务	Group Business	33338	30311	23538	31028	33727	29901	-11.3
人寿保险	Life Insurance	14085	15903	8817	10798	14277	7051	-50.6
意外伤害险	Accident Injury Insurance	10890	7485	6002	9030	11396	15121	32.7
健康险	Health Insurance	8363	6923	8719	11199	8054	7730	-4.0
有效保单件数(万件)	**Cases of Virtual Guarantee Slip(10000cases)**	**233**	**238**	**289**	**354**	**416**	**459**	**10.3**
赔款及给付支出	**Claim and Payment**	**57610**	**91702**	**97339**	**102861**	**113982**	**132696**	**16.4**
个人业务	Personal Business	44473	76691	84798	87775	74656	93250	24.9
赔款支出	Benefit Paid	8058	8978	8041	5131	7753	9495	22.5
年金给付	Payment for Annuity	22348	4177	5350	8878	11862	14179	19.5
满期给付	Payment for Expiration	8108	56461	63116	64447	43237	54158	25.3
死伤医疗给付	Payment for Death and Injured person	5959	7075	8291	9320	11804	15418	30.6
团体业务	Group Business	13137	15011	12541	15086	39326	39446	0.3
赔款支出	Benefit Paid	9287	11625	9621	12719	13253	10766	-18.8
年金给付	Payment for Annuity	1064	2253	1874	1311	3283	2465	-24.9
满期给付	Payment for Expiration	1876	1025	875	700	21412	25039	16.9
死伤医疗给付	Payment for Death and Injured Person	911	108	171	357	1378	1177	-14.6

注：本表数据包含国寿、太保寿险、平安寿险、新华人寿、泰康人寿、平安养老、太平人寿、人保寿险8家人寿保险分公司数据(下表同)。

Note:data in this table include figures of the Guizhou Branches of China Life Insurance Company,Pacific Life Insurance Company, Ping'an Life Insurance Company, Xinhua Life Insurance Company, Taikang Life Insurance Company and Ping'an pension Insurance (the same applies to the next table) .

19-7 人寿保险主要指标(2011)
Major Indicators on Life Insurance

单位：万元 (10000 yuan)

指标项目	Item	合 计 Total	寿险业务 Life Insurance Business	普通寿险 Normal Life Insurance	个人业务 Personal	团体业务 Group	分红寿险 Share out Bonus	个人业务 Personal	团体业务 Group
保费收入	Premium	700228	631959	91417	84341	7076	531278	531278	
期末有效保险金额(亿元)	Virtual Insurance Value at the year-end(100 million yuan)	5659.75	1661.26	830.57	812.62	17.95	654.24	377.89	276.35
期末有效承保人次(万人)	Virtual Insurance Person-time at the year-end (10000 persons)	2586	720	586	570	15	112	102	11
期末有效承保保单件数(万件)	Cases of Virtual Guarantee Slip at the year-end (10000 cases)	459	276	160	156	4	95	94	1
赔款和给付支出	Expenditure for Claim and Payment	132696	109175	48077	40312	7765	59368	59367	1
#赔款支出	Settled Claim	20262							
死伤医疗给付	Payment for Death,Injury or Medical Treatmnet	16595	13382	8552	7376	1176	3788	3788	
满期给付	Mature Payment	79196	79150	29164	25039	4125	49297	49297	
年金给付	Payment for Annuity	16643	16643	10361	7897	2464	6282	6282	1
退保金	Insurance withdrawed	75923	74912	6252	5805	447	68639	68639	
在售产品数量（个）	Amount of Products under Selling(unit)	1049	402	150	121	29	209	202	7

19-7 续表 continued

单位：万元 (10000 yuan)

指标项目	Item	投资连结产品 Life Insurance Product in inve-stment	万能寿险 Omnip-otence Life Insu-rance	健康险业务 Health Insu-rance	个人业务 Personal	团体业务 Group	意外伤害保险业务 Unforeseen Injury Insurance
保费收入	Premium	237	9027	39541	31811	7730	28729
期末有效保险金额(亿元)	Virtual Insurance Value at the year-end(100 million yuan)	4.52	171.93	1165.44	770.65	394.79	2833.05
期末有效承保人次(万人)	Virtual Insurance Person-time at the year-end(10000 persons)	1	21	983			883
期末有效承保保单件数(万件)	Cases of Virtual Guarantee Slip at the year-end(10000 cases)	1	19	83			99
赔款和给付支出	Expenditure for Claim and Payment	432	1299	13630	8023	5560	9891
#赔款支出	Settled Claim			10371	4810	5560	9891
死伤医疗给付	Payment for Death,Injury or Medical Treatmnet	30	1011	3213	3213	…	
满期给付	Mature Payment	402	287	46			
年金给付	Payment for Annuity						
退保金	Insurance withdrawed	1	21	1010	1010		
在售产品数量（个）	Amount of Products under Selling (unit)	11	32	404	270	134	243

19–8 贵州上市公司股票发行情况(A股)(2011)

Summary List of Stocks Publicly Issued by Guizhou Enterprises(A Shares)

单位：万股　　(10000 shares)

上市公司名称	Listed Companies	上市时间 Listed Time	板块类别 Setor of Listed Companies	总股本 Total Capital Stock
中天城投	CENTURY ZHONGTIAN INVESTMENT JIONT STOCK CO.,LTD.	1994年2月2日	主板	127881
黔轮胎	GUI ZHOU TYRE CO., LTD.	1996年3月8日	主板	48890
中航重机	GUIZHOU LIYUAN HYDRAULIC COMPONENTS CO.,LTD.	1996年11月6日	主板	77800
振华科技	CHINA ZHENHUA(GROUP) SCIENCE & TECHNOLOGY CO.,LTD.	1997年7月3日	主板	35812
长征电气	GUIZHOU CHANGZHENG ELECTRICAL APPARATUS CO.,LTD.	1997年11月27日	主板	42434
高鸿股份	GOHIGH DATA NETWORKS TECHNOLOGY CO.,LTD.	1998年6月9日	主板	33290
南方汇通	SOUTH HUITON CO.,LTD.	1999年6月6日	主板	42200
ST国创	ST GUIZHOU GUOCHUANG ENERGY HOLDING(GROUP)CO.,LTD.	1999年9月23日	主板	37769
赤天化	GUIZHOU CHITIANHUA CORP.	2000年2月21日	主板	95039
红星发展	GUIZHOU REDSTAR DEVELOPING CO.,LTD.	2001年3月20日	主板	29120
盘江股份	GUIZHOU PANJIANG REFINED COAL CO.,LTD.	2001年5月31日	主板	110337
贵州茅台	KWEICHOW MOUTAI CO.,LTD.	2001年8月27日	主板	103818
贵航股份	GUIZHOU GUIHANG AUTOMOTIVE COMPONENTS CO.,LTD.	2001年12月27日	主板	28879
益佰制药	GUIZHOU YIBAI PHAMACY CO.,LTD.	2004年3月23日	主板	35276
贵绳股份	GUIZHOU GUISHENG CO.,LTD.	2004年5月14日	主板	16437
航天电器	GUIZHOU SPACEFLIGHT DIANQI CO.,LTD	2004年7月26日	中小板	33000
久联发展	GUIZHOU JIULIAN DEVELOPMENT CO.,LTD.	2004年9月8日	中小板	17303
黔源电力	GUIZHOU QIANYUAN ELECTRIC POWER CO.,LTD.	2005年3月3日	中小板	20360
信邦制药	GUIZHOU XINBANG PHARMACEUTICAL CO.,LTD.	2010年4月16日	中小板	17360
贵州百灵	GUIZHOU BAILING GROUP PHARMACEUTICAL CO.,LTD.	2010年6月3日	中小板	47040

注：1.资料来源于中国证监会贵州监管局。2.ST国创于2011年3月9日迁入贵州。

Note:1.Data in the table are provided by the Guizhou Securities Regulatory Bureau of the CSRC.2.ST GUIZHOU GUOCHUANG ENERGY HOLDING(GROUP)CO.,LTD. Removed to Guizhou on March3,2011.

19-8 续表 Continued

单位：万股 (10000 shares)

上市公司名称	Listed Companies	流通股 Government Share	募集资金总额（万元） Total Amount Issued (10000 yuan)
中天城投	CENTURY ZHONGTIAN INVESTMENT JIONT STOCK CO.,LTD.	127818	4572
黔轮胎	GUI ZHOU TYRE CO., LTD.	48885	183573
中航重机	GUIZHOU LIYUAN HYDRAULIC COMPONENTS CO.,LTD.	77800	344387
振华科技	CHINA ZHENHUA(GROUP)SCIENCE & TECHNOLOGY CO.,LTD.	35812	154376
长征电气	GUIZHOU CHANGZHENG ELECTRICAL APPARATUS CO.,LTD.	42434	109815
高鸿股份	GOHIGH DATA NETWORKS TECHNOLOGY CO.,LTD.	32079	89045
南方汇通	SOUTH HUITON CO.,LTD.	42200	61908
ST国创	ST GUIZHOU GUOCHUANG ENERGY HOLDING(GROUP)CO.,LTD.	37769	
赤天化	GUIZHOU CHITIANHUA CORP.	87018	215400
红星发展	GUIZHOU REDSTAR DEVELOPING CO.,LTD.	29120	37980
盘江股份	GUIZHOU PANJIANG REFINED COAL CO.,LTD.	26631	72000
贵州茅台	KWEICHOW MOUTAI CO.,LTD.	103818	224439
贵航股份	GUIZHOU GUIHANG AUTOMOTIVE COMPONENTS CO.,LTD.	19602	109703
益佰制药	GUIZHOU YIBAI PHAMACY CO.,LTD.	35276	36810
贵绳股份	GUIZHOU GUISHENG CO.,LTD.	16437	51800
航天电器	GUIZHOU SPACEFLIGHT DIANQI CO.,LTD	32980	61250
久联发展	GUIZHOU JIULIAN DEVELOPMENT CO.,LTD.	17303	26640
黔源电力	GUIZHOU QIANYUAN ELECTRIC POWER CO.,LTD	12340	137850
信邦制药	GUIZHOU XINBANG PHARMACEUTICAL CO.,LTD.	9317	71610
贵州百灵	GUIZHOU BAILING GROUP PHARMACEUTICAL CO.,LTD.	11840	148000

注：募集资金总额包括首发、增发、配股、可转债等募集的资金。盘江股份的募集资金总额含资产注入。

Note:Total Raised Capitals, including money raised by the first, issuing, convertible bonds of listed companies.The total amount of funds raised of Guizhou Panjiang Refined coalco.,LTD.indude infusion of funds.

主要统计指标解释

信贷资金 指金融机构以信用方式积聚和分配的货币资金。金融机构信贷资金的来源有各项存款、对国际金融机构负债、流通中货币、银行自有资金及当年结益等；信贷资金的运用有各项贷款、黄金占款、外汇占款、财政借款及在国际金融机构中的资产等。

存款 指企业、机关、团体或居民根据资金必须收回的原则，把货币资金存入银行或其他信用机构保管并取得一定利息的一种信用活动形式。根据存款对象的不同可划分为企业存款、财政存款、机关团体存款、基本建设存款、城镇储蓄存款、农村存款等科目。它是银行信贷资金的主要来源。

城乡居民储蓄存款余额 指某一时点城乡居民存入银行及农村信用社的储蓄金额，包括城镇居民储蓄存款和农民个人储蓄存款，不包括居民的手存现金和工矿企业、部队、机关、团体等单位存款。

贷款 指银行或其他信用机构根据资金必须归还的原则，按一定利率，为企业、个人等提供资金的一种信用活动形式。我国银行贷款分为流动资金贷款、固定资产贷款、城乡个体工商户贷款以及农业贷款等科目。

保险金额 指保险人承担赔偿或者给付保险金责任的最高限额。

保费 指投保人为取得保险人在约定范围内所承担赔偿责任而支付给保险人的费用。

赔款 指保险人根据保险合同的规定，向被保险人支付的赔偿保险责任损失的金额。

给付 包括死伤医疗给付和满期给付。死伤医疗给付是指保险人根据人寿保险及长期健康保险合同的规定，因被保险人在保险期内发生保险责任范围内的保险事故支付给被保险人（或受益人）的金额。满期给付是指被保险人生存期满，保险人按人寿保险合同规定支付给被保险人的满期保险金额。

股票市价总值 指在交易所上市的证券在某一时点按市价与发行数量计算的总金额。计算公式为:

股票市价总值＝Σ（市价 × 发行数量）。

股票流通市值 指在交易所上市的证券在某一时点按市价与上市流通量计算的总金额。计算公式为:

股票流通总值＝Σ（市价 × 可流通量）。

股票成交量 上市公司股票在交易所成交的数量。

股票成交金额 股票成交量乘以成交价格。

Explanatory Notes on Main Statistical Indicators

Credit Funds refer to the funds issued as loans by banking institutions. The sources of credit funds of the banking institutions included deposits, liabilities to international financial institutions, currency in circulation, self-owned funds and current retained profits, etc. The credit funds can be used in forms of loans, gold, foreign exchange, government debt and assets in the international financial institutions.

Deposit is a form of credit by which enterprises, institutions, organizations or households can put money into banks and other credit institutions for safekeeping and interest earning under the principle of free withdrawal. According to different depositors, deposits are divided into enterprise deposits,treasury deposits, deposits of government agencies and organizations,capital construction deposits, urban savings deposits, rural deposits and other deposits. Deposits are major sources of the credit funds of banks.

The Savings Deposits of Urban and Rural Residents refers to the total value of savings deposits of urban and rural households in banks and rural credit cooperatives at a given point of time, including the savings deposit of urban residents and the savings deposit of rural residents. The cash in hand by residents and the deposits of organizations such as enterprises,military units,government agencies, institutions, etc. are not included.

Loan is a form of credit by which banks and other credit institutions provide funds at certain interest rate to enterprises and individuals in the light of the principle of unconditional repayment. Loans from Chinese banks include circulating capital loans, fixed assets loans, loans to urban and rural individuals engaged in industrial and commercial business and agricultural loans.

Amount Insured refers to the maximum that the insurant will get for the claim of the case insured.

Premium is the fee paid by the insurant to the insurer to obtain the obligation of compensation from the insurance within the agreed terms.

Settled Claim is the compensation paid by the insurer to the insurant in accordance with the insurance contract.

Payment includes payment for death, injury or medical treatment and mature payment. Payment for death, injury or medical treatment refers to the money paid to the insurant (or the beneficiary) in accordance with the life or health insurance contract when the insurant encounters accidents within the insured period covered in the contract. Mature payment refers to the mature payment to the insurant in accordance with the life insurance contract at the end of the insured period.

Total Market Capitalization this figure represents the aggregate taken at a given time of the market price the listed volume for each security in the market.

Σ(Marked Price×Listed Volume)

Negotiable Market Capitalization this figure represents the aggregate taken at a given time of the market price the negotiable volume for each security in the market.

Σ(Marked Price×Negotiable Volume)

Trading Volume refers to trading volume of shares of listed companies.

Total Turnover refers to the value derived from the current stock price per share times the traded shares.

20 Twenty

教育和科技

Education, Science and Technology

20-1 各级各类学校数

Number of Schools by Level and Type

单位：所 (unit)

指 标	Item	2006	2007	2008	2009	2010	2011
学校数	**Number of Schools**						
研究生培养机构	Institutions Providing Postgraduate Programs	7	8	8	8	8	8
普通高等学校	Regular Institutions of Higher Education	36	37	37	47	47	48
成人高等教育	Adult Higher Education						
#成人高等学校	Adult Institutions of Higher Education	6	5	5	4	4	4
中等职业教育	Vocational Secondary Education	219	244	259	255	249	227
调整后中等职业教育	Adjusted Vocational Secondary Schools	28	36	36	36	35	32
普通中等专业教育	Regular Specialized Secondary Schools	57	60	61	61	63	54
职业高中	Vocational Senior Secondary Schools	113	129	141	136	130	126
成人中等专业教育	Adult Specialized Secondary Education						
#成人中等专业学校	Adult Specialized Secondary Schools	21	19	21	22	21	15
普通中学	Regular Secondary Schools	2633	2674	2626	2614	2592	2641
高 中	Senior Secondary Schools	482	485	456	451	444	447
初 中	Junior Secondary Schools	1675	1652	1635	1622	1617	1635
九年一贯制学校	Schools of Nine-year Consistent System	476	537	535	541	531	559
小 学	Primary Schools	14076	13645	13107	12862	12422	12008
幼儿园	Kindergartens	1721	1838	1960	2063	2196	2677
特殊教育	Special Education	39	40	49	49	53	52
工读学校	Schools for Juvenile Delinquents	3	4	4	4	4	4
成人中学	Adult Secondary Schools	4	5	45	22	33	13
成人技术培训学校	Adult Technical Training Schools	11850	11747	12999	11852	7711	8202
成人小学	Adult Primary Schools	10198	8972	9433	9377	5405	5059

注：资料来源于省教育厅(以下相关表同)。
Note:Data in the table are Provided by the Provinvial Department of Education(The relative tables in the chapter are the same).

20-2 各级各类学校专任教师数
Number of Full-time Teachers by Level and Type of School

单位：人 (person)

指 标	Item	2006	2007	2008	2009	2010	2011
专任教师	**Number of Full-time Teachers**						
培养研究生的单位	Institutions Providing Postgraduate Programs	1923	2196	2236	2398	2760	2971
普通高等学校	Regular Institutions of Higher Education	15398	16964	18037	19634	20351	21855
成人高等教育	Adult Higher Education						
#成人高等学校	Adult Institutions of Higher Education	1112	1131	555	282	296	314
中等职业教育	Vocational Secondary Education	8404	9954	10237	10889	11291	11635
调整后中等职业教育	Adjusted Vocational Secondary Schools	727	1015	863	1015	1211	1339
普通中等专业教育	Regular Specialized Secondary Schools	3532	3763	3647	3708	3857	3677
职业高中	Vocational Senior Secondary Schools	2837	3662	4396	4698	4883	5354
成人中等专业教育	Adult Specialized Secondary Education						
#成人中等专业学校	Adult Specialized Secondary Schools	975	1064	1148	1201	1190	1233
其它机构	Other Institutions	333	450	183	267	150	32
普通中学	Regular Secondary Schools	128274	131087	135360	139302	142508	147396
高 中	Senior Secondary Schools	28121	29226	30284	31413	33072	36223
初 中	Junior Secondary Schools	100153	101861	105076	107889	109436	111173
小 学	Primary Schools	188762	191991	200024	199189	197913	197094
幼儿园	Kindergartens	10596	11293	12095	13105	14623	18120
特殊教育	Special Education	620	627	695	740	796	901
工读学校	Schools for Juvenile Delinquents	37	75	73	75	76	65
成人中学	Adult Secondary Schools	25	60	125	30	169	33
成人技术培训学校	Adult Technical Training Schools	4662	5902	6277	5201	3983	5515
成人小学	Adult Primary Schools	3742	7972	6324	5781	4463	3403

20-3 各级各类学校招生数

Number of New Students Enrollment by Level and Type of School

单位：人 (person)

指　标	Item	2006	2007	2008	2009	2010	2011
招生数	**New Students Enrollment**						
研究生	Institutions Providing Postgraduate Programs	2848	3017	3327	3908	4246	4417
普通高等教育	Regular Institutions of Higher Education	72693	84208	94530	99026	101548	107841
成人高等教育	Adult Higher Education	30266	29795	32254	26966	26580	26054
#成人高等学校	Adult Institutions of Higher Education	6677	7299	8483	2431	2345	3041
中等职业教育	Vocational Secondary Ecucation	138395	166093	161156	162831	155527	148242
调整后中等职业教育	Adjusted Vocational Secondary Schools	17282	20361	10000	14556	13675	16283
普通中等专业教育	Regular Specialized Secondary Schools	61756	64706	66640	65367	62260	61181
职业高中	Vocational Senior Secondary Schools	53106	74722	75470	72514	62199	64443
成人中等专业教育	Adult Specialized Secondary Education	6251	6304	9046	10394	17393	4042
#成人中等专业学校	Adult Specialized Secondary Schools	5577	6288	7757	8302	14584	1788
普通中学	Regular Secondary Schools	902968	910979	960665	981374	1004948	1022950
高　中	Senior Secondary Schools	198389	201185	212253	219062	240208	277290
初　中	Junior Secondary Schools	704579	709794	748412	762312	764740	745660
小　学	Primary Schools	787895	735245	722009	698976	656919	626379
幼儿园	Kindergartens	614530	616014	623254	623660	627154	632789
特殊教育	Special Education	1715	2331	2265	2616	2755	2858
工读学校	Schools for Juvenile Delinquents	164	630	571	253	432	660

20−4 各级各类学校在校生数

Number of Students Enrollment by Level and Type of School

单位：人 (person)

指　标	Item	2006	2007	2008	2009	2010	2011
在校生数	**Students Enrollment**						
研究生	Institutions Providing Postgraduate Programs	7508	8366	9083	10169	11406	12436
普通高等教育	Regular Institutions of Higher Education	221546	241692	267526	299072	323293	344100
成人高等教育	Adult Higher Education	110418	89554	87963	86209	86630	79615
#成人高等学校	Adult Institutions of Higher Education	19684	19133	17617	5612	5827	6064
中等职业教育	Vocational Secondary Education	277404	333383	356725	386865	375740	379908
调整后中等职业教育	Adjusted Vocational Secondary Schools	27525	34766	23873	29514	32084	39497
普通中等专业教育	Regular Specialized Secondary Schools	146100	163002	171559	177178	169033	170659
职业高中	Vocational Senior Secondary Schools	88852	122322	144393	159943	145853	151786
成人中等专业教育	Adult Specialized Secondary Education	14927	13293	16900	20230	28770	17966
#成人中等专业学校	Adult Specialized Secondary Schools	13900	12151	14752	18028	24855	14057
普通中学	Regular Secondary Schools	2563108	2559983	2617812	2694521	2756820	2827096
高　中	Senior Secondary Schools	530899	545873	562138	581604	620221	689042
初　中	Junior Secondary Schools	2032209	2014110	2055674	2112917	2136599	2138054
小　学	Primary Schools	4743780	4663136	4697910	4568716	4334971	4087382
幼儿园	Kindergartens	724607	732590	737988	747351	769144	877824
特殊教育	Special Education	14815	15867	15186	16507	16231	14474
工读学校	Schools for Juvenile Delinquents	196	579	727	271	233	400
成人中学	Adult Secondary Schools	1160	2127	4779	5637	16869	1203
成人技术培训学校	Adult Technical Training Schools	2595343	2727306	2750734	2627205	2058138	2180591
成人小学	Adult Primary Schools	309146	323074	303429	302286	239936	128006

20-5 各级各类学校毕业生数
Number of Graduates by Level and Type of School

单位：人 (person)

指 标	Item	2006	2007	2008	2009	2010	2011
毕业生数	**Graduates**						
研究生	Institutions Providing Postgraduate Programs	1453	2080	2458	2706	2910	3335
普通高等教育	Regular Institutions of Higher Education	53233	61743	66050	64212	74777	83016
成人高等教育	Adult Higher Education	32844	44795	28919	28147	24365	29953
#成人高等学校	Adult Institutions of Higher Education	9804	6930	7199	1547	2015	2166
中等职业教育	Vocational Secondary Education	47250	62027	75594	82599	100997	90966
调整后中等职业教育	Adjusted Vocational Secondary Schools	2956	4168	6012	3548	7101	6933
普通中等专业教育	Regular Specialized Secondary Schools	30938	32756	42624	45361	50118	46622
职业高中	Vocational Senior Secondary Schools	10666	21637	24230	30096	39099	35230
成人中等专业教育	Adult Specialized Secondary Education	2690	3466	2728	3594	4679	2181
#成人中等专业学校	Adult Specialized Secondary Schools	2506	3033	2560	3077	4643	1913
普通中学	Regular Secondary Schools	787383	794744	785763	780888	807515	830799
高 中	Senior Secondary Schools	137065	149254	161279	165392	171704	180203
初 中	Junior Secondary Schools	650318	645490	624484	615496	635811	650596
小 学	Primary Schools	731361	751878	763062	784574	798173	773003
幼儿园	Kindergartens	364175	366027	349472	334120	328152	365936
特殊教育	Special Education	924	1212	1116	1799	1350	1244
工读学校	Schools for Juvenile Delinquents	164	458	544	930	393	652
成人中学	Adult Secondary Schools	592	1500	3541	4453	7701	3243
成人技术培训学校	Adult Technical Training Schools	2350012	2562038	2643529	2517318	2065482	2195836
成人小学	Adult Primary Schools	268373	272343	236418	243022	214867	3243

20–6 教师职称

Technical Rank of Teachers

单位：人 (person)

类　别	Item	2006	2007	2008	2009	2010	2011
高等学校教师数	**Regular Institutions of Higher Education**	**16510**	**18095**	**18592**	**19916**	**20647**	**22169**
正高级	Senior	1109	1285	1467	1615	1801	2038
副高级	Sub-senior	4324	4871	5410	5673	5913	6544
中　级	Middle	6238	6887	7226	7757	8403	8863
初　级	Junior	3609	3908	3326	3302	3288	3383
无职称	No Rank	1230	1144	1163	1569	1242	1341
中等职业学校教师数	**Vocational Secondary Schools**	**8404**	**9954**	**10237**	**10889**	**11291**	**11635**
正高级	Senior	47	87	69	70	60	68
副高级	Sub-senior	1449	1731	1771	1954	2065	2101
中　级	Middle	3345	3960	4106	4375	4583	4605
初　级	Junior	2913	3347	3366	3547	3457	3492
无职称	No Rank	650	829	925	943	1126	1369
普通中学教师数	**Regular Secondary Schools**	**128274**	**131087**	**135360**	**139302**	**142508**	**147396**
中学高级	Senior-rank of Secondary Teacher	10039	11460	12531	13568	14825	16522
中学一级	First-rank of Secondary Teacher	32214	35573	38573	40760	43329	46402
中学二级	Second-rank of Secondary Teacher	53868	56549	59778	62704	64060	63548
中学三级	Third-rank of Secondary Teacher	17653	16355	13837	10311	8491	6640
未评职称	No Rank of Secondary Teacher	14500	11150	10641	11959	11803	14284
小学教师数	**Regular Primary Schools**	**188762**	**191991**	**200024**	**199189**	**197913**	**197094**
中学高级	Senior-rank of Secondary Teacher	108	177	120	173	205	763
小学高级	Senior-rank of Primary Teacher	49855	56460	66357	71854	77589	82258
小学一级	First-rank of Primary Teacher	91796	92422	89232	86256	80881	76802
小学二级	Second-rank of Primary Teacher	29158	26918	24348	22228	21409	18572
小学三级	Third-rank of Primary Teacher	3429	3005	2943	1996	1141	971
未评职称	No rank of Primary Teacher	14416	13009	17024	16682	16688	17728

20-7 各级学校女学生和女教师数

Female Students and Teachers by Level and Type of School

单位：人 (person)

指 标	Item	2006	2007	2008	2009	2010	2011
在校女生数	**Number of Female Students Entrollment**						
普通高等教育	Regular Institutions of Higher Education	101764	116680	130225	151165	163824	178663
成人高等教育	Adult Higher Education	50627	42803	40792	40018	39923	40274
中等职业教育	Vocational Secondary Education	134716	162419	174100	186657	184525	193289
普通中学	Regular Secondary Schools	1157587	1175084	1218257	1269927	1310999	1356343
#高 中	Senior Secondary Schools	227270	238471	250847	267571	290983	330129
初 中	Junior Secondary Schools	930317	936613	967410	1002356	1020016	1026214
小 学	Primary Schools	2262072	2221262	2232813	2160956	2038362	1913008
女教师数	**Number of Female Teachers**						
普通高等学校	Regular Institutions of Higher Education	7036	7865	8428	9261	9712	10690
成人高等学校	Adult Higher Education	524	526	280	153	157	167
中等职业学校	Vocational Secondary Education	3537	4133	4254	4527	4746	5053
普通中学	Regular Secondary Schools	43209	44948	47339	49549	51868	55196
#高 中	Senior Secondary Schools	10040	10737	11282	11805	12618	14186
初 中	Junior Secondary Schools	33169	34211	36057	37744	39250	41010
小 学	Primary Schools	80729	82535	86520	88954	90208	91253

20–8 各级学校师生比
Student-Teacher Ratio by Level of School

单位：学生/教师 (Student/Teacher)

类　别	Item	2006	2007	2008	2009	2010	2011
普通高等学校	Regular Institutions Of Higher Education	14.39	14.25	14.83	15.23	15.89	15.74
普通高中	Regular Senior Secondary School	18.88	18.68	18.56	18.51	18.75	19.02
普通初中	Regular Junior Secondary School	20.29	19.77	19.56	19.58	19.52	19.23
小　学	Primary School	25.13	24.29	23.49	22.94	21.90	20.74

20–9 各级各类学校学生入学率
Enrollment Rate by Level and Type of School

单位：% (%)

指　标	Item	2006	2007	2008	2009	2010	2011
小学学龄儿童入学率	Enrollment Rate of Primary Schools	98.6	98.6	97.2	98.4	97.9	98.6
小学毕业生升学率	Percentage of Graduates of Primary Schools Entering into Junior Secondary Schools	97.8	95.6	98.7	97.7	96.3	96.5
初中阶段毛入学率	Rate of Primary School Graduates Entering into Junior Secondary Schools	100.5	97.5	95.9	98.2	97.6	94.2
高中阶段毛入学率	Rate of Junior Secondary School Graduates Entering into Senior Secondary Schools	37.7	42.2	47.9	53.4	55.0	58.9
高等教育毛入学率	Rate of Senior Secondary School Graduates Entering into Institution of Higher Learning	11.0	11.5	11.8	18.4	20.0	23.2

20-10 普通高等学校(2011)

Basic Statistics on Regular Institutions of Higher Education

单位：人 (person)

类　别	Sort	学校数(所) Number of Schools (unit)	毕业生数 Graduates with Degrees or Diplomas	招生数 New Enrollment	在校学生人数 Enro-llment	教职员工 Teachers, Staff & Workers	#专任教师 Full-time Teachers	#正、副教授 Senior and Sub-senior Professors
总　计	**Total**	**48**	**83016**	**107841**	**344100**	**31121**	**21855**	**8487**
#综合大学	Comprehensive Universities	18	27987	36183	115598	11656	7809	2852
理工院校	Science & Engineering	6	9626	12658	34113	2433	1924	425
医药院校	Medicine & Pharmacy	9	10929	14649	51214	5516	3869	1718
师范院校	Teacher Training	9	22743	27483	91391	7299	5412	2040
财经院校	Finance & Economics	3	7238	10541	28570	2067	1487	760
政法院校	Politics and Law	1	1846	2209	4582	487	290	123
民族院校	Ethnic Minortities	2	2647	4118	18632	1663	1064	569
#高等职业技术学院	Vocational and Technical Colleges	20	23329	32896	88097	7768	5511	1411

20-11 普通高等学校分科专任教师数(2011)

Number of Full-time Teachers in Institutions of Higher Education by Field of Study

单位：人 (person)

类　别	Sort	专任教师数 Full-time Teachers	正高级 Senior	副高级 Subsenior	中级 Middle	初级 Junior	无职称 No Rank
总　计	**Total**	**21855**	**2022**	**6465**	**8731**	**3308**	**1329**
哲　学	Philosophy	1033	107	337	403	121	65
经济学	Economics	1060	115	329	427	125	64
法　学	Law	1182	128	401	451	151	51
教育学	Education	2164	134	627	936	341	126
文　学	Literature	4172	329	1154	1794	604	291
历史学	History	521	67	166	191	45	52
理　学	Science	2577	222	837	973	350	195
工　学	Engineering	3815	288	1032	1512	772	211
农　学	Agriculture	759	119	227	316	71	26
医　学	Medicine	3253	399	1024	1195	467	168
管理学	Management	1319	114	331	533	261	80

20−12 研究生数

Number of Postgraduates

单位：人 (person)

指标	Item	2006	2007	2008	2009	2010	2011
招研究生数	Number of New Postgraduates Enrollment	2848	3017	3327	3908	4246	4417
#女性	Female	1208	1278	1544	1885	2206	2248
在校研究生数	Number of Postgraduates Enrollment	7508	8366	9083	10169	11406	12436
#女性	Female	3160	3626	4103	4726	5622	6211
毕业研究生数	Number of Postgraduates Graduate	1453	2080	2458	2706	2910	3335
#女性	Female	581	846	1090	1153	1269	1570

20−13 技工学校情况

Statistics on Technical Schools

单位：人 (person)

指标	Item	2010	2011	2011年比2010年增长(%) Increase Rate in 2011 over 2010(%)
学校数（所）	Number of Schools (unit)	29	30	3.4
招生数	Number of Enrollment	16327	16939	3.7
在校学生数	Number of Students	33903	36719	8.3
毕业生数	Number of Graduates	9341	9580	2.6
教职工数	Teachers and Staff	3251	2911	-10.5
专任教师数	Full-time Teachers	2162	2170	0.4
文化技术理论课教师	Classroom Teachers	1623	1210	-25.4
生产实习课指导教师	Practical Training Teachers	539	562	4.3
理论实习一体化教师	Classroom cum Practical Training Teachers	389	398	2.3

注：资料来源于省人力资源社会保障厅。

Note: Date in the table are obtained from provincial department of human resources and social security.

20–14　中等职业学校(机构)数（2011）
Number of Secondary Vocational Schools

单位：个　　　(unit)

项目	Item	总计 Total	地方部门 Local Departments	教育部门 Departments of Education	非教育部门 Departments of Non-Education	民办 Private
中等职业学校	Secondary Vocational Schools	**227**	**165**	**119**	**46**	**62**
调整后中等职业学校	Adjusted Secondary Vocational Schools	32	21	20	1	11
普通中等专业学校	Regular Specialized Secondary Schools	54	54	21	33	
成人中等专业学校	Adult Specialized Secondary Schools	15	12	4	8	3
职业高中学校	Vocational Junior Secondary Schools	126	78	74	4	48
其他机构(教学点)(不计入学校数)	Other Institutions	2	2	1	1	

20–15　中等职业学校(2011)
Basic Statistics on Vocational Secondary Education

单位：人　　　(person)

类别	Item	学校数(所) Schools (unit)	毕业生数 Graduates	招生数 New Students Enrollment	在校学生数 Students Enrolment	教职员工 Teachers, Staff & Workers	#专任教师 Full-time Teachers
总计	**Totel**	**227**	**90966**	**148242**	**379908**	**15680**	**11635**
调整后中等职业学校	Adjusted Vocational Secondary Schools	32	6933	16283	39497	1577	1339
普通中等专业学校	Regular Specialized Secondary Schools	54	46622	61181	170659	5403	3677
成人中等专业学校	Adult Specialized Secondary Educaiton	15	2181	4042	17966	1781	1233
职业高中	Vocational Senior Secondary Schools	126	35230	66736	151786	6868	5354
其它机构(教学点)	Others Institutions					51	32

20−16 中等职业学校（机构)学生分科类情况（2011）

Students in Secondary Vocational Schools by Field of Study

单位：人 (person)

项　目	Item	招生数 New Enrollment	#初中毕业生 Junior Secondary School Graduates	#应届毕业生 Current Year Graduates	在校学生数 Total Enrollment	毕业生数 Graduates	#获得职业资格证书 With Certificate On Professional Competence
总　计	**Total**	**148242**	**139380**	**133013**	**379908**	**90966**	**58055**
农林牧渔类	Agriculture,Forestry,Animal Husbandry and Fishery	16509	14133	13171	48716	7401	3511
资源环境类	Resources and Environment	2483	2257	1619	5920	3176	677
能源与新能源类	Energy and New Energy	868	844	795	2419	400	343
土木水利类	Civil and Hydraulic Engineering	8317	7922	7173	18502	3982	2638
加工制造类	Manufacturing	16769	16171	15097	44236	13795	10085
石油化工类	Petroleum and Chemical	634	634	632	1149	331	288
轻纺食品类	Textile and Foods	1835	1667	1570	4134	678	253
交通运输类	Communication & Transportation	10359	9627	9375	21952	3713	2967
信息技术类	Information Technologies	29859	28701	27806	82272	25251	17936
医药卫生类	Medicine and Health	16040	14695	14119	50709	11049	4432
休闲保健类	Leisure and Health-care	398	398	391	1315	217	189
财经商贸类	Finance and Trade	7084	6723	6522	21499	6215	3731
旅游服务类	Tourism and services	7276	6798	6719	18632	3683	2993
文化艺术类	Culture and Art	3512	3194	3049	8053	1700	1253
体育与健身	Physical Education	648	632	632	1746	474	334
教育类	Education	23001	22376	21808	40151	6367	5057
司法服务类	Justice Service	813	791	784	2839	522	252
公共管理与服务类	Public Management and Service	1244	1224	1160	4151	1742	859
其他	Other	593	593	591	1513	270	257

20−17 民族教育
Minority Nationality Education

类　别	Item	2006	2007	2008	2009	2010	2011
学校数(所)	**Number of Schools(unit)**						
普通高校	Regular Institutions of Higher Education	1	1	1	2	2	2
普通中学	Regular Secondary Schools	97	98	117	119	121	194
小　学	Primary Schools	141	129	151	146	161	637
专任教师数(人)	**Full-time Teachers(person)**						
普通高校	Regular Institutions of Higher Education	3743	3756	3960	4293	4407	5189
成人高校	Adult Institutions of Higher Education	119	126	102	50	42	40
普通中学	Regular Secondary Schools	51222	52834	54958	57007	58519	60519
#高　中	Senior Secondary Schools	10551	11114	11655	12444	13044	14041
中等职业学校	Vocational Secondary Schools	2121	2282	2451	3723	2778	3501
小　学	Primary Schools	78178	79151	82614	83173	82892	80267
在校生数(人)	**Number of Students Enrollment(person)**						
普通高等教育	Regular Institutions of Higher Education	73807	71896	87733	105693	110549	117205
成人高等教育	Adult Institutions of Higher Education	24607	17251	16986	20108	17428	22601
普通中学	Regular Secondary Schools	1010026	1008786	1029863	1067179	1092467	1127199
#高　中	Senior Secondary Schools	212142	216937	220728	228599	243987	275147
中等职业学校	Vocational Secondary Schools	96613	99795	111662	115309	125407	135113
小　学	Primary Schools	1906413	1887449	1901478	1585233	1775808	1697558
毕业生数(人)	**Number of Graduates(person)**						
普通中学	Regular Secondary Schools	301826	315141	312418	306943	315968	325984
#高　中	Senior Secondary Schools	51763	59990	64322	65177	66977	70296
小　学	Primary Schools	281368	294004	299419	315294	316272	304096

20−18 民办教育
Private Education

类　别	Item	2006	2007	2008	2009	2010	2011
学校数(所)	**Number of Schools(unit)**						
普通高等学校	Regular Institutions of Higher Education	1	1	1	9	9	10
中等职业教育学校	Vocational Secondary Schools	36	56	70	66	70	62
普通中学	Regular Secondary Schools	331	376	320	310	319	346
#高　中	Senior Secondary Schools	127	123	99	88	89	94
小　学	Primary Schools	393	384	305	297	259	269
在校学生数(人)	**Number of Students Enrollment(person)**						
普通高等学校	Regular Institutions of Higher Education	30695	37364	44758	50636	54552	58030
中等职业教育学校	Vocational Secondary Schools	14881	34625	50276	63404	49919	41267
普通中学	Regular Secondary Schools	115902	120631	124767	130776	155165	169007
#高　中	Senior Secondary Schools	39337	35890	36082	38134	44672	55248
小　学	Primary Schools	162294	185477	164894	167078	162362	173050
教职员工数(人)	**Teachers, Staff and Workers(person)**						
普通高等学校	Regular Institutions of Higher Education	2053	2392	2674	3062	3251	3818
中等职业教育学校	Vocational Secondary Schools	862	1873	2259	2440	2610	2226
普通中学	Regular Secondary Schools	8932	8321	7978	8710	9719	13771
小　学	Primary Schools	7095	7548	6817	7161	7456	4770
专任教师数(人)	**Full-time Teachers(person)**						
普通高等学校	Regular Institutions of Higher Education	1695	1977	2217	2528	2653	2993
中等职业教育学校	Vocational Secondary Schools	518	1096	1371	1447	1448	1264
普通中学	Regular Secondary Schools	5943	5594	5543	5999	6811	10138
小　学	Primary Schools	5832	6300	5825	5922	6146	3928

20-19 成人教育
Adult Education

类 别	Item	2006	2007	2008	2009	2010	2011
学校数(所)	**Number of Schools(unit)**						
成人高等教育学校	Adult Institutions of Higher Education	6	5	5	4	4	4
成人中等专业教育学校	Adult Specialized Secondary Schools	21	19	21	22	21	15
成人中学	Adult Secondary Schools	4	5	45	22	33	13
成人技术培训学校	Adult Technical Training Schools	11850	11747	12999	11852	7711	8202
成人小学	Adult Primary Schools	10198	8972	9433	9377	5405	5059
在校生数(万人)	**Number of Students Enrollment(10000 persons)**						
成人高等教育	Adult Institutions of Higher Education	11.04	8.96	8.80	8.62	8.66	7.96
成人中等专业教育	Adult Specialized Secondary Schools	1.49	1.33	1.69	2.02	2.88	1.80
成人中学	Adult Secondary Schools	0.12	0.21	0.48	0.56	1.69	0.12
成人技术培训学校	Adult Technical Training Schools	259.53	272.73	275.07	262.72	205.81	218.06
成人小学	Adult Primary Schools	30.91	32.31	30.34	30.23	23.99	12.80
毕业生数(万人)	**Number of Graduates(10000 persons)**						
成人高等教育	Adult Institutions of Higher Education	3.28	4.78	2.89	2.81	2.43	3.00
成人中等专业教育	Adult Specialized Secondary Schools	0.27	0.35	0.27	0.36	0.47	0.22
成人中学	Adult Secondary Schools	0.06	0.15	0.35	0.45	0.77	0.32
成人技术培训学校	Adult Technical Training Schools	235.00	256.20	264.35	251.73	206.55	219.58
成人小学	Adult Primary Schools	26.84	27.23	23.64	24.30	21.49	12.99

20–20 科技活动

Basic Statistics on Scientific and Technological Activities

指　标	Item	2010	2011	2011年比2010年增长(%) Increase Rate in 2011 over 2010(%)
科技活动人员(人)	**Persons Engaged in Scientific and Technological Activities (person)**	**56292**	**60366**	**7.2**
科研机构	**Scientific Research Institutions**			
科研机构数(个)	Number of Institutions(unit)	331	331	持平
科研用仪器设备原价(万元)	Original Cost of Instrument and Equipment for Scientific Research(10000yuan)	303065	435225	43.6
#进口	Import	63738	91212	43.1
研究与实验发展(R&D)	**Research and Development**			
研究与试验发展(R&D)人员(人)	R&D Personnel(person)	23431	24875	6.2
#博士毕业	Doctor	1256	1492	18.8
硕士毕业	Master	3038	4220	38.9
研究与试验发展(R&D)经费支出(万元)	Expenditure on R&D(10000yuan)	299665	363089	21.2
科技产出	**S&T Output**			
专利申请数(件)	Number of Patents Application(unit)	1926	2485	29.0
#发明专利	Inventions	924	1075	16.3
专利授权数(件)	Number of Patents Granted(unit)	151	208	37.7
#发明专利	Inventions	63	91	44.4
有效发明专利数(件)	Number of Valid Patents for Invention(unit)	1308	1560	19.3
专利所有权转让及许可数(件)	Number of Patents Ownership Assigned and Granted (unit)	18	37	105.6
专利所有权转让及许可收入(万元)	Revenue from Patents Ownership Assigned and Granted(10000yuan)	23	31644	135.1倍
集成电路布图设计登记数(件)	Number of IC Layout Design Registrations(unit)		1	
植物新品种权授予数(项)	Number of New Plant Breed Rights Granted(unit)	20	17	-15.0
形成国家或行业标准数(项)	Number of Standards Adopted by State or Industry(unit)	272	286	5.1
发表科技论文(篇)	Scientific Papers Issued(piece)	16326	16514	1.2
出版科技著作(种)	Publication on Science an Technology(kind)	367	400	9.0

20–21 研究与试验发展(R&D)活动

Basic Statistics on Scientific Research and Development

指　　标	Item	2010	2011	2011年比2010年增长(%) Increase Rate in 2011 over 2010(%)
有研究与试验发展(R&D)活动单位(个)	**Number of Institutions Having R&D Activities(unit)**	**282**	**316**	**12.1**
R&D人员	**Bisic Statistics on R&D Personnel**			
R&D人员(人)	R&D Personnel(person)	23431	24875	6.2
#女性	Female	7062	8130	15.1
#研究人员	Research Personnel	13822	14746	6.7
#全时人员	Full-time Personnel	12371	12641	2.2
非全时人员	Part-time Personnel	11060	12234	10.6
#博士毕业	Doctor	1256	1492	18.8
硕士毕业	Master	3038	4220	38.9
本科毕业	Bachelor	8261	9526	15.3
其他学历	Others	10876	9637	-11.4
R&D人员折合全时当量(人年)	Full-time Equivalent of R&D Personnel(person-year)	15087	15886	5.3
#研究人员	Research Personnel	8483	8861	4.5
#基础研究	Basic Research	2055	2436	18.6
应用研究	Applied Research	2578	2337	-9.3
试验发展	Experimental Development	10455	11114	6.3
R&D经费	**R&D Expenditure**			
R&D经费内部支出(万元)	Intramural Expenditure on R&D (10000yuan)	299665	363089	21.2
#基础研究	Basic Research	21805	29228	34.0
应用研究	Applied Research	36002	38962	8.2
试验发展	Experimental Development	241858	294900	21.9
#日常性支出	Daily Expenditure	267770	326471	21.9
#人员劳务费	Personnel Service Fees	60945	71751	17.7
资产性支出	Expenditure on Assets	31895	36620	14.8
#仪器和设备	Insrument and Equipment	25181	32315	28.3
#政府资金	Government Appropration Funds	75265	75230	0.0
企业资金	Self-raised Funds by Enterprises	202654	268920	32.7
境外资金	Overseas Funds	247	238	-3.7
其他资金	Other Funds	21499	18705	-13.0
经费投入强度(%)	**Intensity of Funds Input(%)**	**0.65**	**0.64**	**…**
R&D项目(课题)	**R&D Topics**			
R&D项目(课题)数(项)	Projects of R&D(unit)	9476	10975	15.8
R&D项目(课题)参加人员折合全时当量(人年)	Participants(person-year)	12989	13747	5.8
#研究人员	Research Personnel	7395	8375	13.3
R&D项目(课题)经费内部支出(万元)	Intramural Expenditure (10000yuan)	228606	295405	29.2

20-22 大中型工业企业科技活动
Basic Statistics on Science and Technology Activities of Large and Medium-sized Industrial Enterprises

指　　标	Item	2006	2007	2008	2009	2010	2011
企业基本情况	**Statistics on Industrial Enterprises**						
有R&D活动企业数(个)	Number of Enterprises Having R&D Activities(unit)	74	68	77	90	69	94
有R&D活动企业所占比重(%)	Percentage of Enterprises Having R&D Activities to Total Number of Enterprises(%)	29.5	26.1	21.6	24.1	26.5	16.7
R&D活动情况	**Statitstics on R&D Activities**						
R&D人员全时当量(万人年)	Full-time Equivalent of R&D Personnel (10 000 man-years)	0.55	0.59	0.57	0.67	0.86	0.89
R&D经费内部支出(亿元)	Intramural Expenditure on R&D(100 million yuan)	11.43	10.13	14.10	17.77	21.78	26.01
R&D经费内部支出与主营业务收入之比(%)	Percentage of Intramural Expenditure on R&D to Sales Revenue(%)		0.67	0.66	0.75	1.01	0.75
R&D项目数(项)	Projects of R&D(item)	1002	1112	740	1120	995	1158
R&D项目经费内部支出（亿元）	Intramural Expenditure on R&D Projects(100 million yuan)	10.63	9.38	13.80	14.70	16.71	21.94
企业办R&D机构情况	**Statistics on R&D Institutions**						
机构数(个)	Number of R&D Institutions(unit)	107	104	116	131	109	124
机构人员数(万人)	R&D Personnel(10 000 persons)	0.76	0.91	1.01	1.01	1.14	0.92
机构经费支出(亿元)	Expenditure on R&D(100 million yuan)	12.61	13.41	18.74	19.30	18.88	12.26
新产品开发及生产情况	**Statitstics on New Products Development and Production**						
新产品开发项目数(个)	Number of New Products(unit)	1239	642	1278	1698	1344	1527
新产品开经费支出(亿元)	Expenditure on New Products Development(100 million yuan)	11.69	12.38	17.10	23.60	26.43	34.07
新产品销售收入(亿元)	Sales Revenue of New Products(100 million yuan)	171.24	184.88	177.62	177.48	310.65	424.59
#新产品出口	Export	10.93	16.04	11.71	9.01	21.19	29.88
专利情况	**Statistics on Patent**						
专利申请数(件)	Patent Applications(piece)	428	580	906	1222	1302	1675
#发明专利	Inventions	209	254	405	567	648	654
有效发明专利数(件)	Number of Patents In Force (piece)	253	300	583	629	757	835
技术获取和技术改造情况	**Statistics on Technology Acquisition and Technology Reconstruction**						
引进国外技术经费支出(亿元)	Expenditure for Acquisition of Foreign Technology (100 million yuan)	0.83	0.62	1.34	0.24	1.35	0.45
引进技术消化吸收经费支出(亿元)	Expenditure for Assimilation of Technology(100 million yuan)	0.02	0.54	0.13	0.20	0.29	0.53
购买国内技术经费支出(亿元)	Expenditure for Purchase of Domestic Technology (100 million yuan)	0.31	0.33	0.52	1.03	1.97	0.60
技术改造经费支出(亿元)	Expenditure for Technical Renovation(100 million yuan)	58.65	55.91	71.30	78.40	54.37	66.79

20–23 政府属独立研究与开发机构科技活动
Scientific and Technological Activities of Government-affiliated Independent Research Institutions

指 标	Item	2006	2007	2008	2009	2010	2011	2011年比2010年增长(%) Increase Rate in 2011 over 2010(%)
科技机构数(个)	**Number of S&T Institutions(unit)**	**116**	**111**	**111**	**106**	**107**	**105**	**-1.9**
县级以上研究与开发机构	Scientific Research and Development Institution at County and Higher Levels	73	70	66	62	62	60	-3.2
社会、人文科学研究机构	Research Institutions of Social and Human Studies	3	3	3	3	4	4	持平
县级以上研究与开发转制机构	Conversed Scientific Research and Development Institution at County and Higher Levels	19	21	25	24	24	25	4.2
县级以上部门属科技情报与文献机构	Department of S&T Informations and Literature Institutions at County and Higher Levels	6	6	6	6	6	6	持平
县级政府部门属研究与开发机构	Scientific Research and Development Institutions at County Level	15	11	11	11	11	10	-9.1
科技活动人员数(人)	**Personnel Engaged in S&T Activities(person)**	**5450**	**5523**	**5547**	**4336**	**4594**	**5019**	**9.3**
县级以上研究与开发机构	Scientific Research and Development Institution at County and Higher Levels	3826	3879	3484	2656	2847	3218	13.0
社会、人文科学研究机构	Research Institutions of Social and Human Studies	198	179	203	204	226	223	-1.3
县级以上研究与开发转制机构	Conversed Scientific Research and Development Institution at County and Higher Levels	1188	1256	1675	1280	1300	1348	3.7
县级以上部门属科技情报与文献机构	Department of S&T Informations and Literature Institutions at County and Higher Levels	107	109	92	100	120	128	6.7
县级政府部门属研究与开发机构	Scientific Research and Development Institutions at County Level	131	100	93	96	101	102	1.0
大学本科及以上学历(人)	**University,College and Above(person)**	**3398**	**3938**	**4066**	**2873**	**3103**	**3612**	**16.4**
县级以上研究与开发机构	Scientific Research and Development Institution at County and Higher Levels	2418	2785	2497	1660	1848	2273	23.0
社会、人文科学研究机构	Research Institutions of Social and Human Studies	140	145	158	168	205	200	-2.4
县级以上研究与开发转制机构	Conversed Scientific Research and Development Institution at County and Higher Levels	731	909	1324	913	950	1027	8.1
县级以上部门属科技情报与文献机构	Department of S&T Informations and Literature Institutions at County and Higher Levels	73	79	68	64	74	84	13.5
县级政府部门属研究与开发机构	Scientific Research and Development Institutions at County Level	36	20	19	68	26	28	7.7

注：1、资料来源于省科技厅(以下相关表同)。2、“大学本科及以上学历”2006–2008年为“科学家和工程师”。3、2006–2008年“科技机构数”与2009年及以后的统计口径不一致。

Note:1.Data in the table are obtained from the Department of Science and Technology(The relative tables in the chapter are the same).2.The indicator of university,college and above for the year 2006 to 2008 refer to scientists and engineers.3.The statistical coverage of number of S&T institutions from 2006 to 2008 had been changed from the year 2009.

20-23 续表 continued

指 标	Item	2006	2007	2008	2009	2010	2011	2011年比2010年增长(%) Increase Ratein 2011 over 2010(%)
经费收入总额(万元)	**Funding for S&T Activities(10000 yuan)**	**75377**	**104375**	**123392**	**115296**	**140870**	**175937**	**24.9**
县级以上研究与开发机构	Scientific Research and Development Institution at County and Higher Levels	52697	71422	73498	65448	84360	96246	14.1
社会、人文科学研究机构	Research Institutions of Social and Human Studies	2706	2641	2962	3302	3266	3469	6.2
县级以上研究与开发转制机构	Conversed Scientific Research and Development Institution at County and Higher Levels	18295	28732	44407	43860	50253	72992	45.2
县级以上部门属科技情报与文献机构	Department of S&T Informations and Literature Institutions at County and Higher Levels	1089	1068	2039	2033	1851	1972	6.5
县级政府部门属研究与开发机构	Scientific Research and Development Institutions at County Level	590	513	487	653	1140	1259	10.5
经费支出总额(万元)	**Expenditures on S&T Activities(10000 yuan)**	**71482**	**95949**	**118029**	**125340**	**139117**	**171663**	**23.4**
县级以上研究与开发机构	Scientific Research and Development Institution at County and Higher Levels	50337	67612	64397	70890	73690	87132	18.2
社会、人文科学研究机构	Research Institutions of Social and Human Studies	2087	2549	2623	2869	2724	3262	19.7
县级以上研究与开发转制机构	Conversed Scientific Research and Development Institution at County and Higher Levels	17421	24119	48842	48828	59396	77872	31.1
县级以上部门属科技情报与文献机构	Department of S&T Informations and Literature Institutions at County and Higher Levels	1036	1062	1536	2021	1957	2003	2.3
县级政府部门属研究与开发机构	Scientific Research and Development Institutions at County Level	600	607	631	732	1350	1394	3.3
研究与试验发展经费支出(R&D经费支出)(万元)	**Expenditure on R&D(10000 yuan)**	**16153**	**22806**	**27013**	**30666**	**24771**	**30422**	**22.8**
县级以上研究与开发机构	Scientific Research and Development Institution at County and Higher Levels	12503	18380	20443	26448	19682	20024	1.7
社会、人文科学研究机构	Research Institutions of Social and Human Studies	1264	1103	431	584	839	1001	19.3
县级以上研究与开发转制机构	Conversed Scientific Research and Development Institution at County and Higher Levels	2352	3288	5796	3464	3963	9398	137.1
县级以上部门属科技情报与文献机构	Department of S&T Informations and Literature Institutions at County and Higher Levels	5		257	104	257		
县级政府部门属研究与开发机构	Scientific Research and Development Institutions at County Level	29	35	86	66	30		

20-24 民营科技

Scientific and Technological Research Activities of Non-state-owned Economy

指标	Item	2006	2007	2008	2009	2010	2011
机构数(个)	**Number of Enterprises(unit)**	**238**	**243**	**216**	**260**	**223**	**219**
#集体经济单位	Collective-owned Enterprises	11	8	8	9	10	12
从业人员(人)	**Number of Employed Persons(person)**	**23631**	**27278**	**23170**	**33927**	**37529**	**37016**
#高级职称	Senior Title	474	375	471	509	513	474
中级职称	Middle Title	1795	1744	1475	1725	1926	1470
资产总额(亿元)	Total Assets(100 million yuan)	80.77	94.54	87.12	145.38	177.51	186.69
负债总额(亿元)	Total Liabilities(100 million yuan)	38.79	46.80	42.16	69.22	74.38	92.05
工业总产值(亿元)	Total Output Value of Industry(100 million yuan)	75.85	99.95	80.86	154.54	188.17	202.57
总收入(亿元)	**Total Revenue(100 million yuan)**	**65.38**	**77.51**	**72.91**	**132.57**	**151.27**	**170.38**
#技术性收入	Technical Revenue	0.25	0.13	0.73	2.44	2.28	7.52
产品销售收入	Product Sales Revenue	59.30	69.29	66.28	118.43	143.39	159.06
商品销售收入	Merchandise Sales Revenue	5.34	7.06	3.86	9.77	4.05	2.84
利润总额(亿元)	Total Profits(100 million yuan)	5.15	6.98	5.15	15.57	18.20	18.67
创汇额(万美元)	Total Foreign Exchange(USD 10000)	3096.30	13718.60	741.70	3018.10	2406.40	5396.00
总支出(亿元)	**Total Expenditure(100 million yuan)**	**46.36**	**55.74**	**56.01**	**103.14**	**130.33**	**157.37**
#研究与开发费用	Expenditure on R&D	0.81	2.03	1.10	1.39	3.43	3.20
上缴税金总额	Total Taxes	5.56	7.95	7.07	13.28	14.23	14.31
专利申请数(件)	Number of Patent Applications(unit)	186	163	204	387	279	490
专利授权数(件)	Number of Warrant Patents(unit)	107	81	158	231	200	185
拥有发明专利数(件)	Number of Patents(unit)	141	223	132	278	409	409

20–25　国家级科技计划项目人员

Personnel of National S&T Program Projects

指标	Item	2006	2007	2008	2009	2010	2011
项目参加人员(人)	**Personnel in Project (person)**	**1256**	**1034**	**2948**	**3011**	**3191**	**2533**
按计划类别分	By Type of Progarm						
973计划	973 Program		196	223	216	282	230
863计划	863 Program	95	60	171	190	180	189
支撑计划	Key Technologies R&D Program	433	171	1609	1759	1598	794
火炬计划	Torch Program	414	275	408	354	386	492
星火计划	Spark Program	314	332	537	489	745	828
按职称类别分	By Type of Professional Title						
#高级职称	Senior Title	220	452	984	1045	979	803
中级职称	Middle Title	173	382	1196	1160	1131	733
初级职称	Primary Title	75	16	204	189	132	84
其他人员	Other	60	43	284	361	422	300
按学历分	By Education Background						
#博 士	Doctor	42	144	256	295	295	208
硕 士	Master	83	163	386	347	406	257
工作投入量(人月)	**Personnel Input (man-month)**	**2207**	**2997**	**15665**	**14906**	**13043**	**6694**
973计划	973 Program		1618	2419	1475	2127	1458
863计划	863 Program	356	342	1140	1617	1129	1134
支撑计划	Key Technologies R&D Program	1851	1037	12106	11814	9787	4102

注：1、初级职称和其他人员在火炬计划及星火计划统计中无该两项指标。2、973计划为国家重点基础研究计划，863计划为国家高技术研究发展计划(以下相关表同)。

Note:1.The statistics of Torch Program and Spark Program exclude primary title and other title personel. 2.973 program is the national program on key basic research, and 863 program is the national high technology research and development program(The relative tables in the chapter are the same).

20–26 国家级科技计划项目资金及支出

Funds and Expenditure of National S&T Program

指标	Item	2006	2007	2008	2009	2010	2011
按计划类别分(项)	**By Type of Program (item)**	**89**	**61**	**120**	**124**	**138**	**135**
973计划	National Basic Research Program of China(973 Program)		2	2	10	13	10
863计划	High Technology Research and Development Program of China (863 Program)	5	4	8	10	11	11
支撑计划	Key Technologies R&D Program	16	6	29	34	39	26
火炬计划	Torch Program	40	20	37	34	37	42
星火计划	Spark Program	28	29	44	36	38	46
当年到位资金(万元)	**Funds Arranged (10000 yuan)**	**25970**	**13477**	**119361**	**68180**	**131469**	**83426**
973计划	973 Program		2190	1383	701	1119	376
863计划	863 Program	582	221	3519	1757	798	737
支撑计划	Key Technologies R&D Program	3321	2967	85685	37238	47561	5382
火炬计划	Torch Program	18949	3070	20386	19298	73513	64010
星火计划	Spark Program	3118	5029	8388	9186	8478	12921
项目支出(万元)	**Project Expenditure (10000 yuan)**	**19513**	**8024**	**96684**	**59839**	**97775**	**62601**
973计划	973 Program		888	1814	625	1040	498
863计划	863 Program	1544	401	3511	7737	674	900
支撑计划	Key Technologies R&D Program	3747	1842	72362	34052	49580	10958
火炬计划	Torch Program	11596	3070	12132	9165	38940	39917
星火计划	Spark Program	2626	1823	6865	8260	7541	10328

20–27 国家级科技计划项目培养和引进人才

Cultivated and Introduced Talents of National S&T Program

指标	Item	2006	2007	2008	2009	2010	2011
培养博士和硕士（人）	**Cultivated Master and Doctor (person)**	**48**	**48**	**191**	**299**	**249**	**152**
973计划	973 Program		31	82	45	84	47
863计划	863 Program	18	14	22	35	31	23
支撑计划	Key Technologies R&D Program	30	3	87	219	134	82
引进人才（人）	**Introduction of Talents (person)**	**2**	**3**	**24**	**23**	**27**	**23**
973计划	973 Program				6	9	10
863计划	863 Program			2	3	4	3
支撑计划	Key Technologies R&D Program	2	3	22	14	14	10

20–28 国家级科技计划实施项目效益

Benefit of National S&T Program

单位：万元 (10000 yuan)

指标	Item	2006	2007	2008	2009	2010	2011
新增产值	**Added Value of Output**	**112841**	**80929**	**207698**	**230480**	**236270**	**307027**
支撑计划	Key Technologies R&D Program	25134	1856	57896	82840	71388	93092
火炬计划	Torch Program	85912	74070	119762	122867	130213	183817
星火计划	Spark Program	1795	5003	30040	24773	34669	30118
净利润	**After-Tax Profit**	**16086**	**5976**	**14877**	**15629**	**23024**	**25958**
支撑计划	Key Technologies R&D Program	9913		3196	3121	1484	5455
火炬计划	Torch Program	5741	4693	8251	9032	12006	15981
星火计划	Spark Program	432	1283	3430	3476	9534	4522
实交税金	**Tax**	**5617**	**3587**	**15392**	**8513**	**10760**	**13119**
支撑计划	Key Technologies R&D Program	409	7	8190	1801	796	3893
火炬计划	Torch Program	5135	3354	6000	5744	8799	8176
星火计划	Spark Program	73	226	1202	968	1165	1050

20–29 省部级以上成果登记(完成人员)
Staffs Personnel of Provincial or Ministerial Level and above

单位：人次 (person-time)

指标	Item	2006	2007	2008	2009	2010	2011
合 计	**Total**	**1244**	**1244**	**1279**	**1293**	**1306**	**979**
按学历分	**By Type of Diploma**						
博士	Doctor	106	147	143	134	143	133
硕士	Master	193	253	288	269	279	255
大本	Undergraduate Student	752	700	699	717	720	515
大专	Junior College Student	147	96	111	135	139	68
中专	Senoir Middle School	33	38	31	37	20	8
其他	Below Senoir Middle School	13	10	7	1	5	
按年龄结构分	**By Type of Age**						
35岁以下(含35岁)	Thirty-five and below	233	284	366	379	388	328
36–45岁	Thirty-six to forty-five	491	434	486	476	500	353
46–55岁	Forty-six to fifty-five	367	384	321	338	341	238
56–65岁	Fifty-six to sixty-five	96	100	78	69	55	45
65岁以上	Above sixty-five	57	42	28	31	22	15
按技术职称分	**By Type of Title**						
院士	Academicians		1		2		
正高	Senior Title	228	281	266	272	277	198
副高	Sub-senior Title	423	406	378	377	380	302
中级	Middle Title	371	413	451	452	486	345
初级	Primary Title	141	98	133	142	134	91
其他	No Rank	81	45	51	48	29	43

20−30 省部级以上成果登记(数量及投资额)
Number of Achievements and Investment of Projects at Provincial or Ministerial Level and above(number & investment)

指 标	Item	2006	2007	2008	2009	2010	2011
成果登记(项)	**Achievement Registration(item)**	**141**	**144**	**130**	**137**	**125**	**90**
发明专利授权数(件)	Invention of Patent Authorigations Granted (piece)	7	21	34	46	67	240
制订标准数(个)	Number of Standards for Formulation (unit)	6	19	19	27	12	8
按成果类别分(项)	By Type of Achievement Sort (item)						
基础研究	Basic Research	27	30	23	14	16	19
应用研究	Applied Research	114	114	107	123	109	71
按成果应用属性分(项)	By Type of Achievement Application Property (item)						
#原始性创新	Original Invention	26	63	65	68	63	22
国外引进消化 吸收创新	Absorb and Digest Invention of Foreign Indraught	17	21	20	22	15	11
国内技术二次开发	Twice Development of Inner Technology	71	30	22	33	31	38
项目投资额(万元)	**Project Investment (10000 yuan)**	**29736**	**119313**	**104868**	**108623**	**95331**	**212819**
国家资金	Government Funds	2982	3757	4418	2847	12317	6127
部门资金	Department Funds	643	34253	4635	5396	18234	947
地方资金	Local Funds	4821	34538	21585	26710	31433	6223
基金投入	Fund Input	565	152	69	862	158	135
自有资金	Self-raised Funds	15009	37418	16082	53927	23420	195620
银行贷款	Loans from Bank	320	720	1000	15646		200
国外资金	Foreign Funds.	12	117	3			12
其他资金	Other Funds	5384	8358	57076	3235	9769	3555
净利润(万元)	**After-Tax Profit (10000 yuan)**	**72427**	**29188**	**60115**	**201281**	**78889**	**354367**
实交税金(万元)	**Tax (10000 yuan)**	**18655**	**21520**	**19269**	**17970**	**17699**	**104371**

20–31 事业、企业单位各类专业技术人员

Specialized Technical Personnel in Enterprises and institutions

单位：万人 (10000 persons)

指　标	Item	2006	2007	2008	2009	2010	2011	2011年比2010年增长(%) Increase Rate in 2011 over 2010(%)
总　计	**Total**	**58.32**	**58.54**	**58.63**	**58.82**	**56.43**	**59.27**	**5.0**
#女　性	Female	23.00	23.30	23.48	23.85	23.19	24.01	3.5
按专业分	**By Specialized Subject**							
#工程技术人员	Engineering Technical Personnel	6.23	5.82	6.24	6.23	5.86	6.27	7.0
农业技术人员	Agricultural Technical Personnel	2.69	2.67	2.60	2.60	2.41	2.65	10.0
卫生技术人员	Medical Technical Persomnel	7.38	7.47	7.38	7.45	7.27	7.61	4.7
科学研究人员	Scientific Research Personnel	0.14	0.14	0.14	0.15	0.15	0.15	持平
教学人员	Teaching Personnel	35.91	36.48	36.87	37.11	36.12	37.94	5.0
按专业技术职务分	**By Professional Titles**							
#高　级	Senior	2.64	2.98	3.12	3.37	3.24	3.77	16.4
中　级	Medium	14.56	15.83	16.53	17.29	17.38	18.69	7.5
初　级	Junior	36.72	35.82	34.81	34.00	33.61	32.61	-3.0
按学历分	**By Education Background**							
#大学本科以上	University,College and above	11.92	13.61	14.91	14.95	18.86	20.41	8.2
大学专科	Specialized Institutions of Higher Education	25.23	26.97	27.36	27.37	26.16	27.76	6.1
中专以下	Senior Middle School and the Level below	21.17	18.14	16.33	16.32	11.41	11.10	-2.7

注：1、资料来源于省人力资源社会保障厅。2、本表数据不含非公经济单位，按岗位统计。3、2010年事业单位专业技术人员不含在管理岗位兼职的人员。

Note: 1.Data in the table are obtained from the Provinvial Department of Human Resources and Social Security. 2.Data in the table exclude non-public economy and they are counted on working post.3.The statistical Coverage of specialized technical personnel in institutions was adjuted in 2010 which excludes the part time personnel on the management post.

20–32 专利申请受理及授权

Patent Application Accepted and Granted

单位：件 (item)

指 标	Item	2006	2007	2008	2009	2010	2011	2011年比2010年增长(%) Increase Rate in 2011 over 2010(%)
受理专利总计	**Total Patent Applications Accepted**	**2674**	**2759**	**2943**	**3709**	**4414**	**7510**	**70.1**
按种类分	**Grouped by Sort**							
发 明	Inventions	923	874	873	1336	1322	2087	57.9
实用新型	Utility Models	1220	1287	1403	1659	2441	2769	13.4
外观设计	Designs	531	598	667	714	651	2654	307.7
按对象分	**Grouped by Applicant**							
非职务发明创造	Non-service Creations and Inventions	1271	1223	1160	1114	1631	1954	19.8
职务发明创造	Service Creations and Inventions	1403	1536	1783	2595	2783	5556	99.6
#大专院校	Universities and Colleges	72	70	133	139	172	276	60.5
科研单位	Research Institutions	438	437	446	388	633	342	-46.0
工矿企业	Industrial and Mineral Enterprises	878	992	1192	2047	1937	4840	149.9
机关团体	Government Agencies and Organizations	15	37	12	21	41	98	139.0
授权专利总计	**Total Patent Authorigations Granted**	**1337**	**1727**	**1728**	**2084**	**3034**	**3386**	**11.6**
按种类分	**Grouped by Sort**							
发 明	Inventions	188	233	270	322	434	596	37.3
实用新型	Utility Models	862	1120	1183	1234	1904	1885	-1.0
外观设计	Designs	287	374	275	528	696	905	30.0
按对象分	**Grouped by Applicant**							
非职务发明创造	Non-service Creations and Inventions	640	834	704	712	961	992	3.2
职务发明创造	Service Creations and Inventions	697	893	1024	1372	2073	2394	15.5
#大专院校	Universities and Colleges	15	40	31	50	116	141	21.6
科研单位	Research Institutions	276	299	322	337	366	378	3.3
工矿企业	Industrial and Mineral Enterprises	400	539	660	972	1569	1841	17.3
机关团体	Government Agencies and Organizations	6	15	11	13	22	34	54.5

注：资料来源于省知识产权局。

Note: Data in the table are obtained from the Provincial Intellectual Property Right Bureau.

主要统计指标解释

普通高等学校 指按照国家规定的设置标准和审批程序批准举办，通过国家统一招生考试，招收高中毕业生为主要培养对象，实施高等教育的全日制大学、独立设置的学院和高等专科学校、短期职业大学。

成人高等学校 指按照国家有关规定审批，招收通过全国成人高教统一招生考试的具有高中毕业或同等学历的在职从业人员，利用脱产、半脱产、业余或函授等多种形式对其实施高等学历教育，培养高等教育专科或本科毕业水平的专门人才，修业年限、课程设置和总学时数均按高等学历教育要求付诸实施的学校。包括广播电视大学、职工高等学校、农民高等学校、管理干部学院、教育学院、独立设置的函授学院等。

小学学龄儿童入学率 指调查范围内已入小学学习的学龄儿童占校内外学龄儿童总数（包括弱智儿童，不包括盲聋哑儿童）的比重。计算公式为:

$$小学学龄儿童入学率=\frac{已入学的小学学龄儿童数}{校内外小学学龄儿童总数}\times 100\%$$

科技活动 指在自然科学、农业科学、医药科学、工程与技术科学、人文与社会科学领域（简称科学技术领域）中，与科技知识的产生、发展、传播和应用密切相关的有组织的活动。可分为研究与试验发展 (R&D)、研究与试验发展成果应用及相关的科技服务三类活动。该定义是联合国教科文组织考虑成员国特别是发展中国家开展科技统计工作的需要，而对科技活动所作的统计界定。

科技活动人员 指直接从事科技活动、以及专门从事科技活动管理和为科技活动提供直接服务，累计的实际工作时间占全年制度工作时间 10% 及以上的人员。(1) 直接从事科技活动的人员包括：在独立核算的科学研究与技术开发机构、高等学校、各类企业及其他事业单位内设的研究室、实验室、技术开发中心及中试车间（基地）等机构中从事科技活动的研究人员、工程技术人员、技术工人及其它人员；虽不在上述机构工作，但编入科技活动项目（课题）组的人员；科技信息与文献机构中的专业技术人员；从事论文设计的研究生等。(2) 专门从事科技活动管理和为科技活动提供直接服务的人员，包括：独立核算的科学研究与技术开发机构、科技信息与文献机构、高等学校、各类企业及其他事业单位主管科技工作的负责人，专门从事科技活动的计划、行政、人事、财务、物资供应、设备维护、图书资料管理等工作的各类人员，但不包括保卫、医疗保健人员、司机、食堂人员、茶炉工、水暖工、清洁工等为科技活动提供间接服务的人员。该指标用来反映投入科技活动人力的规模。

科学家与工程师 指科技活动人员中具有高、中级技术职称（职务）的人员和不具有高、中级技术职称（职务）的大学本科及以上学历人员。该指标用来反映投入科技活动人力的素质。

研究与试验发展（R&D） 指在科学技术领域，为增加知识总量、以及运用这些知识去创造新的应用进行的系统的创造性的活动，包括基础研究、应用研究、试验发展三类活动。国际上通常采用 R&D 活动的规模和强度指标反映一国的科技实力和核心竞争力。

基础研究 指为了获得关于现象和可观察事实的基本原理的新知识（揭示客观事物的本质、运动规律，获得新发现、新学说）而进行的实验性或理论性研究，它不以任何专门或特定的应用或使用为目的。其成果以科学论文和科学著作为主要形式。用来反映知识的原始创新能力。

应用研究 指为获得新知识而进行的创造性研究，主要针对某一特定的目的或目标。应用研究是为了确定基础研究成果可能的用途，或是为达到预定的目标探索应采取的新方法（原理性）或新途径。其成果形式以科学论文、专著、原理性模型或发明专利为主。用来反映对基础研究成果应用途径的探索。

试验发展 指利用从基础研究、应用研究和实际经验所获得的现有知识，为产生新的产品、材料和装置，建立新的工艺、系统和服务，以及对已产生和建立的上述各项作实质性的改进而进行的系统性工作。其成果形式主要是专利、专有技术、具有新产品基本特征的产品原型或具有新装置基本特征的原始样机等。在社会科学领域，试验发展是指把通过基础研究、应用研究获得的知识转变成可以实施的计划（包括为进行检验和评估实施示范项目）的过程。人文科学领域没有对应的试验发展活动。主要反映将科研成果转化为技术和产品的能力，是科技推动经济社会发展的物化成果。

研究与试验发展人员 指参与研究与试验发展项目研究、管理和辅助工作的人员， 包括项目（课题）组人员，企业科技行政管理人员和直接为项目（课题）活动提供服务的辅助人员。反映投入从事拥有自主知识产权的研究开发活动的人力规模。

研究与试验发展人员全时当量 指全时人员数加非全时人员按工作量折算为全时人员数的总和。例如：有两个全时人员和三个非全时人员（工作时间分别为20%、30%和70%），则全时当量为2+0.2+0.3+0.7=3.2人年。为国际上比较科技人力投入而制定的可比指标。

专业技术人员 指从事专业技术工作和专业技术管理工作的人员，即企事业单位中已经聘任专业技术职务从事专业技术工作和专业技术管理工作的人员，以及未聘任专业技术职务，现在专业技术岗位上工作的人员。包括工程技术人员，农业技术人员，科学研究人员，卫生技术人员，教学人员，经济人员，会计人员，统计人员，翻译人员，图书资料、档案、文博人员，新闻出版人员，律师、公证人员，广播电视播音人员，工艺美术人员，体育人员，艺术人员及企业政治思想工作人员，共十七个专业技术职务类别。用来反映科技人力资源情况。

科技活动经费筹集 指从各种渠道筹集到的计划用于科技活动的经费，包括政府资金、企业资金、事业单位资金、金融机构贷款、国外资金和其他资金等。反映各社会经济主体对促进科技进步所做的努力。

政府资金 指从各级政府部门获得的计划用于科技活动的经费，包括科学事业费、科技三项费、科研基建费、科学基金、教育等部门事业费中计划用于科技活动的经费以及政府部门预算外资金中计划用于科技活动的经费等。

企业资金 指从自有资金中提取或接受其他企业委托的、科研院所和高校等事业单位接受企业委托获得的，计划用于科研和技术开发的经费。不包括来自政府、金融机构及国外的计划用于科技活动的资金。

金融机构贷款 指从各类金融机构获得的用于科技活动的贷款。

科技活动经费内部支出 指报告年内用于科技活动的实际支出，包括劳务费、科研业务费、科研管理费，非基建投资购建的固定资产、科研基建支出以及其他用于科技活动的支出。不包括生产性活动支出、归还贷款支出及转拨外单位支出。反映科技投入实际完成情况。

劳务费 指以货币或实物形式直接或间接支付给从事科技活动人员的劳动报酬及各种费用。包括各种形式的工资、津贴、奖金、福利、离退休人员费用、人民助学金等。反映改善科技人员待遇情况。

固定资产购建费 指报告年内使用非基建投资购建的固定资产和用于科研基建投资的实际支出额，即固定资产实际支出和科研基建投资实际完成额之和。固定资产是指长期使用而不改变原有实物形态的主要物资设备、图书资料、实验材料和标本以及其他设备和家具、房屋、建筑物。反映用于改善科研条件和科研手段方面的投入情况。

新产品 指采用新技术原理、新设计构思研制、生产的全新产品，或在结构、材质、工艺等某一方面比原有产品有明显改进，从而显著提高了产品性能或扩大了使用功能的产品。既包括政府有关部门认定并在有效期内的新产品，也包括企业自行研制开发，未经政府有关部门认定，从投产之日起一年之内的新产品。用来反映科技产出及对经济增长的直接贡献。

专利 是专利权的简称，是对发明人的发明创造经审查合格后，由专利局依据专利法授予发明人和设计人对该项发明创造享有的专有权。包括发明、实用新型和外观设计。反映拥有自主知识产权的科技和设计成果情况。

发明 是专利法及其实施细则所称的发明，指对有关产品、方法或其改进所提出的新的技术方案。

实用新型 是专利法及其实施细则所称的实用新型，指对产品的形状、构造或者其结合所提出的适于实用的新的技术方案。

外观设计 专利法及其实施细则所称的外观设计，指对产品的形状、图案、色彩或者其结合所作出的富有美感并适于工业上应用的新设计。

Explanatory Notes on Main Statistical Indicators

Regular Institutions of Higher Education refer to educational establishments set up according to the government evaluation and approval procedures, enrolling graduates from senior secondary schools and providing higher education courses and training for senior professionals.They include full-time universities, colleges, high professional schools and short-term professional universities.

Institutions of Higher Education for Adults refer to educational establishments, set up in line with relevant rules approved by the government, enrolling staff and workers with senior secondary school or equivalent education ,and providing higher education courses in many forms of full time, part time, spare time, or correspondence for adults. Professionals thus trained receive a qualification equivalent to graduates studying regular courses at regular universities, colleges and professional colleges. Institutions of higher learning for adults include Radio and TV universities, schools of high education for staff and workers and peasants, colleges for management cadres, pedagogical colleges, independent correspondence colleges.

Enrollment Rate of Primary School Age Children refers to the proportion of school age children enrolled at schools to the total number of school age children both in and outside schools (including retarded children ,but excluding blind, deaf and mute children). The formula is:

$$\text{Enrollment Rate of Primary School Age Children}=\frac{\text{Total Primary School Age Children at Schools}}{\text{Total Primary School Age Children Both at and Outside Schools}}\times 100\%$$

Scientific and Technological Activities(S&T Activities) refer to organized activities which are closely related with the creation, development, dissemination and application of the scientific and technical knowledge in the fields of natural sciences, agricultural science, medical science, engineering and technological science, humanities and social sciences (referred to as scientific and technological fields). S&T activities can be classified in to 3 categories: research and development (R&D) activities, application of R&D results, and related S&T services. This statistical definition is made by UNICHIEF for scientific and technological activities to meet the need of carrying out statistical work in this field for its member countries in particular those developing countries.

Personnel Engaged in S&T Activities refer to personnel directly engaged in S&T activities, in the management of S&T activities, and in providing direct service to S&T activities, who spend over 10% of the total working hours in a year in S&T activities. (1) Personnel directly engaged in S&T activities include researchers, engineers, technicians and other related personnel engaged in S&T activities in independent-accounting R&D institutions, institutions of higher learning, and in research institutes, laboratories, technology development centers and central experiment workshops under enterprises and institutions. Also included are people working in S&T research project teams, professional and technical personnel working in S&T information archiving institutes, and graduate students working on the design of their thesis. (2) Personnel engaged in the management of S&T activities and in providing direct service to S&T activities include senior management people responsible for S&T activities in independent-accounting R&D institutions, S&T information archiving institutes, institutions of higher learning, and in enterprises and institutions where S&T activities are undertaken. Also included are people responsible for the planning, administration, personnel management, financial management, logistics supply, equipment maintenance, information and library management that are related with S&T activities. People providing indirect services are excluded, such as security, medical service, drivers, plumbers, cleaners and those providing catering and related service. This indicator reflects the size of personnel engaged in S&T activities.

Scientists and Engineers refer to persons engaged in S&T activities who have obtained titles of senior and middle level professional positions, and those without such position but having completed university or higher education. This indicator reflects the quality of personnel engaged in S&T activities.

Research and Development(R&D) refers to systematic and creative activities in the field of science and technology aiming at increasing the knowledge and using the knowledge for new application. R&D includes 3 categories of activities: basic research, applied research and experiments and development. The scale and intensity of R&D are widely used internationally to reflect the strength of S&T and the core competitiveness of a country in the world.

Basic Research refers to empirical or theoretical research aiming at obtaining new knowledge on the fundamental principles of phenomena of observable facts to reveal the nature and law of movement of objects and to acquire new discoveries or new theories. Basic research takes no specific or designated application as the aim of the research. Results of basic research are mainly released or disseminated in the form of scientific papers or monographs. This indicator reflects the original innovation capacity of knowledge.

Applied Research refers to creative research aiming at obtaining new knowledge on a specific objective or target. Purpose of the applied research is to identify the possible use of results from basic research, or to explore new (fundamental) methods or new approaches. Results of applied research are expressed in the form of scientific papers, monographs, fundamental models or invention patents. This indicator reflects the exploration of ways to apply the results of basic research.

Experiments and Development refer to systematic activities aiming at using the knowledge from basic and applied researches or from practical experience to develop new products, materials and equipment, to establish new production process, systems and services, or to make substantial improvement on the existing products, process or services. Results of experiment and development activities are embodied in patents, exclusive technology, and monotype of new products or equipment. In social sciences, experiment and development activities refer to the process of converting the knowledge from basic or applied researches into feasible programmes (including conduct of demonstration projects for assessment and evaluation). There are no experiment and development activities in the science of humanities. This indicator reflects the capability of transferring the results of S&T into technique and products, which is the materialized measurement of S&T pushing forward the economic and social development.

R&D Personnel refer to persons engaged in research, management and supporting activities of R&D, including persons in the project teams, persons engaged in the management of S&T activities of enterprises and supporting staff providing direct service to the research projects. This indicator reflects the size of personnel engaged in R&D activities with independent intellectual property.

Full-time Equivalent of R&D Personnel refers to the sum of the full-time persons and the full-time equivalent of part-time persons converted by workload. For instance, if there are 2 full-time persons and 3 part-time workers (20%, 30% and 70% of working hours respectively on R&D activities), the full-time equivalent is 2+0.2+0.3+0.7=3.2 person-years. This is an internationally comparable indicator of input of personnel in S&T activities.

Professional and Technical Personnel refer to persons engaged in professional and technical work or in the management of professional and technical activities, i.e., people with professional or technical positions who are engaged in professional and technical work or in the management of professional and technical activities, and people without professional or technical positions but are working on professional or technical posts. They include professionals and technicians working in 17 categories of technical occupations including engineering, agriculture, scientific researches, medical service, teaching, economic research and application, accounting, statistics, translation, libraries, archives, cultural and museum service, journalism and publication, lawyers, notarization service, radio and television broadcasting, handicraft and fine arts, sports, performing art, and political workers in enterprises. This indicator reflects the condition of human resources in S&T.

Government Funds refer to funds obtained from government agencies at all levels to be used for S&T activities, including fund for scientific undertakings, 3 kinds of fund for S&T activities, fund for capital construction for scientific researches, science fund, funds from education expenditures by education departments for S&T activities, and extra-budget fund from government agencies for S&T activities.

Self-raised Funds by Enterprises refers to self-raised funds by enterprises from their own expenditure or from other enterprises and funds received by universities or research institutions from enterprises for scientific research or technical development projects. Excluded in this category are funds from government agencies, financial institutions or from foreign institutions.

Loans from Financial Institutions refer to loans from various financial institutions for S&T activities.

Internal Expenditures on S&T activities refer to the actual expenditures on S&T activities during the reference year, including service fees, expenditure on research activities, expenditure on research management, purchase or construction of fixed assets not included in the investment for capital construction, expenditure on capital construction for scientific researches, and other expenditures on S&T activities. Not included are expenditure on production activities, repayment of loans and transfer expenditure. This indicator reflects the real accomplishment of input in S&T.

Service Fees refer to direct or indirect payment, in cash or in kind, made to personnel engaged in S&T activities as remuneration and other fees. They include, in various forms, salaries, subsidies, bonus, benefits, retirement pension, stipend, etc. This indicator reflects the improvement of treatment toward S&T personnel.

Purchase or Construction of Fixed Assets refers to the fixed assets purchased or constructed using funds other than the investment in capital construction, and the actual expenditure on capital construction for scientific researches. In other words, it is the sum of the actual expenditure on fixed assets and the accomplished investment in capital construction for scientific researches. Fixed assets refer to main materials and equipment, literatures and documents in libraries, materials for experiments, specimen, instruments, furniture, buildings and constructions that can be used for a long time without changing the form and shape of those articles or constructions. This indictor reflects the input in improving the condition of S&T and the means of scientific research.

New Products refer to new products produced with new technology and new design, or products that represent noticeable improvement in terms of structure, material, or production process so as to improve significantly the character or function of the older versions. They include new products certified by relevant government agencies within the period of certification, as well as new products designed and produced by enterprises within a year without certification by government agencies. This indictor reflects the direct contribution of S&T output to economic growth.

Patent is an abbreviation for the patent right and refers to the exclusive right of ownership by the inventors or designers for the creation or inventions, given from the patent offices after due process of assessment and approval in accordance with the Patent Law. Patents are granted for inventions, utility models and designs. This indicator reflects the achievements of S&T and design with independent intellectual property.

Inventions refer to the inventions as specified by the patent law and its detailed rules and regulations for implementation. They refer to the new technical proposals to the products or methods or their modifications.

Utility Models refer to the utility models as specified by the patent law and its detailed rules and regulations for implementation. They refer to the practical and new technical proposals on the shape and structure of the product or the combination of both.

Designs refer to the designs as specified by the patent law and its detailed rules and regulation for implementation. They refer to the aesthetics and industry applicable new designs for the shape, pattern and color of the product, or their combinations.

21

Twenty-one

文化、体育和卫生

Culture, Sports and Public Health

21-1 文化事业机构和人员

Number of Institutions and Personnel in Cultural Industry

指　标	Item	2006	2007	2008	2009	2010	2011	2011年比2010年增长(%) Increase Rate in 2011 over 2010(%)
机构总计(个)	**Total Number of Institutions(unit)**	**1699**	**1838**	**1869**	**1966**	**2041**	**2075**	**1.7**
#艺术事业	Art Institutions	61	61	59	76	65	56	-13.8
文物事业	Cultural Relics	108	111	113	153	145	130	-10.3
图书馆事业	Libraries	91	92	92	93	93	94	1.1
群众文化事业	Mass Culture	1419	1443	1470	1514	1524	1579	3.6
文艺科研	Cultural and Art Research Institutions	4	4	4	5	4	4	持平
其他文化事业	Other Culture Units	10	129	137	125	210	212	1.0
人员总计(人)	**Total Number of Persons Engaged(person)**	**8431**	**10013**	**10714**	**12520**	**12949**	**14945**	**15.4**
#艺术事业	Art Institntions	2555	2147	2184	2965	2421	2259	-6.7
文物事业	Cultural Relics	923	979	1133	1466	1665	1691	1.6
图书馆事业	Libraries	883	895	913	946	937	950	1.4
群众文化事业	Mass Culture	3732	4106	4400	4808	4790	5223	9.0
文艺科研	Cultural and Art Research Institutions	27	27	27	36	31	33	6.5
其他文化事业	Other Culture Units	281	1577	1955	2299	3105	4789	54.2

注：1、资料来源于省文化厅(以下相关表同)。2、2008年及以后数据含电影机构和人员。3、2008年及以后其他文化事业数据含其他艺术和执法机构。4、机构和人员数不含文化市场新分的机构和人员数。

Note:1.Data in the table are provided by the Provinvial Department of Culture(The relative tables in the chapter are the same).2.Data in the table include the cinema institution and staff from 2008. 3.The data of Other Culture Units in the table include the Other Culture institution and market executing the law institution from 2008. 4.Number of Institutions and Personnel in the table exclude newly increased Institutions and Personnel.

21–2 文化事业单位数
Basic Statistics on Culture Establishment

单位：个 (unit)

类　别	Item	2006	2007	2008	2009	2010	2011
艺术表演场所	Arts Centers	11	11	11	9	7	11
公共图书馆	Public Libraries	91	92	92	93	93	94
博物馆、纪念馆	Museums and Memorials	13	18	23	53	59	53
群众艺术馆、文化馆	Mass Art Centers and Cultural Centers	95	95	95	95	95	97
档案馆	Archives	98	98	107	107	107	107

21–3 文化娱乐业(2011)
Culture and Entertainment Industry

类　别	Sort	机构数(个) Institutions (unit)	从业人员(人) Number of Employed Persons(person)	营业收入(万元) Operating Revenue (10000 yuan)	主营业务利润(万元) Primary Business Profit (10000 yuan)
总　计	**Total**	**4748**	**28950**	**184178**	**69929**
歌舞娱乐场所	Song and Dance Centers	1242	14878	90852	32597
游戏电子游艺经营场所	Computer Game Management Centers	1231	3632	17977	8026
其他娱乐场所	Other Entertainment Centers	19	264	1286	468
网　吧	Internet Bar	2223	9714	65521	28462
网络游戏经营单位	Online Games Operating Centers	1	5	18	-19
演出经纪机构	Performance Broker Institution	32	457	7520	560

21–4 艺术表演场所(2011)
Art Preformances Places

类　别	Sort	机构数(个) Number of Instit-utions (unit)	从业人员(人) Number of Staff and Workers (person)	座席数(个) Seats (unit)	演(映)出场次(场) Number of Perfo-rmances (show)	#艺术演出场次 Art Perfo-rmance	观众人次(万人次) Number of Spectators (10000 person-times)
总　计	**Toatl**	**11**	**362**	**6918**	**753**	**329**	**52.2**
#省　级	Province Level	4	84	1465	162	162	8.2
地　级	Prefectural Level	2	109	1860	338	155	32.5
县　级	County Level	5	169	3593	253	12	11.5
#文化系统	Cultural Organizations and Institutions	11	362	6918	753	329	52.2

21-5 文化部门艺术剧团(2011)
Art Troupes of Culture Sector

指标	Item	剧团数(个) Number of Troupes (unit)	从业人员(人) Number of Employed Persons (person)	国内演出(场) Number of Domestic Performances (show)	#在农村演出 Shows in Rural Areas	国内观众人数(万人次) Number of Domestic Spectators (10000 person-times)
总计	**Total**	**45**	**1897**	**3800**	**1400**	**418**
按隶属关系分	Grouped by Ownership					
#国有剧团	State-owned Troupes	38	1693	2900	1100	383
按剧种分	Grouped by Art Troupes	45	1897	3800	1400	418
话剧、儿童剧、滑稽剧团	Drama, Children's Plays and Comedy Troupes	1	70	100		10
乐团、歌舞团、轻音乐团	Philharmonic, Song and Dance Troupe, Light Music Troupes	24	811	1900	600	219
戏曲剧团	Local Opera Troupes	6	432	700	300	54
曲艺、杂技、木偶、皮影团	Recitation and Ballad Troupes,Acrobatics and Circus Troupes,Puppet Show Troupes and ShadowPlay Troupes	2	183	200		13
文工团	Cultural and Performance Troupes	10	238	600	400	106
综合性艺术表演团体	General Art Performing Troupes	2	163	300	100	16

21-6 群众艺术馆和文化馆(站)(2011)
Mass Art Centers and Culture Centers(Stations)

指标	Item	合计 Total	群众艺术馆 Mass Art Centers	文化馆 Culture Centers	文化站 Culture Stations
馆(站)个数(个)	**Number of Centers(unit)**	**1579**	**9**	**88**	**1482**
组织各类讲座次数(次)	Organizing Lectures(time)	209	21	188	
组织文艺活动次数(次)	Organizing Art Performances(time)	11988	180	4146	7662
举办业余文艺训练班(班次)	Conducting Amateur Art Training Courses(class)	13760	247	4363	3287
#结业人数(万人次)	Number of Persons Completed(10000 person-times)	35.00	2.04	11.29	23.70
举办展览次数(次)	Number of Exhibitions(unit)	1457	26	402	1029

21-7 广播、电视

Radio and Television Industry

指　　标	Item	2006	2007	2008	2009	2010	2011
广播	**Radio**						
广播电台(座)	Radio Stations(unit)	4	4	4	4	4	4
广播节目综合人口覆盖率(%)	Radio Coverage Rate of the Population(%)	83.7	84.1	86.1	86.6	87.5	88.0
#农村	Rural	81.3	81.9	84.2	84.4	85.6	86.1
广播节目自办套数(套)	Number of Radio Programs with Ownership(set)	23	23	23	24	27	31
#公共广播	Public Radio	23	23	23	24	27	31
广播节目制作时间(万小时)	Length of Radio Programs Produced(10 000 hours)	8.61	6.73	6.69	7.37	6.23	10.58
公共广播节目播出时间(万小时)	Length of Public Radio Programs Broadcasted (10 000 hours)	12.38	11.37	13.58	14.34	15.78	18.92
电视	**Television**						
电视台(座)	Television Stations(unit)	5	5	5	5	5	5
广播电视台(座)	Broadcasting and Television Stations(unit)	77	77	77	78	79	79
电视节目综合人口覆盖率(%)	TV Coverage Rate of Population(%)	90.7	91.1	91.3	91.3	92.5	92.8
#农村	Rural	89.6	90.0	90.0	90.0	91.4	91.7
有线广播电视用户数(万户)	Number of Users of Cable Radio and TV (10 000 households)	326.84	335.35	338.23	340.61	335.23	396.57
#农村	Rural	129.29	166.20	113.92	93.07	91.26	210.53
数字电视用户数(万户)	Number of Users of Digital TV(10 000 households)	32.21	69.01	130.05	208.19	234.51	349.67
有线广播电视入户率(%)	Popularization Rate of Cable Radio and TV(%)	28.6	29.3	31.1	31.4	29.9	34.3
#农村	Rural	15.6	20.1	14.4	10.5	9.9	22.0
电视节目自办套数(套)	Number of TV Programs with Ownership(set)	99	99	99	100	101	101
#公共电视	Public TV	99	99	99	100	101	101
电视节目制作时间(万小时)	Length of TV Programs Produced(10 000 hours)	5.55	3.71	3.98	3.74	4.35	3.10
公共电视节目播出时间(万小时)	Length of Public TV Programs Broadcasted (10 000 hours)	28.92	29.94	24.78	23.49	24.69	22.71
电视剧播出数(万部)	Number of TV Plays Broadcasted(10 000 sets)	0.23	0.30	0.27	0.26	0.30	0.26
#进口电视剧播出数(部)	Imported TV Plays(set)	277	355	153	84	140	127
电视剧播出数(万集)	Number of TV Plays Broadcasted(10 000 parts)	5.73	6.22	5.59	6.28	7.24	6.45
#进口电视剧播出数	Imported TV Plays	0.48	0.97	0.50	0.32	0.38	0.26

注：资料来源于省广电局(下表同)。

Note:Data in the table are provided by the provinvial Radio and TV Administration(The relative tables in the chapter are the same).

21–8 广播、电视节目播出时间(2011)

Broadcasting Hours of Radio and Television Programs

单位：小时 (hour)

指 标	Item	全 年 公共节目播出时间 Broadcasting Hours	#新闻咨询类节目 News	#专题服务类节目 Special Subject	#综合益智类节目 General Entertainment
广播电台	**All Radio Broadcasting Stations**	**189225**	**39460**	**46445**	**52546**
省 级	Province Level	43800	2372	14235	19527
地 级	Prefectural Level	114367	24178	26929	28396
县 级	County Level	31058	12910	5281	4623
电视台	**All Television Stations**	**227163**	**64231**	**20680**	**10002**
省 级	Province Level	58970	4814	11192	3516
地 级	Prefectural Level	115445	16142	6475	5113
县 级	County Level	52748	43275	3013	1373

21–9 图书出版

Number of Books Published

类 别	Sort	2006	2007	2008	2009	2010	2011
出版图书(种)	**Number of Publications(kind)**	**996**	**861**	**1549**	**943**	**830**	**856**
#新出版	New Publications	584	502	602	500	647	545
总印数(万册)	Printed Copies(10000 copies)	9402	8626	10457	9263	8069	8492
总印张数(万印张)	Printed Sheets(10000 sheets)	57522	47107	39635	57032	55778	57278

注：资料来源于省新闻出版局(以下相关表同)。
Note: The data in the table are provided by the provinvial Press and Publication Administration(The relative tables in the chapter are the same).

21-10 杂志出版
Number of Magazines Published

类 别	Sort	2006	2007	2008	2009	2010	2011
出版杂志(种)	**Number of Publications(kind)**	**87**	**87**	**88**	**89**	**88**	**88**
每期平均印数(万册)	Average Printed Copies Per Issue(10000 copies)	90	91	98	93	85	78
总印数(万册)	Printed Copies(10000 copies)	1380	1376	1420	1358	1300	1413
总印张数(万印张)	Printed Sheets(10000 sheets)	8379	7784	8145	9243	7117	7257

21-11 报纸出版
Number of Newspaper Published

类 别	Sort	2006	2007	2008	2009	2010	2011
出版报纸(种)	**Number of Publications(kind)**	**44**	**45**	**44**	**44**	**44**	**44**
每期平均印数(万份)	Average Printed Copies Per Issue(10000 copies)	132	135	138	149	162	175
总印数(万份)	Printed Copies(10000 copies)	32026	34676	35110	36286	37004	44931
总印张数(万印张)	Printed Sheets(10000 sheets)	116421	129069	139002	142079	145831	200712

21-12 报纸分类出版数量(2011)
Number of Newspaper Published by Category

类 别	Sort	出版报纸(种) Number of Publications (kind)	每期平均印数(万份) Average Publication Per Issue (10000 copies)	总印数(万份) Total Printed (10000 copies)	总印张数(万印张) Total Printed Sheets (10000 sheets)
总 计	**Total**	**44**	**175**	**44931**	**200712**
#贵州日报	Guizhou Daily	1	14.60	5323.90	13608.90
贵州都市报	Guizhou Urban Newspaper	1	20.70	7164.70	45141.90
贵阳晚报	Guiyang Evening Newspaper	1	29.90	10725.10	77202.70
文 摘	Tabloid	1	4.80	489.60	979.20
每周广播电视报	Broadcasting and Television Weekly Newspaper	1	1.70	91.20	410.20

21-13 体育运动员
Athletes

单位：人 (person)

指标	Item	2006	2007	2008	2009	2010	2011
优秀运动员	**Excellent Athletes**	**264**	**244**	**136**	**145**	**145**	**189**
#女运动员	Female	85	66	49	50	50	67
专职教练员	**Full-time Coaches**	**224**	**200**	**207**	**215**	**215**	**219**
#女专职教练员	Female	58	52	52	56	56	61
等级运动员发展人数	**Number of Certified Athletes**	**314**	**213**	**256**	**332**	**450**	**488**
等级裁判员发展人数	**Number of Certified Referees**	**234**	**242**	**29**	**24**	**153**	**5130**

注：1、资料来源于省体育局(以下相关表同)。2、表中等级裁判员数据，2006和2007年为当年一级以上裁判员登记数，2008年后为当年发展数。

Note: 1.The data in the table are provided by the provinvial Sport Administration(The relative tables in the chapter are the same).2.The data of Referee in the table refers to data of current newly increase referee in the year 2008 to 2011,it refers to data of current registrated Referees in the year 2006 and 2007.

21-14 体育运动获奖
Medals Won by Guizhou Athletes in Domestic and International Competitions

单位：项 (unit)

指标	Item	2006	2007	2008	2009	2010	2011
国内外大赛第一名	Number of the First-Order	12	30	31	19	16	12
国内外大赛第二名	Number of the Second-Order	18	18	26	19	19	21
国内外大赛第三名	Number of the Third-Order	23	21	27	22	12	28

21–15 公共体育场地

Number of Public Stadiums and Gymnasiums

单位：个 (unit)

指　标	Item	2006	2007	2008	2009	2010	2011
总　计	**Total**	**21546**	**21547**	**21547**	**21550**	**21588**	**21596**
#体育场	Stadiums	49	49	49	52	56	61
体育馆	Gymnasiums	21	21	21	21	24	27
游泳池	Swimming Pools	89	89	89	89	90	90
有固定看台的灯光球场	Illuminated Fields with Fixed Seating	172	173	174	174	202	202

注：本表数据含全民健身场地数。
Note:The data in the table includes national fit-keeping fields in rural area.

21–16 群众体育活动

Activities of Mass Sports

指　标	Item	2006	2007	2008	2009	2010	2011
举办县级以上运动会(万次)	Number of Sports Meeting at County level and above(10000 times)	0.08	0.14	0.19	0.21	0.29	0.21
参加运动会的运动员(万人次)	Number of Athletes Attending Sports Meeting (10000 person-times)	166.84	203.12	283.14	210.86	323.13	410.12
青少年体育俱乐部(个)	Athletic Club for Youngsters(unit)	48	56	70	81	86	94
全民健身工程(条)	Body-building Activities of The Whole Nation(unit)	15	75	75	84	180	640

21−17 卫生事业

Health Care

指　　标	Item	2006	2007	2008	2009	2010	2011	2011年比2010年增长(%) Increase Rate in 2011 over 2010(%)
卫生机构(个)	**Number of Health Institutions(unit)**	**6147**	**5907**	**5848**	**5736**	**5637**	**5683**	**0.8**
#医院、卫生院	Hospitals and Township Hospitals	1855	1939	1934	1982	2005	2071	3.3
床位数(万张)	**Number of Beds(10000 beds)**	**6.65**	**7.58**	**8.31**	**9.75**	**10.53**	**11.75**	**11.6**
#医院、卫生院床位	Number of Hospital and Township Hospitals Beds	6.26	7.14	7.81	9.12	9.75	10.80	10.8
卫生人员合计(万人)	**Number of Employed Personnel in Health Care Institutions (10000 persons)**	**9.56**	**10.11**	**10.60**	**11.34**	**12.13**	**13.29**	**9.6**
#卫生技术人员	Medical Technical Personnels	8.23	8.53	8.93	9.53	10.25	11.22	9.5
#执业(助理)医师	Certified Doctors	4.11	4.21	3.88	4.02	4.22	4.40	4.3
#注册护士		2.36	2.65	2.86	3.18	3.60	4.16	15.6
医疗机构病床使用率(%)	**Utilization Rate in Medical Institutions(%)**	**71.9**	**75.9**	**79.3**	**79.8**	**79.7**	**79.6**	**-0.1**
人均卫生费(元)	**Expenditure for Health of each Person(yuan)**	**43.05**	**62.57**	**77.45**	**113.79**	**158.38**	**188.91**	
平均每千人拥有:	**Per 1000 Person:**							
床位数(张)	Beds(set)	1.79	2.07	2.30	2.73	3.00	2.77	
#医院、卫生院床位	Number of Hospital Beds	1.69	1.95	2.16	2.56	2.78	2.55	
卫生人员(人)	Number of Employed Personnel in Health Care Institutions(person)	2.58	2.76	2.93	3.18	3.46	3.14	
#卫生技术人员	Medical Technical Personnels	2.22	2.33	2.47	2.67	2.92	2.65	
#执业(助理)医师	Certified Doctors	1.11	1.15	1.07	1.13	1.20	1.04	
医院服务情况	**Hospital Services**							
诊疗人次(万人次)	Visits (10000 person-times)	4368.52	5012.44	2054.31	2413.97	2536.82	2910.53	14.7
入院人数(万人)	Inpatients (10000 persons)	157.36	244.30	148.12	194.43	211.91	243.34	14.8
出院人数(万人)	Patients Discharged from Hospital (10000 persons)	159.22	244.77	147.29	193.14	208.93	240.59	15.2
危重病人抢救成功率(%)	Survival Rate of Patients in Critically Situations(%)			94.2	94.6	94.7	89.2	-5.5
每百门诊急诊入院人数(人)	Numer of Inpatients Per 100Outpatients and Emergency Cases (person)	6.00	6.70	7.40	8.40	8.50	8.70	2.4
病床使用率(%)	Utilization Rate of Beds (%)	71.9	75.9	79.3	84.0	86.4	87.1	0.7
出院者平均住院日(天)	Average Stay Days in Hospital(day)	10.30	10.10	9.80	9.40	9.70	9.20	-5.2

注：1、资料来源于卫生厅(以下相关表同)。2、表中数据不含村卫生室(下表同)。3、2005年至2007年医院服务情况包括全部医疗机构，从2008年及以后指医院类别的医疗服务情况。4、每千人口指标和人均卫生费2011年以前按常住人口数计算，2011年按户籍人口数计算。

Note:1.Data in the table are provided from the Department of Health(The relative tables in the chapter are the same).2.Data in this table excluole excluding health clinics of village(the same applies to the next table).3.The Hospital Services include all medical institutions from 2005 to 2007, but since 2008 only refer to hospitals' services.4.Indicators of per thousand population and expenditure for health of each Person were calculated by the permanent resident population before 2011,but that were calculated by the household registered population in 2011.

21−18 卫生机构、床位、人员数(2011)

Number of Health Institutions,Beds and Personnels

类别	Item	机构数(个) Institutions (unit)	床位数(张) Hospital Beds (Bed)	人员数(人) Number of Personels (person)	#卫生技术人员数 Medical Technical Personels
合计	**Total Number of Institutions**	**5683**	**117534**	**132920**	**112210**
医院	Hospitals	621	78368	83847	69320
市	City	317	44450	53938	44169
县	County	304	33918	29909	25151
综合医院	Genaral Hospital	472	62005	68239	56856
#县医院	Hospitals at County Level	70	16965	16336	14221
中医医院	Hospital Specialized in TCM	67	9406	9149	7636
中西医结合医院	Combine Hospitals of Chinese and Western Medicine	4	430	255	222
其他专科医院	Other Specialized Hospitals	73	6161	5903	4369
民族医院	Nationality Medicine Hospital	4	306	261	216
疗养院(所)	Sanitariums	2	229	390	299
社区卫生服务中心(站)	Total Health Service Centers for Community	398	3900	5090	4340
#社区卫生服务中心	Health Service Centers for Community	111	1915	2467	2128
社区卫生服务站	Health Service Stations for Community	287	1985	2623	2212
卫生院	Health Centers	1450	29661	23203	20730
#农村乡镇卫生院	Health Centers of Villages and Towns in Country	1436	29541	23047	20604
中心卫生院	Health Centers Focus Villages and Towns	534	15744	11635	10357
乡卫生院	Health Centers of Commonly Villages and Towns	902	13797	11412	10247
门诊部、诊所、医务室	Outpatient Department Clinic and Infirmary	2849	698	8572	8160
#私人办诊所	Private Clinique	2522		6573	6426
专科防治所(站)	Specialized Disease Prevention and Treatment Centers	9	280	243	191
疾控中心(卫生防疫站)	CDC(Epidemic Prevention Station)	103		4542	3629
#县疾控中心	CDC at County Level	69		2425	2032
卫生监督所	Sanitation Supervise Centers	96		1732	1311
#县卫生监督所	Sanitation Supervise Centers at County Level	68		1013	808
妇幼保健院(所、站)	MCH Center	94	4398	3888	3341
#县妇幼保健院(所、站)	MCH Centers at County level	57	1627	1738	1534
医学科学研究机构	Research Institution of Medicine Science	2		196	167
其他卫生机构	Other Health Project Institution	59		1217	722
卫生部门	Health Department	2052	86268	93579	80098
工业及其他部门	Industrial and Other Department	407	14561	16378	12881
集体所有制	Collective-owned	126	649	1010	851
私人办	Private	3098	16056	21953	18380

21-19 卫生防疫防治和妇幼卫生事业

Sanitation and Epidemic Prevention,Maternity and Child Care

类　　别	Sort	2006	2007	2008	2009	2010	2011
防治所、站机构数(个)	**Prevention and Treatment Centers or Stations(unit)**	**8**	**8**	**8**	**8**	**8**	**9**
人员总数(人)	Number of Personnels(person)	191	155	158	182	186	243
#卫生技术人员数	Medical Technical Personnels	157	125	126	140	144	191
床位数(张)	Hospital Beds(bed)	247	136	144	213	199	280
疾病预防控制中心(个)	**CDC(unit)**	**105**	**105**	**105**	**103**	**103**	**103**
人员总数(人)	Number of Personnels(person)	4742	4674	4637	4643	4561	4542
#卫生技术人员数(人)	Medical Technical Personnels(person)	3925	3811	3787	3795	3689	3629
妇幼保健机构合计(个)	**Institutions of Maternity and Child Care(unit)**	**79**	**90**	**90**	**88**	**89**	**94**
人员总数(人)	Number of Personnels(person)	2774	3269	3322	3595	3692	3888
#卫生技术人员数(人)	Medical Technical Personnels(person)	2353	2742	2802	3060	3151	3341
床位数(张)	**Hospital Beds(bed)**	**1864**	**2176**	**2442**	**2928**	**3049**	**4398**

21-20 县及县以上医院、卫生院(2011)

Basic Statistics on Hospitals and Health Centers at County Level and above

类 别	Sort	机构合计(个) Insti-tutions (unit)	诊疗人次数(万人次) Number of Visits and Inpatients (10000 person-times)	#门 诊(万人次) Number of Visits in Clinics (10000 person-times)	入院人数(万人次) Inpatients (10000 person -times)	出院人数(万人次) Outpatients (10000 person -times)	出院病人治愈率(%) Recovering Rate (%)
县及县以上医院合计	**Hospitals at County Level and above**	**621**	**2910.53**	**2531.35**	**243.34**	**240.59**	**67.4**
#综合医院	Comprehensive Hospitals	472	2330.25	2016.45	199.07	197.45	67.0
中医医院	Hospital of Chinese Medicine	67	432.55	388.29	30.27	29.50	67.3
妇幼保健院(所、站)	**Maternity and Child Care Hospital(Centers orStations)**	**94**	**226.01**	**187.99**	**14.52**	**13.83**	**89.4**
#妇幼保健院	Maternity and Child Care Hospital	30	151.88	124.72	10.97	10.32	86.5
卫生院合计	**Township Hospitals**	**1450**	**1868.99**	**1706.22**	**161.99**	**160.71**	**87.4**
#农村乡镇卫生院	Rural Township Hospitals	1436	1861.16	1698.67	161.75	160.47	87.4
中心卫生院	Central Township Hospitals	534	940.72	847.54	87.39	87.30	86.9
乡卫生院	Ecumenic Township Hospitals	902	920.44	851.13	74.36	73.17	87.9

21-20 续表 (continued)

类 别	Sort	平均开放病床数(张) Average Sickbeds Setup (bed)	病床周转次数(次/年) Turnover of Beds (time/year)	病床工作日(日) Number of Days Per Bed in Use (day)	病床使用率(%) Utili-zation Rate of Beds(%)	出院者平均住院日(天) Average Stay Days in Hospital (day)	每100次门(急)诊入院人数(人) Hospital Admissions Per 100 Out-Patient Times and Emergency Patient-Times (person)
县及县以上医院合计	**Hospitals at and above County Level**	**74190.7**	**32.4**	**318.0**	**87.1**	**9.2**	**8.7**
#综合医院	Comprehensive Hospitals	58552.0	33.7	323.9	88.7	9.0	8.8
#中医医院	Hospital of Chinese Medicine	8985.1	32.8	323.6	88.7	9.2	7.3
妇幼保健院(所、站)	**Maternity and Child Care Hospital(Centers orstations)**	**3187.7**	**43.4**	**259.9**	**71.2**	**5.8**	**6.9**
#妇幼保健院	Maternity and Child Care Hospital	2021.3	51.0	320.0	87.7	6.3	7.4
卫生院合计	**Township Hospitals**	**27864.7**	**57.7**	**233.4**	**63.9**	**3.7**	**9.2**
#农村乡镇卫生院	Rural Township Hospitals	27763.5	57.8	233.4	64.0	3.7	9.2
中心卫生院	Central Township Hospitals	14939.0	58.4	237.4	65.0	3.7	9.9
乡卫生院	Ecumenic Township Hospitals	12824.5	57.1	228.8	62.7	3.7	8.5

21−21 县、乡、村三级医疗、预防、保健

Health Organization at County,Town and Village Level

指 标	Item	2006	2007	2008	2009	2010	2011	2011年比2010年增长(%) Increase Rate in 2011 over 2010(%)
县医院个数(个)	**Number of Hospitals at County Level(unit)**	**71**	**69**	**72**	**70**	**70**	**70**	**持平**
平均每院病床数(张)	Average Number of Beds Per Hospital(bed)	142.79	159.32	173.69	211.40	230.01	242.36	5.4
平均每院人员数(人)	Average Personnels Per Hospital (person)	161.63	173.60	171.20	180.11	193.10	233.37	20.9
#平均每院卫生技术人员数	Average Medical Technical Personnels Per Hospital	138.73	146.49	146.17	155.79	167.53	203.16	21.3
县妇幼保健院(所、站)机构数(个)	**Maternity and Child Care Centers at County Level(unit)**	**62**	**67**	**62**	**61**	**58**	**57**	**-1.7**
平均每院(所、站)床位数(张)	Average Number of Beds Per Station (bed)	16.48	17.85	20.60	23.72	26.91	28.54	6.1
平均每院(所、站)人员数（人）	Average Personnels Per Station (person)	25.00	26.95	26.40	27.39	28.98	30.49	5.2
#每院(所、站)卫生技术人员数	Medical Technical Personnels Per Stati on	21.66	23.32	22.73	23.98	25.47	26.91	5.7
县卫生防疫站机构数(个)	**Institutions of Epicemic Prevention Station at County Level(unit)**	**75**	**77**	**70**	**69**	**69**	**69**	**持平**
平均每所站人员数(人)	Personnels Per Station(person)	37.14	36.74	34.40	35.06	35.01	35.14	0.4
#平均每站卫生技术人员数	Average Medical Technical Personnels Per Station	31.91	31.26	29.20	29.94	29.83	29.45	-1.3
农村乡镇卫生院机构数(个)	**Institutions of Rural Township Hospitals(unit)**	**1451**	**1451**	**1448**	**1439**	**1437**	**1436**	**-0.1**
农村乡镇卫生院床位数（张）	Number of Beds of Rural Township Hospitals(bed)	15360	19136	21201	25841	28123	29541	5.0
平均每院床位数(张)	Average Number of Beds Per Hospital(bed)	10.58	13.19	14.64	17.96	19.57	20.57	5.1

21-21 续表 continued

指 标	Item	2006	2007	2008	2009	2010	2011	2011年比2010年增长(%) Increase Rate in 2011 over 2010(%)
平均每千农业人口乡镇卫生院床位数(张)	Average Number of Beds of Rural Township Hospitals Per 1000 Rural Personnels(bed)	0.54	0.57	0.65	0.75	0.80	0.83	3.8
农村乡镇卫生院人员数(人)	Personnels of Rural Township Hospitals (person)	18867	19257	19531	20317	20893	23047	10.3
平均每院人员数(人)	Average Personnels Per Hospital(person)	13.01	13.27	13.49	14.12	14.54	16.05	10.4
平均每千农业人口乡镇卫生院人员数(人)	Average Medical Technical Personnels of Rural Township Hospitals Per 1000 Rural Personnels(person)	0.66	0.58	0.60	0.59	0.59	0.65	10.0
村卫生室个数(个)	**Number of Villages with Medical Treatment Sations(unit)**	**19660**	**19057**	**19031**	**18971**	**19783**	**20260**	**2.4**
村卫生室覆盖率(%)	Coverage Rate of Township Hospitals(%)	98.2	96.9	96.1	88.3	90.1	93.8	3.7(百分点)
开展合作医疗的村数(个)	Number of Villages of Carrying out Rural Cooperative Medical Treatment(unit)	7594	19669	19803	17568	17672	17583	-0.5
开展合作医疗的村覆盖率(%)	Coverage Rate of Villages of Carrying out Rural Cooperative Medical Treatment(%)	37.9	100.0	100.0	100.0	100.0	100.0	持平
平均每村设置医疗点数(个)	Average Number of Medical Treatment Stations Per Village(unit)	0.98	0.97	0.96	1.08	1.12	1.15	2.9
乡村医生和卫生员数(人)	Doctors and Health Workers(person)	26027	27073	25469	32450	31517	34587	9.7
#乡村医生所占比例(%)	Proportion of Rural Doctors(%)	82.5	82.1	83.0	71.6	78.0	76.7	-1.3(百分点)
平均每村乡村医生和卫生员数(人)	Average Number of Doctors and Health Workers Per Village(person)	1.32	1.37	1.29	1.85	1.78	1.97	10.5
平均每千农业人口乡村医生和卫生员数(人)	Average Number of Doctors and Health Workers Per 1000 Rural Personnels (person)	0.91	0.81	0.78	0.95	0.90	0.97	8.2

注：2008年及以前的“村卫生室覆盖率”=村卫生室个数/行政村数，2009年后“村卫生室覆盖率”=设置村卫生室的村数/行政村总数。

Note:For the year 2008 and before,"the coverage rate of township hospitals"=number of village medical treatment sations/the number of administrative villages,While after 2009,"the coverage rate of township hospitals"=number of villages with medical treatment sations/the number of administrative villages.

21-22 28种传染病报告发病及死亡人数(2011)

List of 28 Infectious Diseases Reported and Number of Death

单位：人 (person)

顺 位 No.	发病 疾病名称 Diseases	Disease Incidence 发病人数 Fersons	死亡 疾病名称 Diseases	Death 死亡人数 Persons
1	肺结核 Pulmonary Tuberculosis	46378	狂犬病 Hydrophobia	207
2	病毒性肝炎 Viral Hepatitis	26908	艾滋病 AIDS	294
3	细菌性和阿米巴性痢疾 Dysentery	7286	肺结核 Pulmonary Tuberculosis	193
4	梅毒 Syphilis	6225	乙脑 Encephalitis B	10
5	淋病 Gonorrhea	1523	新生儿破伤风 Newborn Tetanus	10
6	伤寒副伤寒 Typhoid and Paratyphoid Fever	915	病毒性肝炎 Viral Hepatitis	17
7	疟疾 Malaria	153	细菌性和阿米巴性痢疾 Dysentery	1
8	猩红热 Scarlet Fever	653	梅毒 Syphilis	10
9	艾滋病 AIDS	472	流行性脑脊髓膜炎 Epidemic Encephalitis	3
10	狂犬病 Hydrophobia	207	伤寒副伤寒 Typhoid and Paratyphoid Fever	
11	流行性乙型脑炎 Encephalitis B	217	疟疾 Malaria	
12	流行性出血热 Hemorrhage Fever	94	麻疹 Measles	
13	麻疹 Measles	46	甲型H1N1流感 A(H1N1)Flu	
14	新生儿破伤风 Newborn Tetanus	53	炭疽 Anthrax	
15	甲型H1N1流感 A(H1N1)Flu	172	流行性出血热 Hemorrhage Fever	1
16	百日咳 Pertussis	67	钩端螺旋体病 Leptospirosis	1
17	流行性脑脊髓膜炎 Epidemic Encephalitis	10	人感染高致病性禽流感 Highly Pathogenic Bird Flu	
18	钩端螺旋体病 Leptospirosis	12	鼠疫 The Plague	
19	炭疽 Anthrax	5	血吸虫病 Schistosomiasis	
20	登革热 Dengue Fever		百日咳 Pertussis	
21	布鲁氏菌病 Brucellosis	6	淋病 Gonorrhea	
22	血吸虫病 Schistosomiasis		布鲁氏菌病 Brucellosis	
23	霍乱 Cholera		猩红热 Scarlet Fever	
24	鼠疫 The Plague		登革热 Dengue Fever	
25	人感染高致病性禽流感 Highly Pathogenic Bird Flu		霍乱 Cholera	
26	传染性非典型肺炎 SARS		传染性非典型肺炎 SARS	
27	脊髓灰质炎 Poliomyelitis		脊髓灰质炎 Poliomyelitis	
28	白喉 Diphtheria		白喉 Diphtheria	

21–23 28种传染病报告发病率、死亡率及病死率(2011)

List of Incidence,Death and Mortality Rates of 28 Infectious Disease Reported

顺位 No.	发病 Disease Incidence 疾病名称 Diseases	发病率(1/10万) Incidence (1/100 000)	死亡 Death 疾病名称 Diseases	死亡率(1/10万) Death Rate (1/100 000)	病死 Mortality Rate 疾病名称 Diseases	病死率(%) Mortality Rate(%)
1	肺结核 Pulmonary Tuberculosis	133.4800	狂犬病 Hydrophobia	0.5929	狂犬病 Hydrophobia	99.5200
2	病毒性肝炎 Viral Hepatitis	77.4400	艾滋病 AIDS	0.8461	艾滋病 AIDS	62.2881
3	细菌性和阿米巴性痢疾 Dysentery	20.9700	肺结核 Pulmonary Tuberculosis	0.5550	流脑 Epidemic Encephalitis	30.0000
4	梅毒 Syphilis	17.4400	流行性乙型脑炎 Encephalitis B	0.0289	新生儿破伤风 Newborn Tetanus	18.8979
5	淋病 Gonorrhea	4.3832	新生儿破伤风 Newborn Tetanus	0.0175	乙脑 Encephalitis B	4.6083
6	伤寒+副伤寒 Typhoid and Paratyphoid Fever	2.6334	肝 炎 Viral Hepatitis	0.0500	炭疽 Anthrax	
7	疟疾 Malaria	0.4400	细菌性和阿米巴性痢疾 Dysentery	0.0030	甲型H1N1流感 A(H1N1)Flu	0.0137
8	猩红热 Scarlet Fever	1.8793	梅毒 Syphilis	0.0288	麻疹 Measles	
9	艾滋病 AIDS	1.3584	流脑 Epidemic Encephalitis	0.0086	肺结核 Pulmonary Tuberculosis	0.4200
10	狂犬病 Hydrophobia	0.5957	甲型H1N1流感 A(H1N1)Flu		疟疾 Malaria	
11	流行性乙型脑炎 Encephalitis B	0.6245	麻疹 Measles		伤寒+副伤寒 Typhoid and Paratyphoid Fever	
12	流行性出血热 Hemorrhage Fever	0.2705	炭疽 Anthrax		梅毒 Syphilis	0.1600
13	麻疹 Measles	0.1324	伤寒+副伤寒 Typhoid and Paratyphoid Fever		痢疾 Dysentery	
14	新生儿破伤风 Newborn Tetanus	0.0926	疟疾 Malaria		病毒性肝炎 Viral Hepatitis	0.0600
15	甲型H1N1流感 A(H1N1)Flu	0.4950	流行性出血热 Hemorrhage Fever	0.0029	人禽流感 Highly Pathogenic Bird Flu	
16	百日咳 Pertussis	0.1928	钩端螺旋体病 Leptospirosis	0.0029	鼠疫 The Plague	8.3300
17	流脑 Epidemic Encephalitis	0.2288	人禽流感 Highly Pathogenic Bird Flu		钩体病 Leptospirosis	
18	钩端螺旋体病 Leptospirosis	0.0345	血吸虫病 Schistosomiasis		出血热 Hemorrhage Fever	1.0638
19	炭疽 Anthrax	0.0144	鼠疫 The Plague		百日咳 Pertussis	
20	登革热 Dengue Fever		百日咳 Pertussis		血吸虫病 Schistosomiasis	
21	布鲁氏菌病 Brucellosis	0.0173	淋病 Gonorrhea		淋病 Gonorrhea	
22	血吸虫病 Schistosomiasis		布鲁氏菌病 Brucellosis		布病 Brucellosis	
23	霍乱 Cholera		猩红热 Scarlet Fever		猩 红 热 Scarlet Fever	
24	鼠疫 The Plague		登革热 Dengue Fever		登革热 Dengue Fever	
25	人禽流感 Highly Pathogenic Bird Flu		霍乱 Cholera		霍 乱 Cholera	
26	传染性非典型肺炎 SARS		传染性非典型肺炎 SARS		传染性非典型肺炎 SARS	
27	脊灰 Poliomyelitis		脊灰 Poliomyelitis		脊 灰 Poliomyelitis	
28	白喉 Diphtheria		白喉 Diphtheria		白 喉 Diphtheria	

21—24 5岁以下儿童和孕产妇死亡率

Mortality Rate of the Maternal and Children Aged under 5

指 标	Item	2006	2007	2008	2009	2010	2011
新生儿死亡率(‰)	**Newborn Mortality Rate(‰)**	**15.1**	**13.2**	**12.7**	**12.2**	**7.1**	**5.1**
城 市	Urban	7.6	7.2	5.6	6.6	6.3	4.7
农 村	Rural	17.1	15.8	14.9	13.9	7.3	5.1
婴儿死亡率(‰)	**Infant Mortality Rate(‰)**	**22.9**	**21.2**	**21.1**	**17.7**	**11.9**	**8.6**
城 市	Urban	11.1	10.4	11.0	9.4	10.9	8.4
农 村	Rural	26.1	25.4	24.3	20.3	12.2	8.9
5岁以下儿童死亡率(‰)	**Mortality Rate of Children under 5(‰)**	**29.0**	**27.3**	**27.1**	**22.3**	**15.0**	**11.2**
城 市	Urban	12.3	12.7	13.0	11.8	14.0	10.8
农 村	Rural	33.5	31.9	31.5	25.6	15.3	11.3
孕产妇死亡率(1/10万)	**Maternal Mortality Rate(1/100 000)**	**73.9**	**62.6**	**67.3**	**49.8**	**35.4**	**24.5**
城 市	Urban	18.5	56.6	51.6	42.8	35.7	30.2
农 村	Rural	93.6	62.3	70.6	51.0	35.3	22.5

注：2010年及以后的数据取自妇幼卫生年报表，涵盖全省88个县(市、区)。
Note:Data are obtained from the Annual Report of Maternal and Child Health and covering the 88 counties(cities, districts) of the province.

21—25 新型农村合作医疗

Conditions of New Cooperative Medical System

指 标	Item	2006	2007	2008	2009	2010	2011
开展新农合县（市、区、特区)数(个)	Number of Counties Implementing of NCMS (unit)	34	88	88	88	88	88
参加新农合人数(万人)	Number of Enrollees(100 million persons)	918.81	2608.93	2831.87	2912.38	3029.17	3074.80
参合率(%)	Enrollment Rate(%)	72.3	84.9	92.1	94.3	96.3	97.1
当年筹资总额(亿元)	Total Fund Raised at Current Year (100 million yuan)	3.68	12.63	25.15	30.13	44.35	68.73
人均筹资(元)	Per Capita Premiums(yuan)	45	50	90	100	140	230
当年基金支出(亿元)	Payout at Current Year(100 million yuan)	2.22	8.11	16.21	30.78	37.12	52.25
补偿受益人次(万人次)	Number of Beneficiaries from Reimbursement (10000 person-times)	526.22	1314.90	1874.61	3573.96	3949.88	4408.91

主要统计指标解释

文化事业机构　指从事专业文化工作和为专业文化工作服务的独立建制的单位。不包括这些单位另外举办独立核算的其他机构和各部门的业余文化组织。

艺术表演团体　指从事戏曲、音乐、舞蹈、杂技等专业艺术表演，有独立帐户的单位，不包括半工半艺、半农半艺和民间职业剧团。

电影放映单位　指具有放映机器设备、固定或不固定的放映场所与专职或兼职的放映技术人员，经有关部门登记批准，经常为一定的观众对象放映电影的机构。包括经批准对外开放进行营业，并与电影发行放映管理机构分帐的专用放映单位和军委系统租片单位。

艺术表演观众人数（人次）　指售票、包场演出或民族地区免费演出的艺术表演观众人次数，不包括彩排审查和内部观摩演出的观看人次数。

广播节目综合人口覆盖率　指根据国家广电总局制定的《广播电视人口覆盖率统计技术标准和方法》进行统计调查的，在对象区内采用无线、有线、卫星等技术手段能够收听到包括中央、省、地市、县广播节目其中任意一套的人口数占全国总人口数的百分比。

电视节目综合人口覆盖率　指根据国家广电总局制定的《广播电视人口覆盖率统计技术标准和方法》进行统计调查的，在对象区内采用无线、有线、卫星等技术手段能够收看到包括中央、省、地市、县级电视节目中任意一套的人口数占全国总人口数的百分比。

等级运动员人数　指经考核正式批准授予等级运动员称号的人数。运动员等级分为国际级运动健将、运动健将、一级运动员、二级运动员、三级运动员、少年级运动员。

等级裁判员人数　指经考核正式批准授予等级裁判员称号的人数。裁判员等级分为国际裁判、国家级裁判、一级裁判、二级裁判、三级裁判。

体育场　指有 400 米跑道（中心含足球场），有固定道牙，跑道 6 条以上，并有固定看台的室外田径场地。体育场按看台容纳观众人数分为：甲级 25000 人以上，乙级 15000-25000 人，丙级 5000-15000 人，丁级 5000 人以下。

体育馆　指有固定看台，可供篮球、排球、羽毛球、乒乓球、体操等项目训练比赛活动用的室内运动场地。体育馆按看台容纳观众人数分为：甲级 6000 人以上，乙级 4000-6000 人，丙级 2000-4000 人，丁级 2000 人以下。

卫生机构　指从卫生行政部门取得《医疗机构执业许可证》，或从民政、工商行政、机构编制管理部门取得法人单位登记证书，为社会提供医疗保健、疾病控制、卫生监督服务或从事医学科研和教育等工作的单位。卫生机构包括医院、疗养院、社区卫生服务中心（站）、卫生院、门诊部、诊所（卫生所、医务室）、急救中心（站）、采供血机构、妇幼保健院（所、站）、专科疾病防治院（所、站）、疾病预防控制中心（防疫站）、卫生监督所、卫生监督检验（监测、检测）机构、医学科研机构、医学在职培训机构、健康教育所（站）等其他卫生机构。

医疗机构　指从卫生行政部门取得《医疗机构执业许可证》的机构，包括医院、疗养院、社区卫生服务中心（站）、卫生院、门诊部、诊所（卫生所、医务室）、妇幼保健院（所、站）、专科疾病防治院（所、站）、急救中心（站）和临床检验中心。

医院　包括综合医院、中医医院、中西医结合医院、民族医院、各类专科医院和护理院。

社区卫生服务中心（站）　指为本社区居民提供预防、医疗、保健、康复、健康教育、计划生育技术服务等的基层卫生机构。包括社区卫生服务中心和社区卫生服务站。

执业医师　指具有《医师执业证》及其"级别"为"执业医师"且实际从事医疗、预防保健工作的人员，不包括实际从事管理工作的执业医师。执业医师类别分为临床、中医、口腔和公共卫生。

执业助理医师　指具有《医师执业证》及其"级别"为"执业助理医师"且实际从事医疗、预防保健工作的人员，不包括实际从事管理工作的执业助理医师。执业助理医师类别同样分为临床、中医、口腔和公共卫生四类。

甲乙类法定报告传染病发病率　是指某年某地区每 10 万人口中甲、乙类法定报告传染病发病情况。即：

$$法定报告传染病发病率=\frac{甲、乙类法定报告传染病发病数}{人口数}\times 100000。$$

孕产妇死亡率　$$孕产妇死亡率=\frac{孕产妇死亡人数\times 10万}{活产数\times 10万}。$$

5 岁以下儿童死亡率 $5岁以下儿童死亡率 = \frac{5岁以下儿童死亡数}{活产数} \times 1000‰$。

新生儿死亡率 指某地区一年内出生未满 28 天（0–27 天）的新生儿死亡人数与该地区当年全部活产数的比率。

参加新农合人数 指根据本地新农合实施方案到年内新农合筹资截止时已缴纳新农合资金的人口数。

卫生技术人员 指卫生机构中医生、护理人员、药剂人员、检验人员等卫生技术人员。

Explanatory Notes on Main Statistical Indicators

Cultural Institutions refer to units which have their own organizational system and independent accounting system and specialize in or serve cultural development. They exclude other establishments run by these cultural institutions and amateur cultural groups established by various departments.

Art Troupe refers to the troupe which is engaged in drama, opera, music, dance, acrobatics or other art performance, opens independent accounts with banks and has self-supporting accounting system; excluding the troupes which are engaged partly in industrial or agricultural activities, partly in art performance and the professional troupes organized by the people.

Film Projection Units refer to units with film projection equipment, full or part time projectionists, permanent or non permanent places,approved by related administrative departments to show films regularly for certain groups of audience, including those film projection units which have been approved to give commercial shows and run business with independent accounting system as well as those filmrenting units of the military system.

Number of Spectators at Art Performance refers to the number of attendants at commercial shows, completely booked shows or free shows given in minority national areas,and does not include the number of spectators at rehearsals for examination and internal shows for study.

Radio Coverage of Population refers to the percentage of population, which can listen to one of central, provincial, city, prefecture, and county radio programs by wireless, cable, satellite and other technical means, in the surveying area, to national total population, according to Statistical Standard and Method on Television and Radio Coverage of Population established by the State Administration of Broadcasting, Film and Television.

Television Coverage of Population refers to the percentage of population, which can watch one of central, provincial, city, prefecture, and county television programs by wireless, cable, satellite and other technical means, in the surveying area, to national total population, according to Statistical Standard and Method on Television and Radio Coverage of Population established by the State Administration of Broadcasting, Film and Television.

Number of Athletes in Grades refers to the number of athletes who have been given titles through examination. The titles of athletes include international masters of sports, masters of sports, first-grade, second-grade and third-grade sportsmen and young athletes.

Number of Referees in Grades refers to the number of referees who have been given titles after examination. They are classified as international referees, national referees and referees of the first, second and third grades.

Stadiums refer to stadiums for track and field events with six lane 400-meter tracks around soccer fields, permanent track marks and permanent bleachers. Stadiums are classified according to seating capacity. They include: Class A stadiums seating 25000 people each. Class B stadiums seating 15000 to 25000 people each. Class C stadiums seating 5000 to 15000 people each, and Class D stadiums seating fewer than 5000 people.

Gymnasiums refer to indoor sports grounds with permanent seats in which basketball, volleyball. badminton, table tennis and gymnastics competitions can be held. Gymnasiums are classified according to seating capacity. They include Class A gymnasiums seating over 6000 people. Class B gymnasiums seating 4000 to 6000 people. Class C gymnasiums seating 2000 to 4000 people, and Class D gymnasiums seating fewer than 2000 people.

Health Care Institutions refer to the units which have been qualified the Certification of Health Care Institution by the administration of public health, or qualified the Certification of Corporate Unit by the civil affairs, administration for industry and commerce, commission office for public sector reform, and engaging in medical care, disease prevention and control, health supervision and inspection, medicine research and health education, etc., including: hospitals, sanatoriums, community health service centers (stations), health centers, clinics (health stations and infirmaries), first-aid centres (stations), blood gathering and supplying institutions, women and children care agencies (centres and stations), special disease prevention and curing agencies (centres and stations), disease prevention and control centres (epidemic prevention stations), health supervision and inspection agencies, sanitary inspection institutions, medicinal scientific research and on-job training institutions, health education centres and so on.

Medical Organizations refer to the institutions which have been qualified the Certification of Health Care Institution by the administration of public health, including: hospitals, sanatoriums, community health service centers (stations), health centers, clinics (health stations and infirmaries), women and children care agencies (centres and stations), special disease prevention and curing agencies (centres and stations), first-aid centres (stations) and clinic inspection centers.

Hospitals include: polyclinics, traditional Chinese medical hospitals, hospitals integrated with traditional Chinese therapeutics and western therapeutics, ethical hospitals, various specialties hospitals and nursing hospitals.

Community Health Service Centres (stations) refer to the primary units that provide the health care for community residents, such as disease prevention and control, medical treatment, health care, rehabilitation, health education, family planning technical services, including community health service centres and community health service stations.

Licensed Doctors refer to the medical workers who have obtained the licenses of qualified doctors and are employed in medical treatment, disease prevention or healthcare institutions, excluding the licensed doctors engaged in management job. The classification of licensed doctors is clinician, Chinese medicine, dentist and public health.

Licensed Assistant Doctors refer to the medical workers who have obtained the licenses of qualified assistant doctors and are employed in medical treatment, disease prevention or healthcare institutions, excluding the licensed assistant doctors engaged in management job. The classification of licensed assistant doctors is clinician, Chinese medicine, dentist and public health.

Incidence Rate of Notifiable Infectious Diseases refer to the incidence cases notifiable class A and class B infectious diseases per 100 thousand population in the reference region in the reference year. The formula is:

$$\text{Incidence Rate of Notifiable Infectious Diseases}=\frac{\text{Incidence Cases Notifiable Class A and Class B Infectious Diseases}}{\text{Population}}\times 100000.$$

Maternal Mortality Rate $\text{Maternal Mortality Rate}=\frac{\text{number of maternal deaths}\times 100{,}000}{\text{live births}\times 100{,}000}.$

Mortality Rate of Children under 5 $\text{Mortality Rate of Children under 5}=\frac{\text{death number of children under 5}}{\text{live birth}}\times 1000‰.$

Newborn Mortality Rate refers to the ratio of neonatal deaths of newbirth under the age of 28 days (0-27 days) in a year of the region to the total number of live births of this region.

Number of Persons Participated in the New Rural Cooperative Medical System refers to the number of persons who have given payment to the new cooperative medical system by the deadline of fundraising during the year according to the implementation plan of the new system.

Medical Technical Personnel refers to doctors, assistant nurses, pharmacists, and laboratory technicians working in medical institutions.

22

Twenty-two

社会服务及其他

Social Services and Others

22-1 律师、公证、调解工作
Basic Statistics on Lawyers,Notarization and Mediation

指标	Item	2006	2007	2008	2009	2010	2011
律师工作	**Lawyers**						
法律律师事务所(个)	Number of Law Offices(unit)	195	196	206	222	244	267
专职律师(人)	Full-time Lawyers(person)	1211	1421	1371	1562	1809	2030
辅助工作人员(人)	Assistant(person)	443	386	693	829	952	879
聘请常年法律顾问(个)	Number of Permanent Legal Advisors(person)	1877	2052	2366	5726	7392	8973
全年办理(件)	Number of Cases in Whole Year(case)	64250	82019	59379	79533	81398	84788
刑事案件诉讼代理	Agent of Criminal Cases	4791	6271	6301	7011	6532	5698
民事诉讼代理	Agent of Civil Cases	9020	11672	12397	12966	13437	14156
行政诉讼代理	Agent of Administrative Action	519	588	438	429	572	431
经济案件诉讼代理	Agent of Economic Cases	1661	5828	4180	4463	5300	5783
非诉讼法律事务	Agent of Non-litigious Legal Affairs	1831	1484	1445	1062	1367	1860
解答法律询问	Agent of Legal Advisory Services	35990	52009	33637	52070	52623	55172
代写法律事务文书	Agent of Legal Document Written on Behalf of Clients	10438	9264	4632	5518	6076	6620
调解成功	Successful Mediation	335	731	529	477	791	851
公证工作	**Notarization**						
公证处(个)	Number of Notarial Offices(unit)	97	97	97	97	97	97
公证员(人)	Notaries(person)	178	173	164	189	226	256
公证辅助人员(人)	Notarial Assistant(person)	148	58	106	56	92	63
办理公证文书(件)	Number of Notarized Documents(case)	90787	79498	76217	156768	79398	75353
#经济合同公证	Notarized Documents on Economic Affairs	35485	27326	25431	22323	17630	15335
#涉外公证	Foreign-related Notarization	8884	10544	10237	35823	10189	10023
国内公证	Domestic Notarization	80396	67471	52988	93941	67451	63482
公证费收入(万元)	Income of Notarization(10000 yuan)	1239	2072	1027	1596	935	1280
人民调解工作	**People's Mediation**						
人民调解委员会(个)	Number of People's Mediation Committees(unit)	25366	23762	23762	23762	22275	22976
人民调解人员(人)	Number of Mediators(person)	118097	111707	105060	111068	109270	115699
调解民间纠纷(件)	Number of Civil Disputes Mediated(case)	103284	113531	98515	113568	134667	198778
调解成功率(%)	The Rate of Success of Mediation(%)	97.7	96.0	95.9	95.2	97.1	96.7
基层法律服务工作	**Law Service at Basic Level**						
法律服务所(个)	Offices for Law Service(unit)	562	567	501	485	484	451
法律工作者(人)	Law Staffs(person)	2395	2372	2241	2103	2138	1431
代理案件(件)	Cases Deputed(case)	13353	11128	11699	13817	9914	12654
避免经济损失(万元)	Number of Avoided Economical Loss(10000 yuan)	4743	15931	15448	14010	12472	24869
刑释解教人员安置帮教工作	**Settling and Assisting and Teaching Work for People That Has Been Released After Serving a Sentence**						
设立工作机构(个)	Institutions Established(unit)	98	99	96	98	99	99
工作人员(人)	Staffs(person)	1534	1498	313	457	279	194
安置人数(人)	Number of Persons Settled Down(person)	9158	15945	14701	15029	16973	24209
帮教人数(人)	Number of Persons Assisted and Teached(person)	11677	14547	15715	15150	15794	27642

注：资料来源于省司法厅(下表同)。
Note:Data in the table are obtained from provinvial department of justice(the same applies to the next table).

22-1 续表 continued

指 标	Item	2006	2007	2008	2009	2010	2011
#涉外公证	Foreign-related Notarization	8884	10544	10237	35823	10189	10023
国内公证	Domestic Notarization	80396	67471	52988	93941	67451	63482
公证费收入(万元)	Income of Notarization(10000 yuan)	1239	2072	1027	1596	935	1280
人民调解工作	**People's Mediation**						
人民调解委员会(个)	Number of People's Mediation Committees(unit)	25366	23762	23762	23762	22275	22976
人民调解人员(人)	Number of Mediators(person)	118097	111707	105060	111068	109270	115699
调解民间纠纷(件)	Number of Civil Disputes Mediated(case)	103284	113531	98515	113568	134667	198778
调解成功率(%)	The Rate of Success of Mediation(%)	97.7	96.0	95.9	95.2	97.1	96.7
基层法律服务工作	**Law Service at Basic Level**						
法律服务所(个)	Offices for Law Service(unit)	562	567	501	485	484	451
法律工作者(人)	Law Staffs(person)	2395	2372	2241	2103	2138	1431
代理案件(件)	Cases Deputed(case)	13353	11128	11699	13817	9914	12654
避免经济损失(万元)	Number of Avoided Economical Loss(10000 yuan)	4743	15931	15448	14010	12472	24869
刑释解教人员安置帮教工作	**Settling and Assisting and Teaching Work for People That Has Been Released After Serving a Sentence**						
设立工作机构(个)	Institutions Established(unit)	98	99	96	98	99	99
工作人员(人)	Staffs(person)	1534	1498	313	457	279	194
安置人数(人)	Number of Persons Settled Down(person)	9158	15945	14701	15029	16973	24209
帮教人数(人)	Number of Persons Assisted and Teached(person)	11677	14547	15715	15150	15794	27642

22-2 国内公证文书分类
Domestic Notarial Documents by Type

单位：件 (piece)

指　标	Item	2006	2007	2008	2009	2010	2011
总　计	**Total**	**53787**	**67471**	**55728**	**91281**	**48987**	**48138**
经济合同公证合计	**Notarized Documents on Economic Affairs**	**28952**	**19857**	**25431**	**23450**	**17644**	**15335**
#购销	Purchases and Sales of Products	434	497	478	510	529	157
联营	Joint Business	54	68	94	145	24	45
贷款	Loans	27030	18246	22573	21194	16863	14447
招标、投标	Bidding	59	99	247	51	29	271
劳务合同	Labor Contracts	400	176	531	54	3	
建筑工程承包	Construction Project Countracts	48	12	69	4	4	4
农、林、牧、副、渔业承包	Farming,Forestry, Animal Husbandry,Sideline Production and Fishery Contracts	175	100	329	69	70	60
财产租赁	Property Leases	15	14	12	17	11	5
法人(代表)资格	Legal Person(Agent)Identification	20		21	35	90	10
委托书	Legal Person Trust Deeds	717	645	1077	1440	21	336
民事法律关系公证合计	**Notarized Documents on Civil Legal Relations**	**24902**	**40145**	**30297**	**67831**	**31343**	**32803**
#收养	Child Adoption	150	133	52	80	40	32
解除收养	Adoption Renouncement	52	14	15	131	3	1160
继承权	Right of Inheritance	2828	4460	5923	33818	6150	5883
遗嘱	Testaments	760	602	829	3213	552	510
产权	Property Right	423	119	297	1213	208	142
亲属关系	Kinship Confirmation	947	1020	1421	2204	515	459
房屋买卖	Purchases and Sales of Houses	3001	2621	3124	1263	3209	2457
房屋租赁	House Leases	26	49	92	45	54	42
留学协议	Foreign Study Contracts	67	137	197	86	34	44
遗赠抚养协议	Donations and Family Fostering	546	61	74	28	71	82
其他民事协议	Other Civil Agreements	3752	2110	6715	3942	2632	2616
委托书	Trust Deeds	3819	5147	3930	8696	9840	9384
赠与书	Presentation Documents	4941	5602	3447	9031	3823	4099
声明书	Declarations	3436	4133	4035	3892	4073	5679
建房宅基使用协议	Right to Housing Site	154	146	164	189	139	214

22-3 消费者协会受理投诉

Cases Accepted and Heard by Consumer Association

单位：件 (piece)

指 标	Item	2006	2007	2008	2009	2010	2011
总 计	**Total**	**5606**	**9333**	**7900**	**8099**	**5981**	**4986**
家用电器类	Household Appliances	1865	2021	2192	1935	1517	1228
#电视机	Televison	256	373	375	303	253	218
电冰箱	Refrigerators	85	106	118	94	110	77
洗衣机	Washing Machines	83	152	21	95	93	86
空调器	Air-Conditioner	59	77	68	91	58	77
家用机械类	Household Machinery	219	352	319	435	324	281
#摩托车	Motorcycles	40	72	52	85	47	53
百货类	Daily Use Goods	1746	2923	2069	2136	1577	1409
#药品	Materia Medica	57	48	32	56	47	35
医疗辅助用品	Assistant Things of Medical Treatment	24	9	2	5	7	13
服装鞋帽	Garment,Shoes and Caps	686	1254	674	799	712	550
家具	Furniture	82	126	66	83	75	58
食品	Foods	378	592	548	463	325	368
房屋及装修建材	Houses and Fitment Material	340	483	821	667	469	364
#房屋	Houses	181	204	530	283	151	87
装饰材料	Fitment Material	93	194	149	228	191	170
服务类	Services	921	2291	1651	2112	1434	1204
#电信	Telecome	138	972	629	663	589	641
邮政	Mail	13	10	316	230	46	35
农用生产资料类	Agricultural Production Materials	152	186	195	257	168	93
其他类	Others	363	1077	653	557	492	407

注：资料来源于省消费者协会。

Note: Data in the table are obtained from provinvial consumers association.

22-4 检察院主要业务

Cases of Procuratorate

年份 year	职务犯罪(件) Crime by Taking Advantage of Duty(case)			批捕、决定批捕 Total of Arrests		决定起诉 Total of Public Prosecutions	
	受案 Cases Accepted	立案 Cases Registered	结案 Cases Settled	(万件) (10000 cases)	(万人) (10000 persons)	(万件) (10000 cases)	(万人) (10000 persons)
2000	2365	1111	1064	1.60	2.54	1.49	2.22
2001	2284	1130	1089	1.98	3.09	1.94	2.88
2002	2288	1163	1106	1.85	2.79	1.98	2.85
2003	2110	1138	1073	1.72	2.63	1.71	2.51
2004	2356	1160	1133	1.69	2.60	1.79	2.64
2005	2155	1122	1118	1.67	2.58	1.83	2.71
2006	1920	1104	1068	1.63	2.54	1.79	2.67
2007	1709	1060	1071	1.67	2.71	1.80	2.78
2008	1457	981	1020	1.84	2.99	1.96	3.00
2009	1469	1002	967	2.06	3.30	2.18	3.45
2010	1223	983	978	1.94	3.07	2.28	3.59
2011	1003	929	908	1.88	2.89	2.24	3.42

注：资料来源于省人民检察院。
Note:Data in the table are obtained from the provincial people's procuratorate.

22-5 人民法院刑事一审案件收案

First Trail Criminal Cases Accepted by Courts

单位：件 (case)

类别	Sort	2006	2007	2008	2009	2010	2011	2011年比2010年增长(%) Increase Rate in 2011over 2010(%)
总计	**Total**	**19137**	**19098**	**20154**	**22480**	**23294**	**22570**	**-3.1**
#危害国家安全罪	Offences Against State Security	3	1	1		2	2	持平
危害公共安全罪	Offences Against Public Security	1847	1969	2269	1974	2368	2334	-1.4
破坏社会主义市场经济秩序罪	Offences Against Socialist Economic Order	217	281	294	332	399	360	-9.8
侵犯公民人身权利民主权利罪	Offences Against Citizens' Personal and Democratic Rights	4873	4469	4490	5338	5327	4944	-7.2
侵犯财产罪	Offences Against Properties	8260	8401	8565	9819	9854	9320	-5.4
妨害社会管理秩序罪	Offences Against Social Management of Order	2956	2958	3497	4121	4250	4688	10.3
危害国防利益罪	Offences Against National Defense		4		2			
贪污贿赂罪	Offences on Corruption and Bribery	856	854	877	769	938	801	-14.6
渎职罪	Offences on Abuse and Dereliction of Duty	114	148	153	119	143	116	-18.9
其他	Other	11	13	8	6	13	5	-61.5

注：资料来源于省高级人民法院(以下相关表同)。
Note:Date in the table are obtained from provincial higher people's court(The relative tables in the chapter are the same).

22-6 人民法院刑事一审案件结案

First Trail Criminal Cases Settled by Courts

单位：件 (case)

类　别	Sort	2006	2007	2008	2009	2010	2011	2011年比2010年增长(%) Increase Rate in 2011 over 2010(%)
总　计	**Total**	**18808**	**18803**	**19934**	**22201**	**23143**	**22412**	**-3.2**
#危害国家安全罪	Offences Against State Security	3	1	1		2	1	-50.0
危害公共安全罪	Offences Against Public Security	1829	1955	2259	1964	2362	2326	-1.5
破坏社会主义市场经济秩序罪	Offences Against Socialist Economic Order	215	275	288	323	393	352	-10.4
侵犯公民人身权利民主权利罪	Offences Against Citizens' Personal and Democratic Rights	4699	4310	4409	5200	5275	4898	-7.1
侵犯财产罪	Offences Against Properties	8204	8362	8527	9781	9839	9295	-5.5
妨害社会管理秩序罪	Offences Against Social Management of Order	2904	2929	3463	4084	4232	4655	10.0
危害国防利益罪	Offences Against National Defense		4		2			
贪污贿赂罪	Offences on Corruption and Bribery	832	815	829	727	894	776	-13.2
渎职罪	Offences on Abuse and Dereliction of Duty	111	139	150	114	133	104	-21.8
其他	Other	11	13	8	6	13	5	-61.5

22-7 人民法院刑事案件中青少年犯罪

Juvenile Delinquency Among Criminal Cases

单位：人 (person)

指　标	Item	2006	2007	2008	2009	2010	2011	2011年比2010年增长(%) Increase Rate in 2011 over 2010(%)
刑事罪犯总数	**Number of Criminals**	**22434**	**23987**	**24979**	**26834**	**28735**	**28171**	**-2.0**
#青少年罪犯	Juvenile Criminals	8144	9330	9207	9594	10106	9266	-8.3
#不满18岁	Less Than 18	3028	3294	3492	3155	3516	3014	-14.3
18-25岁	Aged 18-25	5116	6036	5715	6439	6590	6252	-5.1
青少年罪犯占刑事罪犯(%)	Proportion of Juvenile Criminals to Total Criminals(%)	36.3	38.9	36.9	35.8	35.2	32.9	-2.3 (百分点)

22-8 生产安全

Production Safety

项　目	Item	2006	2007	2008	2009	2010	2011
各类事故死亡人数合计(人)	**Number of Deaths for Production Security Accidents(person)**	**2787**	**2588**	**2427**	**2183**	**1936**	**1655**
工矿商贸企业	Enterprises of Industry,Mining,Commerce and Trade	1023	985	863	776	659	523
煤矿	Coal Mine	698	554	453	434	388	256
金属与非金属矿	Metallic and Non-metallic Mine	104	147	136	84	47	69
建筑业	Construction	103	102	100	90	105	81
其他	Others	118	182	174	168	119	117
火灾	Fire Accidents	53	81	77	77	64	54
道路交通	Roadway Traffic Accidents	1422	1356	1348	1210	1136	1020
铁路交通	Railway Traffic Accidents	246	150	120	95	75	49
其他	Others	43	16	19	25	2	9
亿元生产总值生产安全事故死亡人数(人/亿元)	Number of Deaths of Production Security Accidents Per of GDP (person/100 million yuan)	1.22	0.96	0.73	0.56	0.42	0.29
工矿商贸企业从业人员10万人死亡率(人/10万人)	Number of Deaths Per 100000 Persons of Employed Personels of Enterprises of Industry,Mining,Commerce and Trade(person/100000 persons)	10.75	9.77	8.56	7.65	6.45	5.08
煤矿百万吨死亡人数(人/百万吨)	Number of Deaths Per Unit of Yields of Coal Mine (person/per million tons)	5.91	4.99	3.84	3.17	2.43	1.64
道路交通万车死亡人数(人/万车)	Number of Deaths of Roadway Traffic Accidents Per Unit of Vehicles(person/10000 sets)	11.26	9.33	7.30	5.36	4.01	3.32

注：资料来源于省安全生产监督管理局。

Note: Data in the table are obtained from provincial production safety supervision management administration.

22-9 火灾(2011)
Fire Accidents

指 标	Item	合计 Total	较大 Comparatively Serious	一般 Ordinary
实际发生数(起)	**Number of Fire Accidents(case)**	**1170**	**4**	**1166**
按火灾原因分	Grouped by Cause			
生产作业	Operation	67		67
电 气	Electric	503	2	501
吸 烟	Smoking	35		35
生活用火不慎	Not Careful with Cooking Fire	217	2	215
玩 火	Playing with Fire	69		69
自 燃	Natural Fire	21		21
不 明	Uncertain	61		61
其 他	Others	137		137
死亡人数(人)	Number of Deaths(person)	55	16	39
受伤人数(人)	Number of Injuries(person)	10	1	9
直接财产损失(万元)	Losses Converted into Cash(10000 yuan)	6625	91	6535
平均每起事故损失(万元)	Average Loss Per Fire(10000 yuan)	5.66	22.62	5.60

注：资料来源于省公安厅(下表同)。
Note: Data in the table are obtained from provincial department of public security(the same applies to the next table).

22-10 交通事故(2011)
Traffic Accidents

指 标	Item	发生数(起) Number of Traffic Accidents(case)	死亡人数(人) Number of Deaths (person)	受伤人数(人) Number of Injuries (person)	损失折款(万元) Losses Converted into Cash(10000 yuan)
总 计	**Total**	**1566**	**1020**	**2270**	**1611.39**
#重大事故	Extraordinarily Serious	746	1019	908	1112.00
特大事故	Serious	71	265	201	361.85
机动车	Motor Vehicles	1509	985	2240	1581.57
#汽车	Automobiles	1038	751	1603	1424.95
摩托车	Motorcycles	430	208	585	140.29
拖拉机	Tractors	41	26	52	16.33
非机动车	Non-motor-driven Vehicles	9	4	9	2.11
#自行车	Bicycles	2	1	1	1.50
行人乘车人	Pedestrians and Passengers	48	31	21	32.99

22-11 社会保险

Social Insurance

指标	Item	2006	2007	2008	2009	2010	2011
社会保险基金	**Social Security Fund**						
社会保险基金收入(万元)	Reveneu(10 000 yuan)	737174	908562	1405024	1713974	2015569	2569408
社会保险基金支出(万元)	Expenses(10 000 yuan)	677705	805721	982387	1227311	1514129	1817403
社会保险基金累计结余(万元)	Balance at year-end(10 000 yuan)	993917	1288714	1478754	2185113	2679319	3431325
基本养老保险	**Basic Pension Insurance**						
基本养老保险参保人数(万人)	Number of Persons Joining Basic Pension Insurance(10 000 pesons)	193.25	205.93	215.89	235.61	257.31	282.06
#参保职工	Number of Employees	139.14	149.39	156.57	172.14	190.29	210.71
基本养老保险基金收入(万元)	Reveneu(10 000 yuan)	702903	802072	1010780	1254653	1448518	1792486
基本养老保险基金支出(万元)	Expenses(10 000 yuan)	573742	617958	759845	905614	1077376	1275654
离退休人员社区管理服务率(%)	Rate of Community Management and Services for Retirees(%)	36.13	40.68	47.17	50.03	57.00	61.08
城镇职工基本医疗保险	**Urban Employees Basic Medical Care Insurance**						
基本医疗保险参保人数(万人)	Number of Persons Joining Basic Medical Care Insurance(10 000 pesons)	199.22	228.22	257.35	279.53	293.52	314.06
#农民工	Tagelöhners	2.15	8.79	20.20	17.70	14.01	14.76
城镇职工基本医疗保险基金收入(万元)	Reveneu(10 000 yuan)	146751	190368	280802	345101	416370	543111
城镇职工基本医疗保险支出(万元)	Expenses(10 000 yuan)	109134	136191	180866	253089	330762	424424
失业保险	**Unemployment Insurance**						
失业保险参保人数(万人)	Number of Persons Joining Unemployment Insurance(10 000 pesons)	131.07	134.55	141.36	144.60	152.48	160.52
领取失业金人数(万人)	Beneficiaries of Unemployment Insurance Fund(10 000 pesons)	1.50	1.42	1.26	1.07	1.21	1.08
失业保险基金收入(万元)	Reveneu(10 000 yuan)	48581	58409	70287	63297	75812	116416
失业保险基金支出(万元)	Expenses(10 000 yuan)	15980	34635	20783	58250	52890	23398
#失业金	Jobless Claims	4982	7187	7233	6705	7101	8217
职业培训补贴支出(万元)	Expenses of Professional Training(10 000 yuan)	1194	1797	1092	720	1352	1369
工伤保险	**Work Injury Insurance**						
工伤保险参保人数(万人)	Number of Persons Joining Injury Insurance (10 000 pesons)	90.47	110.50	129.02	143.35	162.18	193.96
#农民工	Tagelöhners	13.54	28.87	38.37	49.19	59.65	69.78
工伤保险基金收入(万元)	Reveneu(10 000 yuan)	17024	23442	33670	40381	62577	91227
工伤保险支出(万元)	Expenses(10 000 yuan)	8728	10451	18213	28896	48354	65486
生育保险	**Maternity Insurance**						
生育保险参保人数(万人)	Number of PersonsJoining in Basic Maternity Insurance(10 000 pesons)	72.11	88.70	135.95	152.49	164.30	198.09
生育保险基金收入(万元)	Reveneu(10 000 yuan)	3817	5295	9485	10542	12292	14739
生育保险支出(万元)	Expenses(10 000 yuan)	814	1679	2680	3735	4747	6107

注：资料来源于省人力资源社会保障厅。
Note: Date in the table are obtained from provincial department of human resources and social security.

22-12 社会福利机构

Social Welfare Institutions and Enterprises

单位：个 (unit)

项　目	Item	2006	2007	2008	2009	2010	2011	2011年比2010年增长(%) Increase Rate in 2011over 2010(%)
总　计	**Total**	**1444**	**1417**	**1434**	**1432**	**1454**	**1722**	**18.4**
收养性福利单位	Adopting Social Welfare Institutions	904	900	919	948	974	1185	21.7
社会福利企业	Social Welfare Enterprises	207	143	128	90	84	81	-3.6
优抚事业单位	Administration Agencies for Martyrs	47	52	54	56	59	62	5.1
救助类单位	Collecting and Repatriation Units	31	55	56	58	61	64	4.9
殡仪服务单位	Funeral and Interment Institutions	94	102	105	111	116	119	2.6
彩票发行单位	Lottery Issue Units	8	10	11	11	13	15	15.4
社区服务单位	Community Service Institutions	153	155	161	158	147	196	33.3

22-13 社会福利机构工作人员

Staff Employed by Social welfare Institutions and Enterprises

单位：人 (person)

项　目	Item	2006	2007	2008	2009	2010	2011	2011年比2010年增长(%) Increase Rate in 2011over 2010(%)
总　计	**Total**	**16870**	**15638**	**15675**	**13800**	**13433**	**14679**	**9.3**
收养性福利单位	Adopting Social Welfare Institutions	2638	2873	3118	3124	3522	4274	21.4
社会福利企业	Social Welfare Enterprises	9887	8478	8211	6268	5512	5216	-5.4
优抚安置事业单位	Administration Agencies for Martyrs	386	375	342	299	293	466	59.0
救助类单位	Collecting and Repatriation Units	301	333	337	329	339	347	2.4
殡仪服务单位	Funeral and Interment Institutions	2688	2652	2691	2589	2669	2925	9.6
彩票发行单位	Lottery Issue Units	86	101	115	119	147	160	8.8
社区服务单位	Community Service Institutions	884	826	861	1072	951	1291	35.8

22−14　社会服务及设施和民政事业发展主要指标

Main Indicators of Social Services & Facilities and Civil Administration Career Development

指　标	Item	2006	2007	2008	2009	2010	2011	2011年比2010年增长(%) Increase Rate in 2011 over 2010(%)
城镇社区服务设施数(个)	**Number of Urban Community Service Facilities(unit)**	**4870**	**4936**	**5102**	**5176**	**5920**	**6593**	**11.4**
#社区服务单位数	Number of Community Service Institutions	153	155	161	158	147	196	33.3
城镇便民利民服务网点(个)	Number of Urban Service Points for Civilian(unit)	11140	17698	22340	22661	25715	26587	3.4
乡镇敬老院覆盖率(%)	Coverage Rate of Villages and Town Elderly Welfare Homes(%)	56.1	55.0	55.8	56.4	56.5	68.3	11.8(百分点)
收养性福利单位床位数(张)	Number of Beds of Welfare Home (unit)	18054	19121	21343	23396	28358	44025	55.2
收养性福利单位床位利用率(%)	Using Rate of Bed(%)	60.4	64.9	64.0	65.0	60.2	61.8	1.6(百分点)
享受城镇低保人数(万人)	Number of Persons Receiving Lowest Cost of living in Urban Area (10000 persons)	51.17	53.28	54.52	55.50	53.98	54.34	0.7
城镇低保生活保障支出(万元)	Expenditure of Lowest Cost of living in Urban Area(10000 yuan)	51644	63749	87999	104354	101685	143028	40.7

注：资料来源于省民政厅(以下相关表同)。
Note:The data in the table are provided by the provinvial department of civil affairs(The relative tables in the chapter are the same).

22−15　社会福利救济主要支出

Major Expenditures of Welfare Relief Funds

单位：万元　　(10000 yuan)

指　标	Item	2006	2007	2008	2009	2010	2011	2011年比2010年增长(%) Increase Rate in 2011 over 2010(%)
总　　计	**Total**	**123815**	**231788**	**319061**	**433055**	**522166**	**646883**	**23.9**
优抚对象补助金额	Funds for Family Members of Martyrs and Disabled Veterans	33231	39157	56748	66113	81660	95162	16.5
#国家支出	Government Funds	33231	39157	56748	66113	81660	95162	16.5
传统救济对象的国家救济金额	Funds for Family Members of Traditional Relief	30304	69833	11873	12575	14628	29995	105.1
最低生活保障支出	Expenditure for Persons Receiving Lowest Cost-of-living	54068	115493	243291	346696	419143	692908	65.3
城　镇	For Urban Areas	51644	63749	87999	104354	101685	143028	40.7
农　村	For Rural Areas	2424	51744	155292	242342	317458	549880	73.2
收养性社会福利单位支出	Funds for Adopting Social Welfare Institution	6212	7305	7149	7671	6735	12407	84.2
#国家支出	Government Funds	6212	7305	7149	7671	6735	12407	84.2

注：2006—2007年传统救济对象的国家救济金额含农村低保支出。
Note: Funds for family menbers of traditional relief include the expenditure for rural lowest cost-of-living areas in the years from 2006 to 2007.

22-16 享受补助、救济人员

Persons Receiving Subsidies and Relief Funds

单位：万人 (10000 persons)

指 标	Item	2006	2007	2008	2009	2010	2011	2011年比2010年增长(%) Increase Rate in 2011 over 2010(%)
城乡居民最低生活保障人数	**Number of Persons Receiving Lowest Cost-of-living in Urban Area and Rural Area**	**58.85**	**309.72**	**377.86**	**379.48**	**588.72**	**585.23**	**-0.6**
城 镇	Urban Area	51.17	53.28	54.52	55.50	53.98	54.34	0.7
农 村	Rural Area	7.68	256.44	323.34	323.98	534.74	530.89	-0.7
传统救济人数	Number of Persons Receiving Traditional Relief Funds	110.60	1.89	1.81	1.72	1.70	1.71	0.6
收养性福利单位收养三无对象人数	Number of Persons Adopted by Adopting Social Welfare Institutions	0.94	1.05	1.12	1.14	1.35	2.25	66.7

注：2007年全省全面建立实施农村居民最低生活保障制度，原传统救济对象符合条件的均转为农村低保人数。

Note:Rural lowest cost-of living system was set up in Guizhou in 2007. The persons receiving traditional relief funds who meet the standard of rural lowest cost-of-living are counted in the nuber of persons receiving rural lowest cost-of-living allowance.

22-17 享受国家定期抚恤、补助、救济人员数

Persons Receiving Regular Subsidy and Commiseration of Country

单位：人 (person)

指 标	Item	2006	2007	2008	2009	2010	2011	2011年比2010年增长(%) Increase Rate in 2011over 2010(%)
合 计	**Total**	**106818**	**187395**	**192744**	**195265**	**191988**	**223071**	**16.2**
#伤残抚恤人数	Number of Persons Receiving Disability Commiseration	15070	14982	15153	15830	15844	15809	-0.2
#"三属"抚恤人数	Number of Persons Comfort and Compensated Bereaved Family	5257	5183	5069	5307	5121	4931	-3.7
烈士家属	Family Numbers of Martyr	3071	3023	2936	3129	3019	2911	-3.6
牺牲、病故军人家属	Family Numbers of Immolate & Die of Illness Armyman	2186	2160	2133	2178	2102	2020	-3.9
定期补助人数	Number of Persons Receiving Regular Subsidies	86491	167230	172522	174128	171023	202331	18.3
复退军人定补人数	Number of Ex-servicemen	86238	88090	86965	87102	83506	80397	-3.7
参战、参试定补人数	Number of Persons Receiving Regular Subsidies for War and Test		78909	85178	86626	87034	88530	-1.7

注：参战、参试定补人数指参加对越自卫反击战及核试验等人员，2007年开始核查并接受定期补助。

Note:Persons receiving regular subsidies for sar and sest refer to these persons taking part in acting in self-defence war and nuclear test, who have obtained regular subsidies from the government since 2007.

22-18 残疾人事业基本情况

Basic Information of Person with Disablility

单位：人　　　　(person)

项目	Item	2011年
康复	**Rehabilitation**	
视力残疾康复	Rehabilitation of Persons with Sight Disability	
贫困白内障患者免费手术(例)	Free Surgeries for Poor Cataract Patients(case)	5679
低视力者配用助视器	Vision-aids Provided for Persons of Low-vision	397
盲人定向行走训练	Blindman Trained with Direction Walking	213
聋儿康复	Rehabilitation of Children with Hearing Disability	
年收训聋儿	Hearing and Speech Training	356
培训家长	Parents Trained	463
精神病防治康复	Prevention and Treatment of Psychiatric Diseases	
开展精神病防治康复工作市县数(个)	Counties Carried on the Works of Prevention and Treatment of Psychiatric Diseases(unit)	63
接受治疗的精神病患者	Treatment Provided for Patients with Sever Psychiatric Diseases	18109
孤独症儿童训练	Trained Persons with Infantile Autism	46
肢体残疾康复	Rehabilitation of Persons with Physical Disability	
肢体残疾人社区康复训练	Persons Rehabilitated at Community	384
脑瘫儿童机构康复训练	Rehabilitation of Children with Cerebral Palsy at Community	254
贫困肢体残疾儿童矫治手术	Rehabilitation of Children with Physical Disability in Poverty	163
智力残疾康复	Rehabilitation of Persons with Intellectual Disability	
智残儿童社区康复训练	Children Rehabilitated at Community	178
智残儿童机构康复训练	Children Rehabilitated at Institutions	216
辅助器具供应服务数(件)	Sabsidiary Implement Provided for the Disabled (unit)	5322
贫困残疾人假肢装配例数(例)	Artificial limb Assembled (case)	444
#大腿	for Ham	197
小腿	for Shank	230
特殊假肢	Special Artificial limb	17
社区康复协调员培训	Workers Trained for Disabled porsn at Community	3330

注：资料来源于省残联。
Note :Data in the table are provided by Disabled Federation of Gui zhou Province.

22-18 续表 Continued

单位：人 (person)

项目	Item	2011年
教育	**Education**	
未入学适龄残疾儿童少年	School-age Disabled Children without Schooling	8225
职业教育与培训	Vocational Education and Training	
机构数(个)	Facilities (unit)	22
教育与培训人数(人次)	Number or Educated and Trained (person-time)	3810
就业	**Employment**	
城镇残疾人就业状况	Employment of Urban Handicapped	
当年安排就业	Persons Employed in the Year	5666
#按比列就业	Employed by Quote Scheme	834
公益性岗位安置	Employed at Public Institution	77
集中就业	Employed at Welfare Enterprises	2230
个体及其他形式就业	Self-employed and Others	2525
农村残疾人就业状况	Employment of Rural Handicapped	
就　业	Employed	865595
残疾人就业服务机构(个)	Employment Service Institutions for Handicapped (unit)	
省	Provinces	1
市、州	Prefectures	9
县、市、区	County、Cities	60
盲人按摩	**Massage by Persons with Visual Disability**	
保健按摩人员培训	Massage Therapists Training	265
医疗按摩人员培训	Keep-fit Massage Training	115
扶贫	**Poverty Alleviation**	
本年度脱贫人数	Disabled Persons Overcoming Poverty	57637
农村贫困残疾	Rural Disabled persons in Poverty	685906
当地低收入残疾	Disabled Persons at the Local Low-income Level	472877
残联组织建设	**Organization of the Disabled Persons' Federation**	
残疾人工作者	Workers Working for the Disabled	2703

22−19 婚姻
Marriages and Divorces

指 标	Item	2006	2007	2008	2009	2010	2011
准予登记结婚(对)	**Registered Marriages(couple)**	**213081**	**234938**	**263238**	**307940**	**375051**	**373423**
#初婚(人)	First Marriages(person)	393641	432161	486029	567633	692590	679348
再婚(人)	Remarriages(person)	32521	37715	40447	48247	57512	67498
#女性	Female	14871	18794	19223	22707	27696	34236
涉外婚姻(对)	Registered Marriages with Foreigner and the Citizen of Hong Kong,Macao,Taiwan(couple)	683	586	491	467	369	500
#国内公民(人)	Domestic Citizen(person)	683	586	491	467	369	500
#女性	Female	657	559	458	440	330	457
离婚人数(人)	Divorces(person)	84256	91674	102440	115914	127938	144420
#民政部门批准	Permitted by Civil Administration Department	51906	56772	65140	76146	89384	104032

主要统计指标解释

公证人员 指在国家公证机关依法办理公证事务的司法人员，包括公证员、助理公证员和在公证处工作的其他人员。

办理公证文书 指公证处在一定时期内办结的公证文书件数。公证文书按司法部规定或批准的格式制作，包括国内公证和涉外公证两部分。国内公证分为经济合同公证和民事法律关系公证两大类。

调解人员 指在人民调解委员会担负调解民间一般民事纠纷和轻微违法行为引起纠纷的工作人员，包括调解委员会的委员和调解小组的调解员。

调解民间纠纷 指调解委员会依照法律规定，根据自愿原则，用说服教育的方法调解民间发生的有关民事权利和义务的争执，促成当事双方达到协议和谅解，解决纠纷。包括婚姻家庭纠纷，财产权益纠纷等，不包括法院受理调解的民事案件数。

特大火灾 指造成 30 人以上死亡，或者 100 人以上重伤，或者 1 亿元以上直接财产损失的火灾。

重大火灾 指造成 10 人以上 30 人以下死亡，或者 50 人以上 100 人以下重伤，或者 5000 万元以上 1 亿元以下直接财产损失的火灾。

较大火灾 指造成 3 人以上 10 人以下死亡，或者 10 人以上 50 人以下重伤，或者 1000 万元以上 5000 万元以下直接财产损失的火灾。

一般火灾 指造成 3 人以下死亡，或者 10 人以下重伤，或者 1000 万元以下直接财产损失的火灾。

人民检察院直接立案侦查案件 指按照管辖的规定，由人民检察院直接立案侦查的贪污贿赂犯罪、渎职犯罪、国家机关工作人员利用职权实施的侵犯公民人身权利和民主权利的犯罪以及经省级人民检察院决定立案侦查的国家机关工作人员利用职权实施的其他重大犯罪案件。

要案 指县、处级以上干部的犯罪案件。该指标主要反映职务犯罪案件中县、处级以上干部被人民检察院依法立案侦查的情况。

批准逮捕 指人民检察院对公安机关、国家安全机关、监狱管理机关提出逮捕的犯罪嫌疑人进行审查，根据事实，依法做出逮捕决定。该指标主要反映人民检察院对提请逮捕犯罪嫌疑人进行审查后依法做出批准逮捕决定的情况。

青少年罪犯 指人民法院在报告期内判决发生法律效力的有罪判决中 14 周岁以上不满 25 周岁的罪犯。其中 14 周岁以上不满 18 周岁的罪犯为未成年罪犯。

行政案件 指公民、法人和其他组织不服行政机关作出的具体行政行为，向人民法院提起行政诉讼，人民法院依法审理的案件。

城镇居民最低生活保障人数 指在报告期末家庭平均收入在当地规定的最低生活保障线以下的城镇居民数。包括＂三无＂对象，失业人员和在职、下岗、退休人员等。

农村居民最低生活保障人数 指报告期末在建立农村最低生活保障制度的地区，得到当地政府或集体给予最低生活保障的农业人口家庭人数。

五保户 指无法定抚养义务人，或者虽有法定抚养义务人，但是抚养人无抚养能力的；无劳动能力的；无生活来源的老年人、残疾人和未成年人。

农村传统救济人数 指未开展最低生活保障制度的农村地区，仍沿用传统救济制度救济的贫困人口数量。

社会福利企业 指以集中安置有一定劳动能力的残疾人员就业为目的（残疾职工占生产人员 10% 以上）、带有社会福利性质的企业总称。主要包括福利工厂、假肢厂和其他福利企业。

城镇社区服务设施数 指报告期末城镇（街道办事处、居委会）设立的以非盈利为目的，为本社区居民服务，特别是为老年人、残疾人、儿童服务的社区服务中心、活动站、服务站、养老院、老年公寓（托老所），残疾人工疗站、残疾儿童日托所、家务服务站、婚姻介绍所等福利性设施以及职工社会保险管理服务的机构数。几种不同类型的社区服务单位，共用一个场所的，只能统计为一个社区服务设施。成为社区服务设施的条件：（1）是独立核算单位；（2）有固定的从业人员；（3）有一定的服务项目；（4）有一定的场所。

城镇职工基本养老保险

1、（参保）职工人数 指报告期末按照国家法律、法规和有关政策规定参加基本养老保险并在社保经办机构已建立缴费记录档案的职工人数，包括中断缴费但未终止养老保险关系的职工人数，不包括只登记未建立缴费记录档案的人数。

2、（参保）离退休人员人数 指报告期末参加基本养老保险的离休、退休和退职人员的人数。

3、基本养老保险基金收入 指根据国家有关规定，由纳入基本养老保险范围的缴费单位和个人按国家规定的缴费基数和缴费比例缴纳的养老保险基金，以及通过其他方式取得的形成基金来源的收入。包括单位和职工个人缴纳的基本养老保险费、基本养老保险基金利息收入、上级补助收入、下级上解收入、转移收入、财政补贴和其他收入。

4、基本养老保险基金支出 指按照国家政策规定的开支范围和开支标准从养老保险基金中支付给参加基本养老保险的个人的养老金、丧葬抚恤补助，以及由于保险关系转移、上下级之间调剂资金等原因而发生的支出。包括离休金、退休金、退职金、各种补贴、医疗费、死亡丧葬补助费、抚恤救济费、社会保险经办机构管理费、补助下级支出、上解上级支出、转移支出、其他支出等。

5、基本养老保险基金累计结余 指截止报告期末基本养老保险基金收支相抵后的累计余额。

基本医疗保险

1、参保人数 指报告期末按国家有关规定参加基本医疗保险的人数。包括参加保险的职工人数和退休人员人数。

2、基金收入 指根据国家有关规定，由纳入基本医疗保险范围的缴费单位和个人，按国家规定的缴费基数和缴费比例缴纳的基金，以及通过其他方式取得的形成基金来源的款项，包括：单位缴纳的社会统筹基金收入、个人缴纳的个人账户基金收入、财政补贴收入、利息收入、其他收入。

3、基金支出 指按照国家政策规定的开支范围和开支标准从社会统筹基金中支付给参加基本医疗保险的职工和退休人员的医疗保险待遇支出，和从个人帐户基金中支付给参加基本医疗保险的职工和退休人员的医疗费用支出，以及其他支出。包括：住院医疗费用支出、门急诊医疗费用支出、个人账户基金支出、其他支出。

4、基金累计结余 指截止报告期末基本医疗保险的社会统筹和个人帐户基金累计结余金额。包括银行存款、财政专户、债券投资和其他。

失业保险

1、参保人数 指报告期末按照国家法律、法规和有关政策规定参加了失业保险的城镇企业事业单位的职工及地方政府规定参加失业保险的其他人员的人数。

2、失业保险基金收入 指按照规定从企业、事业及其他单位筹集的失业保险费及其他并入失业保险基金收入的总额。包括单位和个人缴纳的失业保险费、失业保险基金利息收入、上级补助收入、下级上解收入、转移收入、财政补贴和其他收入。

3、失业保险基金支出 指报告期内为保障失业人员和下岗职工基本生活、促进其再就业等支出的基金总额。包括失业救济金、医疗费、死亡丧葬补助费、抚恤救济费、转业训练费支出、失业保险经办机构管理费、补助下级支出、上解上级支出、转移支出和其他支出。

4、基金累计结余 指截止报告期末失业保险基金收支相抵后的累计余额。

工伤保险

1、参加保险人数 指报告期末依据国家有关规定参加工伤保险的职工人数。

2、享受保险待遇人数 指劳动者因工负伤致残、死亡或因患职业病致残，根据有关规定享受工伤保险待遇职工或供养直系亲属人数。包括伤残人数、职业病人数、因工死亡人数、供养直系亲属人数。

3、基金收入 指根据国家有关规定，由参加工伤保险的单位按国家规定的缴费基数和缴费比例缴纳的工伤保险基金，以及通过其他形式取得的形成基金来源的款项。包括：单位缴纳的社会统筹基金收入、财政补贴收入、利息收入、其他收入。

4、基金支出 指按照国家政策规定的开支范围和开支标准从工伤保险基金中支付给参加工伤保险的人员及供养直系亲属工伤保险待遇支出及其他支出。包括工伤医疗费、伤残补助金、工亡补助金、护理费、丧葬补助费、工伤预防费用、职业康复费用和其他支出。

5、基金累计结余 指截止报告期末工伤保险基金累计结余金额。包括银行存款、财政专户、债券投资和其他。

生育保险

1、参保人数 指报告期末依据有关规定参加生育保险的职工人数。

2、基金收入 指根据国家有关规定，由参加生育保险的单位按照国家规定的缴费基数和缴费比例缴纳的生育保险基金，以及通过其他方式取得的形成基金来源的款项，包括：单位缴纳的基金收入、利息收入和其他收入。

3、基金支出 指按照国家政策规定的开支范围和开支标准，从生育保险基金中支付给参加生育保险的职工，因妊娠、分娩和计划生育手术而享受的待遇及其他支出。包括：生育津贴、医疗费用支出及其他支出。

4、基金累计结余 指截止报告期末生育保险基金累计结余金额。包括银行存款、财政专户、债券投资和其他。

Explanatory Notes on Main Statistical Indicators

Notary Personnel refers to judicial workers of the state notary offices handling notarization work according to law. They include notaries, assistant notaries, and other people working for notary offices.

Notarized Documents refer to the documents settled by notary offices in a year. The notary documents are drawn up in accordance with the regulations of the Ministry of Justice, including domestic documents and foreign-related documents. Domestic documents are divided into two major categories, documents on economic contracts and documents on civil legal relations.

Mediators refer to workers on peoples mediation committees responsible for mediating in civil disputes and cases of slight infraction of the law. They include members of the mediation committees and mediators of mediation groups.

Serious Fire Case refers to a case which has caused over 10 to 30 deaths; or over 50 to 100 serious injuries; or a direct property loss over 50 million to 100 million yuan.

Comparatively Serious Fire Case refers to a case which has caused over three to ten deaths; or over 10 to 50 serious injuries; or a direct property loss over 10 million to 50 million yuan.

Ordinary Fire Case refers to a case which has caused less than three deaths; or less than 10 serious injuries; or a direct property loss less than 10 million yuan.

Cases Registered and Handled Directly by People's Procuratorate Offices refer to those serious criminal cases that, according to the functional jurisdiction, are registered and handled by the People's Procuratorate Offices, including the ones on bribery and corruption, the ones on abuse and dereliction of duty, offences against citizens' personal and democratic rights by government officials abusing their powers; and that are registered and handled by the provincial Procuratorate offices in relation to other major crimes committed by government officials by abusing their powers.

Key Cases refer to crimes committed by county and director-level officials. This indicator reflects the situation of those county and director-level officials involved in criminal cases registered and handled by People's Procuratorate offices.

Approval for Arrest refers to the decision made by people's procuratorate office, in accordance with the law and relevant facts, to approve the arrest of the suspect(s) as proposed by the public security departments, state security departments or prisons authority. This indicator reflects approved arrests made by people's procuratorate offices that are proposed by related departments.

Juvenile Criminals refers to the offenders within the age range of 14 to 25 convicted guilty by the court during the reporting period while those between 14 and 18 are defined as minor offenders.

Administrative Cases refers to the cases filed by citizens, corporations and other organizations against the specific administrative conducts of administrative authorities and handled by the court.

Number of Urban Residents Entitled to Minimum Living Allowances refers to the number of those whose average family income is below a minimum local standard by the end of the reporting period, including both the employed and unemployed, laid off and retired, and those jobless people without stable residence or valid IDs.

Number of Rural Residents Entitled to Minimum Living Allowances refers to the number of those receiving the minimum living allowances from the local government or community in the rural areas where this allowances system is in place as of the end of the reporting period.

Households Enjoying Five Guarantees refers to those senior citizens, handicapped or under-aged who, without labour ability, can not make a living by themselves and whose statutory providers are unable to support them or who have no statutory providers at all.

Number of Rural Recipients of Traditional Relief refers to the poor people entitled to traditional relief in rural areas where the minimum living allowances system is not in place.

Social Welfare Enterprises refers to those welfare-oriented enterprises employing a significant number of handicapped people with certain labour ability (handicapped employees shall exceed 10% of the production staff), including welfare factories, artificial limb plants as well as other welfare enterprises.

Number of Service Facilities in Urban Communities refers to the number non-profit welfare facilities set up by urban communities (community offices and residents' committees) to serve the community residents, including, among others, community-based centers that serve senior citizens, the handicapped or children, recreational centers, service centers, nursing homes, apartments for the elderly (nursery for the aged), work and treatment stations for the handicapped, day-care centers for handicapped children, domestic help agencies and dating services, as well as social insurance management agencies for the employees. Different types of community service providers that share the same premise are regarded as one community service facility. The requirements for a social service facility of communities include: (1) independent accounting; (2) fixed employees; (3) provision of services; and (4) premises.

Basic Pension Insurance

1.Number of staff and workers covered refer to staff and workers participating in the basic pension insurance programme according to national laws, regulations and related policies at the end of the reference period, who have already had payment records in social security management agencies, including those who have interrupt payment without terminating the insurance programme. Those who have registered in the programme but with no payment records are not included.

2. Number of retirees participating in the basic pension insurance programme refer to the number of retirees participating in basic pension insurance programmes by the end of the reference period.

3. Revenue of the basic pension insurance programme refers to payments made by employers and individuals participating in the pension insurance programme in accordance with the basis and proportion stipulated in State regulations, and income from other sources that become source of pension insurance fund, including the premium paid by employers and staff and workers, interest income, subsidies from higher level agencies, income as transfer from subordinate agencies, transferred income, government financial subsidies and other income.

4. Expenditure of basic pension insurance programme refers to payment made on pensions and funeral subsidies to those retired and resigned people covered in pension insurance programmes according to related national policies on scopeand standard of expenditure. Also included are expenditure which arises due to shift of the insurance relationship or adjustment of funds among agencies. More specifically, included are pensions for resigned people, pensions for retired people, pension for people quitting jobs, various subsidies, medical fees, funeral subsidies, compensation payments, management fees for social security agencies, expenses on subsidies to lower subordinates, expenses as transfer to agencies at higher level, transferred expenditure and other expenditure.

5. Balance of basic pension insurance programme refers to the balance of basic pension insurance funds at the end of the reference period after deducting expenses from revenue.

Basic Medical Care Insurance

1. Number of people participating in the insurance programme refers to people participating in the basic medical care insurance programme according to related regulations as at the end of reference period, including number of staff and workers and retirees participating in this insurance programme.

2. Revenue of the insurance programme refers to payments made by employers and individuals participating in the medical care insurance programme in accordance with the basis and proportion stipulated in State regulations, and income from other sources that become source of medical insurance fund, including income of social comprehensive funds paid by employers, income from individual accounts, government financial subsidies, interest income and other income.

3. Expenditure of the insurance programme refers to payment made from social comprehensive funds to those retired and resigned people covered in basic medical care insurance within the scope and standards of expenditure according to related national policies, and medical care payment made from individual accounts to staff and workers and retirees, and other expenses, including medical expenses of hospital inpatients, medical expenses for outpatients and emergency patients, payment from individual accounts and other expenditure.

4. Balance of the basic medical care insurance programme refer to the balance of medical care insurance of social comprehensive funds and individual accounts at the end of the reference period, including bank savings, special fiscal accounts, investment in bonds and others.

Unemployment Insurance

1. Number of people covered refers to staff and workers in urban enterprises or institutions who have participated in the unemployment insurance programme according to relevant policies and regulations, and other people who have participated according to local government regulations, as at the end of reference period.

2. Revenue of the unemployment insurance programme refers to payments made by employers and individuals participating in unemployment insurance programme in accordance with relevant regulations and other income contributed to this programme, including unemployment insurance premium made by employers and individuals, interest income, subsidies from higher level agencies, income as transfer from subordinate agencies, transferred income, government financial subsidies and other income.

3. Expenditure of the unemployment insurance programme refers to total expenses during the reference period to guarantee the basic livelihood of unemployed people and laid-off staff and workers and to encourage their re-employment. Included are unemployment relief, medical fees, funeral subsidies, compensation payments, training expenses, management fees for unemployment insurance agencies, subsidies to lower level agencies, expenses as transfer to higher level agencies, transferred expenditure and other expenditure.

4. Balance of the unemployment insurance programme refers to the balance of revenue of the programme after deducting expenses at the end of the reference period.

Work Injury Insurance

1. Number of people covered refers to staff and workers who have participated in the work injury insurance programme according to relevant national regulations.

2. Number of beneficiaries refers to staff and workers and their direct dependents who can, in accordance with relevant regulations, benefit from work injury insurance, as a result of work injury leading to disability or death of the staff/worker, or occupational disease leading to disability. Included in this category are number of injured and disabled people, number of people with occupational diseases, number of deaths at work places, and number of direct dependents.

3. Revenue of the work injury insurance programme refers to payments made by employers participating in the work injury insurance programme in accordance with the basis and proportion stipulated in State regulations, and income from other sources that become source of work injury insurance fund, including income of social comprehensive funds paid by employers, government financial subsidies, interest income and other income.

4. Expenditure of the work injury insurance programme refers to payments made from work injury insurance funds to those who participated in the work injury insurance programme and their direct dependents within the scope and standards of expenditure according to related national policies, and other expenditure, including medical fees for work injury, injury and disability subsidies, death subsidies, nursing fees, funeral subsidies, injury prevention fees, occupational rehabilitation fees and other expenditure.

5. Balance of the work injury insurance programme refers to the balance of the work injury funds at the end of the reference period, including bank savings, special fiscal account, investment in bonds and others.

Maternity Insurance

1. Number of people covered refers to staff and workers who have participated in the maternity insurance programme according to relevant regulation at the end of the reporting period.

2. Revenue of maternity insurance refers to payments made by employers participating in the maternity insurance programme in accordance with the basis and proportion stipulated in State regulations, and income from other sources

that become source of maternity insurance fund, including income of funds paid by employers, interest income and other income.

3. Expenditure of the maternity insurance programme refers to payments made from maternity insurance funds to staff and workers who participate in the maternity insurance programme within the scope and standards of expenditure in accordance with related national policies, expenses paid for pregnancy, child delivery or surgeries related to family planning, and other expenditure, including allowance for child bearing, medical fees and other expenditure.

4. Balance of the maternity programme refers to the balance of the maternity insurance funds at the end of reference period, including bank savings, special fiscal account, investment in funds and others.

23 Twenty-three

非公有制经济

Non-public Sectors of the Economy

23-1 非公有制经济生产总值

Value-added of Non-public-owned Economic Unit

单位：亿元 (100 million yuan)

指 标	Item	2006	2007	2008	2009	2010	2011
非公有制经济生产总值	**Gross Domestic Product**	**723.63**	**904.03**	**1152.42**	**1295.10**	**1610.76**	**2103.98**
第一产业	Primary Industry	86.20	101.77	134.80	139.77	165.63	197.77
第二产业	Secondary Industry	322.81	380.81	472.35	525.39	674.31	856.50
工业	Industry	286.98	339.66	418.36	455.97	579.44	728.81
建筑业	Construction	35.83	41.15	53.99	69.42	94.87	127.69
第三产业	Tertiary Industry	314.62	421.45	545.27	629.94	770.82	1049.71
#交通运输、仓储和邮政业	Transport,Storage and Post	81.04	124.94	170.50	183.89	234.88	320.63
批发和零售业	Wholesale and Retail Trade	72.93	90.05	114.46	135.02	178.61	234.14
住宿和餐饮业	Hotel and Catering Services	43.94	70.72	103.55	121.96	148.74	193.28
房地产业	Real Estate	67.40	80.14	91.39	118.72	124.70	146.60
其他服务业中营利性服务业	Profit-making Services in Other Services	31.86	42.45	54.24	62.60	76.89	116.88

23-2 非公有制经济生产总值比重

Value-added of Non-public-owned Economic Unit as Percentage to GDP

单位：% (%)

指 标	Item	2006	2007	2008	2009	2010	2011
非公有制经济生产总值比重	**Gross Domestic Product**	**30.9**	**31.3**	**32.4**	**33.1**	**35.0**	**36.9**
第一产业	Primary Industry	22.6	22.8	25.0	25.4	26.5	27.2
第二产业	Secondary Industry	33.4	33.9	34.5	35.6	37.5	39.0
工业	Industry	34.2	34.7	35.0	36.4	38.2	39.8
建筑业	Construction	27.9	28.2	30.9	31.0	33.5	35.0
第三产业	Tertiary Industry	31.8	32.1	33.0	33.4	35.4	37.7
#交通运输、仓储和邮政业	Transport,Storage and Post	42.0	44.3	46.0	46.0	48.9	54.3
批发和零售业	Wholesale and Retail Trade	45.1	45.3	46.0	46.0	48.6	52.2
住宿和餐饮业	Hotel and Catering Services	77.0	78.5	79.4	79.5	82.3	86.1
房地产业	Real Estate	84.0	86.0	87.2	87.2	89.3	91.5
其他服务业中营利性服务业	Profit-making Services in Other Services	25.1	25.2	25.4	25.0	27.1	29.4

23-3 全社会非公有制经济完成投资额

Investment of Non-public-owned Economic Unit in the Whole Province

单位：亿元 (100 million yuan)

指 标	Item	非公有制经济完成投资额 Amount of Finishied Investment of Non-public-owned Economic Unit						非公有制经济完成投资额占全省比重(%) Proportion of Finished Investments of Non-public-owned Economic Unit to Total Investments(%)					
		2006	2007	2008	2009	2010	2011	2006	2007	2008	2009	2010	2011
总计	**Total**	**582.25**	**773.85**	**928.53**	**1187.14**	**1550.08**	**2429.74**	**48.6**	**52.0**	**49.8**	**48.4**	**48.6**	**47.6**
农、林、牧、渔业	Agriculture,Forestry,Animal Husbandry and Fishing	21.53	15.60	25.15	32.04	36.23	48.42	79.6	53.2	49.4	43.6	44.9	29.7
采矿业	Mining	55.22	84.50	122.75	228.43	319.13	457.75	60.8	70.3	68.0	84.0	85.2	87.6
制造业	Manufacturing	117.26	205.68	232.66	270.36	322.03	720.95	70.6	81.1	71.9	76.1	75.2	75.7
电力、燃气及水的生产和供应业	Production and Supply of Electricity,Gas and Water	86.29	91.33	71.66	55.86	50.78	88.04	33.6	33.7	25.3	20.1	18.7	25.4
建筑业	Construction	0.93	1.71	3.27	4.25	3.30	4.51	31.5	57.4	45.4	63.4	24.7	14.6
交通运输、仓储和邮政业	Transport,Storage and Post	22.24	21.68	18.01	35.62	38.38	29.84	12.6	11.2	7.0	8.1	6.2	3.7
信息传输、计算机服务和软件业	Information Transmission, Computer Service and Software	10.71	11.90	15.57	30.58	27.05	17.17	24.2	31.0	32.9	50.4	48.3	37.2
批发和零售业	Wholesale and Retail Trade	9.10	10.42	13.92	16.14	14.90	39.13	64.7	63.4	75.8	77.8	70.1	78.6
住宿和餐饮业	Hotels and Catering Services	7.88	13.79	11.41	14.57	19.49	43.52	81.7	91.7	81.0	88.5	87.8	82.6
金融业	Financial Intermediation	0.49	0.77	1.61	5.02	2.13	1.18	14.3	27.2	37.4	66.7	34.1	25.6
房地产业	Real Estate	224.59	288.97	372.93	459.90	666.69	864.72	89.7	86.1	86.6	84.5	85.9	72.2
租赁和商务服务业	Leasing and Business Services	0.89	2.19	11.43	4.14	2.65	5.87	73.9	60.5	88.0	55.7	38.3	43.9
科学研究、技术服务和地质勘查	Scientific Research, Technical Services, and Geological Prospecting	1.11	0.86	0.52	1.23	2.12	2.71	33.1	18.7	10.9	14.6	24.9	25.5
水利、环境和公共设施管理业	Management of Water Conservancy, Environment and Public Facilities	11.89	13.25	14.86	13.33	26.61	67.11	15.8	11.9	11.4	5.9	7.8	9.9
居民服务和其他服务业	Services to Households and Other Services	1.89	2.58	4.87	5.92	5.42	7.09	69.3	84.7	95.0	92.2	81.3	62.1
教育	Education	3.13	2.02	2.91	2.41	3.97	8.21	12.8	8.0	9.6	5.9	7.4	9.6
卫生、社会保障和社会福利业	Health, Social Securities and Social Welfare	1.41	1.12	0.75	0.65	1.52	5.18	16.5	11.3	6.3	3.8	6.4	13.2
文化、体育和娱乐业	Culture, Sports and Entertainment	3.28	4.37	3.00	3.38	5.40	16.47	27.6	33.4	20.5	21.4	22.8	51.6
公共管理和社会组织	Public Management and Social Organization	2.41	1.13	1.22	3.31	2.28	1.87	8.5	3.0	3.4	6.2	4.1	3.2

注:本表数据根据投资单位登记注册类型汇总。

Note:Data in the table are calculated by investment unit's registration status.

23–4 规模以上非公有制经济工业企业主要经济指标(2011)

单位：万元

指 标	Item	企业单位数（个）Number of Enterprises (unit)
总 计	**Total**	**2970**
#亏损企业	Loss Making Enterprises	818
按轻重工业分	**Grouped by Type of Light and Heavy Industry**	
轻工业	Light Industry	711
重工业	Heavy Industry	2259
按企业规模分	**Grouped by Size of Enterprise**	
大型企业	Large	18
中型企业	Medium	301
小型企业	Small	2651
按登记注册类型分	**Grouped by Registration Categories**	
内资企业	Domestic Funded Enterprises	2883
股份合作企业	Share-holding Cooperative Enterprises	39
联营企业	Joint Owned Enterprises	20
有限责任公司	Companies with Limited Liabilities	891
股份有限公司	Share-holding Companies with Limited Liabilities	91
私营企业	Private Enterprises	1781
其他企业	Others	61
港、澳、台商投资企业	Enterprises with Funds from Hong Kong, Macao and Taiwan	41
合资经营企业(港或澳、台资)	Joint-venture Enterprises(with Funds from Hong Kong,Macao and Taiwan)	18
港澳台商独资经营企业	Enterprises with Sole Funds from Hong Kong, Macao and Taiwan	23
外商投资企业	Foreign Funded Enterprises	46
中外合资经营企业	Joint-venture Enterprises	21
中外合作经营企业	Cooperative Enterprises	1
外资企业	Enterprises with Sole Foreigner	19
外商投资股份有限公司	Share-holding Companies with Funds from Foreigner	5

Main Economic Indicators of Non-public-owned above Designated Size Industrial Enterprises

(10000 yuan)

工业总产值 (当年价) Gross Industial OutputValue (current price)	固定资产原价 Original Value of Fixed Assets	主营业务收入 Revenue from Principal Business	利润总额 Total Profits	从业人员平均人数(万人) Annual Average Number of Employed Persons (10000 persons)
27035243	**8434228**	**22889883**	**2247592**	**42.58**
4574708	3049830	3782459	-307185	9.49
6652816	1336370	5514410	699828	8.70
20382426	7097858	17375473	1547765	33.88
2458849	631885	1969635	436649	3.52
6969667	2986308	6669533	997068	14.15
17606727	4816035	14250715	813876	24.91
25151156	7144838	21263943	2081459	39.92
378022	99893	278071	39000	0.94
131050	25469	109127	16413	0.18
9558080	2541786	7903955	664183	11.76
1591568	776981	1278889	173013	2.35
13260281	3633241	11452491	1172859	24.22
232155	67468	241410	15991	0.47
635455	706236	579094	-15719	0.75
332542	602063	295424	-22676	0.34
302914	104173	283670	6957	0.41
1248632	583154	1046845	181853	1.91
373484	161648	355039	45613	0.45
179360	117262	179156	93439	0.08
447584	237771	408931	30295	0.62
248203	66472	103719	12506	0.77

23-4 续表

单位：万元

指标	Item	单位数（个）Number of Enterprises (unit)
按工业行业分	**Grouped by Industrial Sector**	
煤炭开采和洗选业	Mining and Washing of Coal	916
黑色金属矿采选业	Mining and Processing of Ferrous Metal Ores	41
有色金属矿采选业	Mining and Processing of Non-Ferrous Metal Ores	40
非金属矿采选业	Mining and Processing of Nonmetal Ores	66
农副食品加工业	Processing of Food from Agricultural Products	189
食品制造业	Manufacture of Foods	67
饮料制造业	Manufacture of Beverages	167
烟草制品业	Manufacture of Tobacco	1
纺织业	Manufacture of Textile	12
纺织服装、鞋、帽制造业	Manufacture of Textile Wearing Apparel,Footware and Caps	10
皮革、毛皮、羽毛(绒)及其制品业	Manufacture of Leather, Fur, Feather and Related Products	3
木材加工及木、竹、藤、棕、草制品业	Processing of Timber, Manufacture of Wood,Bamboo, Rattan, Palm and Straw Products	67
家具制造业	Manufacture of Furniture	6
造纸及纸制品业	Manufacture of Paper and Paper Products	51
印刷业和记录媒介的复制	Printing, Reproduction of Recording Media	23
文教体育用品制造业	Manufacture of Articles For Culture, Education and Sport Activities	3
石油加工、炼焦及核燃料加工业	Processing of Petroleum, Coking, Processing of Nuclear Fuel	34
化学原料及化学制品制造业	Manufacture of Raw Chemical Materials and Chemical Products	164
医药制造业	Manufacture of Medicines	99
橡胶制品业	Manufacture of Rubber	11
塑料制品业	Manufacture of Plastics	55
非金属矿物制品业	Manufacture of Non-metallic Mineral Products	403
黑色金属冶炼及压延加工业	Smelting and Pressing of Ferrous Metals	166
有色金属冶炼及压延加工业	Smelting and Pressing of Non-ferrous Metals	84
金属制品业	Manufacture of Metal Products	36
通用设备制造业	Manufacture of General Purpose Machinery	66
专用设备制造业	Manufacture of Special Purpose Machinery	29
交通运输设备制造业	Manufacture of Transport Equipment	35
电气机械及器材制造业	Manufacture of Electrical Machinery and Equipment	51
通信设备、计算机及其他电子设备制造业	Manufacture of Communication Equipment, Computers and Other Electronic Equipment	9
仪器仪表及文化、办公用机械制造业	Manufacture of Measuring Instruments and Machinery for Cultural Activity and Office Work	8
工艺品及其他制造业	Manufacture of Artwork and Other Manufacturing	6
废弃资源和废旧材料回收加工业	Recycling and Disposal of Waste	4
电力、热力的生产和供应业	Production and Supply of Electric Power and Heat Power	41
燃气生产和供应业	Production and Supply of Gas	2
水的生产和供应业	Production and Supply of Water	4

Continued

(10000 yuan)

工业总产值 (当年价) Gross Industial OutputValue (current price)	固定资产 原 价 Original Value of Fixed Assets	主营业务 收 入 Revenue from Principal Business	利 润 总 额 Total Profits	从业人员数 (万人) Annual Average Number of Employed Persons (10000 persons)
7579654	2129177	6210694	856767	17.40
137934	43218	130413	17427	0.37
189659	56925	166287	14838	0.33
379998	75295	336182	65470	0.50
1361206	165412	1210940	56810	1.34
770570	138806	730122	157205	0.95
1239983	346188	916233	155010	1.92
8439	1077	9490	11	0.01
72510	10846	59952	628	0.27
17374	5940	17827	1124	0.14
19538	1933	19140	2436	0.05
403894	59468	343980	29286	0.96
61714	5095	55939	16254	0.06
348491	53799	317172	23548	0.40
137884	98128	120464	30454	0.20
13106	2072	10794	158	0.08
595960	116951	504706	21982	0.86
2037120	625923	1951620	242737	2.15
2224505	446602	1712182	238234	2.57
41412	17458	32025	-163	0.15
374134	63800	318331	16609	0.58
2543815	1552058	2188649	70540	4.54
3091252	459783	2663911	74496	2.70
1475041	524702	1242234	147353	1.36
141754	17209	119403	6415	0.22
339572	70905	278516	18404	0.62
215205	34167	181243	12294	0.35
363990	128834	336993	12176	0.39
543026	64192	417502	15900	0.60
29731	10822	19651	1238	0.13
43803	5328	41191	519	0.09
21528	731	21875	178	0.03
41149	3035	38086	856	0.04
156040	1084686	142278	-60234	0.18
8355	6744	6027	445	0.02
5902	6852	9393	99	0.02

23–5 资质以上非公有制经济建筑企业主要经济指标(2011)

单位：万元

指　　标	Item	有工作量企业数(个) Number of Enterprises(unit)
总　　计	**Total**	**339**
按登记注册类型分组	**Grouped by Registration Categories**	
内资企业	Domestic Funded Enterprises	339
联营企业	Joint Owned Enterprises	1
其他联营企业	Others	1
有限责任公司	Companies with Limited Liabilities	183
其他有限责任公司	Others	183
股份有限公司	Share-holding Companies with Limited Liabilities	24
私营企业	Private Enterprises	131
私营独资企业	Enterprises Investments with Sole Private	1
私营合伙企业	Cooperative Enterprises	1
私营有限责任公司	Companies with Limited Liabilities	119
私营股份有限公司	Share-holding Companies with Limited Liabilities	10
按建筑业行业中类分组	**By Sector**	
房屋和土木工程建筑业	Housing Construction and Civil Engineering Industry	222
建筑安装业	Construction and Installation Industry	62
建筑装饰业	Construction and Descoration Industry	42
其他建筑业	Other Construction Industries	13
按企业资质等级分组	**By Qualification Standard**	
施工总承包	Chief Construction Contract	235
一级	First Grade	9
二级	Second Grade	77
三级及以下	Third and Lower Grade	149
专业承包	Professional Contract	104
一级	First Grade	7
二级	Second Grade	59
三级及以下	Third and Lower Grade	38

Main Economic Indicators of Non-public-owned above Designated Size Construction Enterprises

(10000 yuan)

建筑业总产值 Gross Output Value of Construction	固定资产原价 Original Value of Fixed Assets	工程结算收入 Prime Operating Revenue	利润总额 Total Profits	平均人数(人) Annual Average Number of Employed Persons(person)
1989788	**291580**	**1907291**	**55857**	**102607**
1989788	291580	1907291	55857	102607
4299	2134	4299	-1462	168
4299	2134	4299	-1462	168
1367399	169983	1276135	38466	66329
1367399	169983	1276135	38466	66329
105520	27981	106479	4610	6387
512571	91481	520378	14244	29723
216	251	216	33	41
6347	42	6354	76	392
406302	78912	403534	13619	23361
99706	12277	110273	516	5929
1621950	247216	1602940	33693	91630
162965	26530	140136	5469	6994
39298	5512	38724	75	3104
165575	12322	125491	16620	879
1666212	247637	1623382	34921	93504
739757	43561	690850	7332	24151
558946	111060	565261	13790	37270
367509	93015	367271	13799	32083
323576	43943	283909	20936	9103
120336	2899	89088	14945	827
139527	25817	137837	2924	5797
63713	15227	56984	3067	2479

23–6 限额以上非公有制经济批发零售企业主要经济指标(2011)

单位：万元

指　标	Item	企业个数(个) Number of Enterprises(unit)
批发业	**Wholesale Trade**	**249**
按登记注册类型分组	**by Types of Registration**	
内资企业	Domestic Funded Enterprises	248
国有企业	State-owned Enterprises	12
集体企业	Collective-owned Enterprises	3
股份合作企业	Share-holding Cooperative Enterprises	1
有限责任公司	Limited Liabilities Corperatioms	167
国有独资公司	State Sole Funded Corperatioms	
其他有限责任公司	Other Limited Liabilities Corperatioms	167
股份有限公司	Share-holding Corperatioms Ltd.	9
私营企业	Private Enterprises	54
私营独资企业	Private-funded Enterprises	5
私营合伙企业	Private Partnership Enterprise	1
私营有限责任公司	Private Limited Liabilities Corperations	45
私营股份有限公司	Private Share-holding Corperations Ltd.	3
其他企业	Other Enterprises	2
港、澳、台商投资企业	Enterprises with Funds from Hong Kong, Macao and Taiwan	
合资经营企业(港或澳、台资)	Joint-venture Enterprises(with Funds from Hong Kong, Macao and Taiwan)	
港澳台商投资股份有限公司	Share-holding Cooperative Enterpriseswith Funds from Hong Kong, Macao and Taiwan	
外商投资企业	Foreign Funded Enterprises	1
中外合资经营企业	Joint-venture Enterprises	1
外资企业	Enterprises with Sole Fund	
按批发行业分组	**by Wholesale Trade Sector**	
农畜产品批发业	Wholesale of Farm Produce and Livestack Products	2
食品、饮料及烟草制品批发	Food, Beverages, Tobacco	29
纺织、服装及日用品批发	Textiles Products,Gaments and Commodity	6
文化、体育用品及器材批发	Culture&Sports Articles and Equipments	4
医药及医疗器材批发	Medicines and Special Appliances of Medicines	42
矿产品、建材及化工产品批发	Mineral Products,Materials of Construction and Chemical Products	108
机械设备、五金交电及电子产品批发	Mechinery Equipments,Hardwares,Electric Appliances and Eletronic Products	51
其他批发	Others	7

Main Economic Indicators of Non-public-owned Enterprises above Designated Size of Wholesale and Retail Trade

(10000 yuan)

固定资产原价 Original Value of Fixed Assets	主营业务收入 Prime Operating Revenue	主营业务税金及附加 Tax and associate charge	利润总额 Total Profits
81571	**3103491**	**6599**	**27302**
79220	3091002	6567	27881
1130	11478	233	566
235	3098	3	12
727	5944	0	-2268
58559	2546773	4261	22432
58559	2546773	4261	22432
5627	112589	1154	2633
12759	394401	860	4460
315	33815	92	-518
1	10984	2	3
12430	330856	755	4962
13	18747	11	12
182	16721	54	46
2351	12489	33	-580
2351	12489	33	-580
149	8004	3	21
15416	180683	823	9341
1115	53129	65	286
1135	13689	31	-11
18749	468920	1097	4546
31073	1372582	3083	5698
12814	987155	1291	7688
1121	19328	207	-266

23-6 续表

单位：万元

指　标	Item	企业个数(个) Number of Enterprises(unit)
零售业	**Retail Trade**	**468**
按登记注册类型分组	**By Types of Registration**	
内资企业	Domestic Funded Enterprises	451
国有企业	State-owned Enterprises	2
集体企业	Collective-owned Enterprises	3
股份合作企业	Share-holding Cooperative Enterprises	2
有限责任公司	Limited Liabilities Corperatioms	235
其他有限责任公司	Other Limited Liabilities Corperatioms	235
股份有限公司	Share-holding Corperatioms Ltd.	5
私营企业	Private Enterprises	196
私营独资企业	Private-funded Enterprises	27
私营合伙企业	Private Partnership Enterprise	7
私营有限责任公司	Private Limited Liabilities Corperations	150
私营股份有限公司	Private Share-holding Corperations Ltd.	12
其他企业	Other Enterprises	8
港、澳、台商投资企业	Enterprises with Funds from Hong Kong, Macao and Taiwan	8
与港澳台商合资经营	Joint-venture Enterprises(with Funds from Hong Kong,Macao and Taiwan)	5
与港澳台商合作经营	Cooperative Enterprises(with Funds from Hong Kong, Macao and Taiwan)	
港澳台商独资经营企业	Enterprises with Sole Funds from Hong Kong,Macao and Taiwan	2
港澳台商投资股份有限公司	Share-holding Cooperative Enterpriseswith Funds from Hong Kong, Macao and Taiwan	1
外商投资企业	Foreign Funded Enterprises	
中外合资经营企业	Joint-venture Enterprises	
外资企业	Enterprises with Sole Fund	
按零售行业小类分组	**By Retail Trade Sector**	
综合零售	Comprehensive Retail Sale	84
食品、饮料及烟草制品专门零售	Food, Beverages, Tobacco	16
纺织、服装及日用品专门零售	Textiles Products,Gaments and Commodity	19
文化、体育用品及器材专门零售	Medicines and Special Appliances of Medicines	8
医药及医疗器材专门零售	Automobiles,Motocycles,Fuels and Their Parts	25
汽车、摩托车、燃料及零配件专门零售	Household Electrical Appliances and Electronic Products	215
家用电器及电子产品专门零售	Hardwares,Furnitures and Materials of Decoration	85
五金、家具及室内装修材料专门零售	Hardware,Furniture and Interior Decoration Materials	7
无店铺及其他零售	Non-shop and Other Retails	9

continued

(10000 yuan)

固定资产原价 Original Value of Fixed Assets	主营业务收入 Prime Operating Revenue	主营业务税金及附加 Tax and associate charge	利润总额 Total Profits
273933	**3235047**	**12109**	**66188**
224230	2823073	9618	37400
105	371	0	0
102	8142	7	5
273	5289	17	596
180423	1888471	7217	23941
180423	1888471	7217	23941
706	13734	38	438
40010	878199	2241	12677
2949	33749	284	1299
1102	13346	59	350
33486	758725	1765	11480
2473	72378	133	-452
2610	28867	99	-257
13327	218970	1043	12760
12101	192572	869	13116
313	9225	26	-586
913	17172	149	230
147709	726216	6408	30701
2573	61800	116	1991
20215	98351	642	2471
1072	18266	217	-81
5748	83981	325	1267
83748	1838590	2996	20660
6559	354980	1146	7294
1716	23022	55	139
4593	29342	203	1744

23-7 限额以上非公有制经济住宿餐饮企业主要经济指标(2011)

单位：万元

指　标	Item	企业个数(个) Number of Enterprises(unit)
住宿业	**Quartering Services**	**211**
按登记注册类型分组	**by Types of Registration**	
内资企业	Domestic Funded Enterprises	206
国有企业	State-owned Enterprises	14
集体企业	Collective-owned Enterprises	
股份合作企业	Share-holding Cooperative Enterprises	
有限责任公司	Limited Liabilities Corperatioms	84
国有独资公司	State Sole Funded Corperatioms	
其他有限责任公司	Other Limited Liabilities Corperatioms	84
股份有限公司	Share-holding Corperatioms Ltd.	2
私营企业	Private Enterprises	98
私营独资企业	Private-funded Enterprises	37
私营合伙企业	Private Partnership Enterprise	15
私营有限责任公司	Private Limited Liabilities Corperations	40
私营股份有限公司	Private Share-holding Corperations Ltd.	6
其他企业	Other Enterprises	8
港、澳、台商投资企业	Enterprises with Funds from Hong Kong, Macao and Taiwan	4
合资经营企业(港或澳、台资)	Joint-venture Enterprises(with Funds from Hong Kong, Macao and Taiwan)	2
港、澳、台商独资经营企业	Cooperative Enterprises(with Funds from Hong Kong, Macao and Taiwan)	2
外商投资企业	Foreign Funded Enterprises	1
中外合资经营企业	Joint-venture Enterprises	1
按住宿行业分组	**by Quartering Services Sector**	
旅游饭店	Tourism Hotels	146
一般旅馆	General Hotels	60
其他住宿服务	Other Hotel Services	5
餐饮业	**Catering Services**	**140**
按登记注册类型分组	**by Registration Categories**	
内资企业	Domestic Funded Enterprises	139
国有企业	State-owned Enterprises	
股份合作企业	Share-holding Cooperative Enterprises	1
有限责任公司	Companies with Limited Liabilities	47
其他有限责任公司	Others	47
股份有限公司	Share-holding Companies with Limited Liabilities	1
私营企业	Private Enterprises	77
私营独资企业	Enterprises Investments with Sole Private	35
私营合伙企业	Cooperative Enterprises	13
私营有限责任公司	Companies with Limited Liabilities	26
私营股份有限公司	Share-holding Companies with Limited Liabilities	3
其他企业	Others	13
港、澳、台商投资企业	Enterprises with Funds from Hong Kong, Macao and Taiwan	
合资经营企业(港或澳、台资)	Joint-venture Enterprises(Hong Kong, Macao or Taiwan)	
港、澳、台商独资经营企业	Corporations soly Funds from Hong Kong, Macao or Taiwan	
港、澳、台商投资股份有限公司	hare-holding Corporations Ltd. Funds from Hong Kong, Macao or Taiwan	
外商投资企业	Foreign Funded Enterprises	1
中外合资经营企业	Joint-venture Enterprises	
外资企业	Enterprises with Sole Foreigner	1
按餐饮行业分组	**by Catering Services Sector**	
正餐服务	Restaurant	137
快餐服务	Snack Counter	3
饮料及冷饮服务	Beverages and Cold Drinks	
其他餐饮服务业	Others	

Main Economic Indicators of Non-public-owned Enterprises above Designated Size of Catering and Quartering Services

(10000 yuan)

固定资产原价 Original Value of Fixed Assets	主营业务收入 Prime Operating Revenue	主营业务税金及附加 Taxes and Other charges on Principal Business	利润总额 Total Profits
268901	**180034**	**10271**	**-2905**
250967	166867	9517	-3070
3987	2916	183	53
148653	94156	5210	-3801
148653	94156	5210	-3801
4198	1422	79	-56
91589	64205	3770	1047
34999	25427	1428	2671
8463	7713	530	138
44057	25137	1519	-1652
4071	5928	293	-110
2539	4169	275	-312
13265	9678	550	146
12350	7784	443	107
915	1894	108	39
4669	3489	203	20
4669	3489	203	20
222567	141683	7953	-2719
39980	35979	2168	36
6354	2372	149	-222
72266	**139575**	**8182**	**743**
72266	137023	8037	743
182	226	13	12
33734	72074	4133	-989
33734	72074	4133	-989
666	725	30	71
32455	53627	3298	2228
17595	17693	1190	730
4780	11157	583	616
9626	18039	1142	690
454	6738	384	192
5229	10370	563	-579
	2552	146	
	2552	146	
72133	135410	7948	757
133	4165	234	-14

24

Twenty-four

民族自治地方

Minority Nationality Autonomous Areas

24-1 民族自治地方行政区划(2011)

Administrative Division of Minority Nationality Autonomous Areas

单位：个 (unit)

民族自治州(县)名称	Autonomous State(County)	地级 Prefectural Level	县级 County Level	#县级市 City at County Level	成立时间 Time of Comeinto Existence	土地面积(平方公里) Total Land Area(sq.km)
黔西南布依族苗族自治州	Qianxinan(Bouyei & Miao)Autonomous State	1	8	1	1982年5月1日	16804
黔东南苗族侗族自治州	Qiandongnan(Miao & Dong)Autonomous State	1	16	1	1956年7月23日	30337
黔南布依族苗族自治州	Qiannan(Bouyei & Miao)Autonomous State	1	12	2	1956年8月8日	26197
道真仡佬族苗族自治县	Daozhen(Gelao & Miao)Autonomous County		1		1987年11月29日	2156
务川仡佬族苗族自治县	Wuchuan(Gelao & Miao)Autonomous County		1		1987年11月26日	2773
镇宁布依族苗族自治县	Zhenning(Bouyei & Miao)Autonomous County		1		1963年9月11日	1703
关岭布依族苗族自治县	Guanling(Bouyei & Miao)Autonomous County		1		1981年12月31日	1468
紫云苗族布依族自治县	Ziyun(Miao & Bouyei)Autonomous County		1		1966年2月11日	2284
威宁彝族回族苗族自治县	Weining(Yi,Hui & Miao)Autonomous County		1		1954年11月11日	6296
玉屏侗族自治县	Yuping(Dong)Autonomous County		1		1984年11月7日	516
印江土家族苗族自治县	Yinjiang(Tujia & Miao)Autonomous County		1		1987年11月20日	1961
沿河土家族自治县	Yanhe(Tujia)Autonomous County		1		1987年11月23日	2469
松桃苗族自治县	Songtao(Miao)Autonomous County		1		1956年12月31日	2861
三都水族自治县	Sandu(Shui)Autonomous County		1		1957年1月2日	2384

24-2 少数民族分布

Geographic Distribution of Minority Nationalities

民 族	Nationality	分布的主要地区	Main Geographic Distribution
苗 族	Miao	黔东南州、黔南州、黔西南州、松桃县、印江县、威宁县	Qiandongnan,Songtao,Weining
布依族	Bouyei	黔南州、黔西南州	Qiannan,Qianxinan
侗 族	Dong	黔东南州、玉屏县	Qiandongnan,Yuping
土家族	Tujia	铜仁地区	Tongren
彝 族	Yi	毕节地区、六盘水市	Bijie,Liupanshui
仡佬族	Gelao	遵义市、安顺市	Zunyi,Anshun
水 族	Shui	三都县	Sandu
回 族	Hui	威宁县、兴仁县、平坝县	Weining,Xingren,Pingba
白 族	Bai	毕节地区	Bijie
瑶 族	Yao	黔东南州、三都县	Qiandongnan,Sandu
壮 族	Zhuang	从江县、黎平县、独山县、荔波县	Congjiang,Liping,Dushan,Libo
畲 族	She	凯里市、麻江县、都匀市、福泉市	Kaili,Majiang,Duyun,Fuquan
毛南族	Maonan	平塘县、独山县、惠水县	Pingtang,Dushan,Huishui
蒙古族	Mongoloid	毕节地区、石阡县	Bijie,Shiqian
仫佬族	Mulam	凯里市、麻江县、黄平县	Kaili,Majiang,Huangping
满 族	Man	黔西县、大方县、金沙县	Qianxi,Dafang,Jinsha
羌 族	Qiang	石阡县、江口县	Shiqian,Jiangkou

24-3 民族自治地方经济社会主要指标

Major Social and Economic Indicators of Minority Nationality Autonomous Areas

指　标	Item	2010	2011	2011年比2010年增长(%) Increase Rate in 2011 over 2010(%)
人口	**Population**			
年末常住人口(万人)	Number of Resident Population at Year-end(10000 persons)	1355.93	1347.16	-0.6
#少数民族人口	Minority Population	796.28	866.89	8.9
生产总值	**Gross Domestic Product**			
生产总值(亿元)	Gross Domestic Product(100 million yuan)	1261.89	1560.50	16.1
固定资产投资	**Investment in Fixed Assets**			
固定资产投资总额(亿元)	Total Investment in Fixed Assets(100 million yuan)	742.24	1311.02	76.6
财政、金融	**Government Finance and Banking**			
财政一般预算收入(亿元)	Local Financial Revenue(100 million yuan)	99.34	155.85	56.9
财政一般预算支出(亿元)	Financial Expenditure(100 million yuan)	500.77	653.56	30.5
金融机构年末存款余额(亿元)	Total Savins Deposit Balance at Year-end(100 million yuan)	1610.35	1941.49	20.6
金融机构年末贷款余额(亿元)	Total Loan Balance at Year-end(100 million yuan)	919.30	1130.50	23.0
城乡居民储蓄余额(亿元)	Urban and Rural Resident Savings Deposit Balance(100 million yuan)	867.48	1098.81	26.7
农　业	**Agriculture**			
常用耕地面积(千公顷)	Cultivated Area(1000 hectares)	761.30	759.33	-0.3
农业总产值(亿元)	Gross Agricultural Output Value(100 million yuan)	478.82	534.26	11.6
粮食产量(万吨)	Output of Grain(10000 tons)	573.39	385.85	-32.7
油菜籽产量(万吨)	Output of Rapeseeds(10000 tons)	18.27	23.42	28.9
牛年底头数(万头)	Large Animals(year-end)(10000 heads)	300.28	257.06	-14.4
猪年底头数(万头)	Hogs(year-end)(10000 heads)	765.81	679.96	-11.2
羊年底头数(万只)	Sheep and Goats(year-end)(10000 heads)	226.04	151.31	-33.1
工　业	**Industry**			
原煤产量(万吨)	Output of Coal(10000 tons)	2478.98	2968.78	19.8
发电量(亿千瓦小时)	Output of Electricity(100 million kwh)	265.74	263.01	-1.0
生铁产量(万吨)	Pig Iron(10000 tons)	20.36	33.18	63.0
运输邮电	**Transportation and Post**			
公路里程(公里)	Length of Highways(km)	50125	61528	22.8
邮路总长度(公里)	Length of Postal Routes(km)	19090		
商　业	**Trade**			
社会消费品零售总额(亿元)	Total Retail Sales of Consumer Goods(100 million yuan)	381.51	456.92	19.8
教　育	**Education**			
在校学生数(万人)	Students Enrollment(10000 persons)			
高等学校	Institutions of Higher Education	5.84	5.85	0.1
中等学校	Secondary Schools		110.52	
小学	Primary Schools	179.04	169.23	-5.5
专任教师(万人)	Full-time Teachers(10000 persons)			
高等学校	Institutions of Higher Education	0.30	0.34	13.3
中等学校	Secondary Schools		5.91	
小　学	Primary Schools	8.46	8.40	-0.7
人均水平	**Per Capita Standard of Living**			
人均生产总值(元)	Per Capita Gross Domestic Product(yuan)	9911	11546	16.9
人均财政一般预算收入(元)	Per Capita Local Financial Revenue(yuan)	734	1153	57.1
城乡居民人均储蓄(元)	Per Capita Urban and Rural Resident Savings(yuan)	6407	8130	26.9

注：表中人均水平数据按常住半年人口计算。

Note:Data of Per Capita Standard of Living are calculated according to resident population staying at home for 6 months.

24-4 民族自治地方经济发展主要指标(2011)
Major Economic Indicators of Minority Nationality Autonomous Areas

指 标	Item	民族自治地方 Minority Nationality Autonomous Areas	民族自治州 Minority Nationality Autonomous State	民族自治县 Minority Nationality Autonomous County
生产总值(亿元)	**Gross Domestic Product(100 million yuan)**	**1560.50**	**1202.71**	**376.79**
第一产业	Primary Industry	322.50	215.02	113.20
第二产业	Secondary Industry	545.67	449.01	100.07
第三产业	Tertiary Industry	692.34	538.68	163.52
农 业	**Agriculture**			
乡村从业人口(万人)	Rural Employment(10000 persons)	925.95	638.92	306.20
年末实有耕地面积(千公顷)	Cultivated Areas(year-end)(1000 hectares)	759.33	512.25	260.70
农用机械总动力(万千瓦)	Total Agricultural Machinery Power(10000 kw)	853.60	650.16	217.12
化肥使用量(折纯量)(万吨)	Consumption of Chemical Fertilizers(10000 tons)	35.95	24.89	11.42
有效灌溉面积(千公顷)	Irrigated Areas(1000 hectares)	508.07	401.07	114.99
农作物播种面积(千公顷)	Total Sown Areas (1000 hectares)	2081.40	1428.94	695.99
#粮 食	Grain Crops	1249.99	855.93	419.87
油菜籽	Rapeseeds	195.70	139.65	61.57
粮食总产量(万吨)	Total Grain Yield(10000 tons)	385.85	254.13	139.37
油菜籽产量(万吨)	Output of Rapeseeds(10000 tons)	23.42	16.76	7.45
烤烟产量(万吨)	Output of Flue -cured Tobacco (10000 tons)	13.95	7.00	6.95
茶叶产量(万吨)	Output of Tea (10000 tons)	2.43	1.60	0.88
当年造林面积(千公顷)	Afforested Areas in 2004(1000 hectares)	160.90	109.11	54.93
牲畜当年存栏数	Animals in Hand			
猪(万头)	Hogs(10000 heads)	679.91	422.61	269.76
牛(万头)	Large Animals(10000 heads)	257.06	177.32	85.82
羊(万只)	Sheep and Goats(10000 heads)	151.31	83.39	68.32
牲畜当年出栏数	Number of Slaughtered Animals			
猪(万头)	Hogs(10000 heads)	753.04	511.40	256.37
牛(万头)	Large Animals(10000 heads)	53.90	35.89	19.37
羊(万只)	Sheep and Goats(10000 heads)	108.98	50.45	58.98
肉类总产量(万吨)	Output of Meat(10000 tons)	76.78	50.19	28.01
水产品产量(万吨)	Total Aquatic Products(10000 tons)	6.73	5.09	1.82
农林牧渔业总产值(亿元)	Gross Output Value of Farming,Forestry,Animal Husbandry and Fishery(100 million yuan)	534.26	362.22	180.76
#农 业	Farming	281.54	185.53	100.95

24-4 续表 continued

指 标	Item	民族自治地方 Minority Nationality Autonomous Areas	民族自治州 Minority Nationality Autonomous State	民族自治县 Minority Nationality Autonomous County
林 业	Forestry	37.12	32.29	5.56
牧 业	Animal Husbandry	190.64	125.67	67.51
渔 业	Fishery	13.84	11.30	2.82
工业(规模以上)	**Industry(above designated size)**			
企业单位数(个)	Number of Industrial Enterprises(unit)	1137	883	263
工业总产值(亿元)	Total Gross Industrial Output Value(100 million yuan)	1273.05	1096.02	179.60
工业销售产值(亿元)	Sales Output Value of Industry(100 million yuan)	2179.56	1061.11	1120.45
工业增加值(亿元)	Value-added of Industry(100 million yuan)	378.52	331.65	47.36
利润总额(亿元)	Total Profits and Taxes(100 million yuan)	85.56	53.19	32.10
主要工业产品产量	Output of Major Industrial Products			
原 煤(万吨)	Coal(10000 tons)	2968.78	2634.00	334.78
生 铁(万吨)	Pig Iron(10000 tons)	33.18	14.76	18.42
水 泥(万吨)	Cement(10000 tons)	2000.79	1622.51	421.49
发电量(亿千瓦小时)	Electricity(100 million kwh)	263.01	205.83	57.52
固定资产投资	**Investment in Fixed Assets**			
固定资产投资完成额(亿元)	All Investment in Fixed Assets in the Whole Province (100 million yuan)	1311.02	1051.74	278.16
商 业	**Trade**			
社会消费品零售总额(亿元)	Total Retail Sales of Consumer Goods(100 million yuan)	456.92	367.21	96.43
财政、金融	**Government Finance and Banking**			
财政一般预算收入(亿元)	Local Financial Revenue (100 million yuan)	155.85	129.99	27.13
财政一般预算支出(亿元)	Financial Expenditure(100 million yuan)	653.56	494.64	170.50
全部金融机构存款余额(亿元)	Deposits Balance(100 million yuan)	1941.49	1559.29	407.00
#城乡居民储蓄余额	Urban and Rural Resident Savings Deposit Balance	1098.81	871.34	242.56
全部金融机构贷款余额(亿元)	Loans Balance(100 million yuan)	1130.50	923.14	221.82

24-5 民族自治地方财政一般预算收入(2011)
Total Financial Revenue of Minority Nationality Autonomous Areas

单位：万元 (10000 yuan)

指 标	Item	民族自治地方 Miniority Nationality Autonomous Area	民族自治州 Nationality Minority Autonomous State	民族自治县 Minority Nationality Autonomous County
总 计	**Total**	**1558484**	**1299924**	**271332**
税收收入	**Tax Income**	**991273**	**824246**	**175251**
#增值税	Value-added Tax	95303	79275	16407
营业税	Business Tax	327276	265910	65176
企业所得税	Enterprises' Income Tax	97562	83976	14285
个人所得税	Personal Income Tax	84596	74885	10164
资源税	Resource Tax	23571	19761	3924
城市维护建设税	Urban Maintenance and Development Tax	67339	58000	9948
烟叶税	Tobacco Tax	40366	21436	18930
非税收入	**Income from Non -tax**	**567211**	**475678**	**96081**
#国有资产经营收益	State-owned Assets Profit	8540	1847	6693
国有资源(资产)有偿使用收入	Planning Subsidies to Loss-suffering Stated-owned Enterprises Income from Administrative Fees	165923	141076	27632
行政事业性收费收入	Penalty and Confiscatory Income	108102	85730	23295
罚没收入	Expert Project Income	76640	65089	11984
专项收入	Expert Project Income	91917	70790	21525

注：资料来源于省财政厅(下表同)。

Note:Data in the table are obtained from Guizhou Provincial Finance Department(the same applies to the next table).

24–6 民族自治地方财政一般预算支出(2011)
Total Financial Expenditure of Minority Nationality Autonomous Areas

单位：万元 (10000 yuan)

指 标	Item	民族自治地方 Miniority Nationality Autonomous Area	民族自治州 Minority Nationality Autonomous State	民族自治县 Minority Nationality Autonomous County
总 计	**Total**	**6535594**	**4946373**	**1705040**
一般公共服务	General Public Service	1100427	876502	242514
国 防	National Defense	9111	7211	1986
公共安全	Public Security	295492	235122	64772
教 育	Education	1349023	987229	391633
科学技术	Science and Technology	27649	25380	2564
文化体育与传媒	Culture,Sports and Media	70136	58443	12785
社会保障和就业	Social Security and Jobs	630794	465995	178007
医疗卫生	Health Care	658834	487120	184245
节能环保	Energy Conservation and Environmental Protection	204886	148927	58684
城乡社区事务	Urban and Country Community Affairs	205311	164412	43903
农林水事务	Affairs of Agriculture,Forest and Water	1050829	766050	306466
交通运输	Transport	130574	102771	28452
其他支出	Other Expenditures	802528	621211	189029

24–7 少数民族教育(2011)
Education of Minority Nationality

单位：人 (person)

类 别	Sort	毕业生 Graduates	招 生 New Students Enrollment	在校生 Total Students Enrollment	专任教师 Full-time Teachers	独立设置的少数民族学校 Minority Nationality Schools	
						学校数 Number of Schools	在校学生 Students Enrollment
普通中学	Regular Secondary Schools	325984	408341	1127199	60519	194	244056
#高 中	Senior	70296	111556	275147	14041		85292
初 中	Junior	255688	296785	852052	46478		158764
小 学	Primary Schools	304096	269822	1697558	83908	637	338377
特殊教育学校	Special Education Schools	161	380	1373	352		
幼儿园	Kindergartens	128626	215186	310383	5697	19	

注：资料来源于省教育厅。
Note:Data in the table are provided by the provinvial Department of Education.

24-8 民族自治地方社会发展主要指标(2011)
Major Indicators on Social Development of Minority Nationality Autonomous Areas

指　标	Item	民族自治地方 Minority Nationality Autonomous Areas	民族自治州 Minority Nationality Autonomous State	民族自治县 Minority Nationality Autonomous County
人　口	**Population**			
年末常住半年人口(万人)	Number of Population at The Year-end (10000 persons)	1347.16	947.00	428.30
#少数民族人口	Minority Population	866.89	641.66	260.16
人口密度(人/平方公里)	Population Density(person/sq.km)	137.71	129.13	159.39
交通运输	**Traffic**			
公路线路里程(公里)	Length of Highways(km)	80145	57043	24348
邮电、通讯	**Post and Telecommunications**			
邮政所总数(处)	Number of Post Offices(unit)	483	344	153
邮路总长度(公里)	Length of Postal Routes(km)	22387	12918	9577
农村投递线路总长度(公里)	Length of Rural Delivery Routes(km)	28323	9849	18583
固定电话年末用户(万户)	Number of Telephone Sets at the Year-end (10000 units)	138	104	36
教　育	**Education**			
普通高等学校	Regular Institutions of Higher Education			
学校数(所)	Number of Schools(unit)	9	9	
在校学生数(人)	Total Students Enrollment(person)	58479	58479	
招生数(人)	New Students Enrollment(person)	16641	16641	
毕业生数(人)	Graduates(person)	15514	15514	
专任教师数(人)	Full-time Teachers(person)	3422	3422	
高中学校	Specialized Secondary Schools			
学校数(所)	Number of Schools(unit)	155	118	39
在校学生数(人)	Total Students Enrollment(person)	254119	189827	68378
招生数(人)	New Students Enrollment(person)	104128	77187	28872
毕业生数(人)	Graduates(person)	68084	50537	18319
专任教师数(人)	Full-time Teachers(person)	13676	10372	3559
初中学校	Regular Secondary Schools			
学校数(所)	Number of Schools(unit)	880	634	265
在校学生数(万人)	Total Students Enrollment(10000 persons)	85.11	56.96	29.80
招生数(万人)	New Students Enrollment(10000 persons)	29.12	19.22	10.51
毕业生数(万人)	Graduates(10000 persons)	26.96	18.32	9.11
专任教师数(万人)	Full-time Teachers(10000 persons)	4.55	3.16	1.48
小　学	Primary Schools			
学校数(所)	Number of Schools(unit)	5290	3568	1833
在校学生数(万人)	Total Students Enrollment(10000 persons)	169.23	106.53	66.51
招生数(万人)	New Students Enrollment(10000 persons)	26.00	16.41	10.23
毕业生数(万人)	Graduates(10000 persons)	30.94	19.89	11.70
专任教师数(万人)	Full-time Teachers(10000 persons)	8.40	5.57	3.00

24-9 民族自治州经济发展主要指标(2011)
Major Indicators on Economic Development of Minority Nationality Autonomous States

指标名称	Item	黔西南州 Qianxinan	黔东南州 Qiandongnan	黔南州 Qiannan
生产总值(亿元)	**Gross Domestic Product(100 million yuan)**	**375.48**	**383.63**	**443.59**
第一产业	Primary Industry	60.10	81.02	73.91
第二产业	Secondary Industry	141.84	123.72	183.45
第三产业	Tertiary Industry	173.54	178.90	186.24
农　业	**Agriculture**			
乡村从业人员(万人)	Rural Employment(10000 persons)	183.55	240.08	215.30
年末常用耕地面积(千公顷)	Cultivated Areas(year-end)(1000 hectares)	159.41	178.56	174.28
农用机械总动力(万千瓦)	Total Agricultural Machinery Power (10000 kw)	178.66	219.18	252.33
化肥使用量(折纯量)(万吨)	Consumption of Chemical Fertilizers(10000 tons)	7.20	7.67	10.02
有效灌溉面积(千公顷)	Effective Irrigated Areas(1000 hectares)	107.48	150.70	142.89
农作物播种面积(千公顷)	Sown Areas of Farm Crops(1000 hectares)	367.41	542.19	519.34
#粮　食	Grain Crops	235.19	305.57	315.17
油菜籽	Rapeseeds	23.49	49.67	66.49
粮食总产量(万吨)	Total Grain Yield(10000 tons)	63.28	90.79	100.06
油菜籽产量(万吨)	Output of Rapeseeds(10000 tons)	2.71	5.83	8.23
烤烟产量(万吨)	Output of Flue -cured Tobacco (10000 tons)	2.60	1.58	2.82
茶叶产量(万吨)	Output of Tea (10000 tons)	0.33	0.58	0.69
当年造林面积(千公顷)	Afforested Areas in 2004(1000 hectares)	44.83	32.40	31.88
牲畜当年存栏数	Animals in Hand			
猪(万头)	Hogs(10000 heads)	129.48	132.06	161.07
牛(万头)	Large Animals(10000 heads)	53.40	63.50	60.43
羊(万只)	Sheep and Goats(10000 heads)	38.70	23.93	20.77
牲畜当年出栏数	Number of Slaughtered Animals			
猪(万头)	Hogs(10000 heads)	138.26	175.21	197.93
牛(万头)	Large Animals(10000 heads)	11.48	12.01	12.40
羊(万只)	Sheep and Goats(10000 heads)	20.13	14.98	15.35
肉类总产量(万吨)	Output of Meat(10000 tons)	14.81	16.85	18.53
水产品产量(万吨)	Aquatic Products(10000 tons)	2.49	1.44	1.15
农林牧渔业总产值(亿元)	Gross Output Value of Farming,Forestry,Animal Husb andry and Fishery(100 million yuan)	96.25	133.72	132.25
#农　业	Farming	48.27	67.27	69.99

24-9 续表 continued

指标名称	Item	黔西南州 Qianxinan	黔东南州 Qiandongnan	黔南州 Qiannan
林　业	Forestry	5.30	21.37	5.62
牧　业	Animal Husbandry	37.05	37.04	51.58
渔　业	Fishery	4.11	4.81	2.38
工业(规模以上)	**Industry(above designated size)**			
企业单位数(个)	Number of Industrial Enterprises(unit)	374	318	337
工业总产值(亿元)	Total Gross Industrial Output Value(100 million yuan)	356.08	278.75	461.19
工业销售产值(亿元)	Sales Output Value of Industry(100 million yuan)	376.71	248.27	436.13
工业增加值(亿元)	Value-added of Industry(100 million yuan)	140.10	69.86	121.69
利润总额(亿元)	Total Profits(100 million yuan)	25.88	8.78	18.52
主要工业产品产量	Output of Major Industrial Products			
原煤(万吨)	Coal(10000 tons)	1989.00	238.00	407.00
生铁(万吨)	Pig Iron(10000 tons)	13.69	1.06	0.01
水泥(万吨)	Cement(10000 tons)	389.51	407.00	826.00
发电量(亿千瓦小时)	Electricity(100 million kwh)	136.55	43.21	24.62
固定资产投资	**Investment in Fixed Assets**			
固定资产投资完成额(亿元)	All Investment in Fixed Assets in the Whole Province (100 million yuan)	301.17	350.55	400.02
商　业	**Trade**			
社会消费品零售总额(亿元)	Total Retail Sales of Consumer Goods(100 million yuan)	105.26	144.83	117.12
财政、金融	**Treasury and Finance**			
财政一般预算收入(亿元)	Local Government Financial Revenue(100 million yuan)	45.52	45.27	39.20
财政一般预算支出(亿元)	Local Government Financial Expenditure(100 million yuan)	137.57	194.66	162.40
全部金融机构存款余额(亿元)	Deposits Balance(100 million yuan)	471.60	562.64	525.04
#储蓄存款	Urban and Rural Resident Savings Deposit Balance	225.49	352.77	293.08
全部金融机构贷款余额(亿元)	Loans Balance(100 million yuan)	273.15	353.43	296.57

24-10 民族自治州社会发展主要指标(2011)

Major Indicators on Social Development of Minority Nationality Autonomous State

指标名称	Item	黔西南州 Qianxinan	黔东南州 Qiandongnan	黔南州 Qiannan
人　口	**Population**			
年末常住半年人口(万人)	Number of Population at The Year-end (10000 persons)	280	346	321
#少数民族人口	Minority Population	136.86	270.82	233.98
人口密度(人/平方公里)	Population Density(person/sq.km)	166.63	114.05	122.53
交通运输	**Traffic**			
公路线路里程(公里)	Length of Highways(km)	14753	26731	15560
邮电、通讯	**Post and Telecommunications**			
邮政所总数(处)	Number of Post Offices(unit)	124	71	149
邮路总长度(公里)	Length of Postal Routes(km)	3381	3530	6007
农村投递线路总长度(公里)	Length of Rural Delivery Routes(km)	4111	2326	3412
固定电话年末用户(万户)	Number of Telephone Sets at the Year-end(10000 units)	22.58	42.57	37.09
教　育	**Education**			
普通高等学校	Regular Institutions of Higher Education			
学校数(所)	Number of Schools(unit)	2	3	4
在校学生数(人)	Students Enrollment(person)	11593	25933	20953
招生数(人)	New Student Enrollment(person)	3475	7176	5990
毕业生数(人)	Graduates(person)	3400	5899	6215
专任教师数(人)	Full-time Teachers(person)	730	1548	1144
高中学校	Specialized Secondary Schools			
学校数(所)	Number of Schools(unit)	40	44	34
在校学生数(人)	Students Enrollment(person)	52421	73334	64072
招生数(人)	New Student Enrollment(person)	20191	30240	26756
毕业生数(人)	Graduates(person)	14993	19688	15856
专任教师数(人)	Full-time Teachers(person)	2900	4103	3369
初中学校	Regular Secondary Schools			
学校数(所)	Number of Schools(unit)	195	231	208
在校学生数(人)	Students Enrollment(person)	178192	199566	191814
招生数(人)	New Student Enrollment(person)	61347	68927	61895
毕业生数(人)	Graduates(person)	55301	61746	66190
专任教师数(人)	Full-time Teachers(person)	9571	11681	10365
小　学	Primary Schools			
学校数(所)	Number of Schools(unit)	1091	1269	1208
在校学生数(万人)	Students Enrollment(10000 persons)	36.31	37.85	32.37
招生数(万人)	New Student Enrollment(10000 persons)	5.76	5.77	4.87
毕业生数(万人)	Graduates(10000 persons)	6.40	7.07	6.41
专任教师数(万人)	Full-time Teachers(10000 persons)	1.73	2.06	1.79

24-11 民族自治县经济发展主要指标(2011)

指 标	Item	道真县 Daozhen	务川县 Wuchuan
生产总值(万元)	**Gross Domestic Product(10000 yuan)**	**206579**	**232332**
第一产业	Primary Industry	62602	77728
第二产业	Secondary Industry	33338	37240
第三产业	Tertiary Industry	110639	117364
农 业	**Agriculture**		
乡村从业人员(万人)	Rural Employment(10000 persons)	18.37	26.65
年末常用耕地面积(千公顷)	Cultivated Areas(year-end)(1000 hectares)	23.50	28.29
农用机械总动力(万千瓦)	Total Agricultural Machinery Power (10000 kw)	16.10	20.30
化肥使用量(折纯量)(万吨)	Consumption of Chemical Fertilizers(10000 tons)	1.07	0.43
有效灌溉面积(千公顷)	Effective Irrigated Areas(1000 hectares)	6.76	6.53
农作物播种面积(千公顷)	Sown Areas of Farm Crops(1000 hectares)	62.04	90.04
#粮食	Grain Crops	38.17	57.76
油菜籽	Rapeseeds	4.94	6.88
粮食总产量(吨)	Total Grain Yield(ton)	110893	128700
油菜籽产量(吨)	Output of Rapeseeds(ton)	6325	8253
烤烟产量(吨)	Output of Flue -cured Tobacco (ton)	11706	14737
茶叶产量(吨)	Output of Tea (ton)	1329	211
当年造林面积(千公顷)	Afforested Areas in this Year(1000 hectares)	2.59	5.06
牲畜当年存栏数	Animals in Hand		
猪(万头)	Hogs(10000 heads)	16.76	18.60
牛(万头)	Large Animals(10000 heads)	3.66	8.72
羊(万只)	Sheep and Goats(10000 heads)	3.05	7.61
牲畜当年出栏数	Number of Slaughtered Animals		
猪(万头)	Hogs(10000 heads)	19.70	19.81
牛(万头)	Large Animals(10000 heads)	0.66	1.95
羊(万只)	Sheep and Goats(10000 heads)	1.48	5.48
肉类总产量(吨)	Output of Meat(ton)	18204	22058
水产品产量(吨)	Aquatic Products(ton)	375	850
农林牧渔业总产值(万元)	Gross Output Value of Farming,Forestry,Animal Husb andry and Fishery(10000 yuan)	103827	137680
#农 业	Farming	64550	89009

Major Indicators on Economic Development of Minority Nationality Autonomous Counties

镇宁县 Zhenning	关岭县 Guanling	紫云县 Ziyun	威宁县 Weining	玉屏县 Yuping	印江县 Yinjiang	沿河县 Yanhe	松桃县 Songtao	三都县 Sandu
326807	**310180**	**203815**	**790698**	**307914**	**314051**	**391737**	**493801**	**190007**
50442	67276	76936	277751	40801	129021	139013	153243	57162
101470	78622	34254	222261	171168	60330	66421	161439	34182
174895	164282	92625	290686	95945	124700	186303	179119	98663
19.85	18.91	22.45	75.23	8.24	23.87	32.05	41.41	19.17
14.60	15.05	16.17	72.01	5.79	18.59	26.33	26.75	13.63
18.05	15.90	15.52	28.67	21.30	15.20	27.30	25.10	13.68
0.79	0.49	0.56	3.82	0.15	0.80	1.48	1.47	0.36
9.80	5.71	12.76	33.39	4.31	9.96	3.37	14.40	7.99
34.29	33.46	42.97	163.15	17.24	56.46	82.39	70.42	43.53
20.62	22.08	24.19	79.90	8.94	37.05	57.26	48.08	25.81
5.81	3.35	9.00	0.16	2.85	8.11	6.27	8.69	5.52
77015	82803	81218	378012	30303	103762	135794	188727	76447
7715	3937	4546	141	3066	13110	7809	11646	7935
		1754	27219		5706	6019	2313	
152	39	141	65	25	3391	350	2568	540
0.74	3.48	2.20	6.64	4.15	3.93	10.86	12.14	3.14
10.39	13.69	26.55	78.23	5.65	18.15	34.66	34.68	12.40
6.10	7.90	10.83	17.72	1.72	4.23	12.12	6.74	6.09
0.51	2.20	2.78	22.59	0.88	3.18	20.20	4.93	0.40
9.12	13.51	26.74	60.83	8.74	24.01	26.99	32.18	14.94
1.21	1.87	2.27	3.98	0.63	1.57	2.08	1.80	1.36
0.28	1.51	2.03	14.86	1.09	5.87	17.73	8.20	0.45
10967	16264	29801	69809	9029	26619	29548	33548	14231
1800	600	800	351	1300	3002	3803	3531	1769
76613	104896	118518	443868	69251	193916	228614	243255	87152
42141	58381	36471	265420	34916	100125	136257	132850	49366

24-11 续表

指 标	Item	道真县 Daozhen	务川县 Wuchuan
林 业	Forestry	5610	4752
牧 业	Animal Husbandry	32397	40654
渔 业	Fishery	780	1407
规模以上工业	**Industry above designated size**		
企业单位数(个)	Number of Industrial Enterprises(unit)	13	13
工业总产值(万元)	Total Gross Industrial Output Value(10000 yuan)	53480	62000
工业销售产值(万元)	Sales Output Value of Industry(10000 yuan)	52710	57200
工业增加值(万元)	Value-added of Industry(10000 yuan)	17962	15077
利润总额(万元)	Total Profits(10000 yuan)	-2600	492
主要工业产品产量	Output of Major Industrial Products		
原煤(万吨)	Coal(10000 tons)	24.42	4.84
生铁(万吨)	Pig Iron(10000 tons)		
水泥(万吨)	Cement(10000 tons)	36.70	5.26
发电量(亿千瓦小时)	Electricity(100 million kwh)	5.6	3.6242
固定资产投资	**Investment in Fixed Assets**		
固定资产投资额(万元)	All Investment in Fixed Assets in the Whole Province(10000 yuan)	137550	193791
商 业	**Trade**		
社会消费品零售总额(万元)	Total Retail Sales of Consumer Goods(10000 yuan)	67686	67960
财政、金融	**Treasiury and Finance**		
财政一般预算收入(万元)	Local Government Financial Revenue(10000 yuan)	15188	24254
财政一般预算支出(万元)	Local Government Financial Expenditure(10000 yuan)	112311	126181
全部金融机构存款余额(亿元)	Deposits Balance(100 million yuan)	40.59	38.18
#储蓄存款	Urban and Rural Resident Savings Deposit Balance	27.75	22.93
全部金融机构贷款余额(亿元)	Loans Balance(100 million yuan)	14.59	15.16

continued

镇宁县 Zhenning	关岭县 Guanling	紫云县 Ziyun	威宁县 Weining	玉屏县 Yuping	松桃县 Songtao	印江县 Yinjiang	沿河县 Yanhe	三都县 Sandu
2545	4449	7892	1545	3529	7127	3981	6825	7362
29033	40916	70781	158582	25561	76496	75018	90235	25430
2536	944	1422	509	2120	5014	5467	5209	2838
29	20	21	30	38	31	23	36	9
110500	94500	58500	333505	553967	124356	53068	326430	25706
104400	93400	55000	331084	5283784	1399731	652115	3155057	19992
19679	17415	10637	145507	115937	30766	21514	74210	4901
12600	1200	1800	9368	-59600	65900	35600	258900	-2706
3.90	33.20	7.20	211.00		3.87	46.35		
			18.42					
1.71	7.08	14.28	23.00	113.19	95.16	17.56	64.34	43.21
3.08	2.59	0.79	0.23	39.91	0.47	0.42	0.46	0.35
176309	119732	95044	679512	195936	246979	355210	392719	188808
100214	111435	78136	148637	49212	64869	91189	117769	67166
27706	19473	10689	56276	21357	15469	36507	31641	12772
125907	117637	111425	391777	88438	140308	180022	195215	115819
33.79	31.67	25.83	53.02	22.54	38.40	42.75	55.44	24.80
16.24	16.02	12.09	30.48	14.90	26.00	28.14	32.93	15.09
26.73	21.17	13.20	18.72	31.61	19.34	21.11	25.74	14.47

24-12 民族自治县社会发展主要指标(2011)

指 标	Item	道真县 Daozhen	务川县 Wuchuan
人 口	**Population**		
年末常住人口(万人)	Number of Populations at The Year-end(10000 persons)	24.13	31.70
#少数民族人口	Minority Populations	17.92	29.10
人口密度(人/平方公里)	Population Density(person/sq.km)	111.91	114.31
交通运输	**Traffic**		
公路线路里程(公里)	Length of Highways(km)	2338	2111
邮电、通讯	**Post and Telecommunications**		
邮政所总数(处)	Number of Post Offices(unit)	11	13
邮路总长度(公里)	Length of Postal Routes(km)	285	1372
农村投递线路总长度(公里)	Length of Rural Delivery Routes(km)	454	968
固定电话年末用户(万户)	Number of Telephone Sets(10000 units)	2.52	2.95
教 育	**Education**		
普通高中	Regular Senior Secondary Schools		
学校数(所)	Number of Schools(unit)	2	3
在校学生数(人)	Students Enrollment(person)	5841	6460
招生数(人)	New Student Enrollment(person)	2498	2635
毕业生数(人)	Graduates(person)	1598	1609
专任教师数(人)	Full-time Teachers(person)	321	336
普通初中	Regular Junior Secondary Schools		
学校数(所)	Number of Schools(unit)	21	26
在校学生数(人)	Students Enrollment(person)	14409	26878
招生数(人)	New Student Enrollment(person)	5493	9060
毕业生数(人)	Graduates(person)	4094	8684
专任教师数(人)	Full-time Teachers(person)	783	1417
小 学	Primary Schools		
学校数(所)	Number of Schools(unit)	89	139
在校学生数(人)	Students Enrollment(person)	27411	41453
招生数(人)	New Student Enrollment(person)	3765	6068
毕业生数(人)	Graduates(person)	5332	9115
专任教师数(人)	Full-time Teachers(person)	1529	2133

Major Indicators on Social Development of Minority Nationality Autonomous Counties

镇宁县 Zhenning	关岭县 Guanling	紫云县 Ziyun	威宁县 Weining	玉屏县 Yuping	印江县 Yinjiang	沿河县 Yanhe	松桃县 Songtao	三都县 Sandu
28.15	29.95	26.82	126.00	11.75	28.29	44.88	48.49	28.14
16.29	19.08	17.54	29.14	9.27	23.17	40.30	23.42	34.93
165.34	204.02	117.44	200.12	227.76	144.26	181.79	169.47	118.06
1505	1247	1733	4807	1535	2709	1532	3586	1246
7	9	11	14	4	13	21	14	15
336	235	332	1488	160	1074	1478	591	647
281	354	536	3278	160	848	1013	591	559
2.10	1.98	4.57	4.20	1.59	3.57	3.30	3.25	2.16
1	3	1	8	3	6	4	6	2
2257	3530	2603	15820	2651	7895	6926	10309	4086
960	1442	914	6692	1120	3364	2865	4451	1931
626	1320	920	3676	744	2311	1940	2803	772
117	190	138	787	201	395	343	476	255
18	18	18	53	8	17	30	37	19
15413	14174	22772	88032	5732	20308	36764	37052	16501
5220	4468	6930	34375	2070	7310	11960	12098	6113
4875	5092	7497	24007	1741	6100	11693	12555	4805
814	780	904	3759	387	1104	1840	2053	958
106	125	138	426	44	126	224	305	111
38268	31557	33717	244707	11516	40150	84373	73889	38097
5613	4860	5030	36424	1961	6725	13253	12227	6391
5874	5488	7844	40419	2051	7065	13694	13635	6439
1706	1557	1900	9606	652	2266	3309	3565	1763

25

Twenty-five

经济强县

Economically Strong Counties

25-1 经济强县主要指标(一)(2011)

Major Indicators of Economically Strong County (1)

单位：万元 (10000 yuan)

县(市、区) 名 称	County (City,Section)	生产总值 Gross Domestic Product	第一产业 Primary Industry	第二产业 Secondary Industry	第三产业 Tertiary Industry	2011年比2010年增长(%) Increase Rate in 2011 over 2010(%)	人均生产总值(元) Per Capita Gross Domestic Product(yuan)	2011年比2010年增长(%) Increase Rate in 2011 over 2010(%)
云岩区	Yunyan	3829820	4007	1577202	2248611	17.4	39597	14.0
南明区	Nanming	3016973	18167	608483	2390323	17.2	36015	14.6
花溪区	Huaxi	987869	79124	392352	516393	18.1	27274	17.1
乌当区	Wudang	1255118	83284	591658	580176	20.3	32609	15.5
白云区	Baiyun	766482	27389	420690	318403	20.3	28729	16.1
小河区	Xiaohe	806261	8863	481915	315483	20.4	31969	11.7
清镇市	Qingzhen	1170698	114659	564715	491324	20.3	24972	20.8
修文县	Xiuwen	576733	87062	235097	254574	20.2	23023	20.9
息烽县	Xifeng	646484	69645	381315	195524	20.3	30323	21.3
开阳县	Kaiyang	819314	133314	453254	232746	20.5	22892	22.3
红花岗区	Honghuagang	1971334	80965	628974	1261395	19.7	29738	17.8
汇川区	Huicuan	1373513	51157	701969	620387	18.8	30977	16.0
仁怀市	Renhuai	2580241	117942	1689201	773098	21.3	47154	21.2
赤水市	Chishui	412932	70630	185754	156548	19.4	17372	20.3
遵义县	Zunyi	1684811	283889	852420	548502	19.6	17946	22.0
桐梓县	Tongzi	626879	125700	242606	258573	18.8	12065	21.1
钟山区	Zhongshan	2182987	20096	1221187	941704	17.1	35312	14.6
盘　县	Panxian	2499770	140004	1850041	509725	17.4	24145	18.8
西秀区	Xixiu	1182160	123974	474903	583283	16.0	15495	24.7
平坝县	Pingba	509575	61561	290660	157354	18.0	17149	13.7
都匀市	Duyun	935385	70222	360271	504892	19.7	21146	21.0
福泉市	Fuquan	661313	63572	328649	269092	18.4	23364	19.7
凯里市	Kaili	963638	70287	347586	545765	20.0	20047	19.1
兴义市	Xingyi	1640295	169543	637057	833695	16.6	20926	16.1
七星关区	Qixingguan	1527090	254742	601634	670714	19.0	13463	20.7
金沙县	Jinsha	1082753	111611	647383	323759	19.6	19309	20.2
碧江区	Bijiang	703421	95439	253006	354976	18.6	21394	19.5

25–2 经济强县主要指标(二)(2011)
Major Indicators of Economically Strong County (2)

县(市、区)名称	County (City,Section)	社会消费品零售总额(亿元) Total Retail Sales of Consumer Goods(100 million yuan)	2011年比2010年增长(%) Increase Rate in 2011 over 2010(%)	城镇居民人均可支配收入(元) Per Capita Annual Disposable Income of Urban Households (yuan)	2011年比2010年增长(%) Increase Rate in 2011 over 2010(%)	农民人均纯收入(元) Per Capita Net Income of Rural Residents (yuan)	2011年比2010年增长(%) Increase Rate in 2011 over 2010(%)
云岩区	Yunyan	218.80	20.7	19420	17.0	9124	20.2
南明区	Nanming	192.49	20.6	19420	17.0	9031	19.9
花溪区	Huaxi	22.57	20.0	19318	18.5	7508	26.1
乌当区	Wudang	53.38	20.5	19332	17.0	8332	22.0
白云区	Baiyun	22.84	20.4	19394	11.0	8887	20.3
小河区	Xiaohe	49.32	20.1	19357	17.0	8947	20.3
清镇市	Qingzhen	21.81	20.3	18261	16.4	6898	26.2
修文县	Xiuwen	12.16	20.0	18721	18.8	6470	25.6
息烽县	Xifeng	10.39	20.1	17528	19.4	6434	26.5
开阳县	Kaiyang	19.84	20.2	19314	18.6	6781	25.7
红花岗区	Honghuagang	106.98	20.2	17426	14.0	6970	18.1
汇川区	Huicuan	59.29	20.1	17426	14.0	7190	17.7
仁怀市	Renhuai	40.16	26.5	17001	17.6	5777	18.0
赤水市	Chishui	13.14	20.1	12589	18.4	5598	17.7
遵义县	Zunyi	36.45	20.1	17056	15.5	6514	15.8
桐梓县	Tongzi	14.03	20.1	13522	18.3	5121	15.4
钟山区	Zhongshan	87.34	20.2	16371	17.6	5789	19.9
盘　县	Panxian	41.45	19.9			4305	16.4
西秀区	Xixiu	33.06	19.8	16300	12.4	5530	26.7
平坝县	Pingba	12.46	19.6			4635	27.0
都匀市	Duyun	37.67	20.9	16983	9.8	5611	16.3
福泉市	Fuquan	12.35	20.1			4834	18.7
凯里市	Kaili	57.72	21.1	16410	16.7	5176	21.0
兴义市	Xingyi	73.16	20.7	17004	7.4	5396	10.7
七星关区	Qixingguan	54.65	20.6	17135	19.8	4412	21.7
金沙县	Jinsha	15.96	19.3	17149	20.0	4910	22.4
碧江区	Bijiang	25.90	20.2	13846	25.9	5339	22.7

26

Twenty-six

扶贫与开发

Anti-poverty and Development

26-1 扶贫开发重点县主要指标占全省比重(2011)
Major Indicators of Basilic County of Anti-poverty and Development and Its Percentage to Provincial Total

单位：亿元 (100 million yuan)

指 标	Item	全 省 合 计 Provincial Total	扶贫开发重点县合计 Poverty Counties Total	扶贫开发重点县占全省比重(%) As Percentage to Provincial Total(%)
国土面积(万平方公里)	Area of Territory(10000 sq.km)	17.61	11.63	66.0
常用耕地面积(千公顷)	Cultivated Area for Frequently Use (1000 hectares)	1754.90	1042.80	59.4
年末常住人口(万人)	Permanent Resident Population at the Year-end (10000 persons)	3469	1776.21	51.2
生产总值	Gross Domestic Product	5701.84	1906.94	33.4
财政一般预算收入	Local Financial Revenue	773.08	162.91	21.1
财政一般预算支出	Financial Expenditure	2249.40	752.61	33.5
农林牧渔业总产值	Gross Output Value of Farming,Forestry, Animal Husban dry and Fishery	1165.46	668.32	57.3
粮食产量(万吨)	Output of Grain(10000 tons)	876.90	524.10	59.8
规模以上工业增加值	Value-added of Industry above Designated Size	1723.58	512.87	29.8
社会消费品零售总额	Total Retail Sales of Consumer Goods	1751.62	417.54	23.8
储蓄存款	Savings Deposit	3934.48	1093.50	27.8

26-2 贫困人口及发生率(2011)

Number of Poverty Population and it's Arisen Rate

县(市、区、特区)名称	County (City,Section, Special Region)	农村贫困人口(万人) Poverty Population (10 000 persons)	农村贫困发生率(%) Arisen Rate of Poverty (%)	县(市、区、特区)名称	County (City,Section, Special Region)	农村贫困人口(万人) Poverty Population (10 000 persons)	农村贫困发生率(%) Arisen Rate of Poverty (%)
全省合计	**Provincial Total**	**1149.00**	**33.4**	△正安县	Zhengan	18.69	31.2
扶贫开发重点县小计	**Basilic Counties of Antipoverty and Development**	**866.40**	**40.6**	△道真县	Daozhen	10.34	32.9
				△务川县	Wuchuan	14.66	35.1
贵阳市	**Guiyang**	**32.32**	**16.8**	凤冈县	Fenggang	7.30	18.4
南明区	Nanming	0.06	1.0	湄潭县	Meitan	7.77	17.5
云岩区	Yunyan	0.06	0.7	余庆县	Yuqing	5.65	20.2
花溪区	Huaxi	4.68	20.8	△习水县	Xishui	23.17	35.4
乌当区	Wudang	2.03	8.8	赤水市	Chishui	4.44	19.2
白云区	Baiyun	0.57	7.9	仁怀市	Renhuai	9.34	16.4
小河区	Xiaohe	0.28	9.9	**安顺市**	**Anshun**	**74.65**	**30.8**
开阳县	Kaiyang	6.77	20.1	西秀区	Xixiu	8.83	13.7
息烽县	Xifeng	5.12	25.4	平坝县	Pingba	6.68	22.2
修文县	Xiuwen	5.62	21.4	△普定县	Puding	15.22	36.0
清镇市	Qingzhen	7.13	17.1	△镇宁县	Zhenning	13.34	38.0
六盘水市	**Liupanshui**	**97.52**	**38.3**	△关岭县	Guanling	14.65	43.1
钟山区	Zhongshan	4.76	29.1	△紫云县	Ziyun	15.93	43.9
△六枝特区	Liuzhi	19.09	33.8	**毕节市**	**Bijie**	**250.05**	**35.5**
△水城县	Shuicheng	34.70	45.4	七星关区	Qixingguan	32.40	28.4
△盘　县	Panxian	38.97	37.0	△大方县	Dafang	34.82	39.4
遵义市	**Zunyi**	**144.99**	**21.9**	黔西县	Qianxi	20.25	27.3
红花岗区	Honghuagang	2.43	11.7	金沙县	Jinsha	12.10	24.2
汇川区	huichuan	2.86	13.3	△织金县	Zhijin	41.25	41.7
遵义县	Zunyi	20.49	17.7	△纳雍县	Nayong	33.64	42.6
桐梓县	Tongzi	10.56	16.3	△威宁县	Weining	47.42	36.7
绥阳县	Suiyang	7.29	14.6	△赫章县	Hezhang	28.17	40.6

26-2 续表 continued

县(市、区、特区)名 称	County (City,Section, Special Region)	农村贫困人口(万人) Poverty Population (10 000 persons)	农村贫困发生率(%) Arisen Rate of Poverty (%)	县(市、区、特区)名 称	County (City,Section, Special Region)	农村贫困人口(万人) Poverty Population (10 000 persons)	农村贫困发生率(%) Arisen Rate of Poverty (%)
铜仁市	**Tongren**	**145.21**	**38.8**	镇远县	Zhenyuan	7.20	40.2
碧江区	Bijiang	4.24	25.7	△岑巩县	Cengong	8.97	41.2
万山区	Wanshan	4.32	33.0	△天柱县	Tianzhu	15.34	42.6
△江口县	Jiangkou	8.12	39.6	△锦屏县	Jinping	9.72	46.5
玉屏县	Yuping	3.91	31.0	△剑河县	Jianhe	10.72	45.3
△石阡县	Shiqian	16.65	43.4	△台江县	Taijiang	7.04	46.1
△思南县	Sinan	24.03	37.7	△黎平县	Liping	18.47	37.0
△印江县	Yinjiang	15.94	39.5	△榕江县	Rongjiang	15.14	45.4
△德江县	Dejiang	17.75	42.3	△从江县	Congjiang	14.54	45.5
△沿河县	Yanhe	25.13	41.3	△雷山县	Leishan	6.39	43.4
△松桃县	Songtao	25.12	37.7	△麻江县	Majiang	10.08	49.7
黔西南州	**Qianxinan**	**109.18**	**36.2**	△丹寨县	Danzhai	7.47	49.2
兴义市	Xingyi	11.27	16.5	**黔南州**	**Qiannan**	**127.72**	**36.0**
△兴仁县	Xingren	15.15	36.7	都匀市	Duyun	7.73	24.4
△普安县	Puan	10.96	35.1	福泉市	Fuquan	7.65	30.0
△晴隆县	Qinglong	16.19	56.2	△荔波县	Libo	7.32	45.7
△贞丰县	Zhenfeng	14.47	38.2	贵定县	Guiding	7.72	30.0
△望谟县	Wangmo	15.22	50.8	瓮安县	Wengan	9.20	20.9
△册亨县	Ceheng	12.51	54.8	△独山县	Dushan	13.01	40.5
△安龙县	Anlong	13.41	32.7	△平塘县	Pingtang	15.38	50.2
黔东南州	**Qiandongnan**	**167.29**	**42.1**	△罗甸县	Luodian	15.01	48.4
凯里市	Kaili	7.49	24.5	△长顺县	Changshun	11.50	47.1
△黄平县	Huangping	15.74	44.2	龙里县	Longli	5.15	27.3
△施秉县	Shibing	3.97	38.3	惠水县	Huishui	11.18	27.2
△三穗县	Sansui	9.01	45.7	△三都县	Sandu	16.87	50.1

注：△为新阶段扶贫开发工作重点县。
Note: These counties with '△' refer to basilic counties of antipoverty and development.

26–3 扶贫开发重点县主要指标(2011)

单位：万元

扶贫开发重点县名称	County	年末总人口(万人) Population (year-end) (10000 persons)	生产总值 Gross Domestic Product	财政一般预算收入 Local Financial Revenue	财政一般预算支出 Financial Expenditure	常用耕地面积(公顷) Cultivated Area for Frequently Use (hectare)	农林牧渔业总产值 Gross Output Value of Farming, Forestry, Animal Husbandry and Fishery
扶贫开发重点县合计	**Total**	**1776.21**	**19069389**	**1629107**	**7526074**	**1042796**	**6683168**
六盘水市	**Liupanshui**						
六枝特区	Liuzhi	49.36	678722	49850	215664	25829	110261
水城县	Shuicheng	70.29	890583	98937	261376	33097	171266
盘　县	Panxian	103.47	2499770	258719	487797	45842	236148
遵义市	**Zunyi**						
正安县	Zhengan	38.14	296899	20823	150572	31157	184243
※道真县	Daozhen	24.13	206579	15188	112311	23502	103827
※务川县	Wuchuan	31.70	232332	24254	126181	28293	137680
习水县	Xishui	51.77	619104	42380	186524	40626	180817
安顺市	**Anshun**						
普定县	Puding	37.54	367838	29994	119385	16654	104807
※镇宁县	Zhenning	28.15	326807	27706	125907	14598	76613
※关岭县	Guanling	29.95	310180	19473	117637	15048	104896
※紫云县	Ziyun	26.82	203815	10689	111425	16166	118518
毕节市	**Bijie**						
大方县	Dafang	78.00	910432	79763	274026	50421	282953
织金县	Zhijin	78.00	742292	97092	270162	39807	216447
纳雍县	Nayong	67.00	888425	83448	224883	30996	189755
※威宁县	Weining	126.00	790698	56276	391777	72011	443868
赫章县	Hezhang	65.00	444009	22756	206068	38807	218155
铜仁市	**Tongren**						
江口县	Jiangkou	17.21	177112	12008	94967	10965	94565
石阡县	Shiqian	30.27	249625	15809	158339	22037	167894
思南县	Sinan	49.72	493060	23119	196002	28786	272205
※印江县	Yinjiang	28.29	314051	15469	140308	18593	193916
德江县	Dejiang	36.62	397805	23254	161263	21347	226882
※沿河县	Yanhe	44.88	391737	36507	180022	26327	228614
※松桃县	Songtao	48.49	493801	31641	195215	26751	243255

Major Indicators on Basilic county of Anti-poverty and Development

(10000 yuan)

粮食产量 (万吨) Output of Grain (10000 tons)	人均粮食 (公斤) Per Capita Output of Grain (kg)	农民人均纯收入 Per Capita Annual Net Income of Rural Households	规模以上工业增加值 Value-added of Industry above Designated Size	储蓄存款 Savings Deposit	固定资产投资 Investment in Fixed Assets	社会消费品零售总额 Total Retail Sales of Consumer Goods
524.10			**5128675**	**10935002**	**15063101**	**4175440**
15.31	271	4026	150196		502019	195945
16.59	217	4010	658513	352085	956755	92208
22.61	214	4305	1264882	933500	1653224	414477
16.07	268	3701	25065	324098	207426	108205
11.09	353	3539	17962	277480	137550	67686
12.87	308	3463	15077	229303	193791	67960
16.60	254	3397	274511	389011	669857	133252
8.69	205	4088	135929	165940	140534	94376
7.70	220	3998	19679	162434	176309	100214
8.28	243	4022	17415	160158	119732	111435
8.12	224	3966	10637	120923	95044	78136
24.12	273	4239	191201	413788	628992	135136
25.25	255	4029	108364	360952	781439	148500
18.87	239	3918	313582	253673	755690	120472
37.80	293	4068	145507	304752	679512	148637
18.35	264	3892	58907	278557	386711	88639
6.66	325	3918	14295	160579	211309	44808
7.52	196	3874	10616	195206	154393	52170
16.37	256	3683	44350	357943	437584	121052
10.38	257	3719	30766	260004	246979	64869
9.95	237	3503	29137	218939	228455	84436
13.58	223	3713	21514	281411	355210	91189
18.87	283	3680	74210	329275	392719	117769

26-3 续表

单位：万元

扶贫开发重点县名称	County	年末总人口（万人）Population (year-end) (10000 persons)	生产总值 Gross Domestic Product	财政一般预算收入 Local Financial Revenue	财政一般预算支出 Financial Expenditure	常用耕地面积（公顷）Cultivated Area for Frequently Use (hectare)	农林牧渔业总产值 Gross Output Value of Farming, Forestry, Animal Husbandry and Fishery
黔西南州	**Qianxinan**						
兴仁县	Xingren	41.70	500265	75929	184244	20429	123702
普安县	Puan	**25.40**	**292260**	35240	113583	**16545**	**76709**
晴隆县	Qinglong	24.60	240560	25582	116658	14059	72201
贞丰县	Zhenfeng	30.30	425464	55008	147521	20591	113589
望谟县	Wangmo	25.10	155879	8924	135509	24903	86746
册亨县	Ceheng	19.00	140822	8413	95317	13403	73930
安龙县	Anlong	35.70	415578	32009	130776	20703	149076
黔东南州	**Qiandongnan**						
黄平县	Huangping	26.14	196737	14372	117582	15923	103534
施秉县	Shibing	13.02	153652	18124	78352	8267	64337
三穗县	Sansui	15.50	160835	12600	82918	8097	59823
岑巩县	Cengong	16.04	176248	10741	83333	12265	63626
天柱县	Tianzhu	25.80	327680	24334	132635	15926	117254
锦屏县	Jinping	15.26	166648	13943	95698	8422	53598
剑河县	Jianhe	18.02	167599	12463	94076	9023	77933
台江县	Taijiang	11.02	116865	10730	77090	6199	42602
黎平县	Liping	38.70	305664	18512	160605	18535	129214
榕江县	Rongjiang	28.60	228462	16366	115292	13101	120489
从江县	Congjiang	29.07	225809	15719	122715	13326	114280
雷山县	Leishan	11.63	113627	10272	84976	6705	43780
麻江县	Majiang	16.52	173551	11819	93273	10654	70895
丹寨县	Danzhai	12.17	115379	10084	88230	7148	49551
黔南州	**Qiannan**						
荔波县	Libo	14.39	208770	16766	89420	8009	54283
独山县	Dushan	26.34	292408	17870	108906	15057	116733
平塘县	Pingtang	22.71	182818	13822	113611	14343	95062
罗甸县	Luodian	25.55	277978	18475	127923	16218	117970
长顺县	Changshun	18.98	192148	13063	112201	13658	97513
※三都县	Sandu	28.14	190007	12772	115819	13626	87152

continued

(10000 yuan)

粮食产量 (万吨) Output of Grain (10000 tons)	人均粮食 (公斤) Per Capita Output of Grain (kg)	农民人均纯收入 Per Capita Annual Net Income of Rural Households	规模以上工业增加值 Value-added of Industry above Designated Size	储蓄存款 Savings Deposit	固定资产投资 Investment in Fixed Assets	社会消费品零售总额 Total Retail Sales of Consumer Goods
11.38	276	4196	181700	223523	430156	95164
4.17	133	3609	128900	161039	210436	41836
4.90	170	3456	81700	134751	230647	35026
7.66	202	4003	272779	209928	279217	48522
6.52	217	3156	3441	91365	115612	23585
3.45	151	3317	6001	97554	88851	13624
11.06	270	3880	109499	274301	222956	63263
7.22	203	3709	15587	199008	138064	56477
4.39	424	4229	23227	113357	120556	42022
4.01	203	3955	23013	146083	135095	73594
4.78	220	3953	42782	134222	134701	57287
8.69	241	4125	57959	307838	275448	102734
4.35	208	3638	49671	174893	97094	55420
4.87	206	3771	10686	156617	122414	45091
3.23	211	3631	14379	98464	114225	31466
10.14	203	3849	46164	312011	236297	106077
6.14	184	3704	30270	205073	182544	67434
8.10	253	3965	25655	143622	185532	61240
3.61	245	3880	11469	95912	80590	34260
4.94	244	3764	46942	134415	154494	38801
3.32	219	3706	25621	98328	145727	30429
3.87	242	4375	58898	136652	210089	58041
8.81	275	4412	75077	238843	194932	84620
8.48	277	4210	22439	129241	191803	45664
8.56	276	4576	62437	131290	254958	59009
8.16	334	4341	65164	105740	210621	56018
7.64	227	4236	4901	150917	188808	67166

市（州）概貌

General pictures of the municipalities

爽爽的贵阳

The bright and clear Guiyang

行政中心
Administrative center

贵阳市面积8034平方公里，辖六区一市三县，一个国家级经济技术开发区，一个国家级高新技术开发区，一个省级经济技术开发区和金阳新区。人口439.33万人。城镇化率69.20%。

2011年是“十二五”规划的开局之年。一年来，全市上下深入贯彻落实科学发展观，牢牢把握“加速发展、加快转型、推动跨越”主基调，始终遵循“走科学发展路、建生态文明市”总路径，大力实施工业强市和城镇化带动主战略，经济社会发展取得了显著成绩，实现了“十二五”良好开局。

经济发展明显加快，增比进位成绩显著。全市经济社会发展呈现出“速度加快、效益较好、位次前移、后劲增强、民生改善”的良好态势，生产总值、固定资产投资、城乡居民收入等指标增幅创历史新高，部分主要指标增幅在26个省会城市中位居前列，在全省地州市经济发展增比进位综合测评中排位第一。全市完成生产总值1383.07亿元，同比增长17.1%，比上年加快2.8个百分点，高于全省2.1个百分

牛郎关立交
Cowboy overpass

5月22日，省委书记栗战书在全省项目建设年现场观摩会高新区观摩点
May 22, Provincial Party Secretary Li Zhanshu in the province project construction year on-site demonstrations of high-tech zones to observe the point

10月11日，省委副书记、省长赵克志调研高新区
October 11,Provincial Committee Deputy Secretary, Governor Zhao Kezhi to have research in High-tech Zone

Guiyang City has an area of 8,034 square kilometers, jurisdiction over 6 districts 1 city and 3 counties, a state-level Economic and Technological Development Zone, a state-level High-tech Development Zone, a provincial-level economic and technological development zones and the Jinyang New District. Population of 4,393,300. Urbanization rate of 69.20%.

2011 is the first year of the "12th Five-Year Plan". Over the past year, the city's upper and lower depth implement the scientific development concept, firmly grasp the "accelerate the development, accelerate the transition, promote leapfrog" the main tone, always follow the "path of scientific development road, building ecological civilization city" path, vigorously implementation industry stong the city and urbanization driven by the main strategic, economic and social development achieved remarkable results, "the 12th Five-Year" received a good start.

5月16日，省委常委、市委书记李军调研高新区
May 16th, Provincial Standing Committee, Municipal Party Committee Secretary Li Jun had research in high-tech zones

Economic development has accelerated markedly, increased significantly than the binary results. Showing the city's economic and social development "faster speed, better efficiency, ranking forward, increased stamina, improved living conditions" the good momentum, increase in GDP, fixed asset investment, urban and rural residents' income and other indicators of a record, some of the major indicators the increase in the top in 26 capital cities, and increased economic development in the province prefectures ranked first of comprehensive evaluation of binary. The city completed a GDP of 138.307 billion yuan, up 17.1% over the previous year, on 2.8 percentage points, higher than the 2.1 percent across the province, an increase of a record. Industries, the first industry was 6.255 billion yuan, an increase of 2.8%; the secondary industry was 58.684 billion yuan, an increase of 21.3%; the tertiary industry was 73.368 billion yuan, an increase of 15.2%. Three industries 4.6:42.4:53.0. The total financial revenue reached 40.136 billion yuan, an increase of 31.8%, to increase nearly 10 billion yuan; local financial revenue reached 18.709 billion yuan, an increase of 37.3%, to increase to 5.1 billion yuan. The state tax department to complete a total revenue of 20.439 billion yuan, an increase of 27.2%,

3月10日，贵阳市委副书记、市长李再勇调研高新区
March 10,Guiyang Municipal Committee Deputy Secretary, Mayor Li Zaiyong to have research in High-tech Zone

奥体中心室内效果图
Olympic Sports Center Interior Drawings

通过创建后评选的市级绿色社区
Created after the selection of municipal green community

点，增幅创历史新高。分产业看，第一产业增加值62.55亿元，增长2.8%；第二产业增加值586.84亿元，增长21.3%；第三产业增加值733.68亿元，增长15.2%。三次产业结构为4.6:42.4:53.0。实现财政总收入达401.36亿元，同比增长31.8%，增收近100亿元；地方财政收入达187.09亿元，同比增长37.3%，增收51亿元。国税部门完成总收入204.39亿元，同比增长27.2%，地税部门完成总收入163.82亿元，同比增长23%；国税和地税增幅创近五年来最高。全市地方财政支出达277.38亿元，同比增长35.7%。城市居民人均可支配收入达19420元，同比增长17.0%；农民人均纯收入达7381元，同比增长23.5%。

固定资产投资大幅增长，重大项目建设进展加快。全社会固定资产投资完成1600.59亿元，同比增长57.1%，增幅创1986年以来新高。其中基本建设投资完成727.10亿元，增长71.7%；更新改造投资完成343.39亿元，增长59.3%；房地产开发投资完成467.36亿元，增长50.5%。168个省级重大工程和重点项目累计完成投资461.6亿元。建成花溪国家城市湿地公园等27个项目，超竣工项目目标任务58.8个百分点，新开工建设贵航军转民高新技术产业园等82个项目。全年累计到位资金1719.82亿元，同比增长34.9%。通过贷款、发行债券、BT等方式融资，自筹资金到位997.47亿元，同比增长76.9%。全市施工项目3288个，同比增长45.2%；投产项目2354个，同比增长45.4%。新开工项目达2657个，同比增长54.6%。

花溪一号大桥侧影
The Huaxi NO.1 Bridge silhouette

高新区、白云区总投资123亿元的27个项目集中开工
High-tech Zone, Baiyun Total investment 12.3 billion yuan, 27 projects focused on start

投资18亿元的中京国际项目奠基
Laid the foundation stone of investment of 1.8 billion yuan of Zhongjing International projects

local tax departments to complete a total revenue of 16.382 billion yuan, an increase of 23%; tax and land tax increase in nearly five years to the highest. The city's local fiscal expenditure amounted to 27.738 billion yuan, an increase of 35.7%. Urban residents per capita disposable income reached 19,420 yuan, up 17.0%; the per capita net income of farmers reached 7,381 yuan, an increase of 23.5%.

The fixed assets investment has growth signifigantly, to accelerate construction of major projects progress. The whole society fixed assets investment was 160.059 billion yuan, an increase of 57.1%, an increase of a new high since 1986. Invested in infrastructure construction completed 72.71 billion yuan, an increase of 71.7%; renovation investment of 34.339 billion yuan, up 59.3%; real estate development and investment of 46.736 billion yuan, an increase of 50.5%. 168 provincial major projects and key projects accumulated investment of 46.16 billion yuan. Completion of 27 the Huaxi national urban wetland park project and so on, surpass the completion of the project objectives and tasks 58.8%, new construction of 82 projects of the construction of Guizhou aircraft conversion Hi-Tech Industrial Park. Annual accumulated capital in place of 171.982 billion yuan, an increase of 34.9%. Through loans, issue bonds, BT and other ways of financing, self-financing in place to 99.747 billion yuan, an increase of 76.9%. 3,288 the city's construction projects, an increase of 45.2%; put into the project of 2,354, an increase of 45.4%. New projects for 2,657, an increase of 54.6%.

Industrial economic growth accelerated, the outlook continues to improve. The city's above-scale industrial output value completed 146.629 billion yuan, up 28.9%; above-scale industrial added value of 37.822 billion yuan, an increase of 23.4%. Rate of 39% of the industrial contribution to GDP, an increase of 9 percentage points over the previous year, to spur economic growth by 6.7 percentage points. High-tech industry accounted for above-scale industrial added value accounted for 32%, an increase of 10.9 percent. Six characteristic industries totaled 27.088 billion yuan of industrial added value of enterprises above designated size, an increase of 24.8%, accounting for 74.2% of the above-scale industrial added value and boost the city's industrial growth by 22.7 percentage points. Industrial investment totaled 56.097 billion yuan, an increase of 109.3%. Implemented a total of 890 technological transformation projects, an increase of 44.7%, of which new construction project 762, an increase of 58.0%, new projects total completed investment of 17.329 billion yuan, an increase of 56.1%. Ten industrial parks infrastructure invested a total of 21.5 billion yuan, the industrial projects invested a total of 22.474 billion yuan, gross industrial output value of 83 billion yuan, 382 enterprises into the park, to provide employment to 89,000.

建设中的高校聚集区
Colleges and universities gathered in the construction

新中广线开工仪式
New Zhongguang line groundbreaking ceremony

贵州开磷40万吨硫磺制酸
Guizhou Kailin 400,000 tons of sulfuric acid

息烽磷化工基地一角
The Xifeng phosphorus chemical base corner

息烽环保袋生产车间一角
The Xifeng enviromental-friendly bags production workshop corner

工业经济增速加快，前景持续向好。全市规模以上工业总产值完成1466.29亿元，同比增长28.9%；规模以上工业增加值完成378.22亿元，同比增长23.4%。工业对地区生产总值的贡献率达39%，比上年增加了9个百分点，拉动经济增长6.7个百分点。高新技术产业增加值占规模以上工业增加值的比重达32%，同比提高10.9个百分点。六大特色产业累计完成规模以上工业增加值270.88亿元，同比增长24.8%，占规模以上工业增加值的74.2%，拉动全市工业经济增长22.7个百分点。工业投资累计完成560.97亿元，同比增长109.3%。共实施技术改造项目890个，同比增长44.7%，其中新开工项目762个，同比增长58.0%，新开工项目累计完成投资173.29亿元，同比增长56.1%。十大工业园区基础设施累计投入达215亿元，产业项目累计投入224.74亿元，实现工业总产值830亿元，入园区企业382家，提供就业8.9万人。

服务业保持较快增长，重点行业快速发展。以会展、物流、旅游和金融为代表的现代服务业快速发展。会展经济成效明显，全年共举办各类会展活动382个（场），实现综合经济效益7.2亿元。旅游业保持较快增长，全年共接待游客5250.42万人（次），同比增长33.0%，实现旅游总收入612.37亿元，同比增长43.8%。社会消费旺盛，社会消费品零售总额完成584.33亿元，同比增长20.5%。物流业发展加快，建成贵阳铁路枢纽改貌货运中心、花溪地利农产品物流园、孟关国际汽贸城，启动建设二戈寨、金阳、扎佐、清镇四大物流园区。金融业取得新进展，贵阳商业银行更名为贵阳银行，组建成立贵阳农村

湿地公园美如画
Wetland Park in picturesque surroundings

前来贵州省现代农业展示区观光游览的小朋友围抱巨型南瓜
Children come to Guizhou Province modern agriculture exhibition area sightseeing around to take a giant pumpkin

苗家的夜场
Miao Night

Service industry to maintain rapid growth, the rapid development of key industries. The rapid development of modern service industry exhibition, logistics, tourism and financial. The effectiveness of the exhibition economy, organizing various conferences and exhibitions throughout the year a total of 382 (field) to achieve overall economic efficiency of 720 million yuan. To maintain a rapid growth in tourism, total tourists 5,254,200 (times), an increase of 33.0%, total tourism income of 61.237 billion yuan, an increase of 43.8%. Strong social consumer, retail sales of social consumer goods the total value of 58.433 billion yuan, an increase of 20.5%. The development of the logistics industry to accelerate the completion of the cargo center of Guiyang railway hub change appearance, the Huaxi location logistics park of agricultural products, Meng Guan International Car Trade City, to start construction of Er Ge Zhai, Jinyang, Zhazuo, Qingzhen four logistics parks. The financial industry has made new progress, Guiyang Commercial Bank renamed Bank of Guiyang, founded the Guiyang rural commercial banks, listed on the Guizhou equity managed trading center and Guiyang commodity exchanges opened, started construction of the the Guiyang international financial center. RMB deposits in the city at the end of the year financial institutions was 360.365 billion yuan, an increase of 19.5% compared with the beginning of the year. Balance of RMB loans of financial institutions was 301.286 billion yuan, up 17.3% compared with the beginning of the year.

漂亮的苗家姑娘
Beautiful girl of Miao

Adjustment of agricultural structure was further optimized, significantly improved agricultural efficiency. The per capita net income of farmers reached 7,380 yuan, an increase of 23.5%, the fourth consecutive year above the national average. Vegetable sown area of 1.4 milion mu (sub), the output reached 1,782,400 tons

天河潭风景区
Tianhetan Scenic Area

2011第六届中国（贵州）国际装备制造业博览会
2011 sixth International Equipment Manufacturing Exposition of China (Guizhou)

2011年贵州省“全国安全生产月”系列活动之一——第十届中国贵州安全生产技术装备展览会
2011 Guizhou Province, "National Safety Month" activities series, one of the activities - the tenth in Guizhou, China safety production technology and equipment exhibition

2011中国•贵阳国际特色农产品交易会开幕式
The opening ceremony of 2011 China•Guiyang International Specialties Agricultural Products Fair

2011首届贵阳（夏季）品牌服装及丝绸博览会
2011 the first brand clothing and Silk Fair in Guiyang (summer)

商业银行，贵州股权托管交易中心和贵阳大宗商品交易所挂牌开业，开工建设贵阳国际金融中心。全市年末金融机构人民币各项存款余额3603.65亿元，比年初增长19.5%。金融机构人民币各项贷款余额3012.86亿元，比年初增长17.3%。

农业结构调整进一步优化，农业效益明显提高。农民人均纯收入达7380元，同比增长23.5%，连续第四年超出全国平均水平。完成蔬菜播面140万亩（次），蔬菜产量达178.24万吨，食用菌产量达1.83万吨。规模养殖场已达1960个，畜牧业总产值占农业总产值31%。完成农产品加工业总产值200亿元，同比增长20%。共实施基本农田基础设施建设3.11万亩，全市农机总动力达131.29万千瓦。完成贵阳市五里冲农副产品批发市场的整体搬迁，初步构成以贵阳地利物流园为龙头，南明永乐、修文兴隆等产地批发市场为支撑，各地农贸市场和社区直销点为终端的市场网络体系。

城市建设明显加快，综合承载力进一步提升。开工建设贵阳龙洞堡国际机场二期扩建工程；“一环一射两联线”的市域快速铁路建设顺利推进。贵清高速公路全线通车，二环路全线贯通，“三环十六条射线”道路路网建设基本形成。建成金阳客运站、客运东站，以及修文、息烽、清镇3个县级客运站。完成三县一市液化气储配站布点建设，液化气的供应保障能力提升。全面完成1000公里串户路、70个大中型沼气池、12个蔬菜标准园和20个乡村清洁工程等实事项目，鱼洞峡水库工程大坝进入主体施工阶段，鱼简河水库渠系配套工程建设已基本完工，9座小型病险水库除险加固工程全部完工。

招商引资成绩显著，外贸进出口较快增长。全年引进内资项目1539个，到位资金691.31亿元，同比增长52.4%。全年批准外资企业28个，实际直接利用外资2.79亿美元，增长106.9%。外贸进出口总额完成37.69亿美元，同比增长65.7%。

体制改革取得新突破，发展环境进一步优化。城市基层管理体制改革试点工作取得重要进展，30个新的社区服务中心挂牌运行；开展了《贵阳市居住证》集中办理试点工作；花溪区、乌当区、清镇市和开阳县被列为省级城乡统筹综合配套改革试点；国家基本药物制度已覆盖全市，覆盖人口数占全市总人口数的64%；完成了贵阳五金交电化工总

2011贵阳避暑季开幕式
2011 the Guiyang summer season opening

EFG2011生态文明贵阳会议
EFG2011 ecological civilization Guiyang Conference

贵阳市第五届旅游产业发展大会
Guiyang City, the fifth Tourism Development Conference

贵阳石板农产品物流园开业典礼
Guiyang Shiban agricultural logistics park opening ceremony

of vegetables, mushroom production reached 18,300 tons. Large-scale farms has reached 1,960, animal husbandry output value of total agricultural output value of 31%. Agricultural product processing industry total output value of 20 billion yuan, an increase of 20%. Implemented a total of 31,100 mu of basic farmland infrastructure construction, the city's gross agricultural machinery amounted to 1.3129 million kilowatts. Completion of Guiyang City, Wulichong relocation of agricultural and sideline products wholesale markets, preliminary form as a leader of Guiyang location Logistics Park, Nan Ming Yongle, Xiuwen Xinglong wholesale market support, and around farmers' markets and community-based direct selling point terminal market network system.

Urban construction has accelerated markedly, to further enhance the comprehensive carrying capacity. Started construction of the Phase II expansion project of the the Longdongbao International Airport; the smooth progress of "a ring and a shot two lines" Regional Express Railway Construction. Guiqing Freeway, the Second Ring Road across the board, through the "three-ring 16 rays" of the road network construction is basically formed. Completion of the Jinyang bus terminal, passenger East Railway Station, and Xiuwen, Xifeng, Qingzhen three county-level passenger terminal. Completion of construction of the three counties and one city of liquefied petroleum gas storage and distribution station, distribution of liquefied gas supply security capacity is improved. Completion of full of 1,000 km Kushido Road, 70 large and medium-sized digesters, 12 standard vegetables gardens, and 20 rural sanitation projects things for the project, the Yudong Gorge Reservoir dam into the main construction phase, Yujianhe Reservoir Canal supporting project construction has been completed, nine small reservoirs reinforcement project is fully completed.

Investment performance significantly, the faster growth of import and export. Full-year 1,539 domestic investment projects, put in place a capital of 69.131 billion yuan, an increase of 52.4%. 28 approved foreign-funded enterprises throughout the year, actual direct foreign investment of $ 279 million, an increase of 106.9%. The total foreign trade volume was $ 3.769 billion, an increase of 65.7%.

机关干部上山植树
Cadres go to the mountains to have tree planting

贵阳市开展65世界环境日宣传
Guiyang City 65 World Environment Day to promote

贵阳市开展地球一小时熄灯活动
Guiyang City Earth Hour lights-out activities

贵阳市开展饮水思源活动
Guiyang City to start the drink from the source activity

公司中兴大厦、贵州省贵阳市进出口公司改革重组工作，启动了贵阳电池厂等10余户已获改革重组批复企业的职工分流安置工作；新组建成立了市地产集团和市农业担保公司两家投融资平台。

节能减排成效明显，生态建设全面推进。完成石漠化综合治理面积50.36平方公里，岩溶面积214.8平方公里，治理小流域河流13条；完成巩固退耕还林补植补造7.84万亩，建成区园林绿地面积20839.5公顷，绿化覆盖面积达7055.88公顷，人均公共绿地面积达10.32平方米。主要污染物控制在省下达的排放目标之内，地面水环境质量保持良好状况，“两湖一库”重要水源稳定在Ⅱ、Ⅲ类水质。支持企业发展循环经济项目23个，安排循环经济专项资金820万元，全年淘汰炼铁、水泥等行业23户企业的落后产能181.25万吨，高耗能产业增加值占工业增加值的比重由45.8%下降到37.17%。被国家发展改革委列为全国餐厨废弃物资源化利用和无害化处理试点城市。

民生工程扎实推进，社会事业全面发展。全年财政用于民生的投入达162亿元，比上年增加了2.2个百分点。全年城镇新增就业8.5万人。城市和农村低保标准平均提高13%，新型农村合作医疗参合率达97.6%，参保人数170.5万人。新建幼儿园40所，新建和改扩建小学、初中各11所。建成3个县级医院、5个中心乡镇卫生院、18个社区卫生服务中心。新开工公租房315.8万平方米，竣工保障性住房41.2万平方米。两次向低收入群体发放临时价格补贴共计3676万元，惠及30余万城市困难群众。

文广、卫生和体育事业蓬勃发展。全市共有艺术表演团体9个、群众艺术文化馆12个、公共图书馆10个，图书馆藏书量212.67万册。全市有广播电台2座，调频转播发射台6座，广播综合人口覆盖率100%，农村广播人口覆盖率100%，无线广播综合人口覆盖率98.19%。电视台2座，电视发射及转播台6座，电视人口覆盖率99.69%，农村电视人口

贵阳新庄污水处理厂
Guiyang Xinzhuang sewage treatment plant

Restructuring made new breakthroughs, the development environment has been further optimized. Urban grass-roots management system pilot project made important progress, 30 new community service center listed on the run; for the "Guiyang City residence permit" centralized handle pilot work; Huaxi District, Wudang District, Qingzhen City and Kaiyang column provincial urban and rural comprehensive reform pilot; the national essential medicines system has covered the city, all the coverage of the population accounted for 64% of the total population in the city; completed the reform of Guiyang Wujinjiaodian Chemical Corporation, Zhongxing Building, Guiyang City, Guizhou Province Import and Export Corporation reorganization, started the reform and reorganization, Guiyang battery factory and more than 10 families have been approved by the workers shunt placement; founded City Real Estate Group and the Agricultural Guarantee Corporation two investment and financing platform.

贵阳市实施了十个城镇污水处理厂的建设工程，图为金阳污水处理厂正在运行的氧化沟
Guiyang City 10 urban sewage treatment plant construction projects, the picture shows the Jinyang sewage treatment plant is running oxidation ditch

The effectiveness of energy saving and emission reduction, ecological construction comprehensively promote. Rocky desertification comprehensive management area of 50.36 square kilometers, the karst area of 214.8 square kilometers, the small watershed rivers 13; to complete the consolidation of returning farmland to forest replanting to fill to build 78,400 mu, built-up area of garden green area of 20,839.5 hectares, green covers an area of 7,055.88 hectares. The public green area per capita reached 10.32 square meters. The main pollutant control emissions targets issued in the province within the surface water quality to maintain in good condition, "two lakes one reservior" water stabilized at □, Grade III. Support the business development of circular economy projects 23, the arrangement of circular economy 8.2 million yuan of special funds, the annual out of 23 enterprises of the iron-smelting, cement and other industries lag behind production capacity of 1.8125 million tons, and high energy-consuming industry accounts for the industrial added value accounted for by down from 45.8% to 37.17%. National Development and Reform Commission listed as a food kitchen waste utilization and safe disposal of pilot cities.

Livelihood projects push forward, the comprehensive development of social undertakings. The annual budget was spent on the people's livelihood and the investment reached 16.2 billion yuan, an increase of 2.2 percentage points over the previous year. Average increase of 13% in urban and rural minimum standard, the new rural cooperative medical participation rate of 97.6%, the number of insured 1,705,000. 40 new nursery, new construction and renovation

花溪石板镇花街村林木寨新貌
Huaxi Shiban town Huajie village Linmu Zhai new look

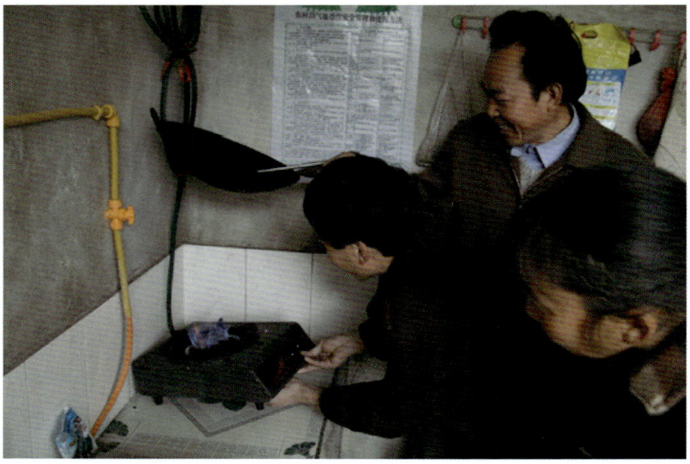

息烽农村生态能源——沼气
The Xifeng rural eco-energy - biogas

覆盖率99.41%。全年出版图书1450种，总印数9100.58万册；印刷出版杂志88种，总印数1301.23万册；印刷出版报纸33种，总印数35632.68万册。全市年末拥有卫生机构2919个，卫生机构床位24347张，卫生技术人员28638人，执业医师10491人，注册护士12284人，药师1336人。完成第九届全国少数民族传统体育运动会协办工作，成功举办中朝国际足球赛。参加第九届全国少数民族运动会获7个一等奖、16个二等奖、8个三等奖，参加全国第七届城市运动会，取得金牌1枚、银牌2枚、1个团体第四名。积极开展全民健身活动，贵阳奥体中心对外开放，全年共开展大中型全民健身活动50多次。

科学技术和教育水平不断提升。全年安排市级应用技术研究与开发资金1.38亿元，实施科技计划项目440多项，其中重大科技专项8项。全年专利申请受理量为3549件，比上年增长20.1%。制定了《贵阳市人民政府关于大力发展学前教育的实施意见》（筑府发〔2011〕29号）和《贵阳市学前教育三年行动计划》，设立了学前教育发展资金，投入3000万元学前教育建设专款。在2011年中国社科院颁布的《公共服务蓝皮书》中，我市基础教育满意度在全国38个主要城市中排名第三。2011年贵阳市高考成绩仍居全省前列。

交通、邮电继续稳步发展。全年各种运输方式完成货物运输量13885.90万吨，比上年增长33.6%。完成旅客发送量38286.90万人次，比上年增长26.0%。全市年末民用车辆拥有量64.47万辆，比上年末增长6.7%。私人汽车拥有量41.62万辆，比上年末增长16.1%。全市邮电业务总量44.68亿元，比上年增长5.9%。

苗家儿女喜事多（摄影/曹廷飞）
Miao children happy event (Photo / Cao Tingfei)

党武乡党武村摆贡寨生态文明建设文艺演出
Dangwu Township Dangwu Village Baigong Zhai ecological civilization art performances

and expansion elementary school, junior high school 11. Completion of the 3 county-level hospitals, 5 Center township health centers, 18 community health service centers. New construction of public rental of 3.158 million square meters, the completion of 412,000 square meters of affordable housing. The issuance of temporary price subsidies to low-income groups twice a total of 36.76 million yuan, benefiting more than 300,000 urban poor people.

Culture and broadcast, health and sports to flourish. The city owns a total of 9 performing arts groups, 12 arts cultural center of the masses, 10 public libraries, the library collection of 2.1267 million books. The city has two radio stations, FM broadcast transmitting station 6, Radio broadcasting coverage rate of 100%, 100% of the population coverage of rural broadcasting, radio broadcasting coverage rate of 98.19%. Two television stations and 6 television transmitting and relay stations, the TV population coverage of 99.69%, 99.41% of the TV population coverage in rural areas. The publication of a full year of 1,450 kinds of books, a total print run of 91,005,800; 88 kinds of printing and publication of magazine, a total print run of 13,012,300; 33 kinds of printing and publishing newspapers, a total print run of 356,326,800. The city with health agencies at the end of the year 2,919, 24,347 beds in health institutions, health and technical personnel of 28,638 people, 10,491 practicing physicians, 12,284 registered nurses pharmacist 1,336. Completion of the work of the Ninth National Traditional Ethnic Minority Sports Association, successfully held the international football match between China and the DPRK. Ninth National Minority Games to participate in 7 of the first prize, second prize of 16, 8 of the third prize, to participate in 7th National City Games, a gold medal, two silver medals, the fourth of a group. Active in the fitness programs, Guiyang Olympic Sports Center opening up to the public, and the year to carry out large and medium-sized national fitness activities 50.

Science and technology and level of education has been increasing. Arrangements for a full year of 138 million yuan of the municipal application technology research and development funds, the implementation of more than 440 technology projects, including eight major science and technology special funds. The annual patent applications accepted for 3,549, an increase of 20.1% over the previous year. "Guiyang Municipal People's Government on vigorously developing pre-school education, the implementation views" (building department issue [2011] No.29) and "Guiyang City the pre-school three-year action plan was formulated", the establishment of pre-school development funds, invested 30 million yuan of pre-school education construction funds. Chinese Academy of Social Sciences in 2011 promulgated the "Blue Book of public services", the satisfaction of basic education in our city ranked third in the country's 38 major cities. Guiyang City, the college entrance examination entrance examination results in 2011 continued to be the top in the province.

Transportation, post and telecommunications continued to develop steadily. The various modes of transport for the whole year to complete cargo transportation volume of 138.859 million tons, an increase of 33.6% over the previous year. The passenger traffic volume of 382,869,000 passengers, an increase of 26.0% over the previous year. The city at the end of the year civilian vehicles have 644,700, an increase of 6.7% over the previous year. Private car ownership is 416,200, an increase of 16.1% over the previous year. The city's total business volume of Posts and Telecommunications of 4.468 billion yuan, an increase of 5.9% over the previous year.

遵 义 市

Zunyi City

高速公路建设
Highway construction

城镇化图
Urbanization map

2011年，全市上下围绕“增比、进位、突破”的要求和“提速赶超、转型跨越”主基调，以决战开局、起步冲刺的决心，以深入开展“三个建设年”等活动为抓手，大力实施工业强市、城镇化带动和农业产业化战略，攻坚克难，奋力拼搏，年度计划任务顺利完成，实现了“十二五”开好局、起好步的目标。

2011年完成地区生产总值1121.16亿元，比上年增长17%；全社会固定资产投资814亿元，增长47.5%；财政总收入202.21亿元，一般预算收入84.62亿元，分别增长43.1%和46.9%；全社会消费品零售总额350.62亿元，增长20.8%；城镇居民人均可支配收入17426元，农民人均纯收入5216元，分别增长14.1%和17.6%；年末金融机构存贷款余额分别为1403亿元和712亿元，分别增长21.2%和19%。三次产业结构调整为13.5：44：42.5。

工业经济发展壮大，园区建设成效显著。一是工业经济总量和质量提升。全年完成规模工业增加值421.8亿元，增长22.5%；大中型骨干企业和规模工业生产经营状况良好，476户规模以上工业企业实现销售收入840亿元，同比增长40%；企业单位能耗下降4%，节能降耗和淘汰落后产能成效显著，淘汰落后产能118.25万吨。二是工业园区建设有效推进。遵义湘江工业园、遵义和平工业园、仁怀名酒工业园、桐梓循环经济工业园、重庆楚米产业园、湄潭绿色食品工业园等园区建设成效显著，完成工业投资300亿元。三是工业重点项目建设进展顺利。长征风电设备制造、桐梓煤化工、桐梓花秋二矿一期工程、容光煤矿一期工程、正安瑞溪水泥厂、中电投绥阳水泥厂等基本建成并投入试生产，桐梓电厂、海螺盘江水泥项目加快推进，习水二郎电厂、厦门以晴集团茶叶加工项目开工建设，长征电气、遵义碱厂、贵州钢绳集团、遵义铁合金厂异地技改步伐加快。

赤水大瀑布

Chishui large waterfall

In 2011, the city's up and down around the "growth, the binary, breakthrough" requirements and "catch up and speed up, accelerate the transition leapfrog" the main keynote, to battle as the start, the determination of the starting sprint, to carry out the "three building year" and other activities for grasping hand, vigorously implement the industry strong city, driven by urbanization and agriculture industrialization strategy, to tackle tough, work hard, successful completion of the annual plan tasks to achieve the goal of "12th Five-Year" a good beginning, a good first step.

In 2011, GDP of 112.116 billion yuan, an increase of 17% over the previous year; total fixed asset investment of 81.4 billion yuan, up 47.5%; total fiscal revenue of 20.221 billion yuan, general budget revenues 8.462 billion yuan, an increase of 43.1%, and 46.9%, respectively; society as a whole, total retail sales of 35.062 billion yuan, up 20.8%; per capita disposable income of urban residents was 17,426 yuan and rural per capita net income of 5,216 yuan, an increase of 14.1% and 17.6% respectively; financial institutions at the end of the year the deposit and loan balances were 140.3 billion yuan and 71.2 billion yuan, an increase of 21.2% and 19% respectively. The three industrial restructuring for 13.5:44:42.5.

Industrial economic development got growth, the construction of the park with remarkable results. First, the total industrial economy and quality improvement. Last year's large-scale industrial added value of 42.18 billion yuan, an increase of 22.5%; large and medium-sized backbone enterprises, and scale of industrial production and management is in good condition, 476 above-scale industrial enterprises realized a sales income of 84 billion yuan, an increase of 40%; enterprise unit energy consumption decreased 4%, saving energy and eliminate backward production capacity, with remarkable results with the elimination of backward production capacity of 1,182,500 tons. Second, is to effectively promote the construction of industrial parks. Zunyi Xiangjiang Industrial Park, Zunyi Heping Industrial Park, Renhuai Wines Industrial Park, Tongzi Circular Economy Industrial Park, Chongqing Chu Rice Industrial Park, Meitan Green Food Industrial Park, construction of the park with remarkable results, the industrial investment of 30 billion yuan. Third, the industrial

茅台酒包装车间
The Maotai packaging workshops

生产中的贵州赤天化纸业股份有限公司
Production of Guizhou Chitianhua production Paper Co., Ltd.

城镇化进程加快，服务业加快发展。一是大力实施城区倍增计划，积极推进城镇化。中心城区按照“东扩西控、南北充实”的空间布局，大力推进旧城区改造和新蒲新区、南白龙坑片区、汇川大道片区、新火车站片区建设；全市城市化率达到37%。二是城市基础设施建设取得成效。中心城区道路柔化改造全面完成，共青大道竣工通车，新火车站迎宾大道、新蒲新南快线、南白青山水厂、南部污水处理厂等市政工程建设进展顺利；黔北汽车城交易展示中心建成投用，“万村千乡市场工程”等一批专业市场建成运行；城市数字管理平台基本建成，国家文明城市和环境模范城市创建活动深入推进。三是第三产业发展加快。红色旅游、生态旅游、乡村旅游发展势头良好，全年接待游客2625万人次，旅游综合收入240.8亿元，分别增长57.9%和71%；文化产业发展取得新进展，成功申报全国公共文化服务体系示范区，文化信息资源共享工程加快；交通运输、金融、保险、邮政、通信、社区服务、现代物流等行业保持较快增长态势。完成第三产业增加值476.88亿元，增长16.6%。

凤冈60万吨水泥厂
Fenggang 600,000 tons of cement plant

凤冈缫丝厂
Fenggang filature plant

key projects progressed smoothly. Changzheng wind power equipment manufacturing, the Tongzi coal chemical, Tongzi Huaqiu II Mine phase I project, Rongguang coal mine phase I project, Zheng'an Ruixi Cement Plant, China Power Investment Suiyang cement plants built and put into trial production, the Tongzi power plants, Hailuo Panjiang cement projects are speeding up, the Xishui Erlang power plant, Xiamen Yiqing Group tea processing project started construction, Changzheng Electric, Soda Plant in Zunyi, Guizhou Wire Rope Group, Zunyi Ferroalloy Factory offsite pace of technological transformation to accelerate.

The urbanization process accelerated, the service sector to accelerate development. First, vigorously implement the city's plan to double, to actively promote the urbanization. Central urban area in accordance with the "eastward expansion western control, north-south to enrich" the space layout, vigorously to advancing old city area transformation and Xinpu New Area, South the Bailong pit Area, Huichuan Avenue Area, Railway Station Area construction; the city's urbanization rate to 37%. Second, the success of urban infrastructure construction. Road softens the transformation of the central urban area full completion, the Gongqing Avenue opened to traffic, the new railway station Yingbin Avenue, New Xinpu Xinnan Express, Southern Baiqingshan water plant, south of the sewage treatment plant and other municipal construction projects are progressing smoothly; Qianbei Motor City transactions show center put into use, "Village Market Project" and a group of professional market up and running; urban digital management platform is basically completed, and further promote the activities of national civilized city, and environmental model city created. Third, the accelerated development of tertiary industry. Red tourism, eco-tourism, rural tourism development momentum is good, the whole annual tourists of 26.25 million visitors, a tourism revenue of 24.08 billion yuan, an increase of 57.9% and 71% respectively; the development of cultural industries has made new progress, declare the success of public cultural service system demonstration area, and cultural information resources sharing project to speed up; traffic, transportation, finance, insurance, postal services, communications, community service, modern logistics industry to maintain a rapid growth. Complete the tertiary industry added value was 47.688 billion yuan, up 16.6%.

桐梓重庆工业园一期标准厂房小广场
Tongzi Chongqing Industrial Park phase I, a small square of the standard factory

农业产业化积极推进，新农村建设成效明显。一是八大农业产业稳步推进。粮食因旱减产，全年粮食产量227.1万吨，下降21.4%；油菜产量23.04万吨，增长20.8%；畜牧业稳步发展，肉类总产量43.73万吨，禽蛋产量3.76万吨，分别增长0.1%和2%；烤烟、茶叶、辣椒、蔬菜、高粱、中药材、竹种植面积扩大，分别达到86万亩、110万亩、132.5万亩、114.5万亩、62.11万亩、122.52万亩、300万亩。二是农业产业化经营水平提高。145家市级龙头企业实现销售收入95亿元，收购农产品价值达30多亿元；培育和发展农民专业合作社1650个，组织农产品销售超过60亿元。三是"四在农家"创建活动深入推进，农村生产生活条件得到改善。治理病险水库50座，完成烟水配套工程10万亩，解决50万农村人口的饮水困难，建设通村公路2300公里（其中通村油路1000公里），完成营造林64.93万亩，新建沼气池2万口，治理水土流失面积120.86平方公里和石漠化面积129平方公里。

桐梓蒙渡大桥立体交叉图
The Tongzi Mengdu bridge interchange Chart

画壁天然

Wall paintings natural

The industrialization of agriculture is actively promoted and achieved remarkable success of the new rural construction. First, the eight agricultural industries pushed steadily. For drought, food production reduced, the annual grain production of 2.271 million tons, down 21.4%; rape yield was 230,400 tons, an increase of 20.8%; the steady development of livestock, meat output of 437,300 tons, 37,600 tons of egg production, increased by 0.1 % and 2%; tobacco, tea, pepper, vegetables, sorghum, herbs, bamboo planting area to expand, respectively, to reach 860,000 mu, 1.1 million mu, 1.325 million mu, 1.145 million mu, 621,100 mu, 1.2252 million mu and 3 million mu. Second, is to raise the level of industrial management of agriculture. 145 municipal leading enterprises realized sales revenue of 9.5 billion yuan, acquisition of agricultural products worth over 3 billion yuan; nurture and develop specialized farmer cooperatives 1,650, the organization of agricultural products sold over 6 billion yuan. Third, "four in the farm" creation activities further promote, rural production and living conditions have improved. Governance dangerous reservoirs of 50, smoke water supporting projects of 100,000 mu, to solve the drinking water problem for 500,000 rural people, building a village road 2,300 km (1,000 km of which the village oil), afforested 649,300 mu, the new biogas pool 20,000, water and soil erosion area of 120.86 square kilometers and rocky desertification area of 129 square kilometers.

Projects to achieve new results, continue to reinforce the foundation for development. First, firmly grasp the project is to focus on economic, grasping the investment is to grasp the concept of development, efforts to promote the project construction and management, investment intensity, intensity, speed are all unprecedented, total fixed assets investment completed 81.4 billion yuan. Second, implementation of projects "three basics", innovative project management institutional mechanisms, to take the focus started, the leadership of the Hanging Wall, evaluations and other effective measures for the work, and actively promote the construction of key projects, throughout the year, to focus on projects under construction 814, supporting and driving the rapid growth in investment. Third, is to accelerate the transportation, water conservancy and other major infrastructure projects. Accelerate the formation of three-dimensional transportation network, the beltway, Ren-Chi high-speed, Hang-Rui high-speed the Zunyi segment construction are progressing smoothly, Qianbei high-speed, altar plant to the Maotai highway started construction, the Maotai airport preliminary work to speed up; construction was speeded up the backbone of water projects, water conservancy construction, ecological construction, rocky desertification "Trinity" is planning to full implementation.

绥阳——双河洞景区洞内风光
Suiyang - the Shuanghe holes scenic cave scenery

绥阳——镖水岩瀑布
Suiyang - Biaoshuiyan Falls

项目建设取得新成效，发展基础不断夯实。一是牢固抓项目就是抓经济、抓投资就是抓发展的理念，着力推进项目建设与管理，投资强度、力度、速度前所未有，全社会固定资产投资完成814亿元。二是推行项目建设“三基本”，创新项目管理体制机制，采取集中开工、领导挂帮、考核奖惩等切实有效工作措施，积极推进重点项目建设，全年集中开工建设项目814个，支撑和带动投资较快增长。三是交通、水利等一批重大基础设施项目加快推进。立体交通网络加快形成，绕城高速、仁赤高速、杭瑞高速遵义段建设进展顺利，黔北高速、坛厂至茅台高速公路开工建设，茅台机场前期工作加快；骨干水源工程建设步伐加快，水利建设、生态建设、石漠化综合治理“三位一体”规划全面实施。

社会事业全面进步，民生不断改善。一是教育事业巩固发展。24个高中阶段教育突破工程建设进展顺利，高中阶段毛入学率达54.6%；全面落实城乡免费义务教育政策及农村家庭生活困难寄宿生活补助政策；1629个农村学校食堂全面完成，65个学前教育突破工程全部开工，开工建设67个农村“薄改工程”、5个特教学校建设。二是医疗卫生事业不断发展。224个乡镇卫生院、6个政府举办的社区卫生服务中心及村卫生室实施国家基本药物制度，新型农村合作医疗参合率达96.11%；市中医院、市妇幼保健院、县级医院、乡村卫生院（室）、社区卫生服务中心建设加快推进；食品药品监管、疾病防控、卫生监督、血液保障力度不断加强。三是就业、社会保障、人口、扶贫工作进一步加强。全年新增城镇就业5.9万人，失业人员再就业1.65万人，城镇登记失业率3.26%；基本医疗、基本养老、失业保险参保人数分别达到693.5万人、33.1万人、17.6万人，均比上年提高；低保人数达 72.1万人，发放基本生活保障金7.72亿元，81.6万人次得到城乡医疗救助，安排冬春群众生活资金1.76亿元，开工建设65个敬老院；完成2700户异地扶贫搬迁，20547套保障性住房全面开工，13500户城市低收入家庭享受住房租赁补贴，45881户农村危房改造基本完成；人口自增率为5.27‰，符合政策生育率为94.8%；投入扶贫资金2.6亿元，全年减少贫困人口15万人。四是文化体育广电事业进一步发展。积极推进全国公共文化服务体系示范区建设，“全国文明城市”创建获得中央精神文明委提名资

绥阳——香树湾风光

Suiyang - Xiangshuwan scenery

Comprehensive social progress, and continuous improvement of people's livelihood. First, the consolidation and development of educational undertakings. 24 senior high school education breakthrough projects progressed smoothly, high school gross enrollment rate of 54.6%; the full implementation of the urban and rural free compulsory education policy and rural family life difficult boarding a living allowance policy; 1,629 rural school cafeteria got full completion, the 65 pre-school education breakthrough works are all in the work, started construction of 67 rural "thin change project", five special education school construction. Second, is the continuous development of medical and health services. 224 township hospitals, 6 government-run community health service centers and village health implementation of the national essential drug system, the new rural cooperative medical participation rate of 96.11%; City Hospital, the maternity and child care, county hospitals, rural health hospital (room), the construction of community health service centers are accelerating; food and drug regulation, disease control, health surveillance, blood protection efforts continue to strengthen. Third, employment, social security, population, poverty alleviation was further strengthened. Throughout the year, added to 59,000 urban jobs, the workers re-employed 16,500, the registered urban unemployment rate of 3.26%; basic medical care, basic pension, unemployment insurance reached 6.935 million, 331,000 people, 176,000 than the previous year; guaranteeing a total of 721,000 people, payment of basic living allowance for 772 million yuan, 816,000 people get medical assistance in urban and rural areas, arrangements for the winter and spring the life of the masses capital of 176 million yuan, started construction of 65 homes for the elderly; completed 2,700 off-site relocation of poverty alleviation, 20,547 units of affordable housing at full capacity, 13,500 low-income urban families to enjoy the housing rental subsidies, 45,881 rural renovation of dilapidated buildings basically completed; the population growth rate of 5.27 ‰, compliance with the policy fertility rate was 94.8%; into anti-poverty funds 260 million yuan, and poverty reduction throughout the year 150,000 people. Fourth, Further development of cultural and sports broadcasting career. Actively promote the construction of public cultural service system demonstration area, "National Civilized City" creating won the Central Committee of spiritual civilization eligible to be nominated, and the completion of the main project of public fitness center, 88 township cultural stations, 60 digital "Farm Book House" and 9 townships, 218 Village Fitness Project, and every village access to radio and television projects are completed. Fifth, production safety, peace building achieved remarkable results. 223 from a production safety accident, 199 people died, 11 years in a row to achieve the "double down"; municipal tranquil county to create up to 100%. At the same time, the cause of the propaganda law, ethnic and religious, women and children, the elderly, the disabled, the meteorological make new achievements.

烤烟制种基地——何坝
Flue-cured tobacco seed production bases - He Dam

苍龙街道下坝新农村风光
Canglong street Xiaba new countryside scenery

格，市民健身中心主体工程完工，88个乡镇综合文化站、60个数字“农家书屋”及9个乡镇、218个村体育健身工程和村村通广播电视工程全面完成。五是安全生产、平安建设取得明显成效。发生生产安全事故223起、死亡199人，连续11年实现“双降”；市级平安县创建率达100%。同时，普法、民族宗教、妇女儿童、老龄人、残疾人、气象等各项事业取得新成效。

改革开放不断深化，发展活力持续增强。一是政府机构改革、农村综合改革、投融资体制改革、文化体制改革、医药卫生体制改革等重点改革稳步推进，经济社会发展的体制和政策环境进一步改善。二是对外交流合作不断扩大。遵渝战略合作取得实质性进展，重庆楚米产业园初具规模、习水二郎电厂开工建设；与广东省、山东省及佛山市工商联、中建、中铁、保利、中电投、中石油、中石化等合作加强，与重庆大渡口、上海杨浦、江苏苏州等地结为友好城市，承接长三角、珠三角等地产业转移取得实效；招商引资和对外贸易工作取得新成绩，全年招商引资到位资金938亿元，增长246%；进出口总额2.53亿美元，增长29.4%。三是积极贯彻国家和省促进非公有制经济发展的政策措施，清理并取缔限制非公有制经济发展的政策，加大对中小企业的资金扶持，非公有制经济发展加快，占GDP的比重提高到47%。

茶海之心旅游景区——仙人岭
Tea sea the heart of tourist attractions - the Immortal Ridge

2011年乡村旅游节
2011 Rural Tourism Festival

The reform and opening up drive deepens, development activity has continued to improve. First, the reform of government institutions, the comprehensive rural reform, investment and financing system reform, cultural system reform, medical and health system reform and other key reform pushed steadily, to further improve the economic and social development of the institutional and policy environment. Second, expanding foreign exchanges and cooperation. Zunyi Chongqing strategic cooperation made substantial progress, in Chongqing Chumi industrial park beginning to take shape, Xishui Erlang power plant started construction; Guangdong Province, Shandong Province, and Foshan City Federation of Industry and Commerce, China construction, China iron, Paul Lee, CPI, the oil, the petrochemical strengthened cooperation such as Chongqing big crossing port, Shanghai Yangpu, Jiangsu Suzhou became sister cities, to undertake the industrial transfer of the Yangtze River Delta, Pearl River Delta to achieve tangible results; investment and foreign trade has made new achievements in the whole year investment capital in place 93.8 billion yuan, an increase of 246%; imports and exports totaled $ 253 million, an increase of 29.4%. Third, actively implement the national and provincial policies and measures to promote non-public economic development, clean up and banned to limit non-public economic development policy, increase funding support to SMEs, non-public economic development accelerated, the proportion of GDP increased to 47% .

安 顺 市

Anshun City

西秀石塔
Xixiu Stone Tower

安顺市位于贵州省中西部，距贵州省省会贵阳90公里，素有“黔之腹、滇之喉、粤蜀之唇齿”之称。面积9267平方公里，人口228万人，其中少数民族人口占全市总人口的39%。

文庙全景
Confucian Temple panorama

安顺文化底蕴深厚，是贵州历史上开发最早的区域，是贵州省历史文化名城，具有穿洞文化、夜郎文化、牂牁文化、屯堡文化、三国文化、攀岩文化、三线文化等独特的文化优势。普定穿洞古人类文化遗址被誉为“亚洲文明之灯”，中国古代八大神秘文字之一的关岭“红崖天书”世称千古之谜，明代军事遗存屯堡村落和关岭古生物化石群堪称世界唯一，安顺蜡染被誉为“东方第一染”，安顺地戏被称为“中国戏剧活化石”。安顺是我党老一辈无产阶级革命家、全国“100位为新中国成立做出突出贡献的英雄模范人物”王若飞同志的故乡，也是中国国民党中常委“谷氏三兄弟”谷正伦、谷正刚、谷正鼎的故地。

虹山湖
Hongshan Lake

光照电站大坝
Guangzhao Power Station Dam

开发区标准化厂房效果图
Development Zone, standardized plant renderings

Anshun City is located in the central and western regions of Guizhou Province, 90 kilometers from the provincial capital Guiyang in Guizhou Province, known as "abdomen of Guizhou, throat of Yunnan, and lip and tooth of Sichuan and Guangdong". Area of 9,267 square kilometers, population 2,280,000, of which the minority population accounts for 39% of the total population of the city.

Anshun owns rich cultural heritage, and Guizhou history of the earliest development of regional, historical and cultural city in Guizhou Province, has a unique cultural advantages of the Chuandong culture, Yelang culture, the culture of Yangke, the Tunbao culture, the Sanguo culture, rock climbing culture, three-line culture and so on. The Puding Chuandong ruins of ancient human culture known as "the light of civilization in Asia", one of eight Chinese ancient mystical text Guanling "Redcliffe bible", the Ming Dynasty military remains of the Tunbao villages and Guanling fossils group called the world's only, Anshun batik as the "Oriental first batik" Anshun Di drama is called "Chinese drama living fossil". Anshun is our party's older generation of proletarian revolutionaries, the National "100 for the new China was established to do the outstanding contributions to the hero exemplary character" Wang Ruofei comrade's homeland, China the Kuomintang in the Standing Committee of the "Gu three brothers" Gu Zhenglun, Gu Zhenggang, Gu Zhengding's old haunt.

平坝宝鑫公司
Pingba Bao Xin Company

普定明达水泥立窑厂厂区
Puding Mingda cement kiln plant factory

黄果树酒业公司
Huangguoshu Wine Corporation

安顺素有“中国瀑乡”、“屯堡文化之乡”、“蜡染之乡”、“西部之秀”的美誉。境内气候宜人，城市空气质量优良率达到100%，是国家最早确定的甲类旅游开放城市之一，是“中国优秀旅游城市”和贵州省优先发展重点旅游区及西线旅游中心。全市风景区面积占幅员面积的12％以上，远高于全国1%和贵州省4.2%的比例。境内有三个国家级风景区，其中世界著名的黄果树大瀑布和龙宫风景区为国家5A级旅游景区，还有格凸河国家级风景区、古生物化石群国家地质公园、九龙山国家森林公园，以及花江大峡谷、夜郎湖、斯拉河等省级风景名胜区。

安顺电厂全景

A panoramic view of the Anshun Power Plant

夏云工业园大门

Xiayun industrial park door

The Anshun is known as the "waterfall Township in China", the "Tunbao cultural village", and "batik village", " Westward beauty". The territory of a pleasant climate, excellent rate of 100% in the urban air quality, one of the first identified tourism open cities by the national CPI, "China Excellent Tourism City" and the priority development of major tourist areas in Guizhou Province and the tourist center of west line. The city's scenic area covers an area of 12%, far higher than the national ratio of 1% and 4.2% of Guizhou Province. There are three National Scenic Area, including the world-famous Huangguoshu Waterfall and Dragon Palace Scenic Area for the national 5A scenic spots, but also have the Getu River National Scenic Area, paleontological fossils National Geological Park, Jiulong Mountain National Forest Park, as well as Huajiang Grand Canyon, Yelang Lake, Sila River on provincial-level scenic spots.

夏云工业园新貌

Xiayun Industrial Park new look

Anshun has always had the first of the reform and opening up, is the birthplace of the contract responsibility system of "production quotas to the group", " Dingyun experience", known as "North FengYang, South Dingyun"; in 1988 when he was of the Guizhou Provincial secretary Comrade Hu Jintao personally guide created "deepening reform, to promote prosperity in various economic components to accelerate the development" reform test area; the "civil aviation industry, the national high-tech industrial base"; is a provincial committee, government to determine the "Guizhou to speed up development of special economic zones".

关岭水泥厂

Guanling cement plant

龙宫美景如画
Dragon Palace picturesque scenery

本寨石塔楼
Benzhai Stone tower

民用无人飞机
Civilian unmanned aircraft

安顺历来得改革开放之先，是“定产到组”联产承包责任制“顶云经验”的发源地，有“北凤阳、南顶云”之称；是1988年时任贵州省委书记胡锦涛同志亲自指导创建的“深化改革，促进多种经济成分共生繁荣，加快发展”改革试验区；是“民用航空产业国家高技术产业基地”；是省委、省政府确定的“贵州加快发展的经济特区”。

在新的历史起点上，安顺市委、市人民政府将带领全市各族人民“提速发展、奋力赶超”建设“实力安顺、宜居安顺、开发安顺、和谐安顺”，努力实现安顺经济社会发展的历史性跨越。

非物质文化遗产——安顺地戏
Intangible Cultural Heritage - Anshun Di Drama

王若飞故居陈列馆
Wang Ruofei former residence gallery

In the new historical starting point, Anshun City Committee, the Municipal People's Government will lead the city's people of all nationalities "accelerate the development, struggling to catch up with the development" building "the strength of Anshun, livable Anshun, developed Anshun, harmonious Anshun", make efforts to achieve the Anshun economic and social development of historic leap.

龙宫
Dragon Palace

天落湾
Tianluo Bay

天星桥
Tianxing Bridge

格凸河大穿洞
Getu river large holes

前进中的毕节试验区

Bijie Test Prefecture in advance

省委书记栗战书视察金沙工业园区
Provincial Party Committee Secretary Li Zhanshu visited the Jinsha Industrial Park

2011年，毕节市各族人民紧紧围绕“加速发展、加快转型、推动跨越”的主基调和“工业化、城镇化”带动主战略，紧扣“推动改革发展双领先、实现试验区新跨越”的主旋律，全面推进社会经济有序、和谐、可持续发展。

区域综合经济实力进一步增强，经济运行质量不断提高。全市生产总值737.41亿元，同比增长16.8%。财政总收入181.66亿元，同比增长42.40%；其中财政一般预算收入80.76亿元，同比增长30%。全社会固定资产投资830.9亿元，同比增长83.9%。

三次产业协调发展，产业结构进一步优化。全市以稳定优化第一产业、壮大提升第二产业、加快发展第三产业为着力点，推进工业、农业和服务业协调发展，在做大经济总量中调整结构、促进发展方式转变。大力实施“3321”工程、“三万农业示范工程”，规划建设“十带百园”农业示范基地和标准化养殖场基地，提高了特色农业产业化、标准化、集约化经营水平。继续实施“工业强区战略”，煤炭、电力、“两烟”、装备制造、建材、白酒、化工、食品、冶金和轻纺等产业多元协调发展。2011年工业增加值295.60亿元，同比增长23.6%，工业增加值占生产总值的比重从上年的37.7%上升到40.1%。加快发展以旅游业为龙头的现代服务业，打响了“洞天湖地、花海鹤乡、避暑天堂”旅游品牌。旅游总收入153.54亿元，同比增长51.87%。社会消费品零售总额150.4亿元，同比增长19.3%。服务业在三次产业中的比重达到35.4%。三次产业结构比为18.2∶46.4∶35.4。

建设中毕节市威宁新城区
The construction of the Bijie City Weining new city district

毕节力帆时骏振兴集团载重汽车生产基地大门

The Bijie Lifan Shijun Zhnexing revitalization Group truck production base door

毕节市金沙工业园区电子城生产场景

Bijie City Jinsha Industrial Park, Electronic City production scene

In 2011, A new leap forward , Bijie people of all ethnic groups closely around the "accelerate the development, accelerate the transition, promote leapfrog" the main tone and "industrialization, urbanization" driven the main strategy, closely linked to "promote the reform and development leading pairs, to achieve the test area" the main theme, and comprehensively promote the socio-economic order, harmony, and sustainable development.

Regional comprehensive economic strength has been further enhanced, to continuously improve the quality of economic operation. The city's GDP was 73.741 billion yuan, an increase of 16.8%. Total fiscal revenue of 18.166 billion yuan, an increase of 42.40%; the general budgetary revenue of 8.076 billion yuan, an increase of 30%. The total fixed asset investment of 83.09 billion yuan, an increase of 83.9%.

Three industries got coordinated development, the industrial structure was further optimized. The city optimizing the first industry to stabilize, grow and improve the second industry, accelerate the development of the third industry as a focal point, promote the coordinated development of industry, agriculture and service industries, in the bigger development of the total economy, to have structural adjustment, promote the transformation of development mode. Vigorously implement the "3321" project, "30,000 agricultural demonstration project", the planning and construction of "ten drive the one hundred Park" agricultural demonstration base and standardized breeding farm base, improve the characteristic agricultural industrialization, standardization, intensive management level. Continue to implement the multi-coordinated development of the "Industrial Strong Area Strategy", coal, electricity, the "two smoke", equipment manufacturing, building materials, liquor, chemicals, food, metallurgy and textile and other industries. In 2011, industrial added value 29.56 billion yuan, an increase of 23.6%, the industrial added value of GDP increased from 37.7% last year rose to 40.1%. Accelerate the development of tourism as the leading modern service industry, started the "cave heaven lake place, flowers sea crane township, summer paradise" tourism brand. The total tourism income of 15.354 billion yuan, an increase of 51.87%. 15.04 billion yuan of total retail sales of social consumer goods, an increase of 19.3%. Services in three industries, the proportion reached 35.4%. Three industrial structure to 18.2:46.4:35.4.

毕节市黔西县城新貌
The Bijie Qianxi county new look

大力实施“十大民生工程”，社会事业取得全面进步。全市大力实施扶贫脱贫攻坚、就业和创业、劳动者素质提升、城乡社会保障体系建设、“一危三棚”改造和保障性住房建设、基础设施向县乡延伸、农村生活环境改善、公共文化服务体系建设、公共卫生事业建设、社会管理创新和平安创建等“十大民生工程”。城乡低保覆盖率达100%。转移农村劳动力120万人，城镇新增就业8万人，新型农村合作医疗参合率达98.9%，城镇居民基本医疗保险参保率为99%，建立各类医疗卫生机构634个，基本形成覆盖城乡的公共卫生和医疗服务体系。人口自然增长率下降到6.01‰。教育“两基”通过“国检”，学前教育三年毛入园（班）率达43.93%，高中阶段教育毛入学率达56.2%，人均受教育年限达到6.8年。城镇居民人均可支配收入16132元，扣除价格因素，同比增长11.5%，农民人均纯收入4210元，扣除价格因素，同比增长19.6%。

切实保护生态环境，着力构建“两型”社会。认真做好生态保护和修复工作，继续实施石漠化防治、退耕还林、湿地恢复保护、中小河流治理和“三江源”保护等工程，治理石漠化面积170平方公里，治理水土流失面积206.5平方公里，营造林85万亩，森林覆盖率达41.5%。抓好重点污染源治理，强化对煤炭采选、金属矿采选、建材等重点行业的污染治理。积极转变资源开发利用方式，加强重点节能减排工程建设，确保各县市污水处理厂、垃圾填埋场正常运行，规划建设一批重点集镇、工矿区、旅游景区污水、垃圾处理设施，完成落后产能淘汰工作，大力发展农村沼气池，积极推广农村节能节材灶和秸杆气化灶，推进资源节约型、环境友好型社会建设。

碧阳大桥夜景
Bi Yang Bridge Night

织金小区建设
The Zhijin residential is being built

2012年4月23日，旅游发展大会在百里杜鹃召开
April 23, 2012, the Tourism Development Conference held in Baili Rhododendron

Vigorously implement the "Ten livelihood projects", the social undertakings has made progress. The city vigorously took the implementation of poverty alleviation and tackling poverty, employment and entrepreneurship, workers enhance the quality, urban and rural social security system construction, the transformation of "one risk and three shed" construction of affordable housing, infrastructure extension to counties and townships, rural living environment improvement, the construction of the public cultural services system, the construction of the cause of public health, social management innovation and to build peace "Ten livelihood projects". Urban and rural low insurance coverage rate up to 100%. Transfer of rural labor force 1.2 million people, 80,000 new urban jobs, the new rural cooperative medical participation rate of 98.9%, 99% of urban residents basic medical insurance, the establishment of 634 health care institutions of all kinds, the basic form that covers both urban and rural areas public health and medical services system. The natural population growth rate dropped to 6.01 ‰. Education "two basics" "CIQ", pre-school years gross admission rate of 43.93% (class), high school education gross enrollment rate of 56.2%, per capita years of schooling up to 6.8 years. The per capita disposable income of urban residents was 16,132 yuan, after deducting price factors, an increase of 11.5%, and rural per capita net income of 4,210 yuan, after deducting price factors, an increase of 19.6%.

Effectively protect the ecological environment, focused on building a "two-oriented" society. Do a good job of ecological conservation and restoration work, the continued implementation of rocky desertification prevention and control, the project of returning farmland to forests, protection of wetland restoration, medium and small rivers and the "Sanjiangyuan" protection and so on, governance rocky desertification area of 170 km2, water and soil erosion area of 206.5 square kilometers, 850,000 mu of afforestation, the forest coverage rate reached 41.5%. The county will focus on pollution sources, and strengthen the key industries of coal mining, metal mining, building materials pollution control. Positive change in the development and utilization of resources, to strengthen the important energy conservation construction projects, to ensure that county and municipal sewage treatment plant, landfill normal operation, planning and construction of a number of key market towns, industrial and mining areas, tourist attractions sewage, solid waste disposal facilities to complete the backward production capacity out of work, vigorously develop rural biogas digesters, and actively promote rural energy and wood stoves and straw gasification stove, promote resource-conserving, environment-friendly society.

建设中的威宁县百草坪风电场
Weining County in the construction of Baicaoping wind-power farm

黔东南州城乡规划局

Qiandongnan Urban and Rural Planning Bureau

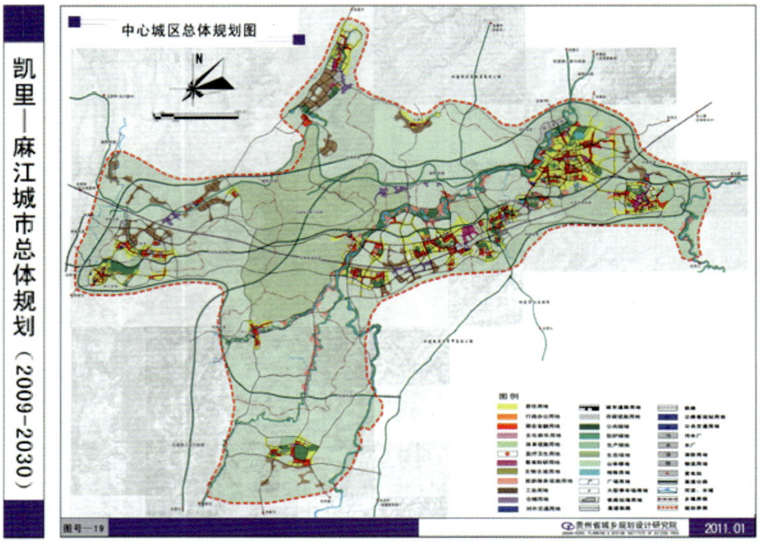

中心城区总体规划图
Center City overall plan map

跨行政区域编制凯麻城市总体规划。全州首次组织编制跨行政区域的《凯里-麻江城市总体规划（2009-2030年）》经省政府审批实施。在凯麻总规基础上，启动了包括凯里麻江城市总体规划区凯麻新区分区规划、重点建设片区控制性详细规划和沪昆客专凯里南站片区城市设计等3个重要规划编制，并于2011年底全部完成。

组建了黔东南州城乡规划局，作为州人民政府工作部门主管全州城乡规划编制管理工作。

炉碧经济开发区规划建设引来大型企业落户。根据凯里-麻江城市总体规划和炉碧经济开发区180平方公里总体规划的要求，完成了园区核心区24平方公里控制性详细规划、园区产业发展规划、园区土地利用规划、园区产业发展规划、环境评价报告。截止2011年底，园区共落户企业50户，协议总投资达450亿元以上，招商引资项目的到位资金49.1亿元。

Cross-administrative regions of the preparation of the overall urban planning of Kai Ma. The whole state first to organize the formulation of administrative regions "Kaili- Ma Jiang's overall urban planning (2009 - 2030)" approved by the provincial government implementation. On the basis of Kai Ma regulation, the start including Kaili Ma Jiang city overall planning of Kai Ma New Area district planning, controlled detailed planning of key construction projects Area and the Shanghai-Kunming passenger specifically Kaili Southern Station Area Urban design and other 3 important planning, and completed by the end of 2011.

The formation of the Qiandongnan urban and rural planning bureau, as the state people government work of the department in charge of statewide urban and rural planning and the preparation of management.

The Lubi Economic Development Zone the planning and construction lead to large enterprises have settled down. According to the Kaili-Ma Jiang overall urban planning and Lubi Economic Development Zone, 180 square kilometers of the overall planning requirements, the regulatory detailed planning of the park core area of 24 square kilometers, the park industry development plan, the park land-use planning, industrial development zone planning, environmental assessment report. By the end of 2011, the park settled a total of 50 enterprises, agreement total investment of more than 45 billion yuan, 4.91 billion yuan of investment projects of the capital in place.

已建成的贵州其亚铝业有限公司
Guizhou Qiya Aluminum Co., Ltd. has been built

黔东南州发展和改革委员会

Qiandongnan State Development and Reform Commission

丹寨金钟经济开发区落户企业厂房建设
Danzhai Jinzhong Economic Development Zone located in the corporate plant construction

2011年，黔东南州发展和改革委员会以"高水平谋划发展、高质量促进发展、高效率服务发展"为主线，以"敢于策划项目、善于研究政策、舍得前期投入"为动力，紧扣发展大局，创新方法举措，深化协调服务，优化工作质量，有力地促进了全州经济社会又好又快、更好更快发展。

一是加强经济运行调节调度和预测预警工作。二是认真编制全州年度国民经济和社会发展计划和积极推进中长期规划编制工作。三是加强固定资产投资和重点项目工作力度。四是认真开展了节能降耗、抗旱救灾、以交通水利等为重点的基础设施建设、物价管理、重大项目稽查等专项工作。五是积极争取项目资金。2011年，争取到国家和省级资金支持各类项目1269个，累计获得国家和省补助资金18亿元。

In 2011, Qiandongnan State Development and Reform Commission to "high-level plan for the development, high quality to promote the development, efficient services to the development" the main line, "Dare to planning projects, good at research policy, willing initial investment" as the driving force, closely linked to the development of measure of the overall situation and innovative approaches, deepen coordination services, optimize the quality of work, and to promote statewide economic and social good and fast, better and faster development.

First, the improved economic regulation and the work of the scheduling and forecasting warning. Second, seriously the preparation of the statewide annual national economic and social development plans and to actively promote medium-and long-term planning work. Third, efforts to strengthen the investment in fixed assets and key projects. Fourth, conscientiously carry out energy-saving, drought relief, special transportation, water conservation, such as the key infrastructure construction, price management, major project audit work. Fifth, actively seek project funding. In 2011, to win the national and provincial funds to support 1,269 various projects, the cumulative national and provincial grant funding of 1.8 billion yuan.

丹寨县金钟经济开发区机械装备制造科技园厂房紧张施工
Danzhai County Jinzhong Economic Development Zone machinery and equipment manufacturing plant tense construction of the science park

黔东南州交通运输局

Qiandongnan Transportation Bureau

黔东南州交通运输局局长吴汉碧一行在旅游公路施工现场检查指导工作
Director of Qiandongnan Transportation Bureau Wu Hanbi and his party to inspect and guide the work in the tourist highway construction site

黔东南州交通运输系统积极抢抓国家新一轮西部大开发和“交通优先发展”的战略机遇，紧紧围绕交通发展主题，突出重点、统筹兼顾、协调发展。2011年，全州完成交通固定资产投资124.19亿元，建设旅游公路702公里，建成通乡油路172公里，完成通村公路1123公里，完成乡镇客运站9个、乡镇渡口码头45个。2011年底，全州公路总里程达26512公里，全州基本实现乡乡通油路、村村通公路目标。

着力加强行业管理，推进公路养护责任目标管理，加强农村公路养护、路政管理，治理超限运输，保护路产路权。加强交通运输管理，交通运输秩序进一步规范。积极探索创新公交管理模式，推行国有公车公营，引导各县市优先发展城市公交。认真开展交通安全生产工作，落实安全管理责任制，加强监管，排除安全隐患。

组织干部职工到凯里监狱接受警示教育
The staff and workers to Kaili to accept the warning education in prison

吴汉碧局长在公路建设第一线检查指导工作
Wu Hanbi director to inspect and guide the work in the first line of the highway construction

2011年9月，帮扶八开引山泉水进寨
September 2011, helping Bakai quoted mountain spring water into the village

The Qiandongnan transportation system actively seize the strategic opportunities of the country's new round of western development and the "traffic priority development" strategy, closely focus on the transportation theme of development, focused the keys, balanced and coordinated development. In 2011, the statewide transportation investment in fixed assets 12.419 billion yuan, the construction of 702 km, of tourist roads, built through the township oil 172 km to complete the 1,123 km of village road, the township bus terminal 9, 45 township ferry pier. By the end of 2011, the statewide total mileage of 26,512 km, the whole state basic realization of the townships oil, every village access roads goal.

Efforts to strengthen the management of industry, to promote the responsibility of road maintenance management by objectives, and to strengthen the rural road maintenance, road administration, governance load transportation to protect the road property right of way. Strengthen transport management, transport order to further standardize. Actively explore innovative traffic management model, the implementation of public, state-owned bus, guide cities and counties to give priority to the development of urban public transport. Earnestly carry out the production work of the traffic safety, the implementation of safety management responsibility system, strengthen supervision, and to exclude security risks.

黔东南州林业局

Qiandongnan Forestry Administration

2011年8月1日，贵州省黔东南州林业科技奖励签约仪式

August 1, 2011, Guizhou Province, Qiandongnan Forestry Science and Technology Award signing ceremony

2011年，全州林业系统按照“保生态、增资源、调结构、强产业、惠林农”的总体要求，开拓创新、真抓实干，实现林业总产值73.8亿元，同比增长37.2%，实现了“十二五”良好开局。

投入不断加大，2011年全州林业总投入达5.72亿元，总投资比2010年增长27.3%。重点工程顺利实施。特色产业基地培育取得实质进展，为林业的持续、高效发展夯实了基础。低产林改造加快推进。林产工业加速发展，2011年全州规模以上林产工业企业达到33户，占全州规模以上工业企业数的20%，年加工能力达80万立方米。抓好公益林区划界定和生态效益补偿资金兑现。加强林业执法力度。切实简政放权，2011年已将林木采伐许可证等6项行政审批下放到县（市）办理。

2011年11月3日，全州蓝莓产业发展推进会在凯里召开

November 3, 2011, the state blueberry industry promoting development meeting was held in Kaili

In 2011, the statewide forestry system in accordance with the overall requirements of the "ecological security, increasing resources, adjust the structure, strong industry, benefit forest farmers", pioneering and innovative, solid work, forestry output value 7.38 billion yuan, an increase of 37.2%, to achieve a good start of "12th Five-Year".

Increasing investment, in 2011, the statewide forestry total investment of 572 million yuan, total investment of 27.3% growth over 2010. The smooth implementation of key projects. Characteristic industry base cultivation real progress, for the sustainable and efficient development of forestry to lay a solid foundation. The transformation of low-yield forest is accelerating. The forest products industry to accelerate the development, in 2011 the statewide forestry industrial enterprises above designated size reached 33, the total state 20% of industrial enterprises above designated size, the processing capacity of 800,000 cubic meters. Defined forest division and the ecological benefit compensation fund to honor a good job. Strengthen forest law enforcement. Effective decentralization, in 2011, the tree cutting licenses and other 6 administrative examination and approval have set to the county (city) on the handle.

剑河县天保工程封山育林区

Jianhe County Tianbao Project closing mountain for forest protection district

黔东南州商务局

Qiandongnan Commerce Bureau

省商务厅市场体系建设处领导检查该州家电下乡推广工作

Commerce Department of Market System Development Department leadership to check the state of home appliances to the countryside promote work

消费规模持续扩大。2011年，全州社会消费品零售总额完成144.8亿元，同比增长19.8%。

对外贸易快速增长。2011年，全州外贸进出口总额4041万美元，同比增长366.5%，进出口增幅居全省第一。

利用外资创历史新高。2011年，新批外商投资企业6家，合同利用外资1.94亿美元，同比增长65.6%。

“家电下乡”工作有力推进。2011年，全州下乡产品销售28.3万台，销售金额6.01亿元，较上年增长63.6%，“家电下乡”工作荣获全省一等奖。

加快市场体系建设。2011年“万村千乡市场工程”农家店建设改造项目500个，完成和在建农贸市场41个。

黔东南州国际投资贸易推介会取得成功。邀请了来自23个国家和地区的多方代表签订了多项合作备忘录、合作框架协议、投资意向协议书。

口岸规划建设工作逐步推进。麻江、黎平机场已纳入全省无水港规划，黔东、洛贯、三穗等区域的无水港前期工作也在积极推进。

正在建设和规划中的麻江无水港

Under construction and planning Majiang dry port

剑河县革东镇“万村千乡”农家店商品展示区

Jianhe County Ge Dong town "Ten Thousand Villages" farm shop product

Consumption continues to grow. In 2011, statewide retail sales of social consumer goods total value of 14.48 billion yuan, an increase of 19.8%.

The rapid growth of foreign trade. In 2011, the statewide total foreign trade volume of $ 40,410,000, an increase of 366.5%, import and export increase ranking first in the province.

Utilization of foreign investment to a record high. In 2011, newly approved 6 foreign-invested enterprises, contracted foreign investment of $ 194 million, an increase of 65.6%.

"Home appliances to the countryside" work force advancing. In 2011, the statewide countryside products to sell 283,000 units, the sales amount of 601 million yuan, up 63.6% over the previous year, won the province's first prize in the "Home appliances to the countryside".

Accelerate the market system construction. In 2011 "Ten Thousand Villages Marketing Project" 500 farm shop construction and renovation projects, completed and under construction in 41 farmers' markets.

The Qiandongnan International Investment and Trade Promotion will won success. Invited from 23 countries and regions, multi-party agreement signed by a number of memoranda of cooperation, cooperation framework agreement, investment agreement of intent.

Port planning and construction of a gradual manner. Ma Jiang, Liping airport have been incorporated into the province anhydrous Hong Kong Planning, eastern Guizhou, Luo Guan, Sansui and other regional dry port preliminary work is also actively promoting.

黔东南州住房和城乡建设局

Qiandongnan Housing and Urban-Rural Construction Bureau

在金泉湖山顶鸟瞰的凯里城市建设风貌
Bird's eye view of the Kaili city construction style in the Jinquan Lake Peak

竣工通车后的凯里市宁波东路延伸段
Kaili City, Ningbo East Road, extension segment is completed and opened to traffic

住房建设。2011年，全州农村危房改造竣工并入住113734户，完成投资27亿元；保障性住房完成投资11.11亿元，其中：新建廉租住房10238套，房地产开发新建商品房销售面积205.79 万平方米，完成投资51.4亿元。

城镇建设。2011年，全州整体城镇化率为28.2%；基础设施建设完成固定资产投资82.14亿元，新、改、扩建城市道路308公里，供水管网铺设73.4公里，新建垃圾中转站21座。

建筑市场监管。2011年，完成勘察设计合同登记项目925个，施工图审查项目408个，共251.44万平方米；审查登记建筑节能项目408个，共236.96万平方米；完成建设工程发包366个项目。

“村落花园化、人居环境舒适化”的新农村建设示范旅游村——台江县台拱镇红阳大寨村庄整治后的情景
"The village garden, living environment comfortable" the new rural construction model tourist village - Taijiang County Taigong Town Hongyangdazhai village scene after remediation

整治后的台江县交宫村庄
After remediation Taijiang County Jiaogong Village

Housing construction. In 2011, the statewide rural dangerous buidings transformation completed and stay at 113,734, completed an investment of 2.7 billion yuan; affordable housing completed an investment of 1.111 billion yuan, which: 10,238 sets of new low-rent housing, real estate development and new housing sales area of 2.0579 million square meters, complete investment of 5.14 billion yuan.

Towns construction. In 2011, the statewide overall urbanization rate of 8.2%; infrastructure construction investment in fixed assets of 8.214 billion yuan, new, revision, extension of 308 km of urban roads, water supply pipe network of 73.4 kilometers, the new solid waste transfer station 21.

Supervision of the construction market. In 2011, to complete the survey and design contracts registration of 925, the construction drawing review project 408, a total of 2.5144 million square meters; review of 408 registered building energy efficiency projects, a total of 2.3696 million square meters; completed construction works contract 366.

黔南州

Qiannan State

省委书记栗战书莅临永红考察指导工作
Provincial Party Secretary Li Zhanshu come to Yonghong examine to guide work

近年来，黔南工业经济在省委、省政府和州委、州政府的正确领导下，大力实施“工业化、城镇化、农业产业化”带动战略，积极探索符合黔南州情的新型工业化发展道路，迎难而上，奋力拼搏，千方百计促生产，全力以赴保增长，努力克服各种自然灾害和要素偏紧等因素影响，改革创新、开拓进取、扎实工作，以强化经济运行调度为重点、以加快项目和园区建设为载体、以培育工业重点产业为手段、以繁荣民营经济和中小企业为动力，着力抓好科技创新、节能减排、淘汰落后、两化融合等各项重点工作，全力推进全州工业经济平稳较快增长。通过围绕优势资源开发，加快工业结构调整，培育和发展特色优势产业，工业总体规模迅速壮大。过去五年，全州工业经济提速增效。建设17个产业园区，其中国家级1个、省级4个，入园企业494户，建设投产345户，实现产值328亿元。扶持磷化工、烟草、特色食品等产业发展壮大，规定卷烟厂、瓮福集团、川恒化工、永红食品等企业成为财源建设骨干企业，规模以上企业320户，产值过亿的

省长赵克志莅临永红考察指导工作
Provincial Governor Zhao Kezhi to visit Yonghong to have inspection and guidance

领导和嘉宾为项目开工剪彩
Leaders and guests cut the ribbon for the project started

In recent years, under the correct leadership of the provincial committee, government and state committee, state government, the Qiannan industrial economy vigorously implement the "industrialization, urbanization, agricultural industrialization" driven strategy, and actively explore the development of new-type industrialization Qiannan loveroad, rose to the challenge, worked hard, and do everything possible to promote production, go all out to maintain growth, efforts to overcome a variety of natural disasters and the elements of tight factors, reform and innovation, pioneering spirit, solid work, in order to strengthen the economic operation scheduling focus to speed up the project and construction of the park as the carrier, to train the industrial key industries as a means to the prosperity of the private economy and small and medium-sized enterprises, focus their efforts on scientific and technological

"工业园区开发建设与管理"专题讲座
"Industrial park development and construction management" seminar

中国建材惠水泰安联合重组协议签字仪式
China Building Materials Huishui Taian joint reorganization agreement signing ceremony

奠基
Lay foundation

97户。开工建设2×60万千瓦福泉电厂；启动惠水龙塘山、龙里草原风力发电项目建设；建成双河口、团坡等一批水电站，新增水电装机33.98万千瓦。全州17家小额贷款公司注册资金3.3亿元，9家担保公司注册资金2.25亿元，为中小企业解决贷款近10亿元。信邦制药上市融资7.1亿元。依法关闭172家污染企业，单位生产总值能耗下降20.2%，有力地促进了全州国民经济持续快速健康发展。

贵州天虹志远电线电缆有限公司
Guizhou Tianhong Zhiyuan Electric Wire & Cable Co., Ltd.

宏福总公司生产厂区
Hongfu Corporation production factory

innovation, energy conservation, elimination of backward, integration of the two important points, efforts to promote the statewide industry stable and rapid economic growth. Around the advantages of resource development, to speed up the adjustment of industrial structure, nurture and develop industries with local advantages, the industry overall size is growing rapidly. Over the past five years, the industrial economy of the statewide speed efficiency. Construction of 17 industrial parks, national 1, provincial 4, 494 enterprises in the park, put in operation 345, the output value of 32.8 billion yuan. To support the industrial development and expansion of the phosphorus chemical, tobacco, specialty foods and other, Guiding Cigarette Factory, Wengfu Group, Chuanheng Chemical, Yonghong food enterprises to become the financial resources building backbone enterprises, 320 enterprises above designated size, 97 enterprises the value of billions yuan. Start the construction of 2 × 600,000 kilowatts of Fuquan Power Plant; start Huishui Longtang Hill, Longli the prairie wind power project construction; built Shuanghekou, Tuanpo on a number of hydropower station, to new hydropower installed capacity of 339,800 kilowatts. The statewide 17 small loan companies registered capital of 330 million yuan, 9 guarantee company registered capital of 225 million yuan, to solve nearly 1 billion loan for small and medium-sized enterprises. The Xinbang Pharmaceuticals listing and financing of 710 million yuan. 172 polluting enterprises to close down by law, the unit GDP energy consumption fell by 20.2%, and vigorously promote the sustained, rapid and healthy development of the statewide.

贵州永红食品有限公司新厂区外景
Guizhou Yonghong Food Co., Ltd. new factory location

“185农业产业化工程”是中共黔南州委、州政府在学习实践科学发展观、加快经济发展方式转变活动中，针对黔南农业和农村存在的突出矛盾和问题，按照“三实三创”的要求，提出的一项富民强农的重大工程。其主要内涵是：坚持以国家新一轮西部大开发和产业化扶贫为契机，以市场为导向，以科技为支撑，以体制创新为动力，以提高农民组织化程度、促进土地有序流转和龙头企业带动为突破口，实行区域化布局、标准化生产、规模化经营、产业化发展，按照一年多熟制，种养加配套等立体高效农业生产模式，形成特色优势产业下田、上山、入水、升空等生产的新格局，不断提高土地、林地、水面、棚架等生产载体的产出率和经济效益，在一个农业生产年度内，使单位面积亩产值达到一万元、八千元、五千元以上。它是一种货币量化的种养模式，是一种产供销一条龙的经营方式，是思路，是理念，是方向，是发展特色高效生态农业的优选路径，是黔南农业“加速发展、加快转型、推动跨越”的有力抓手，对促进农业结构优化调整、农民收入稳步增加、农业产业化扎实推进、农村经济健康发展意义重大。

福泉黄丝江边现代农业基地全景
Fuquan Huangsi riverside modern agricultural base panorama

罗甸龙滩水库红星水产养殖基地
The Luodian Longtan Reservoir Hongxing aquaculture base

福泉喷灌设施
Fuquan irrigation facilities

福泉新合养殖合作社，年产鸭蛋237万枚，年产值197万元
Fuquan new contract farming cooperatives, with an annual duck egg production 2,370,000, the annual output value of 1.97 million yuan

西红柿标准化生产技术
Tomatoes standardized production technology

惠水县涟江大坝生姜基地
Huishui County Lianjiang dam ginger base

波尔山羊
Boer goats

"185 agriculture industrialization project" is the CPC Qiannan Committee, the state government in the study and practice the scientific concept of development, to speed up the economic development mode transformation event, Qiannan agriculture and rural areas exsiting the prominent contradictions and problems, according to the "three real three creat" requirements, propose a wealthy and strong agricultural major projects. Its main connotations: adhere to the country's new round of large-scale development of the western region and the industrialization of poverty alleviation as an opportunity, to market-oriented, technology support, and institutional innovation as a driving force, to improve the organization of farmers, promote land orderly transfer of leading enterprises as a breakthrough, the implementation of the layout of the area, standardization of production and operation of large-scale industrial development, in accordance with the multiple cropping system, supporting three-dimensional cultivation, breeding and efficient agricultural production mode, forming characteristics and advantages of the industrial fields, the mountains, into the water, took off production of new mode, and constantly improve the land, forest land, water surface, scaffolding and other production yields and economic benefits of the carrier, in a year of agricultural production, the per unit area yield values reaches 18,000, 8,000, 5,000 yuan or more. It is a currency quantify the breeding mode, the mode of operation of a production for the marketing of such products, ideas, philosophy, direction and development of specialized and efficient ecological

独山打羊乡草地养羊
The Dushan Dayang Township grass sheep

福泉市林下散养金谷鸡
The Fuquan city understory backyard Jingu chicken

绵羊
Sheeps

五万亩西红柿基地
50,000 mu tomato base

大棚育苗
Greenhouse nursery

蔬菜设施保护栽培
Protected cultivation of vegetables Facilities

精细蔬菜移植小苗长势喜人
The fine vegetable transplant seedlings gratifying

“185农业产业化工程”的建设实施，有力促进了黔南工业与农业、城市与乡村有机结合，使农户、企业、市场紧密联系在一起，使农村劳动力合理流动和转移，提高了农村劳动力资源的开发与利用，与省委提出的工业强省战略、城镇化带动战略一脉相承、有机衔接。预计到2015年，全州“185农业产业化工程”建设达300万亩以上，力争培育国家级龙头企业5家，省级龙头企业60家，州级龙头企业200家。

鲜用椒亩产达3000公斤以上
Fresh with pepper production up to 3,000 kg per mu

独山牟尼河茶场
Dushan Muni River tea plantation

agriculture preferred path, Qiannan Agriculture "accelerate the development, accelerate the transition, to promote across leapfrog" a powerful starting point, adjustment of promoting agricultural structure optimization, a steady increase in farmers' income, and push forward the industrialization of agriculture, and the healthy development of the rural economy is significant.

Construction and implementation of the "185 agriculture industrialization project", a strong impetus to the of Qiannan industry and agriculture, urban and rural organic combination, farmers, enterprises, markets are closely linked to the rational flow and transfer of rural labor, rural labor development and utilization of resources, the industrial province with the provincial strategy, the urbanization strategy spearheaded by the same strain, organic convergence.Expected to 2015, statewide "185 agriculture industrialization project" construction of 3 million mu, and strive to cultivate a national leading enterprises 5, 60 leading enterprises at the provincial level, the state 200 leading enterprises.

三都县水晶葡萄
Sandu County Crystal grapes

独山县基长拉董2000亩淮山药种植基地
Dushan County Jizhang Ladong 2,000 mu of yam and medicine planting base

六盘水市

Liupanshui City

市委书记王晓光在老鹰山煤化工基地调研

Party secretary, Wang Xiaoguang has research in Eagle Mountain coal chemical base

何刚市长参加全市领导干部统计知识培训班

He Gang mayor ia jionning into the city's leading cadres of statistical knowledge training courses

六盘水市位于贵州省西部，1978年经国务院批准正式建市，是以能源原材料为主要产业的重工业城市。面积9915平方公里，辖六枝特区、盘县、水城县和钟山区4个县级行政区，98个乡、镇、办事处，人口321万。

2011年，全市生产总值完成613.39亿元，同比增长16.6%；财政总收入和一般预算收入分别完成128.46亿元和70.84亿元，同比增长20.7%和43.7%；全社会固定资产投资完成550.63亿元，同比增长64.1%；社会消费品零售总额157.61亿元，同比增长20.0%；城镇居民可支配收入16370.89元，比上年增长17.6%。农民人均纯收入4437.38元，比上年增长23.2%。

六盘水资源富集，矿产资源十分丰富。有煤、铁、铅、锌、铜、银、金等30多种矿产资源。其中煤炭资源远景储量844亿吨，已探明储量174亿吨，煤种全、煤质好、易开采，因此六盘水素有“江南煤都”、“江南煤海”之称。市内有水城钢铁（集团）公司、盘江煤电（集团）公司、水城矿业（集团）公司、六枝工矿（集团）公司、水城水泥股份公司、盘县发电厂、盘南发电厂、野马寨发电厂等骨干企业，煤炭、电力、冶金、建材、机械制造是全市的经济支柱。2009年9月，《国务院办公厅关于应对国际金融危机保持西部地区经济平稳较快发展的意见》（国办发〔2009〕55号）将六盘水市列为资源富集区开展循环经济区试点。

六盘水气候宜人。冬无严寒、夏无酷暑，是消夏避暑的胜地。2005年8月，中国气象学会向六盘水市政府颁发了“中国凉都•六盘水”证书。

六盘水风光旖旎，旅游资源丰富，民族文化丰富多彩，南、北盘江流域两岸、八担山片区孕育着苗、彝、布依等少数民族丰富多彩的民族风情和民间文化。境内有国家级森林公园1个，国家级地质公园 1 个，在建省级森林公园3个，国家重点文物保护单位 1 个，省级风景名胜区 5 个，省级重点文物保护单位 6 个，全国工业旅游示范点1个，全国农业旅游示范点2个。

六盘水区位优势明显，位于川、滇、黔、桂结合区域中部，是“攀西——六盘水资源综合开发区”的重要组成部分，境内有贵昆铁路、内昆铁路、水柏铁路、株六复线、盘西铁路、六盘水南编组站，六沾复线正在建设。以水黄高等级公路、GZ65号国道主干线、水盘公路、盘百公路为主干，县乡村三级公路纵横交错的公路网络已经形成，六盘水市在西南地区重要的交通枢纽地位将更加凸显。

玉舍森林公园——森林晨曦
Yushe Forest Park - Forest Dawn

保基陆家寨民族风光
Baoji Luojiazhai national scenery

北盘江大峡谷
Beipanjiang Grand Canyon

Liupanshui City is located in the western part of Guizhou Province, approved by the State Council in 1978 to build the city, the city of heavy industry based on energy and raw materials for major industries. Area of 9,915 square kilometers, jurisdiction Liuzhi Special Zone, Panxian, Shuicheng County and Zhongshan District, four county-level administrative regions, 98 townships, towns, offices and a population of 3.21 million.

In 2011, the GDP of 61.339 billion yuan, up 16.6%; total fiscal revenues and general budget revenue, respectively, completed 12.846 billion yuan and 7.084 billion yuan, an increase of 20.7% and 43.7%; the whole society fixed assets investment of 55.063 billion yuan, up 64.1%; total retail sales of 15.761 billion yuan, an increase of 20.0%; urban residents' disposable income of 16,370.89 yuan, up 17.6% compared with the previous year. Rural per capita net income was 4,437.38 yuan, up 23.2% over the previous year.

Liupanshui resource-rich, very rich in mineral resources. Coal, iron, lead, zinc, copper, silver, gold over 30 kinds of mineral resources. Coal resources, prospective reserves of 84.4 billion tons of proven reserves of 17.4 billion tons, full type of coal, excellent coal quality, easy to exploit, so Liupanshui known as "Jiangnan coal capital", "Jiangnan coal sea". The city owns Shuicheng Iron and Steel (Group) Company, Panjiang Coal Power (Group) Company, Shuicheng Mining (Group) Company, Liuzhi Mining (Group) Company, Shuicheng Cement Joint Stock Company, Panxian power plants, Pannan power plants, Yemazhai power plants ect backbone enterprises, coal, electricity, metallurgy, building materials, machinery manufacturing, is the city's economic pillars. In September 2009, "the State Council on the international financial crisis and to maintain the western region stable and rapid economic development views"(State Office Issued [2009] No. 55) took Liupanshui City as a resource-rich region to carry out pilot recycling economy zone.

保基风光
Baoji landscape

峰岩石林一景
Peak rock stone forest scence

The Liupanshui owns climate pleasant. No cold winter, no hot summer, is the summer resort of Summer, in August 2005, the Chinese Meteorological Society issued the "China cool Capital •Liupanshui" certificate to Liupanshui municipal government.

Liupanshui has beautiful scenery and rich tourism resources, rich and colorful ethnic culture, North and South Panjiang basin on both sides, Badan Hill Area gave birth to the rich and colorful ethnic customs and folk culture of the Miao, Yi, Buyi minority. The territory of a national forest park, a national geological park, under construction in the three provincial forest park, a national key cultural relics protection units, and five provincial-level scenic spots, 6 provincial key cultural relic protection units, 1 the National industrial tourism demonstration sites, 2 national agricultural tourism demonstration sites.

步步高
Rising

Liupanshui District advantage is obvious. Is located in Sichuan, Yunnan, Guizhou and Guangxi to the middle of the binding region, is an important part of the "Panxi - Liupanshui the Comprehensive Development Zone", the territory of the Guiyang-Kunming railway, Neikun Railway, Shuibai Railway, Zhuliu double-track, Panxi Railway, the Liupanshui South marshalling yard, Liuzhan double-track is under construction. Shuihuang high-grade highways, the GZ65 national trunk road, Shuipan roads, Panbai road as highway trunk, county township village level highways criss-cross the highway network has been formed, Liupanshui city is an important transport hub will become even more prominent in the southwest region.

妥乐银杏村
Tuole Ginkgo Village

乘九届全国民族运动会东风　推进民族文化事业繁荣发展
贵阳市民族宗教事务委员会

By the Chance of the Ninth National Games　Promote the prosperity and development of cultural undertakings
Guiyang City Ethnic and Religious Affairs Committee

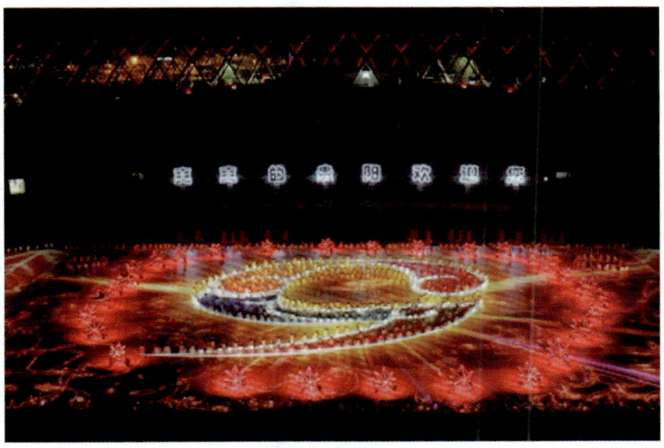

第九届全国民族运动会开幕式——爽爽的贵阳欢迎您
The Ninth National Games opening ceremony - Welcome to Cool Guiyang

2011年9月10日至18日，第九届全国少数民族传统体育运动会在贵阳顺利举行，展示了中华各民族风采，弘扬了民族团结进步事业，实现了贵州和贵阳在全国乃至全世界面前的精彩亮相。贵阳市负责的开幕式、闭幕式、民族大联欢等“协办”工作，不仅收获了成功、圆满、精彩，而且凝炼出热爱贵阳、建设贵阳、不甘落后、奋勇争先、真抓实干、敢打善拼、万众一心、团结协作的“协办精神”，极大的丰富了“知行合一、协力争先”贵阳精神的时代内涵。贵阳市民族宗教事务委员会努力参与协办工作，被省委、省政府授予“承办工作先进集体”称号，被市委、市政府授予“协办工作突出贡献单位”荣誉。

繁荣发展少数民族文化事业，是民族工作一项长期而重大的战略任务。经历第九届全国民族运动会这台文化盛宴的洗礼，贵阳少数民族文化事业进入了新的发展阶段。

各民族入场仪式
National admission ceremony

红枫竞舟
Maple Boating

September 10 to 18, 2011, the Ninth National Traditional Ethnic Minority Sports was successfully held in Guiyang, showing the various ethnic style in China, promote national unity and progress, realize the brilliant appearance of the Guizhou and Guiyang in front of the country and the world. Guiyang city is responsible for the opening ceremony, closing ceremony, national parties and other "co-work", not only success, successful, exciting, and condensed out of the love of Guiyang, the construction of Guiyang, not far behind, courageously rushed, do solid work, the courage to fight the good, fight with one heart and one mind, "Co-spirit" of unity and cooperation, which greatly enriched "the knowledge and action into one, cooperation and fight for the first" Guiyang spirit connotation of the times. Guiyang City Ethnic and Religious Affairs Committee made effrots to participate in co-work, the provincial committee, government granted the title of "contractor collective work unit", the Municipal Party Committee and Municipal Government granted the honor of "outstanding contributions to co-work unit".

Prosperity and development of minority culture, which is the ethnic work in a long-term and significant strategic task. Experienced the baptism of the Ninth National Games this cultural feast, the Guiyang ethnic minority culture has entered a new stage of development.

贵州钢绳股份有限公司

Guizhou Wire Rope Co., Ltd.

已投入使用的贵绳公司建设指挥部办公楼
Have been put into use Guizhou rope company construction headquarters office building

贵州钢绳股份有限公司是一家从事钢丝、钢丝绳产品及相关设备、材料、技术研究、生产、加工销售及进出口业务的上市公司，也是国内最大的金属制品专业化生产企业之一。公司拥有一流的设备、先进的生产工艺和完善的质量管理体系，生产能力、技术水平及产品市场占有率在行业内一直处于领先地位。

公司始终坚持“技术为本、质量第一”的原则，专业致力于各种直径、规格、特殊用途的钢丝绳研发，注重技术革新及人才培育。率先通过了ISO9001：2000质量体系、ISO14000环保体系、中国船级社、挪威船级社（DNV）、法国船级社（BV）、国军标等多项国内国际认可、认证。并承担我国载人航天工程研制建设相关协作配套任务，为天宫一号与神舟八号交会对接任务的圆满完成做出了贡献。公司曾先后多次获得贵州名牌产品、冶金产品实物质量“金杯”奖、“中国名牌产品称号”等荣誉称号。

股份公司行政办公大楼
AG executive office building

整洁明亮的生产车间
Clean and bright production workshop

Guizhou Wire Rope Co., Ltd. is a company engaged in wire, the wire rope products and related equipment, materials, technical research, production, processing, sales and import and export business of listed companies, is one of the largest metal products specialized production enterprise in China. The company has first-class equipment, advanced production technology and perfect quality management system, production capacity, technical level and product market share in the industry has been a leading position.

The company has always adhered to the principle of "technology-oriented, quality first", professional commitment of various diameters, specifications, special-purpose wire rope developed, focusing on technical innovation and personnel training. The first through the ISO9001: 2000 quality system, ISO14000 environmental protection system, China Classification Society, Det Norske Veritas (DNV), the French Classification Society (BV), Guojun marked a number of domestic and international recognized certification. And commitment to China's manned space engineering research and construction of the cooperation task, contributed to Temple One and the Shenzhou VIII rendezvous and docking tasks satisfactorily completed. The company has won several Guizhou brand-name products, metallurgical products quality "Gold Cup" award, the honorary title of "Chinese Famous Brand".

27

Twenty-seven

市（州）、县（市、区、特区）资料

Main Statistics of City(State,Prefecture) and County(City,District,Special Region)

27-1 各市(州)生产总值及构成(2011)

Gross Domestic Product and Its Composition by Region

市(州)名称	City (State,Prefecture)	生产总值 Gross Domestic Product	第一产业 Primary Industry	第二产业 Secondary Industry	#工业 Industry	第三产业 Tertiary Industry	2011年比2010年增长(%) Increase Rate in 2011 over 2010(%)	人均生产总值(元) Per Capita Gross Domestic Product (yuan)	按生产总值绝对量排位 Order by Gross Domestic Product
绝对数(亿元)	**Absolute Figure (100 million yuan)**								
贵阳市	Guiyang	1383.07	62.55	586.84	454.90	733.68	17.1	31712	1
六盘水市	Liupanshui	613.86	32.07	384.69	353.06	197.10	16.6	21522	4
遵义市	Zunyi	1121.46	151.57	493.02	430.98	476.88	17.0	18335	2
安顺市	Anshun	285.64	44.42	112.63	96.09	128.59	15.1	12472	9
毕节市	Bijie	737.88	134.16	342.23	295.60	261.50	16.8	11295	3
铜仁市	Tongren	357.96	103.74	99.90	74.08	154.31	15.5	11622	8
黔西南州	Qianxinan	375.48	60.10	141.84	122.28	173.54	15.6	13386	7
黔东南州	Qiandongnan	383.63	81.02	123.72	92.32	178.90	16.8	11047	6
黔南州	Qiannan	443.59	73.91	183.45	148.92	186.24	15.5	13765	5
构成(%)	**Composition(%)**								
贵阳市	Guiyang	100.0	4.6	42.4	32.9	53.0			
六盘水市	Liupanshui	100.0	5.2	62.7	57.5	32.1			
遵义市	Zunyi	100.0	13.5	44.0	38.4	42.5			
安顺市	Anshun	100.0	15.6	39.4	33.6	45.0			
毕节市	Bijie	100.0	18.2	46.4	40.1	35.4			
铜仁市	Tongren	100.0	29.0	27.9	20.7	43.1			
黔西南州	Qianxinan	100.0	16.0	37.8	32.6	46.2			
黔东南州	Qiandongnan	100.0	21.1	32.3	24.1	46.6			
黔南州	Qiannan	100.0	16.7	41.3	33.6	42.0			

注：表中绝对数按当年价格计算，增长速度按可比价格计算。

Note:Data of absolute Figure in the table are calculated at current prices,Increase Rate are calculated at comparable prices.

27-2 各市(州)年末常住人口

Permanent Population at the year-end by Region

单位：万人 (10000 persons)

市(州)名称	City (State,Prefecture)	2005	2006	2007	2008	2009	2010	2011
贵 阳 市	Guiyang	388.09	396.66	405.26	413.44	423.12	432.93	439
六盘水市	Liupanshui	293.33	292.67	290.59	290.45	287.96	285.43	285
遵 义 市	Zunyi	679.55	667.85	653.98	641.63	627.37	613.29	610
安 顺 市	Anshun	252.26	248.64	243.68	240.28	235.14	230.04	228
毕 节 市	Bijie	688.82	685.35	676.71	673.58	664.09	654.57	652
铜 仁 市	Tongren	364.79	354.17	341.73	333.78	321.55	309.63	308
黔西南州	Qianxinan	298.19	296.07	291.74	290.38	285.70	281.02	280
黔东南州	Qiandongnan	395.66	387.52	377.18	369.17	358.76	348.52	346
黔 南 州	Qiannan	369.32	361.07	351.12	343.28	333.30	323.51	321

注：2006年—2009年数据根据第六次人口普查结果进行修订。

Note:Data from the year 2006 to 2009 had been adjusted according to the result of the Sixth National Population Census.

27-3 各市(州)户籍人口

Household Registered Population by Region

市(州)名称	City (State,Prefecture)	总户数(万户) Total Number of Household (10000 households) 2010	2011	平均每户人数(人) Population of Per Household(person) 2010	2011	年末人口数(万人) Total Population at The Year-end(10000 persons) 2010	2011
贵阳市	Guiyang	108.73	112.13	3.43	3.46	373.16	376.12
六盘水市	Liupanshui	92.41	96.55	3.45	3.48	319.20	321.41
遵义市	Zunyi	211.94	221.60	3.61	3.64	764.16	771.94
安顺市	Anshun	79.77	80.78	3.51	3.54	279.79	282.26
毕节市	Bijie	213.05	225.95	3.91	4.00	833.89	851.73
铜仁市	Tongren	116.19	121.85	3.63	3.68	421.70	427.20
黔西南州	Qianxinan	92.17	98.90	3.69	3.74	339.81	344.74
黔东南州	Qiandongnan	122.34	127.18	3.71	3.75	453.50	458.18
黔南州	Qiannan	116.85	119.43	3.46	3.46	403.79	404.87

注：资料来源于省公安厅(下表同)。
Note:Data in the table are obtained from Guizhou Provincial Department of Public Security.

27-3 续表 Continued

单位：万人 (10000 persons)

市(州)名称	City (state,Prefecture)	按农业与非农业分 By Agricultural and Non-Agricultural: 农业 Agricultural 2010	农业 Agricultural 2011	非农业 Non-Agricultural 2010	非农业 Non-Agricultural 2011	按性别分 Grouped by sex: 男 Male 2010	男 Male 2011	女 Female 2010	女 Female 2011
贵阳市	Guiyang	187.88	189.83	185.27	186.29	190.89	192.05	182.27	184.07
六盘水市	Liupanshui	247.40	248.84	71.80	72.57	167.63	168.95	151.56	152.46
遵义市	Zunyi	639.99	644.51	124.17	127.43	395.94	400.34	368.22	371.6
安顺市	Anshun	238.25	240.74	41.54	41.52	144.46	145.74	135.33	136.52
毕节市	Bijie	772.79	788.93	61.10	62.80	435.72	444.68	398.16	407.05
铜仁市	Tongren	373.10	376.16	48.60	51.04	221.24	223.81	200.47	203.39
黔西南州	Qianxinan	305.83	310.16	33.99	34.58	175.15	177.53	164.66	167.21
黔东南州	Qiandongnan	399.32	402.96	54.19	55.22	239.99	242.56	213.51	215.62
黔南州	Qiannan	348.37	349.08	55.42	55.79	209.35	210.1	194.44	194.77

27-4 各市(州)第六次人口普查各民族人口数

Population of all Ethnic group on the Sixth National Population Census by Region

单位：人 (person)

市(州)名称	City (State,Prefecture)	合计 Total	男 Male	女 Female	汉族 Han	男 Male	女 Female	蒙古族 Mongolian	男 Male	女 Female
贵阳市	Guiyang	4322611	2221896	2100715	3610233	1856295	1753938	4368	2291	2077
六盘水市	Liupanshui	2851332	1493973	1357359	2125906	1114273	1011633	3262	1871	1391
遵义市	Zunyi	6127082	3116640	3010442	5450132	2767218	2682914	515	278	237
安顺市	Anshun	2297612	1186013	1111599	1478796	768409	710387	1093	597	496
毕节市	Bijie	6537498	3387605	3149893	4845699	2515970	2329729	21899	12404	9495
铜仁市	Tongren	3093204	1577421	1515783	927216	460657	466559	7682	4228	3454
黔西南州	Qianxinan	2804612	1439828	1364784	1700052	880556	819496	1182	677	505
黔东南州	Qiandongnan	3481891	1817730	1664161	756587	396364	360223	318	182	136
黔南州	Qiannan	3232714	1664365	1568349	1449535	758131	691404	1242	675	567

27-4 续表1 continued

单位：人 (person)

市(州)名称	City (State,Prefecture)	回族 Hui	男 Male	女 Female	苗族 Miao	男 Male	女 Female	彝族 Yi	男 Male	女 Female
贵阳市	Guiyang	10052	5093	4959	247100	126525	120575	43314	21803	21511
六盘水市	Liupanshui	17682	9390	8292	198330	103640	94690	251629	129842	121787
遵义市	Zunyi	1766	950	816	261673	133186	128487	3432	1692	1740
安顺市	Anshun	13968	7136	6832	306551	154207	152344	8450	4454	3996
毕节市	Bijie	106601	54569	52032	447975	226554	221421	469925	241028	228897
铜仁市	Tongren	2655	1427	1228	450786	236545	214241	765	386	379
黔西南州	Qianxinan	27269	14047	13222	198491	100704	97787	44024	23382	20642
黔东南州	Qiandongnan	2448	1203	1245	1447257	751306	695951	5749	3125	2624
黔南州	Qiannan	2347	1194	1153	410237	208265	201972	7173	3841	3332

27−4 续表2 continued

单位：人 (person)

市(州)名称	City (State,Prefecture)	壮族 Zhuang	男 Male	女 Female	布依族 Bouyei	男 Male	女 Female	满族 Man	男 Male	女 Female
贵阳市	Guiyang	6086	3220	2866	202751	101969	100782	6708	3355	3353
六盘水市	Liupanshui	1265	648	617	82401	42935	39466	1752	872	880
遵义市	Zunyi	1599	713	886	4959	2342	2617	945	477	468
安顺市	Anshun	1443	718	725	346739	176769	169970	1400	748	652
毕节市	Bijie	2336	1157	1179	55123	28413	26710	9327	4942	4385
铜仁市	Tongren	875	418	457	1745	861	884	435	229	206
黔西南州	Qianxinan	4416	2200	2216	773004	388771	384233	775	449	326
黔东南州	Qiandongnan	24618	12838	11780	34599	17849	16750	637	335	302
黔南州	Qiannan	9939	4588	5351	1009244	511142	498102	1107	525	582

27−4 续表3 continued

单位：人 (person)

市(州)名称	City (State,Prefecture)	侗族 Dong	男 Male	女 Female	瑶族 Yao	男 Male	女 Female	白族 Bai	男 Male	女 Female
贵阳市	Guiyang	32645	17471	15174	1236	665	571	16048	8218	7830
六盘水市	Liupanshui	3511	1875	1636	210	112	98	46274	25189	21085
遵义市	Zunyi	5895	2982	2913	315	139	176	725	363	362
安顺市	Anshun	2560	1368	1192	623	333	290	9082	5045	4037
毕节市	Bijie	1491	785	706	316	176	140	103422	55052	48370
铜仁市	Tongren	361132	189551	171581	4058	2324	1734	414	208	206
黔西南州	Qianxinan	2172	1158	1014	2813	1402	1411	1994	1035	959
黔东南州	Qiandongnan	1010352	528230	482122	21732	11263	10469	495	250	245
黔南州	Qiannan	12170	6788	5382	9576	5014	4562	1056	563	493

27-4 续表4 continued

单位：人 (person)

市(州)名称	City (State,Prefecture)	土家族 Tujia	男 Male	女 Female	畲族 She	男 Male	女 Female	水族 Shui	男 Male	女 Female	仫佬族 Mulam	男 Male	女 Female
贵阳市	Guiyang	60076	31812	28264	511	262	249	4768	2464	2304	758	394	364
六盘水市	Liupanshui	4076	2257	1819	40	26	14	11064	5965	5099	180	93	87
遵义市	Zunyi	94154	50668	43486	99	45	54	469	218	251	161	75	86
安顺市	Anshun	3116	1758	1358	58	31	27	365	206	159	79	42	37
毕节市	Bijie	2265	1218	1047	107	64	43	5460	2851	2609	142	75	67
铜仁市	Tongren	1229710	624967	604743	168	115	53	251	145	106	26	7	19
黔西南州	Qianxinan	2737	1475	1262	49	31	18	1147	530	617	88	39	49
黔东南州	Qiandongnan	33676	18498	15178	31397	16477	14920	55357	29827	25530	21395	11600	9795
黔南州	Qiannan	7167	3873	3294	4129	2045	2084	269865	138111	131754	2127	968	1159

27-4 续表5 continued

单位：人 (person)

市(州)名称	City (State,Prefecture)	羌族 Qiang	男 Male	女 Female	毛南族 Maonan	男 Male	女 Female	仡佬族 Gelao	男 Male	女 Female	其他未识别的民族 Undetermined called People Community	男 Male	女 Female
贵阳市	Guiyang	177	94	83	412	209	203	25457	13639	11818	42839	22524	20315
六盘水市	Liupanshui	20	9	11	21	6	15	11693	6380	5313	82135	43483	38652
遵义市	Zunyi	41	23	18	35	12	23	297964	154186	143778	603	304	299
安顺市	Anshun	25	16	9	14	8	6	24718	13311	11407	16281	8641	7640
毕节市	Bijie	36	25	11	55	27	28	20585	10945	9640	440578	229271	211307
铜仁市	Tongren	1179	673	506	12	6	6	102849	54147	48702	464	201	263
黔西南州	Qianxinan	23	14	9	23	11	12	4705	2543	2162	693	381	312
黔东南州	Qiandongnan	61	22	39	56	27	29	3201	1590	1611	28189	14771	13418
黔南州	Qiannan	43	23	20	26704	13937	12767	4010	2194	1816	998	549	449

注：表中数据来源于第六次人口普查机器汇总数。
Note:Data in this table are obtained from the Sixth Population Census.

27−5 各市(州)非私营单位在岗职工年平均人数、年平均工资(2011)

Number of Staff and Workers and Their Annual Average Wages in Non-private units by Region

市(州)名称	City (State,Prefecture)	合计 Total	国有经济 State -owned units	城镇集体经济 Urban Collective-owned Units	其他经济类型 Units of Other Types of Ownership	2011年比2010年增长(%) Increase Rate in 2011 over 2010(%)
在岗职工年平均人数(万人)	**Number of Staff and Workers(10000 persons)**					
贵阳市	Guiyang	70.91	39.76	2.33	28.82	1.5
六盘水市	Liupanshui	20.62	12.78	0.26	7.58	13.6
遵义市	Zunyi	29.81	23.09	0.78	5.94	8.5
安顺市	Anshun	13.75	9.09	0.68	3.98	0.1
毕节市	Bijie	23.21	18.19	0.76	4.26	7.5
铜仁市	Tongren	12.69	11.16	0.72	0.81	4.6
黔西南州	Qianxinan	12.43	9.39	0.35	2.69	4.5
黔东南州	Qiandongnan	17.25	14.15	0.59	2.51	6.0
黔南州	Qiannan	15.68	12.32	0.52	2.84	16.1
年平均工资(元)	**Annual Average Wages (yuan)**					
贵阳市	Guiyang	38674	43820	23045	32842	24.0
六盘水市	Liupanshui	39448	38442	63882	40302	16.1
遵义市	Zunyi	39699	40508	31862	37591	20.6
安顺市	Anshun	35343	36158	34478	33631	14.1
毕节市	Bijie	33102	33176	33933	32637	16.2
铜仁市	Tongren	34125	33976	27593	41966	12.4
黔西南州	Qianxinan	32281	33748	32137	27173	16.1
黔东南州	Qiandongnan	34299	38812	46995	28610	18.4
黔南州	Qiannan	35575	36975	33888	29811	11.7

27–6　各市(州)固定资产投资(2011)

Investment in Fixed Assets by Region

单位：亿元　　(100 million yuan)

市(州) 名 称	City (State,Prefecture)	合 计 Total	2011年比2010年增长(%) Increase Rate in 2011 over 2010(%)
贵 阳 市	Guiyang	1416.62	53.4
六盘水市	Liupanshui	440.07	54.0
遵 义 市	Zunyi	685.31	44.4
安 顺 市	Anshun	165.56	101.5
毕 节 市	Bijie	630.82	87.6
铜 仁 市	Tongren	300.01	53.3
黔西南州	Qianxinan	301.17	53.5
黔东南州	Qiandongnan	350.55	91.1
黔 南 州	Qiannan	400.02	81.0

注：本表统计口径为计划总投资50万元及以上城镇投资、农村非农户投资和房地产开发投资，不含跨区域项目固定资产完成投资。

Note:Data in the table refer to those projects planned to invest 500,000 yuan at least in urban areas,projects funded by rural non-farm households and real estate development,but not include investment in cross-regional projects.

27-7 各市(州)按建设性质和构成分固定资产投资(2011)

Investment in Fixed Assets by Type of Construction and Composition of Funds by Region

单位：亿元　　(100 million yuan)

市(州)名称	City (State,Prefecture)	合计 Total	按建设性质分 By Type of Construction #新建 #New Construction	#扩建 #Expansion	#改建和技术改造 #Reconstruction and Technical Rennovation
贵阳市	Guiyang	1416.62	562.03	173.73	178.47
六盘水市	Liupanshui	440.07	198.77	55.57	141.49
遵义市	Zunyi	685.31	382.27	87.23	122.71
安顺市	Anshun	165.56	80.07	11.7	32.68
毕节市	Bijie	630.82	418.04	41.09	103.73
铜仁市	Tongren	300.01	212.32	10.15	20.00
黔西南州	Qianxinan	301.17	189.38	28.62	55.55
黔东南州	Qiandongnan	350.55	224.18	16.16	42.82
黔南州	Qiannan	400.02	213.13	42.38	51.54

27-7 续表 continued

单位：亿元　　(100 million yuan)

市(州)名称	City (State,Prefecture)	按构成分 By Composition of Funds 建筑工程 Construction	安装工程 Installation	设备工器具购置 Purchase of Equipment and Instruments	其他费用 Others
贵阳市	Guiyang	905.97	49.26	146.63	314.76
六盘水市	Liupanshui	245.01	33.21	91.8	70.05
遵义市	Zunyi	476.91	43.83	82.32	82.25
安顺市	Anshun	94.1	14.2	28.92	28.34
毕节市	Bijie	384.52	34.96	109.45	101.89
铜仁市	Tongren	203.48	12.58	36.63	47.32
黔西南州	Qianxinan	183.97	15.56	54.28	47.36
黔东南州	Qiandongnan	256.52	17.21	42.92	33.9
黔南州	Qiannan	253.85	21.11	77.5	47.56

27-8 各市(州)能源利用效率(2011)

Basic Statistics on Energy Consumption by Region

市(州) 名 称	City (State,Prefecture)	单位生产总值能耗 (吨标准煤/万元) Energy Consumption Per Unit of GDP(ton of SEC/10000 yuan)	单位生产总值能耗比上年增长(%) Growth Rate of Energy Consumption Per Unit of GDP over Preceding Year(%)	单位工业增加值能耗 (吨标准煤/万元) Energy Consumption Per Unit of Industrial Value-added (ton of SEC/10000 yuan)
贵 阳 市	Guiyang	1.4156	-3.45	2.226
六盘水市	Liupanshui	2.8332	-3.45	5.717
遵 义 市	Zunyi	1.3370	-3.44	1.428
安 顺 市	Anshun	2.1339	-3.38	4.204
毕 节 市	Bijie	1.8754	-3.32	6.129
铜 仁 市	Tongren	1.6369	-3.34	4.221
黔西南州	Qianxinan	1.7091	-3.20	2.607
黔东南州	Qiandongnan	1.9242	-3.16	4.195
黔 南 州	Qiannan	1.7750	-3.20	2.374

27-8 续表 continued

市(州) 名 称	City (State,Prefecture)	单位工业增加值能耗比上年增长(%) Growth Rate of Energy Consumption of Industrial Value-added over Preceding Year(%)	单位生产总值电耗 (千瓦小时/万元) Electricity Consumption Per Unit of GDP(ton of SEC/10000 yuan)	单位生产总值电耗比上年增长(%) Growth Rate of Electricity Consumption Per Unit of GDP over Preceding Year(%)
贵 阳 市	Guiyang	-14.79	1787.8	-9.6
六盘水市	Liupanshui	-7.11	1903.2	-8.7
遵 义 市	Zunyi	-8.57	1468.3	-1.8
安 顺 市	Anshun	-9.05	2239.3	-6.9
毕 节 市	Bijie	-13.38	1367.2	-1.2
铜 仁 市	Tongren	-4.44	2010.1	-6.4
黔西南州	Qianxinan	22.86	2042.5	-4.6
黔东南州	Qiandongnan	-10.71	2298.4	-2.6
黔 南 州	Qiannan	-3.22	1885.8	-11.2

注：1、单位生产总值能耗与单位工业增加值能耗均按2010年可比价计算。2、规模以上单位工业增加值能耗增长幅度是用规模以上工业增加值增幅和规模以上工业能耗增幅计算，不用两年的单位工业增加值计算。

Note:1.Both energy consumption per unit of GDP and Energy consumption per unit of industrial value-added are calculated at 2010 comparable prices
2.Growth rate of energy consumption of industrial value-added over preceding year is caculated based on growth rate of industrial value-added and growth rate of energy consumption,but it isn't caculated based on two years of unit industrial Value-added.

27–9 各市(州)财政一般预算收入(2011)

Total Local Government Budgetary Revenue by Region

市(州)名称	City (State,Prefecture)	合计(亿元) Total (100 million yuan)	#增值税 Value-added Tax	#营业税 Operation Tax	#企业所得税 Enterprises' Income Tax	#个人所得税 Personal Income Tax	#城市维护建设税 Urban Maintenance and Development Tax	2011年比2010年增长(%) Increase Rate in 2011 over 2010(%)	人均财政一般预算收入(元) Per Capita Local Financial Revenue(yuan)
贵阳市	Guiyang	187.09	11.87	59.15	23.34	9.27	13.77	37.3	4291
六盘水市	Liupanshui	70.40	7.43	12.10	3.45	4.46	3.52	42.8	2468
遵义市	Zunyi	84.62	8.86	19.44	4.82	4.54	8.09	46.9	1383
安顺市	Anshun	26.51	2.11	9.05	1.71	1.13	1.20	33.6	1157
毕节市	Bijie	80.76	5.86	10.55	3.06	5.46	4.09	30.0	1236
铜仁市	Tongren	28.39	1.78	6.95	1.43	0.83	1.34	56.3	919
黔西南州	Qianxinan	45.52	3.42	7.76	3.89	3.83	2.26	58.2	1623
黔东南州	Qiandongnan	45.27	1.81	9.85	2.13	2.00	1.45	72.9	1304
黔南州	Qiannan	39.20	2.70	8.98	2.37	1.66	2.09	44.4	1216

注：资料来源于省财政厅(下表同)。
Note:Data in the table were obtained from Guizhou Provincial Financial Department(the same applies to the next table).

27–10 各市(州)财政一般预算支出(2011)

Total Local Government Budgetary Expenditure by Region

市(州)名称	City(State, Prefecture)	合计(亿元) Total (100 million yuan)	#一般公共服务 Common Public Service	#教育 Education	#科学技术 Science and Technology	#文化体育与传媒 Culture, Sports and Communication	#社会保障和就业 Social Security and Jobs	#医疗卫生 Health Care	#节能环保 Environmental Protection	#农林水事务 Affairs of Agriculture, Forest and Water	2011年比2010年增长(%) Increase Rate in 2011 over 2010(%)	人均财政支出(元) Per Capita Financial Expenditure(yuan)
贵阳市	Guiyang	277.38	45.83	48.38	5.05	4.35	20.03	17.87	7.13	19.53	35.7	6362
六盘水市	Liupanshui	146.37	18.54	28.78	0.79	1.19	13.30	10.60	4.13	15.57	31.7	5132
遵义市	Zunyi	256.36	39.22	54.68	2.44	3.97	23.15	29.63	8.18	36.72	32.0	4191
安顺市	Anshun	101.02	14.86	18.77	0.73	1.01	12.15	10.73	3.12	13.51	28.1	4411
毕节市	Bijie	249.28	32.68	57.16	1.01	2.48	23.79	23.63	6.40	35.76	21.3	3816
铜仁市	Tongren	163.04	23.79	30.79	0.40	1.67	18.45	17.98	5.70	28.13	29.9	5279
黔西南州	Qianxinan	137.57	20.77	28.84	0.65	1.62	12.16	13.71	4.47	20.70	32.5	4904
黔东南州	Qiandongnan	194.66	35.45	39.06	0.81	2.56	19.19	18.67	5.16	30.60	34.7	5606
黔南州	Qiannan	162.40	31.43	30.83	1.08	1.67	15.25	16.34	5.26	25.30	25.5	5040

27-11 各市(州)税收收入(2011)

Taxation Revenue by region

单位：万元 (10000 yuan)

市(州)名称	City(Stat, Prefecture)	税收总计 Total	国税 National Taxation	地税 Local Taxation	2011年比2010年增长(%) Increase Rate in 2011 over 2010(%) 总计 Total	国税 National Taxation	地税 Local Taxation
贵阳市	Guiyang	3682165	2043935	1638230	28.4	27.2	29.9
六盘水市	Liupanshui	1158931	575902	483029	8.4	-0.3	21.1
遵义市	Zunyi	1787771	1133297	654474	37.7	40.5	33.1
安顺市	Anshun	415411	200988	214423	30.1	21.7	39.2
毕节市	Bijie	1111553	641613	469940	27.3	23.9	32.2
铜仁市	Tongren	404658	194359	210299	36.7	24.2	50.7
黔西南州	Qianxinan	617727	355671	320408	22.7	19.0	27.1
黔东南州	Qiandongnan	539559	196203	343356	40.5	23.4	52.6
黔南州	Qiannan	657032	344009	313023	24.8	17.5	33.9

注：1.资料来源于省国税局、省地税局。2.地税税收收入中不含契税、耕地占用税。

Note:1.Data in the table are provided by Guizhou Provincial National Taxation Bureau and Local Taxation Bureau of Guizhou Province.2.The Local Taxation doesn't include deed tax and farm land occupation tax.

27-12 各市(州)所在城市分类价格指数

Urban Residents Consumer Price Indices of Major Cities by Region

(上年=100) (preceding year=100)

城市名称	City	居民消费价格指数 Residents Consumer Price Index 2010	2011	商品零售价格指数 Retail Price Index of Commodities 2010	2011
贵阳市	Guiyang	102.9	105.5	103.2	105.0
六盘水市	Liupanshui	103.3	105.4	103.3	104.7
遵义市	Zunyi	103.3	105.4	102.8	105.4
安顺市	Anshun	103.1	105.0	102.8	104.4
毕节市	Bijie	102.7	105.0	103.2	106.9
铜仁市	Tongren	102.3	104.6	101.6	104.4
兴义市	Xingyi	103.5	105.5	103.1	105.4
凯里市	Kaili	101.9	105.6	102.3	105.9
都匀市	Duyun	102.6	104.8	102.1	106.0

27-13 各市(州)所在城市城镇居民家庭人均年收支(2011)
Per Capital Annual Disposable Income and Expenditure of Urban Households of Major Cities

单位：元 (yuan)

城市名称	City	城镇居民家庭人均可支配收入 Per Capita Annual Disposable Income of Urban Households	位次 Order	2011年比2010年增长(%) Increase Rate in 2011 over 2010(%)	城镇居民家庭人均消费性支出 Per Capita Annual Consumption Expenditnre of Urban Households	位次 Order	2011年比2010年增长(%) Increase Rate in 2011 over 2010(%)
贵阳市	Guiyang	19420.14	1	17.0	14300.11	1	10.5
六盘水市	Liupanshui	16370.89	7	17.6	9482.09	8	13.5
遵义市	Zunyi	17425.66	2	14.0	11952.64	3	10.3
安顺市	Anshun	16300.38	8	12.4	11897.43	4	15.6
毕节市	Bijie	17135.07	3	19.8	12291.01	2	18.1
铜仁市	Tongren	13846.46	9	25.9	9385.42	9	32.3
兴义市	Xingyi	17003.90	4	13.3	10552.72	6	8.9
凯里市	Kaili	16410.38	6	16.7	10522.77	7	0.2
都匀市	Duyun	16982.73	5	15.0	11547.94	5	5.5

注：表中增长速度未扣除同期价格因素。
Note:The Increase Rate in the table are calculated at current price.

27-14 各市(州)农村居民家庭人均年收支(2011)
Per Capita Net Income and Living Expenditure of Rural Households by Region

单位：元 (yuan)

市(州)名称	City (State、Prefecture)	农村居民人均纯收入 Per Capita Net Income of Rural Households	位次 Order	农村居民人均年现金收入 Annual Per Capita Cash Income of Rural Households	位次 Order	农村居民人均年消费性支出 Annual Per Capita Living Expenditures of Rural Households	位次 Order
贵阳市	Guiyang	7381	1	8162	1	5494	1
六盘水市	Liupanshui	4437	4	4592	5	4115	3
遵义市	Zunyi	5216	2	5719	2	3875	2
安顺市	Anshun	4367	5	4817	4	3388	8
毕节市	Bijie	4210	6	4348	6	3583	5
铜仁市	Tongren	4002	7	4104	8	3735	4
黔西南州	Qianxinan	3900	9	4237	7	3321	9
黔东南州	Qiandongnan	3949	8	3678	9	3500	7
黔南州	Qiannan	4633	3	4965	3	3511	6

27–15　各市(州)常用耕地面积(2011)

Cultivated Area by Region

单位：千公顷　　(1000 hectares)

市(州)名称	City (State、Prefecture)	常用耕地面积 Cultivated Area	#水田 Paddy Fields
贵阳市	Guiyang	96.74	39.18
六盘水市	Liupanshui	108.14	19.64
遵义市	Zunyi	390.02	199.50
安顺市	Anshun	106.22	54.35
毕节市	Bijie	365.81	44.46
铜仁市	Tongren	175.72	103.98
黔西南州	Qianxinan	159.41	52.45
黔东南州	Qiandongnan	178.56	134.27
黔南州	Qiannan	174.28	104.42

27–16　各市(州)乡村从业人员数(2011)

Rural Employment by Region

单位：万人　　(10000 persons)

市(州)名称	City(State、Prefecture)	合计 Total	农业 Agric-ulture	工业 Indu-stry	建筑业 Constru-ction	交通运输仓储和邮政业 Trans-port, Storage and Post	信息传输、计算机服务和软件业 Information Transmission, Computer Services and Software	批发与零售业 Whole-sale and Retail Trade	住宿和餐饮业 Hotel and Resta-urants	其他行业 Other Sectors
贵阳市	Guiyang	118.41	61.10	9.65	7.52	4.02	0.59	5.32	4.57	25.64
六盘水市	Liupanshui	139.90	86.17	9.65	4.69	3.44	0.14	3.32	1.27	31.23
遵义市	Zunyi	400.42	198.53	21.46	18.44	6.50	1.16	13.08	5.28	135.97
安顺市	Anshun	143.47	86.53	7.16	7.22	2.84	0.26	3.40	1.96	34.10
毕节市	Bijie	449.69	235.36	30.50	19.16	8.09	1.28	12.76	7.35	135.19
铜仁市	Tongren	224.65	122.54	9.90	10.70	3.38	0.52	5.63	2.76	69.21
黔西南州	Qianxinan	183.55	115.15	8.21	7.30	3.40	0.36	4.78	2.63	41.72
黔东南州	Qiandongnan	240.08	132.79	9.81	8.80	3.24	0.31	4.99	3.16	76.98
黔南州	Qiannan	215.30	127.16	9.79	7.35	3.08	0.34	4.84	2.49	60.26

27-17 各市(州)农业机械总动力及拥有量(2011)

Total Power and Possession of Agricultural Machinery by Region

市(州)名称	City (State、Prefecture)	农业机械总动力(万千瓦) Total Power of Agricultural Machinery (10000 kw)	大中型拖拉机(万台) Large and Medium Agricultural Tractors(10000 units)	小型拖拉机(万台) Mini Agricultural Tractors(10000 units)	农用水泵(万台) Agricultural Water Pump(10000 units)
贵阳市	Guiyang	138.02	0.295	0.350	2.106
六盘水市	Liupanshui	152.65	0.125	0.420	0.968
遵义市	Zunyi	286.79	0.503	0.812	8.130
安顺市	Anshun	134.15	0.246	0.349	4.549
毕节市	Bijie	243.96	0.486	2.114	2.599
铜仁市	Tongren	245.68	0.277	1.116	6.156
黔西南州	Qianxinan	178.66	0.281	0.479	4.001
黔东南州	Qiandongnan	219.18	0.336	0.342	4.423
黔南州	Qiannan	252.33	0.574	0.654	7.657

注：资料来源于省农委。

Note:Data in this table are obtained from the Agricultural Committee of Guizhou Province.

27-18 各市(州)农林牧渔业总产值(2011)

Gross Output Value of Farming,Forestry, Animal Husbandary, Fishery and Their Services by Region

单位：亿元 (100 million yuan)

市(州)名称	City(State、Prefecture)	合计 Total	农业 Farming	林业 Forestry	牧业 Animal Husbandary	渔业 Fishery	农林牧渔服务业 Services of FFAF	2011年比2010年增长(%) Increase Rate in 2011 over 2010 (%)
贵阳市	Guiyang	96.55	62.21	0.86	31.39	1.36	0.73	2.9
六盘水市	Liupanshui	56.50	29.66	1.98	23.16	0.14	1.56	4.9
遵义市	Zunyi	253.40	152.05	12.23	81.08	4.47	3.56	1.9
安顺市	Anshun	70.01	33.66	1.98	32.53	1.36	0.49	3.8
毕节市	Bijie	212.45	126.31	4.79	75.95	1.31	4.09	2.5
铜仁市	Tongren	167.30	93.72	4.36	59.85	3.89	5.48	2.9
黔西南州	Qianxinan	96.25	48.27	5.30	37.05	4.11	1.52	1.5
黔东南州	Qiandongnan	133.72	67.27	21.37	37.04	4.81	3.22	4.2
黔南州	Qiannan	132.25	69.99	5.62	51.58	2.38	2.67	1.8

27−19　各市(州)农用化肥施用量(2011)

Consumption of Chemical Fertilizers for Agricultural Use by Region

单位：吨　(ton)

市(州)名称	City(State、Profecture)	合计 Total	氮肥 Nitrogenous Fertilizer	磷肥 Phosphate Fertilizer	钾肥 Potash Fertilizer	复合肥 Compound Fertilizer	2011年比2010年增长(%) Increase Rate in 2011 over 2010(%)
贵阳市	Guiyang	65503	31225	6193	8276	19809	3.1
六盘水市	Liupanshui	66428	42847	7216	3829	12536	-2.9
遵义市	Zunyi	206036	114365	22703	20220	48748	33.3
安顺市	Anshun	60395	28382	10891	3550	17572	-0.2
毕节市	Bijie	206672	112383	20145	16078	58066	0.6
铜仁市	Tongren	86653	40751	11574	8224	26104	0.5
黔西南州	Qianxinan	72037	47692	8933	5886	9526	29.1
黔东南州	Qiandongnan	76672	29865	9323	5137	32347	0.8
黔南州	Qiannan	100240	61411	11677	8073	19079	5.9

注:本表按折纯法计算。
Note:Consumption of chemical fertilizers is required in calculation to convert the gross weight into weight containing 100% effective component.

27−20　各市(州)主要农作物播种面积(2011)

Sown Areas of Major Farm Crops by Region

单位：千公顷　(1000 hectares)

市(州)名称	City (State、Profecture)	总计 Total	粮食作物 Sown Areas of Grain Arops	#夏粮 Summer Grain Crops	按品种分 #稻谷 Rice	#小麦 Wheat	#玉米 Corn	#大豆 Soja	油菜籽 Rapeseeds	烤烟 Flue-cured Tobacco
贵阳市	Guiyang	268.35	116.93	30.53	35.20	6.88	40.03	7.16	37.01	11.29
六盘水市	Liupanshui	242.78	182.48	77.23	16.20	29.89	69.08	7.85	5.99	5.61
遵义市	Zunyi	1204.28	758.80	238.64	156.12	35.55	159.75	32.19	133.46	58.60
安顺市	Anshun	255.25	143.24	33.45	53.52	10.69	44.63	5.12	53.97	6.89
毕节市	Bijie	1061.44	642.54	264.90	39.59	64.98	171.50	34.74	56.48	49.97
铜仁市	Tongren	560.18	355.66	102.22	95.41	23.34	76.17	16.84	62.43	19.37
黔西南州	Qianxinan	367.41	235.19	62.71	49.78	46.66	92.71	7.65	23.49	20.11
黔东南州	Qiandongnan	542.19	305.57	78.24	127.88	4.68	46.43	9.92	49.67	10.36
黔南州	Qiannan	519.34	315.17	84.64	107.84	34.96	87.52	11.31	66.49	17.81

27−21 各市(州)主要农产品产量(2011)
Output of Major Farm Crops by Region

单位：万吨 (10000 tons)

市(州)名称	City(State、Profecture)	粮食 Grain	#夏粮 Summer Grain Crops	2011年比2010年增长(%) Increase Rate in 2011 over 2010	油菜籽 Rapeseeds	烤烟 Fluecured Tobacco	茶叶 Tea	水果 Fruits
贵阳市	Guiyang	40.24	8.14	-25.5	5.47	1.82	0.25	13.55
六盘水市	Liupanshui	56.46	18.35	-15.2	0.68	0.99	0.04	2.95
遵义市	Zunyi	227.12	59.36	-20.6	23.04	10.00	2.46	24.65
安顺市	Anshun	53.28	6.38	-22.8	5.86	1.00	0.15	7.42
毕节市	Bijie	191.91	52.88	-12.1	10.74	8.40	0.09	9.12
铜仁市	Tongren	97.46	25.95	-25.4	9.25	3.29	1.23	15.83
黔西南州	Qianxinan	63.28	12.53	-26.4	2.71	2.60	0.33	8.93
黔东南州	Qiandongnan	90.79	15.62	-28.3	5.83	1.58	0.58	25.74
黔南州	Qiannan	100.06	16.93	-23.6	8.23	2.82	0.69	19.84

27−22 各市(州)牲畜出、存栏量(2011)
Amount of Livestocks in Hand and Slaughtered by Region

单位：头、只 (head)

市(州)名称	City (State、Profecture)	出栏 Amount of Slaughtered Livestocks			存栏 Amount of Livestock in Hand		
		猪 Hogs	牛 Cattle and Buffalo	羊 Sheep and Goats	猪 Hogs	牛 Cattle and Buffalo	羊 Sheep and Goats
贵阳市	Guiyang	1237134	45185	19461	904715	235108	32542
六盘水市	Liupanshui	1020149	65570	108133	1086775	313374	176626
遵义市	Zunyi	4400165	178138	502983	3265793	851062	579598
安顺市	Anshun	1139600	103399	43251	1157025	456154	62940
毕节市	Bijie	2739545	173899	286745	2932621	796441	499676
铜仁市	Tongren	2103141	122997	647084	2120035	529414	561090
黔西南州	Qianxinan	1382578	114805	201256	1294804	533965	386958
黔东南州	Qiandongnan	1752144	120110	149760	1320594	634987	239287
黔南州	Qiannan	1979286	124022	153520	1610660	604258	207651

27–23　各市(州)主要畜产品、水产品产量(2011)

Output of Major Livestock Products and Aquatic Products by Region

市(州) 名 称	City (State、Profecture)	肉类总产量(万吨) Total Output of Meat (10000 tons)	2011年比 2010年增长(%) Increase Rate in 2011 over 2010	禽 蛋 (万吨) Poulty and Eggs (10000 tons)	水产品 (吨) Aquatic Products(ton)
贵 阳 市	Guiyang	13.94	0.3	2.24	8600
六盘水市	Liupanshui	10.91	0.3	0.57	873
遵 义 市	Zunyi	43.73	0.1	3.77	25401
安 顺 市	Anshun	13.05	0.3	1.29	4485
毕 节 市	Bijie	31.98	0.2	2.48	4063
铜 仁 市	Tongren	22.20	0.3	2.04	14528
黔西南州	Qianxinan	14.81	0.1	1.85	24865
黔东南州	Qiandongnan	16.85	0.3	1.03	14446
黔 南 州	Qiannan	18.53	0.1	0.96	11541

注：表中“水产品产量”数据由省农委提供。
Note:Output of aquatic products in this table are obtained from the Agricultural Commission of Guizhou province.

27–24　各市(州)主要林产品产量(2011)

Output of Major Forestry Products by Region

单位：吨　　(ton)

市(州) 名 称	City (State、Profecture)	生 漆 Lacquer	油桐籽 Tung- Oil Seed	油茶籽 Tea- Oil Seed	乌桕籽 Tallow- seeds	五倍籽 Nutgall	棕 片 Palm - flake	核 桃 Walnuts	板 栗 Chestnut
贵 阳 市	Guiyang	21	43	142	3	20	55	127	147
六盘水市	Liupanshui	176	53	98			212	2642	531
遵 义 市	Zunyi	612	5242	8808	1269	720	1256	1275	2078
安 顺 市	Anshun	13	4950	293	109	10	114	208	274
毕 节 市	Bijie	700	119	9	3	36	108	9238	976
铜 仁 市	Tongren	121	5346	1670	821	354	401	1014	1684
黔西南州	Qianxinan	138	41617	3870	30	90	1693	940	7949
黔东南州	Qiandongnan	111	8448	7795	252	221	351	852	1934
黔 南 州	Qiannan	109	9951	481		173	340	1068	7080

27−25 各市(州)规模以上工业增加值(2011)

Total Gross Industrial Value-added above Designated Size by Region

单位：亿元 (100 million yuan)

市(州)名称	City (State、Prefecture)	工业增加值 Industrial Value-added	轻工业 Light Industry	重工业 Heavy Industry
贵阳市	Guiyang	365.23	168.41	196.82
六盘水市	Liupanshui	282.01	15.73	266.28
遵义市	Zunyi	427.11	294.03	133.08
安顺市	Anshun	72.34	9.46	62.88
毕节市	Bijie	194.84	33.16	161.68
铜仁市	Tongren	50.60	10.54	40.07
黔西南州	Qianxinan	140.10	5.20	134.88
黔东南州	Qiandongnan	69.86	6.38	63.47
黔南州	Qiannan	121.69	32.50	89.19

27−26 各市(州)规模以上工业企业主要工业产品产量(2011)

Ouput of Major Industrial Products above Designated Size by Region

市(州)名称	City (State、Prefecture)	原煤(万吨) Coal (10000 tons)	发电量(万千瓦小时) Electricity (10000 kwh)	化肥(吨) Chemical Fertilizer(ton)	水泥(万吨) Cement (10000 tons)
贵阳市	Guiyang	248	758752	2355464	956
六盘水市	Liupanshui	4874	3472614		457
遵义市	Zunyi	823	1698627	441447	933
安顺市	Anshun	1244	821431	129410	315
毕节市	Bijie	4123	4134082	272637	478
铜仁市	Tongren	69	660947		489
黔西南州	Qianxinan	1989	1365481	343202	389
黔东南州	Qiandongnan	238	432103		407
黔南州	Qiannan	407	246206	104488	826

27−27　各市(州)公路里程(2011)

Length of Highways by Region

单位：公里　　(km)

市(州)名称	City (State、Profecture)	公路里程 Total Length of Highways	#等级公路 Standard Highway	#高速公路 Expressway	#有铺装路面(高级) Paved Road (advanced)	#沥青混凝土 Asphalt concrete
贵阳市	Guiyang	9215.51	8255.43	289.64	4750.88	591.05
六盘水市	Liupanshui	11904.12	8403.50	87.20	866.48	565.99
遵义市	Zunyi	24024.75	11496.13	303.12	2777.62	795.98
安顺市	Anshun	9228.16	3330.48	184.14	590.74	379.96
毕节市	Bijie	24894.93	13281.78	32.43	802.09	255.63
铜仁市	Tongren	21509.31	7104.73	84.97	1103.16	241.77
黔西南州	Qianxinan	14752.67	9801.19	259.44	944.13	462.11
黔东南州	Qiandongnan	26731.08	8730.28	354.86	1771.17	730.69
黔南州	Qiannan	15559.63	9239.98	426.23	1253.10	488.50

注：资料来源于省交通厅。
Note:Data in the table are obtained from Guizhou Provincial Department of Transportation.

27−28　各市(州)电信主要指标(2011)

Major Indicators of Telecommunications by Region

市(州)名称	City (State、Profecture)	年末固定电话用户数(万户) Number of Telephone Subscribers at Year-end (10000 subscribers)	移动电话用户(万户) Number of Mobile Telephone Subscribers (10000 subscribers)	互联网宽带接入用户(万户) Number of Subscribers of Internet Service (10000 subscribers)	互联网上网人数(万人) Number of Internet Users (10000 persons)
贵阳市	Guiyang	99.34	544.05	68.24	355.18
六盘水市	Liupanshui	29.75	182.50	12.31	126.36
遵义市	Zunyi	80.73	392.54	36.58	262.20
安顺市	Anshun	23.81	125.72	10.75	90.86
毕节市	Bijie	39.38	258.60	17.23	193.00
铜仁市	Tongren	28.72	146.68	11.36	102.07
黔西南州	Qianxinan	22.58	155.58	11.14	115.39
黔东南州	Qiandongnan	42.57	196.06	22.16	148.59
黔南州	Qiannan	37.09	173.48	15.06	125.03

注：资料来源于省通信管理局。
Note:Data in the table are obtained from the provincial communications authority bureau.

27–29 各市(州)电信、邮政主要指标(2011)

Major Indicators of Telecommunications and Post by Region

市(州)名称	City (State、Profecture)	交换机总容量(万门) Capacity of Telephone Exchanges (10000 line)	报刊、杂志累计订销数(万份) Issue of Newspapers and Magazines (10000 copies)	邮政储蓄期末余额(亿元) Post Deposits at the Year-end (100 million yuan)
贵阳市	Guiyang	1030	8817.85	53.92
六盘水市	Liupanshui	327	2535.53	23.28
遵义市	Zunyi	815	6577.48	111.75
安顺市	Anshun	322	1729.92	16.23
毕节市	Bijie	513	3937.74	39.91
铜仁市	Tongren	324	2582.35	51.97
黔西南州	Qianxinan	506	2349.43	26.47
黔东南州	Qiandongnan	621	3742.11	53.18
黔南州	Qiannan	357	2783.18	54.85

注：资料来源于省通信管理局、省邮政公司。
Note:Data in the table are obtained from the provincial communications authority bureau and the provincial post company.

27–30 各市(州)社会消费品零售总额(2011)

Total Retail Sales of Consumer Goods by Region

单位：亿元 (100 million yuan)

市(州)名称	City (State、Profecture)	合计 Total	按销售地区分 Grouped by Distribution Area	
			城镇 Urban	乡村 Rural
贵阳市	Guiyang	584.33	559.76	24.57
六盘水市	Liupanshui	157.61	127.89	29.72
遵义市	Zunyi	350.62	276.10	74.52
安顺市	Anshun	83.93	67.90	16.03
毕节市	Bijie	150.38	96.22	54.16
铜仁市	Tongren	89.88	55.83	34.05
黔西南州	Qianxinan	105.26	87.93	17.33
黔东南州	Qiandongnan	144.83	110.70	34.13
黔南州	Qiannan	117.12	99.37	17.75

27-31 各市(州)金融机构人民币存贷款余额(2011)

Saving Deposits and Loans Balance of Financial Institutions by Region

单位：亿元 (100 million yuan)

市(州)名称	City(State、Prefecture)	金融机构人民币存款余额 Total Deposits	#储蓄存款 Savings Deposit	金融机构人民币贷款余额 Total Loans
贵阳市	Guiyang	3603.65	1251.04	3012.86
六盘水市	Liupanshui	577.02	264.96	416.97
遵义市	Zunyi	1402.98	743.74	711.74
安顺市	Anshun	427.97	205.74	268.63
毕节市	Bijie	624.34	331.00	350.01
铜仁市	Tongren	448.87	266.36	300.52
黔西南州	Qianxinan	471.60	225.49	273.15
黔东南州	Qiandongnan	562.64	352.77	353.43
黔南州	Qiannan	525.04	293.08	296.57

注：资料来源于中国人民银行贵阳中心支行。

Note:Data in the table are obtained from the People's bank of China Guiyang Branch.

27-32 各市(州)教育事业主要指标(2011)

Major Indicators of Education by Region

市(州)名称	City(State, Prefecture)	高等教育 Higher Education		普通中学 Secondary Schools		小学 Primary Schools	
		学校数(所) Number of schools (unit)	在校学生(人) Students Enrollment (person)	学校数(所) Number of schools (unit)	在校学生(人) Students Enrollment (person)	学校数(所) Number of schools (unit)	在校学生(人) Students Enrollment (person)
贵阳市	Guiyang	28	276883	306	259010	742	334305
六盘水市	Liupanshui	2	7764	219	251254	785	322742
遵义市	Zunyi	6	48644	486	517122	2006	615088
安顺市	Anshun	4	14249	149	163821	924	264846
毕节市	Bijie	2	16164	473	574318	2512	1045088
铜仁市	Tongren	2	13968	255	301915	1471	440046
黔西南州	Qianxinan	2	11593	235	230613	1091	363079
黔东南州	Qiandongnan	3	25933	276	273157	1269	378479
黔南州	Qiannan	4	20953	242	255886	1208	323709

注：1、资料来源于省教育厅。2、高等教育学校数包括：中科院地化所、普通高等学校、成人高等学校，高等教育在校学生包括：研究生、普通高等教育、成人高等教育。

Note:1.Data in the table are obtained from Guizhou Provincial Department of Education.2.Institutions of higher education include Localization of Chinese Academy of Sciences,regular schools of higher education,and adult institutions of higher education.Students enrollment include those students enrolling in postgradu-ates education,ragular institutions of higher education and adult institution of higher education.

27–33 各市(州)卫生人员数(2011)

Number of Employed Persons in Health Care Institutions by Region

单位：人 (person)

市(州)名称	City (State、Prefecture)	总计 Total	卫生技术人员 Medical Technical Personnel	#执业(助理)医师 Licensed (Assistant) Doctors	执业医师 Licensed Doctor	#注册护士 Registered Nurse	#药师(士) Pharmacist	#技师(士) Laboratory Technician	乡村医生和卫生员 Village Doctors and Assistants	其他技术人员 Other Technical Personnel	管理人员 Administrative Personnel	工勤技能人员 Logistics Technical Workers
贵阳市	Guiyang	36551	28638	11338	10491	12284	1336	1591	2029	1757	1901	2226
六盘水市	Liupanshui	14207	9334	3579	2839	3457	330	477	2595	592	775	911
遵义市	Zunyi	30353	20552	7881	6232	7570	976	1149	6214	1031	1042	1514
安顺市	Anshun	9282	6156	2535	2000	2337	272	345	1908	243	541	434
毕节市	Bijie	22527	12673	4971	3608	4025	472	594	7665	736	668	785
铜仁市	Tongren	13857	7711	3310	2524	2228	348	518	4891	327	524	404
黔西南州	Qianxinan	11286	7754	2877	2274	2804	290	376	2415	322	390	405
黔东南州	Qiandongnan	17435	11266	4675	3345	3771	396	638	4315	504	849	501
黔南州	Qiannan	13600	9717	4249	3236	3113	478	591	2555	248	554	526

注：资料来源于省卫生厅，含村卫生室。
Note:Data in the table are obtained from Guizhou Provincial Department of Health and including health clinics of Village.

27–34 各市(州)每千人拥有卫生技术人员数(2011)

Medical Technical Personnel by Region

单位：人 (person)

市(州)名称	City (State、Prefecture)	每千人口拥有卫生技术人员 Medical Technical Personnel Per 1000 Persons	每千人口拥有执业(助理)医师 Lecensed(Assistant) Doctors Per 1000 Persons	每千人口拥有注册护士 Registered Nurses Per 1000 Persons
贵阳市	Guiyang	7.61	3.01	3.27
六盘水市	Liupanshui	2.90	1.11	1.08
遵义市	Zunyi	2.66	1.02	0.98
安顺市	Anshun	2.18	0.90	0.83
毕节市	Bijie	1.49	0.58	0.47
铜仁市	Tongren	1.81	0.77	0.52
黔西南州	Qianxinan	2.25	0.83	0.81
黔东南州	Qiandongnan	2.46	1.02	0.82
黔南州	Qiannan	2.40	1.05	0.77

注:表中数据含村卫生室；每千人口指标按户籍人口计算。
Note: Data in the table include health clinics of village;The indicator of per 1000 population is calculated by household registered population.

27−35 各市(州)医院服务情况(2011)

Services in Hospitals by Region

市(州)名称	City (State、Prefecture)	诊疗人次(万人次) Visits (10 000 person-times)	入院人数(万人) Inpatients (10 000 persons)	出院人数(万人) Patients Discharged from Hosptials (10 000 persons)	危重病人抢救成功率(%) Survival Rate of Patients in Critical Situations (%)	每百门诊急诊入院人数(人) Number of Inpatients Per 100 Outpatients and Emergency Cases (person)	病床使用率(%) Utilization Rate of Beds (%)	出院者平均住院日(天) Average Stay Days in Hospital (day)
贵阳市	Guiyang	827.89	42.82	42.37	88.1	5.3	79.2	12.4
六盘水市	Liupanshui	177.38	17.61	17.75	95.7	10.3	81.3	9.7
遵义市	Zunyi	532.80	46.92	47.06	95.0	9.1	103.6	9.5
安顺市	Anshun	174.27	15.50	15.30	93.3	9.1	86.3	8.3
毕节市	Bijie	292.10	33.06	32.43	98.3	12.0	79.0	7.5
铜仁市	Tongren	197.31	20.70	19.80	69.3	10.9	85.3	8.3
黔西南州	Qianxinan	209.43	19.39	19.16	93.3	9.6	90.8	7.3
黔东南州	Qiandongnan	234.02	26.98	26.46	94.0	12.1	92.3	8.3
黔南州	Qiannan	265.33	20.36	20.26	95.5	7.8	88.3	9.2

27−36 各市(州)社区卫生服务中心(站)医疗服务情况(2011)

Medical Services of Community Health Service Centers(Stations) by Region

市(州)名称	City (State、Prefecture)	社区卫生服务中心 Community Health Service Centers						社区卫生服务站 Community Health Service Stations	
		诊疗人次(万人次) Visits (10 000 person-times)	入院人数(人) Inpatients (person)	病床使用率(%) Utilization Rate (%)	出院者平均住院日(日) Average Stay Days in Hospital (day)	医师日均担负诊疗人次(人次) Daily Visits Each Doctor (person-time)	医师日均担负住院床日(日) Daily Inpatients Each Doctor (day)	诊疗人次(万人次) Visits (10 000 person-times)	医师日均担负诊疗人次(人次) Daily Visits Each Doctor (person-time)
贵阳市	Guiyang	54.78	0.57	49.5	10.5	7.06	0.93	73.34	11.88
六盘水市	Liupanshui	1.69	0.15	51.3	10.6	4.21	1.86	29.04	7.82
遵义市	Zunyi	25.80	5.02	77.3	1.7	7.73	1.78	62.90	9.60
安顺市	Anshun	3.59	0.36	77.5	6.2	5.51	2.33	12.97	4.92
毕节市	Bijie	9.80	1.42	49.4	3.2	3.55	1.46	12.09	10.03
铜仁市	Tongren	5.55	0.14	28.1	4.2	6.91	0.61	0.67	6.66
黔西南州	Qianxinan							22.35	10.12
黔东南州	Qiandongnan	4.33	0.92	43.7	1.0	3.52	0.53		
黔南州	Qiannan	15.10	2.25	67.8	1.1	8.72	0.88	6.64	22.06

注：黔西南州无社区卫生服务中心，黔东南州无社区卫生服务站。

Note: Qianxinan has no community health service centers, and Qiandongnan has no community health service stations.

27–37 各市(州)农村乡镇卫生院医疗服务情况(2011)

Situations of Medical Services in Township Health Centers by Region

市(州)名称	City (State、Prefecture)	诊疗人次(万人次) Visits (10000 person- times)	病床使用率(%) Utilization Rate (%)	出院者平均住院日(日) Average Stay Days in Hospital(day)
贵阳市	Guiyang	155.34	42.1	4.9
六盘水市	Liupanshui	93.32	57.4	4.4
遵义市	Zunyi	310.05	75.4	4.0
安顺市	Anshun	60.40	64.1	2.3
毕节市	Bijie	284.92	67.0	4.2
铜仁市	Tongren	226.08	66.5	4.5
黔西南州	Qianxinan	226.09	67.4	2.6
黔东南州	Qiandongnan	221.05	58.6	3.7
黔南州	Qiannan	283.93	47.2	3.2

27–38 各市(州)火灾(2011)

Fires by Region

市(州)名称	City (State,Prefecture)	火灾(起) Number (case)	死亡(人) Deaths (person)	受伤(人) Injuries (person)	直接财产损失(万元) Direct Property Losses(10000 yuan)
贵阳市	Guiyang	518	6		1688
六盘水市	Liupanshui	51	1		101
遵义市	Zunyi	96	17	3	1353
安顺市	Qiandongnan	94	5		632
毕节市	Bijie	29	6		328
铜仁市	Tongren	84	3	6	565
黔西南州	Qianxinan	78			745
黔东南州	Qiannan	105	10	1	883
黔南州	Anshun	115	7		331

注：资料来源于省公安厅。
Note:Data in the table are obtained from Guizhou Provincial Department of Public Security.

27–39 各县(市、区、特区)生产总值(2011)

Gross Domestic Product by County(City,District,Special region)

单位：万元　　(10000 yuan)

县(市、区、特区)名　称	County (City, District, Special region)	生产总值 Gross Domestic Product	第一产业 Primary Industry	第二产业 Secondary Industry	#工业 Industry	第三产业 Tertiary Industry	按生产总值排　位 Order by Gross Domestic Product	2011年比2010年增长(%) Increase Rate in 2011 over 2010(%)
南明区	Nanming	3016973	18167	608483	364758	2390323	2	17.2
云岩区	Yunyan	3829820	4007	1577202	1429095	2248611	1	17.4
花溪区	Huaxi	987869	79124	392352	236173	516393	15	18.1
乌当区	Wudang	1255118	83284	591658	359947	580176	11	20.3
白云区	Baiyun	766482	27389	420690	390821	318403	25	20.3
小河区	Xiaohe	806261	8863	481915	411622	315483	23	20.4
开阳县	Kaiyang	819314	133314	453254	337688	232746	22	20.5
息烽县	Xifeng	646484	69645	381315	357053	195524	30	20.3
修文县	Xiuwen	576733	87062	235097	181750	254574	33	20.2
清镇市	Qingzhen	1170698	114659	564715	300853	491324	13	20.3
钟山区	Zhongshan	2182987	20096	1221187	1123508	941704	5	17.1
六枝特区	Liuzhi	678722	70000	330844	297544	277878	28	19.7
水城县	Shuicheng	890583	90000	585582	517533	215001	20	21.3
盘　县	Panxian	2499770	140004	1850041	1684231	509725	4	17.4
红花岗区	Honghuagang	1971334	80965	628974	539395	1261395	6	19.7
汇川区	Huicuan	1373513	51157	701969	641916	620387	10	18.8
遵义县	Zunyi	1684811	283889	852420	732214	548502	7	19.6
桐梓县	Tongzi	626879	125700	242606	178105	258573	31	18.8
绥阳县	Suiyang	410959	138700	103068	78294	169191	43	14.6
正安县	Zhengan	296899	107536	52562	29829	136801	59	11.4
※道真县	Daozhen	206579	62602	33338	20438	110639	70	13.1
※务川县	Wuchuan	232332	77728	37240	19935	117364	66	10.1
凤冈县	Fenggang	268100	92065	51274	32399	124761	63	8.4
湄潭县	Meitan	366219	100950	91860	71312	173409	48	16.1
余庆县	Yuqing	307537	80992	82302	52100	144243	56	3.7
习水县	Xishui	619104	108958	257387	198572	252759	32	15.1
赤水市	Chishui	412932	70630	185754	157036	156548	42	19.4
仁怀市	Renhuai	2580241	117942	1689201	1635823	773098	3	21.3
西秀区	Xixiu	1182160	123974	474903	431688	583283	12	16.0
平坝县	Pingba	509575	61561	290660	244610	157354	34	18.0
普定县	Puding	367838	63981	183065	162973	120792	47	16.1
※镇宁县	Zhenning	326807	50442	101470	57823	174895	52	18.0
※关岭县	Guanling	310180	67276	78622	35979	164282	54	16.1
※紫云县	Ziyun	203815	76936	34254	24684	92625	71	16.5
七星关区	Qixingguan	1527090	254742	601634	517271	670714	9	19.0
大方县	Dafang	910432	156990	417258	354368	336184	18	18.3
黔西县	Qianxi	905136	124974	418412	340297	361750	19	15.2
金沙县	Jinsha	1082753	111611	647383	568729	323759	14	19.6
织金县	Zhijin	742292	136205	306014	241581	300073	26	17.1
纳雍县	Nayong	888425	120364	498778	453761	269283	21	17.6
※威宁县	Weining	790698	277751	222261	184664	290686	24	19.2
赫章县	Hezhang	444009	142462	116294	84398	185253	39	17.4
碧江区	Bijiang	703421	95439	253006	182294	354976	27	18.6
万山区	Wanshan	91506	13595	52486	45789	25425	88	20.5

27−39 续表 continued

单位：万元 (10000 yuan)

县(市、区、特区)名 称	County (City, District, Special region)	生产总值 Gross Domestic Product	第一产业 Primary Industry	第二产业 Secondary Industry	#工 业 Industry	第三产业 Tertiary Industry	按生产总值排 位 Order by Gross Domestic Product	2011年比2010年增长(%) Increase Rate in 2011 over 2010(%)
江口县	Jiangkou	177112	57717	46869	247912	72526	76	15.7
※玉屏县	Yuping	307914	40801	171168	155316	95945	55	16.0
石阡县	Shiqian	249625	99683	35136	20449	114806	64	15.4
思南县	Sinan	493060	163204	111453	73013	218403	38	16.5
※印江县	Yinjiang	314051	129021	60330	45097	124700	53	17.0
德江县	Dejiang	397805	145722	74494	47803	177589	44	16.8
※沿河县	Yanhe	391737	139013	66421	36447	186303	45	15.8
※松桃县	Songtao	493801	153243	161439	134852	179119	37	16.5
兴义市	Xingyi	1640295	169543	637057	572870	833695	8	16.6
兴仁县	Xingren	500265	76426	197511	157447	226328	35	18.0
普安县	Puan	292260	47857	141547	120127	102856	61	17.8
晴隆县	Qinglong	240560	43913	93637	73790	103010	65	16.5
贞丰县	Zhenfeng	425464	74183	239447	211909	111834	40	16.8
望谟县	Wangmo	155879	50850	15492	7905	89537	82	15.3
册亨县	Ceheng	140822	45745	17324	12241	77753	84	15.3
安龙县	Anlong	415578	92436	139202	120043	183940	41	16.5
凯里市	Kaili	963638	70287	347586	253725	545765	16	20.0
黄平县	Huangping	196737	64542	23764	15730	108431	72	15.2
施秉县	Shibing	153652	39892	41677	35129	72083	83	17.9
三穗县	Sansui	160835	32095	48378	33225	80362	81	18.8
镇远县	Zhenyuan	302746	67659	141256	123032	93831	58	20.1
岑巩县	Cengong	176248	40538	63168	58901	72542	77	18.6
天柱县	Tianzhu	327680	72441	133571	113715	121668	51	18.6
锦屏县	Jinping	166648	27541	61423	56735	77684	80	16.8
剑河县	Jianhe	167599	47147	31403	22554	89049	79	18.1
台江县	Taijiang	116865	29095	28834	20643	58936	85	16.9
黎平县	Liping	305664	68971	93806	49913	142887	57	17.1
榕江县	Rongjiang	228462	80757	56586	29000	91119	67	17.0
从江县	Congjiang	225809	69761	66951	26593	89097	68	17.2
雷山县	Leishan	113627	28810	26621	18614	58196	87	18.5
麻江县	Majiang	173551	42302	63523	56017	67726	78	18.0
丹寨县	Danzhai	115379	31137	30757	20200	53485	86	17.0
都匀市	Duyun	935385	70222	360271	238577	504892	17	19.7
福泉市	Fuquan	661313	63572	328649	273735	269092	29	18.4
荔波县	Libo	208770	31683	77605	68053	99482	69	15.5
贵定县	Guiding	348080	49536	165739	146653	132806	49	15.3
瓮安县	Wengan	496573	87173	215507	207800	193893	36	17.5
独山县	Dushan	292408	76318	111710	107806	104380	60	14.0
平塘县	Pingtang	182818	60258	42885	30487	79675	75	14.3
罗甸县	Luodian	277978	70518	112442	95354	95018	62	15.3
长顺县	Changshun	192148	47006	66229	60022	78913	73	16.1
龙里县	Longli	373469	35917	263572	232327	73980	46	17.7
惠水县	Huishui	343562	91224	135300	122123	117038	50	15.8
※三都县	Sandu	190007	57162	34182	19164	98663	74	14.1

注：1、※为少数民族自治县(以下相关表同)。2、表中绝对数按当年价格计算，增长速度按可比价格计算。

Note:1.Counties with ※ are autonomous counties(The relative tables in this chapter are the same).2.Absolute Figures in the table are calculated at prices,and increase rates are calculated at comparable prices.

27-40 各县(市、区、特区)人均生产总值(2011)

Per Capita Gross Domestic Product by County (City，District，Special region)

单位：元 (yuan)

县(市、区、特区)名称	County (City，District，Special region)	人均生产总值 Per Capita Gross Domestic Product(yuan)	位次 Order
南明区	Nanming	36015	3
云岩区	Yunyan	39597	2
花溪区	Huaxi	27274	11
乌当区	Wudang	32609	5
白云区	Baiyun	28729	10
小河区	Xiaohe	31969	6
开阳县	Kaiyang	22892	17
息烽县	Xifeng	30323	8
修文县	Xiuwen	23023	16
清镇市	Qingzhen	24972	13
钟山区	Zhongshan	35312	4
六枝特区	Liuzhi	13723	32
水城县	Shuicheng	12649	38
盘　县	Panxian	24145	14
红花岗区	Honghuagang	29738	9
汇川区	Huichuan	30977	7
遵义县	Zunyi	17946	24
桐梓县	Tongzi	12065	40
绥阳县	Suiyang	10829	55
正安县	Zhengan	7702	80
※道真县	Daozhen	8512	74
※务川县	Wuchuan	7274	84
凤冈县	Fenggang	8648	73
湄潭县	Meitan	9761	65
余庆县	Yuqing	13131	35
习水县	Xishui	11897	42
赤水市	Chishui	17372	25
仁怀市	Renhuai	47154	1
西秀区	Xixiu	15495	27
平坝县	Pingba	17149	26
普定县	Puding	9754	67
※镇宁县	Zhenning	11556	47
※关岭县	Guanling	10314	59
※紫云县	Ziyun	7564	81
七星关区	Qixingguan	13463	33
大方县	Dafang	11692	45
黔西县	Qianxi	13054	37
金沙县	Jinsha	19309	23
织金县	Zhijin	9487	69
纳雍县	Nayong	13251	34
※威宁县	Weining	6261	87
赫章县	Hezhang	6830	85
碧江区	Bijiang	21394	18
万山区	Wanshan	11410	48
江口县	Jiangkou	10261	60
※玉屏县	Yuping	26072	12
石阡县	Shiqian	8222	75
思南县	Sinan	9889	64
※印江县	Yinjiang	11070	49
德江县	Dejiang	10831	54
※沿河县	Yanhe	8715	72
※松桃县	Songtao	10158	61
兴义市	Xingyi	20926	20
兴仁县	Xingren	11975	41
普安县	Puan	11726	44
晴隆县	Qinglong	9757	66
贞丰县	Zhenfeng	14012	31
望谟县	Wangmo	6197	88
册亨县	Ceheng	7400	83
安龙县	Anlong	11633	46
凯里市	Kaili	20047	22
黄平县	Huangping	7498	82
施秉县	Shibing	11783	43
三穗县	Sansui	10343	58
镇远县	Zhenyuan	14884	29
岑巩县	Cengong	10927	51
天柱县	Tianzhu	12550	39
锦屏县	Jinping	10832	53
剑河县	Jianhe	9285	71
台江县	Taijiang	10500	56
黎平县	Liping	7852	78
榕江县	Rongjiang	7977	77
从江县	Congjiang	7760	79
雷山县	Leishan	9728	68
麻江县	Majiang	10423	57
丹寨县	Danzhai	9446	70
都匀市	Duyun	21146	19
福泉市	Fuquan	23364	15
荔波县	Libo	14452	30
贵定县	Guiding	15108	28
瓮安县	Wengan	13095	36
独山县	Dushan	11059	50
平塘县	Pingtang	8024	76
罗甸县	Luodian	10875	52
长顺县	Changshun	10088	62
龙里县	Longli	20722	21
惠水县	Huishui	10060	63
※三都县	Sandu	6726	86

27-41 各县(市、区、特区)年末常住人口

Permanent Population at Year-end by County(City,District,Special region)

单位：万人 (10000 persons)

县(市、区、特区)名 称	County (City, District, Special region)	2005	2006	2007	2008	2009	2010	2011
南明区	Nanming	71.79	73.78	74.39	76.28	80.79	83.07	84.47
云岩区	Yunyan	72.95	76.29	84.93	88.38	92.04	95.83	97.60
花溪区	Huaxi	35.19	36.09	36.97	37.69	35.80	36.05	36.39
乌当区	Wudang	33.36	35.06	32.97	34.57	36.18	37.75	39.22
白云区	Baiyun	19.60	20.86	22.21	23.57	25.00	26.49	26.87
小河区	Xiaohe	14.94	16.22	17.64	19.19	21.93	24.85	25.60
开阳县	Kaiyang	40.63	39.77	38.82	37.82	36.84	35.85	35.74
息烽县	Xifeng	23.13	22.82	22.47	22.10	21.71	21.31	21.33
修文县	Xiuwen	27.34	26.92	26.48	25.98	25.47	24.93	25.17
清镇市	Qingzhen	49.16	48.86	48.39	47.84	47.35	46.80	46.96
钟山区	Zhongshan	48.81	51.37	53.73	56.75	59.22	61.76	61.88
六枝特区	Liuzhi	60.02	58.01	55.76	54.03	51.78	49.56	49.36
水城县	Shuicheng	71.83	71.95	71.60	71.69	71.14	70.52	70.29
盘　县	Panxian	112.67	111.34	109.50	107.98	105.82	103.59	103.47
红花岗区	Honghuagang	59.95	61.37	62.48	63.79	64.78	65.74	66.83
汇川区	Huichuan	37.70	39.03	40.23	41.56	42.73	43.90	44.78
遵义县	Zunyi	106.12	104.06	101.71	99.53	97.04	94.52	93.24
桐梓县	Tongzi	59.34	58.06	56.60	55.26	53.75	52.23	51.68
绥阳县	Suiyang	47.02	45.25	43.38	41.65	39.82	38.04	37.87
正安县	Zhengan	52.06	49.35	46.60	44.02	41.43	38.97	38.14
※道真县	Daozhen	29.58	28.63	27.56	26.52	25.46	24.42	24.13
※务川县	Wuchuan	39.95	38.49	36.86	35.34	33.74	32.19	31.70
凤冈县	Fenggang	38.36	37.01	35.56	34.17	32.73	31.32	30.67
湄潭县	Meitan	42.50	41.68	40.71	39.83	38.80	37.77	37.27
余庆县	Yuqing	26.04	25.63	25.10	24.62	24.06	23.49	23.34
习水县	Xishui	61.20	59.55	57.73	56.01	54.15	52.32	51.77
赤水市	Chishui	25.87	25.51	25.07	24.68	24.20	23.72	23.82
仁怀市	Renhuai	53.86	54.23	54.39	54.65	54.68	54.66	54.77
西秀区	Xixiu	81.08	80.52	79.51	78.97	77.81	76.63	75.95
平坝县	Pingba	33.98	33.26	32.36	31.68	30.76	29.85	29.58
普定县	Puding	39.16	39.04	38.68	38.55	38.22	37.88	37.54
※镇宁县	Zhenning	34.27	33.16	31.89	30.86	29.62	28.41	28.15
※关岭县	Guanling	31.95	31.73	31.33	31.12	30.66	30.20	29.95
※紫云县	Ziyun	31.82	30.94	29.91	29.10	28.07	27.07	26.82
七星关区	Qixingguan	123.72	122.23	120.02	118.76	116.33	113.86	113.00
大方县	Dafang	93.35	90.76	87.28	84.61	81.15	77.74	78.00
黔西县	Qianxi	80.21	78.34	76.03	74.39	72.02	69.68	69.00
金沙县	Jinsha	57.17	57.21	56.91	57.04	56.61	56.15	56.00
织金县	Zhijin	89.03	87.20	84.91	83.31	80.89	78.48	78.00
纳雍县	Nayong	74.39	73.24	71.62	70.59	68.84	67.09	67.00
※威宁县	Weining	109.33	113.76	116.77	120.68	123.61	126.56	126.00
赫章县	Hezhang	61.62	62.62	63.17	64.19	64.63	65.01	65.00
碧江区	Bijiang	32.55	33.39	33.99	34.95	35.59	36.23	29.52
万山区	Wanshan	4.80	4.74	4.64	4.97	4.88	4.79	11.25

27-41 续表 (continued)

单位：万人 (10000 persons)

县(市、区、特区)名 称	County (City, District, Special region)	2005	2006	2007	2008	2009	2010	2011
江口县	Jiangkou	21.06	20.34	19.48	18.88	18.08	17.30	17.21
※玉屏县	Yuping	13.24	13.01	12.70	12.50	12.18	11.86	11.75
石阡县	Shiqian	34.43	33.78	32.87	32.31	31.38	30.45	30.27
思南县	Sinan	62.31	59.96	57.29	54.96	52.44	49.99	49.72
※印江县	Yinjiang	38.98	36.75	34.45	32.63	30.48	28.44	28.29
德江县	Dejiang	43.49	42.27	40.81	39.79	38.30	36.84	36.62
※沿河县	Yanhe	52.88	51.42	49.72	48.56	46.78	45.01	44.88
※松桃县	Songtao	61.05	58.52	55.78	54.24	51.45	48.72	48.49
兴义市	Xingyi	72.04	73.69	74.79	76.60	77.57	78.53	78.20
兴仁县	Xingren	44.99	44.60	43.78	43.49	42.67	41.85	41.70
普安县	Puan	28.03	27.51	26.94	26.66	26.07	25.47	25.40
晴隆县	Qinglong	27.99	27.78	26.89	26.36	25.53	24.70	24.60
贞丰县	Zhenfeng	34.09	33.50	32.65	32.15	31.29	30.42	30.30
望谟县	Wangmo	27.65	27.18	26.70	26.40	25.80	25.20	25.10
册亨县	Ceheng	21.47	21.07	20.53	20.19	19.63	19.07	19.00
安龙县	Anlong	41.92	40.74	39.46	38.52	37.14	35.79	35.70
凯里市	Kaili	44.90	45.73	46.27	47.03	47.49	47.92	48.22
黄平县	Huangping	32.60	31.41	30.06	28.93	27.61	26.34	26.14
施秉县	Shibing	12.98	13.07	13.07	13.13	13.10	13.06	13.02
三穗县	Sansui	16.55	16.44	16.23	16.10	15.85	15.60	15.50
镇远县	Zhenyuan	23.11	22.66	22.08	21.62	21.01	20.40	20.28
岑巩县	Cengong	20.55	19.71	18.77	17.98	17.09	16.22	16.04
天柱县	Tianzhu	36.04	34.06	31.97	30.18	28.25	26.42	25.80
锦屏县	Jinping	18.72	18.13	17.44	16.86	16.18	15.51	15.26
剑河县	Jianhe	21.13	20.59	19.94	19.40	18.73	18.08	18.02
台江县	Taijiang	12.65	12.42	12.12	11.88	11.56	11.24	11.02
黎平县	Liping	47.94	46.29	44.40	42.82	40.97	39.16	38.70
榕江县	Rongjiang	31.23	30.87	30.31	29.91	29.30	28.68	28.60
从江县	Congjiang	31.04	30.82	30.39	30.12	29.63	29.13	29.07
雷山县	Leishan	12.42	12.34	12.19	12.10	11.92	11.73	11.63
麻江县	Majiang	19.81	19.27	18.62	18.08	17.42	16.78	16.52
丹寨县	Danzhai	13.98	13.69	13.32	13.02	12.64	12.26	12.17
都匀市	Duyun	46.50	46.30	45.86	45.50	45.03	44.43	44.04
福泉市	Fuquan	29.41	29.31	29.07	29.12	28.81	28.44	28.17
荔波县	Libo	16.31	16.01	15.62	15.30	14.90	14.50	14.39
贵定县	Guiding	27.19	26.39	25.49	24.92	24.02	23.13	22.95
瓮安县	Wengan	44.56	43.43	42.08	40.80	39.49	38.10	37.74
独山县	Dushan	33.35	31.98	30.48	29.31	27.89	26.53	26.34
平塘县	Pingtang	28.17	27.14	26.00	25.02	23.93	22.86	22.71
罗甸县	Luodian	31.78	30.58	29.26	28.21	26.93	25.68	25.55
长顺县	Changshun	22.42	21.81	21.09	20.53	19.81	19.12	18.98
龙里县	Longli	19.22	19.08	18.84	18.67	18.39	18.09	17.95
惠水县	Huishui	40.72	39.49	38.08	36.77	35.35	34.27	34.04
※三都县	Sandu	29.69	29.56	29.24	29.14	28.77	28.36	28.14

注：表中数据为常住半年及以上人口数，其中2006年-2009年数据根据第六次人口普查结果修订。
Note:Poulations in the table refer to permanent population in the scope at least half a year;Data from the year 2006 to 2009 had been adjusted according to the result of the Sixth National Population Census.

27-42 各县(市、区、特区)户籍人口(2011)
Household Registered Population by County (City，District，Special region)

单位：万人 (10000 persons)

县(市、区、特区)名称	County (City, District, Special region)	户籍人口 Permanent Population at the year-end	县(市、区、特区)名称	County (City, District, Special region)	户籍人口 Permanent Population at the year-end
南明区	Nanming	56.17	万山区	Wanshan	6.57
云岩区	Yunyan	64.55	江口县	Jiangkou	23.73
花溪区	Huaxi	32.59	※玉屏县	Yuping	15.29
乌当区	Wudang	33.76	石阡县	Shiqian	41.02
白云区	Baiyun	20.04	思南县	Sinan	67.71
小河区	Xiaohe	16.64	※印江县	Yinjiang	43.59
开阳县	Kaiyang	43.74	德江县	Dejiang	53.18
息烽县	Xifeng	25.99	※沿河县	Yanhe	66.10
修文县	Xiuwen	31.01	※松桃县	Songtao	71.09
清镇市	Qingzhen	51.65			
			兴义市	Xingyi	82.20
钟山区	Zhongshan	49.73	兴仁县	Xingren	52.93
六枝特区	Liuzhi	69.59	普安县	Puan	33.19
水城县	Shuicheng	83.34	晴隆县	Qinglong	33.53
盘　县	Panxian	118.75	贞丰县	Zhenfeng	40.85
			望谟县	Wangmo	32.06
红花岗区	Honghuagang	51.75	册亨县	Ceheng	23.67
汇川区	Huichuan	35.73	安龙县	Anlong	46.32
遵义县	Zunyi	121.43			
桐梓县	Tongzi	71.01	凯里市	Kaili	50.10
绥阳县	Suiyang	54.20	黄平县	Huangping	38.65
正安县	Zhengan	64.13	施秉县	Shibing	16.81
※道真县	Daozhen	34.24	三穗县	Sansui	22.06
※务川县	Wuchuan	45.60	镇远县	Zhenyuan	26.84
凤冈县	Fenggang	43.79	岑巩县	Cengong	22.65
湄潭县	Meitan	49.46	天柱县	Tianzhu	40.62
余庆县	Yuqing	30.30	锦屏县	Jinping	22.73
习水县	Xishui	72.15	剑河县	Jianhe	25.50
赤水市	Chishui	31.15	台江县	Taijiang	15.99
仁怀市	Renhuai	67.00	黎平县	Liping	52.76
			榕江县	Rongjiang	35.47
西秀区	Xixiu	87.51	从江县	Congjiang	34.46
平坝县	Pingba	35.50	雷山县	Leishan	15.25
普定县	Puding	46.66	麻江县	Majiang	21.46
※镇宁县	Zhenning	38.42	丹寨县	Danzhai	16.82
※关岭县	Guanling	37.06			
※紫云县	Ziyun	37.11	都匀市	Duyun	48.26
			福泉市	Fuquan	32.83
七星关区	Qixingguan	151.40	荔波县	Libo	17.50
大方县	Dafang	109.84	贵定县	Guiding	29.11
黔西县	Qianxi	93.46	瓮安县	Wengan	46.50
金沙县	Jinsha	67.85	独山县	Dushan	34.94
织金县	Zhijin	111.65	平塘县	Pingtang	32.26
纳雍县	Nayong	96.04	罗甸县	Luodian	34.02
※威宁县	Weining	143.12	长顺县	Changshun	25.85
赫章县	Hezhang	78.36	龙里县	Longli	22.27
			惠水县	Huishui	45.28
碧江区	Bijiang	38.93	※三都县	Sandu	36.04

注：资料来源于省公安厅。
Note:Data in the table above are obtained from the Public Security Department of Guizhou Province.

27-43 各县(市、区、特区)第六次人口普查主要指标

Basic Statistics on the Sixth National Population Census by County

单位：人 (person)

县(市、区、特区)名称	County (City, District, Special region)	普查时点常住人口 Permanent Population	出生率(‰) Birth Rate (‰)	死亡率(‰) Death Rate (‰)	自然增长率(‰) Natural Growth Rate (‰)	城镇人口占比(%) Urbanization Rate (%)
南明区	Nanming	829706	9.11	3.72	5.39	95.66
云岩区	Yunyan	957343	8.16	3.25	4.91	97.31
花溪区	Huaxi	359141	11.87	4.91	6.95	43.71
乌当区	Wudang	377146	13.60	4.18	9.42	55.80
白云区	Baiyun	264621	11.80	3.99	7.80	76.05
小河区	Xiaohe	248185	11.88	3.11	8.78	96.07
开阳县	Kaiyang	358403	11.83	6.41	5.42	30.93
息烽县	Xifeng	212992	13.57	6.64	6.93	28.90
修文县	Xiuwen	249034	15.67	6.35	9.32	29.35
清镇市	Qingzhen	467992	13.16	5.77	7.38	35.93
钟山区	Zhongshan	616178	10.71	2.72	7.99	79.74
六枝特区	Liuzhi	495135	14.40	7.69	6.71	26.16
水城县	Shuicheng	704579	12.88	7.08	5.80	2.41
盘　县	Panxian	1035288	12.96	6.76	6.20	17.25
红花岗区	Honghuagang	656584	10.29	3.92	6.37	64.59
汇川区	Huichuan	438274	11.13	3.68	7.45	66.21
遵义县	Zunyi	942893	12.26	7.06	5.20	29.71
桐梓县	Tongzi	521834	14.97	6.60	8.37	28.31
绥阳县	Suiyang	380078	15.39	7.73	7.66	27.38
正安县	Zhengan	389629	13.29	9.69	3.60	24.99
※道真县	Daozhen	244156	11.62	8.86	2.76	26.62
※务川县	Wuchuan	321653	12.66	7.45	5.21	26.55
凤冈县	Fenggang	313124	11.78	8.12	3.66	26.21
湄潭县	Meitan	377353	11.85	6.79	5.06	27.82
余庆县	Yuqing	234736	13.72	7.56	6.16	33.01
习水县	Xishui	523174	13.71	6.53	7.18	25.74
赤水市	Chishui	237049	13.77	8.56	5.21	34.00
仁怀市	Renhuai	546471	10.91	6.56	4.35	31.45
西秀区	Xixiu	765309	13.68	5.79	7.89	48.97
平坝县	Pingba	297954	16.49	6.79	9.70	33.62
普定县	Puding	378406	13.87	6.23	7.64	19.66
※镇宁县	Zhenning	284029	12.37	7.66	4.71	25.70
※关岭县	Guanling	301327	15.91	7.45	8.46	19.31
※紫云县	Ziyun	270312	17.82	8.20	9.62	15.42
七星关区	Qianxiguan	1137189	15.12	6.39	8.73	37.14
大方县	Dafang	776191	15.55	6.70	8.86	25.58
黔西县	Qianxi	695827	17.15	7.62	9.52	32.57
金沙县	Jinsha	560482	15.68	6.83	8.85	30.04
织金县	Zhijin	783984	13.10	6.61	6.49	25.82
纳雍县	Nayong	670156	15.65	6.00	9.65	24.95
※威宁县	Weining	1263299	15.02	6.32	8.70	18.93
赫章县	Hezhang	649242	14.31	6.31	8.00	16.83
碧江区	Bijiang	361579	12.47	4.74	7.73	57.01
万山区	Wanshan	47804	16.81	9.24	7.57	26.21

27-43 续表 continued

单位：人 (person)

县(市、区、特区)名 称	County (City，District，Special region)	普查时点常住人口 Permanent Population	出生率 (‰) Birth Rate (‰)	死亡率 (‰) Death Rate (‰)	自然增长率 (‰) Natural Growth Rate (‰)	城镇人口占比 (%) Urbanization Rate (%)
江口县	Jiangkou	172716	14.75	6.08	8.66	23.45
※玉屏县	Yuping	118491	17.29	8.35	8.94	39.52
石阡县	Shiqian	304305	12.95	8.15	4.80	24.04
思南县	Sinan	499192	12.51	7.48	5.04	23.12
※印江县	Yinjiang	284142	12.83	8.07	4.76	23.23
德江县	Dejiang	367819	15.11	6.73	8.38	21.89
※沿河县	Yanhe	449690	17.08	6.65	10.43	17.19
※松桃县	Songtao	486626	16.04	6.74	9.29	17.46
兴义市	Xingyi	783467	16.83	5.79	11.04	43.01
兴仁县	Xingren	418106	15.50	6.79	8.71	26.57
普安县	Puan	254361	11.72	6.23	5.49	20.29
晴隆县	Qinglong	246918	17.56	7.66	9.90	19.59
贞丰县	Zhenfeng	304020	14.91	7.45	7.46	22.52
望谟县	Wangmo	252074	13.11	8.20	4.91	18.25
册亨县	Ceheng	190498	16.30	8.26	8.04	17.77
安龙县	Anlong	356414	17.35	6.54	10.80	26.18
凯里市	Kaili	478835	11.91	5.39	6.53	59.34
黄平县	Huangping	263272	13.36	7.83	5.53	18.57
施秉县	Shibing	130416	13.52	7.43	6.09	29.80
三穗县	Sansui	155679	20.55	8.84	11.71	27.97
镇远县	Zhenyuan	203548	16.78	8.36	8.42	33.84
岑巩县	Cengong	162385	15.49	8.82	6.67	20.05
天柱县	Tianzhu	263753	16.99	8.57	8.42	22.94
锦屏县	Jinping	154812	18.22	8.99	9.22	26.99
剑河县	Jianhe	180557	15.61	8.46	7.15	19.65
台江县	Taijiang	112281	15.19	7.79	7.40	21.83
黎平县	Liping	390905	16.64	8.60	8.04	18.76
榕江县	Rongjiang	286216	16.99	6.52	10.47	16.34
从江县	Congjiang	290851	18.30	8.77	9.53	13.55
雷山县	Leishan	117147	17.04	9.89	7.15	23.44
麻江县	Majiang	167578	14.37	8.67	5.70	20.07
丹寨县	Danzhai	122390	15.50	8.37	7.13	20.16
都匀市	Duyun	443511	11.85	6.39	5.46	50.85
福泉市	Fuquan	283768	15.67	6.79	8.88	33.77
荔波县	Libo	144793	14.91	7.68	7.22	23.80
贵定县	Guiding	231009	14.27	7.40	6.87	34.89
瓮安县	Wengan	380135	14.62	6.29	8.33	33.04
独山县	Dushan	265086	14.20	7.88	6.32	23.14
平塘县	Pingtang	228447	14.58	8.97	5.62	21.19
罗甸县	Luodian	257111	14.94	8.57	6.38	17.70
长顺县	Changshun	191038	14.16	6.90	7.26	25.30
龙里县	Longli	180780	16.57	7.89	8.69	31.09
惠水县	Huishui	342480	14.47	7.26	7.21	22.43
※三都县	Sandu	283001	17.82	7.57	10.24	14.08

27-44 各县(市、区、特区)固定资产投资(2011)

Investment in Fixed Assets by County(City,District,Special region)

单位：万元 (10000 yuan)

县(市、区、特区)名称	County (City,District, Special region)	固定资产投资 Investment in Fixed Assets
南明区	Nanming	1476787
云岩区	Yunyan	1750400
花溪区	Huaxi	1129330
乌当区	Wudang	901946
白云区	Baiyun	1331860
小河区	Xiaohe	1347574
开阳县	Kaiyang	1117756
息烽县	Xifeng	847425
修文县	Xiuwen	848509
清镇市	Qingzhen	1232584
钟山区	Zhongshan	1120785
六枝特区	Liuzhi	502019
水城县	Shuicheng	956755
盘　县	Panxian	1653224
红花岗区	Honghuagang	1149859
汇川区	Huicuan	597783
遵义县	Zunyi	1117542
桐梓县	Tongzi	770636
绥阳县	Suiyang	284204
正安县	Zhengan	207426
※道真县	Daozhen	137550
※务川县	Wuchuan	193791
凤冈县	Fenggang	121952
湄潭县	Meitan	325354
余庆县	Yuqing	254658
习水县	Xishui	669857
赤水市	Chishui	405533
仁怀市	Renhuai	616958
西秀区	Xixiu	739191
平坝县	Pingba	185027
普定县	Puding	140534
※镇宁县	Zhenning	176309
※关岭县	Guanling	119732
※紫云县	Ziyun	95044
七星关区	Qixingguan	1040316
大方县	Dafang	628992
黔西县	Qianxi	744568
金沙县	Jinsha	902956
织金县	Zhijin	781439
纳雍县	Nayong	755690
※威宁县	Weining	679512
赫章县	Hezhang	386711
碧江区	Bijiang	671034
万山区	Wanshan	106498

27-44 续表 continued

单位：万元 (10000 yuan)

县(市、区、特区)名称	County(City,District, Special region)	固定资产投资 Investment in Fixed Assets
江口县	Jiangkou	211309
※玉屏县	Yuping	195936
石阡县	Shiqian	154393
思南县	Sinan	437584
※印江县	Yinjiang	246979
德江县	Dejiang	228455
※沿河县	Yanhe	355210
※松桃县	Songtao	392719
兴义市	Xingyi	1110136
兴仁县	Xingren	430156
普安县	Puan	210436
晴隆县	Qinglong	230647
贞丰县	Zhenfeng	279217
望谟县	Wangmo	115612
册亨县	Ceheng	88851
安龙县	Anlong	222956
凯里市	Kaili	1173673
黄平县	Huangping	138064
施秉县	Shibing	120556
三穗县	Sansui	135095
镇远县	Zhenyuan	143210
岑巩县	Cengong	134701
天柱县	Tianzhu	275448
锦屏县	Jinping	97094
剑河县	Jianhe	122414
台江县	Taijiang	114225
黎平县	Liping	236297
榕江县	Rongjiang	182544
从江县	Congjiang	185532
雷山县	Leishan	80590
麻江县	Majiang	154494
丹寨县	Danzhai	145727
都匀市	Duyun	810488
福泉市	Fuquan	469075
荔波县	Libo	210089
贵定县	Guiding	262186
瓮安县	Wengan	474100
独山县	Dushan	194932
平塘县	Pingtang	191803
罗甸县	Luodian	254958
长顺县	Changshun	210621
龙里县	Longli	365100
惠水县	Huishui	368056
※三都县	Sandu	188808

注：1、本表统计口径为50万元以上的城镇固定资产投资和农村非农户投资。2、本表不包括跨县(市、区)域项目，也不包括220KV及以上输电线路投资。

Note:1.Data in the table refer to those projects planned to invest 500,000 yuan at least in urban areas,projects funded by rural non-farm households and real estate development.2.Data in the table do not include investment in cross-regional projects,nor investment in power transmission and distribution projects as the voltage reach 220KV and above.

27–45 各县(市、区、特区)财政一般预算收入(2011)

Total Local Government Budgetary Revenue and by County (City,District,Special region)

县(市、区、特区)名称	County (City,District,Special region)	财政一般预算收入(万元) Local Government Financial Revenue (10000 yuan)	#增值税 Value Added Tax	位次 Order	2011年比2010年增长(%) Increase Rate in 2011 over 2010(%)	人均财政一般预算收入(元) Per Capita Local Financial Revenue(yuan)
南明区	Nanming	186108	12190	3	45.5	2222
云岩区	Yunyan	205007	16250	2	37.4	2120
花溪区	Huaxi	65184	4003	26	49.3	1800
乌当区	Wudang	87671	5513	16	45.0	2278
白云区	Baiyun	94996	11434	13	55.0	3561
小河区	Xiaohe	83148	6024	18	45.1	3296
开阳县	Kaiyang	71139	7389	23	42.0	1988
息烽县	Xifeng	43944	1668	33	42.8	2061
修文县	Xiuwen	38682	3588	36	38.3	1544
清镇市	Qingzhen	78405	5133	20	41.6	1673
钟山区	Zhongshan	110302	7065	8	28.9	1784
六枝特区	Liuzhi	49850	1787	30	75.0	1008
水城县	Shuicheng	98937	9087	11	60.5	1405
盘　县	Panxian	258719	38037	1	31.7	2499
红花岗区	Honghuagang	99581	4942	10	40.5	1502
汇川区	Huichuan	67253	4547	25	26.0	1517
遵义县	Zunyi	104683	8294	9	36.3	1115
桐梓县	Tongzi	39402	2498	35	49.8	758
绥阳县	Suiyang	24371	901	48	47.7	642
正安县	Zhengan	20823	559	58	42.9	540
※道真县	Daozhen	15188	718	71	47.7	626
※务川县	Wuchuan	24254	912	50	72.2	759
凤冈县	Fenggang	15836	637	67	45.8	511
湄潭县	Meitan	26877	1007	46	40.0	716
余庆县	Yuqing	21259	1445	57	23.5	908
习水县	Xishui	42380	4635	34	45.0	814
赤水市	Chishui	27168	1426	45	48.3	1143
仁怀市	Renhuai	161370	45704	4	53.7	2949
西秀区	Xixiu	89885	9264	14	28.9	1178
平坝县	Pingba	36039	2865	38	37.6	1213
普定县	Puding	29994	2685	42	34.1	795
※镇宁县	Zhenning	27706	1269	43	40.2	980
※关岭县	Guanling	19473	860	60	25.3	647
※紫云县	Ziyun	10689	447	83	36.5	397
七星关区	Qixingguan	77496	2779	21	35.8	683
大方县	Dafang	79763	5525	19	22.9	1024
黔西县	Qianxi	70874	5612	24	27.5	1022
金沙县	Jinsha	158229	16091	6	45.4	2822
织金县	Zhijin	97092	4298	12	42.4	1241
纳雍县	Nayong	83448	6634	17	43.7	1245
※威宁县	Weining	56276	3567	28	42.5	446
赫章县	Hezhang	22756	2711	55	19.0	350
碧江区	Bijiang	46884	1334	32	54.2	1426
万山区	Wanshan	8256	969	88	54.7	1029

27-45 续表 continued

县(市、区、特区)名称	County (City,District,Special region)	财政一般预算收入(万元) Local Government Financial Revenue (10000 yuan)	#增值税 Value Added Tax	位次 Order	2011年比2010年增长(%) Increase Rate in 2011over 2010(%)	人均财政一般预算收入(元) Per Capita Local Financial Revenue(yuan)
江口县	Jiangkou	12008	436	79	26.2	696
※玉屏县	Yuping	21357	2352	56	55.3	1809
石阡县	Shiqian	15809	393	68	39.2	521
思南县	Sinan	23119	1275	54	43.0	464
※印江县	Yinjiang	15469	630	70	30.9	545
德江县	Dejiang	23254	865	53	52.8	633
※沿河县	Yanhe	36507	2253	37	73.0	812
※松桃县	Songtao	31641	3020	41	70.3	651
兴义市	Xingyi	160016	11270	5	38.8	2042
兴仁县	Xingren	75929	5269	22	87.3	1818
普安县	Puan	35240	4077	39	36.3	1385
晴隆县	Qinglong	25582	1289	47	44.0	1038
贞丰县	Zhenfeng	55008	3212	29	68.3	1812
望谟县	Wangmo	8924	1380	86	7.2	355
册亨县	Ceheng	8413	914	87	21.9	442
安龙县	Anlong	32009	3929	40	59.5	896
凯里市	Kaili	143510	3790	7	119.6	2986
黄平县	Huangping	14372	595	72	51.0	548
施秉县	Shibing	18124	706	63	53.1	1390
三穗县	Sansui	12600	389	77	72.4	810
镇远县	Zhenyuan	23615	2037	51	80.7	1161
岑巩县	Cengong	10741	1110	81	82.5	666
天柱县	Tianzhu	24334	852	49	75.7	932
锦屏县	Jinping	13943	931	73	52.7	906
剑河县	Jianhe	12463	646	78	87.4	690
台江县	Taijiang	10730	431	82	61.4	964
黎平县	Liping	18512	1008	61	74.3	476
榕江县	Rongjiang	16366	668	66	83.9	571
从江县	Congjiang	15719	804	69	66.7	540
雷山县	Leishan	10272	410	84	85.3	879
麻江县	Majiang	11819	1388	80	72.7	710
丹寨县	Danzhai	10084	564	85	73.4	826
都匀市	Duyun	89546	3140	15	70.4	2024
福泉市	Fuquan	56923	3158	27	42.1	2011
荔波县	Libo	16766	1581	65	23.9	1161
贵定县	Guiding	20516	1461	59	46.1	890
瓮安县	Wengan	47139	3420	31	39.4	1243
独山县	Dushan	17870	1189	64	31.9	676
平塘县	Pingtang	13822	378	74	40.2	607
罗甸县	Luodian	18475	2358	62	28.9	721
长顺县	Changshun	13063	928	75	39.1	686
龙里县	Longli	27188	2208	44	35.8	1509
惠水县	Huishui	23330	2100	52	67.6	683
※三都县	Sandu	12772	379	76	61.4	452

注：资料来源于省财政厅(下表同)。
Note:Data in the table are obtained from Guizhou Provincial Financial Department(the same applies to the next table).

27–46 各县(市、区、特区)财政一般预算支出(2011)

Total Local Government Budgetary Expenditure by County (City,District,Special region)

县(市、区、特区) 名称	County (City,District,Special region)	财政支出(万元) Local Government Financial Expenditures (10000 yuan)	#教育支出 Operating Expenses for Education	位次 Order	2011年比2010年增长(%) Increase Rate in 2011 over 2010	人均财政支出(元) Per Capita Financial Expenditure(yuan)
南明区	Nanming	207553	56101	17	24.4	2478
云岩区	Yunyan	223941	63913	14	25.7	2315
花溪区	Huaxi	137362	30883	41	41.1	3793
乌当区	Wudang	145006	22928	36	38.1	3768
白云区	Baiyun	135605	29717	42	26.2	5083
小河区	Xiaohe	102962	18801	71	34.4	4082
开阳县	Kaiyang	164568	31307	29	34.5	4598
息烽县	Xifeng	115592	24235	60	33.2	5422
修文县	Xiuwen	110409	25432	68	22.9	4407
清镇市	Qingzhen	172828	41780	27	32.3	3687
钟山区	Zhongshan	189019	35855	22	25.1	3058
六枝特区	Liuzhi	215664	41870	15	36.3	4360
水城县	Shuicheng	261376	53533	9	33.7	3712
盘　县	Panxian	487797	121531	1	20.5	4712
红花岗区	Honghuagang	177345	40027	26	31.2	2675
汇川区	Huichuan	140096	28592	40	32.6	3160
遵义县	Zunyi	302387	87631	4	31.3	3221
桐梓县	Tongzi	165732	37270	28	37.2	3190
绥阳县	Suiyang	126875	31920	49	22.5	3343
正安县	Zhengan	150572	35456	34	11.1	3906
※道真县	Daozhen	112311	24764	64	24.9	4627
※务川县	Wuchuan	126181	29219	50	21.6	3950
凤冈县	Fenggang	111746	27036	66	26.2	3605
湄潭县	Meitan	140284	28847	38	31.3	3739
余庆县	Yuqing	97270	23664	72	36.0	4154
习水县	Xishui	186524	44838	23	31.6	3584
赤水市	Chishui	121549	20367	54	40.8	5114
仁怀市	Renhuai	242171	54300	11	43.7	4426
西秀区	Xixiu	250641	53473	10	28.8	3285
平坝县	Pingba	135563	23786	43	30.6	4562
普定县	Puding	119385	25237	55	29.4	3166
※镇宁县	Zhenning	125907	20535	51	35.8	4452
※关岭县	Guanling	117637	20846	56	13.4	3911
※紫云县	Ziyun	111425	25118	67	27.4	4135
七星关区	Qixingguan	327450	89863	3	18.8	2887
大方县	Dafang	274026	60269	6	19.2	3519
黔西县	Qianxi	214868	45971	16	25.7	3099
金沙县	Jinsha	268416	57715	8	7.2	4787
织金县	Zhijin	270162	56782	7	21.1	3453
纳雍县	Nayong	224883	55933	13	14.5	3354
※威宁县	Weining	391777	115374	2	36.4	3102
赫章县	Hezhang	206068	51652	18	19.9	3170
碧江区	Bijiang	140111	23993	39	29.0	4262
万山区	Wanshan	74142	8641	88	6.2	9244

27-46 续表 continued

县(市、区、特区)名称	County (City,District,Special region)	财政支出(万元) Local Government Financial Expenditures (10000 yuan)	#教育支出 Operating Expenses for Education	位次 Order	2011年比2010年增长(%) Increase Rate in 2011 over 2010	人均财政支出(元) Per Capita Financial Expenditure(yuan)
江口县	Jiangkou	94967	17779	76	30.2	5504
※玉屏县	Yuping	88438	14857	80	50.1	7492
石阡县	Shiqian	158339	30298	32	28.9	5215
思南县	Sinan	196002	44715	20	22.7	3932
※印江县	Yinjiang	140308	32991	37	28.4	4947
德江县	Dejiang	161263	34012	30	34.7	4390
※沿河县	Yanhe	180022	35557	25	30.1	4005
※松桃县	Songtao	195215	42533	21	22.4	4016
兴义市	Xingyi	295671	64144	5	37.0	3773
兴仁县	Xingren	184244	39802	24	34.1	4411
普安县	Puan	113583	23916	63	32.3	4465
晴隆县	Qinglong	116658	25176	58	26.8	4733
贞丰县	Zhenfeng	147521	30122	35	44.6	4859
望谟县	Wangmo	135509	28477	44	25.2	5388
册亨县	Ceheng	95317	17063	75	29.6	5008
安龙县	Anlong	130776	33368	47	7.9	3659
凯里市	Kaili	230293	51196	12	50.4	4791
黄平县	Huangping	117582	24131	57	35.9	4481
施秉县	Shibing	78352	12331	86	28.7	6008
三穗县	Sansui	82918	15585	85	28.9	5332
镇远县	Zhenyuan	95445	18514	74	32.4	4692
岑巩县	Cengong	83333	17986	84	30.7	5166
天柱县	Tianzhu	132635	30823	46	35.2	5080
锦屏县	Jinping	95698	18637	73	21.4	6222
剑河县	Jianhe	94076	17281	77	28.7	5212
台江县	Taijiang	77090	14276	87	38.9	6927
黎平县	Liping	160605	37835	31	23.4	4125
榕江县	Rongjiang	115292	27625	61	27.3	4025
从江县	Congjiang	122715	26281	53	18.3	4217
雷山县	Leishan	84976	16475	83	31.3	7273
麻江县	Majiang	93273	18242	78	44.1	5602
丹寨县	Danzhai	88230	18780	81	34.0	7224
都匀市	Duyun	199581	30099	19	39.8	4512
福泉市	Fuquan	122820	25593	52	27.9	4339
荔波县	Libo	89420	19200	79	33.0	6190
贵定县	Guiding	107796	20034	70	21.5	4678
瓮安县	Wengan	151043	28333	33	21.1	3983
独山县	Dushan	108906	26015	69	17.7	4119
平塘县	Pingtang	113611	20473	62	23.2	4986
罗甸县	Luodian	127923	27820	48	25.2	4994
长顺县	Changshun	112201	18980	65	47.9	5890
龙里县	Longli	87310	15626	82	17.4	4845
惠水县	Huishui	134333	27629	45	31.8	3933
※三都县	Sandu	115819	29839	59	28.4	4100

27-47 各县(市、区、特区)农民人均纯收入(2011)

Per Capita Net Income of Rural Households by County(City,District,Special region)

单位：元 (yuan)

县(市、区、特区)名称	County (City,District, Special region)	农民人均纯收入 Per Capita Annual Net Income of Rural Households	位次 Order
南明区	Nanming	9031	2
云岩区	Yunyan	9124	1
花溪区	Huaxi	7508	6
乌当区	Wudang	8332	5
白云区	Baiyun	8887	4
小河区	Xiaohe	8947	3
开阳县	Kaiyang	6781	10
息烽县	Xifeng	6434	13
修文县	Xiuwen	6470	12
清镇市	Qingzhen	6898	9
钟山区	Zhongshan	5789	15
六枝特区	Liuzhi	4026	52
水城县	Shuicheng	4010	54
盘　县	Panxian	4305	40
红花岗区	Honghuagang	6970	8
汇川区	Huichuan	7190	7
遵义县	Zunyi	6514	11
桐梓县	Tongzi	5121	26
绥阳县	Suiyang	5779	16
正安县	Zhengan	3701	76
※道真县	※Daozhen	3539	83
※务川县	※Wuchuan	3463	85
凤冈县	Fenggang	4447	35
湄潭县	Meitan	5841	14
余庆县	Yuqing	5268	23
习水县	Xishui	3897	63
赤水市	Chishui	5598	19
仁怀市	Renhuai	5777	17
西秀区	Xixiu	5530	20
平坝县	Pingba	4635	32
普定县	Puding	4088	49
※镇宁县	※Zhenning	3998	56
※关岭县	※Guanling	4022	53
※紫云县	※Ziyun	3966	57
七星关区	Qixingguan	4412	36
大方县	Dafang	4239	42
黔西县	Qianxi	4276	41
金沙县	Jinsha	4910	28
织金县	Zhijin	4029	51
纳雍县	Nayong	3918	61
※威宁县	※Weining	4068	50
赫章县	Hezhang	3892	64
碧江区	Bijiang	5339	22
万山区	Wanshan	3593	82
江口县	Jiangkou	3918	61
※玉屏县	※Yuping	5216	24
石阡县	Shiqian	3874	67
思南县	Sinan	3683	77
※印江县	※Yinjiang	3719	71
德江县	Dejiang	3503	84
※沿河县	※Yanhe	3713	72
※松桃县	※Songtao	3680	78
兴义市	Xingyi	5396	21
兴仁县	Xingren	4196	46
普安县	Puan	3609	81
晴隆县	Qinglong	3456	86
贞丰县	Zhenfeng	4003	55
望谟县	Wangmo	3156	88
册亨县	Ceheng	3317	87
安龙县	Anlong	3880	65
凯里市	Kaili	5176	25
黄平县	Huangping	3709	73
施秉县	Shibing	4229	44
三穗县	Sansui	3955	59
镇远县	Zhenyuan	4169	47
岑巩县	Cengong	3953	60
天柱县	Tianzhu	4125	48
锦屏县	Jinping	3638	79
剑河县	Jianhe	3771	69
台江县	Taijiang	3631	80
黎平县	Liping	3849	68
榕江县	Rongjiang	3704	75
从江县	Congjiang	3965	58
雷山县	Leishan	3880	65
麻江县	Majiang	3764	70
丹寨县	Danzhai	3706	74
都匀市	Duyun	5611	18
福泉市	Fuquan	4834	29
荔波县	Libo	4375	38
贵定县	Guiding	4612	33
瓮安县	Wengan	4930	27
独山县	Dushan	4412	36
平塘县	Pingtang	4210	45
罗甸县	Luodian	4576	34
长顺县	Changshun	4341	39
龙里县	Longli	4783	30
惠水县	Huishui	4668	31
※三都县	※Sandu	4236	43

27–48 各县（市、区、特区）乡村从业人员(2011)

Number of Rural Employment by County (City,District,Special region)

单位：人 (person)

县(市、区、特区)名称	County (City,District, Special region)	合计 Total	第一产业 Primary Industry	第二产业 Secondary Industry	第三产业 Tertiary Industry	2011年比2010年增长(%) Increase Rate in 2011 over 2010(%)
南明区	Nanming	38496	21185	6610	10701	3.0
云岩区	Yunyan	62684	7875	21585	33224	22.1
花溪区	Huaxi	133209	71003	18617	43589	-0.4
乌当区	Wudang	141469	56351	24033	61085	-4.8
白云区	Baiyun	47661	26319	10441	10901	1.7
小河区	Xiaohe	20745	11099	1751	7895	-4.6
开阳县	Kaiyang	187745	93633	22072	72040	-3.4
息烽县	Xifeng	122209	64815	18287	39107	0.6
修文县	Xiuwen	168099	89499	16611	61989	0.6
清镇市	Qingzhen	261770	169234	31629	60907	-1.4
钟山区	Zhongshan	82965	48795	17140	17030	0.7
六枝特区	Liuzhi	321034	162532	35643	122859	3.1
水城县	Shuicheng	402628	245432	34833	122363	0.3
盘　县	Panxian	592351	404905	55765	131681	4.3
红花岗区	Honghuagang	126421	59568	19140	47713	0.0
汇川区	Huicuan	116591	57451	20415	38725	-8.4
遵义县	Zunyi	716596	322768	91109	302719	1.6
桐梓县	Tongzi	368920	164009	45605	159306	6.2
绥阳县	Suiyang	314808	175136	20997	118675	1.1
正安县	Zhengan	381698	155147	29189	197362	0.8
※道真县	Daozhen	183650	84269	12915	86466	0.9
※务川县	Wuchuan	266531	157131	8793	100607	2.2
凤冈县	Fenggang	255069	151800	20007	83262	1.4
湄潭县	Meitan	264413	156698	18217	89498	-3.6
余庆县	Yuqing	173677	90624	15268	67785	0.1
习水县	Xishui	361477	161284	43042	157151	1.3
赤水市	Chishui	139032	74792	12490	51750	3.0
仁怀市	Renhuai	335340	174631	41819	118890	0.6
西秀区	Xixiu	380283	205508	56277	118498	0.6
平坝县	Pingba	194464	133821	17795	42848	-0.5
普定县	Puding	247770	137251	24298	86221	3.3
※镇宁县	Zhenning	198525	125096	14834	58595	4.7
※关岭县	Guanling	189140	123931	11155	54054	1.6
※紫云县	Ziyun	224475	139662	19459	65354	3.6
七星关区	Qixingguan	789150	366000	97996	325154	3.5
大方县	Dafang	662654	373976	70616	218062	5.6
黔西县	Qianxi	505363	221477	66945	216941	3.3
金沙县	Jinsha	356445	177991	43857	134597	5.9
织金县	Zhijin	543043	291862	66944	184237	-0.1
纳雍县	Nayong	504145	225642	63490	215013	1.9
※威宁县	Weining	752329	484237	52217	215875	2.1
赫章县	Hezhang	383786	212412	34561	136813	1.7
碧江区	Bijiang	161302	83849	16338	61115	0.6
万山区	Wanshan	29722	13845	4698	11179	-3.1

27-48 续表 continued

单位：人 (person)

县(市、区、特区)名称	County (City,District, Special region)	合计 Total	第一产业 Primary Industry	第二产业 Secondary Industry	第三产业 Tertiary Industry	2011年比2010年增长(%) Increase Rate in 2011 over 2010(%)
江口县	Jiangkou	118715	71056	8555	39104	…
※玉屏县	Yuping	82365	38501	12858	31006	1.0
石阡县	Shiqian	238157	136786	15498	85873	0.5
思南县	Sinan	383992	206197	50301	127494	2.9
※印江县	Yinjiang	238674	109039	29821	99814	1.9
德江县	Dejiang	258944	151562	22181	85201	0.6
※沿河县	Yanhe	320532	186126	19634	114772	1.6
※松桃县	Songtao	414072	228399	26157	159516	1.6
兴义市	Xingyi	408400	267519	44972	95909	1.5
兴仁县	Xingren	252884	165768	15775	71341	1.0
普安县	Puan	173673	105668	15196	52809	-3.5
晴隆县	Qinglong	172389	108900	10256	53233	4.8
贞丰县	Zhenfeng	227951	144127	20487	63337	1.6
望谟县	Wangmo	167631	100968	10118	56545	2.9
册亨县	Ceheng	135057	78788	10566	45703	1.4
安龙县	Anlong	297479	179757	27697	90025	8.4
凯里市	Kaili	175010	85880	22329	66801	1.0
黄平县	Huangping	208002	130812	20213	56977	-0.2
施秉县	Shibing	61261	44669	4135	12457	0.6
三穗县	Sansui	124655	47148	10542	66965	0.5
镇远县	Zhenyuan	121320	67632	16796	36892	-1.0
岑巩县	Cengong	125588	69681	5004	50903	2.2
天柱县	Tianzhu	224486	106213	7461	110812	0.2
锦屏县	Jinping	123747	58421	13660	51666	1.0
剑河县	Jianhe	141092	83176	8897	49019	0.1
台江县	Taijiang	98980	48721	13673	36586	12.2
黎平县	Liping	303298	161803	20884	120611	1.4
榕江县	Rongjiang	193945	125552	9301	59092	1.8
从江县	Congjiang	185431	128635	10110	46686	-1.3
雷山县	Leishan	93543	51961	6374	35208	-1.3
麻江县	Majiang	126050	77533	9804	38713	3.9
丹寨县	Danzhai	94351	40066	6895	47390	-1.0
都匀市	Duyun	191442	102040	17340	72062	0.5
福泉市	Fuquan	146834	90851	22846	33137	0.5
荔波县	Libo	99188	57832	6844	34512	-1.5
贵定县	Guiding	162948	92646	14139	56163	6.8
瓮安县	Wengan	280948	134902	22786	123260	2.8
独山县	Dushan	198212	115324	17506	65382	0.6
平塘县	Pingtang	194244	135283	8572	50389	1.0
罗甸县	Luodian	175344	102235	11188	61921	0.5
长顺县	Changshun	134007	87802	7494	38711	-1.6
龙里县	Longli	113610	85654	6380	21576	0.2
惠水县	Huishui	264562	155784	27185	81593	6.5
※三都县	Sandu	191669	111223	9086	71360	1.8

27-49 各县(市、区、特区)常用耕地面积(2011)

Cultivated Areas for Frequently Use by County(City,District,Special region)

单位：公顷 (hectare)

县(市、区、特区)名称	County (City,District,Special region)	常用耕地面积 Cultivated Area for Frequently Use	#水田 Paddy Fields
南明区	Nanming	1554	433
云岩区	Yunyan	565	124
花溪区	Huaxi	10831	6080
乌当区	Wudang	8081	4633
白云区	Baiyun	2351	1253
小河区	Xiaohe	417	115
开阳县	Kaiyang	23191	9265
息烽县	Xifeng	15208	4827
修文县	Xiuwen	17469	6279
清镇市	Qingzhen	17070	6169
钟山区	Zhongshan	3373	3
六枝特区	Liuzhi	25829	9676
水城县	Shuicheng	33097	3570
盘　县	Panxian	45842	6393
红花岗区	Honghuagang	9207	4389
汇川区	Huicuan	9895	5790
遵义县	Zunyi	65476	39977
桐梓县	Tongzi	36277	12536
绥阳县	Suiyang	27387	14131
正安县	Zhengan	31157	15796
※道真县	Daozhen	23502	15293
※务川县	Wuchuan	28293	11058
凤冈县	Fenggang	26517	14525
湄潭县	Meitan	31026	19195
余庆县	Yuqing	19162	11425
习水县	Xishui	40626	14610
赤水市	Chishui	13728	10922
仁怀市	Renhuai	27768	9850
西秀区	Xixiu	27488	18323
平坝县	Pingba	16265	8823
普定县	Puding	16654	7066
※镇宁县	Zhenning	14598	8101
※关岭县	Guanling	15048	5396
※紫云县	Ziyun	16166	6641
七星关区	Qixingguan	58419	5618
大方县	Dafang	50421	4661
黔西县	Qianxi	40849	8429
金沙县	Jinsha	34500	10900
织金县	Zhijin	39807	9867
纳雍县	Nayong	30996	3650
※威宁县	Weining	72011	329
赫章县	Hezhang	38807	1010
碧江区	Bijiang	12429	7780
万山区	Wanshan	2698	1539

27-49 续表 continued

单位：公顷 (hectare)

县(市、区、特区)名称	County (City,District,Special region)	常用耕地面积 Cultivated Area for Frequently Use	#水田 Paddy Fields
江口县	Jiangkou	10965	7131
※玉屏县	Yuping	5788	3920
石阡县	Shiqian	22037	12916
思南县	Sinan	28786	17676
※印江县	Yinjiang	18593	11867
德江县	Dejiang	21347	13183
※沿河县	Yanhe	26327	11074
※松桃县	Songtao	26751	16890
兴义市	Xingyi	28781	10540
兴仁县	Xingren	20429	8265
普安县	Puan	16545	3699
晴隆县	Qinglong	14059	4577
贞丰县	Zhenfeng	20591	6854
望谟县	Wangmo	24903	4583
册亨县	Ceheng	13403	4281
安龙县	Anlong	20703	9655
凯里市	Kaili	12719	8963
黄平县	Huangping	15923	11670
施秉县	Shibing	8267	4705
三穗县	Sansui	8097	5509
镇远县	Zhenyuan	12251	7375
岑巩县	Cengong	12265	7373
天柱县	Tianzhu	15926	11600
锦屏县	Jinping	8422	6617
剑河县	Jianhe	9023	7558
台江县	Taijiang	6199	4832
黎平县	Liping	18535	17606
榕江县	Rongjiang	13101	10791
从江县	Congjiang	13326	11683
雷山县	Leishan	6705	5487
麻江县	Majiang	10654	6801
丹寨县	Danzhai	7148	5702
都匀市	Duyun	13356	10402
福泉市	Fuquan	15444	7902
荔波县	Libo	8009	6351
贵定县	Guiding	11700	6628
瓮安县	Wengan	24219	11153
独山县	Dushan	15057	12518
平塘县	Pingtang	14343	8592
罗甸县	Luodian	16218	7092
长顺县	Changshun	13658	5834
龙里县	Longli	10860	6622
惠水县	Huishui	17788	11370
※三都县	Sandu	13626	9953

27-50 各县(市、区、特区)农林牧渔业总产值(2011)

Gross Output Value of Farming,Forestry,Animal Husbandry and Fishery and Its Order by County(City,District,Special region)

单位：万元 (10000 yuan)

县(市、区、特区)名称	County (City,District, Special region)	合计 Total	农业 Farming	林业 Forestry	牧业 Animal Husbandry	渔业 Fishery	农林牧渔服务业 Services	位次 Order	2011年比2010年增长(%) Increase Rate in 2011 over 2010(%)
南明区	Nanming	28568	21006		7450	12	100	85	3.2
云岩区	Yunyan	6003	4129	91	1762	6	15	88	-47.4
花溪区	Huaxi	120535	82234	1229	35340	163	1569	42	4.1
乌当区	Wudang	127875	91121	2889	31150	1112	1603	38	3.7
白云区	Baiyun	45333	31321	195	13187	211	419	82	4.5
小河区	Xiaohe	14506	12008		2152	256	90	87	3.1
开阳县	Kaiyang	200424	110406	1778	85529	1142	1569	15	4.3
息烽县	Xifeng	105558	65755	626	32754	5593	830	52	4.5
修文县	Xiuwen	144737	101450	843	41459	595	390	33	3.9
清镇市	Qingzhen	171964	102688	957	63087	4527	705	26	4.2
钟山区	Zhongshan	47335	18746	293	27009	52.4	1235	81	4.5
六枝特区	Liuzhi	110261	68885	3683	31370	647	5676	51	7.7
水城县	Shuicheng	171266	95614	3149	69777	95.4	2630	27	0.5
盘　县	Panxian	236148	113348	12639	103456	639	6066	8	-4.2
红花岗区	Honghuagang	132298	66613	578	59802	1403	3902	36	2.2
汇川区	Huicuan	89556	45253	568	37154	641	5940	63	2.4
遵义县	Zunyi	493049	330746	5280	128470	22337	6216	1	2.1
桐梓县	Tongzi	205381	130046	12138	59864	2739	594	14	1.9
绥阳县	Suiyang	227445	173537	3448	45888	2412	2160	10	2.1
正安县	Zhengan	184243	110938	20789	49786	1240	1490	22	0.2
※道真县	Daozhen	103827	64550	5610	32397	780	490	56	1.8
※务川县	Wuchuan	137680	89009	4752	40654	1407	1858	34	1.0
凤冈县	Fenggang	160324	88404	16536	52610	894	1880	30	-0.8
湄潭县	Meitan	167513	113875	3529	44091	2868	3150	29	1.5
余庆县	Yuqing	135946	82182	4238	46478	1743	1305	35	-12.1
习水县	Xishui	180817	77164	5401	94448	1619	2185	23	-0.7
赤水市	Chishui	117571	50538	33551	28954	2660	1868	46	1.4
仁怀市	Renhuai	198321	97693	5883	90196	1949	2600	18	0.8
西秀区	Xixiu	199314	100417	1731	93110	3190	866	16	3.7
平坝县	Pingba	95986	51893	1982	38717	2715	679	60	3.5
普定县	Puding	104807	47255	1238	52718	2759	837	55	3.8
※镇宁县	Zhenning	76613	42141	2545	29033	2536	358	70	4.1
※关岭县	Guanling	104896	58381	4449	40916	944	206	53	3.3
※紫云县	Ziyun	118518	36471	7892	70781	1422	1952	44	4.4
七星关区	Qixingguan	399947	233809	22842	133230	620	9446	3	8.9
大方县	Dafang	282953	180861	8718	87632	1226	4516	4	6.3
黔西县	Qianxi	199114	111620	2257	79581	1392	4264	17	-12.2
金沙县	Jinsha	174232	99661	3771	61562	4468	4770	25	-3.2
织金县	Zhijin	216447	122528	1699	83613	3525	5082	13	-4.5
纳雍县	Nayong	189755	111977	3273	71498	1021	1986	21	-0.7
※威宁县	Weining	443868	265420	1545	168582	509	7812	2	13.3
赫章县	Hezhang	218155	137195	3823	73829	306	3002	12	-1.1
碧江区	Bijiang	154464	92004	3569	48490	5550.9	4850	31	3.1
万山区	Wanshan	21943	10575	1206	8323	708.8	1130	86	3

27-50 续表 continued

单位：万元 (10000 yuan)

县(市、区、特区)名称	County (City,District, Special region)	合计 Total	农业 Farming	林业 Forestry	牧业 Animal Husbandry	渔业 Fishery	农林牧渔服务业 Services	位次 Order	2011年比2010年增长(%) Increase Rate in 2011 over 2010(%)
江口县	Jiangkou	94565	51130	4813	31827	3126	3668	62	3.5
※玉屏县	Yuping	69251	34916	3529	25561	2120	3125	74	3.2
石阡县	Shiqian	167894	90144	5589	64630	2618	4913	28	2.5
思南县	Sinan	272205	151842	3307	102065	6138	8853	5	2.8
※印江县	Yinjiang	193916	100125	7127	76496	5014	5155	19	2.8
德江县	Dejiang	226882	137397	3613	75859	2984	7030	11	2.6
※沿河县	Yanhe	228614	136257	3981	75018	5467	7890	9	2.6
※松桃县	Songtao	243255	132850	6825	90235	5209	8136	7	3.1
兴义市	Xingyi	266501	140123	6080	98999	15899	5400	6	-12
兴仁县	Xingren	123702	73559	3329	46115	149	550	40	-4.2
普安县	Puan	76709	39448	4767	31387	277	830	69	-5.2
晴隆县	Qinglong	72201	34456	3046	29578	4042	1079	72	-1.5
贞丰县	Zhenfeng	113589	53050	2119	57024	347	1050	50	0.9
望谟县	Wangmo	86746	36758	10105	33082	5201	1600	65	12.6
册亨县	Ceheng	73930	33395	13651	22113	3272	1500	71	7.0
安龙县	Anlong	149076	71865	9920	52188	11904	3200	32	-3.2
凯里市	Kaili	124332	69494	6617	43621	3171	1429	39	-0.3
黄平县	Huangping	103534	62124	10918	25864	1646	2982	57	2.3
施秉县	Shibing	64337	47280	3724	11829	519	985	75	8.6
三穗县	Sansui	59823	28127	6494	23062	793	1347	77	1.3
镇远县	Zhenyuan	101976	57449	19747	21986	2144	650	58	0.7
岑巩县	Cengong	63626	32381	4236	19812	677	6520	76	3.6
天柱县	Tianzhu	117254	62191	14565	38562	1262	675	47	2.3
锦屏县	Jinping	53598	18686	13042	15454	4752	1664	79	1.5
剑河县	Jianhe	77933	29819	14150	26746	6459	760	67	6.7
台江县	Taijiang	42602	17021	11100	10339	3252	890	84	1.6
黎平县	Liping	129214	50987	32834	34274	9047	2072	37	7.4
榕江县	Rongjiang	120489	57340	37146	21213	4121	669	43	8.9
从江县	Congjiang	114280	52856	25104	26806	7877	1637	49	5.8
雷山县	Leishan	43780	26974	3617	10776	866	1547	83	9.2
麻江县	Majiang	70895	36454	3611	23134	812	6884	73	3.4
丹寨县	Danzhai	49551	23540	6830	16922	748	1511	80	5.9
都匀市	Duyun	123028	51195	4269	63789	2195	1580	41	2.2
福泉市	Fuquan	104885	58252	3115	42065	1128	325	54	2.1
荔波县	Libo	54283	27562	6250	16568	2070	1833	78	1.1
贵定县	Guiding	80123	46263	2773	26326	1881	2880	66	1.8
瓮安县	Wengan	178450	85313	3097	86096	1794	2150	24	2.1
独山县	Dushan	116733	71542	3567	39755	1136	733	48	1.9
平塘县	Pingtang	95062	62091	4579	26875	411	1106	61	2.0
罗甸县	Luodian	117970	71837	6232	30267	7999	1635	45	1.7
长顺县	Changshun	97513	43573	2730	46414	546	4250	59	3.7
龙里县	Longli	77148	40853	1046	33870	456	923	68	3.1
惠水县	Huishui	190133	92076	11150	78372	1349	7186	20	2.0
※三都县	Sandu	87152	49366	7362	25430	2838	2156	64	1.8

27-51 各县(市、区、特区)粮食、肉类产量(2011)
Output of Grain, Meat and Its Order by County(City,Section,Special region)

县(市、区、特区)名称	County (City,Section, Special region)	粮食产量(吨) Output of Grain (ton)	位次 Order	2011年比2010年增长(%) Increase Rate in 2011 over 2010(%)	人均粮食产量(公斤) Per Capita Output of Grain (kg)	位次 Order	肉类产量(吨) Output of Meat (ton)	位次 Order	2011年比2010年增长(%) Increase Rate in 2011 over 2010(%)
南明区	Nanming	4140	86	-7.8	70	86	3082	86	-1.2
云岩区	Yunyan	844	88	16.4	10	88	676	88	-65.4
花溪区	Huaxi	49277	68	-25.8	219	63	15208	51	-0.2
乌当区	Wudang	37200	77	-24.9	160	81	11620	63	1.2
白云区	Baiyun	10268	85	-27.1	142	83	4809	83	1.3
小河区	Xiaohe	1637	87	-39.5	57	87	987	87	0.8
开阳县	Kaiyang	87780	39	-28.7	261	37	40077	9	1.2
息烽县	Xifeng	60766	64	-22.1	302	20	14166	54	1.1
修文县	Xiuwen	71442	56	-22.0	271	31	17599	45	2.4
清镇市	Qingzhen	79028	50	-27.7	189	77	31213	18	1.7
钟山区	Zhongshan	19482	83	-0.2	119	85	12155	59	10.9
六枝特区	Liuzhi	153097	20	-4.2	271	32	19237	40	-0.6
水城县	Shuicheng	165874	16	-20.1	217	65	28351	23	1.3
盘　县	Panxian	226148	6	-19.0	214	66	49358	5	-2.3
红花岗区	Honghuagang	62929	60	-14.7	304	18	16088	47	2.1
汇川区	Huicuan	60084	65	-12.7	280	25	19280	39	0.5
遵义县	Zunyi	509953	1	-11.2	439	2	86760	1	2.5
桐梓县	Tongzi	196170	8	-18.3	304	19	37008	11	1.8
绥阳县	Suiyang	207317	7	-17.2	415	4	24805	29	7.3
正安县	Zhengan	160708	19	-22.8	268	35	21626	33	-10.9
※道真县	Daozhen	110893	28	-13.2	353	7	18204	43	1.3
※务川县	Wuchuan	128700	24	-18.4	308	17	22058	32	5.6
凤冈县	Fenggang	99476	34	-39.8	251	44	26082	26	0.5
湄潭县	Meitan	170495	14	-25.0	384	6	25632	27	4.0
余庆县	Yuqing	95635	36	-42.2	342	10	26959	24	-15.2
习水县	Xishui	166019	15	-35.4	254	42	56754	3	-0.1
赤水市	Chishui	111304	27	-15.6	480	1	13035	57	5.5
仁怀市	Renhuai	191522	9	-9.8	335	12	42984	6	-0.2
西秀区	Xixiu	119387	25	-36.3	185	78	38035	10	0.1
平坝县	Pingba	85537	43	-16.1	284	23	15456	50	0.2
普定县	Puding	86867	41	-20.2	205	71	19985	37	0.6
※镇宁县	Zhenning	77015	51	-23.8	220	61	10967	67	0.4
※关岭县	Guanling	82803	45	-10.9	243	49	16264	46	0.5
※紫云县	Ziyun	81218	48	-17.0	224	57	29801	20	0.2
七星关区	Qixingguan	337042	3	1.3	295	21	56097	4	0.6
大方县	Dafang	241157	5	-17.2	273	30	35150	13	0.7
黔西县	Qianxi	164033	17	-42.9	221	59	33094	16	0.6
金沙县	Jinsha	174195	13	-27.1	348	9	30344	19	0.6
织金县	Zhijin	252543	4	-14.4	255	41	34758	14	0.8
纳雍县	Nayong	188697	11	-21.4	239	53	29363	22	-0.3
※威宁县	Weining	378012	2	14.2	293	22	69809	2	-0.9
赫章县	Hezhang	183455	12	10.2	264	36	31226	17	0.4
碧江区	Bijiang	98127	35	-20.1	403	5	19420	38	0.3
万山区	Wanshan	12973	84	-20.9	246	45	3212	85	0.3

27-51 续表 continued

县(市、区、特区)名称	County (City,District, Special region)	粮食产量(吨) Output of Grain (ton)	位次 Order	2011年比2010年增长(%) Increase Rate in 2011 over 2010(%)	人均粮食产量(公斤) Per Capita Output of Grain (kg)	位次 Order	肉类产量(吨) Output of Meat (ton)	位次 Order	2011年比2010年增长(%) Increase Rate in 2011 over 2010(%)
江口县	Jiangkou	66608	58	-14.1	325	14	13638	56	0.4
※玉屏县	Yuping	30303	82	-15.2	240	52	9029	74	0.3
石阡县	Shiqian	75151	54	-48.8	196	76	21605	34	0.3
思南县	Sinan	163661	18	-23.6	256	40	40089	8	0.3
※印江县	Yinjiang	103762	31	-21.1	257	38	26619	25	0.3
德江县	Dejiang	99537	33	-34.1	237	54	25312	28	0.3
※沿河县	Yanhe	135794	23	-25.1	223	58	29548	21	0.3
※松桃县	Songtao	188727	10	-17.6	283	24	33548	15	0.3
兴义市	Xingyi	141357	22	-29.2	207	69	42598	7	0.3
兴仁县	Xingren	113818	26	-20.2	276	28	20647	35	0.3
普安县	Puan	41706	74	-43.2	133	84	11429	64	0.1
晴隆县	Qinglong	48957	69	-34.1	170	80	10761	68	-0.6
贞丰县	Zhenfeng	76649	52	-20.2	202	75	13720	55	0.2
望谟县	Wangmo	65185	59	-7.7	217	64	15481	49	-0.4
册亨县	Ceheng	34492	79	-38.5	151	82	9405	72	-0.2
安龙县	Anlong	110603	29	-24.8	270	33	24033	30	0.4
凯里市	Kaili	68994	57	-30.2	225	56	20595	36	-1.4
黄平县	Huangping	72213	55	-28.8	203	74	10638	69	0.1
施秉县	Shibing	43918	72	-26.4	424	3	6206	81	0.5
三穗县	Sansui	40060	75	-28.9	203	73	11047	66	1.2
镇远县	Zhenyuan	61015	63	-28.1	341	11	9163	73	-1.0
岑巩县	Cengong	47822	71	-27.3	220	60	8590	76	0.3
天柱县	Tianzhu	86934	40	-29.7	241	51	18799	41	0.4
锦屏县	Jinping	43479	73	-27.4	208	68	7847	78	0.3
剑河县	Jianhe	48716	70	-25.2	206	70	11946	62	0.4
台江县	Taijiang	32276	81	-28.2	211	67	4278	84	1.5
黎平县	Liping	101439	32	-29.8	203	72	14726	52	0.7
榕江县	Rongjiang	61359	62	-29.5	184	79	10189	70	0.1
从江县	Congjiang	80997	49	-26.0	253	43	12085	61	0.6
雷山县	Leishan	36075	78	-24.8	245	46	5216	82	2.1
麻江县	Majiang	49390	67	-28.5	244	48	10109	71	0.7
丹寨县	Danzhai	33238	80	-29.5	219	62	7101	80	0.9
都匀市	Duyun	81284	47	-24.1	256	39	22165	31	0.9
福泉市	Fuquan	88659	37	-23.2	348	8	12363	58	…
荔波县	Libo	38746	76	-28.5	242	50	8470	77	-0.2
贵定县	Guiding	62891	61	-26.2	245	47	8850	75	2.7
瓮安县	Wengan	142613	21	-21.4	323	15	36085	12	-0.7
独山县	Dushan	88127	38	-25.9	275	29	15900	48	0.2
平塘县	Pingtang	84797	44	-24.3	277	26	12115	60	0.9
罗甸县	Luodian	85584	42	-22.2	276	27	18509	42	-1.1
长顺县	Changshun	81556	46	-17.9	334	13	11303	65	…
龙里县	Longli	59380	66	-27.5	315	16	7448	79	-0.1
惠水县	Huishui	110533	30	-24.0	269	34	17871	44	0.2
※三都县	Sandu	76447	53	-21.9	227	55	14231	53	…

27−52 各县(市、区、特区)油菜籽、烤烟产量(2011)
Output of Rapeseed and Flue-cured Tobacco and Its Order by County(City,District,Special region)

县(市、区、特区)名称	County (City,District, Special region)	油菜籽产量(吨) Output of Rapeseed (ton)	位次 Order	2011年比2010年增长(%) Increase Rate in 2011 over 2010(%)	烤烟产量(吨) Output of Fluecured Tobacco (ton)	位次 Order	2011年比2010年增长(%) Increase Rate in 2011 over 2010(%)
南明区	Nanming	155	83	-1.9			
云岩区	Yunyan						
花溪区	Huaxi	3608	64	54.9	12	69	-78.2
乌当区	Wudang	4282	53	15.7			
白云区	Baiyun	924	76	60.7			
小河区	Xiaohe	130	85				
开阳县	Kaiyang	19519	7	24.0	9584	8	-20.3
息烽县	Xifeng	10999	20	21.4	1848	48	-26.1
修文县	Xiuwen	7558	29	19.9	2325	38	-39.2
清镇市	Qingzhen	7551	30	37.3	4444	33	-15.1
钟山区	Zhongshan						
六枝特区	Liuzhi	5476	44	355.6	211	62	-44.2
水城县	Shuicheng	77	86	92.5	4936	28	-6.5
盘　县	Panxian	1212	73	213.2	4709	30	-51.3
红花岗区	Honghuagang	6601	40	7.5	45	64	-10.0
汇川区	Huicuan	7138	34	1.6	2082	44	5.7
遵义县	Zunyi	70008	1	34.5	17622	3	-13.0
桐梓县	Tongzi	15794	12	20.3	8572	11	10.4
绥阳县	Suiyang	26586	3	18.2	9182	10	12.4
正安县	Zhengan	17693	8	22.9	10098	7	16.8
※道真县	Daozhen	6325	42	6.0	11706	5	14.8
※务川县	Wuchuan	8253	24	4.7	14737	4	-1.9
凤冈县	Fenggang	15088	13	15.9	6251	17	-17.3
湄潭县	Meitan	20110	6	8.6	8117	12	-3.8
余庆县	Yuqing	16424	11	7.7	9284	9	-3.4
习水县	Xishui	7148	33	38.7	18	67	5.9
赤水市	Chishui	268	81	50.6			
仁怀市	Renhuai	12994	17	36.0	2320	39	-19.9
西秀区	Xixiu	25437	4	209.8	5375	23	-13.0
平坝县	Pingba	9925	21	60.7	2200	43	-6.3
普定县	Puding	7050	36	147.7	665	58	-6.7
※镇宁县	Zhenning	7715	28	136.4			
※关岭县	Guanling	3937	61	204.7			
※紫云县	Ziyun	4546	50	28.3	1754	51	11.9
七星关区	Qixingguan	4718	47	68.4	10583	6	-9.9
大方县	Dafang	7360	32	167.4	17697	2	-18.4
黔西县	Qianxi	58436	2	351.7	5846	19	-51.5
金沙县	Jinsha	25022	5	25.3	5744	20	-15.2
织金县	Zhijin	11255	19	51.8	4306	34	-21.7
纳雍县	Nayong	273	80	33.8	4580	32	-26.5
※威宁县	Weining	141	84	54.9	27219	1	13.1
赫章县	Hezhang	188	82	116.1	8050	13	12.3
碧江区	Bijiang	6645	38	8.0	260	59	-10.3
万山区	Wanshan	1134	74	43.7			

27-52 续表 continued

县(市、区、特区)名 称	County (City,District, Special region)	油菜籽产 量(吨) Output of Rapeseed (ton)	位 次 Order	2011年比2010年增长(%) Increase Rate in 2011 over 2010(%)	烤 烟 产 量(吨) Output of Fluecured Tobacco (ton)	位 次 Order	2011年比2010年增长(%) Increase Rate in 2011 over 2010(%)
江口县	Jiangkou	4153	57	2.9	1933	46	19.3
※玉屏县	Yuping	3066	65	-16.5			
石阡县	Shiqian	14282	14	46.5	5265	24	-7.4
思南县	Sinan	17658	9	10.5	4650	31	-21.6
※印江县	Yinjiang	13110	15	14.0	5706	21	-10.0
德江县	Dejiang	13046	16	14.0	6744	16	-10.6
※沿河县	Yanhe	7809	27	6.1	6019	18	0.1
※松桃县	Songtao	11646	18	6.6	2313	40	-0.9
兴义市	Xingyi	8653	23	395.9	7579	14	-43.7
兴仁县	Xingren	5074	45	939.8	4922	29	-37.7
普安县	Puan	793	77	957.3	5556	22	-42.1
晴隆县	Qinglong	989	75	963.4	907	56	-38.8
贞丰县	Zhenfeng	4160	56	980.5	2021	45	-28.0
望谟县	Wangmo	1724	70	171.5			
册亨县	Ceheng	1714	72	99.1			
安龙县	Anlong	3969	60	757.2	5016	26	-1.3
凯里市	Kaili	2528	66	5.5	906	57	-35.4
黄平县	Huangping	4403	51	0.2	1418	54	-39.5
施秉县	Shibing	3846	63	14.3	4941	27	-23.9
三穗县	Sansui	2172	68	-2.9	256	60	-29.5
镇远县	Zhenyuan	6750	37	9.3	2944	36	-38.0
岑巩县	Cengong	3988	59	-3.1	2250	41	34.4
天柱县	Tianzhu	4673	48	4.3	1205	55	-13.2
锦屏县	Jinping	3892	62	7.5	66	63	78.4
剑河县	Jianhe	1717	71	2.1	14	68	-33.3
台江县	Taijiang	1795	69	6.8			
黎平县	Liping	7074	35	4.8	21	66	61.5
榕江县	Rongjiang	5616	43	15.1			
从江县	Congjiang	4651	49	2.2			
雷山县	Leishan	364	79	15.6			
麻江县	Majiang	4161	55	6.7	1581	52	6.3
丹寨县	Danzhai	659	78	16.2	217	61	-27.7
都匀市	Duyun	7848	26	31.5	2212	42	83.1
福泉市	Fuquan	9490	22	25.0	4056	35	-12.9
荔波县	Libo	4035	58	20.2	38	65	8.6
贵定县	Guiding	6622	39	22.0	1774	49	20.7
瓮安县	Wengan	16480	10	15.0	6822	15	-10.4
独山县	Dushan	6403	41	13.0	1758	50	-17.0
平塘县	Pingtang	7441	31	21.0	2920	37	-5.8
罗甸县	Luodian	2450	67	30.4			
长顺县	Changshun	4942	46	48.5	5261	25	5.2
龙里县	Longli	4210	54	21.4	1510	53	-11.7
惠水县	Huishui	4396	52	44.1	1854	47	-3.8
※三都县	Sandu	7935	25	11.0			

27–53 各县(市、区、特区)规模以上工业增加值(2011)

Value-added of Industry above Designated Size and Its Order by County(City,District,Special region)

单位：万元 (10000 yuan)

县(市、区、特区)名称	County (City,District, Special region)	工业增加值 Value-added of Industry	轻工业 Light Industry	重工业 Heavy Industry	位次 Order
南明区	Nanming	403928	147821	256107	11
云岩区	Yunyan	255422	79312	176110	20
花溪区	Huaxi	173583	69629	103954	30
乌当区	Wudang	395355	173699	221656	12
白云区	Baiyun	320648	47801	272847	15
小河区	Xiaohe	1238445	1010089	228356	3
开阳县	Kaiyang	359619	1223	358396	14
息烽县	Xifeng	187157	31509	155648	28
修文县	Xiuwen	193845	91746	102099	24
清镇市	Qingzhen	246493	45130	201363	21
钟山区	Zhongshan	746488	98572	647916	4
六枝特区	Liuzhi	150196	33789	116407	35
水城县	Shuicheng	658513	24240	634273	5
盘　县	Panxian	1264882	677	1264205	2
红花岗区	Honghuagang	305310	100665	204645	17
汇川区	Huicuan	621954	463855	158099	7
遵义县	Zunyi	643584	142963	500622	6
桐梓县	Tongzi	159566	1168	158398	33
绥阳县	Suiyang	61879	27188	34691	53
正安县	Zhengan	25065	10307	14758	70
※道真县	Daozhen	17962	1825	16137	76
※务川县	Wuchuan	15077	2877	12200	79
凤冈县	Fenggang	26041	14001	12040	67
湄潭县	Meitan	69362	58642	10720	50
余庆县	Yuqing	53897	1447	52450	57
习水县	Xishui	274511	199450	75061	18
赤水市	Chishui	122372	78366	44006	40
仁怀市	Renhuai	1874514	1837580	36934	1
西秀区	Xixiu	366230	64355	301875	13
平坝县	Pingba	173466	21165	152301	31
普定县	Puding	135929	3893	132035	37
※镇宁县	Zhenning	19679	5012	14666	75
※关岭县	Guanling	17415		17415	77
※紫云县	Ziyun	10637	162	10475	84
七星关区	Qixingguan	435563	308793	126770	9
大方县	Dafang	191201		191201	26
黔西县	Qianxi	202194	3607	198587	23
金沙县	Jinsha	426164	18683	407482	10
织金县	Zhijin	108364		108364	44
纳雍县	Nayong	313582		313582	16
※威宁县	Weining	145507	566	144941	36
赫章县	Hezhang	58907		58907	54
碧江区	Bijiang	127717	59543	68174	39
万山区	Wanshan	37472	1537	35935	63

27-53 续表 continued

单位：万元 (10000 yuan)

县(市、区、特区)名称	County (City,District, Special region)	工业增加值 Value-added of Industry	轻工业 Light Industry	重工业 Heavy Industry	位次 Order
江口县	Jiangkou	14295	4616	9679	81
※玉屏县	Yuping	115937	3083	112854	42
石阡县	Shiqian	10616	3373	7243	85
思南县	Sinan	44350	3553	40797	61
※印江县	Yinjiang	30766	9067	21699	64
德江县	Dejiang	29137	14379	14758	66
※沿河县	Yanhe	21514	4637	16877	74
※松桃县	Songtao	74210	1671	72539	49
兴义市	Xingyi	617105	43808	573297	8
兴仁县	Xingren	181700	2293	179407	29
普安县	Puan	128900		128900	38
晴隆县	Qinglong	81700	1025	80675	47
贞丰县	Zhenfeng	272779	2772	270007	19
望谟县	Wangmo	3441	1280	2161	88
册亨县	Ceheng	6001	796	5205	86
安龙县	Anlong	109499	378	109121	43
凯里市	Kaili	189616	12607	177009	27
黄平县	Huangping	15587	1472	14115	78
施秉县	Shibing	23227	4605	18622	71
三穗县	Sansui	23013	11898	11115	72
镇远县	Zhenyuan	85516	20379	65137	46
岑巩县	Cengong	42782	564	42218	62
天柱县	Tianzhu	57959	214	57745	56
锦屏县	Jinping	49671		49671	58
剑河县	Jianhe	10686	805	9881	83
台江县	Taijiang	14379	175	14204	80
黎平县	Liping	46164	2886	43278	60
榕江县	Rongjiang	30270		30270	65
从江县	Congjiang	25655	182	25473	68
雷山县	Leishan	11469	3437	8032	82
麻江县	Majiang	46942		46942	59
丹寨县	Danzhai	25621	4598	21023	69
都匀市	Duyun	156960	27903	129057	34
福泉市	Fuquan	229203	714	228489	22
荔波县	Libo	58898	138	58760	55
贵定县	Guiding	167194	152298	14896	32
瓮安县	Wengan	193634	378	193256	25
独山县	Dushan	75077	3340	71737	48
平塘县	Pingtang	22439	6122	16317	73
罗甸县	Luodian	62437	41293	21144	52
长顺县	Changshun	65164	24241	40923	51
龙里县	Longli	121367	51600	69767	41
惠水县	Huishui	92958	25436	67522	45
※三都县	Sandu	4901	518	4383	87

27-54 各县(市、区、特区)社会消费品零售总额(2011)

Total Retail Sales of Consumer Goods by County (City,District,Special Region)

单位：万元 (10000 yuan)

县(市、区、特区)名称	County (City,District,Special Region)	社会消费品零售总额 Total Retail Sales	城镇 Urban	乡村 Rural
南明区	Nanming	1924899	1924899	
云岩区	Yunyan	2187991	2187991	
花溪区	Huaxi	225696	225696	
乌当区	Wudang	533751	293595	240156
白云区	Baiyun	228392	228392	
小河区	Xiaohe	493233	493233	
开阳县	Kaiyang	198426	76940	121486
息烽县	Xifeng	103948	60473	43475
修文县	Xiuwen	121560	50981	70579
清镇市	Qingzhen	218140	160746	57394
钟山区	Zhongshan	873439	709084	164355
六枝特区	Liuzhi	195945	158911	37035
水城县	Shuicheng	92208	74781	17427
盘　县	Panxian	414477	336140	78336
红花岗区	Honghuagang	1069797	905001	164796
汇川区	Huicuan	592886	475714	117172
遵义县	Zunyi	364469	325882	38587
桐梓县	Tongzi	140288	90473	49815
绥阳县	Suiyang	106337	77148	29189
正安县	Zhengan	108205	58464	49741
※道真县	Daozhen	67686	32946	34740
※务川县	Wuchuan	67960	37930	30031
凤冈县	Fenggang	92372	58764	33608
湄潭县	Meitan	141111	89840	51271
余庆县	Yuqing	88890	58598	30292
习水县	Xishui	133252	109040	24212
赤水市	Chishui	131360	85140	46220
仁怀市	Renhuai	401571	356034	45537
西秀区	Xixiu	330567	298570	31997
平坝县	Pingba	124561	94105	30456
普定县	Puding	94376	65311	29066
※镇宁县	Zhenning	100214	71889	28325
※关岭县	Guanling	111435	95664	15771
※紫云县	Ziyun	78136	53472	24665
七星关区	Qixingguan	546507	345960	200547
大方县	Dafang	135136	89417	45718
黔西县	Qianxi	156374	99801	56574
金沙县	Jinsha	159562	101169	58393
织金县	Zhijin	148500	97794	50706
纳雍县	Nayong	120472	77973	42499
※威宁县	Weining	148637	92964	55673
赫章县	Hezhang	88639	57114	31526
碧江区	Bijiang	258995	204773	54222
万山区	Wanshan	14318	7803	6515

27-54 续表 continued

单位：万元 (10000 yuan)

县(市、区、特区)名称	County (City,District,Special Region)	社会消费品零售总额 Total Retail Sales	城镇 Urban	乡村 Rural
江口县	Jiangkou	44808	24417	20391
※玉屏县	Yuping	49212	26816	22395
石阡县	Shiqian	52170	29298	22872
思南县	Sinan	121052	67134	53918
※印江县	Yinjiang	64869	36056	28813
德江县	Dejiang	84436	46767	37669
※沿河县	Yanhe	91189	50053	41136
※松桃县	Songtao	117769	65219	52549
兴义市	Xingyi	731599	602002	129598
兴仁县	Xingren	95164	93253	1912
普安县	Puan	41836	32795	9041
晴隆县	Qinglong	35026	25700	9325
贞丰县	Zhenfeng	48522	41290	7232
望谟县	Wangmo	23585	17107	6478
册亨县	Ceheng	13624	10229	3395
安龙县	Anlong	63263	56922	6342
凯里市	Kaili	577240	467720	109520
黄平县	Huangping	56477	45282	11195
施秉县	Shibing	42022	33749	8273
三穗县	Sansui	73594	51495	22099
镇远县	Zhenyuan	68702	55431	13271
岑巩县	Cengong	57287	45888	11399
天柱县	Tianzhu	102734	55113	47621
锦屏县	Jinping	55420	44233	11187
剑河县	Jianhe	45091	32785	12306
台江县	Taijiang	31466	25207	6259
黎平县	Liping	106077	85067	21010
榕江县	Rongjiang	67434	45210	22224
从江县	Congjiang	61240	41506	19733
雷山县	Leishan	34260	22555	11705
麻江县	Majiang	38801	31425	7375
丹寨县	Danzhai	30429	24353	6076
都匀市	Duyun	376732	342259	34473
福泉市	Fuquan	123521	101287	22234
荔波县	Libo	58041	47594	10447
贵定县	Guiding	72665	59585	13080
瓮安县	Wengan	89989	73791	16198
独山县	Dushan	84620	69389	15232
平塘县	Pingtang	45664	37444	8220
罗甸县	Luodian	59009	48387	10622
长顺县	Changshun	56018	45935	10083
龙里县	Longli	54840	44968	9871
惠水县	Huishui	82903	67980	14923
※三都县	Sandu	67166	55076	12090

27-55 各县(市、区、特区)金融机构人民币存贷款余额(2011)

Urban and Rural Resident Savings Deposit Balance and Its Order by County(City,District,Special region)

单位：亿元 (100 million yuan)

县(市、区、特区)名称	County (City,District, Special region)	金融机构人民币存款余额 Total Deposits	#储蓄存款 Saving Deposit	金融机构人民币贷款余额 Total Loans
开阳县	Kaiyang	55.49	31.55	53.29
息烽县	Xifeng	35.34	20.07	35.50
修文县	Xiuwen	32.87	19.87	22.89
清镇市	Qingzhen	74.68	45.04	46.33
六枝特区	Liuzhi	69.54	35.21	38.25
盘　县	Panxian	205.52	93.35	103.76
遵义县	Zunyi	135.03	87.44	101.20
桐梓县	Tongzi	61.69	42.08	34.90
绥阳县	Suiyang	46.09	33.00	17.93
正安县	Zhengan	48.51	32.41	16.88
※道真县	Daozhen	40.59	27.75	14.59
※务川县	Wuchuan	38.18	22.93	15.16
凤冈县	Fenggang	35.84	24.10	15.84
湄潭县	Meitan	53.72	38.58	25.94
余庆县	Yuqing	35.85	25.07	22.95
习水县	Xishui	70.34	38.90	21.62
赤水市	Chishui	58.52	38.46	45.15
仁怀市	Renhuai	246.28	74.18	48.18
平坝县	Pingba	64.36	33.94	46.10
普定县	Puding	30.12	16.59	42.07
※镇宁县	Zhenning	33.79	16.24	26.73
※关岭县	Guanling	31.67	16.02	21.17
※紫云县	Ziyun	25.83	12.09	13.20
七星关区	Qixingguan	205.51	92.18	115.24
大方县	Dafang	67.29	41.38	42.57
黔西县	Qianxi	60.08	36.66	50.24
金沙县	Jinsha	70.70	40.98	45.58
织金县	Zhijin	73.24	36.10	33.57
纳雍县	Nayong	51.87	25.37	29.66
※威宁县	Weining	53.02	30.48	18.72
赫章县	Hezhang	42.63	27.86	14.44
碧江区	Bijiang	128.35	65.92	100.34
万山区	Wanshan	13.26	5.20	3.63

27-55 续表 continued

单位：亿元 (100 million yuan)

县(市、区、特区)名 称	County (City,District, Special region)	金融机构人民币存款余额 Total Deposits	#储蓄存款 Saving Deposit	金融机构人民币贷款余额 Total Loans
江口县	Jiangkou	28.28	16.06	15.11
※玉屏县	Yuping	22.54	14.90	31.61
石阡县	Shiqian	32.23	19.52	19.12
思南县	Sinan	55.22	35.79	45.68
※印江县	Yinjiang	38.40	26.00	19.34
德江县	Dejiang	32.39	21.89	18.84
※沿河县	Yanhe	42.75	28.14	21.11
※松桃县	Songtao	55.44	32.93	25.74
兴义市	Xingyi	227.76	106.24	161.85
兴仁县	Xingren	45.27	22.35	24.87
普安县	Puan	29.12	16.10	19.08
晴隆县	Qinglong	24.23	13.48	10.06
贞丰县	Zhenfeng	47.16	20.99	18.40
望谟县	Wangmo	27.42	9.14	9.66
册亨县	Ceheng	22.53	9.76	14.37
安龙县	Anlong	48.12	27.43	14.85
凯里市	Kaili	188.17	101.62	147.74
黄平县	Huangping	30.11	19.90	10.90
施秉县	Shibing	15.64	11.34	12.02
三穗县	Sansui	21.92	14.61	10.01
镇远县	Zhenyuan	25.90	19.17	15.94
岑巩县	Cengong	21.55	13.42	15.81
天柱县	Tianzhu	42.03	30.78	14.60
锦屏县	Jinping	29.00	17.49	9.99
剑河县	Jianhe	23.46	15.66	9.10
台江县	Taijiang	14.13	9.85	20.20
黎平县	Liping	45.24	31.20	23.42
榕江县	Rongjiang	30.25	20.51	24.33
从江县	Congjiang	22.64	14.36	12.87
雷山县	Leishan	13.96	9.59	9.53
麻江县	Majiang	21.15	13.44	10.80
丹寨县	Danzhai	17.48	9.83	6.17
都匀市	Duyun	166.53	82.97	95.40
福泉市	Fuquan	47.48	28.35	44.79
荔波县	Libo	22.65	13.67	10.50
贵定县	Guiding	32.70	21.13	13.13
瓮安县	Wengan	53.96	35.78	24.25
独山县	Dushan	36.64	23.88	20.45
平塘县	Pingtang	19.92	12.92	10.54
罗甸县	Luodian	30.93	13.13	17.14
长顺县	Changshun	22.60	10.57	10.57
龙里县	Longli	33.30	16.09	18.95
惠水县	Huishui	33.53	19.49	16.36
※三都县	Sandu	24.80	15.09	14.47

注：资料来源于中国人民银行贵阳中心支行。
Notes:Data in the table are obtained from Guiyang Central Branch of PBC.

27–56 各县(市、区、特区)普通中学(2011)

县(市、区、特区)名称	County (City,Distric, SpecialRegion)	学校数(所) Total Schools (unit)	#初中 Junior Secondary Shools	毕业生数(人) Graduates(person)	
				初中 Junior Secondary Shools	高中 Junior Secondary Shools
南明区	Nanming	67	54	8416	2328
云岩区	Yunyan	55	39	9516	4409
花溪区	Huaxi	37	29	4766	1559
乌当区	Wudang	17	15	2515	900
白云区	Baiyun	11	8	3640	1423
小河区	Xiaohe	16	11	2417	674
开阳县	Kaiyang	24	17	7619	2684
息烽县	Xifeng	14	11	4263	980
修文县	Xiuwen	17	12	4545	1262
清镇市	Qingzhen	30	23	8983	2479
钟山区	Zhongshan	49	37	9512	5476
六枝特区	Liuzhi	44	39	8979	1997
水城县	Shuicheng	52	49	11261	1635
盘　县	Panxian	74	65	25922	4776
红花岗区	Honghuagang	37	26	8775	4188
汇川区	Huicuan	32	24	6751	2559
遵义县	Zunyi	71	63	18874	6307
桐梓县	Tongzi	48	40	11509	2212
绥阳县	Suiyang	32	26	7270	1607
正安县	Zhengan	40	36	9284	1900
※道真县	Daozhen	23	21	4766	1548
※务川县	Wuchuan	29	26	7921	1226
凤冈县	Fenggang	25	22	7413	1774
湄潭县	Meitan	25	22	7585	2048
余庆县	Yuqing	17	14	4309	2511
习水县	Xishui	42	35	11532	2573
赤水市	Chishui	19	16	3552	1138
仁怀市	Renhuai	37	31	11030	3010
西秀区	Xixiu	38	29	11516	3494
平坝县	Pingba	24	17	5004	1654
普定县	Puding	15	13	6152	973
※镇宁县	Zhenning	19	18	5058	609
※关岭县	Guanling	21	18	5271	1324
※紫云县	Ziyun	19	18	4973	1034
七星关区	Qixingguan	124	106	21850	6554
大方县	Dafang	53	39	14221	3963
黔西县	Qianxi	53	41	12776	3651
金沙县	Jinsha	39	32	7117	2943
织金县	Zhijin	47	40	14372	3445
纳雍县	Nayong	36	29	12633	1999
※威宁县	Weining	61	53	21573	3199
赫章县	Hezhang	54	46	16414	2616
碧江区	Bijiang	23	16	5126	3809
万山区	Wanshan	9	8	2034	238

Statistics on Regular Secondary Schools by County

招生数(人) New Enrollment(person)		在校学生数(人) Students Enrollment(person)		专任教师(人) Full-time Teachers(person)	
初中 Junior Secondary Shools	高中 Junior Secondary Shools	初中 Junior Secondary Shools	高中 Junior Secondary Shools	初中 Junior Secondary Shools	高中 Junior Secondary Shools
9081	2976	26811	8051	1626	554
10072	4860	31240	14716	1940	1031
5192	2692	14867	6657	966	389
2750	865	7860	2453	538	174
4609	2612	13040	6540	611	426
3358	1568	9499	4125	469	286
6856	3434	21487	8970	1069	456
3522	1553	11324	4114	591	239
3832	1763	12795	4681	671	290
8873	3391	26908	8766	1338	581
13614	8641	37083	22391	1578	1072
11700	3294	32732	8149	1438	331
14354	3261	42655	7612	1986	243
24767	8613	79936	20696	3722	934
9393	4854	27550	13889	1494	737
7410	3179	21622	8930	1182	556
20044	9671	60252	24280	3240	1029
11355	3539	31494	8947	1876	394
8769	2211	25557	5756	1595	383
10114	2793	28946	7263	1699	446
5493	2498	14409	5841	783	321
9060	2635	26878	6460	1417	336
8995	3259	25573	8239	1263	450
9756	2914	26224	7204	1258	372
5353	2399	14833	6699	691	332
9470	3933	26212	10058	1818	618
3629	1630	10962	4212	696	249
13582	4267	37689	11055	1897	629
13113	4990	35945	12297	1864	638
5507	2035	15979	4906	865	291
6830	1394	18789	3579	1103	185
5220	960	15413	2257	814	117
4468	1442	14174	3530	780	190
6930	914	22772	2603	904	138
32757	12635	89621	27913	3546	1435
19576	7204	50736	16654	2415	609
15479	5499	39457	14578	2287	677
10751	4006	27797	10350	1402	516
20417	5903	51690	14117	2277	793
17553	5708	45411	11396	2041	393
34375	6692	88032	15820	3759	787
19103	5299	55797	11732	2414	472
5791	5343	16723	14271	945	698
2451	270	6983	739	344	65

27-56 续表

县（市、区、特区）名称	County (City,Distric, SpecialRegion)	学校数(所) Total Schools (unit)	#初中 Junior Secondary Shools	毕业生数(人) Graduates(person) 初中 Junior Secondary Shools	高中 Junior Secondary Shools
江口县	Jiangkou	17	14	3154	1263
※玉屏县	Yuping	11	8	1663	706
石阡县	Shiqian	26	23	6493	2215
思南县	Sinan	40	35	11719	4154
※印江县	Yinjiang	23	17	6017	2024
德江县	Dejiang	29	25	8594	2249
※沿河县	Yanhe	34	30	10245	1948
※松桃县	Songtao	43	37	12692	2418
兴义市	Xingyi	66	45	13790	7389
兴仁县	Xingren	33	28	9086	1146
普安县	Puan	26	24	5408	1113
晴隆县	Qinglong	24	22	5211	1408
贞丰县	Zhenfeng	20	18	6886	965
望谟县	Wangmo	19	17	3833	904
册亨县	Ceheng	18	16	3938	335
安龙县	Anlong	29	25	7149	1733
凯里市	Kaili	38	26	6939	3799
黄平县	Huangping	15	13	4004	1662
施秉县	Shibing	11	9	2352	629
三穗县	Sansui	12	10	2332	706
镇远县	Zhenyuan	19	17	2749	962
岑巩县	Cengong	15	13	3481	839
天柱县	Tianzhu	23	20	5027	2100
锦屏县	Jinping	18	15	3523	1409
剑河县	Jianhe	14	11	3074	982
台江县	Taijiang	9	8	2225	654
黎平县	Liping	27	24	8119	1911
榕江县	Rongjiang	24	21	4445	972
从江县	Congjiang	22	21	6167	810
雷山县	Leishan	8	7	2002	567
麻江县	Majiang	11	8	3257	925
丹寨县	Danzhai	9	8	2050	761
都匀市	Duyun	31	21	6881	3121
福泉市	Fuquan	19	16	5595	1581
荔波县	Libo	9	8	3053	792
贵定县	Guiding	16	14	4362	818
瓮安县	Wengan	28	23	7536	2751
独山县	Dushan	17	14	6558	1308
平塘县	Pingtang	18	17	5924	903
罗甸县	Luodian	22	20	5611	949
长顺县	Changshun	19	17	4320	726
龙里县	Longli	15	14	3153	565
惠水县	Huishui	27	25	8271	1529
※三都县	Sandu	21	19	4926	813

continued

招生数(人) New Enrollment(person)		在校学生数(人) Students Enrollment(person)		专任教师(人) Full-time Teachers(person)	
初中 Junior Secondary Shools	高中 Junior Secondary Shools	初中 Junior Secondary Shools	高中 Junior Secondary Shools	初中 Junior Secondary Shools	高中 Junior Secondary Shools
3626	1822	10661	4455	626	200
2070	1120	5732	2651	387	201
7029	2771	20098	7482	1220	413
14391	5899	40966	15297	1835	742
7310	3364	20308	7895	1104	395
9874	3293	28799	7804	1636	463
11960	2865	36764	6926	1840	343
12098	4451	37052	10309	2053	476
15622	8231	44391	24234	2608	1343
9823	2361	28365	5308	1486	357
6316	1555	17282	3891	938	218
5763	1420	15686	4213	722	222
6774	1318	21406	3244	1041	179
5472	1656	15126	3596	793	179
3860	1038	13051	2272	712	124
7717	2612	22885	5663	1271	278
8889	5862	24741	14582	1396	789
5881	2106	15533	5278	701	283
2617	1064	7189	2296	436	134
2811	1182	7952	2759	559	182
3779	1521	10110	3741	596	219
3785	1336	11178	3091	574	199
4922	3271	14105	7992	1066	410
3465	2032	10553	5235	616	279
3678	1328	9880	3337	618	152
2318	1050	6795	2405	463	134
8386	2835	23605	7490	1274	382
4565	1777	16403	3763	958	265
5304	942	18653	2586	922	143
2474	1079	7242	2450	417	149
3559	1753	9291	3921	635	219
2494	1102	6336	2408	450	164
6424	4159	19330	11304	1101	540
4868	1895	15542	5127	976	252
2969	1661	9171	3687	452	201
4518	1147	13479	2942	709	167
6864	4035	21312	10387	1043	518
5625	3463	18135	6344	952	372
5040	1261	15624	3595	897	177
4461	2085	15747	4743	917	260
3784	1741	13206	3738	631	181
3289	1116	9609	2627	563	139
7940	2262	24158	5492	1166	307
6113	1931	16501	4086	958	255

27–57 各县(市、区、特区)小学(2011)

Statistics on Primary Schools by County

县(市、区、特区)名称	County (City,Distric, Special Region)	学校数(个) Schools (unit)	毕业生数(人) Gruaduates (person)	招生数(人) New Enrollment (person)	在校学生数(人) Students Enrollment (person)	专任教师(人) Full-time Teachers (person)	学龄儿童入学率(%) Enrollment Ratio of Primary Schools(%)	学龄女童入学率(%) Enrollment Ratio of School Girls(%)
南明区	Nanming	82	11079	10957	65678	2810	221.60	218.58
云岩区	Yunyan	86	11509	11936	67925	2974	212.06	210.01
花溪区	Huaxi	81	4835	3813	24942	1530	123.58	125.16
乌当区	Wudang	48	2612	2514	15202	897	126.25	125.17
白云区	Baiyun	53	4331	3798	24053	1174	182.42	178.78
小河区	Xiaohe	29	3419	3799	21949	865	111.01	111.12
开阳县	Kaiyang	93	6662	3648	25885	1545	96.94	96.75
息烽县	Xifeng	59	3426	2564	16658	1088	93.14	95.39
修文县	Xiuwen	49	3611	2730	16877	1180	93.28	95.97
清镇市	Qingzhen	131	8534	5552	36970	1886	107.14	109.58
钟山区	Zhongshan	93	12375	11208	76359	2818	122.93	123.64
六枝特区	Liuzhi	163	12484	10938	67088	2759	99.07	101.60
水城县	Shuicheng	221	16807	12064	86032	3781	93.33	96.71
盘　县	Panxian	308	24347	9596	93263	4745	98.06	96.99
红花岗区	Honghuagang	69	9732	7808	49882	2005	132.72	129.87
汇川区	Huicuan	82	7066	5912	36392	1690	132.13	134.89
遵义县	Zunyi	304	19087	11753	78080	5199	88.64	91.70
桐梓县	Tongzi	189	11064	8318	54143	2645	84.08	84.25
绥阳县	Suiyang	167	8806	5587	41012	2246	78.57	80.43
正安县	Zhengan	148	10005	6385	42535	2655	77.03	78.33
※道真县	Daozhen	89	5332	3765	27411	1529	83.95	84.41
※务川县	Wuchuan	139	9115	6068	41453	2133	79.28	82.31
凤冈县	Fenggang	111	8534	5051	35198	1656	92.35	93.30
湄潭县	Meitan	105	9447	5085	38389	2155	87.39	89.79
余庆县	Yuqing	105	5111	3916	24469	1151	83.21	84.08
习水县	Xishui	218	9375	8710	55661	2578	90.14	92.61
赤水市	Chishui	57	3624	3304	18919	1440	76.91	77.87
仁怀市	Renhuai	195	13827	7657	64066	3262	93.39	92.64
西秀区	Xixiu	193	12484	11761	67508	3500	95.46	96.30
平坝县	Pingba	144	5996	5643	33950	1714	100.52	102.45
普定县	Puding	165	8531	7619	44975	2266	99.98	98.98
※镇宁县	Zhenning	106	5874	5613	38268	1706	105.08	107.74
※关岭县	Guanling	125	5488	4860	31557	1557	97.97	97.44
※紫云县	Ziyun	138	7844	5030	33717	1900	93.12	95.60
七星关区	Qixingguan	406	34482	29459	181638	6355	99.90	99.56
大方县	Dafang	319	19378	17777	106451	4815	87.81	86.58
黔西县	Qianxi	258	15344	10775	77306	4103	98.33	99.73
金沙县	Jinsha	193	10874	10464	63369	2855	99.39	93.15
织金县	Zhijin	330	21833	17542	123508	4827	93.05	93.96
纳雍县	Nayong	241	18480	20771	126733	4775	103.32	103.78
※威宁县	Weining	426	40419	36424	244707	9606	101.93	102.17
赫章县	Hezhang	294	22943	15495	112166	4648	93.40	93.77
碧江区	Bijiang	89	5094	4524	28693	1585	95.11	93.70
万山区	Wanshan	63	2342	1904	11339	701	93.71	93.29

27–57 续表　continued

县（市、区、特区）名称	County (City,Distric, Special Region)	学校数（个）Schools (unit)	毕业生数（人）Guaduates (person)	招生数（人）New Enrollment (person)	在校学生数（人）Students Enrollment (person)	专任教师（人）Full-time Teachers (person)	学龄儿童入学率(%) Enrollment Ratio of Primary Schools(%)	学龄女童入学率(%) Enrollment Ratio of School Girls(%)
江口县	Jiangkou	97	3509	4163	21292	1009	99.79	99.72
※玉屏县	Yuping	44	2051	1961	11516	652	90.62	92.95
石阡县	Shiqian	105	7082	6384	40610	2285	95.23	97.05
思南县	Sinan	212	13813	10022	67253	3361	93.66	94.19
※印江县	Yinjiang	126	7065	6725	40150	2266	98.73	99.55
德江县	Dejiang	206	10645	8872	60931	2755	95.19	92.46
※沿河县	Yanhe	224	13694	13253	84373	3309	98.14	100.36
※松桃县	Songtao	305	13635	12227	73889	3565	99.34	99.33
兴义市	Xingyi	232	14420	13027	77200	3987	103.83	102.49
兴仁县	Xingren	175	10090	9258	55836	2515	99.48	99.47
普安县	Puan	105	6466	7296	37926	1632	86.46	88.37
晴隆县	Qinglong	96	6013	5851	35924	1473	98.72	99.41
贞丰县	Zhenfeng	137	8665	6638	51925	2429	99.38	99.19
望谟县	Wangmo	123	6354	6724	41114	1959	98.69	98.30
册亨县	Ceheng	69	4069	3224	23654	1053	97.63	98.21
安龙县	Anlong	154	7947	5621	39500	2216	88.97	89.94
凯里市	Kaili	81	8562	7997	49721	2113	116.11	117.70
黄平县	Huangping	81	5973	5372	33729	1460	101.42	99.23
施秉县	Shibing	58	2779	2237	15202	879	93.85	94.19
三穗县	Sansui	47	2877	2650	16560	920	90.99	93.05
镇远县	Zhenyuan	48	3788	3196	22336	1181	90.88	92.19
岑巩县	Cengong	80	3759	3018	20696	1133	84.84	87.17
天柱县	Tianzhu	63	4989	4279	23120	1656	85.53	90.05
锦屏县	Jinping	112	3476	2293	15054	893	80.38	81.69
剑河县	Jianhe	65	3815	3186	21852	1140	86.19	88.33
台江县	Taijiang	41	2960	2568	14687	931	91.15	87.55
黎平县	Liping	216	8620	5223	37541	2339	95.31	96.13
榕江县	Rongjiang	102	4832	4710	31851	1629	94.55	93.35
从江县	Congjiang	118	5817	4707	31719	1653	95.80	95.69
雷山县	Leishan	58	2452	1926	12928	783	82.64	83.37
麻江县	Majiang	56	3485	1984	15744	1019	99.04	98.20
丹寨县	Danzhai	37	2549	2337	14568	850	91.47	92.17
都匀市	Duyun	104	6570	4451	31526	2046	99.62	93.40
福泉市	Fuquan	94	5015	3083	20827	1452	95.06	94.62
荔波县	Libo	71	3031	2291	14150	880	95.89	96.63
贵定县	Guiding	89	5039	3689	24441	1351	94.84	93.21
瓮安县	Wengan	117	6993	5274	32024	1868	89.01	90.50
独山县	Dushan	118	5452	2690	19979	1581	92.67	95.47
平塘县	Pingtang	118	5082	4172	26815	1270	89.75	92.04
罗甸县	Luodian	93	4671	4992	32286	1493	95.54	97.38
长顺县	Changshun	85	3858	2754	21813	1159	86.75	83.50
龙里县	Longli	75	3459	2608	17140	1101	98.28	96.46
惠水县	Huishui	133	8529	6347	44611	1924	101.32	102.73
※三都县	Sandu	111	6439	6391	38097	1763	99.06	98.96

28

Twenty-eight

全国各省（区、市）资料

Main Statistics of Provinces (autonomous regions, municipalities) in the Whole Country

28–1 全国及各省(区、市)人口、生产总值(2011)

单位：亿元

地区	Region	年末总人口(万人) Total Population (year-end) (10000 persons)	位次 Order	地区生产总值 Gross Domestic Product	位次 Order	第一产业 Primary Industry	位次 Order
全　国	**National Total**	**134735**		**471564**		**47712**	
北　京	Beijing	2019	26	16011.43	13	136.21	29
天　津	Tianjin	1355	27	11190.99	20	159.09	27
河　北	Hebei	7241	6	24228.18	6	2905.73	5
山　西	Shanxi	3593	18	11100.18	21	641.41	25
内蒙古	Inner Mongolia	2482	23	14246.11	15	1304.91	17
辽　宁	Liaoning	4383	14	22025.92	7	1915.57	11
吉　林	Jilin	2749	21	10530.71	22	1277.43	18
黑龙江	Heilongjiang	3834	15	12503.83	16	1705.58	12
上　海	Shanghai	2347	24	19195.69	11	124.94	30
江　苏	Jiangsu	7899	5	48604.26	2	3064.77	3
浙　江	Zhejiang	5463	10	32000.10	4	1580.57	14
安　徽	Anhui	5968	8	15110.31	14	2020.26	10
福　建	Fujian	3720	17	17410.21	12	1610.61	13
江　西	Jiangxi	4488	13	11583.80	19	1391.10	16
山　东	Shandong	9637	2	45429.21	3	3973.80	1
河　南	Henan	9388	3	27232.04	5	3512.06	2
湖　北	Hubei	5758	9	19594.19	10	2569.30	8
湖　南	Hunan	6596	7	19635.19	9	2733.66	6
广　东	Guangdong	10505	1	52673.59	1	2659.83	7
广　西	Guangxi	4645	11	11714.35	18	2047.30	9
海　南	Hainan	877	28	2515.29	28	659.15	24
重　庆	Chongqing	2919	20	10011.13	23	844.52	21
四　川	Sichuan	8050	4	21026.68	8	2983.45	4
贵　州	**Guizhou**	**3469**	**19**	**5701.84**	**26**	**726.22**	**22**
云　南	Yunnan	4631	12	8750.95	24	1407.81	15
西　藏	Tibet	303	31	605.83	31	74.35	31
陕　西	Shanxi	3743	16	12391.30	17	1220.90	19
甘　肃	Gansu	2564	22	5000.47	27	678.22	23
青　海	Qinghai	568	30	1634.72	30	155.44	28
宁　夏	Ningxia	639	29	2060.79	29	184.13	26
新　疆	Xinjiang	2209	25	6474.54	25	1139.02	20

注：除贵州外，全国及各省(区、市)资料均来源于《中国统计摘要—2012》(以下相关表同)，各省生产总值及相关指标为初步核算数据。

The Population and GDP of the Whole Country and All Provinces

(100 million yuan)

第二产业 Secondary Industry	位次 Order	第三产业 Tertiary Industry	位次 Order	地区生产总值比上年增长(%) Increase Rate of GDP in 2011 over 2010(%)	位次 Order	人均生产总值(元) Per Capita Gross Domestic Product(yuan)	位次 Order
220592		**203260**		**9.2**		**35083**	
3744.37	24	12130.85	5	8.1	31	80394	3
5878.02	19	5153.88	14	16.4	1	84337	1
13098.11	6	8224.34	7	11.3	25	33571	14
6577.84	17	3880.93	20	13.0	12	30974	18
8092.07	13	4849.13	16	14.3	5	57515	6
12150.73	7	7959.62	8	12.1	20	50299	7
5601.20	21	3652.08	21	13.7	8	38321	11
6317.29	18	4480.96	17	12.2	18	32615	16
7959.69	14	11111.06	6	8.2	30	82560	2
25023.78	2	20515.71	2	11.0	26	61649	4
16404.18	4	14015.35	4	9.0	29	58665	5
8226.41	12	4863.64	15	13.5	10	25340	26
9167.54	11	6632.06	13	12.2	18	46972	10
6592.21	16	3600.49	23	12.5	15	25884	25
24037.38	3	17418.03	3	10.9	27	47260	9
15887.39	5	7832.59	9	11.6	24	28981	21
9818.76	9	7206.13	11	13.8	7	34131	13
9324.73	10	7576.80	10	12.8	13	29828	19
26205.30	1	23808.46	1	10.0	28	50295	8
5736.78	20	3930.27	19	12.3	17	25315	27
714.50	30	1141.64	28	12.0	21	28797	23
5542.80	22	3623.81	22	16.4	1	34500	12
11027.94	8	7015.29	12	15.0	3	26133	24
2194.33	**27**	**2781.29**	**25**	**15.0**	**3**	**16413**	**31**
3990.97	23	3352.17	24	13.7	8	18957	30
209.54	31	321.94	31	12.7	14	20077	28
6836.27	15	4334.13	18	13.9	6	33142	15
2524.25	26	1798.00	27	12.5	15	19517	29
939.10	29	540.18	30	13.5	10	28891	22
1076.00	28	800.66	29	12.0	21	32392	17
3289.84	25	2045.68	26	12.0	21	29496	20

Note:Data in the table were obtained from China Statistical Digest 2012 except the data of Guizhou Province (the same applies to relative tables below). Data of GDP and its related indicators of all provimces are preliminarily estimated.

28-2 全国及各省(区、市)固定资产投资、房地产开发(2011)

地 区	Region	固定资产投资额(亿元) Investment in Fixed Assets(100 million yuan)	位 次 Order	房地产投资(亿元) Real Estate Investment (100 million yuan)	位 次 Order
全国总计	**National Total**	**301932.85**		**61739.78**	
北 京	Beijing	5519.86	23	3036.33	7
天 津	Tianjin	7040.48	20	1080.04	22
河 北	Hebei	15795.22	6	3069.55	6
山 西	Shanxi	6837.41	21	789.92	25
内蒙古	Inner Mongolia	10291.69	12	1650.02	16
辽 宁	Liaoning	17431.46	3	4487.56	3
吉 林	Jilin	7221.64	18	1165.39	21
黑龙江	Heilongjiang	7206.33	19	1219.37	20
上 海	Shanghai	4877.01	24	2170.31	12
江 苏	Jiangsu	26299.40	1	5552.69	1
浙 江	Zhejiang	13651.48	8	4137.25	4
安 徽	Anhui	11986.02	10	2590.07	10
福 建	Fujian	9692.55	13	2402.61	11
江 西	Jiangxi	8756.10	15	852.69	24
山 东	Shandong	25928.45	2	4108.08	5
河 南	Henan	16932.15	4	2620.01	9
湖 北	Hubei	12223.71	9	2063.21	13
湖 南	Hunan	11360.51	11	1896.66	15
广 东	Guangdong	16688.44	5	4899.19	2
广 西	Guangxi	7563.89	16	1500.46	17
海 南	Hainan	1611.41	28	663.05	26
重 庆	Chongqing	7366.15	17	2015.09	14
四 川	Sichuan	13705.29	7	2836.71	8
贵 州	**Guizhou**	**3734.08**	**27**	**878.67**	**23**
云 南	Yunnan	5927.01	22	1272.72	19
西 藏	Tibet	516.31	31	5.13	31
陕 西	Shanxi	9123.72	14	1420.53	18
甘 肃	Gansu	3865.99	26	362.88	28
青 海	Qinghai	1365.99	30	144.77	30
宁 夏	Ningxia	1583.46	29	330.55	29
新 疆	Xinjiang	4444.99	25	518.26	27

注：本表统计口径为计划总投资500万元及以上城镇投资、非农户投资和房地产开发投资，分省数据不含跨省项目。

The Investment in Fixed Assets and Real Estate Development of the Whole Country and All Province

房屋施工面积（万平方米）Floor Space under Construction(10000 aq.m)	位次 Order	房屋竣工面积（万平方米）Floor Space Completed (10000 aq.m)	位次 Order	商品房销售面积（万平方米）Floor Space of Commercial Houses(10000 aq.m)	位次 Order
507959.39		**89244.25**		**109945.56**	
12065.38	18	2245.24	16	1440.04	25
9075.39	23	2105.32	19	1643.11	24
26835.37	7	5145.32	6	5901.36	7
9325.63	22	2084.20	20	1263.19	26
16378.10	13	2453.11	15	3620.12	13
34511.89	4	6359.15	2	7561.39	4
8963.42	24	1656.17	22	2364.25	19
12065.32	19	2992.61	13	3395.42	14
12983.32	16	2240.62	17	1771.30	22
40738.08	1	8040.88	1	7982.67	2
30318.08	5	4423.32	7	3827.08	12
20744.07	10	3063.87	12	4581.55	9
19212.77	12	2614.88	14	2696.16	18
8210.88	25	1777.42	21	2335.36	20
36293.30	3	6226.85	3	9579.60	1
25280.95	8	5307.13	5	6304.41	6
13923.90	15	3083.54	11	4190.09	11
20746.32	9	3933.97	9	4877.65	8
36311.94	2	5800.52	4	7761.34	3
14448.23	14	2183.90	18	2934.05	17
3659.88	29	375.91	30	888.19	27
20397.24	11	3424.33	10	4533.50	10
27315.44	6	4308.71	8	6664.70	5
10395.27	**21**	**1462.44**	**23**	**1889.95**	**21**
10597.88	20	1450.76	24	3107.12	15
48.73	31	21.69	31	19.36	31
12179.97	17	1104.45	26	3068.63	16
3810.00	28	655.99	28	815.89	29
1659.03	30	505.91	29	348.20	30
4040.83	27	942.77	27	842.89	28
5422.77	26	1253.27	25	1736.98	23

Note:Data in the table refer to those projects planned to invest 500,0000 yuan at least in urban areas,projects funded by rural non-farm households and real estate development, but Provincial data don't include inter-provincial project.

28-3 全国及各省(区、市)进出口总额(2011)

Imports and Exports of the Whole Country and All Provinces

单位：亿美元 (USD 100 million)

地 区	Region	进出口总额 Total Exports and Imports	位 次 Order	#出口额 Exports	位 次 Order	#进口额 Imports	位 次 Order
全国总计	**National Total**	**36421**		**18986**		**17435**	
北 京	Beijing	3895	4	590	7	3305	2
天 津	Tianjin	1034	8	445	9	589	7
河 北	Hebei	536	10	286	11	250	10
山 西	Shanxi	148	23	55	23	93	21
内蒙古	Inner Mongolia	119	26	47	25	72	24
辽 宁	Liaoning	960	9	511	8	449	9
吉 林	Jilin	220	20	50	24	170	13
黑龙江	Heilongjiang	385	12	177	16	208	11
上 海	Shanghai	4373	3	2097	4	2276	3
江 苏	Jiangsu	5398	2	3127	2	2271	4
浙 江	Zhejiang	3094	5	2164	3	930	6
安 徽	Anhui	313	16	171	17	142	14
福 建	Fujian	1436	7	929	6	507	8
江 西	Jiangxi	316	15	219	12	97	19
山 东	Shandong	2360	6	1258	5	1102	5
河 南	Henan	326	14	192	15	134	16
湖 北	Hubei	335	13	195	14	140	15
湖 南	Hunan	190	21	99	20	91	22
广 东	Guangdong	9135	1	5320	1	3815	1
广 西	Guangxi	233	18	124	19	109	17
海 南	Hainan	128	25	26	27	102	18
重 庆	Chongqing	292	17	198	13	94	20
四 川	Sichuan	478	11	291	10	187	12
贵 州	**Guizhou**	**49**	**28**	**30**	**26**	**19**	**28**
云 南	Yunnan	161	22	95	21	66	25
西 藏	Tibet	14	30	12	30	2	30
陕 西	Shanxi	146	24	70	22	76	23
甘 肃	Gansu	87	27	21	28	66	26
青 海	Qinghai	9	31	7	31	2	31
宁 夏	Ningxia	23	29	16	29	7	29
新 疆	Xinjiang	228	19	168	18	60	27

注：表中数据按经营单位所在地分。
Note:Data in the table are estimated according to the enterprise's location of business activity.

28-4　全国及各省(区、市)主要农产品产量(2011)

The Output of Main Agricultural Products of the Whole Country and All Provinces

单位：万吨　　(10000 tons)

地　区	Region	粮食产量 Output of Grain	位 次 Order	油料产量 Oil-bearing Crops	位 次 Order	肉类产量 Output of Pork, Beef and Mutton	位 次 Order	蔬菜产量 Vegetables Products	位 次 Order
全国	**National**	**57120.85**		**3306.76**		**7957.84**		**67929.67**	
北　京	Beijing	121.77	29	1.39	30	44.42	26	296.87	29
天　津	Tianjin	161.83	27	0.66	31	42.92	27	431.30	27
河　北	Hebei	3172.60	6	141.78	8	418.18	6	7384.30	2
山　西	Shanxi	1193.00	19	18.70	25	71.30	25	981.90	22
内蒙古	Inner Mongolia	2387.51	11	133.88	9	237.42	15	1440.17	15
辽　宁	Liaoning	2035.50	13	119.76	10	408.17	7	2832.51	9
吉　林	Jilin	3171.01	7	69.56	14	243.91	14	971.38	23
黑龙江	Heilongjiang	5570.60	1	23.27	24	201.21	16	789.93	24
上　海	Shanghai	121.95	28	1.86	29	27.59	29	408.24	28
江　苏	Jiangsu	3307.76	4	144.05	7	375.92	10	4586.88	4
浙　江	Zhejiang	781.60	23	39.85	21	175.95	20	1815.61	13
安　徽	Anhui	3135.50	8	213.75	6	375.47	11	2213.99	11
福　建	Fujian	672.80	24	27.46	23	182.96	18	1623.41	14
江　西	Jiangxi	2052.79	12	113.59	11	295.60	13	1165.75	21
山　东	Shandong	4426.29	3	341.00	2	711.05	1	9180.93	1
河　南	Henan	5542.50	2	532.36	1	641.65	3	6709.74	3
湖　北	Hubei	2388.53	10	304.72	3	381.93	9	3358.60	6
湖　南	Hunan	2939.35	9	215.29	5	489.48	4	3337.40	7
广　东	Guangdong	1360.95	16	91.90	12	434.68	5	2850.99	8
广　西	Guangxi	1429.93	15	50.14	19	391.08	8	2246.40	10
海　南	Hainan	188.04	26	9.94	27	71.64	24	469.06	25
重　庆	Chongqing	1126.90	20	46.51	20	196.28	17	1407.97	17
四　川	Sichuan	3291.60	5	278.45	4	651.17	2	3573.65	5
贵　州	**Guizhou**	**876.90**	**22**	**78.85**	**13**	**179.97**	**19**	**1250.05**	**20**
云　南	Yunnan	1673.60	14	60.75	17	324.36	12	1340.00	18
西　藏	Tibet	93.73	31	6.35	28	26.14	30	60.07	31
陕　西	Shanxi	1194.70	18	58.97	18	99.60	22	1432.50	16
甘　肃	Gansu	1014.60	21	63.52	16	83.75	23	1320.60	19
青　海	Qinghai	103.36	30	33.29	22	28.84	28	144.61	30
宁　夏	Ningxia	358.95	25	18.41	26	25.24	31	438.71	26
新　疆	Xinjiang	1224.70	17	66.76	15	119.98	21	1866.15	12

28–5 全国及各省(区、市)主要工业产品产量(2011)

The Output of Main Industrial Products of the Whole Country and All Provinces

地 区	Region	发电量 (亿千瓦时) Electricity (100 million kwh)	成品钢材 (万吨) Products Steel (10000 tons)	水 泥 (万吨) Cement (10000 tons)	农用化肥 (万吨) Chemical Fertilizers (10000 tons)	家用电冰箱 (万台) Refrigerator (10000 sets)	十种有色金属 (万吨) Ten Kinds of Nonferrous Metals (10000 tons)	电解铝 (万吨) Electrolyzed Aluminum (ton)	铁合金 (吨) Ferroalloy (ton)
全国总计	**National Total**	**46037**	**88131**	**206317**	**6027**	**8699**	**3424**	**1756**	**2842**
北 京	Beijing	263	287	912		74			1
天 津	Tianjin	619	5164	766	6	49	2		
河 北	Hebei	2281	19227	13972	175		14		34
山 西	Shanxi	2300	3369	3936	364		143	105	169
内蒙古	Inner Mongolia	2971	1417	6397	126		239	166	342
辽 宁	Liaoning	1367	5740	5690	63	96	77	21	85
吉 林	Jilin	702	1069	4221	28		2		58
黑龙江	Heilongjiang	824	597	4214	68				
上 海	Shanghai	947	2483	806	3	185	17		
江 苏	Jiangsu	3756	9994	14900	244	1195	69	11	82
浙 江	Zhejiang	2716	3135	12122	26	627	54	15	18
安 徽	Anhui	1633	2743	9205	258	3114	142		5
福 建	Fujian	1579	1560	6571	52		22	15	37
江 西	Jiangxi	688	2247	6782	30	117	115		1
山 东	Shandong	3162	7034	15036	610	719	263	191	58
河 南	Henan	2572	3551	13666	474	406	564	388	145
湖 北	Hubei	2052	3570	9343	1018	220	95	36	31
湖 南	Hunan	1294	1943	9228	208	26	266	30	396
广 东	Guangdong	3607	3177	12607	52	1409	19		0
广 西	Guangxi	1014	1759	8640	96		133	63	312
海 南	Hainan	169	23	1509	67				
重 庆	Chongqing	530	948	4935	170	194	34	23	42
四 川	Sichuan	1845	2233	14501	471	67	99	58	201
贵 州	**Guizhou**	**1344**	**462**	**5000**	**360**	**170**	**95**	**88**	**261**
云 南	Yunnan	1376	1351	6457	322		268	88	78
西 藏	Tibet	22		233					
陕 西	Shanxi	1209	1035	6431	92	32	130	31	51
甘 肃	Gansu	1013	813	2747	62		212	110	129
青 海	Qinghai	437	141	1043	263		183	169	114
宁 夏	Ningxia	937	77	1456	93		130	118	178
新 疆	Xinjiang	810	980	2994	227		38	29	15

28-5 续表 continued

地 区	Region	轮胎外胎 (万条) Tires (10000 tires)	磷肥 (万吨) Phosphate Fertilizers (10000 tons)	磷矿石 (万吨) Phosphorite Mineral (10000 tons)	卷 烟 (亿支) Cigarettes (100 million pieces)	白 酒 (万千升) Liquor (10000 kiloliter)	中成药 (万吨) Traditional Chinese Medicine (10000 tons)
全 国	**National Total**	**83209.1**	**1462.4**	**8122.3**	**24474.0**	**1025.8**	**238.4**
北 京	Beijing	375.4			208.9	20.6	3.6
天 津	Tianjin	3618.9			226.0	4.3	0.4
河 北	Hebei	58.2	11.2	37.7	807.5	32.4	4.2
山 西	Shanxi	164.9	10.0		155.0	14.6	0.8
内蒙古	Inner Mongolia		21.4		287.5	52.3	1.2
辽 宁	Liaoning	1669.7	4.2		274.5	68.1	0.9
吉 林	Jilin	4.6			430.0	42.4	41.6
黑龙江	Heilongjiang	441.0			436.1	20.9	15.0
上 海	Shanghai	908.3	0.5		896.1	1.1	1.4
江 苏	Jiangsu	10767.6	18.7	9.8	991.1	67.9	1.0
浙 江	Zhejiang	9673.1	0.6		885.2	2.1	2.1
安 徽	Anhui	7918.4	49.9	13.2	1258.3	39.5	4.7
福 建	Fujian	3000.2	1.8		884.3	3.3	0.7
江 西	Jiangxi	438.0	18.8		584.0	14.6	8.6
山 东	Shandong	30451.4	17.0		1361.3	99.2	12.1
河 南	Henan	2217.6	16.1		1676.1	105.3	15.1
湖 北	Hubei	519.0	575.9	2768.7	1347.5	29.8	20.8
湖 南	Hunan	2.3	34.5		1816.2	12.9	12.5
广 东	Guangdong	6123.3	46.4		1345.6	10.0	19.1
广 西	Guangxi	10.0	31.0		741.5	7.3	15.8
海 南	Hainan				95.0	0.4	
重 庆	Chongqing	2503.0	64.7	43.5	516.0	17.3	6.7
四 川	Sichuan	1531.2	91.1	959.3	944.2	309.4	39.0
贵 州	**Guizhou**	**536.8**	**193.1**	**2052.8**	**1226.2**	**24.7**	**4.7**
云 南	Yunnan		214.6	2236.1	3649.9	5.9	2.4
西 藏	Tibet						0.1
陕 西	Shanxi		24.8	1.2	860.0	8.0	2.7
甘 肃	Gansu		11.1		410.0	3.0	0.6
青 海	Qinghai					1.7	0.1
宁 夏	Ningxia	188.4	3.2			1.5	0.1
新 疆	Xinjiang	87.8	1.8		160.0	5.3	0.4

注：本表统计口径为年主营业务收入2000万元及以上工业企业。
Note:Data in the table refer to the revenue from principal business of 20 million yuan and above of industry enterprises.

28–6 全国及各省(区、市)贸易和旅游(2011)

The Trade and Tourism of the Whole Country and All Provinces

地区	Region	社会消费品零售总额(亿元) Total Retail Sales of Consumer Goods (100 million yuan)	位次 Order	国际旅游外汇收入(亿美元) Foreign Exchange Earnings (USD 100 million)	位次 Order	入境旅游人数(万人次) Number of International Tourists Received (10000 person-times)	位次 Order	#接待外国人 Foreigners	位次 Order
全国总计	**National Total**	**183919**		**484.60**		**13542.40**			
北京	Beijing	6900	10	54.16	4	520.40	7	447.40	5
天津	Tianjin	3395	23	17.56	9	200.44	16	63.60	23
河北	Hebei	8036	9	4.48	23	114.14	24	98.30	20
山西	Shanxi	3903	19	5.67	20	155.32	20	98.30	20
内蒙古	Inner Mongolia	3992	17	6.71	18	151.52	21	147.60	14
辽宁	Liaoning	8095	7	27.13	7	410.30	10	339.40	6
吉林	Jilin	4120	16	3.85	25	99.32	25	85.50	22
黑龙江	Heilongjiang	4750	15	9.18	17	206.52	15	197.80	9
上海	Shanghai	6815	12	57.50	2	668.61	6	555.00	2
江苏	Jiangsu	15988	3	56.53	3	737.33	5	537.90	3
浙江	Zhejiang	12028	4	45.42	5	773.69	3	515.00	4
安徽	Anhui	4955	14	11.79	12	265.17	13	151.70	13
福建	Fujian	6276	13	36.34	6	427.42	8	140.00	15
江西	Jiangxi	3485	22	4.15	24	135.83	22	44.00	26
山东	Shandong	17156	2	25.51	8	424.40	9	312.30	7
河南	Henan	9454	5	5.49	21	168.29	18	104.30	19
湖北	Hubei	8275	6	9.40	16	213.52	14	160.10	12
湖南	Hunan	6885	11	10.14	14	1692.30	2	119.80	17
广东	Guangdong	20298	1	139.06	1	24500.00	1	749.30	1
广西	Guangxi	3908	18	10.52	13	302.79	11	171.50	11
海南	Hainan	760	28	3.78	26	81.46	26	56.20	24
重庆	Chongqing	3488	21	9.68	15	186.40	17	132.60	16
四川	Sichuan	8045	8	5.94	19	163.97	19	113.70	18
贵州	**Guizhou**	**1752**	**25**	**1.35**	**27**	**58.51**	**27**	**23.60**	**28**
云南	Yunnan	3000	24	16.08	10	763.72	4	281.00	8
西藏	Tibet	219	31	1.20	28	27.00	28	24.90	27
陕西	Shanxi	3790	20	12.95	11	270.41	12	189.90	10
甘肃	Gansu	1648	26	0.17	30	9.11	29	5.50	29
青海	Qinghai	411	30	0.27	29	5.17	30	4.10	30
宁夏	Ningxia	478	29	0.06	31	1.95	31	1.40	31
新疆	Xinjiang	1616	27	4.65	22	132.50	23	48.80	25

29

Twenty-nine

历年资料

Historical Statistics

29-1 全省生产总值
Gross Domestic Product

单位：亿元 (100 million yuan)

年 份 Year	地 区 生产总值 Gross Domestic Product	第 一 产 业 Primary Industry	第 二 产 业 Secondary Industry	工 业 Industry	建筑业 Construction	第 三 产 业 Tertiary Industry	#交通运输、仓储、邮政业 Transportation, Storage, Post and Telecommunications	人均生 产总值 (元) Per Capita Gross Domestic Product(yuan)
1978	46.62	19.42	18.73	15.24	3.49	8.47	1.68	175
1979	55.28	23.29	22.41	18.33	4.08	9.58	1.86	204
1980	60.26	24.86	24.00	19.37	4.63	11.40	2.01	219
1981	67.89	29.90	24.95	20.36	4.59	13.04	2.56	242
1982	79.39	37.37	27.44	22.58	4.86	14.58	2.74	278
1983	87.38	37.76	33.14	28.16	4.98	16.48	3.76	302
1984	108.27	45.73	43.51	36.85	6.66	19.03	4.66	371
1985	123.92	50.45	49.88	41.96	7.92	23.59	5.86	420
1986	139.57	56.46	50.96	43.57	7.39	32.15	7.34	467
1987	165.50	66.46	60.11	49.93	10.18	38.93	7.74	546
1988	211.79	85.20	78.63	68.32	10.31	47.96	9.78	683
1989	235.84	92.88	86.74	77.26	9.48	56.22	12.36	750
1990	260.14	100.10	92.83	82.15	10.68	67.21	11.69	810
1991	295.90	115.71	101.54	88.96	12.58	78.65	13.98	896
1992	339.91	121.18	122.08	106.41	15.67	96.65	19.00	1034
1993	417.69	133.41	155.03	135.40	19.63	129.25	25.45	1234
1994	524.46	183.56	194.80	173.03	21.77	146.10	18.02	1527
1995	636.21	227.13	232.52	208.75	23.77	176.56	22.77	1826
1996	723.18	254.53	255.09	225.36	29.73	213.56	26.79	2048
1997	805.79	271.96	288.99	251.10	37.89	244.84	23.51	2250
1998	858.39	265.04	319.40	273.82	45.58	273.95	29.14	2364
1999	937.50	267.75	350.41	294.42	55.99	319.34	59.17	2545
2000	1029.92	271.20	391.20	328.73	62.47	367.52	75.86	2759
2001	1133.27	274.41	433.52	360.73	72.79	425.34	88.47	3000
2002	1243.43	281.10	481.96	395.45	86.51	480.37	102.48	3257
2003	1426.34	298.69	569.37	473.38	95.99	558.28	119.26	3701
2004	1677.80	334.50	681.50	577.40	104.10	661.80	134.90	4317
2005	2005.42	368.94	821.16	707.35	113.81	815.32	138.65	5394
2006	2338.98	382.06	967.54	839.13	128.41	989.38	192.95	6305
2007	2884.11	446.38	1124.79	978.86	145.93	1312.94	282.04	7878
2008	3561.56	539.19	1370.03	1195.30	174.73	1652.34	370.65	9855
2009	3912.68	550.27	1476.62	1252.67	223.95	1885.79	399.77	10971
2010	4602.16	625.03	1800.06	1516.87	283.19	2177.07	480.32	13119
2011	5701.84	726.22	2194.33	1829.20	365.13	2781.29	590.91	16413

注：1、1978–2004年按老行业分类标准计算，2005–2009年按新行业分类标准计算，第三产业中“交通运输、仓储、邮电通信业”从2005年起按新标准分类为“交通运输、仓储和邮政业”。2、2005–2011年人均生产总值按人口普查数已修订。3、2005–2011年按常住半年人口计算，以往年份按常住一年人口计算(以下相关表同)。

Note:1.From 1978 to 2004,data in the table were calculated by the Old Industry Classification Standard;from 2005 to 2009, data in the table were calculated by the New Industry Classification Standard;from 2005,acording to the New the Industry Classification Standard, the data of Transportation, Storage,Post and telecommunications refers to data of Transportation, Storage and Post.2.From 2005 to 2011,the data of per capital GDP have been adjusted according to the result of national population census.3.Data from 2005 to 2011 were calculated by permanent population in half a year scope,while they were calculated by permanent population in a year scope in the past(the same applies to relative tables below).

29-2 全省生产总值指数(上年=100)

Indices of Gross Domestic Product(Preceding year=100)

单位：% (%)

年份 Year	地区生产总值 Gross Domestic Product	第一产业 Primary Industry	第二产业 Secondary Industry	工业 Industry	建筑业 Construction	第三产业 Tertiary Industry	#交通运输、仓储、邮电通信业 Transportation, Storage, Post and Telecommunications	人均生产总值 Per Capita Gross Domestic Product
1978	123.7	106.6	137.3	139.7	123.7	132.7	133.6	121.4
1979	111.0	102.8	117.3	119.1	105.2	111.4	107.2	109.1
1980	104.4	100.4	104.3	106.9	85.6	111.7	106.5	102.7
1981	106.5	109.9	101.7	99.1	112.7	109.5	109.8	104.7
1982	115.8	123.0	109.3	111.4	101.3	112.6	103.6	113.8
1983	112.6	104.6	122.9	126.4	108.8	112.3	134.6	111.2
1984	119.8	118.2	123.8	123.8	123.5	114.9	137.6	118.6
1985	107.9	98.8	112.8	112.0	116.6	117.8	124.3	106.7
1986	105.6	106.1	98.0	99.7	90.5	120.9	108.7	104.3
1987	110.8	102.9	116.2	113.8	128.6	114.8	113.9	109.3
1988	108.6	99.0	113.2	115.5	103.1	115.0	108.3	106.2
1989	104.5	106.3	103.9	106.8	89.4	103.3	113.0	103.1
1990	104.3	101.7	106.1	105.6	108.8	104.6	84.9	102.1
1991	109.2	113.2	103.5	103.5	103.8	111.2	106.8	106.2
1992	108.1	99.3	115.0	116.0	108.0	112.6	121.2	108.6
1993	110.4	103.9	113.5	115.8	95.2	114.8	115.1	108.8
1994	108.4	103.7	111.8	112.4	105.8	109.8	111.9	106.9
1995	107.5	102.4	110.5	111.1	104.0	109.3	107.8	105.9
1996	108.9	103.8	112.6	112.1	117.8	109.2	111.1	107.4
1997	109.0	104.2	112.3	111.8	118.0	109.3	112.5	107.5
1998	108.5	101.5	111.8	110.4	126.4	110.5	117.5	106.9
1999	108.8	103.4	113.2	111.8	125.1	107.3	114.5	107.3
2000	108.4	103.6	107.6	107.5	108.3	113.7	117.5	107.0
2001	108.8	101.1	109.4	109.2	110.7	113.6	112.0	107.5
2002	109.1	102.2	113.2	111.0	124.5	109.4	105.4	107.9
2003	110.1	104.6	113.3	113.3	113.5	110.1	110.9	109.1
2004	111.4	105.3	114.2	115.9	106.5	112.0	116.0	110.4
2005	112.7	105.2	112.0	113.0	107.4	117.6	126.5	117.9
2006	112.8	104.6	113.4	113.8	111.2	116.0	129.6	113.1
2007	114.8	103.3	113.2	114.0	107.8	121.1	129.4	116.4
2008	111.3	106.8	108.1	108.6	104.7	115.8	119.4	112.8
2009	111.4	104.3	112.1	110.2	125.6	113.1	105.3	112.9
2010	112.8	104.7	116.6	115.7	122.1	112.1	115.2	114.7
2011	115.0	101.2	117.9	117.8	118.3	116.5	115.3	116.1

29-3 全省生产总值指数(1978=100)

Indices of Gross Domestic Product(year of 1978=100)

单位：% (%)

年份 Year	地区生产总值 Gross Domestic Product	第一产业 Primary Industry	第二产业 Secondary Industry	工 业 Industry	建筑业 Construction	第三产业 Tertiary Industry	人均生产总值 Per Capita Gross Domestic Product
1978	100.0	100.0	100.0	100.0	100.0	100.0	100.0
1979	111.0	102.8	117.3	119.1	105.2	111.4	109.1
1980	115.9	103.2	122.3	127.3	90.1	124.4	112.0
1981	123.4	113.4	124.4	126.2	101.5	136.3	117.3
1982	142.9	139.5	135.9	140.5	102.9	153.4	133.5
1983	160.9	145.9	167.1	177.6	111.9	172.3	148.4
1984	192.8	172.5	206.8	219.9	138.2	198.0	176.0
1985	208.0	170.4	233.4	246.3	161.1	233.2	187.9
1986	219.6	180.8	228.7	245.6	145.8	281.9	195.9
1987	243.4	186.0	265.8	279.4	187.5	323.7	214.1
1988	264.3	184.2	300.9	322.8	193.3	372.2	227.5
1989	276.2	195.8	312.6	344.7	172.8	384.5	234.4
1990	288.1	199.1	331.7	364.1	188.0	402.2	239.4
1991	314.6	225.4	343.3	376.8	195.1	447.2	254.2
1992	340.1	223.8	394.8	437.1	210.8	503.6	276.1
1993	375.3	232.5	448.3	506.1	200.6	578.3	300.5
1994	407.0	241.2	501.1	568.7	212.2	635.2	321.2
1995	437.4	246.8	553.7	632.0	220.6	693.9	340.3
1996	476.1	256.3	623.4	708.7	259.8	757.9	365.3
1997	519.0	267.1	700.3	792.3	306.6	828.6	392.8
1998	562.9	271.0	783.1	874.8	387.6	915.3	420.0
1999	612.4	280.0	886.4	978.4	485.0	982.5	450.5
2000	663.7	290.2	953.4	1051.5	525.1	1117.4	481.8
2001	721.8	293.4	1043.5	1148.3	581.5	1269.5	517.9
2002	787.2	300.0	1181.3	1274.5	724.2	1388.3	558.7
2003	866.6	313.8	1338.4	1443.5	821.8	1528.6	609.4
2004	965.4	330.4	1528.4	1673.0	874.9	1711.4	673.1
2005	1088.0	347.6	1711.8	1890.5	939.6	2012.6	793.6
2006	1227.3	363.6	1941.2	2151.4	1044.8	2334.6	897.6
2007	1408.9	375.6	2197.4	2452.6	1126.3	2827.2	1044.8
2008	1568.1	401.1	2375.4	2663.5	1179.2	3273.9	1178.5
2009	1746.9	418.3	2662.8	2935.2	1481.1	3702.8	1330.5
2010	1970.5	438.0	3104.8	3396.0	1808.4	4150.8	1526.1
2011	2266.1	443.3	3660.6	4000.5	2139.3	4835.7	1771.8

29–4 年末常住人口

Permanent Population at the year-end

单位：万人 (10000 persons)

年 份 Year	合 计 Total	按城镇、乡村分 Grouped by Urban and Rural 城 镇 Urban	乡 村 Rural	按性别分 Grouped by Sex 男 Male	女 Female	性别比 Sex Ratio (女=100) (female=100)	年平均人口 Annual Average Population
1978	2686.40	323.97	2362.43	1364.82	1321.58	103.27	2663.27
1979	2730.99	520.82	2210.17	1386.93	1344.06	103.19	2708.70
1980	2776.67	543.18	2233.49	1409.61	1367.06	103.11	2753.83
1981	2826.78	528.41	2298.37	1439.89	1386.89	103.82	2801.73
1982	2875.21	542.13	2333.08	1470.43	1404.78	104.67	2851.00
1983	2901.46	550.96	2350.50	1484.73	1416.73	104.80	2888.33
1984	2931.85	854.14	2077.71	1501.55	1430.30	104.98	2916.65
1985	2972.18	883.18	2089.00	1522.93	1449.25	105.08	2952.02
1986	3025.86	909.55	2116.31	1550.90	1474.96	105.15	2999.02
1987	3072.58	1002.93	2069.65	1576.23	1496.35	105.34	3049.22
1988	3127.27	951.23	2176.04	1599.01	1528.26	104.63	3099.93
1989	3171.00	1000.26	2170.74	1628.85	1542.15	105.62	3149.14
1990	3267.53	1083.67	2183.86	1684.53	1583.00	106.41	3219.27
1991	3314.63	1238.48	2076.15	1709.31	1605.32	106.48	3291.08
1992	3360.96	2256.05	1104.91	1735.46	1625.50	106.76	3337.8
1993	3408.69	2324.92	1083.77	1761.65	1647.04	106.96	3384.83
1994	3458.41	2371.06	1087.35	1789.32	1669.09	107.20	3433.55
1995	3508.08	2408.78	1099.30	1815.63	1692.45	107.28	3483.25
1996	3555.41	2457.33	1098.08	1840.38	1715.03	107.31	3531.75
1997	3605.81	2503.75	1102.06	1866.48	1739.33	107.31	3580.61
1998	3657.60	2539.76	1117.84	1893.29	1764.31	107.31	3631.70
1999	3710.06	2539.80	1170.26	1920.40	1789.66	107.30	3683.83
2000	3755.72	896.49	2859.23	1968.00	1787.72	110.08	3732.89
2001	3798.51	910.12	2888.39	1973.41	1825.10	108.13	3777.12
2002	3837.28	932.11	2905.17	1993.15	1844.13	108.08	3817.90
2003	3869.66	958.52	2911.14	2010.22	1859.44	108.11	3853.47
2004	3903.70	1025.89	2877.81	2022.22	1881.48	107.48	3886.68
2005	3730	1002.25	2727.75	1920.55	1809.45	106.14	3717.61
2006	3690	1013.27	2676.73	1908.85	1781.15	107.17	3710
2007	3632	1025.68	2606.32	1879.70	1752.30	107.27	3661
2008	3596	1046.79	2549.21	1868.73	1727.27	108.19	3614
2009	3537	1057.21	2479.79	1827.56	1709.44	106.91	3567
2010	3479	1176.25	2302.75	1797.43	1681.57	106.89	3508
2011	3469	1212.76	2256.24	1801.21	1667.79	108.00	3474

注：1、2000年以后的城镇、乡村人口的划分标准按国家统计局1999年发布的《关于统计上划分城乡的规定》计算，以前年份数据不可比。
2、2005年及以后为常住半年口径(下表同)。3、2006年～2009年常住总人口数据已根据第六次人口普查数据进行修订(下表同)。

Note:1.Data on grouped by residence from 2000 was calculated on the basis of Statistical Partition Ordain about Urban or Rural that had been issued by National Bureau of Statistial of China, So the date are not comparable with the preceding years. 2.Population since 2005 have refer to permanent population in half a year scope(the same applies to the next table).3.Data from 2006 to 2009 had been verified according to the Six National Population Census(the same applies to the next table).

29-5 人口自然变动

Natural Change of Population

单位：万人 (10000 persons)

年 份 Year	出 生 Birth		死 亡 Death		自然增长 Natural Increase	
	人 数 Number of Persons	率(‰) Rate	人 数 Number of Persons	率(‰) Rate	人 数 Number of Persons	率(‰) Rate
1978	76.22	28.62	19.65	7.38	56.57	21.24
1979	72.84	26.89	19.23	7.10	53.61	19.79
1980	68.02	24.70	19.39	7.04	48.63	17.66
1981	66.46	23.72	21.07	7.52	45.39	16.20
1982	70.73	24.81	21.67	7.60	49.06	17.21
1983	60.11	20.81	26.46	9.16	33.65	11.65
1984	54.98	18.85	21.29	7.30	33.69	11.55
1985	59.97	20.33	17.43	5.91	42.54	14.42
1986	72.04	24.11	18.08	6.05	53.96	18.06
1987	71.77	23.69	25.87	8.54	45.90	15.15
1988	73.76	23.81	18.62	6.01	55.14	17.80
1989	67.08	21.23	21.58	6.83	45.50	14.40
1990	74.13	23.09	25.36	7.90	48.77	15.19
1991	72.96	22.42	26.39	8.11	46.57	14.31
1992	73.61	22.40	28.00	8.52	45.61	13.88
1993	74.96	22.60	28.19	8.50	46.77	14.10
1994	76.93	22.92	27.32	8.14	49.61	14.78
1995	76.14	21.86	26.47	7.60	49.67	14.26
1996	77.88	22.05	27.16	7.69	50.72	14.36
1997	79.31	22.15	27.46	7.67	51.85	14.48
1998	79.97	22.02	28.18	7.76	51.79	14.26
1999	80.75	21.92	28.29	7.68	52.46	14.24
2000	76.86	20.59	28.11	7.53	48.75	13.06
2001	70.10	18.56	27.31	7.23	42.79	11.33
2002	68.57	17.96	27.53	7.21	41.04	10.75
2003	61.31	15.91	26.47	6.87	34.84	9.04
2004	58.61	15.08	24.68	6.35	33.93	8.73
2005	54.00	14.59	25.00	7.21	29.00	7.38
2006	51.83	13.97	24.89	6.71	26.94	7.26
2007	48.62	13.28	24.16	6.60	24.46	6.68
2008	48.75	13.49	24.47	6.77	24.28	6.72
2009	48.68	13.65	23.86	6.69	24.82	6.96
2010	48.52	13.96	22.76	6.55	25.76	7.41
2011	46.24	13.31	24.07	6.93	22.17	6.38

29–6 户籍人口

Household Registered Population

单位：万人 (10000 persons)

年 份 Year	年末总人口 Total Population at the Year-end	按农业非农业分 Grouped by Agriculture and Non-agriculture		占总人口比重(%) Proportion	
		农 业 Agriculture	非农业 Non-agriculture	农 业 Agriculture	非农业 Non-agriculture
1978	2686.40	2380.52	305.88	88.6	11.4
1979	2730.99	2416.67	314.32	88.5	11.5
1980	2776.67	2456.37	320.30	88.5	11.5
1981	2826.78	2500.74	326.04	88.5	11.5
1982	2875.21	2544.10	331.11	88.5	11.5
1983	2901.46	2564.92	336.54	88.4	11.6
1984	2931.85	2588.11	343.74	88.3	11.7
1985	2967.91	2609.04	358.87	87.9	12.1
1986	3007.99	2643.57	364.42	87.9	12.1
1987	3051.39	2678.60	372.79	87.8	12.2
1988	3143.94	2760.47	383.47	87.8	12.2
1989	3184.05	2793.35	390.70	87.7	12.3
1990	3236.97	2840.21	396.76	87.7	12.3
1991	3271.40	2868.27	403.13	87.7	12.3
1992	3300.97	2887.95	413.02	87.5	12.5
1993	3332.30	2910.71	421.59	87.3	12.7
1994	3380.58	2927.54	453.04	86.6	13.4
1995	3419.54	2957.32	462.22	86.5	13.5
1996	3459.54	2979.85	479.69	86.1	13.9
1997	3495.50	3004.76	490.74	86.0	14.0
1998	3536.54	3032.50	504.04	85.7	14.3
1999	3582.05	3063.23	518.82	85.5	14.5
2000	3676.63	3144.98	531.65	85.5	14.5
2001	3710.20	3156.33	553.87	85.1	14.9
2002	3747.68	3175.17	572.51	84.7	15.3
2003	3786.84	3196.70	590.14	84.4	15.6
2004	3831.19	3224.62	606.57	84.2	15.8
2005	3867.73	3258.05	609.68	84.2	15.8
2006	3921.91	3295.08	626.83	84.0	16.0
2007	3985.04	3346.09	638.95	84.0	16.0
2008	4036.75	3385.66	651.09	83.9	16.1
2009	4090.78	3429.36	661.43	83.8	16.2
2010	4189.00	3512.92	676.07	83.9	16.1
2011	4238.44	3551.18	687.26	83.8	16.2

注：1984年前为公安、统计共同使用的数据，1984年后为公安户籍人口统计口径。

Note: Data after 1984 in the table are obtained from the Public Security Department of Guizhou Province,while data before 1984 are used by Statistics Beaura and Public Security Department of Guizhou Province.

29-7 就业人员

Employed Persons

单位：万人 (10000 persons)

年份 Year	就业人员 Employed Persons	第一产业 Primary Industry	第二产业 Secondary Industry	第三产业 Tertiary Industry
1978	1053.67	872.89	108.26	72.52
1979	1060.62	873.88	105.63	81.11
1980	1109.63	919.69	102.01	87.93
1981	1152.95	954.55	102.64	95.76
1982	1207.06	989.78	109.53	107.75
1983	1234.18	1014.15	109.99	110.04
1984	1285.32	1037.71	122.12	125.49
1985	1335.17	1018.38	185.98	130.81
1986	1383.17	1053.26	197.09	132.82
1987	1435.85	1115.35	180.53	139.97
1988	1501.32	1172.51	185.80	143.01
1989	1570.84	1228.64	163.19	179.01
1990	1651.75	1292.30	169.10	190.35
1991	1701.47	1329.56	177.72	194.19
1992	1739.03	1359.00	173.35	206.68
1993	1779.01	1374.00	171.00	234.01
1994	1828.30	1365.00	181.90	281.40
1995	1812.20	1312.80	268.80	230.60
1996	1783.20	1235.60	278.50	269.10
1997	1796.70	1251.10	256.60	289.00
1998	1844.43	1284.72	251.57	308.14
1999	1832.50	1299.90	201.40	331.20
2000	1866.28	1305.28	221.80	339.20
2001	2068.01	1692.33	133.88	241.80
2002	2106.14	1698.39	108.89	298.86
2003	2145.00	1671.20	120.49	353.31
2004	2186.00	1672.29	124.60	389.11
2005	1944.29	1497.26	164.00	283.04
2006	1953.24	1487.40	174.17	291.67
2007	1872.64	1388.02	172.31	312.31
2008	1867.20	1350.32	180.73	336.15
2009	1841.92	1299.29	197.60	345.03
2010	1770.90	1209.55	203.52	357.82
2011	1792.80	1194.39	215.86	382.55

注：就业人员数2010年根据第六次人口普查长表数据推算，2005–2009年根据人口普查结果，采用趋势离差法修订，2011年按同口径进行推算。

Note:Date of employed persons were estimated according to the 6th National Population Census in 2010,From 2005 to 2009,according to the result of National Population Census,the total number of employed persons were revised by the trend deviation method,and the same to 2011.

29–8 非私营单位职工人数

Number of Staff and Workers in Non-private units

单位：万人 (10000 persons)

年份 Year	合计 Total	国有单位 State-owned Unit	集体单位 Collective-owned Unit	其他单位 Other Ownership Unit
1978	171.19	137.66	33.53	
1979	175.56	142.32	33.24	
1980	178.18	146.14	32.04	
1981	185.73	153.50	32.23	
1982	191.03	158.08	32.95	
1983	193.33	160.54	32.79	
1984	197.13	159.53	37.60	
1985	202.33	162.11	40.03	0.19
1986	206.69	167.81	38.78	0.10
1987	211.92	172.58	38.88	0.46
1988	214.43	176.32	37.56	0.55
1989	216.70	180.10	35.90	0.70
1990	225.48	185.35	39.19	0.94
1991	231.88	190.45	40.49	0.94
1992	235.80	193.61	40.94	1.25
1993	233.11	192.83	38.35	1.93
1994	230.88	194.47	34.87	1.54
1995	226.55	193.36	29.63	3.56
1996	231.64	196.60	30.45	4.59
1997	232.80	196.08	31.33	5.39
1998	207.01	167.14	23.98	15.89
1999	197.80	156.86	21.03	19.91
2000	193.96	153.55	19.00	21.41
2001	189.18	148.87	15.73	24.58
2002	188.47	146.96	14.39	27.12
2003	188.70	141.75	13.71	33.24
2004	192.67	139.57	12.77	40.33
2005	202.02	140.50	9.81	51.71
2006	201.87	137.86	8.86	55.15
2007	207.53	141.48	8.10	57.95
2008	199.76	140.97	7.42	51.37
2009	206.44	141.79	6.69	57.96
2010	210.67	146.81	6.41	57.45
2011	225.90	158.26	7.17	60.47

29–9 非私营单位在岗职工平均工资
Average Wages of Staff and Workers in Non-private units

单位：元 (yuan)

年 份 Year	在岗职工平均工资 Average Wages of Staff and Workers	国有单位 State-owned Unit	集体单位 Collective-owned Unit	其他单位 Other Ownership Unit
1978	616	642	450	
1979	654	692	448	
1980	755	797	502	
1981	774	804	535	
1982	783	815	562	
1983	801	830	608	
1984	913	949	708	
1985	1066	1132	787	
1986	1216	1297	859	1236
1987	1319	1395	961	1204
1988	1531	1627	1072	1389
1989	1676	1777	1158	1647
1990	1947	2070	1347	2281
1991	2090	2214	1489	2527
1992	2406	2543	1717	3286
1993	2823	2958	2104	3375
1994	3870	4085	2618	4475
1995	4475	4672	3061	5369
1996	4917	5125	3456	5613
1997	5206	5434	3556	6461
1998	5775	5819	4426	7289
1999	6595	6695	5008	7456
2000	7453	7594	5444	8325
2001	8991	9308	6218	8831
2002	9810	10150	6566	9680
2003	11037	11390	7504	10975
2004	12431	12870	8630	12103
2005	14344	14681	10506	14161
2006	16815	17638	12873	15365
2007	20668	22106	16893	17668
2008	24602	25874	20914	21659
2009	28245	29956	22167	24772
2010	31458	32718	24703	29006
2011	37331	38914	31601	33851

29-10 全社会固定资产投资

Total Investment in Fixed Assets in the Whole Province

单位：亿元 (100 million yuan)

年 份 Year	全社会固定资产投资 Total Investment in Fixed Assets in the Whole Province	增长速度(%) Growth Rate(%)	按经济类型分 (Grouped by Ownership) 国有经济 State-owned Units	集体经济 Collective-Owned Units	其 他 Others
1978	10.93		9.73	0.56	0.64
1979	11.94	9.2	10.20	0.61	1.13
1980	13.97	17.0	11.59	0.83	1.55
1981	15.16	8.5	12.06	0.99	2.11
1982	15.52	2.4	11.56	1.08	2.88
1983	17.07	10.0	11.88	1.23	3.96
1984	23.02	34.9	15.02	0.98	7.02
1985	33.14	44.0	21.24	1.76	10.14
1986	35.99	8.6	24.09	1.71	10.19
1987	42.97	19.4	27.10	3.61	12.26
1988	45.42	5.7	33.05	2.74	9.63
1989	44.08	-3.0	32.29	2.73	9.06
1990	51.51	16.9	36.95	2.14	12.42
1991	58.44	13.5	42.97	3.67	11.80
1992	78.82	34.9		3.59	16.41
1993	106.30	34.9	77.84	6.81	21.65
1994	140.95	32.6	93.74	9.77	37.44
1995	173.66	23.2	108.85	12.94	51.87
1996	207.10	19.3	133.19	14.75	59.16
1997	247.23	19.4	149.75	15.09	82.39
1998	304.91	23.3	188.93	19.34	96.64
1999	333.90	9.5	210.80	22.19	100.91
2000	402.50	20.5	259.95	28.45	114.10
2001	533.74	32.6	357.69	22.45	153.60
2002	632.44	18.5	423.88	18.86	189.70
2003	754.13	19.2	457.10	39.26	257.77
2004	869.25	15.3	507.74	38.41	323.10
2005	1018.25	17.1	545.37	12.61	460.27
2006	1197.68	17.6	602.50	12.93	582.25
2007	1488.80	24.3	697.68	17.27	773.85
2008	1864.45	25.2	910.69	25.23	928.53
2009	2450.99	31.5	1250.42	29.70	1170.87
2010	3186.28	30.0	1605.82	29.01	1551.45
2011	5101.55	60.1	2412.97	57.23	2631.36

29−11 财政收支

Financial Revenue and Expenditure

单位：亿元　　(100 million yuan)

年份 Year	财政总收入 Total Government Financial Revenue		财政一般预算收入 Local Government Financial Revenue		财政一般预算支出 Local Government Financial Expenditure	
	绝对数 Absolute Numbers	增长速度(%) Growth Rates(%)	绝对数 Absolute Numbers	增长速度(%) Growth Rates(%)	绝对数 Absolute Numbers	增长速度(%) Growth Rates(%)
1978	14.20	48.2	6.26	157.6	12.30	39.9
1979	14.26	0.4	6.54	4.5	13.30	8.1
1980	13.23	-7.2	6.69	2.3	12.66	-4.8
1981	13.74	3.9	6.32	-5.5	13.28	4.9
1982	16.00	16.4	7.70	21.8	15.11	13.8
1983	18.26	14.1	9.56	24.2	16.38	8.4
1984	21.81	19.4	11.81	23.5	22.28	36.0
1985	26.71	22.5	15.17	28.5	24.55	10.2
1986	31.38	17.5	17.01	12.1	30.43	24.0
1987	36.80	17.3	21.37	25.6	31.43	3.3
1988	39.55	7.5	25.96	21.5	36.14	15.0
1989	45.37	14.7	32.14	23.8	45.89	27.0
1990	49.36	8.8	35.37	10.0	47.87	4.3
1991	55.71	12.9	42.80	21.0	53.42	11.6
1992	60.98	9.5	47.28	10.5	60.63	13.5
1993	68.43	12.2	56.50	19.5	67.39	11.1
1994	77.30	13.0	31.24	-44.7	74.23	10.1
1995	87.40	13.1	38.80	24.2	85.33	15.0
1996	103.92	18.9	49.46	27.5	99.58	16.7
1997	116.19	11.8	57.90	17.1	113.79	14.3
1998	136.31	17.3	65.34	12.8	133.09	17.0
1999	133.75	-1.9	74.26	13.7	170.72	28.3
2000	153.04	14.4	85.23	14.8	201.57	18.1
2001	177.04	15.7	99.75	17.0	275.20	36.5
2002	203.03	14.7	108.28	8.6	316.67	15.1
2003	236.64	16.6	124.56	15.0	332.35	5.0
2004	296.48	25.3	149.29	19.9	418.42	25.9
2005	366.16	23.5	182.50	22.2	520.73	24.5
2006	448.88	22.6	226.82	24.3	610.64	17.3
2007	556.98	24.1	285.14	25.7	795.40	30.3
2008	674.58	21.1	349.55	22.6	1055.39	32.7
2009	779.59	15.6	416.48	19.1	1372.27	30.0
2010	969.57	24.4	533.73	28.2	1631.48	18.9
2011	1329.99	37.2	773.08	44.8	2249.40	37.9

注：资料来源于省财政厅。
Note:Data in the table are obtained from provincial financial department.

29-12 人民生活

单位：元

年 份 Year	城镇居民人均可支配收入 Urban Households Per Capita Disposable Income	指 数 (上年=100) Index (preceding year=100)	指 数 (1978=100) Index (year of 1978=100	城镇居民人均消费性支出 Urban Households Per Capita Living Expenditures	#食 品 #Food
1978	261.26	101.2	100.0	246.53	150.15
1979	279.66	105.2	105.2	273.60	176.64
1980	343.83	111.9	117.7	334.32	202.32
1981	434.10	122.5	144.1	393.24	237.60
1982	459.73	103.8	149.6	403.92	243.96
1983	483.33	103.5	154.8	426.36	258.72
1984	558.00	112.3	173.8	480.36	279.48
1985	682.27	110.9	192.7	617.52	324.24
1986	824.40	113.6	218.8	722.28	381.84
1987	912.26	100.9	220.7	788.76	431.40
1988	1101.84	99.4	219.4	1050.24	554.52
1989	1275.45	98.2	215.4	1102.56	640.20
1990	1399.36	108.5	233.8	1163.25	658.19
1991	1593.54	109.6	256.2	1338.86	750.79
1992	1887.51	109.7	281.0	1564.34	886.89
1993	2300.38	105.1	295.4	1876.24	1021.42
1994	3196.06	114.1	337.2	2531.78	1353.13
1995	3916.25	102.2	344.5	3250.55	1752.41
1996	4210.74	97.1	334.4	3572.78	1923.49
1997	4438.05	101.8	340.4	3555.69	1819.90
1998	4566.17	102.3	348.3	3799.38	1839.64
1999	4935.47	109.0	379.6	3964.35	1683.38
2000	5121.22	105.1	399.0	4278.28	1847.63
2001	5451.91	103.9	414.5	4492.25	1832.26
2002	5944.02	109.8	455.1	4598.30	1788.61
2003	6568.91	109.5	498.4	4947.62	1967.67
2004	7322.04	107.7	536.8	5494.43	2260.46
2005	8147.13	110.6	593.7	6156.27	2457.09
2006	9116.61	110.1	653.7	6848.39	2649.02
2007	10678.40	110.6	723.0	7758.69	3122.46
2008	11758.76	102.9	744.0	8349.21	3597.94
2009	12862.53	110.9	825.1	9048.29	3755.61
2010	14142.74	107.0	882.9	10058.29	4013.67
2011	16495.01	110.8	978.3	11352.88	4565.85

注:表中指数已扣除价格因素。

People's Living Conditions

(yuan)

农村居民人均纯收入 Rural Households Per Capita Net Income	指 数 (上年=100) Index (preceding year=100)	指 数 (1978=100) Index (year of 1978=100)	农村居民人均生活消费支出 Rural Households Per Capita Living Expenditures	#食 品 #Food
109.30	103.5	100.0	104.52	72.20
131.09	115.4	115.4	116.23	82.44
161.50	116.6	120.7	139.24	96.45
208.87	127.3	171.2	162.51	105.16
223.13	105.3	180.3	187.02	121.67
224.87	100.5	181.1	185.20	126.01
262.81	115.5	209.1	208.87	144.00
302.14	108.8	204.1	254.58	177.83
303.57	96.1	218.6	271.60	190.60
341.84	106.4	232.5	304.22	212.90
397.74	99.2	230.7	359.73	254.32
430.34	92.7	213.9	407.28	282.92
435.14	98.7	189.2	403.28	281.92
465.53	103.5	218.4	420.44	286.60
506.13	102.0	222.9	454.47	309.77
579.67	98.6	219.8	550.11	390.45
786.84	106.6	234.2	684.27	484.41
1086.62	106.6	223.8	930.59	661.85
1276.67	105.5	263.3	1068.09	774.62
1298.54	104.2	274.4	1065.70	742.16
1334.46	104.4	286.5	1094.39	757.55
1363.07	104.7	299.9	1069.81	722.16
1374.16	103.6	278.6	1096.59	687.32
1411.73	103.7	289.0	1098.39	659.37
1489.91	104.3	301.5	1137.56	661.35
1564.66	104.7	315.7	1185.17	674.71
1721.55	105.6	333.3	1296.34	754.39
1876.96	105.2	350.7	1552.39	819.87
1984.62	104.7	367.4	1627.07	838.42
2373.99	111.6	410.3	1913.50	998.39
2796.93	108.9	446.6	2165.70	1119.64
3005.41	109.2	487.7	2421.95	1093.94
3471.93	112.6	549.1	2852.48	1319.43
4145.35	114.0	626.0	3455.76	1646.51

Note:The Indices in the table are calculated at constant prices.

29-13 农林牧渔业总产值

Gross Output Value of Farming, Forestry, Animal Husbandry and Fishery

单位：亿元 (100 million yuan)

年 份 Year	合 计 Total	农 业 Farming	林 业 Forestry	畜牧业 Animal Husbandry	渔 业 Fishery	农林牧渔服务业 Services of Farming, Forestry,Animal Husbandry and Fishery
1978	27.46	21.72	1.07	4.64	0.03	
1979	31.74	24.54	1.27	5.90	0.03	
1980	36.44	28.05	1.46	6.89	0.04	
1981	41.93	32.07	2.08	7.69	0.09	
1982	51.49	38.93	2.49	9.95	0.12	
1983	52.66	38.17	3.48	10.84	0.17	
1984	63.09	45.43	4.44	12.94	0.28	
1985	70.24	47.42	5.37	17.05	0.40	
1986	79.34	53.54	5.27	20.05	0.48	
1987	92.25	61.95	5.50	24.23	0.57	
1988	123.39	78.90	6.13	37.55	0.81	
1989	133.69	85.64	5.90	41.30	0.85	
1990	145.53	95.23	7.95	41.38	0.97	
1991	165.34	112.08	9.44	42.68	1.14	
1992	176.73	116.03	12.22	47.18	1.30	
1993	201.40	126.20	11.85	62.33	1.02	
1994	277.13	180.26	13.61	81.18	2.08	
1995	344.85	224.16	15.29	102.54	2.86	
1996	388.29	265.57	14.99	104.57	3.16	
1997	417.54	289.20	15.39	109.37	3.58	
1998	402.32	274.55	15.48	108.12	4.17	
1999	407.12	278.67	16.02	108.07	4.36	
2000	412.97	279.61	18.04	110.67	4.65	
2001	418.61	279.95	15.08	118.46	5.13	
2002	431.39	278.88	18.17	128.80	5.54	
2003	466.72	275.46	25.87	139.48	6.08	19.83
2004	524.64	317.69	23.25	168.79	7.02	7.89
2005	571.84	335.53	23.91	194.20	9.41	8.79
2006	601.54	347.97	25.85	189.79	7.44	30.49
2007	697.01	392.20	27.77	231.60	9.04	36.40
2008	843.80	464.80	35.63	291.65	10.49	41.23
2009	875.20	501.52	36.92	281.53	11.06	44.17
2010	997.82	587.31	41.01	304.16	13.82	51.52
2011	1165.46	655.30	46.66	381.95	19.90	61.65

注：1、2006年数据为第二次农业普查修订数(以下相关表同)。2、农林牧渔服务业2004、2005年计算口径有变化(以下相关表同)。

Note:1.Data were adjusted according to the Second National Agricultural Census in 2006.2.Calculate the caliber of Farming,Forestry,Animal Husbandry and Fishery have changed in the year of 2004 and 2005(The same applies to the relative tables below).

29-14 农林牧渔业总产值指数(上年=100)

Indices of Gross Output Value of Farming, Forestry, Animal Husbandry and Fishery (preceding year=100)

单位：% (%)

年 份 Year	合 计 Total	农 业 Farming	林 业 Forestry	畜牧业 Animal Husbandry	渔 业 Fishery	农林牧渔服务业 Services of Farming, Forestry,Animal Husbandry and Fishery
1978	102.9	100.7	107.7	113.2	99.5	
1979	101.0	98.9	102.4	111.0	101.4	
1980	104.3	103.7	106.2	106.1	159.3	
1981	106.9	107.3	86.6	109.9	96.3	
1982	119.8	120.9	113.8	116.9	104.4	
1983	102.6	98.6	139.8	108.2	136.9	
1984	111.4	109.0	123.1	115.6	148.9	
1985	100.4	96.9	100.9	112.6	112.5	
1986	108.4	109.4	88.4	112.3	102.6	
1987	104.0	103.3	101.1	107.0	102.6	
1988	102.3	101.2	94.4	107.4	105.2	
1989	104.8	105.9	97.6	103.5	97.1	
1990	102.4	102.9	106.4	100.2	106.6	
1991	113.1	116.5	109.2	106.3	109.9	
1992	100.8	98.4	114.0	103.6	102.4	
1993	104.2	105.9	90.1	103.9	120.2	
1994	103.7	104.0	100.7	103.6	109.7	
1995	103.0	100.8	100.3	108.9	116.6	
1996	104.5	105.6	94.5	103.9	107.2	
1997	104.9	105.0	101.4	104.8	120.2	
1998	100.3	97.3	102.2	107.1	119.2	
1999	103.6	103.6	99.5	104.0	109.6	
2000	103.8	103.1	111.0	103.7	113.4	
2001	101.2	99.9	84.1	106.9	110.2	
2002	102.5	98.6	116.7	108.5	108.1	
2003	105.4	104.9	101.0	108.8	106.4	
2004	105.5	105.4	85.6	109.2	108.7	105.2
2005	105.9	104.3	99.9	109.8	106.7	107.3
2006	104.8	102.4	104.4	108.2	119.8	109.2
2007	103.3	103.4	102.3	102.1	106.5	106.4
2008	106.8	106.1	115.5	107.1	101.5	106.9
2009	104.6	102.8	100.7	108.5	102.6	104.7
2010	105.2	102.7	109.7	108.2	111.6	109.2
2011	101.4	99.8	107.4	101.2	125.1	110.3

29−15 农林牧渔业总产值指数(1978=100)

Indices of Gross Output Value of Farming, Forestry, Animal Husbandry and Fishery(year of 1978=100)

单位：% (%)

年 份 Year	合 计 Total	农 业 Farming	林 业 Forestry	畜牧业 Animal Husbandry	渔 业 Fishery	农林牧渔服务业 Services of Farming, Forestry,Animal Husbandry and Fishery
1978	100.0	100.0	100.0	100.0	100.0	
1979	101.0	98.9	102.4	111.0	101.4	
1980	105.3	102.6	108.7	117.8	161.5	
1981	112.6	110.0	94.2	129.4	155.6	
1982	134.9	133.0	107.2	151.3	162.4	
1983	138.4	131.2	149.8	163.7	222.3	
1984	154.2	143.0	184.4	189.2	331.0	
1985	154.8	138.6	186.1	213.1	372.4	
1986	167.8	151.6	164.5	239.3	382.1	
1987	174.5	156.6	166.3	256.1	392.0	
1988	178.5	158.5	157.0	275.0	412.4	
1989	187.1	167.8	153.2	284.6	400.5	
1990	191.6	172.7	163.0	285.2	426.9	
1991	216.7	201.2	178.0	303.2	469.2	
1992	218.4	198.0	203.0	314.1	480.4	
1993	227.6	209.6	182.9	326.3	577.5	
1994	236.0	218.0	184.2	338.1	633.5	
1995	243.1	219.8	184.7	368.2	738.6	
1996	254.1	232.1	174.6	382.5	791.8	
1997	266.5	243.7	177.0	400.9	951.8	
1998	267.3	237.1	180.9	429.4	1134.5	
1999	276.9	245.6	180.0	446.5	1243.4	
2000	287.5	253.2	199.8	463.0	1410.0	
2001	290.9	253.0	168.0	495.0	1553.8	
2002	298.2	249.4	196.1	537.1	1679.7	
2003	314.3	261.6	198.1	584.4	1787.2	100.0
2004	331.6	275.7	169.5	638.1	1942.7	105.2
2005	351.1	287.6	169.4	700.7	2072.8	112.9
2006	368.0	294.5	176.8	758.1	2483.3	123.3
2007	380.1	305.1	180.9	774.8	2647.2	131.2
2008	406.0	323.7	207.0	829.8	2686.9	140.3
2009	424.6	332.8	208.4	900.3	2756.8	146.9
2010	446.7	341.8	228.6	974.1	3076.6	160.4
2011	453.0	341.1	245.5	985.8	3848.8	176.9

29-16 主要农产品产量

Output of Major Farm Crops

单位：万吨 (10000 tons)

年份 Year	粮食 Grain	油料 Oil-Bearing Crops	烤烟 Flue-cured Tobacco	水果 Fruits	肉类总产量 Total Yield of Meat	水产品 Aquatic Products
1978	643.36	9.89	8.11	4.82	12.80	0.37
1979	623.05	10.90	9.54	4.68	22.84	0.38
1980	648.35	15.59	5.56	4.97	26.67	0.55
1981	567.36	34.04	11.93	6.23	31.61	0.58
1982	654.00	48.10	16.41	6.58	35.26	0.60
1983	703.00	28.50	13.62	7.19	38.58	0.81
1984	757.80	30.59	21.48	9.23	44.76	1.22
1985	594.96	31.97	26.55	10.14	50.46	1.35
1986	672.34	41.90	19.24	13.88	57.09	1.40
1987	673.17	46.34	21.19	15.19	62.26	1.80
1988	635.68	39.87	29.15	15.63	68.73	1.86
1989	708.25	32.93	31.58	16.80	71.82	2.01
1990	721.00	43.87	28.66	16.68	74.47	2.24
1991	885.50	61.79	38.53	17.17	81.65	2.29
1992	788.90	53.38	44.90	14.18	85.59	2.36
1993	869.50	43.28	49.66	16.53	88.91	2.55
1994	938.70	47.32	33.04	16.47	95.02	2.80
1995	948.85	58.83	33.53	20.97	105.69	3.27
1996	1002.60	55.62	52.27	19.46	103.65	3.50
1997	1025.90	58.97	68.66	25.14	106.77	4.21
1998	1100.00	62.24	29.19	27.50	113.33	5.02
1999	1125.21	67.31	32.32	32.57	117.09	5.50
2000	1161.30	74.34	31.09	58.33	124.06	6.24
2001	1100.30	71.32	26.38	62.93	131.70	6.89
2002	1034.20	72.48	30.65	71.57	145.02	7.46
2003	1104.30	72.31	28.72	78.75	156.99	7.96
2004	1149.58	82.71	29.98	87.17	171.06	8.85
2005	1152.06	84.89	34.45	95.96	187.01	9.46
2006	1038.00	68.24	30.71	109.19	163.70	6.71
2007	1100.86	69.66	31.22	112.86	150.60	7.68
2008	1158.00	68.39	37.71	114.28	161.46	7.80
2009	1168.27	78.68	36.92	119.74	169.60	8.03
2010	1112.30	60.34	37.02	123.47	179.09	8.79
2011	876.90	78.85	32.50	128.03	179.97	10.88

注：1、肉类总产量1978—1984年为猪牛羊肉产量,1985—1988年为猪牛羊禽肉产量,1989年以后为猪牛羊禽肉产量和其它肉(如：马肉、狗肉、兔肉等)产量。2、2000年以后的水果包含果用瓜。

Note:1.The Data of Total Yield of Meat included output of pock,beef and mutton from 1978 to 1984;it included Output of Pock,Beef,Mutton and Meat of Poultry from 1985 to 1988;after 1989,it includes output of pock,beef,mutton,meat of poultry and other meat(e.g.horse,dog,rabbit meat and so on). 2.After 2000,the data of yield of fruits included output of melon used as fruits.

29-17 工业总产值
Gross Output Value of Industry

单位：亿元 (100 million yuan)

年 份 Year	规模以上工业总产值 Gross Output Value of Industry above Designated Size	轻工业 Light Industry	重工业 Heavy Industry
1996	514.10	191.40	322.70
1997	575.49	211.58	363.91
1998	507.91	185.66	322.25
1999	551.93	187.05	364.88
2000	631.60	206.30	425.30
2001	696.63	220.11	476.52
2002	797.90	253.00	544.90
2003	977.64	279.50	698.14
2004	1394.91	307.81	1087.10
2005	1690.40	380.85	1309.55
2006	2066.77	449.67	1617.10
2007	2520.36	527.16	1993.20
2008	3111.13	641.78	2469.34
2009	3426.69	758.14	2668.55
2010	4206.37	914.19	3292.18
2011	5794.83	1253.14	4541.70

注：1、1998年以前为乡及乡以上数据，1998年及以后为规模以上年主营业务收入500万元及以上企业数据(以下各表同)。2、2004年数据为经济普查数据(以下各表同)。

Notes:1.Before 1998,Industrial Statistics were based on type of industrial enterprises above county level.After 1998,industrial statistics were based on type of industrial enterprises above designated size(The relative tables in the chapter are the same). 2.Data in the table refer to the data of the First Economic Census in 2004(The relative tables in the chapter are the same).

29-18 工业增加值

Value-added of Industry

单位：亿元 (100 million yuan)

年 份 Year	全部工业增加值 Value-added of Industry	#规模以上工业增加值 Value-added of Industry above Designated Size	轻工业 Light Industry	重工业 Heavy Industry
1996	225.36	188.43	74.71	113.72
1997	251.10	204.72	75.27	129.45
1998	273.82	181.80	76.48	105.32
1999	294.42	196.04	77.46	118.58
2000	328.73	216.99	82.16	134.83
2001	360.73	236.57	87.66	148.91
2002	395.45	271.09	88.20	182.89
2003	473.38	346.49	116.72	229.77
2004	577.40	476.75	147.79	328.96
2005	707.35	585.85	177.19	408.66
2006	839.13	747.38	218.52	528.86
2007	978.86	890.48	267.87	622.61
2008	1195.30	1051.26	302.25	749.01
2009	1252.67	1170.29	352.38	817.91
2010	1516.87	1227.17	413.99	813.18
2011	1829.20	1723.58	563.48	1160.10

29-19 工业增加值指数(上年=100)
Indices of Value-added of Industry (preceding year=100)

单位：% (%)

年 份 Year	全部工业 增 加 值 Value-added of Industry	#规模以上 工业增加值 Value-added of Industry above Designated Size	轻工业 Light Industry	重工业 Heavy Industry
1996	112.1	110.3	111.0	109.8
1997	111.8	109.0	106.0	111.1
1998	110.4	110.2	108.1	111.5
1999	111.8	106.2	100.8	109.3
2000	107.5	113.8	112.2	114.7
2001	109.2	112.6	106.4	113.6
2002	111.0	116.2	113.4	117.6
2003	113.3	116.9	109.8	120.3
2004	115.9	120.1	122.1	119.2
2005	113.0	117.0	125.3	113.3
2006	113.8	117.5	113.1	119.7
2007	114.0	116.8	113.9	118.1
2008	108.6	110.1	114.0	108.4
2009	110.2	110.6	111.6	110.2
2010	115.7	115.8	115.9	115.7
2011	117.8	122.6	123.7	122.1

29-20 规模以上工业主要经济指标

Major Economic Indicators of Industrial Enterprises above Designated Size

单位：亿元 (100 million yuan)

年 份 Year	主营业务收入 Revenue from Principal Business	轻工业 Light Industry	重工业 Heavy Industry	利税总额 Total Profits and Taxes	轻工业 Light Industry	重工业 Heavy Industry
1996	434.00	129.12	304.88	50.61	29.73	20.88
1997	419.82	128.07	291.75	60.82	38.42	22.40
1998	463.24	149.81	313.43	62.25	37.38	24.87
1999	507.55	162.34	345.21	65.81	40.47	25.34
2000	593.80	178.54	415.26	87.44	45.66	41.78
2001	646.01	193.35	452.66	94.30	51.27	43.03
2002	752.97	213.50	539.47	104.43	57.76	46.67
2003	974.30	248.48	725.82	135.87	72.15	63.72
2004	1325.95	274.04	1051.91	201.21	85.43	115.78
2005	1577.16	338.02	1239.14	232.49	113.50	118.99
2006	1948.57	389.38	1559.19	299.09	137.05	162.04
2007	2430.62	486.28	1944.34	403.49	187.27	216.22
2008	2922.35	567.80	2354.55	453.53	233.66	219.87
2009	3234.59	674.36	2560.23	470.60	252.25	218.35
2010	3926.01	807.13	3118.88	671.39	326.72	344.67
2011	5290.90	1132.83	4158.07	924.04	465.59	458.45

29-20 续表 continued

年 份 Year	利润总额 Total Profits	轻工业 Light Industry	重工业 Heavy Industry	资产合计 Total Assets	轻工业 Light Industry	重工业 Heavy Industry
1996	-3.57	-2.47	-1.10	960.79	257.78	703.01
1997	0.76	0.65	0.11	1076.72	294.65	782.07
1998	1.64	-0.65	2.29	1166.76	312.79	853.97
1999	0.65	1.14	-0.49	1328.55	357.12	971.43
2000	12.56	4.48	8.08	1517.13	371.83	1145.30
2001	18.59	6.98	11.61	1698.58	412.57	1286.01
2002	21.41	10.82	10.59	1797.46	404.54	1392.92
2003	37.52	19.00	18.52	1958.57	409.35	1549.22
2004	61.99	18.03	43.96	2441.52	430.64	2010.88
2005	70.79	34.31	36.48	2734.05	458.41	2275.64
2006	110.91	48.52	62.39	3214.39	514.26	2700.13
2007	174.41	81.29	93.12	3521.19	541.49	2979.70
2008	181.83	108.56	73.27	4566.10	700.92	3865.18
2009	191.73	109.42	82.31	5066.17	819.69	4246.48
2010	317.63	149.62	168.01	5960.13	1007.10	4953.03
2011	464.89	221.28	243.61	7384.82	1271.92	6112.90

29-21 主要工业产品产量

Output of Major Industrial Products

年 份 Year	卷 烟 (万箱) Cigarettes (10000 cases)	茅台酒 (吨) Mao-Tai Chiew (ton)	原煤 (万吨) Coal (10000 tons)	发电量 (亿千瓦小时) Electricity (100 million kwh)	粗钢 (万吨) Steel (10000 tons)	成品钢材 (万吨) Steel Products (10000 tons)	水泥 (万吨) Cement (10000 tons)	农用化肥 (万吨) Chemical Fertilizer (10000 tons)	磷矿石 (万吨) Phosphorite Material (10000 tons)
1978	31.60	1067	1669	41.43	8.73	4.95	130.93	11.57	169.02
1979	34.30	1143	1636	44.90	9.11	6.48	148.38	21.8	124.61
1980	44.00	1200	1398	45.17	8.66	7.75	144.47	30.34	188.02
1981	48.70	1055	1416	43.55	8.60	5.17	145.82	30.22	170.03
1982	56.10	1181	1695	57.86	10.62	9.43	161.07	30.98	207.98
1983	64.40	1189	1847	69.51	11.63	13.73	182.26	32.37	216.72
1984	85.70	1320	2027	76.46	13.87	18.93	206.94	36.85	214.34
1985	106.10	1266	2344	78.07	19.28	20.47	231.26	30.31	92.77
1986	102.10	1267	2554	82.52	26.34	21.45	247.31	34.99	162.58
1987	146.40	1331	3170	84.90	32.67	25.30	258.10	39.32	248.39
1988	188.40	1300	3210	90.12	33.17	23.13	293.38	39.23	281.82
1989	205.10	1727	3496	96.53	37.78	22.96	295.51	43.49	285.46
1990	208.00	1879	3695	103.87	47.11	25.36	278.29	46.73	323.86
1991	194.00	1959	3723	116.03	52.71	31.87	308.13	51.65	342.96
1992	202.90	2089	4162	129.35	64.19	48.83	370.44	51.54	348.42
1993	193.60	2281	4529	146.56	70.67	53.03	406.68	60.06	307.00
1994	204.90	3390	5128	197.21	69.89	56.14	463.10	53.60	341.43
1995	202.90	3978	5472	231.55	65.94	51.69	468.34	61.02	390.81
1996	197.70	4365	6143	248.80	59.47	51.60	522.00	57.50	446.40
1997	205.30	4468	6597	255.75	78.77	57.65	632.00	69.17	509.91
1998	195.80	5072	6561	291.77	100.28	77.28	559.42	72.82	436.51
1999	187.60	5074	4025	334.46	140.09	118.77	710.29	73.12	493.92
2000	187.40	5397	3677	404.70	166.90	150.93	783.88	84.05	588.70
2001	180.80	7317	3731	480.25	146.99	138.61	920.01	86.75	669.91
2002	177.80	9625	5001	547.12	194.65	177.79	1121.11	158.49	729.20
2003	183.19	10869	7816	636.60	206.10	192.97	1324.66	186.89	783.68
2004	194.74	12836	9757	713.04	208.07	203.22	1428.80	213.78	801.98
2005	208.21	8885	10615	786.78	237.83	214.85	1557.97	268.28	878.79
2006	211.73	9719	11817	974.66	332.51	256.57	1799.40	338.76	1034.60
2007	220.71	10789	10864	1166.32	349.36	328.14	1943.10	321.84	1198.83
2008	226.74	11308	11798	1192.08	345.64	337.52	2048.94	262.21	1317.18
2009	232.24	12161	10001	1363.09	343.10	337.62	2664.78	347.28	1360.66
2010	239.24	12911	12656	1358.69	360.48	391.04	3694.84	384.92	1579.21
2011	245.23	15523	14015	1359.01	434.01	462.77	5250.89	364.66	2084.18

注：1、表中工业产品产量1998年前为全社会口径，1998年及以后为规模以上工业企业数据，其中原煤产量2008年以后为规模以上工业企业数据。2、茅台酒产量从2001年后计量单位为千升，2005年开始按包装量统计。

Note:1.Before 1998, output of industrial products refer to the caliber of total society,but from 1998,it refer to the output of industrial enterprises above designated size.And output of coal refer to the output .of industrial enterprises above designated size after 2008. 2.Measurement units of Mao-Tai chiew since 2001 has been changed into kiloliter,Output of Mao-Tai was counted by packing quantity from the year 2005 and later.

29–22 建筑业总产值和房屋建筑面积

Gross Output Value of Construction and Floor Space of Building

年份 Year	建筑业总产值(亿元) Gross Output Value of Construction Enterprises (100 million yuan)	#国有及国有控股 State-owned and State-controlled	施工面积(万平方米) Floor Space of Building Under Construction (10000 sq.m)	竣工面积(万平方米) Floor Space of Building Completed (10000 sq.m)
1978	4.40	3.55	313	164
1979	4.44	3.40	371	185
1980	4.55	3.37	380	198
1981	4.76	3.27	392	213
1982	5.34	3.46	450	236
1983	6.22	3.85	501	258
1984	7.54	4.79	551	293
1985	9.81	6.34	662	342
1986	11.27	7.21	720	368
1987	12.93	8.62	725	378
1988	15.30	10.43	823	326
1989	15.57	11.07	765	305
1990	16.98	11.85	699	328
1991	20.32	14.09	739	335
1992	26.20	18.13	906	393
1993	37.65	26.63	1250	597
1994	48.69	36.65	1119	467
1995	55.40	44.58	1191	477
1996	66.49	52.45	1216	510
1997	76.70	59.78	1278	585
1998	83.20	62.42	1457	592
1999	96.65	70.91	1671	694
2000	109.06	77.04	1792	824
2001	150.20	110.40	1946	892
2002	181.12	133.62	2309	1054
2003	212.29	164.02	2520	980
2004	255.45	191.63	2820	1251
2005	271.23	207.88	3153	1150
2006	312.34	247.90	3369	1108
2007	348.79	271.69	3813	1204
2008	393.88	303.28	4230	1216
2009	523.91	408.00	4953	1244
2010	622.96	496.00	5756	1350
2011	824.72	659.29	6779	1530

29–23 交通运输
Transportation

年 份 Year	铁路营业里程(公里) Length of Railways(km)	公路线路里程(公里) Length of Highways(km)	客运量(万人) Passenger Traffic (10000 persons)	铁 路 Railway	公 路 Highway	水 运 Waterway	货运量(万吨) Freight Traffic (10000 tons)	铁 路 Railway	公 路 Highway	水 运 Waterway
1978	1365	25954	3294	977	2260	57	3467	1320	2083	64
1979	1373	26166	4608	1083	3462	63	3599	1314	2209	76
1980	1374	27367	5950	1164	4700	86	3424	1395	1953	76
1981	1373	27422	7175	1224	5873	78	3541	1481	1991	69
1982	1396	27499	8026	1288	6648	90	3825	1581	2164	80
1983	1396	27675	8259	1456	6707	96	4233	1665	2488	80
1984	1411	27872	9915	1620	8184	111	4600	1777	2735	88
1985	1419	27999	10874	1638	9102	134	5717	1874	3758	85
1986	1419	28383	11033	1458	9387	188	6551	1949	4510	92
1987	1420	29823	13512	1461	11854	197	7613	2043	5479	91
1988	1420	30445	14361	1633	12564	164	8570	2074	6413	83
1989	1420	30716	14923	1530	13125	268	9459	2178	7170	111
1990	1420	31157	17048	1256	15682	110	9840	2315	7414	111
1991	1419	31588	19081	1255	17718	108	10008	2365	7551	92
1992	1423	31889	21641	1251	20262	128	11349	2498	8752	99
1993	1423	32092	23494	1366	22010	118	11495	2537	8851	107
1994	1423	32398	27076	1515	25313	248	12189	2599	9453	137
1995	1423	32487	36151	1572	34304	275	12586	2657	9806	123
1996	1423	32700	42429	1843	40245	341	12182	2770	9192	220
1997	1640	33211	46644	1957	44416	271	13077	2739	10117	221
1998	1648	33604	48468	2048	45987	433	13577	3044	10219	314
1999	1654	33973	49457	2194	46807	456	14065	3272	10449	344
2000	1641	34643	53032	2251	50313	468	15615	3577	11684	354
2001	1644	34618	54665	2017	52154	494	16344	3875	12114	355
2002	1893	44220	55980	1947	53478	555	17399	4356	12685	358
2003	1900	45304	55074	1796	52695	583	18224	4971	12886	367
2004	1891	46128	58707	1855	56077	775	19439	5504	13541	394
2005	1986	46893	64450	2191	61414	845	21771	6169	15082	520
2006	2014	113278	69270	2536	65786	948	24709	6826	17284	599
2007	2012	123247	74440	2979	70377	1084	26788	7289	18834	665
2008	1962	125365	80056	3199	75350	1507	33576	6683	26156	737
2009	1983	142561	84981	3204	80044	1733	34844	6997	27031	816
2010	2002	151644	97793	3437	92426	1930	40310	7991	31409	910
2011	2070	157820	120554	3939	114429	2186	44890	7219	36684	987

注：1、资料来源于省交通厅、成都铁路分局(下表同)。2、2006年起，公路线路里程包括村道里程；2008年公路水路运输量采用全国公路水路运输量专项调查数据(下表同)。

Notes:1.Data in the table are obtained from provincial transports department and Chengdu Railway Branch.2.Since 2006,the data of total length of highways have been included the length of village road;the data of highways and waterways freight traffic refers to data of highways and waterways freight traffic special investigation in 2008 (the same applies to the next table).

29−24 旅客周转量和货物周转量
Passenger-kilometers and Freight Ton-kilometers

年 份 Year	旅客周转量 (亿人公里) Passenger-kilometers (100 million passenger-km)	铁 路 Railway	公 路 Highway	水 运 Waterway	货物周转量 (亿吨公里) Freight Ton-kilometers (100 million ton.km)	铁 路 Railway	公 路 Highway	水 运 Waterway
1978	25.50	16.04	9.26	0.20	79.60	72.30	6.57	0.73
1979	31.54	19.66	11.68	0.20	93.99	86.49	6.59	0.91
1980	37.69	22.77	14.67	0.25	96.03	88.99	5.91	1.13
1981	43.28	25.32	17.73	0.23	100.43	93.19	6.23	1.01
1982	46.93	26.70	19.99	0.24	109.69	98.99	9.50	1.20
1983	52.35	30.69	21.40	0.26	117.22	104.86	10.97	1.39
1984	61.04	36.21	24.55	0.28	132.72	119.19	11.61	1.92
1985	74.07	45.11	28.64	0.32	151.42	133.22	16.32	1.88
1986	76.45	47.39	28.70	0.36	171.03	148.13	20.44	2.46
1987	93.19	53.22	39.60	0.37	186.09	156.33	26.87	2.89
1988	105.67	61.20	44.14	0.33	196.04	159.75	33.50	2.79
1989	105.73	58.08	47.16	0.49	216.45	174.59	38.96	2.90
1990	102.90	49.20	53.34	0.36	224.31	179.72	41.84	2.75
1991	117.61	54.84	62.52	0.25	232.91	186.96	42.51	3.44
1992	136.77	66.62	69.84	0.31	268.80	214.88	49.84	4.08
1993	156.26	80.86	75.12	0.28	292.96	239.40	49.12	4.44
1994	173.71	88.72	84.53	0.46	298.44	243.87	50.06	4.51
1995	180.09	91.23	88.32	0.54	301.28	245.76	51.34	4.18
1996	185.94	88.32	96.84	0.78	317.70	261.99	51.07	4.64
1997	191.02	97.97	92.52	0.53	336.08	277.95	54.06	4.07
1998	201.77	101.13	99.97	0.67	330.30	270.40	54.84	5.06
1999	229.20	118.37	109.95	0.88	370.03	305.68	60.28	4.07
2000	238.36	120.79	116.54	1.03	404.07	334.11	65.86	4.10
2001	251.06	124.22	125.76	1.08	439.30	364.71	70.36	4.23
2002	250.79	116.10	133.60	1.09	486.03	407.26	74.25	4.52
2003	248.55	112.08	135.31	1.16	547.01	465.92	76.63	4.46
2004	278.21	125.87	150.79	1.55	610.88	520.70	84.27	5.91
2005	312.40	145.71	164.91	1.78	646.55	544.31	94.15	8.09
2006	349.82	160.98	186.91	1.93	680.96	557.70	114.48	8.78
2007	369.20	160.51	206.40	2.29	721.26	583.85	127.99	9.42
2008	407.59	163.00	241.15	3.44	809.93	564.31	234.96	10.66
2009	430.56	162.41	264.06	4.09	897.38	644.41	241.60	11.37
2010	514.41	189.38	320.46	4.57	1012.20	706.45	293.00	12.75
2011	631.74	204.58	422.01	5.15	1060.69	696.36	350.10	14.23

29–25 内外贸易

Domestic Trade,Foreign Trade and Economic Cooperation

年 份 Year	社会消费品零售总额（亿元） Total Retail Sales of Consumer Goods (100 million yuan)	进出口总额（万美元） Total Imports and Exports (USD 10000)	#出口额 Exports	实际利用外资额（万美元） Foreign Capital Actually Utilized (USD 10000)	#国外贷款 Foreign Loans	#外商直接投资 Direct Foreign Investments
1978	21.23	1645	285			
1979	23.57	2111	703			
1980	26.73	2797	1641			
1981	30.48	4782	3617			
1982	34.55	5455	4522			
1983	38.43	5238	4186			
1984	43.64	6997	4548	61	61	
1985	52.25	8720	4010	286	12	148
1986	57.25	8605	6361	1276	38	74
1987	66.39	12488	9296	376	127	101
1988	83.40	15527	11586	1408	425	440
1989	83.84	18681	13322	2102	826	747
1990	85.90	21802	15358	2983	1925	463
1991	92.92	24614	18958	2845	1436	1034
1992	106.75	33907	22424	3574	1595	1979
1993	143.09	36470	24491	4922	628	4294
1994	165.01	53595	37346	8363	2000	6363
1995	204.45	68144	43023	9637	3934	5703
1996	241.57	64240	43554	10628	7490	3138
1997	274.68	67660	48239	13834	8857	4977
1998	299.97	62243	38794	18100	13565	4535
1999	324.67	54763	35780	19532	15442	4090
2000	355.58	66002	42060	19545	17044	2501
2001	391.14	64978	42170	14010	11181	2829
2002	430.64	69141	44181	9383	5684	3700
2003	474.57	98477	58834	13191	7565	5626
2004	535.31	151442	86709	13932	7399	6533
2005	615.75	140425	85925	19568	8800	10768
2006	710.00	161745	103874	18413	9029	9384
2007	858.15	227285	146513	15333	2682	12651
2008	1075.24	337037	190084	17379	2475	14904
2009	1247.25	230732	135856	18027	4663	13364
2010	1482.68	314680	192018	34026	4480	29546
2011	1751.62	488440	298531	71674	4353	51541

注：1、进出口总额1997年及以前数据来源于原省对外贸易经济合作厅，1998年及以后数据来源于贵阳海关。2、实际利用外资额数据来源于省发改委、省商务厅。

Note:1.The yrar 1997and before,total imports and exports were obtained from the former provincial department of foreign trade and economic cooperation.After 1998 they obtained from Guiyang Customs.2.Data of foreign capital actually utilized are obtained from provincial development and reform commission and department of commerce.

29−26 旅 游

Tourism

年 份 Year	国内旅游人数 (万人次) Total Number of Domestic Tourists (10000 person-times)	国内旅游收入 (亿元) Earnings from Domestic Tourism (100 million yuan)	入境旅游人数 (万人次) Total Number of International Tourists Inbound (10000 person-times)	#外国人 Foreigners	国际旅游外汇收入(万美元) Foreign Exchange Income from Tourism(USD 10000)
1980			0.17	0.07	0.70
1981			0.23	0.06	2.49
1982			0.51	0.18	5.73
1983			0.71	0.19	8.03
1984	204	0.07	1.02	0.27	15.86
1985	244	0.07	1.13	0.29	61.95
1986	248	0.05	1.40	0.46	100.19
1987	261	0.07	1.88	0.77	137.22
1988	296	0.18	2.36	0.75	162.54
1989	397	0.18	1.37	0.47	136.75
1990	399	0.19	2.41	0.74	180.90
1991	630	0.66	3.75	1.04	307.35
1992	1426	2.21	7.63	1.87	686.13
1993	1647	4.29	10.25	4.26	1049.45
1994	1700	4.28	12.08	7.61	2109.63
1995	1750	7.18	13.65	7.78	2897.73
1996	1800	8.53	12.53	6.67	3811.95
1997	1850	30.81	15.02	7.81	4429.10
1998	1880	35.14	15.13	6.77	4831.18
1999	1910	43.75	16.70	6.57	5501.54
2000	1980	57.95	18.39	7.12	6092.23
2001	2100	75.81	20.55	7.85	6873.23
2002	2200	99.86	22.81	8.45	7950.63
2003	1835	114.36	7.70	2.40	2893.91
2004	2480	161.02	23.10	7.63	8020.27
2005	3099	242.83	27.62	9.26	10141.36
2006	4716	377.79	32.14	10.70	11515.66
2007	6220	504.04	43.00	15.48	12917.55
2008	8151	643.82	39.54	18.22	11697.37
2009	10400	797.69	39.95	16.28	11044.40
2010	12863	1052.64	50.01	18.61	12957.88
2011	16961	1420.70	58.51	23.62	13507.18

注：资料来源于省旅游局。
Note:Data in the table are obtained from provincial tourism bureau.

29-27 金融机构存贷款余额

Saving Deposits and Loans Balance of Financial Institutions

单位：亿元 (100 million yuan)

年 份 Year	各项存款 合 计 Total Deposits	#储蓄存款 Saving Deposit	人均储蓄余额 (元) Per Captia Savings Deposit (yuan)	各项贷款 合 计 Total Loans
1978	18.05	1.84	6.91	21.62
1979	19.82	2.42	8.93	23.31
1980	24.43	3.73	13.54	24.94
1981	25.75	5.28	18.85	30.10
1982	30.75	7.26	25.46	33.99
1983	35.25	8.86	30.68	36.07
1984	45.33	12.33	42.27	46.22
1985	52.27	16.61	56.27	63.41
1986	69.76	22.21	74.06	89.67
1987	83.79	30.37	99.60	107.76
1988	91.92	34.99	112.87	125.17
1989	107.35	44.54	141.44	142.73
1990	144.39	61.27	190.32	183.91
1991	187.06	80.30	243.99	234.56
1992	232.80	102.07	305.80	290.01
1993	291.22	141.88	419.16	357.00
1994	364.84	181.05	527.30	421.07
1995	478.21	247.62	710.89	513.41
1996	586.26	311.19	881.12	610.51
1997	712.80	362.87	1013.43	761.88
1998	815.43	423.08	1164.96	840.63
1999	945.80	484.51	1315.23	899.83
2000	1106.64	539.49	1445.23	1064.82
2001	1341.11	641.67	1698.83	1212.23
2002	1553.00	759.05	1988.13	1403.92
2003	1898.62	912.84	2368.88	1714.04
2004	2322.27	1094.55	2816.16	2020.04
2005	2777.54	1350.90	3633.79	2303.93
2006	3300.08	1596.86	4304.20	2696.11
2007	3826.37	1790.14	4889.76	3128.63
2008	4736.93	2237.05	6189.96	3569.27
2009	5898.26	2676.09	7503.41	4656.50
2010	7363.92	3244.99	9250.26	5747.53
2011	8742.79	3934.48	11325.50	6841.92

注：1、资料来源于中国人民银行贵阳中心支行。2、2005年及以后各年人均储蓄余额采用按人口普查修订后常住半年的年平均人口计算，以前年份按常住一年口径计算。3、表中储蓄存款及人均储蓄2010年及以前为城乡居民储蓄存款和城乡居民人均储蓄。

Note:1.Data in the table are obtained from Guiyang Central Branch of PBC. 2.Per captia savings deposit are calculated by permanent population in half a year scope since 2005,and by permanent population in one year scope before 2005.3.The year 2010 and before,savings deposit refer to resident savings deposit of urban and rural.

29-28 教 育

年份 Year	在校学生数(万人) Students Enrollment(1 0000 persons)			小学毕业生升学率(%) Percentage of Graduates of Primary Schools Entering into Junior Secondary Schools(%)
	普通高等学校 Regular Institutions of Higher Education	普通中学 Regular Secondary Schools	小学 Primary Schools	
1978	1.33	137.17	423.60	76.1
1979	1.78	126.07	413.71	70.0
1980	1.71	110.24	404.22	62.6
1981	1.81	96.58	403.49	56.7
1982	1.67	89.53	412.30	53.8
1983	1.68	82.39	415.79	51.5
1984	2.03	85.13	436.56	53.1
1985	2.30	91.59	447.68	54.2
1986	2.52	99.00	461.99	53.8
1987	2.60	102.35	458.27	47.7
1988	2.73	98.63	449.70	56.6
1989	2.76	93.31	440.36	67.1
1990	2.70	96.54	435.05	60.8
1991	2.57	100.23	433.85	59.6
1992	2.67	103.99	435.94	59.9
1993	2.93	100.55	439.81	63.9
1994	3.23	103.08	455.30	70.5
1995	3.47	108.43	475.34	72.7
1996	3.57	113.47	489.32	71.5
1997	3.85	121.54	503.82	75.8
1998	4.26	127.10	505.36	75.1
1999	5.65	138.63	500.96	77.8
2000	7.55	157.20	500.21	78.7
2001	10.82	184.60	490.17	84.4
2002	12.27	212.81	484.28	88.2
2003	14.94	235.30	476.87	92.4
2004	17.99	249.34	479.41	96.0
2005	20.68	254.96	473.76	97.4
2006	22.15	256.31	474.38	97.8
2007	24.17	256.00	466.31	95.6
2008	26.75	261.78	469.79	98.7
2009	29.91	269.45	456.87	97.7
2010	32.33	275.68	433.50	96.3
2011	34.41	282.71	408.74	96.5

注：资料来源于省教育厅。

Education

学龄儿童入学率(%) Percentage of School-Aged Children Enrolled(%)	专任教师数(人) Number of Full-time Teachers(person)		
	普通高等学校 Regular Institutions of Higher Education	普通中学 Regular Secondary Schools	小学 Primary Schools
89.5	2753	54227	155930
86.1	3357	55532	151860
80.8	3638	51950	155708
78.5	3606	46892	159494
78.3	3986	44646	152176
81.2	4183	43821	152338
83.6	4555	41879	155715
84.9	4830	45159	157622
86.9	5177	47119	162105
89.2	5559	50216	161689
89.9	5588	51618	163514
88.8	5530	53279	164298
91.3	5469	55528	166662
90.3	5371	57074	168364
92.4	5542	59006	166769
93.8	5550	60453	165276
95.1	5540	63059	168842
96.0	5599	64292	168358
96.7	5600	66842	166526
97.4	5699	69355	168493
97.7	5929	72865	167823
98.2	6050	76654	170680
98.5	7240	81156	174822
98.2	9007	88079	173238
98.2	11079	97641	177920
98.2	11775	107312	179367
97.8	13792	115616	180793
98.3	14353	122721	183679
98.6	15398	128274	188762
98.6	16964	131087	191991
97.2	18037	135360	200024
98.4	19634	139302	199189
97.9	20351	142508	197913
98.6	21855	147396	197094

Note:Data in the table are obtained from Provincial Education Department.

29–29　卫生
Health Care

年 份 Year	卫 生 机构数 (个) Number of Health Institutions (unit)	#医 院、卫生院 Hospitals	卫生机构床位数 (张) Number of Beds in Health Institution (bed)	#医院、卫生院 Hospitals	卫生技术人员数 (人) Medical Technical Personnels (person)	#执业(助理)医 师 Doctors	每万人口拥有 Per 10000 persons 床位数 (张) Number of Beds(bed)	每万人口拥有 Per 10000 persons 执业(助理)医师数(人) Number of Doctors (person)
1978	6274	4510	40274	37533	58190	21228	14.0	7.9
1979	6267	4516	42812	40001	60635	21868	14.6	8.0
1980	6246	4529	43627	40835	63766	26491	14.7	9.5
1981	6634	4588	44752	41314	68918	26798	14.6	9.5
1982	6595	4605	46226	42301	70671	27097	14.7	9.4
1983	6605	4602	47555	43292	72988	28433	14.9	9.8
1984	6673	4643	49271	44123	75808	29309	15.0	10.0
1985	6480	3295	49805	45226	76722	29153	15.2	9.8
1986	6760	3358	50893	46259	79776	30475	15.3	10.1
1987	6716	3349	52595	48059	81599	31305	15.6	10.2
1988	7021	3896	54193	49543	84904	35249	15.8	11.3
1989	6926	3620	57428	52063	84891	35646	16.4	11.2
1990	6949	3721	59013	53074	86120	37185	16.2	11.4
1991	6908	3630	59168	53978	87774	37978	16.3	11.5
1992	4734	1624	57767	52405	87927	38537	15.6	11.5
1993	3908	1623	57720	51888	84409	38060	15.2	11.2
1994	3930	1660	59648	53766	88053	40358	15.5	11.7
1995	3934	1692	60295	54475	87005	40260	15.5	11.5
1996	10932	1870	58205	54051	84273	43548	15.2	12.2
1997	8955	1870	57560	53627	84348	43236	14.9	12.0
1998	9113	1877	57844	54492	84400	44138	14.9	12.1
1999	9703	1874	58624	55138	85613	45473	14.9	12.3
2000	8992	1878	58380	55148	85397	45673	14.8	12.2
2001	8791	1872	59120	55876	86103	46412	14.8	12.3
2002	7027	1857	59850	57742	79727	36964	15.1	11.3
2003	6499	1866	59281	56273	77557	36911	14.9	11.2
2004	6664	1850	61313	58113	76699	36911	14.9	12.2
2005	6571	1843	61784	58398	77805	35521	16.6	9.5
2006	6147	1855	66452	62586	82324	41147	17.9	11.1
2007	5907	1939	75806	71400	85298	42100	20.7	11.5
2008	5848	1934	83132	78129	89313	38830	23.0	10.7
2009	5736	1982	97527	91164	95270	40171	27.3	11.3
2010	5637	2005	105277	97490	102527	42158	30.0	12.0
2011	5683	2071	117534	108029	112210	44037	27.7	10.4

注：1、资料来源于省卫生厅。2、表中数据不含村卫生室。3、每万人口指标2010年及以前按常住人口数计算，2011年按户籍人口数计算。
Note:1.Data in the table are obtained from provincial health department.2.The number of health institutions do not include health clinices of village.
3.Indicators of per 10000 population was calculated by the permanent resident population before 2011,but that was calculated by the household registered population in 2011.

中国统计出版社最新图书简目

（仅供参考，以最后出书为准）

统计资料

中国统计年鉴 -2012
中国统计摘要 -2012
国际统计年鉴 -2012
2012 中国发展报告
中国第三产业统计年鉴 -2012
中国区域经济统计年鉴 -2012
中国劳动统计年鉴 -2012
中国社会统计年鉴 -2012
中国城市统计年鉴 -2009
中国建筑业统计年鉴 -2012
中国人口和就业统计年鉴 -2012
中国工业经济统计年鉴 -2012
中国商品交易市场统计年鉴 -2012
中国房地产统计年鉴 -2012
中国能源统计年鉴 -2012
中国民政统计年鉴 -2012
中国贸易外经统计年鉴 -2012
2012 中国地区经济监测报告
中国科技统计年鉴 -2012
中国农村统计年鉴 -2012
中国农产品价格调查年鉴 -2012
中国高技术产业统计年鉴 -2012
中国教育经费统计年鉴 -2010
中国农村贫困监测报告 -2012
全国农产品成本收益资料汇编 -2012
中国科学技术协会统计年鉴 -2012
工业企业科技活动资料 -2012
大中型批发零售和住宿餐饮企业统计年鉴 -2012
中国城市（镇）生活与价格年鉴 -2012
中国县（市）社会经济统计年鉴 -2012
中国农村住户调查年鉴 -2012（中、英文）
中国农村全面建设小康监测报告 -2012
第二次全国 R&D 资源清查资料汇编 - 综合卷
第二次全国 R&D 资源清查资料汇编 - 工业企业卷
中国零售和餐饮连锁企业统计年鉴 - 2012
中国民族统计年鉴 2011、2012
2010 年中国第六次人口普查公报

2012 年省级综合统计年鉴系列

北京 天津 河北 山西 内蒙古
辽宁 吉林 黑龙江 上海 江苏
浙江 安徽 福建 江西 山东
河南 湖北 湖南 广东 广西
海南 重庆 四川 贵州 云南
西藏 陕西 甘肃 青海 宁夏
新疆 新疆生产建设兵团

2012 年市（县）级综合统计年鉴系列

天津滨海新区
石家庄 唐山 邯郸 太原 大同
长治 阳泉 晋城 朔州 晋中
运城 忻州 临汾 呼和浩特
包头 沈阳 大连 长春 吉林市
四平 哈尔滨 黑龙江垦区
上海浦东新区
苏州 无锡 常州 徐州 南通
盐城 镇江 江阴 丹阳
杭州 宁波 绍兴 台州 温州
金华 嘉兴 衢州
福州 福州经济技术开发区
厦门经济特区 南昌 上饶
济南 青岛 潍坊 郑州
洛阳 三门峡 南阳 武汉 宜昌
十堰 荆州 咸宁 长沙 广州
东莞 惠州 深圳 桂林 南宁
柳州 来宾 河池 海口 成都 绵阳
贵阳 昆明 庆阳 西安
兰州 银川 乌鲁木齐

2010 年人口普查资料系列

中国 2010 年人口普查资料
北京 天津 河北 山西 内蒙古
辽宁 吉林 黑龙江 上海 江苏
浙江 安徽 福建 江西 山东
河南 湖北 湖南 广东 广西
海南 重庆 四川 贵州 云南
西藏 陕西 甘肃 青海 宁夏
新疆 新疆生产建设兵团
河南省各市 2010 年人口普查资料丛书
中国分县 2010 年人口普查资料
中国分乡镇、街道 2010 年人口普查资料
中国分民族 2010 年人口普查资料

“十一五”规划教材

非参数统计　医学统计学
概率论与数理统计　统计学
现代金融投资统计分析
多元统计分析　经济计量学教程
应用时间序列分析
统计指数理论及应用
统计数据处理概论
质量管理统计方法　社会统计学
多元统计分析实验
企业经营管理统计
市场调查与预测
统计学原理（非统计专业使用）
统计学：从数据到结论
国民经济核算教程（国民经济统计学）
概率论与数理统计（经济、管理类专业使用）

重点图书

挑大学选专业 2012—高考志愿填报指南　挑大学选专业 2012—考研择校指南

欲购以上图书请与中国统计出版社发行部联系
电话：（010）63376907,63376908　同榻行书店电话：68783171,68783172
通讯地址：北京市西城区三里河月坛南街 57 号　邮政编码：100826
网址：http://csp.stats.gov.cn

增比进位、后发赶超
——奋进中的县（市、区、特区）

Incrementary ratio and ranking, Catching-up and surpassing -Counties (cities, districts and special regions) in advance

仁怀市

Renhuai City

省委书记栗战书、省长赵克志到仁怀调研基层党组织建设，要求在全省推广仁怀党员创业带富工程的经验和做法

Provincial Party Committee Secretary Li Zhanshu, vice governor Zhao Kezhi to Renhuai have research of the grass-roots party organizations, have requirements to promote Renhuai party members and entrepreneurs with rich engineering practices and experience in the province

仁怀市行政区域面积1788平方公里，辖6个乡、12个镇和3个街道，总人口67万。主要矿藏有煤炭、硫铁矿等，森林覆盖率44.6%。地区生产总值完成258.02亿元,同比增长21.3%；财政总收入65.4亿元，同比增长44.6%，其中一般预算收入16.14亿元，同比增长53.7%；全社会固定资产投资71.92亿元，同比增长49.0%；社会消费品零售总额40.1亿元，同比增长26.4%；金融机构各项存款余额246.28亿元，贷款余额48.18亿元，同比分别增长49.9%和40.6%；农民人均纯收入和城镇居民人均可支配收入分别达5777元、17001元，同比分别增长22.9%和18.1%。

茅台酒包装车间

The Maotai packaging workshops

2011年，仁怀名酒工业园区入驻30个产业项目，获遵义市2011年园区年度考核一等奖，并被省经信委批准为省级一类工业园区

In 2011, the Renhuai wine Industrial Park settled in 30 industrial projects by 2011 Zunyi City Park, the first prize of the annual assessment, and be the provincial first class industrial park approved by the Province Information Commission

酒都文化广场
Wine Capital Cultural Square

红军四渡赤水纪念园
The Red Army across the Chishui for Four Times Memorial Park

仁怀市国酒大道
Renhuai City National Liquor Avenue

酒都城市新形象
Wine city a new image (Photography

Renhuai City owns administrative area of 1,788 square kilometers, 6 townships, 12 towns and 3 streets, the total population of 670,000. The main mineral deposits such as coal, pyrite and so on, 4.6% of forest coverage. Regional GDP of 25.802 billion yuan, up 21.3%; total fiscal revenue of 6.54 billion yuan, an increase of 44.6%, of which general budget revenue of 1.614 billion yuan, up 53.7%; the whole society fixed assets investment of 7.192 billion yuan, an increase of 49.0%; total retail sales of 4.01 billion yuan, an increase of 26.4%; financial institutions 24.628 billion yuan of outstanding deposits, outstanding loans of 4.818 billion yuan, an increase of 49.9% and 40.6% respectively; the per capita net income of farmers and urban residents disposable income of 5,777 yuan, 17,001 yuan, an increase of 22.9% and 18.1% respectively.

发展中的仁怀一中全景图
Renhuai in the development of a panorama

深入推进转方式、调结构，全市经济社会持续健康发展。工业经济显著增强，2011年全市白酒产量达22万千升，产值达232亿元，规模工业增加值达180亿元，成为全省工业强县市的排头兵；农业产业化发展步伐加快，农业生产基础不断增强，新农村建设深入推进，农民收入持续增加，农村经济稳步增长；旅游兴市战略深入推进，第三产业健康发展，2011年接待游客208万人次，旅游综合收入达27.2亿元；城乡建设实现新突破，城市建成区面积达14.5平方公里，城区人口达17.4万人，城镇化率提高到43%。全市三次产业结构由5.8:62.2:31.6调整为4.6:65.5:29.9。市域经济综合实力列全省经济强县市第1位、西部百强县（市）第31位。仁怀入选“中国小康成长型百佳县市”、“全国县域经济科学发展十大范例县市”、“中国西部最具投资潜力市”。

仁怀市污水处理厂
Renhuai City sewage treatment plant

实施病险水库除险加固后的仁怀流沙岩水库
Implementation of the dam reinforcement Renhuai quicksand rock reservoir

苍龙街道下坝新农村风光

Canglong street Xiaba new countryside scene

群众文化生活日益丰富多彩

Increasingly rich and colorful cultural life of the masses

坛厂镇茅台酒有机原料基地

Tanchang town Maotai organic raw material base

Further promote the transfer mode, adjust the structure, the city's economic and social got sustainable and healthy development. Significantly enhanced in the industrial economy, in 2011 the city's white wine production reached 220,000 kiloliters, the output value reached 23.2 billion yuan, the scale of industrial added value of 18 billion yuan, becoming the vanguard of the province's strong industrial cities and counties; to accelerate the pace of development of agricultural industrialization, agricultural production base continuously enhance and further promote the construction of new countryside, farmers' income continued to increase, the steady growth of the rural economy; the tourism prospers the city strategic depth to push forward, the healthy development of the tertiary industry, 2.08 million people of the 2011 annual tourists, tourism revenue reached 2.72 billion yuan; urban and rural construction to achieve new breakthroughs, the urban built-up area of 14.5 square kilometers, the city has a population of 174,000, the urbanization rate has increased to 43%. Three of the city's industrial structure from 5.8:62.2:31.6 adjust to 4.6:65.5:29.9. City in comprehensive economic strength out of the province's 1st economic strong counties a western hundred counties (cities) 31th. Renhuai was selected "Chinese well-off growth hundred counties", "National County's economic and scientific development, the top ten examples of cities and counties", "the most investment potential city in western China".

金三角下的一颗明珠——盘县

Pearl in the Golden Triangle - Panxian

中共六盘水市委常委、副市长、盘县县委书记陈少荣
CPC Liupanshui Municipal Committee, vice mayor, Panxian county party secretary Chen Shaorong

盘县位于贵州西部，已有2100多年的历史。盘县素有“滇黔锁钥”之称，总面积4056平方公里，辖37个乡镇，450个行政村，52个社区居委会，总人口103.6万。

盘县自然资源富集，其中煤炭资源以储量大、品种全、质量优、易开采而著称，被誉为“金三角下的一颗明珠”。旅游资源丰富，自然景观、人文景观遍布境内，有徐霞客笔下“形如天柱”的丹霞山等。交通便捷。工业化进程快速推进。

2011年全县地方生产总值完成249.98亿元，增长17.4 %；固定资产投资完成225.25亿元，增长90.87 %；财政总收入完成70.63亿元，增长20.44%，县级一般预算收入完成25.87亿元，增长31.67 %。在中国西部百强县（市）排名中列第19位，贵州经济强县（市）排名中列第2位，获“中国最具投资潜力百强”、“中国最具区域带动力百强”和“中国金融生态县”等项殊荣。“十二五”期间，盘县将继续强力推进工业强县和城镇化带动战略，围绕“发展提速、转型加快、效益较好、民生改善、后劲增强”的目标，开拓创新、扎实工作、全力推进全县经济社会又好又快、更好更快发展，力争进入中国西部百强前十，冲刺中国百强。

盘县人民政府县长邓志宏
Panxian people's government Magistrate Deng Zhihong

红果新城一角
Corner of Hongguo New City

佛教名山——盘县丹霞山
Famous Buddhist mountains - Panxian Danxiashan Mountain

贵州最具魅力村寨——盘县妥乐村
Guizhou most attractive villages - Panxian Tuole village

Panxian located in western Guizhou Province, owns more than 2,100 years of history. Panxian is known as "Yunnan-Guizhou lock and key," a total area of 4,056 square kilometers, jurisdiction over 37 townships and 450 administrative villages, 52 neighborhood communities, the total population of 1.036 million.

Panxian owns rich natural resources, which the coal resources reserves is the most, all varieties, superior quality, easy to exploit, known as the "Pearl in the Golden Triangle". It has rich tourism resources, natural landscape, cultural landscape throughout the territory, Xuxiake wrote "shaped like Tianzhu" Danxiashan mountain and so on. And convenient transportation. The rapid progress of industrialization process.

In 2011, the local GDP of the county completed 24.998 billion yuan, up 17.4%; investment in fixed assets of 22.525 billion yuan, an increase of 90.87%; total fiscal revenue of 7.063 billion yuan, an increase of 20.44%, county-level general budget revenue of 2.587 billion yuan, up 31.67%. It ranked 19 in western China top 100 counties (cities), Guizhou Economic county (city) ranked 2rd, awarded "China Top 100 most investment potential counties", "China's most regional driving force top 100" and "Chinese financial ecological county" other items of honor. During the "12th Five-Year Plan" period, Panxian will continue to strongly promote the industrial county and urbanization led strategy, focusing on "the development of speed transformation to accelerate and better efficiency, improved living conditions, increased stamina" the objective, pioneering innovative, solid work, to promote the county's economic and social good and fast, better development, and strive to enter the Chinese western 100 top ten, sprint Chinese top 100.

盘南240万千瓦电厂
Pannan 2.4 million kilowatts power plants

金 沙 县

Jinsha County

2012年4月24日，省委书记栗战书（前排右一）在市县领导陪同下考察金沙窖酒酒业有限公司
April 24, 2012, Provincial Party Committee Secretary Li Zhanshu (first from right in the front row), accompanied by city and county leaders investigated Jinsha cellar wine Wine Co., Ltd.

2011年4月26日，省长赵克志到金沙产业园区视察
April 26, 2011, Governor Zhao Kezhi went to the Jinshan industrial park have inspections

金沙县位于贵州省西北部，地处黔中经济区、成渝经济圈、泛珠三角经济圈，是贵州省经济强县、中国西部百强县之一。金沙于1941年立县，昔属黔北四大集镇之冠，享“黔北粮仓”美誉，2009年被中国茶叶流通协会命名为“中国贡茶之乡”。面积2528平方公里，辖26个乡镇、244个村（居、社区），人口67.8万人。

金沙境内山川毓秀，气候宜人，资源富集。森林覆盖率达43.3%。主要矿藏有煤、铁、硫、磷、硅等19种，其中煤炭储量约80亿吨，是全国重点产煤县、“西电东送”工程能源基地之一。主要农产品有水稻、小麦、油菜、辣椒、烤烟、茶叶、花生、马铃薯等。主要特色商品有贵州十大名酒、中国驰名商标“金沙回沙酒”系列、第11届亚运会指定饮用水“岩孔矿泉水”、香韵独特的“禹谟醋”、绿色环保的“康星油”和历史悠久的“清池贡茶”等。主要旅游资源有冷水河省级森林公园和三丈水省级森林公园等自然风光景点，石场敖家坟石刻、后山东汉古墓群石刻、茶园万寿宫戏楼等文物古迹，位于后山乡的贵州省经典红色旅游景区、贵州省爱国主义教育基地、国家安全教育基地——钱壮飞烈士墓等人文景观，还有彝族“火把节”、苗族“踩山节”、仡佬族“吃新节”、布依族“对歌节”等，民族风情浓郁。

金沙回沙酒业公司全景
Jinsha Huisha Wine Co.,Ltd. panoramic view

2012年6月8日，省委常委、毕节市委书记秦如培到金沙调研

June 8, 2012, Provincial Standing Committee, Bijie party secretary Qin Rupei has research in Jinsha

2012年5月6日，张吉勇市长一行在县委书记丁翊强等陪同下听取金沙窖酒酒业公司介绍扩建工程情况

May 6, 2012, Zhang Jiyong mayor and his team accompanied by the county party secretary Ding Yi and other listen to Jinsh cellar wine Wine Co., Ltd. to introduce the expansion project

县城一角

County corner

Jinsha County is located in the northwest of Guizhou Province, located in central Guizhou Economic Zone, Chengdu-Chongqing economic circle, the Pan-Pearl River Delta economic circle, is one of thetop 100 economic county in Guizhou Province and top 100 counties in western China. Jinsha county was established in 1941, formerly belongs to Qianbei the highest of the four market towns, to enjoy the reputation of "Qianbei granary", in 2009, the China Tea Marketing Association named it as "tribute tea Township". Area of 2,528 square kilometers, jurisdiction over 26 townships, 244 villages (neighborhood, community), the population of 678,000.

Jinsha territory of mountains, a pleasant climate and rich resources. The forest coverage rate reached 43.3%. The main deposits of 19 kinds of coal, iron, sulfur, phosphorus, silicon, of which about 8 billion tons of coal reserves, is a national key coal-producing counties, one of the energy base of the "West Electricity to East" project. The main agricultural products are rice, wheat, rape, pepper, tobacco, tea, peanuts, potatoes and so on. The main features of goods are Guizhou top ten famous wines, China Famous Brand "Jinsha Huisha wine" series, the 11th Asian Games in designated drinking water "Yankong mineral water", unique nuances of "Yu Mo vinegar" green "Kangxing oil" and the historic "Qingchi tribute tea". The main tourism resources of Lengshuihe provincial forest parks and Sanzhangshui provincial level forest parks and other natural beauty spots, the Ao Jiafen of quarry stone carvings, Houshan Dong Han tombs carved stone, the Tea Garden Palace in Peking Opera Theater and other cultural relics, in the Houshan Township, Guizhou Province classic Red Tourism, Guizhou Province bases for patriotic education, national security education base - Qian Zhuangfei martyr tomb, such as cultural landscape, Yi "Torch Festival", Miao "Caishan Festival", Gelao "Chixin Festival", Buyi "Antiphonal Festival", and so on, with deep ethnic features.

金沙县产业园区标准化厂房一角
Jinsha County Industrial Park the standardized plant corner

新农村建设
New rural construction

在“十二五”新征程中，紧紧围绕“加速发展、加快转型、推动跨越”主基调和“工业化、城镇化”两大战略，确立了以科学发展观为统领，以科学规划为先导，以工业发展为支撑，以城市和园区建设为载体，以产业结构调整为主线，以改善民生为目的，以新农村建设为着力点，以发展现代服务业为突破口，突出“工业立县、项目支撑”理念，强力推进基础设施建设、招商引资、农业产业化等重点工作，加快产业向园区集中、人口向城镇和新型农村社区集中、土地向适度规模经营集中，全力打造“活力金沙”、“宜居金沙”、“幸福金沙”，努力建成全省经济发展一流县、统筹城乡发展一流县、城镇建设一流县、生态文明一流县、社会和谐一流县，实现金沙经济社会科学发展、和谐发展、率先发展的发展思路。规划建设了“以商贸、新兴产业为主的产业园区，以煤盐电化为主的循环经济园区，以中小企业为主的民营经济聚集区，以红色旅游、生态旅游、交通物流、农产品集散为一体的乌江旅游开发区，冷水河民族风情生态观光区，以农业产业化聚集发展为主的现代农业科技示范园区，以煤炭物流为主的新安矿产工贸园区”的“七大特色经济板块”。

2011年，全县完成生产总值108.28亿元，同比增长19.6%；财政总收入30.17亿元，同比增长39.99%，其中地方财政收入16.5亿元，同比增长39.04%；农民人均纯收入4910元，同比增长22.45%；城镇居民人均可支配收入17149元，同比增长20.03%。先后被授予全国人口与计划生育先进县、全国计划生育优质服务先进县、全国科技工作先进县、全国科普示范县、全国水土保持生态环境建设示范县、全国社会治安综合治理先进县、国家级食品安全示范县、全国社会主义新农村建设档案工作示范县、全国农业标准化示范县，全省计划生育工作依法行政先进县、全省科技进步先进县、全省绿化模范县、全省平安建设先进县、全省双拥模范县、全省村民自治模范县等荣誉称号。

县城一角
County corner

冷水河省级森林公园
Lengshuihe Provincial Forest Park

金沙县红色旅游景点——钱壮飞烈士陵园
Jinsha County Red attractions - Qian Zhuangfei martyrs' cemetery

Closely around a new journey in the "12th Five-Year", to "accelerate the development, accelerate the transition to promoteleapfrog" main tone and "the industrialization and urbanization" two strategic, established the scientific development concept as a guide the scientific planning for the pilot, industrial development as a support, the city and the construction of the park as the carrier, the main line to industrial restructuring, to improve people's livelihood for the purpose, the new rural development as a focal point, for the development of modern service industry as a breakthrough, highlighting the "industrial build the county. the project supporting" concept, and vigorously promote the construction of infrastructure, investment, agriculture industrialization and other key tasks, speed up industrial park focused, concentrated population to the towns and the new rural community, the land business focus to the appropriate scale, to create "dynamic Jinsha" "livable Jinsha", "happiness Jinsha", and strive to build first-class counties of the province's economic development, urban and rural development first-class counties, cities and towns first-class counties, first-class county of ecological civilization, social harmony first-class counties, to achieve the Jinsha economic and social scientific development, harmonious development take the lead in the development of ideas. Planning and construction "trade, emerging industries based industrial park, mainly coal-salt power of circular economy park, mainly to small and medium private economic areas, red tourism, eco-tourism, transport and logistics, agricultural products distribution as one of the Wujiang River Tourism Development Zone, Lengshuihe ethnic customs eco-tourist areas, agricultural industrialization gathered based on the development of modern agricultural demonstration zone, based coal logistics the Xin'an Mineral Industry and Trade Park", "the seven characteristics of economic blocks".

In 2011, the county completed a GDP of 10.828 billion yuan, up 19.6%; total fiscal revenue of 3.017 billion yuan, an increase of 39.99%, which the local revenue of 1.65 billion yuan, an increase of 39.04%; rural per capita net income of 4,910 yuan. an increase of 22.45%; per capita disposable income of urban residents was 17,149 yuan, an increase of 20.03%. Has been awarded advanced counties of the national population and family planning, advanced county of national family planning services, advanced county of national science and technology, national scientific and technological demonstration counties, the National Ecological Environment Construction demonstration counties, the national social security comprehensive management of advanced counties, national food safety demonstration counties, the new socialist countryside construction of archival work demonstration counties, agricultural standardization demonstration counties, advanced counties of the province's family planning work of administration by law, the province's scientific and technological progress advanced counties, the province's green model county, the province's peace building advanced counties, provincial double-support model county, the province villagers' autonomy model county and other honorary titles.

南 明 区

Nanming District

省人大代表一行调研南明区农副产品直销进社区

Provincial People's Congress representatives had research of the Nanming agricultural products direct sales into the community

省政协主席会议视察团视察南明区进城农民工子女教育工作开展情况

Chairman meeting team of the CPPCC Provincial Committee, had visiting mission to inspect the Nanming migrant workers children's education work

贵阳市市委书记李军抗凝除冰

Guiyang municipal party committee secretary Li Jun anticoagulant de-icing

贵阳市市委副书记、市长李再勇慰问南明区老党员

Guiyang City Committee deputy decretary, Mayor Li Zaiyong condolences Nanming veteran party members

南明区是贵阳市的中心城区之一，省委办公所在地，因南明河蜿蜒贯穿全区而得名。南明区是全省、全市的政治、经济、文化、科技和教育中心，也是全省最为重要的通信枢纽、旅游胜地和客流、物流集散中心。面积209.34平方公里，辖4个乡、29个村，13个街道办事处，3个社区服务中心，141个居委会。人口为56.17万人。

2011年，南明区生产总值达到301.7亿元，比上年增长17.2%；财政总收入达到30.44亿元，比上年增长33.57%；地方财政收入达到18.61亿元，比上年增长45.51%；全社会固定资产投资达到175.46亿元，比上年增长47.70%；规模以上工业总产值达到196亿元，比上年增长25.82%；社会消费品零售总额达到192.49亿元，比上年增长20.60%；招商引资实际到位资金85.23亿元，比上年增长42.05%；城镇居民人均可支配收入达19420元，比上年增长17.01%；农民人均纯收入达9031元，比上年增长20%。

2011年，南明区商贸服务业全面扩容升级，发展质量和水平再上台阶。以金融、物流、旅游、电子商务、楼宇经济等为特色的现代服务业和以商贸、餐饮、住宿等为主的传统服务业快速增长，全年入驻楼宇的企业达1700余户，新增1000万元以上服务业项目59个。此外，根据全市市场产业转移升级的工作要求，对花溪大道（南明段）汽车市场和五里冲农副产品批发市场实施了关闭搬迁，新的产业规划布局调整初步完成。

区委书记柯德来听取水口寺社区服务中心负责人介绍社区情况

Party Secretary KeDe to listen to the Shuikousi Community Service Center responsible person introduce the situation in the community

区委副书记、区长朱丽霞在南明老干妈风味食品有限公司调研

District Deputy secretary, mayor Zhu Lixiahad research in Nanming Laoganma flavor food Co., Ltd.

南明区检察院“办案及专业技术用房”落成

Completion of the Nanming District Prosecutor's "Office handling the case and the professional and technical space" was built

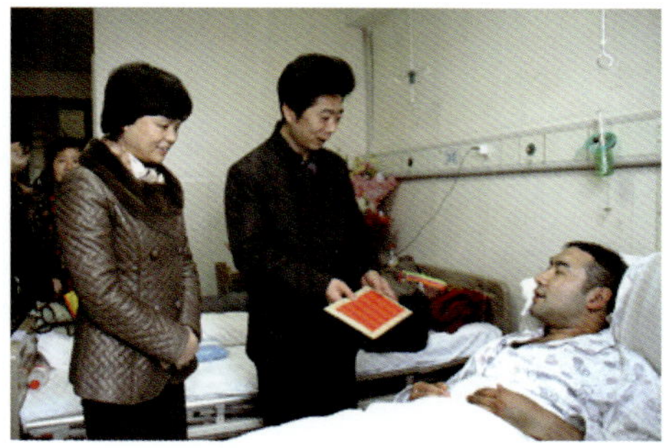

南明区委区政府领导慰问英勇干警韩奇

Nanming District Government leadership condolences to the heroic police officers Han Qi

彭家湾片区市政路网项目开工仪式

Pengjiawa Area municipal road network project groundbreaking ceremony

The Nanming district is one of the central districts of Guiyang City, the seat of the Provincial Party Committee Office, named Nanming River meandering through the region. Nanming is the province, the city's political, economic, cultural, technological and educational center, the province's most important communications hub, tourist destination and passenger traffic, logistics and distribution center. Area of 209.34 square kilometers, the jurisdiction of the 4 townships, 29 villages, 13 neighborhood offices, 3 community service centers, 141 neighborhood committees. The population of 561,700.

In 2011, Nanming GDP reached 30.17 billion yuan in 2011, an increase of 17.2% over the previous year; total fiscal revenue reached 3.044 billion yuan, an increase of 33.57% over the previous year; local financial revenue reached 1.861 billion yuan, an increase of 45.51% over the previous year; The total investment in fixed assets reached 17.546 billion yuan, an increase of 47.70% over the previous year; scale industrial output value reached 19.6 billion yuan, an increase of 25.82% over the previous year; total retail sales of social consumer goods reached 19.249 billion yuan, an increase of 20.60% over the previous year; The investment funds actually realized 8.523 billion yuan, an increase of 42.05% over the previous year; urban residents per capita disposable income reached 19,420 yuan, an increase of 17.01% over the previous year; rural per capita net income reached 9,031 yuan, an increase of 20% over the previous year.

In 2011, the commercial service of the Nanming comprehensive upgrade and expansion of the higher level of development quality and level. Finance, logistics, tourism, e-commerce, building and economic characteristics of the modern service industry and the traditional service-based commerce, catering, accommodation, rapid growth, and settled in buildings throughout the year more than 1,700 enterprises, new 59 service projects in more than 10 million yuan. In addition, according to the requirements of industrial transfer of the city market to upgrade, Huaxi Avenue (Nanming segment) car market and Wulichong agricultural products wholesale market implemented close relocation, new industrial planning and layout to adjust the initial completion.

In 2011, the Nanming industrial economy developed steadily. Strength to push forward the construction of the Longdongbao food industrial park, spread out across the 1st Road, Henger Road, Zongyi Road, the Longshui road etc road network within the industrial park, the pipe network and ancillary facilities, and has invested a total of 3.6 billion yuan, enterprises into the park got the accelerating pace. Support the strong supporting the superior, implementation of the various support measures, the scale industries in the region is growing, 31 new industrial enterprises above designated size throughout the year, of which 19 output value of more than 10 million yuan, 10 enterprises output value with more than 100 million yuan.

花果园湿地公园
Hua Guoyuan Wetland Park

全省农业产业化龙头企业南明老干妈风味食品有限公司带动一大批农民增收致富，图为“老干妈”公司二期工程的主厂房车间
The province's agricultural industrialization leading enterprises, Nanming Laoganma style Food Co., Ltd. is driven by a large number of farmers to get rich, the picture shows the the "Laoganma" second phase of the main plant workshop

2011年，南明区工业经济稳步发展。强力推进龙洞堡食品工业园建设，全面铺开工业园区内一号路、横二路、纵一路、龙水路等园区路网、管网及附属设施建设，已累计完成投资36亿元，企业入驻园区步伐不断加快。通过扶强扶优，落实各项扶持措施，全区规模工业日益壮大，全年新增31家规模以上工业企业，其中19家产值超过千万元，10家企业产值过亿元。

紧紧围绕新城开发和旧城改造，南明区城市面貌实现较大提升。一是全力推进新城建设。以机场路、西南环线为主轴线，以龙洞堡国际机场改扩建、“四路四沟”、青年路、市一医分院、贵阳首开城等项目的建设为契机，全面启动了龙洞堡新城开发。二是加大旧城改造力度。以旧城棚户区改造项目为重点，继彭家湾旧城改造项目之后又启动了汤家坡城中村改造项目、五里冲棚户区改造项目和二戈寨片区的改造。三是城市管理提标扩面。狠抓重点领域、重点区域专项整治，“脏乱”现象得到有效治理，完成了38个农贸市场升级改造，城区面貌有了较大改观。

2011年，南明区始终坚持发展社会事业，努力促进社会进步。一是坚持优先发展教育。进一步加大教育投入，提高教育教学基础设施的水平和质量，2011年教育一般预算支出已达6.37亿元；建设了甲秀小学学区等5个优秀学区，发挥了优质学校的示范引领作用；解决了辖区4609名农民工子女入学问题。二是坚持促进卫生事业发展。加强新型农村合作医疗制度建设，参保率达到99.3%；认真执行国家基本药物制度，基层卫生院全部使用基本药物并实行零差率；完成7个社区卫生服务中心的项目建设。2011年未发生暴发疫情及突发公共卫生事件。三是坚持发展科技、文体工作。加大各级各类科技项目的申报工作力度，广泛开展“讲文明、除陋习、树新风”活动，进一步加大了文体公共设施投入，丰富了辖区群众的业余文化生活。

南明区高度重视进城务工人员子女的就学问题，图为二戈寨小学的同学们正在上民歌音乐课

The Nanming attaches great importance to the schooling of the children of migrant workers, the picture shows the Ergezhai Primary School students are on a folk song music lessons

南明区西湖社区服务中心挂牌

The Nanming Xihu Community Service Center listed

南明区广大干部职工、青年志愿者积极投身"三创一办"，图为"绿丝带"在为过往市民宣传"创模"内容

Nanming cadres and workers, youth volunteers play an active part in the "three creation one doing", The picture shows the "Green Ribbon "propaganda for the content of " model" to past members of the public

南明区连续5年举办的茶文化活动，图为炒制现场

The Nanming tea cultural activities organized in five consecutive years, The picture shows the frying site

近年来，南明区加大力度发掘民间文化，扶持文化产业发展。图为艺人们正仔细对作品进行雕琢

In recent years, Nanming made greater efforts to explore the folk culture, to support the development of cultural industries. The picture shows the artists are carefully crafting the works

Tightly around the new town development and urban renewal, the Nanming appearance of the city to achieve larger increase. First, efforts to promote the new town construction. The main axis of the Airport Road, Southwest Link, Rebuilding the Longdongbao International Airport, the construction of the "fouth road four ditch", Qingnian road, City Medical Branch, Guiyang Shoukai City project as an opportunity, to fully launch the Longdongbao Metro developed. Second, is to intensify transformation of the old city. By urban shantytowns project, started Tangjiapo city reconstruction project, the Wulichong shantytowns projects and the transformation of the Ergezhai Area reconstruction after the Pengjiawan old city redevelopment project. Third, mentioned standard extending the coverage of urban management. Pay close attention to key areas, key areas of special rectification, "dirty" phenomenon has been effectively controlled, 38 farmers' markets to upgrade, the city outlook has been greatly improved.

In 2011, Nanming always adhere to the development of social undertakings, and efforts to promote social progress. First, give priority to the development of education. Further increase investment in education, improve the level and quality of education and teaching infrastructure, education in general budget expenditures had reached 637 million yuan in 2011; the construction of the 5 excellent primary areas of outstanding school district, played a lead role model of high-quality schools; solve the area 4,609 of the schooling of children of migrant workers. Second, is to insist on promoting health development. Strengthen the construction of new rural cooperative medical care system, insurance rates have reached 99.3%; earnestly implement the national essential drug system, primary health centers all use of essential medicines and zero slip; completed seven community health service center projects. At the end of 2011, outbreaks of epidemic and public health emergencies. Third, the development of science and technology, cultural and sports work. Reporting efforts of the various projects at all levels, extensive "civilized, in addition to bad habits, and fostering new activities", and further increase the input of the stylistic public facilities and rich area masses of amateur cultural life.

凯里市

Kaili City

州政协副主席、凯里市委副书记、市长洪金洲对市人民政府上半年整体工作进行全面回顾，并对下半年工作进行全面安排和部署

State Vice Chairman, deputy secretary of Kaili Municipal Committee, mayor Hong Jinzhou conducted a comprehensive review of work of the City People's Government in the first half of the year, and the overall arrangement and deployment of work in the second half of the year

黔东南州凯里市行政区域面积1306平方公里，辖2个乡、7个镇、7个街道办事处，201个村民委员会、17个社区，14个居（家）委。凯里市是省级“双拥模范城”、省级“文明城市”、省级“卫生与秩序”创建先进市、“中国优秀旅游城市”、“全国绿化模范城市”、“中国特色魅力城市”、“全国科技进步考核先进市、“全国计划生育优质服务先进县”、“全国幼儿教育先进县”、 中国十佳风貌城市、“中国100个最具幸福城市”、全国41个“绿都”和20座“公众心目中的中国和谐之城”之一。

2011年，全市生产总值（GDP）963638万元，同比增长20%。其中第一产业完成70285万元，同比增长0.1%；第二产业完成347585万元，同比增长29.9%；第三产业完成545767万元，同比增长16.9%。辖区规模工业总产值完成617073万元，同比增长49.3%，辖区规模工业增加值完成147843.4万元，增长37.3%，签约项目88个，签约资金 960.5亿元，到位资金86.12亿元； 农林牧渔业总产值124330万元，同比增长0.52%；全市实现财政总收入200642万元，同比增长82.09%，年末金融机构存款余额1881727万元；社会固定资产1055593万元，同比增长71.35%；接待游客776.96万人次，同比增长56.85%，旅游总收入95.2亿元，增长59.44%，创汇1684.2万美元，增长23.73%；全社会商品销售额完成2126839.2万元，增长31.7%；居民消费价格同比上涨5.6%，消费品价格上涨7.2%，服务项目价格上升1.1%，商品零售价格上涨5.9%；城镇居民人均可支配收入16410.38元，同比增长16.73%；农民人均纯收入5176.31元，增长26.84%；全年，凯里炉山工业园区共落户企业36户，其中：2011年落户企业31户，建成投产企业5户，企业项目完成固定资产投资36亿元，完成工业总产值11726万元，实现税收552.9万元。

州政协副主席、市委副书记、市长洪金洲到炉山工业园区视察项目推进建设情况

State Vice Chairman, deputy secretary of Kaili Municipal Committee, mayor Hong Jinzhou to inspect the project promoting construction situation in Lushan Industrial Park

凯里市“十一五”期间城市基础设施进一步完善，为城市扩容奠定了坚实基础。图为凯里中心繁华区

Kaili City, during the "Eleventh Five Year" urban infrastructure further improved, laid a solid foundation for urban expansion. The picture shows Kaili Centre prosperous and bustling area

“健康凯里·人人运动”行动启动仪式暨凯里地区第三个“全民健身日”健身项目展示活动

"Health Kaili • Everyone Movement Action" Launching Ceremony cum Kaili the third area of "National Fitness Day" fitness program exhibition

Qiandongnan State Kaili City has administrative area of 1,306 square kilometers, administers 2 townships, 7 towns, 7 street offices, 201 village committees, 17 community, 14 neiberghood (home) Committee. Kaili City is the provincial "double support model city", provincial "civilized city", the provincial "health and order" create advanced city, "China Excellent Tourism City", "National Model Green City", "Chinese characteristics attractive city", "advanced city of the national scientific and technological progress assessment", "the national family planning services advanced counties", "the National Early Childhood Education Advanced County", Top Ten style city in China, "China's 100 most happiness city", one of 41 "Green Capital" and 20 "Chinese Harmony city in the eyes of the public".

In 2011, the city's gross domestic product (GDP) was 9.63638 billion yuan, an increase of 20%. The first industry to complete 702.85 million yuan, an increase of 0.1%; secondary industry completed 3.47585 billion yuan, an increase of 29.9%; the tertiary industry was 5.45767 billion yuan, an increase of 16.9%. Area-scale industrial output value completed 6.17073 billion yuan, an increase of 49.3%, area scale industrial added value of 1.478434 billion yuan, an increase of 37.3%, and 88 contracted projects, contracted to 96.05 billion yuan of funds, a capital of 8.612 billion yuan in place; agriculture, forestry, animal husbandry and fishery output value of 1.2433 billion yuan, an increase of 0.52%; the city's total fiscal revenue of 2.00642 billion yuan, an increase of 82.09%, the balance of deposits with financial institutions at the end of the year was 18,817,270,000 yuan; 10.55593 billion yuan in fixed assets, an increase of 71.35%; tourists 7,769,600 passengers, an increase of 56.85%, total tourism income of 9.52 billion yuan, an increase of 59.44%, earning $ 16,842,000, an increase of 23.73%; the whole society goods sales was 21,268,392,000 yuan, an increase of 31.7%; consumer prices rose 5.6%, consumer goods prices rose 7.2%, prices of services rose by 1.1%, retail prices rose 5.9%; per capita disposable income of urban residents was 16,410.38 yuan, an increase of 16.73%; rural per capita net income was 5,176.31 yuan, up 26.84%; throughout the year, Kaili Lushan Industrial Park settled a total of 36 enterprises, including: 31 enterprises settled in 2011, 5 enterprises put into operation, enterprise projects completed investment in fixed assets of 3.6 billion yuan, industrial output value of 117.26 million yuan, tax of 5.529 million yuan.

加速发展　加快转型
强力推进经济强县建设工作——白云区

Accelerate development　Accelerate transformation

Strongly promote the construction of economic County -Baiyun District

4月22日，中共中央政治局委员、广东省委书记汪洋和广东省委副书记、省长黄华华率广东党政代表团，在贵州省委书记、省人大常委会主任栗战书，省委副书记、省长赵克志等陪同下，到中铝贵州企业考察

April 22, the CPC Central Committee, Guangdong Provincial Party Secretary Wang Yang and deputy secretary of Guangdong Province, Guangdong governor Huang Huahua lead the party and government delegation, accompanied by the Guizhou Provincial CPC Committee, director of the Provincial People's Congress Li Zhanshu, the provincial party committee deputy secretary and governor Zhao Kezhi, to investigate China Aluminum Group Guizhou enterprises

10月10日，贵州省委副书记、省长赵克志（右一）在省、市、区各级领导的陪同下，深入贵阳数字内容产业园调研

October 10, deputy secretary of the Guizhou Province, governor Zhao Kezhi (the first from right) accompanied by the province, city and district leaders at all levels, had in-depth research in Guiyang digital content industry park

11月6日，省政协主席王正福率省政协常委视察团到白云铝及铝加工基地视察

November 6, Province CPPCC Chairman Wang Zhengfu lead the provincial CPPCC Standing Committee of the visiting mission to the Baiyun aluminum and aluminum base inspection

2011年8月，省委常委、市委书记李军调研白云区高新区重点工业项目建设情况

August 2011, the Provincial Standing Committee, Party Secretary Li Jun had research of Baiyun District High-tech Zone of key industrial projects construction

2011年4月，区委副书记、区长黄昌祥到贵州金苹果铝棒有限公司考察试产情况

April 2011, District deputy secretary, mayor Huang Changxiang to the Guizhou golden apple aluminum rod Co., Ltd. to examine the trial production

2008年以来的第三轮经济强县建设中，白云区经历了前所未有的困难，经受了巨大的挑战。四年来，白云区委、区政府克服"两个百年不遇"所带来的强大冲击，团结和带领全区人民抢抓机遇，攻坚克难，突出"转型、升级、提速"这一主题，解放思想、求真务实、开拓奋进，充分依托高新区和驻区国有大中型企业两大发展平台，最大限度抓发展机遇，最大限度聚集发展要素，最大限度凝聚力量，破解难题，真抓实干，加快发展，强县工作取得了一定的成绩。

艰难之中奋力突困。在第三轮强县建设中，白云区先后经受了百年不遇的低温雨雪冰冻灾害、国际金融危机和连续两年的干旱冲击。经过努力，到2010年底，全区经济发展总体上恢复至灾前水平。

经济发展小幅增长。全区生产总值四年年均增长11.4%。其中，一产增加值年均增长9.4%，二产增加值年均增长10.4%，三产增加值年均增长16.3%。大部分经济指标园满完成强县建设目标任务。

发展后劲明显增强。紧紧围绕"项目落实年"、"项目推进年"、"项目建设年"等活动，全力推动项目建设。项目建设带动固定资产投资强劲增长，预计2011年全社会固定资产投资完成146亿元，是2007年的4.9倍，四年年均增长37.2%。

城乡居民收入大幅提高。城镇居民可支配收入从2007年的12066元提升到19402元，增加7336元，四年年均增长12.9%；农民人均纯收入从2007年的5019元提升到8936元，增加3917元，四年年均增长15.5%。

下一步，白云区将认真贯彻落实全省建强办主任会议精神，突出"增比、进位、突破"工作主题，坚定信心不动摇，聚精会神搞建设，一心一意谋发展，进一步做好建强工作，推动建强县经济社会发展再上新台阶。

11月11日，贵阳高新区党工委书记、白云区委书记宗文一行深入贵州永青仪电有限公司调研

November 11, Guiyang High-tech Zone Party Work Committee, Baiyun District secretary Zong Wen had in-depth research of Guizhou Yongqing Instrument and Electronics Co., Ltd.

2010年12月31日，省委副书记、省长赵克志宣布高新区、白云区工业园区重点项目集中开工暨15万吨铝板带项目开工

December 31, 2010, deputy secretary of the Guizhou Province, governor Zhao Kezhi announced that the High-tech Zone, Baiyun District, Industrial Park, key projects focus on start-cum-15 million tons of aluminum with the project started

12月17日，高新区、白云区27个重大项目集中开工暨中国南车集团贵阳新产业基地奠基仪式举行，省委常委、市委书记李军宣布开工并表示祝贺

December 17, focus on 27 major projects of the High-tech Zone, Baiyun District, started that is China South Locomotive Group the new industrial base in Guiyang foundation stone laying ceremony was held, the Standing Committee of the Provincial Party Committee, Party Secretary Li Jun announced the start and congratulated

Since 2008 the third round of economic county construction, Baiyun District has experienced unprecedented difficulties, and withstood a huge challenge. In the past four years, Baiyun district committee, the district government to overcome the powerful impact of the "two difficulties that are rare for hundred years", unite and lead the region's people seize the opportunity to tackle tough, highlighting the "transition, upgrade, speed up" the subject, emancipate the mind pragmatic, forging ahead, fully rely on two major development platforms High-tech Zone and Garrison large and medium-sized state-owned enterprises, to maximize grasp the development opportunities, to maximize aggregate development factors, the maximum cohesion force to crack the problem, do solid work, speed up development, the county has made some achievements.

Difficults among the struggling suddenly trapped. In the third round of the county construction, Baiyun District has withstood the rare snow disaster, the international financial crisis, and for two consecutive years of drought impact. Through efforts to the end of 2010, the region's economic development in general return to pre-disaster level.

The slight increase in economic development.GDP in the region for four years the average annual increase of 11.4%. Among which, the first industry added value average annual growth of 9.4%, the secondary industry added value average annual growth of 10.4%, the tertiary industry added value average annual growth of 16.3%. Most economic indicators park full completion of the county building objectives and tasks.

Development potential is significantly enhanced. Focus on "implementation of the project year," "advancing project year", "year of construction projects" and other activities, to promote the project construction. Projects driven by strong growth in fixed asset investment, expected 2011 total fixed asset investment of 14.6 billion yuan, 4.9 times that of 2007, average annual growth of 37.2% for four years.

12月11日，贵州大众橡胶与美国岱高合作项目奠基仪式在白云区麦架镇隆重举行

December 11, Guizhou Dazhong Rubber and USA Dai Gao cooperation projects groundbreaking ceremony was held at Baiyun District Maijia town

8月27日，第五届亚洲青年动漫大赛COSPLAY决赛在白云区举行

August 27, the 5th Asian Youth Animation Competition the COSPLAY finals field in the Baiyun District

A substantial increase in the income of urban and rural residents. Urban residents disposable income from the year 2007 of 12,066 yuan to 19,402 yuan, an increase of 7,336 yuan, average annual growth of 12.9% for four years; farmers per capita net income increased to 8,936 yuan from 5,019 yuan in 2007, an increase of 3,917 yuan, an increase of 15.5% for four years .

Next, the Baiyun District will conscientiously implement the spirit of the meeting of the province to build strong Affairs Office, highlight the "increasing ratio of binary breakthrough" theme of the work, strengthen their confidence without wavering, concentrate on construction and focus on development, do a better job to build a strong work, promote the economic and social development in built county to a new level.

乌当区

Wudang District

来仙秘境
To Sin Fam

乌当区面积686平方公里，人口32万。新天城区距龙洞堡国际机场8公里，距贵阳火车站10公里。交通网络四通八达，便捷顺畅。

2011年，地区生产总值达到125.51亿元；规模以上工业总产值达到98亿元；城镇居民人均可支配收入达到19332元；农民人均纯收入达到8605元；全社会固定资产投资总额累计完成100.3亿元，取得了经济发展增比进位综合测评排名全省第九、全市第三的好成绩。

现代制药、先进制造、电子信息、新材料、特色食品加工是乌当区的五大支柱产业，2011年总产值完成了84亿元。全区规模以上工业企业发展到87家，高新技术产业增加值达到21亿元。乌当是全省高新技术企业聚集度最高的区（市、县）。

2011年，乌当城市化率达到了56%，准备五年后城市化率达到66%。过去五年，乌当招商引资累计完成内资186.18亿元、外资8174万美元。

乌当既是国家级高新开发区，又是国家级农业科技园区，同时还是省级城乡统筹和新型工业化综合配套改革两个试点。下一步，将大力推动新天园区、农业园区扩区调位，以制药工业为开端，加快块状经济向现代产业集群的转变。调整种植业结构12.65万亩，粮经比达到10:90，建成贵州山区现代农业示范区。积极打造偏坡乡、羊昌镇、新堡乡、工水田镇四个特色小城镇。

暮色乌当
Twilight Wudang

国泰民安
Peace and prosperity life

贵御温泉
Yugui Spa

银杏恋歌
Ginkgo Love Song

Wudang District has an area of 686 square kilometers, population of 320,000. The new city district is 8 km from the the Longdongbao International Airport, 10 km away from Guiyang Railway Station. Transportation network is smooth and convenient.

In 2011, the GDP reached 12.551 billion yuan; scale industrial output value reached 9.8 billion yuan; per capita disposable income of urban residents reached 19,332 yuan; farmers per capita net income reached 8,605 yuan; in fixed assets total investment totaled 10.03 billion yuan, has made economic development to increase the province's ninth, the city's third good results than the binary comprehensive evaluation.

Modern pharmaceuticals, advanced manufacturing, electronic information, new materials, characteristics of food processing is the five pillar industries of Wudang District, in 2011, the total output value of 8.4 billion yuan. Development of industrial enterprises above designated size of the region to 87, high-tech industries to increase turnover to 2.1 billion yuan. Wudang is the highest degree of aggregation of the high-tech enterprises in the province (city, county).

In 2011, Wudang urbanization rate reached 56%, prepare to reach the urbanization rate of 66% after five years. In the past five years, Wudang investment totaled 18.618 billion yuan of domestic capital, foreign capital of $ 81,740,000.

Wudang is not only the state-level High-tech Development Zone, but also is the National Agricultural Science and Technology Park, also the provincial urban and rural areas and new industrialization comprehensive reform of the two pilot sites. Next, it will vigorously promote the Xintian park and agricultural park expansion tune bit, as the start of the pharmaceutical industry, to speed up the massive economic transformation to a modern industrial clusters. Adjust planting structure of 126,500 mu, the grains are more than 10:90, the completion of Guizhou mountain modern agriculture demonstration area. Actively to create a Pianpo county, Yangchang town, Xinbao county, Gongshuitian town four characteristics of small towns.

乡村秋色
Village Autumn

偏坡夫妻树
Pianpo couples tree

小 河 区

Xiaohe District

省第二轮第一次项目建设调研
The provincial second round of the projects building research

省委常委、贵阳市委书记李军调研小孟工业园区建设情况
Provincial Standing Committee of Guiyang municipal party committee secretary Li Jun had research of Xiaomeng Industrial Park construction

2011年，小河区牢牢把握省委、省政府关于“加速发展、加快转型、推动跨越”的主基调，紧紧围绕“纵深推进生态文明、率先实现全面小康，加快建设新型工业化和现代都市新区”的总体目标，大力实施“工业强区”和“开放带动”两大战略，积极推进经济结构调整和重点项目建设，全区经济总体实现平稳较快发展，财政收入大幅增长，工业经济平稳较快增长，城乡居民收入稳步提高，社会消费持续增长，民生保障不断加强，实现了“十二五”规划的良好开局。

2011年，小河区经济总量大幅攀升，综合实力明显增强，全区生产总值实现80.63亿元，比上年同期增长20.4%。工业经济呈现良好增长势头，装备制造、烟草医药及绿色食品、电子信息等三大主导产业集聚发展，规模以上工业总产值完成175.48亿元，同比增长36.2%。全社会固定资产投资保持高速增长，完成145.06亿元，同比增长53.7%。全区正在实施建设的项目达170个，其中工业项目60个，纳入省、市重点项目共27个，是开发区建区历史上同期开工项目最多的一年。小孟工业园区建设快速推进，已开工项目31个，工业项目占地面积5206亩，新建厂房约为340万平方米，总投资超过170亿元，建成后将新增工业产值400亿元以上，实现税收30亿以上，提供就业岗位2万余个。财政总收入完成14.87亿元，同比增长36.3%。招商引资实际到位资金85.23亿元，同比增长30.2%。社会消费品零售总额完成49.32亿元，同比增长20.1%。城镇居民可支配收入和期内农民现金收入分别完成19357元、9000元，同比分别增长17%、21.5%。

建设中的标准厂房项目
Standard factory construction projects

海子街镇红堰村新农村建设见成效
The Haizijie town Hongyan village new rural construction got initial achievement

The Bijie Qixingguan District, governed by Pingyijun in Han Dynasty, and Pingmanjun in Dongjin Dynasty, belonged to Luzhou legacy in Tang, Song Dynast, built station in Yuan Dynasty, the Ming Dynasty set up Wei, Qing Emperor Kangxi 26 years (AD 1687) to build the county, in Decemeber 1993, the State Council approved to move county to build the city, in November 2011,withdraw county level Bijie City, the establishment of Bijie City Qixingguan District, the original county-level Bijie city administrative region for Qixingguan District administrative areas.

修葺一新的人民公园免费向市民开放
Repair of a new People's Park is open to the public free of charge

The Bijie Qixingguan District is located in the northwest of Guizhou Province, located in Sichuan, Yunnan and Guizhou provinces interchange, is the political, economic, technological, cultural and information center of Bijie City. East bordering Jinsha and Dafang two counties, south bordering Nayong County, west bordering Hezhang County, Zhenxiong County in Yunnan Province, and Weixin County, to the north junction of Sichuan Gulin, Xuyong counties, is the material distribution center in southwest area. Covering an area of 3,410.98 square kilometers, jurisdiction over 27 towns, 8 townships, 6 offices, inhabited by 23 ethnic groups of Han, Yi, Bai, Miao, Buyi, a population of 1.51 million people. Domestic terrain high in the west low in the east, with an average altitude of 1,511 m, mild climate, abundant rainfall, humid subtropical climate, the region without cold winter and hot in summer, known as the "top ten summer tourist cities in China".

小坝镇中屯街上房屋改造工程
Xiaoba town Zhongtun street housing renovation project

In 2011, GDP in the region completed 15.271 billion yuan, an increase of 19.0%, investment in fixed assets of 14.625 billion yuan, an increase of 55.31%; total fiscal revenue of 2.157 billion yuan, an increase of 86.68%; total retail sales of social consumer goods reached 5.465 billion yuan, an increase of 20.6%; rural per capita net income of 4,412 yuan, an increase of 21.74%. With the continuous deepening of reform and opening up, the region's economy has entered a golden period of rapid development. Has now become the most dynamic regions of the western region.

清镇市

Qingzhen City

国家发改委莅临清镇调研
National Development and Reform Commission to come to Qingzhen have research

贵阳市市长李再勇调研职教城
Guiyang City Mayor Li Zaiyong has research in Vocational Education City

贵阳市副市长马长青陪同国家发改委在清镇调研
Guiyang City Vice Mayor Ma Changqing accompanied by the National Development and Reform Commission have research in Qingzhen

清镇市地处黔中腹地，境内有全国最大的猫场铝矾土连片矿区，有国家4A级风景名胜区红枫湖和省级风景名胜区百花湖，区位优势明显、交通便利、资源丰富。面积1383平方公里，人口52万人，规划建设有西部工业园区、南部物流园区、北部职教园区和城市新区、东部生态宜居区等，是南贵昆经济带和黔中经济区及贵阳循环经济产业区的重要工业基地、交通枢纽，系贵州省27个经济强县和全国西部百强县之一。

近年来，随着贵州省、贵阳市新一轮城市的发展战略，清镇大部地区已被纳入贵阳市“百花生态新城”、贵州省“贵安新区”的规划范围，作为国发2号文件重点建设的“贵安新区”中重要的节点城市，发展后劲巨大。其中，国发2号文件提出的清镇-织金-黔西煤电铝、煤电化一体化基地核心主体就位于清镇市，贵阳市规划的铝精深加工、煤精细化工基地也主要位于清镇市。目前，清镇工业开发区已被列为贵州省一级开发区。

2011年，全市生产总值完成117.07亿元，同比增长20.3%。财政总收入完成13.04亿元，同比增长31.2%。地方财政收入完成7.84亿元，同比增长41.6%。全社会固定资产投资完成150亿元，同比增长53%。招商引资实际到位资金54亿元。在全国西部百强县中排名第85位。先后荣获“国家可持续发展实验区”、“全国科普示范市”、“全国人口和计划生育优质服务先进市”、“中国西部投资软环境最佳区（市、县）”、“省级文明城市”、“省级卫生城市”、“省级双拥模范市”等称号。

市委书记杨明晋、市长刘军陪同贵阳市长李再勇调研工业园区
Party secretary Yang Mingjin, Mayor Liu Jun accompanied by Guiyang Mayor Li Zaiyong have research in industrial park

清镇市委书记杨明晋、常务副市长杨亚林调研物流园区
Qingzhen party secretary Yang Mingjin, Deputy Mayor Yang Yalin have research in logistics park

Qingzhen City is located in the hinterland in central Guizhou, the territory of the country's largest cat the bauxite contiguous mining area, there are obvious national 4A level scenic spots Hongfeng Lake and Baihua Lake of provincial-level scenic spots, advantages of area location and convenient transportation, abundant resources. Area of 1,383 square kilometers, population 520,000, planning and construction of the western industrial park, southern logistics park, the northern vocational park and the new urban area, the eastern ecological livable area etc, is the the NGK economic zone and central Guizhou Economic Zone and Guiyang cycle economic and industrial zones important industrial base and transportation hub, is one of the 27 economic County Department of Guizhou Province and the country western hundred counties.

省纪委书记宋璇涛、贵阳市委书记李军调研清镇环保工作
Provincial Commission for Discipline Inspection Song Xuantao, Guiyang municipal party committee secretary Li Jun have research of the Qingzhen environmental work

In recent years, Guizhou Province, Guiyang City, a series new city development strategies, Qingzhen most areas have been included in Guiyang City "Baihua eco-town planning new city", range of Guizhou Province, "Gui'an New Area", as the National Development No.2 important node in the document focuses on building "Gui'an New Area"city, a huge development potential. Among them, the National Development document No.2 Qingzhen - Zhijin - Western Guizhou coal-fired aluminum, coal-fired integrated base of the core subject in Qingzhen City, Guiyang City Planning aluminum deep processing, fine coal chemical industry base mainly located Qingzhen City. At present, the Qingzhen Industrial Development Zone has been identified as a first class Development Zone of Guizhou Province.

刘晓凯调研职教城
Liu Xiaokai has research in Vocational Education City

In 2011, the GDP completed 11.707 billion yuan, an increase of 20.3%. The total fiscal revenue of 1.304 billion yuan, an increase of 31.2%. The local financial revenue of 784 million yuan, an increase of 41.6%. The total fixed asset investment of 15 billion yuan, an increase of 53%. The investment funds actually in place of 5.4 billion yuan. Ranked 85 in the National Western hundred counties. Has won the "National Sustainable Development Experimental Zone", "the National Popular Science Demonstration City ", "advanced city of the country's population and family planning services", "China's soft environment for investment in the west area (city, county)", "provincial civilized city", "provincial health city", "provincial double-support model city" title and so on.

遵 义 县

Zunyi County

黔北国际汽车博览城
Qianbei International Motor Expo City

正合铝业成品车间一角
Zhenghe Aluminium finished Workshop

遵义县国土面积4094平方公里，耕地面积65476公顷，辖29个镇、2个民族乡、225个村民委员会、14个居民委员会和27个社区居民委员会。人口121.43万人，其中少数民族1.53万人，非农业人口17.25万人。

2011年，实现地区生产总值168.48亿元，增长19.6%；工业增加值73.22亿元，增长25.7%，其中规模工业增加值62.65亿元，增长31.4%；固定资产投资158.22亿元，增长44.7%；财政总收入19.06亿元，增长30.6%；地方财政收入10.47亿元，增长36.3%；社会消费品零售总额36.45亿元，增长20.1%；城镇居民人均可支配收入17056元、农民人均纯收入6514元，分别增长15.5%、15.8%。金融机构存款余额135.03亿元、贷款余额101.20亿元，分别增长26.4%、17.2%。

着力抓项目建园区，工业经济加快提速。建立重点项目推进机制，实行建设进度媒体公示制度，一手抓在建项目的协调服务，力促其加快施工进度，一手抓现有企业的生产调度，推动其满负荷生产。

着力扩投资夯基础，发展后劲明显增强。坚持把扩大有效投资作为拉动经济增长的第一抓手，采取BT等模式强力推进交通、城建等基础设施建设，固定资产投资保持高速增长。招商引资取得明显成效，签约引进项目198个，实际到位资金139.02亿元。

着力抗大旱调结构，农业生产平稳推进。着力改民生促和谐，社会事业全面进步。

遵义县城夜景
Zunyi county night scene

遵义新世界建材城开业
Zunyi New World Building Material City opened

Honghuagang District is the main city of the historical and cultural city of Zunyi, located in the northern Guizhou Province, an area of 624 square kilometers. Governs 8 towns, 8 offices, 45 villagers' committees, 63 residents' committees and a population of 656,700.

In 2011, to complete the GDP of 19.692 billion yuan, an increase of 19.7%. The total fixed asset investment of 11.499 billion yuan, an increase of 56.3%. Investment capital in place of 16.99 billion yuan, an increase of 265.4%. Total fiscal revenue of 1.484 billion yuan, an increase of 41.43%; local general budgetary revenue of 996 million yuan, an increase of 40.5%. The per capita disposable income of urban residents was 17,426 yuan, an increase of 14%; per capita net income of farmers was 6,970 yuan, an increase of 22.9%.

In 2011, allowed the establishment of the Guizhou Honghuagang Economic Development Zone, which is maturing in industrial park infrastructure and supporting facilities, the relocation of the off-site technical innovation of "six companies" progressed smoothly, energy saving and emission reduction tasks are completed according to plan. The annual scale industrial output value, added value completed 15.8 billion yuan, 3.03 billion yuan respectively, up 40.4%, 36.7%. The total value of annual retail sales of social consumer goods completed 10.698 billion yuan, an increase of 20.2%; total number of tourist, the total tourism revenue reached 5.9392 million people, and 6.106 billion yuan, an increase of 64.24%, 53.1%, respectively.

城市建设美如画
Urban construction is beautiful like picture

大板水森林公园风光一瞥
Dabanshui forest park scenery glimpse

The whole year summer grain output is 9,971 tons, an increase of 4.5%; new perennial vegetable area of 64,200 mu, scale pig farms up to 105 households; new land transfer area of 3,853 mu, agricultural professional cooperatives of 47, agricultural product processing enterprises reached 25. "Four in farm" create coverage of 93.2%, and 45,000 farm houses, 175,000 farmers have benefited.

Preparation of the southern new city, east area, the old city shanty town and the town new village construction planning; accelerating the southern new city road network, the construction of new railway station area and other projects; built-up area expanded to 37 square kilometers, the urbanization rate has reached 68.15%; Community into a "four people community" boutique community of 15; continue to beautify the city environment.

Implemented the School Milk Subsidy Scheme, to start the rural students receiving compulsory education lunch program; co-ordinate employment and training of 7,813 people, 8,085 people of the transfer of rural labor force, new added of 11,400 urban jobs.

高原明珠　生态花溪

Pearl of the plateau　Ecological Huaxi

湿地公园美如画
Wetland Park in picturesque surroundings

花溪区位于黔中腹地，贵阳市南郊，辖9乡、2镇和3个街道办事处，143个村委会，27个社区居委会。人口为36.39万人，少数民族人口约占总人口的33%。花溪区已经成功创建国家级生态区，被国家环保部授予“国家级生态示范区”称号，成为贵阳市唯一获此殊荣的区（县、市），成功申报并建成全省唯一的花溪国家城市湿地公园，是全省著名的风景旅游区和文化区，素有“高原明珠”的美誉。

2011年，全区主要经济指标的增长速度均高于全国、全省和全市的增速，生产总值、规模以上工业总产值、全社会固定资产投资、财政总收入、一般预算收入、城镇居民人均可支配收入、农民人均纯收入、旅游总收入分别比上年增长18.1%、31.5%、53.0%、36.6%、49.3%、18.5%、26.1%、55.3%。在2011年全省88个县（市、区、特区）经济发展增比进位中成效显著，排位由上年的32位跃升至第10位，是贵阳市进位最快的区（县、市）。

贵阳金石产业园建成投产
Guiyang Jinshi Industrial Parkis put into operation

生态民居——七里香溪
Eco-houses - Qilixiang Creek

贵州（花溪）大学城——贵州财经学院新校区
Guizhou (Huaxi) University City - the new campus of the Guizhou College of Finance and Economics

Huaxi District is located in the hinterland of central Guizhou, the southern suburbs of Guiyang City, the jurisdiction over 9 townships, 2 towns and 3 subdistrict offices, 143 village committees, 27 community neighborhood committees. The population of 363,900 people, the ethnic minority population accounts for 33% of the total population. Huaxi District has successfully created a national ecological zones, to be awarded the title of "National Ecological Demonstration Area" by the State Ministry of Environmental Protection, the only award of the district (county, city) in Guiyang City, declare the success and completion of the sole province's Huaxi National Urban Wetland Park, the province's famous tourist area and cultural district, known as the "pearl of the plateau" reputation.

In 2011, the growth rate of the region's main economic indicators are higher than the national, provincial and city-wide growth, GDP, industrial output value of enterprises above designated size, the total fixed asset investment, total fiscal revenue, the general budget revenue, urban residents disposable income, farmers per capita net income, total tourism income increased by 18.1%, 31.5%, 53.0%, 36.6%, 49.3%, 18.5%, 26.1%, 55.3% over the previous year. In 2011 the province's 88 counties (cities, districts, the development of the SAR) economic growth than in the binary effectiveness significantly, ranking from 32nd last year jumped to 10th, is the fast binary district (county, city)in Guiyang City.

六盘水市钟山区

Liupanshui City Zhongshan District

2011年11月16日，贵州省委、省政府第二次全省项目建设年现场观摩会在六盘水市召开，会议期间，省委书记栗战书，省委副书记、省长赵克志率领与会人员到水钢观摩水钢建设及生产情况

November 16, 2011, the Guizhou Provincial Party Committee, Provincial Government the second province's project building year onsite demonstrations held in Liupanshui City, during the meeting, the provincial party secretary Li Zhanshu, Provincial Committee vice secretary, governor Zhao Kezhi led the participants to observe the water steel construction and production of the water steel

2011年11月16日，全省产业园区（开发区）发展大会暨项目建设年现场观摩会期间，省委书记、省人大常委会主任栗战书，省委副书记、省长赵克志到红桥新区观摩

November 16, 2011, during the periodof the development of the province's industrial park (Zone) Conference and project building year onsite demonstrations, the provincial party committee secretary, director of the Provincial People's Congress Li Zhanshu, Provincial Committee vice secretary, governor Zhao Kezhi to observe the Hongqiao new district

2011年，全区上下在区委的正确领导下，着力扩大固定资产投资规模，投资对经济增长的拉动作用明显增强；着力调整优化经济结构，经济发展质量和效益稳步上升；着力实施“十大民生工程”，群众生活水平稳步提高；着力开展“三个建设年”活动，发展环境不断优化，全区经济社会呈现出“投资加大、增速加快、活力增强、民生改善、环境趋好”的发展态势。

经济保持平稳较快增长，2011年全区生产总值完成220亿元，同比增长16%。结构调整取得重要进展，服务业稳步发展，工业结构更加优化。城市形象魅力不断提升。统筹城乡实现稳步发展。新农村建设扎实推进。农村基础设施不断夯实。农村生活环境大幅改善。重点项目建设稳步推进。招商引资力度不断加大。生态环境建设成效显著。保障和改善民生全面加强。就业和社会保障工作稳步推进。城乡社会保障体系日趋完善。公共卫生事业发展快速推进。

钟山区凤凰新区

Zhongshan District Phoenix New Area

In 2011, the whole region under the correct leadership of the District committee, efforts to expand the scale of investment in fixed assets, investment on economic growth is significantly enhanced; efforts to adjust and optimize the economic structure, quality and efficiency of economic development has steadily increased; focus on the implementation of the "Ten people's livelihood project", the people's living standards improved steadily; efforts to carry out "three constructions year" activities, the development environment constantly optimize, the region's economic and social shows "investment increase, accelerated and increased vitality, improved living conditions, the environment is getting better and better" development trend.

The economy has maintained steady and rapid growth, the region's GDP of 22 billion yuan in 2011, an increase of 16%. Restructuring made important progress, the service sector developed steadily, the industrial structure optimization. City Charm is rising. Urban and rural got steady development. Push forward new countryside construction. Constantly reinforce rural infrastructure. Substantial improvement of rural living environment. The steady progress of key projects. The investment has intensified. The construction of ecological environment with remarkable results. Protect and improve people's livelihood is fully strengthened. Employment and social security work pushed steadily. Urban and rural social security system is maturing. The development of public health is rapidly advancing.

钟山区广场人民广场夕照

Zhongshan Square People's Square of Sunset

修 文 县

Xiuwen County

国务院扶贫办党组书记、主任范小建到谷堡乡猕猴桃扶贫产业基地考察
The State Council Leading Group Office of Poverty Alleviation party secretary and director Fan Xiaojian visits Cubao village kiwi pro-poor industrial base

省领导莅临视察调研
Provincial leaders to come to inspect research

阳明文化产业园投资建设
The Yangming cultural industrial park got investment and construction

贵州商贸物流港（扎佐建材家居物流中心）开工建设
Guizhou Trade Logistics Port (Zazuo home building materials logistics center) started construction

修文县位于贵州省中部，面积1075.7平方公里，辖4镇、6乡(其中1个民族乡)、1个社区服务中心，有217个村民委员会、10个居民委员会。

2011年，全县完成地方生产总值57.7亿元，同比增长20.2%。完成规模以上工业总产值75.1亿元，同比增长36.1%。完成财政总收入7.12亿元，同比增长30.9%，其中地方级财政收入3.87亿元，同比增长38.3%。完成全社会固定资产投资90.3亿元，同比增长76.7%。完成非公经济增加值36.77亿元，同比增长28.0%。完成人均地方生产总值23023元，同比增长20.9%；城镇居民人均可支配收入和农民人均纯收入18721元、6667元，同比增长18.8%、29.4%。

一是工业经济势头强劲。园区项目布局区域已达17平方公里，入园企业85户，总投资328.56亿元，在全省经济强县建设中排名第21位。二是现代农业特色明显。立足于区位优势，突出抓好“猕猴桃、奶业、蔬菜、中药材”等四大产业，完成农业总产值14.1亿元，修文猕猴桃获得了国家“地理标志”证明商标。三是第三产业发展迅猛。2011年，全县累计接待游客458.5万人（次），实现旅游收入27.5亿元，完成社会消费品零售总额12.4亿元。四是城市面貌日新月异。县城规划面积由6平方公里扩大到22平方公里，城区建成面积达8平方公里，全县城镇化率达38.5%，“一城三片区”城市规划成果在全省城镇化推进大会上展示交流。五是社会事业协调发展。修文中学达到省级二类示范性高中标准，县医院创“二甲”通过专家评估验收，群众安全感名列全市第1位、全省名列第15位，政务环境测评全省排第1位，创建“全国计划生育优质服务先进县”通过评估验收，第六次人口普查工作全面完成。

修文县城市面貌焕然一新

Xiuwen County city has a new look

工业项目达产增效

Industrial projects production got efficiency

Xiuwen County is located in central Guizhou Province, with an area of 1,075.7 square kilometers,jurisdiction 4 towns, 6 townships (one ethnic townships), 1 Community Service Center, 217 villagers' committees, 10 residents' committees.

In 2011, the county local GDP of 5.77 billion yuan, an increase of 20.2%. Scale industrial output value of 7.51 billion yuan, an increase of 36.1%. The total fiscal revenue of 712 million yuan, an increase of 30.9%, including local fiscal revenue of 387 million yuan, an increase of 38.3%. The total fixed asset investment of 9.03 billion yuan, an increase of 76.7%. Complete non-public economic added value of 3.677 billion yuan, an increase of 28.0%. Local GDP per capita of 23,023 yuan, an increase of 20.9%; urban residents per capita disposable income and rural per capita net income of 18,721 yuan, 6,667 yuan, an increase of 18.8% and 29.4% respectively.

美丽的绿色石林

Beautiful green Shilin

First, the strong momentum of the industrial economy. Park project layout area of 17 square kilometers, 85 enterprises in the park with a total investment of 32.856 billion yuan, in the construction of the province's economic County ranked 21. Second, the obvious characteristics of modern agriculture. Based on the geographical advantages, give prominence to the "kiwi fruit, dairy, vegetables, herbal medicines" four major industries, agricultural output value 1.41 billion yuan, the Xiuwen Kiwi won the national "geographical indications" certification mark. Third, the tertiary industry is developing rapidly. In 2011, the county accumulated tourists 4,585,000 people (times), tourism revenue of 2.75 billion yuan, 1.24 billion yuan of total retail sales of social consumer goods. Fourth, the ever-changing urban landscape. To expand the county planning area of 6 square kilometers to 22 square kilometers, the urban built area of 8 square kilometers, the county's urbanization rate of 38.5%, displayed urban planning achievements of the "one city, three districts" in the province of urbanization promote the General Assembly exchange. Fifth, the coordinated development of social undertakings. Xiuwen Middle School reached the provincial model high schools II standards, the county hospital record "II A" through the acceptance of an expert assessment, the safety of the masses is ranked first in the city, the province ranked 15th, the government environment evaluation of the province ranked first, create the "National Family Planning Services Advanced County" evaluation and acceptance, fully completed sixth census work.

桃园河魔幻漂流

Taoyuan River Magic drifting

镇 远 县

Zhenyuan County

省委书记栗战书在镇远古城聆听游客们心声

Provincial Party Committee Secretary Li Zhanshu listened to the voices of visitors in Zhenyuan ancient city

第九届全国少数民族运动会火距传递

Ninth National Minority Games fire torch pass

镇远县面积1878平方公里，辖6个乡（其中1个民族乡）、6个镇，110个村民委员会、16个居民委员会。人口26.84万人，人口较多的少数民族有苗族、侗族、土家族。主要矿藏有磷、铅、锌、铜、重晶石、锰等，森林覆盖率58.04%。

镇远历史悠久，文化底蕴深厚。自汉高祖五年（公元前202年）镇远开始置县，至今已有2280多年历史，1986年被国务院命名为中国历史文化名城。近年来，镇远县始终坚持“工业强县、农业稳县、城镇带县、文化旅游兴县”四大战略，按照省、州的战略部署和确定的主基调，进一步强化以加速发展为核心，大力实施工业强县和文化旅游兴县两大重点战略，努力实现建成建设经济强县、文化旅游大县、撤县建市三大目标，着力打造东部产业承接转移基地、白酒产业基地、黔东物流基地和国内外知名旅游休闲度假基地四个基地的发展思路，在加速发展中加快转型、奋力赶超、推动跨越，继续保持了全县经济社会又好又快、更好更快发展。

中国贵州黔东南超100公里跑国际挑战赛

China Guizhou Qiandongnan 100 km run International Challenge Race

经济社会快速发展，综合实力稳步提升。全县生产总值完成30.2亿元，比上年（下同）增长20.1%；农林牧渔业总产值10.2亿元，增长0.7%；工业总产值36.7亿元，增长33.78%；财政总收入4.41亿元，增长45.76%；其中地方财政收入2.36亿元，增长80.65%；财政总支出9.54亿元，增长30.89%；固定资产投资14.3亿元，同比增长160.1%；社会消费品零售总额6.87亿元；城镇居民人均可支配收入达12099元，人均消费支出8586元；农民人均纯收入达4169元。按照全省88个县市区经济发展增比进位综合测评由2010年的第58位上升为2011年的第24位。

两台机组同时并网保养运行

Two units at the same time have network maintenance run

江南民居——付家大院正门

Southern residential areas - the main entrance to Fu Home Grand Courtyard

Zhenyuan County has an area of 1,878 square kilometers, governs 6 rural townships(including 1 ethnic townships) 6 towns, 110 villagers 'committees, 16 residents' committees. Population of 268,400, more populous ethnic minority is Miao, Dong, Tujia. The main mineral phosphorus, lead, zinc, copper, barite, manganese, 58.04% of forest coverage.

Zhenyuan has a long history, rich cultural heritage. From the Han emperor five years (202 BC) Zhenyuan start to establish county, has been 2,280 years of history, to be named by the State Council in 1986 for the Chinese historical and cultural city. In recent years, Zhenyuan always adhere to the "industrial stong county, agriculture stable county, cities and towns drive the county, culture and tourism propers the county" four major strategies, in accordance with provincial, state strategic plan and identify the main tone, further strengthening to accelerate the development as the core, vigorously implement the industrial strong county, and cultural tourism propers the county two key strategic, efforts to achieve the completion of the construction of county economic, cultural tourism county established city from county three major objectives, and strive to build the eastern industry to undertake the transfer of the base, the liquor industry base, Qiandong logistics base and the base of the well-known domestic and international tourism and leisure development ideas of the four bases, in the accelerated development to accelerate transformation, struggling to catch up, to promote leapfrog, continue to maintain the county's economic and social good and fast, better and faster development.

和谐镇远夜景

Night view of harmony Zhenyuan

高过河激情漂流

Gaoguo River passion drift

Rapid economic and social development, the comprehensive strength has been improving steadily. Completion of the county's GDP by 3.02 billion yuan, up 20.1% over the previous year; agriculture, forestry, animal husbandry and fishery output value 1.02 billion yuan, up 0.7%; industrial output value 3.67 billion yuan, up 33.78%; total fiscal revenue of 441 million yuan, up 45.76%; local fiscal revenue of 236 million yuan, an increase of 80.65%; total fiscal expenditure of 954 million yuan, an increase of 30.89%; investment in fixed assets of 1.43 billion yuan, an increase of 160.1%; 687 million yuan of total retail sales of social consumer goods; urban residents per capita disposable income reached 12,099 yuan, 8,586 yuan of per capita consumption expenditure; the per capita net income of farmers reached 4,169 yuan. Increase in accordance with the economic development of the province's 88 counties and districts carry comprehensive evaluation increased from 58th in 2010 to 24th in 2011.

万亩杂交水稻制种基地
Thousand mu of hybrid rice seed production bases

江古现代烟草示范基地
Jianggu modern tobacco demonstration base

报京三月三喜庆歌堂（摄影/何昌华）
Reported in Beijing March 3 festive songs Church (Photography / He Changhua)

土家农历“八月八”，以唢呐、长号、傩戏最为特色，充满了神秘的土家色彩，图为刀梯绝活
Tujia Lunar "August 8", the most characteristic, suona, trombone, Nuo opera, full of mysterious the Tujia color, photo shows Daoti unique skills

腾龙虎跃
Dragon Tiger Leap

园区功能逐步增强，工业经济发展壮大。2011年启动基础设施项目16个，开工建设项目12个，完成各类投资约9.85亿元；新引进技改及工业项目共21个，总投资14.94亿元；实施技改扩建项目10个，完成投资5.25亿元。进一步加大招商引资力度，全年招商引进工业新项目、大项目项目55个，开工建设项目46个，开工率达83.6%，完成协议资金270.47亿元，到位资金29.56亿元。加大非公有制企业的扶持力度，全面落实企业奖励扶持政策，全年兑现扶持奖励资金2082.2万元。

农业农村发展加快，农民增收渠道拓宽。全县完成农业总产值9.99亿元，增长5.9%。收购烤烟5.88万担，实现产值4961.5万元。积极抓好科技示范工作。完成了2500亩水稻制种基地建设、5600亩烟水配套工程和1310亩土地整治。完成了农业生态观光园和农业生态养殖园大鲵养殖基地、冷水养鱼基地建设。

配套设施不断完善，文化旅游蓬勃发展。通过加强旅游基础设施和城市配套功能建设，村旅游发展加快，丰富古城文化内涵，全力推出“古韵镇远”文化品牌。全年接待游客231.9万人次，实现旅游综合收入20.5亿元，分别同比增长45.92%和39%。

社会事业加强、民生工作改善。一是教育事业全面推进。二是卫生事业不断巩固提升。三是民生保障力度加大。

龙潭《梦泽》
Longtan "Mengze"

“五月五”龙舟节
"May 5th" Dragon Boat Festival

㵲阳河孔雀开屏
Wuyang river peacock

铁溪龙池
Tiexi Longchi

The park features gradually increase, the industrial economy to grow and develop. In 2011, start 16 infrastructure projects, 12 projects under construction, to complete the various types of investment of about 985 million yuan; the introduction of new technical innovation and a total of 21 industrial projects with a total investment of 1.494 billion yuan; implementation of technical innovation expansion project 10 , completed to invest 525 million yuan. To further increase investment, the annual investment to the introduction of 55 new industrial projects, large projects, 46 projects under construction, start rate was 83.6%, complete agreement funds of 27.047 billion yuan, 2.956 billion yuan of funds in place. Increase efforts to support non-public enterprises, the full implementation of corporate incentive support policies, the annual honor to support the reward fund of 20.822 million yuan.

Agriculture and rural development to accelerate, increasing farmers' income to widen the channel. The county agricultural output value of 999 million yuan, an increase of 5.9%. 58,800 Tam acquisition of flue-cured tobacco, the output value of 49.615 million yuan. Good grasp of science and technology demonstration. Completion of the 2,500 mu of rice seed production bases, supporting projects of the 5,600 mu of tobacco water and 1,310 mu of land remediation. The agro-ecological tourist park and agro-ecological farming, garden giant salamander breeding base, cold water fish farming bases construction.

Supporting facilities constantly improve, cultural tourism is booming. By strengthening the tourism infrastructure and urban support functions building, village tourism development accelerated, rich in ancient cultural connotation, and the full launch of "old rhyme Zhenyuan" cultural brand. 2.319 million of annual tourists trips, tourism income of 2.05 billion yuan, an increase of 45.92% and 39% respectively.

Social undertakings to strengthen, improve people's livelihood. First, the education comprehensively pushed. Second, continue to consolidate and improve health services. Third, livelihood security intensified.

剑 河 县

Jianhe County mn

在州委、州政府和县委的正确领导下，全县上下认真贯彻落实科学发展观，坚持把抢抓机遇、加快发展作为富民兴县的第一要务，经济社会发展步入了一个崭新的阶段。

产业结构明显优化，经济实力显著增强。坚持按照“做优一产、做大二产、做强三产”的目标，不断优化产业结构，三次产业结构逐渐趋于合理，2011年全县三次产业比重调整为26.3:19.9:53.8；农业经济亮点纷呈；工业经济逐渐崛起；第三产业迅猛发展。

基础设施明显改善，城乡面貌焕然一新。交通网络更加畅通，建成通村公路897公里，通乡油路248公里，全县通车总里程达1590公里；水利建设不断加强；实施饮水安全工程120处，有效解决10.5万人的饮水安全；城镇建设步伐加快。

2012年4月19日，县委书记江朝伦陪同省委巡视四组尹新黔组长一行到屯州工业园区视察

April 19, 2012, the county party secretary Jiang Zhaolun accompanied by the provincial party committee inspecting No.4 groups head Yin Xinqian and his team to inspect Tunzhou Industrial Park

2012年2月9日，县委书记江朝伦一行到贵州昌昊中药材发展有限公司钩藤GAP实验基地调研

February 9, 2012, the county party secretary Jiang Zhaolun and his team to have research in Guizhou Chang Hao Chinese Herbal Medicines Development Co., Ltd. the Uncaria GAP experimental base

2012年3月1日，县委常委、常务副县长龙开泉陪同省统计局冯育毅副局长等一行到屯州工业园区进行调研

March 1, 2012, the County Committee, Deputy Mayor Long Kaiquan accompanied by the Deputy Secretary of the Provincial Bureau of Statistics Feng Yuyi and his team to have research in Tunzhou Industrial Park

改革开放步伐加快，发展后劲日益增强。集体林权制度改革、国有企业改革改制全面完成；政府机构改革、医药卫生体制改革不断深化；招商引资工作力度不断加大。

民生保障扎实推进，人民生活更加殷实。累计投入国债资金、财政扶贫资金26873万元，实施扶贫项目339个，减少低收入贫困人口2.13万人；认真落实各项惠农政策，累计发放涉农补助补贴资金5538万元；着力完善城乡救助体系；建立健全城镇低保和农村低保制度，狠抓农村救灾救济工作。

社会事业全面进步，和谐氛围日渐浓厚。加快教育事业发展；大力发展医疗卫生事业；妥善解决人口计生问题；积极繁荣文化事业；着力推进国防后备力量建设，2011年被授予省级“双拥”模范县；深入开展文明卫生创建活动；着力维护社会和谐稳定。

40万立方米板材建设项目开工仪式

400,000 cubic meters of sheet construction project groundbreaking ceremony

民主法制进程加快，行政能力明显提升。着力推进依法行政；转变政府职能；清理行政许可，削减行政审批；依法决策、科学决策、民主决策进一步加强。

剑河县重大项目开工建设动员大会
Jianhe County major projects started construction mobilization meeting

正在建设中的城西路网
Under construction of the west city road network

投资3700万元，正在建设中的清水江大桥
Investment of 37 million yuan, the construction of Qingshuijiang Bridge

Under the correct leadership of the state committee, state government, the county up and down earnestly implement the scientific concept of development, adhere to seize opportunities, accelerate the development as the top priority of riching people prospering the county, economic and social development has entered a brand new stage.

剑河县久仰乡党义村集中建设
Jianhe County Jiuyang town Dangyi village to concentrate on building

Industrial structure has optimized, the economic strength has markedly increased. Adhere to "excellent first industry, bigger capacity of the second industry, and strengthen the tertiary industry" the goal, and continuously optimize the industrial structure, three industrial structure gradually tends to be reasonable, in 2011, the proportion of three industries in the county to adjust for 26.3:19.9:53.8; agriculture economic got bright scene; the gradual rise of the industrial economy; the rapid development of tertiary industry.

Infrastructure construction improved significantly, the new look of urban and rural areas.More smooth flow of traffic network, built through the village of road 897 km, 248 km oil road through the township, the county total mileage of 1,590 km; continue to strengthen water conservancy construction; implementation of the Drinking Water Safety Project 120, an effective solution to the safety of drinking water of 105,000 people; the accelerated pace of urban construction.

The accelerated pace of reform and opening up, increasing potential for further development. Reform of collective forest right system, the reform and restructuring of state-owned enterprises fully completed; reform of government institutions, medical and health system continued to deepen; investment efforts continue to increase.

Livelihood security made solid progress, and the people lead a better life. Invested a total of treasury bonds, financial funds are to 268.73 million yuan, the implementation of the Poverty Alleviation Project 339, to reduce low-income poor population of 21,300; conscientiously implement preferential agricultural policy, the cumulative release of 55.38 million yuan of funds for agriculture-related grants subsidies; efforts to improve the urban and rural rescue system; improve the urban low and rural subsistence allowances system, pay close attention to relief work in rural areas.

Comprehensive social progress, harmonious atmosphere is growing strong. Accelerate the development of education; vigorously develop the cause of medical and hygiene; properly resolve the problem of population and family planning; positive prosperity of cultural undertakings; efforts to promote the national defense reserve force building, in 2011 was awarded the provincial "double support" model of a county; to create depth of civilization health activities; efforts to maintain social harmony and stability.

Democracy and the legal process to speed up, the administrative capacity has improved significantly. Efforts to promote the administration according to law; transformation of government functions; clean up the administrative license, the reduction of administrative examination and approval; decision-making according to law, scientific decision-making, democratic decision making to further strengthen.

三 穗 县

Sansui County

县委书记袁尚勇（右二）到雪洞镇调研农业产业化工作
County party secretary Yuan Shangyong (second from right) to the Xuedong town have research of the industrialization of agriculture

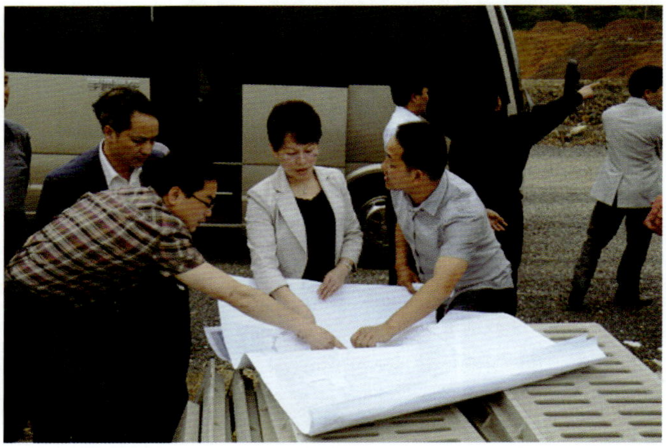

县长付乐欣（中）调研园区建设情况
Magistrate Fu Lexin (middle) has research of park construction

三穗县位于贵州省东部，是贵州省“东联”经济发展的前沿阵地，素有“黔东要塞”和“千里苗疆门户”之称。面积1035.8平方公里，辖5镇、4乡，159个村、5个居民社区，人口22万人，其中少数民族占75%。三穗交通区位优势明显，是贵州入湘及东出两广的重要喉舌通道，国家60号高速公路、320国道横贯县境，随着三（穗）黎（平）高速公路、长昆快速铁路客运专线及其三穗站的规划建设，交通区位优势将更加凸显。

2011年，全县上下认真贯彻落实科学发展观，致力于“项目突破、经济突围、面貌突破”奋斗目标，紧紧围绕建设黔东中心城市、黔东旅游服务中心、黔东商贸物流中心和黔东产业承接基地、黔东返乡创业基地、黔东轻工产业基地的“一城、两中心、三基地”目标定位，坚定不移实施“工业强县、城镇带县、商贸活县”战略，着力调结构、提质量、抓改革、惠民生，全县经济社会持续快速健康发展。

2011年，全县生产总值160835万元，比上年增长18.8%；财政总收入18393万元，比上年增长62.2%；年末金融机构各项存款余额219202万元，各项贷款余额100136万元，比上年分别增长22.5%和21.5%；全县社会消费品零售总额73594万元，比上年增长18.7%；农民人均纯收入3954.90元，比上年增长27.3%。在2011年全省88个县（市、区、特区）经济发展增比进位综合测评中，由2010年的67位上升到32位，进位35个位次。

《银色的穗城》
Silver Sansui City

《生态三穗鸭——飞跃》
"Ecological Sansui duck - leap"

新农村
New rural

寨头苗族二月二穰桥节
Cold head Miao February 2 Rangqiao Festival

Sansui County is located in the eastern part of Guizhou Province, Guizhou Province "East Communication" of the economic development of the forward position, known as "Qiandong fortress" and " housands of miles Miao portal" said. Area of 1,035.8 square kilometers, jurisdiction 5 towns, 4 townships, 159 villages 5 residents' community, population 220,000, which minority people accounted for 75%. Sansui traffic advantage is obvious, is an important mouthpiece of the channel of Guizhou into Hunan and east to Guangdong and Guangxi, National Highway No. 60, 320 National Highway running through the county, with San(Sui), Li (Ping), highway, Chang-Kun railway passenger special line and Sansui station planning and construction, traffic advantages will become more prominent.

In 2011, the whole county to seriously implement the scientific concept of development, is committed to "project breakthrough, economic breakthrough, the face breakthrough" goal, closely around the construction Qiandong center city, Qiandong tourism service center, Qiandong trade and logistics center, and Qiandong industry to undertake base, Qiandong home business base, Qiandong Light Industry base "one city, the two centers, three bases" targeting, firmly implement the strategy of "industrial strong the county, cities and towns push the county, trade live county", focus on adjusting the structure, to improve the quality, focus on reform and improve people's livlihood, the county's economic and social got sustained, rapid and healthy development.

斗笠人家
Hats people

In 2011, the county's GDP was 1.60835 billion yuan, an increase of 18.8% over the previous year; total fiscal revenue of 183.93 million yuan, an increase of 62.2% over the previous year; the balance of deposits of financial institutions at the end of the year was 2.19202 billion yuan, the loan balance 1.00136 billion yuan, an increase of 22.5% and 21.5% respectively over the previous year; county retail sales of social consumer goods of a total of 735.94 million yuan, an increase of 18.7% over the previous year; rural per capita net income was 3,954.9 yuan, an increase of 27.3% over the previous year. In 2011 the province's 88 counties (cities, districts, DC) economic development growth than carry comprehensive evaluation increased from 67 in 2010 to 32, decimal 35.

铜仁市碧江区

Tongren City Bijiang District

陈代文书记调研廉租房
Chen Daiwen secretary has survey of low-rent housing

杨彪区长现场指挥抢险工作
Yang Biao Mayor direct rescue work scene

铜仁市碧江区于2011年11月14日根据《省人民政府关于撤销铜仁地区设立地级铜仁市的通知》（黔府发［2011］34号）规定而设立， 以原县级铜仁市（不含谢桥办事处、茶店镇、鱼塘乡、大坪乡）的行政区域为碧江区的行政区域。碧江区下辖4个办事处（市中、环北、河西、灯塔），4镇（川洞、坝黄、漾头、云场坪），5乡（和平、滑石、桐木坪、瓦屋、六龙山），20个社区（居）委会，69个村委会。面积1012平方公里。2011年户籍人口为30万人，常驻人口为29.52万人。

碧江区位于贵州省东北部，是镶嵌在武陵深处的一颗黔东明珠。碧江区东接湖南、北邻重庆，素有“黔东重镇、黔东门户”之美称。区内机场、铁路、高等级公路，以成为连接湘、黔、渝、鄂四省市的交通枢纽城市。

碧江区地方生产总值为63.15亿元，人均生产总值21394元；全社会固定资产完成79.32亿元；社会消费品零售完成24.39亿元；财政总收入完成6.26亿元，其中：地方财政收入完成4.2亿元；城镇居民人均可支配收入为13846元；农民人均纯收入为5339元。

通过近几年文明卫生城市创建活动的开展，碧江区城市品位迅速提升，先后荣获“中国西部名城”、“中国天然钓都”、“全国绿化模范先进（县）市”、“全国计划生育优质服务县”、“中国传统龙舟之乡”、“2009中华十大生态亲水美景”等称号。特别是在2010年成功举办第五届省旅发大会在铜仁召开后，全区上下正在创建“优秀旅游城市目的地”。

碧江区——金滩
Bijiang District - Gold Beach

碧江风景
Bijiang landscape

梦幻锦江夜景
Dream Jinjiang night scene

Tongren City Bijiang District on November 14, 2011 according to "the Provincial People's Government on the revocation of Tongren Prefecture, the establishment of the prefecture-level city of Tongren (Guizhou Government Issue[2011] No. 34), provides the establishment of Bijiang District. Took the original county-level city of Tongren city (without Xieqiao offices, Chadian Town, Yutang Township, Daping Township) administrative region as the Bijiang district administrative areas. Bijiang under the jurisdiction of the 4 offices (Shizhong, Huanbei, Hexi, Dengta), 4 towns (Chuandong, Bahuang,Yangtou, Yuchangping), 5 townships (Heping, Huashi, Tongmuping, Wawu, Liulongshan), 20 community (neighborhood) committees, 69 village committees. An area of 1,012 square kilometers. The 2011 household population of 300,000 people with a permanent population of 295,200.

2012碧江区端午龙舟赛
The 2012 Bijiang Dragon Boat Race

Bijiang District is located in the northeast of Guizhou Province, is a mosaic pearl in depths Wuling in Qiandong. The Bijiang east of Hunan Province, north of Chongqing, known as the "city of eastern Guizhou, eastern Guizhou portal" reputation. Airports in the region, railway, highway, to become a transportation hub connecting the four provinces of Hunan, Guizhou, Chongqing, Hubei.

Bijiang District Local GDP of 6.315 billion yuan, per capita GDP of 21,394 yuan; total fixed assets are completed 7.932 billion yuan; social consumer goods retail completed 2.439 billion yuan; total fiscal revenue of 626 million yuan, of which: local fiscal revenue 420 million yuan; per capita disposable income of urban residents was 13,846 yuan; rural per capita net income of 5,339 yuan.

Health and civilized cities activities carried out in recent years, Bijiang urban quality in rapid increase, has won the "China's western famous city", "the natural fishing capital", "National Model Green advanced (County) City", "National Family Planning quality services county", "the hometown of the Chinese traditional Dragon Boat", "2009 China top ten eco-hydrophilic beauty," and so on. In 2010, successfully held the fifth province Tourism General Assembly convened in Tongren, the whole region is being created "outstanding tourist city destination".

夜郎故地——六枝特区

The Yelang old haunt - Liuzhi SAR

市人大常委会副主任、六枝特区党委书记高玉林在六盘水市2012年二季度200个项目集中开工暨六枝路喜循环经济园区开工仪式上讲话

Municipal People's Congress Standing Committee, deputy director, Liuzhi SAR party secretary Gao Yulin made speech on 200 projects are concentrated starting in Liupanshui City the second quarter of 2012, Liuzhi road circular economy park groundbreaking ceremony

特区党委副书记、政府区长舒勇（左一），副区长周金平（左三）在永盛冶炼有限公司调研

Deputy party secretary of the SAR, Government Mayor Shu Yong (first from left), Deputy Mayor Zhou Jinping (third from left) in Yongsheng Smelting Limited have research

特区党委副书记、政府区长舒勇（左四），人大副主任王箐（右一）在木岗工业园区检查工作

Deputy party secretary of the SAR, Government Mayor Shu Yong (fourth from left), the National People's Congress, deputy director Wang Qing (first from right) in the Mugang Industrial Park checking the work

六枝气候宜人，四季如春。这里是中国凉都•六盘水市的东大门，古夜郎腹地，距省会贵阳172公里，距六盘水市中心98公里，距黄果树大瀑布45公里，具有良好的交通网络和区位优势。这里矿产资源富集，已探明煤炭储量33亿吨，是全国重点产煤县。这里水能和生物资源丰富，水能资源理论蕴藏量14.96万千瓦，森林覆盖率25.26%，有天麻、杜仲等87科、158个物种，是贵州省地道中药材种植基地县。这里旅游资源独具特色，喀斯特地貌发育典型，自然风光秀丽，少数民族风情浓郁。境内还有牂牁江省级风景名胜区、月亮河省级森林公园、亚洲第一座生态博物馆——梭戛生态博物馆、中国唯一布依生态园——凉都•月亮河夜郎布依文化生态园。

2011年全区生产总值达67.87亿元，增长19.7%，人均生产总值13728元；财政总收入达6.66亿元，增长25.66%，公共财政预算收入4.99亿元增长75%；全社会固定资产投资75.2亿元，增长150.67%；工业总产值94.32亿元，增长50.95%；社会消费品零售总额19.59亿元，增长20%；农民人均纯收入达4026元。

近年来，六枝加快改革步伐，走出了一条独具特色的经济发展路子，全面实施"农业稳区、工业强区、生态立区、城镇亮区、科教兴区、旅游活区、民营富区"的发展战略，经济和社会各项事业稳步推进，改革开放和现代化建设步入新阶段，呈现出前所未有的蓬勃发展局面。

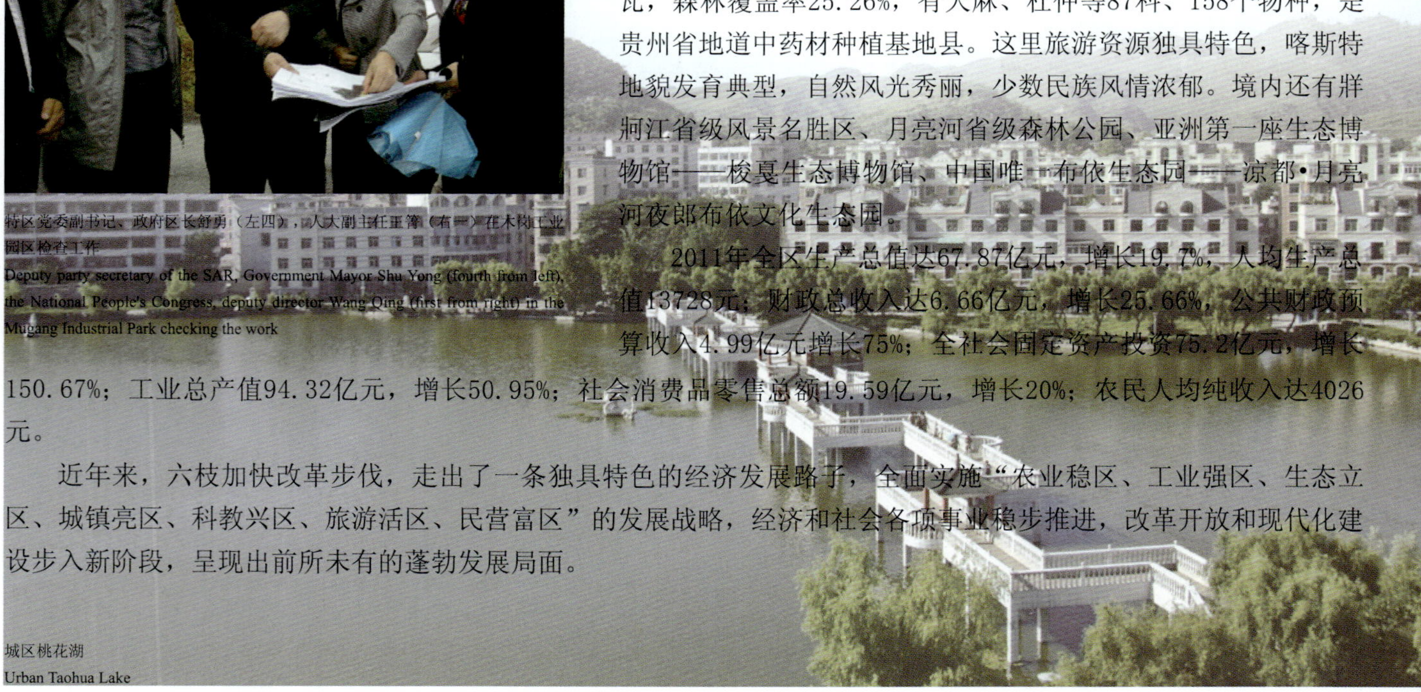

城区桃花湖

Urban Taohua Lake

特区政府副区长李仕强（左一）在龙场乡检查廉租房建设工作
SAR Government, deputy mayor Li Shiqiang (first from left) to check low-rent housing construction work in Longchang Township

古朴神秘的六枝特区梭戛长角苗习俗——拦路酒与拦路歌
Ancient and mysterious Liuzhi SAR Suojia Chaojiao Miao customs - highway wine and highway song

月亮河森林公园——神鼓之韵
Moon River Forest Park - God drum Rhyme

Liuzhi has pleasant climate year-round spring. This is the east gate of China cool capital•Liupanshui City, ancient Yelang the hinterland, away from the provincial capital Guiyang 172 kilometers, from Liupanshui city center 98 km, 45 km away from Huangguoshu Great Falls, has a good transportation network and regional advantages. Rich mineral resources, has proven coal reserves of 3.3 billion tons, is a national key coal-producing counties. Where hydro and rich biological resources and reserves of 149,600 kilowatts of hydropower resources in theory, the forest coverage rate of 25.26%, Tianma, Eucommia and 87 families, 158 species, is the traditional Chinese medicinal materials planting base county in Guizhou Province. Here unique tourism resources, karst development is typical, beautiful natural scenery, folk customs of ethnic minorities. Territory Zangke river provincial scenic spots, Moon River provincial forest park, Asia's first eco Museum - Suojia Eco-museum, the only Buyi Ecological Park - cool capital• Moon River Yelang Buyi culture ecological park.

In 2011, the region's GDP reached 6.787 billion yuan, up 19.7%, per capita GDP of 13,728 yuan; total fiscal revenue reached 666 million yuan, an increase of 25.66%, the public budget revenue increased by 75% from 499 million yuan; fixed assets investment of 7.52 billion yuan, an increase of 150.67%; industrial output value of 9.432 billion yuan, an increase of 50.95%; total retail sales of 1.959 billion yuan, an increase of 20%; per capita net income of farmers reached 4,026 yuan.

In recent years, Liuzhi speed up the pace of reform, out of a unique economic development path, full implementation of the "metastable zone of agriculture, industry strong area, ecological build area, the town highlights area, science and education prospers area, tourist living area, private business rich area" development strategy, economic and social various undertakings made steady progress, reform and opening up and modernization drive has entered a new stage, showing an unprecedented booming situation.

国家地质公园——六枝特区牂牁江风景名胜区美景
National Geological Park - Liuzhi SAR Zangke river beauty of the scenic spots

兴 义 市

Xingyi City

兴义市桔山新城区
Xingyi City Jushan New District

兴义市位于贵州省西南部，是黔西南布依族苗族自治州州府所在地和全州政治、经济、文化、信息中心，面积2911平方公里，耕地面积3.04万公顷，森林覆盖率37%。辖5个乡、17个镇、8个街道办事处。人口84万人，其中少数民族人口占23.4%，人口较多的少数民族有布依族、苗族、回族。兴义钟灵毓秀，物产丰饶。

2011年，全市生产总值完成166.22亿元，财政总收入突破26.81亿元，固定资产投资完成123.1亿元，全社会消费品零售总额完成75.71亿元，农民人均纯收入达到5396元，城镇居民人均可支配收入达到17004元，全市招商引资到位资金达到56亿元。

工业经济增势强劲，工业化进程日益加快。城市建设日新月异，城镇化水平不断提升。农业农村经济发展，扶贫攻坚取得新突破。旅游产业优势凸显，发展后劲不断增强。基础设施投入加大，发展环境日趋优化。

穿云洞公园
Chuanyundong Park

八一公园夜景
Bayi Park night view

万峰湖——湖光叠翠
Wanfeng Lake - lake Pinnacle

马岭河峡谷——百里画廊
Maling River Gorge- Barry Gallery

Xingyi City is in the southeast of Guizhou Province, is the state capital of Southwest Guizhou Buyi and Miao Autonomous Prefecture and the center of statewide political, economic, cultural and information, with an area of 2,911 square kilometers, 30,400 hectares of arable land, forest coverage rate of 37%. Jurisdiction over 5 townships, 17 towns and 8 subdistrict offices. Population of 840,000 people, including ethnic minority population accounted for 23.4%, the more populous minority is Buyi, Miao, Hui. The Xingyi is pregnant with beauty and rich products.

In 2011, the GDP of 16.622 billion yuan, the total fiscal revenue exceeded 2.681 billion yuan, fixed assets investment of 12.31 billion yuan, total retail sales of the society completed 7.571 billion yuan and rural per capita net income reached 5,396 yuan, per capita disposable income of urban residents reached 17,004 yuan, the city's investment of funds in place to reach 5.6 billion yuan.

Industrial economy have been strong, ever-accelerating process of industrialization. The rapid urban construction, urbanization got rising standards. Agricultural and rural economic development, aiding the poor to achieve new breakthroughs. The tourism industry highlighting the advantages, continuously enhance the potential for further development. Infrastructure increased investment and development environment is becoming increasingly optimized.

毕节市七星关区

The Bijie Qixingguan District

市委常委、区委书记宫晓农
Municipal Committee, Party Secretary Gong Xiaonong

区委副书记、区长刘建平
District committee deputy secretary, mayor Liu Jianping

宫晓农书记（左五）、刘建平区长（左二）到德溪新区调研
Gong Xiaonong secretary (fifth from left), Liu Jianping mayor(second from left) to Dexi new district have research

毕节市七星关区，汉为平夷郡治，东晋为平蛮郡治，唐、宋属禄洲治所，元代建驿，明代设卫，清康熙二十六年（公元1687年）建县，1993年12月经国务院批准撤县建市，2011年11月撤销县级毕节市，设立毕节市七星关区，以原县级毕节市行政区域为七星关区行政区域。

毕节市七星关区位于贵州省西北部，地处川、滇、黔三省交汇处，是毕节市的政治、经济、科技文化和信息中心。东与金沙、大方两县接壤，南与纳雍县毗邻，西与赫章县及云南省镇雄县、威信县相连，北与四川省古蔺、叙永两县交界，是西南地区重要的物资集散地。全区面积3410.98平方公里，辖27个镇、8个乡、6个办事处，聚居着汉、彝、白、苗、布依等23个民族，人口151万人。境内地势西高东低，平均海拔1511米，气候温和，雨量充沛，属亚热带湿润气候，区内冬无严寒、夏无酷暑，被誉为“中国十大避暑旅游城市”。

2011年全区生产总值完成152.71亿元，同比增长19.0%，固定资产投资完成146.25亿元，同比增长55.31%；财政总收入完成21.57亿元，同比增长86.68%；社会消费品零售总额达到54.65亿元，同比增长20.6%，农民人均纯收入4412元，同比增长21.74%。随着改革开放的不断深入，全区经济已进入高速发展的黄金期。现已成为西部地区最具活力的地区。

新村晨曦
New Village Dawn

居乐新村
Jule new village

The rich ethnic customs and quaint. Annual passionate Yi Torch Festival, a solemn Hui Guierbang Festival, cheerfu Miao Huashan festival; folk song "Axilixi" is widely sung, comedy living fossil "summarized Tai Kut" was included in the national Directory of non-material culture, reflect Miao history, "mass migration Dance" Rhyme long; Buyi "planting song" is original and quaint. There are hair products, paper cutting, batik and other kinds of folk crafts.

远眺岩格新村
Overlooking the Yange Village

In 2011, Weining comprehensive evaluation of ranking among the 13th of the province, the city's 3rd; year-on-year rise in 2009 were 41th and 6th, a year-on-year in 2010 increased by 8 and 3 respectively. GDP of 7.907 billion yuan, year-on-year (compared with 2009), an increase of 29.03%; investment in fixed assets of 9.5 billion yuan, an increase of 381.01%; total fiscal revenue of 1.03 billion yuan, an increase of 105.26%; attract investment capital in place of 7.05 billion yuan, an increase of 450.78%; large-scale industrial output value completed 4.81 billion yuan, an increase of 191.16%; scale industrial added value 1.455 billion yuan, an increase of 126.99%; the balance of deposits of financial institutions to complete the 5.3 billion yuan , an increase of 56.43%; savings deposits of urban and rural residents to complete 3 billion yuan, an increase of 77.43%; financial institutions, the loan balance was 1.9 billion yuan, an increase of 61.29%; retail sales of social commodities total value of 1.49 billion yuan, up 47.67%; Urban residents per capita disposable income of 14,174 yuan, an increase of 3,440 yuan; rural per capita net income of 4,068 yuan, an increase of 1,515 yuan.

In 2011, Weining County, was grant by the State Council "national food production advanced unit" honorary title, "Twelfth Five Year of the first batch of the most unique charm of tourism county", "advanced unit of national scientific and technological benefits of agricultural Village", "national scientific and technological demonstration County", "National Women civilization station", "the second inventory of research and experimental development work advanced unit", "national civilized village", "the Ninth National Games preparatory work for advanced collective" national honor. The experience of the implementation of the Independent Commission Against Risk Vigilance mechanism in recognition of the Central Commission for Discipline Inspection and the Ministry of Supervision. 23 work at the provincial level in recognition, 66 working for municipal recognition.

雪山镇法地石林
Xueshan town Fadi Stone forest

草海镇大马城村广场
Caohai Town Damacheng Village Square

泰丰园
The Taifeng Garden

建设种羊场
Construction of stud farm

迤那合心村公园
Yinahexin Village Park

秀水乡中海村村公所
Siushui Village Zhonghai Village Office

关怀烤烟生产
Care for flue-cured tobacco production

民族风情浓郁古朴。有一年一度热情奔放的是彝族火把节、庄严肃穆的回族古尔邦节、欢快明朗的苗族花山节；民歌《阿西里西》广为传唱，喜剧活化石“撮太吉”被列入国家非物质文化名录，反映苗族历史的《大迁徙舞》意韵悠长；布依族的《插秧歌》原始古朴。有毛制品、剪纸、蜡染等各类民族民间工艺品。

2011年威宁县综合测评排名位居全省13位、全市3位；同比2009年分别上升了41位和6位、同比2010年分别上升8位和3位。实现生产总值79.07亿元，同比（与2009年相比，下同）增长29.03%；完成固定资产投资95亿元，同比增长381.01%；财政总收入完成10.3亿元，同比增长105.26%；招商引资到位资金70.5亿元，同比增长450.78%；规模工业总产值完成48.1亿元，同比增长191.16%；规模工业增加值完成14.55亿元，同比增长126.99%；金融机构各项存款余额完成53亿元，同比增长56.43%；城乡居民储蓄余额完成30亿元，同比增长77.43%；金融机构各项贷款余额完成19亿元，同比增长61.29%；社会商品零售总额完成14.9亿元，同比增长47.67%；城镇居民人均可支配收入完成14174元，同比增加3440元；农民人均纯收入完成4068元，同比增加1515元。

2011年威宁县被国务院授予“全国粮食生产先进单位”荣誉称号，获得了“全国十二五首批最具特色魅力旅游名县”、“全国科普惠农兴村先进单位”、“全国科普示范县”、“全国巾帼文明岗”、“全国第二次研究与实验发展清查工作先进单位”、“全国文明村寨”、“全国第九届运动会筹备工作先进集体”等国家级荣誉。推行廉政风险预警防范机制的经验被中央纪委和国家监察部表彰。有23项工作获得省级表彰，66项工作获得市级表彰。

西凉山上的风电站
The Xiliang mountain wind power plant

高架如云
Elevated clouds

建成投产中的润基水泥厂
Runji cement plant put into operation

明天更美好
Better tomorrow

Weining Yi Hui and Miao Autonomous County is located in northwest Guizhou, an area of 6,298 square kilometers, with an average elevation of 2,200 m, is the largest and highest county in Guizhou Province. County annual average sunshine of 1,812 hours, known as the city of highland sun. County jurisdiction over 35 townships and 610 administrative villages, 15 neighborhood communities, inhabited by the Yi, Hui, Miao, Buyi and other 19 ethnic groups. Population of 1,434,200 people, is the only province consists of three ethnic minority autonomous counties.

Outstanding traffic advantage. Neijiang-Kunming Railway, Guiyang-Kunming railway wear over the territory, 326 national highway and 102 provincial highway, Weining is not only the "roof" of Guizhou, but also the transportation hub of Yunnan into Sichuan.

Property of a wide range of resources. The Weining is rich in potatoes, buckwheat, corn and other food material and vegetables, tobacco, kidney beans, grinding taro and other cash crops as well as apple, pineapple, walnuts and other fresh and dried fruits. Chinese herbal medicines have Codonopsis, Tianma, Cork, Panax, Pinellia, Eucommia ulmoides, Magnolia, is the famous "Southern potato town", "the hometown of Chinese herbal medicine", "the hometown of Animal" and "South deciduous fruit base".

Rich in mineral resources. More than 30 varieties of coal, iron, lead, zinc, copper, gold, silver, coal resources prospective reserves of 5 billion tons, iron ore reserves of 100 million tons, 598,000 tons of gypsum reserves, 600,000 tons of lead and zinc reserves.

Hydro, solar and wind energy resource development prospects. Hydro resource potential of 525,000 kilowatts; low latitude, high altitude, the geographical characteristics of the solar energy resources and wind energy resources to the highest in Guizhou, wind energy the theories installed capacity of 1 million kilowatts.

Long and glorious history and culture, rich and colorful tourism resources. Weining was Hanyang County of the Qin Dynasty, so far, more than two thousand years of history, much domestic and foreign experts widespread concern Shimenkan, is China's first advocacy and practice of bilingual education, is China's earliest leprosy, to fluoride disease prevention and control area. The first football field, first school swimming sites in Guizhou. Was named the 2005 "China Top Ten Archaeological Discoveries of the ruins" the one in the water, the unearthed cultural relics, to fill the number of gaps in Guizhou Prehistoric Archaeology. Weining not only owns National Nature Reserve - Caohai, but also the Mabai mountains,Baicaoping of the main plateau scenery eco-tourism and Shimenkan ruins, Fengshan Temple, Yuhuangge, historical and cultural tourism.

威宁自治县

Weining Autonomous County

威宁自治县会展中心
Weining Autonomous County Convention and Exhibition Center

住宅小区
Residential district

君怡广场
Juyi Plaza

建设中的奥体花园
Construction of the Olmpic Garden

威宁彝族回族苗族自治县位于贵州西北部，面积6298平方公里，平均海拔2200米，是贵州省面积最大、海拔最高的县。县城年平均日照为1812小时，被誉为高原阳光城。全县辖35个乡镇、610个行政村、15个社区居委会，居住着彝、回、苗、布依等19个民族。人口143.42万人，是全省唯一由三个少数民族自治的县。

交通区位优势突出。内昆铁路、贵昆铁路穿境而过，326国道，102省道在县城交汇，威宁既是贵州的“屋脊”，又是进滇入川的交通要塞。

物产资源种类繁多。威宁盛产马铃薯、荞麦、玉米等粮食作物和蔬菜、烤烟、芸豆、磨芋等经济作物以及苹果、黄梨、核桃等干鲜水果。中药材有党参、天麻、黄柏、三七、半夏、杜仲、厚朴等，是著名的“南方马铃薯之乡”、“中药材之乡”、“畜牧之乡”和“南方落叶水果基地”。

矿产资源丰富。有煤、铁、铅、锌、铜、金、银等30余个品种，其中煤炭资源远景储量达50亿吨，铁矿石储量1亿吨，石膏储量59.8万吨，铅锌储量60万吨。

水能、光能和风能资源开发前景好。水能资源蕴藏量达52.5万千瓦；低纬度、高海拔的地理特征，使这里的光能资源和风能资源为贵州之冠，风能理论装机容量达100万千瓦。

历史文化悠久而辉煌，旅游资源丰富多彩。威宁秦朝为汉阳县地，至今有两千多年的历史，备受国内外专家广泛关注的石门坎，是我国第一个倡导和实践双语教学的地方，是中国最早的麻风病、地氟病防治区。有贵州的第一个足球场、第一个学校游泳遗址。被评为2005年度“中国十大考古新发现”之一的中水遗址，出土的文化遗物，填补了贵州史前考古的多项空白。威宁不仅有国家级自然保护区——草海，而且还有马摆大山、百草坪为主的高原风光生态旅游，以及石门坎遗址、凤山寺、玉皇阁等历史文化旅游。

投资2.5亿元，仅用120天就建成的永靖大道通车仪式
Investment of 250 million yuan, only 120 days on the built Yongjing Avenue Opening Ceremony

省级经济开发区息烽磷煤化工基地一角
Provincial Economic Development Zone of Xifeng Phosphorus coal chemical base corner

In 2011, Xifeng county committee, county People's Government in accordance with the path of "scientific development road, building the ecological civilization county", unswerving implementation of the "industrial strong the county, science and education prosper county, environment build the county, tourism live county" strategy to overcome the serious the impact of natural disasters, work together, work hard, and successfully completed the goals and tasks, to achieve a good start in the "2th Five-Year" Plan.

天下第一汤息烽温泉
The world first soup Xifeng Hot Spring

Local GDP of 6.465 billion yuan, an increase of 20.3%; per capita GDP has crossed the $ 4,000 mark; fixed assets investment was 8.524 billion yuan, up 70.1%; total fiscal revenue reached 709 million yuan, an increase of 28.47%, local fiscal revenue of 439 million yuan, an increase of 42.82%. The urban residents per capita disposable income and rural per capita net income reached 17,528 yuan and 6434 yuan respectively, an increase of 9.4% and 26.6% respectively. Industrial strong county strategy moving forward strongly, to achieve the above-scale industrial output value of 16.599 billion yuan, an increase of 44%. Non-public economy has made rapid progress, to achieve the increase in non-public economy value of 3.128 billion yuan, an increase of 22%. Investment has achieved remarkable results, the capital of 2.626 billion yuan in place, an increase of 32.67%, the direct utilization of foreign capital of $ 9,660,000. The development of the service industry to a new level, to achieve 1.039 billion yuan of total retail sales of social consumer goods, an increase of 20.1%.

全国红色旅游精品线经典景区乌江峡著名景点姊妹峰
Classic red tourist line scenic Wujiang River Gorge famous attractions Zimei Peak

Looking ahead, Xifeng County tightly around the province of the eleventh Congress proposed the "three above, one achieve, five doubled" and the city of the ninth Party Congress's "first priority two ultra an upgrade" goal to continue to promote "self-reliance, hard work, honest and loyalty, to concerted efforts first" the Xifeng spirit, firmly grasp the "accelerated development and accelerate the transition, and promote leap" the main keynote, and vigorously promote the industrialization, urbanization and agricultural modernization "three of linkage" strategy, strive to build a "spiritual high ground", efforts out of the "economic depression", unswervingly take the road of scientific development, better and faster to build ecological civilization county, to further enhance the comprehensive competitiveness of the county economy, efforts to promote the Xifeng economy social development growth than binary.

息烽县小寨坝镇新农村建设示范点
Xifeng County Xiaozhaiba Town new rural construction demonstration

息烽县

Xifeng County

息烽县城夜景一角
Xifeng county night view corner

全国爱国主义教育基地息烽集中营革命历史纪念馆
National patriotism education bases Xifeng Concentration Camp Revolutionary History Memorial Hall

2011年，息烽县委、县人民政府按照“走科学发展路，建生态文明县”的路径，坚定不移实施“工业强县、科教兴县、环境立县、旅游活县”战略，克服严重自然灾害影响，齐心协力、奋力拼搏，圆满完成了各项目标任务，实现了“十二五”规划的良好开局。

地方生产总值完成64.65亿元，增长20.3%；人均生产总值跨过了4000美元大关；固定资产投资完成85.24亿元，增长70.1%；财政总收入达到7.09亿元，增长28.47%，地方财政收入实现4.39亿元，增长42.82%。城镇居民人均可支配收入和农民人均纯收入分别达到17528元和6434元，分别增长19.4%和26.6%。工业强县战略强力推进，实现规模以上工业总产值165.99亿元，增长44%。非公经济得到长足发展，实现非公经济增加值31.28亿元，同比增长22%。招商引资取得显著成绩，到位资金26.26亿元，增长32.67%，直接利用外资966万美元。服务业发展迈上新台阶，实现社会消费品零售总额10.39亿元，增长20.1%。

展望未来，息烽县将紧紧围绕省第十一次党代会提出的“三高于、一达到、五翻番”和市第九次党代会提出的“一先二超一提升”的奋斗目标，继续弘扬“自强不息、艰苦奋斗、赤胆忠诚、协力争先”的息烽精神，牢牢把握“加速发展、加快转型、推动跨越”主基调，强力推进工业化、城镇化和农业现代化“三化联动”战略，着力构筑“精神高地”，努力冲出“经济洼地”，坚定不移走科学发展路，更好更快建生态文明县，进一步提升县域经济综合竞争力，努力推进息烽经济社会发展增比进位。

息烽县西山乡直供港澳蔬菜基地
Xifeng County Xishan Township direct supply of Hong Kong and Macao vegetable base

凯沃重工第一辆整装车下线

Kaiwo Heavy Industries, an entire loading off the assembly line

海信生产线

Hisense production line

In 2011, the Xiaohe District firmly grasp the provincial party committee and the provincial government "to accelerate the development and accelerate the transition, to promote leap" the main tone, closely around the "depth of promoting ecological civilization, the first to achieve a comprehensive well-off, accelerate the construction of new industrialization and modern urban new area" the overall goal, vigorously implement the "Strong Industrial District" and "open-led" two strategic, actively promote economic restructuring and the construction of key projects, the region's economy as a whole to achieve stable and rapid development, and substantial growth in fiscal revenue, industrial economy steady faster growth, the urban and rural residents' income improved steadily, and continued growth of social consumption, livelihood security has been strengthened, to achieve a good start in the "12th Five-Year" Plan.

In 2011, Xiaohe District total economic output rose sharply, the overall strength significantly enhanced, the region's GDP to achieve 8.063 billion yuan, an increase of 20.4% over the same period of last year. The industrial economy has shown a good momentum of growth, the three leading industries of equipment manufacturing, tobacco, medicine and green food, electronics and information gathering to develop, large-scale industrial output value completed 17.548 billion yuan, an increase of 36.2%. The total investment in fixed assets to maintain rapid growth, completed 14.506 billion yuan, an increase of 53.7%. Region is implementing construction 170 projects, including 60 industrial projects, a total of 27 key projects included in the provincial, city key projects, is the most projects on the history of the Development Zone District year in the same period. Xiaomeng construction of industrial parks quickly push, started 31 projects, industrial projects cover an area of 5,206 acres, the new plant is about 3.4 million square meters, with a total investment of more than 17 billion yuan, the project will add more than 40 billion yuan of industrial output, to achieve the tax for more than 3 billion yuan, provide more than 20,000 jobs. The total fiscal revenue of 1.487 billion yuan, an increase of 36.3%. Investment actual funds of 8.523 billion yuan, an increase of 30.2%. The total retail sales of social consumer goods was 4.932 billion yuan, an increase of 20.1%. Cash income of urban residents' disposable income and the period farmers were completed 19,357 yuan, 9000 yuan,respectively, an increase of 17%, 21.5%.

枫叶PE贯彻项目生产线

Maple Leaf PE implementing the project production line

枫叶PE管材项目生产的直径为1.6米的大型管材

Maple Leaf PE pipe produced by the project is 1.6 meters in diameter large pipe

烟厂生产线

Tobacco Factory production line

铜仁市万山区

Tongren City Wanshan District

省委书记栗战书调研万山
Provincial Party Committee Secretary Li Zhanshu had research in Wanshan

工业企业鸟瞰
An aerial view of industrial enterprises

2011年1月，贵州省人民政府将铜仁市谢桥街道办事处划转万山特区管辖。同年11月，国务院批复同意撤销铜仁地区、县级铜仁市和万山特区，设立地级铜仁市，将万山作为地级铜仁市的市辖区，并将原县级铜仁市改为碧江区，将其茶店镇、鱼塘乡、大坪乡划转万山管辖。万山区面积842平方公里，辖一个街道办事处，两个镇，六个乡，人口15.5万人。

2011年，全区实现地方生产总值的9.15亿元，同比增长20.5%；实现财政总收入1.51亿元，同比增长46.2%；实现规模工业总产值16.76亿元，同比增长32.0%；实现全社会固定资产投资11.25亿元，同比增长175.7%；实现社会消费品零售总额1.43亿元，同比增长18.1%；农民人均纯收入3593元，同比增长22.7%；年末金融机构存款余额11.36亿元，贷款余额3.64亿元，分别比年初增长41.2%和32.9%。

工业车间外貌
Industrial workshop appearance

食用菌菌孢基地
Mushroom spores base

西红柿规范化栽培
Tomato standardized cultivation

In January 2011, the Guizhou Provincial People's Government made the Tongren city Xieqiao neighborhood offices transfer to Wanshan Special Administrative Region under the jurisdiction. In November, the State Council approved the revocation of Tongren Prefecture, county level Tongren City and Wanshan SAR, establishment of level of Tongren City, Wanshan as a prefecture-level city of Tongren City area, and the original county-level city of Tongren changed to Bijiang District, and its Chadian town, Yutang Township, Daping Township transferred to Wanshan jurisdiction. Wanshan district has an area of 842 square kilometers, the jurisdiction of 1 neighborhood office, 2 towns, 6 townships, population of 155,000.

In 2011, the region's local GDP of 915 million yuan, an increase of 20.5%; total fiscal revenue of 151 million yuan, an increase of 46.2%; large-scale industrial output value of 1.676 billion yuan, up 32.0%; total fixed assets investment of 1.125 billion yuan, an increase of 175.7%; to achieve 143 million yuan of total retail sales of social consumer goods, up 18.1%; rural per capita net income of 3,593 yuan, an increase of 22.7%; 1.136 billion yuan of the deposits of financial institutions at the end of the year, the loan balance of 364 million yuan, an increase of 41.2% and 32.9% respectively, compared with the beginning of the year.

丹 寨 县

Danzhai County

省委书记栗战书、省长赵克志在金钟经济开发区检查指导工作

Provincial Party Committee Secretary Li Zhanshu, vice governor Zhao Kezhi to inspect and guide the work of the Jizhoang Economic Development Zone

省长赵克志在丹寨调研

Provincial governor Zhao Kezhi has research in Danzhai

开发区建设

Construction of development zones

2011年，丹寨县着力推进“开放兴县、项目立县、城镇带县、开发区强县”，全力推进“宜业宜居、创新创智”美丽新丹寨和开发区“现代企业生态城”建设。全县生产总值 11.54亿元，同比增长17%；财政收入1.64亿元，同比增长49.1%；全社会固定资产投资17.43亿元，同比增长137.6%；社会消费品零售总额30429万元，同比增长18.6%；农民人均纯收入3706元，同比增长20.9%。

开发区建设强势起步。2011年，全部工业增加值为31167万元，同比增长35.9%。金钟经济开发区强势起步。金钟大道、长兴大道等路网及供水供电等基础设施建设已启动建设。招商引资成效明显，共引进项目63个，协议总投资82.1亿元。

城镇化建设步伐加快。初步形成了连接内外、四通八达的快速通道路网，实现了乡乡通油路、村村通公路。龙泉大道以西的城镇建设全面铺开，供水、绿化等市政设施增强，城市功能进一步完善，2011年城镇化率为20.8%。

农业产业化加快推进。推进“三个转变”，实施“三个万元”增收计划，着力抓好“两项重点、八条线”，重点打造黑毛猪、茶产叶，抓好低产林改造、蓝莓、硒米、硒锌茶、中药材、蔬菜、畜牧养殖、文化手工业。以产品变商品为核心，抓龙头、建基地、扩农户、冲市场。

旅游产业蓬勃发展。2011年，接待游客46.23万人次，实现旅游综合收入1.6亿元，比上年增长79.77%。

社会事业全面进步。人民生产生活条件进一步改善，生活水平不断得到提高。

龙泉大道
Longquan Road

龙泉山景区
Longquan Mountain Scenic Spot

In 2011, Danzhai County made efforts to promote "opening up prospers the county, projects build the county, cities and towns drive the county, the development zone strong the county", to promote the "industry and habit should be livable, innovative Powerise" beautiful new Daizhai and development zones "modern enterprise eco-city" building. GDP of the county was 1.154 billion yuan, an increase of 17%; financial income of 164 million yuan, up 49.1%; the whole society fixed assets investment of 1.743 billion yuan, an increase of 137.6%; total retail sales of 304.29 million yuan, an increase of 18.6%; farmers' per capita net income of 3,706 yuan, up 20.9%.

丹寨民族高级中学新校址
Danzhai National High School new campus

Strong start of construction of development zones. In 2011, all industrial added value of 311.67 million yuan, an increase of 35.9%. Jinzhong Economic Development Zone got a strong start. Jinzhong Road, Changxing Road, the road network and water and power supply infrastructure construction has started construction. Investment achieved remarkable success, and attracted a total of 63 projects, total investment of 8.21 billion yuan agreement.

Speed up the pace of urbanization. The initial formation of connections within and outside the fast-pass road network extending in all directions, achievement of the townships oil, every village access roads. Longquan Road, west of the town construction in full swing, enhance water supply, afforestation and other municipal facilities, further improve the functions of cities, the urbanization rate was 20.8%, in 2011.

茶场
Tea plantation

To accelerate the industrialization of agriculture. Promote the "three changes", the implementation of "three million yuan" income plan, and focus their efforts on "two major points, eight lines", focusing on creating a black pork, tea leaf yield to grasp the transformation of low-yield forest, blueberry, selenium rice, zinc and selenium tea, herbs, vegetables, livestock, cultural handicrafts. Grasping the leading product variations goods, build a base, and expansion of farmers, rush into the market.

The tourism industry is flourishing. In 2011, tourists of 462,300 visitors, the tourism income of 160 million yuan, an increase of 79.77% over the previous year.

Round social progress. People living and working conditions to further improve the standard of living is improving.

黎 平 县

Liping County

黔东南州州长李飞跃（右二）在县长唐浩（右一）的陪同下到黎平侗乡木业检查指导工作

The Qiandongnan Governor Li Feiyue (second from right) accompanied by Magistrate Tang Hao (right) to inspect and guide the work of Liping Dong Wood

黔东南州黎平片区100个项目建设集中开工仪式

The Qiandongnan Liping Area 100 projects focus on the groundbreaking ceremony

黎平县是黔、湘、桂三省（区）交界及云贵高原向江南丘陵过渡地区，属中亚热带季风湿润气候。面积4441平方公里，辖25个乡镇、403个行政村、19个居委会、3086个村民小组，人口52.76万人，侗族人口33.57万人占总人口的63.63%，是全国侗族人口聚居最多的县，被誉为“侗乡黎平”和“第一侗乡”，县政府所在地为德凤镇，县城面积8.5平方公里，人口6.85万。

2011年，全县生产总值完成30.57亿元，年均增长14.1%，其中三次产业年均分别增长6.7%、24.3%和13.6%；工业增加值实现4.62亿元，年均增长20.6%；财政总收入完成3亿元，年均增长34.95%；全社会固定资产投资完成47.1亿元，年均增长53.4%；农民人均纯收入达3849元，年均增长11.4%。

侗乡第一航空港——黎平机场

Dong first airport- Liping airport

县城一角

County corner

县境内立体交通格局初步形成，机场航班逐渐加密，厦蓉高速贵阳至水口段建成通车，黎洛高速即将开通，贵广高铁和黎三高速加快建设，全县25个乡镇基本实现通油路，村村通公路，旅游公路建设加快，目前公路里程达3548.3公里。

县境内有丰富的森林资源，是全国28个重点林业县之一，全县林业用地518万亩，有林地面积463万亩，森林覆盖率达74.6%，活立木蓄积量1930万立方米，楠竹面积9.16万余亩，蓄量居全省第二位。

旅游资源十分丰富，人文景观保存完好，是贵州省优先发展的重点旅游区。有世界之最的天然石拱桥——天生桥；有造型独具匠心的侗族古楼、花桥、戏台和民居建筑，鼓楼330座、花桥60多座，地坪风雨桥被列为全国重点保护单位，述洞独柱鼓楼进入“大世界基尼斯之最”；有中共中央政治局会议——黎平会议会址、翘街明清古建筑群、两湖会馆等人文景观。县内有景点73个，其中特级景点2个。

黎平县城全景图

Liping county panorama

祭萨踩堂

Memorial ceremony for Sa and step on the hall

热情好客的侗家人盛情接待远方客人

Hospitable Dongjia people hospitality distant guests

厦蓉高速公路穿境而过

Xiamen-Chengdu expressway through the territory

茶叶加工企业工人精心加工产品

Tea processing enterprise workers carefully processed products

木材加工企业工人在抢抓生产

Wood processing enterprise workers to seize production

Liping County is the Guizhou, Hunan and Guangxi provinces (autonomous regions) border and the Yunnan-Guizhou Plateau to the Jiangnan hills transition region, in the subtropical monsoon humid climate. Area of 4,441 square kilometers, jurisdiction over 25 villages and towns, 403 administrative villages, 19 neighborhood committees and 3,086 village groups, a population of 527,600 people, Dong population of 335,700, 63.63% of the of the total population, the country Dong populated most of any county, known as "Dong Liping" and "Fisrt Dong Village", the county seat for Defeng Town, county area of 8.5 square kilometers and a population of 68,500.

正在修建的黎洛高速公路

Being built Liluo highway

In 2011, the county's GDP of 3.057 billion yuan, an average annual increase of 4.1%, including three industry average annual increase of 6.7%, 4.3% and 3.6%, respectively; industrial realize the added value of 462 million yuan, average annual growth of 20.6%; total fiscal revenue of 300 million yuan, with an average annual growth of 34.95%; the total fixed asset investment of 4.71 billion yuan, average annual growth rate of 53.4%; per capita net income of farmers reached 3,849 yuan, with an average annual increase of 11.4%.

The initial formation of three-dimensional traffic pattern of the county, airport flight encryption, Guiyang outlet segment of the Xiamen-Chengdu Expressway opened to traffic, Li Luo upcoming high-speed opening, accelerate the construction of Gui Guang high-speed rail and Li San high-speed, 25 townships in the county is the basic asphalt roads, every village access roads, to speed up the construction of tourist highway, the highway mileage of 3,548.3 km.

The County is rich in forest resources, is one of the 28 key forestry county, 5.18 million mu of forestry land in the county, forest area of 4.63 billion mu, the forest coverage rate reached 74.6%, 19.3 million m3 of stumpage, Nan Bamboo area of 91,600 mu, the storage capacity ranks second in the province.

Rich in tourism resources, well-preserved cultural landscape, is a major tourist areas of priority to the development of Guizhou Province. The world of the natural stone arch bridge - Tianshengqiao; Kurau shape the distinctive Dong Ancient Tower, Huaqiao, stage and residential buildings, the Drum Tower 330, the Huaqiao over 60 seats, Diping wind and rain bridge was listed as national key protection units, state the hole alone column the Gulou enter "Guinness's World"; the CPC Central Committee Political Bureau meeting - Liping meeting venue, Qiaojie Ming and Qing dynasties of ancient buildings, two lakes Guild cultural landscape. County has 73 attractions, including two special attractions.

平 坝 县

Pingba County

县委书记沈新国到夏云工业园调研
County party secretary Shen Xinguo to the Xia Yun Industrial Park to have research

高新区
High-tech Zone

平坝县地处黔中腹地，因地多平旷而得名，是中国屯堡文化之乡、中国清真美食之乡、中国民间文化艺术之乡。全县辖6镇4乡，206个行政村（居委会、社区）。面积999平方公里，人口36万人，其中少数民族人口7.81万人，人口较多的少数民族有苗族、布依族、回族等族，主要矿藏有煤炭、铝土矿、硫铁矿等30多种。森林覆盖率36.49%。交通便利，生态良好，山川秀丽，资源丰富。

2011年，全县生产总值51亿元，同比增长18%；农林牧渔业总产值75192万元，同比增长8.46%；财政总收入5.8亿元，同比增长26.28%；一般预算收入3.6亿元，同比增长37.65%；固定资产投资30亿元，同比增长123.8%，增幅全市第一；全县社会消费品零售总额完成12.45亿元，同比增长19.5%。

台泥（安顺）水泥厂
Taini(Anshun) cement plant

招商引资工作取得新成效。2011年是平坝县的“招商建设年”，共有招商引资项目166个，协议引资213.93亿元，实际到位资金40.04亿元（含续建），同比增长194.59%。占市目标任务数29亿元的138.05%，提前并超额完成县目标任务数30亿元。新签约项目122个，其中亿元以上项目32个；5000万元以上亿元以下的项目9个；1000万以上5000万元以下的项目46个；1000万元以下项目35个；其中一产项目10个，总投资17.51亿元，实际到位资金1.2亿元；二产项目65个，总投资97.55亿元，实际到位资金16.54亿元；三产项目47个，总投资51.83亿元，实际到位资金5.98亿元。

沪昆高速与迎宾大道交接处
Kunming Shanghai high-speed and Yingbin Avenue junction

中山大道
Zhongshan Road

Pingba County is located in the hinterland in central Guizhou, so named due to great falt land, the Chinese tunbao culture Township, the hometown of Chinese Islamic cuisine, the hometown of Chinese folk culture and art. County jurisdiction over 6 towns, 4 townships, 206 administrative villages (neighborhood, community). Area of 999 square kilometers and a population of 360,000 people, including ethnic minority population of 78,100, more populous ethnic minorities Miao, Buyi and Hui, the main mineral is coal, bauxite, pyrite, 30 variety. The forest coverage rate of 36.49%. Convenient transportation, good ecological environment, beautiful scenery, rich in resources.

In 2011, the county's GDP of 5.1 billion yuan, an increase of 18%; agriculture, forestry, animal husbandry and fishery output value of 751.92 million yuan, an increase of 8.46%; total fiscal revenue of 580 million yuan, an increase of 26.28%; general budget income of 360 million yuan, an increase of 37.65%; investment in fixed assets of 3 billion yuan, an increase of 123.8%, an increase of the city's first; county retail sales of social consumer goods the total value of 1.245 billion yuan, an increase of 19.5%.

Attracting funds work made new achievements. 2011 Pingba County "Merchants building year", a total of 166 investment projects, agreements attract investment of 21.393 billion yuan, the actual funds of 4.004 billion yuan (including the continued construction), an increase of 194.59%. Accounted for 138.05% of the 2.9 billion yuan of the City objectives and tasks, ahead of schedule and exceeded 3 billion yuan of county objectives and tasks. 122 newly signed projects, of which 32 projects over 100 million yuan; more than 50 million yuan below 100 million yuan 9 projects; 10 million to 50 million yuan 46 projects; less than 10 million yuan 35 projects: including first industry project 10, a total investment of 1.751 billion yuan, 120 million yuan of funds actually in place; 65 of the secondary industry projects with a total investment of 9.755 billion yuan, 1.654 billion yuan of actual funds; tertiary industry, 47 projects with a total investment of 5.183 billion yuan, the actual funds 598 million yuan.

平坝窖酒
Pingba cellar wine

景观整治
Landscape renovation

迎宾大道夜景
Yingbin Avenue at night

音乐喷泉
Musical Fountain

城镇面貌焕然一新。2011年平坝县逐步完善了城乡规划，优化城镇空间布局，构建了以县城和黔中新区为“两核”，夏云和天龙为“两翼”的县域城镇体系。完成了《黔中经济区黔中新兴产业示范（园）区城乡统筹总体规划》、《平坝夏云工业园区发展规划》等13个规划编制。县城详规覆盖率60%以上。完成了196个村庄规划，实现了村庄规划全覆盖。城镇品位不断提升。县城旧城区改造、城中村改造稳步推进。台泥大道、天马路等一批城市基础设施建设项目顺利推进。完成了迎宾路一期、平安广场、清真街沿线及高新区周边房屋风格风貌改造，规范了城区沿街部分铺面的门窗、广告牌。安装了县城中山大道、天台山大道、塔山路隔离护栏。县城绿化率、亮灯率分别达到25%和98%以上，城镇化率提高到35.7%。“三创三建”工作取得阶段性成效，城市管理水平和文明程度明显提高，荣获省委、省人民政府授予贵州省文明县城称号。

采取措施加快发展白酒传统产业。平坝酿造业的兴盛，至今已有两千多年的历史。解放以来，老牌名酒生产企业贵州平坝酒厂将平坝酒推上过一个辉煌的顶峰，曾被国家轻工部及贵州省确定为名优白酒生产重点企业。1995年金壶牌平坝窖酒、平安牌平安酒双双被评为中国名牌产品，为贵州省白酒制造业第三名。平坝现有各类大小白酒生产厂家66个。初具规模企业有4家，占地面积共155亩，年生产能力5400千升，从业人员近1000人。为发展白酒传统产业，平坝县委、县人民政府成立了白酒办，并将平坝县白酒生态工业园确定为全县的重点工程，成立了平坝县森泰白酒工业园投资发展有限公司，将已获准生产白酒资质的企业集聚，同时引进战略投资者与现有重点白酒企业进行战略重组，全面推动县白酒产业沿着集团化、市场化的方向发展。白酒工业园以贵州省平坝酒厂有限责任公司为中心，总规划面积2123亩，其中工业用地641.15亩。

苗家风情之山歌催得菜花黄
Miao style of folk songs urging the cauliflower yellow

高峰山卍华禅院
GaoFeng Mountain swastika Chinese Buddhist Temple

美丽的斯拉河
Beautiful Sila river

天台古碉楼
Tiantai ancient towers

Urban with a new look. In 2011, Pingba County gradually improve the urban and rural planning, and optimize urban space layout, built to the county and cQianzhong New Area for the "two cores", Xiayun and Tianlong as "two wings" for the county town system. Completed "Qianzhong Economic Zone Qianzhong emerging industrial demonstration (Park) District, urban and rural overall planning", "Pingab Xiayun ndustrial Park Development Plan", and 13 plannings. County detailed rules more than 60% of the coverage. 196 village planning, village planning to achieve full coverage. Towns grade has been increasing. The county old district rennovation got steady progress in the transformation of villages. Taini Avenue, tTianma road, and a number of urban infrastructure construction projects progressed smoothly. Completed Yingbin road phase I, Ping'an Square, Muslim street and around the High-tech Zone housing style transformation, specification of a city street part of the pavement of the doors and windows, billboards. Installation of a county Zhongshan Road, Tiantai Mountain Road, Tashan Road, isolation barrier. County greening rate, lighting rate of 25% and 98%, urbanization rate increased to 35.7%. The "three creation and three built" work to achieve substantive results, the level of city management and the degree of civilization is significantly improved, won the Provincial Party Committee, Provincial People's Government awarded the title of civilized county in Guizhou Province.

Take measures to accelerate the development of traditional liquor industry. The rise of the Pingba brewing industry has been more than two thousand years of history. Since liberation, the old wine production enterprises the Guizhou Pingba winery plant pushed Pingba wine onto a pinnacle of glory, was the national Ministry of Light Industry and Guizhou Province to determine the production of key enterprises to the famous liquor. In 1995, Jinhu brand Pingba wine cellar, Ping'an brand Ping'an wine both as brand-name products in China, is Guizhou Province liquor manufacturing to third. Pingba owns the various sizes of liquor manufacturers 66. Begun to take shape 4, covers an area of 155 mu, the annual production capacity of 5,400 kilo-liters, employing nearly 1,000 people. Traditional industries for the development of white wine, Pingba county committee and county governments set up a liquor office, and Pingba County Liquor eco-industrial park is identified as a key project in the county, set up Pingba County Sentai Liquor Industrial Park Investment and Development Co., Ltd. would have allowed the production of liquor qualified enterprises gather, while the introduction of strategic investors and the strategic restructuring of existing key liquor enterprise, promote the development of the county liquor industry along the direction of the group, market-oriented. Liquor Industrial Park Co., Ltd. of Guizhou Province Pingba winery, with a total planned area of 2,123 mu, of which 641.15 mu of industrial land.

屯堡民居
Tunbao residential

从 江 县

Congjiang County

李飞跃州长“指点”新从江
Li Feiyue governor instructions New Congjiang

从江县人民政府县长张广渊
Congjiang County People's Government Magistrate Zhang Guangyuan

从江县第十六届人代会少数民族代表
Congjiang County sixteenth National People's Congress representatives of ethnic minorities

从江县位于贵州省黔东南苗族侗族自治州东南部。面积3244平方公里。辖14个乡、7个镇（其中民族乡3个），377个村民委员会，4个社区，10个居民委员会，2228个村民小组，28个居民小组。全县常住人口29.08万人。从江是一个以苗族、侗族为主体的多民族聚居县，世居民族有苗、侗、汉、壮、瑶、水6个，少数民族人口占全县总人口的94.1%。主要矿藏有铜、铅、锌、金银多金属矿、花岗石、硅石等，水能资源理论蕴藏量20.88万千瓦，全县森林覆盖率67%。

2011年，全年完成生产总值24亿元，扣除价格上涨因素，比上年增长21%。二、三产业大幅增长，二产增速达到39%，三产增速达23%。全社会固定资产投资完成30亿元，增长223.5% ；财政总收入完成2.63亿元，比上年增长62.83%；社会消费品零售总额完成6.12亿元，增长19%；全县金融机构存贷款余额分别为22.64亿元和12.87亿元；农民人均纯收入4055元，增速达29.8%，增速排名全省第9位。

2011年，全县有规模以上工业企业19家，工业实现增加值16453万元，比上年增长22.5%。全县耕地面积21.57万亩，人均耕地面积0.643亩。2011年启动实施交通建设项目29个，完成续建工程项目12个，全社会交通固定资产投资5.35亿元。2011年投入救灾资金429万元，比上年增长12.9%。全面完成“2009年度薄改工程”。

从江县政务服务中心投入使用
Congjiang County Government Service Center put into use

都柳江流域从江航电枢纽工程开工建设
Duliu river-basin Congjiang Navigation and Hydropower Project started construction

县领导参加一事一议建设
County leaders to participate in the proposed building

建设中的贵州洛贯工业园区
Construction in Guizhou Luo Guan Industrial Park

从贯一级公路施工现场
Congguan first class highway construction site

Congjiang County is located in the southeast of Qiandongnan Miao and Dong Autonomous Prefecture in Guizhou Province. An area of 3,244 square kilometers. Jurisdiction over 14 townships, 7 towns (including nationality townships 3), 377 villagers' committee, the 4 communities, 10 residents' committees, 2,228 villagers' groups, 28 residents groups. County resident population of 29.08 million.Congjiang is a Miao, Dong, multi-ethnic county, native peoples have the Miao, Dong, Han, Zhuang, Yao, Shui, 6 minorities, the ethnic minority population accounts for 94.1% of the total population of the county. The main minerals are copper, lead, zinc, gold and silver polymetallic ore, granite, silica and so on, hydropower resources theoretical potential of 208,800 kilowatts, 67% of forest coverage in the county.

In 2011, the annual GDP of 2.4 billion yuan, after deducting price factors, an increase of 21% over the previous year. Secondary and tertiary industries got substantial growth, in secondary industry growth rate of 39%, the tertiary industry growth rate of 23%. Total fixed assets investment of 3 billion yuan, an increase of 223.5%; total fiscal revenue of 263 million yuan, an increase of 62.83% over the previous year; total retail sales of social consumer goods completed 612 million yuan, an increase of 19%; financial institutions in the county to deposit and loan balances were 2.264 billion yuan and 1.287 billion yuan; rural per capita net income of 4,055 yuan, the growth rate of 29.8%, growth rate ranked 9th of the province.

In 2011, the county has 19 industrial enterprises above designated size, the industrial added value of 164.53 million yuan, an increase of 22.5% over the previous year. 215,700 mu of arable land in the county, per capita arable land area of 0.643 mu. In 2011, to start the implementation of transportation construction projects 29, complete the continued construction projects 12 , traffic investment in fixed assets of 535 million yuan for the whole society. In 2011, invested 4.29 million yuan in relief funds, an increase of 12.9% over the previous year. Full completion of the "2009 Thin improvement works".

开展“亲帮亲、邻帮邻”，危改群众正在立房架
To carry out "pro help pro neighbor help neighbor", dilapidated building masses are putting room frame

第八届原生态侗族大歌节——琵琶歌
The 8th original ecological Dongzutaige of Day - lute songs

黔东南州第十届中学生田径运动会
Qiandongnan Tenth Middle School Students Track and Field Games

县城夜景（摄影/张成文）
County night (Photography / Zhang Chengwen)

西 秀 区

Xixiu District

塔山
Tashan

2011年是实施“十二五”规划的开局之年。一年来，在市委、市政府和区委的领导下，在区人大的依法监督和区政协的民主监督下，区人民政府团结和依靠全区各族人民，锐意进取，攻坚克难，全区经济社会保持较快发展，人民生活持续改善，社会大局和谐稳定。

主要指标顺利完成。全年实现生产总值118亿元，同比增长16%；全社会固定资产投资73.2亿元，同比增长106.8%；规模以上工业增加值26.5亿元，同比增长21.33%；财政总收入17.4亿元，同比增长34.05%，地方财政一般预算收入7.2亿元，同比增长25.82%；社会消费品零售总额33亿元，同比增长19.8%。

三次产业协调发展。深入实施工业强区、城镇化带动战略，推进“三化”同步，经济结构不断优化。第一产业实现增加值12.39亿元，第二产业实现增加值47.49亿元，第三产业实现增加值58.12亿元。全年接待游客370万人次，实现旅游总收入51.5亿元，同比分别增长31%和37%。

市委常委区委书记罗建强、区委副书记区长胡强率队到辖区军工企业调研
Municipal Standing Committee, Party Secretary Luo Jianqiang, deputy secretary of Mayor Hu Qiang led team to the jurisdiction of military industrial enterprises to have research

市委常委区委书记罗建强下基层办实事解难题、强基础惠民生促发展
Municipal Standing Committee, Party Secretary Luo Jianqiang to the grassroots and do practical things and solve problems, strengthen foundation and benefit people's livelihood and promote development

区长胡强集中调研“城中村”改造、“棚户区”改造、重大项目建设和工业发展工作
Mayor Hu Qiang focus on research, “Villages in city” transformation, “shanty towns” transformation, construction of major projects and industrial development

基础条件进一步完善。建成通村油路103.83公里。完成86处农村饮水安全项目，解决了6.5万农村群众的饮水安全问题。治理水土流失33.13平方公里。治理石漠化面积14.89平方公里。安西灌区工程全面完成。营造林34982亩，森林覆盖率31.85%。

对外开放力度加大。全年共签约项目30个，签约金额761.65亿元（其中：全国民营企业助推贵州发展大会签约项目14个，金额584.5亿元）。招商引资到位资金40.37亿元，同比增长146.18%；新开工项目184个，同比增长133%。

贯城河
Guancheng River

虹山水库
Hongshan Mountain Reservoir

西秀区举行端午节纪念活动
Xixiu held Dragon Boat Festival commemoration

住宅新区
Residence district

2011 is the implementation of the first year of the "12th Five-Year Plan". Over the past year, under the leadership of the municipal government and committee, and the district committee, the District of law supervision of the District People's Congress and the democratic supervision of the District Political Consultative Conference, the district people's government of unity and rely on people of all ethnic groups in the region, forge ahead to tackle tough, the region economic and social to maintain a rapid development, the people's living standards continued to improve, the overall social harmony and stability.

Successful completion of key indicators. Annual GDP of 11.8 billion yuan, an increase of 16%; the whole society fixed assets investment of 7.32 billion yuan, an increase of 106.8%; scale industrial added value 2.65 billion yuan, an increase of 21.33%; total fiscal revenue of 1.74 billion yuan, an increase of 34.05%, local general budget revenue of 720 million yuan, an increase of 25.82%; 3.3 billion yuan of total retail sales of social consumer goods, an increase of 19.8%.

Three industries coordinated development. Depth implementation of a strong industrial area, and urbanization led strategy, promoting the synchronization of the "three changes", constantly optimize the economic structure. The primary industry of the added value of 1.239 billion yuan, secondary industry realized added value of 4.749 billion yuan and the tertiary industry added value of 5.812 billion yuan. 3.7 million of annual tourists trips, total tourism income of 5.15 billion yuan, an increase of 31% and 37% respectively.

Further improve the basic conditions. Build 103.83 kilometers through the village of oil road. Completion of the 86 rural drinking water safety projects to address the safety of drinking water for 65,000 rural masses. Water and soil erosion of 33.13 square kilometers. Governance rocky desertification area of 14.89 square kilometers. The Anxi Irrigation Project is fully completed. 34,982 acres of afforestation, the forest coverage rate of 31.85%.

Opening up the intensity to increase. Total of 30 contracted projects, the contracted amount of 76.165 billion yuan (including: private enterprises, boosting Guizhou Development Conference contracted projects 14, the amount of 58.45 billion yuan). 4.037 billion yuan of investment capital in place, an increase of 146.18%; new projects of 184, an increase of 133%.

印江土家族苗族自治县

Yinjiang Tujia and Miao Autonomous County

印江体育场
Yinjiang Stadium

文昌广场一角
Wenchang corner of the square

印江土家族苗族自治县位于贵州省东北部、铜仁地区西部，地处武陵山脉主峰、佛教名山——梵净山西麓。面积1969平方公里，辖17个乡镇、365个村、9个居委会，人口43.6万人，其中土家族、苗族等少数民族人口占71.2%。2001年被确定为国家新阶段扶贫开发工作重点县。素有“书法之乡”、“长寿之乡”、“名茶之乡”的美誉。

近年来，印江自治县委、县政府抢抓国家实施积极的财政政策和新阶段扶贫开发的历史性机遇，紧扣省委、省政府“两加一推”主基调，围绕市委、市政府构建“两带两圈”产业体系、推进“六个新跨越”战略部署，坚持“三措并举”（大争项目、全员招商、金融支持），推进“四化进程”（新型工业化、特色城镇化、农业现代化、旅游产业化），改善十大民生（就学、就医、就业、增收、社保、住房、基础、环境、文化、稳定），推动了全县经济社会又好又快、更好更快发展。

2011年，全县完成生产总值31.4亿元，同比增长17.0%；实现财政总收入2.46亿元，增长46.3%，其中，地方财政收入1.55亿元，增长30.9%；完成全社会固定资产投资35.6亿元，增长106.0%；农民人均纯收入达到3719元，增长22.9%；城镇居民人均可支配收入达到13040元，增长21.0%；社会消费品零售总额6.5亿元，增长20.1%；经济发展增比进位在全省综合排位从上年的66位上升到47位，提升19位。

印江河风光
Yijing rivers scenery

江城晨曦
Jiangchen Dawn

农业产业化龙头企业

Agricultural industrialization leading enterprises

土家民居

Tujia houses

梵净杜鹃

Fanjing rhododendron

Yinjiang Tujia and Miao Autonomous County is located in the northeast of Guizhou Province, west of Tongren Prefecture, located in Wuling peak, Buddhist mountains - west foot of Fanjingshan. Area of 1,969 square kilometers, jurisdiction over 17 townships, 365 villages, 9 neighborhood, a population of 436,000 people, Tujia, Miao and other ethnic minority population accounts for 71.2%. In 2001, to determine the key counties for poverty alleviation and development for the country a new stage. Known as "calligraphy township", "longevity township" and "famous tea town" reputation.

In recent years, the Yinjiang Autonomous County Committee, the county government to seize the historic opportunity of a proactive fiscal policy and poverty alleviation and development of a new stage of national implementation, closely linked to the provincial committee, government to "two-plus one-push" the main tone, around the City Commission, the municipal government build "two belts two circles" industrial system, to promote the "six new leap forward "strategic plan, adhere to the "three measures simultaneously" (contention project, the full investment, financial support), to promote the "four modernizations process" (new-type industrialization, features urbanization, modernization of agriculture, tourism and industrialization), to improve the top ten people's livelihood (education, medical care, employment, income, social security, housing, infrastructure, environment, culture, stability), and promote the county's economic and social good and fast, more better and faster development.

In 2011, the county completed a GDP of 3.14 billion yuan, an increase of 7.0%; total fiscal revenue of 246 million yuan, an increase of 46.3%, of which the local revenue of 155 million yuan, an increase of 30.9%; completed total fixed asset investment of 3.56 billion yuan, an increase of 106.0%; rural per capita net income reached 3,719 yuan, up 22.9%; urban residents per capita disposable income reached 13,040 yuan, an increase of 21.0%; 650 million yuan of total retail sales of social consumer goods, an increase of 20.1%; the development of economic growth than the binary in the province's comprehensive ranking rose from 66th last year to 47th, improve 19-bit.

梵净茶园

Fanjing tea garden

黄 平 县

Huangping County

赵克志省长在黄平民族中学调研工作
Zhao Kezhi Governor in Huangping Minority Middle School had research work

黄平县位于贵州省东南部，总面积1667.8平方公里，辖9乡、5镇，共243个行政村，3个居民委员会，4个社区居民委员会。总人口38万人，居住着23个民族，少数民族人口占总人口的64%。

黄平交通便利，资源丰富，县内森林覆盖率41.78%，有生物生态资源1000多种，县境内已探明多种贵重金属矿。自然景观、历史文化、民族风情构成了黄平三大旅游资源。

2011年，黄平县紧扣“加速发展、加快转型、奋力赶超、推动跨越”主基调，深入实施“六大战略”，突出抓好“新型工业化、绿色城镇化、文化旅游产业化和农业现代化”四项重点工作，积极推进“诚信黄平、创业黄平、绿色黄平、宜居黄平、和谐黄平”建设进程，推动了全县经济社会又好又快、更好更快发展，加快构建生态文明和谐富裕新黄平。

2011年，全县生产总值完成196737万元，其中：工业增加值完成15730万元，同比增长34.3%， 500万元工业增加值完成15587万元，同比增长38.8%； 、二、三产比重为 32.8、12.1、55.1；财政总收入和一般预算收入分别达到21598万元和14372万元，分别增长43.9%和51.1%；50万元以上固定资产投资完成138064万元，增长129.1%；社会消费品零售总额56477万元，增长18.8%；城镇居民人均可支配收入12351元，同比增长15.9%；农民人均纯收入3708.70元，同比增长23.09%；金融机构年末存、贷款余额分别为301145.14万元、108957.77万元，分别增长27.2%和12.8%。

王晓东常务副省长、李飞跃州长出席凯里黄平民用机场试验段开工典礼
Wang Xiaodong, executive vice governor, Li Feiyue governor attend the groundbreaking ceremony at the Kaili Huangping people used airport test section

凯里黄平民用机场试验段开工典礼
Kaili Huangping people used airport test section groundbreaking ceremony

县城新姿
The county Wonder

素有旧州古镇“银碗”的㵲阳湖

Known as the Old State Town "Silver Bowl" Wuyang Lake

Huangping county is located in the southeastern part of Guizhou Province with a total area of 1,667.8 square kilometers, jurisdiction 9 villages,5 towns, a total of 243 administrative villages, 3 residents'committees, 4 community residents' committees. Total population of 380,000, is home to 23 ethnic minority, minority population accounts for 64% of the total population.

Huangping owns convenient transportation, abundant resources, the county forest coverage rate of 41.78%, biological and ecological resources more than 1,000 kinds, the County has proved a variety of precious metal ores. Natural landscape, history culture, ethnic customs formed the three major tourism resources in Huangping.

In 2011, Huangping County closely to "accelerate the development, speed up the transition, struggling to catch up, and promote leap bound" tone, in-depth implementation of the "six strategic prominence" to the "new-type industrialization, green urbanization, cultural tourism, industrialization and agricultural modernization" four importaces work, actively promote "credit Huangping, poineering work Huangping, green Huangping, livable Huangping, harmonious Huangping" buding course, promote the whole county economy society have good and fast, more better and faster development, speed up the construction of ecological civilization and harmonious affluent new Huang Ping.

In 2011, the county's GDP completed 1.96737 billion yuan, of which: industrial added value of 157.3 million yuan, an increase of 34.3%, 5 million yuan of industrial added value of 155.87 million yuan, an increase of 38.8%; production proportion of first, second, tertiary industry is 32.8 、 12.1 、 55.1;total fiscal revenue and general budget revenue reached 215.98 million yuan and 143.72 million yuan, an increase of 43.9% and 51.1% respectively; 500,000 yuan investment in fixed assets of 1.38064 billion yuan, an increase of 129.1%; social consumer goods retail a total of 564.77 million yuan, an increase of 18.8%; urban residents per capita disposable income of 12,351 yuan, an increase of 15.9%; 3,708.70 yuan per capita net income of farmers, an increase of 23.09%; financial institutions deposit at the end of the year, loan balance of 3,011,451,400 yuan, 1,089,577,700 yuan, an increase of 27.2% and 12.8% respectively.

旧州古城

Old ancient city

正在积极打造成“亚州第一、国际一流”的磨料磨具生产基地的贵州黄平富城实业有限公司

Actively fight the "Asian first, world-class" abrasives production base Guizhou Huangping Fucheng Industrial Co., Ltd.

优质脱毒马铃薯生产基地图景

High-quality virus-free potato production base picture

榕 江 县

Rongjiang County

贵州省委书记栗战书到榕江视察工作
Guizhou Provincial Party Committee Secretary Li Zhanshu to the Rongjiang have inspection work

省长赵克志（前排中）在省交通运输厅厅长程孟仁（前排右一）、贵州高速公路开发总公司总经理耿黔生（左一）陪同下，视察厦蓉高速公路榕江段
Governor Zhao Kezhi (middle in the front row) accompanied by the provincial Department of Transportation Director Cheng Mengren (first from rightin the front row), the Guizhou Expressway Development Corporation general manager Geng Qiansheng (first from left), had inspection of the building in Xiamen-Chengdu expressway Rongjiang section

黔东南州委书记廖少华到榕江检查工作
Qiandongnan state secretary Liao Shaohua to Rongjiang have inspection

李飞跃州长到榕江调研
Li Feiyue governor to Rongjiang have research

2011年11月24日，榕江县第十六届人民代表大会第一次会议在榕江县城召开
November 24, 2011, sixteenth Rongjiang County People's Congress meeting held in Rongjiang County

榕江县位于黔东南南部，面积3315.8平方公里，耕地1.31公顷，辖6镇、13乡（其中6个民族乡），260个行政村、7个居委会、3个社区，1653个村民组、78个居民组，共8.58万户、35.47万人，其中少数民族人口占79.88%。全县共有17个民族，其中侗族、苗族、汉族、水族和瑶族人口超5万以上。主要矿产有锑、铅锑和石煤。森林覆盖率74.71%。

2011年国内生产总值22.85亿元，比上年增长17%。其中一、二、三产业分别为8.26亿元、5.56亿元和9.03亿元，分别较上年增长8.8%、22.7%和21.4%。农村牧渔总产值12.05亿元，较上年增长10.89%。工业总产值15.39亿元，较上年增长45.74%。财政总收入11.53亿元（含专款），增长20.72%。其中地方财政收入2.6亿元，增长62.46%。财政支出11.53亿元，增长27.32%。全社会固定资产投资22亿元。在建重点项目有县城环城东路、 老城区道路（石板街）改造、县人民医院综合大楼等16个。全县通车里程3424.9公里。通信业务实现1.05亿元。县城规划扩展到56.4平方公里，县城建成区实现6.9平方公里。人口城镇化率实现31.4%。

大力发展经济。2011年非公有制工商户和个体工商户发展到13237户，注册资金6.13亿元；保险实现收入0.19亿元；卷烟收入1.47亿元；电力售电收入1.14亿元，纳税1342.32万元；建筑业增加值1.9亿元；旅游收入2.16亿元；招商引资到位6.5亿元；劳务输出收入1.05亿元；金融各项存款余额30.25亿元，现金收入突破5亿元大关；国土出让实现收入2.59亿元。乡镇企业总产值9.5亿元，较上年增长1.2%，实现增加值1.8亿元，税金0.17亿元；科技推出示范基地9000亩，带动10万亩，实现亩产值1.5万元。

厦蓉高速公路榕江段头塘立交桥
Xiamen-Chengdu Expressway the Rongjiang segment Toutang overpass

Rongjiang County is located at the southern of the Qiandongnan, an area of 3,315.8 square kilometers, 1.31 hectares of arable land, exempted 6 towns, 13 townships (including ethnic townships 6), 260 administrative villages, 7 neighborhood, 3 communities, the 1,653 group of villagers' groups, 78 residents' groups, a total of 85,800 households, 354,700 people, including ethnic minority population accounts for 79.88%. The county has a total of 17 ethnic groups, including the Dong, Miao, Han, Shui, and Yao population of over 50,000. The major minerals, antimony, lead, antimony, and stone coal. The forest coverage rate of 74.71%.

榕江县工业园区建设39个项目同时开工奠基仪式
Rongjiang County Industrial Park, 39 project groundbreaking ceremony

贵州宏发木业有限公司生产的产品正在装车外销
Guizhou Hongfa Wood Co., Ltd. products are loading for export

榕江县人民医院
Rongjiang County People's Hospital

In 2011, GDP was 2.285 billion yuan, an increase of 17% over the previous year. The first, second, tertairy industries were 826 million yuan, 556 million yuan and 903 million yuan, an increase of 8.8%, 22.7% and 21.4%, respectively, compared with last year. Rural areas, animal husbandry and fishery output value of 1.205 billion yuan, an increase of 10.89% over last year. Industrial output value 1.539 billion yuan, an increase of 45.74% over last year. Total fiscal revenue of 1.153 billion yuan (including special funds), an increase of 20.72%. Local fiscal revenue of 260 million yuan, an increase of 62.46%. Financial expenditure of 1.153 billion yuan, an increase of 27.32%. The total fixed asset investment of 2.2 billion yuan. The key projects under construction, the county Ring Road East, the old city road (Shiban street), transformation of the county People's Hospital Complex 16. County traffic mileage of 3,424.9 km. Communication services to achieve 105 million yuan. County planning expanded to 56.4 square kilometers, the county built-up areas to achieve 6.9 square kilometers. Population urbanization rate is 31.4%.

Develop the economic development. In 2011, non-public businesses and individual business development to 13,237, with registered capital of 613 million yuan; insurance revenue of 19 million yuan; cigarette revenue of 147 million yuan; power from electricity sales revenue of 114 million yuan, tax 13.4232 million yuan; construction increase value of 190 million yuan; tourism revenue of 216 million yuan; investment in place of 650 million yuan; labor export revenue of 105 million yuan; financial balance of 3.025 billion yuan deposits, cash receipts exceeded 500 million yuan mark; Homeland transfer income of 259 million yuan. The total output value of township enterprises was 950 million yuan, an increase of 1.2% over last year, the added value of 180 million yuan and tax of 17 million yuan; Science and Technology launched the 9,000 mu of demonstration bases, driven by 100,000 mu, 15,000 yuan per mu value.

榕江万亩大坝和千户侗寨
The Rongjiang ten thousand mu dam and one thousand Dongzhai

榕江新城区天佑商城和祥和小区一角
The Rongjiang new city Tianyou mall, and Xianghe district corner

榕江县车江千户侗寨侗族萨玛节抬官人
Rongjiang County Chejiang one thousand Dongzhai Dong Sama Festival lift Husband

榕江县速生丰产杉木林
Rongjiang County fast growing fir

高度关注民生。2011年发放城低保、农低保、基本生活补助、救济款、大病医疗、五项保险和“一折通”兑现各项补贴共3.48亿元，人民生活得到较大改善，全社会消费品零售总额实现7.4亿元，城镇居民人均可支配收入21317.38元，人均消费支出2086.25元；农民人均占有粮255.21公斤，纯收入3623元。

竭诚办好事业。2011年有各级各类学校272所，在校在园学生59529人，教职工3176人。幼儿园、小学、初中和“三残”学生入学率分别为91%、99.1%、97.4%和94.5%；有各级各类医院16所、903张病床，医务人员649人，全年诊断病人25.42万人，住院4.56万人，手术1810台次；广播、电视实现村村通并且数字化；体育、旅游有序发展。

着力科学发展。2011年完成政府机构改革，实现依法管理和规范管理各项事务；完善服务窗口，简化审批程序，高效率的服务社会；重点打击贪污腐败分子和危害社会稳定、扰乱经济秩序的不法分子，取缔反人类反科学的邪教组织，铲除“黄”、赌、毒集团窝点。优化了竞争环境，净化了投资环境，美化了人居环境，社会稳定，物价平稳，人民安居乐业。

新建的榕江大桥
The new Rongjiang Bridge

通往雷公山的旅游公路
Leading to the Leigong Mountain tourist road

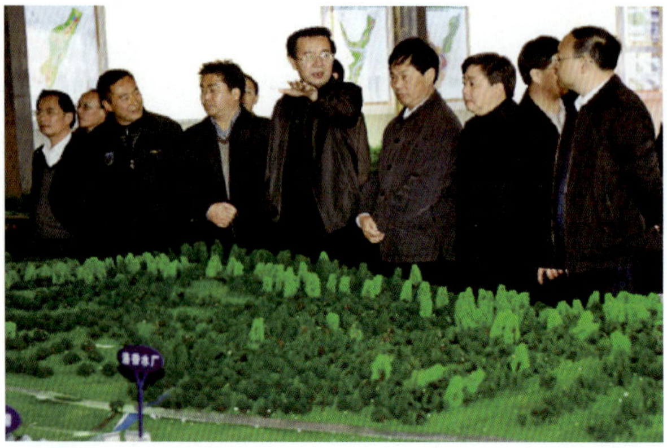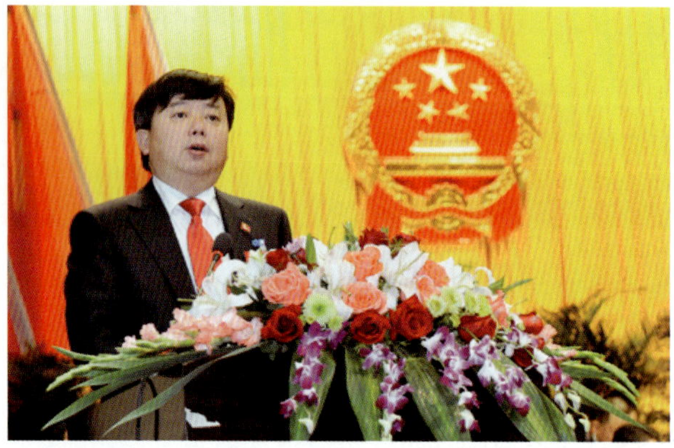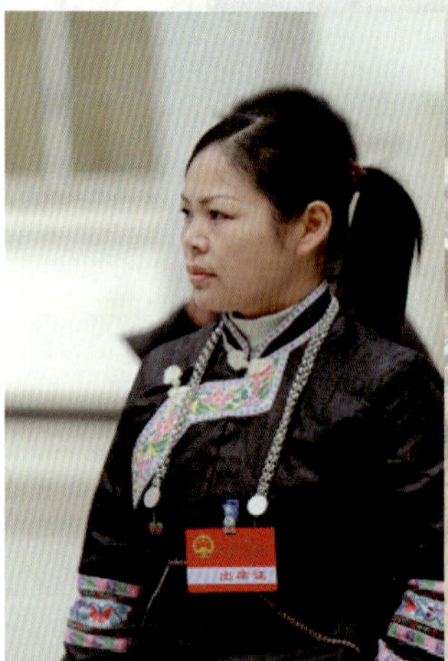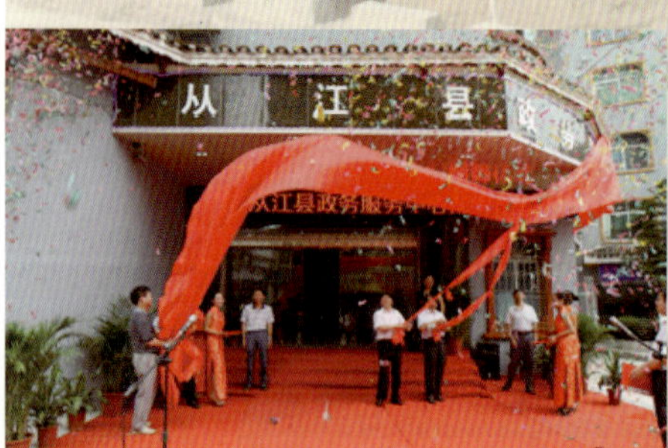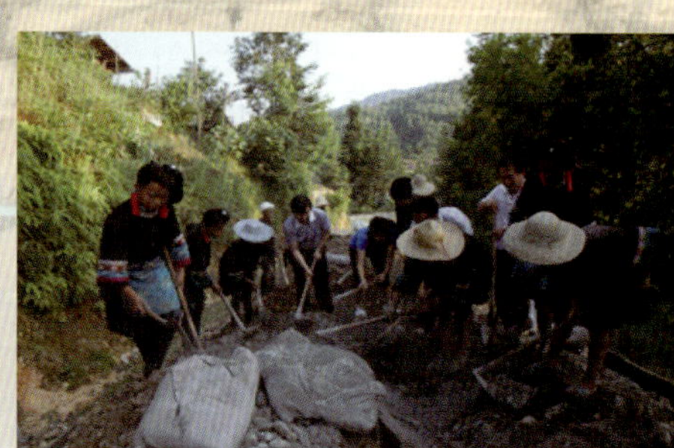

榕江县寨蒿镇新貌
Rongjiang County Zhaigao town new look

榕江县江边寨水乡风光
Rongjiang County Jiangbai village River Scenery

百瀑溪风光
Baipuxi landscape

白玉兰
Michelia alba

榕江县优质蔬菜基地
Rongjiang County high-quality vegetable base

Highly concerned about people's livelihood. In 2011, guaranteeing payment of the city, agricultural guaranteeing the basic living allowance, relief funds, catastrophic health care, five insurance and "one card" to honor the subsidies of 348 million yuan, the People's life has been greatly improved, the whole retail sales of social consumer goods to achieve 740 million yuan in total, per capita disposable income of urban residents was 21,317.38 yuan, 2,086.25 yuan per capita consumption expenditure; farmers' per capita grain of 255.21 kg, the net income of 3,623 yuan.

Dedicated to run the business. In 2011, types of schools at all levels of 272, 59,529 students in the school, faculty 3,176. Kindergarten, elementary, junior high school, and "disabled" student enrollment rate was 91%, 99.1%, 97.4% and 94.5%; types of hospitals at all levels of 16, 903 beds, 649 medical personnel, throughout the year to diagnose and treat patients 254,200, 45,600 people hospitalized, surgery 1,810; radio, television got to every village and digital; sports, tourism had orderly development.

Focus on scientific development. In 2011, to complete the reform of government institutions, and management in accordance with the law and regulate the management of the affairs; improve the service window, simplifying approval procedures, efficient service to the community; focus on combating corruption and corrupt elements and harm social stability, disrupt the economic order criminals to eliminate anti- human anti-science cult to eradicate the "yellow", gambling, drug syndicate dens. Optimize the competitive environment, and purified investment environment, and beautify the living environment, social stability, price stability, the people live peacefully and work happily.

赫 章 县

Hezhang County

赫章县城城南开发区一角

Hezhang county south city the development zone corner

赫章县位于贵州西部，面积3250平方公里，其中耕地面积582104亩，辖1个矿区社区服务管理局、21个乡（其中少数民族乡12个）、6个镇，456个村民委员会、9个社区居民委员会。人口较多的少数民族有彝族、苗族。主要矿藏有铁、铅、锌、煤、铜。

全年生产总值44.4亿元，比上年增长17%，产业结构从传统的“一二三”向“三一二”优化，产业结构比为32.1：26.19：41.71，人均生产总值6830元。农林牧渔业总产值21.82亿元，增长15.36%；工业实现现价工业总产值43.02亿元，同比增长36.9%。全社会固定资产投资完成65.9亿元，同比增长123.76%。全社会消费品零售总额8.9亿元，同比增长21.4%。城镇居民人均可支配收入16126元，同比增长13.9%。农民人均纯收入3892元，同比增长24.5%。城镇居民人均住房面积38.41平方米，同比增长1.03平方米。农村居民人均住房面积29.1平方米，同比增长2.09平方米。全县各项存款余额42.63亿元，同比增长13.59%；贷款余额14.44亿元，同比增长26.56%。

工业经济逐步转型。城镇化建设步伐明显加快。“三农”工作成效明显。基础设施建设明显改观。改革开放稳步推进。文化旅游发展水平不断提升。生态环境建设扎实推进。“和谐赫章”建设取得新进展。

哲庄坝红军战斗遗址纪念碑

Zhe Zhuang dam the Red Army fighting the site of the monument

赫章县珠市装备制造工业园区内建设中的道坤铁业有限责任公司一角

Hezhang County Zhushi Construction equipment manufacturing industrial park Daokun iron industry limited liability company of the iceberg

赫章县农危改与村庄整治示范点——平山乡中寨村中寨组

Hezhang County Farmers dilapidated building and village renovation demonstration - Ping Shan Zhai the Walled group

韭菜坪石林迎宾门
The Joicaoping Shilin Yingbin gate

雨磨山上牛羊成群
Cattle and sheep flocks in Yumo Hill

二台坡上的白云朵
Ertai slope of the white clouds

种植三年挂果的嫁接核桃
Planted three years of fruiting grafted walnut

Hezhang County is located in western Guizhou Province, with an area of 3,250 square kilometers, of which 582,104 acres of arable land, the jurisdiction of a Mining Area Community Services Authority, 21 townships (including minority township 12), 6 towns, 456 of villagers' committee, 9 community members. More population are Yi, Miao ethnic minority. The main mineral deposits of iron, lead, zinc, coal, copper.

The annual GDP of 4.44 billion yuan, an increase of 17% over the previous year, the industrial structure from the traditional "123" to "312" optimize, industrial structure is 32.1:26.19:41.71, 6,830 yuan of per capita GDP. Agriculture, forestry, animal husbandry and fishery output value of 2.182 billion yuan, an increase of 15.36%; industrial price of industrial output value 4.302 billion yuan, an increase of 36.9%. The total fixed asset investment was 6.59 billion yuan, an increase of 123.76%. The total retail sales of the whole society is 890 million yuan, an increase of 21.4%. The urban residents per capita disposable income of 16,126 yuan, an increase of 13.9%. The per capita net income of farmers was 3,892 yuan, an increase of 24.5%. The per capita housing area of urban residents was 38.41 square meters, an increase of 1.03 square meters. Rural residents per capita housing area of 29.1 square meters, an increase of 2.09 square meters. The county the deposit balance of 4.263 billion yuan, an increase of 13.59%; loan balance of 1.444 billion yuan, an increase of 26.56%.

赫章县核桃深加工企业“赫之林”牌核桃乳
Hezhang County Walnut deep processing enterprise "He Zhi Lin" brand walnut milk

赫章标准化半夏示范基地
The Hezhang standardized Pinellia demonstration base

The gradual transformation of the industrial economy. Markedly accelerated the pace of urbanization. "Three rural" work achieved remarkable success. Marked improvement in infrastructure construction. The reform and opening up pushed steadily. The level of development of cultural tourism has been increasing. Push forward the construction of ecological environment. "Harmonious the Hezhang" construction made new progress.

松桃苗族自治县

Songtao Miao Autonomous County

县委书记冉晓东（右四）调研工业化
County party secretary Ran Xiaodong (fourth from right) had research of industrialization

县长叶德恩（右二）调研农业产业化
Magistrate Ye Deen (second from right) had survey of agricultural industrialization

松桃苗族自治县位于贵州省东北部，辖28个乡镇、509个行政村，面积3400平方公里，人口73万，其中以苗族为主的22个少数民族占总人口的68.1%。

2011年，全县地方生产总值实现49.4亿元，比上年增长16.5%。财政总收入完成6.1亿元，比上年增长44.2%。城镇居民可支配收入和农民人均纯收入分别达到12996元和3680元，比上年分别增长20.1%和24.5%。工业经济迅猛发展，农业产业化经营强势推进，城镇建设日新月异，社会各项事业蓬勃发展，全县呈现出经济快速增长、社会繁荣稳定、人民安居乐业的大好局面。

松桃气候宜人，山川秀丽，交通便捷，矿产资源较为丰富。境内有铜仁•凤凰机场，渝怀铁路穿境而过，公路、铁路、航空“三位一体”的交通网络正不断优化升级。境内已探明具有开发价值的矿产资源有20余种，其中锰的远景储量达1.2亿吨，占全国总储量的八分之一，硅矿储量超过1.2亿吨。同时，又是国家页岩气先导区之一，初步探明储量在1万亿立方米以上。

近年来，松桃按照“优化环境、塑造形象，融入湘渝、扩大开放，整合资源、讲求质效，抢抓机遇、建设小康”的总体思路，深入实施“环境立县、产业富县、城镇兴县、民生和县、人才强县”的发展思路，着力推动全县经济社会又好又快、更好更快发展，先后被评为“全国粮食生产大县”、“中央财政现代农业建设示范项目县”、“全国小型农田水利建设重点县”和“贵州省草地生态畜牧业产业化科技扶贫项目示范县”、“贵州省油茶发展核心示范县”、“省级文明卫生县城”、“全国平安建设先进县”、“全国科普示范县”，及“中国民间绝技艺术之乡”、“中国滚龙艺术之乡”和“贵州省苗族花鼓艺术之乡”。

松桃新貌
Songtao new look

生态茶产业
Ecological tea industry

Songtao Miao Autonomous County is located in the northeast of Guizhou Province, jurisdiction over 28 townships, 509 administrative villages, with an area of 3,400 square km, population of 730,000, of which 22 Miao-based minority population accounted for 68.1% of the total population.

连接杭瑞、渝湘高速的迓大二级路
Connecting Hangzhou Ruian, Chongqing Hunan high-speed Yada Second-class road

In 2011, the local GDP of the county to achieve 4.94 billion yuan, up 16.5% over the previous year. The total fiscal revenue of 610 million yuan, an increase of 44.2% over the previous year. The urban residents' disposable income and rural per capita net income reached 12,996 yuan and 3,680 yuan, an increase of 20.1% and 24.5%, respectively, than last year. The rapid development of the industrial economy, the industrial management of agriculture to promote strongly, rapid urban construction, social undertakings flourish, the county showing a rapid economic growth, social prosperity and stability, excellent situation of the people live and work.

Songtao owns pleasant climate, beautiful scenery, convenient transportation, mineral resources are more abundant. Tongren • Phoenix Airport, Chongqing-Huaihua railway passing through the territory, the transport network of road, rail, air, "Trinity" is the optimization and upgrading. Province with proven mineral resources development value of more than 20 species, of which manganese prospective reserves of 120 million tons, accounting for one eighth of the country's total reserves, silicon ore reserves of over 120 million tons. At the same time, one of the national pilot area of shale gas, initial proved reserves of more than 1 trillion cubic meters.

In recent years, Songtao in accordance with "optimize the environment, to shape the image, get into Xiangyu, expand opening up, and integration of resources, emphasis on the quality effect, seize the opportunity, building well-off" the general idea, in-depth implementation of "environmental legislation in the county, industry rich the ocunty, cities and towns prosper the county, livelihood harmony the county, talent strong the county" development ideas, efforts to promote sound and rapid economic and social developmetn in the county, better and faster development, has been rated as "the nation's grain-producing counties", "the central finance modern agricultural construction demonstration project counties", "small water conservancy farmland construction key counties" and "Poverty Reduction Project of Guizhou Province grassland ecological animal husbandry industry, science and technology demonstration counties", "Guizhou Province Camellia core model county", "provincial civilized health county", advanced county of national peace building", "the National Popular Science Demonstration County", and "Chinese hometown of folk skills of art", "the art of rolling dragon township" and "the township of Guizhou Province Miao Drum Art".

黄板500千伏变电站
Huangban 500 kV substation

奋进的锦屏

Jinping Advancing in a Pioneering Spirit

把脉锦屏林业
Pulse Jinping forestry

花脸龙的魅力
Charm of Baikal dragon

锦屏地处黔东南州东部，因境内“青山似锦，秀丽如屏”而得名。面积1596.9平方公里，辖7镇、8乡，人口22.7万人，苗、侗等少数民族占总人口的88%。境内资源丰富，木材蓄积量769万立方米，森林覆盖率72%；矿产主要有黄金、青石、石灰石、硅矿石和陶瓷高岭土等；水能资源理论蕴藏量129万千瓦，装机容量118万千瓦。

2011年，全县上下紧紧围绕“加速发展、扩大总量、奋力赶超、推动跨越”的主基调，重点实施工业强县、城镇带县、旅游活县三大战略，进一步优化发展环境、政策环境和服务环境，依托“三材一电一矿一特（木材、建材、石材，电力，矿产，特产）”资源禀赋，大力发展林业、建材、石材、电力、矿产精细化加工、特色农产品“六大”产业，统筹抓好扩投资、增总量、惠民生等各项工作，全面完成年初确定的各项主要目标任务，为“十二五”开好局、起好步。

经济增长提速进位。2011年，全县生产总值完成16.66亿元，同比增长16.8%；全社会固定资产投资完成11.76亿元，同比增长132.95%；财政总收入完成2.25亿元，同比增长40.51%，其中地方财政收入1.39亿元，增长52.67%。全省县（市、区）经济发展增比进位综合测评上升至58位。

三大战略强势起步。2011年，全县工业增加值完成5.79亿元，工业对经济增长的贡献率达60.8%，成为拉动经济增长的主要力量。锦屏工业园区稳步推进，完成总投资3.47亿元。加强市政基础设施建设，实施“绿化、亮化、美化”工程，城镇化率达28%。积极打造“隆里古城”和“三板溪湖”两张旅游名片，旅游总收入和旅游接待人数分别增长23.2%和19.6%。

基础条件继续改善。交通建设加快，“三黎”高速公路进入实质性建设；完成通村油路建设34.72公里，公路通车里程达1782.2公里。水利建设力度加大，全年新增有效灌溉面积4950亩。生态建设进行一步加快，完成营造林12.73万亩。

发展动力显著增强。全年新开工项目67个；全县金融机构存贷款余额分别达29亿元和10亿元；民间投资达到2亿元以上。对外开放力度加大，成功引进县外资金160.05亿元，实际到位资金17.63亿元。市场主体活力增强，实施民营经济三年倍增计划，民营经济占生产总值的比重达38.7%。

人民生活水平明显提高。实施“十大民生工程”，城镇居民家庭人均可支配收入11925元，增长16.2%；农民人均纯收入3638元，增长22.4%。完成易地扶贫搬迁1066人，减少贫困人口18000人。加大高中基础设施建设力度。建立社会救助和保障标准与物价上涨挂钩联动机制。完成农村危房改造5777户，开工建设保障性住房854套。医疗卫生机构基础设施得到改善，新型农村合作医疗参合率达到90%。

锦屏响水坝（中型）水库灌溉工程开工仪式
The Jinping Xiaoshuiba irrigation dams reservoir irrigation project (medium) groundbreaking ceremony

项目签约
Projects signed

喜庆的夜晚
Festive night

Jinping is located in the eastern part of Qiandongnan, named after the territory of "Castle bright Peak, beautiful like screen". Area of 1,596.9 square kilometers, jurisdiction over 7 towns and 8 rural, population of 227,000 people, the Miao, Dong and other ethnic minorities accounted for 88% of the total population. The rich resources in the territory, 7.69 million cubic meters of wood volume, 72% of forest coverage; mineral gold, bluestone, limestone, silicon ore and ceramic kaolin; reserves of 1.29 million kilowatts of hydropower resources in theory, the installed capacity of 1.18 million kilowatts.

In 2011, the county up and down closely around the "to accelerate the development and expansion of the total, struggling to catch up, to promote leap" the main tone, focusing on the implementation of industrial strong county, cities and towns push the county, tourism living county three major strategies, to further optimize the development environment, policy environment and service environment, relying on "a special three materials one power and one mine one specialty(wood, building materials, stone, power, mining, specialty)" resource endowments, vigorously develop forestry, building materials, stone, electricity, mineral fine processing of local agricultural products the "big six" industry, co-ordinating a good job expanding investment, increase the total amount of benefiting people's livelihood and the full completion of the main objectives and tasks identified at the beginning of the year, made a a good beginning, a good first step for the "12th Five-Year".

Economic growth speed binary. In 2011, GDP in the county completed 1.666 billion yuan, up 16.8%; the whole society fixed assets investment was 1.176 billion yuan, an increase of 132.95%; total fiscal revenue of 225 million yuan, an increase of 40.51%, including local fiscal income of 139 million yuan, an increase of 52.67%. Economic development of the province's counties (cities, districts) growth than the binary comprehensive evaluation up to 58.

锦屏夜景
Jinping night scene

隆里古城花脸龙
Longli ancient city of Baikal dragon

三板溪湖
SanBanXi Lake

Three major strategies for a strong start. In 2011, the industrial added value in the county completed 579 million yuan, the industrial contribution to the economic growth rate of 60.8%, becoming the main force driving the economic growth. Jinping Industrial Park pushed steadily, and completed a total investment of 347 million yuan. Strengthen the construction of municipal infrastructure, the implementation of "Green, lighting, beautification" project, the urbanization rate of 28%. Actively to build the "Longli city" and "Sanban Xihu" two travel card, the total tourism income and the number of tourist increased by 23.2% and 19.6%, respectively.

The basic conditions continue to improve. To accelerate transportation construction, "San-Li" Highway to enter into a substantive construction; completed through the village of oil construction of 34.72 kilometers, the highway mileage of 1,782.2 km. Water conservancy construction intensified, the annual effective irrigation area of 4,950 mu. Ecological construction step to speed up, completion of 127,300 mu of afforestation.

The devekopment momentum has markedly increased. Yearly start projects 67; balance of deposits and loans of financial institutions in the county of 2.9 billion yuan and 1 billion yuan; private investment reached 200 million yuan. Opening to the outside world has been intensified, and the successful introduction of the county outside the capital of 16.005 billion yuan and 1.763 billion yuan of the actual funds. Market players vitality, the implementation of the private economy in a three-year plan to double, the private economy accounted for a proportion of GDP reached 38.7%.

People's living standard has improved significantly. Implementation of the "10 livelihood projects", urban households per capita disposable income of 11,925 yuan, an increase of 16.2%; per capita net income of farmers was 3,638 yuan, an increase of 22.4%. Completion of the ex-site poverty alleviation relocation of 1,066 people, reduce poverty population of 8,000 people. Increase the infrastructure construction in high school. Establishment of social assistance and security standards and price increases linked to the linkage mechanism. Completed rural renovating dilapidated houses in 5,777, started the 854 sets of building affordable housing. The infrastructure of medical and health institutions to improve, the new rural cooperative medical participation rate reached 90%.

县城的早晨
The county morning

贞 丰 县

Zhenfeng County

"三月三"祭山节

"March 3" Memorial Ceremony for Mountain Festival

双乳峰景区

Breasts peak area

布依族"三月三"："三月三"即农历三月初三，是贞丰布依族人民在长期的生产和生活中形成的具有浓厚民族特色和地方特色的传统节日。2010年贞丰布依族"三月三"被国家文化部公布为第三批国家级级非物质文化遗产名录项目。

小屯古法造纸：在贵州的两个偏远山区，至今仍完好地保留着蔡伦式的造纸作坊。其中之一就是贞丰县小屯乡，用构皮作原材料制作白绵纸。2006年贞丰县小屯白棉纸手工制作技艺被国家文化部公布为第一批国家级级非物质文化遗产名录项目。

古法造纸

Ancient papermaking ioo

双乳峰景区：双乳峰景区位于贞丰县者相镇，峰顶海拔1265.8米，高出地面150多米，占地40公顷，被誉为"峰林绝品"、"天下奇观"。双乳峰景区于2009年双乳景区被评为"贵州省十大魅力景区之一"、"中国避暑名山"。

北盘江大桥

The Beipanjiang Bridge

北盘江大峡谷：北盘江，由下九盘进入景区，从鲁贡白泥田出境，由北向南东流贯景区，全长93公里。年均流量378.2m^3/s。入境点海拔493米，出境点海拔331米，在境内的自然落差162米。北盘江峡谷2002年通过国际旅游规划专家实地考察，被评为B级景区。

The Buyi "March 3" : "March 3" that is March third lunar month, is the traditional festivals with a strong ethnic and local characteristics which is the formation of Zhenfeng Buyi people in long-term production and life. Zhenfeng Buyi 2010 "March 3" was announced for the third national-level non-material cultural heritage project by the Ministry of Culture.

Xiaotun ancient papermaking : Two remote mountainous areas of Guizhou, is still well preserved Cai Lun-style paper-making workshop. One of them is Zhenfeng County Xiaotun village, using constitutive skin raw materials for production of white tissue-paper. Zhenfeng County Xiaotun white tissue paper manual production techniques in 2006 announced the first batch of national-level non-material cultural heritage project by the Ministry of Culture.

Breasts peak area : Breasts peak area is located in Zhenfeng County Zhexiang town, the peak elevation of 1,265.8 meters above the sea level, over 150 meter sabove the ground , covers an area of 40 hectares, known as the "peaks delicious," "the world wonders". Breasts peak area in 2009 breasts scenic is granted as "one of the 10 most charming area in Guizhou Province", "one of the summer mountains in China".

Beipanjiang Grand Canyon : Beipanjiang enter the area by Jiupan, and exit from the Lu Gong Bainitian, from north to south east penetration area, a length of 93 kilometers. The average annual flow of 378.2 m/s. The point of entry altitude of 493 m, the exit point 331 meters above sea level, in the territory of the natural drop of 162 meters. Beipanjiang Canyon in 2002 through international travel planning experts' field trips, and was named the B-level scenic spots.

借力国发二号　建设“三化同步”的先行示范区
——好花红故乡惠水

Leveraging the National Development II Construction of "three synchronization" first demonstration area

-The hometown of Haohuahong Huishui

委书记栗战书在惠水县大龙乡考察“185”助民增收示范工程——雅羊生姜种植基地
Provincial Party Committee Secretary Li Zhanshu investigated the "185" and assisting people with incomes demonstration project - Ya Yang ginger planting base in Dalong village Huishui county

惠水位于贵州中南部，县域总面积2470平方公里，辖8镇、17乡，总人口46万人，其中少数民族人口27.81万人。惠水县城坐落在涟江河畔，县城城区面积8.8平方公里。自然生态良好。

惠水人民在县委、县政府的领导下，抢抓机遇，奋发图强，建设“和谐幸福新惠水”，国民经济持续增长，各项社会事业稳步发展。2011年完成地区生产总值34.36亿元，同比增长15.8%，财政总收入4.01亿元，同比增长43.2%，农业总产值19.01亿元，同比增长2%，工业总产值58.34亿元，同比增长55.58%，规模工业增加值增长37.2 %，全社会固定资产投资42.56亿元，同比增长116.86%，社会消费品零售总额达到8.29亿元，同比增长20.3%，农民人均纯收入4668元，同比增长22.01%。

近年来，黔南州委州政府将惠水作为“三化同步”的试点县，又逢国家实施新一轮西部大开发和新阶段扶贫开发战略、黔中经济区建设、省委省政府实施“三化同步”发展战略和国务院出台国发二号文件扶持贵州加快发展优惠政策的有利时机，在科学发展观的统领下，惠水将建设成为黔中经济区“三化同步”的先行示范区，实现增比进位，跨越发展。惠水县将坚持以工业化带动城镇化，以城镇化推进工业化，以农业产业化服务工业化和城镇化。

在中央和省州党委政府的正确领导下，惠水县广大干部群众将坚持干字当头、敢字为先、拼字求胜，以国发二号文件为支点，从后发赶超的现实发力，奋力撬动“三化同步”跨越发展的历史杠杆。

长赵克志在惠水县永红公司调研
Governor Zhao Kezhi had research in Yonghong Company Huishui County

黔南州政协副主席、惠水县委书记吴丹深入基层调研
Qiannan CPPCC Vice Chairman and the secretary of Huishui County Wudan had research of county grassroots

惠水县政府县长万庆华与云南星长征投资开发控股集团有限责任公司成功签约
Huishui County government county magistrate Wan Qinghua signed with Yunnan Star Long March Investment Development Holding Group Co., Ltd. successfully

惠水县"携手强县之路"签约仪式
Huishui County "hand in the strong county road" signing ceremony

Huishui is located in central and southern Guizhou, owns the total area of 2,470 square kilometers, jurisdiction over 8 rural town and 17 villages, with a total population of 460,000, of which the minority population of 278,100. Huishui county located in Lian Jiang River, county urban area of 8.8 square kilometers. Natural ecosystems is good.

Under the leadership of the county committee and government, the people of Huishui seize the opportunity, to work hard and build a "harmonious happiness new Huishui" sustained national economic growth and steady development of various social undertakings. The 2011 GDP of 3.436 billion yuan, an increase of 15.8%, the total fiscal revenue of 401 million yuan, an increase of 43.2%, agricultural output value 1.901 billion yuan, an increase of 2%, industrial output value 5.834 billion yuan, an increase of 55.58, scale industrial added value increased 37.2%, total fixed asset investment of 4.256 billion yuan, an increase of 116.86%, total retail sales of social consumer goods reached 829 million yuan, up 20.3% and rural per capita net income of 4,668 yuan, an increase of 22.01%

In recent years, the Qiannan Committee state government made Huishui as a "three synchronization" pilot counties, has stimulated the national implementation of western development and the new phase of a new round of poverty alleviation and development strategies, the central Guizhou Economic Zone Construction, the implementation of the provincial government "three synchronization" development strategy and the State Council promulgated the National Development II documents to support Guizhou to speed up the development of preferential policies favorable opportunity, under the command of the scientific concept of development, Huishui will be built into the first demonstration of the central Guizhou economic Zone "three synchronization" area, increase than the binary, and leapfrog development. Huishui County will adhere to the industrialization and urbanization drive, promote industrialization, urbanization and the industrialization of agriculture, industrialization and urbanization.

Under the correct leadership of the central and provincial state party committee and government, Huishui County cadres and the masses will adhere to work as the leader, and dare the word first, fight to win , the National Development II documents as a fulcrum, from later catch up with reality force, struggling to leveraging the leverage of the "three synchronization" across the history of the development.

长田工业园区一角
One corner of Changtian Industrial Park

涟江广场夜景
Ripple River Plaza night scene

长 顺 县

Changshun County

领导视察
Leaders inspected

长顺县地处贵州黔中，面积1543平方公里。辖7个镇、10个乡、153个村居，1634个村民组，总人口25.78万人，少数民族人口占56%，主要以布依族、苗族为主。水能资源理论蕴藏量193597千瓦，可开发利用75970千瓦。矿产资源丰富。交通非常便利。自古被称为“夜郎故地，杜鹃之乡”，民风淳朴，风景优美。

2011年，长顺县地区生产总值达到19.21亿元，同比增长16.1%；财政总收入2.11亿元，同比增长38.1%，其中，一般预算收入完成1.3亿元，同比增长39.1%；规模以上工业总产值23.76亿元，同比增长82.9%；固定资产投资21.06亿元，同比增长83.1%；招商到位资金达26.83亿元，同比增长206%；社会消费品零售总额5.60亿元，同比增长20.2%；农民人均纯收入4341元，同比增长22.1%。

长顺以建设“活力园区、生态园区、创业园区、可持续发展园区”为目标，积极打造威远工业园区。截至目前，园区共签约入驻项目46个，签约投资总额为130.51亿元。所有产业项目投产后预计实现年产值100亿元，年创税8.5亿元。

长顺县按照工业新村、文化新村、景区新村和产业新村的不同定位，打造了39个环境优美的新村，形成景色优美、生态良好的山地城市特色景观。

长顺县紧紧抓住农业产业结构调整的历史机遇，扎实稳步开展各项工作，积极推进长顺农业现代化进程。2011年，长顺被列入“全国农产品主产区县”。

农村新风貌
A new look in rural areas

长顺职中规划效果图
Changshun vocational planning renderings

长顺浩瀚酒店
Changshun Haohan Hotel

长顺银杏王
Changshun ginkgo king

Changshun County is located in the central part of Guizhou, with an area of 1,543 square kilometers. Governs 7 towns, 10 townships, 153 villagers committees, 1,634 villagers groups, the total population of 257,800, minority population accounts for 56%, mainly Buyi and Miao. 193,597 kilowatts of the theoretical reserves of hydropower resources, development and utilization of 75,970 kilowatts. Rich in mineral resources. The traffic is very convenient. "Yelang old haunt, the cuckoo town" is named in the history, ancient simple and sincere, and beautiful scenery.

In 2011, Changshun County GDP reached 1.921 billion yuan, up 16.1%; total fiscal revenue of 211 million yuan, up 38.1%, of which general budget revenue of 130 million yuan, up 39.1%; scale industrial output value 2.376 billion yuan, up 82.9%; fixed assets investment of 2.106 billion yuan, up 83.1%; investment capital in place of 2.683 billion yuan, an increase of 206%; 560 million yuan of total retail sales of social consumer goods, an increase of 20.2%; rural per capita net income of 4,341 yuan, an increase of 22.1%.

长顺绿壳鸡蛋
Changshun green shell egg

Changshun takes the construction "energy park, ecological park, business park, sustainable development park," as the goal, and actively build the Weiyuan industrial Park. Up to now, the park signed a total of 46 assigned to the project, signing a total investment of 13.051 billion yuan. All industrial projects put into operation is expected to achieve annual output value of 10 billion yuan, annual tax of 850 million yuan.

Changshun County is in accordance with the different positioning of the Industrial Village, cultural Village, scenic Village and Industry New Village, to create 39 beautiful environment of New Village, a scenic, ecological characteristics of the landscape of mountainous city.

Changshun County firmly seize the historical opportunity of the agricultural structure adjustment, solid and steadily carry out the work, and actively promote the the Changshun agricultural modernization process. In 2011, Changshun is included in the "national agricultural production counties".

长顺高钙苹果
Changshun high calcium apple

中国茶城——湄潭

Chinese Tea City - Meitan

湄潭天下第一壶
The Meitan world first pot

湄潭，位于贵州高原北部，面积1864平方公里，辖9镇、6乡、132个村，总人口近50万，是黔北东部地区重要的交通枢纽。这里冬无严寒，夏无酷暑，森林覆盖率60.8%，素有“高原明珠”、“云贵小江南”之美誉。

湄潭，历史悠久，文化厚重，土地肥沃，物产丰富。2011年，全县生产总值达36. 62亿元，同比增长16. 1%；财政总收入达62113万元，地方一般预算收入达26877万元，同比分别增长56%和40%；金融机构存、贷款余额分别达53. 7亿元和25. 9亿元，同比分别增长19. 7%和34. 1%；城镇居民人均可支配收入达15185元，同比增长16. 2%；农民人均纯收入达5841元，同比增长17. 9%。

茶城人民正激情满怀、开拓奋进，全力打造“文明、高效、开放、平安、花园、清洁”六大湄潭，建成名副其实的“文明中国茶城”。

湄潭新农村
Meitan new rural

茶乡新农村(摄影/卢现艺)
Tea-rural new village (Photography/ Lu Xianyi)

Meitan, located in the northern part of Guizhou Plateau, with an area of 1,864 square kilometers, jurisdiction over 9 towns, 6 townships, 132 villages, with a total population of nearly 500,000, is an important transport hub of the Qianbei eastern part.Here the winter is not cold, summer isn ot hot, the forest coverage rate of 60.8%, known as the "pearl of the plateau", "Yunnan-Guizhou small southern" reputation.

Meitan onws long history, deep culture.Fertile land, abundant products. In 2011, the county's GDP reached 3.662 billion yuan, up 16.1% over the same period of the last year; total fiscal revenue reached 621.13 million yuan, the local general budget revenue amounted to 268.77 million yuan, an increase of 56% and 40% respectively; the balance of deposit and loans of financial institutions reached 5.37 billion yuan and 2.59 billion yuan, an increase of 19.7% and 34.1% respectively; urban residents per capita disposable income reached 15,185 yuan, up 16.2%; the per capita net income of farmers reached 5,841 yuan, an increase of 17.9%.

Tea City people are full of passion, forging ahead to build the "civilized, efficient, open, safe, garden, clean" six Meitan, and built a veritable "civilized Chinese Tea City".

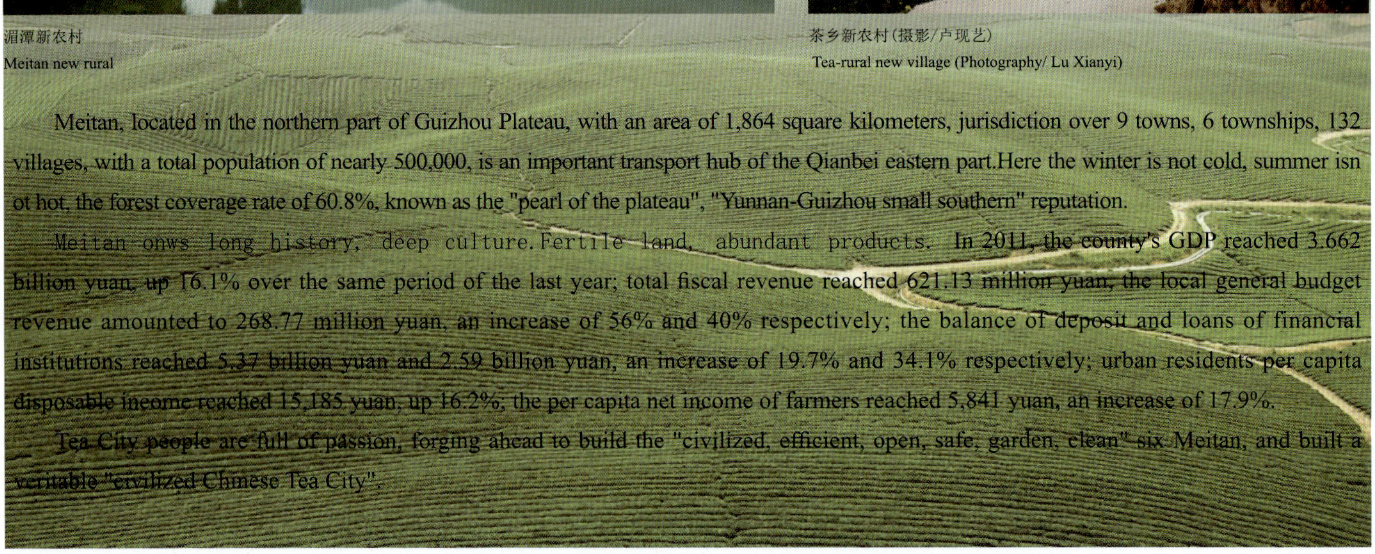

西部茶海景区
Sea area in the western tea

玉屏侗族自治县

Yuping Dong Minority Autonomous County

县委书记王俊铭（中）、县长安孝荣（左一）深入企业调研
County party secretary Wang Junming (middle), county mayor An Xiaorong (first from left) had depth research in the company

招商项目签约
Investment projects signed

企业集团成立
Enterprise Group was established

项目集中开工演出
Projects focused on start performance

完善的电网
Improved power grid

新农村建设
New rural construction

玉屏位于贵州省东部，素有“黔东门户”之称。全县总面积517平方公里，辖4镇2乡、84个村、9个社区，人口15万人，侗族人口占80%，是全国五个、全省唯一的侗族自治县。玉屏交通便捷；电力设施完善，国家电网覆盖全境，已成为贵州“西电东送”工程的一个重要支撑点；自然人文资源丰厚，是驰名中外的中国箫笛之乡、中国油茶之乡。

2011年，全县生产总值达30.8亿元，同比增长16% 。财政总收入4.12亿元，比上年增长46.09%，其中地方财政收入2.15亿元，同比增长42.75%。社会固定资产投资完成41.3亿元，比上年增长96%。其中固定资产投资完成39.29亿元，同比增长94.5%。全年社会消费品零售总额为4.92亿元，同比增长18.97%。农民人均纯收入5216元，同比增长22.6%。

Yuping is located in the eastern part of Guizhou Province, known as "Qiandong portal". County has a total area of 517 square kilometers, governs 4 towns and 2 townships,84 villages and 9 communities, the population of 150,000, Dong population accounted for 80%, is the only one of the country five, province one Dong Autonomous Minority County. Yuping owns convenient transportation; power facilities is good, the national grid covering the whole territory, has become an important support of the "West electricty to east" project in Guizhou; rich natural and cultural resources, is the hometown of the famous Chinese Xiaodi, China Camellia Township.

In 2011, the county's GDP reached 3.08 billion yuan, an increase of 16%. Total fiscal revenue of 412 million yuan, an increase of 46.09% over the previous year, including local fiscal revenue of 215 million yuan, an increase of 42.75%. Fixed asset investment was 4.13 billion yuan, an increase of 96% over the previous year. Fixed asset investment of 3.929 billion yuan, up 94.5%. The annual retail sales of social consumer goods amounted to 492 million yuan, an increase of 18.97%.The per capita net income of farmers was 5,216 yuan, an increase of 22.6%.

玉屏县城夜景
Yuping county night scene

普 定 县

Puding County

县委书记彭贤伦（中）到猴场乡老甲村帮扶点调研

County party secretary Peng Xianlun (middle) to Houchang Township Laojia village helping sataion to have research

县长方东（中）到猫洞乡普茂煤矿检查安全生产工作

Magistrate Fang Dong (middle) to Maodong village Pu Mao coal mine to check the work of production safety

安普城市干道系列项目开工典礼

An'pu city roads series project groundbreaking ceremony

黄桶储备煤基地奠基

Huangtong reserves of coal base foundation

普定县面积1091.6平方公里，辖5镇、6乡（其中4个民族乡）、317个行政村、10个村（居）委会。人口46.66万人，人口较多的少数民族有苗族、布依族、仡佬族、彝族等。主要矿藏有煤、铁、铅锌、铜、硅石等十余种，森林覆盖率40.5%。

2011年，全县生产总值完成36.78亿元，比上年增长（下同）16.1%。其中，农林牧渔总产值10.48亿元，增长3.8%；工业增加值13.59亿元，增长23.8%；第三产业实现增加值12.08亿元，增长17.2%。财政总收入（新口径）4.82亿元，增长21.6%，地方一般预算收入3亿元，增长34.2%。固定资产投资24.5亿元，增长88%。社会消费品零售总额9.44亿元，增长19.9%。金融机构存贷款余额分别达30.12亿元、42.07亿元，增长23.4%和22.93%。农民人均纯收入4088元，增长24.4%。公路通车里程1315.82公里，新建公路83.3公里（其中高速公路38.3公里）。年末固定电话用户22437户、移动电话用户66868户，电话普及率24部/百人，互联网用户9324户。

产业园区集聚功能增强。黄桶物流园区带动效应增强。城镇规划建设加快。农业产业化发展有力推进。招商引资取得新进展。大力推进社会管理创新。

建设中的普定新城

In the construction of Puding Metro

Puding County has an area of 1,091.6 square kilometers, jurisdiction over 5 town, 6 townships (4 ethnic townships), 317 administrative villages, 10 villages (neighborhood) committees. Population of 466,600 people, the more populous ethnic minorities such as Miao, Buyi, Gelao, Yi and so on. The main minerals are coal, iron, lead, zinc, copper, silica, etc. more than ten kinds, forest coverage of 40.5%.

建设中的安普城市大道

In the construction of the An'pu city's Road

In 2011, the county's GDP was 3.678 billion yuan, an increase of 16.1% over the previous year(same below). Among them, agriculture, forestry, animal husbandry and fishery output value of 1.048 billion yuan, an increase of 3.8%; industrial added value of 1.359 billion yuan, up 23.8%; tertiary industry added value of 1.208 billion yuan, an increase of 17.2%. Total fiscal revenue (new caliber) of 482 million yuan, an increase of 21.6%, local general budget revenue of 300 million yuan, an increase of 34.2%. Investment in fixed assets of 2.45 billion yuan, an increase of 88%. Retail sales of social consumer goods totaled 944 million yuan, an increase of 19.9%. Financial institutions to deposit and loan balances were 3.012 billion yuan, 4.207 billion yuan, an increase of 23.4% and 22.93%, respectively. The per capita net income of farmers was 4,088 yuan, an increase of 24.4%. Highway mileage of 1,315.82 km, 83.3 km of new highways (including 38.3 km of expressways). By the end of the year, the fixed phone users 2,2437, 66,868 mobile phone users, the telephone penetration rate of 24/100, internet users 9,324.

Industrial park gathering enhancements. Driving effect to enhance the Huangtong Logistics Park. Urban planning and construction accelerated. Effectively promote the development of agricultural industrialization. The investment made new progress. Great efforts to promote social management innovation.

夜郎湖风光

Yelang lake scenery

黔中首郡——思南

YThe first County in Central Guizhou - Sinan

省长赵克志到思南调研
Governor Zhao Kezhi to Sinan have research

思林水电站建成
Silin hydropower station was built

打火机厂开工
Lighter Plant started

文化产业园开工
Cultural Industrial Park started

思南位于黔东北铜仁地区西部，辖13个镇、14个民族乡，489个行政村、37个社区，地域面积2230.5平方公里，杂居着汉、土家、苗、满、蒙古等18个民族，总人口68万。思南历史源远流长，是乌江中下游地区的商品集散地和经济文化中心，素有"黔中首郡"、"乌江明珠"之称，是贵州开发最早的县份之一。思南文化底蕴深厚，人才辈出。思南资源富集，发展能源产业、现代农业、石材产业有坚实基础。境内山川秀丽，风景优美，是国土资源科普示范基地、乌江喀斯特国家地质公园。县内温泉日总产水量突破10000吨，被授予全国第六个、西南地区第一个全国温泉开发利用示范区。

2011年，全县完成生产总值49.31亿元，同比增长22%。财政总收入4.07亿元，同比增长50.32%。一般预算收入2.32亿元，同比增长43.64%。一般预算支出19.6亿元，同比增长22.71%。农民人均纯收入3683.48元，同比增长23%。完成固定资产投资62亿元，同比增长75%。完成工业总产值24.8亿元，同比增长55%。金融机构存贷款余额分别达到51.6亿元、48.8亿元，同比分别增长25%、20%。社会消费品零售总额12亿元，同比增长25%。

国家实施新一轮西部大开发战略给思南带来了千载难逢的发展机遇。思南县将积极统筹城乡发展，促进经济社会发展与人口、资源、环境相协调，奋力在工业化、城镇化及农业产业化发展方面取得重大突破，努力实现经济社会发展历史性跨越。

建设中的打火机厂、皮具加工厂
Construction of lighter factory, leather factory

思南县灯油坝产业园一角
Sinan County, kerosene dam corner of Industrial Park

Sinan is located in the western part of the northeastern Guizhou Tongren Prefecture, jurisdiction over 13 towns, 14 ethnic townships, 489 administrative villages, 37 communities, the geographical area of 2,230.5 square kilometers, mixed with 18 ethnic groups of Han, Tujia, Miao, Manchu, Mongolian, total population of 680,000. Sinan had a long history, the commodity distribution center and the economic and cultural center of the Wujiang River region, known as the "central Guizhou County", "Wu River Pearl," is one of the earliest development counties in Guizhou. Sinan's rich cultural heritage, talented people. Sinan is rich in resources, the development of energy industries, modern agriculture, stone industry have a solid foundation. The territory of the beautiful mountains and rivers and beautiful scenery, land and resources model base of science, the Wu River Karst National Geopark. County hot springs water production exceeded 10,000 tons, was awarded the sixth in the country, southwest first national spa development and utilization of the demonstration area.

建设中的杭瑞高速思南段乌江特大桥
The construction Hangrui high-speed the Sinan section of Wujiang River Bridge

In 2011, the county completed a GDP of 4.931 billion yuan, an increase of 22%. Total fiscal revenue of 4.07 billion yuan, up 50.32%. The general budget revenue of 232 million yuan, an increase of 43.64%. General budget expenditure of 1.96 billion yuan, up 22.71%. Rural per capita net income of 3,683.48 yuan, an increase of 23%. Investment in fixed assets of 6.2 billion yuan, an increase of 75%. Industrial output value 2.48 billion yuan, up 55%. Deposits and Loans of financial institutions reached 5.16 billion yuan, 4.88 billion yuan, an increase of 25%, 20% respectively. The total retail sales of social consumer goods was 1.2 billion yuan, an increase of 25%.

The national implementation of the new western development strategy to the Sinan bring a golden opportunity for development. Sinan County will actively co-ordinate urban and rural development, promoting economic and social development, population, resources, environmental coordination, struggling to achieve a major breakthrough in terms of industrialization, urbanization and industrialization of agriculture development, and strive to achieve a historic leap in economic and social development.

思南许家坝烤烟示范区
The Sinan Xu Jiaba flue-cured tobacco demonstration area

思南县许家坝种草养畜草场
Sinan County, Xu Jiaba forage for raising livestock pasture

贵定县

Guiding County

贵定县城新貌
Guiding county new look

建设中的昌明经济开发区
Changming economic development zone construction

贵定县云雾贡茶
Guiding County Cloud tribute tea

贵定娃娃鱼
Guiding salamander

贵定县面积1631平方公里，辖12乡、8镇，95个村民委员会，17个居民委员会。人口30.28万人，其中少数民族15.21万人。森林覆盖率48%。矿藏丰富，区位优越，素有“黔中咽喉”和“贵阳门户”之称。

2011年，全县生产总值34.81亿元，同比增长15.30%；农林牧渔业总产值7.53亿元，比上年增长6.02%；工业总产值32.03亿元，比上年增长33.63%；财政总收入4.8亿元，比上年增长37.74%；财政总支出11.89亿元，比上年增长29.91%；固定资产投资35.92亿元，比上年增长18.76%。全县通车里程1318.53公里，河内航道里程12公里，移动数字通讯覆盖20个乡镇。小城镇建设稳步推进，县城基础设施建设不断完善，人居环境不断美化并辐射到周边乡镇。社会消费品零售总额7.27亿元，城镇居民可支配收入12880元，农民人均纯收入4612元。招商引资到位资金20.40亿元，全年共接待旅游人数210万人次，旅游总收入16.5亿元。

Guiding County has an area of 1,631 square kilometers, exempted 12 township, 8 towns, 95 of the villagers' committees, 17 of residents' committees. Population of 302,800, including 152,100 minority population. Forest coverage rate of 48%. Mineral reserve is rich, superior location, known as the "central Guizhou throat" and "the Guiyang portal".

In 2011, the county's GDP was 3.481 billion yuan, an increase of 15.30%; agriculture, forestry, animal husbandry and fishery output value of 753 million yuan, an increase of 6.02% over the previous year; industrial output value 3.203 billion yuan, an increase of 33.63% over the previous year; total fiscal income of 480 million yuan, up 37.74% over the previous year; total fiscal expenditure of 1.189 billion yuan, an increase of 29.91% over the previous year; fixed assets investment of 3.592 billion yuan, an increase of 18.76% over the previous year. County traffic mileage of 1,318.53 km, 12 km Hanoi Waterways, mobile digital communications coverage to 20 towns. Construction of small towns pushed steadily, and county infrastructure construction constantly improved, the living environment continue to beautify and radiation to the surrounding towns. The total retail sales of social consumer goods 727 million yuan, the urban residents' disposable income of 12,880 yuan and rural per capita net income of 4,612 yuan. 2.04 billion yuan of investment capital in place, throughout the year received a total tourist arrivals of 2.1 million people, total tourism income of 1.65 billion yuan.

关岭县

Guanling County

关岭自治县举办“四月八风情节”
Guanling county held "April 8, the wind plot"

关岭位于贵州省中部，隶属安顺市，属国家新阶段扶贫开发重点扶持县之一。面积1468平方公里，耕地面积225725亩，辖8镇、6乡，241个村民委员会，5个居民委员会，5个社区，人口370616万人，少数民族人口23.94万人。全县森林覆盖率40.28%，素有“天然温室”之美誉，是旅游、休闲、度假的理想之地。

2011年，全县实现生产总值31.02亿元，同比增长16.1 %；全社会固定资产投资预计完成15.07亿元，同比增长110.7%；财政总收入3.1亿元（含基金），同比增长25.1%；一般预算收入1.62亿元，同比增长21.2%；社会消费品零售总额预计完成11.14亿元，同比增长19.7%。2011年，关岭县综合评价在全省88个县区排位中赶超进位，从2010年的第83位上升至2011年的62位，实现赶超21个位次。

关岭交通区位优势明显，旅游资源丰富，矿产资源丰富，开发潜力巨大。

2011年关岭旅游推介会
2011 Guanling Tourism Promotion Council

关岭自治县自然风光
Guanling county natural scenery

关岭自治县举办“花树节”活动
Guanling county held the "blooms Festival"

关岭自治县举办第二十届老年人运动会
Guanling county held its twentieth elderly Games

Guanling is located in the middle of Guizhou Province, belongs to the Anshun City, is one of the state new stage of poverty alleviation and development focus on supporting county. Area of 1,468 square kilometers, 225,725 acres of arable land, 8 towns and 6 townships, 241 village committees, 5 residents' committees, 5 communities, a population of 3,706,160,000 people, the minority population of 239,400. 40.28% of forest coverage in the county, known as the "natural greenhouse" reputation, is ideal for tourism, leisure, vacation.

In 2011, the county realized a GDP of 3.102 billion yuan, up 16.1%; total fixed asset investment is expected to be completed 1.507 billion yuan, an increase of 10.7%; total fiscal revenue of 310 million yuan (including the Fund), an increase of 5.1%; general budget revenue of 162 million yuan, an increase of 21.2%; total retail sales of social consumer goods is expected to complete 1.14 billion yuan, an increase of 19.7%. In 2011, Guanling County Comprehensive Evaluation catch up into the province's 88 counties, qualifying from 83 in 2010 rose to 62 in 2011, to achieve catch-up 21 ranking.

Guanling owns obvious traffic advantages, rich tourism resources, rich in mineral resources and huge development potential.

沿河土家族自治县

Yanhe Tujia Autonomous County

县委书记张翊皓（左一）在检查烤烟收购情况
The county party secretary Zhang Yihao (first from left) has the acquisition of checking flue-cured tobacco

县长任廷浬（左二）在企业调研
Magistrate Ren Tingli (second from left) has research in the enterprise

沿河土家族自治县位于贵州省东北角、铜仁市西北部，面积2468.8平方公里，辖22个乡镇，429个村、6个社区、13个居委会，总人口65万，其中以土家族为主体的少数民族人口占总人口的61.2%，是全国四个单一土家族自治县之一，贵州省唯一的单一土家族自治县，也是国家新阶段扶贫开发重点县、革命老区县和对外开放县。境内旅游资源丰富，有国家级自然保护区麻阳河、国家级风景名胜区和水利风景区乌江山峡、国家重点文物保护单位黔东特区革命委员会旧址，民族文化底蕴厚重，被文化部命名为“中国土家族山歌之乡”。

2011年，沿河土家族自治县抢抓西部大开发、新阶段扶贫开发等历史性机遇，围绕“两区一带”（武陵山经济协作区、黔北经济协作区、乌江特色经济产业带）区域发展布局，以融入成渝经济区为战略取向，紧扣“两加一推”主基调，大力实施工业强县和城镇化带动战略，坚持工业化、城镇化、农业产业化“三化”同步推进，加快发展以文化旅游产业为重点的第三产业，着力打好“强基础、兴产业、惠民生”攻坚战，奋力战胜各种自然灾害，实现了“十二五”良好开局，进入加快摆脱贫困、建设全面小康的新阶段。

经济总量实现新增长，2011年全县地方生产总值实现39.17亿元。农业产业化取得新成效。工业发展有了新突破。城乡面貌发生新变化。基础设施得到新改善。民生保障有了新提高。

县城乌江广场
County Wujiang River Plaza

县城丁字口片区
County T-mouth Area

县城夜景
County night scene

洪渡移民集镇新貌
Hungdu the immigrant town new look

工业园区标准厂房
Standard factory of the industrial park

乌江特色产业园区山峡生态工业区规划展示厅
The Wujiang characteristics Industrial Park gorge eco-industrial zone Planning Exhibition Hall

Yanhe Tujia Autonomous County is located in the northeast corner of Guizhou Province, northwest of Tongren City, wiht an area of 2,468.8 square kilometers, jurisdiction over 22 townships, 429 villages, 6 communities, 13 neighborhood committees, with a total population of 650,000, which the Tujia as the main minority accouts for 61.2% of the total population, is one of the four single Tujia Autonomous County, only a single Tujia Autonomous County in Guizhou Province, is also the country's new stage of poverty alleviation counties, old revolutionary counties, and opening up county. It is rich in tourism resources, the National Nature Reserve Mayang River gorge, a national scenic area and the Water Conservancy Scenic Area Wujiang Gorge, Metres of the Revolutionary Committee of the SAR former site of the national key cultural relics protection units. The national culture is thick, the Ministry of Culture named as "the hometown of Chinese Tujia folk song".

In 2011, Yanhe Tujia Autonomous County to seize the historic opportunity of western development, poverty alleviation and development of a new stage, around the vicinity of the "two areas one belt"(economic cooperation zone in Wuling Mountains, Qianbei areas of economic cooperation, the Wujiang characteristics Economic zone) regional development layout, strategic orientation, focuses on the main tone of the "two-plus-one push" into the Chengdu-Chongqing Economic Zone, vigorously implement the strategies for industrial county and urbanization led, to adhere to the industrialization and urbanization, the industrialization of agriculture, "three changes" to proceed, with the accelerate the development of tertiary industry focus on the cultural tourism industry, efforts to lay the "strong foundation, emerging industries, and benefit people's livelihood" battle, struggling to overcome all kinds of natural disasters, which realized a good start for "The 12th Five-Year Plan", enter accelerate out of poverty , a new stage of building a comprehensive well-off.

The total economy to achieve new growth, in 2011 the county local GDP to achieve 3.917 billion yuan. The industrialization of agriculture has made new achievements. The industrial development of new breakthroughs. Urban and rural areas has undergone changes. Infrastructure has been improved. Livelihood security has a new improved.

建设中的乌江沙沱电站
The Wujiang Shatuo power plant construction

年产10万立方米商品混凝土生产线
Annual output of 100,000 cubic meters of concrete production line of goods

塘坝金竹贡米基地
The Tangba Jinzhu rice base

洪渡蛋鸡养殖场
Hungdu egg hen breeding farms

山水册页 幸福亨通

Landscape album happiness prosper

穿境而过的汕昆高速公路（板江段）建成通车
Through Habitat Shantou Queensland highway (Banjiang section) was opened to traffic

投资3.5亿元的册亨南华糖厂建成投产
Ceheng nanhua sugar mills to invest 350 million yuan put into operation

册亨县位于黔西南州东南部，面积2598平方公里，辖9镇、5乡，总人口23.4万人，其中布依族占76%，建州前是全国唯一的布依族自治县。2011年，全县生产总值达14.38亿元，财政总收入达1.8186亿元，城镇居民人均可支配收入达12468元，农村居民人均纯收入达3317元。册亨交通区位优势明显，自然资源、矿产资源、旅游资源丰富，民族文化独特，发展潜力巨大，是贵州省实施南下开放带动战略的前沿码头。

近年来，全县上下坚持以科学发展观为统领，牢固树立“贫困县有亮点、小县能办大事”的发展理念，扎实推进“创建生态文明县、打造册亨绿色品牌”发展战略，着力发展蔗糖、林业、畜牧、蔬菜、水产五大产业，坚持走新型工业化道路，不断深化拓展创新党的基层组织建设，社会和谐稳定，人民群众安居乐业，被评为“平安县”、“无毒县”、“十佳和谐县”、“中华布依第一县”称号。

“花-菜-稻”模式初见成效
"Flowers - vegetables - rice" mode got initial success

Ceheng County is located in the southeast of Qianxinan state, with an area of 2,598 square kilometers, jurisdiction over 9 towns and 5 townships, with a total population of 234,000, which Buyi minority accounted for 76%, before the statehood, it is the only Buyi Autonomous County in the country. In 2011, the county's GDP reached 1.438 billion yuan, the total fiscal revenue reached 1.8186 million yuan, urban residents per capita disposable income reached 12,468 yuan, the per capita net income of rural residents reached 3,317 yuan. Ceheng owns obvious traffic advantages, is rich in natural resources, mineral resources, tourism resources, and unique national culture and huge development potential, is the cutting-edge pierin of Guizhou Province to the south open to drive the strategy.

In recent years, the whole county adhere to the scientific development concept as a guide, firmly establish the "highlight of the poverty-stricken counties, small counties can do big things," the concept of development, push forward "create an ecological civilization county, to build Ceheng green brand" development strategy, focus development of sugar, forestry, livestock, vegetables, aquatic products, five industrial, adhere to the new path of industrialization, continuously deepened to expand the innovation of the party's grassroots organizations, social harmony and stability, people live and work, was named the "Peaceful County", "drug-free County" "Top Ten harmony County", "China Buyi first county" title.

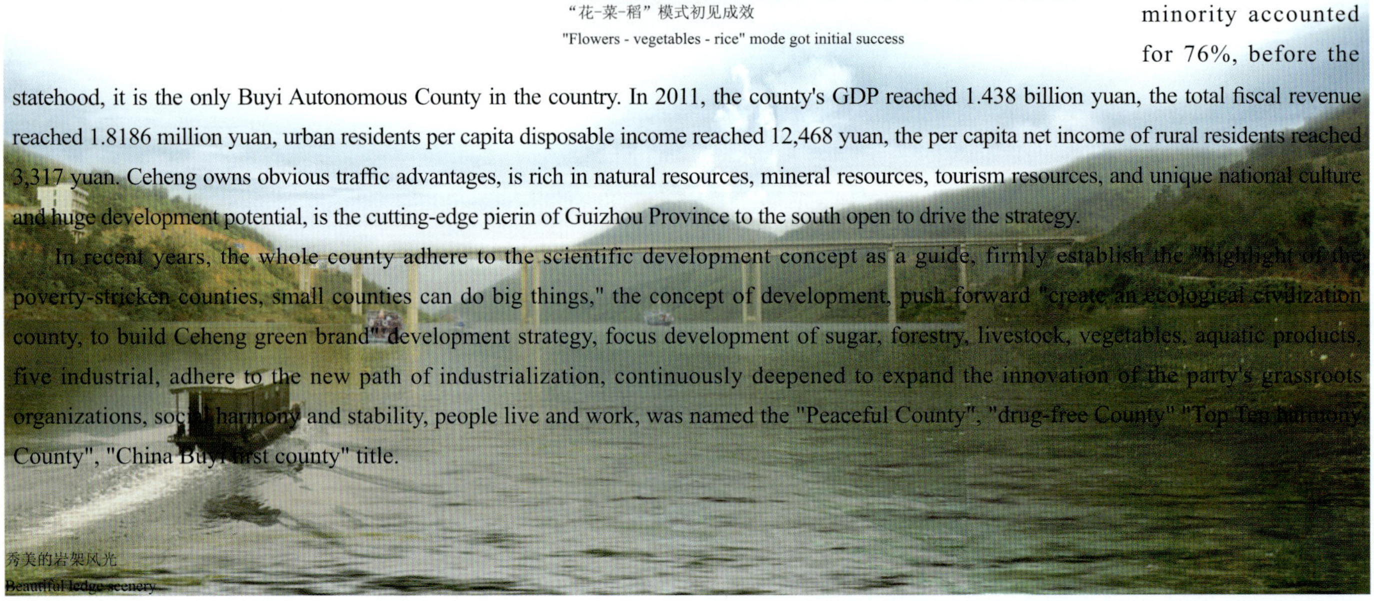

秀美的岩架风光
Beautiful ledge scenery

正 安 县

Zheng'an County

10月15日，正安县和正安县顶箐方竹有限公司分别荣获“中国特色竹乡”、“中国竹产业龙头企业”称号
October 15, Zheng'an County and Zheng'an County Dingjing Chimonobambusa Co., Ltd. won the title of "Chinese characteristics Bamboo Township", "Chinese bamboo industry leading enterprises"

11月23日，贵州省道真至瓮安高速公路开工仪式
November 23, the Guizhou province Daozhen to Weng'an highway groundbreaking ceremony

5月16日，县城七号路建设正式启动
May 16, the county VII road construction officially launched

1月14日，县南门三期旧城改造招商签约仪式
January 14, County South Gate III transformation of the old Merchants signing ceremony

2011年，正安县国土面积2595.2平方公里，耕地面积46.74万亩，林地面积138万亩，森林覆盖率46.3%。辖11镇、8乡，152个村，年末总人口64.1万人。境内有铝土矿、含钾页岩、萤石等矿藏16种，大小河流393条。全年完成地区生产总值29.32亿元，同比增长11.9%；其中一产10.47亿元，同比增长0.8%；二产5.3379亿元，同比增长26.4%；三产13.51亿元，同比增长15.9%；三次产业比为35.7∶18.2∶46.1。地方财政收入3.0211亿元，同比增长41.49%；一般预算收入2.0823亿元，同比增长42.94%；一般预算支出15.0389亿元，同比增长10.9%。农民人均纯收入3701元，同比增长22.5%；城镇居民可支配收入12574元，同比增长14.7%。社会消费品零售总额10.82亿元，同比增长20.1%。金融机构年末各项存款余额48.5亿元，同比增长22.2%；各项贷款余额16.88亿元，同比增长13.53%。

3月29日，八岔林水库前期工程动工仪式
March 29, Bachalin reservoir early commencement of works ceremony

6月12日，年产120万吨新型干法水泥生产线点火投产仪式
June 12, an annual output of 1.2 million tons of cement production line put into the ignition ceremony

12月16日，正安白茶大连旗舰店开业
December 16, Zheng'an white tea Dalian flagship store opening

In 2011, Zheng'an County land area is 2,595.2 square kilometers, 467,400 mu of arable land, forest land area of 1,380,000 mu, the forest coverage of 46.3%. Jurisdiction over 11 towns and 8 rurals, 152 villages, total population of 64.1 million by the end of the year. There are 16 kinds of bauxite, potassium shale, fluorspar and other minerals, and 393 rivers and streams. The total GDP of 2.932 billion yuan, up 11.9%;among which the first industry had a production of 1.047 billion yuan, an increase of 0.8%; the second industry produced 533.79 million yuan, up 26.4%; the teritary output of 1.351 billion yuan, up 15.9%; three industries ratio was 35.7:18.2:46.1. The local financial revenue of 302.11 million yuan, an increase of 41.49%; general budget revenue of 208.23 million yuan, an increase of 42.94%; general budget expenditures of 1.50389 billion yuan, an increase of 10.9%. Rural per capita net income of 3,701 yuan, an increase of 22.5%; urban residents' disposable income of 12,574 yuan, an increase of 14.7%. The total retail sales of social consumer goods was 1.082 billion yuan, up 20.1%. At the end of the year, financial institutions deposit balance of 4.85 billion yuan, up 22.2%; the loan balance of 1.688 billion yuan, an increase of 13.53%.

望 谟 县

Wangmo County

国家减灾委领导到望谟调研
National Disaster Reduction Committee leadership to Wangmo have research

国家水利和生态调研组领导到望谟调研
National Water and ecological research group leaders to Wangmo have research

黔西南州副州长、中共望谟县委书记邓家富向来宾介绍工业园区建设情况
Qianxinan Lieutenant Governor, the CPC Wangmo county party secretary Deng Jiafu briefed the construction of industrial parks to the guests

县长农文海陪同省设计院领导到蔗香港调研
Magistrate Nong Wenhai accompanied by the leadership of the province Design Institute to Zhe Xianggang have research

望谟县位于贵州省南部，黔西南布依族苗族自治州东部。面积3005.5平方公里，辖17个乡镇、161个行政村、2个社区，居住着布依、苗、瑶、壮、汉等19个民族。人口32万人，其中少数民族占80.09%。属亚热带季风湿润气候，素有“贵州天然温室”之称。

望谟资源丰富，境内富含金矿、铅锌矿、铁矿、锑矿、萤石矿、大理石、辉绿岩、煤矿等10多种矿藏；有流域面积大于20平方公里的河流13条，水能理论蕴藏量11.58万千瓦；生态植被完好，有百万亩的油桐林，被国家林业部授予“中国油桐之乡”称号，森林覆盖率53.2%，被评为全国林业先进县；有奇异壮观的天坑溶洞群，谷深林茂的峡谷地缝，布依、苗文化风情浓郁，红色旅游资源丰富。

国民经济持续健康发展。2011年，全县生产总值15.67亿元，同比增长15.3%。财政总收入预计完成2.19亿元，同比增长16.47%。其中：地方财政收入完成0.89亿元，同比增长6.9%；地方一般预算支出完成13.55亿元，同比增长25.23%。全社会固定资产投资完成11.56亿元，同比增长122.74%。社会消费品零售总额完成2.36亿元，同比增长15.7%。城镇居民人均可支配收入完成12980元，同比增长8.26%。农民人均纯收入完成3156元，同比增长22.04%。金融机构各项存贷款余额分别为25.8亿元、9.7亿元，同比分别增长33.3%、36%。

基础设施建设步伐加快。一是交通建设进度加快。全县公路通车里程达到2530公里，基本实现村村通公路。西南水运出海中线通道完成航运整治，500吨级试航成功，开通航运通道122公里。二是水利建设全面铺开。三是城镇建设逐步完善。制定了《关于加快城镇化建设的实施意见》，抓好城镇化建设规划，着力实施城镇化带动发展战略。2011年城镇化率达22.3%。

望谟山水

Wangmo mountain and water landscape

2011年6月6日灾情

Disaster on June 6, 2011

洪水无情人有情

Flood without mercy but people owns mercy

平洞工业园区开工仪式

Pingdong Industrial Park groundbreaking ceremony

新农村建设

New rural construction

Wangmo County is located in the southern Guizhou Province, in the east part of Qianxinan Buyi and Miao Autonomous Prefecture. Area of 3,005.5 square kilometers, jurisdiction over 17 townships and 161 administrative villages, 2 communities, inhabited by Buyi, Miao, Yao, Zhuang, Han and other 19 ethnic groups. Population of 320,000 people, including ethnic minorities accounted for 80.09%. It is a humid subtropical monsoon climate, known as "the Guizhou natural greenhouse".

Wangmo is rich in resources, the territory is rich in gold, lead and zinc, iron ore, antimony ore, fluorite ore, marble, diabase, coal, etc. more than 10 kinds of mineral deposits; drainage area greater than 20 square kilometers of rivers 13, the water reserves of 115,800 kilowatts; ecological vegetation intact,million acres of tung trees, the State Forestry Department granted the title of "the hometown of the Chinese tung tree, forest coverage of 53.2%, was rated as advanced national forestry county; singular and spectacular sinkhole caves, deep valleys heavy forest Canyon to sew, the folk customs of Buyi, Miao culture, red and rich tourism resources.

Sustained and healthy of national economy development. In 2011, the county's GDP 1.567 billion yuan, an increase of 15.3%. The total fiscal revenue expected to be completed 219 million yuan, an increase of 16.47%. Of which: local fiscal revenue completed 89 million yuan, an increase of 6.9%; local general budget expenditures to complete 1.355 million yuan, an increase of 25.23%. The whole society fixed assets investment was 1.156 billion yuan, an increase of 122.74%. The total retail sales of social consumer goods was 236 million yuan, an increase of 5.7%. The urban residents per capita disposable income of 12,980 yuan, an increase of 8.26%. Rural per capita net income of 3,156 yuan, an increase of 22.04%. Financial institutions, the deposit and loan balances were 2.58 billion yuan, 970 million yuan, an increase of 33.3%, 36% respectively.

The accelerated pace of infrastructure construction. First, the progress of transportation construction accelerated. The county road mileage of 2,530 km, the basic realization of the village accessible by road. Southwest Water Transport at sea midline channel to complete the shipping regulation, 500-ton trial is successful, the opening of the shipping channel of 122 km. Second, water conservancy construction is in full swing. Third, the gradual improvement of cities and towns. Develop "Implementation opinions on accelerating urbanization", do a good job of urbanization planning, focus on the implementation of the urbanization drive the development strategy. Urbanization rate of 22.3% in 2011.

布依族“三月三”
Buyi "March 3"

望谟麻山绝技——上刀梯
The Wangmo Masha stunt - Shang Daoti

农业产业化建设稳步推进。全县农作物种植面积65.29万亩，秋冬农作物面积22.65万亩，夏粮面积6.74万亩，产量6577吨，增长217.88%，秋粮总产量71961吨。全年粮食总产量75951吨，比上年减少6549吨。完成蔬菜种植面积10万亩，产量达11万吨，投入294万元发展火龙果种植3070亩，全县水果产量达6533吨。投资260万元建成2010年度石漠化草地畜牧业发展项目，新增种草面积10000多亩，新增圈舍建设面积12035平方米，水产养殖逐步规范化、规模化、科学化，水产品产量达到3412吨，同比增长5.47%。在农业产业化的推动下，今年望谟县第一产业增加值达5.29亿元，完成年计划的102.72%，同比增长15.5%。

布依少女
Buyi girl

改善民生工作力度加大，社会事业全面协调发展。一是继续深入开展新阶段扶贫开发工作。二是狠抓各项惠民利民政策的落实。三是不断加强就业和社会保障工作。四是加大危房改造督查力度，明确目标任务，层层落实工作责任，全力推进农村危房改造工作。

抗灾救灾取得胜利，灾后重建成效明显。2011年6月6日，望谟县遭受了特大山洪泥石流灾害，造成了重大的人员伤亡和巨大的财产损失。在抗灾救灾工作中，全县广大干部群众在县委、县政府的坚强领导下，团结一致，齐心协力与灾害顽强抗争，把群众的损失降到最低限度，抗灾救灾和灾后重建取得重大胜利。

苗族织麻手工工艺
Miao minority weave craftsmanship

苗族歌舞
Miao minority song and dance

山寨人
Cottage people

丰收
Harvest

纳朝风光
Nachao scenery

The construction of agricultural industrialization pushed steadily. 652,900 mu of crop acreage in the county, area of 226,500 mu of winter crops, summer grain area of 67,400 mu, and production of 6,577 tons, an increase of 217.88%, autumn grain output of 71,961 tons. Annual grain output of 75,951 tons, 6,549 tons less than last year. Vegetable cultivation area of 100,000 mu, the output reached 110,000 tons, invested 2.94 million yuan to develop 3,070 mu of dragon fruit cultivation, fruit production in the county up to 6,533 tons. Rocky desertification of grassland animal husbandry development projects completed in 2010 to invest 2.6 million yuan, the new grass area of 10,000 mu, the new sheds construction area of 12,035 square meters, aquaculture is gradually standardized, large-scale scientific and aquatic production reached 3,412 tons, an increase of 5.47%. Under the promotion of the industrialization of agriculture, the primary industry of Wangmo County to increase the value of 529 million yuan, 102.72% of the annual plan, an increase of 15.5%.

Improve the livelihood work, to increase the social cause of comprehensive and coordinated development. First, continue to carry out the work of poverty alleviation and development of a new stage. Second, pay close attention to the benifit people implementation of the policy. Third, is to continue to strengthen employment and social security work. Fourth, is to increase the renovation of dilapidated buildings supervision, clear objectives, tasks, and levels of work responsibility, to promote the renovation of dilapidated buildings in rural areas.

Disaster relief to win, achieved remarkable success of post-disaster reconstruction. June 6, 2011, Wangmo County suffered a large torrential debris flows, resulting in significant casualties and huge property losses. In disaster relief work, the cadres and masses in the county under the strong leadership of the county committee, government, united, work together and heroic struggle against disaster, made the mass loss to a minimum, disaster relief and reconstruction achieved a major victory.

麻山黑山羊
Ma Mountain Black goats

甘蔗林
Cane forest

平 塘 县

Pingtang County

张永锋主席陪同省政协副主席班程农调研平塘扶贫开发工作
Zhang Yongfeng President, accompanied by provincial CPPCC Vice Chairman Ban Chengnong has research of Pingtang poverty alleviation and development work

县委书记严肃到通州工业园区视察工作
The county secretary Yan Su to inspect the work in the Tongzhou Industrial Park

2011年，平塘县委、县政府在省、州党委政府的正确领导下，认真贯彻落实科学观，抢抓中央实施西部大开发和扩大内需等重大机遇，强力实施工业化、城镇化、新农村、旅游业“四大战略”，全县经济社会统筹发展、协调发展、跨越发展。

2011年实现全县地区生产总值18.2818亿，较上年增长14.3%；农业总产值95862万元，较上年增长14.5%；规模工业总产值8.0715亿元，较上年增长68.1%，规模工业增加值较上年增长28.3%；全社会固定资产投资20.6803亿元，较上年增长52.78%，其中固定资产投资较上年增长48.56%，财政总收入1.8658亿，较上年增长37.82%，地方财政收入较上年增长40.2%；社会消费品零售总额4.5664亿，较上年增长20.8%，农民人均纯收入4210元，较上年净增782元，增长22.81%。

县委副书记、县长毛有智视察甲茶电站建设情况

County deputy secretary, county director Mao Youzhi has inspection of Jiacha power plant construction

县人大常委会主任孟玉凤深入苗族村寨调研三农工作

The director of the county People's Congress Standing Committee Meng Yufeng has depth research of three rural work Miao minority village

In 2011, Pingtang county committee, the county government under the correct leadership of the province, state party committees and governments, earnestly implement the scientific concept, significant opportunities to seize the central implementation of western development and the expansion of domestic demand, strong implementation of the industrialization, urbanization and new rural tourism "the four major strategies", the county's economic and social co-ordinate the development of coordinated development of leapfrog development.

In 2011, the GDP in the county of 1.82818 billion yuan, representing an increase of 14.3% over last year; agricultural output value of 958.62 million yuan, representing an increase of 14.5% over last year; large-scale industrial output value of 807,15 million yuan, representing an increase of 68.1% over last year, large-scale industry value-added growth of 28.3% over the previous year; total fixed asset investment 2.06803 billion yuan, representing an increase of 52.78% over last year, including fixed asset investment growth of 48.56% over the previous year, total fiscal revenue 186.58 million yuan, representing an increase of 37.82% over last year, local fiscal revenue increase of 40.2% over the previous year; total retail sales of 456.64 million yuan, up 20.8% over the previous year, the per capita net income of farmers was 4,210 yuan, a net increase of 782 yuan, an increase of 22.81% over the previous year.

晴 隆 县

Qinglong County

晴隆县位于贵州省西南面，总面积1331.1平方公里。辖6个乡（其中1个民族乡），8个镇，5个社区，91个行政村。人口335328人。主要矿藏有煤炭、黄金、锑、铅、萤石、贵翠等，森林覆盖率34.6%。

2011年，全县生产总值（GDP）243486万元，比上年增长16.5%。实现人均生产总值9894元，比上年增加1977元。第一产业、第二产业、第三产业增加值占生产总值的比重分别由上年的18.6%、36.2%和45.2%，调整为18.04%、39.66%和42.31%。财政收入完成4.0218亿元，全社会固定资产投资完成25亿元，城镇居民人均可支配收入14570元，农民人均纯收入3450元。

2011年，农、林、牧、渔业总产值实现72201万元，比上年增长4.6%；工业经济保持较快发展，全年实现工业总产值234360万元，比上年增长19.31%；固定资产投资快速增长，全社会固定资产投资总额完成230647万元，同比增长52.21%；消费品市场继续保持稳步发展的良好态势，全县实现社会消费品零售总额35026万元，比上年增长16.03%；交通运输继续发展，交通运输能力继续提高；邮电通信业快速发展；财政收支增长较快；教育事业全面发展；卫生医疗条件逐步改善；人民生活水平不断提高；社会保障覆盖面不断扩大。

二十四道拐抗战公路景观
Twenty-four Shui War Highway Landscape

镇胜65号高速公路
Zhensheng NO.65 Highway

光照湖区风光
Light Lakes scenery

江满草场
JiangMan pasture

三望坪草场
SanWangPing pasture

发祥煤矿煤炭资源
FaXiang coal mine coal resources

桃园草场果、草、畜配套发展，图为牧民放羊时的情景
The Taoyuan pastures and fruit, grass, animals, supporting the development, the photo shows the scene when the herders sheep

沙子水库茶场一角
Sand reservoir tea plantation corner

Qinglong County is located in the southwest of Guizhou Province, with the total area of 1,331.1 square km. Jurisdiction over 6 rural (including 1 ethnic township), 8 towns, 5 communities, 91 administrative villages. Population of 335,328 people. The main minerals are coal, gold, antimony, lead, fluorite, Guicui and other, forest coverage of 34.6%.

In 2011, the county gross domestic product (GDP) was 2,434,860,000 yuan, an increase of 16.5% over the previous year. GDP per capita of 9,894 yuan, 1,977 yuan more than last year. The proportion of primary industry, secondary industry and tertiary industry accounted for GDP from the previous year 18.6%, 36.2% and 45.2%, adjusted to 18.04%, 39.66% and 42.31% respectively. Financial income of 402.18 million yuan, the total fixed asset investment of 2.5 billion yuan, per capita disposable income of urban residents was 14,570 yuan, 3,450 yuan per capita net income of farmers.

沙子茶场新品种491茶叶
The sand tan factory new varieties of 491 tea

In 2011, the total output value of agriculture, forestry, animal husbandry, fisheries to achieve 722.01 million yuan, an increase of 4.6% over the previous year; to maintain a rapid development of industrial economy, the annual industrial output value of 2.3436 billion yuan, up 19.31% over the previous year; fixed assets rapid growth in investment, total fixed asset investment in the total value of 2.30647 billion yuan, an increase of 52.21%; consumer goods market continued to maintain the good momentum of steady development, the county total retail sales of 350.26 million yuan, an increase of 16.03% over the previous year; transportation continue to develop, continue to improve the transport capacity; post and telecommunications industry has developed rapidly; rapid growth in financial revenue and expenditure; education undertakings has full development; the gradual improvement of health and medical conditions; constantly improve people's living standards; expanding social security coverage.

飞龙胜境 苦丁之乡——余庆

dragow Beautiful Scenery Kuding Tea Town - Yuqing

天下第一长龙
World first long dragon

余庆位于黔中腹地，面积1623.7平方公里，辖9镇、1乡，69个村，总人口30万人，其中农业人口26.28万人，总耕地面积28.74万亩，是典型的西部山区农业县。

2011年，余庆县委、政府围绕省委“两加一推”，市委、市政府“提速赶超、转型跨越”主基调，全力落实保增长、保民生、保稳定的目标任务，实现了经济社会平稳较好发展。

全县生产总值完成30.75亿元，增长5%；全社会固定资产投资32亿元，同比增长8.7%；财政总收入预计完成3.43亿元，同比增长22.7%；地方一般预算收入预计完成2.13亿元，同比增长23.5%；社会商品零售总额8.89亿元，同比增长20%；农民人均纯收入5268元，同比增长1%，城镇居民可支配收入11425元，同比增长10.8%。

2011年招商引资项目金地鞋业生产车间一角
One corner of the 2011 investment projects Golden shoe production workshop

第二届旅游节文艺演出现场
Theatrical performances at the scene of the Second Tourism Festival

遵义市四在农家现场会在余庆召开
Zunyi City, Sizai farm meetings held in the Yuqing on site

Yuqing is in the hinterland of Guizhou, with an area of 1,623.7 square kilometers, jurisdiction over 9 towns,1 rural, 69 villages, with a total population of 300,000, which agricultural population of 262,800, the total cultivated land area of 287,400 mu, is typical of the western mountain agricultural county.

In 2011, Yuqing county committee, governments around the provincial party committee "two plus a push", to catch up with the municipal government "accelerate and excel, transformation span" the main tone, is fully committed the objectives and tasks to maintain growth, safeguard people's livelihood, maintaining stability, to achieve a smooth and better economic development.

County GDP of 3.075 billion yuan, an increase of 5%; total fixed asset investment 3.2 billion yuan, an increase of 8.7%; total fiscal revenue expected to be completed 343 million yuan, an increase of 22.7%; local general budget revenue is expected to complete 213 million yuan, up 23.5%; total volume of retail sales of 889 million yuan, an increase of 20%; rural per capita net income of 5,268 yuan, an increase of 1%, urban residents' disposable income of 11,425 yuan, an increase of 10.8%.

美丽村落
Beautiful villages

毕节学院

Bijie College

2010年8月，教育部部长袁贵仁出席联系点毕节学院创先争优活动座谈会

August 2010, Minister of Education Yuan Guiren at contact point The Bijie College of competing for excellence activities forum

毕节学院是2005年3月经国家教育部批准，由原毕节师范高等专科学校、毕节教育学院合并组建的一所全日制综合性普通本科院校。现任党委书记陈永祥教授，院长张学立教授。

学校现有教职工841人，其中专任教师556人，副高以上职称198人，博士、硕士328人。教师中有国家一级学会专业委员会主任、副秘书长，省管专家、省高校哲学社会科学学术带头人、省级教学名师等30人，有1人受聘担任西南大学博士研究生导师，10人受聘担任省内外高校硕士研究生导师。设有14个教学学院，开设33个本科专业，18个专科专业。有来自25个省、区、市的全日制在校学生10174人，成人教育在册本专科学生4509余人。学校先后荣获“三下乡”、“扶残助残”、“国防教育”、“预征工作”等全国先进集体称号。学校注重对外交流与合作，先后与澳大利亚、印尼、美国等10多个国家和地区的大学与科研机构建立了长期合作与交流关系。

绣山实验楼

The Xiushan laboratory building

艺术楼正面

The front of the Art Building

乌蒙书画院

The Wumeng calligraphy college

The Bijie College was approved by the National Ministry of Education in March 2005, the former Bijie Normal College and Bijie Institute of Education merged to form a full-time regular undergraduate institutions. The current party secretary, Professor Chen Yongxiang, president of Professor Zhang Xueli.

The school's existing staff of 841 people, including 556 full-time teachers, 198 associate professors, Ph.D., Master of 328 people. Teachers at the national level the Society of Professional Committee, Deputy Secretary-General, the provincial experts, academic leaders of the province of Philosophy and Social Science, provincial teaching teacher, etc. 30 people, one person was appointed to the Southwestern University doctoral student mentor, and 10 people employed as outside the province of university postgraduate tutor. There are 14 teaching colleges, the creation of 33 undergraduate programs, 18 specialties. There are full-time 10,174 students from 25 provinces, autonomous regions and municipalities in schools, adult education and junior college students more than 4,509 people. The school has won the title of the "countryside", "help and assist disabled", "National Defense Education", "warning sings of the work" National Advanced Collective. Schools focus on international exchanges and cooperation, has established long-term cooperation and exchange relations with more than 10 countries and regions, including Australia, Indonesia, the United States and other universities and research institutions.

学校北大门

Schools northern gate

遵义医学院

Zunyi Medical College

教育部副部长鲁昕视察该校
Lu Xin, Vice Minister of Education visited the school

原省委书记石宗源视察该校
The former Provincial Party Secretary Shi Zongyuan visited the school

副省长刘晓凯视察该校
Provincial Vice Governor Liu Xiaokai has inspection of the school

遵义医学院坐落于风光秀丽的历史文化名城遵义，创建于1947年，是中国共产党创办的第一所本科医学院校。1969年更名为遵义医学院。经过65年的建设和发展，学校已成为一所以医学为主、文理渗透的多学科、多层次、办学特色鲜明、办学实力雄厚、拥有全日制在校生14000多人的省属重点建设高校。

学校由校本部、珠海校区和新蒲校区组成，占地面积3000多亩，建筑面积266345㎡。设有21个教学院系，学科涵盖6大门类，包含27个本科专业及专业方向。学校本科教学质量省内一流，在国内有较大影响。学校拥有一支阵容整齐、结构合理、锐意创新的师资队伍。现有专任教师701人，其中教授153人，副教授271人。学校坚持开放办学的方针，不断加强对外交流与合作。

2009年至2011年，全校获得国家自然科学基金50项，连续3年位居贵州省高等学校第二位，国家社会科学基金取得了历史性突破的好成绩。

Zunyi Medical College is located in the beautiful historical and cultural city of Zunyi, founded in 1947, the Chinese Communist Party founded the first undergraduate medical schools. Renamed Zunyi Medical College in 1969. After 65 years of construction and development, the school has become one of medicine-based, arts and science penetration of multi-disciplinary, multi-level, school with distinctive features, the strength of school, the provincial key universities has more than 14,000 full-time students.

School is composed by self-ampus, Zhuhai Campus and Xinpu Campus, an area of 3,000 mu, building area of 266,345 square meters. There are 21 teaching departments, disciplines covered by the six major categories, including 27 undergraduate programs and professional direction. School owns first class quality of undergraduate teaching in the province, have a greater impact in the country. The school has a neat line-up, reasonable structure, and innovation of the teaching staff. Existing full-time teachers 701 people, including 153 professors, 271 associate professors. Schools adhere to the principle of open schools, continue to strengthen international exchanges and cooperation.

In 2009-2011, the school get the National Natural Science Foundation of 50, for three consecutive years in the Guizhou Province Higher School ranked 2rd, National Social Science Foundation made a historic breakthrough in the good results.